ISBN 978-1-5284-3511-6
PIBN 10917491

DEPARTMENT OF THE INTERIOR
BUREAU OF EDUCATION

BULLETIN, 1916, No. 24

MONTHLY RECORD
OF CURRENT EDUCATIONAL
PUBLICATIONS

OCTOBER, 1916

WASHINGTON
GOVERNMENT PRINTING OFFICE
1916

ADDITIONAL COPIES
OF THIS PUBLICATION MAY BE PROCURED FROM
THE SUPERINTENDENT OF DOCUMENTS
GOVERNMENT PRINTING OFFICE
WASHINGTON, D. C.
AT
5 CENTS PER COPY

MONTHLY RECORD OF CURRENT EDUCATIONAL PUBLICATIONS.

Compiled by the Library Division, Bureau of Education. /

CONTENTS.—Publications of associations—Educational history and biography—Current educational conditions—Educational theory and practice—Educational psychology: Child study—Special subjects of curriculum—Rural education—Secondary education—Teachers: Training and professional status——Higher education—School administration—School management—School hygiene and sanitation—Physical training—Play and playgrounds—Social aspects of education—Moral education—Religious education—Manual and vocational training—Vocational guidance—Agricultural education—Home economics—Commercial education—Professional education—Military training—Boy scouts—Exceptional children—Libraries and reading—Bulletin of the Bureau of Education.

NOTE.

This office can not supply the publications listed in this bulletin, other than those expressly designated as publications of the Bureau of Education. · Books, pamphlets, and periodicals here mentioned may ordinarily be obtained from their respective publishers, either directly or through a dealer, or, in the case of an association publication, from the secretary of the issuing organization. Many of them are available for consultation in various public and institutional libraries.

Publications intended for inclusion in this record should be sent to the library of the Bureau of Education, Washington, D. C.

PUBLICATIONS OF ASSOCIATIONS.

1091. North central association of colleges and secondary schools. Proceedings of the twenty-first annual meeting . . . held at Chicago, Ill., March 24-25, 1916. Published by the Association, 1916. 246 p. 8°. (Henry E. Brown, secretary, Kenilworth, Ill.)

Contains: 1. T. A. Clark: College and character, p. 5–19. 2. Accredited schools, p. 97–121. 3. David Felmley: What is a reasonable limit to which an institution may go in enrolling students in the first and second years and yet retain the right to be classified as a senior college? p. 130–40. 4. J. S. Brown: The junior high school, the senior high school and the junior college, p. 140–51. 5. J. H. T. Main: No institution of college grade, which offers few advanced courses, should be classified as a senior college, p. 152–58. 6. Committee recommendations regarding the organization and administration of junior high schools, p. 171–74. 7. Digest of the responses to the questionnaire on the junior high school (or intermediate school) p. 174–92. 8. The definition of units, p. 192–229.

3

1092. **Vermont state teachers' association.** Report of the sixty-sixth annual convention, Rutland, Vermont, October 28–30, 1915. 116 p. 8°. (Etta Franklin, secretary, Rutland.)

> Contains: 1. Caroline S. Woodruff: The call of the school, p. 9–12. 2. G. A. Trueman: The use of the Binet-Simon measuring scale for intelligence, p. 31–39. 3. Lillian B. Poor: The kindergarten as the foundation of the elementary school, p. 51–55. 4. Ruth Farr: Story-telling in the primary grades, p. 55–60. 5. Dorothy C. Fisher: An open-air school for normal children, p. 71–74. 6. J. L. McConaughy: The superfluous in education, p. 98–102.

EDUCATIONAL HISTORY AND BIOGRAPHY.

1093. **Littell, Harold.** Development of the city school system of Indiana— 1851–1880. Indiana magazine of history, 12: 193–213, September 1916.

> To be concluded.

1094. **Memorial service for Miss Blow held in St. Louis.** Kindergarten and first grade, 1: 322–24, September 1916.

> Held in the Soldan high school auditorium on May 29.

1095. **Winship, A. E.** Irwin Shepard (Educators as I have known them— XXIV) Journal of education, 84: 201–202, September 7, 1916.

CURRENT EDUCATIONAL CONDITIONS.

1096. **Audollent, Aug.** La guerre et l'enseignement supérieur en France. Revue internationale de l'enseignement, 36: 241–53, July–August 1916.

> Deals with the service the German universities have rendered that country and shows that the French universities must prepare to use all their power after the war to preserve, defend and perpetuate "la tradition française."

1097. **Bourne, Randolph S.** The Gary public schools. Scribner's magazine, 30: 371–80, September 1916.

> With an introductory note by William Wirt, director of the Gary schools.

1098. **Brelet, Henri.** L'enseignement secondaire et la réforme de 1902. Revue internationale de l'enseignement, 36: 254–79, July–August 1916.

1099. **Cortright, Edward Everett.** Patent medicine formulas in our public school curriculum. Education, 37: 20–28, September 1916.

> The author states that the present curriculum does not take into account individual differences and so "doesn't and hasn't worked."

1100. **Gilman, Isabel Ambler.** The Alaska school service. Granite monthly, 48: 248–55, August 1916.

1101. **McCormick, S. B.** [Educational needs] National association of corporation schools bulletin, 3: 18–21, September 1916.

> An address before the fourth annual convention of the National association of corporation schools, defining the agencies that will play an important part in the future developments of the educational system of the United States.

1102. **Marquardt, W. W.** Child welfare work in the Philippines. Child, 6: 602–6, September 1916.

1103. **More, Louis Trenchard.** Education and the melting-pot. Nation, 103: 229–31, September 7, 1916.

> Writer says that American public schools emphasize vocational work above mental discipline, and standardize education down to the needs of the melting-pot, for the assimilation of immigrant children. If this should be continued, the children of the intelligent classes will more and more be sent to private schools, a result which would be unfortunate for the country.

1104. New possibilities in education; ed. by Ambrose L. Suhrie. Philadelphia, The American academy of political and social science, 1916. 331 p. 8°. (The annals of the American academy of political and social science. vol. LXVII. Whole no. 156)

CONTENTS.—1. Ambrose L. Suhrie: The educational program of a democracy, p. xi–xxvi. 2. A. Duncan Yocum: Appreciation of music, literature and art as a social aim, p. 1–12. 3. Irving King: Social training through school group activities, p. 13–25. 4. J. Lynn Barnard: Training in the schools for social efficiency, p. 26–33. 5. Edward H. Griggs: The moral training of children, p. 34–39. 6. Carrie A. Lyford: The science and art of home making, p. 40–46. 7. Thomas C. Blaisdell: Education for parenthood, p. 47–53. 8. John M. Brewer: Vocational guidance in school and occupation, p. 54–63. 9. Frederick G. Bonser: Education for life work in non-professional occupations, p. 64–76. 10. B. H. Crocheron: Manual labor and the achievement of national ideals, p. 77–81. 11. Jessie Field: Education for home life on the farm, p. 82–86. 12. John M. Gillette: Training for rural leadership, p. 87–96. 13. Louis W. Rapeer: Health as a means to happiness, efficiency and service, p. 97–106. 14. George E. Johnson: Play and recreation, p. 107–14. 15. J. George Becht: Training children to a wise use of their leisure, p. 115–22. 16. Annie C. Moore: Children, libraries and the love of reading, p. 123–29. 17. L. J. Hanifan: The rural school community center, p. 130–38. 18. Mrs. Frederic Schoff: The National congress of mothers and parent-teacher associations, p. 139–47. 19. Walter L. Philips: An urban home and school league, p. 148–55. 20. Payson Smith: The rural school improvement league, p. 156–61. 21. L. R. Alderman: School credit for home work, p. 162–66. 22. George E. Vincent: The spread of the school manse idea, p. 167–69. 23. Arthur J. Jones: Continuation schools, p. 170–81. 24. Louis Reber: University extension, p. 182–92. 25. James A. Moyer: The "People's university" of Massachusetts, p. 193–201. 26. Lee Galloway: Correspondence school instruction by non-academic institutions, p. 202–209. 27. Henry M. Leipziger: Education for adults through public lectures in New York city, p. 210–17. 28. Peter W. Dykema: The spread of the community music idea, p. 218–23. 29. Bradford Knapp: Education through farm demonstration, p. 224–40. 30. Mary E. Creswell: The home demonstration work, p. 241–49. 31. Arthur E. Bostwick: The library extension movement in American cities, p. 250–56. 32. Sarah Askew: Library work in the open country, p. 257–66. 33. Ellen C. Lombard: The home reading courses of the United States Bureau of education, p. 267–69. 34. Alfred W. Abrams: Visual instruction in New York state, p. 270–72. 35. H. H. Wheaton: The United States Bureau of education and the immigrant, p. 273–83. 36. William H. Allen: Education through official publicity, p. 284–90. 37. Clyde L. King: The public services of the college and university expert, p. 291–96.

1105. Rankin, Janet R. School service in Wisconsin. Educational review, 52: 144–51, September 1916.

Writer says that the new feature in the Wisconsin plan is "its aggressiveness in bringing home to every teacher the fact that the presence of problems and difficulties does not connote inefficiency; that the state desires to aid in transforming difficulties into achievements; and that prompt help may be received for the asking."

1106. Sargeant, Ide G. Is the Gary system the panacea for our educational ills? Forum, 56: 323–26, September 1916.

Writer says: "Briefly the Gary plan will reduce the per capita cost for school buildings and for supervision, take care of the children for a longer day through the use of the auditorium, playground, and shop in connection with the special academic subjects, give the child a more attractive and profitable school life, and at the same time provide better facilities for recreation and continuation work for adults."

1107. Sarraut, Albert. L'instruction publique et la guerre. Paris, H. Didier, 1916. xxxi, 266 p. 12°.

EDUCATIONAL THEORY AND PRACTICE.

1108. Bowman, Ernest Lavern. The lesson-plan for inexperienced teachers. Industrial-arts magazine, 5: 377–79, September 1916.

1109. **Furst, Clyde.** Liberal education. Midland schools, 31: 7–11, September 1916.

> "Liberal education represents a full adjustment of the individual to society, attending alike to body, mind, and spirit."

1110. **Guénot, H.** Contre l'identification des programmes masculins et des programmes féminins. Revue universitaire, 7: 118–26, July 1916.

1111. **Henry, T. S.** A comparison of two recent contributions to the theory of education. School and home education, 36: 14–17, September 1916.

> A review of Dewey's Democracy and education and Yocum's Culture, discipline and democracy. The author thinks that Yocum's is the more important contribution.

1112. **Wilson, *Mrs.* Louise Jones.** The average boy and how to teach him. School news and practical educator, 30: 41–42, September 1916.

> Some suggestions for teachers in dealing with boys in the schoolroom.

EDUCATIONAL PSYCHOLOGY: CHILD STUDY.

1113. **Cary, Charles P.** Measuring school achievement. Wisconsin journal of education, 48: 186–88, September 1916.

> The author explains the necessity for scales or standards by which to measure achievement.

1114. **Coxe, Warren W.** The Woolley tests applied to a prevocational class of boys. School review, 24: 521–32, September 1916.

1115. **Fordyce, Charles.** Educational measurements. Middle-west school review, 9: 17–18, September 1916.

> The author gives some of the reasons for having a scale by which to judge the work of pupils.

1116. **Gray, William S.** Descriptive list of standard tests. Elementary school journal, 18: 24–34, September 1916.

1117. **Kayfetz, Isidore.** A critical study of the Harvard-Newton composition scales. Pedagogical seminary, 23: 325–47, September 1916.

> Bibliography: p. 346–47.

1118. **McFarland, W. H.** Relation between spelling judgment and spelling ability. Midland schools, 31: 19–21, September 1916.

> A study to determine whether "all one needs in order to learn to spell is a spelling conscience and a dictionary habit." The conclusion drawn is that "the 'conscience and dictionary' scheme cannot be relied upon."

1119. **McManis, John T.** The study of the behavior of an individual child; syllabus and bibliography. Baltimore, Warwick & York, inc., 1916. 54 p. 12°.

> Bibliography at end of each chapter.

1120. **Scofield, F. A.** Difficulty of Ayres's spelling scale as shown by the spelling of 560 high school students. School and society, 4: 339–40, August 26, 1916.

1121. **Shaw, Elizabeth Ross.** A suggestion for child study. Kindergarten and first grade, 1: 304–308, September 1916.

> Tests given at the Francis Parker School to 5-year-old children. The questions were based on a list standardized by Professor Sommer of Giessen University with the substitution of six questions from the Binet scale.

1122. **Springer, Isidore, *ed.*** Teachers' year book of educational investigations; a manual giving the tests and standards that have been devised for the purpose of measuring the efficiency of school instruction and administration. Issued by the Division of reference and research, Department of education, the city of New York. 58 p. fold. chart. 8°. (Pub. no. 14)

1123. **Studebaker, John W.** Spelling; results of an investigation of pupils' ability to spell. New York, Boston [etc.] Newson & company [1916]. 57 p. 8°.

An investigation of the schools of Des Moines, Ia.

1124. **Wang, Chang Ping.** The general value of visual sense training in children. Baltimore, Warwick & York, inc., 1916. 85 p. illus. 12°. (Educational psychology monographs, no. 15)

Bibliography: p. 81–82.

1125. **Woodrow, Herbert.** The faculty of attention. Journal of experimental psychology, 1: 285–318, August 1916.

1126. **Woody, Clifford.** Measurements of some achievements in arithmetic. School and society, 4: 299–303, August 19, 1916.

1127. **Ziedler, Richard.** Tests in silent reading in the rural schools of Santa Clara county, California. Elementary school journal, 18: 55–62, September 1916.

SPECIAL SUBJECTS OF CURRICULUM.

1128. **Bolenius, Emma Miller.** The story in school. Popular educator, 34: 38–40, 47, September 1916.

The author gives "(1) information about the story . . . (2) special suggestions . . . (3) devices that enliven work with the short story."

1129. **Brawley, Benjamin.** The course in English in the secondary school. Southern workman, 45: 494–502, September 1916.

A discussion of the English course for negro schools.

1130. **Hamm, Franklin P.** Outline and suggestive methods and devices on the teaching of elementary arithmetic. Designed to increase the efficiency of teachers of the fifth and sixth years. Also an aid to teachers of succeeding grades in maintaining uniformity in methods and forms throughout the course. Philadelphia, J. B. Lippincott company [1916] 40 p. 16°.

1131. **Hauvette, Henri.** A propos de l'allemand et de quelques autres langues étrangères. Revue de l'enseignement des langues vivantes, 83: 289–96, July 1916.

The author takes issue with those who would stop the teaching of German after the war, claiming that the study of foreign languages keeps a nation in touch commercially and intellectually with foreign countries, and that this is necessary for the welfare of the nation.

1132. **Krause, Carl A.** The direct method in modern languages; contributions to methods and didactics in modern languages. New York, Chicago [etc.] C. Scribner's sons [1916] 139 p. 12°.

Bibliography of American writers, 1912–14: p. 117–39.

1133. **Lewis, G. W.** Present methods of teaching primary reading. Catholic school journal, 16: 181–88, September 1916.

Short sketch of the various methods but describes especially the Lewis story method.

1134. **Mackay, Constance D'Arcy.** Festival history and festival ideas for the school. Popular educator, 84: 14–15, 58, September 1916.

1135. Norris, F. A. The incidental teaching of English in school shops. Manual training magazine, 18: 13–15, September 1916.

1136. Noyer, Ralph. How to judge a debate. Rural school messenger, 6: 27–28, September 1916.

> Gives an outline which the author has "often found helpful in arriving at a decision."

1137. Sears, Isabel and Diebel, Amelia. A study of the common mistakes in pupils' oral English. Elementary school journal, 18: 44–54, September 1916.

> Results of an investigation to determine the errors of speech made by Cincinnati school children.

1138. Smith, David E. The development of the American arithmetic. Educational review, 52: 109–18, September 1916.

> Traces the development of the American arithmetic, particularly with regard to the influences exerted in turn by various European countries. Discusses the influences that will bear upon text books by the junior high school. "This school," says the writer, "offers the most encouragement to mathematics that has been seen in many years."

1139. Sutton, H. O. General science in the high school. Nebraska teacher, 19: 24–26, September 1916.

> A brief discussion of the reasons for a course in general science, the nature of the course, and the results obtained.

1140. Sypherd, Wilbur Owen. A bibliography on "English for engineers", for the use of engineering students, practicing engineers, and teachers in schools of engineering, to which are appended brief selected lists of technical books for graduates in civil, electrical, mechanical, and chemical engineering. Chicago, New York, Scott, Foresman and company [1916] 68 p. 12°.

> Printed on one side of leaf only.

1141. Tatlock, John S. P. Literature and history. University of California chronicle, 18: 309–28, July 1916.

> The Phi beta kappa address delivered at the University of California, May 16, 1916.
> Discusses the historical aspect of literature.

1142. Tryon, R. M. The high school history recitation. History teacher's magazine, 7: 236–42, September 1916.

> Suggests some methods which a teacher may profitably employ in her attempts to improve the technique of her high-school history recitations.

1143. Walker, Curtis Howe. The sketch-map as an aid in the teaching of historical geography. School review, 24: 497–514, September 1916.

> A paper read before the High school history teachers' association of Chicago, October 30, 1915, slightly revised.

1144. Whitney, Frederick L. Measuring the value of first grade readers. American school board journal, 53: 24, 77–78, September 1916.

KINDERGARTEN AND PRIMARY SCHOOL.

1145. Aguayo, Alfredo M. La escuela primaria como debe ser. 1 ed. Habana, Imp. "La Propagandista," 1916. 165 p. 12°.

1146. Alder, Louise. Kindergartens in the schools of Kansas. Kansas teacher, 3: 5–8, July and August 1916.

> History and present status of the kindergarten in Kansas. Kansas ranks "as the 33d state in the union in regard to the number of children enrolled in kindergartens per thousand of population of kindergarten age."

1147. **Bradstreet, Marjora.** A kindergarten upon the Florida keys. Kindergarten and first grade, 1 : 299–300, September 1916.

Description of a kindergarten at Key West.

1148. **Dobbs, Ella Victoria.** Meeting of National council of primary education. Kindergarten and first grade, 1 : 309–10, September 1916.

Meeting held July 6, 1916, at New York.

1149. **Hill, Patty S.** Kindergartens of yesterday and tomorrow. Kindergarten-primary magazine, 29 : 4–6, September 1916.

Paper delivered at the National education association meeting, July 1916.

1150. **Palmer, Luella A.** Practical means of unifying the work of kindergarten and primary grades. Kindergarten point of view. Kindergarten-primary magazine, 29 : 7–10, September 1916.

RURAL EDUCATION.

1151. **Benson, P. H.** Rural supervision in a California county. American school board journal, 53 : 42–43, September 1916.

1152. **Clark, Taliaferro; Collins, George L.,** *and* **Treadway, W. L.** Rural school sanitation, including physical and mental status of school children in Porter county, Indiana. Washington, Government printing office, 1916. 127 p. illus. 8°. (Treasury department. U. S. Public health service. Public health bulletin no. 77)

1153. **Fairview's hired man.** Rural school messenger, 6 : 7–23, September 1916.

"A humorous story of real progress [in a rural school] supposedly told by a conservative farmer. From the Saturday evening post."

1154. **[Williams, Henry G.]** A course of study for rural schools. Ohio teacher, 37 : 4–5, August 1916.

Gives some features of the redirected rural school. The course of study will be published in the September issue.

1155. **Williams, J. Harold.** Reorganizing a county system of rural schools. Report of a study of the schools of San Mateo county, California. Washington, Government printing office, 1916. 50 p. illus., plates. 8°. (United States. Bureau of education. Bulletin, 1916, no. 16.)

SECONDARY EDUCATION.

1156. **California high school teachers' association.** Proceedings of the fourth annual convention, Berkeley, July 10–14, 1916. Sierra educational news, 12 : 1–206, August 1916.

Contains: 1. M. E. Hill: Education for the larger life, p. 9–12. 2. A. F. Lange: The new high school and the new high-school teacher, p. 12–18. 3. W. C. Wood: Effect of recent regulations of the state board of education on the relation of the high school to the normal school, p. 27–37. 4. D. S. Hill: Educational research in public schools. p. 39–48. 5. C. E. Rugh: Moral implications in subjects, activities and government of a modern high school, p. 49–55. 6. J. B. Sears: The legal status and growth of California high schools, p. 55–64. 7. M. E. Deutsch: Where the fastenings are weakest (Latin in high schools) p. 78–86. 8. S. I. Miller, jr.: The teaching of economics in the high school, p. 106–12. 9. A. L. Gould: Can the junior college be made to serve its community primarily and be an end in itself? p. 116–18. 10. W. A. Cooper: Collegiate training of high-school teachers of German, p. 127–34. 11. W. C. Wood: Forming and informing in the rural high school, p. 143–50. 12. A. F. Lange: The reorganization of rural education, p. 155–58. 13. B. H. Paddock: The proposed rural school survey, p. 159–66. 14. R. G. Boone: Some implications of vocational guidance, p. 170–72. 15. J. C. Templeton: Report of the committee on high-school architecture and grounds, p. 178–81. 16. Report of the vocational guidance committee. Progress of vocational guidance in California, and suggestions for its introduction into school systems, p. 190, 193–94, 197–98, 201.

1157. **Abelson, Joseph.** A study of the junior high school project. Education, 37. 1–19. September 1916.

1158. **Andrew, William E.** A study in high-school cost of production. American school board journal, 53: 12, September 1916.

> "Set of standards . . . derived from a study of the official records of seventeen high schools in thirteen counties in Central Illinois."

1159. **Brown, George A.** [Junior high schools] School and home education, 36: 6–8, September 1916.

> The author criticises the junior high school idea unfavorably.

1160. **Gillan, S. Y.** Classifying high-school pupils. Western teacher, 25: 9–12, September 1916.

> Advocates a plan of organisation for high schools which discards the plan of promoting by classes and lets each pupil do as much as he is able to do well, and no more.

1161. **Herrick, Cheesman A.** What high-school studies are of most worth. School and society, 4: 305–309, August 26, 1916.

> Paper read at the meeting of the Secondary department, National education association, July 4, 1916.
> Changes in secondary education, the author states, "should be made with the following as a guiding principle: Those high-school studies are of most worth which are worth most to the individual pupil, which will best fit him for meeting the many-sided demands of the life which he is to live"

1162. **Mooney, William Barnard.** The relation of secondary schools to higher schools in the United States. Pedagogical seminary, 23: 387–416, September 1916.

1163. **Nelson, A. M.** The six-six plan in practice. Wisconsin journal of education, 48: 197–98, September 1916.

> Result of a brief summary made under Professor M. V. O'Shea in his educational seminar at the University of Wisconsin.

1164. **Osborn, William Q.** The story of a big school in a little town. American school board journal, 53: 15–17, 76, September 1916.

> The Eatonville high school, Eatonville, Washington.

1165. **Reinoehl, F. W.** Some fundamentals of the junior high school problem. American school board journal, 53: 19–20, September 1916.

> Read at a conference of superintendents and principals of schools at the University of North Dakota, May 18th, 1916.

TEACHERS: TRAINING AND PROFESSIONAL STATUS.

1166. **Barnum, Charlotte E.** Systematic guidance for teachers-in-training in the grades. Pedagogical seminary, 23: 348–59, September 1916.

> States that systematic guidance should be given in the formation of good teaching habits.

1167. A code of ethics for teachers. American school board journal, 53: 62–63, September 1916.

> Adopted by the New Jersey state teachers' association.

1168. **Deihl, J. D.** Directed teaching and directed observation—a correction and an explanation. School review, 24: 515–20, September 1916.

> A correction of statements made in an article by John C. Weigel in regard to the training of teachers of German at the University of Wisconsin.

1169. **Furst, Clyde.** Pensions for public school teachers. American school board journal, 53: 30–34, September 1916.

> Gives the fundamental principles "applicable to all pension systems which involve large groups"

1170. **Mississippi Valley historical association.** Normal school relation to high school teaching. Report of committee, presented at Nashville, April 28, 1916. History teacher's magazine, 7: 244–48, September 1916.

The place of the normal school in preparing high school history teachers.

1171. The professor of pedagogy—once more. Unpopular review, 6: 58–72, July–September 1916.

A reply to the defense of the professor of pedagogy in the April Unpopular review (item 667).

1172. **Stoutemyer, J. Howard.** The social status of the teaching profession. Pedagogical seminary, 23: 417–40, September 1916.

Bibliography: p. 489–40.
The conclusion is that the "social status varies directly with the professional training and fitness on the part of the teacher, and adequate return in salary and social esteem on the part of the state."

1173. **Thomas, J. M.** Training for teaching composition in colleges. English journal, 5: 447–57, September 1916.

1174. **Wolfe, A. B.** The graduate school, faculty responsibility, and the training of university teachers. School and society, 4: 423–33, September 16, 1916.

1175. **Young, Walter H.** Effects of unstable tenure of office. Journal of education, 84: 202–205, September 7, 1916.

Unstable tenure is shown to be one of the greatest hindrances to the progress of education.

HIGHER EDUCATION.

1176. **Bovingdon, John.** Can we improve upon the college lecture system? School and society, 4: 393–97, September 9, 1916.

The lecture system, since it does not meet the demands made upon education by the state, namely, teaching the pupil how to make decisions by himself and with others, should be abandoned for the discussion method, which provides "an environment more conducive to the training which life requires of men."

1177. **Britton, N. L.** The New York botanical garden and Columbia university. Columbia university quarterly, 18: 352–59, September 1916.

Describes the agreement for coöperative educational facilities between the Garden and the University.

1178. **Brush, H. R.** The junior college and the universities. School and society, 4: 357–65, September 2, 1916.

Paper read before the Faculty club of the University of North Dakota, February, 1916.
The author claims that the junior college will have a beneficial effect on universities by taking care of a class of student which the university cannot benefit.

1179. **Clark, Charles Upson.** What are colleges for? North American review, 204: 413–20, September 1916.

Discusses the effects upon college education of the elective system, the vocational movement, and extra-curriculum activities, and suggests raising the standards by a revised course of studies.

1180. **The College art association of America.** School and society, 4: 384–87, August 26, 1916.

Report of the committee appointed to investigate the condition of art instruction in universities and colleges of the United States.

1181. **Gildersleeve, Virginia C.** The purpose of college Greek. Educational review, 52: 174–82, September 1916.

1182. **Hartman, L. W.** Grading systems again. School and society, 4: 388-92, September 9, 1916.

A plan for standardizing grading in colleges, too small for the "Missouri plan," suggested by a committee appointed by the senate of the University of Nevada.

1183. **Hervey, William Addison.** The amateur graduate student. Columbia university quarterly, 18: 323-31, September 1916.

An address to the students of the Division of modern languages and literatures at the Spring conference, held April 18, 1916.

The author claims that in graduate work the practical, utilitarian motive must not be controlling; the student should be "an amateur while he is on the field, whether a professional before, or after, matters not."

1184. **Illinois. University.** University of Illinois directory, listing the 35,000 persons who have ever been connected with the Urbana-Champaign departments, including officers of instruction and administration and 1897 deceased, ed. by Vergil V. Phelps. . . . Urbana-Champaign, University of Illinois, 1916. cxii, 1284 p. front., plates, ports. 8°.

1185. **Jordan, David Starr.** Does the American college pay dividends on the investment? Forum, 56: 311-16, September 1916.

This article declares that the college system does justify itself, but it could be made more effective for the same money.

1186. **Lowell, Abbott Lawrence.** Liberty and discipline, a talk to freshmen; an address delivered to the freshman class of Yale college, October 15th, 1915, on the Ralph Hill Thomas memorial lectureship foundation. New Haven, Yale university press, 1916. 16 p. 8°.

1187. **Nettleton, George Henry,** *ed.* The book of the Yale pageant, 21 October 1916, in commemoration of the two hundredth anniversary of the removal of Yale college to New Haven. New Haven, Conn., Yale university press, 1916. x p., 1 l., 243, [1] p. front., illus. (incl. facsims.) plates, ports., plan. 4°.

CONTENTS.—The pageant.—Essays on Yale.

1188. **Phillips, John C.** A study of the birth-rate in Harvard and Yale graduates. Harvard graduates' magazine, 25: 25-34, September 1916.

Based on the class reports for graduates during the last half century. Shows a decrease in the birth-rate during that period.

1189. **Poole, Murray Edward.** A story historical of Cornell university, with biographies of distinguished Cornellians. Ithaca, N. Y., The Cayuga press, 1916. 227, [33] p. 8°.

1190. State higher educational institutions of Iowa; a report to the Iowa State board of education of a survey made under the direction of the Commissioner of education. Washington, Government printing office, 1916. 223 p. 8°. (U. S. Bureau of education. Bulletin, 1916, no. 19)

SCHOOL ADMINISTRATION.

1191. Brief and report on state uniformity and state publication of high-school textbooks by a joint committee representing California high-school teachers' association, California high-school principals' convention, California council of education, California teachers' association. 16 p. 8°. (Bulletin of the California teachers' association, Supplement to the Sierra educational news, September 1916)

1192. Brooks, E. C. The new textbooks adopted for five years. North Carolina education, 11: 3–4, September 1916.

Textbooks adopted by the North Carolina Sub textbook commission and the State board of education.

1193. Cubberley, Ellwood P. School organization and administration; a concrete study based on the Salt Lake City school survey. Yonkers-on-Hudson, N. Y., World book company, 1916. xiv, 346 p. 12°.

By E. P. Cubberley, assisted by J. B. Sears, L. M. Terman, J. H. Van Sickle, and J. H. Williams.

1194. Denver civic and commercial association. *Civic and legislative bureau. Committee on preparation of revised educational code.* Tentative outline of proposed educational code for the state of Colorado. [Denver, 1916] 27 p. 8°.

1195. Educational administration and supervision, vol. 2, no. 7, September 1916. (Junior high school number)

Contains: 1. C. H. Johnston: The junior high school, p. 418–24. 2. David Snedden: Reorganisation of education for children from 12 to 14 years of age, p. 425–32. 3. H. S. Weet: Rochester's junior high schools: a first step in establishing the six-three-three organization, p. 433–47. 4. C. R. Stacy: The training of teachers for intermediate schools, p. 448–55. 5. F. R. Park: The six and six plan of organization for the small school, p. 456–60. 6. E. H. Taylor: The course in mathematics in the junior high school, p. 460–65.

1196. Grey, A. A. School attendance. American school board journal, 53: 18–19, September 1916.

The author maintains that although a school census and better compulsory education and truancy laws would help in bettering school attendance, the real difficulty lies in the industrial conditions which result in poverty and necessitate child labor.

1197. Rowland, S. P. Standardization after one year. Kansas teacher, 3: 8–10, September 1916.

The county superintendent of Reno county, where almost one-third of the total number of the standard schools of Kansas are located, states that the experiment with standardization has been a success.

1198. Snedden, David. Scientific methods in educational administration. American school board journal, 53: 13, September 1916.

"From the Massachusetts state board of education report for 1915."

1199. Wilde, Arthur H. The high-school teacher's responsibility to the school budget. American school board journal, 53: 14, 79, September 1916.

The teacher should equip his department well, should know the relation of his department to others, and should understand the financial resources of the community.

SCHOOL MANAGEMENT.

1200. Fitzgerald, William J. Classroom management. Catholic educational review, 12: 97–108, September 1916.

Paper read before the convention of the Catholic educational association, Baltimore, Md., June 28, 1916.

1201. Foster, William Trufant. Should students study? Harper's monthly magazine, 133: 609–18, September 1916.

1202. **Heck, William H.** Correlation between amounts of home study and class marks. School review, 24: 588–49, September 1916.

1208. **Hunter, Fred M.** The socialized recitation. Nebraska teacher, 19: 80–82, September 1916.

1204. **Jones, Adam L.** Comprehensive examinations. Educational review, 52: 166–73, September 1916.

> Says that "comprehensive examinations unintelligently administered would be productive of as great harm as 'piecemeal' examinations similarly administered."

1205. **Lovett, A. J.** The school program. Oklahoma journal of education, 6: 2–4, September 9, 1916.

1206. **McAndrew, William.** Our old friend, the examination. American education, 20: 15–18, September 1916.

> Address before the secondary school section of the National education association.

SCHOOL HYGIENE AND SANITATION.

1207. **Ashcraft, F. R.** School hygiene is race hygiene. Associate teacher, 18: 19–21, September 1916.
> A plea for more thorough medical inspection of school children.

1208. **Greeg, F. M.** The most essential school subject. Middle-west school review, 9: 15–16, September 1916.
> The author considers hygiene the most essential subject.

1209. **Sundwall, John.** Organization and activities of a university health service. School and society, 4: 848–51, September 2, 1916.

> "It is the purpose of this communication to outline a plan of organization which is proving effective in the initiation and maintenance of activities concerned with student health" at the University of Kansas.

PHYSICAL TRAINING.

1210. **Mason, Samuel K.** The importance of teaching school children to swim. American city, 15: 314–16, September 1916.
> Gives the method of coöperation between the Bath department and the School department in Brookline, Mass.

1211. **Young, Charles V. P.** What American universities are doing. Physical culture, 36: 32–88, September 1916.
> By the director of physical training, Cornell university.

PLAY AND PLAYGROUNDS.

1212. **Foster, Warren Dunham.** Organized recreation. Pennsylvania school journal, 65: 61–64, August 1916.
> Address before the National education association, New York, July 8, 1916.
> A working plan for organizing recreation in city or country.

1218. **Rogers, James E.** Report of the recreation conditions and problems of Peoria, with recommendations and suggested system. Child welfare bulletin, 4: 147–78, August 1916.

1214. **Starks, Grace Evelyn.** The school playground. Popular educator, 34: 35–37, 58, September 1916.

> Suggestions for the teacher in a rural school where there is no trained director for the playground.

SOCIAL ASPECTS OF EDUCATION.

1215. **Flexner, Abraham.** Parents and schools. Atlantic monthly, 118: 25–33, July 1916.

1216. **Larson, Ruby P. M.** Entertainments and social events. Nebraska teacher, 19: 11–18, September 1916.

> Tells how to "create a closer fellowship between the school and the community, to unite them in a common interest."

MORAL EDUCATION.

1217. **Archer, William.** Knowledge and character. Educational review, 52: 119–43, September 1916.

> An address delivered at the annual meeting of the Moral education league, London, February 6, 1914. Based upon a paper read at a previous session, by Principal Griffiths, of the University of South Wales, which lamented that the present system of education "subordinated the development of character to the acquisition of knowledge."

1218. **Davis, Jesse B.** Recent progress in moral training and instruction in public high schools. American city, 15: 288–92, September 1916.

> A survey to show how suggestions made by a committee of the Religious education association in 1911 have been carried out.

1219. **Séailles, Gabriel.** L'éducation morale de la démocratie. Bibliothèque universelle et revue suisse, 83: 201–24, August 1916.

> Writer is a professor in the Sorbonne.

1220. **Stacy, Emma A.** Morning exercises for moral and civic training. Popular educator, 34: 9–12, 44, September 1916.

RELIGIOUS EDUCATION.

1221. **Leo,** *Brother.* The religious basis of pedagogy. Catholic school journal, 16: 169–71, 96, September 1916.

> The author examines "some of the ways in which the religious spirit vitally enters into the art of teaching."

1222. **Schoff,** *Mrs.* Frederic. Spiritual guidance of children: duty of home and church. Child-welfare magazine, 11: 18–20, September 1916.

> Given at the International training school for Sunday-school leaders. To be continued.

1223. **Shields, Thomas Edward.** Some relations between the Catholic school and the public school system. Catholic educational review, 12: 185–46, September 1916.

> Paper read at the annual convention of the Catholic educational association, Baltimore, June, 1916.

1224. **Wardle, Addie Grace.** Handwork in religious education. Chicago, Ill., The University of Chicago press [1916] 143 p. illus. 12°.

> "Books for reference": p. 136–40.

MANUAL AND VOCATIONAL TRAINING.

1225. **National society for the promotion of industrial education.** Proceedings ninth annual meeting, Minneapolis, January 20-22, 1916. New York City, 1916. 405 p. 8°. (Alvin E. Dodd, secretary, 140 West 42d street, New York City)

> With this is bound the Proceedings of Employment managers' conference, held under the auspices of the National society for the promotion of industrial education and the Minneapolis civic and commerce association, January 19-20, 1916. Bulletin of the United States Bureau of labor statistics, number 196. 82 p.
>
> Contains: 1. David Snedden: Some predictions as to the future of vocational education, p. 21-40. 2. Lucinda W. Prince: Present accomplishments and some future possibilities in training for department store work, p. 41-49. 3. Sara A. Conboy: Trade union ideals and vocational education, p. 50-56. 4. The Minneapolis survey, p. 85-125. 5. W. H. Henderson: Report of Minneapolis survey on trade agreements, p. 129-35. 6. F. D. Crawshaw: Report of survey on private schools giving industrial education, p. 136-40. 7. L. H. Carris: The county unit plan in the development of vocational education, p. 141-45. 8. W. E. Clark: The relation of the industrial teacher to the labor and manufacturing interests of the community, p. 146-53. 9. H. A. Hutchins: Publicity methods or the advertising of evening vocational schools, p. 154-63. 10. H. S. Schnell: Evening school organization and administration, p. 164-72. 11. Anna M. Cooley: The training of the teacher of household arts for the vocational school, p. 182-86. 12. Mrs. H. M. Hickok: Business of home-making, p. 187-95. 13. W. E. Hicks: A description of the continuation schools of Wisconsin, p. 203-11. 14. Violet Coen: Shop methods and the utilisation of product, p. 215-19. 15. Florence M. Marshall: Trade extension and part-time courses for girls in New York city, p. 220-25. 16. Sara A. Conboy: The value of the trade union movement to industrial education and wage workers, p. 233-36. 17. W. H. Henderson: The Wisconsin plan, p. 237-41. 18. C. R. Allen: The Massachusetts plan for the training of teachers for vocational schools, p. 242-46. 19. S. S. Edmands and W. A. O'Leary: What Pratt institute is doing to train teachers of trades, p. 249-60. 20. M. W. Murray: Broadening the training of industrial teachers in the service by industrial employment during vacation, p. 265-70. 21. Antoinette Roof: Provision for commercial experience during the period of training, p. 271-77. 22. H. W. Schmidt: Commercial shop experience for teachers, p. 281-88. 23. G. A. Works: Apprentice teacher training, p. 291-301. 24. A. C. Monahan: The status of teacher-training for agriculture in the United States, p. 302-305. 25. C. G. Selvig: The home project as the center vs. the home project as the outgrowth of agricultural instruction, p. 306-11. 26. L. S. Hawkins: Plans and records of home project instruction, p. 312-24. 27. R. C. Keople: The relation of the pre-vocational school to the rest of the school system, p. 325-34. 28. F. V. Thompson: Problems of industrial education under public administration, p. 337-46. 29. G. E. Barnett: Trade agreements and industrial education, p. 347-61. 30. A. S. Hurrell: How the high school can best serve industrial education, p. 366-73. 31. Cleo Murtland: Recommendations of the survey on women's work, p. 374-83.

1226. **Colegrove, C. P.** The educative value of manual training. West Virginia school journal and educator, 45: 182-83, September 1916.

> The author maintains that the educative value of manual training is proved by testing it by three fundamental principles of education.

1227. **Indlekofer, John N.** Cultural phases of vocational training. Manual training magazine, 18: 5-7, September 1916.

1228. **Johnston, Charles H.** Public instruction and public training. Educational review, 52: 152-65, September 1916.

> Discusses various phases of vocational instruction as presented by the Cooley bill and Teachers' substitute bill, proposed in Illinois as legislative solutions of industrial education.

1229. Leonard, R. J. Research for purposes of vocational education in Indiana. School and society, 4: 272–79, August 19, 1916.

The Indiana state board of education has appropriated funds for vocational research. The question of the scope of the problems to be studied and the methods of study are considered by the writer.

1230. Redfield, William C. Industrial education. American education, 20: 12–14, September 1916.

Address delivered at the general session of the National education association, New York city, July 5, 1916.

1231. Snedden, David. Vocational education in Massachusetts; some achievements and some prospects. Manual training magazine, 18: 1–4, September 1916.

Notes of an address given at a Conference of vocational school teachers, Worcester, Mass., May 26th, 1916.

1232. ———. What is vocational education? West Virginia school journal and educator, 15: 188–89, September 1916.

VOCATIONAL GUIDANCE.

1233. Bess, Elmer Allen. Training for vocation. School and society, 4: 433–39, September 16, 1916.

Discusses the need of specialists in vocational guidance, their qualifications and duties.

1234. Bonner, H. R. Necessity for vocational guidance. West Virginia school journal and educator, 45: 190, 204, 206, September 1916.

The author bases his contention on the answers to a questionnaire sent to three high schools in West Virginia.

1235. Gruenberg, Benjamin C. What's in a job? Scientific monthly, 3: 263–76, September 1916.

By the secretary of the Vocational guidance association of New York, who concludes: "Men and women should rejoice in their work, for that is the most of their life."

AGRICULTURAL EDUCATION.

1236. Heald, F. E. School credit for home practice in agriculture. Washington, Government printing office, 1916. 27 p. 8°. (U. S. Department of agriculture. Bulletin no. 385)

This bulletin is intended to assist superintendents and teachers of rural schools who desire to use home practice in agriculture as an educational feature, giving proper rank and credit on the school records. It may be procured from the Superintendent of documents, Washington, D. C., at 5 cents per copy.

1237. Meisnest, C. W. Harvest fairs in county and township schools. American city (Town and county ed.) 15: 255–58, September 1916.

1238. Nolan, A. W. Going up the road to the country. School news and practical educator, 30: 2–4, September 1916.

Initiatory ceremonies for boys' and girls' country life clubs leading to the degree of Master country man, in which Father Wisdom, Master Toil, and Country Gentleman examine the candidates.

HOME ECONOMICS.

1239. **Henegren, Marie.** Household arts and domestic science. Catholic school journal, 16 : 190–91, September 1916.

1240. **Keen, Charlotte.** Home economics in the Detroit schools. Journal of home economics, 8 : 479–87, September 1916.

1241. **Sellers, Edith.** An antediluvian on the education of working-class girls. Nineteenth century and after. 80 : 337–49, August 1916.

> Says that the English educational system gives too much time to teaching girls how to paint, dramatise, and botanise, and not enough to teaching them how to cook.

COMMERCIAL EDUCATION.

1242. **Smith, E. Newton.** Commercial education. Education, 37 : 51–61, September 1916.

> "The chief aim of commercial education should be to produce the highest possible degree of efficiency, to increase production, to make a just distribution in commercial labor, to make self-respecting, self-supporting, and contributing members of society, and thereby help in promoting social justice to all mankind."

PROFESSIONAL EDUCATION.

1243. **Dixon, Brandt V. B.** The present status of woman's education with special application to a better nursing education. American journal of nursing, 16 : 1072–76, August 1916.

> Address at a public meeting of the National league of nursing education, New Orleans, La., May 2, 1916.

1244. **Dunning, William B.** The Columbia university school of dentistry. Columbia university quarterly, 18 : 345–51, September 1916.

> Gives besides a description of the school a brief sketch of the growth of dental education.

1245. **Hammett, Frederick S.** Medical education in chemistry. Medical record, 90 : 503–6, September 16, 1916.

> Writer says it is lamentably self-evident that the average physician possesses little if any applicable knowledge of chemistry. This condition should be remedied.

MILITARY TRAINING.

1246. Schools and preparedness. School, 28 : 5, September 7, 1916.

> Three letters from principals of secondary schools to the New York Times in answer to its invitation for opinions on the new military training law of the state.

BOY SCOUTS.

1247. **West, James E.** [Boy scouts of America] Midland schools, 31 : 11–14, September 1916.

> Address at the National education association meeting, July 1916.

EXCEPTIONAL CHILDREN.

1248. **Hoag, Ernest Bryant.** Is your child a misfit? Mother's magazine, 11 : 29–30, September 1916.

> Give him special guidance. He is worth personal attention and individual training. Many of the world's greatest men have been thought misfits as children because they did not march in time with the public school lockstep.

1249. **Koch, Felix J.** Teaching the boys and the girls who can't hear. Ohio teacher, 37 : 10–12, August 1916.

> Interesting public school in the middle west which teaches deaf children.

1250. **Morris, Elise.** For the children of Nashville 100% efficiency. Mother's magazine, 11 : 31–33, September 1916.

> Physical, mental, and moral peculiarities are diagnosed, and the deformed, diseased, delinquent, and abnormal receive skilled treatment and individual training, to bring them to maximum efficiency.

1251. **Treloar,** *Sir* **William.** The vocational training of crippled boys : the work of the Lord Mayor Treloar cripples' college at Alton. Child, 6 : 591–601, September 1916. illus.

LIBRARIES AND READING.

1252. **Bostwick, Arthur E.** General principles involved in high-school library control. Library journal, 41 : 646–47, September 1916.

> Advocates administration of the school library by the public library.

1253. **Budlong,** *Mrs.* **Minnie Franklin (Clarke).** A plan of organization for small libraries; methods of work, lists of supplies and aids. Rev. ed. [Bismarck, N. Dak.] North Dakota Public library commission, 1916. 65 p. 8°.

1254. **Hopkins, Florence M.** A plea for the library in public schools. Education, 37 : 35–41, September 1916.

1255. **Johnston, Charles Hughes.** The need for an aggressive campaign for better school libraries. Library journal, 41 : 633–39, September 1916.

> Also in School and society, 4 : 381–88, September 9, 1916.
> Address delivered before the joint meeting of the Department of secondary education and the Library department of the National education association, New York city, July 1916.

DEPARTMENT OF THE INTERIOR
BUREAU OF EDUCATION

BULLETIN, 1916, NO. 25

COMMERCIAL EDUCATION

A REPORT ON THE
COMMERCIAL EDUCATION SUBSECTION OF THE
SECOND PAN AMERICAN SCIENTIFIC CONGRESS
DECEMBER, 1915–JANUARY, 1916

BY

GLEN LEVIN SWIGGETT
BUREAU OF EDUCATION
MEMBER COMMITTEE ON EDUCATION, NATIONAL FOREIGN TRADE COUNCIL
UNITED STATES CHAMBER OF COMMERCE

WASHINGTON
GOVERNMENT PRINTING OFFICE
1916

ADDITIONAL COPIES

OF THIS PUBLICATION MAY BE PROCURED FROM
THE SUPERINTENDENT OF DOCUMENTS
GOVERNMENT PRINTING OFFICE
WASHINGTON, D. C.
AT
10 CENTS PER COPY

CONTENTS.

3

CONTENTS.

LETTER OF TRANSMITTAL.

DEPARTMENT OF THE INTERIOR,
BUREAU OF EDUCATION,
Washington, August 28, 1916.

SIR: The program of the subsection on commercial education of the education section of the Pan American Scientific Congress, held in Washington City December 27, 1915, to January 8, 1916, was so comprehensive and the papers of such value that I requested Dr. Glen Levin Swiggett, assistant secretary general of the congress and chairman of the committee on commercial education, to prepare these papers for publication as a bulletin of the Bureau of Education. This he has done in such way as to preserve the best of the substance of these papers with as little repetition as possible. Because of the increasing general interest in commercial education in all parts of the country, and especially in the centers of urban population, I recommend that the manuscript transmitted herewith be published as a bulletin of this bureau.

Respectfully submitted.

P. P. CLAXTON,
Commissioner.

The SECRETARY OF THE INTERIOR.

5

COMMERCIAL EDUCATION.

The Second Pan American Scientific Congress convened in Washington, D. C., December 27, 1915, and adjourned January 8, 1916. The congress was held under the auspices of the Government of the United States and was recognized officially by the 21 Governments constituting the Pan American Union, all of which were represented by 111 official delegates.

This congress had its origin in the Latin-American Scientific Congress that was held in Buenos Aires in 1898 under the auspices of the Government of Argentina, on the occasion of the celebration of the Silver Jubilee of the distinguished Sociedad Científica Argentina. Subsequent congresses were held in Montevideo, 1901; Río de Janeiro, 1905; and Santiago de Chile, 1908. The last-named was called the First Pan American Congress owing to the generous invitation extended to the United States and that Nation's participation in the congress.

There has been a remarkable growth of interest in this organization on the part of the Governments and scientific and learned societies of the Western Hemisphere. The first congress emphasized a relatively larger degree of interest in pure science than have the subsequent ones, which have placed an increasingly larger emphasis upon questions bearing on the practical application of science. The latter received a preponderant attention in the Second Pan American Scientific Congress. There were 868 papers presented before this congress. The total membership was 2,566; from the United States, 1,899; from Latin America, 667. The following persons constituted the executive committee and officers of organization:

Executive Committee.

WILLIAM PHILLIPS, Third Assistant Secretary of State, chairman ex officio.
JAMES BROWN SCOTT, Secretary Carnegie Endowment for International Peace, vice chairman.
WILLIAM H. WELCH, President National Academy of Sciences, honorary vice chairman.
JOHN BARRETT, Director General Pan American Union.
W. H. BIXBY, Brigadier General United States Army, retired.
PHILANDER P. CLAXTON, Commissioner of Education.

WILLIAM C. GORGAS, Surgeon General United States Army.
WILLIAM H. HOLMES, Head Curator Smithsonian Institution.
HENNEN JENNINGS, former President London Institution Mining and Metallurgy.
GEORGE M. ROMMEL, Chief Animal Husbandry Division, Bureau of Animal Industry, Department of Agriculture.
L. S. ROWE, President American Academy of Political and Social Science.
ROBERT S. WOODWARD, President Carnegie Institution of Washington.

Organization Officers.

JOHN BARRETT, LL.D, secretary general.
GLEN LEVIN SWIGGETT, Ph. D., assistant secretary general.

The program of the congress was divided into nine main sections, which were in turn subdivided into 45 subsections. The program of each subsection was in charge of an officially appointed committee. The Commissioner of Education of the United States was the chairman of Section IV, Education. This section was one of the largest of the congress. Section IV and the 10 subsections, with their respective committees, were as follows:

SECTION IV—EDUCATION.

Chairman.—P. P. CLAXTON, Commissioner of Education of the United States.
Vice chairman.—S. P. CAPEN, Specialist in Higher Education, Bureau of Education, Washington, D. C.

SUBSECTION 1.—*Elementary Education.*

JOHN H. FINLEY, Commissioner of Education, State of New York, Albany, N. Y., chairman.
PAUL MONROE, Teachers' College, Columbia University, New York, N. Y.
ERNEST CARROLL MOORE, Department of Education, Harvard University, Cambridge, Mass.
M. P. SHAWKEY, State Superintendent of Schools, Charleston, W. Va.

SUBSECTION 2.—*Secondary Education.*

ELMER E. BROWN, Chancellor New York University, New York, N. Y., chairman.
JESSE BUTRICK DAVIS, Principal Central High School, Grand Rapids, Mich.
ALEXIS F. LANGE, Head of the Department of Education, University of California, Berkeley, Cal.
BRUCE R. PAYNE, President George Peabody College for Teachers, Nashville, Tenn.

SUBSECTION 3.—*University Education.*

EDMUND JANES JAMES, President University of Illinois, Urbana, Ill., chairman.
JOHN GRIER HIBBEN, President Princeton University, Princeton, N. J.
BENJAMIN IDE WHEELER, President University of California, Berkeley, Cal.
HARRY BURNS HUTCHINS, President University of Michigan, Ann Arbor, Mich.
WILLIAM OXLEY THOMPSON, President Ohio State University, Columbus, Ohio.

Subsection 4.—*Education of Women.*

Sarah Louise Arnold, Dean Simmons College, Boston, Mass., chairman.
Margaret Schallenberger, Commissioner of Elementary Education, State Department of Education, Sacramento, Cal.
Marion Talbot, Dean of Women, University of Chicago, Chicago Ill.
Mary E. Parker, Western Reserve University, Cleveland, Ohio.
Susan M. Kingsbury, Bryn Mawr College, Bryn Mawr, Pa.

Subsection 5.—*Exchange of Professors and Students.*

Nicholas Murray Butler, President Columbia University, New York, N. Y., chairman.
Edwin A. Alderman, President University of Virginia, Charlottesville, Va.
George E. Vincent, President University of Minnesota, Minneapolis, Minn.
Henry Suzzallo, President University of Washington, Seattle, Wash.

Subsection 6.—*Engineering Education.*

Arthur A. Hammerschlag, Director Carnegie Institute of Technology, Pittsburgh, Pa., chairman.
Frederick A. Goetze, Dean School of Mines, Columbia University, New York,
G. C. Anthony, Dean Engineering School, Tufts College, Mass.
R. M. Hughes, President Miami University, Oxford, Ohio.
Herman Schneider, Dean College of Engineering, University of Cincinnati, Cincinnati, Ohio.
Carl L. Mees, President Rose Polytechnic Institute, Terre Haute, Ind.
John B. Whitehead, Johns Hopkins University, Baltimore, Md.

Subsection 7.—*Medical Education.*

William Cline Borden, Dean Medical School, George Washington University, Washington, D. C., chairman.
C. E. Munroe, George Washington University, Washington D. C.
Paul Bartsch, George Washington University, Washington, D. C.
B. M. Randolph, George Washington University, Washington, D. C.
F. A. Hornaday, George Washington University, Washington, D. C.

Subsection 8.—*Agricultural Education.*

Winthrop Ellsworth Stone, President Purdue University, Lafayette, Ind., chairman.
Andrew M. Soule, President Georgia Agricultural College, Athens, Ga.
Robert J. Aley, President University of Maine, Orono, Me.
Raymond A. Pearson, President Iowa State College of Agriculture, Ames, Iowa.

Subsection 9.—*Industrial Education.*

William T. Bawden, Specialist in Industrial Education, Washington, D. C., chairman.
Charles A. Bennett, Bradley Polytechnic Institute, Peoria, Ill.
Charles A. Prosser, Director Dunwoody Industrial Institute, Minneapolis, Minn.
David Snedden, former Commissioner Massachusetts Board of Education, Boston, Mass.

Subsection 10.—*Commercial Education.*

Glen Levin Swiggett, Bureau of Education, Washington, D. C., chairman.
J. Paul Goode, University of Chicago, Chicago, Ill.
Frederick C. Hicks, Dean University of Cincinnati, Cincinnati, Ohio.

JEREMIAH W. JENKS, Director Division of Public Affairs, New York University, New York, N. Y.

L. C. MARSHALL, Dean College of Commerce and Administration, University of Chicago, Chicago, Ill.

DEVELOPMENT OF COMMERCIAL EDUCATION.

The subcommittee in charge of commercial education considered carefully the task of constructing a program and decided finally to invite the preparation of papers under topics that would give to these papers, when printed in the proceedings of the congress, the character of a dependable monograph on commercial education, a book for which there is great need, not only in the United States, but throughout Latin America as well. Commercial education has been the last of the so-called technical phases of education to receive attention and careful study on the part of educators. This is particularly true with reference to courses of study that prepare for foreign service, commercial and consular. The National Education Association has a department on business education and committees on vocational education and foreign relations, but the association has not given special attention to this phase of training. It has been left largely to extramural agencies, business and public activities, to awaken and stimulate the desire for the immediate introduction in schools and colleges of adequate preparatory courses of study on domestic and foreign trade. The National Foreign Trade Council has already prepared, through its committee on education, of which Mr. Wallace D. Simmons is chairman, a report based on a questionnaire submitted to the leading business men of the United States. Copies of this printed report may be obtained through the secretary, Mr. Robert Patchin, India House, Hanover Square, New York City. The Chamber of Commerce of the United States has appointed recently a committee of experts on vocational education, which is to include commercial education. The chairman of this committee is Mr. Frederick A. Geier, president of the Cincinnati Milling Machine Co. Information concerning the work of this committee may be obtained through Mr. Geier or through the secretary of the Chamber of Commerce of the United States, Mr. Elliot H. Goodwin, Riggs Building, Washington, D. C. The Commissioner of Education of the United States recently called a conference of representative educators, business men, and Government experts interested in the foreign aspect of business training. This conference was held Friday, December 31, 1915, during the sessions of the Second Pan American Scientific Congress. The president of the National Foreign Trade Council, Mr. James A. Farrell, presented on that occasion a notable address under the title "Preparation for Trade, Domestic and Foreign, from the Standpoint of the Business Man." A complementary paper, discussing the same question from the standpoint of the educator, was presented earlier in the same week by the dean of the graduate school of business administration of Harvard University. An abstract of Dean Gay's paper will be found in this bulletin, page 24. Pursuant to a resolution introduced at this conference, the Commissioner of Education has appointed a committee of 15 members to investigate the status of commercial education in the United States and other commercial nations, to recommend a course of study, and to suggest ways and means for its early establishment in educational institutions. Inquiries concerning the work of this committee should be addressed to the chairman, care of the Bureau of Education, Washington, D. C.

The following are members of this committee:

E. D. Adams, Professor of History, Leland Stanford University.
Morton A. Aldrich, Dean College of Commerce and Business Administration, Tulane University.
John Clausen, Manager Foreign Department, Crocker National Bank, San Francisco.
James C. Egbert, Director School of Business, Columbia University, New York City.
William Fairley, Principal Commercial High School, Brooklyn, N. Y.
J. F. Fish, President Northwestern Business College, Chicago, Ill.
Frederick C. Hicks, Dean College of Commerce, University of Cincinnati.
Lincoln Hutchinson, Professor of Commerce, University of California, and former American commercial attaché, Rio de Janeiro.
Jeremiah W. Jenks, Professor of Government, New York University.
Samuel MacClintock, Director La Salle Extension University, Chicago, Ill.
Samuel B. McCormick, Chancellor University of Pittsburgh.
Leo S. Rowe, Head Professor of Political Science, University of Pennsylvania.
John E. Treleven, Chairman School of Business Training, University of Texas.
Charles H. Sherrill, Counsellor at Law and Chairman Committee on Foreign Relations, United States Chamber of Commerce, New York City.
Glen Levin Swiggett, Bureau of Education, Chairman of the Committee.

The papers on commercial education of the Second Pan American Scientific Congress present a new body of material from which to proceed for further study and incorporation in the proceedings of subsequent congresses. In the earlier congresses the theme of commercial education was well-nigh negligible. The same remark holds true largely of vocational education in general, but applies in particular to commercial education. The program of the First Pan American Congress, at Santiago de Chile, contains titles of two papers on this subject by Prof. Francisco Araya Bennett, of Valparaiso, Chile. The titles of these papers are as follows:

1. "The desirability of introducing commercial education into the primary, secondary, and higher grades to meet the various requirements of business. The necessity also of maintaining supplementary courses for persons actually engaged in business."

2. "In what form should commercial instruction be carried on in professional schools for girls."

The earlier congresses seem to have omitted completely any consideration of this question. Deeming it, however, of paramount importance at this time, not only for economic reasons of higher efficiency in the organization of business and the marketing of products at home and abroad, but for less apparently selfish reasons of acquiring by study the international way of looking at things and of assisting in establishing international amity, the committee on commercial education, as mentioned above, constructed a program that would permit the definition of commercial education through a series of graded papers by persons expert in the particular phase of the subject which they were invited to discuss. Beginning with introductory papers presented by men prominent in business, education, and government, and proceeding through a symposium of brief talks which would show the intimate relations between the fields of education, business, and government in the establishment of commercial education, the program discussed carefully the general phases of this type of education in elementary, secondary, and higher schools, whether a part of, or separate from, the regular public-school system, and treated under separate headings each of the well-recognized subjects taught or to be taught in the curriculum of commercial education. Further, in view of the fact that certain private educational agencies, established solely for the purpose or as a part of a mercantile, manufacturing, or exporting system, have been prominent in the United States in offering specific or general courses of business, the committee included in its program papers from most of these agencies. The executive committee of organization of the Second Pan American Scientific Congress authorized the framing of certain topics, the discussion of which by a representative from each of the participating countries would create a series of Pan American conferences, with the idea that some joint action might be taken now or at some subsequent congress leading to mutual benefit in the carrying out of the resolutions consequent upon the discussion of the particular topics. The committee on commercial education submitted for discussion the following Pan American theme:

How can a nation prepare in the most effective manner its young men for a business career that is to be pursued at home or in a foreign country?

    (*a*) *In schools that are a part of the public-school system.*

    (*b*) *In schools of private endowment.*

    (*c*) *In special business schools of private ownership.*

Outline a course of study that will best prepare young men to engage in such a business career. Each suggested outline should consider not only the character of the educational system of the country for which the course of study is intended, but the desirability and practicability of a uniform course of business education for all Pan American countries.

The program on commercial education, prepared by the committee in charge, follows.

TUESDAY AFTERNOON, DECEMBER 28, 1915, 2.30 O'CLOCK.

Pan American Union Building.

Chairman: PHILANDER P. CLAXTON.

Joint session of Sections IV and IX, with program furnished by subsections on commercial education and commerce.

INTRODUCTORY REMARKS.

WILLIAM C. REDFIELD, Secretary of Commerce, Washington, D. C.
ANDREW J. PETERS, Assistant Secretary of the Treasury, Washington, D. C.
JOHN H. FAHEY, President, United States Chamber of Commerce, Boston, Mass.
EDMUND J. JAMES, President University of Illinois, Urbana, Ill.

GENERAL TOPIC.

Preparation for Trade, Domestic and Foreign.
  (a) *From the Standpoint of the Business Man.*[1]
      J. A. FARRELL, President, National Foreign Trade Council, New York, N. Y.
  (b) *From the Standpoint of the Educator.*
      EDWIN F. GAY, Dean, Graduate School of Business Administration, Harvard University, Cambridge, Mass.

WEDNESDAY MORNING, DECEMBER 29, 9.30 O'CLOCK.

Pan American Union Building.

Acting Chairman: S. P. CAPEN.

Is There a Profession of Business, and Can We Train for It?
    ELLIOT H. GOODWIN, Secretary, U. S. Chamber of Commerce, Washington, D. C.
The Proper Use of Business Experts in Class Instruction on Domestic and Foreign Commerce. (Symposium—five-minute talks.)
    ROGER W. BABSON, President, Babson's Statistical Bureau, Wellesley Hills, Mass.
    EDWARD N. HURLEY, Chairman, Federal Trade Commission, Washington, D. C.
    WALLACE D. SIMMONS, Chairman, Committee on Education, National Foreign Trade Council, Philadelphia, Pa.
    B. OLNEY HOUGH, Editor, "American Exporter," New York, N. Y.
    WILBUR J. CARR, Director, Consular Service, Washington, D. C.[1]
    HARRY ERWIN BARD, Secretary, Pan American Society for the United States, New York, N. Y.
    J. F. CROWELL, Executive Officer, Chamber of Commerce of State of New York, New York, N. Y.

[1] Presented before the Conference on Foreign Service Training, Friday, Dec. 31.

The Proper Use of Business Experts, etc.—Continued.

JOHN CLAUSEN, Manager, Foreign Department, Crocker National Bank, San Francisco.

E. T. GUNDLACH, Gundlach Advertising Co., Chicago, Ill.

WEDNESDAY AFTERNOON, DECEMBER 29, 2.30 O'CLOCK.

Pan American Union Building.

Acting Chairman: ROGER W. BABSON.

Commercial Education.

In Latin America—

EDGAR E. BRANDON, Dean, Miami University, Oxford, Ohio.

In England—

I. L. KANDEL, Carnegie Foundation for the Advancement of Teaching, New York, N. Y.

In Germany—

FREDERICK ERNEST FARRINGTON, Special Collaborator, Bureau of Education, Washington, D. C.

THURSDAY MORNING, DECEMBER 30, 9.30 O'CLOCK.

Pan American Union Building.

Acting Chairman: ROGER W. BABSON.

Modern Business and the New Orientation of Commercial Education.

ISAAC GRINFELD, Director, International Correspondence Schools, Buenos Aires, Argentine Republic.

(*a*) *Preparation for a Business Career in Chile.*

(*b*) *Latin-American Standpoint on Business Education.*

FRANCISCO ARAYA BENNETT, Attorney at Law, University Professor of Political Economy and Principal Commercial Institute, Valparaiso, Chile.

The Arguments for a Separate or Combined Course of Commercial Study.

ROSWELL C. McCREA, Dean, The Wharton School, University of Pennsylvania, Philadelphia, Pa.

What Can the Small College Do in Training for Business?

GEORGE W. HOKE, Miami University, Oxford, Ohio.

How to Procure Adequately Prepared Instructors for Colleges and Universities.

JAMES C. EGBERT, Director School of Business, Columbia University, New York, N. Y.

THURSDAY AFTERNOON, DECEMBER 30, 2.30 O'CLOCK.

Pan American Union Building.

Acting chairman: ROGER W. BABSON.

The Problem of Commercial Education in (*a*) *Elementary Schools.* (*b*) *Secondary Schools.* (*c*) *Colleges.*

(*a and b*) *Elementary and Secondary Schools—Foundation; Subjects: Articulation, Correlation, and Methods.*

(*a*) F. G. NICHOLS, Director Business Education, Department of Public Instruction, Rochester, N. Y.

(*b*) PAUL MONROE, Teachers College, Columbia University, New York, N. Y.

DAVID SNEDDEN, former Commissioner of Education of Massachusetts, Boston, Mass.

(c) Colleges—Entrance Requirements.

DAVID KINLEY, Dean Graduate School, University of Illinois, Urbana, Ill.

W. F. GEPHART, Professor of Economics, Washington University, St. Louis, Mo.

MONDAY MORNING, JANUARY 3, 9.30 O'CLOCK.

Pan American Union Building.

Acting chairman: ALBERT A. SNOWDEN.

The Teaching of Special Subjects in the Collegiate Course of Study for Business, Domestic and Foreign.

Languages—

GLEN LEVIN SWIGGETT, Bureau of Education, Washington, D. C.

Geography—

J. PAUL GOODE, University of Chicago, Chicago, Ill.

History—

WM. R. SHEPHERD, Columbia University, New York, N. Y.

Government—

JESSE S. REEVES, University of Michigan, Ann Arbor, Mich.

Mathematics—

EVERETT W. LORD, Boston University, Boston, Mass.

Banking and Finance—

CHARLES LEE RAPER, University of North Carolina, Chapel Hill, N. C.

Business Law—

WARD W. PIERSON, the Wharton School, University of Pennsylvania, Philadelphia, Pa.

Business Ethics and Psychology—

JAMES E. LOUGH, New York University, New York, N. Y.

Organization and Administration—

ARTHUR E. SWANSON, Northwestern University, Evanston, Ill.

Statistics—

E. DANA DURAND, University of Minnesota, Minneapolis, Minn.

Accounting—

JOHN B. GEIJSBEEK, Foster Building, Denver, Colo.

DONALD F. GRASS, Leland Stanford Junior University, California.

MONDAY AFTERNOON, JANUARY 3, 2.30 O'CLOCK.

Pan American Union Building.

Acting chairman: ALBERT A. SNOWDEN.

Special Schools of Secondary Grade: Raison d'être; character and method of instruction.

Commercial High School—

WILLIAM FAIRLEY, Principal, Commercial High School, Brooklyn, N. Y.

Young Men's Christian Association—

EDWARD L. WERTHEIM, Director, West Side Y. M. C. A., New York City.

Business Colleges—

C. C. GAINES, President, Eastman Business College, Poughkeepsie, N. Y.

Value of Commercial Education—

WILLIAM JENNINGS BRYAN.

TUESDAY MORNING, JANUARY 4, 9.30 O'CLOCK.

Pan American Union Building.

Acting Chairman: FREDERICK C. HICKS.

Special Schools of Commercial Education of College and University Grade.
Tulane University.
> DEAN MORTON A. ALDRICH, College of Commerce and Business Administration, New Orleans, La.

University of Cincinnati: Continuation and Evening Courses.
> DEAN FREDERICK C. HICKS, College of Commerce, Cincinnati, Ohio.

University of Oregon: Problems of the Detached School.
> HARRY B. MILLER, Director, School of Commerce, Eugene, Oreg.

New York University: Two-Year Course and Individualization of Training for Business.
> JEREMIAH W. JENKS, Director, Division of Public Affairs, New York University, New York, N. Y.

The Graduate School of Business:
> *Amos Tuck School of Administration and Finance, Dartmouth College.*
> DEAN H. S. PERSON, Hanover, N. H.
> *Harvard Graduate School of Business Administration.*
> DEAN EDWIN F. GAY, Cambridge, Mass.

TUESDAY AFTERNOON, JANUARY 4, 2.30 O'CLOCK.

Pan American Union Building.

Acting Chairman: ROGER W. BABSON.

Special Courses for Commercial Study. Statement as to Aims and Achievements since Establishment.
Correspondence Schools.
> T. J. FOSTER, President, International Correspondence Schools, Scranton, Pa.
> SHERWIN CODY, Director, National Associated Schools of Scientific Business, Chicago, Ill.

University Extension Work for Men in Business.
> SAMUEL MACCLINTOCK, Director, La Salle Extension University, Chicago, Ill.

Alexander Hamilton Institute.
> JOSEPH FRENCH JOHNSON, Dean School of Commerce, Accounts, and Finance, New York University, New York, N. Y.

National Association of Corporation Schools.
> LEE GALLOWAY, Secretary, Alexander Hamilton Institute, New York, N. Y.

Commercial Museum.
> W. P. WILSON, Director, Commercial Museum, Philadelphia, Pa.

The National City Bank.
> F. C. SCHWEDTMAN, Educational Director, the National City Bank, New York, N. Y.

Bureau of Commercial Economics.
> FRANCIS HOLLEY, Director, Bureau of Commercial Economics, Washington, D. C.

FRIDAY AFTERNOON, JANUARY 7, 2.30 O'CLOCK.

New Willard Hotel.

Chairman: JOSÉ MARIA GÁLVEZ.

Discussion of the Pan American Topic:

How can a nation prepare in the most effective manner its young men for a business career that is to be pursued at home or in a foreign country?

   (a) In schools that are a part of the public-school system.

   (b) In schools of private endowment.

   (c) In special business schools of private ownership.

Outline a course of study that will best prepare young men to engage in such a business career. Each suggested outline should consider not only the character of the educational system of the country, for which the course of study is intended, but the desirability and practicability of a uniform course of business education for all Pan American countries.

Papers presented by—

   SANTIAGO H. FITZSIMON, Professor International Correspondence Schools, Buenos Aires, Argentina.

   AGUSTÍN T. WHILAR, Lima, Peru.

   ANTONIO L. VALVERDE, Professor, School of Commerce, Habana, Cuba.

   A. AUBERT, Managua, Nicaragua.

   M. DELLEY, Caracas, Venezuela.

   FRANCISCO ARAYA BENNETT, Valparaiso, Chile.

In the belief that the main facts of the papers presented before the subsection on commercial education should be made known as early as possible, the Commissioner of Education of the United States requested the publication of the abstracts of these papers in advance of the publication of the latter in the proceedings of the Second Pan American Scientific Congress. These abstracts have been made by the writers of the papers or by the compiler of this bulletin. In a few cases the statement is taken from the official stenographic report.

FIRST SESSION.

The Secretary of Commerce of the United States, under whose direction the Department of Commerce has shown a keen interest in the early establishment of commercial education in schools and colleges, was the first speaker at the opening session of this subsection. Mr. Redfield spoke, in part, as follows:

It is a sad fact that in business of all lands science and commerce have been greatly divorced. They have looked at each other askance, and not in this country alone, for there have been in America, and there still are, men who speak of the "practical" things as distinguished from the scientific thing; who argue that the scientific mind is the most modest of all minds if it be truly scientific, because it is that mind which seeks ever for the new truth. And this antagonism between the so-called practical and the scientific method has been deeply hurtful to American commerce; has resulted too much in the reign, now largely passing, of what we may call the "rule of thumb." I find in a newspaper published this week what will strike you, I am sure, strangely as the title of the article. It reads, "Adapting Science to Commerce." As if science, after all, was to come to be a servant and handmaiden of this thing we call commerce! I hope there yet may be a larger development of this thought, and that we shall come to recognize our own beginnings, at least, of a science of commerce, that we shall consider commerce itself as a matter requiring in very truth a scientific training.

And now, how do we make the science with which we have to deal the servant of commerce? I purpose to touch only very briefly on a little of what the scientific work of the Government does, so far as we have to do with it. First, as to how it affects the commerce of the country; for, to my thinking, we shall never reach what the commerce of America ought to be; it will never be the friend of our country and the other countries that it is possible it may be; it will never spread its influence abroad as it ought to do until we picture the United States aiding her commerce with the light that science can shed upon it. We need our industries; we greatly need the aid and constant thought of scientific men. We are as yet bunglers in much of our commercial work. We are attempting to do a great deal of commercial work all over the land with untrained and untaught instruments. We have not yet developed a class of trained commercial men. If you knew the difficulty we have to get men fit to go into the lands at the south, fit to be seen in the presence, as the equals in mind and training, of the great merchants and bankers and business men of the great South and Central Americas, you would realize this more fully. The simple question: What modern languages does this gentleman speak? mows down like a scythe the great mass of applicants for commercial work. In what particular branch of commerce is the gentleman trained? acts like a sickle. The few we are able to get are pitifully few as compared with the needs that exist for trained men, speaking the languages of the living world, and not the dead languages, and knowing something at least of what commerce means in all its broad significance. For the modern conquistador of commerce leaves no ruins in his path. He is a builder up of things. He is not the man who tramples with the iron heel of war, but he is a true constructor. He draws nations together; and just as the conquistador of old had to be trained for his fierce and cruel war, so the conquistador of to-day needs to be trained for his work of useful living, of helpful service. And we know perfectly well that to send men out into the great commercial arenas of this world untaught, untrained, with what we are pleased sometimes to call a general education, is to send him to defeat, and to submit the nation to harm because the man is not equipped for the task. That is a branch of commercial education which has its manifold phases. I could not as much as touch upon them all here to-day, but I may lift a corner of the veil which shows how true it is that the scientific man of this hour is the servant and supporter of commerce, and how upon his work commerce is building. If it were not for applied biology, there would be no pearl-button industry in America. I presume there are a great many pearl buttons in this audience. You take them and use them, pay a few cents for them without one thought that it requires constant active work of biological scientists to provide so simple a matter as a pearl button. And yet if we did not have applied biology your pearl buttons would be very high-priced, because the supply of them now comes from the rivers of the Mississippi Valley and the supply was long ago threatened to be exhausted. How was the supply replenished? That meant that some one, somewhere, must find where the fresh-water clam came from, for it is his shell that provides the raw material from which the pearl button is obtained.

I should like to talk to you about the researches in the Bureau of Standards; to go into the great facts, the great truths which underlie our industries. There we keep something like 400 young scientific men working all the time. Did it ever strike you that there is no such thing as a standard of color? That your views and your fellowman's views as to what was red, yellow, or green may be different? There is no such thing as a standard red. Did you ever realize that there are great industries depending upon accurate colors? And there is no standard by which these things can be positively determined; so that I doubt if there is anyone in this room who could say with accuracy as to red, green, blue, or yellow. If I asked you to bring me red, I am sure 20 different shades, if not 200, would be brought. These things have to be known. There are industries depending upon a definite known standard of color, such as oleomargarine, butter, cottonseed oil. We are working at the department on what standards of color are. It is our duty to go into many facts which are a little beyond the ordinary things of living and bring them out and see if we can determine the lines by which nature operates and make them useful to mankind.

In all this we are simply the servants of commerce, and it rejoices us day by day and more and more to see the recognition of this service coming from the men who are the great producers of the commercial world, until we have come to believe that the veil is lifting and the scientific man is finding his place, and that we shall add to the science of commerce as it should be done by trained men in science, in all its bearings, backing up commerce by scientific truth and supporting commerce in its final phases.

The Assistant Secretary of the Treasury, Hon. Andrew J. Peters, followed the Secretary of Commerce, and in his remarks, particularly timely because of his intimate knowledge of the very successful achievements of the recent Pan American financial conference, convoked in the city of Washington by the Secretary of the Treasury, addressed himself, among other things, to the question of training for foreign trade. Mr. Peters said:

Since the outbreak of the European war interest in foreign trade in the United States has been something entirely unparalleled in our previous experience. During the last half century, when our foreign trade has been growing steadily from year to year, we have not had the same attitude toward foreign trade which the people in the principal nations of Europe have had. In the first place, we have not possessed a merchant marine. Thus our foreign trade has been physically in the hands of the people of other commercial nations. We have exported chiefly raw materials and agricultural products which practically sold themselves, and consequently did not have to go out and study foreign markets and possible foreign outlets for our principal export products. Instead, the representatives of foreign merchandising concerns and the foreign merchants came to us and took off our hands what we had to supply, and there was the end of the transaction. All the merchandising problems, with a few notable exceptions, were solved for us by the mere force of economic conditions. We were anxious to sell only to the same extent that foreign buyers were anxious to buy.

The result of it all has been that foreign trade has not offered a career to a large number of Americans in the same way that foreign trade has offered a career to a large number of Englishmen, a large number of Dutchmen, Germans, and Frenchmen. The peoples of those nationalities have for years been marketing manufactured products, and manufactured products which required the cultivation of sales ability and vigorous penetration into foreign markets. Those countries have been developing their merchant marines and have been actually handling their own export commodities up to the time when they reached the consumers in foreign lands. Foreign commerce in those countries has consequently for years offered a career. In England young men starting in business have been confronted with specific opportunities to go to the colonies and to go to foreign countries representing English industrial concerns. In France the development has been along the same lines, though on a smaller scale. In our country we have thought of " the learned professions," the Army and Navy, and possibly some other branches of Government service under the conception of a career. Certainly the ordinary employee beginning with a commercial concern has had no such lofty idea as that of a career ahead of him. He has had a job, no very definite aims or ambitions; if another line of employment offered a better job he would take it no matter how far removed it might be from the line he was in before, if he thought he could hold down the new job, liked the firm, etc.

We must acknowledge that Germany is indisputably ahead of us in the whole matter of vocational training, and though the development of the fine network of schools of commerce in that country is recent, the system has brought and is bringing such good results that the appropriations for the extension of this kind of instruction have not been begrudged. It is in these schools that the Germans get the training which fits them for commerce as a career; those who select foreign commerce, world commerce, receive the proper training for their chosen work. Before 1880 the commercial schools (Handelsschulen) were almost unknown even in their elementary forms, and it is only since 1890 that their development has been really notable. The commercial schools were at first looked upon as superfluous or as specializing too early or too highly. Gradually, however, the various governments, the trade organizations, the chambers of commerce, came to realize the importance of this class of instruction, and to-day in Germany the higher institutions of learning devoting special attention to the training of men to meet the vast problems of world trade are better established and better equipped than those of any other country. The trade schools teach the artisan how to apply science and skill in the handicraft-employments, and the commercial schools educate the merchant, the wholesaler, the world dealer, the great banker, the consular officer—in short, the men who stand at the head of the commerce of the Empire. It is felt that both systems of education are necessary for the successful development of the manufacturing industry and the marketing of commodities, upon which, in truth, the success of the manufacturing industry so largely depends. A few years ago United States Deputy Consul Meyer made an interesting report on the development of these schools and on the attitude toward them in Germany. This report was published by the Department of Commerce as Special Consular Reports, volume 33. Mr. Meyer has pointed out that in Germany education invests a man with a peculiar social prestige, irrespective of his personality. The social standing of the mercantile classes has been elevated by a higher education in the schools of the type of the commercial high schools. Instruction in these schools is given not only by the regular professors, but is in a very large measure given by practical men of affairs. The effort has constantly been made to safeguard the instruction from becoming too academic and including too practical aspects; that is, to keep the instruction from becoming of a typical professorial sort. In one or another of the schools practically all the languages of the civilized world are taught, not only the ordinary commercial languages which are a subject of instruction in our universities, but even the most outlandish tongues, such as the bantu and other negro dialects which prevail in some sections of Africa where the Germans have been seeking foreign trade.

In our Government service we have recently expanded our foreign trade work in consequence of the ever-increasing demand for such work on the part of American manufacturers. I have been informed that the Department of Commerce and the Department of State have experienced difficulty particularly in getting men with the proper education and training to do this class of work. In language training most candidates have been decidedly deficient. The Bureau of Foreign and Domestic Commerce of the Department of Commerce has been conducting examinations practically every month during the year 1915. Candidates have reported that they have studied French, German, or Spanish for so-and-so many years in our universities, and when the tests have come it has been shown that they are woefully deficient in practical knowledge of the languages. Their training in commercial geography and in matters relating to the technique of the export trade has been equally deficient. Perhaps the most discouraging feature in this problem is that the leaders in our schools and colleges seem unable or unwilling to see the need, or, having seen it, are unable or unwilling to give the thorough instruction necessary. If ever the educator had a definite, concrete problem to solve, it is this. Up to the present time there are no appreciable results. Several of the commercial schools and colleges are giving excellent instruction to young men intending to engage in business in this country, and some are offering good courses in foreign trade. But these courses have not been grouped so as to give the all-around training necessary for success in export trade; the language work is inadequate, and no opportunity is provided to acquire the requisite practical experience.

Mr. Fahey, president of the Chamber of Commerce of the United States, called attention in his paper to the increasing interest on the part of the business men in the United States in the schools of the country; and to the fact that emphasis is being laid upon education for business and commerce as never before. Referring to the successful High School of Commerce in Boston, he said:

This school has been established something like nine years now, and at present is educating a little less than 1,600 pupils. The course is a four-year course. The average number of graduates is in the neighborhood of 200; and as an evidence of the value of this type of education, the fact that there is a demand for it, you will be interested to know that fully 70 per cent of the graduates have positions waiting for them two and three months before completing their education, and most of the others are quickly snapped up by the business houses of Boston and Massachusetts. The system has been developed to a point where, in the view of our local business men, it is meeting their needs in a most satisfactory way. The school has an advisory committee composed of business men among the business men of our community who give their time willingly in superintending the courses of study and the detail work. Moreover, they are devoting their time to series of lectures on the part of the business men to the pupils of the school. The young men in the school do a certain amount of continuation work in that a large proportion of them secure positions during the holiday season and during the summer vacations in business houses in and about Boston. The records they have made there have been most satisfactory. There is being developed in connection with the school a rather promising commercial museum. We are likewise raising the funds for scholarships to send young men abroad to take up special courses of study, fitting them for their life work. As evidence of very practical work, there is maintained now within the school a savings bank, as a branch of a local bank, all the detail work being done by the pupils of the school, and only the results when accumulated turned over to the banking institution. That has given not only a mental training, but a physical training is not overlooked. It has been realized by our men that these youngsters who are trained at our schools serve their purposes in life most when they are personally strong as well as mentally fit. An elaborate system of gymnastics, therefore, is encouraged, with satisfactory results.

Work along these lines is also being done with most satisfactory results in the New York High School of Commerce; also at Detroit, Springfield, and Providence, and a number of other cities. It is being taken up rapidly by one town after another. As a result more business men, chambers of commerce, and boards of trade have cooperated with educational systems.

For one, I believe that the cooperation which has already gone on can go still further; first of all, so far as business organizations are concerned, I think that every city of any size in this country ought to have an intelligent, efficient organization as a part of the system, a business organization. Moreover, some scheme might be developed that would lead to a great international cooperation between schools and between the business men themselves. There is an appreciation of that need, not only on the part of legal business organizations, but on the part of the national federation which is represented by the chamber of commerce, in that we have a committee on education, and that, aside from that, we are just completing a special committee to undertake to go into university needs and to devise better means for the promotion of cooperation between them than have existed so far. Organized methods should be devised for the interchange of students between the countries of North and South America, and better organized methods should likewise be worked out for a closer cooperation between the business men of the countries. So far as the students are concerned, I know some demands have already been made on the part of the South American countries to place young men in the business houses and manufacturing establishments in this country, and because it has been more or less haphazard it has not been as successful as it should be. Much better results will be secured if they undertake to organize. I know the Chamber of Commerce of the United States will be glad to cooperate with the chambers of commerce and other business bodies of South America to help in this direction.

President Edmund J. James, of the University of Illinois, and Dean Edwin F. Gay, of the Harvard Graduate School of Business Administration, who rank easily among the best-informed educators in the United States on the subject of business training, presented papers at this session, speaking largely from the standpoint of the educator.

President James said in part:

Thirty-two years ago this autumn I joined the faculty of the Wharton School of Finance and Economy of the University of Pennsylvania. This school was an integral part of the college department of the University of Pennsylvania. So far as I know, it represented in its origin and development the first real attempt either in Europe or America to develop a center of higher learning in intimate connection with the other important faculties of our historic universities, to provide a curriculum of university grade and university character which it would be worth the while of the future business man to complete before beginning the practical work of his career.

Many of the subjects which entered into the curriculum of this school had, of course, been for a long time objects of cultivation in university centers, both in Europe and America. Economics in the widest sense of the term, politics, history, had been, of course, important subjects of study in university centers since their establishment. More practical subjects, like bookkeeping and accounting, commercial geography, and similar subjects, had been utilized in the secondary schools and in special technical preparatory schools in all countries. A course in commercial education had been organized and conducted for a brief period in the University of Illinois in the latter part of the seventies, but it did not succeed, according to the ideas of the men responsible for the conduct of the institution, and was soon dropped.

The great commercial schools in Europe, such as those at Antwerp, Leipzig, Vienna, and Paris, had no intimate connection, and, generally speaking, no connection at all, with the universities or university life of their respective countries. In fact, it was felt that there was nothing in the business career, nothing in the subjects with which a business man busied himself, which offered any good ground for including them within the university curriculum or locating their cultivation at the university centers.

In this sense, therefore, the Wharton School of Finance and Economy represented a real departure. Its organization, development, and great success marked an epoch in the development of this important side of higher learning. The Wharton School of Finance and Economy has been a pioneer and has influenced the policy, not merely of this country, but of foreign countries as well. I think it is not too much to say that the establishment of the commercial courses at Manchester and the other provincial English universities, the affiliation of the great schools of commerce in Berlin, Leipzig, and Munich with the universities can be traced pretty directly toward the movement inaugurated and ever pressed by this original university school of business.

If the university, therefore, is to become a center of training for the future business man, it must have a set of sciences by the acquisition of which it can give this fundamental training which shall prepare a man for the largest success in a business way.

This was to a considerable extent the greatest obstacle which we had to overcome in initiating the work of the Wharton School of Finance and Economy. There was little or no valuable literature accessible to the student bearing on the subjects which he might wish to pursue as a part of his training for business. One reason why the movement has received such a great impetus in the second 15 years as compared with what was possible in the first 15 years of this development is to be found in the fact that we are finally developing a literature worth studying, worth reading in the English university sense of the term "reading."

I expect to see the university in the United States of America a center for the scientific study of business and for valuable scientific contributions to our knowledge of business. I expect to see our practical people turning more and more toward the university as the place from which thoughtful logical analysis and criticism of business methods and business practices shall proceed. I expect to see further the business world coming to an ever greater realization of the fact that they can find in the young men who have had this business training of the university most valuable assistants, men who can do in 5

years or 10 years what untrained men can not do in a generation, and many
times can not do at all. If this comes about, the young man who is looking
forward to a business career, who is expecting to become a banker or a railroad officer, or an insurance officer, or the head of a merchandising firm, will
think as little of going into any one of these businesses without a preparatory
university training as the youngster thinks to-day of following a medical career
without going to a medical school, or a legal career without attending a law
school, or an engineering career without completing the course of an engineering
school.

The following is an abstract of Dean Edwin F. Gay's paper:

The educational organization has not kept pace with the industrial organization since the great changes wrought by the industrial revolution. In the
earlier period the educational system, including apprenticeship as well as
formal schooling, was adapted vocationally to the social needs. The factory
system undermined apprenticeship, the type of education evolved under the
handicraft system, and has put nothing in its place. The readjustment of the
educational organization has been retarded in taking over this work not only
by its traditional conservatism, but by the pressure, imposed by political
democracy, of extending elementary education to include all classes. This
great task having been successfully undertaken, attention has been turned in
recent decades to the problem of vocational training. In this direction industrial education has earlier worked out a clearer program for future progress
than commercial education. Training within the business, such as that provided by the older apprenticeship system and more recently by the corporation
school, is inadequate for present conditions. The older established commercial
courses in the high school have been limited to clerical education. The secondary schools and colleges are now called upon to develop their commercial
training, and they have made a promising commencement in this work. In
relation to the whole field, the schools of business administration have the
especial function of leadership in research. A fuller content and a more advanced theoretical basis must be given to the courses of study leading to a
business career, and it is for this reason that emphasis should be laid for the
present upon the opportunity and responsibility of the schools of college grade.
The growing international competition is likely to compel a more serious attention to educational problems, especially in their vocational aspects.

SECOND SESSION.

The second session of this subsection was held Wednesday morning, December 29, in the building of the Pan American Union. This
session was carried on as a symposium in which several experts took
part, speaking to the topic, " *The proper use of business experts from
the business world in class instruction on domestic and foreign commerce.*" Introducing this symposium, the secretary of the Chamber
of Commerce of the United States, Mr. Elliot H. Goodwin, presented
a paper on "*Is there a profession of business and can we really train
for it?*" In Mr. Goodwin's opinion the feasibility of training for
business must be decided by the business men themselves; for the

result which advocates of commercial training seek is an increased demand by business heads for trained subordinates, a demand that will be based upon an increasing success of school-trained over office-trained men and must lead to an increased number of students. Enlightened business opinion, he said, has been the incentive and moving force which has created the growth and support of commercial education in this country and has led to the installation of courses of business administration.

Mr. Goodwin said in part:

Whatever skepticism on the part of business men may have existed in the past in regard to the practicability of commercial training certainly has been greatly lessened in the face of the crisis through which we are now passing. The lessons of the war in regard to business come home particularly to those engaged in intercourse between North and South America. What more than any other one thing stands in the path of complete development of commercial relations between the nations of the south, cut off from their usual sources of financial aid and industrial supplies, and that rich nation of the northern continent, seeking new markets for its oversupply above domestic consumption? In the face of the emergency and the opportunity bitterly must we, north and south, in Pan America regret that lack of real commercial education which goes beyond languages, commercial usages, international banking, credits, and foreign trade—needs which we are endeavoring to supply by emergency schools and classes—to those fundamentals of successful commercial intercourse, knowledge of geography, racial conditions, history, customs, and social life. The cataclysm of the European war caught the Americas, North and South, commercially unprepared, and that unpreparédness lies mainly in the lack of commercial education.

Competition in business is becoming keener, success is requiring a greater degree of knowledge, breadth, and ability. The development of foreign trade has brought the American merchant in touch with foreign competitors, and the lessons thus learned as to new methods of doing business have been reflected at home. It is one thing to compete with your fellow countryman in the home market behind the protection of a tariff wall, and a totally different thing to break into the foreign market where a foreign competitor has already intrenched himself and compete with him with no protection of any kind. The lessons thus learned have their application to domestic competition. The field for business education is there. How it shall be taught and how far it can practically be carried, are the main questions. Clearly the school of practical experience produces but a small proportion of men with large business capacity. As a method of training it is wasteful. It is equally clear that the college or university commercial training can not be expected to graduate only those of marked business ability any more than law schools produce great lawyers or medical schools produce great surgeons. Much remains with the man himself, his inborn capacity and power to expand. Yet professional training for lawyers and doctors is now universally accepted. What is there about business capacity or executive ability that would place them beyond the pale of those things for which a special education is valuable? Is it the power to handle men? Then, the traning of the army officer or the professor should be equally futile. Is it the imagination, the power to grasp and arrange in an ordinary manner and execute? If these can not be trained or trained in part, what practical purpose does education serve? To what end the study of history and biography, if it does not enable us to apply the experience and the ingenuity of others to our own problems? In spite of the example of men in all walks of life who have started at the bottom and risen to the highest places, there is nothing so sad in business and industry as the consideration of that 90 per cent of those who are competent for the positions they fill, but who lack the education or the almost superhuman will to make up for its lack, which will permit them to rise above a certain dead level. In commercial education lies the hope for the future of American business.

Mr. Goodwin's paper was discussed at length by Mr. Albert A. Snowden, of the National Association of Manufacturers, and Mr. J. F. Crowell, of the Chamber of Commerce of the State of New York, an expert on foreign trade.

Mr. Snowden said in part:

The National Association of Manufacturers is composed of about 4,000 concerns engaged in business. All of these member concerns have something like 6,000,000 employees. The extent of the organization is shown by the fact that our members produce more goods than any other industry in the country. We are interested in industrial education rather than in commercial. Perhaps there are hundreds of thousands of students getting instruction in industries and in industrial and commercial education in various forms of schools—State, municipal, private, and other forms. The students in our institutions are receiving education in a peculiar way. They are our employees, and while they are earning money they are receiving instruction in a practical way. I feel as though we ought to have a complete and thorough organization for finding out what has been done in similar organizations in other countries of the world. We have a very large audience through our publications in connection with these industrial matters. A perusal of these publications will show you that this body is greatly interested in commercial and industrial training.

There is a wonderful lack of space in this congress devoted to manufactured goods. It is in education along this line that we are interested. In the promotion of foreign trade it is absolutely essential that the trader may have knowledge of the manufactured goods in detail and the conditions of sale of such goods, etc. From our point of view, at least, it is considered quite practical that these courses, especially studies which are supplementary to the regular courses usually given in schools, include continuous instruction in matters connected with exports, the banking business, etc. There ought to be some classification of manufactured articles—from experiments myself I know there are somewhere between 35 and 40—and a part of the program should be given over to the treatment of manufactured goods.

Mr. J. F. Crowell remarked:

I wish to say a few words on the general question of whether business is a profession. It seems to me, from the experience I have had in the field, that it is not yet what it may aspire to, because the business man, taken as a class, has not developed any such privileged position as the lawyer, the physician, or the engineer. Again, the field of commercial knowledge is in no sense organized, as it is in medicine or in law or in engineering or in theology. In the third place, the sense of economic responsibility by which all business conduct can be referred to a common standard, is not so highly developed in the business man of to-day as is the ethical which we find in the ministry or in the law or other professions. Fourthly, a professional career is not primarily a career whose end is economic profit. The business man's aim and end is primarily profit. The professional man works to attain and maintain a privileged position and a high standing in his community. Any profit connected with that work is, in a measure, incidental. The standing he attains in his community is a part of his reward. Furthermore, he works for progress in his profession—medicine, theology, or whatever it may be. The business man devotes himself to his business for gain, for profit, primarily; while the professional man follows his pursuit for the attainment of a privileged position. These distinctions seem to me to be conclusive as against the claim that you can train business men up to the high plane occupied by the professional man. Certainly business has not yet attained to anything like a professional status. I believe, howeyer, that with the development of education there will be a marked rise in the standards of business men in business pursuits.

PROPER USE OF BUSINESS EXPERTS IN CLASS INSTRUCTION ON DOMESTIC AND FOREIGN COMMERCE (SYMPOSIUM).

The following are the authors' abstracts of papers presented at this symposium:

Mr. ROGER W. BABSON, president of Babson's Statistical Bureau, Wellesley Hills, Mass.—The president of one of our country's great industrial organizations asked me concerning the best college to which to send his son, whom he desired to fit to become vice president of the great corporation and eventually to have entire charge of its investments, property, and employees. I suggested a general four-year course at some university and two additional years at the Massachusetts Institute of Technology, or four years at the institute and then two years at the Harvard School of Business Administration. He agreed that either of these would be an ideal combination, but he believed six years was, in this instance, too long. This incident well illustrates the position which many men take relative to higher education for administrative positions, and I hope to see some institution soon make definite provision for meeting this well-justified demand. The first year of such a course might be identical with the courses at any college, while in the second year the student might take up, with the general work common to the engineering courses, the study of bookkeeping and business mathematics and begin the study of applied economics. The third year he might specialize along the lines of options and begin the practical engineering work most applicable to the special option chosen. If the student decided to enter manufacturing, he should then take up some fairly advanced studies in mechanical engineering. If he decided to enter the transportation business, he should take strong courses in railroad engineering and electrical engineering. If he intended to go into banking or general business, he should study the financial side of railroad and industrial enterprises, as well as the more advanced features connected with general banking.

The main reason why I am anxious to have schools establish such courses of commercial training is because at the present time there are no such combined courses provided. The establishment of such courses in any school would greatly help the institution on the public and financial side by causing the leaders of industry to interest themselves more directly in its work and by attracting young men of wealth seeking to prepare themselves for administrative positions. There is, however, a far greater reason why all of us should aid in establishing a course in commercial training. I refer to our Nation's need for men trained along these lines. Every feature of mechanical, electrical, and chemical engineering has been taught in its minutest details; but to the great fundamental factors of trade, upon which the ultimate progress of all our industrial, electrical, and transportation enterprises rests, we have given only the briefest consideration. For this reason, probably more than any other, we so long had to endure one of the poorest monetary and credit systems on the face of the globe. Young men are graduated from our universities utterly unable to discuss intelligently the fundamental principles of credit, trade, and conservation. Our people are wasting their resources, misdirecting their efforts, and playing at politics because the graduates of our colleges are not thoroughly grounded in applied economics.

Mr. EDWARD N. HURLEY, chairman of the Federal Trade Commission of the United States.—Professional and business activities were once limited by national boundaries, but to-day the pursuit of any profession or occupation is likely to lead into the foreign field. Only political boundaries now remain; economic and industrial frontiers have been swept away. The business man, more frequently than any other now, becomes a 'citizen of the world. As foreign trade increases, the question of industrial efficiency and of the fitness of the business man of to-day becomes more important. This touches particularly the college student, to whom the business man of the present, versed in the requirements of the domestic market, must eventually pass over the reins. A manufactured article never sells itself abroad as does a bushel of wheat. It must either fill a new demand or displace a like product from another country. And the early detection of the new demand requires as much, if not more, skill and organization than does the attainment of superiority in quality over the rival British or German article.

While the boys of the United States have been educated to the responsibilities of domestic trade, a large percentage of the youth of Europe has been specially trained for foreign commerce. In languages, in world-business practice, in banking, and in shipping law they have been painstakingly instructed, and thus each of our great competitors has a huge army of capable young foreign traders familiar with the rules and phraseology of world trade, subjects of which all but a comparatively few Americans are ignorant.

Nothing would enable the college student to grasp the significance of foreign trade so quickly as a contact in the classroom with men prominent in the foreign business of the United States. Men who are directly in touch with foreign competition can furnish detailed and practical information obtainable nowhere else, and in addition they will inspire the student with the enthusiasm which comes only from personal touch with big affairs. My intention is not to undervalue the systematic teaching of foreign languages, banking and shipping laws, commercial geography, and the intelligent use of statistics, cost accounting and bookkeeping, and, in fact, a general systematic course in foreign trade. These are, of course, essential. I think, however, that such a course should be supplemented from time to time by lectures of experts from the business world. These men will make the student realize the vital relation between his studies and the conquest of foreign markets and give him enthusiasm for achievement over our foreign competitors.

Mr. E. T. GUNDLACH, of the Gundlach Advertising Co., Chicago, Ill.—Recent college experiments in the use of business men as class lecturers prove, in spite of many failures, that the innovation can be made a success. But the talent must be carefully sifted, then coached in advance, and properly restricted. This conclusion may be stated with considerable confidence, for it is the unanimous verdict, both as regards the value and the limitation of the plan, of 15 leading universities. In several institutions, notably at Harvard University, experiments were begun early and have ripened into a system. This past experience, combining encouragement and warning, may serve as a guide to other colleges which, it is hoped, will begin similar work.

But before business experts can be used more largely and more successfully in our universities, attention must be called to the difficulties. In the first place, courses entirely in the hands of business experts, through a series of lectures, are nearly all failures. A regular teacher must take charge, mapping out the course and assigning subjects. In other words, there must be a master mind, a director, continuously in charge. In the second place, the detail of each subject must be sketched out. It appears almost necessary to tell each business expert exactly the limits within which he is to speak, perhaps even giving him the questions in trade or manufacture to which the lecture is to be a reply. Many outsiders, upon appearing before a class of students, proceed to air their views on business ethics and on life in general. It is important to tell these business men that they are asked to speak because they know a subject, that other subjects are covered by other lecturers, and that each speaker will please confine himself strictly to his theme. In the third place, the lecturers must be thoroughly prepared. They must be notified long in advance, and they must be asked to work up not one lecture of an hour, but, let us say, one lecture of three or four hours, and then to condense it into 50 or 55 minutes; for one of the most common complaints made by the universities appears to be that half the lecturers come without having much of anything to say, merely talking in a general way and sometimes closing before the hour is half over.

Mr. WALLACE D. SIMMONS, chairman, committee on education of the National Foreign Trade Council, New York City.—The National Foreign Trade Council, through its committee on education for foreign trade, has obtained from several hundred American manufacturers, merchants, exporters, bankers, etc., expressions with reference to our present methods of education and the extent to which they offer to our young people an adequate opportunity to get a thorough grounding for successful service in connection with foreign trade, either in work in the home office or in the foreign field. The opinions expressed and the suggestions made cover a wide field and a great variety of ideas. One can not help being impressed, however, with the extent to which a large percentage of the replies point to certain few fundamental defects in our educational systems which exist to-day in most of the school districts of this country. These defects appear both in our elementary and our secondary schools. The opinion was generally expressed that the changes most needed are (1) an improvement in the ability to write a business letter expressed in terse grammatical English, (2) the ability to figure accurately and rapidly, and (3) a thorough knowledge of geography both of our own country and of the world at large.

Through the cooperation of business men, it may be possible for the educators of the country to impress our students more thoroughly with the importance of these fundamental things, and also to impress their parents with the relative value of thoroughness in them. The field of opportunity in this direction is so vast and the present variety of available information so great as to make it an exceedingly puzzling problem to know how to begin to coordinate our efforts in some general movement that will make for effectiveness. Other nations have been giving this subject very much more thought and attention than we have during the past one or two generations. If we can not at first cover the whole field in such a way as to enable us to get as favorable results, we should find a way to concentrate on a few fundamentals and expand from them. If we can get the educators of this whole country to teach these few things and teach them as well as they are being taught to the youth of other nationalities, we shall have made a long step forward, and will make possible further development approaching the standards of our competitors for the trade of the world.

Dr. Harry E. Bard, secretary of the Pan American Society of the United States.—In the preparation for a career in foreign commerce four things seem to me to be of essential importance: (1) A complete course of study of constructive character, which would represent the experience and wisdom of various competent authorities in the field; (2) special methods for the different subjects which go to make up the course of study, including a complete outline of subject matter, proper method of presentation, classroom technique, etc., for each; (3) professionally trained teachers, having each a mastery of the subject matter, special method, etc., of the subject he is to teach and a good understanding of the relation of this subject to the whole; (4) business experts competent to supplement the efforts of the professionally trained teachers by lecturing on special topics in accordance with the general plan and method under the immediate guidance and direction of the teacher in charge, bringing to the students something of the knowledge and experience gained in practical foreign commerce life.

The number of different subjects which merit consideration in preparing a satisfactory course of study is large, and the work of choosing the most important and of organizing these so as to meet at once the demands of pedagogical science and the practical requirements of foreign commerce is such as to engage the best thought and efforts of those most competent for the task.

The work of developing a special method for each of the subjects included in the course of study is even more important. The selection and organization in detailed outline of the subject matter and the development of proper method of treatment and classroom technique can not ordinarily be left entirely to the individual teacher, although room should be left always for the exercise by the teacher of personal initiative and some reasonable measure of original thought. The work of business experts must be considered, and careful thought given to the nature of the subject matter which these experts will be expected to present and its proper relation to the whole.

The business expert will, of course, be a person practically engaged in the field of foreign commerce, who has a special message and is competent to present it. The topic of his lecture will have very definite relation to the subject as a whole. The students will be prepared to appreciate his message by previous instruction and assigned reading, which will be further driven home by subsequent classroom discussions and examinations. Occasional lectures on unrelated topics, even by the most competent business experts, will not give satisfactory results.

Mr. B. Olney Hough, editor of the American Exporter and author of the well-known textbook on exporting.—Schools, and especially colleges, too often disdain not only the motions, but the very spirit of work in the business world for which they profess to be preparing boys and young men, devoting themselves wholly to what may be called the higher aspects of commerce, to theories of tariff and finance, to pure economics, if there is such a thing, instead of to applied business science. On the other hand, it is certain that few business men have either the inclination or the time to take any active or personal interest in the progress of the employees in their own offices. Our apprenticeship system, lacking or woefully weak in the trades, absolutely does not exist in the office.

Undoubtedly the business man can profitably be utilized in schemes for more practical business education, especially in view of the intensifying consciousness of civil and national responsibilities, which is so encouraging a characteristic of the times. Business men are to be found who not only are masters in a broad way, as well as in detail, of the principles and minutiæ of their own affairs, but who are generously disposed to do what they can to raise the plane of the country's business life. But none of them are teachers. To ask business men to take into their offices for practical work boys or young men who are spending a part of their day in the schools is, theoretically, an ideal plan, coupling educational equipment, textbook training in theory and the "reasons why" with actual, routine, day-to-day business transactions, and furthermore cultivating habits of method and application. Such opportunities may be earnestly sought and eagerly embraced, but are almost certain to be few. It is to be doubted if any considerable number of employers will be willing to suffer the really-severe tax on their time and the inevitable disruption in their offices which such a course is bound to occasion, if the young men are to receive real assistance, even attention. On the other hand, if business men are only to be relied upon as lecturers, supplementing school and college courses, then it will probably be the part of the professional teacher to take his business man in hand, and, through a joint study of the situation, in a spirit of mutual helpfulness, together map out clearly and definitely the exact lines of the business lecture.

The criticism which I have had to make of certain experiments during the last year or two, with business men's talks on export trade to classes in New York, has been that lecturers have been given, or have been allowed to choose, subjects at once too broad and too deep—subjects whose adequate discussion would probably involve a series of 10 or 20 lectures.

The benevolence of manufacturers and merchants of the United States has —freely been bestowed on trade and technical schools. Can it not be wisely extended to schools of commerce of a broader description? I have always been particularly attracted by the *bourses de voyage* offered by many a European chamber of commerce to prize students in local business schools. I especially remember reading two really interesting and informing theses submitted after a year of business experience, respectively, in Hamburg and Manchester by students holding such prizes from the chamber of commerce of Algiers. Why should not our American, North, Central, and South American, business men and chambers of commerce similarly encourage commercial students, encourage them by making it easy to acquire that actual acquaintance with and experience in other lands which is indispensable to the closer understanding, sympathy, and community of interests which we preach and seek? To the personal assistance of individual business men to higher commercial education let there be added the broader interests of manufacturers' associations and local chambers of commerce. Support, help, encouragement of individuals is necessary and good. Better, maybe, the official recognition by important bodies. of business men of business students' diligence and success. Students from Latin America, following many different courses, are plentiful in schools of all descriptions in the United States; the working, business, postgraduate student from North American commercial colleges is unknown in Latin America.

DR. JOHN F. CROWELL, Chamber of Commerce of the State of New York.—The expert should not be put in charge of directing and instructing those contemplating a commercial career. Commercial education is not well enough organized, however, on the part of teachers to dispense with the specialist. The kind of specialist will depend somewhat on the course of instruction included in the curriculum. For the undergraduate school the general results of expert experience should be emphasized rather than the special results. Undergraduate commercial instruction should include the following topics:

1. A statistical expert on population, including occupational classes.
2. A statistical expert on natural resources.
3. An expert on the products and distribution of the products of agriculture, manufactures, etc.
4. An expert on the different branches of commerce, including raw materials, manufactured commodities, and miscellaneous.
5. An expert on inland transportation.
6. An expert on maritime transportation.
7. Engineering experts in various fields of construction.
8. An expert on financing commerce, both domestic and foreign.

Instruction in commerce should always be given from the international viewpoint. There should be close cooperation between teacher and expert. In engaging a specialist for an individual talk or two, it is in general a safe thing to ask him to keep in mind three or four main topics and to have a good illustration or two upon each topic. The use of the expert will be very much enhanced if students be held responsible for having certain information on the subject, either by reading beforehand or within a certain period thereafter. Excellent results may be obtained through the use of a single page outline or syllabus of the main topic which the speaker is to discuss. This may cover probably a third of the page of the syllabus; the second third may be occupied with references to several books on the reserve shelves of the library; the third feature should contain a list of 10 questions to show how much the student carried away with him.

JOHN CLAUSEN, manager foreign department, Crocker National Bank, San Francisco.—The people of this country are awakening to an appreciation of the importance for more intimate relations—in business, social, and intellectual activities—with our sister Republics in Central and South America. In the development of closer relational ties our first thought and attention must, therefore, be given to the necessity of acquainting ourselves with the customs and languages of the peoples of those Republics—as also of other foreign countries. Our attention is daily called to the scarcity of available young men who in a competent and honorable manner are qualified to occupy positions of trust and responsibility. To meet this crying demand of the commercial world too little importance is given to the necessity of finding a common ground on which the business man and the educator can meet and solve the great problem for a better cooperation in the national movement of fostering trade relations.

It would seem that the first forward step to devise effective courses of study and developed methods of commercial attainments would be to unite the educational agencies in promoting the move of specialization in instruction for the most direct preparatory training, as covered by the following principal class subjects, viz:

1. History.
2. Modern languages and literature (preference to be given to Spanish and Portuguese).
3. Industrial economics.
4. Commercial economics.
5. Political economy.

A young man with a theoretical commercial training and the additional linguistic attainments brought about by such a course would assuredly prove of infinitely more value to his employer in many fields than one who lacks such qualifications. For the benefit of the scholar a merit system should be encouraged for appointments, into the staff of commercial and banking institutions engaged in foreign trade, of worthy graduates who in their sphere of endeavor have demonstrated their fitness to occupy such positions of junior posts.

The laudable activities of institutions such as the Young Men's Christian Association and the American Institute of Banking can well be considered criterions in the demonstration of the desire for education along commercial lines, when it is considered that even members of advanced age studiously devote their evenings in acquiring the essential points of business training which were not afforded in their younger years of schooling.

It is of interest here to note that the San Francisco Chapter of the American Institute of Banking offers every opportunity to its members for the acquisition of a broader knowledge in banking and finance, commercial laws, accounting, public speaking, as also in the study of the Spanish language, which only recently was inaugurated in the interest of better Pan Americanism, and the institute now boasts a class of 135 pupils who are enthusiastically lending every effort to the successful mastery of this linguistic attainment.

The paper of Mr. Wilbur Carr, director of the consular service of the United States, invited for this session, was presented before the above-mentioned educational conference on foreign service training, and will be found in the report on that conference. Keen interest was shown at all times in the papers of this session, several of which were discussed at great length from the floor.

Mr. JOHN F. CROWELL remarked:

The expert is the hard man to find. This is not because he does not exist, but because he is working in a particular field. One of the main difficulties is that the average school-teacher is not acquainted with a large number of business men. The man who teaches commercial education and does not make at least two new acquaintances in the business world every day is a failure. But when we come to specialists, we have to hunt for him in the business world. We should go to him and tell him to come up before our boys and tell them what he does in the handling of a particular line of goods. He will come before the pupils and tell them where the article originates, how it is distributed, what depots there are for meeting the national and international needs, and why they are located at Shanghai rather than at Hongkong or Harbin; what is the object of maintaining this kind of organization rather than that kind; what kind of implements are sent to this country or to that, and why. The youth will grasp the idea. He will talk to them in such a way that the boys will have a mental picture of the country, of the conditions, and they will, as the bent of the boys naturally is, want to go to that field.

When you come to the problem of transportation you can go out and get a man like the traffic manager of one of our trunk lines and bring him before a group of boys, and he will tell them of how tens of thousands of cars are handled, how they are moved from, for instance, Pittsburgh to the seaboard. He will tell the students of a concrete instance where a man arranges for the sale of a large quantity of commodities, say, 10, 20, or 30 carloads, but is unable to get them to destination and close the sale, and may be compelled to dispose of them by auction in order to protect himself. These things mean something to the boys. There is not an expert that can not light up the dull theme of arithmetic, for example, by applying its principles to the huge business of transportation.

Take the marine expert. You can get a man who has spent all his life in the shipping business, and he will come to a class and ask what is the average tonnage of ships built in the United States in a year. Teachers, as a rule, do not impart to boys such information as that. Their mind has not been trained in that direction. The mind of the expert has. Therefore, while you, on the one hand, do not put such questions as the one I have suggested, the expert in marine shipping would naturally think of such a question at the very outset of his talk with boys.

Prof. JOHN E. TRELEVEN, representing the University of Texas, spoke of the effort made by that institution to use the expert in its business training courses. In part he said:

We have first tried to select our men with unusual care before we have extended an invitation to an expert to address our students. We have selected the expert with an eye to the probability, as near as it could be determined, of his delivering to them a logical, practical, and beneficial talk. In the second place, we have been trying to prepare our students to listen to the lecturer. We have been trying to prepare them by some systematic course in the same line as that upon which the expert will address them when he comes into the classroom, and by means of assigned readings. In the third place, we have made it a point to have a conference with each person who is to come in contact with the boys. We have also made it a point to talk to the latter themselves before the lecture is given by the expert. Usually, when our professor visits the expert, he does so in his own office; that is, the office of the expert. He talks with him about his work, finds out the things in which he is particularly interested, and helps the expert to furnish the materials which he will use in the presentation of his lecture to our classes. We have found that if we take the expert out of the formal atmosphere of a classroom, he does better work. Then, in the smaller classes, we ask him in to a round-table discussion, either in the homes of professors or in the lounging rooms of the school. In the larger classes, we ask the expert to meet our classes in the lobby, where there are easy-chairs, and where the expert does not feel that he is delivering a formal lecture. The professor is furnished beforehand with a line of questions to which he wishes answers. This line of questions furnishes the basis for the expert's talk, and this serves to keep the lecture within the bounds intended.

Mr. E. L. Wertheim, of the Young Men's Christian Association, West Side Branch, New York City, said:

Out of 3,600 students last year who came to us to study something along definite commercial lines there was collected over $90,000. That is one association.

The matter of getting men to lecture is of especial interest and importance. The expert has a contribution to make to the cause of education, and if we can guide him we are doing something that is well worth while. You will find that if you ask an expert to come in and speak, he thinks it necessary to go immediately to the library and read up on his question, rather than take something he is dealing with constantly, daily, and that will be of much more interest than anything he could prepare on. The man who tells of the things that are of everyday occurrence with him is the man who will be the most beneficial to the men and boys.

I am afraid we have not in the past sufficiently recognized the dignity of commercial education. We have not sufficiently recognized, in practice, the fact that men fail in business because of the lack of proper training. I wonder whether commercial education will receive very much attention in the future unless we begin now to give more attention to it. We have schools, secondary schools, which prepare boys for college. There we have preparation. Why is it not just as possible to spend a portion of the preparatory period for training the boys to take their places in the commercial world, rather than to step from the secondary schools into the college? Isn't the one as feasible as the other?

Mr. S. P. Capen, the acting chairman, specialist in higher education of the Bureau of Education of the United States, remarked:

It seems to me that the profession of business, which is becoming recognized as a learned profession, is itself undergoing the experience of older learned professions. Originally all professional training was in the hands of the practitioner, and you must suppose for the professions a condition very similar to that in which commercial training now finds itself, commercial training being largely in the hands of the practitioner or the expert. This is for two reasons chiefly: First, that you have not enough trained teachers, or teachers trained in exactly the right way for your needs in training others in the profession of business; and, secondly—and this seems to me most important—as I judge from what has been said here, that you have as yet no recognized teaching content. Is not that the case? Isn't it necessary, first of all, to know just exactly what knowledge shall make up your higher courses of commercial training, and isn't it necessary to organize that knowledge into a system, to organize, in a word, a teaching content, and turn that over to the teacher? It is only the occasional expert which you now get in schools of medicine and in schools of law. In medical schools the teachers give almost their entire time to the work of teaching. The same is also true of the law schools. I anticipate it will be true of the schools of commerce and business administration in a very short time.

THIRD SESSION.

The third session was held Wednesday afternoon, December 29, at 2.30 o'clock, in the Pan American Union Building. Mr. Roger W. Babson presided.

Papers of a general character on commercial education in Latin America, Germany, and England were presented.

COMMERCIAL EDUCATION IN LATIN AMERICA.[1]

By EDGAR E. BRANDON.

The traditional form of education in Latin America, in both the secondary schools and the universities, was distinctly cultural. This type descended in direct line from the old colonial universities, modeled after the medieval universities of Spain, and continued in the national universities after the independence of Latin America. It was an education that looked forward distinctly to the so-called liberal professions, the priesthood, the law, and somewhat later, medicine. The curriculum of the secondary schools was formed in harmony with this tradition. In former times it included the classics, studies in literature and philosophy, with a relatively small amount of mathematics and

---

[1] Author's abstract.

little science. In more modern times the classics have been generally replaced by modern languages, but the study of mathematics and science has always remained overshadowed by the so-called cultural and liberal studies.

This being the status of the traditional university education, it became absolutely necessary in the commercial period of the latter half of the nineteenth century to establish schools distinctly devoted to the study of commerce and business administration. The crying need of such institutions was emphasized by the commercial development of Latin America. As long as this section of the globe remained in the semi-isolation that was its lot until the middle of the nineteenth century, the old classical and liberal education satisfied the needs of the country, but with the development of commerce a reform was imperative, and it seemed much easier to educators to institute a distinctive type of commercial schools than to engraft the idea of a more practical education on the older and established forms.

The Latin-American mind lends itself readily to commercial education, which in its broadest form must be liberal as well as technical, and include the modern commercial languages, a very considerable amount of history, geography, and political institutions, as well as economics and accounting. When once the need was fully recognized and commercial schools began to be established, they met with unusual favor. Their establishment and development in the different countries of Latin America has been in direct ratio with the commercial advance of the country. In very few cases was their origin similar to that of the so-called business colleges of the United States, and likewise it was not often that their establishment was due to individual initiative. On the contrary, in almost every case it was by act of government that the schools were established, and they have been from the very first an integral part of the national educational system. As at present constituted, they are of different types or grades. At the top of the list are the colleges or higher schools of commerce, such as the one at Buenos Aires which is a part of the University of Buenos Aires, and the one at Santiago, Chile, which, although not connected with the University of Chile, is of a rank that almost, if not quite, equals that of a university faculty. The more common grade, however, is the secondary school of commerce. This grade does not always require a completion of the studies of the elementary schools for admission. There are often two or three classes below the ordinary rank of high school, and two or three classes above the entrance grade of a high school. This is the type of the ordinary schools of commerce in Chile. Nearly every town of importance in this Republic has a commercial school of this grade.

In some countries the commercial school is a section of the regular high school. This system of organization is in vogue in Cuba and Peru, for example. The entrance requirements to the section is the same as for the other sections, but the course of study is distinctly of the commercial type. The commercial high school or the commercial school, which is a combination of the upper elementary grades and the lower high-school grades, usually attracts a different class of students than the traditional and literary high school. The latter remains the school of the upper classes, since it leads on to a university career. The former is patronized by the middle and lower middle classes who are engaged in commerce.

It is for this reason that the separate installation of the separate school is usually thought preferable in Latin America, and it has only been for reasons of economy that the commercial section has been introduced into the regular high school rather than erecting a separate institution. There is the fear that the older type of secondary education will absorb the newer and prevent it reaching its fullest development. This is a condition imposed by the social structure of Latin America.

No part of the public education in Latin America has to-day a greater appeal to the whole public than has the commercial school, notwithstanding the facts mentioned in the preceding paragraph. A liberal profession may still be looked forward to by parents as the desirable one for their own sons, but none fail to recognize that it is the practical education which will bring the greatest material benefit to society. For this reason business men of means and commercial associations take an active part in fostering the commercial schools in their locality, and in aiding the institutions to acquire an installation and equipment adequate for this purpose. Gifts of material, of money, and of service are often made, and local business houses apply to the schools for trained young men for positions in their business.

Commercial education in Latin America is of recent foundation, while there were some ephemeral institutions toward the middle of the nineteenth century. It was not until about 1890 that the Governments took up the matter in a serious way, and the national schools of Chile and Argentina date from the last decade of the nineteenth century. The same is true of Mexico, and the other countries followed at an even later date. At the present time there are either separate commercial schools or commercial sections in the high school in practically all the countries of Latin America.

COMMERCIAL EDUCATION IN GERMANY.[1]

By Frederic E. Farrington.

Germany has long been a fruitful source of educational inspiration to the American student, but this has largely been confined to the traditional subjects. Commercial education represents a field hitherto little noted by American investigators.

During the 25 years from 1882 to 1907 Germany underwent a marvelous transformation from an agricultural to an industrial nation. The education of the German youth for commerce has played its part in this change. In Germany specialization is the order of the day. Every effort is made to find out early what a lad can do best, and he is then trained thoroughly for that particular work and for no other. All this results in a vocational stratification which parallels the social stratification so characteristic of German life.

Germany has two distinct educational systems, one for the masses and the other for the classes. Commercial education cross-sects them both, and appears in three degrees or levels—lower commercial schools, middle commercial schools, and higher commercial schools. The first, beginning at 14 years of age, is represented by the continuation school, a part-time school demanding the pupil's time for six hours per week for three years. Here one finds a high degree of specialization, the youth being trained for a particular line of commercial work. The instruction is more or less theoretical, paralleling closely the practical training the youth is receiving pari passu with his employer. Compulsory continuation schools for boys are found in 12 of the 26 States of the Empire, and for girls in 4. In 1907, of the 460 German cities with 10,000 and more inhabitants, 291 had continuation schools, and in 220 of these attendance was compulsory. Commodities of commerce and training for citizenship are noteworthy subjects of study.

------

[1] Author's abstract.

Middle or secondary commercial schools are chiefly attached to the regular secondary school system, although class prejudice has prevented this grade of commercial school from attaining the prevalence or the success which characterize the lower and the higher commercial schools. A variant of this middle commercial school is found in some half dozen centers wherein a more advanced and more highly specialized type of training is given. This represents a protest against the narrower humanistic influence of the older type of regular secondary schools and responds more closely to the changing needs of modern life.

In the highest group of commercial schools appear the colleges of commerce, schools which are well worthy to rank alongside the old-line universities, with which they are legally on a par. The establishment of the commercial college is the result, rather than a contributory cause, of Germany's commercial progress, but it bids fair in the future to enhance that progress even more. Training for the civil and municipal service, together with opportunities for modern language training, are perhaps the most striking features of colleges of commerce. Private and semipublic activity figure largely in their foundation and support and show one phase of the spirit of cooperation which brings out the most important lesson we can learn from a consideration of German commercial education.

COMMERCIAL EDUCATION IN ENGLAND.[1]

By I. L. KANDEL.

The provision of commercial education in England is of recent origin, and dates from the beginning of the present century. The causes for this slow development have been the great success of English trade and commerce during the nineteenth century, which was due not to specialized training but to a wealth of natural resources and a native bent for mercantile pursuits. To this was added the opposition of educators, on the one hand, to early specialization and vocational preparation and their belief in the value of a general education as a foundation for life occupations, and, on the other, of employers who prefer to train their own employees through the actual routine of the shop and office and see no value in theoretical training. The present development of commercial education has been due to the agitation of a few men at the close of the nineteenth century, to the increasing severity of foreign competition, and to the success attained by competitors largely through training. An important element has been the establishment of examinations in commercial subjects conducted by such national bodies as the London Chamber of Commerce, the Royal Society of Arts, and the Union of Lancashire and Cheshire Institutes.

The facilities for commercial organization are not systematized, but they follow three main directions—the training of boys and girls who can remain at school until the age of 15 or 16, courses in evening continuation schools for those who are engaged during the day, and courses of university grade leading to degrees. It will be noticed that the secondary schools hardly provide instruction in commercial subjects, and this for the reason mentioned above—the educational opposition to providing special preparation in schools whose chief function is conceived to be the imparting of a general education. The first type mentioned above is in an experimental stage and has attained completeness only in London in what are known as "central schools," to which boys and girls are drafted from local elementary schools at the age of 11 for four-year

----

[1] Author's abstract.

courses, one of which may have a commercial bias. The preparation is of a general character, only the elements of the technical branches being taught. The evening continuation schools furnish, among other courses, organized commercial courses of four or five years' duration. The schools are open for about 30 weeks a year, and students may attend on three evenings a week. Efforts are made to secure the cooperation of employers. The work of the first two years is general in character, and in the third and fourth years there may be specialization according to the different branches of commerce. The last year offers advanced work in language and special branches. The course includes commercial arithmetic, English, geography, shorthand or bookkeeping, commercial correspondence, a modern language, and office routine, with economics, accountancy, commercial administration, banking, commercial law, etc., in the advanced courses.

Finally, the present century has seen the development of faculties of commerce in the new universities and university colleges like Manchester, Liverpool, Birmingham, London School of Economics, Nottingham, Reading, and Southampton. The courses are organized in connection with the faculties of commerce and the advice of local chambers of commerce, and other commercial interests is enlisted. Diplomas are awarded usually after two years' work, and degrees at the close of three. The subjects of study include modern languages, statistics, accounting, banking and exchange, commercial geography and history, economics, the organization of commerce and industry, and commercial law.

Progress has been slow in England in this field, but the development has begun and a new stimulus has been furnished by recent events, and increasing attention is being given to the subject by the Government and unofficial authorities which will undoubtedly lead to more rapid advance and increasing recognition of the value of training in the future.

FOURTH SESSION.

The fourth session of this subsection was held Thursday morning, December 30, 9.30 o'clock, in the Pan American Union Building. Mr. Roger W. Babson presided.

The following is a résumé of Director Grinfeld's paper:

MODERN BUSINESS AND COMMERCIAL EDUCATION.

By ISAAC GRINFELD.

In spite of the nature of modern commercial transactions, the underlying motives for preparation are the same to-day as they have always been. The technique of buying and selling is, however, so intricate and the latter carried on on so vast a scale that educational preparation, presented in a scientific and adequate manner, is absolutely necessary. Three men play an essential part in a commercial transaction to-day the success of which depends upon their training as experts; e. g., buyer, salesman, and the organizing and administrative head. The expert buyer must have a thorough knowledge of the articles manufactured or sold by his firm, and the sources of production, markets, and prices for the same. Schools must aid, supplementing actual practice, in furnishing this knowledge. This information can be best given in special schools, as this is a day of specialization. For example, industrial chemistry, applied mechanics, and electricity, necessary for certain buyers, can be better taught in technical institutes, provided they be taught in a special group of commercial technology, than through courses in these same subjects in regular schools of commerce. Most schools, whatever their character, can offer a course in buying and selling with reference to the products in the study of which the school is engaged. In view of the present-day specialties, such a procedure would be best. Commercial preparation is only possible, however, in a school organized for that purpose where due respect is given to economic considerations and less to industrial and legal. This view needs to be encouraged in the Latin-American countries, where too much attention is given to the legal aspects.

Preparation for the salesman and the advertising expert is no less important a branch, but has been considered of even less importance in the Latin-American countries. The agent or broker carries on here the work of buying and selling. This system of brokerage, however, is a failure largely through the inadequate preparation of the broker and the character of the class from which the agent is recruited for this work. On the other hand, no subject is given greater attention in the United States. Extra-mural courses, like those of the International Correspondence Schools and the Alexander Hamilton Institute, demonstrate that buying and selling can be taught. Further, large industrial and manufacturing concerns have established highly successful schools in connection with their plants, where their salesmen are not only instructed thoroughly about their own products, but are given a fairly satisfactory course in commercial training. The training course in publicity or advertising is one of the most important subjects to be considered in these special training schools. Thousands of dollars are lost annually through the incompetency of those engaged in this work. More and more such loss is being reduced in the United States through the employment of men trained in the salesmen's training schools. The profession of salesmanship must be given greater dignity. Pupils engaged in the study of it must be given a clear comprehension of general business principles, supplemented later by a specific knowledge of each particular business.

Of greatest importance is the training of the organizing and administrative heads. The qualifications for these two branches of business service are different, but the same person is frequently called upon to act in this double capacity. The knowledge of general principles in reference to the economic forces that affect his business are of greater importance to the organizing chief than to the administrator, to whom the knowledge of accounting, office practices, and daily trade movements are necessary.

Elementary schools of commerce prepare largely clerks; the higher schools, experts in buying, selling, and advertising, organizing and administrative chiefs. The latter schools, owing to the complex character of society to-day, must include studies that will furnish culture and arouse in the students lofty aspirations. The lower schools must inculcate the spirit of patriotism, the higher schools establish a sense of social and industrial justice. The instruction given, however, must be practical above all. Practical courses must be given whereby students may be trained to observe and coordinate phenomena of interest to them, and to test their own productions by comparing them with actual results. The problems studied should be similar to those with which the students will be confronted in the practical business world.

The acting chairman read the following abstract of the paper by Prof. Bennett:

PREPARATION FOR A BUSINESS CAREER IN CHILE: LATIN-AMERICAN STANDPOINT ON BUSINESS EDUCATION.

By FRANCISCO A. BENNETT.

The Instituto Nacional of Santiago de Chile, established in 1813, holds to-day a leading position among the secondary training schools. The Memoria Ministerial of 1889 contains plans for the establishment of training schools of commerce. Vocational training in agriculture and mining had been developed prior to this date. The Instituto Comercial of Santiago was established with the hope of creating a college of commerce similar to the college of commerce of Antwerp and the college of advanced commercial studies of Paris. A Belgian gentleman was invited to organize and take charge of the school. The idea of establishing a commercial university was then abandoned, and a plan proposed to establish instead practical schools like the Italian technical institutes. The disparity in plans proposed has resulted in creating a type of school similar to that which the chamber of commerce of Paris maintains in the Avenue Trudaine, or to the German, Austrian, and Italian schools of the same grade. There are at present in Chile schools of commerce in Santiago, Valparaiso, Iquique, Antofagasta, Concepcion, Arica, Vallenar, Coquimbo, Talca, San Carlos, and Talcahuano. The Instituto Comercial of Santiago is called the Instituto Superior de Comercio. The institute has a training course for professors and teachers of commercial subjects.

Commercial education is under the general direction of a council, the president and secretary of which are, respectively, the minister of public instruction and the visitor of commercial institutes. A more or less uniform content of instruction for these commercial institutes is the following: English, Spanish, bookkeeping, typewriting and stenography, commercial geography and history, commercial arithmetic, natural sciences with direct reference to commercial products, political economy, commercial law, commercial writing and commercial practices.

In the Commercial Institute of Valparaiso, which we shall take as a model, the course is one of four years. The first is devoted to studies of general knowledge; in the second are introduced elements of commerce and commercial arithmetic; the third is given up to commercial theory; and in the fourth the studies are of a more practical nature and are completed by work in the "model office." Students and graduates of the institute easily find remunerative positions in commercial houses.

In Chile, as in the larger part of South America, importing and exporting business is carried on largely by foreigners. In view of this fact the commercial institutes prefer to give courses that will train the native clerk, merchant, and clerks for foreign commerce. The idea of the institute of Valparaiso is to prepare young men to enter commercial establishments, and, after they have learned the methods practically, to enable them to organize on their own account and later to help enlarge Chilean business enterprise. Some of these schools also consider for their graduates work in connection with the customs, consular service, railway administration, the teaching of commercial branches, etc. For the present there does not exist the official position of commercial expert.

The Latin-American point of view in regard to commercial education is rather that of the German Handelsschule than the American business college, which stresses the application and use of certain technical acquirements. A young man, possessing a thorough training and a well-informed mind, can use his novitiate in any mercantile branch to greater advantage and advancement. The young Latin American with lively imagination wishes to know always cause and effect in the pursuit of his studies and labors. The Institute of Commerce, further, believes the literary course and school prejudicial to a successful commercial career, and is opposed very much to receiving students from the " liceos." It prefers to take students between 10 and 11 years of age and give them the necessary general training basic to later courses of a more special commercial character which will enable them at the age of 15 or 16 to take a position as a " junior " in commerce. For those unable to take this course of training in this manner there are schools similar to the American business college. Some schools of commerce and nearly all of the private schools have night schools for this type of student.

Commercial education on the whole only occupies at present, as a branch of public instruction, a secondary place in Chile. In time, as this phase of education improves, the commercial schools will prepare through systematic and organized knowledge for a higher professional career.

THE ARGUMENTS FOR A SEPARATE OR COMBINED COURSE OF COMMERCIAL STUDY—THE CURRICULUM OF A SCHOOL OF COMMERCE.[1]

By ROSWELL C. McCREA.

The organization of the curriculum of a graduate school of commerce and business administration is relatively simple. The curriculum of such a school may well be highly technical, narrowly confined to business problems, and conducted by methods of instruction which largely follow the research plan. The ideals and methods of such a school are strictly professional. The school of commerce of undergraduate type likewise has professional ends, but its ideals are less strictly vocational, and its methods more closely approximate those of a college of liberal arts. The main variation from the scheme of the college is in the content of courses. A school of commerce may so organize its four years of study as to realize most of the primary aims of college instruction in discipline and breadth of view, and at the same time lay foundations for speedy adaptation to the requirements of later business life. There should be training in the fundamentals of business science and practice. But general educational aims should ever be in the foreground. Courses other than strictly technical ones must be woven into the curriculum in such a way as to develop on the part of the student liberality of view, intellectual perspective that extends beyond and behind purely contemporary phenomena, a socially minded attitude toward public problems, and a mental discipline and grasp of. scientific and philosophic methods.

To be more specific, the curriculum of a four-year student should include not only required courses dealing with broad fundamental aspects of commercial and industrial organization and activity, but as well properly devised courses in English, history, psychology, economics, politics, sociology, and biology or chemistry.

I have omitted mathematics and foreign language work from the list of required studies. From the standpoint of utility, college mathematics is ordi-

---

[1] Author's abstract.

narily not of fundamental importance in the equipment of the business man. For purposes of mental discipline there are various substitutes for mathematics. For training in analysis there is ample scope in the study of accounting, of political science and business law, where the case method is used, and of economic theory.

Foreign-language study is usually urged because of the discipline it affords, because of its utility in intercourse with foreigners, and because it opens a new avenue to an understanding of the literature and life of other people. From the disciplinary standpoint the disadvantage is that results are hardly commensurate with the time spent in study. Equivalent discipline may be secured more readily in other ways. From the standpoint of practical serviceableness the great difficulty is that not more than 1 student in 25 gets enough out of his course to put it to practical use. For the few who may have subsequent use for a language, ample provision should be made; but the many should not be forced into a meaningless routine looking toward ends that are not realized. The opening of new fields of culture is quite as vain for the usual student as the utilitarian ideal.

With reference to the order of presentation of studies, advantages preponderate on the side of a mixed scheme. In the freshman year the student should be placed in intellectual touch with his environment—physical, economic, social—and taught how to use its component parts. The second year should emphasize mental processes so that he can turn to principles developed in the first year's work and apply them more fully to practical affairs. Two such years should develop a viewpoint, often so sadly lacking in the amorphous preparatory years, and should awaken enthusiasm and help toward an interpretation of the world of affairs. The last two years should be both more general and more specialized. The business man must have breadth as well as special training, for he touches at some point the social, economic, and cultural problem of his time. It would seem unwise to exhaust the first two years of his course in elementary liberal studies, and then compress in the last two years the routine tasks that prepare for his future career.

Let a study of the fundamentals of the physical and business environment exert its influence during the first years while the boy's preparation for his career is receiving initial impetus; and do not narrow the horizon in the last two years by an intense specialization that will result in efficiency at the cost of a restricted intellectual growth.

The university school of commerce is a modern college. Its function is to stand side by side with the modernized college of arts and sciences in the effort to revivify and extend culture studies, to afford special training and to yield a clearer insight into the complicated relations of modern life, whether in business, the old professions, or in the broader field of social service.

HOW TO SECURE PROPERLY PREPARED INSTRUCTORS FOR COLLEGES AND UNIVERSITIES IN COURSES ON DOMESTIC AND FOREIGN COMMERCE.[1]

By James C. Egbert.

The expression "domestic and foreign commerce" may be described in general as standing for the interrelations of trade as maintained at home and

[1] Author's abstract.

abroad. When, however, it is considered as a subject of instruction in our institutions of learning, it evidently has a wider significance, inasmuch as it apparently includes the study of business, a term used in its broadest sense. It will be well, therefore, to modify the title of our theme by substituting the word "business" for commerce.

We must consider first the development of commercial study in the American college and then the place it holds in such institutions. Early schools of business were developed in large cities; they were private institutions. Then followed the high schools of commerce. These prepared many young people for a business career, but served another purpose in calling attention to the need of training of a more advanced character.

Political economy was the predecessor of the various related subjects of economics now admitted into the college curriculum. Finally the graduate courses were established. Then it was realized that a more complete and independent treatment was necessary, and schools of commerce of a collegiate and university grade were begun. There are three types of these schools to-day: The school of commerce, which takes the period usually assigned to the college; then the professional school of business, built on a partial collegiate career; the third type is the graduate school, as existing now at Harvard.

In our desire to secure instructors for such schools we must understand that these schools must be operated for a double purpose, the training of students for a business career and the preparation of those who will serve as teachers in the higher institutions of learning devoted to business as the subject of instruction. The preparation of a larger number of instructors in these subjects is vitally necessary. We can not expect in general to draw our teachers from business life. The teacher must be trained and must be qualified to impart knowledge. Three important facts should be recognized: First, the colleges have been preparing students for instruction in the secondary schools and not for the colleges; again, graduate students tend at present toward the theory of business. The laboratory method is almost entirely neglected. We must first establish a profession of business and receive more recognition in the colleges. The professional school of business must form the background in the education of teachers. The practical or laboratory work must not be forgotten. Business houses may cooperate with the schools of commerce and afford an apprenticeship to the students, who may there receive practical experience. Colleges of business must be carefully organized with an understanding as to the possibilities of specialization. The problem will be solved by regulating, adapting, and developing agencies now existing and emphasizing the profession as the center of interest.

If we consider our theme as concerned with the special subject of foreign and domestic commerce, we should recognize the importance of securing instructors trained in commercial geography and the colloquial use of modern language, and particularly in the institutions of the countries with which trade is desired. The cooperation of business firms will be invaluable in this particular. Finally, we must secure suitably trained instructors by requiring a general education, followed by professional training, with opportunity for specialization and for practical experience.

WHAT CAN THE SMALL COLLEGE DO IN TRAINING FOR BUSINESS?[1]

By George W. Hoke.

Three points are prominent in this discussion:

(1) The function of the college is to develop ability in its students to give efficient and versatile response to environment.

(2) One-sided response of the college product is due to the fact that experience in the promotion and administration of affairs has no adequate representation in the training given by the college.

(3) Certain readjustments are necessary to meet this situation: (a) The organization of a system of academic and vocational guidance; (b) the establishment of functional relations between the various departments of the college; and (c) the grouping of a series of prebusiness courses.

The chief obstacle to training for business is the conservatism of the college faculty. They do not seem to realize that such training is not an innovation, but a return to the functional responsibility of the college, made necessary by the acute maladjustment of its product to life. Three instances are selected to show the need of training for productive service:

(1) The conservation of resources is too serious a responsibility to intrust to men without adequate training and foresight.

(2) The organization of modern business demands a type of management that can be provided only by men trained in psychology and scientific methods.

(3) Changes in standards of behavior, incident to our complex régime of mutual dependence, require a trained insight into problems of conduct and responsibility.

Six general qualifications are necessary for the efficient conduct of affairs:

(1) Vision, i. e., the ability to see the signs of opportunity and responsibility.

(2) Mastery of scientific method, i. e., ability to organize a situation with economy and efficiency.

(3) Understanding of human nature, i. e., ability to anticipate mental reactions.

(4) Capacity for self-expression, i. e., ability to deliver an acceptable message by word or deed.

(5) Capacity for recreation, i. e., ability to take leisure after labor, and make it profitable.

(6) Capacity for productive service, i. e., ability to recognize standards of worth more fundamental than financial profits.

From the day that a boy enters college he should have sympathetic advice, and his course should be routed to meet his specific needs. The departments of the college should remember that they are conducting partial processes only and that their work should conform to the standards of quantity and quality set up for the final product. The college should insist that every student acquire, before graduation, interest and knowledge in some specific field of the world's work. Upon graduation the college should do all in its power to place the student where he will do the most good.

---

[1] Author's abstract.

FIFTH SESSION.

The problem of commercial education, as this refers directly to elementary, secondary, and higher schools, was discussed at the fifth session, which was held Thursday afternoon, December 30, at 2.30 o'clock in the Pan American Union Building. Mr. Roger W. Babson presided.

ELEMENTARY SCHOOL COMMERCIAL EDUCATION.[1]

By F. G. NICHOLS.

There is at present a growing demand for an elementary school commercial course to take its place with other seventh and eighth grade vocational courses. The purposes of such a course may be stated as follows: To provide vocational education for a part of the great number of children who leave school before the high school is reached; to hold boys and girls in school a year or two longer; to interest more pupils in a complete education for business; to increase the pupil's knowledge of the opportunities that are open to him; to develop in boys and girls, by concrete instruction, business habits so essential to the largest measure of success in any field of human endeavor; and, in short, to make the seventh and eighth years count for more in the child's education.

It must be kept in mind by those who would frame such a course that it must be essentially vocational; that it not only must be vocational, but it must be within the easy comprehension of the boys and girls of the seventh and eighth grades; it must also be suited to the occupations that are open to such boys and girls; it must be planned with regard for local requirements; it may well be differentiated for the two sexes, in view of the existing differences in occupational opportunities open to each; it may also be planned with reference to urban or rural requirements. It is also important to remember that while early choice is extremely desirable, irrevocable choice at such an early age will always produce much harm unless the paths from one course to the other are kept open as long as possible. Further, it is well to recognize the fact that secondary education can not be forced downward into the lower school without such modification of subject matter as the immaturity of the grammar-school children makes imperative. It may also be suggested in this connection that the traditional business course of the secondary school is rapidly undergoing reorganization to meet the demands of modern business. It must, therefore, be apparent that the old bookkeeping and shorthand course will not meet the needs of the grammar-school boy and girl.

In the junior high schools of this country elementary commercial courses have been organized. Almost without exception they include commercial arithmetic, bookkeeping, shorthand, typewriting, commercial geography, business writing, and English. They do not differ materially from the secondary school commercial course, notwithstanding the important fact that much of the subject matter is beyond the comprehension of grammar-school children, or the more important fact that boys and girls of grammar-school age are not wanted as bookkeepers and stenographers.

A better course of study that is in harmony with the principles set forth above is one that includes the following subjects: (1) English, with special emphasis on spelling, vocabulary building, punctuation, simple business letters,

---

[1] Author's abstract.

and easy descriptive work both oral and written; (2) business arithmetic, with special emphasis on topics suggested by local conditions; (3) business writing that will insure the mastery of a good business hand; (4) commercial geography, with special emphasis on place geography in general and on local vocational geography in particular; (5) civics, elementary in character and for the sole purpose of developing a high type of citizenship; (6) typewriting for its vocational value, and also to develop accuracy, concentration, neatness, etc.; (7) first lessons in business, to inculcate business habits, to teach simple record keeping, to acquaint the pupils with simple business practice; and at the end of the course to link up the elementary commercial course with the high-school commercial course in such a way that every pupil in the former will want to continue in the latter. Physical training, physiology and hygiene, industrial work for boys and household arts for girls will all receive the usual attention in this course.

· ———

COMMERCIAL EDUCATION IN SECONDARY SCHOOLS.[1]

By PAUL MONROE.

There are two hindrances to the development of adequate provision for commercial education in the secondary schools of the United States: (1) The general prejudice in favor of the traditional literary education; (2) the feeling against any differentiation in our school organization which involves special treatment of different groups of pupils. The first feature implies emphasis on preparation for the leisure activities of life; the second renders difficult the consideration of technical preparation of any sort.

It is this differentiation of the school system into a variety of kinds of schools that is the chief characteristic of the system of Continental Europe, and to a less extent of South America. In place of this we have in the United States a prolonged elementary course and a briefer secondary course which is but slightly differentiated and is of the same length for all.

These two characteristic features are now undergoing changes which may ultimately be quite radical. These changes, so far as they have progressed, will explain the present status of commercial education.

Commercial, like industrial, education is education stated in terms of production, rather than in the ordinary cultural terms of consumption. In the United States natural resources and opportunity have been so great that it has been unnecessary until recently to organize education in terms of production. Now, with our approach to the marginal standards of the older countries and with the great influx of unskilled labor, a new attitude is necessary.

For fifty or seventy-five years we have had numbers of private commercial schools which afforded routine training for routine business procedure. At present there are probably 2,000 such schools giving training to 200,000 students. For some twenty-five years we have supplemented this means of preparation with business courses in our public high schools. Nearly 2,000 public schools now offer some such courses and reach about as many students as do the private schools. The public school has the broader curriculum, but the private school has the advantage of closer contact with business.

The problem for ·the immediate future is such an organization of secondary education as will place within the reach of every youth in the country the op-

———

[1] Author's abstract.

portunity for a commercial or an industrial education which shall not only prepare him for the business of life but at the same time be a genuine education. The problem is a wholly different one from that of the private business school. The new curriculum must include a greater variety of subjects. It must consider business from the social and the national as well as the individual point of view. Many problems in the organization and control of these schools have arisen and few have been finally solved. Satisfactory solutions await a longer experience.

A further need is for the awakening of the public to the necessity and the problems of commercial and industrial education. There can be no permanent progress until the people as a whole realize that economic advance, as well as political and social stability, depends upon an adequate preparation through education for dealing with industrial and business processes. Modern democracy demands as a guarantee of its well-being an increased attention to these types of practical or vocational education.

The following is a résumé of a paper on the same subject by David Snedden, former commissioner of education of the Commonwealth of Massachusetts.

COMMERCIAL EDUCATION IN SECONDARY SCHOOLS.

By DAVID SNEDDEN.

At least 350,000 pupils are studying in commercial departments or courses in the schools of the United States. These figures express quite definitely the demand for commercial education in the United States. They do not clearly measure the extent to which occupations of a commercial character finally require or absorb all these young people; but they bear eloquent testimony to the fact that parents see in these occupations desirable opportunities for their sons and daughters. Let us analyze, first, the character of the thousands of pupils taking commercial courses and, secondly, the general character of the instruction offered.

For upward of half a century private and public commercial schools and departments in high schools have offered the most accessible and inexpensive opportunities available for an education of secondary grade that seemed to have a definite vocational outcome.

Hence, a vast army of young people, attracted and sometimes fascinated by the alleged large possibilities of success in business careers, have sought the instruction and training offered through commercial courses. Often these youths have been under economic necessity to seek employment early; often, too, they have either lost or else never developed interest in or capacity for the general studies of high school and college. Classes in commercial studies generally show a large percentage of students of mediocre ability and also a considerable percentage pathetically eager to get the equipment necessary to early entrance on wage-earning employment. Into these classes have been forced or have drifted pupils not bright enough for the college preparatory work of the high school. What have these pupils received? At all times the larger part of the education could be divided into two kinds—(a) a variety of definite forms of training in skill and (b) a variety of forms of instruction in organized bodies of knowledge of a commercial character.

Judged by any adequate standards, commercial education in the United States during the last half century has, in spite of its seeming successes, been in large measure characterized by poor organization, ill-defined, confused, and unscientific aims, and ignorance, sometimes willful, of the general quality of its output. It has thrived on the credulity of a public deprived of opportunities for thorough and intelligent vocational education and tempted by the allurements of modern business enterprise.

The present is obviously a period of rapid transition in secondary commercial education. Partly under the influence of the general movement for vocational education during recent years, the aims and methods of commercial education are in process of becoming more clearly defined. An increasing number of educators recognize that any form of commercial education which rests largely upon abstract processes, as so often found in high schools now, must in the long run prove wasteful and ineffective. More attention is being paid to training in skill in the various divisions of commercial occupations that are being defined. Systematic comparison of various methods of teaching is being made, with a view to ascertaining which offers greatest economy and effectiveness.

It will be found that there are many commercial occupations which are not yet definitely analyzed, but for which, when analyzed and defined, systematic training can be given. The beginnings of this movement we find now in the interest developing in the direction of training for salesmanship, for office administration, for field salesmanship, for advertising, and the like.

Very probably commercial education in the future will make extensive use of so-called "part-time training," by means of which, after a brief introductory period, the novice will spend part of his time in the lower stages of the commercial occupations and the remaining part in schools, seeking systematically to correlate the practical experience gained in the commercial pursuit with the technical knowledge and training which the school is able to impart.

ENTRANCE REQUIREMENTS TO COLLEGES OF COMMERCE.[1]

By DAVID KINLEY.

The principles which control and which, on the whole, should be observed in framing a curriculum preparatory to a college commercial course are these: The subjects of study should afford adequate mental training; they should have proper relation to the civilization, form of government, and opinion of the community; they should stimulate the interest of the students; they should, to a proper extent, have a vocational relation to the subsequent course of study; the subjects should be susceptible of good teaching, and a supply of capable teachers must be at hand.

Not every subject that should be in the curriculum meets all the above tests in the same degree, but every subject should meet one or more of them as fully as possible, and, to a certain extent, should meet all of the others. The general subjects which do so are the languages, mathematics, science, history, economics, and civics. The vocational subjects which meet these tests most fully are bookkeeping, business law, and commercial geography. For a college course in commerce, stenography and typewriting are not educationally necessary,

---

[1] Author's abstract.

although useful, for the reason that those who take college or university courses in commerce are preparing themselves not for clerical, but for managerial. positions. The educational value of commercial arithmetic is so doubtful and its scope so unsettled as to make its inclusion doubtful.

Practice in the United States conforms pretty closely to the above theories. Taking the Universities of Illinois, Wisconsin, California, and Pennsylvania as fairly representative of the institutions which have undergraduate collegiate courses in commerce, we find that their entrance requirements agree substantially with one another, and also in placing the emphasis as above indicated. All accept approximately from one to four units, or years' work, of high-school grade for admission to their courses. The other units, or most of the high-school work, are in general subjects.

The prospect is that the college commercial course will become more intensely vocational and technical. We must look, therefore, for an increase in the amount of vocational study in the high schools preparatory thereto. Probably the next subjects to be recognized in the high-school course for this purpose will be business organization and practice, salesmanship, and advertising. But while the next few years will see more highly specialized high-school courses preparatory to college and technical courses, there is little probability that these subjects will ever become the main part of the program of the high-school boy. He will still be obliged to have his mother tongue, his history, his science, and, for reasons aside from its obvious utility, his foreign language.

Dean Kinley's paper was discussed by W. F. Gephart, professor of economics, Washington University. The author's abstract of this paper follows:

The demand for formal training for business is due, first, to the wonderful economic development of the United States, with its accompanying complexities in modern business organization and conduct; second, to the rapid development of interest in foreign markets; third, to the splendid results achieved in devising formal training for technical and professional ends.

The particular subjects admitted for entrance credit should not be decided by an attempt to evaluate an assumed worth of a particular subject of study in secondary schools. Any institution which desires to organize a college of commerce should recognize that there are certain well-defined differences in business activity. The chief courses of separate training are for foreign business, domestic business, with its important subdivisions, for technical business positions, such as accountants, and for teachers of business subjects. Thus, with a difference in ends to be achieved, the value of a subject of study in the secondary schools will be determined. The entrance requirements will have a very limited number of required subjects and a large number of electives, depending upon what line of business the applicant expects to enter. Modern language will be required of those who expect to enter the foreign-trade business. A larger amount of subjects called vocational, such as bookkeeping, may be accepted from those who expect to enter accountancy.

Since in many lines of business the facts have not been, and can not for some time be, correlated and scientifically treated in a deductive manner, subjects in the high school which have a large measure of mental discipline should be emphasized.

SIXTH SESSION.

The sixth session of the subsection on commercial education was held Monday morning, January 3, at 9.30 o'clock, in the Pan American Union Building. .Mr. Albert A. Snowden presided. The teaching of certain fundamental and special subjects of the collegiate business training curriculum was discussed in brief papers by specialists in those subjects._ Abstracts prepared by the writers of these papers follow.

LANGUAGES.

By GLEN LEVIN SWIGGETT.

The teaching of modern languages is perhaps the most unsatisfactory of all subjects in the course of commercial education. This is due to a lack of texts prepared with this kind of instruction in view and to the prevailing method of classroom instruction in these subjects. Foreign-language study in the schools and colleges of the United States has been largely for the purpose of discipline in the earlier school years and culture in the later. This attitude persists in the face of the well-recognized and insistent demand on the part of business men and high Government officials that the modern commercial languages be so taught that students engaging in foreign service, consular and commercial, be given the ability to speak one or more of these languages.

It is difficult to give this ability to students in our schools and colleges as constituted and controlled. Faculty direction of courses of study, the attitude of the teachers of modern languages, and the method of class assignment of students are strong factors still within the school that act in opposition to the growing demand for a more satisfactory and practical plan and method of teaching modern languages. The latter can only be achieved through a larger spirit of cooperation within the faculty, the growth of an interdepartmental esprit de corps, prompted by a larger sense of public service, the emphasis upon a speaking knowledge of the language in the appointment of teachers, and through a larger freedom within the departments of modern languages that will permit either the dropping of students from these courses, after it is plainly shown that they have neither interest nor ability to pursue a course carried on by the conversational method, or their reassignment to special courses carried on by the traditional method.

The number of texts that place value upon the practical teaching of modern languages is steadily increasing. Teachers' courses in these languages are placing an increasing emphasis upon the ability to speak as a necessary requirement in the study of a modern language. Methods have greatly improved. There is still lacking, however, suitable texts prepared to give through content the essential knowledge of foreign countries and prepared by a method that is both interesting and progressive through a period of study of several years. This lack of suitable texts, together with the inability on the part of the teacher to condition a student's opportunity to pursue a modern language by the latter's native ability to take it, are a serious menace and present insurmountable obstacles for the present, except in a few favored institutions, in the teaching of modern languages for commercial purposes.

The study of Latin should precede, if possible, that of the modern languages. To do this the two elementary years of Latin should be placed in the grammar-school period. Sound pedagogy and precedent argue for this. The study of modern languages in the high school and in the college, on the basis of election and permission, can then proceed naturally and effectively and the real aim and purpose in the study of all living languages achieved; e. g., the ability to speak them.

GEOGRAPHY.

By J. PAUL GOODE.

Of all the subjects in the school curriculum, geography has, next to language, the largest possibilities for service in the way of a liberal education for business. The phase of geography which is being developed in this service takes its point of view from both physiography and economics, and attempts to find the physical or geographic influences underlying industry and commerce. It is a fascinating field for both teacher and student. Though its principles may be firmly rooted in the nature of things, its data are in continual flux with the everyday changes in market conditions and international relations. For these reasons it is not an easy subject to prepare in or to teach. But the reward of such a study is found in the exhilaration of a constantly widening horizon and of migration out of a provincial frame of mind.

The subject as thus conceived lends itself very readily to a year's profitable work as a general course in the later years of high school or to trade schools and first-year college work. The interest thus roused and taste acquired lead naturally to the more specialized courses in industry and commerce now being developed in colleges and schools of commerce. A brief synopsis of the ground covered here follows:

I. The geographic influences underlying industry:
    Position on the earth, as determining climate, area, and form of the lands under study.
    Land relief-barriers of mountain or dissected land.
        Passes and valley routes through highland barriers.
        Plains and their influence.
    Mineral resources: Character, areal distribution, accessibility.
    Climate as an influence on life.
    Plant life, wild and cultivated, as a basis of commerce.
    Human life and development, especially as to stage of development, education and training, population density, government participation in industry and commerce.

II. The chief commodities of commerce: A general view.
    Products of the farm, orchard, and range—The cereals, sugar, fruits, vegetables, beverages, drugs, animal products.
    Products of hunting and fishing—Furs and fish.
    Products of the forest—Lumber, rubber and other gums, cork, dyes, etc.
    Products of mines, quarries, and wells—The mineral fuels, iron and other common metals, the precious metals and stones, building stones, cement, clay products, etc.
    Power as a commodity.

III. The geographic influences in commerce.
    Advantage of position with reference to trade.
    Winds and currents and the great ocean routes.
    The organization of ocean commerce.
    The development of land routes of trade.
    The development of market foci.

IV. Commercial countries and their commerce.
　　Selected important countries studied as to commercial development and possibilities.
　　The growth of world trade and the part played by leading lands.

The last two sections as outlined above may well be developed as advanced collegiate work, and even a single country may profitably occupy the time of a college course. The work thus developed opens up almost numberless avenues of special research of university grade. In high-school work a textbook is used, almost of necessity. But even here much reading may profitably be done on library references, especially in periodical literature as in the recent official publications by various Governments.

No subject offers a better opportunity for education by way of the eye, since photographs, stereographs, and lantern slides, or, better still, motion pictures, bring vividly before the student the foreign lands and strange peoples at work on the production of commodities, or the transportation of these wares along the highways of world trade. Fortunate, too, are those schools in the great commercial centers, where access is easy to commercial museums; or better still, where the great industries may be visited, and the actual work be observed in the handling and transforming of the raw products into the finished wares of commerce. Then, too, the subject calls for a large and constant use of maps. The ingenuity of teacher and student will also be well repaid by the conversion of statistics into graphs, which bring vividly before the eye the trend of commerce and the growth of nations.

HISTORY.

By WILLIAM R. SHEPHERD.

Too often is history conceived and written, taught and studied, with the idea that it is an adjunct of belles-lettres and mathematics. But the new concept of history as a record of the totality of human endeavor, as the story of the growth of mankind broadly considered, is giving to the knowledge of the past an organic vigor, a live practical utility, a genuine power of application to the problems of to-day, which differ more commonly in degree than they do in kind from those of yesterday.

In habitual conversation the world over, men and women have talked and continue to talk about business, politics, and the weather, domestic relations, children, and servants, to the utter exclusion of what is ordinarily supposed to constitute material for history. These men and women were and are living creatures, not animated books; their habitat was and is the bright and busy earth at large and not the dark and motionless shelving of a library. What they have done and thought are the things in general that interested them then, interest them now, and will continue to interest them until the end of time. Such things are the veritable stuff out of which history as a living record of human conduct is made.

History, as the word goes and as the child finds it, is only too apt to be dull, and hence profitless for the youthful if not also for the adult mind. Yet it can be made interesting, and hence valuable, simply by humanizing it.

What people to-day really care to know about their predecessors on this planet is what the latter did in the ordinary affairs of life; just how, in fact, they lived and moved and had their being. Obviously, then, studies aimed at affording a practical familiarity with the methods of gaining a livelihood in the realm of business should include the story of what our ancestors have accomplished in the same realm, pointing out the respects in which they failed and in which they succeeded, and why. The manifold relationships in the actual dealings of people with one another, in their application of the treasures of earth to human welfare, these are the themes on which emphasis should be laid. How our forbears procured the wherewithal to eat and wear and shelter themselves, how such things were produced, exchanged, and consumed; how our parents through the ages contrived to fashion themselves into an ordered society, and how they cooperated to render this world a better place in which to dwell, are questions rising in the youthful mind which call for an adequate answer.

Politics and war, the topics that hitherto have crammed the pages of "history," and commonly made them as dead as the personages of whom they treated, should be relegated to the few who have the leisure and the inclination to learn about them. What the teacher in the modern school of commerce has to present is social history, in the broad acceptation of the term. This will embrace a record of doings in the fields of industry, trade, and transportation not only, but in those of the evolution of groups and classes in the community, their characteristics and relationships, their thoughts, and their deeds, as affecting the development of mankind, quite apart from the spectacular achievements of the soldier and the lawgiver.

The scarcity of available textbooks on organic history of the sort need not daunt the teacher who realizes the value of it. If he will search through the conventional works, he will find many a chapter, many a paragraph, and even a sentence to serve his purpose; for even the mere narrator of wars and politics could not avoid altogether the less spectacular or extraordinary, and hence the more human, and the more interesting, in his record. Diligently to seek them out, and to set them forth means the study of a genuine history that "teaches," and does "repeat itself."

GOVERNMENT.

By JESSE S. REEVES.

In this paper consideration is given to conditions in the colleges and universities of the United States only.

1. Prerequisites, not only for the study of government, but also for general preparation in foreign commerce:

(a) Familiarity with foreign languages and literatures. The deficiency noted is that instruction in the modern languages is too often delayed until after entrance into college.

(b) A knowledge of geography. The ignorance of college students in this field is notorious. It is a burden upon the college instructor in the fields of history, economics, and political science, as well as in higher commercial education in the narrower sense.

(c) College training in history and economics to the extent of at least one year's course in each.

2. Training in government is admitted to be of less direct vocational value in the field of higher commercial education than is training in economics, finance, and transportation.

3. The courses suggested:

(a) An elementary course in government which should cover the field of American political institutions, but it is suggested that there should be included within such a course a treatment of the governments of other countries, European and American, in order to obtain a less provincial point of view and a broader horizon.

(b) Commercial law, which should be based not upon the English common law, but upon the legal ideas common to all civilized countries.

(c) Private international law, in order that the fundamental differences in the great legal systems of the world may be appreciated.

(d) Public international law, in order that the student of international commerce may become familiar with the greater legal conceptions which bind states together, and so develop broader sympathies and a conception of the international mind.

Finally, while these studies are primarily cultural, it is suggested that they may ultimately be of the highest vocational value.

MATHEMATICS.

By EVERETT W. LORD.

Between the colleges and the business world there has been a gulf which sometimes has seemed impassable. Not a few eminent men of affairs have maintained that the college course tended rather to unfit a young man for business than to aid his advancement. At the same time, the average college professor has considered the world of commerce wholly apart from his sphere and has disdained any connection with business men other than that sometimes necessary when the latter were allowed to contribute toward an educational endowment. In spite of this feeling, an increasingly large number of college men in the past few years have gone into business. These men have insisted that the colleges should recognize the importance of business as a profession, and that business men should acknowledge the possibility of learning something from college courses. One after another, leading educational institutions have offered courses in business or have even established departments of business administration or commerce. The teaching of mathematics has formed but a small part of these business courses. There seemed to be no particular connection between higher mathematics, trigonometry, calculus, or even higher algebra, and the routine mathematical transactions of buying and selling. A study of the catalogues of the various schools of commerce and business administration shows that few of them have included college mathematics in their course. As a rule, these colleges have limited their teaching to higher accountancy, to statistics, and phases of mathematics included in marketing and economic courses. The study of banking and foreign exchange has involved some mathematics, although little more than phases of commercial arithmetic, and the study of insurance has brought in a specialized type of mathematical work—the theory of probabilities and actuarial mathematics.

The school with which I am most intimately familiar, the college of business administration of Boston University, includes in its complete course, leading to the degree in business administration, not only the mathematics of accounting, but applications of algebra and geometry, a study of logarithms, and, in one of its divisions, the same work in solid geometry and trigonometry that is required of freshmen in a course in liberal arts. The applications of algebra and geometry are found to be of direct help to the young business man, while the training in solid geometry and trigonometry is warranted as the stimulant to scientific observation and accurate record—two things of the utmost importance to the business man. When making up the course of this college, the writer conferred with many business men, including bankers and merchants in various lines, asking them for their opinion on the subjects to be required of the college student who aspired to excel in business. In no case did one of these business men suggest the higher mathematics; indeed, several of them were inclined to believe that any mathematical study beyond that needed for work in accounting was little more than a superfluity. College men, when consulted about the same matter, varied in their opinions largely according to their individual tastes for or against mathematics. In spite of the unanimity of opposition or of indifference shown by active business men in the teaching of mathematics, we have found that the modicum of mathematical training included in our course gives good results. We shall not extend the requirements to include any other of the traditional college mathematics, but we shall continue to allow our students to elect higher mathematical subjects as part of their general course, and we shall encourage such elections when students show marked mathematical ability.

BANKING AND FINANCE.

By Charles Lee Raper.

The fact that in many countries the great majority of trades are made on the basis of credit, that much of the productive work rests upon credit, should easily convince us of the vital importance of banking and credit. To make a course on banking and finance vital, the important steps and instruments in the process of banking practice, as well as the chief factors in commerce and industry, must receive large consideration. The study should make clear and real the functions and workings of the bank, the chief credit institution which we have, as it accumulates its resources—capital, surplus, deposits, and credit—and as it makes loans of these resources to the active producers of commodities. The part which bank reserves play in banking practice and in credit and business stability should be intelligently grasped by the students. How large they should be for the sake of the safety of the bank and of its depositors and note holders, and where they should be mobilized for use when the call comes for them, are fundamental questions which bankers have to answer; and the answers should always be in terms of the actual business and political conditions.

The work performed by the various types of banks should be known. Special effort should be made to obtain a clear understanding of the work and the results of centralized banking and of the decentralized system. The weakness of the completely decentralized system which has prevailed in the United States should constantly be contrasted with the strong points of the most effective European banks. To discover how much of governmental regulation and what its form should be, to make the banking practice sufficiently safe and stable, at the same time allowing the managers to perform their work with elasticity, according to business and financial conditions, is one of the precious discoveries of a country. Because the bank should always be prepared to meet the obligations which it owes to its depositors and note holders, and because it should always accommodate business with the maximum loan of its resources, the problem of converting its assets into cash when it most needs it is highly important. One solution of such a problem is to be found in the investment of a considerable part of its resources in the most salable forms of loans.

Three more or less distinct fields are open for the investment of bank credit: (1) Local, (2) national, (3) international. The banking system of a country should perform services in all of these fields; it must do so before it can render the most complete service. And banking in the international field, as well as in the national and local, stimulates the broadest possible intercourse and confidence and promotes solidarity of business. The student should know the function and the working of the more important instruments of bank credit and finance—the check, bank draft, documentary bill of exchange, commercial bill, finance bill, etc.

To understand the money market and rate is no easy task, but the student must have a firm grasp of these before he can hope to know banking and finance. The money market and rate may at times be largely controlled by Government finance, as is evidenced now in many of the European countries. Ordinarily private finance—the discounting of commercial and industrial paper or lending on promissory notes secured by stock-exchange securities—plays the larger part in the control of the money market and rate. The money market and rate may be local, national, or international, and their scope exercises a large influence upon banking and finance. No one can make the most effective study of banking and finance without an intimate knowledge of the whole field of business, of the making of the raw materials and their finished goods, as well as their exchange. Banking and finance are fundamentally attached to the forces of the production, distribution, and consumption of commodities.

Textbooks should be used as the general guide, but they must be supplemented by much reading in general economics and government. To make the course closely connected with the real currents of life, the daily newspapers and the weekly bank statements, such as are issued by the New York Clearing House and by the Federal Reserve Board, must be read. By a combination of texts, readings, and his own enthusiastic interest, the teacher may bring to the minds of the students the leading principles of banking and finance and the more important facts of the operation of these principles in everyday business life. The task is a large one, but it will pay a large percentage on the investment.

STATISTICS.

By E. DANA DURAND.

This paper has reference to the teaching of statistics in institutions of collegiate or university rank which aim to prepare students for a business career. The enormous part played by statistics in modern industrial and commercial life shows their importance in the curriculum. Many of the courses ordinarily offered in schools for business training include statistical information as part of their subject matter; for example, courses in commercial and industrial geography, corporation problems, transportation, money and banking, and the like. Students in such courses should be made familiar by actual use with the more important sources of statistical information and taught the critical use of the data.

There is need, however, for specialized courses dealing with the statistical method. Practically all students preparing for business might well be given at least one such course, as in after life they will often need to use statistical material and should be able to grasp it readily, interpret it clearly, and present it effectively to others. There is also increasing demand both in public and private employment for expert statisticians, and advanced statistical courses should be offered for those who aim to become such.

It is not necessary that statistical courses in the majority of institutions should enter into very advanced mathematical regions. Instruction in the higher statistical mathematics may be confined to a few institutions. On the other hand, a school of business training should not aim to turn out skilled statistical clerks. Practice in the simpler mathematical and graphical processes should be chiefly incidental to practice in the application of analytical methods.

The most important desideratum in statistical work is accuracy in the original data, and much place should be given to instruction in methods of preparing schedules of inquiries and instructions for filling them, and in methods of collecting data in the field. Practical experience is essential in connection with such instruction, as in fact in connection with all parts of a statistical course. Instruction in methods of compilation should lay stress upon the close connection between the methods applicable to a given set of data and the final methods of presentation and analysis to which it is intended to subject the results. Stress should be laid upon form of tabular and graphical presentation, as well as upon analysis. Much of the value of statistics is lost because people can not understand them. Absolute clearness of form and proper perspective are essential. Finally, courses in statistics should obviously train the student to apply adequate methods of mathematical and graphic analysis. Much of published statistics is only raw material, from which lessons of great value might be drawn by trained men.

In every course in statistical method students should be given abundant practice work. There should be a well-equipped laboratory. Much instruction by lecture or textbook will leave the student incapable of actually doing successful statistical work in his later career.

Papers on the teaching of the very important subject of accounting were presented from the standpoint of the teacher and the practicing public accountant. The following is an abstract of the paper by Prof. Grass, of Leland Stanford Junior University:

THE TEACHING OF ACCOUNTING.

By DONALD F. GRASS.

Collegiate instruction in business subjects is a late development in the United States, due to overcrowded curricula and inertia in the educational field. Growth in size of business unit is the most important factor in the increased study of business. Combination, large-scale production, and in some cases, monopoly, bring problems demanding greater efficiency and men of greater mental and moral grasp. These problems awaken people to the greater need of accountability of business men. Government activities in the field of business call for highly and broadly trained men. Peculiarly so in a democracy, as they must be intelligently responsive to the people's will.

Political questions like railroad rates, tariff rates, and questions of monopoly price call for accounting knowledge in the equipment of the statesmen who would handle them intelligently. The response to call for collegiate instruction in business is heartily met when need becomes clear. To-day there is scarcely an institution of higher rank that does not give instruction in accounting and allied subjects.

Accounting should be considered from the collegiate point of view. This is due to the fact that business activities are economic activities. The real work of the accountant is the tracing of values through all their mutations in the business world. Principles of valuation are economic principles.· All the economic forces at work upon these business values must be understood by the accountant. Their intricate play must be made a matter of accurate record just as they occur. The fundamental studies of the accountant should be the principles of economic theory and the social organization of the forces of production in each business unit. Legal knowledge is also necessary to a comprehension of the business and its transactions in relation to the rest of the social organization. Law is the expression of human experience in adjusting equitably these relationships.

Last and least in importance from the standpoint of university study is the technical material of accounting. Technical means and method in the handling of accounting are infinite in variety and vary with growth and development. Study of all important technical devices is necessary, but is incidental to the study of accounting principles and problems. The aim is to give knowledge of underlying principles, and capacity to meet comprehensively a new problem.

A résumé of Mr. Geijsbeek's paper follows. Mr. Geijsbeek was for four years chairman of the committee on education of the American Association of Public Accountants, which has made a very careful and continuous study of this question since 1911.

ACCOUNTING.

By John B. Geijsbeek.

1. *What kind of accounting is meant.*—The accounting here treated is the work of the expert accountant, who aids materially in the management of business by furnishing financial statement and data, after the work of the entry clerk is complete.

2. *The education of a person desiring to become an accountant.*—The accountant should receive just as ample an education as the manager. This is to enable him to execute his duties with the greatest sureness and effectiveness. His education must be accomplished in a very much shorter time and through altogther different routes from that of experience.

3. *The necessity for such an education.*—The public and high schools furnish no education of help to the accountant, as the commercial courses in these schools only give good instruction in typewriting and bookkeeping, in which he is not interested. Very little knowledge is obtained in the lower schools that is of real value to the student, and it is the author's opinion that the curricula of American schools should be greatly changed, so as to really furnish a practical instruction. The necessity for commercial education is more important than ever on account of the present war, which will affect the American trade by greatly increasing it.

4. *It should be a college education.*—As the accountant must be able to cope with the mature mind of the management of the firm, it is necessary for him to have a mature education, and this can only be received in a college.

5. *The methods of teaching the subject.*—The greatest difficulty is to make the courses as practical as they will be found in actual business. The author suggests a method similar to the clinic service of the doctor. He suggests letting the student work under guidance on the books of charitable institutions and

small business concerns. The progress would be much greater and the knowledge obtained more profound.

6. *The qualifications of the student.*—Before beginning the study of accounting, the student should possess a thorough general education which will enable him to understand the use of technical terms and fully grasp the instruction offered him. He should have a good foundation in commercial history, commercial geography, commercial law, commercial economics, and like subjects; and, above all, he should be master of the language he is to use and have a good knowledge of other foreign tongues. It is thus easily seen that accounting can not be fruitfully taught before the third year of a collegiate education.

7. *The postgraduate course seems better.*—The postgraduate course seems more adequate to prepare a man for this work, as only a graduate possesses that knowledge of the world so lacking in the college man. As business ability consists chiefly in grappling seriously with the daily problems, it is necessary that the training in directing ability should only be given to graduates and not to undergraduates. The author does not mean by this that instruction should only be given to the college graduate, but desires rather that the course be one of college education for business men than of business education for college men, and concludes by regretting the formalities required of business men who seek to enter colleges after having acquired sound experience in the world of business and practical affairs.

The subdivisions of the courses in accounting are very numerous, but in general may be enumerated as follows: Philosophy of accounts; practical accounting; accounting procedure; accounting systems; simple accounting problems; advanced accounting problems; auditing; advanced auditing; private auditing; accountants' reports; corporation finance; accountancy of investments; and cost accounting.

BUSINESS LAW.

By WARD W. PIERSON.

An investigation recently completed by the business law department of the Wharton School of Finance and Commerce of the University of Pennsylvania brought to light interesting data concerning the teaching of business law in the colleges and universities of the United States. The following is the distribution of educational institutions reporting: Universities, 86; colleges, 149; technical schools, 14; agricultural schools, 8; total, 257.

Ninety-eight of the above institutions offer courses in business law. Taking these numbers as a basis of computation, we find that over 38 per cent, or a little more than one out of every three institutions of higher education in the United States, offer business law as a regular study.

Of the 86 universities reporting, 20 have a separate commercial course of which business law is an integral part; 20 others offer it as a subject under their general curriculum, while 46 universities as yet give no instruction whatsoever in the subject. Of the 149 colleges reporting, 12 have a distinct commercial course, including business law, 31 offer it under the general curriculum, while the remaining 106 do not offer business law in any form. Business law forms an important study in technical and agricultural schools. Reports from 14 engineering schools show that 13 offer courses in agency and contracts, and these courses are required for a degree. Out of 8 agricultural schools reporting, 8 require it before graduation. As to time given over to teaching of business law, only 2 institutions offer courses covering four full years, these being the University of Pennsylvania and New York University. Four others offer 8 one-year courses, 10 offer two-year courses, and 25 have one-year courses, while 44 offer business law in the form of a short course of one term or less.

In engineering schools the subjects of contracts and agency are emphasized, while in universities the course is broader and the study more detailed. The subject in the latter includes contracts, negotiable instruments, agency, partnerships, corporations, bailments, sales, personal property, crimes, decedent's estates, bankruptcy, suretyship, guaranty, and evidence.

Fifty-two institutions require the subject of business law before graduation, while 46 carry it as a free elective. Thirty-seven institutions reported that they used the combination method, including a study of court decisions, class discussions, and the lecture system. Seventeen used lectures and quizzes, 5 used simply a textbook, supplemented by lectures; while 4 reported courses given through medium of lectures alone. The remaining number offer combination of various forms too detailed and numerous to mention. Forty-three institutions reported that the subject was taught by practicing attorneys. Three reported that, though not practitioners, the instructors were law-school graduates. In 52 schools it is given by instructors holding merely a college degree.

The subject of business law was first introduced in the United States 44 years ago. However, only 13 institutions have taught it more than 30 years. Twenty-five have taught it between 10 and 20 years, while during the last 10 years, 49 have introduced courses in the subject. This proves that the number of institutions where business law is taught has increased in the last 20 years sevenfold, and in the last 10 years it has doubled. Out of 257 institutions reporting, 159 offer no instruction in the subject. Of these, however, 16 are contemplating the introduction of such a course within the next two years. Against this number there are but 8 which at one time taught the subject, but have dropped it.

The investigation proves beyond doubt the growing importance of business law as a college subject. A knowledge of the legal status of corporations, the forms and functions of negotiable instruments, and the laws in regard to property fill a need in the lives of thousands of people engaged in business or professional pursuits. There is probably no other subject which fills so wide a gap in the college curriculum, which has sprung into existence in so short a time, and which gives greater promise of genuine service to the world at large, than does the teaching of the subject of business law.

BUSINESS ETHICS AND PSYCHOLOGY.

By James E. Lough.

Until recently business organizations and business operations were frequently regarded as existing and functioning under conditions entirely peculiar to each individual case. We now realize that business is a science and that it is founded on certain general principles. These principles apply to all business operations and include among other topics business ethics and business psychology. Business ethics must not be confused with business etiquette, or with the conventions of business. Business ethics deals with the principles of morality governing business operations and with the duties and obligations of business organizations to other organizations, competitors, employees, investors, and the public. The same principles of conduct that govern the action of the individual apply equally to the activities of business. The obligations of honesty, uprightness, truthfulness, etc., must be recognized by the corporation as well as by the individuals constituting the corporation.

The aim of a course in business ethics, therefore, will be to teach students to apply the general principles of ethics to business operations. The course should include:

1. The consideration of the evolution of morality.
2. The causes which have produced morality.
3. The necessity of morality.
4. A study of the virtues and duties with special reference to business.
5. Following the discussion of the more formal topics of ethics, consideration should be given to the practical development of ethics as shown in the interest of the larger corporations in welfare work among the employees, the organization of cooperative clubs, vacation clubs, etc.; the general tendency on the part of large corporations to look on the employee as a human being rather than as a mechanism.

The method of instruction is a matter of the greatest consequence. It is most important that the instructor himself should be a man thoroughly familiar with business conditions and who also holds the highest reputation for business integrity. The course must be inductive in nature, must avoid academic discussion and formal definitions, and rich in illustrative material drawn from business.

The general course in business psychology must first of all present in systematic order the essential facts of psychology so far as these apply to business operations. For example, attention, apperception, sensory elements, types of imagination, judgment and reason, emotions and will. This should be followed by a study of the individual, his natural and acquired capacities, and other traits that constitute the elements of his personality.

The following traits should be included in the general course: (1) Physique; (2) knowledge; (3) mental ability, as distinguished from knowledge; (4) disposition; (5) the will; (6) trait chart.

Following this the course should present practical suggestions and exercises for increasing the strength of undeveloped traits. If time permits, some of the more exact methods of psychological measurement may be introduced in connection with the trait chart, or this subject may be treated in a more advanced course. The psychology of salesmanship, the psychology of advertising, etc., constitute special developments of the psychology of business and should be given only a very general treatment in the introductory course.

BUSINESS ORGANIZATION AND ADMINISTRATION.

By Arthur E. Swanson.

A survey of the courses now being offered in 34 universities and colleges under the head of business organization, management, or administration indicates that there is little uniformity in the subject matter taught in these courses. This is to be explained principally by the newness of the subject, since most of the courses have made their appearance within the last five years.

The study of business organization and administration means a study of business enterprises, their structure, methods, and policies, with particular attention to the ascertainment of the principles underlying and determining successful business organization and administration, and an additional study of the observed facts and principles of other fields of knowledge as they bear on this subject. These peripheral fields include especially economics, psychology, sociology, and accounting. Too much emphasis has been placed on the study of organization and administration of ownership in courses in business organization and administration. This is especially true if it can be assumed that students have taken courses in business law and corporation finance.

In the study of operative organization and administration a course in fundamentals should precede and serve as an introduction to the applied courses. The fundamentals to which I have reference appear to me to be as follows: (a) The functions of organization and administration; (b) the limitations; (c) the dependence of organization and administration on the purposes of a business; (d) the delegation of authority; (e) the fixing of duties and responsibility; (f) the conditions necessary to administrative control; (g) the specialization functionally or divisionally of authority and administrative direction, and of the work to be performed; (h) the standardization of materials, methods, and policies; (i) the assembling, classification, dissemination, and recording of information; (j) the personal correlation of men and departments, and the mechanical correlation of materials and equipment; (k) discipline; (l) incentives, including all forms of compensation and other inducements; (m) employment and discharge.

Following this elementary study, strictly applied courses should be given in production and distribution in which a presentation can be made of specific problems of organization and administration in the light of the fundamentals. In the field of production a course in factory organization and administration can well be supplemented with specialized courses in such subjects as motion study, efficiency standards as applied to production and production costs. In the field of distribution a course in merchandising or marketing can be supplemented with specialized courses in foreign trade, advertising, sales organization and management, credits and collections.

Theoretically, the value of special training in business organization and management can be supported on the basis that there are ascertainable facts in this field which can be classified and studied. This process is essentially educational. Supporting this assumption, experience proves clearly that business organizers and managers find courses in business organization and administration very valuable.

SEVENTH SESSION.

The seventh session was held in the Pan American Union Building January 3, at 2.30 o'clock. Mr. Albert J. Snowden presided. The subsection on commercial education was most highly honored on this occasion with an address by the Hon. William Jennings Bryan, to whom an invitation was extended to address the Second Pan American Scientific Congress, the plan and purpose of which he had indorsed and encouraged cordially and constantly during his tenure of the portfolio of State. Electing to speak in a general way to the establishment of relations through educational preparedness, the address of Mr. Bryan was assigned to this subsection as such time as he could conveniently attend it. Space does not permit printing Mr. Bryan's remarks in full in this brief report; the importance and significance of which may be readily seen in the following quoted paragraphs:

ADDRESS OF HON. WILLIAM JENNINGS BRYAN.

In casting about for a theme for my brief remarks to-day, it occurred to me that the word "cooperation" might well serve as the point about which to group certain suggestions for which I ask your consideration. Cooperation, is the growing word of the twentieth century. There is noticeable everywhere an increasing tendency on the part of individuals and nations to get together in matters of mutual concern. In the business of life the idea is accentuated by the multiplicity of corporate organizations in which individuals associate themselves for the advancement of joint interests. Nations, too, are more and more considering matters of common interest and learning to give each other the assistance which comes from joint action. While the unprecedented struggle now raging across the Atlantic has, for the time being, interrupted cooperation in that section of the world, it should be regarded as a temporary suspension of cooperation rather than a permanent surrender of an ideal. Cooperation in the Western Hemisphere has been more general because of the greater similarity of institutions and political aims. The present conflict in Europe has tended to draw the Republics of the Western Hemisphere nearer together, as their dependence upon and power to aid each other have become more apparent.

With this introduction, permit me to suggest a few lines of action along which I believe it is possible to cooperate to a larger extent than we do now. First, the language tie which binds nations together is a strong one. The ability to speak and understand each other lies at the foundation of both business and social intercourse. The two languages spoken in the Americas are the growing influences of the present century. The rapid increase of the population of the United States would alone greatly influence the English-speaking population of the world during the next century, and in addition to this the use of the English tongue is rapidly spreading in the Orient, in the commercial centers of the world. As the Central and South American countries are likely to repeat during this century the development witnessed in the United States during the past century, the Spanish language seems destined to fill an increasing place in the world's future. The very best encouragement should therefore be given to the teaching of the English language in Latin America and the teaching of Spanish in the United States. There are several ways in which this encouragement can be given. The exchange of professors would be one. If an arrangement could be had by which colleges and universities of Central and South America would accept American instructors in return for Latin-speaking instructors in the United States, the temporary exchange would not only be helpful in extending the two languages, but larger acquaintances would follow, and acquaintance is, after all, the most essential thing in the improvement of international relations, whether social, business, or political. I would turn aside from my manuscript a moment to still further emphasize this idea. It has, ever since my connection with the Pan American Union, been a growing thought with me, that we have not improved to the full the opportunity to increase acquaintance by this interchange of professors and students, and I hope that those who are here assembled will carry back this thought for consideration and development, because whenever a professor comes to us from any of these Republics the students who knew him there will follow him with their thoughts, and where he goes he is apt to establish a center which will draw more and more of these young men to the United

States, and in this country he will become acquainted with students and he will be able to give to them a better knowledge of the country from which he comes than they can get from books. As this acquaintance is increased and as these ties between us multiply, there will be not only commercial and business advantage, but there will be the advantage that comes from more intimate political relations and more friendly diplomatic relations that rest upon this better knowledge of each other. Encouragement also could be given to the study of the two languages by colleges, especially by those located in the southern part of the United States, and in the northern Republics of the Latin-American countries, where special inducements could be offered to foreign students. The United States, for instance, could establish in Porto Rico, Panama, and accessible points along the Gulf Coast, schools in which special attention would be given to the teaching of the Spanish language and Spanish history, and the Latin-speaking nations could in return offer similar inducements to students from the north. In these special schools young men from the United States intending to go to South America, and young men from South America intending to come to the United States, could meet and while preparing themselves for their work, acquire that personal acquaintance which contributes so largely to success. This thought occurred to me first when nearly six years ago I visited Porto Rico, and again when I visited Panama, and I have not from that time failed to think of the opportunity which we have, as a nation, to extend our ideas as represented in our educational systems where they will be seen and taken advantage of by our neighboring Republics.

The establishment of some monetary unit throughout the Western Hemisphere has long been discussed, and there is no doubt that it would greatly facilitate the exchange between countries. The currency law now in force has, by authorizing the establishment of branch banks in foreign lands, greatly aided in the improvement of trade conditions, but it will require some years to realize to the full the advantages made possible by this law. It is worth while to consider whether it would be wise for the American Governments to facilitate exchange by an arrangement under which they could cable each other deposits made with each to cover foreign purchases.

During my connection with the State Department I had an opportunity to learn of the enormous burden thrown on the small Republics of Central and South America by the high interest rates they are compelled to pay. I became convinced that these high interest rates not only worked an injustice to the countries that paid them, and retarded proper development of those countries, but these loans, the very best that could be secured under existing conditions, sometimes caused insurrection and revolution. I learned of one incident in which the Government had to pay 22 per cent interest. I talked with the representative of that Government which was paying what would seem to us a very excessive rate, and found that the men who loaned the money felt justified in charging the higher rate to cover what they called the "risk." I also found that some of these people, after being paid for the risk, then asked the Government to take the risk off their hands and give them the profits without the risk. I came then to the conclusion that it would be much better for our Government to remove the risk and thus remove the burden instead of allowing the risk to be paid for and then removing it for the benefit of the man who loaned the money.

This Congress has already under consideration the possibility of cooperation in the defense of the Western Hemisphere as embodied in the proposition recently submitted by the President through Secretary Lansing, which contemplates a joint convention providing for the investigation of all diplomatic differences and arbitrary boundary disputes among the Republics of America, a convention which will go far toward removing the possibility of armed conflict between them. This evolution of the Monroe Doctrine enforced by the United States alone into Pan Americanism, supported by Latin America generally, will not only insure a solidarity of sentiment, but will, by the union of strength, lessen the expenditure necessary for protection, in case of a possible attempt of invasion, especially since the danger of invasion has decreased in proportion as the population in Europe has been reduced by the enormous loss of life occasioned by the war.

In conclusion, permit me to express the deep gratification which I feel over the spirit of cooperation and friendship which has made possible the treaties already negotiated between the United States and Latin-speaking republics. The plan, providing for the investigation of disputes of every character, was submitted to all the nations of the world at the same time, but to Latin America fell the honor of first accepting the proposal. The Republic of Salvador signed a treaty of this kind on the 8th of August, 1913. Guatemala, Panama, Honduras, and Nicaragua followed in the order named. It was not until after these five treaties had been concluded with the Latin-American Republics that the first treaty with a European nation was negotiated, namely, that of the Netherlands, signed on the 18th of December following. We now have 30 of these treaties connecting us with nations exercising authority over three-fourths of the peoples of the globe. Nearly all of the Republics of Central and South America are included in the 30, and the plan embodied in these treaties has been followed in a treaty recently entered into between Brazil, Argentina, and Chile. And when could an example set by the western Republics be more timely. While Europe, rent with passion, is in the throes of a struggle more bloody and costly than any the world has known before, peace prevails in the Americas. On the north of us, there is an unfortified boundary line of 3,000 miles, and our Nation has relieved our neighbors on the south of any fears that they may have had of invasion or conquest by us. Nor is our Nation the only one in giving evidence of peaceful intention. On the boundary line between Argentina and Chile there stands an heroic figure, the Christ of the Andes, erected by the joint contributions of the citizens of the two Republics, a proof of present amity and a pledge of future friendship. God grant that all the American Republics, one in their reverence for God and in their worship of His Son, identical in their aspirations, similar in their governmental methods, may, in the spirit of brotherhood and faith, cooperate in the advancement of the material, intellectual, and moral welfare of the western world, honorable rivals in helpfulness and service. They are joint tenants of a new land, neighbors in a new country, and are united by ties of interest as well as by ties of sentiment. What God hath joined together let no man put asunder.

The character and method of the instruction given in special schools of secondary grade were discussed at this session. Papers on the work of the business college, commercial high school, and the Young Men's Christian Association were presented, respectively, by President C. C. Gaines, Prof. William Fairley, and Mr. Edward L. Wertheim.

COMMERCIAL HIGH SCHOOL.

By WILLIAM FAIRLEY.

The most striking recent development in our secondary education has been along commercial lines. The reasons for this are twofold: The demand for a practical bread-winning training for that large proportion of our young people who can not go to college, and the demand of business men for young people in their offices who have some training in business operations. The report of the Commissioner of Education for 1913–14 shows the following ratio of commercial pupils to the entire secondary enrollment: North Atlantic Division, 22 per cent; North Central Division, 10 per cent; South Atlantic Division, 8 per cent; South Central Division, 4 per cent; and Western Division, 14 per cent; in New York City for 1914, 29 per cent. These figures show very clearly that commercial education is in demand very nearly in proportion to the business activity of the several sections.

The aim of the private school is largely confined to the lower ranges of commercial work. The public school should have a larger purpose, manifested in the length and the scope of its instruction. It adds to the technical training some preparation for citizenship. Most of our commercial training is in departments of general schools. A few of our larger centers of trade have developed the specialized commercial high school. The latter type has its distinct advantages. There is a lamentable tendency for the department in a general school to attract the weaker students. Even in the special commercial school there is as yet a too general feeling that its courses and standing are inferior to those of the academic school. The remedy for this can be found only in a change of public sentiment which shall arise from the manifested utility and success of commercial courses. The fact that most girls enter commercial courses simply to get a training for clerical duties creates the need for different training for such boys as wish to prepare earnestly for duties of a more advanced nature. The purposes of a commercial high school are: To fit for the simpler clerical duties, to fit the more earnest and capable to grow into managerial and executive positions, and to fit those who wish it to enter the commercial schools of university grade.

The course of study ranges from two to four years. The most common type is a three-year course. The best schools offer a four-year course. And in view of the subject matter undertaken and the aim in view, this is none too long. The full commercial course should embrace far more than the traditional penmanship, arithmetic, spelling, letter writing, bookkeeping, stenography and typewriting. These prepare only for subordinate clerical work. They are essential, most of them, for the majority of students. But they are only a beginning. Remembering, of course, that we are dealing with boys and girls of from 14 to 18 years of age, there is need of such other studies as shall give them as broad an outlook as possible into the world of men and of affairs. An unfortunate distinction is sometimes made in commercial schools between academic and commercial work. With the possible exception of music, there should be no subject in a commercial school which is not regarded as having a bearing on the future life of the business man; no subject which may well be slighted in the student's estimation because it is not practical. There must be some subjects which will have only an indirect bearing on office procedure, but will have a powerful influence on general intelligence and capacity for seizing and solving problems. Moreover, every business man is to be a citizen as well. The things that make for citizenship have their place as truly in the commercial as in the academic school. As will be shown later, it is this very breadth of training offered by our better commercial schools which the business world is fast learning to value and to demand.

Cooperation of business men and associations, illustrated best in Germany, may be obtained by visits and by helpful criticism of courses and methods, by lectures and addresses, by gifts of specimens and apparatus, and by entering into the "cooperative system"—half time in school and the alternate week in actual business employment. Every commercial school should have as ample a museum of commercial raw materials, products, and processes as possible.

There is one broad, general field which may well be had in mind in secondary work; it is the field of foreign trade. We know, as a matter of fact, that a good many graduates of our commercial schools are being sought now for Latin-American positions. Our schools will do well to have this growing possibility in mind. An English writer has thus stated the preparation for work in foreign fields:

1. An effective knowledge of foreign languages.
2. A knowledge of the modern methods of importing or exporting goods, including freightage and modes of transport.
3. A thorough knowledge of the goods in which he deals and of the sciences bearing on his trade.
4. A knowledge of the markets at home and abroad and the customs of the trade.
5. To understand foreign tariffs, foreign weights, measures, and moneys, and the exchanges.
6. To be acquainted with the technicalities of commercial documents, such as bills of exchange, bills of lading, insurance policies, etc.; and to have some knowledge of commercial law.
7. To know the principles of bookkeeping and accountancy.
8. A knowledge of economics bearing upon commerce, and the use of trade statistics.

YOUNG MEN'S CHRISTIAN ASSOCIATION.

By EDWARD L. WERTHEIM.

The Young Men's Christian Association in the United States has for a long time been engaged in the training of men and boys for commercial pursuits. Its membership, as well as its committees, are made up for the most part of business men. The 4,780 secretaries engaged to carry on the various phases of its work are in the main of the business type.

From simply providing reading rooms and libraries in 1851, the educational work has developed through the gradual additions of lectures, practical talks, educational clubs for study and research, classroom instruction introduced in 1860, definite schools for both day and evening students, etc., until it has produced those necessary lines of practical, vocational training demanded to-day for men and boys. This kind of instruction gradually grew out of the needs of the men, because they could not get this training so well in other institutions. So far as is known definite evening educational instruction of a vocational nature began in the Y. M. C. A. There are educational secretaries who give their whole time to the supervision of the work. Last year in the United States there were 78,000 different men in the classes, with 2,512 paid teachers and 4,700 lecturers. The cost of these activities was $1,045,900, of which $800,024 was paid by the students in tuition fees, aside from the membership fee of $214,190 more.

In addition to the ordinary courses fitting for college and university, 130 different subjects were taught, including every phase of commercial training.

There are many other forms of educational activities, such as educational trips, educational moving pictures, clubs, etc.

The association educational work is for men by men; it is given at any place or time in or outside the building to any kind or group of men; the teachers are selected for reasons of special fitness; courses of a practical nature are preferred; classes in English for foreigners are given free; and, as a whole, the work is conducted so as to be as nearly as possible self-sustaining.

Courses are offered as soon as need for them has been observed; for example, exporting was immediately put on at the time when the agitation for the need of knowledge began at the outbreak of the present war. Spanish at the present time is one of-the most popular subjects, and Russian is one of the most recent languages to be added. Classes in business and personal efficiency, accounting, advertising, and salesmanship are all very popular at the present time. In a majority of the classes the instruction is individual. Discussions and interchange of ideas are encouraged in the larger groups.

Definite educational work is being done by the association to acquaint men with the business opportunities in Latin America and to encourage friendly relationship. Spanish was taught to about 1,000 different men last year. Exporting has been taught in New York and San Francisco. Many associations have had special lectures dealing with opportunities in Latin America. Clubs have been organized for men to meet in discussion and have conversation in Spanish and Portuguese. Definite plans for work among the 60,000 Latin-American men in New York, who are encouraged to come to the local city associations on arriving in the United States, have been made.

The associations, with a membership of 620,799 in North America, with 759 buildings, its 4,400 employed officers, etc., offer an opportunity for diffusing information about Latin America. From its platform talks may be given on Latin-American topics. Books, magazines, trade journals, Government reports, etc., can be introduced into the association libraries and reading rooms, and in many other ways the present activities may be extended to include Latin America.

EIGHTH SESSION.

The program of the eighth session, held in the Pan American Union Building, Tuesday morning, January 4, at 9.30 o'cock, was devoted entirely to the instruction given in special schools of college and university grade. Interesting and valuable experiments are being carried on in the colleges of the United States incident to the establishment, as part of their curricula, of courses in business training. Several of the most fruitful of these experiments, as carried on in different types of schools, were explained at this session by the deans of these courses. Synopses of their papers, prepared by the writers, follow:

TULANE UNIVERSITY.

By MORTON A. ALDRICH.

When certain representative business men of New Orleans made up their minds that their city should have a college of commerce, they found three groups of people to which they could turn for help. First, there was the city's organization of business men, the Association of Commerce; secondly, there was Tulane University; and also there were those individual business men who were especially interested in establishing mature training for a business career. The problem with these men was how to mobilize and combine these three forces so as to secure the active and permanent interest of each group.

The business men of New Orleans have come to think of their college of commerce as an essential part of the commercial equipment of the city. They are of the conviction that they can best use the college of commerce when they think of it along with their exchanges, their railroads, and banks. Thus, the happy situation has developed where the business men think of the college as their asset and their responsibility. The business men do not feel that their responsibility to the college ceases with the signing of a check. Their cooperation is of the solid, active, day-by-day kind, and by bringing their constant interests and practical experience to the support of the college they have prevented waste motion and formalism so as to make every stroke tell.

The Association of Commerce provides ample quarters in its own building for the night courses which the college offers for business men and women (in addition to its four-year day course in the college buildings) and for the public Friday night talks of the college. These Friday night talks, under the joint auspices of the college and the Association of Commerce, have developed in our city one strong business forum. These talks are very informal and are always followed by questioning and discussion. As a result of this close relationship between the Association of Commerce and the college, more of the older members of the association, and more of the members of its vigorous young men's department, are enrolled in the business courses. All this gives the college a business atmosphere which is highly stimulating to young men.

Now, as to the support of individuals: One hundred and four of the leading men of the city have organized themselves into a board of guarantors to guarantee the expenses of the college, and they back up their financial support with their active personal interest. This board meets monthly to hear detailed reports of the work of the college and to lay plans for the further expansion of its usfulness. The college has relied for its success on the conviction that the public spirit and foresight of the modern business man make him ready to support any educational work when he can be shown that it is man's size, concrete, and definite.

UNIVERSITY OF CINCINNATI.

By FREDERIC C. HICKS.

The working plan of the college of commerce of the University of Cincinnati represents the attempt to realize two main objects: First, to provide facilities for commercial education of a high standard, and second, to make the training fit the actual needs of business.

The university is a municipal institution not merely in the sense of one supported and controlled by the city, but also in the sense of one whose work is related directly to the activities of the city.

The college of commerce is new, largely the outgrowth of evening classes started some 14 years ago by the Cincinnati chapter of the American Institute of Banking. These evening classes were organized into an incorporated college in 1906, but the real beginning of the plan outlined here dates from 1912, when the college became a part of the university. The requirements for admission in the case of those contemplating graduation consist of, first, the regular college-entrance requirements, and second, a two-years' precommercial course in the college of liberal arts. The two years' precommercial course may consist either of two full years of liberal-arts work or of a combination of liberal-arts work and approved business experience, such business experience being accepted for one-third of the precommercial course. Students who come into the college of commerce with business experience seem to have a better appreciation of the subjects studied in the college. The subjects studied are in the main prescribed. They include economics, economic history, commercial geography, English composition, mathematics, statistics, business psychology, ethics, money and banking, and railroads. For certain of these studies, subject to the approval of the faculty, work in German, French, or Spanish may be substituted in case the student is contemplating a career to which any of these languages is essential. As a rule, it is expected that the precommercial studies will be completed before the student enters the college of commerce. But it sometimes happens that he needs immediately some of the training offered by the college. In such cases permission is given to pursue precommercial and college of commerce work at the same time. The college is not primarily a degree-giving institution. It exists for the purpose of increasing the efficiency of those who contemplate engaging in business or who have already entered upon such a career. To this end its facilities are available to everyone whose training, either in school or in actual business, is such as to enable him to utilize them with profit. Accordingly, provision is made for admitting special students.

The regular course in the college of commerce covers a period of three years, and leads to the degree of bachelor of commerce. The work here consists of two parts carried on simultaneously; the first consisting of studies in the college; the second, of practice in business. The studies of the first year are prescribed; those of the second year are partly prescribed and partly elective; while those of the third year are wholly elective. The class work mentioned constitutes two-thirds of the work required for graduation. The other third consists of business experience and the study of the business in which the student is engaged. In addition to the above the requirements for graduation include the preparation of a satisfactory thesis relating to the business in which the student has been engaged.

A full year's work in the college can scarcely consist of fewer than 10 hours of class sessions a week, or five two-hour periods. If these sessions are so arranged as to require attendance upon classes five evenings in the week, the student whose days are filled with the duties incident to business activities is unable to maintain the standard which is expected of him. To meet this situation, the college provides classes in the late afternoon as well as in the evening, and no student is allowed to include in his schedule more than three evening sessions, each of two hours' duration. To strengthen still further the quality of the student's work, we hope ultimately to be able to require stated periods for supervised study.

The University of Cincinnati organized its commercial work as a separate college in the belief that it could adapt the work better to meet the practical demands upon it. Long experience shows that deviation of interest results whenever the attempt is made to carry on professional work in the college of liberal arts. The subject matter which must constitute the content of commercial education is still in the experimental stage. Larger freedom can be secured in determining this content in a college of separate organization. Further, when so organized, there can be developed among the students themselves better professional spirit. The teaching force of the college consists of three groups: The faculty staff, staff lecturers, and special lecturers. Most of those constituting the second and third divisions are business men. To utilize effectively the services of men of affairs as special lecturers in class work requires both care in the selection of men and supervision of the subject matter to be presented by them, to the end that it may be given in the proper form and fit the course of which it is a part. It may not be out of place to mention also the fact that we do not accept the services of anyone in connection with regular instruction without paying for it. This is true even in the case of the special lecturers. Though the compensation is relatively small, our experience has been that it serves to give a business tone to the arrangement which greatly increases its usefulness.

To comprehend the principles underlying any vocation, one needs to be in actual contact with those who are daily trying them out. Only in this way can he grasp their significance and appreciate their bearing upon the conduct of affairs. The method we are now employing to secure this combination of theory and practice is to place the class work of the college in the late afternoon and evening, from 5 to 7 and 7.30 to 9.30, so that students may spend the major part of each day in their several business positions. A systematic attempt to enlist the support of employers in this part of our work was begun about a year ago. The results thus far have been most encouraging.

It is sometimes thought that the curriculum of a college of commerce should include studies treating of all the important phases of business. Such is not necessarily the case. However vital an activity may be to business success, it can not be taught until there is something to teach, that is, until the experience in that field has become sufficiently standardized and formulated to supply the requisite subject matter. In the development of our class work, the starting point is business itself. The studies are planned with definite reference to specific vocations, such as the work of the business manager, the salesman, the advertising manager, the credit man, the traffic manager, the general banker, the investment banker, the accountant, etc. An essential part of this phase of our plan is the study of the business in which the student is engaged, to which reference was made in an earlier connection. It is to be carried on under the supervision of the faculty of the college and will involve regular weekly reports and conferences. Specially prepared schedules will guide the student in his investigations. During the first year, attention will be given to the character and organization of the business unit in which the student is employed, and to his relations with it, contractual and other. During the second year the study will cover the character of the industry to which the given business unit belongs, its history and its place in the general field of commerce, both domestic and foreign. The third year will be devoted to special problems that arise in connections with the business.

UNIVERSITY OF OREGON.

By HARRY B. MILLER.

This school was organized in September, 1914, with H. B. Miller, a former United States consular officer, as director and seven leading business men of the State as a board of advisers.

The first principle of the organization of the school is that it should promote the welfare of and interest in the industrial and commercial productions and prosperity of Oregon, the scope of the school to include a broad and comprehensive study of world-wide trade and commerce, the world's markets and methods of distribution, and particularly their utilization and adaptation to the resources and demands of the State.

The development of the resources and industries of Oregon demands a world market, and it was decided that the school of commerce should be actively associated with the Chamber of Commerce of Portland and have the assistance of the Federal Government. The school of commerce has been accorded a recognition that gives it benefits derived from these two departments of government.

The department of commercial and industrial service, whose primary function is to be of service to the commercial and industrial interests of the State, has been established. It is to be the collecting point and source of distribution of information regarding the resources of the State, and it is to devise and adopt such methods of investigation and instruction as will best aid in development of these resources. The plan is to select one of the leading industries and formulate a complete list of questions covering the essential features of the industry, answers to which will aid in creating and enlarging its markets. These questions are handed over to the Departments of State and Commerce and forwarded to the consular and commercial representatives in various parts of the world. From replies, bulletins are issued which give the Oregon producers and manufacturers complete and detailed knowledge of the world's production and consumption of the commodities investigated and the possibilities of Oregon in competition with other States and countries. The school of commerce also has the aid of State organizations in the industry under investigation.

There is also a course of lectures by business men and manufacturers and by representatives of the Federal departments who have made investigations of conditions abroad.

The director and his associates are endeavoring to inaugurate a system for the exchange of professors between this institution and some of the South American universities.

NEW YORK UNIVERSITY.

By JEREMIAH W. JENKS.

The purpose of the New York University school of commerce, accounts, and finance has been to combine with special courses, intended to widen the intellectual vision and to raise the ideals of the students, such a practical training as would fit young men best for the technical work of a business career. Emphasis is laid upon certain fundamental courses, such as accounting, business English, and a practical use in speaking and letter writing of any foreign language required, with, in addition, collateral subjects such as economics, business finance, principles of education, the relation of Government to business and the like. A large percentage of the students are engaged in active business, so that they pursue these courses largely in the evening, although a day school is maintained. Two years are required for day students, three for night students. The teachers themselves have practically all had business experience. The combination of students actively engaged in business and business trained teachers brings about eager enthusiasm and clear conceptions of the scientific principles upon which business is conducted. A considerable number of the students entering are already college graduates, who are expected to do a higher grade of work. Cooperation with the city of New York is maintained through a number of special courses given to young men in the civil service of the city. In addition, a number of courses are given for the engineering department of the city.

Last year a number of "business fellowships" were established in order to bring the university into closer touch with the best business houses, especially with the idea of securing men of ability to meet the crying demand for material to enter the work of developing the foreign trade of the United States. A number of important business houses have arranged to cooperate with the university by offering to a limited number of college graduates positions enabling these men to combine scientific study of business principles with actual business practice. Among the companies cooperating are the United States Steel Products Co., the Western Electric Co., the National City Bank, the American Telephone and Telegraph Co., the Ingersoll Watch Co., the United States Mortgage and Trust Co., the Alexander Hamilton Institute, the Union Pacific Railroad Co., and the Bureau of Foreign and Domestic Commerce. Most houses engaged in foreign trade wish men with knowledge of the language of the country in which they are extending their business. They wish to fit men for work in Russia, South America, India, and China, as well as in the United States. The company usually pays $50 to $75 a month. The holder of the fellowship gives part of his time during the college year, full-time during vacation. In addition, each man devotes his time to a study of business subjects in New York University. His work and his studies are adapted to his needs and those of his employer. The response to this plan was most gratifying. Over 300 applicants for these positions were received. As the work is experimental, only 15 fellows have been appointed. It is an opportunity for young men to secure positions that promise well; for business houses to get the pick of able young college men.

So many college men are now in residence preparing themselves for business careers that the university is considering the organization of a graduate division of the school of commerce, offering a specially planned course.

In these ways the New York University school of commerce, accounts, and finance is attempting to meet the various demands for business training made upon it.

THE AMOS TUCK SCHOOL OF ADMINISTRATION AND FINANCE, DARTMOUTH COLLEGE.

By H. S. Person.

The Amos Tuck School is a specialized, professional school of training for business; a semigraduate, finishing school for college graduates who plan to enter business. Its course consists of two years. The first year is of a grade equivalent to the senior year of an American college, to which are eligible for admission candidates who have completed three years in any college of high standing. The second year is a purely graduate year, at the end of which students receive the degree of master of commerical science. The curriculum of the first year represents a transition from the liberalizing courses of a college to the specialized courses of a professional school of commerce and administration; the curriculum of the second year is a compact group of specialized, professional courses, with a moderate flexibility allowing preparation for special branches of business, including foreign commerce.

The Tuck School has a definite relation to the elementary and secondary schools and to the colleges of the United States. To them it leaves, with respect to the students who may come to it, the cultural and mentally liberalizing influences of their educational processes. Of them it demands a broad foundation of training in the physical sciences, language and literature, and the social sciences; and of the college in particular it demands a thorough training in political science, history, and especially economics.

As a superstructure added to such a foundation, the school offers:

1. In its first year, courses in the primary functions of business common to all business, to insure that, with respect to preparation for business, the student's training shall not be too narrow. These functions comprise the financing of a business, the recording of the results of business operations, the technical organization and management of a business, the production and marketing, equipment and processes of a business.

2. In its second year: (a) More advanced courses in the above business functions, with the addition of a course in commercial law; (b) special courses affording the student opportunity for specific preparation for a particular business (e. g., foreign commerce, banking, etc.); (c) the opportunity for preliminary practical experience through the requirement of a thesis which represents the solution of a real problem in some plant of the business for which he is preparing.

By its entrance requirements, the Tuck School secures an automatically selected group of students more mature than the average of American college students, of higher average ability and capacity for serious work, and with a more uniform and thorough grounding in the sciences fundamental to business; in general a more homogeneous group as to preparation, purpose, and capacity for hard and sustained effort. These facts throw light on the quality of instruction possible in the school, and on the quality of response the school may reasonably demand of its students.

The Tuck School does not presume to train complete business men, but offers to the business community high-grade, mature, adaptable apprentices, broadly informed as to facts and principles of business, intensively informed with respect to the facts and principles of some particular field of business, and capable of assimilating rapidly the results of experience in business.

HARVARD GRADUATE SCHOOL OF BUSINESS ADMINISTRATION.

By EDWIN F. GAY.

The establishment of the business school as a graduate department of Harvard University occurred in March, 1908. The school aims to give a specialized preparation for business. The instructing staff includes men who give their entire time to this work, and men from the business world. The cooperation of business men is of great value and is shown also in their willingness to open their factories as laboratories for our students. Each candidate for graduation writes a graduation thesis and is expected to work in the summer between his two years in the school.

There is a lack of assembled information regarding the business subjects taught. Research alone can collect such material. The work of the bureau of business research of this university is valuable in this connection.

Throughout the work of the school the development of the professional spirit is emphasized in the instruction.

NINTH SESSION.

The ninth session was held in the Pan American Union Building, Tuesday afternoon, January 4, at 2.30 o'clock. Mr. Roger W. Babson presided. This session may be considered easily one of the most important of the program on commercial education in the United States in view of the fact that from the standpoint of priority and efficiency, particularly in reference to preparation for foreign trade, the claims of the extramural educational agencies represented at this session were presented in a series of papers by the directors of these educational activities. Authors' abstracts of the papers follow:

INTERNATIONAL CORRESPONDENCE SCHOOLS.

By T. J. FOSTER.

The International Correspondence Schools had their birth in a desire to improve the conditions of the miners of the State of Pennsylvania. The Mining Herald, a weekly newspaper of Shenandoah, Pa., established a department devoted to questions and answers relative to coal mining for the benefit of its readers. With the aid of competent engineers, a course in coal mining was printed which anyone able to read English could study at home. Within six months after the enrollment of the first student, October 16, 1891, a thousand men were studying the mining course by mail. From this beginning has been developed the present system of correspondence instruction. Created to teach a single subject, the schools now give instruction in 280 courses, covering almost every branch of technical education and dozens of other subjects ranging from advertising and salesmanship to poultry husbandry and agriculture. These courses include 62,000 pages of text and 31,000 illustrations and cost $2,500,000 to prepare. To conduct the work requires the hands and brains of more than 4,000 employees in America alone and hundreds in other countries of the world. They have enrolled more than 1,750,000 persons, representing every occupation in the realm of industry and every country on the globe; and approximately 100,000 new students are being enrolled each year.

The foundation of a system is its textbooks. To teach successfully by correspondence requires an entirely different kind of textbook than that used for classroom work. These books must take nothing for granted save the ability to read. They must begin at the beginning and proceed by easy stages, leading the student forward by natural and carefully graded steps. They must foresee and meet his difficulties by full explanations, demonstrations, and illustrations. Books of this class are used by 218 universities, colleges, Government schools, institutes of technology, and vocational schools in America. Successful home study depends upon a sustained interest on the part of the student. An Encouragement Department watches with a genuine personal interest the progress of their students. Last year the encouragement department of one school sent 1,110,204 letters of inspiration to students. As a result of this work, students to-day are doing 56 per cent more studying than in 1906. In 1914 the students of this school sent in for examination 1,141,430 lessons. The London instruction department handled in one year 358,000 lessons. Recently, to obtain specific information, an investigation was made of the cases of 27,000 typical students in a few Eastern States. Among the cases investigated 2 students were found who now have incomes of $50,000 a year, 6 who have incomes of $25,000 or over, and 20 who receive $10,000 per year or better. Out of these 27,000 students, 14,990, or 54.2 per cent, are receiving $1,500 a year; 2,451, or 9 per cent, are receiving at least $2,500 a year; and 413, or 1.6 per cent, have annual incomes of $5,000 or more.

Some of our best American colleges and universities have frankly admitted and adopted the method. Chicago University offers 52 courses by correspondence. The Universities of Minnesota, Wisconsin, Nebraska, West Virginia, and several others have adopted the method and are achieving some satisfactory results. Latin America has proven a good field for correspondence schools. One school, besides offering courses written in English, also offers courses written in Spanish. This company did a very good business in Mexico before the war and is now doing a considerable business in Cuba and in the South American Republics. This school has a good business in the Argentine Republic and conducts an instruction department at Buenos Aires. This department also handles the work for Chile, Peru, Uruguay, Paraguay, and southern Brazil. Seventeen technical courses in Spanish and 188 in English are now being sold in these countries.

NATIONAL ASSOCIATED SCHOOLS OF SCIENTIFIC BUSINESS.

By SHERWIN CODY.

Something like two years ago the leading mail-order house of New York determined to raise the standard of its office force all along the line and instituted a series of written examinations or tests of ability to perform usual operations in the business office, arranged in four general grades, with rather elaborate variations to fit their different departments. In two years they have very materially raised the entire standard of their office work; they have high-school graduates where before they had grammar-school graduates, and they have first-raters where before they had average mediums. They believe it pays, and they are developing their tests and supplementary training on a larger scale than ever before. At the last annual meeting of the National Association of Corporation Schools, the Curtis Publishing Co. exhibited a series of similar tests which they had been using. A large life insurance company has in regular use a somewhat complicated series of psychological tests. Experiments with systematic tests for office help in business houses have nearly all been tried by trained educators. A thoroughly wide-awake schoolman seems to learn business very much more rapidly than a person of business training solely learns the true science of testing and training young brains. The success along this line has suggested that the business men ought to take hold of our commercial schools and have these tests of ability to perform common operations in the business office substituted for the academic examinations now all too general. The first stand for speed and accuracy on simple and common operations, while the second consist largely of answering questions and giving definitions on the higher theory of the subject. The trouble is that the educators know only in a general way what the business men want. If the employment managers would work out a series of tests on which they would be willing to make appointments, there is no doubt that the educators would promptly adopt them, because their students are all working for jobs, and anything that will help them get jobs will be quickly seized.

The National Associated Schools of Scientific Business has been incorporated as a committee under the laws of Illinois. The organization is not for profit directly or indirectly, but is devoted to the public improvement of office efficiency both in schools and in business offices. Gov. W. N. Ferris is the president and Sherwin Cody the managing director and secretary. This committee has concentrated its attention on developing and trying out a series of elementary tests of ability to perform common operations in the business office, so as to measure speed and accuracy and also to test the fundamental education which all office employment presupposes and without which not even an office boy gives promise of future success. A series of tests was devised and printed in June, 1914, and tried out on employees by the employment managers of the National Cloak & Suit Co., the National Cash Register Co., the Burroughs Adding Machine Co., the Commonwealth Edison Co. of Chicago, Swift & Co., and in a limited way Marshall Field & Co. The object of the tests was to find out what were practical, how long the tests needed to be, what different kinds of tests were required. As a result 20 short, simple tests were devised which met the unanimous approval of the employment managers of the houses that cooperated, and were adapted to trying out in about an hour's time the following common classes of office employees: Office boys and girls, general clerks, stenographers of lowest grade, stenographers of secretarial class or beginning correspondence, and beginning bookkeepers.

The third edition of the National Business Ability Tests now published will give on the record blank, side by side with individual markings, the average of grammar-school graduates under the head of grammar-school education, high-school averages under the head of high-school education, and business-house averages under the head of business efficiency, or minimums that seem to be accepted widely as standard. Any good clerk can easily learn to give the tests and also to grade them by the key with speed and uniform accuracy. In certain things, such as figuring, spelling, typewriter operation, filling out business papers, filing, and copying, the business world demands approximately a 100-per cent standard of accuracy, while the schools have a tendency to operate on a 70-per cent standard appropriate to Latin and Greek where the 100-per cent standard is manifestly impossible. The National Business Ability Tests, if they can be generally established in business offices and schools, will undoubtedly stimulate schools to adopt the 100-per cent standard in some such matters as spelling. Of course this narrow, specialized proficiency is a good thing only in a few certain lines. In other directions the broad power to think in a clear businesslike way is far more important and more difficult to develop; but the practical test on answering letters ought to induce schools to abandon teaching merely the external forms of letter writing and give some attention to handling human nature skilfully and accurately, putting accuracy, tact, and good feeling into letters and cultivating the large outlook of human service in business.

———

UNIVERSITY EXTENSION WORK FOR MEN IN BUSINESS.

By SAMUEL MACCLINTOCK.

Business is becoming increasingly more exact, more scientific, and therefore professional. Knowledge consequently becomes indispensable for its successful conduct, and business knowledge becomes a synonym for commercial power. This is just as true in Cuba, Honduras, and the Argentine as it is in the United States of America.

It is extraordinary, but true, that business is the only great occupation which a man can enter to-day without previous special preparation. No one can become an engineer, a lawyer, an architect; he can not become even a stonemason or a motorman on our street cars without some previous preparation; but he can go into business no matter how inadequately he may. be prepared in the science of business. After entering upon his business career, the average man has been inclined to depend upon his personal experiences as his sole means of advancement. He has looked to precedents. He has tried to do things just as others have done them. There must be, and fortunately there is, some more direct, more scientific, and more economical plan by which every man who will may gain that knowledge and insight into business which makes for power and success. In response to the demand of modern business for exact knowledge, a number of our best universities have established within the past few years special schools of commerce and administration for the preparation of students who want to make professional careers in business. Such schools offer a valuable training, but how many can avail themselves of it? More than 85 per cent of our boys and girls leave school before they are 16, and never do any systematic studying after that. In the whole United States there are only 22 definitely organized schools of commerce and administration. The total number of enrolled students in the regular classes is apparently about 6,000. Consequently, this course of training is only for the favored few.

Some of our leading universities, recognizing the very limited numbers which they are serving, have endeavored to extend their usefulness to those who can not come to the campus by taking the university to the people, at least within their own States. This extension work of the university away from the campus is carried on in several ways, the chief of which are: (1) Classroom instruction, (2) lectures, and (3), above all, correspondence. Classroom instruction is not essential to adults who know how to study and are in earnest in seeking information. The second method—evening lectures—is excellent for the purpose of arousing interest and enthusiasm, but is a poor means of carrying on systematic instruction. Correspondence work remains as the chief means available for carrying on organized instruction for adults engaged in business. The first advantage of this method is that it comes to the student at his home, office, or factory, through the mails and at his convenience. The work is carried on by means of textbooks, lesson assignments, examination papers, and problems. The student sends in his written work to his instructor, who criticizes it, grades it, and returns it with such comment and suggestion as may be needed. In this way the student goes through the subject in orderly fashion, mastering each lesson as he goes and consulting his instructor by correspondence if serious difficulties arise.

The number of colleges and universities having correspondence departments is only 32 in the whole United States, and the total number of students enrolled is approximately 20,000, including the large number taking agricultural work. The number of students thus engaged in studying business subjects is certainly not more than 10 per cent of the total number enrolled—a mere handful of all those in business who could profitably be supplementing their personal work and experience by this broader knowledge of others.

The universities, furthermore, are not the only sources of knowledge of practical value to the business world by any means. But our State and Federal Governments go to great expense to collect information about business and useful for business which, nevertheless, is but little used. The distribution of knowledge is as great a social and economic need as is the discovery of new truths.

The demand for practical business training and the inability of the established educational institutions to supply it have led to the founding, during the last few years, of a considerable number of schools operating on a commercial basis and endeavoring to supply the want. There are possibly over 100 such schools in existence today. Most of them are poorly organized and poorly conducted and have but a limited enrollment.

The reputable correspondence schools use university extension methods in supplying, at a relatively small cost, practical training of a vocational character to all adults who desire to learn something worth while, wherever they may live and whatever their previous education. Over 300 different subjects, including the mechanical trades, professions, arts, sciences, languages, and business subjects, are being successfully taught to-day by the correspondence schools. Their text material, lessons, quizzes, examinations, and practical problems are often prepared with great care and at great expense by business and professional authorities of the highest rank. Such material is characterized by clearness, simplicity, directness, and comprehensiveness. In the high-grade correspondence school the instruction staff likewise is made up of well-trained specialists. The pedagogy of correspondence study is absolutely sound. The student takes the training along with his daily work at the very time when he needs it' most, thus happily combining the theory and the practice of the subject. It must not be supposed, moreover, that the modern extension university confines its work exclusively to formal instruction. In addition to such work it renders a highly useful service through its consulting department. It collects data upon current topics and developments in its various fields of instruction. Such an institution thus becomes a veritable clearing house for business information. The correspondence schools are distinguished from extension divisions of the resident universities primarily by being private enterprises. They are conducted to make a profit by rendering a service worthy of the fees charged and in response to a demand for something which the other educational agencies do not supply. Systematic extension study gives a man a more comprehensive and better rounded-out knowledge of the policies and principles that make for business success than can be obtained from personal experience alone or from any " hit-or-miss " system of unorganized reading. Systematic, organized business knowledge makes a salesman out of a clerk, a merchant out of a storekeeper, a producer out of a credit man, and a business general out of a manager. That it pays goes without saying. American industry has advanced in character and efficiency because correspondence schools, though only in their infancy, have developed the study habit in hundreds of thousands of men and women throughout the country. University extension work is truly one of the biggest ideas in modern education and one of the most hopeful plans for promoting the efficiency of adult workers in all lines of industry. I think I may safely say that in carrying on such work the La Salle Extension University, with nearly 30,000 student subscribers, and other such institutions are rendering to the business men of the country, and thus to the cause of general education and efficiency, a distinctly valuable service.

ALEXANDER HAMILTON INSTITUTE.

By Joseph French Johnson.

The Alexander Hamilton Institute is not a correspondence school. It gives no diploma and no certificate. Appealing to men of a mature type, it was necessary to develop the work along lines distinctly different from anything ever tried before. In the main, such men fall into two groups: First, those who are already executives or in semiexecutive positions, or those who have the education to be in line for such a position; and, second, men holding highly specialized positions who should be in line for work of a more general character. Among the latter are mainly technical men, specialty salesmen, and the like.

Since the institute was organized, there have been enrolled about 35,000 active, ambitious, energetic men. It is interesting to note that the average age of a subscriber is about 32 years, and the average salary about $2,650. A large percentage are college graduates, though a college training is not an indispensable qualification.

In planning the material of the course, it was necessary to keep in mind that there are really only four fundamental activities in every business—producing, marketing, financing, and accounting. The principles underlying these activities are fundamental and apply in all lines of business.

The institute provides for its subscribers a reading course paralleling a university school of commerce course, under the guidance of an active staff of business men and professional teachers. It also supplies, in the form of printed talks, lectures, and problems, as nearly as possible instruction similar to that given in college classrooms. Furthermore, it offers the free services of its staff in the reviewing of problems and in the discussion of such questions as the subscribers themselves seek light upon.

The text volumes form the backbone of the course. They bring to the reader a survey of business principles from the executive's point of view. But they are not the whole of a college or of a nonresident reading course. If we are to follow pedagogical methods developed in resident work, we need to get something to take the place of the instructor. Now, what are the instructor's functions? First of all, in assigning reading on a topic he gives an informal talk on it. Next he takes up some special point and elaborates on it. At the end of each session, through quizzes and examinations, he tests the student's understanding of the subject and his ability to use his knowledge in the solution of definite problems. Finally, he stands ready to assist the young man in case he has trouble in getting things clear in his mind. In planning the modern business course and service we arranged for a staff to do these very things in connection with the subscriber's reading of the textbooks of the course. Every fortnight for two years the subscriber receives by mail a group of pamphlets consisting of the talk, and either a lecture or a problem. The mere receipt of the material serves as a stimulus to regular and systematic reading.

THE COMMERCIAL MUSEUM OF PHILADELPHIA.

By W. P. Wilson.

The first two great international commercial congresses held in the United States were organized and conducted by the Commercial Museum of Philadelphia. To the first, in 1897, were invited, through the State Department, delegates only from the Latin-American nations. All of these countries were represented by 51 delegates. To the second, in 1899, all commercial countries were invited through the State Department, and delegates to the number of 300 responded from every leading nation of the world.

Two lines of educational work have been inaugurated and strenuously carried out by the Commercial Museum: The first, *a foreign trade bureau*, has arduously labored to convince the manufacturer of the urgent necessity of occupying some of the foreign fields of trade before they were possessed by other countries. This .work has been pushed in all parts of the United States and with all lines of manufacturers whose products could find normal sale in any locality abroad. This foreign trade bureau furnishes the manufacturer with all necessary data on the requirements and opportunities of foreign markets and on tariffs existing in different ports of entry; on trade-marks and patent laws, consular relations, shipping routes and rates, and similar information relating to the invoicing and transportation of goods for foreign countries; methods of payment and granting of credits; competition to be met in foreign markets, and names of reliable business houses throughout the world. The bureau has a list of more than 375,000 foreign firms, with information regarding their lines of business and importance in the trade. It conducts a free reference library of commerce and travel, with over 78,000 volumes, containing over 400 foreign and domestic directories, both city and trade, official bulletins of every country publishing them, consular reports from all countries which issue them, 750 of the leading magazines, trade journals, and dailies, of which over one-half are from foreign countries. This library, with its very complete list of foreign documents, is used by a large corps of assistants for the direct benefit of exporting firms, and to give them the needed help they require. This work is done for any manufacturer at actual cost of investigation and compilation.

The second line of educational work done by the Commercial Museum is for the schools of the city of Philadelphia and the State of Pennsylvania. This work includes the following: (a) A special series of lectures in the museum to classes from the schools and colleges of Philadelphia and vicinity. These lectures cover subjects of geographic, commercial, and industrial importance and are adapted to scholars of all ages from the fourth grade up. Classes come to the museum by special appointment to hear these lectures, which are illustrated by colored lantern slides and motion pictures. At the close of every lecture the pupils, under the direction of experienced museum guides, study the exhibits which illustrate the subject of the lecture. These lectures bring more than 35,000 pupils to the museum every year and make the collections a great laboratory for the study of geography and commerce. (b) The loan, free of cost to public school teachers in all parts of Pennsylvania, of sets of colored slides, accompanied by lantern, screen, and typewritten lectures, covering the same field of geography, commerce, and industry. These sets of slides have now a very wide circulation, especially among the rural schools, and every year reach tens of thousands of pupils in all sections of the State. During the past year, 75,000 children from the State public schools attended the lectures. (c) The distribution, free of cost to public schools in all parts of Pennsylvania, of large collections of specimens to aid teachers in geographic and commercial instruction. These collections are not loaned, but remain permanently in the schools to which they are sent. They include the principal articles which make up the bulk of the world's commerce and represent the chief industries of mankind. The specimens are arranged to show the important raw materials and stages through which they pass in the process of manufacture. Thousands of these collections have gone to schools in all parts of Pennsylvania within the past few years. They are distributed under an appropriation made by the State for this purpose.

THE NATIONAL CITY BANK OF NEW YORK.

By F. C. SCHWEDTMAN.

The similarity of situation, political organization, and other characteristics of the American nations makes commercial education, with special reference to the needs of the continent, of the greatest importance to the members of this congress.

The National City Bank has for many years been engaged in fostering commercial education, coordinating theory and practice. The enactment of the recent Federal reserve act has enabled the National City Bank to extend its activities to the rest of the continent. One of the vice presidents, Mr. William S. Kies, together with a large corps of trained commercial experts, has devoted more than a year and a half to the development of industrial and commercial relations between the United States and South America. These educational efforts may be summarized as follows:

(a) The sending of experts to the various Central and South American countries to make careful observations at the different trade centers; (b) the keeping of this information up to date by commercial attachés named by the National City Bank at each of its branch banks, at present established in six Latin-American countries; (c) special systems of acceptances and dollar credits; (d) propaganda as to the importance of international trade in general with special reference to the South American trade; (e) publication of the special magazine known as The Americas; (f) special classes for the training of additional foreign banking and trade experts; (g) an employment office maintained where men suited for foreign commerce and those requiring such men are brought together; (h) the foreign-trade department renders aid and gives advice to all interested in foreign-trade matters; (i) the compilation of the most important facts relating to international trade and credit and which bear on South America—these are furnished free to both customers and non-customers of the bank.

In this work the bank has been inspired not only by commercial, but by patriotic reasons as well, due to the attitude to be assumed in the relations between the United States and Latin America by reason of the present European war, which is now converting the United States into the financial center of the world and the chief consumer of Latin-American products. The United States should be ready to do its part in supplying the necessary capital for the development of South America. To this end are directed the efforts of the National City Bank which is laboring to bring about a better understanding among the peoples of the continent, having ever in mind a unanimity of purpose in attaining the aims desired by all.

NATIONAL ASSOCIATION OF CORPORATION SCHOOLS.

By LEE GALLOWAY.

As we have reached the commercial era which is permeated with the spirit of public service, commercial education is now given a place not only in the schools and colleges, but in the workday program of the business corporation itself. The corporation is assuming its share of responsibility by preparing its employees to do their work more efficiently, not only because it means profit to them, but because they are becoming public-spirited enough to realize that training is the right of the adult individual. The corporation school is particularly well qualified to do this because there is a chance for actual experience in connection with the schooling and the opportunity to interpret abstract things in the light of concrete experience.

Commercial education as given by corporation schools is classified as follows: (1) Salesmanship; (2) general office, including accountancy. The students are mostly adults. Therefore adult psychology and methods of teaching to appeal to the adult only will apply. No matter how much personal hygiene, etc., is taught, this will not train the mind to do some particular thing well.

Classification of salesmanship courses includes: (1) Knowledge of the product and competitor's product; (2) personal methods of selling; (3) business policies; (4) business English; (5) advertising methods; (6) market distribution; (7) economics; and (8) organization and management.

The study of the product constitutes the only topic of many salesmanship courses. It is the chief thing in some businesses. It is intricate or not according to the nature of the product. An illustration of teaching the product may be seen in the method of the Norton Grinding Co., of Worcester, Mass. The length of time for this study, the methods of teaching, the teachers, etc., are considered in the writer's paper.

The change from the policy of *caveat emptor* to the " public-be-pleased " point of view makes the course in personal selling very important. The courses included under this are: (1) The selling process proper; (2) the study of the prospect; (3) psychology of gaining attention and interest; (4) the demonstration of the goods; (5) essential qualifications of the salesman; and (6) ethics of business.

The teaching of personal salesmanship was begun 20 years ago by the National Cash Register Co. It was crude in method, but has developed into quite comprehensive courses.

Business policy must be taught to arouse interest in the company and its merchandise. It is necessary, too, to reflect this policy of the firm by the proper demeanor of its representatives. The slogan of the United Cigar Stores Co. and the Larkin Co., as well as the more comprehensive method of the New York Edison Co., are given by way of illustration.

The study of business English is necessary in these commercial courses in order that the company may be represented accurately and pleasingly. Illustrations from the manual of the Larkin Co. are given to show one method of teaching this. Advertising and market distribution have not yet been taught systematically in corporation schools, although they are important subjects. Elementary economics deserves a place. An illustration of how it may be taught is given from the Goodyear Tire & Rubber Co.'s school. Organization and management are taught in very few schools.

The new movement in department-store education is accomplishing valuable results. There are about 50,000 sales people in New York City alone. The policy of the store was one of the first subjects to be inculcated, so as to get the interest of the individual aroused. Then followed the teaching of the store system, the care and arrangement of stock, the technique of selling, and finally the study of merchandise or knowledge of the goods, and business English. The Department Store Education Association in New York aims to study the methods and conditions of department-store employment and to develop salesmanship to the basis of a skilled occupation and give it a professional standard. An experimental school was held at Lord & Taylor's, and one is now conducted at Stern Bros. under the supervision of an educational director. The association is also trying to coordinate their work with that of the public schools. In Boston, at the Union School, saleswomen attend classes in salesmanship.

The necessity of office-work schools and the method of teaching office routine are explained by the writer, and figures are given to show that the office school is a profitable investment.

In order to economize effort and expense, the National Commercial Gas Association is standardizing commercial courses for the men in the gas business. The distinctive features of such courses must be kept in mind. The gas company is a public utility organization, and the idea of service predominates throughout the course. During the first two years only salesmanship and organization were dealt with; during the third year the knowledge of the product, i. e., the utilization of gas appliances was taught, and now a three years' course is being organized embracing more general subjects. The National Electric Light Association is beginning a similar correspondence course.

In order to interchange ideas concerning corporation schools, the National Association of Corporation Schools was organized by a number of interested companies. The work and problems of this association are described.

BIBLIOGRAPHY.

1. The Proceedings of the National Association of Corporation Schools, Conventions of 1913, 1914, 1915. Published by the Executive Committee, Irving Place and Fifteenth Street, New York City.
2. The Bulletins of the National Association of Corporation Schools, Irving Place and Fifteenth Street, New York City.
3. Industrial Education—The official convention newspaper of the third convention of the National Association of Corporation Schools, 1915. Published by Norton Grinding Co., Worcester, Mass.
4. Answers to the questionnaire of the Codification Committee of the National Association of Corporation Schools.
5. The monthly bulletins of the National Commercial Gas Association, 1913–1915.
6. Outlines of the Courses of Study of the National Commercial Gas Association, 1915.

BUREAU OF COMMERCIAL ECONOMICS.

By FRANCIS HOLLEY.

The Bureau of Commercial Economics is an institution which shows by the graphic method of motion pictures how things in common use are made and produced, and from what sources the raw material is obtained, and under what conditions labor is called upon to serve in their production. It is an institution that has been organized under the general educational law; it has no capital stock; it is not operated for profit, and has been affiliated with 106 of the universities and colleges of the country, including nearly all of our State universities. It shows, for instance, in motion pictures, sheep ranging on the foot-hills and on the plains in both America and Australia. It shows the care and protection of these sheep, the treatment for disease, the dipping and washing and shearing, and then it follows the bale of wool to the making of cloth and clothing of every description. It shows the taking of the hides and the various processes of tanning, the old method and the new, and the making of shoes and gloves. The films then recur to the flesh of the animal and show, in motion pictures, furnished by the great packing houses, the various processes of making it fit for the table, and the final disposition of the by-products. The cattle and hog industry is treated likewise.

The films show the making of glassware, pottery and china, mining, making of all classes of garments, raising of rice and sugar cane, making of silverware, canned goods, cutting of timber, and making of wood pulp and paper, the harvesting of hemp, and the making of cordage, lace, carpets, rugs, oilcloth, and linoleum. The films of the bureau depict the making of all classes of electrical equipment, turpentine and creosote, antitoxins and vaccines, and various types of drugs and medicines. The films of the bureau include a series showing the action and reaction in chemistry—analytical, industrial, and commercial—in the making and production of commercial fertilizers and dyestuffs, and the like, and also a complete series in road building. The silk industry is clearly shown. The films depict the making of the felt hat, show the making of varnish and buttons, the gathering of rubber and the making of pens and tires, the pumping of oil and its treatment, transportation, and uses; the engraving and printing of bonds and securities, and the surveying and construction of railways and railway equipment; the printing and binding of books and magazines, and the manufacture and uses of fiber of all types; the production of roofing material from old rags and the operation of machinery in our city laundries; the care with which milk is obtained from the modern dairy, and the sterilization and pasteurization of it as a protection to the public health and the production of canned milk and other products of the dairy, including the creameries.

In addition to the industrial films which the bureau has in circulation, there is a large number in the series of travelogues. These travelogues show all of the transcontinental lines from the Canadian border to the Mexican border. In our collection which is being made for us now by the Canadian Government we will be able to show the seal and fur industries along the Arctic, and the apple industry of the Province of Ontario; and we are in receipt of all of the films of the Commonwealth of Australia, which have been intrusted to us for use in our crusade for public instruction. The bureau has also the films of the Republic of Bolivia, and will shortly have those from Argentina, showing the trans-Andean lines and all of the activities in stock raising in the great pampas of Argentina.

The work of the bureau is given in the various State universities, with appropriations provided by the legislature of the several States, to encourage extension work, and in many instances, in missions and other organizations which may be benefited by their display. The work of the bureau is also carried on before the chambers of commerce, boards of trade, and commercial bodies, and fraternal organizations, and in the summer time they are given in the parks and playgrounds of the various cities. No film is shown for money. If it is clearly educational, divested of all advertising, and shows a process, it will be displayed free of expense to the producer. It, however, carries a credit line, simply giving the name of the donor. No film is shown where any admission charge is made to the public. The work of the bureau is perpetuated through the election of its directing offices by an advisory council composed of college presidents and men of international distinction in science and letters. The bureau is maintained through contributions and annuities. Contributions are invariably voluntary, and no one is authorized to solicit the same. The surplus funds of the bureau will be used in the production of welfare films, first aid to the injured, including the resuscitation of the drowning and the emergency methods of rescue of imprisoned miners, and the awakening and development of civic pride and patriotic American citizenship.

TENTH SESSION.

The tenth and concluding session of this subsection was held jointly with the several subsections of Section IV, Education, meeting at the New Willard Hotel, Friday afternoon, January 7, 1916, at 2.30 o'clock. Sr. José María Gálvez, of the University of Chile, presided. At this joint session the following Pan American theme was discussed in conference:

How can a nation prepare in the most effective manner its young men for a business career that is to be pursued at home or in a foreign country?
(a) In schools that are a part of the public school system.
(b) In schools of private endowment.
(c) In special business schools of private ownership.
Outline a course of study that will best prepare young men to engage in such a business career. Each suggested outline should consider not only the character of the educational system of the country for which the course of study is intended, but the desirability and practicability of a uniform course of business education for all Pan-American countries.

The following are abstracts of papers presented by the Latin-American contributors:

Francisco Araya Bennett, Director of the Commercial Institute of Valparaiso, Chile.—As a general rule all extensive commercial undertakings in Latin-America are carried on by foreigners. Commercial education in these Republics takes cognizance of this fact, therefore. The Chilean youth, for example, who wishes to succeed in the commercial world seeks a position with some English, American, French, German, or Italian firm. To be admitted into a foreign house, a knowledge of modern languages is necessary, particularly English. For some time past aspirants for a commercial career have prepared themselves in English private training schools, but since it was noted that they had to compete with the foreign employees of these same houses, even more preparation has been deemed necessary.

There was formerly a common belief that a merchant was born not made, that a merchant by vocation knew certain things without being taught. Aside from the profession of a merchant, there were certain trades which might be studied, e. g., stenography, bookkeeping, typewriting, etc. For this purpose, then, instead of commercial institutions there were separate courses given in these branches. The American business colleges have flourished everywhere, offering usually at a high price rapid courses in these branches and guaranteeing lucrative employment on completing the course. We now no longer believe that a merchant is specially gifted, but that a normal man with appropriate training can develop particular skill and achieve satisfactory results in any sphere of activity. All now recognize that the quality is more important than the number of the inhabitants. Everywhere we are endeavoring to improve public education, and to give to our citizens the best possible training for their own well-being, and with it that of the nation. Modern means of locomotion have erased distance, uniting the globe in one market. The example of the merchant, chief agent of the circulation of the world's wealth, reflects better than anything else the transformation in commercial teaching.

The productive power of the British Empire, the United States, Germany, Austria, Belgium, France, and Italy has reached such a stage that the world has been alarmed at the specter of over-production; and one nation, Germany, has proclaimed the necessity for preparing her merchants especially for this congestion, opening with intelligence and perseverance those markets which show possibilities of success. Even those merchants, trained in established traditions, have noted the effects of this systematic preparation and have made ready to arm themselves for the economic struggle. The merchants of Latin America have had a different problem to face from those of Europe and the United States, as these Republics are producers of raw materials, food stuffs, or only partly manufactured supplies. The Latin tendency, inherited from Spain, which tends toward the literary professions, makes even more vital the necessity for a change in public instruction. In the university, instead of studying only a political economy based upon foreign books suggested by observations of other social conditions, one should devote himself to the study of his own national conditions. In general Latin America lacks opportunities for a common study of her interests and ideals. It has common problems, yet each part seeks solutions for its own difficulties without waiting, as it should, for the results obtained by others facing the same conditions. In the educational field the problems differ substantially from those which confront the United States. British tradition is very different from Iberian. English democratic customs are not like those which have been acquired through the inherent absolute monarchical system of Spanish origins. Latin Americans should endeavor to create, like the States of Germany and of the United States, economic relations which would permit them, facing common necessities and recognizing their own peculiar problems, to establish satisfactory and mutually advantageous customs—and trade relations in general.

South America has been colonized upon the coasts and that is why there still exists in the center an immense unpopulated area. It lacks the railroad systems which bind together the States of the United States, a lack which the rivers do not supply. The creation of a Latin-American commercial university would accomplish more than anything else to join the Latin-American Republics in bonds of confraternity and common welfare. For secondary commercial education each State can provide for itself, but when it comes to the university, it seems that no one of the Republics separately can establish it; and all need it. Commerce is a bond of union. The Latin-American countries are in the matter of economic development more or less on the same plane. They are not, generally speaking, competitors of each other. Europe and the United States are the great supply markets for all of them. They appreciate the benefits of this foreign commerce and of foreign capital, but at the same time believe that each country should prepare itself to develop its own resources. The United States and Europe are for them on the same plane commercially. The Latin Americans need, therefore, to study their own interests from their point of view as producers of raw materials. A commercial university should look chiefly toward economic studies which should not be mere abstractions, but should furnish the opportunity for research work in economics applied to the various countries in Latin America. Two plans are proposed for the secondary phase of commercial education: (1) To prepare the future merchant in a school of general character and then send him for his special training to schools where he may study stenography, typewriting and office practice, bookkeeping, accounting, exchange, banking, customs, and fiscal matters; (2) to send him direct to special schools of commerce at any early age for his commercial training. His training should be here both general and special. This plan is followed by the Chilean Government. The plan proposed by the Instituto Comercial of Valparaiso for secondary commercial training seems most acceptable.

With English as the basic modern language, thoroughly taught and acquired, the young "junior" in commerce, on finishing this school at 15 or 16, has through his skill in rapid and accurate figuring in simple commercial practices a great advantage over the clerks carried from England for this purpose and shows great adaptability in his development from a mere clerk to a subordinate independent executive position. The course of study in the institute of Valparaiso offers also history, particularly of Chile, the elements of modern law, customs and exchange, German, and hygiene.

SR. A. AUBERT, Leon, Nicaragua: A commercial career must be the outcome and part of some system of general and industrial training where young men may acquire not only the rudiments of knowledge necessary to any determined and special calling, but a mastery of those elements which must perforce establish an unmistakable superiority and advantage of what may very properly be called "skilled training" over and above the more common and ordinary form of "unskilled labor." Technical training is of great advantage whenever a classification of service exists. Such a classification exists whenever individual efforts are considered as mechanical and administratve. The first refers to unskilled and rudimentary labor and the second to that product of ability and knowledge due to skillful and adequate training for managerial and administrative employments, and obtained and acquired in competent and well-established centers of education. The different callings require different degrees of skill. A clerk behind a counter, an accountant in his office, a manager of a concern, a carpenter, a blacksmith, and a mason furnish examples of this, but the economic results of these degrees of skill depend evidently on efficiency and proper training.

The value of technical education can not be overestimated. It is invaluable both to the individual and to society, becomes a sort of propelling force toward the advancement and progress of any civilized country and State. In the business world this want of skilled training is keenly felt. Governments and municipalities have, further, to face a series of perplexing economic and administrative problems of organization and management in which the counsel, advice, experience, activity, and labor of the trained expert offer incalculable service. Efficiency is demonstrated to-day as never before. A well-known writer recently said: "The average young man of to-day without a trained mind equipped with a previously acquired foundation of facts is not, in the narrow place to which the division of labor assigns him, in a position to grasp the breadth and depth of this business."

A uniform course of commercial instruction for all the countries of the American Continent may be established for the different kinds of schools enumerated in the writer's paper as sections A, B, and C under the following curriculum, which may conveniently be divided in a full course of three years, and for young men who have been previously prepared or who may have acquired beforehand a knowledge of the three R's or the benefits of a high-grade school: Grammar, arithmetic, languages, geography, accounting, bookkeeping, stenography, typewriting, economics, customhouse laws, port regulations, commercial law, shipping and transportation, correspondence, and history. Each subject should be so presented as to afford the necessary scope and extension which will secure the desired end.

SR. M. DELLEY, Director School of Commerce, Caracas, Venezuela.—The prosperity of a country and the peace of the world are due to commerce and to its instrument, credit. Adequate educational preparation for commerce is highly necessary. Latin America, owing to its natural resources and proximity to the Panama Canal, should begin immediately this educational preparation.

Diversified business and division of labor have made it impossible to train young men by the older system of apprenticeship. The German modification of this system, through compulsory supplementary school instruction, is the modern and successful type. The subjects usually taught in the school-apprentice course of three years are accounting, commercial arithmetic, business correspondence, commercial law, economic geography, and one foreign language. Germany has 650 of these schools; Switzerland, 110; and England has 250,000 pupils enrolled in 6,000 classes.

A course of instruction in a school of commerce is absolutely necessary to young men engaged in the practice of commerce to-day, as the special character of work he has to do makes it impossible for him to correlate his work. Elementary commercial schools with a course of two years will give the elementary technical knowledge for an apprentice and will shorten the term of service in actual practice. The higher schools, with courses of 3, 4, or 5 years, will reduce likewise the period of service and will give in addition to the technical training that general knowledge which is helpful in the higher positions. These schools should be supplemented through higher training schools, like collegiate business training courses and universities of commerce.

The Latin-American countries have attempted largely to establish commercial instruction after European models. It would be better to evolve a system according to native needs and conditions. For the present, the great trouble is that of a satisfactory elementary course. The later courses will proceed naturally from this.

Mexico, Panama, El Salvador, Ecuador, Honduras, Bolivia, Chile, Argentina, and Venezuela have shown great interest for this phase of education. There is, however, no uniformity in their plan of instruction. Commercial education is particularly necessary in the Latin-American countries, owing to the fact that the Latin-American boy matures early, is restive under discipline, and has the tendency to enter a business house too early. Uniformity in plan and method of instruction, the establishment of a common type of school in Latin America, may be possible since the work is recently established in these countries. The best type of school for such a purpose is one of three years, beginning with pupils 14 years of age. A suggested course of study is the following:

Schedule and course of study.

Studies.	First year.	Second year.	Third year.
	Hours.	*Hours.*	*Hours.*
Native language	4	2	2
First foreign language	6	6	6
Second foreign language	3	3	3
Arithmetic and algebra	3	3	0
Accounting and commerce	6	3	3
Commercial practices	0	5	6
Local commercial products	0	0	2
Physics and chemistry	2	2	0
Merchandising	0	0	2
Economic geography	1	2	2
History of commerce	0	1	1
Commercial law	0	1	1
Political and commercial economy	0	1	1
Penmanship, typewriting, and stenography	2	1	1
Total	27	30	30

DR. SANTIAGO H. FITZSIMON, Professor, International Correspondence Schools, Buenos Aires Branch, Argentina.—The public school system of Argentina has been influenced greatly by the example of the United States. One of the first measures of President Sarmiento, on returning from the United States in 1860 was the establishment of the Normal School of Paraná under the direction of a North American. In this school the teachers of the public schools have been trained. Further, American scientists, like Gould, have introduced American methods into the higher schools. Not until 1890 was anything done for commercial education, although Alberdi in 1852 urged the establishment of commercial schools in the larger commercial cities. Dr. Victor M. Molina, introduced a bill in Congress in 1889 for the establishment of two schools, in Buenos Aires and in Rosario de Santa Fe. In 1890 the first national school of commerce was established. The course proposed was liberal in character, based on general training studies supplemented by special courses. A succession of distinguished ministers of public instruction have been deeply interested in this school. The course was enlarged and two additional schools established in Buenos Aires, one for males and one for females. Schools have been established likewise in Rosario, La Plata, Bahia Blanca, Concordia, and Tucuman.

His Excellency, Dr. Romulo Naón gave this work his special attention and introduced important reforms as minister of public instruction in 1910. The work is now divided into elementary, secondary, and higher or university. The elementary courses are given at night and prepare business clerks and bookkeepers. The secondary course contains studies that develop intellectual discipline. The university course, given in the faculty of economic sciences of the university, prepares commercial and administrative chiefs and professors of commerce.

The elementary course prepares business clerks in three years, and bookkeepers in four. It includes the following subjects: *Compulsory.*—Arithmetic, business methods and accounting, Spanish and commercial correspondence, history of Argentina, general and commercial geography, penmanship and typewriting. *Elective.*—English or French, commercial products and stenography.

The higher course graduates mercantile experts in five years. It includes the following subjects:

	Years.
Mathematics: Arithmetic, algebra, geometry	5
Drawing	2
Spanish: Grammar, composition, literature, and commercial correspondence	5
Practical business course and accounting	4
Natural sciences: Natural history, physics, chemistry	4
Mercantile technology	2
General and commercial geography	4
Elements of political economy	1
History of Argentina, of the American countries, and history of commerce	4
Customs regulations	1
Elements of commercial law	1
English	5
French	4
Penmanship	2
Stenography and typewriting	2

Gymnastics and athletic sports for pupils of the first three years. For those of the two upper years: Rifle range shooting and drilling.

The writer describes at length the various courses of study pursued. Commercial education in Argentina, he shows, is aided greatly by its Commercial

Museum, where the student is given easy access to, and afforded the largest opportunity for, the study of the products of the world and investigation through printed documents, specimens, and the use of instruments. For the study of geography there is also a special geographical laboratory.

Private schools are generally free from any governmental control. The Buenos Aires branch of the International Correspondence Schools is held in very high esteem. The subjects of greatest importance are: Commercial arithmetic, business correspondence, accounting, penmanship, typewriting and stenography, Spanish, English, and French. The faculty of economic sciences of the university was established by law two years ago. Its curriculum and regulations are printed in a separate program, issue of February, 1915.

Graduates of the higher commercial schools and of the faculty of economic sciences are fitted, in the opinion of the writer, to enter any business or banking establishment in any country where Spanish, English, or French is spoken. The writer urges that special courses in Spanish and Portuguese be added to the curricula of the schools of commerce of the United States, and that stress be laid on the study of the natural resources, geography, and history of the Latin-American countries.

Dr. ANTONIO L. VALVERDE, Professor, School of Commerce, Habana, Cuba.— The course of study in the School of Commerce of Habana, a part of the Institute of Secondary Instruction of Habana, was established by decree November 15, 1900, and consists of the following: Arithmetic and algebra; universal geography; commercial arithmetic; bookkeeping and accounting, commercial and public; commercial practices; industrial and commercial geography; political economy and elements of public finance; statistics; commercial law and commercial international law; history of commerce and commercial products; and English and French. Graduates, after a grouped course of four years, obtain a degree of mercantile professor. This academic title is of small consideration in Cuba, although this country has had a rich development in agriculture and commerce since the establishment of its independence. The personnel of banking houses, etc., is largely office trained.

The course of study is not sufficiently comprehensive and should be enlarged so as to prepare for any career the success of which depends on commercial training, e. g., commercial agents, consuls, custom officials, Government inspectors, accountants for governmental and public utility service, etc. The courses should be so constituted as to include the following: Bookkeeping and general commercial accounting; commercial practices, with particular reference to banks and exchanges; industrial and commercial geography; political economy and finance, with relation to commerce; commercial statistics; commercial law and international commercial law; the elements of civil and administrative law; laws on patents and trade-marks; history of commerce and commercial products; English, French, and German languages; fiscal and customs laws and practices; consular laws and practices; the comparative study of foreign commercial laws; and the writing of public and commercial papers and documents. This curriculum should be made general for all the countries of the continent, and the method of instruction should be uniform in every grade of commercial school. The writer distributes the courses in the different groups so that the careers may be studied of mercantile professor, the doctor or licentiate in commercial science, the commercial agent, the customs inspector and customs agent, a consular and the expert appraiser.

Commercial education has been neglected. Its importance, however, is receiving more and more recognition. The method, content of study, and effort necessary to prepare to engage in commerce is in no sense inferior to that required to prepare a lawyer, physician, or engineer.

Dr. Agustin T. Whilar, Lima, Peru.—Commerce is the instrument of civilization. It is concerned with barter, commissions, marketing, transportation, money, banking, insurance, exchange, food and textile products, building material and articles of luxury, merchandise, public and private commerce. The character and scope of commerce require a high degree of professional and moral training for the merchant. This instruction should be educative and instructive in the largest measure and presented in the most scientific manner. It should include a knowledge of the commercial languages; the history of the various countries—their literature, customs, resources, industries, and commerce; the applied sciences and mathematics; the mechanical practices and methods of business; political economy, business ethics, and psychology; commercial, civil, administrative, and international law; accounting, finance, etc.—in a word, commercial science.

The International Exposition of London, 1851; of Paris, 1867; and of Vienna, 1868, inaugurated an international commercial struggle. This struggle has led to the establishment of commercial museums, export societies, improved consular methods, and a conscious need in the various countries for improved commercial education.

Commercial instruction is of two grades, (1) professional and (2) academic. The special or professional training may be divided into three classes, lower, middle, and upper. These are distinct types and do not grow into each other like elementary, secondary, and higher instruction. The course of study in each type of school is complete. The elementary type is not fixed for the different countries. The practice is more or less general in adding general culture studies in the secondary type. The upper type is best seen in the model College of Commerce of Antwerp and the Commercial Institute of Rome. The academy or university type is more advanced and more highly developed in the United States, England, Switzerland, Belgium, and Italy. The "Luis Bocconi" Commercial University of Milan, Italy, furnishes a fine example of this type of school. The plan of study of the commercial universities of Pan America should correspond to this school, with a compulsory course in general knowledge and elective specialties. The greatest obstacle in America to the establishment of commercial instruction is the dislike for commerce of the upper classes and the prevailing tendency for those who have failed in the academic courses in school or college to undertake the business training courses. Lack of sympathy has further prevented adequate equipment in the way of buildings, teachers, etc.

The author urges the establishment of commercial education in the larger commercial cities, with its introduction according to the two different grades and three classes in the private and public grammar and secondary schools. The preparatory sections thus established should furnish a thorough training in the fundamentals and give to the student a due sense of the value of the profession of business and desire to study for the same in the special elementary, secondary, and higher schools of commerce. He urges, further, public and private subventions for the higher schools and Federal aid for the establishment of the lower and middle schools with a uniform plan of study; aid of the larger commercial and industrial interests in the establishment of a university of commerce in the capital of each Republic; annual visits and award of prizes to the best pupils, whose work should be judged by a committee composed of visiting members appointed by the Government and the chambers of commerce; and the establishment of night schools and of courses of study that will give an international viewpoint to the students engaged in its pursuit; the establishment of scholarships and the demand for a student's certificate of business aptitude for public positions that require technical knowledge; a satisfactory entrance requirement for the various grades of commercial schools; remission of the customary scholastic fees; and the creation of the doctorate in commerce. He urges the creation of a superior council of technical education, to have charge of this phase of education, and insists that the course of training be both theoretical and practical, experimental, educative, as well as instructive; that the instruction should not be given without the necessary material and equipment, such as a museum, laboratories, library, business office, and model bank, and that ample opportunity be given for visits by the students to commercial and industrial plants.

The writer proposes the following courses:

A. A two-year course for elementary commercial education in grammar schools: The native language taught with reference to commerce; commercial organization, national and international; simple accounting; economic geography and commercial arithmetic; penmanship, stenography, and typewriting; drawing and manual training; commercial practices and visits to commercial and industrial plants.

B. A three-year course for secondary schools. This course is similar to course "A." It adds commercial correspondence, bookkeeping, and a modern language, omitting accounting and business organization.

C. A four-year course, including a preparatory year, for the elementary commercial schools: Preparatory year—elementary mathematics, native language, universal history, drawing, and penmanship; second year—native language, business organization, elementary mathematics, typewriting and drawing, physical and military training, and vocal music; third year—native and foreign language, economic geography, bookkeeping, stenography, physical and military training, and vocal music; fourth year—business correspondence, accounting, history of commerce, elements of political economy and common law, stenography, commercial practices and visits to industrial and commercial plants.

D. Four-year course for secondary commercial schools: Native language, business correspondence, commercial languages, literary history, commercial economic geography, history of commerce, statistics, applied mathematics, transportation, merchandising, industrial and agricultural implements, commerce, general accounting, social and business ethics, civil and commercial law, maritime international law, finance, commercial practices, visits to commercial and industrial plants, drawing and vocal music, and training of secretaries and commercial executives.

E. Two-year course for the higher commercial schools: Native language, rhetoric, logic and classical nomenclature, comparative literature, contemporary geography, applied mathematics, merchandising and commerce, public and business accounting, commercial correspondence, commercial economics, commercial and civil law, commercial practices, finance and budgets. Electives in this course: Administrative, constitutional and consular law, the history of diplomacy, commercial treaties, political economy and statistics, and the elements of biology and sociology.

F. Course of study for the universities. The studies are grouped under the different faculties. Economic sciences: Principles of political economy, history of commercial establishments, public finance, statistics, economic history and geography. Juridical sciences: Constitutional, administrative, civil, commercial and international law. Technical sciences: Mathematics applied to finance, accounting, merchandising and training in a model bank. Pedagogical sciences: Applied psychology, theory and practice of commercial education, and methodology.

G. Three-year course for apprentice night schools: Foreign commercial languages, importing and exporting, transportation, merchandising, markets, tariffs, weights and measures, money and exchange, commercial documents and laws, bookkeeping and business correspondence, political and commercial economy, statistics, typewriting and stenography.

INDEX.

O

DEPARTMENT OF THE INTERIOR

U.S. – BUREAU OF EDUCATION

BULLETIN, 1916, No. 26

A SURVEY OF EDUCATIONAL INSTITUTIONS OF THE STATE OF WASHINGTON

WASHINGTON
GOVERNMENT PRINTING OFFICE
1916

ADDITIONAL COPIES
OF THIS PUBLICATION MAY BE PROCURED FROM
THE SUPERINTENDENT OF DOCUMENTS
GOVERNMENT PRINTING OFFICE
WASHINGTON, D. C.
AT
25 CENTS PER COPY
▽

CONTENTS.

LETTER OF TRANSMITTAL.

DEPARTMENT OF THE INTERIOR,
BUREAU OF EDUCATION,
Washington, August 22, 1916.

SIR: I am transmitting herewith for publication as a bulletin of the Bureau of Education the report of a survey of education in the State of Washington, made under my direction at the request of the Commission of Educational Survey created by the legislature of the State, as set forth in the introduction to this report. The survey includes the State institutions of higher education, the University of Washington at Seattle, the State College of Washington at Pullman, and the three normal schools at Cheney, Ellensburg, and Bellingham, and such a study of the elementary and secondary schools of the State and of the preparation of teachers in these schools as was necessary to an intelligent consideration of the functions and standards of the higher schools.

This survey was made by Dr. S. P. Capen, specialist in higher education; Harold W. Foght, specialist in school practice; and Alexander Inglis, assistant professor of education, Harvard University. Their report and conclusions were approved by me.

Accompanying this report is a report of the findings and recommendations of the Commission of Educational Survey as submitted to the governor of the State of Washington. For these neither the survey committee nor the Commissioner of Education is in any way responsible, but it will be observed that in the main the Commission of Educational Survey approves the conclusions of the survey committee.

Respectfully submitted.

P. P. CLAXTON,
Commissioner.

The SECRETARY OF THE INTERIOR.

REPORT AND RECOMMENDATIONS OF THE COMMISSION OF EDUCATIONAL SURVEY OF WASHINGTON.[1]

The Legislature of Washington, by an act passed by the senate and house of representatives March 9, 1915, and approved by the governor March 18, 1915, provided for a commission to make an educational survey of the State of Washington. The scope of the work of this commission is defined and its members named in the following act, chapter 143, session laws of 1915:

AN ACT Creating a commission to make an educational survey, defining its powers and duties, appointing the members thereof, and making an appropriation therefor.

Be it enacted by the Legislature of the State of Washington:

SECTION 1. There is hereby created a commission, consisting of six members, to be known as "The Commission of Educational Survey of Washington," and it shall be the duty of such commission to make a comprehensive survey of the organization and work of the University of Washington, the State College of Washington, and the State Normal Schools at Ellensburg, Cheney, and Bellingham, and a general survey of the public-school system of the State. both urban and rural, elementary and secondary, and of the educational development and possibilities of the State, and to determine more definitely the purpose, sphere, and functions of the university, the State college, and the State normal schools, and the lines along which each should be encouraged to develop for the better service of the State. In the performance of its duties said commission shall have power to employ experts and to fix and authorize the payment of their compensation. Upon the completion of such survey and on or before April 30, 1916, said commission shall make and file with the governor a report of its findings and recommendations, which report shall be published for general distribution throughout the State, and shall contain such recommendations to the legislature in regard to the enactment or amendment of the statutes relating to the several institutions as may be found advisable, including any necessary changes in the distribution of the millage tax for the support of such institutions and such additional appropriations as the commission may deem advisable.

SEC. 2. The members of the subcommittee of the joint committee on educational institutions and education of the fourteenth legislature, to wit, Senators W. J. Sutton, E. E. Boner, and A. H. Imus, and Representatives Tom Brown, Charles Timblin, and Victor Zednick, are hereby appointed members of said commission, who shall receive as compensation five dollars ($5) for each day while actually engaged in the performance of their duties.

SEC. 3. For the payment of the actual and necessary traveling expenses of the members of the said commission, the compensation of the members of said commission, and the experts employed, and expenses incidental to the work of said commission, there is hereby appropriated out of any funds in the State treasury not otherwise appropriated the sum of five thousand dollars ($5,000) or so much thereof as may be necessary.

---

[1] It should be noted that this section (pp. 7 to 19) constitutes the report of the legislative commission, for which the Bureau of Education is in no way responsible. The report of the survey experts begins on p. 21.

At its first meeting, held in North Yakima, Wash., July 5, 1915, the commission decided, in addition to visits to the State institutions of higher education and inquiries conducted by its own members, to cause to be made an expert study of educational conditions in this State in so far as outlined in the legislative enactment. To this end it obtained the services and cooperation of the United States Bureau of Education.

The Commissioner of Education, with the approval of the commission and of the heads of the State institutions of higher education, obtained the following experts to conduct the survey in this State and report to the commission: Dr. Samuel P. Capen, specialist in higher education, United States Bureau of Education; Mr. Harold W. Foght, specialist in rural-school practice, United States Bureau of Education; and Dr. Alexander Inglis, assistant professor of education, Harvard University.

The commission held several meetings for the purpose of adopting a suggestive course of procedure and working out the details, and visited the University of Washington, Washington State College, Ellensburg Normal School, Bellingham Normal School, and Cheney Normal School. The final session convened at Spokane, Wash., April 15, 1916, at which time the report of the experts was received. These expert findings and recommendations are hereto attached and made a part of this report.

At its final meeting the commission studied carefully the expert findings and conclusions, and from these, together with the testimony of the heads of the several institutions and the inquiries of its own members, the commission formulated this report.

In the interest of brevity this report embraces for the most part only recommendations, no supporting arguments or statistical facts being given, except in cases where the commission differs from the conclusions of the experts. These cases, however, are rare, occurring in almost all instances when the commission is of the opinion that the State is unable financially to carry out the program suggested. The reasons and facts supporting the recommendations, when not given herein, are to be found in the report of the experts, which is added hereto, and of which a thoughtful reading is urged. In some few instances recommendations concern subjects not touched upon in the findings of the investigators. The reasons for these, of course, are given.

The commission's recommendations and suggestions appear under four general subdivisions:

1. Common schools, both urban and rural, elementary and secondary.
2. Normal schools.
3. State university and State college.
4. Distribution of the millage tax.

The commission desires to express its appreciation of the helpful cooperation of the presidents, faculties, and administrative officers of the several institutions, and of the State superintendent of public instruction. Without their assistance the work could scarcely have been done efficiently in the time allotted. The leadership and services of Dr. P. P. Claxton, United States Commissioner of Education, and of the experts are also gratefully acknowledged.

I. COMMON SCHOOLS.

The commission's survey of the public-school system was not exhaustive. General, rather than comprehensive, it was concerned only with those phases which are closely related to the institutions of higher education. The legislature did not contemplate a more detailed investigation at this time.

One of the most important questions affecting the common schools is that of the proper system of apportioning the current State school fund and the county fund, and of arriving at an equitable basis for scaling up the State and county taxes. These problems were not studied, however, because a legislative committee, created by joint resolution to make this study, is now at work.

With the instructional and administrative side this commission was primarily concerned. It went particularly into the matters of the county superintendency, county organization, county supervision, certification of teachers, and the school curriculum.

COUNTY SUPERINTENDENCY.

The commission recommends:

1. That the eligibility and salary clauses in the educational code be changed so that any person, in order to be eligible to the office of county superintendent, shall hold a professional certificate valid in this State; shall have had at least five years of professional experience; and shall have had not less than two years of advanced preparation of college or normal-school grade, in addition to being graduated from a secondary school.

2. That the minimum salary of the county superintendent shall be $1,200, and that in case an eligible person can not be found in the county he may be chosen from some other county.

3. That the legislature submit to the people a constitutional amendment removing the limitation on the tenure of office of the county superintendent. The commission is firmly of the opinion that the best interests of the county schools can not be subserved by frequent change in county superintendents.

4. That the powers and duties of the county superintendent be enlarged, so that in all school districts, except those of the first and second class, the county school superintendent shall select the teachers, subject to approval by the board of directors.

COUNTY ORGANIZATION.

5. That careful consideration be given by the legislature to the permissive county organization plan as outlined in the report of the committee of experts, hereto attached and made a part of this report.

COUNTY SUPERVISION.

6. That the legislature carefully consider the question of a more adequate supervision of the rural schools by subdividing the county into supervision districts, as discussed in the report of the committee of experts.

CERTIFICATION.

7. That a new system of certificates be substituted for that now in force, in order that the standards for entering the teaching profession in this State shall rank among the highest in the Union.   In any case the commission most emphatically recommends that third-grade certificates be abolished at a very early date, and that the experience provision of the code for the renewal of second-grade certificates be discontinued, and that the professional requirements for the renewal of the same, as set forth in the code, be somewhat increased.

The new system of certification recommended for enactment follows:

STANDARDS RECOMMENDED.

1. The minimum basis for certification of all teachers shall be at least graduation from a four-year high school or its equivalent.

2. Beginning with September 1, 1918, the basis shall be changed and include not only graduation from a four-year high school, but in addition one semester of 18 weeks of professional training.   Teachers holding certificates in force at the time of the passage of this proposed act and whose certificates will expire by regular limitation shall be exempt from this requirement until September 1, 1920.

3. Beginning with September 1, 1920, the basis shall again be increased and include graduation from a four-year high school, with one year of 36 weeks of professional training.   Teachers holding certificates in force at the time of the passage of this proposed act and whose certificates will expire by regular limitation will be exempt from this requirement until September 1, 1922.

4. Beginning with September 1, 1922, the basis shall again be changed to include graduation from a four-year high school and one and a half years (54 weeks) of professional training.   Teachers holding certificates in force at the time of the passage of this proposed act

and whose certificates will expire by regular limitation shall be exempt from this requirement until September 1, 1924.

5. Beginning with September 1, 1924, the basis shall again be raised to include graduation from a four-year high school and two years (72 weeks) of professional training. Teachers holding certificates in force at the time of the passage of this proposed act and whose certificates will expire by regular limitation shall be exempt from this requirement until September 1, 1926.

The professional requirements above mentioned shall be such as are provided in the regular courses in the State normal schools, the regular courses provided in the departments of education in the State college and in the university, and such equivalent courses in other institutions as may be approved by the State board of education. Experience credits may be accepted to the extent and under such rulings as the State board of education may provide. All practice teaching necessary to meet the foregoing requirements must be done under conditions approved by the State board of education.

TYPES OF CERTIFICATION STIPULATED.

1. Common-school certificates based upon examination:
    - *a.* Primary certificates.
    - *b.* Grammar-school certificates.
    - *c.* Rural-school certificates.
    - *d.* High-school certificates.
    - *e.* Administration certificates.
2. Normal school certificates:
    - *a.* Elementary-school certificates—
        - (a) Primary certificates.
        - (b) Grammar-school certificates.
        - (c) Rural-school certificates.
    - *b.* Special certificates—
        - (a) Supervisory certificates.
        - (b) Certificates of special subjects.
        - (c) Certificates of administration.
3. University and State college certificates:
    - *a.* High-school certificates.
    - *b.* Special high-school certificates.
    - *c.* Special supervisors' certificates.
    - *d.* High-school administration certificates.
    - *e.* General administration certificates.

CERTIFICATION LIMITED AND DEFINED.

Common-school certificates.—All common-school certificates based upon examination shall meet the requirements prescribed by the State board of education and shall be issued by the superintendent of public instruction. All examinations must be given in accordance with the present prescribed law and shall be based upon all subjects included in the scope of work contemplated by the certificate.

Primary certificates.—Primary certificates shall entitle the holder to teach in the first four grades of the elementary schools.

Grammar-school certificates.- Grammar-school certificates shall entitle the holder to teach in the grammar grades of the elementary schools.

Rural-school certificates.—Rural-school certificates shall entitle the holder to teach in any or all of the eight grades of the elementary schools.

High-school certificates.—High-school certificates shall entitle the holder to teach in any of the high schools of this State.

Normal-school certificates.—The normal-school certificates issued by the State normal schools shall primarily cover the work of the elementary schools, shall provide for special teachers and supervisors for the elementary schools, and shall provide special administration certificates for the elementary and rural schools. Special certificates issued by the normal schools shall be sufficient in the named limited field of work in any of the common schools of the State.

University and State college certificates.—Certificates issued by the university and State college shall primarily cover the work of the high-school field, including high-school teachers, principals, and specialists in a definite limited field of work, and shall prepare special teachers and supervisors for the elementary schools.

Administration certificates.—Certificates of administration may be granted either by the normal schools, by the State college, or by the university upon a stipulated basis provided for by the State board of education.

Special certificates.—Special certificates of all types shall be issued by the institutions training for them under conditions approved by the State board of education.

Provision for the extended recognition of certain certificates in nine-year schools.—In nine-year schools, normal-school certificates to teach in elementary grades shall be recognized as covering the first high-school year, and university and State-college certificates to teach in the high schools shall be recognized as covering the upper elementary grades.

TENURE OF OFFICE FOR SCHOOL-TEACHERS.

The commission favors long tenure of office for school-teachers, but does not believe that the "bonus" plan, as advocated in the report of the committee of experts, is the most desirable or effective stimulus to that end, and believe that it is impracticable from a financial viewpoint.

TEACHERS' EXAMINATIONS.

The commission recommends that the certification laws be so amended as to require an examination of the teacher in every subject he is required to teach.

COURSES OF STUDY.

In that part of the report dealing with the common schools the experts recommend that the training of city and rural school children be differentiated, the object being to adapt the training to the child's environment.

It is the opinion of the commission, however, that a too rigid interpretation should not be put on this recommendation, for it might have the effect of producing a too diversified course of study, which in the interest of the child it is most desirable to avoid, for the following reasons: [1]

1. A child in the elementary grades needs drilling in the five essential branches of education, which are taken to be reading, writing, spelling, arithmetic, and grammar, rather than to know a mass of facts. To keep this main object in view is of vital importance in elementary education at all times. That a child should read distinctly, spell correctly, write legibly and grammatically, are matters of first importance; but that he should know the details of the Missouri Compromise, the scientific name of every bone in his hand, the exact location of the source of the Nile, is not a matter of first importance in this stage of his career.

2. The chief question to be asked in this connection is: What is of highest value in elementary education? That question settled, the rest is easy and will follow in logical order. To educate the child to the highest degree of efficiency, it is necessary to see that his energy be not wasted on matters of secondary importance, but that it be conserved at every stage of his school career. To aim for this is to aim to secure the maximum of economy for the State's work.

3. In order to secure the advantages of this program and preserve vital interest in it, the following mode of procedure is earnestly recommended, viz, that the examination given by the State to children in the rural schools on completion of the elementary curriculum be extended to include urban and all State schools of the same grade, and that only those who give proof of competency be allowed to pass into the high schools of the State. It is also recommended in order to preserve a unified plan, with the same objects of economy and efficiency in view, that a similar test be applied to students of the high schools of the State on the completion of their course before being allowed to pass into the State's higher institutions of learning.

MILITARY INSTRUCTION.

The commission recommends that the next legislature carefully consider the question of military instruction, with a view to making it compulsory in the high schools of this State.

[1] It should be noted that these are the opinions of the commission, and not of the survey committee. For the committee's statement, see pp. 150 et seq.

II. NORMAL SCHOOLS.

To the end that unwarranted duplication be now and hereafter eliminated, the commission defines rigidly the scope and functions of the university and State college in the preparation of teachers on the one hand and of the normal schools on the other. It draws a clean line of demarcation between them, indicating the class of teachers each group is to train. This is done in the interests both of economy and of turning out the most efficient product possible. It has been decided that the training of elementary-school teachers is the function of the normal schools; that the preparation of high-school teachers is the function of the university and college. This differentiation is definitely made in this report.

Questions of entrance requirements for the normal schools, the length of course they should give, the subjects to be taught, means of promoting harmonious development, and plans of extension service and kindred questions have been given careful consideration.

On the report of the experts, the views of the normal-school principals, and personal inquiries by its members the commission bases the following recommendations:

1. That requirements for matriculation in the normal schools be those stated in the experts' report.

2. That the normal schools develop a full three-year course in accordance with the suggestion of the experts.

3. That they go on a full four-year basis, not earlier than 1920, provided they have in the meantime arrived at the point where a full four-year course in an accredited high school is required for entrance and they have developed the three-year course referred to above on a basis to warrant the expenditure this fourth year of work will entail.

4. That the State university and State college confine their training of teachers for the common schools strictly to the high-school grades, but that graduates of such institutions be allowed to teach the upper elementary grades, when taught in connection with ninth-grade work in strictly one-year high schools.

5. That the State normal schools confine their training of teachers for the common schools strictly to the elementary grades, but that graduates of such institutions be allowed to teach the ninth grade when taught in connection with the upper elementary grades in strictly one-year high schools.

6. That school superintendents and directors, in this class of schools where both the upper elementary grades and one year of high-school work are taught, give preference to those applicants having both a university or State college and a normal-school training.

7. That, in consonance with the suggestions of the experts, the training of rural-school teachers through the normal schools be further developed, but that the question of the location of model rural schools be left to the governing boards of the normal schools.

8. That the normal schools devote much serious effort to provide teachers for rural communities.

9. That the three-year course of study for the normal schools of the State, as suggested in the experts' report, be adopted.

10. That, for the purpose of.promoting a harmonious development along parallel lines, a joint meeting of the respective boards of trustees of the three normal schools be held annually.

11. That the membership of the State board of education be increased to 10, and shall consist of the superintendent of public instruction, the president of the University of Washington, the president of the State College of Washington, the principals of each of the three State normal schools of Washington, and four persons holding life diplomas issued under the authority of the State and actively engaged in educational work, appointed by the governor, one of whom shall be a superintendent of a district of the first class, one a county superintendent of schools, one a principal of a fully accredited four-year high school in a district of the first class, and one a principal of a fully accredited four-year high school in a district other than of the first class.

12. The commission believes that the needs of the State will soon require a fourth normal school, as suggested in the report of the experts, and recommends that one be established as soon as financial conditions of the State will justify.

13. The commission is convinced of the advisability of having the normal schools engage in extension service, such as is suggested in the report of the experts. This work, however, conducted on a scale as broad as that suggested, would involve an expenditure which the State can not afford at the present time. After considering carefully the value and cost of teachers' institutes in this State and after taking up this matter and the extension service question with the normal-school principals, a number of county superintendents, and other educators, the commission has come to the conclusion that this extension service would be of more value to the teachers of the State than are the institutes. In the light of this fact, and because money is not available for both, and also because of the value of this extension service, the commission recommends that the legislature provide by enactment for such service in lieu of the institute work now prescribed by law.

14. As the law now stands, the children attending the training departments of the normal schools are not allowed to draw State school money per diem. This gives cause for much complaint by

the people of the cities where the normal schools are located, who demand that this discrimination be removed, as they suffer financial loss by sending their children to the training departments. The commission, therefore, recommends that the law be changed to allow school money to be apportioned to the local district for all children attending normal-school training departments, as this provides a necessary service to the State at large.

III. UNIVERSITY AND STATE COLLEGE.

The commission advises the enactment of legislation in accordance with the following recommendations:

1. That agriculture (in all its branches and subdivisions), veterinary medicine, mining, pharmacy, economic science in its application to agriculture and rural life, and the training of high-school teachers (especially in agriculture, home economics, and mechanic arts), school supervisors, and school administrators be major lines at the State college.

2. That law, medicine, architecture, forestry, pharmacy, mining, commerce, journalism, library economy, graduate work in liberal arts and pure science, professional training of high-school teachers, school supervisors, and school superintendents be major lines at the State university.

3. That duplication be recognized in liberal arts, pharmacy, mining, home economics, and in certain branches of engineering.

4. That civil, electrical, and mechanical engineering be taught at both the State college and the State university.

5. That chemical engineering be taught at the State university exclusively.

6. That agriculture and its various subdivisions be taught at the State college exclusively.

7. That the development of further departments or branches of engineering be submitted to a joint conference of the respective governing boards before their establishment at either institution.

8. That degree courses in liberal arts, with the training of high-school teachers in the various branches of the same, be continued at the State college, but that no graduate work in these lines be offered.

9. That home economics be developed for the present without restriction at both the State university and the State college, but no extension work in home economics be undertaken by the university outside of King County.

10. That professional courses in marine engineering and fisheries be established at the State university as soon as its resources permit.

11. That graduate work in engineering branches, when developed, be developed at the university exclusively.

12. That both the State college and the State university continue their respective departments of mining engineering, but that the cooperation of the two institutions be secured so that each department will best serve the State. To this end we recommend that the university place special emphasis on coal and clay mining and ceramic engineering and that the State college place special emphasis on metalliferous mining.

13. That the work of the department of elementary science at the State college, which work in our opinion is making a most important contribution to the life of the State, be still further strengthened and extended, and that to this end there be brought about a partial reorganization of the administrative relationship of this department to the college, whereby this department shall have a teaching staff entirely its own and shall be separately housed.

14. That the administrative officers of both institutions take under consideration the matter of small classes, as discussed in the report of the experts.

15. That the officers of the State college and the university consider the total number of hours required in the major subject, since it is often excessive and unduly limits the opportunity of the student to obtain the desired breadth of training.

16. That high-school graduation be required of all students entering the State college or the university, except those 21 years of age or older, and except students in the elementary science department of the State college. This restriction will not apply to summer schools, short courses, or extension work in either institution.

17. That in order to promote harmony, economy, and efficiency in the management of the institutions of higher education the regents of the State university and the State college hold joint meetings at least once a year.

IV. DISTRIBUTION OF THE MILLAGE TAX.

The phenomenal growth of population in the State of Washington, hardly realized by the average citizen, becomes astounding when viewed in connection with the State's higher educational institutions. All have grown, some having doubled, while others have even trebled their attendance during the current six-year millage period which will terminate in 1917.

The experts make it clear in their report that if this demand is to be met, even in fairly full measure, a much larger increase of support must be provided for.

46564°—16——2

Contrary to general belief, Washington's contribution to higher education is not excessive, as is evidenced by the following excerpt from the report of the experts:

Attention is here especially called to the fact that Washington ranks twenty-fourth in Table 4, on the basis of the amount spent on higher education for each $1,000 of wealth. It ranks twenty-third in Table 6, on the basis of apportionment per capita of the receipts of higher institutions of collegiate grade. It ranks fifteenth in Table 8, on the basis of apportionment per capita of the receipts of higher education, including normal schools. These figures should allay the apprehension of those citizens who have believed that Washington is unduly extravagant in its support of higher education.

The increased demands in the budgets of the different institutions correspond in the main with their respective enrollments.

It is necessary to provide for maintenance on a much larger scale; for larger and better buildings; and to meet the insistent demand for industrial research work in the university, and for extension work and research along agricultural lines in the State college.

The growth of the normal schools is equally remarkable. Particularly is this true with respect to two of them, the normal school at Cheney and the normal school of Bellingham.

The corollary to all this is the insistent demand for an increase in maintenance, buildings, land, and equipment.

The legislature of 1911 passed an act providing a fund for the maintenance of the State institutions of higher education. It was decided to divide this fund in the following manner: Forty-seven and one-half one-hundredths ($47\frac{1}{2}$/100) of 1 mill for the State university fund; thirty-two and one-half one-hundredths ($32\frac{1}{2}$/100) of 1 mill for the Washington State college fund; nine one-hundredths ($\frac{9}{100}$) of 1 mill for the Cheney normal school fund; seven one-hundredths ($\frac{7}{100}$) of 1 mill for the Ellensburg normal school fund; and nine one-hundredths ($\frac{9}{100}$) of 1 mill for the Bellingham normal school fund. The sum of this is 1 mill and five one-hundredths (1.05) of 1 mill.

But this millage can no longer yield an amount sufficient to maintain these institutions and allow them to expand.

After carefully studying their budgets and paring down the demands of the institutions to their lowest possible requirements, the commission recommends the allotment to each institution of the following portions of the millage tax for the next six-year millage period:

To the university ninety one-hundredths ($\frac{90}{100}$) of 1 mill—eighty-five one-hundredths ($\frac{85}{100}$) of 1 mill for maintenance and five one-hundredths ($\frac{5}{100}$) of 1 mill for buildings, which with tuition fees and rental from univeraity properties is to be devoted to a building fund. Because of the unusually large and pressing building needs of the university, due to the growth of the student body and the rapid deterioration of the buildings inherited from the Alaska-Yukon-

Pacific Exposition, it is necessary to meet this continuing emergency by additional provision outside the usual resources. To this end, the commission recommends that those provisions of the act creating the University of Washington building fund, which authorize the charge of a tuition fee of $10 per student each semester, be continued in force.

To the State college fifty-five one-hundredths ($\frac{55}{100}$) of 1 mill— fifty-one one-hundredths ($\frac{51}{100}$) of 1 mill for maintenance and four one-hundredths ($\frac{4}{100}$) of 1 mill for buildings and repairs to buildings.

To the Cheney normal school fourteen and one-fourth one-hundredths ($14\frac{1}{4}/100$) of 1 mill—twelve one-hundredths ($\frac{12}{100}$) of 1 mill for maintenance, and two and one-fourth one-hundredths ($2\frac{1}{4}/100$) of 1 mill for buildings.

To the Ellensburg normal school twelve and three-fourths one-hundredths ($12\frac{3}{4}/100$) of 1 mill—nine one-hundredths ($\frac{9}{100}$) of 1 mill to be given for maintenance and three and three-fourths one-hundredths ($3\frac{3}{4}/100$) of 1 mill for land, buildings, and improvements.

To the Bellingham normal school eighteen one-hundredths ($\frac{18}{100}$) of 1 mill—fourteen one-hundredths ($\frac{14}{100}$) of 1 mill for maintenance and four one-hundredths ($\frac{4}{100}$) of 1 mill for buildings, land, and equipment.

The sum total of this millage is 1 mill and ninety one-hundredths ($90/100$) of 1 mill.

In conclusion, the commission is of the opinion that, in connection with its work, there is no more complex or difficult problem relating to the State's higher educational institutions than the question of finance. How to maintain them without placing an unduly heavy burden on the taxpayers of the State is a most important and difficult matter. The commission feels certain, however, that with the limited means at hand this effort to meet the needs of the immediate future will be regarded as a serious attempt at the solution of a great problem, even if the result obtained can not be regarded with complacency.

Dated this 27th day of April, 1916.

W. J. SUTTON,
Chairman.

E. E. BONER.
A. H. IMUS.
TOM BROWN.
CHARLES TIMBLIN.
VICTOR ZEDNICK,
Secretary.

REPORT OF THE SURVEY COMMITTEE.[1]

INTRODUCTION.

The 1915 Legislature of the State of Washington had before it several bills affecting higher educational institutions. Before final action on these was taken the governor and members of the legislature invited the Commissioner of Education to come to the State and give the legislature the benefit of his advice. In the early part of March the commissioner and the specialist in higher education visited four of the five institutions and attended various hearings held before a subcommittee of the joint committee of the committees on educational institutions and education. The commissioner then made a brief report to the joint committee, in which he recommended a comprehensive survey of the higher institutions, with such general survey of the public school system as might be necessary before legislative action limiting the sphere of any of the institutions was taken. To have charge of the survey he recommended the creation of a legislative commission which should work through experts, and he offered the services of the Bureau of Education in the prosecution of the survey.

In compliance with these recommendations the legislature passed an act creating a survey commission and naming as its members the subcommittee before which the hearings had been held. The commission was instructed to conduct a survey as outlined by the Commissioner of Education and to report to the governor on or before April 30, 1916.

Immediately upon organization the survey commission called upon the Bureau of Education to furnish the expert assistance promised and to take charge of the survey. The Commissioner of Education met with the members of the commission in North Yakima July 5, 1915, and submitted to it an outline of the procedure to be followed. This outline was approved by the commission with a few slight emendations. (It was further slightly amended by the commission in December.) It has served as the basis of this report, practically all matters agreed upon being treated at greater or less length in the following pages.

During the summer and fall of 1915 various members of the Bureau of Education compiled statistics and gathered documentary material bearing on the questions under consideration. A questionnaire was issued to all the public school teachers in the State, asking information concerning certain other matters of importance in estimating the quality of the State's teaching staff. The recording officers of both the State university and the State college were requested to prepare summaries showing the enrollment in various courses, the teaching hours of the faculties, and the geographical distribution of the students in the different departments, together with certain other statistical material.

In February, 1916, the Commissioner of Education, with the approval of the commission and of the heads of the State higher institutions, appointed the following committee to have charge of the survey on the ground:

Samuel P. Capen, specialist in higher education, United States Bureau of Education, chairman.

Harold W. Foght, specialist in rural school practice, United States Bureau of Education.

Alexander Inglis, assistant professor of education, Harvard University.

The committee began its work in the State on the 4th of March. The task was apportioned among its members in accordance with what appeared to be the peculiar aptitude of each, gained through previous teaching or administrative experience. In view of the fact that the questions which had given rise to the survey related for the most part to the State university and the State college, and that the issues affecting these institutions were the most difficult of adjustment, the majority of the committee's membership was assigned to the study of these institutions. All members of the committee visited each of the five institutions and the office of the State superintendent of public instruction. Messrs. Capen and Inglis devoted the bulk of their attention, however, to the State college and State university, spending somewhat more than a week at each institution. Mr. Foght addressed himself chiefly to the problems of the three normal schools and to the collection of material bearing on the administration of the public school system.

At each institution the committee held conferences with the presidents, deans, financial and recording officers, and heads of departments. It examined the buildings and equipment and reviewed the records of financial and educational operations.

On the 1st of April the Commissioner of Education and the members of the committee met with the survey commission in Seattle, outlined the scope of the report which the committee proposed to make, and exhibited some of the evidence which it intended to use in support of its recommendations. The presidents of several of the State higher institutions were also in attendance. The plans of the committee were approved by the survey commission.

The period between the 1st and the 14th of April was devoted to the preparation of the committee's report, each of the members and the Commissioner of Education contributing one or more chapters. All recommendations were passed upon by the Commissioner of Education and the committee acting in conference. Nearly all were unanimously indorsed.

On the 14th of April the committee met the heads of the five State institutions in Seattle and submitted to them the first draft of the report. The purpose of the conference was to make certain that all statements of fact were, as far as possible, correct, and that no phraseology which might be susceptible of misinterpretation was used. The chairman of the committee continued the conference with the presidents of the State university and the State college in Spokane on the 16th of April, and with the presidents of the normal schools on the 19th of April. As the result of these conferences a few minor verbal changes were made in the report. No recommendation was substantially modified.

On the 15th, 17th, and 18th of April the chairman of the committee met with the commission in Spokane and presented the report.

In the preparation of the statements and recommendations contained in the following pages the committee has held certain considerations constantly in view. In its opinion these may be appropriately summarized by way of introduction.

In the first place, it has taken full account of the legal status of the institutions. The committee has examined, with especial care, the various legislative enactments specifying the functions of the State university and the State college, and has convinced itself that neither institution has exceeded the limits prescribed for it or allowed it by the legislature of the State.[1] Wherever either has offered courses already given by the other, there has been sanction for such duplication in the laws and statutes under which the institutions operate.

Secondly, the committee has been actuated by the conviction that above mere legal justification lie the interests of the State. The determination of the way in which its institutions may serve the State most efficiently is the primary purpose of the investigation in which the committee has been called to assist. The framers of the several acts establishing and prescribing the spheres of the college, the university, and the normal schools sought to provide for the social needs of their time as these needs were then interpreted. The committee has endeavored to study present needs and those of the immediate future which the higher institutions must meet. Several factors have been kept always in mind. Although these are familiar to most citizens, the committee ventures to enumerate them here. They are: (1) The vast

---

[1] For a detailed account of these prescriptions, see ch. 6, p. 82 et seq.

natural resources of the State, the development of which will demand unusually large numbers of persons scientifically trained in agriculture and engineering, and will depend upon the continued progress of scientific knowledge in these fields; (2) the great size of the State; (3) the separation of its population by a barrier of mountains and arid territory into two relatively compact groups and the consequent development of strong sectional consciousness; (4) the germination of what promises to be a phenomenally varied and dynamic industrial and commercial activity in one of these groups; (5) the demonstrable need of a larger number of well-trained elementary teachers, especially for the schools of the open country

In the light of these facts, and guided by its conviction that the service of the State is the touchstone by which every educational policy must be tested, the committee offers a number of recommendations which contemplate the clearer definition of the spheres of the State institutions and the partial redistribution of their functions. It is persuaded that these recommendations will, if adopted, be the means of saving some future expense. But, more especially, the committee believes that these recommendations will effect a unity both of organization and of purpose in the State system of higher education that has not characterized the system thus far.

In delivering its findings to the survey commission, which has authorized its investigation, the committee would like to record its grateful appreciation of the consideration with which it has everywhere been received. The officers of the institutions examined have answered inquiries with the greatest frankness and have shown a constant desire to help the committee arrive at the truth. The registrars, bursars, and other executives have been indefatigable in the preparation of the information called for. Indeed, without their ready and efficient cooperation the preparation of this report in the time allotted would have been impossible. The commission itself has placed every possible facility at the committee's disposal, has allowed it to conduct the investigation without interference or suggestion, and has accorded its members every courtesy.

SECTION I.—RELATIONS OF THE STATE UNIVERSITY AND THE STATE COLLEGE TO THE STATE SYSTEM OF PUBLIC EDUCATION AND TO EACH OTHER.

Chapter I.

GENERAL CONSIDERATION OF HIGHER EDUCATION IN WASHINGTON, WITH INCIDENTAL TREATMENT OF SECONDARY EDUCATION.

All institutions, whether publicly or privately controlled, which undertake the education of the children of a State and to which the children are admitted without distinction of class or creed must be reckoned among the State's educational resources. The attempt is made in this introductory chapter to give a brief account, chiefly statistical, of Washington's agencies for secondary and higher education, both public and private, and to show in a general way what the contribution of each group has been. In this review special attention is naturally accorded to the State-supported higher institutions, because it is with these that the report is mainly concerned. The committee is of the opinion, however, that these institutions can not be fairly judged unless seen in their full educational setting. In particular must they be viewed against the background of the secondary schools. The State-supported higher institutions of Washington are part of the system of public education. Their connection with both the public and the private secondary schools of the State is close and definite. The character of the courses which they offer to entering students is conditioned by the work of the secondary schools. All but a small percentage of their students are drawn from these schools. Indeed, the number of students entering the State higher institutions is determined, for the most part within limits that can be foreseen, by the number enrolled in the various types of secondary schools. In other words, State higher education in Washington, as in many other States, rests almost entirely upon facilities for secondary education provided *within the State*. Fundamental, therefore, to any consideration of higher education is the knowledge of certain important facts concerning the secondary schools of the State.

SECONDARY EDUCATION IN WASHINGTON.

The population of Washington was 357,232 in 1890; 518,103 in 1900; 1,141,990 in 1910; and 1,407,865 (estimated) in 1914.[1]

---

[1] The year 1914 is used here instead of 1915 because it is possible to get more complete educational statistics for the former year.

In the period between 1905 and 1910 it increased 91 per cent, and in the period between 1910 and 1914 it increased 23 per cent, a truly phenomenal growth for nine years. Within this interval of nine years, however, the school population did not increase so rapidly. Between 1905 and 1910 the school population increased 70½ per cent, and between 1910 and 1914, 23 per cent.

For the past 19 years the enrollment in public and private secondary schools of the State has increased quite out of proportion to the rate of growth of the school population, and at a rate which far outstrips

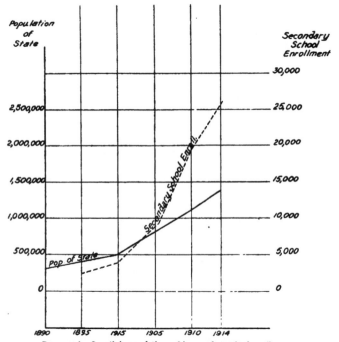

DIAGRAM 1.—Growth in population and in secondary-school enrollment

even the rapid rate of increase in the population itself. Indeed, the relative growth in secondary-school enrollment in Washington surpasses that recorded in any other one of 15 States recently studied by the Bureau of Education, all of which were known to have made particularly rapid progress in the development of facilities for secondary education. Between 1895 and 1900 secondary-school enrollment in Washington increased 65 per cent; between 1900 and 1905, 119 per cent; between 1905 and 1910, 112 per cent; and between 1910 and 1914, 36 per cent. Stated in actual figures, the increase is no less astonishing. There were 2,564 pupils in secondary schools in 1895; 3,989 in 1900; 8,732 in 1905; 19,522 in 1910; and 26,036 in 1914.[1]

Appended are a table, diagram, and map, illustrating the facts just presented. Table 1 shows the percentage of change in population,

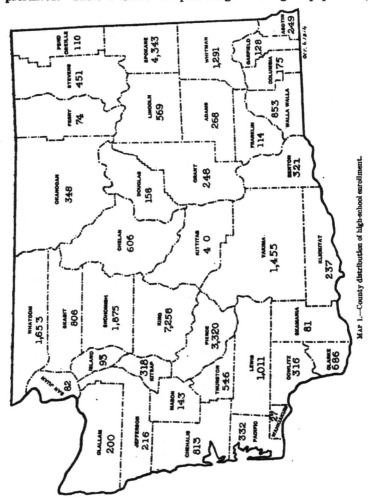

MAP 1.—County distribution of high-school enrollment.

school population, and secondary-school enrollment in 15 States from 1895 to 1914. Diagram 1 shows the curve of secondary-school enrollment from 1895 to 1914 applied to the curve of population.

---

[1] Figures reported by the U. S. Commissioner of Education.

In spite of the extremely rapid growth in secondary-school enrollment, Washington did not show in 1913–14, the last year recorded in the published statistics of the Bureau of Education, as large a percentage of the whole number of pupils in secondary schools as California, the District of Columbia, or Massachusetts. In California 11.7 per cent, in the District of Columbia 11.18 per cent, and in Massachusetts 10.88 per cent of the whole number of pupils were enrolled in secondary schools; in Washington, 10.45 per cent. Moreover, 12 other States reported in the same year a larger percentage of the total population enrolled in the secondary schools.[1] Remarkable as has been the numerical growth of secondary education in Washington therefore, the State has not yet attained preeminence even in point of numbers.

TABLE 1.—*Gain and loss in population, school population, and secondary enrollment, 1895 to 1914.*

[Italic figures show percentage of loss.]

Years.	Population.	School population.	Secondary enrollment.	Population.	School population.	Secondary enrollment.	Population.	School population.	Secondary enrollment.
	IOWA.			GEORGIA.			NORTH CAROLINA.		
1895	2,064,000	622,600	26,413	1,954,000	603,700	12,201	1,719,000	607,740	8,543
1900	2,231,853	662,520	35,575	2,216,331	736,920	11,250	1,893,810	669,530	9,570
Per cent	8.13	6.41	34.68	13.42	13.44	7.79	10.17	10.17	12.02
1905	2,391,633	681,376	39,529	2,405,821	802,582	12,297	2,031,740	675,980	10,108
Per cent	7.16	2.84	11.11	8.55	1.99	9.31	7.28	0.96	5.62
1910	2,224,771	634,000	46,262	2,609,121	830,180	16,635	2,206,287	680,050	15,617
Per cent	6.97	6.94	17.00	8.45	3.36	35.22	8.59	2.08	54.55
1914	2,221,755	583,655	51,929	2,776,513	886,818	21,501	2,339,452	761,900	21,192
Per cent	0.13	7.94	12.25	6.41	6.82	29.34	6.03	10.41	35.72
	TENNESSEE.			ILLINOIS.			MINNESOTA.		
1895	1,857,000	624,500	14,472	4,387,000	1,240,000	36,460	1,626,000	470,500	11,679
1900	2,020,616	691,570	15,697	4,821,550	1,362,700	47,825	1,751,394	506,770	15,685
Per cent	8.81	10.74	8.47	9.90	9.89	31.16	7.71	7.71	33.87
1905	2,147,166	636,878	13,248	5,319,150	1,455,851	57,278	1,971,949	579,359	22,099
Per cent	6.26	0.68	15.61	10.32	6.83	19.77	12.59	14.32	41.34
1910	2,184,789	697,132	20,063	5,638,591	1,409,648	75,979	2,075,708	610,358	32,062
Per cent	1.75	1.49	51.59	6.01	3.17	32.65	5.26	5.33	45.60
1914	2,254,754	677,102	24,525	5,986,781	1,473,347	89,329	2,213,919	599,529	42,886
Per cent	3.20	2.87	22.12	6.17	4.52	17.57	6.66	1.78	32.19
	MICHIGAN.			WASHINGTON.			CALIFORNIA.		
1895	2,241,641	618,500	24,354	474,900	107,800	2,980	1,390,000	329,700	12,976
1900	2,384,000	661,940	30,991	518,103	108,660	4,924	1,485,053	352,270	17,173
Per cent	6.35	7.35	27.26	9.09	0.80	65.06	6.84	6.85	32.35
1905	2,257,275	691,743	35,969	598,538	151,370	9,719	1,690,883	370,048	28,464
Per cent	7.77	4.50	16.06	15.53	39.33	97.38	9.15	5.05	65.75
1910	2,810,173	758,747	43,200	1,141,990	258,066	20,574	2,377,549	540,081	41,558
Per cent	9.89	9.89	20.10	90.80	70.50	111.70	46.69	45.94	48.00
1914	2,976,030	732,103	54,322	1,407,855	308,463	27,980	2,757,895	536,135	61,263
Per cent	5.90	3.51	25.45	23.28	19.52	36.00	16.00	0.73	47.43

[1] In this connection it should be noted that the per cent of children of school age in the total population of Washington is unusually small.

TABLE 1.—*Gain and loss in population, school population, and secondary enrollment, 1895 to 1914*—Continued.

Years.	Population.	School population.	Secondary enrollment.	Population.	School population.	Secondary enrollment.	Population.	School population.	Secondary enrollment.
	UTAH.			MASSACHUSETTS.			NEW YORK.		
1895.................	264,900	85,960	3,300	2,474,000	565,600	33,689	6,390,000	1,570,000	50,889
1900.................	276,749	81,810	4,400	2,805,346	641,500	42,691	7,268,012	1,786,000	82,607
Per cent...........	4.47	· 4.48	33.33	13.39	13.42	26.72	13.72	13.76	62.43
1905.................	309,734	100,911	5,824	3,083,546	686,275	53,308	7' 901,754	1,890,100	100,613
Per cent...........	11.92	12.36	32.36	10.16	6.98	24.87	8.72	5.83	21.72
1910.................	373,351	121,712	8,146	3,366,416	727,344	63,072	9,113,614	2,067,017	131,165
Per cent...........	20.54	20.62	39.87	8.99	5.98	18.32	15.34	9.36	30.37
1914.................	414,518	120,376	10,969	3,605,522	804,752	81,389	9,899,761	2,251,206	162,902
Per cent...........	11.03	1.10	34.65	7.10	10.64	24.14	8.63	8.91	24.20
	OHIO.			CONNECTICUT.			PENNSYLVANIA.		
1895.................	3,788,000	1,074,700	42,182	799,500	188,160	8,660	5,826,000	1,626,000	35,117
1900.................	4,157,545	1,179,600	56,290	908,355	213,800	10,931	6,302,115	1,759,300	46,837
Per cent...........	9.76	9.76	33.47	13.27	13.63	26.22	8.17	8.20	33.39
1905.................	4,400,155	1,163,841	65,781	989,500	226,892	12,536	6,824,115	1,810,438	60,049
Per cent...........	5.84	1.54	16.86	8.93	6.12	14.69	8.28	2.91	28.30
1910.................	4,767,121	1,075,686	70,889	1,114,756	258,270	16,526	7,665,111	1,891,608	78,906
Per cent...........	8.34	7.58	6.61	12.66	13.81	31.84	10.97	4.48	31.24
1914.................	5,026,896	1,188,359	82,267	1,202,688	275,897	22,874	8,245,967	2,054,894	104,870
Per cent...........	5.45	10.48	16.05	7.89	8.07	38.43	7.56	8.63	33.84

It should be observed that secondary education in Washington is thus far principally public education. Private secondary schools are not numerous and enroll considerably less than 10 per cent of all pupils. In the foregoing summaries private secondary schools are included; nevertheless, the Washington system may be regarded as predominantly a public system.

The incompleteness of the development of Washington's public secondary-school facilities is still further manifest when its secondary institutions are considered from another angle. In the last scholastic year, 1914–15, there were 511 public high schools, enrolling a total of 32,244.[1] For the purpose of this study they may be classified as follows:

Four-year accredited high schools... 153
High schools accredited for less than four years.............................. 30
Unaccredited high schools.. 328

Somewhat more than 27,000 pupils are enrolled in the four-year accredited schools, approximately 85 per cent of the total number of high-school pupils.

It appears, then, that the standards and equipment of more than two-thirds of the high schools of Washington do not yet justify their

[1] Taken from the report of the State superintendent of public instruction. The enrollment figures of the superintendent are, for all the years cited in the foregoing summaries, somewhat larger than the figures appearing in the report of the Commissioner of Education. For the sake of comparisons that may be made with other States, however, the figures reported by the United States Commissioner of Education have generally been used in this report.

approval by the State board of education. It is a fair deduction from this fact that more than two-thirds of the communities maintaining high schools are served by schools which are, up to the present, high schools in little more than name. Later in the report this phase of Washington's educational system will be discussed at greater length. At this point it is sufficient to indicate that the State may look forward with reasonable certainty to the continuance of the rapid development of its high-school facilities and to large increases in high-school enrollments. The character of its population and the generous support that they have always accorded to the public schools furnish ample grounds for the belief that the State will be satisfied with nothing less than a system of secondary schools which puts the opportunity for a complete high-school education within the reach of every boy and girl of appropriate age. The statistics just cited imply that this condition does not yet obtain.[1]

HIGHER EDUCATION IN WASHINGTON.

The Bureau of Education lists six institutions of collegiate rank in Washington.[2] These are the College of Puget Sound, Gonzaga University, the State College of Washington, the University of Washington, Whitworth College, and Whitman College. By acts of the legislature the State normal schools at Bellingham, Cheney, and Ellensburg are designated as parts of the State's system of higher education and are classed with the State college and State university. Although normal schools are not generally included in the bureau's list of collegiate institutions, and although the Washington normal schools do not in one respect meet the definition just cited, they will in this discussion be added to the institutions mentioned above. The accompanying map shows the location of all these institutions, the population of the several counties according to the census figures of 1910, and the locations of some of the largest cities. It is interesting to note that each of the three principal cities has one or more colleges located within its limits and that the grouping of higher institutions (normal schools being included) follows much more closely than is the case in most States the centers of gravity in population. Five are situated on the east side, one in the center, and three on the west side of the State. One normal school is conveniently placed in each of the three chief geographical divisions.

Various lines of higher liberal, specialized, and professional training are offered by these nine institutions. The extent to which they

---

[1] The map on p. 27 shows the distribution of the high-school enrollment, by counties.
[2] To be included in the bureau's collegiate list an institution must be authorized to give degrees, must have definite standards of admission, must give at least two years' work of standard college grade, and must have at least 20 students in regular college status.

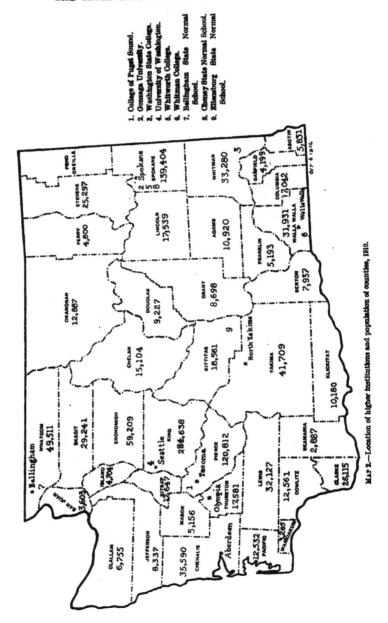

1. College of Puget Sound.
2. Gonzaga University.
3. Washington State College.
4. University of Washington.
5. Whitworth College.
6. Whitman College.
7. Bellingham State Normal School.
8. Cheney State Normal School.
9. Ellensburg State Normal School.

MAP 2.—Location of higher institutions and population of counties, 1910.

provide similar or identical courses leading to the several higher degrees and certificates is indicated by the following summary:

Colleges of arts and sciences (liberal arts)...............	6 (2 State institutions.)
Colleges of law...	2 (1 State.)
Colleges of veterinary medicine.........................	1 (State.)
Colleges or departments of pharmacy....................	2 (State.)
Schools or departments of civil engineering..............	3 (2 State.)
Schools or departments of chemical engineering...........	2 (State.)
Schools or departments of electrical engineering..........	3 (2 State.)
Schools or departments of mechanical engineering........	3 (2 State.)
Schools or departments of mining engineering...........	3 (2 State.)
Colleges of agriculture.................................	1 (State.)
Colleges or departments of forestry......................	2 (State.)
Departments of architecture.............................	2 (State.)
Departments of journalism..............................	1 (State.)
Departments of music (degree courses)....................	3 (2 State.)
Schools or departments of home economics................	4 (2 State.)
Schools of education or courses in education preparing for State certificates.....................................	7 (5 State.)
Summer schools...	6 (5 State.)

Four of the collegiate institutions, one of them a State institution, maintain subcollegiate departments. All three normal schools are under the law required to offer courses for tenth-grade students.

Several significant facts appear at once from this summary. First, more institutions, public and private, are engaged in the training of teachers than in any other branch of higher education. Second, aside from liberal arts and teacher training, the only fields of higher education entered by private institutions are law, engineering, music, and home economics; and but one private institution offers degree courses in each of the first three of these subjects. Third, the important fields of veterinary medicine, pharmacy, agriculture, forestry, architecture, and journalism are cultivated by State institutions alone. Fourth, the two State institutions of collegiate rank give professional courses in pharmacy, all branches of engineering, forestry, architecture, music, and home economics. In other words, there is duplication of specialized training at State expense in nine different professional lines. The wisdom of this duplication will be discussed later.

The increase in the enrollment in Washington higher institutions has been no less amazing than the growth of secondary schools. The following table shows the numbers in State and private colleges and in normal schools at five-year periods from 1895 to 1914. The diagrams appended, 2, 3, and 4, illustrate various aspects of these increases and indicate the relation between the higher institutional enrollments and the growth in population.

TABLE 2.—*Students in higher educational institutions.*

Years.	Collegiate students.			Normal.	Grand total.
	State.	Private.	Total.		
1894–95	233	228	461	225	686
1899–1900	500	200	700	330	1,030
1904–5	1,001	399	1,400	1,112	2,512
1909–10	2,438	472	2,910	1,286	4,196
1913–14	3,070	562	3,632	1,569	5,201

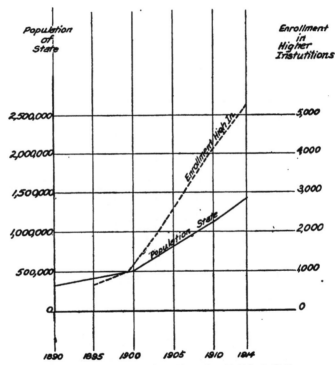

DIAGRAM 2.—Growth in population and in enrollment in higher institutions.

It is, however, when the enrollment in the higher institutions is compared with that in secondary schools that the most surprising developments are observed. It appears, then, that between 1900 and 1905, the period of most rapid growth in secondary education, both the State and private colleges increased approximately 100 per cent, that the normal schools increased almost 350 per cent, and that the higher institutions taken together increased almost 150 per cent.

In the following lustrum, while the per cent of increase for all higher education taken together is less (67 per cent), State institutions increased about 140 per cent.   Between 1910 and 1914 the per cent of increase both for State institutions and for private institutions, although not so great as in the two preceding five-year periods, is still large.   The great growth in secondary and higher institutions, it will be observed, has been simultaneous, and higher institutions have

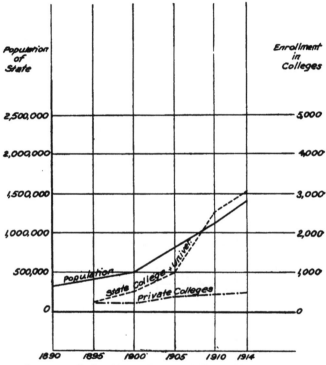

DIAGRAM 3.—Enrollment in growth in population and in State and private colleges.

increased at an even more rapid rate than secondary schools.   This development is entirely unexpected and quite unlike the usual course of evolution of a State educational system.   As a rule the expansion of collegiate enrollments follows a few years behind the growth of secondary-school enrollment.

Comparing Washington with other States, it appears that in spite of this swift and sudden growth Washington does not rank high in the percentage of students enrolled in higher institutions.   In 1913, 15 other States showed a larger per cent of the whole number of pupils in higher institutions, and 20 other States recorded a larger per cent of the total population receiving higher education.[1]

The summary on page 33 and diagram 3 reveal one other fact of far-reaching importance, namely, the higher education in Washington is thus far preponderatingly State education. This fact is really fundamental to whatever recommendations the survey commission

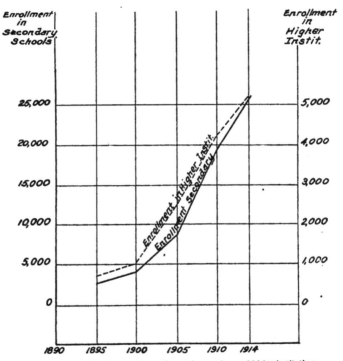

DIAGRAM 4.—Relative increases in enrollments in secondary and higher institutions.

may see fit to make and to the treatment the legislature may decide to accord to the State-supported higher institutions. More than 80 per cent of all the students enrolled in higher institutions are in State institutions. The working income of private institutions (exclusive of additions to endowment) is but 12 per cent of the total sum spent for higher education in Washington. The rate of growth of private institutions has thus far been relatively sluggish.

---

[1] But, as has been noted, the percentage of persons of school age is low in Washington.

An interesting forecast of what the State may expect in the way of numerical increase of both secondary and higher education is found by continuing upward to 1925 the curves shown in diagrams 5 and 6. While precisely these conditions may not obtain, it is a safe assumption that these projected curves represent approximately what the

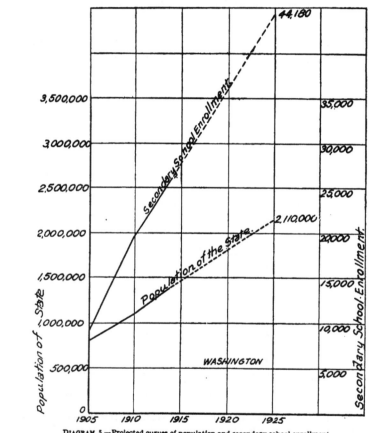

DIAGRAM 5.—Projected curves of population and secondary school enrollment.

State may look forward to. Unless the committee has been misinformed, all previous estimates made by school officers of the increases to be anticipated within a given biennium have been too low. In any event the State must contemplate very large additions to its expenditures for both secondary and higher education if it desires to maintain its position among the educationally progressive States of the Union.

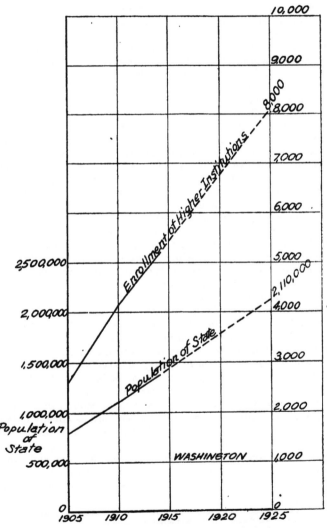

DIAGRAM 6.—Population of State and enrollment in higher institutions.

In this outline of the State's provision for higher education the relations between the higher institutions and secondary schools properly demand brief mention. Admission to the degree courses of the State university and State college is based on graduation from an accredited high school or equivalent preparation, except in the case of the schools of pharmacy, veterinary science, and music at the State college. The entrance requirement for these schools is but two years of high-school work.[1] The normal schools under the law are required to admit graduates of the eighth grade, if of sufficient maturity. As a matter of practice, however, the lowest regularly established courses in the normal schools presuppose the completion of the tenth grade, and the great majority of applicants for admission to the normal schools are high-school graduates. Of the privately supported colleges all but one maintain preparatory departments. The principal object of each of these departments is to fit students for the college to which it is attached. As far as the relation of the college departments of these institutions to the public secondary schools is concerned, the tendency of all but one appears to be to follow the standard set up for the degree courses of the State institutions and to demand for entrance the completion of the course in an accredited high school or its equivalent. While there is substantial parity between the higher institutions, except the normal schools,[2] with respect to the *amount* to be required for entrance, there is wide variation in the subjects actually demanded of entering students. It may possibly be wise institutional policy for colleges maintaining technical curricula or dedicated to the attainment of individual and peculiar educational purposes through the medium of courses in liberal arts to impose special entrance requirements different from those of neighboring institutions, which are fed by the same secondary schools; but the committee is unable to see the justification for essential variation in the requirements laid down by two State institutions for admission to identical courses.

From facts brought out in the foregoing pages certain generalizations can safely be made. Both systems, the secondary and the higher, have grown so fast that it has thus far been impossible to render either thoroughly substantial. The majority of schools in the secondary system are still small and undeveloped, but, as already noted, 85 per cent of the students are enrolled in accredited schools. The growth of the higher institutions, especially the university and two of the normal schools, could hardly have been foreseen and must have proved a veritable embarrassment to any institution, however soundly established. In the chapter of accidents which have deter-

---

[1] This is the usual requirement in similar schools elsewhere.
[2] See the proposals of the committee regarding changes in entrance requirements for the normal schools made on p. 174 et seq. These changes have the indorsement of the schools.

mined the location of higher institutions in the United States, Washington has fared much better than its neighbors. Nearly all of its higher schools have undisputed spheres of influence, which bear somewhat logical relations to geographical conditions and the distribution of population. The State's higher institutions of collegiate rank, however, duplicate to an extent scarcely paralleled in the United States technical and professional courses and courses in the liberal arts. Academic standards as evidenced by entrance requirements are similar for both public and private institutions, except the normal schools. Yet the special requirements of individual institutions present unnecessary variations, tending to defeat the unity of purpose in State higher education. Private institutions of both higher and secondary grade are in a small minority. Both higher and secondary education are, to an extent found only in a few States, publicly supported and controlled.

Too much emphasis can hardly be laid upon this last-mentioned fact, and upon its bearing on the substance of this report. Whatever the future may bring forth, Washington must recognize that for the present, and, probably, indeed for a long time to come, the higher education of its citizens is to be accomplished mainly through the agency of State institutions. The responsibility rests upon the State to provide opportunities for higher education equal to the demand, commensurate with the provision for other forms of education and with the outlay for higher education in other States, consonant with the progressive spirit and high ideals of the people. A well-supported, well-coordinated State university system is called for.[1] Has the State such a system to-day? Certain of the broader phases of this question are discussed in the following chapters.

Chapter II.

SUPPORT OF HIGHER EDUCATION IN WASHINGTON AND IN OTHER STATES.

The figures presented in the accompanying tables and diagrams furnish a striking revelation of the extent to which Washington is supporting its higher institutions in comparison with other States. Expenditures for both private and public higher institutions are included. In many of the older States higher education has been left largely to private initiative; and is endowed and supported for the most part by private benefactions. Nevertheless, the institutions on private foundations are as truly public agencies for higher training as are State-supported institutions. The existence of them

---

[1] For a fuller discussion of the term "University system" see Chs. VII and VIII.

relieves the State of the necessity of providing similar facilities at public expense. Moreover, the fact should not be overlooked that to a large degree the citizens of the State pay for private as well as public institutions. The fees and other charges imposed upon students are met by the students themselves or by their parents, and such collections constitute a considerable portion of the resources of most private institutions. Even the benefactions upon which privately supported institutions also rely are likely to come from the citizens of the State. The taxation for the support of private higher institutions may be indirect and so distributed in time as to escape recognition. Yet, it is in a very real sense a fiscal burden which the citizens of the State must bear. On the other hand, States which have few private institutions must, of necessity, meet the demands of their people by the provision of public institutions. Allowing for variations produced by certain peculiar State conditions,[1] the following tables make possible a fairly reliable comparison of the generosity of the States in the matter of the support of higher education.

Table 3 shows the total wealth of the States in 1912, the last year for which it was possible to secure an estimate, the amount spent for higher education in the following academic year, and the amount spent for higher education for each $1,000 of wealth. Table 4 shows the rank of the States with respect to the expenditure recorded in column 3 of Table 3. Table 5 shows the population of each State, the receipts of higher educational institutions (excluding normal schools),[2] and the apportionment per capita among the citizens of the States of the receipts of higher institutions.[3] Table 6 shows the rank of the States with respect to per capita apportionment of receipts of higher education. Tables 7 and 8 show the per capita apportionment of the receipts of higher education with the inclusion of the expense of normal schools.

Attention is here especially called to the fact that Washington ranks twenty-fourth in Table 4 on the basis of the amount spent on higher education for each $1,000 of wealth. It ranks twenty-third in Table 6 on the basis of apportionment per capita of the receipts of higher institutions of collegiate grade. It ranks fifteenth in Table 8 on the basis of the apportionment per capita of the receipts of higher education, including normal schools. These figures should

---

[1] For example, the high rank of Delaware in Tables 4, 6, and 8 is due to the fact that the State in the year under consideration made large appropriations for the sound establishment of the State college. The high rank of Massachusetts in the same tables is not altogether significant, because Massachusetts contains many long-established wealthy institutions and in turn educates a large proportion of the young people of the whole Northeast.

[2] In the summaries prepared by the United States Commissioner of Education, from which the material for these tables has largely been drawn, normal schools are not included with higher institutions.

[3] The figures on the map on p. 57 show the apportionment for 1913.

allay the apprehension of those citizens who have believed that Washington is unduly extravagant in its support of higher education.

In nearly all States which maintain large State institutions the State expenditure for higher education has increased rapidly in the last 25 years. Legislatures have frequently felt some reluctance to make the ever-increasing appropriations requested by institutional authorities. Nevertheless, with surprising unanimity the State law-making bodies have in the end granted the larger part of these demands. Indeed, not only have State appropriations for higher education grown steadily from year to year, or from biennium to biennium, in nearly all the Western and middle Western States, but the proportion of the total State appropriations which is devoted to higher education has increased steadily also. The accompanying diagrams indicate for the States of Ohio, Indiana, Illinois, Iowa, Michigan, Wisconsin, Minnesota, Kansas, Montana, Texas, Oregon, and Washington the relation which State expenditures for higher education have borne to total State expenditures from 1890 to 1914.[1] The significant aspect of these diagrams is the divergence between the curve for State expenditures and that for higher education. It will be observed that in most States the rate of increase in expenditure for State-supported higher education has been very much more rapid than the rate of increase in total State appropriations reported by the State treasurer. It will be noted also that the relative rate of increase in Washington has been much less than, for instance, in Illinois, Iowa, Kansas, Nebraska, or Wisconsin.

---

[1] The reader of this document should be cautioned not to draw from the figures or the percentages which form the basis of these diagrams any conclusions as to the ratio which the expenditures for higher education bear to the total outlay for public purposes within a given State. Variations between the States in methods of collecting and disbursing public funds ha e made impossible any comparison of the whole amounts spent for public purposes by two or more States, including all their administrative divisions. The only statements of State expenditures available were those contained in State treasurers' reports. These include widely varying lists of items, according as the disbursements for certain purposes are or are not made through the office of the State treasurer. Nevertheless, in most cases the group of expenses handled through the State treasurer's office remains the same from year to year.

TABLE 3.—*Amount expended for higher education for each $1,000 of wealth.*

[Based on the estimated true value of all taxable property, United States Census, 1912, and total receipts of universities, colleges, and normal schools as shown in the Report of the Commissioner of Education.]

States.	Total wealth in 1912.	Spent for higher education, 1913-14.	Spent per $1,000.
Alabama	$2,050,000,000	$1,323,000	$0.65
Arizona	487,000,000	601,000	1.23
Arkansas	1,758,000,000	524,000	.30
California	8,023,000,000	5,488,000	.68
Colorado	2,286,000,000	1,142,000	.50
Connecticut	2,154,000,000	2,706,000	1.25
Delaware	294,000,000	1,142,000	3.88
Florida	1,015,000,000	449,000	.44
Georgia	2,299,000,000	1,407,000	.61
Idaho	591,000,000	417,000	.71
Illinois	14,596,000,000	9,774,000	.68
Indiana	4,951,000,000	2,089,000	.42
Iowa	7,437,000,000	3,815,000	.51
Kansas	4,394,000,000	2,327,000	.53
Kentucky	2,152,000,000	1,077,000	.50
Louisiana	2,057,000,000	1,122,000	.55
Maine	1,030,000,000	948,000	.92
Maryland	2,002,000,000	1,898,000	.95
Massachusetts	5,735,000,000	8,445,000	1.47
Michigan	5,169,000,000	3,799,000	.73
Minnesota	5,267,000,000	4,140,000	.79
Mississippi	1,306,000,000	1,140,000	.87
Missouri	5,546,000,000	2,314,000	.42
Montana	1,113,000,000	540,000	.48
Nebraska	3,605,000,000	1,842,000	.51
Nevada	441,000,000	208,000	.47
New Hampshire	613,000,000	1,130,000	1.84
New Jersey	5,362,000,000	2,066,000	.39
New Mexico	502,000,000	301,000	.60
New York	21,913,000,000	16,139,000	.74
North Carolina	1,745,000,000	1,644,000	.94
North Dakota	2,038,000,000	1,250,000	.61
Ohio	8,552,000,000	4,817,000	.56
Oklahoma	4,321,000,000	845,000	.19
Oregon	1,843,000,000	1,232,000	.67
Pennsylvania	14,137,000,000	7,673,000	.54
Rhode Island	893,000,000	503,000	.56
South Carolina	1,301,000,000	1,569,000	1.21
South Dakota	1,331,000,000	960,000	.72
Tennessee	1,834,000,000	1,461,000	.80
Texas	6,552,000,000	3,223,000	.49
Utah	735,000,000	515,000	.70
Vermont	797,000,000	482,000	.60
Virginia	2,175,000,000	2,980,000	1.37
WASHINGTON	3,855,000,000	1,954,000	.64
Wisconsin	4,282,000,000	5,428,000	1.27
Wyoming	345,000,000	193,000	.56
West Virginia	2,180,000,000	871,000	.39

TABLE 4.—*Amount expended for higher education for each $1,000 of wealth in order of rank, by States, 1913-14.*

1.	Delaware	$3.88	25.	North Dakota	$0.61
2.	New Hampshire	1.84	26.	Georgia	.61
3.	Massachusetts	1.47	27.	Vermont	.60
4.	Virginia	1.37	28.	New Mexico	.60
5.	Wisconsin	1.27	29.	Ohio	.56
6.	Connecticut	1.25	30.	Rhode Island	.56
7.	Arizona	1.23	31.	Wyoming	.56
8.	South Carolina	1.21	32.	Louisiana	.55
9.	Maryland	.95	33.	Pennsylvania	.54
10.	North Carolina	.94	34.	Kansas	.53
11.	Maine	.92	35.	Iowa	.53
12.	Mississippi	.87	36.	Nebraska	.51
13.	Tennessee	.80	37.	Kentucky	.51
14.	Minnesota	.79	38.	Colorado	.50
15.	New York	.74	39.	Texas	.49
16.	Michigan	.73	40.	Montana	.48
17.	South Dakota	.72	41.	Nevada	.47
18.	Idaho	.71	42.	Florida	.44
19.	Utah	.70	43.	Indiana	.42
20.	California	.68	44.	Missouri	.42
21.	Illinois	.68	45.	West Virginia	.39
22.	Oregon	.67	46.	New Jersey	.39
23.	Alabama	.65	47.	Arkansas	.30
24.	WASHINGTON	.64	48.	Oklahoma	.19

TABLE 5.—*Per capita apportionment of receipts of higher educational institutions,*
1913-14.

States.	Population.	Receipts.	Per capita.
Alabama	2,138,000	$628,000	$0.29
Arizona	204,000	267,000	1.31
Arkansas	1,574,000	371,000	.24
California	2,378,000	4,402,000	1.85
Colorado	799,000	1,099,000	1.38
Connecticut	1,115,000	2,578,000	2.31
Delaware	202,000	1,142,000	5.65
Florida	751,000	449,000	.60
Georgia	2,609,000	1,183,000	.45
Idaho	326,000	285,000	.87
Illinois	5,639,000	8,787,000	1.56
Indiana	2,701,000	1,934,000	.72
Iowa	2,225,000	3,789,000	1.70
Kansas	1,691,000	1,938,000	1.15
Kentucky	2,290,000	845,000	.37
Louisiana	1,656,000	908,000	.55
Maine	742,000	762,000	1.03
Maryland	1,295,000	1,843,000	1.42
Massachusetts	3,366,000	7,837,000	2.33
Michigan	2,810,000	3,121,000	1.11
Minnesota	2,076,000	3,580,000	1.72
Mississippi	1,797,000	973,000	.54
Missouri	3,293,000	1,755,000	.53
Montana	376,000	480,000	1.28
Nebraska	1,192,000	1,528,000	1.28
Nevada	82,000	208,000	2.54
New Hampshire	431,000	975,000	2.25
New Jersey	2,537,000	1,709,000	.67
New Mexico	327,000	224,000	.69
New York	9,113,000	15,568,000	1.70
North Carolina	2,206,000	1,332,000	.60
North Dakota	577,000	785,000	1.36
Ohio	4,767,000	4,567,000	.96
Oklahoma	1,657,000	622,000	.38
Oregon	673,000	1,185,000	1.76
Pennsylvania	7,665,000	6,254,000	.81
Rhode Island	543,000	423,000	.78
South Carolina	1,515,000	1,298,000	.86
South Dakota	584,000	680,000	1.16
Tennessee	2,185,000	1,216,000	.55
Texas	3,897,000	2,740,000	.70
Utah	373,000	515,000	1.38
Vermont	356,000	457,000	1.28
Virginia	2,062,000	2,017,000	.98
WASHINGTON	1,142,000	1,320,000	1.16
West Virginia	1,221,000	526,000	.43
Wisconsin	2,334,000	3,825,000	1.64
Wyoming	146,000	193,000	1.32

TABLE 6.—*Rank of States as to per capita receipts of higher educational institutions,*
excluding normal schools, 1913-14.

1. Delaware	$5.65	25. Michigan	$1.11
2. Nevada	2.	26. Maine	1.02
3. Massachusetts	2.	27. Virginia	.97
4. Connecticut	2.	28. Ohio	.95
5. New Hampshire	2.	29. Idaho	.87
6. California	1.	30. South Carolina	.85
7. Oregon	1.53	31. Pennsylvania	.81
8. Minnesota	1.98	32. Rhode Island	.77
9. New York	1.70	33. Indiana	.72
10. Iowa	1.	34. Texas	.70
11. Wisconsin	1.	35. New Mexico	.68
12. Illinois	1.70	36. New Jersey	.67
13. Maryland	1.42	37. North Carolina	.60
14. Colorado	1.38	38. Florida	.60
15. Utah	1.38	39. Tennessee	.55
16. North Dakota	1.	40. Mississippi	.54
17. Wyoming	1.32	41. Louisiana	.54
18. Arizona	1.31	42. Missouri	.53
19. Vermont	1.28	43. Georgia	.45
20. Nebraska	1.28	44. West Virginia	.43
21. Montana	1.27	45. Oklahoma	.37
22. South Dakota	1.16	46. Kentucky	.36
23. WASHINGTON	1.16	47. Alabama	.29
24. Kansas	1.14	48. Arkansas	.24

TABLE 7.—*Receipts of higher educational institutions, including normal schools, for the school year 1913-14.*

	Universities and colleges.	Normal schools.	Total.	Per capita.
Alabama	$628,000	$695,000	$1,323,000	$0.62
Arizona	267,000	334,000	601,000	2.94
Arkansas	371,000	153,000	524,000	.33
California	4,402,000	1,056,000	5,458,000	2.30
Colorado	1,099,000	43,000	1,142,000	1.43
Connecticut	2,578,000	128,000	2,706,000	2.43
Delaware	1,142,000	0	1,142,000	5.65
Florida	449,000	0	449,000	.60
Georgia	1,183,000	224,000	1,407,000	.54
Idaho	285,000	132,000	417,000	1.28
Illinois	8,787,000	1,187,000	9,974,000	1.77
Indiana	1,934,000	155,000	2,089,000	.77
Iowa	3,789,000	26,000	3,815,000	1.71
Kansas	1,938,000	389,000	2,327,000	1.38
Kentucky	845,000	232,000	1,077,000	.47
Louisiana	908,000	214,000	1,122,000	.68
Maine	762,000	186,000	958,000	1.28
Maryland	1,843,000	55,000	1,898,000	1.46
Massachusetts	7,837,000	608,000	8,445,000	2.51
Michigan	3,121,000	678,000	3,799,000	1.35
Minnesota	3,580,000	560,000	4,140,000	1.99
Mississippi	973,000	167,000	1,140,000	.63
Missouri	1,755,000	559,000	2,314,000	.70
Montana	480,000	60,000	540,000	1.44
Nebraska	1,528,000	314,000	1,842,000	1.54
Nevada	208,000	0	208,000	2.53
New Hampshire	975,000	155,000	1,130,000	2.62
New Jersey	1,709,000	357,000	2,066,000	.81
New Mexico	224,000	77,000	301,000	.92
New York	15,568,000	571,000	16,139,000	1.77
North Carolina	1,332,000	312,000	1,644,000	.75
North Dakota	785,000	465,000	1,250,000	2.17
Ohio	4,567,000	250,000	4,817,000	1.01
Oklahoma	622,000	223,000	845,000	.51
Oregon	1,185,000	47,000	1,232,000	1.83
Pennsylvania	6,254,000	1,419,000	7,673,000	1.00
Rhode Island	423,000	80,000	503,000	.93
South Carolina	1,298,000	271,000	1,569,000	1.04
South Dakota	680,000	280,000	960,000	1.64
Tennessee	1,216,000	245,000	1,461,000	.67
Texas	2,740,000	483,000	3,223,000	.83
Utah	515,000	0	515,000	1.38
Vermont	457,000	25,000	482,000	1.35
Virginia	2,017,000	963,000	2,980,000	1.45
WASHINGTON	1,320,000	634,000	1,954,000	1.71
West Virginia	526,000	345,000	871,000	.71
Wisconsin	3,825,000	1,603,000	5,428,000	2.33
Wyoming	193,000	0	193,000	1.32

TABLE 8.—*Rank of States as to per capita receipts of higher educational institutions, including normal schools, 1913-14.*

1.	Delaware	$5.65	25.	Michigan	$1.35
2.	Arizona	2.94	26.	Wyoming	1.32
3.	New Hampshire	2.62	27.	Idaho	1.279
4.	Nevada	2.53	28.	Maine	1.277
5.	Massachusetts	2.51	29.	South Carolina	1.04
6.	Connecticut	2.43	30.	Ohio	1.01
7.	Wisconsin	2.33	31.	Pennsylvania	1.00
8.	California	2.30	32.	Rhode Island	.93
9.	North Dakota	2.17	33.	New Mexico	.92
10.	Minnesota	1.99	34.	Texas	.83
11.	Oregon	1.83	35.	New Jersey	.81
12.	New York	1.770	36.	Indiana	.77
13.	Illinois	1.768	37.	North Carolina	.75
14.	Iowa	1.714	38.	West Virginia	.71
15.	WASHINGTON	1.711	39.	Missouri	.70
16.	South Dakota	1.64	40.	Louisiana	.68
17.	Nebraska	1.54	41.	Tennessee	.67
18.	Maryland	1.46	42.	Mississippi	.63
19.	Virginia	1.45	43.	Florida	.60
20.	Montana	1.44	44.	Alabama	.57
21.	Colorado	1.43	45.	Georgia	.54
22.	Kansas	1.38	46.	Oklahoma	.51
23.	Utah	1.38	47.	Kentucky	.47
24.	Vermont	1.35	48.	Arkansas	.33

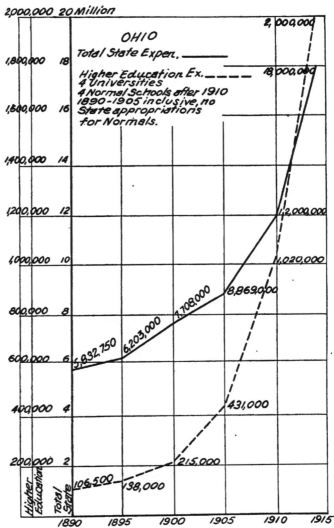

OHIO

Total State Expen. _____

Higher Education Ex. _ _ _ _
4 Universities
4 Normal Schools after 1910
1890-1905 inclusive, no
State appropriations
for Normals.

2,000,000

1,800,000

1,020,000

8,869,000

1,708,000

6,203,000

5,832,750

431,000

215,000

106,500

138,000

DIAGRAM 7.—State expenditures for higher education in Ohio compared with total State
expenditures.

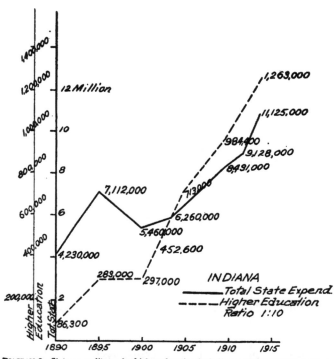

DIAGRAM 8.—State expenditures for higher education in Indiana compared with total State expenditures.

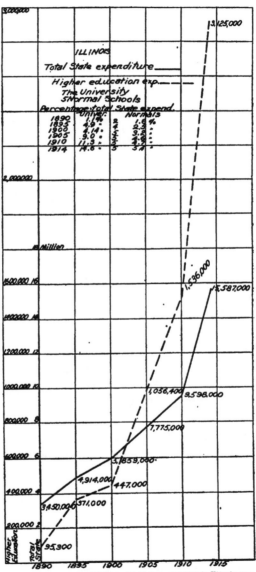

DIAGRAM 9.—State expenditures for higher education in Illinois compared with total State expenditures.

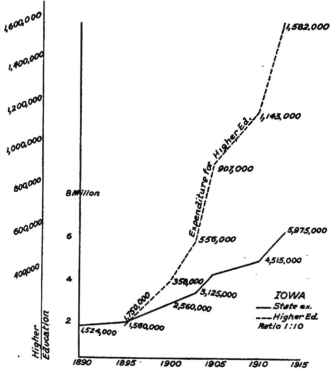

DIAGRAM 10.— State expenditures for higher education in Iowa compared with total State expenditures.

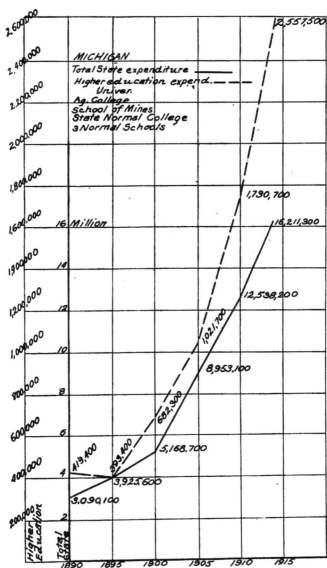

DIAGRAM 11.—State expenditures for higher education in Michigan compared with total State expenditures.

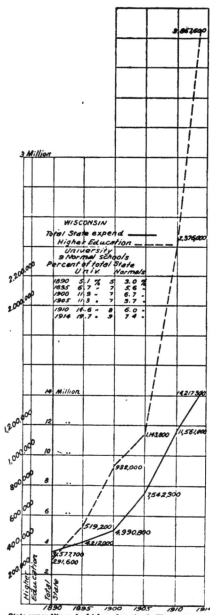

DIAGRAM 12.—State expenditures for higher education in Wisconsin compared with total
State expenditures.

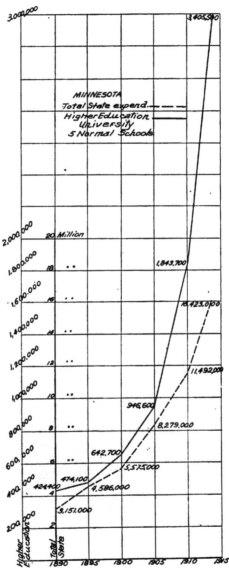

DIAGRAM 13.—State expenditures for higher education in Minnesota compared with total State expenditures.

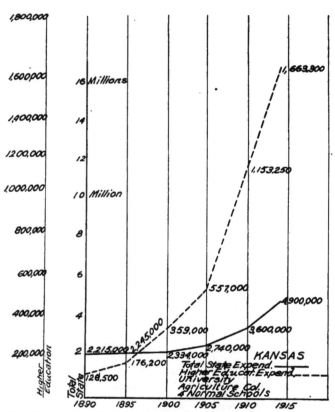

DIAGRAM 14.—State expenditures for higher education in Kansas compared with total State expenditures.

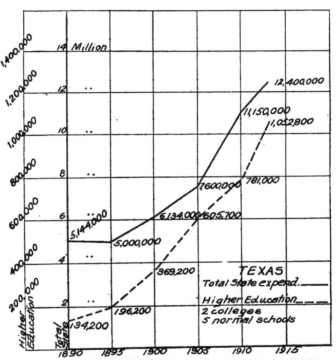

DIAGRAM 15.—State expenditures for higher education in Texas compared with total State expenditures.

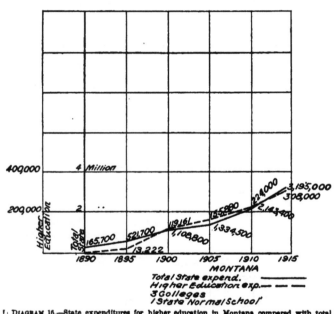

[ ] DIAGRAM 16.—State expenditures for higher education in Montana compared with total
State expenditures.

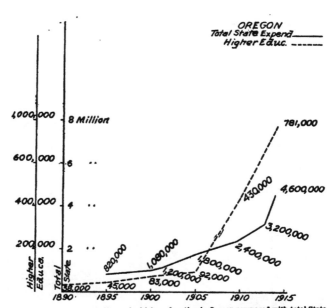

DIAGRAM 17.—State expenditures for higher education in Oregon compared with total State expenditures.

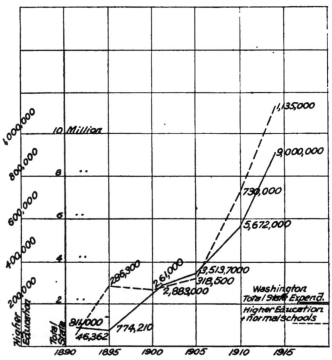

DIAGRAM 18.—State expenditures for higher education in Washington compared with total
State expenditures.

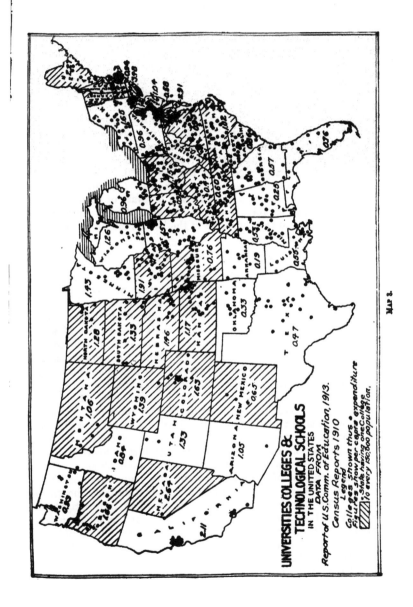

UNIVERSITIES COLLEGES &
TECHNOLOGICAL SCHOOLS
IN THE UNITED STATES
DATA FROM
Report of U.S.Comm. of Education, 1913.
Census Reports 1910
Legend
Colleges shown thus •
Figures show per capita expenditure
State having one College
to every 150,000 population.

MAP 3.

Chapter III.

STATE OFFICIALS AND ADMINISTRATIVE MACHINERY.

A well-coordinated State system of higher education may be secured either through the control of administrative officials charged with the duty of overseeing the State's educational policies as a whole or through the common agreement of officers of individual institutions who deliberately join forces for the formulation of a State policy. It is worth while to inquire how far either or both of these conditions prevail in Washington.

The administration of Washington's higher institutions is intrusted directly to six different boards. Indirectly two others are concerned in the financial management of the institutions. The six boards are the State board of education, the board of regents of the State university, the board of regents of the State college, and the three boards of trustees of the State normal schools. One State administrative officer exercises ex officio a certain measure of authority over higher institutions, namely, the superintendent of public instruction. The constitution and the functions of the boards mentioned are very briefly summarized below.

STATE BOARD OF EDUCATION.

The State board of education consists of the superintendent of public instruction, the president of the University of Washington, the president of the State College of Washington, the principal of one of the normal schools elected by the principals of the State normal schools, and three persons appointed by the governor, one of whom shall be superintendent of city schools, one a county superintendent, and one a principal of an accredited high school. The appointed and elected members hold office for two years. The members of the board receive no compensation except when on special committee duty. In general, the powers of the board are: The approval of entrance requirements for State higher institutions, the approval of teacher-training courses in State higher institutions, the accrediting of higher institutions whose graduates may receive teachers' certificates without examinations, the accrediting of secondary schools, the prescription of the course of study for the common schools and the rules for the government of such schools, and the preparation of examinations for teachers' certificates and for graduation from the graded schools. The law also provides that the board shall investigate the work required as a condition of entrance to and graduation from normal schools, colleges, universities, and other institutions of higher education. Apparently this provision is intended merely to facilitate the accrediting of higher institutions, but possibly it is susceptible of a broader construction.

BOARD OF REGENTS OF THE UNIVERSITY OF WASHINGTON.

The board of regents of the university consists of seven members appointed by the governor each for a term of six years. Broadly, its duty is to control the university and its property. Its powers extend to the appointment of all officers, teachers, and employees of the institution, the prescription of courses of study, the conferring of degrees, and the management of its finances. The board serves without compensation. It is required to meet quarterly.

BOARD OF REGENTS OF THE STATE COLLEGE.

The board of regents of the State college consists of five persons appointed by the governor for terms of six years. The president of the college serves ex officio as secretary of the board without vote. The governor of the State is ex officio an advisory member without vote. Each regent must give bond in the sum of $5,000 and the treasurer in the sum of $40,000. Briefly, the powers of the regents are to control the funds of the college and experiment stations, to employ and fix salaries of all officials and teachers, and to grant degrees. The board is expected to meet annually. It serves without compensation.

THE BOARDS OF TRUSTEES OF THE NORMAL SCHOOLS.

Each of the three normal schools is under the control of a separate board of trustees consisting of three members appointed by the governor for terms of six years. The secretary of the board is not a member. The powers of each of these boards extend to the election and dismissal of all officers, teachers, and employees of their respective schools, the adoption of textbooks, the management of school property, and the purchase of supplies. Each board is expected to meet twice a year and to make a biennial report to the governor prior to the meeting of the legislature.

THE STATE BOARD OF FINANCE AND THE STATE BOARD OF EQUALIZATION.

Upon the State board of finance is conferred the authority to invest the permanent funds of any State educational institution. The State board of equalization is charged with the levying upon taxable property in the State of the millage tax for the support of the higher instituti s.

THE STATE SUPERINTENDENT OF PUBLIC INSTRUCTION.

The State superintendent of public instruction in his capacity as president of the State board of education comes in contact with certain phases of the management of the State higher institutions. As has been indicated above, the board exercises a larger measure of authority over normal schools than over the other higher institutions. Its jurisdiction over the State university and the State college is limited in practice to the approval of entrance requirements and the work of departments of education.

As is usual the various boards of regents and trustees deal merely with the affairs of their respective institutions. The powers and duties of the boards of normal school trustees are prescribed in one act and in the same terms for all three boards. Their functions, while similar to, are not identical with those of the boards of regents of the university and the State college. Neither are the latter two boards exactly the same in constitution and functions. The Washington State Board of Education is in its constitution almost unique. It will be observed that it is a board of experts. But one other State, West Virginia, has an expert board of education, although the State boards in Arizona and Indiana are composed mainly of experts. The prevailing theory in administration favors the lay board working through expert executives, on the assumption that by this means the desires of the public will best be represented and will reach their accomplishment in educational practice. However, there is nothing fixed and immutable about administrative procedure. The pragmatic test is after all the final test. Within the limits of its past and current activities the Washington State board of education appears to have met this test. It is universally well spoken of. Nevertheless, the committee is inclined to believe that it has not fully realized its possibilities. It seems to have confined itself to the somewhat mechanical discharge of the functions prescribed for it in the law. In particular it has failed to perform—perhaps circumstances of which the committee is unaware have prevented its performing—one great educational service which the State of Washington sadly needs. This service is discussed and certain constructive suggestions are offered in the following chapter.

Chapter IV.

THE FORMULATION OF STATE POLICIES IN HIGHER EDUCATION.

It is evident from the discussion in the preceding chapter that there is at present no machinery for the formulation of State policies in higher education. The result of this lack is painfully apparent and has in fact given rise in a large measure to the difficulties which the present survey is designed to remedy. A State's educational institutions exist primarily to furnish training for those activities which must be carried on by the citizens of the State. They grow in response to definite public demands. Their expansion and the development of new courses follow in general the existence of a public need for specific types of training. Yet the correlation between the demand and the facilities provided for training in a given line is not always close. Particularly is this true in highly specialized or professional lines. A State institution may provide too little or it may provide too much. Rarely are its excursions into new fields of professional training based upon a scientific study of the actual call for workers in those fields. The existence of a large demand is frequently inferred when really a few trained workers will suffice. On the other hand, even the most progressive and pushing institutions are often surprisingly blind to the necessity for the development of certain types of professional training. They fail to interpret the as yet inarticulate call. When two institutions whose functions are not sharply differentiated compete for the same educational territory these maladjustments are most apt to appear. The close correlation of State institutions with actual needs and conditions becomes all the time more important as States grow and their economic and sociological problems develop in complexity. Every State can afford to furnish for its citizens the types of training actually required. No State can afford to waste its money in oversupplying a limited professional market. The value of some central coordinating machinery is that it can study State educational problems in a nonpartisan spirit for the purpose of determining what is and what is not needed and that it can bring State institutions to comply with its conclusions.

Even such a superficial consideration as the committee has had time to give to the relation of the types of training now offered by Washington State higher institutions to the occupations, industries, and prospective growth of the State shows that these statements are applicable to the local situation. As has already been indicated in the summary on page 32, the State higher institutions are tending in the direction of oversupplying professional needs. One important line of specialized training appears to need further development—commerce; and for that the demand has now become insistent. Against the defect of inadequate provision for the development of advanced commercial training of university grade should be placed the maintenance of two schools of mining, one of the most expensive of professional departments; two departments of architecture[1] to supply a profession numbering 505 in the census of 1910; two schools of forestry to recruit a calling which numbered 536 in the same census year and for the practice of which in Washington men come from all over the United States. However, the detailed discussion of expensive duplication appears in Chapters VI, VII, and VIII. Mention is here made of these cases merely by way of illustration to show the disadvantages of the lack of a coherent State program.

[1] At the State college the head of the department of architecture discharges also the duties of college architect.

In the judgment of the committee the most important reform which may be wrought in public education in Washington is the provision for the definite and permanent coordination of higher institutions. This may be accomplished in any one of at least three ways. Two of them entail no organic change in the present machinery of administration. The third is also simple and involves no structural reorganization. They are as follows:

1. The committee is of the opinion that joint meetings of the boards of regents of the State university and the State college at regular intervals for the discussion of the interrelations of these institutions and for the determination of measures to promote harmony and economy in the management of the State higher institutions would probably accomplish the major part of the desired purpose. The committee has been much impressed by the possibilities of such oint meetings, one of which, on the initiative of the boards themselves, has already been called. It believes that this very simple device may prove a solution of the State's most vexed educational difficulties, that it may result in welding together into a common constructive program in which the interests of the State shall be held paramount the conflicting aims of two institutions which are, but should not be, rivals. The boards of trustees of the normal schools could be included in the joint conferences whenever occasion required.

2. The committee believes that the law allows the extension of the activities of the State board of education to include such a formulation of State higher educational policies as is here under discussion. The law provides that the board is to investigate the work required as a condition of entrance to and graduation from normal schools, colleges, universities, and other institutions of higher education. Although this section of the act defining the powers of the board probably contemplates only such investigation as may be necessary to determine the eligibility of higher institutions for accrediting, the committee—no member of which, however, is a lawyer—believes that it might be broadly construed to include a consideration of the programs and tendencies of higher institutions. The recommendations which it might see fit to make in the light of such consideration, even though the board has no power to enforce them, would probably have the effect of a mandate, particularly if they were made public. If on examination by competent legal authorities it appears that the present law does not permit such action by the board as is here suggested, the committee judges that only a slight amendment of the act defining the powers of the board will be necessary to give it this wider range. We think that this question, together with the other alternatives proposed in connection with it, is worthy the consideration of your commission.

The extension of the functions of the board to include this wider field would have certain distinctive advantages. It would help to emphasize the unity of the State's educational enterprise. It would tend to bring together various constituencies and lead to the interpretation of one group of educational problems in the light of the educational needs of the whole system. The Washington board, being an expert board, is peculiarly qualified to render this service. All educational interests are represented on it. No one preponderates. Moreover the board has the confidence and respect of the educators and of the State at large.

3. It will be remembered that, in his report to the legislature of 1915, the United States Commissioner of Education recommended the creation of a State council of education—

to consist of two representatives of the board of regents of the university, two representatives of the board of regents of the State college, one representative of the board of trustees of each of the State normal schools, two representatives of the State board of education, the president of the university, the president of the State college, the principals of the normal schools, and the State superintendent of public instruction. Each board should elect its representation and no person should represent more than one board or institution. This council should hold at least one meeting each year, the necessary expenses being paid out of the public funds, and should be required to report the results of its deliberations to the several boards or institutions represented.

It will be observed that the professional membership of this proposed council coincides almost exactly with the membership of the State board of education.

SUMMARY OF RECOMMENDATIONS.

1. The provision for the formulation of State policies in higher education—

    a. Through joint meetings of boards of regents, or

    b. Through the extension of the functions of the State board of education, or

    c. Through the creation of a State council of education.

Chapter V.

COSTS OF STATE UNIVERSITY AND STATE COLLEGE.

Thus far State higher education in Washington has been considered as a unit. The remaining chapters in this section deal with the details of financial and educational management of the State college and State university and present the committee's recommendations concerning these institutions. This chapter is devoted to the presentation of certain material bearing both on the costs of the college and the university and on some phases of their educational administration.

The first group of exhibits in connection with the chapter consists of tabulations of the expenses of these two institutions for the academic years 1913–14 and 1914–15.[1] The expenditures of higher institutions differ greatly, and the forms in which such expenditures are reported differ still more. In a recent study by the Bureau of Education of the Iowa State institutions, financial reports of all three of these institutions were secured in the same form as is here used. Within this limited group of five institutions, therefore, substantially accurate comparisons may be made. In order that the tabulation may be clear, the following explanation is offered.[2]

The total expenditures for the year are first divided into two main groups: *Educational expenditures* and *extension and service expenditures*. The *educational expenditures* are then divided into three separate categories: *Construction and land, special and rotating funds*, and *operating expenditures*.

The category *construction and land* includes expenditures for direct additions to the plant to provide for growth in enrollment, together with outlays for the ordinary furniture of new buildings. *Special and rotating funds* include expenditures from prize funds, boarding and rooming departments, and special funds available only for specified purposes apart from instruction. These two classes of expenditures are in a certain sense entirely independent of the cost of the operation of the educational plant.

The category *operating expenditures* includes all expenses for the annual maintenance of the institution, aside from dormitories and boarding departments. It is further analyzed into *educational equipment and supplies, instruction*, and *general operating expenses*. The latter may perhaps more aptly be termed *overhead expense*. The following may make this clear:

Total expenditures { Educational { Construction and land. / Special and rotating fund. / Operating expenditures { Educational equipment and supplies. / Instruction. / General operating expenses (overhead expense). } } / Extension and service. }

Under *operating expenditures* the first subdivision, *educational equipment and supplies*, includes in addition to purely departmental supplies the expenditures for books and library supplies. The second subdivision, *instruction*, includes the salaries of the deans and faculty members, but not those of the president, other purely administrative officers, and librarians. The third, *general operating or overhead expense*, includes the salaries of administrative officers, janitors, etc., in addition to other expenditures essential to the maintenance of the work of the institution.

---

[1] Summaries only are included in this chapter. The detail tables appear in the appendix.

[2] The explanation of the form for the reporting of expenditures and the discussion of student clock hours in this chapter are taken for the most part from the report of the survey of the Iowa State institutions.

TABLE 9.—*University of Washington, expenditures, 1913–14.*

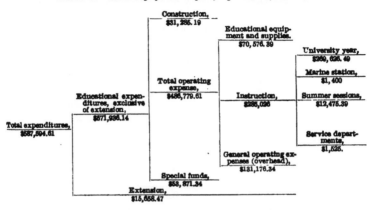

TABLE 10.—*University of Washington expenditures, 1914–15.*

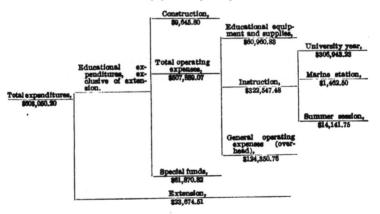

TABLE 11.—*State College of Washington expenditures, 1913-14.*

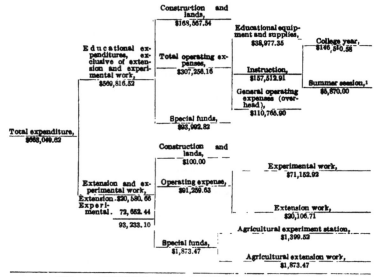

[1] Difference of $5,132.33 is for summer school of 1914-15. See report for that year.

TABLE 12.—*State College of Washington expenditures, 1914-15.*

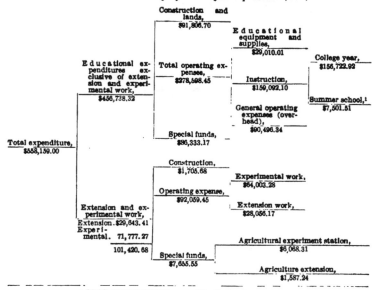

[1] Of this amount $5,132.33 was paid in the fiscal year 1913-14.

There follow next two tables, one relating to the State college and one to the State university, which deserve somewhat careful explanation and which repay study. They show the departments represented in each institution, the total number of instructors in each department (part-time teachers being reduced to a full-time basis), the average salary for each department, the total number of student clock hours, and the average number of student clock hours for each department. The student clock hour is a relatively new unit in academic measurements. It may be defined thus: One student under instruction in lecture, quiz, or laboratory for at least 50 minutes net represents one student clock hour. For example, therefore, 20 students meeting four hours a week in recitation represent 80 student clock hours. The student clock hour is, it will be observed, a different unit from the "credit hour" or the "semester hour." Usually two or three hours of laboratory work are required as the equivalent of one hour of recitation in reckoning semester or credit hours. The student clock hour does not discount laboratory hours, but reckons laboratory, lecture, and quiz exercises equally hour for hour. For example, a student taking a course in chemistry and spending one hour in lecture, one hour in quiz, and four hours in laboratory in a week would be counted as receiving six student clock hours of instruction.

The Bureau of Education has already suggested certain standards to govern the size of university and college classes. They are as follows:

1. In a lecture a professor may meet effectively as many as can comfortably hear and see him.

2. In a recitation or quiz 30 in a section is probably the largest number that can be effectively handled, but the desirable maximum for classes of this type would be from 20 to 25.

3. In laboratory work it is commonly agreed that one instructor should be provided for every 15 or 16 students.

The number of lecture, laboratory, and quiz sections which an instructor can meet in a week depends to a considerable degree upon the character of the work and the amount of labor which it involves outside of the classroom. It also is contingent to some extent upon the amount of outside writing and research which the instructor is expected to do. An examination of any department indicates that no definite number of student clock hours can be fixed for each instructor. An average for a department may, however, be safely set up. The Bureau of Education has estimated that in an institution where research work is encouraged and expected it is reasonable to expect also a departmental average of 250 student clock hours per instructor. This, it is believed, might be a fair working average for a modern State university. In a distinctively undergraduate college, on the other hand, where research is limited and where little or no graduate work is conducted, a departmental average of 300 student clock hours per instructor is regarded as a reasonable norm. In this connection it is worth while to note that usually an institution whose program is made up largely of laboratory work will generally record a larger number of student clock hours per instructor than an institution whose program consists chiefly of nonlaboratory courses.

TABLE 13.—*University of Washington—Salaries and student clock hours for the year ending June 30, 1915.*

Departments.	Number of instructors.	Total salaries.	Average salary.	First semester.		Second semester.	
				Total student clock hours.	Average student clock hours.	Total student clock hours.	Average student clock hours.
COLLEGE OF LIBERAL ARTS.							
English	14	$22,600	$1,619	3,871	276.5	3,247	231.9
French	6⅞	11,937	1,736	1,962	285.4	1,845	268.4
German	7¾	12,362	1,595	2,267	292.5	2,078	277.0
Greek	2¼	5,300	2,355	441	252.0	361	240.0
History	6¾	12,900	1,911	2,908	504.9	2,870	499.1
Journalism	5⅜	9,645	1,794	580	178.4	659	181.7
Latin	2¾	6,000	2,182	395	143.6	465	155.0
Library economy	1	1,714	....	168	....	198	....
Oriental history	1	2,600	....	310	....	296	....
Philosophy	3	5,700	1,900	941	313.7	957	319.0
Political and social science	9	16,350	1,817	3,469	385.4	3,107	345.2
Public speaking and debate	2	3,900	1,950	290	145.0	521	260.5
Scandinavian languages and literature	1	2,100	....	112	....	132	....
Spanish	3¾	6,825	1,820	1,053	280.8	1,091	290.9
COLLEGE OF SCIENCE.							
Botany	6½	10,500	1,615	2,926	457.3	2,172	334.2
Chemistry	13	18,975	1,460	7,299	561.4	[1] 5,761	443.1
Geology	4	5,950	1,487	1,252	313.0	[2] 1,324	331.0
Home economics	5	7,800	1,560	1,252	350.0	1,324	264.2
Mathematics	10½	18,050	1,719	3,139	298.9	2,691	256.3
Philosophy (psychology)	2⅝	3,825	1,457	966	368.0	829	315.8
Physical training	5½	7,300	1,327	2,127	386.7	2,507	455.8
Physics	5⅜	9,100	1,699	1,568	291.7	1,455	270.7
Zoology	4¾	7,850	1,653	2,838	597.5	3,080	648.4
COLLEGE OF ENGINEERING, ETC.							
Civil engineering	10¼	18,445	1,800	3,117	336.9	[3] 4,137	367.7
Electrical engineering	3½	6,975	1,993	916	261.7	920	262.8
Mechanical engineering	5	9,800	1,960	2,350	470.0	1,962	392.4
College of Mines	4	8,150	2,037	376	94.0	[4] 443	110.8
College of forestry	4⅛	8,850	2,145	1,051	254.8	[5] 721	174.8
College of pharmacy	5¾	8,595	1,495	998	285.1	1,096	292.2
School of education	5	10,500	2,100	1,375	275.0	1,633	326.6
School of law	5¾	14,200	2,457	2,565	448.7	2,197	382.1
College of fine arts	6⅜	10,700	1,678	2,312	362.0	2,033	318.9
Military training	2	600	600	1,624	812.0	1,388	694.0
Total	174½	306,099	1,754	58,813	337.0	57,652	330.3

[1] In a short course, 48, making the total 5,809, and average hours 474.2.
[2] In a short course, 138; making the total 1,462, and average hours 365.5.
[3] In a short course, 262; making the total 4,399, and average hours 391.
[4] In a short course, 310; making total 753, and average hours 188.3.
[5] In a short course, 494, making total of 1,215, and average hours 494.5.

TABLE 14.—*State College of Washington—Summary by departments, year ending June, 1915.*

FIRST SEMESTER.

Departments.	Total clock hours.	Total number instructors.	Average clock hours.	Total salaries.	Average salary.
Agriculture	2,176	8¾	248.6	$15,686	$1,790
Botany	1,247	3¼	383.6	6,150	1,892
Chemistry	2,021	6	336.8	10,240	1,707
Civil engineering and mathematics	1,098	6¼	175.6	12,000	1,920
Economic science and history	1,639	5	327.8	8,140	1,628
Education	453	2	226.5	3,800	1,600
English	1,862	8	232.5	11,200	1,400
Home economics	994	3	331.3	4,300	1,433
Horticulture	554	4	138.5	6,950	1,737
Mechanical engineering and electrical engineering (mechanical arts, physics, and architecture included)	1,951	11½	169.6	17,925	1,559
Modern languages	1,571	8	196.3	9,920	1,240
Manual arts	28	½	46.6	773	1,290
Latin	37	1	37.0	2,200	2,200
Geology	208	2	104.0	4,200	2,100
Mining engineering	161	2	80.5	4,100	2,050
Pharmacy	214	1	214.0	1,800	1,800
Photography	32	⅒	320.0	90	900
Zoology	284	1⅔	171.0	2,800	1,681
Veterinary science	738	2⅔	276.7	5,900	2,213
Forestry	22	1	22.0	2,200	2,200
Music	342	8	43.0	6,500	812
Total	17,682	....	194.3	....	1,640

SECOND SEMESTER.

Agriculture	2,183	8⁴⁄	259.1	$15,550	$1,849
Botany	744	3¼	228.9	6,025	1,854
Chemistry	2,117	6⁶⁄	347.04	10,340	1,695
Civil engineering and mathematics	1,069	6¼	171.04	12,000	1,400
Economic science and history	1,066	6	177.7	10,340	1,723
Education	720	2	360.0	3,800	1,900
English	1,974	8	246.7	11,200	11,400
Home economics	838	3¼	257.8	4,600	1,415
Horticulture	350	4	87.5	6,950	1,737
Mechanical engineering and electrical engineering (mechanical arts, physics, and architecture included)	1,662	10¼	162.1	17,950	1,751
Modern languages	1,474	8	195.5	9,920	1,240
Manual arts	86	1	86.0	1,200	1,200
Latin	146	1	146.0	1,400	1,400
Geology	319	2	159.5	4,200	2,100
Mining engineering	103	2	51.5	4,100	2,050
Pharmacy	360	1	360.0	1,800	1,800
Photography	36	⅒	360.0	90	900
Zoology	389	1⅔	234.3	2,800	1,681
Veterinary science	1,064	4⅔	228.3	9,220	1,979
Forestry	71	1	71.0	2,200	2,200
Music	589	8	736.0	6,500	812
Total	17,315	....	234.5	....	1,623

The relation of the distribution of student clock hours to the salary paid in a given institution is close, and it is a matter of considerable importance to the teaching staff. For example, if the curriculum of an institution demands that each student shall be under instruction on the average for 20 hours a week, then for every 500 students 10,000 student clock hours of instruction must be provided. If instructors carry an average of 300 student clock hours each, 33 or 34 instructors will be required to serve this student body of 500. Suppose the institution has $67,000 to spend on teachers' salaries and employs 40 instead of 33 instructors, the average load of student clock hours will, of course, be reduced, but so will the average salary.

The Bureau of Education is also on record concerning the salaries which collegiate institutions, especially the stronger State institutions, should try to pay. It has declared that for the time being an average salary of $2,000 for a department should be regarded as the reasonable minimum.[1] The practice of the stronger institutions throughout the country indicates that this average will be necessary to command men of the desired quality. In departments which expect to retain men of distinction a higher average salary must be paid.

With the aid of one more factor in addition to those already exhibited, certain fairly definite information concerning the average cost per student may be obtained. This factor is the average number of students in attendance. This is not the same as the catalogue enrollment. The usual catalogue statement of enrollment includes all students who have attended the institution during any part of the year of 12 months. Often the summer enrollment is large. As a rule the number of students in actual attendance rises from the opening of college in September for about two weeks to a maximum and then declines, because of withdrawals, until the close of the term. The second term usually opens with increased numbers, again reaching a maximum shortly after the opening date and then gradually declining until the close of the year. An average of the two high tides in enrollment may under very liberal interpretation be regarded as the average attendance. The difference between this average attendance and the reported catalogue enrollment may be seen by referring to Table 15. The average attendance computed in the fashion described for the year 1913–14 at the University of Washington was 2,318. The catalogue enrollment was 3,340. For the year 1914–15 the average attendance was 2,684. The catalogue enrollment was 4,050.

To determine, then, the average cost per student the items listed in the first tabulations under the heading of *operating expenditures* (including the *total educational, equipment and supplies*, the *total general operating expenses* and *cost of instruction*), less the expenditures for the summer term, are taken. The average attendance for the same year is then used as a divisor. The two following tables (Tables 15 and 16) show the average cost per student at the State university and the State college for the years 1913–14 and 1914–15.

Tables 17 and 18 in this chapter were secured in answer to the specific and repeated requests of members of the commission that some calculations be submitted showing the cost per department. The actual cost of different departments the committee has found it exceedingly difficult, perhaps impossible, to determine. The nearest approach that could be made seemed to be to secure the cost of a student clock hour in each department. This has been done for both institutions and appears in the last column of Tables 17 and 18.

[1] This does not apply to subcollegiate departments, where a lower average may properly prevail.

It was obtained by adding the total amount paid for salaries in each department and the amount spent for departmental equipment and supplies. The general operating expense or overhead expense was then divided among the separate departments in accordance with the ratio which the salary budget for each department bore to the general salary budget. This amount, as its proportion of the overhead, was then added to the two departmental items already mentioned, and the total divided by the number of student clock hours for the department. A word of caution should be added against the drawing of too wide inferences from this table. As contributory evidence, however, it may have some value.

TABLE 15.—*University of Washington—Cost per student, based on enrollment two weeks after day of registration, for the years 1913–14 and 1914–15.*[1]

Students enrolled:

October 1, 1913, first semester..	2, 263
February 16, 1914, second semester...................................	2, 373
Total..	4, 636
Average attendance for year.....................................	2, 318
Total expenses..	$517, 505
Cost per student of average attendance.................................	$223. 49

Students enrolled:

October 1, 1914, first semester..	2, 724
February 15, 1915, second semester...................................	2, 645
Total..	5, 369
Average attendance for year.....................................	2, 684. 5
Total expense...	$517, 505
Cost per student of average attendance.................................	$192. 77

TABLE 16.—*Washington State College—Cost per student, based on enrollment two weeks after day of registration, for the years 1913–14 and 1914–15.*[2]

Students enrolled:

October 1, 1913, first semester..	947
February 16, 1914, second semester...................................	972
Total..	1, 919
Average attendance for year.....................................	959. 5
Total expense...	$343, 865
Cost per student of average attendance.................................	$358. 37

Students enrolled:

October 1, 1914, first semester..	1, 013
February 15, 1915, second semester...................................	956
Total..	1, 969
Average attendance for year.....................................	984. 5
Total expenses..	$285, 299
Cost per student of average attendance.................................	$289. 79

[1] In both years the only expense items used were (1) "Total operating expenses"—which include educational equipment, instructional salaries, and overhead—and (2) such items of "construction" as correspond to comparable items in the State college. Buildings and all special funds, as well as all extension division items, were excluded.

[2] In both years the only expense items used were (1) "Total operating expenses"—which include educational equipment, instructional salaries, and overhead—and (2) such items of "construction" as correspond to the items in the university's budget of repairs and betterments and campus improvement and upkeep. Buildings and all special funds, as well as all extension and experiment station items, were excluded.

TABLE 17.—*University of Washington—Student clock hour cost based on class reports of the first and second semesters, 1914-15.*

Departments	Salaries	Department equipment — Undergraduate	Department equipment — Graduate	Overhead	Total	Student clock hours per week — First semester	Student clock hours per week — Second semester	Total for year	Student clock hour costs
College of Liberal Arts:									
English	$20,483.04	$794.88		$7,132.07	$28,399.79	3,671	3,247	128,124	$0.2217
French	12,040.32	299.98		4,404.49	17,233.07	1,062	1,246	68,628	.2562
German	12,278.33	474.17		4,275.19	17,169.84	2,287	2,078	78,210	.2195
Greek	14,763.33	100.00		1,665.55	6,725.00	441	361	14,428	.466
History	12,678.06	787.47	$141.85	4,464.26	18,076.81	2,908	2,570	103,914	.1777
Journalism	8,427.89	1,113.48	180.21	2,984.26	12,675.48	580	699	22,302	.5684
Latin	6,453.25	185.74	560.16	2,340.05	9,917.48	345	465	15,499	.6781
Library economy	1,659.97		87.44	670.93	3,210.80	195	195	9,633	.3330
Oriental languages and literature	2,491.59	185.49		867.57	3,544.65	310	300	24,114	.2266
Philosophy	5,653.25	1,178.97		1,943.96	8,706.28	941	957	115,265	.1888
Political and social science	15,920.61	166.40		5,543.55	22,067.28	3,499	3,107	14,896	.8470
Public speaking and debating	3,897.39	166.40		1,345.02	5,270.47	520	521	4,992	.7296
Scandinavian	2,083.25	813.27	76.80	725.41	3,200.91	113	132	28,582	.2105
Spanish	5,970.68	43.16	20.84	2,078.99	8,122.07	1,058	1,091		
College of Science:									
Botany	10,867.17	4,380.97	362.11	3,730.71	19,620.96	2,928	2,172	91,794	.2116
Chemistry	19,944.76	16,830.36		6,944.41	43,719.53	7,390	5,761	235,080	.1850
Short course							48	578	.1855
Geology	6,461.54	930.88		2,340.90	9,632.32	1,302	1,234	46,382	.2075
Short course							138	1,466	.2004
Home economics	13,080.19	6,488.66	449.24	4,736.88	17,355.67	1,263	1,824	46,982	.1778
Mathematics and astronomy	13,173.17	1,242.66	732.07	6,527.84	26,191.70	2,129	2,091	104,940	.2401
Philosophy (psychology)	14,940.99	810.43		2,681.96	8,081.25	946	529	32,310	.3601
Physical training	7,415.48	1,744.40		2,181.80	11,741.40	2,127	2,607	58,412	.1466
Physics	9,008.95	3,188.52		2,154.48	15,996.15	1,598	1,455	54,414	.3820
Zoology	7,138.02	2,342.50		2,631.61	12,466.73	2,588	3,090	106,624	.1175
College of Engineering:									
Civil engineering	18,408.08	1,613.89	20.00	6,411.49	26,452.16	3,117	4,157	130,577	.2588
Short course							252	3,144	.1970
Electrical engineering	15,303.97	1,220.42	42.61	3,981.24	12,458.44	916	920	33,048	.1770
Mechanical engineering	9,185.68	1,578.01		3,085.37	16,844.38	2,350	1,962	77,616	.2043
		2,046.94		3,085.38	12,580.80	376	443	14,742	.9311
College of mines								3,720	.7566
Short course							310	21,800	.4588
College of forestry	9,076.14	1,272.13	70.40	3,108.11	13,574.77	1,061	721		
Short course							464	5,626	.8889
College of pharmacy	7,920.72	525.44	14.74	2,757.99	10,981.89	998	1,089	37,062	.8814
School of education	10,457.64	438.54	88.45	3,644.53	14,640.46	1,375	1,653	64,144	.7704

School of law	14,491.68	831.11		5,045.96	19,537.60	2,505	2,197	85,716
College of fine arts	10,443.98	704.27		3,696.59	14,911.68	2,312	2,033	78,210
Military training	1,066.00			370.63	2,189.90	1,624	1,388	54,216
Total Including short course	306,948.28	54,926.03	2,980.15	106,876.30	471,006.30	58,513	55,500 55,763	2,057,634 2,072,658
Marine station	1,462.60	606.74	187.30	606.34	3,560.48			
Library	8,982.00	2,705.47		3,100.07	14,997.64			
Summer school	14,141.75	1,960.36		4,924.00	21,025.01			
Grand total	331,478.48	59,632.09	3,047.35	115,418.41	509,568.33			

1 Does not show the accurate distribution with reference to instructional duties. The proportional assignment of salaries to instruction has been made in the report referred to in the accompanying note. The difference between the salary amounts credited to the departments in this report and the report entitled "Table showing salaries and student clock hours for the year ending June 30, 1915," is, in the main, the difference between salary authorizations and actual expenditures between July 1, 1914, and June 30, 1915. The faculty are paid in 12 installments, beginning with August; so in all cases where new men were brought into departments in 1914-15 the figures show only 11 months' salary, the twelfth month being shown only for 11 months. A smaller difference is accounted for by increases in salaries, the increase being shown only after June 30.

The cost per student at the university is exceedingly, almost disastrously, low. On the other hand, at the State college the cost per student is higher than in other institutions for which the bureau has been able to get comparable figures.[1] For example, in the year 1914–15 the cost per student at the Iowa State University was $274.50. At the Iowa State College it was $271, and at the Iowa State Teachers College $170. Institutions that are largely technical are generally expensive, and allowance must be made for extra cost of laboratory instruction where such preponderates.[2] Agricultural and mechanical colleges, being for the most part technical institutions and having also expensive tracts of land to operate, probably cost more per student throughout the country than do State universities of similarly good equipment. Nevertheless, it is the opinion of the committee that the State college can reduce its student cost by such readjustments as will raise the departmental and institutional average of student clock hours.

TABLE 18.—*State College of Washington—Expenditures by departments, 1914–15.*

Departments.	Salaries.	Equipment and supplies.	Overhead.	Total.	Student clock hours (year).	Student clock-hour costs.
Agriculture	$14,549.86	$2,432.81	$7,791.05	$24,773.72	78,402	$0.3160
Architecture	4,512.50	310.87	2,001.96	6,825.33	6,354	1.0742
Botany	8,362.29	3,651.97	3,684.32	15,698.58	35,838	.4380
Chemistry	14,244.44	5,675.53	6,255.85	26,175.82	74,484	.3514
Economic science and history	7,829.96	314.62	3,451.70	11,596.28	48,600	.2382
Education	3,790.92	604.97	1,690.15	6,095.04	21,114	.2887
English	11,374.88	220.64	4,970.82	16,566.34	69,048	.2399
Forestry	2,149.95	215.57	969.11	3,334.63	1,674	1.9930
Geology	4,199.88	370.03	1,840.28	6,410.19	9,486	.6758
Home economics	4,670.69	2,337.59	2,071.10	9,079.38	32,976	.2750
Horticulture	6,717.46	454.03	3,180.38	10,351.87	16,272	.6362
Latin	3,519.96	77.97	1,538.25	5,136.18	3,290	1.5611
Mathematics and civil engineering	10,298.92	568.26	4,531.10	15,398.28	39,006	.3947
Mechanical and electrical engineering	13,574.83	1,444.12	5,961.17	20,980.12	58,680	.3575
Mining and metallurgy	4,127.92	1,118.05	1,833.95	7,079.92	4,752	1.4898
Modern languages	9,892.14	126.51	4,322.80	14,341.45	54,810	.2617
Music and fine arts	4,611.00	134.52	1,559.50	6,305.02	16,758	.3762
Pharmacy	1,650.00	427.56	751.05	2,828.61	10,332	.2738
Veterinary science	8,669.80	1,777.90	4,635.98	15,083.68	32,436	.4650
Zoology	3,324.99	1,090.91	1,767.07	6,182.97	12,114	.5104
Total	142,081.39	23,354.43	64,807.59	230,243.41	626,516	.3675
Elementary science	14,641.53	919.94		21,990.02		
Physical education			2,301.79	2,301.79		
Summer school	7,501.51	1,338.76		8,840.27		
Extension			6,843.56	6,843.56		
Experimental station			10,114.85	10,114.85		
Grand total	164,224.43	29,010.01	71,236.14	280,333.90		

By way of conclusion certain generalizations may be made.

The average salary paid at both institutions is far too low. The salaries at the State college are lower than those at the university.

---

[1] As already noted, the Bureau of Education has used the methods outlined in this chapter for the study of costs, student clock hours, and average enrollment only in investigations of the State institutions of Iowa and Washington.

[2] Laboratory instruction constitutes 54.3 per cent of the student clock hours at the university and 68.7 per cent of the student clock hours at the college.

In the long run neither can hope to get or keep men of distinction for such small remuneration. Below are tables showing the salary scales of all State higher institutions and the number receiving each grade of salary at the Washington institutions.

The instructing staff at the university is badly overloaded with student clock hours. The committee does not see how it is possible for it to do work of real university grade under such conditions.

The instructing staff at the State college is, on the whole, carrying a very light load of student clock hours. The average for the institution is lower than that of any other institution that the Bureau of Education has studied. For example, the average for the year 1914–15 at the Iowa State Teachers College was 321. At the Iowa State College of Agriculture and Mechanic Arts it was 312, and at the Iowa State University 252. The average in certain departments at the Washington State College is very low indeed. This is in spite of the fact that for some years 20 credit hours of teaching a week has been considered a normal program for each instructor.[1]

---

[1] Credit hours, as the term is used here, means the number of hours a week that instructors hold class exercises (laboratory exercises usually counting one hour for three). No institution that valued its reputation for high standing, except a State institution—which is often the victim of circumstances and must sometimes compromise its principles in the face of legislative prejudice—would dare to demand such a large number of teaching hours of its instructors. If the members of the staff of the Washington State College had actually obeyed what was understood to be the rule and had taught 20 hours a week each, the effect on the standards of the college would have been serious. Fortunately, the rule has been more honored in the breach than in the observance.

TABLE 19.—*Salaries of the teaching force in State universities and State colleges.*

Names of institutions.	President.	Deans.		Professors.		Associate professors.		Assistant professors.		Adjunct professors.		Instructors.		Assistants.		Tutors and others.		House in addition to salary.	
		Maximum.	Minimum.	Maximum.	Minimum.	Maximum.	Minimum.	Maximum.	Minimum.	Maximum.	Minimum.	Maximum.	Minimum.	Maximum.	Minimum.	Maximum.	Minimum.	President.	Professors.
1	2	3	4	5	6	7	8	9	10	11	12	13	14	15	16	17	18	19	20
1 Alabama Polytechnic Institute	$5,000	$2,600	$2,400	$2,400	$1,800	$1,800	$1,500	$1,800	$1,500	$1,600	$900	$1,400	$700	$800	$350			No.	0
2 University of Alabama	6,000	3,200	2,400	2,500	1,800	1,800												Yes	0
3 University of Arizona	5,000	3,600	2,800	2,500	1,700	2,200	1,200	1,000	1,400									No.	0
4 University of Arkansas	4,000	3,000	2,500	2,300	1,900	2,300	1,800	2,500	1,400	1,200	1,000	1,400	600	1,200	900			No.	0
5 University of California	12,000	8,000	5,000	3,000	1,700	3,000	1,300	2,600	1,400			2,200	800	1,600	100			Yes	1
6 University of Colorado	6,000	3,200		3,000	1,800			1,600	1,500			2,200	1,100	900				Yes	0
7 Colorado State Agricultural College	5,000	3,000	2,000	3,000	2,000	2,500	1,700	1,800	1,300		300	1,400	1,000						0
8 Colorado School of Mines	5,000			3,000	1,600	1,700	1,550	1,800	1,500	1,850		1,700	900					Yes	0
9 State Teachers College of Colorado	5,000	2,500	1,800	2,500	2,000							1,500	800	300	100	$450	$100	Yes	0
10 Connecticut Agricultural College	4,500			3,000	1,600													No.	0
11 Delaware College	3,000	4,000	2,000	3,000	1,800			1,600				1,500	600					No.	0
12 University of Florida	3,600	3,000	1,900	2,900	1,600	1,800	1,800	1,750	1,600			750	400	350	100			No.	0
13 Florida State College for Women	3,450	2,050	2,000	1,800	1,800	1,900		1,200	900	1,500	1,500	1,000						Yes	0
14 University of Georgia	6,000			2,300	2,000			1,450	1,200	1,350	1,350	1,200	1,000	450	25	600	100	Yes	0
15 Georgia School of Technology	6,500	2,700	1,800	3,000	2,000	1,800	1,800	1,500	1,200	1,000		700	800			1,500	800	Yes	0
16 North Georgia Agricultural College	2,500			1,500	1,300	1,200	1,900											No.	0
17 College of Hawaii	6,000	2,800	2,700	2,500	2,400	1,800	1,600	1,800	1,300			1,800	750	600	300	400	300	No.	0
18 University of Idaho	6,000	6,000	4,000	2,800	1,800	2,100	2,100	3,000	1,300	2,000	1,500	1,600	750	900	500	500	150	Yes	1
19 University of Illinois	12,000	5,000	1,600	5,000	2,000	2,300	1,700	1,800	1,300			1,200	700	1,000	500	1,000	50	No.	1
20 Indiana University	6,000	5,000	3,200	3,000	2,250	2,250	1,200	2,000	1,200			1,200	700	900	500			No.	0
21 Purdue University (Ind.)	7,500	4,800	2,100	3,000	1,800	2,500		2,000	1,300	1,500	1,500	1,000	800	1,200	700	500	100	Yes	8
22 Iowa State College of Agriculture and Mechanic Arts																			
23 Iowa State Teachers College	5,000	5,000	1,100	2,400	1,800	2,000	1,250	1,400	1,000			1,400	800	450	450			Yes	0
24 State University of Iowa	7,500	3,500	4,000	4,000	2,200	2,200	1,700	2,500	800			2,300	800	600	50			Yes	0
25 University of Kansas	6,000	3,000	4,000	3,500	2,200	2,100	1,700	1,700	1,200			1,200	800	660				Yes	0
26 Kansas State Agricultural College	4,500	4,000	2,750	3,200	1,650	2,100	1,600	2,250	1,200			1,700	900	2,100	500			No.	0
27 State University of Kentucky	5,500	4,000	2,000	2,250	1,800	1,900	1,500	1,500	1,100			1,000	750	1,000	750		108	Yes	1
28 Louisiana State University and Agricultural and Mechanical College	5,000	4,000	2,200	2,500	1,600	2,500	1,200	2,000	1,200			1,200	800	1,200	300	108	108	Yes	0
29 University of Maine	6,000	2,800	2,700	3,000	1,625	2,000	1,500	1,400	1,200			1,200	600			900	300	Yes	0

No.	Institution																	
30	Maryland Agricultural College	1,400	1,800		1,800			1,620		2,150	1,600						No.	0
31	Massachusetts Agricultural College	5,000	4,000	2,750	3,500			2,500									Yes.	0
32	Massachusetts Institute of Technology																No.	0
33	University of Michigan	10,000	5,000	1,800	4,000	2,000	3,000	2,000		2,000	1,700		1,000	900	540	420	Yes.	6
34	Michigan Agricultural College	5,000	3,500	2,000	3,000	2,200	2,300	2,000	1,350	2,000			1,000	550			No.	31
35	Michigan College of Mines	5,000	7,500	3,000	5,000	2,100	3,000	2,200	1,500	2,500	1,500		900	850	600	90	Yes.	0
36	University of Minnesota	10,000	2,500	2,000	2,500	1,500	1,500	1,500	1,200	2,200	1,200		1,100	600	600			
37	University Agricultural and Mechanical College	3,500	1,500	1,200	1,800	1,000				1,000	800				150		Yes.	3
38	Mississippi Industrial Institute and College	3,500	2,750	2,000	2,000	1,550	1,950	1,800	1,000	1,100	1,000		1,400	1,000	300	100	Yes.	0
39	University of Mississippi	7,500	4,500	2,500	2,600	2,400	2,400		1,500	1,500	1,500		1,500	1,000	300	50	Yes.	2
40	University of Missouri	4,500	4,000	2,400	3,000	2,000	2,000	1,800	1,500	2,000	1,500		1,500	750	400	100	No.	0
41	Montana College of Agriculture and Mechanic Arts				2,000		2,000												
42	Montana State School of Mines	4,000	3,200	1,300	3,000	1,800	1,200	2,200	1,500	2,200		1,600	1,500	1,000	500	60	No.	0
43	University of Montana	6,000	3,000	2,000	2,750	1,500	2,000	900		1,700	900	1,500	1,200	250			No.	0
44	University of Nebraska	6,000	3,000	3,000	2,500	2,200	2,200	1,900	1,500	1,800	1,500	1,600	1,500	100		50	No.	0
45	University of Nevada	6,000	2,500	1,800	2,600	1,200	1,500	1,000	1,500	1,700	1,200	1,500	600				Yes.	0
46	New Hampshire College of Agriculture and Mechanic Arts																	
47	Rutgers College (N.J.)	6,000	4,000	2,000	3,600	1,500	1,800	1,300	1,500	1,800	1,500	1,500	1,500	800	900	450	Yes.	0
48	University of New Mexico	4,000	2,500		1,800	1,500	1,500	1,300		1,500	1,000		1,200	600			No.	0
49	New Mexico School of Mines	3,000			1,800	1,000											No.	0
50	New Mexico College of Agriculture and Mechanic Arts	4,500	2,200	2,200	2,100	1,200	1,600			1,600		900			600		No.	0
51	New York State College for Teachers	6,000	3,500		3,000	2,500				2,400	1,800		1,700	1,200	150		No.	0
52	Cornell University (N.Y.)	10,000	8,000	3,500	6,000	2,000	2,000	1,600	2,000	2,000	1,250		1,300	800	500		Yes.	2
53	University of North Carolina	4,000	2,750	2,500	2,500				1,250	1,250			1,200	600	250	50	No.	0
54	North Carolina College of Agriculture and Mechanic Arts	4,500	2,700		2,700		1,600	1,500	1,400	1,000	1,400		1,300	700	100		No.	0
55	North Dakota Agricultural College	6,000	3,700	3,000	3,000	1,800	1,900	1,700	2,100		1,400		1,600	1,000	150	500	Yes.	0
56	University of North Dakota	6,000	3,200	2,800	3,000	2,150	2,150	1,600	2,000	1,400			1,500	900	500	250	Yes.	0
57	Ohio University	5,000	3,000	1,700	2,100	1,400	1,600	900	2,300	900	1,200		1,000	1,000	700	100	Yes.	0
58	Ohio State University	7,000	5,000	3,000	3,500	1,900	1,800	1,250	1,700	1,900			1,100	900	500	700	Yes.	0
59	Miami University (Ohio)	5,000	3,000	2,000	2,500	2,000	2,000	1,450	1,700	1,700			900	700	700	250	Yes.	0
60	University of Oklahoma	7,500	2,800	2,000	2,000	1,800	1,800	1,400	1,700	1,800			1,300	600	700		No.	0
61	Oklahoma Agricultural and Mechanical College	3,000	3,000	2,000	2,000	1,800	1,500	1,200	1,750	1,500			900	675	600	360		
62	Oklahoma State School of Mines and Metallurgy	2,700			1,800	1,800		1,400		1,400	900		1,300				Yes.	0
63	Oregon State Agricultural College	7,000	3,100	2,400	3,000	1,700	2,100	1,300	2,000	1,400			1,000	900	500		No.	0
64	University of Oregon	5,000	2,750	1,400	2,500	1,600	1,600	2,380	2,300	1,300	600		1,550	800	600		Yes.	11
65	Pennsylvania State College	5,000	6,000	3,000	2,400	1,600	1,600		1,400	1,400			1,850	405			Yes.	2
66	University of Porto Rico	4,500	3,000		2,400	1,600	1,000	1,500	1,550	1,500			1,500	800				
67	Rhode Island State College	4,500			2,400	1,700		1,000	1,300	1,300							Yes.	3
68	The Citadel, the Military College of South Carolina	3,000			2,000	1,700					1,200							
69	Clemson Agricultural College (S.C.)	4,500	3,000	2,500	2,000	1,900	1,700	1,700	1,700	1,500	1,200	1,200	1,200	800	900	1,200	Yes.	12
70	University of South Carolina	5,000	2,500	2,000	2,000	2,000	1,500	1,500	1,300				800	800	300	500	Yes.	

TABLE 19.—*Salaries of the teaching force in State universities and State colleges—Continued.*

	President	Deans Maximum	Deans Minimum	Professors Maximum	Professors Minimum	Associate professors Maximum	Associate professors Minimum	Assistant professors Maximum	Assistant professors Minimum	Adjunct professors Maximum	Adjunct professors Minimum	Instructors Maximum	Instructors Minimum	Assistants Maximum	Assistants Minimum	Tutors and others Maximum	Tutors and others Minimum	House in addition to salary President	House in addition to salary Professors
Names of Institutions.																			
1	2	3	4	5	6	7	8	9	10	11	12	13	14	15	16	17	18	19	20
71	South Dakota State College of Agriculture and Mechanic Arts.	$3,000	$3,000		$3,000	$1,200	$2,100	$1,500	$1,000	$800			$1,500	$700	$1,500	$600			Yes	0
72	South Dakota State School of Mines.	2,800	2,750	$2,200	1,900	1,560			1,400	1,250				800	800	800	200	No.	0
73	University of South Dakota.	3,300	2,800	1,800	2,000	1,600	1,500	1,600	1,500	1,200			1,000	400	800	180	300	125	Yes.	1
74	University of Tennessee.	5,000	4,000	1,900	2,200	1,800	2,500	2,000					1,800	900	450	180	400		No.	0
75	University of Texas.	6,000	3,120	3,000	3,000	2,500	2,000	1,300	1,700	1,000	$1,700		1,650	1,000			1,000	400	Yes.	1
76	Agricultural and Mechanical College of Texas.																			
77	College of Industrial Arts (Tex.).	4,800	2,400	3,000	2,000	1,800	2,100	1,800	1,800	1,000			1,400	800	120	120			Yes.	0
78	Agricultural College of Utah.	5,500	3,600	3,000	2,700	1,800	2,100	1,750	1,700	1,200			1,200	500	600	300	100	100	Yes.	2
79	University of Utah.	5,000	3,000	2,600	2,500	1,900	2,500		1,800	1,300			1,500	250			650		No.	0
80	University of Vermont and State Agricultural College.	7,000	3,000	1,700	3,000	1,200	3,000	2,500	2,000	500									Yes.	0
81	Virginia Polytechnic Institute.	5,000	2,600	2,200	2,100	1,800			1,000	500	1,500		1,700	900	500	250	250	125	Yes.	19
82	University of Virginia.	8,000	4,800		3,300	2,600				785	2,800	1,200	2,500	500	1,000	250	250		Yes.	0
83	Virginia Military Institute.	4,500			2,500	2,300		2,500	1,000		1,300	1,200	800		135				Yes.	10
84	College of William and Mary (Va.).	2,750	2,000	1,800	1,800			1,750	1,000				1,700						Yes.	0
85	State College of Washington.	6,000	3,000	2,300	3,000	1,800		1,500	1,650	1,200			1,800	800	500	500	100	100	Yes.	0
86	University of Washington.	6,000	3,000	2,400	3,000	1,800	2,000	1,600	1,800	1,300			1,500	800	600	400	500	50	Yes.	0
87	West Virginia University.	4,500	3,500	2,400	3,000	2,200	2,000	1,600	1,800	1,550			1,500	900	400	400			Yes.	4
88	University of Wisconsin.	7,000	5,000	2,650	4,500	2,880	3,000	2,250	2,900	1,750			2,000	1,000	900	600			Yes.	0
89	University of Wyoming.	4,700	3,000		2,300	2,100	3,000	2,250	2,000	1,500			1,700	720	600	660	400	100	Yes.	0

Diagram of University of Washington faculty salaries for year ending June 30, 1915.

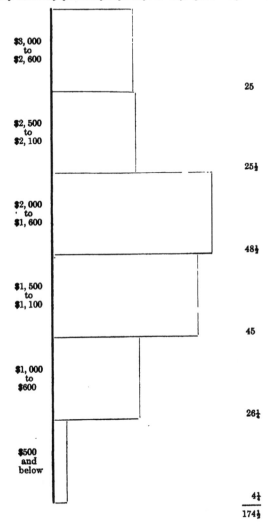

$3,000
to
$2,600

25

$2,500
to
$2,100

25½

$2,000
to
$1,600

48½

$1,500
to
$1,100

45

$1,000
to
$600

26¼

$500
and
below

4¼
———
174½

Washington State College faculty salaries as shown on pay roll for June, 1915.

Professors, heads of departments:

7, at	$3,000
2, at	2,600
2, at	2,400
6, at	2,200
1, at	1,900
3, at	1,800

Professors:

1, at	2,500
1, at	2,100
5, at	2,000
3, at	1,900
4, at	1,800
2, at	1,620
2, at	1,600

Associate professors:

1, at	1,900
1, at	1,700
1, at	1,600

Assistant professors:

2, at	1,800
2, at	1,700
2, at	1,650
3, at	1,600
6, at	1,500
5, at	1,400
5, at	1,320

Instructors:

1, at	1,500
2, at	1,400
2, at	1,320
15, at	1,200
4, at	1,100
2, at	1,000
1, at	900
2, at	750
1, at	600

Chapter VI.

PRESENT SCOPE AND FUNCTIONS OF THE STATE COLLEGE AND STATE UNIVERSITY.

I.—LEGISLATIVE PROVISIONS.

(1) *The university.*—The act of January 24, 1862,[1] which created and incorporated the University of the Territory of Washington, declared that the university should provide the inhabitants of the Territory with the means of acquiring a thorough knowledge of the

---

[1] Laws of Washington Territory, 1861–62 (Jan. 24, 1862, secs. 2, 9).

various branches of literature, science, and arts. To accomplish
this end, the act provided that "at least" four departments should
be established: A department of literature, science, and arts; a
department of law; a department of medicine; a military department. These departments were to be organized and such others
added as the regents should deem necessary and the state of the
university fund should allow.

Concerning the original intent of the Territorial legislature in this
act, in the light of contemporary educational policy, there can be
little doubt that in 1862 a university was designed to cover the entire
field of college or university instruction, and that the expressions
"literature, science, and arts" were to be interpreted in the most
general sense, it being remembered that the changes in the policy of
State higher education fostered by Federal legislation began with the
Morrill Act approved by the National Congress nearly six months
later.

These provisions of 1862 were reenacted by the legislature in a law
approved January 23, 1863,[1] and remained in force throughout the
Territorial period. During that period the university maintained
courses covering the liberal arts and sciences and at times normal
courses and commercial courses, but the work of the institution was,
for the most part, of subcollegiate grade. Within that period no
department of law or medicine was put into operation.

Neither the enabling act nor the State constitution dealt specifically with the functions of the university, but the first State legislature enacted[2] that the object of the university should be to provide
"a liberal education and thorough knowledge of the different branches
of literature, the arts and sciences with their varied applications,"
and that, "so far as practicable," the course of study should begin
"in the collegiate and scientific departments at the points where the
same are completed in the high schools."

By the act of 1893[3] it was provided that:

The aim and purpose of the University of Washington shall be to provide * * *
a liberal instruction in the different branches of literature, science, art, law, medicine,
mechanics, industrial training, military science, and such other departments of
instruction as may be established therein from time to time by the board of regents.

In the code of public instruction enacted in 1897[4] the law of 1893
(above) was reenacted, but with the striking out of the terms "mechanics and industrial training." Meanwhile the following courses
had been announced in the catalogue of the university: Mining engineering, 1894; civil engineering, 1895; electrical engineering, 1895;
pharmacy, 1895; forestry, 1895. Little had been done in any of
these subjects, however.

---

[1] Law of Washington Territory, 1862–63, p. 177.
[2] Session Laws, 1890, p. 395, sec. 2.
[3] Session Laws, 1893, ch. 122, sec. 6 (p. 296).
[4] Session Laws, 1897, Title IV, ch. 1, sec. 183, p. 427.

In the revision of the code of instruction in 1909 [1] the functions of the university were left unchanged, and the provisions of the law of 1897 are therefore still in force.

(2) *Federal legislation affecting higher education.*—In 1862 the Federal Government extended its policy of granting land and money in aid of higher education in the several States and Territories. The first important provision was contained in the first Morrill Act, approved July 2, 1862,[2] which provided that certain lands be appropriated to the several States, the income from which—

shall be inviolably appropriated by each State which may take and claim the benefit of this act to the endowment, support, and maintenance of at least one college where the leading object shall be, without excluding other scientific and classical studies, and including military tactics, to teach such branches of learning as are related to agriculture and the mechanic arts, in such manner as the legislatures of the States may respectively prescribe, in order to promote the liberal and practical education of the industrial classes in the several pursuits and professions in life.

In an act approved July 23, 1866,[3] the first Morrill Act was amended so as to provide:

That when any Territory shall become a State and be admitted to the Union such new State shall be entitled to the benefits of the said act of July 2, 1862, by expressing the acceptance therein required within three years from the date of its admission into the Union, and providing the college or colleges within five years after such acceptance, as prescribed in this act.

The second Morrill Act, approved August 30, 1890 [4]—

to apply a portion of the proceeds of the public lands to the more complete endowment and support of the colleges for the benefit of agriculture and the mechanic arts established under the provisions of an act of Congress approved July 2, 1862—

outlined further the courses of study to be offered in colleges receiving the benefit of Federal funds, the money available through this law—

to be applied only to instruction in agriculture, the mechanic arts, the English language, and the various branches of mathematical, physical, natural, and economic science, with special reference to their applications in the industries of life and to the facilities for such instruction.

By act of Congress (the Nelson Amendment) approved March 4, 1907,[5] "for the further endowment of agricultural colleges" appropriations of funds from the National Treasury were provided for purposes implied in the Morrill Act and in the title of that law, with the further provision:

That said colleges may use a portion of this money for providing courses for the special preparation of instructors for teaching the elements of agriculture and the mechanic arts.

---

[1] Session Laws, 1909, Title II, ch. 1, sec. 2, p. 238.
[2] 12 Stat. L., 503, sec. 4.
[3] 14 Stat. L. 208.
[4] 26 Stat. L., 417.
[5] 34 Stat. L., 1256, 1281.

In the Hatch Act, approved March 2, 1887,[1] provision was made—

to establish agricultural experiment stations in connection with the colleges established in the several States under the provisions of an act approved July 2, 1862, and of the acts supplementary thereto.

Finally the Smith-Lever Act, approved May 8, 1914, was—

to provide for cooperative extension work between the agricultural colleges in the several States receiving the benefits of an act of Congress approved July 2, 1862, and of acts supplementary thereto, and the United States Department of Agriculture.

This act provides:

That, in order to aid in diffusing among the people of the United States useful and practical information on subjects relating to agriculture and home economics, and to encourage the application of the same, there may be inaugurated in connection with the college or colleges in each State now receiving, or which may hereafter receive, the benefits of * * * (the Morrill Acts, etc.) * * * agricultural extension work which shall be carried on in cooperation with the United States Department of Agriculture.

SEC. 2. That cooperative agricultural extension work shall consist of the giving of instruction and practical demonstrations in agriculture and hon e economics to persons not attending or resident in said colleges in the several communities, and imparting to such persons information in said subjects through field demonstrations, publications, and otherwise; and this work shall be carried on in such manner as may be mutually agreed upon by the Secretary of Agriculture and the State agricultural college or colleges receiving the benefits of this act.

Under the provisions of the Smith-Lever law the State of Washington would be eligible to receive as maximum amounts of Federal funds:

1914–15	$10,000	1919–20	$38,266
1915–16	16,523	1920–21	43,702
1916–17	21,958	1921–22	49,138
1917–18	27,394	1922–23	54,571
1918–19	32,830	Thereafter	54,571

However, to secure amounts above $10,000, the State or other parties must make available amounts equal to the amounts appropriated by the Federal Government.

The State of Washington by an act of the legislature approved March 28, 1890, accepted the terms of the Morrill Act of 1862 and of the Hatch Act of 1887. Section 2 (concerning the Morrill Act) reads as follows:

That all moneys derived by virtue of said act of Congress from the sale of lands and of land scrip shall be immediately deposited with the treasurer of the State of Washington, who shall invest and hold the same in accordance with the provisions of the fourth section of the aforementioned act of Congress, approved July 2, anno Domini, 1862, and the moneys so invested shall constitute a permanent and irreducible fund to be entitled "The fund for the promotion of instruction in agriculture and the mechanic arts," and the income derived from said funds shall be expended under the direction of the commission of technical instruction. (An act appointing this commission was appro ed on the same date.)

---

[1] 24 Stat. L., 440. Cf. also 25 Stat. L., 176, 841, and 34 Stat. L., 63.

Section 4 of the same act concerning the Hatch Act provided that—

The treasurer of the State of Washington is hereby authorized to receive all moneys to which the State of Washington may become entitled under the provisions of said act of Congress approved March 2, anno Domini 1887, and moneys so received by the said treasurer shall be applied under the direction of the commission of technical instruction to the uses and purposes of the agricultural experiment station established in connection with the Department of Agriculture of the Washington Agricultural College and School of Science.

Provision was made subsequently to receive the benefit of the other Federal acts above mentioned.

It follows, therefore, that as long as the State of Washington receives the benefits of the Federal appropriations of land and money the State is under obligation in return therefor to provide and support a college or colleges in which—

(1) "The leading object shall be, without excluding other scientific and classical studies, and including military tactics, to teach such branches of learning as are related to agriculture and the mechanic arts" in such manner as the legislature of the State may prescribe, "in order to promote the liberal and practical education of the industrial classes in the several pursuits and professions of life." (First Morrill Act, sec. 4.)

(2) There shall be provided "instruction in agriculture, the mechanic arts, the English language, and the various branches of mathematical, physical, natural. and economic science, with special reference to their application in the industries of life." (Second Morrill Act, sec. 1.)

(3) There may be provided "courses for the special preparation of instructors for teaching the elements of agriculture and the mechanic arts." (Nelson amendment.)

(4) There shall be provided, "under the direction of the college or colleges or agricultural department of colleges, a department to be known and designated as 'an agricultural experiment station.'" (Hatch Act; Adams Act.)

(5) There shall be provided, in connection with the agricultural college, "cooperative agricultural extension work * * * in agriculture and home economics." (Smith-Lever Act, secs. 1 and 2.)

It is to be noted always that the agreement to provide such instruction and to perform such duties as those outlined above is an agreement between the State of Washington and the United States (not between the United States and any institution of the State), and that the legislature of the State is expressly authorized by the terms of the Morrill Act to provide such instruction "in such manner as the legislatures of the States may respectively prescribe." (Morrill Act, sec. 4.)[1]

(3) *The State college.*—December 23, 1864,[2] an act was passed by the legislature of the Territory—

for the location of an agricultural college of Washington Territory, under the provisions of an act of Congress donating lands to the several States and Territories which may provide colleges for the benefit of agriculture and the mechanic arts.

---

[1] For court decisions on this point, see appendix to Ch. VI.
[2] Laws of Washington Territory, 1864-65, p. 30.

Another similar law was passed January 2, 1865.[1] Nothing came of either, nor was any action taken further during the Territorial period.

On March 28, 1890,[2] an act was passed "to create a commission of technical instruction and to establish a State agricultural college and school of science." Section 6 of that act stated—

That the object of said college shall be to train teachers of physical science and thereby to further the application of the principles of physical science to industrial pursuits.

Section 8 read as follows:

That the said commission shall make provisions that all instructions given in the college shall, to the utmost practicable extent, be conveyed by means of practical work in the laboratory. Said commission shall provide, in connection with said college, the following laboratories: One physical laboratory or more, one chemical laboratory or more, and one biological laboratory or more, and suitably furnish and equip the same. Said commission shall provide that all male students shall be trained in military tactics. Said commission shall establish a department of said college to be designated the department of elementary science, and in connection therewith provide instruction in the following subjects: Elementary mathematics, including elementary trigonometry; elementary mechanics; elementary and mechanical drawing; land surveying. Said commission shall establish a department of said college to be designated as the department of agriculture, and in connection therewith provide instruction in the following subjects: First, physics, with special application of its principles to agriculture; second, chemistry, with special application of its principles to agriculture; third, morphology and physiology of plants, with special reference to the commonly grown crops and their fungous enemies; fourth, morphology and physiology of the lower forms of animal life, with special reference to insect pests; fifth, morphology of the higher forms of animal life, and in particular of the horse, cow, sheep, and swine; sixth, agriculture, with special reference to the breeding and feeding of live stock and the best mode of cultivation of farm produce; seventh, mining and metallurgy. * * * Such commission may establish other departments of said college, and provide courses of instruction therein, when those are, in its judgment, required for the better carrying out of the objects of the college.

Failure to agree on the location of the college led to another law, approved March 9, 1891—

to provide for the location and maintenance of the agricultural college, experiment Station, and School of Science of the State of Washington.

This act provided in section 2 that—

The agricultural college, experiment station, and school of science created and established by this act shall be an institution of learning * * * devoted to practical instruction in agriculture, mechanic arts, natural sciences connected therewith, as well as a thorough instruction in all branches of learning upon agriculture and other industrial pursuits.

Section 3 provides that—

The course of instruction of the agricultural college, experiment station and school of science shall embrace the English language, literature, mathematics, philosophy,

---

[1] Laws of Washington Territory, 1864–65, p. 32.
[2] Session Laws, 1890, pp. 260 ff.

civil and mechanical engineering, chemistry, animal and vegetable anatomy and physiology, the veterinary art, entomology, geology, and political, rural, and household economy, horticulture, moral philosophy, history, mechanics, and such other sciences and courses of instruction as shall be prescribed by the regents of this institution of learning.

Section 10 provided that—

The said college and experiment station shall be entitled to receive all the benefits and donations made and given to similar institutions of learning in other States and Territories of the United States by the legislation of the Congress of the United States now in force or that may be enacted.

Section 13 continued the force of section 8 of the law of 1889:

SEC. 13. This act shall not be construed as impairing section eight (8) of the act to establish a commission of technical instruction of the session laws of 1889.

Such are the laws of the State determining the functions and scope of the State College of Washington at the present time.

As the only college at present designated by the State legislature to receive the benefits of the Federal funds, the State college must perform the functions previously outlined.

By specific acts of the State legislature, it must provide instruction in agriculture, the mechanic arts, the natural sciences related thereto, all branches bearing on agriculture and other industrial pursuits, the English language, literature, mathematics, philosophy, civil and mechanical engineering, chemistry, animal and vegetable anatomy and physiology, the veterinary art, entomology, geology, political economy, rural economy, household economy, horticulture, moral philosophy, history, mechanics, mining and metallurgy, elementary science (including elementary mathematics, elementary mechanics, elementary and mechanical drawing, land surveying), and such other courses as the board of regents may have instituted or may institute.

II.—PRESENT SCOPE OF THE WORK OF THE COLLEGE AND OF THE UNIVERSITY.

(1) *The college.*—With the exception of philosophy, the State college at the present time is offering instruction in all the branches of learning specifically mentioned by law as within its scope. In addition, it offers courses in forestry, pharmacy, music, architecture, electrical engineering (which may in some senses be classed as mechanical engineering), foreign languages (French, German, Latin, Spanish, Scandinavian), oral expression, and dramatic art. In the following list are indicated the various groups of subjects offered according to the catalogue of 1915, together with the number of courses offered in each group:

Mathematics (20), civil engineering (27), chemistry (37), botany (35), zoology, including entomology (24), agriculture (54), horticulture (30), forestry (17), English (37), economic science, including some commerce (22), history (12), political science (9), mechanical engineering (36), electrical engineering (21), physics (18), architecture (23),

German (20), French (13), Spanish (5), Scandinavian (8), mining engineering (21), geology (19), home economics (24), pharmacy (12), veterinary science (36), Latin (19), rural law and readings in Blackstone (2 listed in department of Latin), education (including psychology) (12, plus courses in special methods in departments of agriculture, botany, chemistry, home economics, English, history, Latin, mathematics, modern languages, physics, physical education listed in those departments), manual arts (15), music (48), fine arts (21), oral expression and dramatic art (22), elementary science (6 courses, each three years in length, in agriculture, horticulture, mechanic arts, commercial, home economics, general), military science (4), physical education (11), mechanic arts (36)—a total (excluding elementary science, military science, and physical education) of 755 separate courses offered in 1914–15, when (excluding summer-school students and those enrolled in elementary science) 1,021 students were in attendance.

During the first semester of 1914–15 the number of courses of collegiate grade actually given was 274, of which 89 enrolled less than 5 students each. During the second semester the number of courses actually given was 293, of which 98 enrolled less than 5 students each. Of all semester-collegiate courses actually given in 1914–15, nearly one-third enrolled from 1 to 4 students each.[1]

(2) *The university.*—With the exception of medicine, which is represented by certain premedical courses only, the State university at the present time is offering instruction in the branches of learning specifically mentioned in the law. In addition it offers courses in four forms of engineering, in forestry, pharmacy, education, home economics, architecture, music, journalism, commerce, fine arts.

In the following list are indicated the various groups of subjects offered according to the catalogue of 1915, together with the number of courses (in parentheses) offered in each group:

Botany (37), chemistry (37), English (47), French (17), Italian (2), German (29), Greek (14), Latin (20), Spanish (14), Scandinavian (10), geology (30), history (40), home economics (26), journalism (16), mathematics and astronomy (45), oriental history, etc. (8), philosophy and psychology (27), physical education (16), physics (26), political and social science, including commerce (40), public speaking and debate (10), zoology (19), education (32, plus courses in special methods listed in other departments), chemical engineering (16), civil engineering (39), electrical engineering (22), mechanical engineering (34), music (25+), architecture (14), design and drawing (4), forestry (48), law (48), mining engineering and metallurgy (34), pharmacy (17)—a total of 863 separate courses offered in 1914–15 when (excluding summer school students) 3,307 students were in attendance.

During the first semester of 1914–15 the number of courses actually given was 398, of which 95 enrolled less than 5 students each. During the second semester 421 courses were actually given, of which 102 enrolled less than 5 students each. Of all semester courses actually given in 1914–15 nearly one-quarter enrolled from 1 to 4 students each.

---

[1] Cf. Table 21, p. 89.

III.—ENROLLMENTS AT THE STATE COLLEGE AND AT THE STATE UNIVERSITY IN 1914-15.

(1) *Distribution according to major departments.*—With some unimportant allowances for differences in administrative organization and nomenclature, the distribution of students at the State college and at the university according to major departments of study may be seen from the following table:

TABLE 20.—*Enrollments at the State college and university, 1914-15.*[1]

Major courses.	College.				University.				Both.			
	Full standing for 4-year courses.	Short courses.	Special students.	Total.	Full standing.	Short courses.	Special students.	Total.	Full standing.	Short courses.	Special students.	Total.
Liberal arts[2]	205			205	890		96	986	1,095		96	1,191
Science[3]	46			46	268		14	282	314		14	328
Engineering:												
Civil	29			29	146		5	151	175		5	180
Electrical[4]	58			58	180		48	228	238		48	286
Mechanical	36			36	90		1	91	126		1	127
Mining	26			26	70	[5]38	5	113	96	38	5	139
Chemical					64		1	65	64		1	65
Forestry	5	(6)		5	77	[5]20	10	107	82	20	10	112
Pharmacy	17	21		38	70		17	87	87	21	17	125
Education	30			30	76		18	94	106		18	124
Veterinary science	14	[5]26		40					14	26		40
Home economics[7]	96			96	248		9	258	345		9	354
Architecture	13			13	12			12	25			25
Agriculture[8]	258	[9]97		355					258	97		355
Music[10]	23	[9]12		35	98		16	114	121	12	16	149
Journalism[11]					136		4	140	136		4	140
Commerce					102	[12]40	16	158	102	40	16	158
Premedical					66			66	66			66
Preparatory to law					100			100	100			100
Library economics					65			65	65			65
Law					107		83	190	107		83	190
Elementary science			[13]256	256							256	256
Mechanic arts[14]			9	9							9	9
Totals[15]	856	156	[13]265	1,277	2,866	98	343	3,307	3,722	254	608	4,584
Summer school				335				743				1,118
Grand total				1,612				4,050				5,702

[1] Figures taken from data for the State college submitted on sheet headed "Students majoring in the various departments," and data for the university on sheets headed "Enrollment, 1914-15", together with data on pages 510 and 511 of the bulletin of the university of Washington, April, 1915, catalogue. Figures indicate only the numbers of students specializing in certain courses. Figures for those studying in various fields are much greater.

[2] Includes at the State college economic science and history, English (general course), Latin, modern languages, and such other general courses as are not separately listed in the State college enrollment. At the university includes students registered in the college of liberal arts, except home economics, journalism, library economy, commerce, and law preparatory departments.

[3] Includes at the State college botany, chemistry, economic biology, geology, mathematics and physics, zoology. Includes at the State university all enrollment of the school and college of science, except home economics and premedical ocurse.

[4] Includes hydroelectrical engineering.

[5] Three months' course.

[6] Three-year courses, admission to which is based on less than 15 units of secondary school work.

[7] Includes at the State university students in the college of liberal arts majoring in home economics, and in the college of science majoring in home economics.

[8] Includes at the State college horticulture.

[9] Six weeks' course.

[10] Includes at the State college a few others majoring in fine arts in general or other departments.

[11] Some courses offered in the department of English at the State college.

[12] Two-year course.

[13] Work in general of secondary school grade.

[14] Subcollegiate courses in manual arts.

[15] Excludes double registration.

(2) *Students enrolled in various departments.*—The following table indicates the gross enrollment in various departments of the State college and of the State university for 1914–15, each student being counted as many times as his name was found in the class lists in each department.

TABLE 21.—*Gross enrollment in 1914-15.*[1]

Courses.	College.				University.			
	Number of courses given.		Gross enrollment.		Number of courses given.		Gross enrollment.	
	First semester.	Second semester.	First semester.	Second semester.	First semester.	Second semester.	First semester.	Second semester.
Liberal arts [2]........................	69	78	1,430	1,308	136	131	3,977	3,960
Science [3].............................	45	49	813	822	71	78	2,957	2,424
Engineering:								
Civil............................	14	9	132	85	21	27	489	644
Electrical.......................	6	9	39	55	14	15	228	181
Mechanical......................	15	12	216	150	20	23	521	475
Mining..........................	8	7	28	94	12	13	89	115
Forestry.............................	4	8	11	21	14	14	239	167
Pharmacy............................	4	6	37	73	10	12	159	160
Education...........................	7	5	140	116	21	22	492	708
Veterinary..........................	9	13	159	218				
Home economics.....................	11	10	159	141	16	14	512	400
Architecture........................	8	8	35	64	3	4	85	79
Agriculture.........................	24	28	467	483				
Horticulture........................	9	12	117	83				
Music..............................	15	16	125	168	20	21	652	660
Journalism..........................					10	12	200	224
Law...............................					27	30	1,152	1,185
Fine arts (other) [4].................	7	10	48	71	3	5	125	134
Mechanic arts [5]....................	18	18	71	95				
Elementary science [5]..............	69	76	1,252	1,154				
Total........................	343	369	5,079	4,981				
Total collegiate grade..........	274	293	3,827	3,777	398	421	11,877	11,516

[1] These figures are taken from enrollment figures supplied for this purpose by the registrars of the two institutions. In the case of the State college the figures for elementary science were separated from the figures for the other departments.
[2] Including English, foreign languages, history, economic, social, and political science, philosophy, etc.
[3] Including botany, chemistry, geology, mathematics, zoology, etc.
[4] Including painting, drawing, expression and dramatic art, public speaking.
[5] Special noncollegiate course at the State college.

(3) *Geographical distribution of students, 1914-15.*—The geographical distribution of the students in attendance at the State college and at the university in 1914-15 (including summer schools of 1914) was as follows (duplicates excluded):

TABLE 22.—*Distribution of university and State college enrollments in 1914-15 according to counties in which students reside.*

Counties.	College.			University.			Both.		
	Regular session.	Summer session.[1]	Total.	Regular session.	Summer session.	Total.	Regular session.	Summer session.	Total.
Adams	14	3	17	8	2	10	22	5	27
Asotin	17	2	19	8	2	10	25	4	29
Benton	20	2	22	7	4	11	27	6	33
Grays Harbor	11	2	13	45	11	56	56	13	69
Chelan	18	7	25	18	13	31	36	20	56
Clallam	11	2	13	8	2	10	19	4	23
Clarke	10	2	12	15	6	21	25	8	33
Columbia				2	2	4	2	2	4
Cowlitz	15	3	18	16	3	19	31	6	37
Douglas	3	6	9	5	1	6	8	7	15
Ferry	8	4	12				8	4	12
Franklin	4		4	1		1	5		5
Garfield	12	3	15	3	1	4	15	4	19
Grant	13	3	16	1	2	3	14	5	19
Island	5	8	13	2	4	6	7	12	19
Jefferson	10	6	16	18	2	20	28	8	36
King	75	[2] 29	[2] 104	2,003	252	2,255	2,078	281	2,359
Kitsap	11	2	13	25	13	38	36	15	51
Kittitas	20	8	28	24	8	32	44	16	60
Klickitat	6	1	7	5	6	11	11	7	18
Lewis	17	2	19	35	14	49	52	16	68
Lincoln	28	6	34	10	5	15	38	11	49
Mason	4	4	8	12		12	16	4	20
Okanogan	14	7	21	11		15	25	11	36
Pacific	2	1	3	11	7	18	13	8	21
Pend Oreille	1	2	3	1		1	2	2	4
Pierce	56	[2] 92	[2] 148	174	37	211	230	129	359
San Juan	2		2	11	1	12	13	1	14
Skagit	14	7	21	47	11	58	61	18	79
Skamania	2	2	4	1		1	3	2	5
Snohomish	47	9	56	83	33	116	130	42	172
Spokane	157	31	188	105	35	140	262	66	328
Stevens	16	9	25	7	2	9	23	11	34
Thurston	24	7	31	14	9	23	38	16	54
Walla Walla	36	17	53	22	10	32	58	27	85
Wahkiakum	5	2	7				5	2	7
Whatcom	33	4	37	57	20	77	90	24	114
Whitman	296	78	374	11	7	18	307	85	392
Yakima	52	14	66	62	18	80	114	32	146
State	1,089	387	1,476	2,888	547	3,435	3,977	934	4,911
Out of State	127	32	159	357	193	550	484	225	709
Not accounted for			8	62	3	65	62	3	73
Grand total	1,216	419	1,643	3,307	743	4,050	4,523	1,162	5,685

[1] Includes short-course winter session (95 students).
[2] Summer school is maintained at Puyallup, Pierce County.

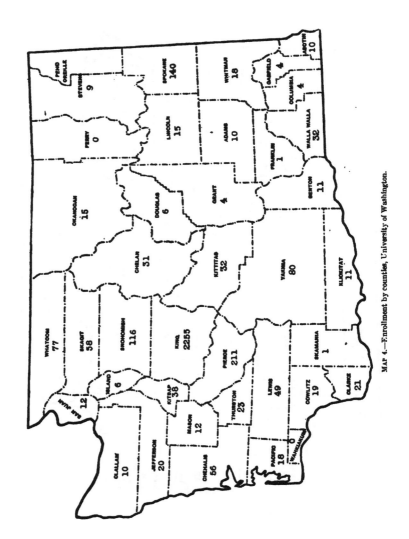

MAP 4.—Enrollment by counties, University of Washington.

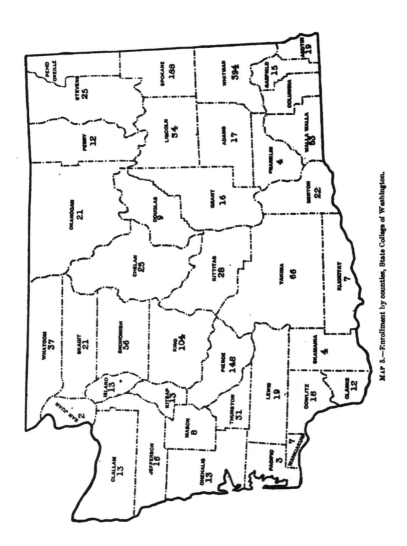

MAP 5.—Enrollment by counties, State College of Washington.

TABLE 23.—*Distribution of university and State college enrollment in 1914-15 according to the three main sections of the State.*

Sections of State.	College.			University.			Both.		
	Regular session.	Summer session.	Total.	Regular session.	Summer session.	Total.	Regular session.	Summer session.	Total.
Western [1]	343	¹ 182	¹ 525	2,552	412	2,964	2,895	594	3,489
Central [3]	157	50	207	160	71	231	317	121	438
Eastern [4]	589	155	744	176	64	240	765	219	984

[1] West of Cascades.
[2] A summer school is maintained at Puyallup, Pierce County.
[3] East of Cascades and west of Ferry, Lincoln, Adams, Franklin, Walla Walla (western boundaries).
[4] Remainder of State.

The fuller meaning of this geographical distribution of students becomes clear when these figures are reduced to per cents. The two tables following present such figures.

TABLE 24.—*Per cents of the total enrollment of the State institutions from each of the three main sections of the State.*

Section of State.	College.			University.			Both.		
	Regular session.	Summer session.	Total.	Regular session.	Summer session.	Total.	Regular session.	Summer session.	Total.
Western	31.5	47.1	35.6	88.4	75.3	86.3	72.8	63.6	71.0
Central	14.5	12.9	14.0	5.6	13.0	6.7	8.0	13.0	9.0
Eastern	54.0	40.0	50.4	6.0	11.7	7.0	19.2	23.4	20.0
Total	100.0	100.0	100.0	100.0	100.0	100.0	100.0	100.0	100.0

TABLE 25.—*Per cents of the total number of collegiate students residing in each of the three main sections of the State enrolled at the university and the State college.*

Institutions.	Western section.			Central section.			Eastern section.		
	Regular session.	Summer session.	Total.	Regular session.	Summer session.	Total.	Regular session.	Summer session.	Total.
College	11.8	30.6	15.0	49.5	41.3	47.3	77.0	71.2	75.5
University	88.2	69.4	85.0	50.5	58.7	52.7	23.0	28.8	24.5

From these figures a number of important facts may be observed, as follows:

(1) Attendance at the State college or university is determined to a considerable extent by geographical factors.

(2) About 85 per cent of the enrollment at the university is from west of the Cascade Mountains.

(3) About one-half of the enrollment at the State college is from the eastern part of the State.

(4) About 70 per cent of the total number of students in the higher institutions of college grade are from west of the Cascade Mountains, about one-tenth from the central portion of the State, and about one-fifth from the eastern part of the State.

(5) Of students attending such institutions from the western part of the State, 85 per cent are at the university and 15 per cent at the State college.

(6) Of students attending such institutions from the eastern part of the State, about three-fourths are at the State college and one-fourth at the university.

(7) Students from the central part of the State are about equally divided between the two institutions.

For purposes of comparison the distribution of the population in the three sections of the State, according to the census of 1910, is added.

TABLE 26.—*Population, by sections, in 1910.*

Sections.	Population.	Per cent.
Western	735, 576	64
Central	124, 303	11
Eastern	285, 397	25
Total	1, 145, 276	100

IV.—TOTAL INSTRUCTION GIVEN IN REGULAR SESSIONS, 1914–15.

The actual work of the two institutions is not indicated by the number of courses offered or given, nor by the numbers of students enrolled in major departments, nor yet by the gross enrollment. Probably the most accurate measure is the aggregate number of student clock hours of instruction. This is determined by multiplying the number of hours (including laboratory, etc.) per week that a course is given for a semester by the number of students enrolled in that course. Thus, a class which meets for any kind of instruction five hours per week (per semester) and in which 20 students are enrolled provides 100 student clock hours.[1]

In the following table are indicated the number of student clock hours actually given in 1914–15 in the State college and in the university,[2] together with the number of "full-time" instructors engaged.[3]

[1] Cf. definition in Ch. V, p. 67.

[2] This table presents a summary of certain portions of Tables 13 and 14.

[3] Certain instructors give but a fraction of their time to the work of instruction or divide their time between two or more departments. In estimating the number of instructors in each department these persons are reckoned as fractional instructors.

TABLE 27.—*Instructors and student clock hours in 1914–15.*

Departments.	College.				University.			
	Number of instructors.		Student clock hours.		Number of instructors.		Student clock hours.	
	First semester.	Second semester.	First semester.	Second semester.	First semester.	Second semester.	First semester.	Second semester.
Agriculture	8¾	8 1/12	2,176	2,183	....		....	....
Architecture	2	2	99	242	(1)	(1)	(1)	(1)
Botany	3½	3½	1,247	774	6⅓	....	2,926	2,172
Chemistry	6	6 1/16	2,021	2,117	18	....	7,299	5,809
Education	2	2	453	720	5	....	1,375	1,633
Mathematics	6½	6½	1,098	1,069	10½	....	3,139	2,691
Civil engineering					10¼	....	3,117	4,399
Mining engineering	2	2	161	103	4	....	376	753
Electrical engineering					3½	....	916	920
Mechanical engineering	9½	8½	1,852	1,440	5	....	2,350	1,962
Physics					5⅔	....	1,568	1,455
English	8	8	1,862	1,974	14	....	3,871	3,247
History	5	6	1,639	1,066	6⅔	....	2,903	2,870
Economic, social, and political science					9	....	3,469	3,107
Modern languages	8	8	1,571	1,474	19½	....	5,394	5,146
Ancient languages	1	1	37	146	5	....	836	826
Home economics	3	3½	994	838	5	....	1,252	1,324
Horticulture	4	4	554	350	....		....	....
Geology	2	2	208	319	4	....	1,252	1,462
Zoology	1⅔	1⅔	284	389	4⅔	....	2,858	3,080
Forestry	1	1	22	71	4⅔	....	1,051	1,215
Pharmacy	1	1	214	360	5⅔	....	998	1,096
Fine arts	8	8	342	589	6⅔	....	2,312	3,033
Law	....	....	....	....	5⅔	....	2,565	2,197
Veterinary	2⅔	4⅔	738	1,064	....		....	....
Philosophy and psychology	(2)	(2)	(2)	(2)	5⅔	....	1,907	1,786
Photography	1/16	1/16	32	36	....		....	....
Manual arts	1	3/16	86	28	....		....	....
Oriental history	....	....	....	....	1	....	310	296
Library economy	....	....	....	....	1	....	168	198
Public speaking	(3)	(3)	(3)	(3)	2	....	290	521
Total[4]	85½	85⅔	17,632	17,315	167	....	55,062	53,757

[1] Cf. fine arts.
[2] Cf. education.
[3] Cf. English.
[4] Excluding physical education and military tactics.

V. GRADUATES OF THE TWO INSTITUTIONS.

(1) *The college.*—The range of the instruction provided at the State college in the past and at present may be noted from the degrees granted to its graduates. Summarized data are available for the years 1897 to 1915 only.[1]

[1] Compiled from catalogue for 1915.

TABLE 28.—*Degrees granted by the State college.*

Courses.	1897–1914		1915		Total.	
	Number.	Per cent.	Number.	Per cent.	Number.	Per cent.
Agriculture....................	67	6.6	27	20.6	94	8.3
Horticulture..................	42	4.2	11	8.4	53	4.6
Engineering:						
Civil....................	91	9.0	4	3.1	95	8.4
Electrical..............	96	9.5	9	6.9	105	9.2
Mechanical.............	19	1.9	1	.8	20	1.8
Mining.................	47	4.7	4	3.1	51	4.5
Home economics...............	69	6.9	12	9.2	81	7.1
Chemistry....................	30	3.0	4	3.1	34	3.0
Zoology......................	14	1.4	....	....	14	1.2
Botany......................	20	2.0	1	.8	21	1.8
Geology.....................	6	.6	....	....	6	.5
English......................	57	5.7	6	4.6	63	5.6
Economic science and history..	88	8.7	10	7.6	98	8.6
B. A. (general)..............	27	2.7	8	6.1	35	3.0
B. S. (general)..............	13	1.2	6	4.6	18	1.6
Education....................	27	2.7	6	4.6	33	2.9
Mathematics and physics......	10	1.0	1	.8	11	1.0
Modern languages............	27	2.7	3	2.3	30	2.6
Latin.......................	9	.9	....	....	9	.8
Forestry....................	1	.1	....	....	1	.1
Architecture.................	1	.1	....	....	1	.1
Pharmacy, B. S. in...........	5	.5	....	....	5	.4
Pharmacy, graduates in.......	164	16.2	7	5.3	171	15.1
Veterinary medicine, B. S. in..	8	.8	2	1.5	10	.9
Veterinary medicine, graduates in........	63	6.2	6	4.6	69	6.2
Music, B. A. in..............	7	.7	....	....	7	.6
Music, graduates in..........	9	.9	3	2.3	12	1.1
Total..................	1,016	....	131	....	1,147	....
Counted twice..........	11	....	....	....	11	....
Net total.............	1,005	100.8	131	100.2	1,136	101.0

Apparently in the early history of the State college a relatively
small proportion of the total number of degrees was granted in the
field of agriculture, a relatively large proportion in engineering,
and a relatively large proportion in the liberal arts. There were
also many degrees of "graduates in pharmacy." It appears from the
degrees granted in 1915, however, that agriculture is coming to its
own in the State college.[1] This becomes more apparent when figures
are grouped as follows:

TABLE 29.—*Per cents of graduates.*

Courses.	1897–1914	1915
	Per cent.	Per cent.
Agriculture and horticulture.....................	10.8	29.0
Engineering......................................	25.1	13.9
Home economics..................................	6.9	9.2
Veterinary.......................................	7.0	6.1
Sciences..	9.2	9.3
Liberal arts.....................................	20.7	20.6
Other departments...............................	21.2	12.2
Total.......................................	100.8	100.2

(2) *The university.*—A similar tabulation of the degrees granted
by the university during the same period appears in Table 30.

---

[1] In the year 1914–15 the total expenditure of the State college for agriculture was $288,289, or 51 per cent of
its total budget. This does not include instruction in botany, zoology, chemistry, and other necessary
scientific foundations for all agricultural study and experimentation.

TABLE 30.—*Degrees granted by the university.*

BACHELOR DEGREES.

Courses.	1876-1914		1915		Total.	
	Number.	Per cent.	Number.	Per cent.	Number.	Per cent.
Bachelor of arts	1,294	54.28	142	40.23	1,436	52.46
Bachelor of arts in education	1	.04			1	.04
Bachelor of science	43	1.80	51	14.45	94	3.43
Bachelor of science in home economics	14	.58			14	.51
Bachelor of science in college of engineering	9	.38	6	1.70	15	.55
Bachelor of science in chemical engineering	13	.55	4	1.13	17	.62
Bachelor of science in civil engineering	80	3.36	10	2.83	90	3.28
Bachelor of science in electrical engineering	76	3.19	16	4.53	92	3.36
Bachelor of science in mechanical engineering	28	1.17	6	1.70	34	1.24
Bachelor of science in college of mines			1	.28	1	.04
Bachelor of science in mining engineering	60	2.52	3	.85	63	2.30
Bachelor of science in geology and mining	7	.29	2	.57	9	.33
Bachelor of science in metallurgical engineering	2	.08			2	.07
Bachelor of science in college of forestry	8	.34	5	1.42	13	.47
Bachelor of science in forestry	21	.88	2	.57	23	.84
Bachelor of science in pharmacy	34	1.43	6	1.70	40	1.46
Graduate in pharmacy, Ph. C	154	6.46	17	4.82	171	6.28
Certificate in pharmacy	13	.55			13	.47
Bachelor of laws	351	14.72	41	11.61	392	14.32
Bachelor of music			5	1.42	5	.18
Business graduates	4	.17			4	.15
Total	2,212	92.79	317	89.81	2,529	92.40

GRADUATE DEGREES.

Master of arts	136	5.71	13	3.68	149	5.44
Master of arts in education	1	.04	3	.85	4	.15
Master of science	11	.46	14	3.97	25	.91
Master of science in education	2	.08			2	.07
Master of science in chemical engineering	1	.04			1	.04
Master of science in civil engineering			1	.28	1	.04
Master of science in electrical engineering	1	.04			1	.04
Civil engineering	4	.17	1	.28	5	.18
Electrical engineering	4	.17	2	.57	6	.22
Mining engineering	2	.08			2	.07
Master of science in forestry	8	.34	1	.28	9	.33
Master of science in pharmacy	1	.04			1	.04
Ph. D	1	.04	1	.28	2	.07
Total graduate degrees	172	7.21	36	10.19	208	7.60
Total bachelor degrees	2,212	92.79	317	89.81	2,529	92.40
	2,384	100.00	353	100.00	2,737	100.00
Counted twice	271		5		276	
Net total	2,113		348		2,461	
Normal diplomas granted	613		108		721	
Life diplomas granted	84		79		163	

The following table indicates the professional distribution of the graduates of the State university, 1876–1915, according to present occupations:

TABLE 31.—*Professional distribution of State university graduates.*

Agriculture	25	Home making	471
Business	119	Law	339
Chemistry	9	Literary and newspaper work	33
Engineering	270	Pharmacy	161
Fine arts	21	Religious and social	21
Forestry	11	Unknown	66
Government science	67		
Education	810	Total	2,461

Particularly noticeable here are the number engaged in "home making," emphasizing the importance of home economics, and the number engaged in teaching, emphasizing the importance of education in the university. ·

APPENDIX TO CHAPTER VI.

The competence of a State legislature to determine the college or colleges to receive the benefits of the Federal acts and to distribute functions as it may see fit has been determined by the State and Federal courts too often to leave any ground for doubt. (156 Mass., 150 (30 N. E., 555); 51 Miss., 361; 39 Southern, 929; 17 R. I., 815 (21 Atl., 916); 14 Wyo., 318 (84 Pac., 90) (206 U. S., 278); 136 U. S., 152.)

Thus in the case of the Wyoming Agricultural College v. Irvine (84 Pac., 90) (decision affirmed by the Supreme Court of the United States) it was held:

(1) That the act of Congress July 2, 1862, and act of Congress August 30, 1890 (first and second Morrill Acts), constituted a grant to the several States, and not to the colleges competent to receive the same in the States to be received through the State as a mere conduit.

(2) It was the duty of the State legislature to select the beneficiary entitled to receive and expend the funds received under the congressional acts.

(3) That the Wyoming Agricultural College * * * was a public corporation whose charter did not constitute a charter which the State was prohibited from impairing.

(4) That under the act of July 2, 1862, a college may be a department or college of the State university whose leading object is instruction in the subjects prescribed by the acts of Congress (Morrill and Hatch Acts), and it makes no difference that a majority of the students are enrolled in other departments.

(5) That the donations are to the State, and not to any institutions of the State.

In the case of the State versus Vicksburg & Nashville Railroad Co. (51 Miss., 361) the court said:

The discretionary power of the legislature over the subject is full. The legislature is free to establish one or more colleges of the character described in the act of Congress and make them the recipients of the interest of their support, or it may bestow it, as it has done, upon the universities. Both of them are subject to change and modification by the legislature. Against the State neither can set up a vested right to property or corporate franchise.

In the case of the State (of Florida) versus Bryan (39 Southern, 929) the court held that the legislature had the power to prescribe what college or colleges should be the recipient or recipients of the interest in the fund derived from the sale of lands donated in the Morrill Act; the power to bestow it for such purposes and upon a university of the State, as it might elect; the power to withdraw the interest from any institution of learning which had been the recipient of it and found another institution at any time it might elect to do so and make it the recipient of said interest for such instruction.

In the case of Massachusetts Agricultural College versus Marden, State Treasurer, et al. (30 N. E., 555), the supreme court of Massachusetts held that:

Under act of Congress August 30, 1890, providing for the payment to the various States of money for the more complete endowment and maintenance of colleges for the benefit of agriculture and the mechanic arts now established, or which may be hereafter established, in accordance with act of Congress July 2, 1862, States are not restricted in the use of the money to one college in each State or to colleges established subsequent to the act of 1862.

Chapter VII.

WARRANTED AND UNWARRANTED DUPLICATION.

THE PRINCIPLE OF MAJOR AND SERVICE LINES.

Nineteen States, of which Washington is one, maintain colleges of agriculture and mechanic arts as separate institutions not connected with the State university. The harmonious and economical adjustment of these two types of institutions to the performance of the State's educational task and the establishment of definite and equitable relations between them constitute possibly the greatest problem in educational administration in the United States. Three elements in the problem have proved most fruitful causes of difficulties. They are, first, the common belief that a college of agriculture and mechanic arts is in its nature a "lower" type of institution than a university and that it can not properly be ranked with a university; second, the confusion of the words "university" and "universal," with the result that many—some university authorities among them—believe that a university is under implied contract with its sponsors to teach everything; and, third, the development of an almost superstitious horror of duplication of courses. This last has been stimulated in many cases by partisan institutional officials for selfish ends. It is worth while to discuss these three matters briefly.

Unquestionably the State university was at first intended to be the ranking institution in the State. It was assumed that all higher training would center in it. But most State universities were established before the differentiation of higher education into separate specialized fields of subject matter. This development has taken place within 50 years. The same period has seen the rise of the land-grant college. Land-grant colleges have indeed borne an important part in the great modern movement which has led to the elevation of applied science among the learned professions; they have contributed largely to this differentiation of professional lines which marks present-day higher education.

In the beginning the land-grant college was undoubtedly not of equal standing with the university. In some States it is still on a lower academic level, but in States where higher education in both the applied subjects and the older scholastic subjects has been best supported and most wisely administered the disparity between these two types of institutions has wholly disappeared. It should be emphasized that it remains with the institutions and with the States to establish the full educational equivalence of the land-grant college and the university. If the land-grant college has as high entrance requirements, as severe educational standards, and as able a corps of instructors, it is a university (no matter what it is called), doing work of equal rank with that offered by the university proper. More especially is this true of the land-grant colleges which have developed graduate courses and encouraged research in the applied sciences. In Washington, it might be remarked in passing, the complete educational parity between the university and the land-grant college has long been established and is generally recognized. Neither institution has yet developed graduate work to any large extent, although the university has now made a beginning in this field. The committee is happy to contribute its testimony as to the high standards set by the State college for entrance and their rigid enforcement, as well as to the serious and valuable character of the research work already done by members of the staff.

It is generally admitted by all who study education that no university, no matter how wealthy, can cover the whole field of human knowledge. No university can longer be universal. Every university must, to a certain degree, specialize; it must give higher training—if possible, the highest—in those subjects and professions which its constituents ought to know or to practice. Some universities can, of course, provide for instruction and research in more different lines than others. But the test of a university's standing and greatness is not the size of the territory over which it spreads. The true tests are the quality of the work which it does and the eminence of the scholars who make up its faculty. A university is an institution where men are taught to think universally, not one that attempts to cover the universe.

Those States which maintain separate land-grant colleges have in effect divided their universities and have created a university system. If they have been wise enough early enough to differentiate the functions of the two institutions, they may have assigned to one the liberal arts and the learned professions, to another the applied sciences and agriculture, or they may have made some other division; but unfortunately few States have possessed this wisdom. In any event it must be recognized that where a State university system exists, instead of a single institution, the field of the university proper is likely to be abbreviated. This is entirely just, and from the point of view of the State may not be a disadvantage. In fact the existence of two or more institutions of collegiate rank undoubtedly increases the total number of students who avail themselves of higher education. Every institution exerts a strong, magnetic pull on its immediate environment.[1]

The word "duplication" has become a bogy. Many believe it designates what is tantamount to a crime in public or institutional management. Duplication, however, is of two kinds. One of these is perfectly harmless, justifiable, desirable, necessary. The other is exceedingly undesirable, first on the ground of expense and second on the ground of the animosities which it engenders.

---

[1] See tables on p. 90 and p. 93, ch. 6.

What is the extent of harmless necessary duplication? First of all, the fundamental subjects, such as English, a limited amount of modern languages, physics, chemistry, biology, history and economics, and many more must be taught in every institution of collegiate grade. The maintenance of a college without them is unthinkable, even if it is a strictly technical institution. These subjects form a sort of universal groundwork. Moreover, the allegation so often made that duplication is expensive and wasteful is probably untenable as applied to such subjects as have just been mentioned. Work in elementary mathematics, in chemistry, or in English composition may be just as economically carried on in two or three places as in one, if the instructors are paid at the same rate, the classes are of the same size, and each plant is full to the point of saturation. Similarly, laboratory space for several hundred elementary students in biology or physics may as well be provided in two places as in one. Duplication of this sort is not unlike that which prevails among all high schools. It constitutes neither an educational nor a fiscal problem for the State. The important thing is to keep clearly in mind the distinction between such duplication as this and the kind of duplication discussed in the next paragraph.

In any but the most populous and wealthy States the proposition that the State should establish out of hand two or more schools of law or medicine or dentistry would not be seriously considered. The demand for men trained in these professions would not warrant it, and the expense, unless justified by the demand, would be an inexcusable extravagance. Probably no State would at present think of establishing two graduate schools to conduct costly research in the same departments for a few students each. In the same way it is doubtful whether any State not already having two or more schools of engineering would seriously contemplate the establishment of more than one. Engineering education constantly becomes more expensive and involves constant additions to institutional equipment in the shape of costly appliances. Training in these and other professional lines is largely a thing by itself. It builds to some extent (in some lines more than in others) on the fundamental subjects mentioned in the preceding paragraph. It does not itself constitute, however, a component part of the training for some other pursuit. In other words, one may have to study chemistry and mathematics before one can study medicine, but one does not have to study medicine in order to study chemistry or law. If the committee were to make a sweeping generalization, it would say that duplication in professional lines (except teacher training, for which few States provide sufficient opportunities) is highly undesirable.

Not only is duplication of professional training expensive, but it has proved in almost every State the source of institutional rivalries, jealousies, and antagonisms which have brought a train of evils in their wake. Higher institutions have been dragged into politics. Issues which should have been settled on their merits have been settled by partisan votes. The true end of State institutions, the service of the State, has been abandoned in favor of petty schemes for personal or institutional aggrandizement. This has been so generally the history of States where professional training is duplicated in two or more institutions as to point unmistakably to the advisability of a clear definition of the field of each higher institution.

In a recent report on the State higher institutions of Iowa (already cited) the Bureau of Education has laid down as a working principle of differentiation what is described as the principle of "major and service lines of work." The following paragraphs discussing this principle are quoted with few modifications from that report:

In accordance with this principle of major and service lines, each State institution should have assigned to it certain major fields which it may be expected to develop to their fullest extent. Agriculture at the State college is such a major line. Latin, German, French, history, political science, psychology at the State university are such major lines. Service lines are such subordinate subjects as are essential to the proper cultivation of a major line. The amount is generally not large. English is such a service line for engineering and agriculture at the State college. Institutions may well overlap as regards the relation of their service lines to one another and more particularly as regards the relation of their major to their service lines. English is a major line at the State university, a service line at the State college, but there should be no material overlapping of major lines.

In many parts of the educational field such a division affords a rational and practicable principle of administration. If, for example, it reserved as major lines to the land-grant college (reference is not now being made to the Washington State College) agriculture, veterinary medicine, home economics, and certain departments of engineering, then all other subjects would be regarded as service subjects, in no case to be developed beyond the point at which the needs of the major subjects are supplied. A moderate amount of elementary collegiate work might be given in the languages and humanities and certain of the sciences, for instance, but they would presumably never go beyond these rudimentary stages. At the State university, on the other hand, agriculture, if cultivated at all, would in the same way have a place only as a service subject contributory to the major lines allotted to the institution.

Certain subjects do not fall readily into line on such a principle of division. Chemistry, for example, has an obvious place at the State university and also at the State college. Chemistry is involved in many agricultural and engineering processes and problems. It is, of course, fundamental also to the work of the experiment stations. Physics, zoology, and botany present similar perplexities. Such cases of overlapping, however, might, if the main principle is accepted, be easily settled by means of conferences of representatives of the faculties of institutions affected, together with representatives of the governing boards.

Once this principle of major and service lines is adopted, the whole situation clears up, not only as regards intramural work, but also as regards extension work. An institution would be permitted to do extension work only in a major line.

In the following chapter the application of this principle of major and service lines to the Washington higher institutions, especially the State college and State university is suggested as far as the committee judges it wise to apply it.

Chapter VIII.

DIFFERENTIATION OF FUNCTIONS OF THE STATE UNIVERSITY AND THE STATE COLLEGE.

The complete differentiation of the functions of the State higher institutions of Washington would have to be based on the following assumptions: That all are parts of a single State system of higher education or State university system; that no one part should attempt to cover the whole field; that the sole object of the system is to serve the State economically and effectively and not to serve any particular institution or locality; that this larger State service can best be accomplished by friendly cooperation, rather than by competition and rivalry; and that no institution should attempt to maintain a particular branch of training when it can be proved that greater benefit would accrue to the State if this branch were cultivated elsewhere. If the problem of differentiation were approached by the university and State college in this spirit, it would doubtless be necessary to disregard the sanction of State laws, which may provide that certain subjects may be taught at one or the other institution, and to consider the question entirely with a view to the higher good of the State. Laws, in so far as they are mandatory, can be easily amended, if the present institutional beneficiaries favor their amendment. If they are merely permissive, institutional policies can be changed without recourse to legislative action.

It is perhaps impossible to bring about at once and by a single drastic action an absolutely complete differentiation of the fields of State institutions in any State where the institutions affected have been long established and have built up extensive patronage and costly equipment. Certain peculiar local factors may also enter into the question, making a sweeping reorganization at least temporarily unwise. In the committee's judgment, Washington is one of the States in which these inhibiting factors to some extent exist. Two of these factors are the great size of the State and the peculiar distribution of the population. Nevertheless, the committee believes that the principles just enunciated and those discussed in the preceding chapter should underlie all future State and institutional policies, and that every reasonable endeavor should be made, as soon as the public mind is adjusted to the idea, to reduce to the lowest minimum the area of duplication in advanced and professional work. On the basis of these assumptions the committee submits the following propositions, stated as briefly as possible, with reference to the appropriate fields of the Washington State higher institutions.

The recommendations are separated into three groups. The first group contains recommendations to which the committee assumes there will be general assent.

1. The Washington State College should develop as major lines agriculture,[1] veterinary medicine, economic science in its applications to agriculture and rural life, and the training of high-school teachers of agriculture, home economics, and mechanic arts. This means the development of work in these subjects to the fullest extent, including not only professional courses, but the prosecution of research and of graduate work (except in the courses for the training of teachers) as the call may arise and the resources of the institution permit. The institution would be, with respect to these departments, of full university rank. It should, moreover, be encouraged to extend these departments freely.[2]

2. Law, medicine (if established at all), graduate work in liberal arts and the pure sciences, commerce, journalism, and the professional training of high-school teachers, superintendents, and educational administrators should be considered major lines for the State university.

The second group of proposals will doubtless arouse some objection, but the committee is convinced that any impartial observer from without the State would come to the same conclusions.

The committee recommends that architecture, forestry, and pharmacy be cultivated as major lines by the university alone. The first two of these subjects, architecture and forestry, might well be retained as service lines at the State college, with special emphasis on rural architecture in the one case and on wood-lot cultivation in the other.

The evidence upon which the committee bases its recommendation with regard to architecture and forestry is of a twofold nature. In the first place, the location of the university is much more favorable to the prosecution of work in these departments. The university is in the center of the great building operations of the State. The State college, on the other hand, is in the midst of a sparsely settled rural district, offering few opportunities to the student for observation of architectural achievements. The university is comparatively close to the principal lumbering industries in the State, and the greater part of the forests are on the western side of the Cascade Range. The State college is located in a region which is, for the most part, treeless. Its students must travel many miles to come into contact with logging operations. Aside from the advantages of location, which indicate to the committee the advisability of concentrating work in these departments at the university, attention is called to the present costs and actual enrollments in these departments at both institutions. Reference to Tables 17 and 18, chapter 5, and to

---

[1] This recommendation does not exclude the encouragement of research and advanced work in the sciences fundamental to agriculture in the direction of their practical applications.

[2] It is understood that the State college should have exclusive control and direction of all agricultural and horticultural extension, experimentation, and demonstration work.

Tables 20, 21, 27, and 28, chapter 6, will furnish further corroboration of the committee's decision.

In the case of pharmacy a different set of reasons dictate the recommendation. The university, to be sure, has a considerable advantage in point of enrollment (see Tables 20, 21, and 27, ch. 6). Nevertheless, pharmacy is not an expensive department when conducted at an institution already well supplied with chemical, biological, and bacteriological laboratories. Reference to the cost tables in chapter 5 will indicate that the cost of the department of pharmacy is not in either institution large enough to constitute a noticeable burden. The principal reasons for the committee's recommendation are, first, that it believes it advisable to restrict wherever possible the area of duplication; second, that pharmacy is closely allied to medical work, and in time, no doubt, the university will develop at least the preliminary years of medical training; and, third, that the largest demand for trained druggists is on the western side of the State. The number of drug stores in the three main divisions of the State are as follows: Western, 406; central, 70; eastern, 208.

The third group of proposals relates to the State's provision for engineering (including mining), the position of liberal arts at the State college, and the position of home economics at the State university. The committee has found it most difficult to determine a principle of division which shall not do more harm than good. It has finally decided to recommend the continuance, for the present, of duplication in these fields with certain minor limitations.

The committee has already recorded its opinion that, if the State did not now have two schools of engineering, it probably would not establish more than one. However, the two schools are very palpable realities. They are vital factors in the institutional organization of both the college and the university. Under these circumstances the elimination of duplication in the field of engineering might prove—indeed in the committee's opinion would most certainly prove—more expensive in its drain on intangible institutional values than it is worth. If a division of the work in engineering to obviate duplication were contemplated, however, the committee conceives that it would be possible in one of three ways.

1. The work in engineering might be divided horizontally, so that one institution (probably the State college) should offer only undergraduate work, possibly only work in the first two or three years, and the other institution should be a strictly graduate engineering school or at least of senior college grade. Whether the line of demarcation be on the higher or lower level suggested, the committee admits that the strict horizontal division would be difficult to enforce.

2. In the report of the Bureau of Education on the Iowa State institution already several times cited, a vertical or topical division of

engineering between the State university and the State college is recommended.   On this principle certain branches of engineering would be assigned to one institution and the others to the other.   The committee at one time hoped that it might be possible to recommend a similar vertical division in Washington.   In conferences with engineering experts, however, the opinion has always been expressed that the peculiar needs of engineers practicing in the northwest would render any such vertical division, especially as affecting the fields of civil, mechanical, and electrical engineering, well-nigh impossible.

3. Another principle of division advocated by some partisans of both institutions is the concentration of all engineering at one institution.   Cogent arguments may be advanced for the union of all engineering work at either place.   In substance they are as follows: For the consolidation of all engineering at the State college, it may be urged that the land-grant college is a college of agriculture and mechanic arts, that mechanic arts has usually been interpreted as synonymous with engineering, and that nearly all the land-grant colleges in the country have developed to a greater or less extent highly specialized courses in engineering.   In two States, Indiana and Oregon, the division under discussion has been made and all engineering work concentrated at the State Agricultural and Mechanical College.   In Washington, State laws also prescribe engineering as among the branches of learning in which the college is to provide instruction.   For the concentration of engineering work at the university it may justly be argued that the university is the center of a populous, rapidly growing, industrial district where there is an ever-increasing demand for trained engineers and where young men undergoing training in engineering branches may have the benefit of observing at close range most of the principal operations which they will later be called upon to perform.   It is further urged that work in the applied sciences is for the modern university a natural and necessary complement of work in the pure sciences and that the applied sciences themselves benefit by close contact with departments devoted to pure research.   It is also pointed out that the enrollment in the various engineering branches in the university is several times as large as that in the college.

The more the committee has studied the question the more it has been impressed with the strength of the position of at least the fundamental branches of engineering in the curricula of both institutions. It believes that while a college of agriculture and mechanic arts may be maintained with engineering on a lower basis than full professional courses, nevertheless in Washington this seems to be exceedingly undesirable.   Unquestionably, also, engineering has established itself as one of the vital departments at Pullman.   On the other hand the committee is equally convinced that the phenomenal development of courses in engineering at the university represents the dynamic drive of a real demand, a demand which could not be met by an institution 400 miles away, a demand which, unless all signs and portents fail, will continue to increase.

In view of these considerations the committee recommends that civil, mechanical, and electrical engineering be continued as major lines at both institutions. It is the more reconciled to this recommendation for two reasons: First, because the plants and engineering equipment of both institutions are now used almost, if not quite, to their full capacity. The concentration of both schools at a single point would entail considerable expense for new equipment. It is probable that, while it costs somewhat more to give the training in two places than in one, the added expense is, under these circumstances, not very great. Second, because the development of the State of Washington has already called, and will undoubtedly in the future call for a larger percentage of trained engineers than are needed in most other States. The accompanying diagram shows the increases in the number of graduates in engineering from the two institutions. The maintenance of two schools of engineering (somewhat differentiated as is suggested below), while an unwarranted extravagance for a State like Iowa or North Dakota, may be justified in the State of Washington.

Granting the justification of duplication of the three fundamental branches of engineering, the committee recommends certain limitations which will prevent the most sweeping future duplications, as follows:

1. Chemical engineering, already established at the university, should be restricted to that institution.[1]

2. Graduate work in engineering branches, when developed, should be developed at the university and not at the State college.

3. The establishment of new lines of engineering at either institution should be authorized by the regents only after a joint conference of representatives of both faculties and both boards.

4. The committee is persuaded that only one school of mining engineering is needed in the State of Washington. It has studied the evidence presented by the officers of the college of mines at the university and of the department of mining engineering at the State college. No one of its members can pretend to expert knowledge in this or an allied line. In view of this fact, and of the weight of evidence brought forward in support of both schools, the committee is unwilling to hazard a decision as to which should be retained. It recommends that the matter be laid before a group of mining experts from

---

[1] A course in chemical engineering is also announced in the 1915 catalogue of the State college. In the year 1914-15 students were enrolled in chemical engineering at the State college as follows: Freshmen, 8; sophomores, 3; juniors, 1.

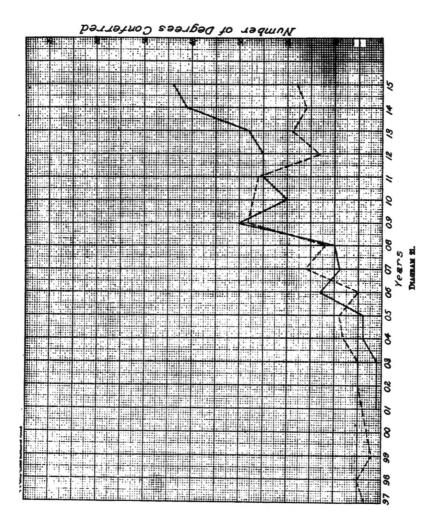

Number of Degrees Conferred

Years

DIAGRAM 21.

outside the State, no one of whom shall have any connection with either institution and the majority of whom shall be members of the American Society of Mining Engineers.

Under different local conditions, the committee would recommend the discontinuance of degree courses in liberal arts at the land-grant college. Liberal arts courses should ordinarily be included in the work of the land-grant college only in such amounts as will wisely reinforce the technical or semitechnical specialized curricula for whose development the institution was constituted. The Bureau of Education has already put itself on record to this effect. However, there are several reasons why the committee believes that courses in liberal arts leading to the bachelor's degree should continue to be given at the Washington State College. In the first place this work has formed a very large part, for a while indeed perhaps the major part, of the work of the State college during the past 25 years. It has, on the whole, had a highly beneficial influence on the life of the institution. Probably it did for a time bulk too large, but this tendency has now righted itself. Work in liberal arts is not now absorbing an undue part of the resources of the college. Confirmation of these statements may be had by referring to Tables 20, 21, 27, 28, and 29, chapter 6, and to the financial tables of chapter 5. But the principal reason for the continuance of these courses is a geographical one. The counties in the eastern part of the State are from 200 to 400 miles from the university. The committee believes that a State the size of Washington can well afford to maintain two liberal arts colleges in widely separated regions. The committee recommends, however, that courses in these departments at the State college be not allowed to expand into graduate work.[1]

In most other States the committee would as unhesitatingly recommend the limitation of home economics at the State university to the scope of a service department. Such a recommendation is in accordance with the custom which has developed professional work in home economics at the land-grant colleges. The preferred position of the land-grant college for this type of training is also recognized by Federal laws. In view, however, of the very great demand for the various kinds of training in home economics that has manifested itself at the university, the committee is led to recommend that home economics be considered a major line at both the State college and the State university. In the extension field it recommends that the university make no attempt to offer instruction in home economics outside of King County. The large and increasing funds which will be at the disposal of the State college for extension work in home economics (see p. 83, ch. 6) render it unwise for the State to spend

[1] The approval of the continuance of a full department of liberal arts in the State college necessarily carries with it the approval of the training of high-school teachers in all liberal arts subjects.

money on this subject through the agency of the university extension division.

Evidence brought to the attention of the committee has demonstrated that the university may well contemplate the development of two other lines of work as major lines. These are departments of marine engineering and of fisheries. Both of these lines relate closely to industries of great importance to the life of the district in which the university is situated. There could be no question as to which of the two State institutions should develop them.

In the event that the propositions made in this chapter receive the indorsement of the commission [1] and are adopted either by the legislature or by the governing boards of the institutions, the committee would suggest one other device to facilitate minor adjustments. This is a conference of representatives of the faculties of both institutions for the purpose of determining the scope of instruction and research in those departments which, through their nature and their connection with other subjects, are likely to overlap. Chemistry and botany, for example, are such departments. This conference might be assembled whenever the need appeared. It should not be formal in character.

The committee believes that the proposals made in this chapter should not be regarded as an undue limitation on the State college; indeed, it is confident that if these suggestions were carried out they would prove the greatest stimulus to the development of the institution. To meet the full needs of the State in only one of the lines allotted to it under such a division would tax the resources of an institution far richer than this. The discontinuance of professional work in the lines suggested should afford relief. The proposal that these subjects be taken over by the university is more likely to prove a temporary embarrassment than a benefit to the latter institution. With its present inadequate support, the university probably would not welcome any addition to its tasks. Nevertheless, the logic of location renders such redistribution of departments as is here proposed essential to a wise and economical State procedure.

But the committee desires to reaffirm its high appreciation, already several times implied, of the great contribution made by the State college to the life of the State. Despite its location, which has always been a handicap, it has evolved into an institution of which every citizen has a right to be proud. For many years it apparently failed to realize the possibility of a college of agriculture in a State of such large agricultural interests and such diversified agricultural conditions. Recently, however, this incomplete realization has been to a great extent remedied and a proportion of the institution's energies devoted to this field more nearly commensurate with the magnitude of the problems to be solved. In the other fields that

---

[1] Referring to the State legislative commission to which the survey report was rendered.

it has entered the State college has been a potent force. Its engineers have made engineering history in the Northwest. It has developed a department of veterinary medicine that ranks with the best in the country. The department of elementary science has met the needs of hundreds of boys and girls whom no other institution could serve. The department of liberal arts has given a sound, general college education in a wholesome environment. In the matter of standards the college has kept faith with itself; indeed it has been among the leaders in the establishment of high standards in the land-grant colleges of the country. In suggesting the readjustments proposed in this chapter the committee is nowise unmindful of these contributions.

SUMMARY OF RECOMMENDATIONS.

1. Agriculture, veterinary medicine, economic science in its application to agriculture, and the training of high-school teachers of agriculture, home economics, and mechanic arts to be major lines at the State college.

2. Law, medicine, graduate work in liberal arts and pure science, professional training of high-school teachers and school superintendents, commerce, journalism, architecture, forestry, and pharmacy to be major lines at the State university.

3. Duplication to be recognized in certain branches of engineering, in home economics, and in liberal arts.

4. Civil, electrical, and mechanical engineering to be taught at both the State college and the State university.

5. Chemical engineering to be a major line at the State university exclusively.

6. The development of further departments or branches of engineering to be submitted to a joint conference before their establishment at either institution.

7. The maintenance of but one school of mining, its location to be determined by the advice of mining experts.

8. Degree courses in liberal arts with the training of high-school teachers in the same, to be continued at the State college, but no graduate work in these lines to be offered.

9. Home economics to be developed for the present without restriction at both the State university and the State college, but no extension work in home economics to be undertaken by the university outside of King County.

10. The approval of the establishment of courses in marine engineering and fisheries at the State university as soon as its resources permit.

11. The appointment of a conference composed of representatives of the faculties of both institutions to meet from time to time to adjust cases of overlapping, especially in the field of graduate work.

Chapter IX.

DEPARTMENTS OF EDUCATION IN THE STATE COLLEGE AND UNIVERSITY.

In this chapter additional comment on the special functions of the State university and the State college in the direction of teacher training is submitted.

The State normal schools prepare teachers for the elementary schools of the country and city, and it is elsewhere urged that this should be considered their chief function, at least until such time as there is an ample supply of teachers for the elementary schools of this State. It is expected that some of the graduates of the normal schools will for the present continue to teach in the high schools of one and two years, especially when these are connected directly with elementary schools and taught in the same buildings, and that some will, after experience in practical work and further study in higher institutions, become teachers in four-year high schools, superintendents, supervisors, and teachers or directors of special subjects. To the university and the State college should be left the work of giving professional training to high-school teachers, supervising school officers and educational investigators, including teachers in normal schools and colleges. The college and the university should be accorded such support as will enable them to give the best possible preparation to sufficient numbers of men and women to supply the constantly increasing demand.

That teachers in high schools and higher institutions should have academic education at least equivalent to that represented by graduation from a standard college has long been admitted. The State Board of Education of Washington has indeed imposed this requirement upon candidates for teaching positions in all accredited high schools. In addition to their knowledge of the subjects taught, teachers of adolescent youth need a broad outlook on economic, industrial, social, and civic life, an understanding of the relation of the subjects which they teach to other subjects taught in the schools, and a breadth of general culture which the college and university can best give. Certainly no less degree of scholarship and professional knowledge should be expected and required of principals and supervisors, who must formulate and direct the work of the teachers under their charge, and of superintendents who are responsible also for the work of elementary schools, and who must determine the policies and administer the business affairs of county and State school systems.

STATE COLLEGE.

The organic act creating the State College of Washington states that one of the objects of the college should be to train teachers of physical science and thereby further the application of the principles of physical science to industrial pursuits. The Nelson amendment to the Morrill Act, increasing by $25,000 the annual appropriation made by the Federal Government to the land-grant colleges, provides that colleges may use part of this fund to maintain courses for the special preparation of instructors in the elements of agriculture and the mechanic arts. The Commissioner of Education has urged that this provision be interpreted to mean a very liberal portion of the fund in those institutions which have not considerable funds for this purpose from other sources. Evidently the intent of the clause in the organic act and the intent of the clause in the Nelson amendment are one and the same, to prepare teachers of industrial subjects and of the sciences in their practical applications to industry. The committee is of the opinion that this should continue to be the principal aim of the department of education in the State college. Every high school in the State should have one or more teachers of these subjects; the larger schools should have several, and the demand for supervisors in country and city and for college and normal-school instructors in these subjects may be expected to increase.

These facts should be constantly borne in mind in arranging courses in the department of education in the college. It should also be remem ere that teachers of the industrial and applied-science subjects need much more than the skill in manipulation which has too often been thought sufficient. They need a firm grasp of the scientific principles involved in the industries, an understanding of the relation of these industries to life and a mastery of those principles of education necessary to give a certainty of success in teaching.

In order to do this work for the State and to comply with the law which requires the college to collect information as to schemes of technical instruction adopted in other parts of the United States and in foreign countries, and to cooperate with the university and the normal schools in the promotion of the educational interests of the State the college department of education will probably need additional equipment. It is especially desirable that those who are preparing to teach industrial subjects may have the opportunity to do actual teaching. Possibly arrangements for this can be made with schools at or near Pullman. The committee recommends that the State college do not prepare teachers for the elementary schools.[1]

UNIVERSITY.

The committee is very definitely of the opinion that the task of preparing young men and women for service as teachers for normal schools and high schools (except for special subjects, preparation in which can better be given at the State college) and the preparation of

---

[1] The committee also suggests that in view of its unusually good courses in music the administration of the State college may well consider the advisability of preparing teachers in this subject. The same person might well teach domestic science and arts and music in a small high school.

superintendents, supervisors, and principals, together with provision for general educational investigation and research, belong to the university. Its college of education should be strengthened as may be needed to enable it to do this work well.

Early in its history the university gave courses in education, serving in a way as a normal school before the normal schools were established. The courses in education were assembled in a "school of education" in 1913, and in 1914 this school was changed into a "college of education." The increase in the number of undergraduate students taking education courses in the past four years has been very rapid. Moreover, there were 51 graduate students enrolled in education courses in 1915–16, as against 24 in 1911–12. Of 148 students in the graduate school this year, 36, nearly 24 per cent, are majoring in education. This is nearly twice as many as are majoring in any other subject and three times as many as the number in the next highest subject but one. This year there are enrolled in the college of education 110 students, distributed as follows: Freshmen 34, sophomores 12, juniors 23, seniors 9, specials 20, unclassified 12.

The contribution which the university and the State college have made to the system of public education of the State is indicated by the fact that in 1915–16 of 1,947 high-school teachers and principals and city superintendents in the State, 514 were trained wholly or partly in the university and 221 in the State college. Almost half of the whole number received part or all of their higher academic and professional preparation in these two institutions.

In the years 1914–15 students from the university went as teachers to all the counties in the State save one. Of 2,484 persons who have graduated at the university, 810 are reported as teaching. This is more than twice as many as are engaged in any occupation except homemaking, two and one-half times as many as are engaged in the practice of law, three times as many as are engaged in engineering, and six and one-half times as many as are in business. Of these 810 persons who are engaged in teaching, 550, or 68 per cent, are teaching in universities, colleges, and high schools, or are serving as superintendents, principals, supervisors, and librarians, while 260, or 32 per cent are in elementary schools. These figures show that the preparation of teachers constitutes a very important part of the work of the university. The fact that of the 714 calls made upon the university for teachers in 1914–15, 60 per cent were for superintendents, principals, and teachers in colleges and high schools indicates the kind of educational service for which the people at large think the university should prepare. Since this is the largest college of education in the Northwest, it will naturally become a source of supply for teachers and school officers not only for the State of

Washington, but to some extent for this entire section and also for Alaska.

The State has already provided in its normal schools, where the service can be performed better and with greater economy, the means of preparing teachers for the elementary schools, and will no doubt extend these means as it becomes conscious of the need of doing so. The committee therefore recommends that the university do not engage in this work.

Every school or college of education should have under its control a school for demonstration, practice, and research on or near its campus. The committee recommends the provision of these facilities at both the university and the State college.

State systems of education present many difficult problems in the solution of which school officers need the kind of expert help which a well-equipped university school of education should be able to give. This is especially true of a new, vigorous, and rapidly developing State like Washington. The committee believes that the college of education of the university should receive such support as will enable it to do this work.

SUMMARY OF RECOMMENDATIONS.

1. The discontinuance of the training of elementary teachers by the State university and the State college.

2. The provision at or near the State university and the State college of facilities for practice, demonstration, and research.

Chapter X.

AGRICULTURAL SCHOOLS.

Until very recently agriculture was not taught in the elementary or secondary schools of the State, and it is taught now only to a very limited extent. According to a ruling of the State board of education, pupils who complete the eighth grade are expected to stand an examination on agriculture, manual training, or domestic science. But teachers of the elementary schools have had little or no preparation for teaching these subjects and are not required to pass examinations on either of them before being granted a certificate, which may be accepted as a license to teach. In 1913–14, according to the report of the State superintendent of public instruction, only 4 per cent of the students in the high schools were studying agriculture. About 8 per cent of the number enrolled in .the first year of the high school took Agriculture I. One per cent of the number in . the second high-school year took Agriculture II. One-third of 1 per cent of the number in the third high-school year took Agriculture III, and one-third of 1 per cent of the number in the fourth high-school year took Agriculture IV. The figures for manual training for that year are somewhat better, being 16 per cent, 11 per cent, 7 per cent, and 5 per cent, respectively, and the figures for domestic science and home economics are still better in the first two high-school years, but not so good as for manual training in the last two high-school years. In 1915-16 about 50 per cent more were taking agriculture in the high schools than in 1913-14. There is also an increase in the number of girls taking home economics. The time may come when the majority of boys and girls in the high schools of the country will study agriculture, manual training, and home economics extensively, but it will not be soon, nor do the majority of boys and girls who live in the country as farmers and farmers' wives attend high school. There are therefore now, and will be for many years, a very large number of older boys and girls and young men and young women who are to live in the country and engage in the pursuits of farming and country homemaking who have had no opportunity of instruction in these important subjects either in the elementary or in the high schools. Most of them are too old to be expected to attend the high schools and take a regular high-school course for the sake of getting the little work offered in agriculture and home economics, and no high school, except the very largest, can afford to offer enough work in these subjects to take all the time of any student even for five or six months in the winter. Again, most' of these boys and girls, though of college age, are not prepared to enter the State college. Opportunity, therefore, for them to get any systematic and practical instruction in these subjects, so important for the welfare of themselves and of the State, must come through schools established and organized for this particular purpose.

In his report to the subcommittee of the joint committees of the committee on educational institutions of the senate and the committee on education of the house of representatives of the legislature, 1915, the Commissioner of Education suggested the advisability of the establishment of two schools of agriculture in the two sections of the State, one in direct connection with the State college at Pullman, the other somewhere in the western part of the State.

The committee hereby reaffirms this recommendation with a slight modification. It has elsewhere commended the work of the department of elementary science at the State college. Work similar to that contemplated in this recommendation is now given by the department of elementary science. As far as the recommendation bears on agricultural work of subcollegiate grade at Pullman, therefore, the committee merely desires to emphasize anew its importance to the State and to urge the still greater development of facilities for prosecuting it. The other school, it is believed, might be located at or near the experiment station at Puyallup.

The committee's conception is that both these schools should admit boys and girls 16 years old and over who have completed an elementary school course, and more mature young men and women of even less school preparation. For the convenience of those students, no doubt a large majority, who must work on the farm during the spring and summer, the sessions of these schools should be limited to six months in the year, as in the agricultural school of the University of Minnesota, or there might be two sessions, a winter session of 5½ months, to be attended mostly by boys and young men, and a summer session of 4½ months, to be attended mostly by girls and young women, although both sexes should be admitted to both sessions. This last arrangement would better enable the schools to keep their faculties employed and to carry on their work through the entire year. Later it may be found desirable to establish another school of this type.

There are many agricultural schools of this grade, and for purposes similar to those to be served here, in other States and countries. A tabulated statement of the organization, attendance, and work of some of these is appended.

TABLE 32.—*Special schools of agriculture.*

Name and location.	Date established.	Value of—		Support by—		Cost of maintenance.	Acres owned by school.	Secondary pupils.	
		Plant.	Equipment.	State.	City.			Men.	Women.
ARKANSAS.									
Fourth District Agricultural School, College Station	1910	$270,000	$6,000	$40,000	....	$20,000	500	163	78
First District Agricultural School, Jonesboro	1910	150,000	15,000	40,000	....	28,000	463	67	48
Third District Agricultural School, Magnolia	1910	180,000	3,000	40,000	....	25,000	400	42	38
Second District Agricultural School, Russellville.	1910	120,000	2,500	40,000	....	14,090	....	98	52
COLORADO.									
Fort Lewis School of Agriculture and Mechanic Arts	1911	200,000	....	30,000	....	17,644	....	27	10
MASSACHUSETTS.									
Smith's Agricultural School, Northampton.	1908	79,000	8,000	4,000	$7,500	11,000	94	34	....
Bristol County Agricultural School, Segreganset.	1913	65,000	10,000	....	....	16,000	110	60	4
MINNESOTA.									
Northwest School of Agriculture, Crookston	1906	325,000	40,000	....	....	....	....	....	...
West Central School and Station, Morris	....	250,350	22,110	24,000	6,065	27,408	....	57	49
NEBRASKA.									
Nebraska School of Agriculture, Curtis	1910	150,000	10,000	30,000	1,500	21,500	160	56	52

TABLE 32.—*Special schools of agriculture*—Continued.

Name and location.	Date established.	Value of—		Support by—		Cost of maintenance.	Acres owned by school.	Secondary pupils.	
		Plant.	Equipment.	State.	City.			Men.	Women.
NEW YORK.									
New York State School of Agriculture at Alfred University, Alfred	1908	$199,642	$32,616	$43,000	....	....	230	138	55
New York State School of Agriculture at St. Lawrence University, Canton	....	....	....	....	....	....	230	92	30
New York State School of Agriculture, Cobleskill ..	1911	75,000	10,000	....	....	$40,000	85	....	....
New York State School of Agriculture, Farmingdale......................	1916	473,000	37,000	....	....	50,380	308	150	
New York State School of Agriculture, Morrisville..	1908	96,050	32,500	46,980	....	37,000	200	120	73
VERMONT.									
Vermont State School of Agriculture, Randolph Center..................	1910	40,000	5,000	10,000	$450	10,000	....	78	....
Vail State School of Agriculture and Industry, Lyndon Center..........	1910	....	....	....	....	....	....	....	....
WISCONSIN.									
Marinette County School of Agriculture, Marinette.	1907	....	....	....	....	7,304	....	....	....
Dunn County School of Agriculture, Menominee....	1902	....	....	1,000	300	10,000	....	50	16
La Crosse County School of Agriculture, Onalaska...	1909	60,000	10,000	6,000	1 1,300	14,500	....	37	19
Racine County School of Agriculture, Rochester...	1912	40,000	10,000	....	....	4,600	....	....	....
Marathon County School of Agriculture, Wausau..	....	....	....	....	....	6,800	....	....	....
Milwaukee County School of Agriculture, Wauwatosa..................	1912	267,600	43,138	67,538	5,279	65,031	136	114	85
Winnebago County School of Agriculture, Winneconne..................	1906	....	....	....	....	9,254	....	....	....

1 $8,000 of this from county.

If such schools are established in Washington, they should be under the immediate control of the regents and the president of the State college.

SUMMARY OF RECOMMENDATIONS.

1. The further development of the facilities of the department of elementary science at the State college for agricultural instruction of subcollegiate grade.

2. The establishment at Puyallup, or somewhere else in the western part of the State, of another school of agriculture of subcollegiate grade under the direction and control of the State college.

Chapter XI.

MINOR QUESTIONS OF ADMINISTRATION AND STATEMENTS AS TO THE SUPPORT OF THE STATE UNIVERSITY AND STATE COLLEGE.

There are several minor matters of administration to which the committee has given some consideration. Three schools at the State college now admit students with two years of high-school preparation (see p. 38). Students, if 19 years of age, are also admitted with 8 units of high-school training to the certificate course in pharmacy at the university. The committee believes that the time is ripe for the requirement of high-school graduation (15 units or 30 credits) of all students entering the college or the university, except for those 21 years of age or older, and except for students in the department of elementary science at the State college. This recommendation has the indorsement of the heads of the schools concerned.

The committee has been much impressed by the value of the work carried on by the department of elementary science at the State college. It is of the opinion that this work is making a most important contribution to the life of the State. Under the wise limitations as to scope which have already been adopted, it believes that this work should be still further strengthened and extended. To this end it recommends the partial reorganization of the administrative relationship of this department to the college. The department should have a teaching staff entirely its own and it should be separately housed.

The surprisingly large number of classes at both institutions having enrollments of less than five students each calls for careful study.[1] In advanced courses enrollments are likely to be small. This is one of the factors in the large expense of advanced work. In elementary and intermediate courses, however, small classes can often be avoided by care on the part of the administration. The committee recommends that the administrative officers of both institutions take this matter of small classes under examination.

At both the State college and the university the number of hours required in the major subject is often excessive in that it unduly limits the opportunity of the student to obtain the desired breadth of training. The committee is of the opinion that the administrators of both institutions may profitably give this problem serious consideration.

Reference has already been made (p. 75, Ch. V) to the number of credit teaching hours required of professors at one institution. State institutions have a tendency to exact a larger number of hours of teaching of their professors than do the well-established private

---

[1] See p. 87, Ch. VI.

universities. Some of the most productive and distinguished men in the larger American universities on private foundations conduct but six or eight classroom exercises a week. Teaching of university grade requires time for sound preparation, for reflection, and for arrangement of material. The physical presence of professors in classrooms can be secured by rule for any number of hours a week, but the amount of effective teaching can hardly be increased by this means. The committee recommends that 15 credit teaching hours a week be regarded as the absolute maximum and that a smaller maximum be encouraged.

The committee has been unable in the time at its disposal to arrive at any but the most general conclusions with reference to the support of the State college and university. It submits these conclusions for what they may be worth. They are:

1. That Washington has not been spending as much money on its State collegiate institutions in proportion to their needs and the State's wealth as many other progressive States, and that both should be more liberally supported.

2. That the State college is for the most part well housed and the pressure on its plant is not extreme. On the other hand, the salaries paid its teachers are considerably below what should be paid to competent men in institutions of this character (see p. 69, Ch. V). In the last two years the amount spent per student has been somewhat higher than the per capita outlay in other institutions which the Bureau of Education has studied. However, the committee especially calls attention to the fact that in order to meet the needs of the State in the direction of agricultural instruction, extension, and experimentation alone, this institution will require largely increased appropriations.

3. That the State university has for a number of years been starved. It is housed, in part, in buildings which are unworthy of a great university in a great and wealthy State. Its expense per student during the last two years is much lower than the similar expense in any institution of university rank which the Bureau of Education has studied. The legitimate expansion of the institution in the directions already noted, especially the development of a college of commerce, demands large increases in its support.

As reinforcement of these conclusions the committee calls attention to the summaries and diagrams representing State expenditures in Chapter I, to the institutional cost sheets in Chapter V, and also to the budgets for the next biennium arranged in the same form as the cost sheets referred to and appended to this chapter.

RECOMMENDATIONS.

1. The requirement of high-school graduation of all students entering the college or university, except for those 21 years of age or older, and except for students in the elementary science department of the State college.

2. The modification of the administrative relationships of the department of elementary science at the State college.

3. The serious consideration by the administrative officers of both institutions of the large number of small classes.

4. The possible revision of the excessive major requirements at both institutions.

5. The establishment of 15 hours of classroom teaching a week as the maximum at the State college and State university and the encouragement of a lower maximum.

1. The provision for the formulation of State policies in higher education—

(a) Through joint meetings of boards of regents, or

(b) Through the extension of the functions of the State board of education, or

(c) Through the creation of a State council of education.

2. Agriculture, veterinary medicine, economic science in its application to agriculture, and the training of high-school teachers of agriculture, home economics, and mechanic arts to be major lines at the State college.

3. Law, medicine, graduate work in liberal arts and pure science, professional training of high-school teachers and school superintendents, commerce, journalism, architecture, forestry, and pharmacy to be major lines at the State university.

4. Duplication to be recognized in certain branches of engineering, in home economics, and in liberal arts.

5. Civil, electrical, and mechanical engineering to be taught at both the State college and the State university.

6. Chemical engineering to be a major line at the State university exclusively.

7. The development of further departments or branches of engineering to be submitted to a joint conference before their establishment at either institution.

8. The maintenance of but one school of mining, its location to be determined by the advice of mining experts.

9. Degree courses in liberal arts with the training of high-school teachers in the same to be continued at the State college, but no graduate work in these lines to be offered.

10. Home economics to be developed for the present without restriction at both the State university and the State college, but no extension work in home economics to be undertaken by the university outside of King County.

11. The approval of the establishment of courses in marine engineering and fisheries at the State university as soon as its resources permit.

12. The appointment of a conference composed of representatives of the faculties of both institutions to meet from time to time to adjust cases of overlapping, especially in the field of graduate work.

122

13. The discontinuance of the training of elementary teachers by the State university and the State college.

14. The provision at or near the State university and the State college of facilities for practice, demonstration, and research.

15. The further development of the facilities of the department of elementary science at the State college for agricultural instruction of subcollegiate grade.

16. The establishment at Puyallup, or somewhere else in the western part of the State, of another school of agriculture of sub-collegiate grade under the direction and control of the State college.

17. The requirement of high-school graduation of all students entering the college or the university, except for those 21 years of age or older, and except for students in the elementary science department of the State college.

18. The modification of the administrative relationships of the department of elementary science at the State college.

19. The serious consideration by the administrative officers of both institutions of the large number of small classes.

20. The possible revision of the excessive major requirements at both institutions.

21. The establishment of 15 hours of classroom teaching a week as the maximum at the State college and State university and the encouragement of a lower maximum.

Instruction.		1915–1917.	1917–1919.
	Bacteriology	$5,500.00	$7,300.00
	Botany	16,200.00	18,900.00
	Chemistry	39,520.00	41,920.00
	Civil engineering	41,400.00	51,900.00
	Commerce	3,400.00	24,000.00
	Education	20,600.00	31,100.00
	Electrical engineering	17,100.00	23,100.00
	English	52,100.00	63,200.00
	Extension	24,000.00	40,000.00
	Fisheries		3,000.00
	Forestry	17,900.00	26,300.00
	Forest products		8,000.00
	French	26,700.00	31,350.00
	Geology	18,900.00	22,200.00
	German	26,700.00	30,550.00
	Greek	11,900.00	12,800.00
	History	26,650.00	34,350.00
	Home economics	16,450.00	21,600.00
	Industrial research		2,500.00
	Journalism	20,040.00	23,840.00
	Latin	11,300.00	12,200.00
	Law	31,400.00	33,200.00
	Library economy	3,490.00	3,790.00
	Marine engineering		6,000.00
	Mathematics	37,400.00	42,900.00
	Mechanical engineering	20,200.00	24,100.00
	Mining	16,100.00	17,900.00
	Military science	3,540.00	3,540.00
	Music and fine arts	25,400.00	36,800.00
	Oriental languages and literature	5,400.00	5,700.00
	Pharmacy	15,720.00	16,920.00
	Philosophy	12,100.00	15,400.00
	Physical training	15,300.00	20,400.00
	Psychology	11,100.00	14,400.00
	Physics	20,650.00	22,600.00
	Political and social science	32,100.00	42,600.00
	Public speaking and debate	5,000.00	5,300.00
	Scandinavian	4,400.00	4,700.00
	Spanish	15,600.00	22,800.00
	Zoology	18,100.00	30,000.00
		691,360.00	899,160.00
	Marine station	2,800.00	4,000.00
	Summer session	16,000.00	22,000.00
		710,160.00	
	New instructors, 1916–1917	4,870.00	
		715,030.00	925,160.00

Summary.		1915–1917.	1917–1919.
	All salaries	$890,000.00	$1,118,500.00
	Instructional equipment	82,100.00	179,400.00
	Overhead, supplies and labor	137,900.00	228,400.00
	Special laboratory construction		62,500.00
		1,110,000.00	1,588,800.00

HERBERT T. CONDON,
Comptroller.

SECTION II.—GENERAL REVIEW OF THE PUBLIC-SCHOOL SYSTEM.

It has been impossible for the committee in the time allotted to survey in detail the public schools of the State. Only those general aspects of the public-school system have been considered which are believed to bɔ of vital importance to the progressive development of the system as a whole.

These are treated very briefly under the following heads:

1. Support of the public schools.
2. County school administration and supervision.
3. Public-school teachers.
4. Special preparation for rural teachers.
5. Certification of teachers.
6. Instruction in the schools.

Chapter XII.

SUPPORT OF THE PUBLIC SCHOOLS.

Washington has been comparatively liberal in the support of its public schools, and in the main the plan used for levying and apportioning the school funds is thoroughly sound.

The State utilizes three units for tax purposes—

(a) The State.
(b) The county.
(c) The local district.

It is eminently fair that the State at large should be taxed to support all the schools of the State, for education is the business of the State just as much as it is the business of a community or an individual. Washington is a large Commonwealth extremely varied in topography and natural wealth. It is rich in grain, fruit, minerals, and lumber, but it has also large sections of semiarid lands, where the population is sparse and poor. In these sections, where the amount raised by local taxation is correspondingly low, it is right that the State at large should give liberal aid. County taxation is justifiable on similar grounds. Since the county is the unit for civil administration, it is reasonable to expect that it should tax itself for the maintenance of all its schools alike, and divide equitably among the schools the taxes from such public carriers as railways

and steamship lines. Finally, a considerable amount of local taxation is necessary to keep alive and foster the local interest in school
affairs and to develop local independence and self-reliance. Since
Washington distributes the burden of school taxes among the three
administrative divisions, the sole question of concern in this State is
·whether or not these three kinds of taxes are scaled in the most equitable way.

The total levies for school purposes for the fiscal year ending June
30, 1914 (the last available figures), amounted to $13,648,534, divided

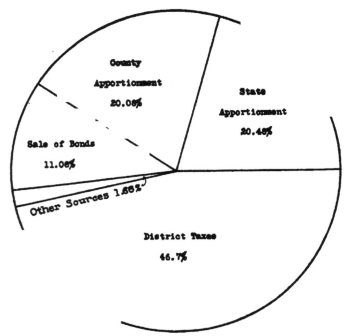

FIG. 1.—Sources of school-district revenues for the year ended June 30, 1914.

as follows: State apportionment, $2,794,806; county apportionment,
$2,739,107; school district taxes, $6,376,886; sale of bonds, $1,510,-
400; other sources, $227,335. In addition there were balances on
hand sufficient to make the total levies and balances $17,465,627.
Of this total, $13,774,643 represents the actual disbursements for
common-school purposes during the year. These facts are shown
graphically in figures 1 and 2.

The graphs disclose that practically 60 per cent of the taxes come
from district levies. There is, however, general agreement through-

out the country that the bulk of the funds for school maintenance should come from State and county rather than from local effort; in other words, that local district taxation should be used only for buildings and similar local advantages, and that State and county should pool their efforts for all other purposes.   California, for example, has a uniformly good system of rural, village, and city schools, in the mountains and the valleys, in the fruit belt, and in the arid sections, because it wisely relies on State and county taxation to maintain all its schools, seldom resorting to local taxation for other than building

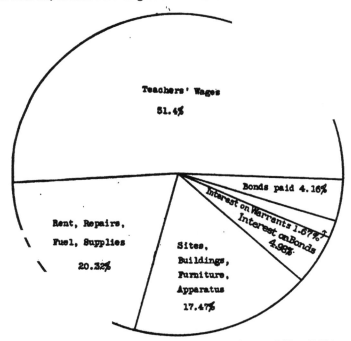

Fig. 2.—Distribution of warrant and capital disbursements for the year ended June 30, 1914.

purposes.   Washington strives to equalize the natural inequalities in the State's taxable wealth for the schools through an excellent method of apportionment, but, unfortunately, this is not sufficient to overcome the fundamental inequalities in the general tax system.

The committee recommends that a careful study of the best tax systems in other States be made to ascertain a fair and equitable basis for scaling up the State and county taxes levied in the State.

The school taxes are applied through three separate funds: The general school fund, the building fund, and the bond-redemption fund. The general school fund includes the following: State appropriations or "current State school fund," county appropriations, and district maintenance levies. The apportionment of the current State school fund for 1916 is graphically shown in figure 3.[1]

The system of apportionment is based on the soundest principle. The two vital factors in school cost are the teaching force and the children actually utilizing the schools, i. e., the children in daily attendance. These two factors have been made the basis in apportioning the general school fund in Washington, the current State school

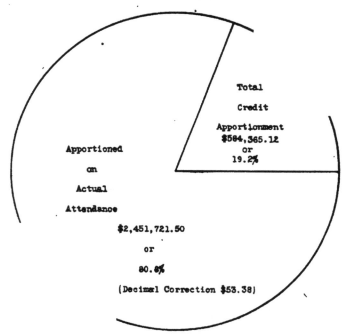

Total

Credit

Apportionment
$584,365.12
or
19.2%

Apportioned

on

Actual

Attendance

$2,451,721.50

or

80.8%

(Decimal Correction $53.38)

FIG. 3.—State current school fund, 1915-16, $3,036,140.

fund being apportioned entirely on the basis of daily attendance, and the county appropriation on the basis of two-thirds for attendance and one-third for teachers needed.

A full analysis follows, showing how the current State school fund for 1916 is apportioned:

303,614 census-children at $10 each equals $3,036,140, if all is collected.
$3,036,140 less $89,300 bonus to high-school grades equals $2,946,840.

1 A full statement of this fund has just been published by the State department of education, Olympia, as Bulletin No. 28.

$2,946,840 divided by 39,918,540 days (basis of apportionment) equals 7.382 cents per day.

    (39,918,540 days at 7.382+ cents per day equals $2, 946,787.)

    ($2,946,840 less $2,946,787 equals $53, correction due to decimal.)

$3,036,140 divided by 33,213,683 days (total actual days, all schools, all credits excluded) equals 9.141+ cents per day.

33,213,683 multiplied by 9.141+ cents equals $3,036,063. Decimal correction, $77

$2,062,555 (direct tax portion) less $89,300 equals $1,973,255.

$1,973,255 (tax portion) divided by 39,918,540 equals 4.94+ cents per day.

39,918,540 multiplied by 4.94+ cents equals $1,971,976. Decimal correction, $1,279.

Actual attendance rate per diem (all credits excluded), 9.141+ cents.

Present basis of apportionment, rate per diem (one-half high-school attendance credit, private-schools credit, institute credit, 2,000-day credit, consolidation credit, defective credit, evening school credit, parental-school credit, sickness credit, actual-attendance credit), equals 7.382 cents+ $89,300 high-school grades.

TABLE 33.—*Credits itemized.*

Basis of apportionment.	Days.	Rate per day (cents).	Amount.	
1. One-half high-school attendance credit........	[1] 2,299,348	7.382	$169,737.87	5.59
2. Private schools............................	1,622,201	7.382	119,750.87	3.94
3. $100 bonus to high-school grades............			89,300.00	2.94
4. Institute...............................	922,586	7.382	68,105.30	2.24
5. 2,000 days' attendance....................	678,127	7.382	50,059.33	1.64
6. Consolidation............................	632,000	7.382	46,654.24	1.53
7. Defective...............................	267,820	7.382	19,770.47	.64
8. Evening schools.........................	177,310	7.382	13,069.08	.43
9. Parental................................	83,346	7.382	6,152.60	.20
10. Sickness...............................	23,644	7.382	1,745.41	.05
Total amount to credits....................			584,365.12	19.20
11. Basis of apportionment.................	[2] 33,212,158	7.382	2,451,721.50	....
Decimal correction........................			53.38	....
Total......................................	39,918,540	7.382	3,036,140.00	....

[1] Excluding 286 for Skamania and 50 for Stevens.
[2] Equals actual attendance (33,213,685 days) less 1,525 days.

Although the underlying principle is correct, in minor details the system should be changed. The attorney general of the State ruled (Oct. 7, 1915) that (1) the 2,000-day credit attendance, (2) the one-half high-school credit attendance, (3) the credit attendance in parental schools, and (4) the credit attendance for defectives should not be counted in "arriving at the basis of attendance for the apportionment of two-thirds of the county apportionment." This needs reconciliation with the State basis. The credit attendance is the growth of years. Many of the items included should be modified or discontinued altogether. The State superintendent of public instruction has urged such modification on various occasions.

The committee is of the opinion that a careful revision of the whole system of apportioning both the current State school fund and the county fund should now be undertaken.

Chapter XIII.

COUNTY SCHOOL ADMINISTRATION AND SUPERVISION.

When Washington organized its school system, the State borrowed its plans largely from the older States. In the early days this organization was adequate for all purposes, but the State is now rapidly outgrowing it. The fact is recognized not only by the educational leaders, but by the laity of the State as well. The present chapter is devoted to a brief outline of the system of administration and supervision so far as it concerns the county and its subdivisions.

Section 1 of paragraph 97 of article 1 of the school code provides that "for purposes of supervision and administration each county in the State shall constitute one county school district." The supervisory and administrative control of the county school district is delegated to a county superintendent and such assistants as may be provided him by law. The superintendent's administrative function, however, is largely neutralized by the powers of the directors of the local districts into which the county is divided, so that in matters of school administration the county loses much of its significance. In practice Washington utilizes the county as the unit of school supervision. For purposes of taxation, also, the county is important.

Three units are used in the United States for local educational administration: The district, the township, and the county. The district unit belonged to the original pioneer system. It came into use by common consent in early days when nothing else was possible and generally preceded all school legislation. Wherever a sufficient number of families gathered in a new settlement they organized their own schools as best they could. The families served by a single school formed the original district unit.

The present small district school organization in Washington is an outgrowth of the early system used in New England and the Middle West. While pioneer conditions prevailed in the State this organization proved satisfactory, but now that Washington has become a flourishing Commonwealth, the small district is less able to provide the most economical kind of school organization. The district unit must either be abandoned or reinforced through other means.

The township unit of administration belongs to New England and a few States westward. It would not be a practicable device for this State, and may be passed by in the discussion.

The county unit, on the other hand, which had its origin in the Southern States and has more recently spread to several Northern and Western States, is better adapted to the changing conditions of such a State as Washington. The county system of organization usually centralizes school effort by placing practically all educational authority in the hands of a small county board of education, which elects a professionally prepared educator as county superintendent and executive secretary. This educator is charged with the selection of all the teachers of the county. Questions of school policy, establishment of new schools, closing of small, ineffective schools or their consolidation into large central schools, and similar matters are decided by the board. The prevention of the duplication of schools and the consequent reduction of the number of teachers, the establishment of careful grading, and the adoption of courses of study appropriate to the community—these are some of the improvements which have usually followed the inauguration of the county system of organization and which tend to make this system both effective and economical.

But even the county system of school administration as just outlined does not prove satisfactory under all conditions. In Washington many of the counties are too large and the population too scattered to warrant the general adoption of such a system. Okanogan County, for example, has an area equal to New Hampshire and is more difficult to traverse. The population is comparatively small, living in great measure under pioneer conditions. The same is true of other large sections of the State. In view of these facts the committee is inclined to advocate for the present a flexible policy of school administration. It is probably better that the sparsely populated counties retain, for the time being at least, the local district organization and seek a remedy for the defects of general administration and supervision in some other way. For such of the Washington counties, however, as have a well-distributed population of, say, not less than 6,000 census children, a permissive county organization might be authorized by law to allow the most compact and best populated sections of the State to experiment with the system.

The early county superintendent in the United States was created as a clerical and financial functionary to apportion locally the school taxes, to make statistical reports to the State department of education, and, incidentally, to visit schools and stimulate interest in educational affairs. The office called for no special qualifications, and could be filled from the general electorate as easily as any other county office. But recently educational problems have changed, and the superintendent's work has become greatly enlarged. Many new powers and functions have been conferred upon the county superintendent. The office can not now be filled satisfactorily except by a well-educated person of broad experience and executive ability.

The Washington school code, dealing with the subject of county superintendent, is in harmony with the old conditions when any layman of reasonable ability could fill the office well. It reads:

No person shall be eligible to hold the office of county superintendent of schools who shall not at the time of his election or appointment have taught in the public schools of this State two school years of nine months each, and who shall not at the time of such election or appointment hold a first grade or higher certificate.

This minimum requirement of experience and preparation does not guarantee to the county persons fit for the important office of superintendent. Entirely too often the incumbents have less preparation for their work than do the majority of the teachers under their direction. This is a serious evil. Again, the State, which otherwise pays rather liberal salaries, provides for the county superintendent a salary utterly inadequate and out of proportion to the importance of the office. In fact the post is so poorly paid that there is no incentive for any person to prepare for it. The salaries range from $480 per annum to $2,000, averaging about $1,138. Consequently, it is not uncommon to find county superintendents who are obliged to preach, to plow, or to keep shop, and to make of their educational office a side issue. As a remedy for this condition the committee recommends that the eligibility and salary clauses in the code be changed so that any person, in order to be eligible to the office of county superintendent, shall hold a professional certificate valid in this State; shall have had at least five years of professional experience, and shall have had not less than two years of advanced preparation of college or normal school grade in addition to being graduated from a secondary school. The minimum salary, it is recommended, shall be $1,200, and the maximum, $3,000. In case eligible persons can not be found in the county, candidates should be chosen from some other county.

Even with the right kind of county superintendent, the problem of providing effective schools would not be solved. In addition to expert administration, there is urgently needed in the schools of the State—and particularly in the rural schools—close professional supervision. Indeed, with adequate supervision, no further reorganization would probably be needed for years to come. Ohio, West Virginia, and other States have attacked the problem by subdividing the county into supervision districts on the basis of one supervisor to not more than 30 teachers (or schools) under his jurisdiction. The supervisor should preferably live in his supervision district, although he should be responsible for his work to the county superintendent, who is his superior officer. In order to equalize educational opportunities the State should pay part of the supervisor's salary. In return the supervisor should be nominated by the State superintendent of schools, or by the State board of education, and his appointment should be ratified finally by the local boards of the districts comprised in the supervision unit.

The committee is convinced that the lack of professional supervision in the rural and village schools is one of the greatest weaknesses in the whole school system, and recommends that legislation be passed to remedy it by subdividing the counties for supervision purposes.

Chapter XIV.

PUBLIC SCHOOL TEACHERS.

STATISTICS OF GENERAL TRAINING, PROFESSIONAL PREPARATION, AND TENURES.

Liberal school support and efficient school administration are essential in a progressive school system; but more important still is a well educated, professionally trained teaching body. The professional preparation and general education of the present body of Washington teachers are discussed in the following paragraphs.

In the year 1912–13 the common schools of Washington employed 8,459 teachers, of whom 6,795 were women; in 1913–14 the number had increased to 8,639, of whom 6,928 were women; in 1914–15 there were 9,068, of whom 7,276 were women.

The committee, working in cooperation with the State department of education, recently sent a questionnaire to every teacher in service to ascertain the preparation each had had, the length of service, and several other important facts. At the time of the filing of this report the questionnaires had not all been returned. Final tables could not therefore, in every instance, be given. However, the data for many counties were complete, and for purposes of comparative statistics the figures are wholly satisfactory. The data on high schools also were complete.

According to the returns there are 1,947 high-school teachers, 987 men and 960 women; 1,737 teachers of one-room schools reported. This number should probably be increased to about 1,800. In addition to the teachers in one-room schools, 4,202 elementary teachers reported. This number should probably be increased to about 5,500. The total of these three groups would give the State a present teaching force of about 9,248 in elementary and secondary schools.

Of more importance than mere numbers is the kind and amount of preparation of the teachers intrusted with the education of the future citizenry of the State. The study has disclosed that Washington teachers on the whole are better prepared for their profession than teachers in many other States. This statement refers only to the amount of time spent in academic and professional institutions, and furnishes no final criterion of the absolute effectiveness of the instruction secured. It appears from Table 34 that in a total of 1,737 teachers of one-room schools reporting, 1,158 have some professional preparation and 302 have none. This is set forth graphically in figures 16 and 17 in Section III. Professional preparation, as the term is used here, ranges from attendance at a university, college, or normal school for one or more summer schools to graduation from advanced courses in these schools. Other elementary teachers make a better showing, only 5 per cent reporting no professional preparation.

Figures compiled by the United States Bureau of Education (Bulletin, 1914, No. 49) give the average number of teachers without any professional preparation in places of less than 2,500 people, as 32.3 per cent, and the average for the Western Division of States as 22.9 per cent. A comparison of these figures with those given in the preceding paragraph is not unfavorable to Washington. Nevertheless, the fact remains that 1 out of 5 rural teachers and 1 out of 20 other elementary teachers in the State have no training for their tasks, and

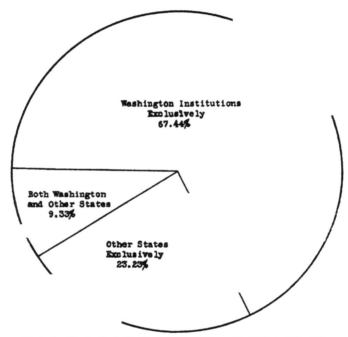

FIG. 4.—Rural teachers trained in Washington Institutions and institutions of other States.

a still larger number do not have as much or as efficient preparation as the public has a right to expect.

The State occupies a unique place in one respect, namely, that it has been able to depend on other States farther east to prepare nearly one-half of its teaching staff. For the future there will probably be a gradual decline in this supply of foreign-trained teachers until a minimum is reached. Teachers from the older States are attracted to Washington by the better salaries paid, and by the apparently greater opportunities for winning worthy positions in life. Out of the total of 1,947 Washington high-school teachers, 949

have had all their preparation in other States, and 274 have
attended schools both outside the State and in it, while only 606
are exclusively from Washington institutions. Probably the time
is at hand to consider carefully the conditions under which extra-
State teachers should be accredited and certificated. Up to the
present their influx into the State has been stimulating to the home
product and has given the young State better teachers than it
could otherwise have received. The ratio of State and extra-State
rural and other elementary teachers is seen in figures 4 and 5.

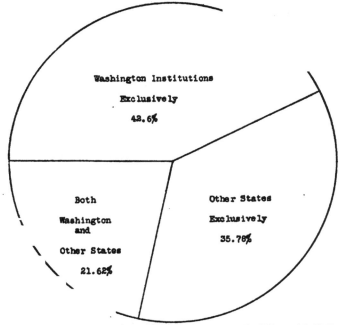

FIG. 5.—Elementary teachers (other than rural) trained in Washington institutions and institutions of other States.

Figures presented elsewhere in this report[1] show certain significant
facts, namely: (1) That the university and colleges devote considerable attention to preparing elementary-school teachers, a task for
which they have poor facilities, and in performing which they duplicate the work of the normal schools; and (2) that a considerable
number of teachers find their way into the service from the university and colleges by the county-examination route. These have
had no professional preparation worth mentioning. The report
later emphasizes the fact that the preparation of elementary school

[1] See Figures 16 and 17 in Section III; also Table 34.

teachers is the peculiar function of the normal schools.   For this they
are better adapted than the colleges.   In the preceding section it was
also recommended that the colleges should be discouraged from offering courses for elementary teachers.[1]

Figures 6 and 7 indicate the institutions attended by rural and
other elementary teachers one term or more.   The comparison naturally favors the elementary group.   Of teachers in one-room schools
8.28 per cent have had elementary-school preparation only, and 15.56

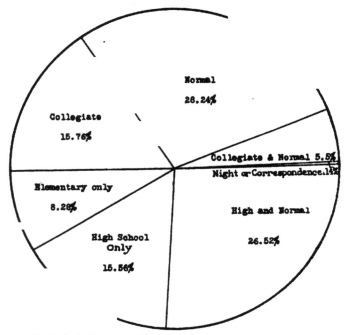

Fig. 6.—Institutions attended one term or more.   (Teachers of one-room schools.)

per cent high-school preparation only (which does not always mean
the completion of high-school courses).   Of the other elementary
teachers, 1.77 per cent report elementary preparation only, and 4.78
per cent high-school preparation only.   While conditions in regard
to the academic preparation of teachers are more serious in some
other States, it is evident that in the interests of its children Washington can not continue to intrust 8 per cent of its one-room schools
to teachers whose formal training has not extended beyond the curriculum of the very school in which they teach.   The committee's con-

[1] See Ch. IX, p. 112 et seq.

ception of the academic and professional preparation which should be required of all teachers is set forth in the section on normal schools.

Figures 8 and 9 call attention to another serious condition. Too many teachers, once they are certificated, are satisfied to remain scholastically *in statu quo*. For example, 47.33 per cent of teachers in one-room schools and about one-third of the other elementary teachers have attended no educational institutions while in service. This is probably due in a large measure to the exceptional ease with

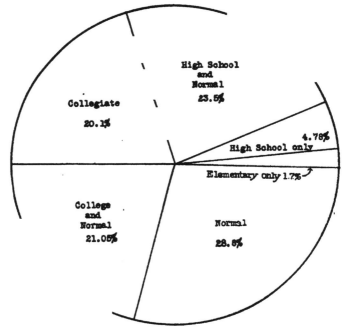

FIG. 7.—Institutions attended one term or more. (Elementary teachers in other than one-room schools.)

which certificates can be renewed in this State. As a remedy the committee suggests that some new compulsory plan be adopted for the further training of all teachers while in service. Such a plan can advantageously be worked out by the normal schools in cooperation with the State department of education. (See Section III, p. 177 et seq.)

Long tenure is an indication of professionalized teaching. The amateur teacher never remains long in the profession or in any one place. The survey has disclosed that teacher tenures in Washington are a trifle better than the average for the United States as a whole. Figures 10 and 11 give the teaching experience of all except high-school teachers. They show (1) that one-fourth of all the teachers in one-room schools do not teach more than one school year, and that the percentage of other elementary teachers reporting similarly brief tenures is much smaller; (2) that one-third of the rural teachers have taught more than five years, and that fully 65 per cent of other elementary teachers teach five years and over.

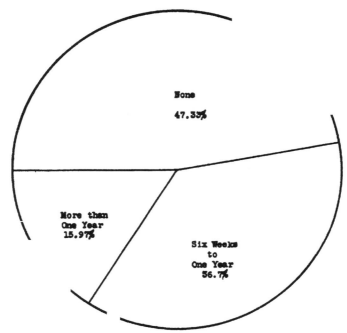

FIG. 8.—Per cent of teachers attending institutions while in service. (One-room teachers.)

The large number of very short tenures in rural schools is due to the fact that these schools alone are willing to accept inexperienced teachers. It is one of the inconsistencies of the American school system that the rural schools, which, with the new demands, are becoming the most difficult of all for a beginner, should continue as practicing grounds for all kinds of apprentices. The cure for this defect lies with the State. Not until the State demands a specialized preparation of rural teachers will the practice cease. On the other hand, the comparatively large number continuing in the profession in Washington for more than five years is probably due to the good salaries and to the efforts made to house teachers properly by providing teachers' cottages. The average salaries paid teachers in the State are $105.79 for men and $83.85 for women. The remuneration is sufficient to secure for the State long and effective service.

The conditions revealed by figures 12 and 13, which disclose the longest tenure in one place. are similar to those already discussed. Long tenure in one place is held to be of such importance that several

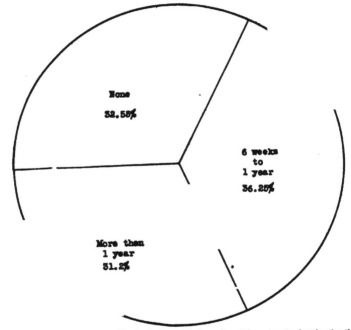

Fig. 9.—Per cent of teachers attending institutions while in service. (Elementary teachers in other than one-room schools.)

States—notably Wisconsin and Indiana—have passed laws recently to encourage teachers to continue indefinitely in the same community. These laws provide that the State, in addition to the salary supplied by the community, shall pay the teacher something like $5 monthly for the second year, $10 monthly for the third year, and $15 monthly for each subsequent year. A penalty clause is also attached to provide against local salary reduction to offset the State's contribution. Such a law is recommended for Washington.

Chapter XV.

SPECIAL PREPARATION FOR RURAL TEACHERS.

The educational needs of rural-school teachers have already been alluded to, but the committee believes the subject is important enough to warrant special discussion.

It is not sufficient that teachers in rural schools should have as much general education and professional skill as teachers in the elementary grades of the city schools. In addition they need a

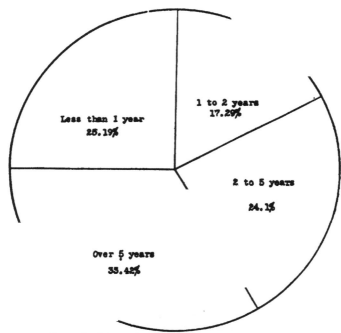

FIG. 10.—Teaching experience in years.   (Teachers in one-room schools.)

wider range of knowledge and a knowledge of some subjects not necessary for the success of teachers in elementary schools in the city. It has long been accepted that the schools must give the tools of learning—reading, writing, arithmetic, and elementary geography—and educate for the duties and responsibilities of citizenship. To direct this work teachers in country and city schools need practically the same educational preparation. Human interests and the fundamental requirements of good citizenship are substantially the same in city and country. But it is now agreed that the schools must also prepare children, to some extent at least, for their vocational life, and the demand that the schools shall perform this function more fully grows from year to year.

While in the cities the occupations of the masses of the people are more varied than in the country, the division of labor has been carried to a very high degree, and the year's work of very many people has been reduced to a constant repetition of a few simple processes, many, if not most, of which may be learned largely by imitation and continued with a fair degree of success without any very comprehensive knowledge of the fundamental principles involved. In the

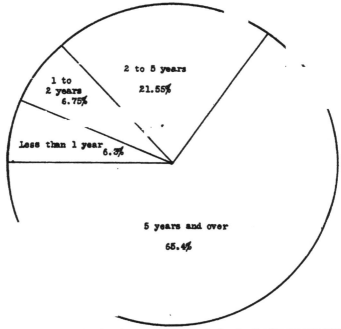

Fig. 11.—Total teaching experience in years. (Elementary teachers in other than one-room schools.

country, on the contrary, most men are engaged in one occupation, that of farming, and most women in making and caring for their country homes. In neither of these occupations has division of labor been carried very far, nor do they readily lend themselves to the application of this principle. The farmer who owns the farm which he cultivates (86.3 per cent of the farms in the State of Washington are operated by their owners, according to the Federal census of 1910, and only 13.7 per cent are operated by tenants) must, in order to do his work intelligently and to be sure of any degree of success, have a mastery of a wide range of very different processes to be applied under varying conditions from day to day and from season to season. He should have also a working knowledge of the physics and chemistry of the soil, of fertilizing and the means of preserving the fertility of the soil, of plant and animal life, of plant and animal breeding, of methods of tillage, and of harvesting, preserving, and storing crops of many kinds, of feeding and caring for different kinds of animals, of plant and animal diseases, of the operation, care, and repairing of all kinds of farm machinery, of such engineering as is required in

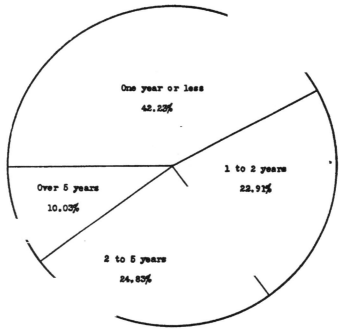

FIG. 12.—Longest tenure in one place. (Teachers in one-room schools.)

road building, terracing, draining, and irrigating, and in controlling small streams, of bookkeeping and accounting, marketing and many forms of rural economy, of the elementary principles of forestry, and of such forms of architecture, carpentry, and stone and brick masonry as are necessary for planning and building houses, barns, silos, sheds, fences, and gates.'

The task of the farmer's wife is to make the country home sanitary, convenient, comfortable—a fit place for herself and her husband to live in happily and for their children to be born and reared in. In this she can not have the help of sanitary inspectors and other useful agents of the more complex urban communities. She must know how to select and prepare a wholesome, balanced ration for the members of her family, how to clothe them most suitably and economically, how to care for the health of herself and her children without the constant help of the physician, and how to guide her children in their early mental and moral development. She must also know how to buy and sell to advantage a large variety of produce and household necessities, how to care for vegetable and flower gardens and poultry. She

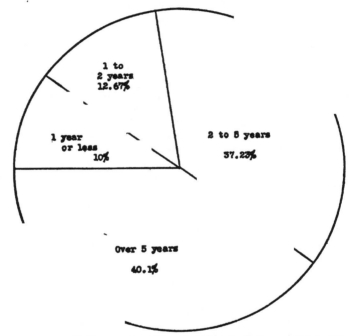

Fig. 13.—Longest tenure in one place. (Elementary teachers in other than one-room schools.)

should have such a knowledge of the general operation of the farm as will enable her to sympathize with her husband's work and to advise him in it; and it is always possible that she may be left the task of managing the farm alone and that the living and education of her children may depend upon her ability to do so successfully. All these things need to be known by the farmer and the farmer's wife, not only in process but also in principle, since through a knowledge of principles alone can one work intelligently under ever-changing conditions.

Only a small per cent of country boys and girls of Washington as yet go through the high schools. Therefore, whatever the schools are to do toward teaching them or putting them in the way of learning these principles and practices of their vocational life must be done in the elementary schools.

If the rural schools are to teach what country people need to know, the teachers of these rural schools must know these things also, and know how to teach them, and the schools in which the teachers are educated and trained must prepare for this work. It may be a large and difficult task, but there is no way to avoid it. It must be met squarely, or else the rural schools will fail in this very important function, demanded by modern life and changing social ideals. To prepare teachers for rural elementary schools, therefore, normal schools should give more extended and more practical courses in all the sciences that pertain to country life. For this they need larger equipment of laboratories and sufficient land for cultivation of farm crops, produce, and vegetables to enable them to demonstrate the more important processes of farming, gardening, and fruit growing. Each normal school should also have the use of a house to be fitted up and kept as a model country home. It should have the use of one or more rural schools to be made as nearly as possible into model schools for observation and practice, and should put itself and its students into close touch with as many schools as may be reached by any practicable means of transportation. The cost of equipment for preparing teachers for rural schools need not be very large, but it is important that it should be provided as early as possible. Already something has been done in this direction at each of the normal schools, but not enough at any one of them.

All persons preparing to teach in rural schools should be encouraged to remain through the entire three years of the normal-school course, as recommended later in this report.[1] Those who leave at the end of two years should be expected to continue their studies in the vocational side of their work and to return from time to time to the normal schools for further instruction. Since approximately half of the elementary teachers of the State are in rural schools, and all of these must be vocational teachers to some extent at least, this special preparation of rural teachers should be accepted by the normal schools as a large and important part of their work.[2]

---

[1] See Section III, p. 177 et seq.

[2] There is a growing demand for special teachers of gardening in city schools, gardening to be done in both school gardens and at the homes of the children, in both cases under the direction of the school. As this is a valuable phase of educational work for city children, and since the demand for teachers to direct such work will probably be permanent, the normal schools might well make provisions for their preparation. This might easily be done in connection with the preparation of rural teachers in agriculture. The State college might also prepare teachers for this work through the cooperation of its departments of agriculture and education.

Chapter XVI.

CERTIFICATION OF WASHINGTON TEACHERS.

Public-school teachers in Washington are certificated in several different ways. The higher institutions of learning are authorized by law to issue certificates and diplomas. City schools issue high-school, grammar-school, primary, and special certificates; and the county superintendents issue temporary and special certificates. The majority of the public-school teachers, however, are certified by the State superintendent of public instruction. The office of the State superintendent issues several thousand certificates annually. The centralization of certification through the superintendent's office on the basis of State-wide examination makes for uniformity and fairness. Nevertheless, the Washington system has serious defects which should be remedied. These are chiefly due to the fact that very few changes have been made in the method of certification since it was first established.

The following are the "common-school certificates" issued by State authority:

(a) Third-grade certificates;
(b) Second-grade certificates;
(c) First-grade primary certificates;
(d) First-grade certificates;
(e) Professional certificates;
(f) Permanent certificates;
    1. Permanent first-grade primary certificates;
    2. Permanent first-grade certificates;
    3. Permanent professional certificates;
(g) Life certificates.

The third-grade certificate is the lowest grade of certificate issued by the State. It may be procured by any person 18 years of age who has passed an examination in the common-school subjects, with minimum grades of 70 per cent in arithmetic and grammar, and 60 per cent in reading, penmanship and punctuation, United States history, physiology and hygiene, geography, theory and art of teaching, orthography, and Washington Manual. Almost any person coming out of the elementary schools can get a third-grade certificate by doing a small amount of outside reading. In the early days of the State's history, when teachers were few and difficult to obtain, such certificates were necessary; but this is no longer the case. It is shown elsewhere (p. 177 et seq.) that the professional schools of the State and other States should hereafter be able to supply enough professionally prepared teachers to obviate the necessity of resorting to recruits of low-grade certification.

A large number of the holders of these third-grade certificates are employed in the one-room rural schools of the State, and far too many find service in the other elementary schools. In a total of 1,737 teachers in one-room schools reporting to the committee (see fig. 14), 20.07 per cent hold third-grade certificates, while in a total of 4,269 other elementary teachers (see fig. 15) a little more than 3 per cent have similar certificates.

The most unfortunate feature of the law relating to certification is that third-grade certificates may, in actual fact, become permanent

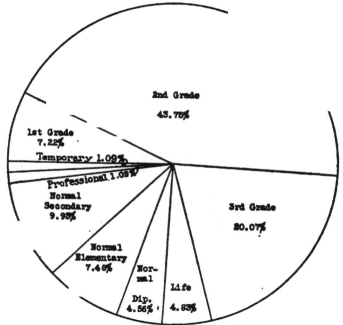

FIG. 14.—Washington certification. (One-room rural teachers.)

certificates if the holder takes advantage of paragraph 316, article 1 of the school code. Teachers who are able to make their third-grade certificates permanent under this "90 per cent clause" should be encouraged to secure a higher form of certificate.[1] However, as has been implied above, the committee is convinced that third-grade certificates are no longer necessary in this State. It recommends that they be discontinued at an early date.

---

[1] See table of examination for teachers' certificates, p. 148.

Respectively 43.7 per cent and 28.6 per cent of rural and other elementary teachers in the State teach on the second-grade certificate. The subjects required are the same as for the third-grade with the addition of music, but the standing required on examination is higher. The second-grade certificate should be the lowest grade of certificate granted hereafter, but the law under which it is renewed should be modified. The act reads:

This certificate shall be valid for two years, but may be renewed if, during the life of the certificate, the holder has complied with any one of the following conditions,

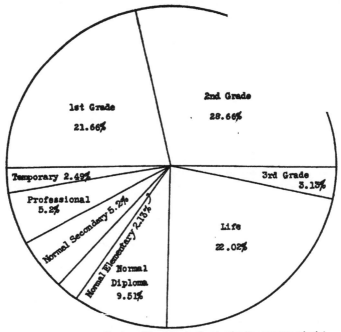

FIG. 15.—Washington certification. (Elementary teachers in other than one-room schools.)

to wit: (1) An attendance of one semester at an accredited school of higher education or of six weeks at an accredited summer school when satisfactory work was done in three subjects and certified to by the principal of such school. (2) Upon 16 months of successful teaching.

The renewal condition based on professional study in a school of higher education is excellent and should be the only basis for renewing the certificate, at least until the State can see its way clear to organize a thorough-going system for the further training of teachers in service.[1] Renewal "upon 16 months of successful teaching" is of

---

[1] See proposals made in Section III, p. 180 et seq.

doubtful value, for no supervising officer will refuse to subscribe to such renewal, except in extreme cases.

No teacher should be permitted to instruct in the new vocational subjects and the other subjects which have recently come to be regarded as essential in the curricula of modern schools who has not himself been examined in these subjects. Such is not the case under the laws of Washington. Many teachers are at the present time obliged to instruct in subjects with which they have little acquaintance and in which they have not been examined. The examination schedules for practically all the certificates issued under State authority are limited, for the most part, to the traditional courses of study. This appears from the analysis made by the State board of examiners set forth below:

Examination schedules for teachers' certificates.

Subjects for examination.	Grade of certificate and length of validity.			
	Temporary.	Third (1 year).	Second (2 years).	First primary (5 years).
All grades of 90 per cent or above on a valid certificate issued by this department or obtained during life of such certificate will be accepted so long as applicant has a certificate in full force.	No examination required; see rules of State board of education, Circular 10, sent upon application.	Reading, grammar, penmanship and punctuation, history of United States, physiology and hygiene, arithmetic, geography, theory and art of teaching, orthography, Washington State Manual.	Same as third grade, and music.	Same as second grade, and any 4 of the following: Nature study, drawing, literature, physical geography, psychology, history of education.

Subjects for examination.	Grade of certificate and length of validity.			
	First (5 years).	Professional (5 years).	Life, unless revoked for cause.	Permanent, unless revoked for cause.
All grades of 90 per cent or above on a valid certificate issued by this department or obtained during life of such certificate will be accepted so long as applicant has a certificate in full force.	Same as second grade, and any 4 of the following: Physics literature, algebra, physical geography, botany. psychology.	Same as first grade, and any 5 of the following not taken in securing a first-grade certificate: Plane geometry, geology, botany, zoology, civil government, psychology, history of education, bookkeeping, composition, general history, Latin, German, political economy.	Same as first grade, and any 10 of the following not taken in securing a first-grade certificate: Plane geometry, geology, botany, zoology, civil government, psychology, history of education, bookkeeping, composition, general history, Latin, German, political economy.	First-grade and professional certificates may be made permanent without additional examination.

Attention is called to the fact that not a single one of these certificates requires examination in the modern vocational subjects, and yet the outlined course of study for the common schools of the State of Washington, adopted February 21, 1910, includes manual training and household economics one hour per week throughout the eighth grade, and forestry, agriculture, or horticulture three days per week in the same year. In addition, nature study is given in the first and second years, and manners and morals are included as a general exercise throughout the year.

The committee recommends that the examination schedules be thoroughly revised to conform to the work actually required of the teachers in the schools.

It was disclosed above that fully one-fifth of all the rural and other elementary-school teachers in the State have no professional preparation. A large number of these persons have gained whatever knowledge they may possess about the business of teaching from pedagogical books, from brief summer institutes, and experimentation in the classroom. In the opinion of the committee the facilities for the training of teachers provided within the State, together with the supply of professionally prepared teachers coming to Washington from other States, are now adequate to warrant the imposition of a minimum professional requirement for all public-school teachers. Other States, for example Nebraska and Missouri, have laws to this effect. Washington might well follow their lead. If it should see fit to do so, the plan adopted should give the teachers in the field ample time to meet the new requirements. In order to work no hardship on anyone, five or six years from the time the act is passed might be allowed in which to procure the required professional preparation. But for specific recommendations as to legislation, see Section III, pp. 177 and 180.

The schools suffer probably as much from the insufficient academic preparation of the teachers as from any other cause. The traditional elementary curriculum does not furnish either the broad culture or the scientific and practical knowledge essential to the comprehension of modern civilization. No person whose academic preparation is limited to the elementary school has a sufficient foundation on which to build his teaching career. Indeed, graduation from an accredited four-year high school ought to be regarded as the minimum requirement for all the teachers in the State. It is the conviction of the committee that within a reasonable time no person should be granted a teacher's certificate who is not a graduate from a four-year high school. As in the case of professional preparation discussed above, teachers should be allowed ample time to meet this additional requirement. The necessary legislative provisions are suggested in Section III, p. 177, et seq.

Chapter XVII.

INSTRUCTION IN THE SCHOOLS.

The committee regrets that it has been unable, by reason of the limited time at its disposal, to study at first hand the content of the public-school courses and the methods and quality of instruction; for these matters furnish, after all, the final evidence of the efficiency of the schools. Under the circumstances the brief discussion in this chapter is necessarily based on documentary evidence mainly.

The common-school course of study.—The course adopted in 1910 for the rural and graded elementary schools of the State contains, in addition to the fundamental studies, a considerable number of subjects of great instructional and inspirational value, such as history and mythology, geography, literature, nature study and agriculture, and manual arts. Mention has already been made of the fact that teachers are not examined in all the subjects they are expected to teach. The extent to which teachers are actually unprepared in certain common-school subjects is indicated in the tables at the end of this section.

It may be said in passing, however, that of the teachers in one-room schools 264 teach agriculture, 85 manual training, 86 music and drawing, 71 high-school subjects, 41 history and civics, without preparation. Table 37 contains a similar statement with regard to the defective preparation of elementary teachers. Moreover, in view of the incompleteness of the reports, the numbers given probably represent only a small part of the teachers who are actually without preparation in the subjects listed.

The people of the open country and rural-minded villages need their own peculiar preparation for successful living. The course of study in use in Washington and in many other States is based largely on urban needs and on tradition. Some agriculture and some manual arts have been added recently to the already crowded course, much as a patch is applied to an old garment. What is needed is to renew the woof and the warp of the cloth, or, to change the figure, to have the new subject matter permeate the whole course of study as yeast leavens an entire lump. The revitalized rural-school curriculum must be based on what the farmer and his wife ought to know. In this way only can Washington expect to develop its greatest resource, the land. Even such a course of study will not and should not keep all the people on the land. Those who are innately city-minded will inevitably find their way to town. But the solution of the greatest problem in this State—the rural or agricultural problem—must lie largely in providing for the rural schools a course of study especially adapted to rural needs, and in permitting no one to teach in rural districts who has not been specifically prepared for this kind of work.

The committee recommends that a thoroughgoing study be made of the rural-school curriculum in the State, with a view to eliminating nonessentials and substituting instead those modern educational elements necessary to prepare people to live contented and remunerative lives in farm communities. The obligation of the normal schools to provide special courses for persons preparing to be rural teachers is discussed in Section III (p. 181).

TABLE 34.—*Rural-teacher preparation in higher academic and professional institutions.*

Counties.	University of Washington		Washington State College		Cheney State Normal School			Ellensburg State Normal School			Bellingham State Normal School			Holy Name Normal		College of Puget Sound			Whitman College		Whitworth College		Other Washington colleges		Prepared in other States — Collegiate rank		Normal school rank		Total number of teachers, prepared and unprepared				Total number required in one-teacher schools
	One or more summer sessions	One to three years regular	Graduate	One or more summer sessions	One to three years regular	Graduate	One or more summer sessions	One to three years regular	Graduate	One or more summer sessions	One to three years regular	Graduate	One or more summer sessions	One to three years regular	Graduate	One or more terms	One or more summer sessions	One to three years regular	Graduate	One or more terms	Graduate	One or more terms	Graduate	One or more terms	Graduate	Graduate	Less than graduate	Graduate	Less than graduate	Outside institutions attended exclusively	Washington institutions attended exclusively	Both State and outside institutions attended	Total professionally prepared	Total with no professional preparation	
Adams		3	1		3		5	5		1	1		1		4	1											3		5	13	26	3	42	7	56
Asotin	1	1		1				3					3	5														2	2	7	4	2	13	8	24
Benton	3	2	2	1			3	1	1	1			5	4						2							1	3		7	7	2	10	3	17
Chelan		1		1							3			3													3			7	17		24	9	38
Clallam								2					3	1	1			2									1			8	14	1	22	8	36
Clarke					2		1	1		2				7															2	7		1	17	17	43
Columbia	6	1	1	2			6	2					1	2													3			1	9		14	4	31
Cowlitz	1	1					4	1		4	1		2	2	1				1								4		5	16	6		14	20	40
Douglas	1	1	3		2		3	3		1			4	6	2		9												6	13	18	1	34	15	76
Franklin	3	1					5	2					4	9	2		1		2							2	2		6	6	21		45	8	62
Garfield	1						5	5		2			2	2				2									1		2	13	15		21	3	27
Grant	3	3	1	1	1					4			4	3				1									5			5	20	1	58	14	88
Gray's Harbor	3	2		1	1		2	2		1			2	2			1	3	1							3			2	18	40	3	59	21	90
Island	1		1	1		2							1	4			1	1											1	1	17		21	10	10
Jefferson	1	1								2			2	2				3				1					1			4	4		7	4	21
King	5	2		1	1		3	3		4			4	2	1		1	1								2	3		2	6	30	3	35	5	51
Kitsap	1	1			1		4	2		2	1		4	5			1		1							1	5			2	10	4	19	3	37
Kittitas	4	3		1				3		4			4	2	2		1		1							5			2	6	10	1	20	4	21
Klickitat	3	2	1							4			5	2	1		1		1							9	2			7	22	4	36	21	64
Lewis	1	1		3	1		3	29		38			5	12			2	5				1		23		6	1		3	9	50	4	58	6	71
Lincoln				2	1		3	3		8			5	4	2		3	1	1			1		6		2	1			8	71	1	24	14	119
Mason	1			1									9	2	1		1	1						5						8	18	1	26	6	31
Okanogan				1				2		1			3	3	1	1		2								1			1	4	20	2	32	9	59
Pacific	1	1	1										1	1		2	1			1		1		2			2			5	7	2	13	6	17
Ferry														6									1				1			3	7	2	15	7	26
San Juan	3	4	1					1					1	6	2		1	1				1		2		1	1			3	15	3	21	1	32

Skagit

Skamania

Snohomish

Spokane

Stevens

Thurston

Wahkiakum

Walla Walla

Whatcom

Whitman

Yakima

Pend Oreille

Total

Grand total

TABLE 35.—*Statistics affecting qualifications of Washington teachers in one-room schools*—PART I.

Counties	Number of teachers and grades taught.			Teachers holding Washington certificates, and number of each grade.									Number of teachers, with institutions attended one term or more.							Attended institute.		Attended institutions while in service.		
	Eight.	Less than eight.	Mixed with high school.	First grade.	Second grade.	Third grade.	Life.	Normal diploma.	Normal elementary.	Normal secondary.	Professional.	Temporary.	Collegiate.	Normal.	Collegiate and normal.	Night or correspondence.	High school and normal.	High school only.	Elementary school only.	Regular.	Irregular.	None.	Six weeks to one year.	More than one year.
Adams	27	20	4	4	18	13	3	4	3	8		2	15	11	2		15	6	2	43	3	21	17	13
Asotin	7	15		2	11	8		1		1	1		6	6	1		9	6	1	18		10	11	8
Benton	8	8	4	2	4	7				3	1	3	3	3			3	2	3	14	3	8	4	7
Chelan	10	21	9	4	18	8		1		3			9	11	2		7	5	1	30	8	18	11	9
Clallam	4	14	7	3	15	7			1	3			5	6		1	7	4		23	3	14	9	8
Clarke	20	23	2	4	17	14	2	1	2	5		3	5	8	2		4	11	10	33	1	28	6	8
Columbia	8	13	1	1	5	10	1	1	1	2		1	3	4	1		3	3	5	17	2	11	14	4
Cowlitz	21	23	6	3	20	13	2	1	1	6		1	4	9	1		14	21	5	35	3	19	17	7
Douglas	8	26	1	1	20	11	1	1	7	2			4	6	1		4	1	1	45	3	24	6	4
Ferry	3	18	2	2	9	7	2	3	4		1	1	4	11	2		8	4		20	1	14	12	3
Franklin	3	17	7	2	8	8	1	2	1	8			4	12	1		6	1	1	19	2	7	6	5
Garfield	18	12	3	1	11	13	7	2	4	6			2	24	2		8	4	2	65		18	12	6
Grant	30	46	1	2	33	13	2	1	8	1		1	17	12	1		6	1		21	8	27	35	13
Grays Harbor	8	11	1	1	6	4		1	6				2	5	1		3	4	2	10		4	6	4
Island	6	11	8	3	22	9			1	2			2	7			3	6		40	10	11	15	5
Jefferson	7	13	9	2	22	3		2	4	7		3	5	9	4		3	1	2	19	5	19	16	8
King	16	23	8	4	12	3	2	1	8	1			6	8	5		9	5	1	20	6	12	18	5
Kitsap	10	8		2	12	3	1	1	6	1			2	9	4		7	10	2	21	4	5	6	5
Kittitas	14	35	8	1	21	26	3	2	4	22			10	11	7	1	16	3	3	53	5	31	16	8
Klickitat	38	48	9	5	36	12	3	1	4				4	23	3		63		2	64	6	31	18	11
Lewis	52	14	4	6	37	12	4	3		3			7	9	2		12	14	2	86	22	46	2	26
Lincoln	9	21	3	6	13	9	2	2	5	3		1	6	13	4		8	6	3	26	4	13	13	8
Mason	13	10	1	1	15	12	3	1	1			1	2	9	4		6	5	3	33	2	10	4	5
Okanogan	5	31	5	1	13	11	4	1	4	1		1	5	19	4		7	1	2	26	4	19	14	6
Pacific	21	14	6	4	23	12	1	2	2				2	6	2		1	2	4	55	2	18	2	7
Pierce	6	9	1	2	9	4	1	2	5	3			1	5	1		3	1	7	23	1	9	8	2
San Juan	6	12	8	1	37	8	1	3	4	3			1	8	1		9	4	3	10		7	7	3
Skagit	12	9	5	2	10	2	4	4	10	1			5	26			26	5	2	24	2	6	3	8
Skamania	94	12	1	4	47	15	4	1	10	1			4	18	1		36	18	4	24	3	8	9	6
Snohomish	40	50	6	4	47	16	4	3	5	4		1	5	18	2		26	9	7	51	1	8	7	9
Spokane	34	31	3	3	35	16		1	5	4	2	1	12		2		22	9	5	66	3	37	19	12

Thurston	15	20	1	8	10	1	1	2	8	4	7						6	14		7		7	4	4	1	16	16	36	1	16	17	2
Wahkiakum	2	8	2	3	4	2	2	1			3			1			1			1	5	3		1	8	9	6	1	2
Walla Walla	9	22	2	4	12	1	5	1	3	1	6						7	6		9		3	1	5	3	31	13	20
Whatcom	17	11	1	8	53	3	20		3	3	5	8			1		1	8	3	15	8	8	3	1	1	107	53	12
Whitman	38	67	8	8	11	4	3		8	6	8	8			1	1	28	21	2	22	2	13	6	20	6	22	8	51	10
Yakima	10	10	2	3	11	1	2		2	1	2	2			1		9	1		7	3	1	1	3	3	22	11	8
Pend Oreille	12	13	3	4	15	3	2		2	3	2	1					3	10	1	9	2	2	3	3		24	10	4	7
Total	665	781	126	306	643	295	71	67	110	146	16	16		81	2	390	229	122	1,344	128	697	540	285
Grand total		1,472						1,470						1,472					1,482			1,472

TABLE 35.—*Statistics affecting qualifications of Washington teachers in one-room schools*—PART II.

Counties	Number of teachers and years taught				Longest tenure in same position				Teachers having persons dependent upon them				Number of teachers teaching certain subjects without preparation									Criticism by teachers on course of study	
	Less than one year	One to two years	Two to five years	Over five years	One year or less	One to two years	Two to five years	Over five years	None	One to two	More than two	Helping	Agriculture	Manual training and domestic science	Music or drawing	Printing	Writing	Horticultural science	History or civics	None	Nature study or geography	Favorable	Unfavorable
Adams	15	8	12	16	21	16	14		31	15	5		9	3	4		2	1	1	31	1	42	4
Asotin	4	2	11	5	7	9	8	1	13	3	3		7	1	2		3			8		17	2
Benton	5	3	6	10	9	7	7	1	9	6	6	3	2	1	5		2	1	1	6		31	2
Chelan	12	5	8	16	19	7	7	1	15	9	6	3	4	1	1		1	5	1	17		21	2
Clallam	7	3	7	10	17	4	2	1	16	7	6	2	8	1	3		1	1	1	21	1	31	3
Clarke	11	7	5	2	25	4	2		10	11	4	1	2	2	2		2	1	2	10		18	
Columbia	6	4	9	9	10	6	5		9	20	2		5	1	1				1	21		37	3
Cowlitz	8	9	7	17	35	3	3	2	14	18	9		9	2	4		1	1	2	35		41	8
Douglas	13	7	4	10	10	12	7		13	7	4		6	6	7		3	5	1	11		17	3
Ferry	6	4	3	10	12	4	1		10	6	4		5	4	1			1		6		27	6
Franklin	3	6	4	9	12	10	2		12	11	5		2	1	4	1		2	2	16		27	1
Garfield	6	2	6	10	26	9	3		36	25	8		6	2	4	1	1	4	1	40		25	
Grant	19	10	2	30	2	16	10	2	12	3	8	1	13	4	2		2	4	2	13		19	1
Grays Harbor	12	3	3	7	3	4	4	6	20	1	12	1	3	4	7	2	1	1	1	23		37	7
Island	3	3	3	11	2	3	7	7	5	5	7		2	3	1			3		11		13	
Jefferson	4	2	6	10	3	5	2	10	8	1	4		3	7	1		4	3		15		33	1
King	10	6	8	13	4	4	6	11	19	6	8		9	2	3		2	1		35		53	1
Kitsap	5	1	1	14	10	7	7	10	10	9	15		8	4	3		1	1	3	67		56	2
Kittitas	8	5	3	15	19	8	3	1	11	14	2	1	2	3	1		2			14		25	8
Klickitat	18	1	6	23	35	5	6		31	14	4		10	7	5	2	1	1		20		28	3
Lewis	13	11	13	9	10	15	21		37	38	3		17	8	4		3	1		34		32	8
Lincoln	26	22	29	27	35	19	37	2	58	15	8	1	20	7	6	4	2	1		19		37	2
Mason	4	8	8	7	3	10	16	6	9	7	2		6	2	2		1	3		12		26	4
Okanogan	9	5	7	17	10	7	12	7	20	13	4		7	4	2		2	3	2	34		28	4
Pacific	2	6	1	5	2	8	1		8	9	3		1	3	1			1		19		12	1
Pierce	17	4	10	25	31	19	7	8	20	12	8	2	14	7	1		4	2	1	12	3	40	3
San Juan	7	2	4	8	7	4	6	4	10	1	3	1	4	2	1	1	2	2		9		15	3
Skagit	6	5	5	8	6	2	6	4	2	4	2		3	1	2	2	1	3		17		14	5
Skamania	3	6	4	5	3	3	6	5	5	3	1		2	1	1		3	1		1		21	4
Snohomish	3	2	3	6	6	12	13		13	23	18		24	4	2	1		2	1	57		22	5
Spokane	20	13	25	28	61	23	13	1	44	32	16	2	24	2	3	1	5		8	17		44	4
Stevens	20	11	9	28	42	13	10		57	19	11	1	16	1	5	1		3	2	24		58	5

Thurston	9	7	7	13	14	14	8		17	12	7		6						1	24		83	8
Wahkiakum	1	2	4	5	4	5	3		7	8	1	1						2	1	11		11	1
Walla Walla	5	9	10	9	10	9	8		13	13	6	1	2	9	3					18	1	30	1
Whatcom	6	8	4	11	13	6	10		14	12	2	1	4			6	5	1	5	17	2	29	
Whitman	33	18	33	30	66	24	23		57	31	21	4	15	6	7		1	3	1	64	1	106	7
Yakima	4	2	6	11	9	10	3		10	8	4		2	1	1					16		19	
Pend Oreille	7	4		11	8	4	10	6	15	6	6	1			2					23	1	23	3
Total	371	256	354	492	633	338	367	148	715	455	306	21	264	85	88	25	46	71	41	863	11	1,306	138
Grand total	1,473			1,476					1,487				1,492							1,483			

TABLE 36.—*Preparation in higher academic and professional institutions of elementary teachers (other than one-room schools).*

Counties:

Adams
Asotin
Benton
Chelan
Clallam
Clarke
Columbia
Cowlitz
Douglas
Ferry
Franklin
Garfield
Grant
Grays Harbor
Island
Jefferson
King
Kitsap
Kittitas
Klickitat

Lewis.
Lincoln.
Mason.
Okanogan.
Pacific.
Pierce.
San Juan.
Skagit.
Skamania.
Snohomish.
Spokane.
Stevens.
Thurston.
Wahkiakum.
Walla Walla.
Whatcom.
Whitman.
Yakima.
Pend Oreille.

Total.

Grand total.

TABLE 37.—*Statistics affecting qualifications of Washington elementary teachers (other than of one-room schools)*—PART I.

Counties.	Number of grades taught.			Washington certification.									Institutions attended one term or more.						Institutions attended while in service.		
	Four or more.	Two to four.	Less than two.	First grade.	Second grade.	Third grade.	Life.	Normal diploma.	Normal elementary.	Normal secondary.	Professional.	Temporary.	Collegiate.	High school and normal.	High school.	Elementary only.	Normal.	Collegiate and normal.	None.	Six weeks to one year.	One year or more.
Adams	11	11	7	3	12		4	4	1	3	2	1	2	10	10		13	4	7	12	10
Asotin	2	10	13	3	11	2	5	1		1	1	1	5	6	6	1	3	8	3	11	11
Benton	8	20	19	4	11	4	9	2	1	6	2	1	8	12	1	2	14	16	14	19	14
Chelan	19	39	20	19	35	4	14	6	1	3	7	1	18	12	1	5	23	30	22	21	46
Clallam	9	13	16	7	7	1	10	2		3	1	1	8	9	2	2	7	9	12	11	14
Clarke	10	74	19	32	45	5	6	4		6	7	1	30	13	14	8	21	14	47	29	27
Columbia	5	15	11	7	15		8	4		1	1		4	7			7	7	6	13	12
Cowlitz	14	32	10	3	26		7	2	1	8	1		10	10		8	10	7	25	18	21
Douglas	8	10	3	11	13	1	9	2	1	2			7	14	10		6	1	9	13	9
Ferry	5	3	6		4	2		1		2				4		2	2	2	9	4	2
Franklin		12	1	8	4		6		1	2				6		5	5	5		10	8
Garfield	8	5	1	3	5	1	5			4	2		2	1	9	2	11	4	12	7	3
Grant	8	26	6	2	8		2	1	1	1	1	1	2	8			13	3	8	15	11
Grays Harbor	11	67	61	37	51	4	20	7	2	6		2	28	25	6		45	30	53	59	23
Island	24	4	6	2	6	6		11	2	2		3	2	3			2	3	3		1
Jefferson	2	4	2	2	2		2	1					2	7		6	3	2	2	3	
King	87	424	474	234	141	10	240	49		10	46	15	272	209	45	6	214	224	283	387	317
Kitsap	8	73	13	13	36	8	19	10	4	9	1		15	18			32	11	29	20	26
Kittitas	8	38	38	11	16	4	21	13	7	5	1	2	13	24	5	2	29	11	20	23	16
Klickitat	6	13	11	5	13	3	13	3	5	1		1	2	3	4	2	2	2	12	11	8
Lewis	10	78	47	19	40	2	20	27	8	17	8	5	21	36	9		52	19	45	53	34
Lincoln	7	31	14	9	14	1	6	10	2	5	1		5	15	5		15	8	12	17	11
Mason	8	9	3	9	8	2	1	4		2	1		4	5	4		10	2	12	7	7
Okanogan	13	27	7	7	14	5	6	4	2	5	1	5	8	7	3	2	22	15	18	14	17
Pacific	6	42	3	14	9	2	6	11	4	4	1	9	11	12	2	4	9	17	8	25	25
Pierce	90	171	121	113	74	10	80	28	4	7	37	2	96	76	12	1	92	83	130	110	123
San Juan		5		1		7	3	19		2				5				1		3	1
Skagit	35	32	32	25	28	5	22	10	4	11	1	21	15	23	4	2	40	19	62	32	25
Skamania	1	10	1	1	7	5	5	3	1		1	3	1	5	1	4	1	1	3	2	3
Snohomish	44	193	39	30	149	6	20	22	4	18	26	1	19	39	14	1	68	88	186	92	68
Spokane	46	229	228	65	22	5	21	19	7	6	2		65	21	31	5	159	62	22	222	69
Stevens	14	20	13	5	21	6	6	3	1	6		2	13	15	8	2	14	22	16	10	21
Thurston	12	47	13	14	16	5	6	12	4	5		3	5	12	6	5	13	8	19	21	25
Wahkiakum	4	5	4		4	1	2			1	2	1	1	2			4	9	9	3	9

Walla Walla	15	53	23	28	3	30	5	1	6	5	4	30	16	3	1	28	24	28	37	40
Whatcom	96	92	37	48	7	70	37	10	31	5	1	23	31	6	2	55	44	64	77	72
Whitman	33	57	26	68	11	17	11	3	5	8	5	17	46	3		40	28	30	50	54
Yakima	20	81	38	70	7	27	19	7	9	8	6	38	42	4		57	49	62	56	74
Pend Oreille	2	9	2	7		6	3	7	1	1		2	1	1	1	2	4	7		3
Total	719	1,568	846	1,118	122	869	371	83	203	203	97	830	970	197	73	1,190	870	1,346	1,499	1,292
Grand total	4,157					3,901						4,130							4,136	

TABLE 37.—*Statistics affecting qualifications of Washington elementary teachers (other than of one-room schools)*—PART II.

Counties	Teaching experience in years — Less than one year	One to two years	Two to five years	Five years and over	Longest tenure in same position — One year or less	One to two years	Two to five years	Over five years	Institution attended — Regular	Irregular	Persons dependent on teacher — None	One or more	Helping	Subjects taught without preparation — Kindergarten	Primary	High school subjects	Manual training	Domestic science	Agriculture	Others	None	Criticism of course — Favorable	Unfavorable	Sex of teacher — Male	Female
Adams																										
Asotin																										
Benton																										
Chelan																										
Clallam																										
Clarke																										
Columbia																										
Cowlitz																										
Douglas																										
Ferry																										
Franklin																										
Garfield																										
Grant																										
Grays Harbor																										
Island																										
Jefferson																										
King																										
Kitsap																										
Kittitas																										
Klickitat																										
Lewis																										
Lincoln																										
Mason																										
Okanogan																										
Pacific																										
Pierce																										
San Juan																										
Skagit																										
Skamania																										
Snohomish																										
Spokane																										
Stevens																										
Thurston																										
Wahkiakum																										

Walla Walla	8	7		6	13	34	50	96	6	68	34	0			1	8	14	84	92	10	12	90
Whatcom	19	57	45	24	35	105	96	252	8	100	120	20	3		5	5	5	108	215	15	34	205
Whitman	5	12	135	12	17	68	43	154	2	81	59	1	1		1	2	2	110	127	7	20	174
Yakima	18	16	73	22	32	68	69	184	7	105	74	12	1		1	2	4	163	180	11	18	173
Pend Oreille	1	2	117	3	2	7	7	18	1	11	8		2		2	1	1	13	18	1	1	18
Total	259	277	887	415	526	1,547	1,667	3,639	502	2,064	1,583	236	25		72	96	138	186	3,510	3,858	259	517	3,662
Grand total			4,116		4,155			4,141			4,143		7	41		4,060				4,109

SUMMARY OF RECOMMENDATIONS DEALING WITH THE PUBLIC-SCHOOL SYSTEM.

1. A comparative study of State systems of taxation to ascertain a fair and equitable basis for scaling up the State and county taxes levied in Washington.

2. A revision of the system of apportioning the current State school fund and the county fund.

3. A revision of the qualifications and salaries of county superintendents.

4. The provision of professional supervision in rural communities and the subdivision of the counties for supervision purposes.

5. The encouragement of long teaching tenures by supplementing salaries on the basis of years taught in the same community.

6. The abolition of third-grade certificates.

7. The revision of the requirements for renewing second-grade certificates until such certificates are finally discontinued.

8. The revision of the examination schedules for the several kinds of certificates.

9. The establishment of minimum professional requirements for all persons teaching in this State.

10. The establishment of minimum academic requirements for all persons teaching in this State.

11. The thoroughgoing revision of the common-school course of study, and the adoption of a distinctively rural course of study for schools of the open country.

Chapter XVIII.

GENERAL CONSIDERATIONS.

The State normal schools of Washington are, in law and common practice, an integral part of the State system of higher education. Their function in this system should properly be determined by State needs rather than by sectional or local desires. Education is the business of the State. The institutions in which its teachers are prepared are supported by all the citizens of the State. The State, therefore, has the right to demand that these institutions be so administered as to give to the people the largest possible returns in well-prepared teachers, without waste of funds or needless duplication of courses and expensive equipment. To the attainment of this end the special fields of the normal schools and also of the departments of education at the University of Washington and the Washington State College must be clearly defined.

With respect to the sphere of the normal schools the State code provides (sec. 11, par. 57, ch. 2) that:

The State board of education shall prescribe courses of study for the normal schools of the State as follows: (1) An elementary course of two years; (2) a secondary course of two years; (3) advanced courses of two and three years; (4) a complete course of five years; (5) an advanced course of one year for graduates from colleges and universities. Upon the satisfactory completion of any one of these courses, a student shall be awarded an appropriate certificate or diploma as follows: Upon the completion of the elementary course, a certificate to be known as an elementary normal school certificate, which shall authorize the holder to teach in any elementary school for a period of two years; upon the completion of the secondary course, a certificate to be known as a secondary normal school certificate, which shall authorize the holder to teach in the common schools of the State for a period of three years; upon the completion of any advanced course, a diploma to be known as a normal school diploma, which shall authorize the holder to teach in the common schools of the State for a period of five years, and upon satisfactory evidence of having taught successfully for three years such person shall receive a life diploma countersigned by the superintendent of public instruction.

Under the code, therefore, only elementary certificates limit the holders to service in the elementary schools. All other certificates authorize the holders to teach in the "common schools" of the State, which (sec. 1, par. 1, ch. 1) include "high and elementary

165

schools, schools for special help and discipline, schools or departments for special instruction."

On the other hand the State board of education—in which is vested the power to examine and accredit secondary schools, as well as to prescribe the courses of study for the normal schools, and to investigate and approve the requirements for entrance to and graduation from the normal schools—can to some extent limit the force of the normal-school certificates and diplomas. By action taken at a meeting held December 29, 1910, the State board virtually excluded normal-school graduates from teaching in fully accredited high schools. An excerpt from the minutes reads:

No school shall be accredited which does not have three or more teachers giving their entire time to the work of instruction. The scholastic preparation of any high-school teacher shall be such as to especially qualify him to give instruction in the subjects which he teaches. The minimum scholastic attainment, except for teachers of special subjects, should be graduation from a standard college, except in the case of instructors who, by reason of native ability, experience, and scholastic training, are considered by the inspector as having qualifications equivalent to such graduation. In no case shall the State board accept the work of an instructor who shall have scholastic training less than graduation from the advanced course of the State normal schools of Washington or its equivalent; *Provided,* That this rule shall not disqualify any teacher employed in high-school work in this State prior to January 1, 1911.

Before examining in detail the present status of the Washington State normal schools and suggesting changes of policy, the committee desires to lay down a few general premises bearing upon the fundamental purposes and limitations of all normal schools.

The first efforts to prepare elementary school teachers in the United States were made about 75 years ago in New York State, which subsidized a few of its private academies for this important task. Shortly afterwards Massachusetts and other States began to prepare elementary and grammar school teachers in the first regular normal schools. At that time teachers needed for the academies (there being practically no other high schools) were trained for the most part in the colleges and universities. The policy thus established has been adhered to consistently down to the present time in the northeastern section of the country. The replies to a recent questionnaire on normal-school functions show that all the normal schools in New England and New York and practically all in Pennsylvania confine their energies to the preparation of teachers for schools below high-school rank, leaving the training of high-school teachers to the departments of education in colleges and universities.

In the Middle West and West the normal schools have generally developed contemporaneously with the State universities and colleges and have often become well established as the chief institutions for teacher training, while the universities were struggling to lay good foundations for college courses in arts and sciences. In some of these States the normal schools have developed into colleges of education, competing for prestige and patronage with the schools of education in the universities and colleges.

From the point of view of the economical and effective use of the State's educational machinery, the policy represented by the northeastern States is unquestionably the wiser one. The teaching force and physical equipment of normal schools all over the country have been selected and the general professional atmosphere developed with a view to one paramount purpose, namely, the training of elementary teachers. Whatever the ambitions of certain institutions, the momentum of the normal school is in this direction. The peculiar and exacting nature of this task prevents the successful adaptation of the normal school to secondary ends. The committee's dictum on this point is based on the study of many normal schools in all parts of the country. It is convinced that not until the normal schools of a State have completely fulfilled their major function, the preparation of elementary teachers, may they profitably devote their surplus energies and equipment to preparing teachers for higher schools. Normal schools have not satisfied this major function so long as the State is obliged to draw for part of its teachers upon the professionally unprepared, who enter the service by the examination route, or so long as the normal schools are unable to give a specialized preparation to both rural and other elementary teachers.

Moreover, certain other considerations should not be forgotten. The physical equipment required in preparing teachers for elementary schools is comparatively inexpensive; but the laboratories and other equipment needed to prepare teachers for high schools are much more costly. For a normal school to provide facilities for higher teacher training often entails an expense out of proportion to the results attained. Schools which embark upon this enterprise generally fall victims also to another tendency equally calculated to defeat their main purpose. The attention of the stronger members of their staffs is concentrated upon a small group of advanced students while the younger pupils are left to the care of the less efficient instructors.

A point may be reached in the growth of any normal school when very great numbers of students result in loss of efficiency through crowded classes, overworked instructors, and particularly through strained training-school facilities. In no school is the intimate touch of instructor and student so important as in the normal school. France limits its normal-school attendance to about 100 students per school; Denmark has 20 normal schools for elementary teachers, the attendance at any one seldom reaching 100 students. Similar conditions prevail in other European countries.

The school of education in the University of Washington antedates the establishment of the normal schools; but so great has been the pressure of the other activities in this institution and in the State college that until recently educational courses have not had much opportunity for development. Even yet the facilities for practice teaching are meager and must be greatly improved if the university and college are to give adequate preparation to high-school teachers. Meanwhile Ellensburg and Cheney State Normal Schools were established and more recently the school at Bellingham. The normal schools have devoted most of their energies to the elementary school field, although quite a number of graduates have gone into important high-school positions and supervisory work. The time is now evidently at hand when the State must determine whether these schools shall be permitted to develop into teachers' colleges—free to prepare teachers of all kinds—or shall be limited to a definite field. In the following chapters the committee sets forth its findings, based on a study of the three normal schools and the present need for well-trained teachers in the State.

Chapter XIX.

TEACHERS TRAINED IN NORMAL SCHOOLS AND OTHER INSTITUTIONS.

The following table, in addition to other interesting information, gives in column 5 the amount spent for normal schools for each 100 children of school age, and in column 6 the amount spent for normal schools for each $1,000 spent for public schools in all the States. It appears that Washington ranks fifth in column 5 and twenty-seventh in column 6. The State is liberal in its support of normal schools, judged on the basis of the number of children to be served. Compared with the support given the other parts of the public-school system, however, the normal schools are not very generously supported.

TABLE 38.—*Value of property in the various States—Expenditures for normal schools.*

States.	Total value of property in millions.	Value of property for each child 5 to 18 years of age (1913).	Number of adults for each 100 children 5 to 18 years of age (1910).	Number of men 21 years and over for each 100 children 5 to 18 years of age (1910).	Amount spent for normal schools for each 100 children 5 to 18 years of age (1913–14).	Amount spent for normal schools for each $1,000 spent for public schools (1912–13).[3]
North Atlantic Division:						
Maine	1,030	$5,900	241	120	$77.57	$25
New Hampshire	613	6,300	252	123	46.95	25
Vermont	497	9,500	237	119	23.89	10
Massachusetts	5,753	7,300	246	116	61.71	19
Rhode Island	893	6,600	231	111	50.71	25
Connecticut	2,154	7,900	231	115	47.35	16
New York	21,913	9,900	239	117	23.41	8
New Jersey	5,362	8,100	222	110	22.63	8
Pennsylvania	14,137	6,900	208	105	12.53	5
North Central Division:						
Ohio	8,552	7,300	227	113	8.18	[1]3
Indiana	4,951	7,200	211	106	20.88	9
Illinois	14,596	10,000	213	108	43.36	14
Michigan	5,169	7,100	214	109	61.14	20
Wisconsin	4,282	6,400	183	93	157.41	58
Minnesota	5,267	8,900	185	99	48.50	17
Iowa	7,437	12,700	195	98	4.40	[1]2
Missouri	5,546	6,300	195	98	39.22	27
North Dakota	2,088	10,900	166	93	93.72	47
South Dakota	1,331	7,500	175	96	85.95	34
Nebraska	3,605	10,700	182	95	77.75	28
Kansas	4,394	9,400	190	98	66.28	24
South Atlantic Division:						
Delaware	294	5,700	215	107	....	10
Maryland	2,002	5,700	196	94	14.07	
Virginia	2,175	3,400	153	74	36.16	28
West Virginia	2,180	5,800	161	84	42.46	35
North Carolina	1,745	2,200	133	63	23.46	37
South Carolina	1,301	2,500	124	58	23.32	43
Georgia	2,299	2,600	137	66	18.30	21
Florida	1,015	4,300	165	87	....	
South Central Division:						
Kentucky	2,152	3,100	160	79	23.74	24
Tennessee	1,834	2,700	152	74	21.16	25
Alabama	2,050	2,900	138	67	14.77	20
Mississippi	1,306	2,100	160	65	7.04	18
Louisiana	2,067	3,800	144	70	18.57	15
Texas	6,552	5,000	142	72	19.89	14
Arkansas	1,758	3,400	139	70	16.60	21
Oklahoma	4,321	7,300	145	78	36.86	34
Western Division:						
Montana	1,113	12,300	261	165	64.77	9
Wyoming	345	10,200	269	179	....	
Colorado	2,286	11,100	231	125	19.36	6
New Mexico	502	4,700	162	88	62.44	52
Arizona	487	8,600	213	129	210.30	52
Utah	735	6,300	160	85	....	
Nevada	441	28,400	269	180	....	
Idaho	591	5,900	190	113	93.09	24
Washington	3,055	10,400	255	151	90.19	16
Oregon	1,843	11,100	253	148	26.05	[2]6
California	8,023	15,500	301	169	108.66	13

[1] Cents not included.
[2] Amounts spent for public normal education not included.
[3] Recent reorganization accounts for low figures.

Several questions will naturally arise in the mind of any citizen. Does the State get proportionately good returns from its investment? Are the teachers trained in the normal schools fitted to serve the farmers' and the fruit growers' children as well as the children of merchants and bankers? All the people of Washington help to maintain the schools and the children of all the people should have equal opportunities to share in the benefits of the State's investment.

The section on the public-school system gives in detail an analysis of the number and kind of teachers necessary to supply the needs of the State. In 1914–15, 9,068 teachers were required for the rural, other elementary, and high schools. The salaries paid are attractive, in 1914–15 averaging $105.79 per month for male teachers and $83.85 per month for women. Teachers remain longer in the profession than formerly, and teaching in the State appears to be approaching a professional status. Although the State is growing in population, and consequently needs annually a larger number of teachers,

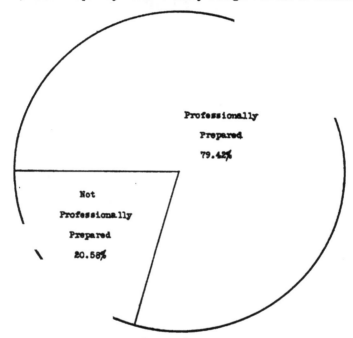

FIG. 16.—Per cent of rural teachers professionally prepared and not prepared.

the actual number of new teachers required is for the present about stationary—ranging from 1,000 to 1,200. Probably this condition will continue, as a result of the growing stability in the profession, the increasing tenures, and good salaries.

It has already been pointed out that large numbers of public school teachers have had insufficient or defective professional training and that many are teaching subjects for which they have had no regular preparation. (See Sec. II, p. 133 and p. 150). Figures 16 and 17 present a graphical recapitulation of some of these facts. They show that 20.58 per cent of all rural teachers and 5 per cent of all other elementary teachers have no professional preparation. It might be added that many others have had only as much as can be secured at an institute or summer school. It seems patent to the committee that, if the State is to rid itself of the very serious handicap to the

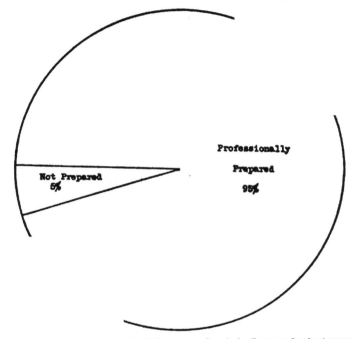

Fig. 17.—Per cent of elementary teachers (other than rural) professionally prepared and not prepared.

effectiveness of its public school system which this large body of untrained teachers imposes, it must provide in, or through the agency of, the normal schools for the further academic and professional training of elementary teachers in the service.

The following table shows the kinds of certificates and the number of each kind in force in the State in 1914:

TABLE 39.—*Teachers' certificates in force in Washington in 1914.*

Kind of certificate.	Number.	Per cent.
1. State certificate...	57	0.66
2. State university normal diploma...........................	215	2.50
3. State college normal diploma..............................	50	.58
4. Normal elementary..	190	2.21
5. Normal secondary...	334	3.90
6. Normal advanced..	555	6.46
7. Life certificate..	709	8.96
8. Professional...	288	3.35
9. Permanent first grade......................................	634	7.38
10. First grade...	1,276	14.85
11. Second grade..	2,471	28.79
12. Third grade..	848	9.87
13. Special..	373	4.34
14. Temporary...	539	6.16
Total...	8,589	100.00

The normal schools have furnished 1,079, or 12.57 per cent, of these certificates and the State university and State college 265, or 3.08 per cent. To be sure many teachers have been in attendance at the normal schools who did not complete any special courses, and therefore have received no school diploma or certificate. The following table gives the total number of diplomas and certificates issued by the normal schools in 1914–15:

TABLE 40.—*Total number of certificates and diplomas issued by the normal schools in 1914–15.*

Schools.	Life diplomas.	Diplomas.	Secondary certificates.	Elementary certificates.	Total.
Cheney.......................................	88	107	100	62	357
Ellensburg...................................	59	61	28	32	180
Bellingham...................................	123	202	179	112	616

This total of 1,153 diplomas and certificates does not represent an equal number of new teachers, since the 270 life diplomas were granted to successful teachers in service. Many of the remaining 883 were former teachers. Probably the number of new candidates who went forth from the normal schools last year did not exceed 600. Of these, only 370 were full graduates with the normal-school diploma. When to these are added less than 100 new candidates entering the profession during the year from the university and State college, it is clearly evident that the field of elementary-teacher training is not fully occupied by the professional schools of the State, without reference to the question as to whether or not the work is properly divided among them.

Figures 18 and 19 show that of the rural and other elementary teachers reporting academic and professional preparation received in the State a surprisingly large number have attended the university and colleges. Thus nearly one-third of all teachers in one-room rural schools have been in attendance some time at the colleges, as have nearly 47 per cent of all other elementary teachers. It has already been recommended that the practice which these figures indicate of relying on the colleges for the professional preparation of elementary teachers should be discontinued. These institutions do not have the training-school facilities or school atmosphere essential to the best results in elementary-teacher training. But it

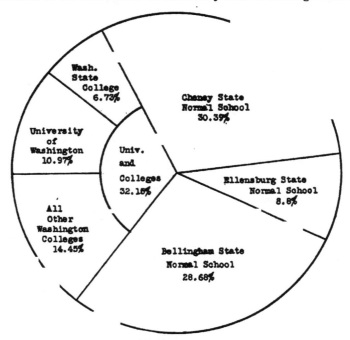

FIG. 18.—Preparation in Washington institutions. (Teachers of one-room schools.)

should at the same time be recognized that the full occupation by the normal schools of the field of elementary-teacher training can not be brought about until the State decides to demand definite standard academic and professional requirements of all persons teaching in the schools of the State.

Meanwhile, it is pertinent to inquire to what extent have the normal schools contributed high-school teachers. The answer is given in the table on the following page.

TABLE 41.—*High-school teachers trained in Washington institutions and in institutions in other States.*

	Male.	Female.	Post-graduate.	Graduate.	Partial course.	Elementary course.	Summer school.	Net total.
Totals......................	967	960	35	1,818	696	67	52	1,947
University of Washington.............			25	351	156		36	582
Washington State College........				147	68		6	278
Other Washington colleges.........				81	82		1	104
Cheney State Normal School........				44		34	3	71
Ellensburg State Normal School.....				11		14		26
Bellingham State Normal School.....				46		19	6	71
Colleges in other States...........				907	237			
Normal schools in other States.....				231	90			
Outside institutions exclusively.....								949
Washington institutions exclusively.								606
Both outside and State institutions.								274
Training not given..............								48
Normal schools not named........								56
Colleges not named..............								14

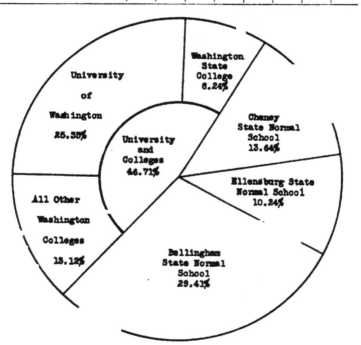

FIG. 19.—Preparation in Washington institutions. (Elementary teachers in other than one-room schools.)

The table shows that 949 Washington high-school teachers have received their preparation in higher institutions outside the State; that only 606 have been prepared wholly in this State; and that

274 have both State and extra-State preparation. But the outstanding fact is that 1,485 high-school teachers are university and college graduates, while only 332 are normal-school graduates. Of the teachers prepared wholly in Washington, 579 are graduates of the university and the various colleges, while only 101 are graduates from the normal schools. Some of both groups have, of course, attended both college and normal school. Up to the present time, therefore, somewhat less than one-fifth of all the secondary-school teachers trained in Washington institutions have had only normal-

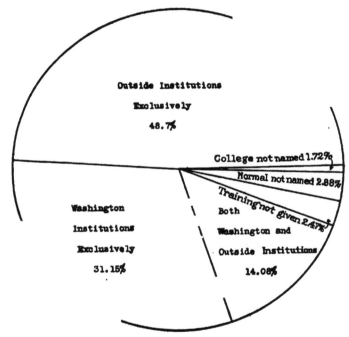

Fig. 20.—Per cents of high-school teachers prepared in Washington institutions and in institutions outside the State.

school preparation. This analysis is reenforced graphically in figures 20 and 21.

Chapter XX.

STANDARDS AND PROPOSED COURSES.

The committee proposes at this point to summarize what seem reasonable standards for a satisfactory State system of teacher preparation, standards which might serve to determine the future policy of this State.   Indeed, it is believed that in their essential features these standards might be applied with profit in most other States also.   The summary is followed in this and the succeeding chapter by a series of recommendations designed to bring the practice of the Washington State normal schools into harmony with the proposed standards.

1. The State should require certain definite academic and professional attainments of all teachers.

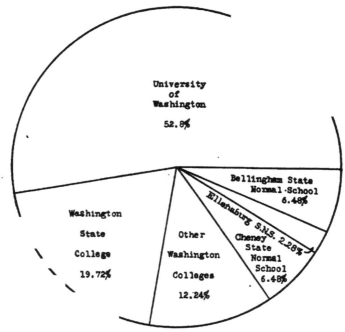

FIG. 21.—Per cents of high-school teachers prepared in various Washington institutions.

2. The entrance requirements of the State normal schools should gradually be raised to graduation from a four-year accredited high-school course.

3. The lowest grade of certificate to be issued by the normal schools after 1921 should represent two years of study above high-school graduation.   After 1922 the normal diploma should be given only to those who have finished satisfactorily a full course of three years.

4. The ultimate standard of attainment for all persons teaching in the State should be graduation from an accredited high school and at least two years of professional preparation.

5. The process of elimination should be gradual, to permit teachers in service to meet the new requirements without undue hardship.

6. The normal schools should organize thoroughgoing extension courses for the teachers in service.[1]

7. The normal schools should recognize a special obligation to provide appropriately trained teachers for rural communities.

8. The normal schools should offer differentiated courses of study representing two and three years of work above high-school graduation.

9. The principal function of the normal schools should be the preparation of elementary teachers; while the principal function of the departments of education of the State university and the colleges should be the preparation of high-school teachers.

To secure the establishment of the first five of these standards, the committee recommends:

1. That, beginning with the first quarter of the school year 1917-18, the first year of the elementary course and the first year of the complete course as now given be discontinued, and that for that year the minimum requirement for admission to any regular course in a State normal school be made the completion of three full years of the course of an accredited high school or its equivalent.

2. That, beginning with the first quarter of the school year 1918-19, the second year of the elementary course, the second year of the complete course as now given, and the first of the secondary course, be discontinued and that thereafter the completion of a course of four years in an accredited high school or its equivalent be required for admission to any regular course in a State normal school.

3. That after the close of the summer session of 1921 all certificates given for the completion of courses representing less than two years of study after the completion of a high-school course of four years be discontinued.

4. That after the close of the summer session of 1922 a certificate be awarded for the completion of a full course of two years, 72 weeks, above the high-school course of four years, or its equivalent, and a normal-school diploma for the completion of a full course of three years, 108 weeks, above the high-school course of four years.

5. That since there will be for a long time in the service of the elementary schools of the State many teachers of less academic and

---

[1] The principal features of the Iowa system of normal-school extension, which is one of the best conceived and most successful, are as follows:

It is exclusively aimed to supplement the previous training of teachers. To this end, study centers are organized in as many localities as possible (94 out of 99 counties now have them). Meetings are held on Saturdays, usually in a high-school building and under the direction of the county superintendent of schools. About four hours in the morning and afternoon combined are devoted to the weekly sessions. Heads of departments at the State Teachers' College, and specially qualified local teachers, city superintendents, and other persons conduct instruction at these centers. The whole extension enterprise is under a director, who is a member of the staff of the State Teachers' College. The subject matter studied comprises the usual subjects of the school curriculum.

professional preparation than will be required by the higher standards in use after 1922, special provision be made at the summer sessions of the normal schools for these teachers, and that such irregular courses be offered as may be necessary to meet their needs. All such teachers should be required to attend the summer sessions of some normal school, university, or college for the full term at least once in two years.

The following figures indicate that but a small number of the present matriculants of the three schools would be affected by the first two of the proposed changes. At Cheney, in a total attendance of 605 students, 57 fall below four-year high-school rank; in a total of 962, at Bellingham, 116 are below high-school graduation, 39 being reported as having preparation equivalent to that of fourth-year high-school pupils; in a total of 322 at Ellensburg, 88 are below high-school graduation, and 30 of these entered as fourth-year pupils. In other words, in an aggregate attendance of 1,899 at the three schools, 261 are below high-school graduation. Many of this class of students are mature people, practical teachers, who in their earlier years were deprived of high-school facilities. Under the new plan, these teachers would be provided for by the normal-school extension service recommended in the next chapter, and need not seek the normal schools unless ready to take the required courses.

Below are suggested differentiated two and three year courses based on graduation from a four-year accredited high school. Courses of this general type are contemplated in standard number 8 above.[1]

TWO-YEAR COURSE.

	Credits.
Professional work	40
Academic work	20
Free electives	20

THREE-YEAR COURSE.

Professional subjects	40
Academic subjects	40
Free electives	40

SPECIALIZED TWO-YEAR COURSES.

Kindergarten course.

Professional subjects:

Observation and practice teaching	10
Educational psychology	5
Educational sociology	5
Kindergarten practice	5
Special methods for kindergarten	10
Class management	5
Total	40
General subjects, including music, drawing, expression, and physical education.	20
Electives	20

---

[1] These courses were prepared in conference by the normal-school presidents of the State.

Primary course.

Professional subjects:	Credits.
Observation and practice teaching	10
Educational psychology	5
Educational sociology	5
Primary methods	5
Special methods for primary grades	10
Class management	5
Total	40
General subjects, including music, drawing, expression, and physical education	20
Electives	20

Grammar-school course.

Professional subjects:	
Observation and practice teaching	10
Educational psychology	5
Educational sociology	5
Grammar-grade methods	5
Special methods for the upper grades	10
Class management	5
Total	40
General subjects, including music, drawing, expression, physical education, sociology, economics, and government	20
Electives	20

Rural-school course.

Professional subjects:	
Observation and practice teaching	10
Educational psychology	5
Rural sociology	5
Rural-school methods	5
Special methods for rural schools	10
Class management	5
Total	40
General subjects, including music, drawing, agriculture, and physical education	20
Electives	20

THREE-YEAR SPECIALIZED COURSES.

Professional subjects:	
Educational psychology	8
Educational sociology	4
Methods of teaching	10
Class management	4
Observation and practice teaching	10
Economics or social science	4
Total	40
Academic work	40
Electives, such as manual training or home economics, public-school music or public-school art, physical education and play, etc	40
Total	120

Chapter XXI.

EXTENSION AND THE FURTHER TRAINING OF TEACHERS IN SERVICE.

If the measures just outlined looking toward the establishment of definite standards of academic and professional training for all public-school teachers in the State are adopted, the State is under obligation to provide means whereby the teachers already in service may meet the new requirements. The committee, therefore, recommends, as a corollary of the recommendation made above on minimum requirements, that the State be divided into extension service districts, one for each normal school, and that each normal school organize an extension service for its district on such lines as may appear best suited to the needs of the district and of the State. The committee is inclined to favor the type of extension service which has recently been successfully established in Iowa by the State Teachers' College,[1] but it believes that the determination of the exact plan of extension to be adopted in Washington should be made by the heads of the normal schools acting in conference.

Further steps leading to the full professionalization of the corps of elementary teachers in the State are proposed in the following recommendations:

1. That for all students who leave the normal school with any kind of certificate or diploma which may be accepted as a license to teach in the schools of the State the State board of education shall, with the assistance of the presidents of the normal schools and the heads of the departments of education in the State university and the State college, prepare such courses of study, including both professional and cultural (scientific and literary) subjects as may be completed within a period of three years by devoting to them not less than 10 hours a week for 10 months of each year; that examinations on portions of these courses be held from time to time, and that no person be granted a permanent license to teach in the public schools of the State until after he has passed a final examination on all courses prescribed. The final examination should be passed not earlier than two nor later than five years after the time of leaving the normal school.

2. That State, county, and city superintendents and supervisors be required to give special attention to young teachers who are pursuing these prescribed courses of study and have not yet been granted a permanent license to teach. Before granting a permanent license to any teacher the State board of education should require, in addition to a statement that such teacher has passed a satisfactory

---

[1] For a brief account of this system, see p. 177.

examination on the prescribed course of study, a specific report from a qualified superintendent, supervisor, or inspector that this teacher has taught satisfactorily not less than 16 months in the schools of the State, and this report should be accompanied by detailed record of the work done, showing its excellencies and its defects, within the past 8 months.

3. That the same policy in regard to permanent licenses to teach in the elementary schools of this State be pursued with teachers entering the service from other States or from other schools than the State normal schools in this State. The first license granted to any such teacher should be a temporary license. To secure a permanent license the candidate should be required to pass examinations on the prescribed courses of study proposed in 1 and 2 above.

4. That when the normal schools have put into operation the standards recommended in this report—namely, (a) graduation from an accredited four-year high school as a prerequisite for admission, (b) two years of work above high-school graduation for the normal school certificate, and (c) three years of work above high-school graduation for the normal-school diploma—the State fix by law minimum salaries for teachers holding normal-school certificates and for teachers holding normal-school diplomas, the difference between the minimum salaries of the two classes being such as may seem justified by the different degrees of preparation, and that it provide by law for a definite increase in the minimum salaries of both classes of teachers when they have complied with the requirements for and have been granted permanent licenses. This law should also be made to apply to teachers from other States and from other schools in this State, but it should not be so construed as to discriminate in any way against the teachers from the State normal schools, on the one hand, or to discourage good teachers from other States and schools from entering the service in this State.

Some beginnings have been made in all the normal schools for preparing rural teachers for their difficult tasks. The preparation can best be accomplished through distinct departments organized for this purpose. The normal schools at Cheney and Bellingham have such departments already organized, with two instructors in each giving their time exclusively to the work. At Ellensburg one instructor gives part of his time only to the special training of rural teachers. The committee recommends that these departments in the normal schools be gradually enlarged and that their organization include (1) a head of department, (2) an extension service, and (3) one or more rural practice and critic teachers.

Chapter XXII.

ATTENDANCE, FACULTIES, AND FUTURE POLICY.

The following table gives the attendance by years in the three normal schools for the last 11 years:

TABLE 42.—*State normal schools—Attendance by years.*[1]

Years.	Cheney.	Ellens-burg.	Belling-ham.
1905–6	305	187	285
1906–7	350	210	327
1907–8	349	164	335
1908–9	417	248	403
1909–10	598	284	465
1910–11	650	353	448
1911–12	582	337	396
1912–13	526	341	478
1913–14	725	324	588
1914–15	858	395	704
1916 [2]	[3] 605	332	[4] 962

[1] Including summer attendance, but counting no names more than once.
[2] To Mar. 31 only.
[3] In addition to these figures, Cheney has 60 correspondence students.
[4] In addition to these figures, Bellingham has 90 correspondence students.

The school at Ellensburg, by reason of its location far from large cities, has been of slow growth. The school at Cheney has had a satisfactory growth, and has reached an attendance commensurate with its instructional force and equipment. The school at Bellingham, on the other hand, has practically outgrown its equipment; it should be given increased appropriations, or some of its students should be diverted to other schools. The committee realizes the difficulty of putting the latter suggestion into practice, since school attendance depends largely on conditions beyond ordinary control.

The following summary, showing (1) preparation and experience of faculty members, (2) salaries paid, (3) total number of subjects taught, (4) total teaching hours per instructor, (5) average students per hour, and (6) average student clock hours per week, furnishes a more exact basis for a comparative study of the three schools: [1]

TABLE 43.—*Comparative study of salaries, teaching hours, etc., in Washington normal schools.*

Institutions.	Regular normal-school instructors.[2]	Average salary of regular instructors.	Total number of subjects taught.	Average teaching hours per week.	Average number students per hour.	Average student clock hours per week.
Ellensburg	14	$1,700	95	19	23	[3] 282
Cheney	24	1,696	72	14	32	[3] 428
Bellingham	39	1,713		17		[3] 559

[1] For the detail tables from which this summary is derived, see Appendix D.
[2] The principals and supervisors whose work is exclusively in the training school are not included; only regular normal-school instructors are counted.
[3] This average would be increased by about one-third if time of regular instructors devoted to training school supervision were included.

The State normal school at Ellensburg has only 14 regular faculty members listed. The school is weak in rural and agricultural work, and should have additional instructors in these departments at least. The Ellensburg school also shows a larger number of hours per instructor than the other schools, because of the larger number of subjects offered and the smaller list of instructors. The average number of students per .hour is smaller than it should be, which accounts for the small number of student clock hours.

The school at Cheney is the best balanced of the schools. The faculty is probably large enough for all present purposes. The average hours per week are few (although here, as in the other schools, the average would be materially increased by counting time devoted to supervision). The average number of students per hour is not excessive, but a smaller number would undoubtedly increase the efficiency of the instruction. The total number of student clock hours is close to the standard.

The instructional staff at Bellingham is larger than at the other schools, but this is justified by the larger attendance. The average number of students per class is not reported, but will exceed that of the other schools.

The committee suggests the following standards of internal administration for the general guidance of the administrative officers:

1. The number of classroom hours per instructor in a normal school should not exceed 20 per week;[1]

2. The average salary (excluding the administrative head) should approach $2,000;

3. Classes should not exceed 30 or 35, except in lecture work;

4. The average number of student clock hours carried by normal-school instructors may range between 300 and 400;[1] the reasonable load in any given case being determined by the type of work required.

Applying these standards to the Washington normal schools, it appears that:

(a) The school at Ellensburg is operated at only about two-thirds of its capacity;

(b) The school at Cheney is operated at a trifle less than its full capacity; and

(c) The school at Bellingham is crowded beyond normal capacity.

The value of normal schools depends more than does the value of schools of other kinds on the number of students who complete the work of their higher classes rather than on the number in lower

---

[1] In Sec. I, p. 121, the committee recommended a smaller maximum number of teaching hours per week for instructors in the university and State college. It should be noted in this connection that teaching periods in normal schools are likely to be shorter and that much of the work is more strictly of a routine character, involving less outside study and research.

classes or on the total enrollment. It is only in the higher classes with students more mature both in scholarship and in age that the most important part of the professional work can be done, including practice teaching in the training schools. Students who leave the normal schools from the lower classes, without having done this work have made little more advance in *professional* preparation than they might have made by attending college an equal length of time. The normal schools should therefore strive to hold students until they have completed one of the regular courses. When the normal schools of Washington have been reorganized, as herein recommended, they might well require a declaration of purpose on the part of the student to remain through the two years at least, as one of the conditions of admission.

But there is a very definite limit to the number of students that can be taught to best advantage in the last year of the normal school. During this last year every student should teach under critical supervision at least an hour a day throughout the entire year, under conditions as nearly as possible like those which must be met in the schools of the State. As a rule, the opportunities for such practice teaching can not be multiplied indefinitely. For this and many other reasons the normal school should not be a large school. As has already been stated, in the normal schools of western European countries the attendance is limited. When more teachers are needed the State establishes more schools, instead of increasing beyond desirable limits the attendance at the schools already in existence. In this country those States in which a similar policy is pursued appear to be more effectively served by their normal schools. (For attendance at public normal schools see Appendix C.) Already two of the normal schools of Washington have as many students as they should have for best results, if not more. It is also quite evident that these three normal schools will never be able to supply to the State all the well-prepared teachers needed, even after making full allowance for all that may come from other States and schools. At present about 1,000 new teachers are needed for the elementary schools each year. Of these, approximately 350 can be had from other States and other schools. The normal schools of this State should, therefore, turn out approximately 650 well-educated, well-trained new teachers every year. Though the school population, and consequently the total number of teachers needed, are both increasing, and though the relative number of teachers coming from other States may be expected to decrease with the receding tide of immigration from the older States, still an annual output of 700 new teachers from the normal schools of this State will probably be sufficient to supply the demand for the immediate future. One reason for the large present demand is the short professional life of a considerable percentage of the teachers. But it is the common experience that if teachers are well prepared and successful, they tend to remain longer in the profession.

To turn out this number of trained teachers annually, at least four normal schools will be needed. The committee therefore recommends that steps be taken for the establishment of another normal school at a very early date, somewhere in western Washington. That the new school should be located in this part of the State is evident, since approximately two-thirds of the people of the State live west of the Cascades, and the school at Bellingham now has more students than both of the others taken together. The millage tax set apart for the support of the new school should be not less than the average tax for the three schools now in existence. Even with this increase in the number of schools, the expenditures of the State for normal schools will be less in proportion to the total expenditures for public schools than in several other States.[1]

---

[1] See p. 168.

SUMMARY OF RECOMMENDATIONS RELATING TO THE NORMAL SCHOOLS.

1. The restriction of the field of the State normal schools to the preparation of elementary teachers until all elementary schools are supplied with professionally trained teachers.

2. The gradual increase of the entrance requirement to graduation from a four-year high school.

3. The granting of no normal school certificate after the summer session of 1921 for less than the completion of two years of normal school work above high-school graduation.

4. The award after the summer session of 1922 of a certificate for the completion of a two-year course and of the normal-school diploma for the completion of a three-year course.

5. The establishment of special summer and irregular courses to enable teachers in service to fulfill the new academic and professional requirements.

6. The provision by the normal schools of differentiated courses of study of two and three years, respectively, above high-school graduation.

7. The division of the State into extension service districts, one for each normal school, within which each normal school shall organize an extension service for the teachers of the State.

8. The preparation of courses of study for the further training of teachers in service, the satisfactory completion of which shall be necessary to secure a permanent license to teach.

9. The eventual establishment by the State of minimum salaries for teachers holding normal-school certificates and normal-school diplomas.

10. The considerable enlargement of the courses and facilities at all three normal schools for the preparation of rural-school teachers.

11. The organization of a fourth normal school.

186

SUMMARY OF RECOMMENDATIONS OF SURVEY COMMITTEE.

I. STATE UNIVERSITY AND STATE COLLEGE.

1. The provision for the formulation of State policies in higher education—

(a) Through joint meetings of boards of regents, or

(b) Through the extension of the functions of the State board of education, or

(c) Through the creation of a State council of education.

2. Agriculture, veterinary medicine, economic science in its application to agriculture, and the training of high-school teachers of agriculture, home economics, and mechanic arts to be major lines at the State college.

3. Law, medicine, graduate work in liberal arts and pure science, professional training of high-school teachers and school superintendents, commerce, journalism, architecture, forestry, and pharmacy to be major lines at the State university.

4. Duplication to be recognized in certain branches of engineering, in home economics, and in liberal arts.

5. Civil, electrical, and mechanical engineering to be taught at both State college and the State university.

6. Chemical engineering to be a major line at the State university exclusively.

7. The development of further departments or branches of engineering to be submitted to a joint conference before their establishment at either institution.

8. The maintenance of but one school of mining, its location to be determined by the advice of mining experts.

9. Degree courses in liberal arts with the training of high-school teachers in the same to be continued at the State college, but no graduate work in these lines to be offered.

10. Home economics to be developed for the present without restriction at both the State university and the State college, but no extension work in home economics to be undertaken by the university outside of King County.

11. The approval of the establishment of courses in marine engineering and fisheries at the State university as soon as its resources permit.

12. The appointment of a conference composed of representatives of the faculties of both institutions, to meet from time to time to adjust cases of overlapping, especially in the field of graduate work.

13. The discontinuance of the training of elementary teachers by the State university and the State college.

14. The provision at or near the State university and the State college of facilities for practice, demonstration, and research.

15. The further development of the facilities of the department of elementary science at the State college for agricultural instruction of subcollegiate grade.

16. The establishment at Puyallup, or somewhere else in the western part of the State, of another school of agriculture of subcollegiate grade under the direction and control of the State college.

17. The requirement of high-school graduation of all students entering the college or the university, except for those 21 years of age or older, and except for students in the elementary science department of the State college.

18. The modification of the administrative relationships of the department of elementary science at the State college.

19. The serious consideration by the administrative officers of both institutions of the large number of small classes.

20. The possible revision of the excessive major requirements at both institutions.

21. The establishment of 15 hours of classroom teaching a week as the maximum at the State college and State university and the encouragement of a lower maximum.

II. THE PUBLIC-SCHOOL SYSTEM.

1. A comparative study of State systems of taxation to ascertain a fair and equitable basis for scaling up the State and county taxes levied in Washington.

2. A revision of the system of apportioning the current State school fund and the county fund.

3. A revision of the qualifications and salaries of county superintendents.

4. The provision of professional supervision in rural communities and the subdivision of the counties for supervision purposes.

5. The encouragement of long teaching tenures by supplementing salaries on the basis of years taught in the same community.

6. The abolition of third-grade certificates.

7. The revision of the requirements for renewing second-grade certificates until such certificates are finally discontinued.

8. The revision of the examination schedules for the several kinds of certificates.

9. The establishment of minimum professional requirements for all persons teaching in this State.

10. The establishment of minimum academic requirements for all persons teaching in this State.

11. The thoroughgoing revision of the common-school course of study, and the adoption of a distinctively rural course of study for schools of the open country.

III. THE NORMAL SCHOOLS.

1. The restriction of the field of the State normal schools to the preparation of elementary teachers until all elementary schools are supplied with professionally trained teachers.

2. The gradual increase of the entrance requirement to graduation from a four-year high school.

3. The granting of no normal-school certificate after the summer session of 1921 for less than the completion of two years of normal-school work above high-school graduation.

4. The award after the summer session of 1922 of a certificate for the completion of a two-year course and of the normal-school diploma for the completion of a three-year course.

5. The establishment of special summer and irregular courses to enable teachers in service to fulfill the new academic and professional requirements.

6. The provision by the normal schools of differentiated courses of study of two and three years, respectively, above high-school graduation.

7. The division of the State into extension-service districts, one for each normal school, within which each normal school shall organize an extension service for the teachers of the State.

8. The preparation of courses of study for the further training of teachers in service, the satisfactory completion of which shall be necessary to secure a permanent license to teach.

9. The eventual establishment by the State of minimum salaries for teachers holding normal-school certificates and normal-school diplomas.

10. The considerable enlargement of the courses and facilities at all three normal schools for the preparation of rural-school teachers.

11. The organization of a fourth normal school.

University of Washington—Salaries and student clock hours for the year ending June 30, 1915.

Department and instructors.	Salary.	Student clock hours.	
		First semester.	Second semester.
COLLEGE OF LIBERAL ARTS.			
English:			
Head professor.............................	$3,000	238	318
Professor...................................	2,400	337	309
Associate professor.........................	2,200	294	247
Associate professor [1].....................	2,200	....	....
Assistant professor.........................	1,900	345	294
Assistant professor.........................	1,700	270	279
Assistant professor.........................	1,700	252	196
Assistant professor.........................	1,600	187	55
Instructor..................................	1,600	432	275
Instructor..................................	1,100	232	206
Instructor [2]..............................	1,100	264	253
Teaching fellow.............................	900	180	220
Teaching fellow.............................	650	192	180
Teaching fellow.............................	450	114	141
Teaching fellow.............................	450	170	138
Teaching fellow.............................	700	237	....
Teaching fellow.............................	450	127	127
Total (instructors, 14) [3].................	22,600	3,871	3,247
Average.....................................	1,619	276	232
French:			
Professor...................................	3,000	144	114
Associate professor.........................	1,900	334	260
Assistant professor.........................	1,700	370	325
Assistant professor [4].....................	800	114	122
Assistant professor.........................	1,600	200	170
Assistant professor.........................	1,500	350	303
Instructor..................................	1,100	274	355
Instructor..................................	337	176	196
Total (instructors, 6½) [3].................	11,937	1,962	1,845
Average.....................................	1,736	285	268
German:			
Head professor.............................	2,800	118	140
Assistant professor.........................	1,700	288	285
Assistant professor.........................	1,600	335	265
Assistant professor.........................	1,600	339	368
Instructor..................................	1,400	302	270
Instructor..................................	1,300	325	328
Instructor..................................	1,200	360	328
Instructor [4]..............................	650	128	94
Graduate assistant..........................	112	72	....
Total (instructors, 7½).....................	12,362	2,267	2,078
Average.....................................	1,595	292	277
Greek:			
Dean..	3,000	51	45
Assistant professor.........................	1,800	309	316
Associate professor [7].....................	500	81	....
Total (instructors, 2½).....................	5,300	441	361
Average.....................................	2,355	252	240
History:			
Head professor.............................	3,000	530	619
Professor...................................	2,400	281	279
Associate professor.........................	2,200	450	452
Associate professor.........................	2,200	998	752
Instructor..................................	1,300	644	768
Research assistant [8]......................	1,200	....	....
One teaching fellow.........................	450	....	....
Student assistant...........................	150	....	....
Total (instructors, 6¾)....................	12,900	2,903	2,870
Average.....................................	1,911	505	499

[1] On leave.
[2] Substitutes for another professor.
[3] Total instructors reduced to full time basis.
[4] See also Spanish.
[5] Half time.
[6] Half time, not included here, given to extension instruction.
[7] See also Latin.
[8] No instruction.

University of Washington—Salaries and student clock hours for the year ending June 30, 1915—Continued.

Department and instructors.	Salary.	Student clock hours.	
		First semester.	Second semester.
COLLEGE OF LIBERAL ARTS—continued.			
Journalism:			
Head professor	$3,500	303	195
Assistant professor	2,100		177
Assistant professor	2,000	113	166
Instructor	1,200	164	121
Pressman [1]	1,620		
Student assistant	150		
Student assistant	75		
Total (instructors, 5½)	9,645	580	659
Average	1,794	178	182
Latin:			
Head professor	3,000	98	90
Associate professor [2]	1,500	124	183
Assistant professor	1,500	183	192
Total (instructors, 2¾)	6,000	395	465
Average	2,182	144	155
Library economy:			
Instructor (¼ time)	750	27	63
Instructor (¼ time)	500	66	88
Instructor (¼ time)	250	51	33
Instructor (¼ time)	125	34	
Instructor (¼ time)	89		14
Total (instructor, 1) [2]	1,714	168	198
Average	1,714		
Oriental history:			
Head professor	2,600	316	296
Philosophy:			
Head professor	3,000	231	660
Instructor	1,500	270	201
Instructor	1,200	440	96
Total (instructors, 3)	5,700	941	957
Average	1,900	314	319
Political and social science:			
Head professor	3,000	492	297
Professor	3,000	566	423
Assistant professor	2,000	339	270
Assistant professor	1,700	258	396
Assistant professor	1,600	342	306
Assistant professor	1,350	450	390
Instructor	1,300	430	353
Instructor	1,200	166	276
Instructor	1,200	432	306
Total (instructors, 9)	16,350	3,460	3,107
Average	1,817	385	345
Public speaking and debate:			
Head professor	2,590	186	262
Professor	1,400	104	259
Total (instructors, 2)	3,900	290	521
Average	1,950	145	260
Scandinavian language and lirature:			
Head professor	2,100	112	122
Spanish:			
Head professor	2,000	270	223
Associate professor	2,000	307	233
Assistant professor	1,900	280	280
Instructor	265		150
Assistant professor [4]	860	196	196
Total (instructors, 3¾)	6,825	1,053	1,091
Average	1,820	281	291

[1] No instruction.　　　　[2] Total instructors reduced to full time basis.
[2] See also Greek.　　　　[4] See also French.

University of Washington—Salaries and student clock hours for the year ending June 30, 1915—Continued.

Department and instructors.	Salary.	Student clock hours.	
		First semester.	Second semester.
COLLEGE OF SCIENCE.			
Botany:			
Head professor	$2,800	400	316
Professor	2,800	872	520
Assistant professor	1,700	708	492
Assistant professor	1,600	320	289
Teaching fellow	450		375
Graduate assistant	450		150
Graduate assistant	600	312	
Student assistant	150	30	30
Student assistant	150	384	
Student assistant	150		
Student assistant	150		
Total (instructors, 6½)	10,500	2,926	2,173
Average	1,615	457	334
Chemistry:			
Head professor	3,000	3,329	2,170
Professor	2,400	391	208
Associate professor	2,000	872	668
Assistant professor	1,800	1,680	1,544
Instructor	1,600	130	72
Instructor	1,400	672	929
Instructor	1,000	222	80
Graduate assistant	450		
Graduate assistant	450		
Graduate assistant	450		
Graduate assistant	450		
Graduate assistant	450		
Graduate assistant	450		
Stockman	900		
Two stockmen (at $600)	1,200		
Stock assistant	200		
Assistant	250		
Stock assistant	50		
Lecture assistant	250		
Graduate assistant	225		
Total (instructors, 13)	18,975	7,299	5,761
Average	1,460	561	443
Short course—			
Professor			48
Geology:			
Dean (science)[1]			
Assistant professor	2,000	570	609
Assistant professor	1,800	168	241
Instructor	1,600	514	474
Student assistant	150		
Student assistant	150		
Student assistant	150		
Lecturer	100		
Total (instructors, 4)	5,950	1,252	1,324
Average	1,487	313	331
Short course—			
Assistant professor			18
Instructor			120
Home economics:			
Head professor	2,100	213	188
Assistant professor	1,700	268	284
Instructor	1,400	484	453
Instructor	1,400	405	222
Instructor	1,200	380	176
Total (instructors, 5)	7,800	1,252	1,324
Average	1,560	350	264
Mathematics:			
Head professor	3,000	123	101
Associate professor	2,400	283	283
Associate professor	2,100	211	240
Assistant professor	1,700	378	350
Assistant professor	1,300	306	218
Assistant professor [2]	1,600		
Assistant professor	1,500	326	177
Instructor	1,400	374	308
Instructor	1,300	360	298

[1] Acting president.   [2] On leave.

University of Washington—Salaries and student clock hours for the year ending June 30, 1915—Continued.

Department and instructors.	Salary.	Student clock hours.	
		First semester.	Second semester.
COLLEGE OF SCIENCE—continued.			
Mathematics—Continued.			
Instructor	$1,300	340	296
Instructor [1]	1,200	336	310
Graduate student	225	76	68
Graduate student	225	76	92
Total (instructors, 10½)	18,050	3,139	2,691
Average	1,719	299	256
Philosophy (psychology):			
Professor	1,050	36	30
Instructor	1,500	858	648
Instructor	1,200	72	151
Teaching fellow	75		
Total (instructors, 2¾)	3,825	966	829
Average	1,457	368	315
Physical training:			
Director	2,400	773	823
Instructor	1,500	230	380
Instructor [2]	1,200		
Instructor	1,000	275	366
Instructor	900	849	882
Assistant	300		16
Total (instructors, 5½)	7,300	2,127	2,507
Average	1,327	387	456
Physics:			
Head professor	3,000	299	545
Assistant professor	2,000	546	424
Assistant professor	1,500	180	320
Instructor	1,400	543	156
Teaching fellow	450		
Teaching fellow	450		
Teaching fellow	225		
Student assistant	75		
Total (instructors, 5¾)	9,100	1,568	1,455
Average	1,699	293	271
Zoology:			
Head professor	3,000	753	1,012
Assistant professor	1,800	513	670
Instructor	1,400	726	744
Instructor	1,200	846	654
Student assistant	150		
Student assistant	150		
Student assistant	150		
Total (instructors, 4¾)	7,850	2,838	3,080
Average	1,653	597	648
COLLEGE OF ENGINEERING.			
Civil engineering:			
Dean (engineering)	3,000	140	114
Professor	2,500	39	129
Professor	2,400	311	340
Associate professor [3]	1,900		362
Assistant professor	1,600	365	474
Assistant professor	1,500	268	190
Assistant professor	1,500	654	606
Instructor	1,400	440	230
Instructor [4]	700	278	553
Instructor	1,200	572	486
Instructor	600		502
Student assistant	85		
Student assistant	60		
Total (instructors, 10½)	18,445	3,117	4,187
Average	1,800	337	368
Short course—			
Professor			
Assistant professor			22
Instructor			200
			40

[1] Substitute for assistant professor.
[2] Rowing; hours not available.
[3] On leave, first semester.
[4] Substitute for assistant professor, first semester.

University of Washington—Salaries and student clock hours for the year ending June 30, 1915—Continued.

Department and instructors.	Salary.	Student clock hours.	
		First semester.	Second semester.
COLLEGE OF ENGINEERING—continued.			
Electrical engineering:			
Head professor	$3,000	152	212
Assistant professor	1,900	245	186
Instructor (¼)	425	88	40
Instructor	1,400	323	332
Graduate assistant	200	108	78
Student assistant	50		72
Total (instructors, 3½)	6,975	916	920
Average	1,993	262	263
Mechanical engineering:			
Head professor	3,000	258	188
Associate professor	2,000	250	270
Assistant professor	1,500	686	490
Instructor	1,700	412	416
Instructor	1,600	744	504
Total (instructors, 5)	9,800	2,350	1,962
Average	1,960	470	392
COLLEGE OF MINES.			
Dean	3,000	88	207
Assistant professor	2,000	82	132
Assistant professor [1]	2,000		
Assistant professor [2]		206	104
Student assistant	250		
Student assistant	250		
Student assistant	250		
Student assistant lecturer	400		
Total (instructors, 4)	8,150	376	443
Average	2,037	94	111
Short course—			
Dean			120
Assistant professor			90
Assistant professor			100
COLLEGE OF FORESTRY.			
Dean	2,700	295	241
Associate professor	2,300	116	180
Assistant clerk	2,200	322	108
Instructor	1,400	318	192
Lecturer	250		
Total (instructors, 4½)	8,850	1,051	721
Average	2,145	255	175
Short course:			
Dean			74
Associate professor			63
Assistant professor			212
Instructor			144
COLLEGE OF PHARMACY.			
Dean	3,000	124	110
Associate professor	1,900	490	546
Instructor	1,000	384	368
Instructor [2]	1,300		72
Assistant [3]	900		
Student assistant	150		
Student assistant	225		
Student assistant	120		
Total instructors, 5½	8,595	998	1,096
Average	1,495	285	292
SCHOOL OF EDUCATION.			
Dean	3,000	529	593
Professor	2,500	124	303
Assistant professor	2,000	414	253
Assistant professor	1,800	193	214
Instructor	1,200	115	270
Total (instructors, 5)	10,500	1,375	1,633
Average	2,100	275	327

[1] On leave.
[2] Substitute for assistant professor.
[3] State food analysis; not counted in teaching except one for one-fourth time second semester.

University of Washington—Salaries and students clock hours for the year ending June 30, 1915—Continued.

Department and instructors.	Salary.	Student clock hours.	
		First semester.	Second semester.
SCHOOL OF LAW.			
Dean	$3,000	340	356
Professor	3,000	441	374
Professor (lecturer, ½)	1,000	258	196
Professor	2,400	459	342
Assistant professor	2,100	557	525
Assistant professor	2,100	362	308
Lecturer (¼)	600	128	96
Total instructors, 5¾	14,200	2,565	2,197
Average	2,457	449	382
COLLEGE OF FINE ARTS.			
Dean	2,500	365	425
Assistant professor (architecture ¼)	1,000	302	56
Assistant professor	1,600	106	158
Assistant professor	1,000	228	196
Assistant professor	600	39	36
Assistant professor	200	68	60
Instructor	500	112	98
Instructor	1,300	504	536
Instructor	400	80	98
Instructor (architecture)	800	375	255
Assistant	300	28	22
Band master	350	105	90
Student assistant	150		
Total (instructors, 6¾)	10,700	2,312	2,022
Average	1,678	362	319
MILITARY TRAINING.			
Commandant		1,624	1,388
Student assistant	150		
Student assistant	150		
Student assistant	150		
Student assistant	150		
Total (instructors, 2)	600	1,624	1,388
Average	600	812	694

Washington State College—Salaries and student clock hours for first semester, year 1914–15.

Title of instructor.	Salary.	No. of course.	Value.	Clock hours.	Students.	Student clock hours.
Soil physicist	[1] $2,000	Agr. 1	4	6	52	312
		Agr. 8	3	4	3	12
		Agr. 21	3	3	15	45
						369
Professor of farm crops	[2] 2,000	Agr. 4	5	7	25	175
Assistant agronomist	[3] 1,400	Agr. 5	2	2	9	18
Professor of agriculture	3,000	Agr. 17	1	1	4	4
Professor of agricultural engineering	1,600	Agr. 20	5	7	7	49
Associate professor of animal husbandry.	1,800	An. Husb. 1	5	7	46	322
		An. Husb. 1	5	7	27	189
		An. Husb. 1	5	7	36	252
		An. Husb. 9	1	2	13	26
						[4] 789
Professor of animal husbandry	2,000	An. Husb. 2	2	2	22	44
		An. Husb. 7	3	3	36	108
		An. Husb. 6 and 17	2	2	45	90
						242
Assistant professor of poultry husbandry.	[5] 1,500	An. Husb. 16	3	4	7	28

[1] Experiment station pays $1,000 of this.
[2] Experiment station pays $500 of this.
[3] Experiment station pays $1,283 of this.
[4] Students in electrical engineering, 35 lacking.
[5] Extension division pays $750 of this.

Washington State College—Salaries and student clock hours for first semester, year 1914-15—Continued.

Title of instructor.	Salary.	No. of course.	Value.	Clock hours.	Students.	Student clock hours.
Assistant professor of architecture.....	$1,650	Arch. 5............ Arch. 13............ Arch. 17............ Arch. 33............	2 4 1 2	2 6 2 4	8 1 1 10	16 6 2 40 64
Professor of architecture...............	3,000	Arch. 11............ Arch. 35............ Arch. 43............ Arch. 51............	2 1 4 1	2 2 8 1	2 4 2 7	4 8 16 7 35
Director of experiment station and professor of botany.	[1] 1,500	Bot. 1............. Bot. 101............ Bot. 70............	4 4 3	6 6 5	36 20 2	216 180 10 406
Associate professor of plant physiology.	1,900	Bot. 4............. Bot. 45............ Bot. 46............ Bot. 91............	4 5 3-5 1	6 8 2	45 1 19 39	270 8 ...... 78 [2] 356
Assistant professor of botany..........	1,400	Bot. 14............ Bot. 45............	5 8	6 8	17 1	102 8 110
Associate professor of botany and assistant in experiment station.	[3] 1,800	Bot. 16............ Bot. 18............ Bot. 71............	5 4 3	8 6 5	41 3 7	328 12 35 375
Associate professor of chemistry.......	1,600	Chem. 1............ Chem. 1............ Chem. 1............	5 5 5	8 8 8	65 33 30	520 264 240 1,024
Dean of faculty and professor of chemistry.	[4] 3,000	Chem. 1............	5	8	52	416
Assistant professor of chemistry.......	1,320	Chem. 3............ Chem. 29............	5 3	8 5	25 2	200 10 210
Assistant professor of chemistry.......	1,320	Chem. 6............ Chem. 19............ Chem. 22............ Chem. 35............	5 3 5 2	9 ...... 9 4	2 39 1 10	18 117 9 40 184
Associate professor of physiological chemistry.	1,800	Chem. 11............ Chem. 41............ Home Econ. 31....	5 5 5	5 10 8	11 7 8	55 70 64 189
Instructor in chemistry................	1,200	Chem. 12............	5	9	6	62
Professor of sanitary engineering......	1,800	Civil Eng. 4....... Civil Eng. 5....... Civil Eng. 9....... Civil Eng. 14...... Civil Eng. 20......	1 1 5 3 3	1 1 5 3 3	15 13 32 3 3	15 13 160 9 9 206

[1] Experiment station pays $1,500 of this.   [2] Experiment station pays $450 of this.
[3] Pickett 3, 4, or 5 hours.   [4] $1,500 of this is salary as dean.

Washington State College—Salaries and student clock hours for first semester, year 1914–15—Continued.

Title of instructor.	Salary.	No. of course.	Value.	Clock hours.	Students.	Student clock hours.
Professor of railway and highway engineering.	$2,100	Civil Eng. 10	5	10	6	68
		Civil Eng. 19	2	2	8	16
		Civil Eng. 21	3	3	3	9
		Civil Eng. 22	2	2	3	6
						91
Vice president and professor of mathematics and civil engineering.	[1] 3,000	Civil Eng. 11	5	7	3	21
		Civil Eng. 13	5	5	5	25
		Civil Eng. 16	2	2	15	30
		Civil Eng. 24	3	3	12	36
						112
Instructor in civil engineering	1,200	Civil Eng. 30	2	4	11	44
Professor of dairying	[2] 1,800	Dairying 1	3	4	53	212
		Dairying 7	2	4	13	52
		Dairying 15	1	2	16	32
						296
Instructor in dairy practice	1,200	Dairying 4	2	3	8	24
Second instructor in dairying	1,200	Dairying 6	5	8	10	80
		Dairying 9	2	3	1	3
						83
Instructor in economic science	1,200	Econ. 9	5	3	9	27
		Econ. 39	5	5	17	85
		Econ. 42	3	3	13	39
		Econ. 43	2	2	9	18
						169
Professor of economic science	2,200	Econ. 31	5	5	59	295
		Econ. 35	3	3	25	75
		Econ. 36	2	2	23	46
						416
Professor of psychology	2,200	Educ. 3	5	5	42	210
		Educ. 11	2	2	22	44
		Educ. 20	3	3	13	39
						293
Assistant professor of education	1,600	Educ. 5	2	2	14	28
		Educ. 6	3	3	25	75
		Educ. 17	3	3	9	27
		Educ. 19	2	2	15	30
						160
Professor of applied electricity	1,900	Elec. Eng. 1	5	5	12	60
		Elec. Eng. 10	2	2	9	18
		Elec. Eng. 15	3	3	5	15
		Elec. Eng. 131 [3]	....	....	4	....
		Elec. Eng. 35	2	4	(4)	....
						93
Professor of mechanical engineering and electrical engineering.	3,000	Elec. Eng. 5	5	5	9	45
		Mech. Eng. 13	3	3	12	36
						81
Assistant professor of English	1,600	English 1	5	5	20	100
		English 28	3	3	23	69
		English 29	3	3	25	75
		English 30	2	2	26	52
		English 31	2	2	16	32
						328

[1] $2,000 of this is salary as vice president.
[2] Experiment station pays $300 of this.
[3] Temporary course.
[4] Students lacking.

Washington State College—Salaries and student clock hours for first semester, year 1914-15—Continued.

Title of instructor.	Salary.	No. of course.	Value.	Clock hours.	Students.	Student clock hours.
Professor of English....................	$2,400	English 4..........	5	2	11	22
		English 11..........	5	3	6	18
		English 28..........	3	3	16	48
		English 40..........	5	3	13	39
		English 30..........	2	2	25	50
						177
Instructor in English..................	1,200	English 4..........	5	3	11	33
		English 28..........	3	3	21	63
		English 29..........	3	3	18	54
		English 30..........	2	2	15	30
		English 30..........	2	2	6	12
		English 31..........	2	2	17	34
		English 38..........	2	2	7	14
						240
Instructor in English..................	1,200	English 18..........	5	3	6	18
		English 28..........	3	3	26	78
		English 28..........	3	3	19	57
		English 30..........	2	2	28	56
		English 34..........	3	3	11	33
						242
Instructor in English.................	1,200	English 28..........	3	3	17	51
		English 28..........	3	3	19	57
		English 30..........	2	2	41	82
		English 51..........	2	2	7	14
						204
Assistant professor of English.........	1,500	English 28..........	3	3	20	60
		English 28..........	3	3	22	66
		English 30..........	2	2	27	64
		English 30..........	2	2	15	30
		English 30..........	2	2	6	12
		English 50..........	2	2	9	18
		English 46..........	3	3	11	33
						283
Assistant professor of English.........	1,700	English 28..........	3	3	19	57
		English 28..........	3	3	29	87
		English 28..........	3	3	20	60
		English 30..........	2	2	15	30
		English 48..........	5	3	3	9
						243
Student assistant in English..........	400	English 28..........	3	3	23	69
		English 30..........	2.	2	24	48
						117
Instructor in expression...............	300	Expression 8......	1	1	2	2
		Expression 5......	2	2	1	2
		Expression 1......	1	1	3	3
		Expression 3......	2	2	5	10
		Expression 4......	2	2	4	8
		Expression 7......	1	1	10	10
		Expression 9......	2	2	2	4
		Expression 10......	2	2	2	4
		Expression 11......	2	2	4	8
		Expression 14......	1	1	9	9
		Expression 16......	1	1	3	3
		Expression 19......	3	1	5	5
		Expression 21......	3	1	1	1
		Expression 30......	1	1	1	1
		English 10..........	2	2	14	28
						98

*Washington State College—Salaries and student clock hours for first semester, year 1914–15—*Continued.

Title of instructor.	Salary.	No. of course.	Value.	Clock hours.	Students.	Student clock hours.
Instructor in fine arts................	$1,000	Fine Arts 1........	2	4	38	152
		Fine Arts 1........	2	4	1	4
		Fine Arts 8........	2	2	3	6
		Fine Arts 16.......	5	10	1	10
		Fine Arts 17.......	5	10	1	10
		Fine Arts 18.......	5	10	2	20
		Fine Arts 20.......	5	10	1	10
		Fine Arts 22.......	{ 1–3 or 5 }	......	1	(1)
						212
Professor of forestry..................	2,200	Forestry 40........	2	2	2	4
		Forestry 45........	2	2	3	6
		Forestry 48........	2	2	2	4
		Forestry 49........	2	2	4	8
						22
Instructor in French.................	1,100	French 2...........	5	5	11	55
		French 10..........	5	5	2	10
		French 19..........	5	5	5	25
						90
Instructor in German and French.....	1,500	French 2...........	5	5	5	25
		French 11..........	5	5	17	85
		German 3..........	5	5	5	25
						135
Professor of geology..................	2,600	Geology 1 and 2 ...	5	5	27	135
		Geology 15	5	6	3	18
						153
Assistant professor of economical geology.	1,600	Geology 3..........	3	3	6	18
		Geology 7..........	3	6	5	30
		Geology 9..........	2	3	4	7
						55
Instructor in German.................	1,100	German 10.........	5	5	32	160
		German 10.........	5	5	7	35
						195
Professor of German..................	2,200	German 4..........	5	5	12	60
		German 9..........	5	5	4	20
		German 10.........	5	5	17	85
		German 11.........	5	5	21	105
		German 17.........	5	5	9	45
		German 11.........	5	5	26	130
						445
Instructor in German.................	1,100	German 10.........	5	5	8	40
		German 11.........	5	5	19	95
		German 14.........	2	2	7	14
		German 21.........	5	5	9	45
		German 27.........	3	3	9	27
						221
Second instructor in German..........	500	German 11.........	5	5	31	85
		German 20.........	5	5	15	45
						130
Professor of political and social science.	1,620	History 2	5	5	37	185
		History 2	5	5	38	190
		History 4	5	3	10	30
		Sociology 7........	5	3	22	66
						471

[1] Clock hours lacking.

Washington State College—Salaries and student clock hours for first semester, year 1914-15—Continued.

Title of instructor.	Salary.	No. of course.	Value.	Clock hours.	Students.	Student clock hours.
Assistant professor of history..........	$1,500	History 11..........	5	3	9	27
		History 24	5	5	44	220
						247
		Economy 31.......	5	5	35	175
						422
Professor of history....................	1,620	History 26..........	5	5	14	70
		History 46..........	5	3	7	21
		History 52..........	5	5	14	70
						161
Instructor in textiles and clothing.....	1,100	Home Econ. 1.....	3	5	44	264
		Home Econ. 20....	5	10	8	80
						344
Professor of home economy............	1,800	Home Econ. 1.....	1	2	17	34
		Home Econ. 4.....	4	8	15	120+3
		Home Econ. 7.....	2	4	10	40
		Home Econ. 37....	5	5	14	70
						264
Assistant professor of foods and cookery	1,400	Home Econ. 11....	3	6	9	54
		Home Econ. 11....	3	6	11	66
		Home Econ. 21....	5	10	39	195
		Home Econ. 34....	3	3	4	12
						322
Associate professor of pomology	1,900	Horticulture 9.....	3	4	18	64
		Horticulture 11....	5	7	42	294
		Horticulture 28....	2	2	15	30
						388
Instructor in horticulture	1,260	Horticulture 18....	2	4	12	48
Professor of horticulture................	2,200	Horticulture 24....	2	2	4	8
		Horticulture 25....	3	4	5	20
						28
Assistant professor of floriculture and gardening.	1,650	Horticulture 26....	3	5	2	10
		Horticulture 34....	3	4	15	60
		Horticulture 38....	3	5	4	20
						90
Professor of Latin.....................	2,200	Latin 3............	5	5	1	5
		Latin 11...........	5	5	3	8
		Rural law.........	2	2	12	24
						37
Instructor in metal work...............	750	Metal Art 1.......	2	4	3	12
		Metal Art 21	4	6	4	24
						36
Instructor in drawing..................	1,500	Drawing 5.........	(1)	....	2	....
		Metal Art 4.......	(1)	....	3	....
Professor of mathematics...............	1,900	Math. 1...........	5	5	10	50
		Math. 2 and 3.....	5	5	19	95
		Math. 5...........	5	5	10	50
		Math. 7...........	2	3	5	15
		Math. 9...........	3	3	5	15
						225

[1] Value not given.

Washington State College—Salaries and student clock hours for first semester, year 1914-15—Continued.

Title of instructor.	Salary.	No. of course.	Value.	Clock hours.	Students.	Student clock hours.
Assistant professor of mathematics....	$1,700	Math. 2 .... Math. 2 and 3 ..... Math. 5 .... Math. 8	5 5 5 5	5 5 5 5	24 20 19 2	120 100 95 10 325
Instructor in mathematics..............	1,200	Math. 2 and 3	5	5	19	95
Instructor in electrical engineering.....	1,200	Manual Arts 1.....	4	4	7	28
Assistant professor of mechanical engineering.	1,400	Mech. Eng. 28...... Metal Arts 3....... Metal Arts 5....... Mech. Eng 7....... Mech. Eng. 21.....	2 2 3 3 5	3 3 4 6 8	7 5 6 12 4	21 16 24 72 32 165
Instructor in mechanical engineering..	450	Mech. Eng. 20..... Metal Arts 7....... Metal Arts 40 ..... Metal Arts 40-41... Metal Arts 43...... Mech. Eng. 11.....	2 3 5 5 3 5	4 3 10 10 6 10	4 5 3 9 3 1	16 15 30 90 18 10 179
Assistant professor of mechanical engineering.	1,500	Mech. Eng. 33..... Mech. Eng. 37..... Mech. Eng. 31..... Metal Arts 37 ..... Mech. Eng. 5...... Mech. Eng. 12....	2 2 2 3 3	2 3 1 3 3	8 4 9 (2) 4 16	24 (1) 27 12 48 111
Assistant professor of manual training.	1,400	Man. Arts 43...... Man. Arts 5....... Man. Arts 11...... Man. Arts 8.......	3 2 4 2	6 4 8	4 2 1 (2)	24 8 8 40
Associate professor of mechanical engineering.	1,600	Mech. Eng. 1...... Mech. Eng. 1...... Mech. Eng. 1...... Mech. Eng. 15..... Mech. Eng. 34.....	5 5 5 5 2	8 8 8 5 2	16 24 33 2 8	128 192 264 10 16 610
Student assistant......................	100	Mech. Eng. 1......	5	8	5	40
Instructor in forge work...............	750	Mech. Eng. 3......	2	4	46	184
Assistant professor of metallurgy.......	1,500	Min. Eng. 1........ Min. Eng. 2........ Min. Eng. 5........ Min. Eng. 10...... Min. Eng. 12......	2 3 2 5 2	2 3 4 9 4	5 3 2 5 4	10 9 8 45 16 88
Professor of mining engineering........	2,600	Min. Eng. 4........ Min. Eng. 7........ Min. Eng. 9........	6 5 5	10 5 9	4 3 2	40 15 18 73
Professor of pipe organ and piano......	1,100	Music 31........... Music 33........... Music 35........... Piano and organ..	5 2 3 2½ or 5	5 2 3 (4)	10 2 2 15	50 4 6 (4) 60

¹ Not catalogued.
² Number of students not given.
³ Report incomplete.
⁴ Private music lessons not estimated.

Washington State College—Salaries and student clock hours for first semester, year 1914-15—Continued.

Title of instructor.	Salary.	No. of course.	Value.	Clock hours.	Students.	Student clock hours.
Instructor in voice......................	[1] $400	Methods...........	2½ or 5	([3])	7	([3])
		Vocal.............	2½ or 5	....	23	....
Instructor in piano.....................	([2])	Piano.............	2½ or 5	([3])	10	([3])
Professor of piano.....................	[1] 1,500	Piano.............	2½ or 5	([3])	3	([3])
		Piano 3...........	2½ or 5	....	3	....
		Piano 1...........	2½ or 5	....	6	....
		Piano 6...........	2½ or 5	....	1	....
		Piano 5...........	2½ or 5	....	1	....
		Piano 7...........	2½ or 5	....	1	....
Professor of violin...................	[1] 500	Violin.............	1, 2, 5	([3])	19	([3])
Instructor in voice.....................	[1] 200	Vocal.............	2½ or 5	([3])	12	([3])
Professor of pharmacy and materia medica.	1,800	Phar. 1...........	5	7	20	140
		Phar. 6...........	3	3	6	18
		Phar. 11..........	2	1	6	6
		Phar. 21..........	5	10	5	50
						214
Instructor in photography.............	450	Photog. 1.........	2	4	8	32
Professor of physics...................	1,800	Phys. 1...........	3	3	40	120
		Phys. 13..........	3	4	7	28
		Phys. 15..........	5	7	3	21
		Phys. 31..........	2	4	36	144
						313
Professor of Scandinavian languages...	1,320	Scan. 1...........	5	5	5	20
		Scan. 3...........	5	5	3	15
						35
Instructor in Spanish.................	1,100	Span. 1...........	5	5	56	280
		Span. 3...........	5	5	2	10
		Span. 4...........	5	5	6	30
						320
Associate professor of anatomy and surgery.	1,700	Clinics...........	1–3	4	30	120
		Vet. 19...........	5	7	18	126
		Vet. 21 and 35....	5	8	11	88
		Vet. 39...........	3	4	14	56
						390
Professor of veterinary science........	3,000	Vet. 22...........	4	5	11	55
		Vet. 24...........	5	6	42	252
						307
Assistant professor of pathology and histology.	[4] 1,800	Vet. 30...........	1	1	11	11
		Vet. 40...........	2	3	10	30
						41
Instructor in zoology.................	1,200	Zool. 3...........	5	8	2	16
		Zool. 21..........	5	8	26	208
						224
Professor of zoology..................	[5] 2,400	Zool. 4...........	5	5	9	27
		Zool. 7...........	3	3	7	21
		Zool. 38..........	3	3	4	12
						60

[1] And tuition fees.
[2] Private music lessons not estimated.
[3] Tuition fees only.
[4] Experimental station pays $600 of this.
[5] Experimental station pays $800 of this.

Washington State College—Salaries and student clock hours for second semester, year 1914-15.

Title of instructor.	Salary.	No. of course.	Value.	Clock hours.	Students.	Student clock hours.
Professor of agricultural engineering.	$1,600	Agr. 2............	5	7	16	112
		Agr. 2............	5	7	16	112
		Agr. 2............	5	7	16	112
		Agr. 2............	5	7	10	70
		Farm Eng........	2	4	15	60
		Tract. Eng.......	2	4	23	92
		Agr. 14..........	2	4	20	80
		Mech. Eng. 58.....	....	4	7	28
						606
Soil physicist.................	1 2,666	Agr. 11	3	3	7	21
		Agr. 23..........	5	3	12	144
						165
Professor of agriculture........	3,000	Agr. 12..........	3	3	27	71
		Agr. 16..........	2	2	6	12
						83
Professor of farm crops.........	2 2,000	Agr. 22..........	5	7	78	546
		Agr. 3...........	5	6	19	114
						660
Professor of animal husbandry.	2,000	An. Husb. 2......	3	3	44	132
		An. Husb. 4.......	2	2	47	94
		An. Husb. 14.....	2	2	20	40
						266
Associate professor of animal husbandry.	1,800	An. Husb. 5.......	2	2	21	42
		An. Husb. 8.......	3	3	22	5 66
						108
Assistant professor of poultry husbandry.	4 1,500	An. Husb. 16......	3	4	10	40
		An. Husb. 13......	3	4	4	16
						56
Professor of architecture.......	3,000	Arch. 18.........	1	2	5	10
		Arch. 25.........	3	6	27	162
		Arch. 44.........	5	10	1	10
						182
Assistant professor of architecture.	1,650	Arch. 36.........	1	2	15	30
		Arch. 6..........	1	1	6	6
		Arch. 42.........	3	6	3	18
		Arch. 14.........	4	6	1	6
						60
Instructor in drawing :........	1,500	Arch. 38.........	1	2	6	12
		Fine Arts 3.......	5	10	18	180
		Metal Arts 5.....	....	(5)	3	(5)
		Metal Arts 4.....	....	(5)	2	(5)
						192
Associate professor of plant physiology.	1,900	Bot. 2...........	4	6	32	192
		Bot. 8...........	5	8	3	24
		Bot. 17..........	2	2	5	10
		Bot. 44..........	1-10	(6)	4	(6)
		Bot. 102..........	4	6	9	54
						280
Professor of plant pathology ..	7 2,750	Bot. 7...........	....	(6)	1	(6)
		Bot. 41..........	....	(6)	9	(6)
		Bot. 44..........	1-10	(6)	1	(6)
		Bot. 51..........	3	8	10	80
						80

1 Experiment station pays $1,000 of this.
2 Experiment station pays $500 of this.
3 Five-sixths time.
4 Experiment station pays $750 of this.
5 Clock hours not given.
6 Not given.
7 Experiment station pays $1,375 of this.

Washington State College—Salaries and student clock hours for second semester, year 1914-15—Continued.

Title of instructor.	Salary.	No. of course.	Value.	Clock hours.	Students.	Student clock hours.
Assistant professor of botany ..	$1,400	Bot. 15............	5	7	16	112
		Bot. 47............	3-5	(¹)	2	(¹)
		Bot. 92............	1	2	34	68
						180
Associate professor of botany and assistant of experiment station.	²1,800	Bot. 18............	4	6	34	204
		Bot. 44............	1-10	(¹)	3	(¹)
						204
Associate professor of chemistry.	1,600	Chem. 2............	5	8	26	208
		Chem. 31..........	5	8	51	408
						616
Dean of faculty and professor of chemistry.	³3,000	Chem. 2............	5	8	47	376
		Chem. 21..........	2	2	7	14
						390
Assistant professor of chemistry.	1,320	Chem. 4............	4	7	11	77
		Chem. 33..........	5	8	94	752
						829
Instructor in chemistry.......	1,000	Chem. 5............	1	1	11	11
Do........................	1,200	Chem. 14..........	5	5	21	105
Associate professor of physiological chemistry.	1,800	Chem. 14..........	5	5	22	110
		Chem. 18..........	1	1½	6	10
						120
Assistant professor of chemistry.	1,320	Chem. 32..........	5	7	5	35
		Chem. 46..........	2	3½	3	11
						46
Instructor in civil engineering..	1,200	Civil Eng. 7.......	5	8	26	208
		Civil Eng. 26	2	2	4	8
						216
Professor of railway and highway engineering.	2,100	Civil Eng. 8.......	4	7	8	56
		Civil Eng. 5.......	5	7	4	28
		Civil Eng. 35......	3	4	3	12
						96
Vice president and professor of mathematics and electric engineering.	⁴3,000	Civil Eng. 15......	2	2	10	20
		Civil Eng. 12......	5	7	3	21
		Math. 1............	5	5	15	75
						116
Professor of sanitary engineering.	1,800	Civil Eng. 29......	4	5	22	110
		Civil Eng. 27......	5	5	5	25
						135
Instructor in dairy production.	1,200	Dairying 3........	2	3	7	21
		Dairying 11.......	2	3	6	18
						39
Instructor in dairying.........	1,200	Dairying 8........	3	5	7	35
		Dairying 10.......	3	5	4	20
						55
Professor of dairying..........	⁵1,800	Dairying 13.......	3	4	14	56
		Dairying 16.......	1	2	6	12
						68
Student assistant.............	100	Manual Arts 1.....	2	4	4	16

¹ Not given.
² Experiment station pays $450 of this.
³ Salary as dean, $1,500, constitutes part.
⁴ Salary as vice president, $2,000, constitutes part.
⁵ Experiment station pays $300 of this.

Washington State College—Salaries and student clock hours for second semester, year 1914–15—Continued.

Title of instructor.	Salary.	No. of course.	Value.	Clock hours.	Students.	Student clock hours.
Instructor in economic science.	$1,200	Econ. 5	5	3	7	21
		Econ. 10	5	3	21	37
		Econ. 60	3	3	3	63
		Econ. 61	2	3	18	54
						165
Professor of economic science.	2,200	Econ. 31	5	5	33	165
		Econ. 31	5	5	30	150
		Econ. 37	5	3	6	18
						333
Assistant professor of history.	1,500	Econ. 33	3	3	10	30
		Econ. 34	2	2	9	18
		Hist. 24	5	5	14	70
		Hist. 25	5	3	18	54
						172
Professor of Latin	2,200	Econ. 41	5	5	26	130
		Econ. 12	5	3	2	6
						136
Assistant professor of education.	1,600	Educ. 1	5	7	28	196
		Educ. 8	3	3	29	57
		Educ. 9	5	5	19	95
						378
Professor of psychology.	2,200	Educ. 3	5	5	46	230
		Educ. 4	5	8	14	112
						342
Professor of applied electricity.	1,900	Elec. Eng. 2	3	3	8	24
		Elec. Eng. 4	3	3	11	33
		Elec. Eng. 32	2	4	(1)	....
		Elec. Eng. 34	3	6	....	....
		Elec. Eng. 36	3	6	....	....
						[2] 57
Professor of mechanical and electrical engineering.	3,000	Elec. Eng. 6	3	3	9	27
		Elec. Eng. 7	2	2	6	12
		Elec. Eng. 16	2	2	9	18
		Elec. Eng. 22	4	4	12	48
						105
Professor of English	2,400	English 4	2	5	17	85
		English 5	5	3	13	39
		English 29	3	3	22	66
		English 31	2	2	23	46
		English 33	5	5	28	140
						376
Instructor in English	1,200	English 4	5	5	17	85
		English 29	3	3	20	60
		English 30	2	2	42	84
		English 31	2	2	15	30
		English 35	3	3	3	9
						268
Assistant professor of English.	1,600	English 14	5	3	5	15
		English 28	3	3	23	69
		English 29	3	3	19	57
		English 31	2	2	22	44
		English 43	5	3	7	21
						206

[1] Not given. [2] So far as given.

Washington State College—Salaries and student clock hours for second semester, year 1914–15—Continued.

Title of instructor.	Salary.	No. of course.	Value.	Clock hours.	Students.	Student clock hours.
Assistant professor of English.	$1,700	English 15........	5	3	5	15
		English 28........	3	3	17	51
		English 29........	3	3	25	75
		English 30........	2	2	27	54
		English 31........	2	2	27	54
		English 49........	5	3	3	9
						258
Do......................	1,500	English 23........	2	2	3	6
		English 25........	3	3	8	24
		English 28........	3	3	13	39
		English 29........	3	3	23	69
		English 31........	2	2	28	56
		English 52........	2	2	14	28
						222
Instructor in English..........	1,200	English 51........	2	2	8	16
		English 28........	3	3	17	51
		English 29........	3	3	31	93
		English 31........	2	2	19	38
		English 51........	2	2	5	10
						208
Do......................	1,200	English 29........	3	3	42	126
		English 31........	2	2	42	84
		English 36........	5	3	5	15
		English 39........	2	2	7	14
						239
Do......................	400	English 29........	3	3	17	51
		English 31........	2	2	23	46
						97
Instructor in expression.......	300	Expression 1......	1	1	3	3
		Expression 2......	1	1	4	4
		Expression 3......	2	2	2	4
		Expression 4......	2	2	4	8
		Expression 5......	2	2	1	2
		Expression 7......	1	1	3	3
		Expression 8......	1	1	6	6
		Expression 10.....	2	2	8	16
		Expression 11.....	2	2	1	2
		Expression 12.....	2	2	1	2
		Expression 13.....	1	1	8	8
		Expression 14.....	1	1	12	12
		Expression 15.....	1	1	1	1
		Expression 16.....	1	1	1	1
		Expression 19.....	3	1	2	3
		Expression 20.....	3	1	2	2
		Expression 22.....	3	1	2	2
						80
Instructor in fine arts.........	1,000	Fine arts 2........	3	6	32	182
		Fine arts 4........	2	4	1	8
		Fine arts 4........	2	4	3	12
		Fine arts 9........	2	2	3	6
		Fine arts 17.......	5	10	1	10
		Fine arts 19.......	5	10	2	20
		Fine arts 20.......	5	10	1	10
		Fine arts 22.......	(1)	....	1	(2)
						248
Professor of forestry..........	2,200	Forestry 33	3	4	2	8
		Forestry 34	5	7	5	35
		Forestry 35	2	2	4	8
		Forestry 37	1	1	1	1
		Forestry 43	1	2	3	6
		Forestry 44	1	1	1	1
		Forestry 48	2	2	1	2
		Forestry 49	2	2	5	10
						71

[1] 1 to 3 or 5.   [2] Not given.

Washington State College—Salaries and student clock hours for second semester, year 1914-15—Continued.

Title of instructor.	Salary.	No. of course.	Value.	Clock hours.	Students.	Student clock hours.
Instructor in French	$1,100	French 4	5	5	14	70
		French 20	5	5	1	5
		French 25	5	5	4	20
						95
	1,500	French 11	5	5	4	20
		French 21	5	5	3	15
		German 8	5	5	1	5
		German 10	5	5	11	55
						95
Professor of German	2,200	French 21	5	5	30	150
		German 2	5	5	9	45
		German 12	2	2	5	10
		German 15	5	5	4	20
		German 19	3	3	3	9
						234
Professor of geology	2,600	Geology 1 & 2	5	5	29	175
		Geology 21	2	2	10	20
		Geology 22	3	5	4	20
						215
Assistant professor of economic geology.	1,600	Geology 4	2	4	6	24
		Geology 5	3	6	7	42
		Geology 11	2	2	4	8
		Geology 13	3	6	5	30
						104
Instructor in German	1,100	German 20	5	5	20	100
		German 20	5	5	45	225
						325
Do	1,100	German 3	5	5	12	60
		German 4	5	5	9	45
		German 17	5	5	3	15
		German 20	5	5	13	65
						185
Do	500	German 3	5	5	1	5
		German 11	5	5	16	80
		German 16	5	5	2	10
		German 21	5	5	24	120
						215
Professor of political and social science.	1,620	History 2	5	5	28	140
		History 2	5	5	17	85
		History 12	5	3	29	87
						312
Professor of history	1,620	History 1	5	5	9	45
		History 20	2	2	6	12
		History 22	5	3	9	27
		History 51	5	(1)	5	(1)
						84
Instructor in textiles and clothing.	1,100	Home Econ. 3	2	2	38	76
		Home Econ. 20	5	10	15	150
						226
Professor of home economics	1,800	Home Econ. 5	3	6	17	102
		Home Econ. 10	2	4	13	52
		Home Econ. 2	1	2	1	2
		Home Econ. 33	3	3	9	27
		Home Econ. 38	5	5	13	65
						248

[1] Not given.

Washington State College—Salaries and student clock hours for second semester, year 1914–15—Continued.

Title of instructor.	Salary.	No. of course.	Value.	Clock hours.	Students.	Student clock hours.
Assistant professor of foods and cookery.	$1,400	Home Econ. 12.... Home Econ. 36...	3 5	6 8	17 9	102 72
						174
Student assistant..............	300	Home Econ. 21....	5	10	9	190
Assistant professor of floriculture and gardening.	1,650	Hort. 1............. Hort. 33............ Hort. 37............ Hort. 39............ Hort. 40............	3 3 3 2 2	4 5 6 3 3	16 5 2 3 4	64 25 12 9 12
						122
Instructor in horticulture.....	1,200	Hort. 3............. Hort. 31............	3 5	4 6	8 2	32 12
						44
Associate professor of pomology.	1,900	Hort. 29............ Hort. 12............ Hort. 24............ Hort. 30............	3 2 2 3	4 7 2 4	9 8 6 12	36 56 12 48
						152
Professor of horticulture.......	2,200	Hort. 32............	3	4	8	32
Assistant professor of Latin...	1,400	Latin 1............. Latin 2............. Pharmacy 4.......	5 5 2	5 5 2	1 1 21	5 5 42
						52
Instructor in metal work......	750	Manual Arts 2.... Manual Arts 14...	2 4	4 8	3 2	12 16
						28
Assistant professor of mechanical engineering.	1,500	Manual Arts 6..... Mech. Eng........ Mech. Eng. 38.....	4 3 3	4 3 4	6 7 3	24 21 12
						57
Instructor in mathematics.....	1,200	Math. 4............ Math. 11........... Math. 13...........	4 1 1	4 1 1	8 8 8	32 8 8
						48
Professor of mathematics......	1,900	Math. 2 and 3..... Math. 4............ Math. 6............ Math. 10........... Math. 13........... Math. 15...........	5 4 5 2 1 3	5 4 5 2 1 3	17 13 12 8 14 4	85 52 60 16 14 12
						239
Assistant professor of mathematics.	1,700	Math. 4............ Math. 4............ Math. 6............ Math. 13........... Math. 14........... Math. 17...........	4 4 5 1 2 3	4 4 5 1 2 3	16 13 11 13 6 5	72 52 55 13 12 15
						219
Instructor in electrical engineering.	1,200	Mech. Arts 2...... Mech. Arts 10.....	4 2	4 2	6 4	24 8
						32
Instructor in mechanical engineering.	450	Mech. Arts 8...... Mech. Arts 40..... Mech. Arts 42..... Mech. Arts 44..... Mech. Arts 50..... Mech. Arts 11.....	5 5 3 5 2 5	5 10 6 10 4 10	7 7 2 5 3 20	35 70 12 50 12 200
						379

Washington State College—Salaries and student clock hours for second semester, year 1914–15—Continued.

Title of instructor.	Salary.	No. of course.	Value.	Clock hours.	Students.	Student clock hours.
Associate professor of mechanical engineering.	$1,600	Mech. Arts 20.....	2	2	2	4
		Mech. Eng. 3......	3	6	17	102
		Mech. Eng. 3......	3	6	22	132
		Mech. Eng. 19.....	3	6	7	42
		Mech. Eng. 17.....	3	3	11	33
		Mech. Eng. 3......	3	6	16	96
						409
Assistant professor of manual training.	1,400	Mn. Eng. 5........	2	4	11	44
		Manual Arts 12....	4	2	9	18
						62
Assistant professor of mechanical engineering.	1,400	Mech. Eng. 25.....	3	6	2	12
		Mech. Eng. 27.....	2	2	2	4
		Mech. Eng. 40.....	1	1	3	3
		Mech. Eng. 42.....	2	2	4	5
						33
Instructor in foundry........	450	Mech. Eng. 34.....	2	2	24	48
Assistant professor of metallurgy.	1,500	Mining 6..........	2	2	4	8
		Mining 6..........	2	2	2	4
		Mining 10.........	5	9	4	36
		Mining 12.........	2	4	3	12
						60
Professor of mining engineering.	2,600	Mining 8..........	5	5	4	20
		Mining 9..........	5	9	2	18
		Mining 11.........	1	1	5	5
						43
Professor of pipe organ and piano.	1,100	Music 10..........	1	1	34	34
		Music 32..........	5	5	8	40
		Music 34..........	2	2	2	4
		Music 36..........	3	3	3	3
		Organ and piano..	2½ or 5	....	21	....
						81
	[1] 400	Music 62..........	5		11	....
		Vocal 26..........	2½ or 5		26	....
Instructor in piano..........	([2])	Piano.............	2½ or 5		18	
Professor of violin..........	[1] 500	Violin............	....		18	
Professor of piano..........	.... [1] 1,500	Piano 2...........	2½ or 5	....	6	....
		Piano 4...........	2½ or 5	....	3	....
		Piano 5...........	2½ or 5	....	2	....
		Piano 6...........	2½ or 5	....	1	....
		Piano 8...........	2½ or 5	....	1	....
		Piano 1...........	2½ or 5	....	1	....
		Piano 3...........	2½ or 5	....	2	....
Instructor in voice..........	[1] 200	Vocal.............	....	....	....	11
Professor of pharmacy and materia medica.	1,800	Pharmacy 3.......	3	3	17	51
		Pharmacy 5.......	5	5	16	80
		Pharmacy 7.......	4	13	6	78
		Pharmacy 8.......	4	13	7	91
						300
Instructor in veterinary science.	1,320	Pharmacy 9.......	3	3	6	18
		Veterinary 34.....	5	6	26	156
		Veterinary 41.....	2	2	41	82
						312
	450	Photography......	2	4	9	36
Professor of physics..........	1,800	Physics 2.........	3	4	32	128
		Physics 16........	5	7	2	14
		Physics 20........	5	7	6	42
		Physics 32........	2	2	28	56
						240

[1] And tuition fees.   [2] Tuition fees only.

Washington State College—Salaries and student clock hours for second semester, year 1914–15—Continued.

Title of instructor.	Salary.	No. of course.	Value.	Clock hours.	Students.	Student clock hours.
Professor of Scandinavian.....	$1,320	Scan. 2............	5	5	3	15
		Scan. 4............	5	5	2	10
						25
Instructor in Spanish.........	1,100	Span. 1...........	5	5	8	40
		Span. 2...........	5	5	23	115
		Span. 2...........	5	5	12	60
		Span. 2...........	5	5	15	75
		Span. 6...........	5	5	2	10
						300
Associate professor of anatomy and surgery.	1,700	Clinics............	1–5	6	32	192
		Vet. 20............	4	6	19	114
		Vet. 26............	5	5	13	65
		Vet. 42............	2	2	46	92
		Vet. 46............	1	1	11	11
						474
Professor of veterinary science.	3,000	Vet. 23............	5	7	11	77
		Vet. 25............	5	6	12	72
						149
Do.......................	2,000	Vet. 29............	5	5	6	30
		Vet. 44............	3	3	6	18
						48
Assistant professor of pathology and histology.	[1] 1,800	Vet. 31............	5	9	11	99
		Zool. 10...........	2	10	19	190
						289
Instructor in zoology.........	1,200	Zool. 22...........	5	8	17	136
Professor of zoology...........	[2] 2,400	Zool. 40...........	1	1	9	9
		Zool. 37...........	4	6	9	54
						63

[1] Experiment station pays $600 of this.   [2] Experiment station pays $800 of this.

APPENDIX C.

Instructors and students in public normal schools.

Location	Institution	Instructors — Number — Male	Female	In teachers' training courses — Male	Female	Students — Number, counting 9 none 9 twice — Male	Female	In teachers' training courses — Male	Female	In business courses — Male	Female	In high-school grades — Male	Female	In elementary grades — Male	Female	Graduates from teachers' training courses — Male	Female	Children in model school — Male	Female	Years in normal course
1	2	3	4	5	6	7	8	9	10	11	12	13	14	15	16	17	18	19	20	21
Daphne, Ala.	Daphne State Normal School	3	6	3	3	48	74	6	47	4	4	38	28	0	0	1	2	15	36	4
Florence, Ala.	State Normal School	6	11	3	11	209	366	145	265	15	9	10	11	39	27	0	11	90	99	4
Jacksonville, Ala.	...do...	9	8	6	8	166	164	160	161	0	0	7	3	0	0	6	8			4
Livingston, Ala.	...do...	3	15	3	16	0	402	0	402	0	0	0	0	0	0	0	16	123	140	4
Montgomery, Ala.	State Colored Normal School	15	26	9	26	413	572	184	329	0	0	229	333	72	67	17	21	60	47	4
Normal, Ala.	Agricultural and Mechanical College for Negroes	10	14	4	2	126	128	10	19	0	0	37	37	79	0	2	2	47	64	4
Troy, Ala.	State Normal School	10	14	3	2	128	169	10	150	0	0	0	0	0	67	14	18	47	64	4
Tuskegee, Ala.	Tuskegee Normal and Industrial Institute (colored)	121	71			896	631	108	40	0	0	208	158	670	433	18	46	81	120	3
Flagstaff, Ariz.	Northern Arizona Normal School	6	9	1	4	54	104	18	10	0	0	44	14	0	0	1	32	55	68	3
Tempe, Ariz.	Tempe Normal School of Arizona	14	11	1	6	78	287	10	285	0	0	0	0	0	0	7	55	84	100	3
Conway, Ark.	Arkansas State Normal School	9	6	4	2	115	197	99	197	0	0	0	2	0	0	8	4	28	47	4
Pine Bluff, Ark.	Branch Normal College (colored)	10	5	3	2	70	100	115	55	0	0	0	0	40	66	6	0			4
Arcata, Cal.	Humboldt State Normal School	5	12	3	12	15	37	30	37	0	0	0	0	0	0	0	7			3
Chico, Cal.	State Normal School	9	7	7	7	51	263	15	216	0	0	0	47	0	0	11	75	172	192	3
Fresno, Cal.	...do...	7	18	1	18	18	239	42	239	0	0	0	0	0	0	0	98	105	98	3
Los Angeles, Cal.	...do...	15	49	15	49	35	1,370	35	1,370	0	0	0	0	0	0	13	549	411	365	3
San Diego, Cal.	...do...	8	18	8	18	7	315	7	315	0	0	0	0	0	0	4	134	189	222	3
San Francisco, Cal.	...do...	18	18	6	18	36	402	36	402	0	0	0	0	0	0	18	82	341	303	3
San Jose, Cal.	...do...	32	32	8	32	28	947	28	947	5	5	39	65	0	0	16	82	301	364	3
Santa Barbara, Cal.	...do...	9	12	2	3	0	224	4	224	0	0	0	0	0	0	1	19			3
Gunnison, Colo.	Bridgeport City Normal School	12	0	1	4	0	143	0	88	0	0	0	0	0	0	0	9	145	131	3
Bridgeport, Conn.	State Normal Training School	0	31	0	31	0	44	0	44	0	0	0	0	0	0	0	107	338	222	2
Danbury, Conn.	...do...	4	8	4	8	0	224	0	224	0	0	0	0	0	0	0	90			2
New Britain, Conn.	...do...	5	57	5	57	0	200	0	200	0	0	0	0	0	0	1	86	146	131	2
New Haven, Conn.	...do...	3	21	2	21	1	267	0	267	0	0	0	0	0	0	0	64	338	222	2
Willimantic, Conn.	...do...	8	20	2	20	1	122	1	122	0	0	0	0	0	0	2	45			2
Washington, D.C.	J. Ormond Wilson Normal School	3	9	3	7	9	114	8	114	0	0	0	9	0	0	2	64	317	289	2
Do.	Myrtilla Miner Normal School (colored)																	193	293	2

* Statistics of 1912–13.

Instructors and students in public normal schools—Continued.

Location	Institution
Athens, Ga.	State Normal School
Milledgeville, Ga.	Georgia Normal and Industrial College*
Valdosta, Ga.	South Georgia State Normal College*
Albion, Idaho.	State Normal School
Lewiston, Idaho.	....do.
Carbondale, Ill.	Southern Illinois State Normal University *
Charleston, Ill.	Eastern Illinois State Normal School
Chicago, Ill.	Chicago Normal School
De Kalb, Ill.	Northern Illinois State Normal School
Macomb, Ill.	Western Illinois State Normal School
Normal, Ill.	Illinois State Normal University
Fort Wayne, Ind.	Normal Training School
Indianapolis, Ind.	Indianapolis Normal School
Terre Haute, Ind.	Indiana State Normal School
Shenandoah, Iowa.	Western Normal College
Emporia, Kans.	State Normal School
Hays, Kans.	Fort Hays Kansas State Normal School
Pittsburg, Kans.	State Manual Training Normal School
Bowling Green, Ky.	Western Kentucky State Normal School
Frankfort, Ky.	State Normal and Industrial Institute for Colored Persons
Richmond, Ky.	Eastern Kentucky State Normal School
Natchitoches, La.	Louisiana State Normal School
New Orleans, La.	New Orleans Normal School
Castine, Me.	Eastern State Normal School
Farmington, Me.	Farmington State Normal School
Fort Kent, Me.	Madawaska Training School *
Gorham, Me.	Western State Normal School
Lewiston, Mo.	Lewiston Normal Training School

Location	School																				
Machias, Me.	Washington State Normal School																				
Presque Isle, Me.	Aroostook State Normal School																				
Baltimore, Md.	Baltimore Teachers' Training School																				
Do.	Colored Training School																				
Do.	Maryland State Normal School																				
Bowie, Md.	Maryland State Normal and Industrial School (colored).*																				
Frostburg, Md.	Maryland State Normal School																				
Boston, Mass.	Boston Normal School																				
Do.	Massachusetts Normal Art School																				
Bridgewater, Mass.	State Normal School																				
Fall River, Mass.	Normal Training School																				
Fitchburg, Mass.	State Normal School																				
Framingham, Mass.	do.																				
Hyannis, Mass.	do.																				
Lowell, Mass.	do.																				
North Adams, Mass.	do.																				
Salem, Mass.	do.																				
Westfield, Mass.	do.																				
Worcester, Mass.	do.																				
Detroit, Mich.	Wales Martindale Normal Training School																				
Kalamazoo, Mich.	Western State Normal School																				
Marquette, Mich.	Northern State Normal School																				
Mount Pleasant, Mich.	Central State Normal School																				
Ypsilanti, Mich.	Michigan State Normal College																				
Duluth, Minn.	do.																				
Mankato, Minn.	do.																				
Moorhead, Minn.	do.																				
St. Cloud, Minn.	do.																				
St. Paul, Minn.	St. Paul Normal School																				
Winona, Minn.	State Normal School																				
Hattiesburg, Miss.	Mississippi Normal College																				
Cape Girardeau, Mo.	State Normal School																				
Jefferson City, Mo.	Lincoln Institute* (colored)																				
Kirksville, Mo.	State Normal School																				
Maryville, Mo.	do.*																				
St. Louis, Mo.	Harris Teachers College																				
Springfield, Mo.	State Normal School																				
Warrensburg, Mo.	do.																				
Dillon, Mont.	Montana State Normal School																				
Chadron, Nebr.	State Normal School																				
Kearney, Nebr.	do.																				
Peru, Nebr.	do.																				
Wayne, Nebr.	do.																				
Keene, N. H.	do.*																				
Plymouth, N. H.	do.																				
Elizabeth, N. J.	Normal and Training School																				
Jersey City, N. J.	Teachers' Training School																				
Montclair, N. J.	New Jersey State Normal School																				
Newark, N. J.	do.																				
Paterson, N. J.	Paterson Normal Training School																				

* Statistics of 1912–13.

Instructors and students in public normal schools—Continued.

Location.	Institution.	Instructors.				Students.													Children in model school.		Years in normal course.
		Number.		In teachers' training courses.		Number, counting none twice.		In teachers' training courses.		In business courses.		In high-school grades.		In elementary grades.		Graduate from teachers' training courses.		Male.	Female.	
		Male.	Female.	Male.	Female.	Male.	Female.	Male.	Female.	Male.	Female.	Male.	Female.	Male.	Female.	Male.	Female.			
1	**2**	**3**	**4**	**5**	**6**	**7**	**8**	**9**	**10**	**11**	**12**	**13**	**14**	**15**	**16**	**17**	**18**	**19**	**20**	**21**
Trenton, N. J.	New Jersey State Normal School	17	40	10	24	94	771	15	613	0	0	79	188	0	0	7	229	110	139	3
El Rito, N. Mex.	Spanish-American Normal School	1	1	1	1	45	35	45	35	0	0	0	0	0	0	0	0	15	35	3
East Las Vegas, N.Mex.	New Mexico Normal University	8	14	4	7	67	117	12	63	22	6	33	50	0	0	9	28	85	78	4
Silver City, N. Mex.	New Mexico Normal School	4	4	2	5	27	74	3	6	7	14	17	54	0	0	0	4	77	68	4
Albany, N. Y.	Teachers' Training School	3	9	1	6	83	67	0	57	0	0	81	119	0	0	0	20	200	210	2
Brockport, N. Y.	State Normal and Training School	11	44	12	16	576	574	4	124	0	0	0	0	0	0	0	79	140	138	3
Brooklyn, N. Y.	Training School for Teachers	4	17	3	4	437	437	98	974	0	0	0	0	0	0	33	404	157	130	3
Buffalo, N. Y.	State Normal School	2	6	0	17	96	437	4	437	0	0	0	0	0	0	0	361	161	168	3
Cohoes, N. Y.	Cohoes Training School	0	3	1	1	0	388	35	388	0	0	28	110	0	0	18	159	188	208	3
Cortland, N. Y.	State Normal and Training School	6	29	8	17	73	207	6	169	0	0	119	61	0	0	4	170	178	144	3
Fredonia, N. Y.	....do....	9	20	7	28	119	296	21	296	0	0	40	92	0	0	6	188	163	175	3
Geneseo, N. Y.	Geneseo State Normal School	7	17	8	16	83	271	8	271	0	0	61	54	0	0	8	289	167	157	3
New Paltz, N. Y.	State Normal School	7	58	10	65	40	780	3	780	0	0	36	0	0	0	5	74	306	307	3
New York, N. Y.	New York Training School for Teachers	10	56	5	16	3	671	3	435	0	0	0	21	0	0	2	210	190	327	3
Oneonta, N. Y.	State Normal School	10	16	10	14	62	188	41	203	0	0	21	26	0	0	14	139	100	151	3
Oswego, N. Y.	Oswego State Normal and Training School	10	16	10	16	85	201	85	201	0	0	30	88	0	0	0	63	90	131	3
Plattsburg, N. Y.	State Normal and Training School	2	17	4	13	117	227	11	105	0	0	106	123	0	0	1	76	137	130	3
Potsdam, N. Y.	State Normal and Training School	3	31	1	11	0	105	0	105	0	0	0	0	0	0	0	83	400	460	3
Rochester, N. Y.	Rochester Training School	2	24	9	9	0	18	0	18	0	0	0	0	0	0	7	7	275	275	3
Schenectady, N. Y.	Teachers' Training School	1	4	1	3	0	14	0	14	0	0	0	0	0	0	301	34			3
Syracuse, N. Y.	Syracuse Training School for Teachers	3	3	3	8	0	44	0	44	0	0	0	0	0	0	34	24			3
Yonkers, N. Y.	Yonkers Training School for Teachers	1	6	1	6	0	65	0	65	0	0	0	0	0	0	0	0	61	60	3
Cullowhee, N. C.	Cullowhee Normal and Industrial School	3	7	3	2	140	125	140	125	0	63	0	0	104	103	12	12	34	123	4
Elizabeth City, N. C.	State Colored Normal School	7	2	7	3	178	260	74	88	0	0	74	0	104	130	8	3	43	47	4
Fayetteville, N. C.	....do....	4	4	2	3	183	203	0	203	0	0	0	0	0	0	0	71	176	161	4
Greensboro, N. C.	State Normal and Industrial College	13	65	13	65	0	240	9	170	0	0	0	0	0	0	0	87			4
Greenville, N. C.	East Carolina Training School	8	13	2	9	0	175	56	125	119	47	0	0	0	0	7	23			4
Ellendale, N. Dak.	North Dakota State Normal and Industrial School	16	10	4	1	174	175	60	126	0	0	0	0	0	0	0	74			4
Mayville, N. Dak.	State Normal School	8	7	3	6	50	200	50	200	0	0	0	0	0	0	2				3

Location	Institution
M, N. Dak.	do
y City, N. Dak.	Perkins Normal School*
Akron, Ohio	Cleveland Normal Training School
ad, Ohio	llis Normal School
us, Ohio	Dayton Normal College
Dayton, Ohio	State Normal College
Zai, Ohio	lite N nd School
Ada, Okla	6th State nll School
d, Okla	Stern State nll School
Pat, Okla	il Ste ell Skool
did, Okla	th State Normal School
Tahlequah, Okla	th State Normal School
Wird, Okla	th tile Normal School
Mt, Oreg	State Normal School
bur, Pa	
Gala, Pa	Southwestern State Normal School
Clarion, Pa	State Normal School
Eas' tsburg, Pa	do
Edinboro, Pa	do
Erie, Pa	Erie Normal Training School
Harrisburg, Pa	Teachers' Training School
ath, Pa	State Normal School
Kutztown, Pa	Keystone State Normal School
Lock Haven, Pa	Central State Normal School
d, Pa	State Normal School
Millersville, Pa	Philadelphia Normal School for Girls
Philadelphia, Pa	Philadelphia School of Pedagogy
Do	Normal and Training School for Girls
Reading, Pa	do
Shippensburg, Pa	Cumberland Valley State Normal School *
Slippery Rock, Pa	State Normal School
West Chester, Pa	do
Providence, R. I	Rhode Island State Normal School
Orangeburg, S. C	Colored Normal, Industrial, Agricultural, and Mechanical College of South Caroli a
Rockhill, S. C	Wop Normal nd lll College
Aberdeen, S. Dak	Northern Normal nl Industrial School
Madison, S. Dak	State Normal School
Spearfish, S Dak	do
Springfield, S. Dak	do
Johnson (Tenn	live State Normal School*
Memphis, Tenn	West Tennessee State Normal School
Murfreesboro, Tenn	Middle Tennessee State Normal School
Nashville, Tenn	State Agricultural of Industrial Normal School for Negroes.*
Canyon City, Tex	West the State Normal College
Denton, Tex	North Texas State Normal College
Huntsville, Tex	Sam 6th State Normal Institute
Prairie View, Tex	Prairie View State Normal and Industrial College (colored).

* Statistics of 1912–13.

Instructors and students in public normal schools—Continued.

Location	Institution	Instructors — Number. Male	Female	In teachers' training courses. Male	Female	Students — Number, counting none twice. Male	Female	In teachers' training courses. Male	Female	In business courses. Male	Female	In high-school grades. Male	Female	In elementary grades. Male	Female	Graduates from teachers' training courses. Male	Female	Children in model school. Male	Female	Years in normal course.
San Marcos, Tex.	Southwest Texas State Normal School	16	16	16	16	151	543	151	563	0	0	0	0	0	0		37	40	80	4
Castleton, Vt.	State Normal School	5	5	2	5	0	63	0	63	0	0	0	0	0	0	0	43	50	80	2
Johnson, Vt.	...do...	5	12	3	6	2	134	2	134	0	0	0	0	0	0	4	40	70	121	2
East Radford, Va.	State Normal School for Women	10	27	10	21	26	480	4	160	0	0	0	0	0	0		130	70	85	2
Farmville, Va.	...do...	5	41	6	11	0	523	0	249	0	0	0	0	0	0	4	30	53	125	2
Fredericksburg, Va.	State Normal and Industrial School for Women	62	68	7	18	717	692	17	77	0	0	0	0	0	0	0	20	198	267	2
Hampton, Va.	Hampton Normal and Agricultural Institute (colored)	10	32	3	11	0	266	0	306	0	0	0	0	465	445	25	60	26	36	2
Harrisonburg, Va.	State Normal and Industrial School for Women	3	11	7	24	141	419	57	191	0	0	187	124	509	0	10	65	130	143	4
Petersburg, Va.	Virginia Normal and Industrial Institute (colored)	10	24	10	7	60	635	88	635	0	0	84	228	0	0	8	98	61	146	3
Bellingham, Wash.	State Normal School	15	14	15	7	80	620	80	620	0	0	0	0	0	0	1	64	61	143	3
Cheney, Wash.	...do.	9	6	7	3	20	259	20	229	0	0	0	0	0	0	9	63	65	75	3
Ellensburg, Wash.	...do.	11	18	11	18	101	262	7	40	0	0	98	180	0	0	1	41	25	36	3
Athens, W. Va.	Concord State Normal School	12	11	12	4	245	206	260	206	0	0	94	169	0	0	16	51	100	105	4
Fairmont, W. Va.	State Normal School	16	30	8	20	260	375	260	300	0	0	20	45	81	55	10	51	2	14	2
Glenville, W. Va.	...do.*	4	8	4	3	125	113	22	121	25	36	53	23	0	0	5	20	0	13	3
Huntington, W. Va.	Marshall College, State Normal School	8	7	3	2	85	123	21	46	0	32	57	53	0	0	17	17	19	12	3
Institute, W. Va.	West Virginia Colored Institute	2	2	2	2	19	41	19	77	0	0	0	0	0	0	8	16	0	9	4
Shepherdstown, W. Va.	Shepherd College, State Normal School	1	1	1	1	42	41	8	41	0	0	0	0	0	0	5	13	5	8	3
West Liberty, W. Va.	Rock Normal School	2	2	2	2	0	42	0	42	0	0	0	0	0	0	8	16			3
Algoma, Wis.	Door-Kewaunee County Training School	2	1	1	1	9	45	9	45	0	0	0	0	0	0	1	18	9	19	2
Alma, Wis.	Buffalo County Training School	1	1	1	0	8	51	0	51	0	0	0	0	0	0	0	19	21	53	2
Antigo, Wis.	Langlade County Training School	2	1	2	1	9	42	9	43	0	0	0	0	0	0	1	18			2
Berlin, Wis.	Green Lake County Training School	1	1	1	1	3	41	3	61	0	0	0	0	0	0	1	25			2
Columbus, Wis.	Columbia County Training School	1	1	1	0	3	34	3	34	0	0	0	0	0	0	1	26			2
Eau Claire, Wis.	Eau Claire County Training School	2	1	1	1	7	31	0	31	0	0	0	0	0	0	1	17	18	24	2
Gays Mills, Wis.	Crawford County Training School	1	2	1	2	0	30	0	30	0	0	0	0	0	0	0	13	18	24	2
Grand Rapids, Wis.	Wood County Training School	1	1	1	1	7	28	0	29	0	0	0	0	0	0	1	11	93	110	2
Janesville, Wis.	Rock County Training School	2	2	1	1	0	30	0	30	0	0	0	0	0	0					2
La Crosse, Wis.	State Normal School	21	16	21	16	164	299	164	299	0	0	0	0	0	0	27	107	96	110	2

Place	Institution																				
Ladysmith, Wis	Rusk County Training School	1	2	1	1					9	34	9	34	0	0	0	0	0	3	4	28
Manitowoc, Wis	Manitowoc County Training School	2	2	1	1					12	30	12	30	0	0	0	0	0	4		11
Medford, Wis	Taylor County Training School*	1	1	1	1					1	27	1	27	0	0	0	0	0	0		2
Menomonie, Wis	Dunn County Training School	3	3	1	1					4	74	4	74	0	0	0	0	0	1		27
Do	Stout Institute	26	26	17	17			16	14	161	417	161	417	0	0	0	0	0	79	147	
Merrill, Wis	Lincoln County Training School*	2	2	2	2			208	211	0	64	0	54	0	0	0	0	0	16	16	
Milwaukee, Wis	State Normal School*	42	43	21	21					153	688	153	688	0	0	0	0	0	18	267	
Monroe, Wis	Green County Training School	3	3	1	1					1	67	1	67	0	0	0	0	0	0	33	
New London, Wis	Waupaca County Training School	1	1	1	1					2	43	2	43	0	0	0	0	0	1	14	
Oshkosh, Wis	State Normal School	23	23	23	23			136	129	171	376	171	376	0	0	0	0	0	350	123	
Phillips, Wis	Price County Training School*	1	1	1	1					0	33	0	33	0	0	0	0	0	0	10	
Platteville, Wis	State Normal School	12	12	13	13			102	108	100	210	100	210	0	0	0	0	0	43	61	
Reedsburg, Wis	Sauk County Training School	3	3	1	1			20	20	2	41	2	41	0	0	0	0	0	1b	19	
Rhinelander, Wis	Oneida County Training School*	1	1	1	1					12	40	12	40	0	0	0	0	0	0	11	
Rice Lake, Wis	Barron County Training School	2	2	1	1					4	65	4	65	0	0	0	0	0	1	28	
Richland Center, Wis	Richland County Training School*	2	2	1	1			18	18	14	43	14	43	0	0	0	0	0	1	18	
River Falls, Wis	State Normal School	13	13	5	5			66	63	141	349	141	349	0	0	0	0	0	21	68	
St. Croix Falls, Wis	Polk County Training School*	1	1	1	1			61	15	2	41	2	41	0	0	0	0	0	0	14	
Stevens Point, Wis	State Normal School	18	18	14	14			124	124	74	331	74	331	0	0	0	0	0	15	90	
Superior, Wis	do.	21	21	13	13			100	61	81	433	81	433	0	0	0	0	0	19	113	
Viroqua, Wis	Vernon County Training School	3	3	1	1					6	54	6	54	0	0	0	0	0	4	19	
Wausau, Wis	Marathon County Training School*	2	2	1	1					7	76	7	76	0	0	0	0	0	0	29	
Wautoma, Wis	Waushara County Training School*	1	1	1	1					2	36	2	36	0	0	0	0	0	1	22	
Whitewater, Wis	State Normal School	16	16	15	15			113	115	84	228	84	228	0	0	0	0	0	14	78	

* Statistics of 1912-13.

STATEMENT OF MAINTENANCE, PHYSICAL EQUIPMENT, AND URGENT NEEDS OF THE THREE NORMAL SCHOOLS.

STATE NORMAL SCHOOL AT CHENEY.

1. *Maintenance.*—The school receives regularly for maintenance nine one-hundredths of 1 mill of the State millage tax. This has thus far proved ample for all purposes, and with the increase in the State's wealth should, for the future, yield an even larger revenue. Enough has been saved from the millage tax during the last few years to construct a modern dormitory for the women students and a satisfactory manual training building. Such portion of the millage tax as has been used in the past to build up the school plant should for the immediate future be used for increased salaries and larger working staff.

2. *Physical equipment.*—The school has practically been rebuilt since 1913, when its old main building was destroyed by fire. The present equipment comprises a new administration building, a manual training building, a training school building, a dormitory for girls, and a central heating plant—all on a campus of 22 acres.

The valuation of the physical plant is given by the school authorities as follows:

Training school building	$77,000	Monroe Hall (girls' home).....	$46,000
Equipment................	9,800	Equipment...............	8,600
Administration building......	300,000	Central heating plant [1].......	3,000
Equipment................	31,000	Equipment..............	13,000
Manual training building......	13,500	Campus (22 acres).............	12,000
Equipment...............	6,000	Total................	519,900

Administration building.—This structure has been in use for a little over a year. It was constructed at a cost of about $300,000 (special legislative appropriation). It is well planned and equipped with necessary furniture, apparatus, etc. The building is fireproof, and from an architectural point of view, wholly satisfactory. Indeed, it is one of the best planned and equipped normal school buildings in the country.

The Manual training building.—This new building is just being put into operation. It is ample for its purpose for some years to come.

The dormitory for girls.—This structure has also recently been completed, at a cost of $46,000. It is well planned and affords good living quarters for the girls. A satisfactory plan of student government secures good management.

The practice school building.—This was built some years ago for practice school purposes; but it seems not to have been intelligently planned and is wholly inadequate for its purpose. This important phase of the normal school work is in charge of a director and critic teachers, but their best efforts are much hampered by the building in which they are obliged to do their work. This building should be reconstructed at an early date.

The heating plant is a temporary structure made of sheet iron and should be replaced by a permanent building.

Recommendation for new equipment:

1. A new practice school building.
2. A school farm.
3. A model rural practice school on the campus.
4. A permanent heating plant.

The normal school sends 64 per cent of all its graduates into the rural schools of the State, many going into the one-teacher schools; the others into the consolidated schools. The modern rural school is rooted to the soil, and no teacher can do the work well who has not had thorough courses in agriculture. This requires land for experimentation and demonstration purposes, which should be in addition to the small area of garden plats now in use by the department of agriculture. It is recommended that

---

[1] Largely temporary.

a normal school farm be procured without delay. It should lie handy to the school premises, and contain not less than 25 acres. It might be operated in cooperation with the extension service of the State College of Agriculture. A large number of the leading normal schools of the country already have similar school farms in successful operation. Rural demonstration schools conducted for the purpose of assisting county superintendents and giving demonstrations in rural-school work are operated by the normal schools in the counties adjacent to Cheney.

The model rural practice school.—The rural school department of the normal school is well organized and is doing a good work. The rural teacher, however, has a difficult field—in many respects more difficult than the town field—and requires a specialized professional preparation. Much of this may be acquired in a rural-practice school. Fifty-nine strong normal schools are already using such model rural schools to excellent advantage. It is recommended that an appropriation not to exceed $5,000 be made for the building and equipment of such a school as soon as possible.

STATE NORMAL SCHOOL AT ELLENSBURG.

1. *Maintenance.*—The school receives for maintenance seven one-hundredths of 1 mill of the State millage tax. This amount has proved insufficient to provide for both operation and maintenance, and also for much needed equipment and new buildings. Probably the institution's present share of the millage tax will be ample for operating expenses, however, until there is a material increase in attendance. It was suggested to the committee in several quarters that the school at Ellensburg, on account of its small attendance, should be able to carry on its work with much smaller appropriations than are required by the other schools. This theory is only partly correct and fails to take account of the fact that a certain standard equipment and a well-balanced faculty are essential whether a school has 300 or 600 students. Nor should a school's influence and value to the people be judged wholly by its numerical strength. It is well to bear in mind that the Ellensburg school lies in the sparsely settled section of the State and can not depend to any extent on large cities for students. Nevertheless, it has its own field to serve, and should be given ample support to perform this service.

2. *Physical equipment.*—The normal school is located in the town of Ellensburg, on grounds which comprise about 8 acres of land, valued at approximately $65,000. The number and value of the buildings and equipment are given by the school authorities as follows.

1. Main building (contains offices, classrooms, laboratories, auditorium, gymnasium, and library of 10,000 volumes)	$120,000
Equipment	15,000
Library	23,000
2. Training school	65,000
Equipment	4,500
8. Science, manual training, and heating plant	30,000
Equipment	2,200
Heating plant	5,200
4. Girls' dormitory	60,000
Equipment	7,000
5. Club house	9,000
Equipment	1,500
Total (including value of land)	407,400
Total value of land	65,000
Total value of buildings	284,000
Total value of equipment	58,400
Total value of all properties	407,400

The main building.—This is the original normal school building. It was built at a time when the emphasis in schoolhouse construction was placed on the achievement of an impressive exterior rather than on sanitation and practical arrangement. The toilet facilities are entirely inadequate and should be improved without delay. The domestic science department of the school—which is rendering excellent service—is housed in the basement of this building. It should have better-quarters. The gymnasium is also in the basement of the main building. It has no equipment worthy the name. The normal school library is housed in this building also. It contains about 10,000 bound volumes, well selected, and suitable to normal school use. The collection of periodicals is also very satisfactory.

The practice school (training school).—This, like the Cheney practice school, was built some years ago and is imperfectly adapted to actual needs. Neither the arrangement of classrooms, nor their sanitation, is satisfactory. The toilet facilities are particularly bad. Moreover, the building is too small for its purpose. The offices of the director and critic teachers are, for example, used regularly for class purposes. The practice school is too important an arm of the normal school to be slighted.

It is recommended that a wing be added to the present building, and that the basement of the structure now standing be entirely remodelled especially with a view to the improvement of its lighting and to the provision of additional lavatories and toilet facilities. The new wing should be of fireproof construction. Indeed, too little regard has been paid to safety and permanency in the construction of all the buildings of this school.

The science and manual training building.—This is an inexpensive building, fairly well planned, but of poor construction. Its deep basement contains the central heating plant of the school. The science laboratories and manual training shops are meagerly equipped with apparatus. Good work is being done with an equipment that should be enlarged and improved as soon as possible.

The dormitory for girls.—This is an attractive building, well kept, and well adapted to its purpose, although not very substantial or very expensive.

Recommendations for added equipment:

    1. A normal school farm.

    2. Either a model rural practice school on the campus or the establishment of
        closer relations with rural schools in the vicinity.

The arguments offered in support of similar recommendations in the discussion of the equipment of the Cheney Normal School are equally applicable in the case of Ellensburg. At Ellensburg only a small patch of ground is available for agricultural experiment and school gardens. The school has no rural practice school equipment. Visitation of outlying schools, as carried on at Ellensburg, is incidental only and of little practical value.

Separate departments in agriculture and rural school subjects.—Special attention is called to the needs of agricultural and general rural education. One instructor is charged with the work of both these departments. It is encouraging to note that the number of students in agriculture has increased from 73 in 1913–14 to 91 in 1914–15, and that the number of students in the rural education classes has increased from 14 in 1913–14, reciting two hours weekly, to 103 in 1914–15, reciting four hours weekly. These facts furnish ample evidence of the demand for the new courses, but, also, of the urgent need of reorganization and enlargement.

It is recommended that the department be divided so that one instructor can give all his time to agricultural education and that as soon as the development of the department shall warrant it he be given one or more assistants for extension work to cooperate with the rural school department. There should then be organized a complete department in rural education in charge of an expert who shall instruct in rural life problems (sociology and rural economics) and in special rural school management and rural school methods. This department should have the use of a practical laboratory—that is, a rural practice school. The committee's preference is for a rural practice school located on the campus, where it can be used hourly. For the practice school is needed a specially prepared teacher, who can also give class periods in special rural school methods.

STATE NORMAL SCHOOL AT BELLINGHAM.

1. *Maintenance.*—This institution, like the one at Cheney, gets nine one-hundredths of 1 mill of the millage tax, an amount which has proved wholly inadequate. The school has in fact been so hampered for funds during the last biennium that it has been forced to make a reduction in salaries amounting to $4,000. If the Bellingham Normal School is to maintain and increase its efficiency, it must either be granted larger appropriations or its student roll must be reduced.

2. *Physical equipment.*—The valuation of the physical equipment of the school is summarized in the following table:

Valuation of physical resources.

Central building, science building, training-school building, training-school
annex, manual-training shop, gymnasium, Edens Hall for women, and
equipment for all... $301,000
Land, estimated value.. 44,000

Total valuation... 345,000

The central building.—This is a large structure, which has been added to from time to time. It is of good appearance and substantial construction. The equipment and sanitary facilities are, for the most part, excellent. The building is satisfactory, although crowded to its capacity.

Gymnasium.—This is a frame annex to the main building. It is inadequate for gymnasium purposes by reason of its small size. Better facilities for gymnasium and play should be provided.

Manual-training building.—This was constructed in 1914, and while not large or expensive, is practically arranged, and will answer the purpose for which built for a number of years.

Edens Hall.—This is a dormitory for girls. It is a plain, frame structure, located on the front part of the campus, where it in a large measure destroys the harmony of an otherwise beautiful arrangement of grounds and buildings. The dormitory has been enlarged several times. As a result it contains dark, labyrinthine halls and inadequate sanitary facilities. Risk from fire is great. The dormitory facilities of the school are, on the whole, inadequate.

3. *Recommendations.*—The committee makes the following recommendations for improvement of the Bellingham school equipment:

    (1) The acquisition of more land.
    (2) The construction of a modern dormitory for girls.
    (3) The provision of a new gymnasium.
    (4) The provision of auditorium and library facilities.
    (5) The erection of a model rural school on campus.
    (6) The use of city-schools for training school purposes.

(*a*) *More land urgently needed.*—The school is situated in a beautiful and healthful environment, but is too crowded. More land is urgently needed for campus purposes, for gardens, and for general agricultural experimentation. The trustees have recently a k en options on 21 acres of land adjoining the premises. Steps should be taken to purchase this land without delay.

(*b*) *A new dormitory.*—The State can not afford to risk the health and lives of its omen students by continuing to house them in such a building as Edens Hall. It is recommended that appropriation be made for a dormitory similar to the one at Cheney, to be erected at a cost of from $85,000 to $100,000, fully equipped.

(c) *A new gymnasium.*—While this is not so urgently needed as the dormitory, the present equipment is far from satisfactory. An appropriation should be made for a new gymnasium to be erected during the next biennium.

(d) The school needs additional auditorium and library facilities. It is suggested that a single building, to cost about $85,000, may be provided to serve both purposes.

(e) *Model rural school.*—The value of a rural practice school as a part of the equipment of a State normal school has already been discussed (see pp. 222 and 223).

(f) *Additional training-school facilities.*—One of the most difficult problems of a large normal school is to provide sufficient training-school facilities. This, in itself, is a strong argument for more and smaller normal schools. At Bellingham the training school is so crowded that the prospective teachers do not get ample opportunity for practice teaching. A solution of the difficulty might be reached if the normal school could arrange with the city of Bellingham to take over one or more of the city schools for training purposes, the city and normal school sharing the expense of operation. At McComb, Ill., for example, the normal school makes use of the entire city system for practice school purposes, the principal of the normal school being also head of the city system. The State, which furnishes part of the funds for the maintenance of all the schools and pays for the training of the teachers for these schools, has the right to utilize schools for practice school purposes whenever the public good requires.

State normal school at Cheney.

[Data relating to regular students only, fourth quarter, 1915–16.]

Instructors, designated by letter.	Salary for regular school year only.	Different subjects taught.	Total teaching hours per week.	Average number of students per hour.	Total student clock hours per week.	Remarks.
A	$2,500	5	14	43.0	602.0	Additional definite assignment as vice president and registration work.
B	2,400	3	18	37.0	666.0	Dean of summer session.
C	2,000	5	20	33.5	670.0	
D	1,600	4	20	30.6	612.0	
E	1,800	1	3	39.0	117.0	Dean of women.
F	2,000	4	16	29.2	467.2	
G	1,700	3	12	22.0	264.0	Two periods a day in training school and one period (40 minutes) in glee club.
H	1,200	4	9	20.6	185.4	Two periods a day in training school (bands and orchestra included).
I	2,000	3	12	60.8	729.6	Appointment committee work, heavy fourth quarter.
J	1,900	1	7	52.2	365.4	Appointment committee work, heavy fourth quarter; secretary of committee.
K	1,500	4	18	25.0	450.0	Two periods per day in training school; German; boys' athletics.
L	1,500	3	9	9.3	83.7	
M	1,600	7	21	10.0	210.0	Two periods per week in training school.
N	1,500	3	9	21.0	189.0	Do.
O	1,400	5	18	25.4	457.2	Two periods per day in training school.
P	1,440	2	8	18.6	148.8	
Q	1,600	1	5	29.0	145.0	Medical inspection and health work.
R	1,200	2	9	47.7	429.3	One period per day in training school.
S	1,800	6	18	17.5	315.0	Do.
T	1,350	1	2	52.0	104.0	Regular eighth-grade teacher in training school.
U	1,460	2	6	22.0	132.0	Senior student assistant.
V	1,460	1	3	36.0	108.0	Supervisor grades 2, 3, and 4 in training school.
W	2,000	1	3	41.0	123.0	Superintendent training school; also appointment committee work.
X	1,800	1	3	50.0	150.0	Business office.
Average of total 24 instructors.	1,696	[1] 72	10.6	32.1	321.8	

[1] Total number of different subjects taught.

State normal school at Ellensburg.

[Data relating to regular students only, year 1914–15.]

Instructors designated by letter.	Salary for regular school year only.	Different subjects taught.	Total teaching hours per week.	Average number of students per hour.	Total student clock hours per week.
A	$3,000	2	4	69	276
B	1,550	5	15	19	297
C	1,500	3	12	40	484
D	1,300	1	4	39	156
E	2,000	8	29	31	906
F	1,500	4	18	15	265
G	1,300	5	12	16	200
H	1,550	8	22	17	371
I	1,200	4	11	21	226
J	750	3	6	25	150
K	1,300	3	9	10	96
L	2,000	6	21	25	535
M	1,200	2	2	29	57
N	1,100	7	14	24	332
O	1,100	5	9	14	128
P	1,300	13	27	18	400
Q	1,500	3	12	10	124
R	1,300	4	10	10	102
S	1,300	3	12	4	48
T	1,200	6	12	32	388
Average of total, 14 instructors [1]	[2] 1,417	[3] 95	19	23	282

[1] The whole number of instructors, when reduced to a full-time basis, is 14.
[2] This is figured on a 10 months' basis only; the average for 12 months would be $1,700.40.
[3] Total number of subjects taught.

State normal school at Bellingham.

[Data affecting regular students only, year 1915–16. This school did not report the number of different subjects taught or the average number of students per hour.]

Instructors designated by letter.	Salary for regular school year only.	Total teaching hours per week.	Total student clock hours per week.
A	$1,620	20	1,040
B	1,500	25	365
C	2,040	23	606
D	2,160	25	940
E	1,320	18	285
F	1,500	[1] 5	560
G	1,080	[1] 5	112
H	600	[2] 20	108
I	1,500	[1] 5	215
J	2,580	16	860
K	1,800	[2] 10	25
L	1,800	25	1,121
M	1,680	20	440
N	1,500	20	496
O	1,900	20	1,241
P	1,260	[1] 15	520
Q	1,620	23	261
R	1,200	20	1,126
S	1,500	[1] 5	560
T	1,380	28	250
U	1,200	[4] 5	384
V	1,980	[1] 12	260
W	1,260	5	1,334
X	2,160	....	....
Y	1,500	[3] 28	308
Z	1,320	20	984
AA	1,860	[3] 24	435
BB	1,260	24	496
CC	1,200	20	....
DD	600	12½	500
EE	1,500	[3] 30	160
FF	1,980	20	621
GG	1,200	19	753
HH	1,620	[4] 5	190
II	1,440	20	804
JJ	900	15	1,050
KK	1,200	25	495
LL	1,500	[1] 5	215
MM	1,680	([5])	....
Average of total, 39 instructors	1,713	17.5	558.8

[1] And as supervisor.
[2] And as athletic coach.
[3] And laboratory work.
[4] And as nurse.
[5] Librarian.

·INDEX.

227

DEPARTMENT OF THE INTERIOR
ソ ', - BUREAU OF EDUCATION

BULLETIN, 1916, No. 27

STATE
HIGHER EDUCATIONAL INSTITUTIONS
OF NORTH DAKOTA

A REPORT TO THE NORTH DAKOTA STATE BOARD OF REGENTS
OF A SURVEY MADE UNDER THE DIRECTION OF THE
UNITED STATES COMMISSIONER OF EDUCATION

WASHINGTON
GOVERNMENT PRINTING OFFICE
1917

ADDITIONAL COPIES

OF THIS PUBLICATION MAY BE PROCURED FROM
THE SUPERINTENDENT OF DOCUMENTS
GOVERNMENT PRINTING OFFICE
WASHINGTON, D. C.
AT
30 CENTS PER COPY

CONTENTS.

4 CONTENTS.

LIST OF ILLUSTRATIONS.

LETTER OF TRANSMITTAL.

DEPARTMENT OF THE INTERIOR,
BUREAU OF EDUCATION,
Washington, November 25, 1916.

SIR: I am transmitting herewith for publication as a bulletin of the Bureau of Education the manuscript of the report of a survey of the system of higher education of the State of North Dakota, including the University of North Dakota; the North Dakota Agricultural College; the normal schools at Mayville, Valley City, and Minot; the Normal and Industrial School at Ellendale; the School of Science at Wahpeton; the School of Forestry at Bottineau; and the State Library Commission, which has its offices in the Capitol at Bismarck. The survey has been made, as stated in the body of the report, under my direction and at the request of the State board of regents. The investigations in the field were made by Dr. William T. Bawden, the bureau's specialist in vocational education; Dr. Edwin B. Craighead, formerly president of the University of Montana, employed by the board of regents; and Dr. Lotus D. Coffman, dean of education of the University of Minnesota, serving at my request.

In this report no attempt has been made to appraise the ability of any individual teacher, the work of any department, or the contents of any particular course of study; only the spheres and functions of the several institutions have received primary consideration.

Respectfully submitted.

P. P. CLAXTON,
Commissioner.

The SECRETARY OF THE INTERIOR.

INTRODUCTORY.

PERSONNEL OF THE SURVEY COMMISSION.

Under date of August 4, 1916, President Lewis F. Crawford, of the North Dakota Board of Regents, addressed a letter to Commissioner Claxton, inquiring whether it would be possible for him to detail one or more members of the staff of the Bureau of Education to assist the board in making "a survey of the State educational institutions," as required by a law recently enacted by the State legislature. After considerable correspondence, the Commissioner of Education notified the board of regents on October 6 that he had assigned to the work of the North Dakota survey Dr. William T. Bawden, specialist in industrial education, of the bureau staff.

On October 20 Secretary Charles Brewer announced that the board of regents had employed Dr. Edwin B. Craighead, formerly president of the University of Montana, to assist in the work of the survey.

After conferring with officers of the board of regents in Bismarck, N. Dak., on November 1, Commissioner Claxton accepted the invitation to have the survey conducted under the direction of the Commissioner of Education. The board of regents authorized the commissioner to select an additional member to assist in the work.

On December 24 Commissioner Claxton announced the appointment of Prof. Lotus D. Coffman, dean of the college of education, University of Minnesota, to serve as the third member of the survey commission.

SUMMARY OF INSTRUCTIONS.

On November 1, 1915, the members of the survey commission received a letter from President Crawford outlining the objects which the board had in view in requesting the survey, and calling attention to the fact that the various institutions in question were established by constitutional provisions, back of which it was not deemed to be the province of this survey to go. The instructions to the commission emphasized the desirability of a report on the conditions as they exist in the several institutions, and especially a careful study of the question of unnecessary duplication of work. It was made clear, however, that the board desired a comprehensive, constructive report, looking toward the future development of a sound and progressive State policy of higher education rather than a mere critical analysis of any defects that might be found to exist.

PROCEDURE.

At the request of the State board of regents, the director and two members of the commission met with the board at Bismarck, N. Dak., on Monday, November 1, 1915. Immediately after this conference the study of the State institutions was begun. The director and all members of the commission visited the university, the agricultural college, and the State normal school at Valley City. Each of the remaining institutions was visited by at least two members of the commission. The aggregate number of days spent in the field visiting these institutions was approximately 100, which was supplemented by time spent in the office of the Bureau of Education in Washington in preparing the report.

In January, 1916, the three members of the commission met with the State board of regents, at which time the presidents of the State schools, the secretary and treasurer of the library commission, the State superintendent of public instruction, and the State inspector of consolidated, graded, and rural schools, were invited to appear and make such statements as they desired to make concerning the functions of the institutions and offices represented, and subsequently to file briefs. Both in the conference and in the formal statements filed in reply to the questions of the commission, these officers displayed a most commendable spirit of cooperation. All seemed eager to work together for the development of an educational system that should bring to all interests of the State the largest possible returns for the money invested.

In April the Commissioner of Education appeared before the State board of regents at Bismarck, N. Dak., and submitted a preliminary general report on the work of the survey.

In June the three members of the commission met with the Commissioner of Education in Washington, to formulate and review the conclusions which had been reached. At this time an outline of the conclusions was forwarded to the State board of regents.

The commission finds it a pleasure to express appreciation of the courtesy and cooperation which have been extended by the citizens of North Dakota, the presidents and members of the faculties of all the schools, the State superintendent of education, the inspector of consolidated, graded, and rural schools, officers of the library commission, State officials at the capital, and many others both in public and private life.

STATE HIGHER EDUCATIONAL INSTITUTIONS OF NORTH DAKOTA.

Chapter I.

THE STATE OF NORTH DAKOTA.

North Dakota, with a land area of 70,183 square miles and a water surface of 654 square miles, is one of the larger States of the Union, ranking sixteenth in size. The entire area lies within the Great Plains, far away from ocean, away from lakes that serve as highways for commerce, and from large navigable streams. It is almost wholly without forests. There are few falls and rapids capable of being developed into water powers. A large portion of the western half of the State is underlaid with lignites, and here also extensive deposits of clays for brick, tiling, and pottery are found. Gold, silver, copper, lead, and iron are unknown. The soil varies from the rich alluvial and lacustrine Red River Valley on the east through the rolling uplands of the Coteau Plateau to the residual prairies and high plains sections of the west and southwest. The total average precipitation varies from about 20 inches in the east to about 15 inches in the west. Most of this comes in the form of rainfall through the growing seasons of spring, summer, and early fall and is in most years sufficient in all parts of the State for maturing crops without irrigation. Only a small fraction of 1 per cent of the land under cultivation is irrigated.

The winters are long, the summers short. This limits the range of profitable farming to the hardy cereals, grasses, fruits, vegetables, and root crops, and to live-stock growing. In 1910, of the total crop acreage, 99.6 per cent was in cereals and other grains, and 91 per cent of the value of all crops came from wheat, oats, flaxseed, barley, hay, and forage. Most of the State may be profitably farmed, and more than half of it is already improved. Of the total area of the State, 63.6 per cent in 1910 was in farms, and 72 per cent of this, or 45.5 per cent of the whole, was improved.

9

POPULATION.

The population of the State is still small, but it is growing rapidly from natural increase, from foreign immigration, and from immigration from other States, mostly from those of the Middle West. The population of the territory now included in North Dakota was 2,405 in 1870; 36,909 in 1880; 190,983 in 1890; 319,146 in 1900; 577,056 in 1910; and is approximately 700,000 in 1916. This indicates a probable population of 2,000,000 by the middle of the century. The population is now about 10 to the square mile. With a population of 2,000,000 there will be a little less than 30 to the square mile. Formerly a very large majority of the people of the State lived in the eastern half, but the population is now more evenly distributed. In 1910, 40 per cent lived west of a line drawn through the western boundary of McIntosh, Logan, Kidder, Wells, Pierce, and Rolette Counties. Probably 45 per cent are now west of this line.

North Dakota is definitely a rural State with rural interests, and although the population of the cities and towns will continue to increase more rapidly in proportion than the population of the rural districts, as it has done for many years, the life and interest of the State will continue to be predominantly rural for decades to come. There are no large cities in the State and none near it. On the north lies Saskatchewan and Manitoba, with their sparse populations; on the south South Dakota, and on the west and southwest Montana, Wyoming, and Idaho, all without large cities and with a population still more sparse than that of North Dakota. The nearest cities with a population as large as 100,000 are St. Paul and Minneapolis, more than 200 miles east of the Red River; and Omaha, Des Moines, Kansas City, Denver, Salt Lake City, and Spokane, from 400 to 1,000 miles to the south, southwest, and west. There will probably be no large cities in the State and few near it within the next quarter or half century, but there will be many small towns, centers of agricultural communities, with their local commerce and varied small local industries.

In 1910 there were only five places with a population of 5,000 or more, and only two with a population greater than 10,000. Only 95,381 people lived in the 34 places of 1,000 population and over. This was only 16.5 per cent of the total population; 83.5 per cent of the population lived in the open country and in towns and villages of less than 1,000. Only 28 per cent lived in the 226 cities, towns, and villages of all sizes, 142 of which had less than 500 inhabitants. Only 11 per cent lived in towns and cities of 2,500 and over; 89 per cent of the total population and 90.3 per cent of the population between 10 and 20 years old were rural as counted by the United States census. Even the people in urban communities lived largely under rural conditions as to housing, as is shown by the fact that in 1910 there were in the State 118,757 separate dwelling houses for a total of 120,910 families.

RACIAL COMPOSITION OF POPULATION.

More than 70 per cent of the population of North Dakota are foreign born or of immediate foreign descent, as may be noted in

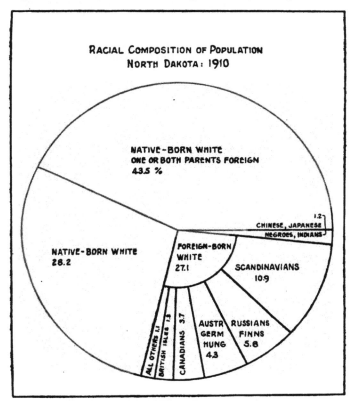

RACIAL COMPOSITION OF POPULATION
NORTH DAKOTA: 1910

NATIVE-BORN WHITE
ONE OR BOTH PARENTS FOREIGN
43.5 %

1.2
CHINESE, JAPANESE
NEGROES, INDIANS

NATIVE-BORN WHITE
28.2

FOREIGN-BORN
WHITE
27.1

SCANDINAVIANS
10.9

ALL OTHERS 1.1
BRITISH ISLES 1.8
CANADIANS 3.7

AUSTR
GERM
HUNG
4.3

RUSSIANS
FINNS
5.8

FIGURE 1.

More than 70 per cent of the population of North Dakota are foreign-born or of immediate foreign descent, the foreign elements consisting largely of immigrants from those strong and virile stocks of northern and western Europe, whose peoples have shown special capacity for adapting themselves to American conditions and ideals. (See Table 1.)

Table 1 and Figure 1. It may be noted further that the foreign elements are of the most desirable types, coming largely from those countries of northern and western Europe whose peoples have shown special capacity for adapting themselves to American conditions and ideals.

Nevertheless, the fact that there are within the State considerable numbers of persons of foreign descent, grouped for the most part in settlements more or less clearly differentiated by language or racial characteristics, inevitably creates special difficulties for the schools. Not only the common schools, but the higher institutions of learning as well, must adapt themselves to the special conditions that exist, if they are to render their full service to the State.

The character of the foreign-born population is shown by the fact that more than one-half of the farm operators are foreign-born, although only 27.1 per cent of the total population are foreign-born.

TABLE 1.—*Racial composition of population, 1910.*

Country of birth.	Number.	Per cent.
Native-born white	162,461	28.2
Native-born white, one or both parents foreign	251,236	43.5
Foreign-born white:		
From Norway, Sweden, Denmark	63,452	10.9
From Russia, Finland	33,096	5.8
From Austria, Germany, Hungary	24,576	4.3
From Canada	21,507	3.7
From England, Scotland, Ireland, Wales	7,486	1.3
From all other countries	6,537	1.1
Chinese, Japanese, Negroes, Indians	7,201	1.2
Total	577,056	100.0

AGE DISTRIBUTION OF POPULATION.

According to the United States census figures for 1910, Table 2, presented graphically in Figure 2, the population of North Dakota contains slightly more than average proportions in the age groups under 25 years, and slightly less than the average in the groups above this age. Comparing North Dakota in this respect with the neighboring agricultural States of South Dakota, Nebraska, and Iowa, it appears that North Dakota contains slightly larger proportions in the age groups under 45 years, and slightly smaller proportions in the groups above this age. (See Figure 3.)

There are apparently no special conditions as regards the age composition of the population which affect the educational problems of the State.

TABLE 2.—*Age distribution of total population, 1910.*

Age groups.	North Dakota.	Average for United States.	South Dakota, Nebraska, and Iowa combined.
	Per cent.	Per cent.	Per cent.
Under 5 years	14.3	11.6	11.6
5 to 14 years	22.4	20.5	21.0
15 to 24 years	20.5	19.7	20.4
25 to 44 years	29.0	29.1	27.9
45 to 64 years	11.3	14.6	14.4
65 years and over	2.2	4.3	3.3
Total	100.0	100.0	100.0

SCHOOL ATTENDANCE AND ILLITERACY.

The percentage of illiteracy in the native white population is 1.5 per cent; in the foreign-born white population, 1.7 per cent, much

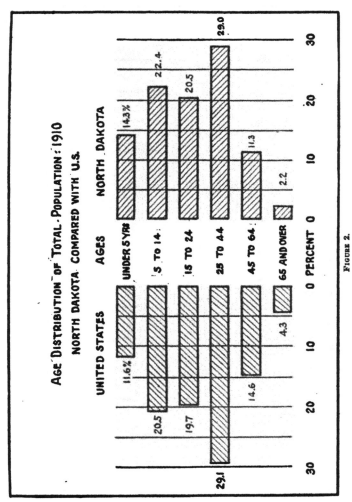

FIGURE 2.

The population of North Dakota contains slightly more than average proportions in the age groups under 25 years, and slightly less than the average in the groups above this age.

less in both classes than the average for the United States. This small percentage of illiteracy is due not only to the schools of North Dakota, but to the fact that the immigration from other States has been mostly from those with good school systems of long standing, while the foreign immigration has been very largely from European States in which elementary education, at least, is practically univer-

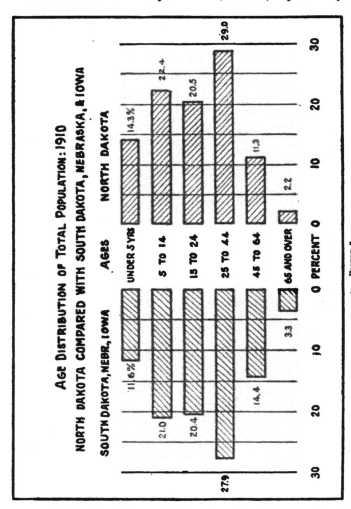

FIGURE 3.

The population of North Dakota contains slightly larger proportions in the age groups under 45 years, and slightly less than the average in the groups above this age, as compared with the neighboring agricultural States of South Dakota, Nebraska, and Iowa. There are apparently no special conditions as regards the age composition of the population which affect the educational problems of the State.

sal. Only 1.7 per cent of the population of all classes between the ages of 10 and 20 were reported as illiterate in 1910. This shows also the effectiveness of the elementary schools of the State in reducing illiteracy.

In 1910, of all children from 6 to 9 years old, 70.6 per cent attended schools; from 10 to 14 years, 90 per cent; from 15 to 17 years, 57.4 per cent; from 18 to 20 years, 17.4 per cent.

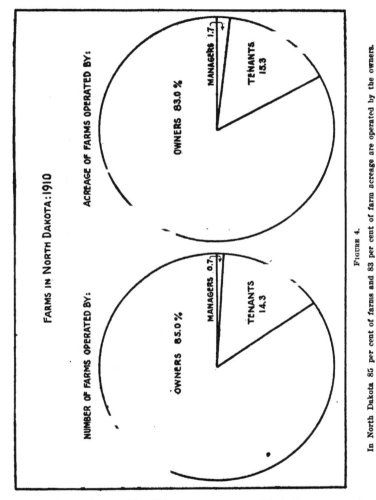

FARMS IN NORTH DAKOTA: 1910

NUMBER OF FARMS OPERATED BY:

OWNERS 85.0%

MANAGERS 0.7

TENANTS 14.3

ACREAGE OF FARMS OPERATED BY:

OWNERS 83.0%

MANAGERS 1.7

TENANTS 15.3

FIGURE 4.

In North Dakota 85 per cent of farms and 83 per cent of farm acreage are operated by the owners.

Of urban children from 6 to 14 years of age, 84.2 per cent attended school; of urban children from 15 to 20 years, 43.1 per cent. Of rural children from 6 to 14 years, 80.4 per cent, and of rural children from 15 to 20 years, 37.7 per cent. (See Table 3.)

TABLE 3.—*Percentages of children of specified ages in North Dakota reported as attending school, 1910.*

Ages.	All children.	Urban children.	Rural children.
6 to 9 years	70.6		
10 to 14 years	90.0		
6 to 14 years		84.2	86.1
15 to 17 years	57.4		
18 to 20 years	17.4		
15 to 20 years		43.1	37.7

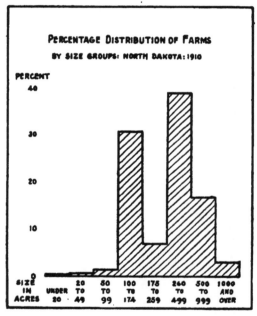

PERCENTAGE DISTRIBUTION OF FARMS
BY SIZE GROUPS: NORTH DAKOTA: 1910

FIGURE 5.

In 1910 less than 5 per cent of the farms contained less than 100 acres each, and only 20.2 per cent contained more than 500 acres.

FARMING AND OTHER INDUSTRIES.

The nature of the farming in North Dakota is indicated by the following facts from the census of 1910:

Of the whole number of farms, 85 per cent are operated by their owners, 14.3 per cent by tenants, 0.7 per cent by managers. (See Table 4 and Figure 4.)

More than 60 per cent of all the farms hired some labor, and nearly $22,000,000 was expended in farm wages.

The farms averaged 382.3 acres, and the average had been increasing for 20 years.

Less than 5 per cent of the farms contained less than 100 acres each, and only 20.2 per cent contained more than 500 acres. (See Table 5 and Figure 5.)

TABLE 4.—*Farms in North Dakota, 1910.*

Farms operated by—	Number.	Per cent.	Area in acres.	Per cent.
Owners	63,212	85.0	23,586,728	83.0
Managers	484	.7	477,213	1.7
Tenants	10,664	14.3	4,362,709	15.3
Total	74,360	100.0	28,426,650	100.0

TABLE 5.—*Distribution of farms by size groups, North Dakota, 1910.*

Size groups.	Number.	Per cent.	Size groups.	Number.	Per cent.
Under 20 acres	229	0.3	260 to 499 acres	29,048	39.1
20 to 49 acres	450	.6	500 to 999 acres	12,662	17.0
50 to 99 acres	1,207	1.6	1,000 acres and over	2,416	3.2
100 to 174 acres	23,003	30.9			
175 to 259 acres	5,345	7.2	Total	74,360	100.0

The percentage of farms operated by tenants in North Dakota, 14.3, is very much less than that for the United States, 37, as shown in Table 6. The same table shows that in 11 States situated in various sections of the country the percentage of farms operated by tenants, 52.9, is nearly four times as great as in North Dakota.

To these considerations should be added the fact that in 1910 the average value of the 74,360 farms in North Dakota, including equipment, was $13,109. Not only is North Dakota overwhelmingly agricultural in its interests, but the people for the most part own their own farms, and each farm represents the investment of a considerable amount of capital. Socially and economically, therefore, the State is made up of a relatively high class of citizens abundantly able to pay for educational advantages and to utilize them fully. Such a population is far more likely to be interested in scientific and practical agricultural education than the tenant classes to be found in some other States.

TABLE 6.—*Tenancy of farms in certain States.*

States.	Percentage distribution of farms operated by—				Percentage distribution of acreage of farms operated by—			
	Owners.	Managers.	Tenants.	Total.	Owners.	Managers.	Tenants.	Total.
Illinois.................	57.6	0.9	41.4	100.0	54.7	1.7	43.6	100.0
Delaware..............	57.0	1.1	41.9	100.0	45.9	2.0	52.1	100.0
North Carolina.........	57.3	.4	42.3	100.0	69.8	2.6	27.6	100.0
South Carolina.........	36.5	.5	63.0	100.0	59.6	4.1	36.4	100.0
Georgia...............	33.9	.5	65.6	100.0	55.1	2.9	42.0	100.0
Tennessee.............	58.6	.3	41.1	100.0	73.2	1.7	25.1	100.0
Alabama..............	39.5	.2	60.2	100.0	64.1	1.3	34.2	100.0
Mississippi............	33.6	.3	66.1	100.0	63.1	3.2	33.7	100.0
Arkansas..............	49.7	.4	50.0	100.0	71.1	1.9	27.0	100.0
Louisiana.............	44.0	.8	55.2	100.0	64.8	9.4	25.7	100.0
Oklahoma.............	44.9	.3	54.8	100.0	55.4	1.5	43.1	100.0
Average of 11 States.....	46.6	.5	52.9	100.0	61.5	3.0	35.5	100.0
Average United States.	62.1	.9	37.0	100.0	68.1	6.1	25.8	100.0
North Dakota.........	85.0	.7	14.3	100.0	83.0	1.7	15.3	100.0

Most farmers grow a variety of crops within the range already indicated. Nearly half report vegetables in small quantities. The total value of vegetables reported was $3,148,304.

A very large per cent report horses, cattle, swine, poultry, and other live stock.

The total value of crops was $180,636,000; of live stock, $110,000,-000; of animals sold and slaughtered, $14,457,000.

The value of milk, cream, butter fat sold and butter and cheese made was $4,872,304.

The value of forest products was almost negligible.

Although the total value of manufactured products increases from year to year, there are as yet no very large industrial plants. The 752 industrial establishments reported in 1910 had a capital of $1,585,000, paid in salaries and wages $2,416,000, and had an output valued at $19,138,000. Fully two-thirds of the value of all manufactured products consisted of the products of flour mills and of butter and cheese, the latter in small amounts. The total value added by the manufacturing process was $5,468,000.

Persons engaged in manufacturing numbered 4,148, only 2,732 of whom were wage earners.

Mining industries are increasing, but as yet are comparatively unimportant. In 1910 only 960 persons were reported as engaged in mining, including proprietors, officials, clerks, and wage earners. The total capital invested was $1,058,649; the amount paid in wages, $570,140; and the value of products, $564,000.

In the year 1910 the capital invested in farming in North Dakota was 84 times that invested in manufacturing and 926 times that invested in mining. (Table 7.) The number of farm operators was 103 times the number of operators of industries and 1,403 times the number of mining operators. The value of farm products was 11 times the value of manufactured products and 37 times the value of manufactured products over the value of raw material used in these products. It was 361 times the value of products of the mines.

TABLE 7.—*Relative magnitude and value of farming, manufacturing, and mining in North Dakota, Federal census of 1910.*

	Farming.	Manufacturing.	Mining.
Capital invested	$974,814,205	$11,585,000	$1,058,642
Operators	74,360	1 723	53
Value of products	$204,000,000	2 $19,138,000	$564,812

1 Proprietors and firm members.
2 Value added to raw material by the manufacturing process, $5,464,000.

SUMMARY OF OCCUPATIONS.

A general view of the gainful occupations followed by the people of North Dakota is afforded by Table 8, which also compares this State with the neighboring States of South Dakota, Nebraska, and Iowa, combined, and with the States of New York, Pennsylvania, New Jersey, and Ohio, combined. (See also Figures 6 and 7.)

In North Dakota, even more than in the three neighboring States referred to, agriculture is preeminent, 60.2 per cent and 45.8 per cent, respectively. The "trade" and "manufacturing" groups are much less important in North Dakota, where, together, they comprise only 18 per cent of all occupations reported, whereas in the three States mentioned they include 27.5 per cent of the total. The differences between North Dakota and these three States in the cases of the remaining occupation groups are not striking.

TABLE 8.—*Distribution by general divisions of persons 10 years of age and over engaged in gainful occupations—North Dakota compared with South Dakota, Nebraska, and Iowa, combined; and with New York, Pennsylvania, New Jersey, and Ohio combined, 1910.*

Division of occupations.	North Dakota.		South Dakota, Nebraska, and Iowa, combined.		New York, Pennsylvania, New Jersey and Ohio, combined.	
	Number engaged.	Per cent.	Number engaged.	Per cent.	Number engaged.	Per cent.
Agriculture, forestry, animal husbandry	130,919	60.2	682,068	45.8	1,240,358	12.2
Extraction of minerals	506	.2	20,642	1.3	400,721	3.9
Manufacturing and mechanical industries	21,339	9.8	258,433	17.4	4,088,100	39.8
Transportation	13,813	6.4	113,423	7.6	805,861	7.9
Trade	17,910	8.2	151,181	10.1	1,183,720	11.7
Public service (not elsewhere classified)	1,597	.7	14,336	.9	139,576	1.4
Professional service	9,851	4.5	86,111	5.8	493,428	4.9
Domestic and personal service	17,318	8.0	113,810	7.6	1,139,632	11.3
Clerical occupations	4,165	1.9	46,500	3.1	686,544	6.8
Total	**217,418**	**100.0**	**1,486,504**	**100.0**	**10,127,940**	**100.0**

North Dakota, 1910.—Total population, 577,056; engaged in gainful occupations, 217,418; per cent of total population, 87.7.

On the other hand, comparison of North Dakota with four of the Eastern States—New York, Pennsylvania, New Jersey, and Ohio—combined serves to emphasize the predominance of agricultural in-

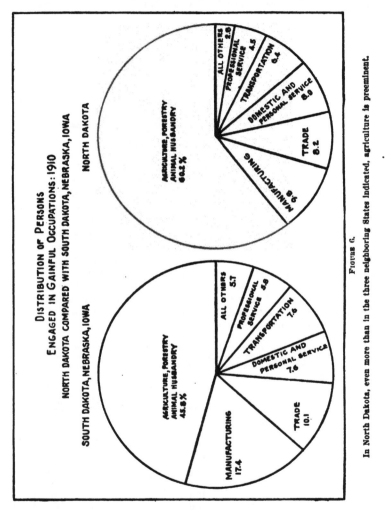

DISTRIBUTION OF PERSONS
ENGAGED IN GAINFUL OCCUPATIONS: 1910
NORTH DAKOTA COMPARED WITH SOUTH DAKOTA, NEBRASKA, IOWA

NORTH DAKOTA

AGRICULTURE, FORESTRY ANIMAL HUSBANDRY 60.2%

ALL OTHERS 2.9

PROFESSIONAL SERVICE 4.5

TRANSPORTATION 6.4

DOMESTIC AND PERSONAL SERVICE 8.0

TRADE 8.2

MANUFACTURING 9.6

SOUTH DAKOTA, NEBRASKA, IOWA

AGRICULTURE, FORESTRY ANIMAL HUSBANDRY 45.8%

ALL OTHERS 5.7

PROFESSIONAL SERVICE 5.9

TRANSPORTATION 7.6

DOMESTIC AND PERSONAL SERVICE 7.6

TRADE 10.1

MANUFACTURING 17.4

FIGURE 6.

In North Dakota, even more than in the three neighboring States indicated, agriculture is preeminent.

terests in the former. Agriculture, forestry, and animal husbandry constitute only 12.2 per cent of the occupations in the four States considered together, as compared with 60.2 per cent in North Dakota. (See Figure 7.)

The predominance of agricultural interests in North Dakota is still further emphasized by an examination of the constituent elements of the occupational group designated by the census report as

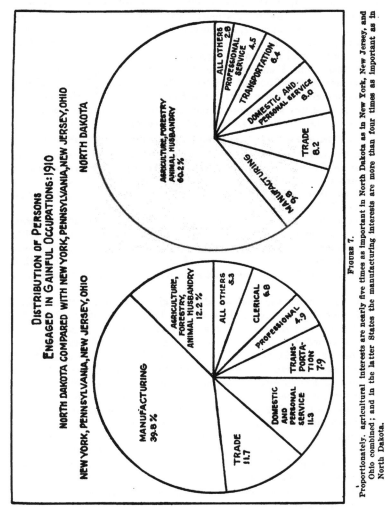

DISTRIBUTION OF PERSONS
ENGAGED IN GAINFUL OCCUPATIONS: 1910
NORTH DAKOTA COMPARED WITH NEW YORK, PENNSYLVANIA, NEW JERSEY, OHIO

NORTH DAKOTA

AGRICULTURE, FORESTRY, ANIMAL HUSBANDRY 60.2%

ALL OTHERS 2.9
PROFESSIONAL SERVICE 4.5
TRANSPORTATION 6.4
DOMESTIC AND PERSONAL SERVICE 8.0
TRADE 8.2
MANUFACTURING 9.8

NEW YORK, PENNSYLVANIA, NEW JERSEY, OHIO

MANUFACTURING 39.8%

AGRICULTURE, FORESTRY, ANIMAL HUSBANDRY 12.2%
ALL OTHERS 5.3
CLERICAL 6.8
PROFESSIONAL 4.9
TRANSPORTATION 7.9
DOMESTIC AND PERSONAL SERVICE 11.3
TRADE 11.7

FIGURE 7.

Proportionately, agricultural interests are nearly five times as important in North Dakota as in New York, New Jersey, and Ohio combined; and in the latter States the manufacturing interests are more than four times as important as in North Dakota.

"Agriculture, forestry, and animal husbandry." Certain of these occupations, clearly distinguishable from agriculture, are of very slight importance in North Dakota. Thus, foresters, lumbermen, raftsmen, woodchoppers, owners and managers of log and timber camps, fishermen, and oystermen (combined), number 21,351 in the four States mentioned, or 1.7 per cent of the occupations reported in this group; in North Dakota, however, there are only 97 persons engaged in all these occupations. Not only do they constitute an almost negligible number, absolutely, but they comprise only seven-hundredths of 1 per cent of the occupations in the " agriculture, forestry, and animal husbandry " group.

In these four Eastern States the " manufacturing " group comprises nearly two-fifths of the total (39.8 per cent), instead of less than one-tenth (9.8 per cent), as in North Dakota. Clerical occupations also occupy a far more important place in the four States (6.8 per cent) than in North Dakota (1.9 per cent).

RESOURCES AVAILABLE FOR EDUCATIONAL PURPOSES.

In the following pages certain tables are presented showing comparative figures for the 48 States of the Union with respect to resources available for educational purposes. The tables are based on data given in the reports of the Census Bureau and the Commissioner of Education.

From Table 9 it appears that North Dakota ranks seventh from the top in average value of property per child of school age. With an average property value of $10,900 on which to draw for the education of each child 5 to 18 years of age, North Dakota has, in this respect, more than five times the resources of the lowest State in the list.

Supplementing the analysis already given of the age distribution of the population in North Dakota (see Table 2 and figures 2 and 3), another view of the conditions as they affect the problem of education is afforded in Table 10, which compares the 48 States by the number of men 21 years of age and over for each 100 children of school age. North Dakota, ranking thirty-first in the list, with 93 men to 100 children, thus has considerably more children to be educated than there are men of income-producing years. Only 16 States have a smaller proportion of men over 21 years of age, while the State ranking highest has nearly twice as many.

Comparing the amounts expended for public schools for each adult male, North Dakota ranks second, with $33.52. (Table 11.) In amount expended for public schools in proportion to wealth it ranks twenty-sixth. (Table 12.) Apparently the State can, without undue stress, tax itself more heavily than it now does for the support of higher education.

According to Table 13, North Dakota, with $34.17, ranks ninth in the amount expended on public schools for each child of school age.

North Dakota ranks ninth also in receipts of higher educational institutions per capita of population, with $2.17. (Table 14.)

TABLE 9.—*Value of property, by States, for each child 5–18 years of age (1913).*		TABLE 10.—*Number of men 21 years of age and over, by States, for each 100 children 5 to 18 years of age (1910).*	
1. Nevada	$28,400	1. Nevada	180
2. California	15,500	2. Wyoming	179
3. Iowa	12,700	3. California	169
4. Montana	12,300	4. Montana	165
5. Colorado	11,100	5. Washington	151
6. Oregon	11,100	6. Oregon	148
7. **North Dakota**	**10,900**	7. Arizona	129
8. Nebraska	10,700	8. Colorado	125
9. Washington	10,400	9. New Hampshire	123
10. Wyoming	10,200	10. Maine	120
11. Illinois	10,000	11. Vermont	119
12. New York	9,900	12. New York	117
13. Vermont	9,500	13. Massachusetts	116
14. Kansas	9,400	14. Connecticut	115
15. Minnesota	8,900	15. Idaho	113
16. Arizona	8,600	16. Ohio	113
17. New Jersey	8,100	17. Rhode Island	111
18. Connecticut	7,900	18. New Jersey	110
19. South Dakota	7,500	19. Michigan	109
20. Massachusetts	7,300	20. Illinois	108
21. Ohio	7,300	21. Delaware	107
22. Oklahoma	7,300	22. Indiana	106
23. Indiana	7,200	23. Pennsylvania	105
24. Michigan	7,100	24. Minnesota	99
25. Pennsylvania	6,900	25. Iowa	98
26. Rhode Island	6,600	26. Kansas	98
27. Wisconsin	6,400	27. Missouri	98
28. New Hampshire	6,300	28. South Dakota	96
29. Missouri	6,300	29. Nebraska	95
30. Utah	6,300	30. Maryland	94
31. Idaho	5,900	31. **North Dakota**	**93**
32. Maine	5,900	32. Wisconsin	93
33. West Virginia	5,800	33. New Mexico	88
34. Delaware	5,700	34. Florida	87
35. Maryland	5,700	35. Utah	85
36. Texas	5,000	36. West Virginia	84
37. New Mexico	4,700	37. Kentucky	79
38. Florida	4,300	38. Oklahoma	78
39. Louisiana	3,800	39. Tennessee	74
40. Arkansas	3,400	40. Virginia	74
41. Virginia	3,400	41. Texas	72
42. Kentucky	3,100	42. Arkansas	70
43. Alabama	2,900	43. Louisiana	70
44. Tennessee	2,700	44. Alabama	67
45. Georgia	2,600	45. Georgia	66
46. South Carolina	2,500	46. Mississippi	65
47. North Carolina	2,200	47. North Carolina	63
48. Mississippi	2,100	48. South Carolina	58

TABLE 11.—*Amount expended for public schools (1912–13), by States, for each adult male (1910).*

1. Utah	$38. 67
2. North Dakota	33. 52
3. Idaho	32. 55
4. New Jersey	29. 36
5. Washington	28. 54
6. Montana	28. 50
7. California	27. 76
8. Nebraska	26. 07
9. Minnesota	24. 54
10. Colorado	24. 02
11. Iowa	23. 57
12. Oregon	23. 50
13. Arizona	23. 34
14. South Dakota	23. 28
15. Indiana	23. 15
16. Massachusetts	22. 96
17. Kansas	22. 23
18. New York	21. 87
19. Illinois	21. 82
20. Michigan	21. 56
21. Ohio	21. 11
22. Pennsylvania	20. 17
. Connecticut	19. 66
Wisconsin	18. 56
. Oklahoma	$17. 99
Vermont	17. 10
. Rhode Island	16. 95
. Wyoming	16. 72
. Missouri	15. 96
Nevada	15. 62
31. Maine	15. 27
32. West Virginia	14. 99
33. Texas	14. 44
34. Maryland	13. 55
35. New Hampshire	13. 55
36. Florida	12. 29
37. New Mexico	11. 79
38. Kentucky	11. 77
39. Louisiana	11. 76
40. Arkansas	10. 81
41. Tennessee	10. 61
42. Virginia	10. 47
43. Delaware	9. 85
44. Georgia	8. 70
45. North Carolina	8. 03
46. Alabama	7. 94
47. South Carolina	7. 68
48. Mississippi	6. 57

TABLE 12. — *Amount expended for higher education, by States, for each $1,000 of wealth.*

[Based on the estimated true value of all property, U. S. Census, 1912, and total receipts of universities and normal schools as shown in the Report of the Commissioner of Education, 1913–14.]

1. Delaware	$3. 88
2. New Hampshire	1. 84
3. Massachusetts	1. 47
4. Virginia	1. 37
5. Wisconsin	1. 27
6. Connecticut	1. 25
7. Arizona	1. 23
8. South Carolina	1. 21
9. Maryland	. 95
10. North Carolina	. 94
11. Maine	. 92
12. Mississippi	. 87
13. Tennessee	. 80
14. Minnesota	. 79
15. New York	. 74
16. Michigan	. 73
17. South Dakota	. 72
18. Idaho	. 71
19. Utah	. 70
20. California	. 68
21. Illinois	. 68
22. Oregon	. 67
23. Alabama	. 65
24. Washington	. 64
25. Georgia	. 61
26. North Dakota	. 61
27. New Mexico	. 60
28. Vermont	. 60
29. Ohio	. 56
30. Rhode Island	. 56
31. Wyoming	. 56
32. Louisiana	. 55
33. Pennsylvania	. 54
34. Kansas	. 53
35. Iowa	. 51
36. Nebraska	. 51
37. Colorado	. 50
38. Kentucky	. 50
39. Texas	. 49
40. Montana	. 48
41. Nevada	. 47
42. Florida	. 44
43. Indiana	. 42
44. Missouri	. 42
45. New Jersey	. 39
46. West Virginia	. 39
47. Arkansas	. 30
48. Oklahoma	. 19

TABLE 13.—*Amount expended on public schools, by States, for each child 5 to 18 years of age (1913–14).*

1.	California	$49.58
2.	Montana	41.48
3.	Nevada	40.72
4.	Washington	40.57
5.	Arizona	37.15
6.	Utah	34.68
7.	Oregon	34.63
8.	New Jersey	34.47
9.	North Dakota	34.17
10.	Idaho	33.71
11.	Wyoming	33.13
12.	Massachusetts	31.68
13.	Colorado	31.02
14.	Minnesota	30.78
15.	Nebraska	29.86
16.	Ohio	29.60
17.	Connecticut	29.39
18.	New York	29.29
19.	Indiana	28.73
20.	Iowa	28.17
21.	Illinois	26.48
22.	Kansas	25.87
23.	Michigan	25.66
24.	Pennsylvania	25.57
25.	South Dakota	24.77
26.	Maine	23.68
27.	Vermont	23.36
28.	New Hampshire	21.59
29.	Rhode Island	20.97
30.	Wisconsin	20.59
31.	Missouri	19.88
32.	Maryland	15.70
33.	West Virginia	14.00
34.	Oklahoma	12.65
35.	New Mexico	12.02
36.	Florida	11.81
37.	Delaware	11.76
38.	Texas	10.86
39.	Kentucky	9.76
40.	Louisiana	8.69
41.	Tennessee	8.67
42.	Virginia	8.54
43.	Arkansas	8.24
44.	North Carolina	6.64
45.	Alabama	6.22
46.	Georgia	6.21
47.	South Carolina	5.60
48.	Mississippi	4.53

TABLE 14.—*Receipts of higher educational institutions, including normal schools, per capita of population (1913–14).*

1.	Delaware	$5.65
2.	Arizona	2.94
3.	New Hampshire	2.62
4.	Nevada	2.53
5.	Massachusetts	2.51
6.	Connecticut	2.43
7.	Wisconsin	2.33
8.	California	2.30
9.	North Dakota	2.17
10.	Minnesota	1.99
11.	Oregon	1.83
12.	New York	1.77
13.	Illinois	1.768
14.	Iowa	1.714
15.	Washington	1.711
16.	South Dakota	1.64
17.	Nebraska	1.54
18.	Maryland	1.46
19.	Virginia	1.45
20.	Montana	1.44
21.	Colorado	1.43
22.	Kansas	1.38
23.	Utah	1.38
24.	Vermont	1.35
25.	Michigan	$1.35
26.	Wyoming	1.32
27.	Idaho	1.279
28.	Maine	1.277
29.	South Carolina	1.04
30.	Ohio	1.01
31.	Pennsylvania	1.00
32.	Rhode Island	.93
33.	New Mexico	.92
34.	Texas	.83
35.	New Jersey	.81
36.	Indiana	.77
37.	North Carolina	.75
38.	West Virginia	.71
39.	Missouri	.70
40.	Louisiana	.68
41.	Tennessee	.67
42.	Mississippi	.63
43.	Florida	.60
44.	Alabama	.57
45.	Georgia	.54
46.	Oklahoma	.51
47.	Kentucky	.47
48.	Arkansas	.38

Chapter II.

BRIEF OUTLINE OF EDUCATIONAL NEEDS, AS INDICATED BY CHARACTER AND RESOURCES OF THE STATE.

The foregoing brief survey of the State and its resources, of the people and their occupations, and of their industrial, social, and economic status, indicates, in broad outline at least, the educational needs of the people and what should be expected of the institutions under the control of the board of regents and included in this survey.

A vigorous, democratic, progressive, pioneer people, with an unusually high average of wealth, with little poverty and no class of idle rich, offers the best possible opportunity for universal education of a high standard, ideal and cultured on the one hand and scientific and practical on the other. To this end there is need of a strong and efficient system of elementary and secondary schools in the State, the elementary schools consolidated sufficiently to make possible the best results and the most economical use of funds, and the high schools numerous enough to be within reach of all. The uniformity of conditions and the small variety of occupations emphasize the need for strength and efficiency in the work of the schools rather than for large variety in vocational and prevocational courses. The predominance of rural and agricultural life indicates the need for a larger proportion of teachers trained for the work of the rural schools and for making the work of the schools such as to prepare for success in agricultural pursuits and for intelligent, joyous living in the open country and in small villages and towns. It also indicates the need for some system of public libraries that will serve effectively a rural population.

The large number of rural schools in the State as compared with the number of urban schools, and the character of work needed to be done in these schools, show clearly the task of the normal schools, the school of education in the university, and the department of education in the agricultural college.

The comparatively small number of persons engaged in the professions other than teaching and the ministry indicates the unwisdom of maintaining at present in more than one institution schools or courses intended to prepare men and women for any one of these professions. This would seem to apply with special force to the various forms of professional engineering, in none of which, except those connected with or growing immediately out of agriculture, is there present or probable immediate future need for any large number of highly trained men. On the other hand, an unusually large number of people engaged in agriculture on a comparatively large scale, on their own farms and not as hirelings or tenants, makes an unusual demand for a very large number of men possessed of such scientific knowledge and training as will enable them to cultivate their farms, market their crops, breed and feed and otherwise care for their live stock, and perform all the other duties of agriculturists intelligently and profitably without other guidance than their own knowledge and their own powers of intelligent observation and judgment.

Again, the limited range of variety in soil and climate and in staple crops shows the importance of providing comparatively few strong and fundamental courses in agriculture for the largest possible number of students, rather than a large variety of intensively specialized courses for fewer students. The same conditions call for a similar policy in regard to students in courses in home economics, domestic science, and homemaking.

The increasing need for highways to be constructed across country devoid of the need of difficult engineering feats, the growing demand for agricultural engineering, including the care and use of power machinery, etc., and for tradesmen possessed of a high degree of scientific knowledge and trained skill create a corresponding need and demand for courses of instruction in these subjects for large numbers of students, some of which courses at least should be of college grade. The large number of young men and women in the State who have not had high-school education and who will not attend college creates at least a temporary demand for serious and systematic instruction in agriculture, in the trades and industries, and in home economics in courses below college grade, much of which should be given in comparatively short courses and under conditions which will make attendance as inexpensive as possible.

The ideals and the educational and cultural traditions of the people of the State are responsible for the justifiable demand for a large element of cultural education in all these schools, but the need for special and professional courses in the fine arts, literature, and the languages does not appear to be sufficient to justify an attempt to give them at more than one place.

The commercial interests of the State are already sufficiently large to justify commercial courses of higher or lower grade in the university and the agricultural college, and the commercial nature of farming in this State creates a demand for courses in farm accounting in the agricultural college and possibly in the university, in the schools at Wahpeton and Bottineau, and in the rural high schools. It also makes it desirable that simple farm accounting should be taught in the rural elementary schools. The normal schools should therefore offer instruction in this subject and in those simple forms of bookkeeping which relate to the home and to household affairs. There seems, however, to be no reason why the normal schools should give courses in those commercial branches that are not, and can not be, taught in the elementary schools.

To these purposes and tasks should the institutions herein considered adjust themselves in generous and hearty cooperation and with such division of work as will result in the greatest economy and the largest and most efficient service.

Chapter III.

THE UNIVERSITY OF NORTH DAKOTA.

The early interest of the people of North Dakota in higher education is shown by the fact that provision for a university was made by the Territorial assembly, February 23, 1883, more than six years before the Territory became a State (Special Session Laws of the Territorial legislature, ch. 40, secs. 13–15). These laws authorize the support and endowment of the university by means of a "university fund income and all other sums of money appropriated by any law to the university fund income of North Dakota."

The university thus provided for was located at Grand Forks, and first opened its doors to students on September 8, 1884. It is the oldest of the State's institutions for higher education. During the first year of the existence of the university its faculty consisted of four instructors: A president, who was professor of metaphysics; a vice president, who was professor of natural sciences; an assistant professor of Greek and Latin; and a preceptress and instructor in English and mathematics. It is said that all the 79 students of this year were below college grade. During the first seven years the teaching staff of the university increased to 13 and the number of students to 151.

From the beginning the university has been open to both men and women.

CONSTITUTIONAL PROVISIONS.

In November, 1887, the people of the Territory of Dakota voted in favor of the division of the Territory into the two Territories of North Dakota and South Dakota. In November, 1889, North Dakota, with boundaries as at present, became a State of the Union. The constitution of the State, adopted in 1889, provides for a system of public education. Article 19 of this constitution provides for the establishment of the State university and school of mines in the city of Grand Forks. The Revised Code of 1905 (ch. 10, sec. 1040) provides that "the University of North Dakota as now established and located at Grand Forks shall continue to be the university of the State." The same chapter records the provision for a board of five trustees, to be appointed by the governor of the State, to have charge of the affairs of the university, and outlines the powers and duties of this board. This was the method of control of the university until the creation of the present State board of regents in July, 1915.

By the terms of the enabling act admitting the Territory to statehood, Congress granted the university 72 sections (46,080 acres) of public lands which had been reserved for university purposes in an act of February 18, 1881, and in addition thereto apportioned to it 40,000 acres of the 500.000 acres given to the State in lieu of grants provided in the acts of September 4, 1841, and September 28, 1850. The school of mines was granted 40.000 acres. Thus the total grant of land to the university through the enabling act was 86,080 acres, and the grand total to the university and the school of mines was 126,080 acres. Of this amount, by July, 1910. 89,567.82 acres had been sold for $1,163,324.26, and the portion paid in had been invested in such a way that, together with the interest at 6 per cent on unpaid land contracts and rentals and hay permits on unsold lands, it yielded an annual income of $65,026.09.[1]

Chapter 40 of the Special Session Laws of 1883 provided for a special annual appropriation of one-tenth of 1 mill for the support of the university. This appropriation was subsequently changed, as follows: In the Revised Code of 1899, two-fifths of 1 mill; in the Session Laws of 1907, thirty-three one-hundredths of 1 mill; in the Session Laws of 1913, two-fifths of 1 mill; in the Session Laws of 1915, a fixed sum. $102,720, was appropriated in lieu of the university's portion of the millage tax.

In the biennial period 1915 and 1916 the total income of the university from all sources and for all purposes, including the State public health laboratory and its branches, the mining substation, the biological station, and the geological survey, amounted to $400,743.55, of which $270.760 is classed as " educational."[2]

The growth of the university, like that of the State, has been rapid and sure. As already stated, the first faculty consisted of only 4 members, and only 79 students, all below college grade, were enrolled the first year; but during the first seven years of the life of the school the faculty increased to 13 and the student enrollment to 151. In 1915–16 the faculty contained a total of 168 members and the total enrollment of students was 1,241, of whom 675 were regular college students in residence. Of these, only a very few had entered with less than 15 units and none with less than 14. It is, however, quite evident that the influence of the university has not yet reached all parts of the State as it should. (See map, fig. 8, showing distribution of resident students.)

---

[1] See Report of the Temporary Educational Commission to the Governor and Legislature of the State of North Dakota, Dec. 27, 1912, pp. 31 and 32.
[2] See Appendix VIII, Table 48.

CAMPUS AND BUILDINGS.

The material growth of the university has, to some extent at least, kept pace with the increase in faculty and students, and the consequent demand for room and equipment. To the original small campus additions have been made by purchase and gift until it now contains about 120 acres. A dormitory for men was built in 1883, and a dormitory for women was authorized in 1887 and erected in

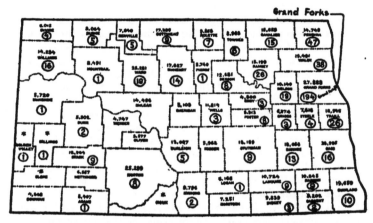

Fɪɢ. 8.—Distribution of resident students enrolled in the University of North Dakota, at Grand Forks, exclusive of summer sessions, 1914–15. (See Table 31, p. 136.)

The figures above the county name in each case give the population in 1910. At that date the population of Golden Valley County (later divided into Golden Valley, Billings, and Slope Counties) was 10,186; and the population of Morton County (later subdivided into Morton and Sioux Counties) was 25,289.

The figures inclosed in the circle in each case indicate the number of students from the county who are enrolled at the university.

This institution drew 583 students from 42 of the 52 counties in North Dakota (of whom 83.2 per cent came from Grand Forks County), and 104 from without the State; total, 687.

In 1910 the population of North Dakota was 577,056. Approximately 60 per cent of the population was found in that portion of the State located east of the western boundary lines of the Counties of Rolette, Pierce, Wells, Kidder, Logan, and McIntosh, which divide the State into two nearly equal parts, and 40 per cent was found in the portion west of this line; whereas, of the 583 North Dakota students in residence at the university, approximately 78 per cent came from the territory east of the line indicated, and only about 22 per cent from west of this line.

1889. On the campus at present are: Merrifield Hall, in which are located administration offices, study and recitation rooms, etc.; Science Hall, in which are located the departments of geology and mineralogy, physics, and biology, including special work of the school of medicine; the Mechanical Engineering Building, in which are located machine and forge shops, foundry, mechanical laboratory, woodworking shop, machine drawing, drafting and class rooms, library and offices; the Mining Engineering Building, devoted to the technical work of the college of mining engineering and to the university museum; Woodworth Hall, which houses the school of education, the model high school, and associated work; the Carnegie Library; the Gymnasium and Assembly Hall; the Commons Building; Davis Hall, a dormitory for women with rooms for the Women's League, literary societies, and amusement; Macnie Hall, a dormitory for women; Budge Hall, a dormitory for men; the president's house; and a power house containing central heating and lighting plants.

There is already need for other buildings, and as the work and attendance of the university grow still others will be needed. Here, as elsewhere, it is very important that all buildings should be located and erected after a definite plan, and that they should be built for permanency and with the future development of the institution in mind.

The library of the university, which contained less than 1,000 volumes the first year of the opening of the university, had grown by gift and purchase to 8,000 volumes in 1902, 30,000 volumes and pamphlets in 1908, and 55,843 volumes, including the 8,612 volumes of the law library, in 1916. It is added to at the rate of about 2,500 volumes annually. The Scandinavian collection of more than 3,500 volumes and the James J. Hill railway transportation collection are of special interest. Departmental libraries of biology and medicine, geology, physics, mechanical engineering, civil engineering, mining engineering, and chemistry are installed in the buildings with these departments.

There are laboratories for the biological department and the school of medicine; the public health laboratory; chemical, metallurgical, and mining laboratories; geological, mineralogical, and physical laboratories; mechanical engineering shops and laboratories; and surveying laboratories, all of which are constantly replenished with new apparatus. The university museum contains material for work in geology, zoology, and botany.

For the care of the sick, one room with bath is set aside in each residence hall, and a trained nurse maintains office hours daily. The hospitals of Grand Forks are also easily accessible, but, as the school grows, there will probably be need for a special building for an infirmary on the grounds.

DEPARTMENTS AND COURSES OF STUDY.

The few courses in philosophy, science, and language offered to students below college grade in 1884 have expanded until the catalogue of the university for 1915-16 lists the following colleges, schools, and divisions:

A. The College of Liberal Arts.
B. The Division of Education:
   The School of Education.
   The Model High School.
C. The School of Law (1900).
D. The Division of Engineering:
   The College of Mining Engineering (The School of Mines) (1900).
   The College of Mechanical and Electrical Engineering (1900).
   The Course in Civil Engineering (1913).
E. The Division of Medicine:
   The School of Medicine.
   The Course for Nurses.
   The Public Health Laboratory.
F. The Graduate Department.
G. The Summer Session.
H. The Extension Division:
   The Bureau of Educational Cooperation.
   The Bureau of Public Service.

In these departments more than 700 courses were offered in the announcement for 1915-16, exclusive of the model high school and the summer session. These courses, except for the division of medicine, the school of law, and the graduate department, are summarized briefly as follows:

In the *College of Liberal Arts*, astronomy, bacteriology and hygiene, biology (botany and zoology), ceramics, chemistry, commercial subjects, economics and political science, education, English language and literature, art and design, music, geology, German language and literature, Greek language and literature, history, home economics, Latin language and literature, law, library science, manual training and mechanical drawing, mathematics, metallurgy and industrial chemistry, philosophy and psychology, physical education, physics, physiology, French language and literature, Spanish language and literature, Italian language and literature, Scandinavian languages and literatures, sociology.

In the *School of Education*, special courses for the training of teachers in biology, chemistry, commercial subjects, arts and design, domestic science and art, English, French, German, history and civics, Latin, manual training, mathematics, music, physics, physiography, supervision and administration.

In the *Law School*, all the usual subjects of a first-class legal curriculum.

In the *School of Medicine*, in addition to the premedical subjects prescribed for the first two years, courses are given in the professional subjects of anatomy, general and special pathology, organic chemistry, embryology, advanced physiology, pharmacology, materia medica, physical diagnosis, surgery, hygiene and sanitation, dietetics, principles of nursing, hospital economics.

In the *School of Mines*, metallurgy, ore treatment and milling, industrial chemistry, building materials and masonry, mining engineering.

In the *School of Mechanical and Electrical Engineering*, descriptive geometry, mechanical drawing, shopwork, bridge design, sanitary engineering, mechanical engineering, electrical engineering.

In the *Course in Civil Engineering*, surveying, hydraulics, municipal engineering, water supplies.

In addition to the extramural work of the extension division through the bureau of educational cooperation and the bureau of public service, as stated elsewhere, the university also has under its immediate direction the public health laboratory at Grand Forks and its branches at Bismarck and Minot, the biological station at Devils Lake, the mining substation at Hebron, the State geological survey, the United States weather bureau at Grand Forks, and the bureau of public accountancy.

That the expansion of the work of the university has been affected by the growth of the State, and that the university has endeavored to meet all demands as they have risen, is shown by the number of additions made within the last seven years, since the inauguration of the present president—years that have also been years of rapid growth and development for the State. Among the additions are the following:

1909. The mining station at Hebron and the biological station at Devils Lake established.
The university quarterly journal established.
1910. A director of music appointed.
A department of ceramics established.
Courses for nurses inaugurated and a university nurse appointed.
Branches of public health laboratory established at Bismarck and Minot.
Medical school faculty enlarged.
University extension division organized.
Federal support obtained for weather bureau.
1911. Course in home economics inaugurated.
Course in art and design inaugurated.
Law course extended from two years to three years.
College section of summer session established.
1913. Course in civil engineering established.

In the meantime the preparatory school has been separated from the university and made into a model high school and practice school for the school of education, the graduate department has been developed, a five-year course in engineering has been inaugurated, fellowships and scholarships established, all faculties have been enlarged, material equipment of buildings and laboratories have been added to extensively, and plans for future development have been outlined. The chief danger has been that in the enthusiasm of youth and through the very laudable desire to respond to all demands of a new and growing State, new courses, divisions, and departments would be provided before the demands were sufficient to justify the expense and to the detriment of other work for which there was greater need. It is not the opinion of the survey commission that any of these should now be abandoned except possibly some minor divisions of specialized subjects for which there will probably not be much demand at any time soon. For some work of this kind a new State like North Dakota should not attempt to provide. It is cheaper for the very few students who might be interested in these courses to go for them where they can be given in a more satisfactory manner, with better equipment and probably at less cost. It is important, however, that for the present and the immediate future, the energies of the university should be used in building up departments and courses already in existence.

THE COLLEGES.

The college of liberal arts offers four-year curricula leading to the degrees of bachelor of arts and bachelor of science.[1] The courses offered in economics and commerce, in connection with other subjects, provide a university training for business careers.

The school of education provides preparation for teaching, especially in secondary schools. It regularly requires for entrance two years of college work, and its courses of two years lead to the degree of bachelor of arts and the bachelor's diploma in teaching. The latter is valid in law as a first-grade professional certificate. The school of education also grants the teacher's certificate to those who complete two years of college work, academic and professional, above the high school, and this certificate is valid in law as a second-grade professional certificate. Special certificates in music, art and design, manual training, home economics, and commercial subjects are granted to those who have specialized in these lines and who have completed at least two years of college work.

The model high school is under the direction of the school of education and is used for observation and practice teaching, for the study of problems of secondary education, and as a model of high-school organization and instruction.

---

[1] The revised code of 1905 provides for courses of instruction in the university as follows:

"SECTION 1051. *Courses of instruction.*—The college or department of arts shall embrace courses of instruction in mathematical, physical, and natural sciences, with their application to industrial arts such as agriculture, mechanics, engineering, mining and metallurgy, manufactures, architecture, and commerce; and such branches included in the college of letters as shall be necessary to properly fit the pupils in the scientific and practical courses for their chosen pursuits and in military tactics. In the teachers' college the proper instruction and learning in the theory and art of teaching and all the various branches and subjects needful to qualify for teaching in the common and high schools; provided, that all instruction in the teachers' college shall be above the grade of secondary schools, and as soon as the income of the university will allow, in such order as the wants of the public shall seem to require, the courses of science and their application to the practical arts shall be expanded into distinct colleges of the university, each with its own faculty and appropriate title. The college of letters shall be coexistent with the college of arts and philosophy, together with such courses or parts of courses in the college of arts as the trustees shall prescribe."

In other sections provision is made for instruction in Scandinavian languages, for a comprehensive geological survey of the State, for the tabulation of meteorological statistics and barometrical observations, for the making of official topographical and statistical maps of the State, and for the collection, preparation, and preservation of botanical, zoological, and mineralogical specimens for the university museum.

The school of law offers a three years' course of study, to which persons who are 18 years of age and graduates of high schools are admitted. The course leads to the degree of bachelor of laws. Students in the college of liberal arts are permitted to offer one year of law toward the degree of bachelor of arts. A graduate in liberal arts from a reputable college or university may receive the degree of Juris Doctor upon the completion of a three years' graduate course in law.

The college of mining engineering offers a four years' course for prospective mining engineers, surveyors, metallurgists, and manufacturing supervisors, leading to the degree of bachelor of science in mining engineering. A five years' course leads to the degree of engineer of mines.

The college of mechanical and electrical engineering offers four-year courses leading to the degrees of bachelor of science in mechanical engineering and bachelor of science in electrical engineering and five-year courses leading to the degrees of mechanical engineer and electrical engineer.

In connection with the colleges of mechanical and electrical engineering and mining engineering, a course in civil engineering is offered covering four years and leading to the degree of bachelor of science in civil engineering. A five years' course leads to the degree of civil engineer.

The school of medicine offers the first two years only of the medical course. The university has announced that the final two years of medical training will not be offered until the clinical facilities of the institution are adequate to meet the demands of advanced professional training in a satisfactory manner. When these are offered they should be of such nature as to prepare physicians for the rural communities of the State as well as for the more specialized work of the cities. Students are not permitted to begin the first year of medical work until they have completed two years of the liberal arts curriculum. During these two years special emphasis is placed on physics, chemistry, and biology. At the end of the four years the student receives the degree of bachelor of arts and a certificate showing that he has completed two years of the medical course. This certificate is accepted by medical colleges with which the university is affiliated.

The course for nurses, two years in length, offers instruction in the academic and technical subjects which precede the hospital work in the training of nurses.

The graduate department includes in a single organization the advanced work of all the colleges and departments of the university which offer courses leading to the higher degrees. The administration of the department is intrusted to a committee on graduate work, under the general direction of the president. Graduate students are permitted to select major subjects only in the college of liberal arts or the school of education. The roster of students for the year 1915–16 contains the names of 12 students in the graduate department. Two degrees of master of arts and two degrees of master of science were conferred in June, 1915. It is stated that the university has thus far conferred but one degree of doctor of philosophy.

· The summer session, six weeks in length, is organized in two sections, a college section and an elementary section. In the college section courses are offered in nearly all departments of the university, including special courses in library science, physical education, and fine arts, and credit is given toward university degrees. The elementary section is maintained strictly for the training of teachers. Courses in all the required certificate subjects are offered, as well as in home economics, manual training, agriculture, and music.

The extension division of the university has been instrumental in organizing lyceum entertainment and educational courses throughout the State, and in stimulating the demand for courses of better quality. During the year 1915–16 the division filled 430 lyceum dates, with an aggregate attendance of approximately 90,000 persons. For the year 1916–17 the number of courses booked is 121, with a total of 586 dates. Under this division are enrolled also 127 correspondence students. It also provides for the establishment and maintenance of conferences and community institutes in various parts of the State. The appropriation for this division is at present $2,500 annually.

Graduates of the University of North Dakota are admitted without conditions to the graduate schools of the leading universities of the country; the school of medicine of the university is listed in "Class A" by the American Council for the Advancement of Medical Education; the law school is a member of the Association of American Law Schools; a chapter of Phi Beta Kappa was established in the college of liberal arts of the university in 1914; and the university is included in the list of American universities recommended to the German Government for the admission of graduate students to foreign universities.

The organization of the university is quite elaborate and in one instance at least the division of authority seems to be extended too far. The survey commission can see no reason why there should be two deans in the division of engineering, one of the college of mining engineering and another of the college of mechanical and electrical engineering. The large number of elements common to all the branches of engineering given in the university and the small number of students in each branch make it all the more desirable that they should be united under one head. The commission has recommended elsewhere that all the engineering be put under the direction of a single dean. The three branches should be merged into one college of engineering under the direction of a dean who shall have under him heads of the different branches.

The fact that the president of the university is a member ex officio of the State high-school board, that the annual high-school conference has been held at the university since 1901, and that the inter-scholastic athletic meets have been held since 1903, have all served to bring together the university and the high schools of the State and to identify their interests. Laboratories and branch laboratories, the substation of the school of mines at Hebron, the university extension work, the work which the university does through the United States Weather Bureau, and more recently through the radio station, not only help the university to serve better and more fully the people of the State, but they have tended also to bring the university and the people closer together and to keep alive the interest of each in the other.

AFFILIATED COLLEGES.

In 1906 the policy of affiliation with other colleges was inaugurated by the location of Wesley College on a campus opposite the campus of the university and by making provision for an exchange of credits on the usual collegiate basis.

This policy seems to be in the interest of true economy and efficiency and to be worthy of extension. It is commended to State universities and denominational colleges of other States. Through this arrangement students of the denominational college receive the full advantage of opportunities for instruction offered by the university which the college might not be able to offer, and those who attend the university may do so without being deprived of the religious teaching and fellowship of a denominational college.

SALARY SCHEDULE.

Members of the teaching staff and administrative officers are employed in different ways. Full professors are appointed permanently, associate professors are appointed for five years, assistant professors for three years, instructors for one year. The general schedule of salaries is as follows:

```
Deans_____ $3,000 to $3,500
Full professors_____   2,500 to  3,000
Associate professors_____   2,000 to  2,500
Assistant professors_____   1,400 to  2,000
Instructors_____     900 to  1,500
```

The general policy of the university relative to salary schedules is as follows: That instructors shall receive an increase of pay up to $1,500 at the rate of $100 a year. The same shall be true of other grades of appointment; that is, assistant professors shall have an increase at the rate of $100 a year up to $2,000, etc. It has not been possible to hold regularly to this schedule, due to the fact that the increase in the income of the university has not been sufficiently large to maintain it. In 1905 the dean having the highest salary received $2,500; in 1915 the highest amount paid was $3,200 and the dean having the lowest salary received $2,900. In 1905 the highest paid professor received $2,000 and in 1915, $3,000. In 1905 the highest paid instructor received $1,200 and the lowest paid, $400. In 1915 the highest paid instructor received $1,500 and the lowest paid, $1,100.

Salaries paid at the university have been reasonably liberal as compared with other institutions in this section, but it is evident that the best interests of the university will demand larger salaries and especially a larger number of professors and associates of the higher grades.

Chapter IV.

THE NORTH DAKOTA AGRICULTURAL COLLEGE.

The first legislative assembly of the State of North Dakota established the North Dakota Agricultural College by an act of March 2, 1890), by accepting the provisions of the Morrill Act of July, 1862. The college, which had been located at Fargo by provision of the State constitution, adopted in 1889, was organized immediately and opened, in rented quarters, October 15, 1890.

LEGAL PROVISIONS FOR THE ESTABLISHMENT OF THE NORTH DAKOTA AGRICULTURAL COLLEGE.

The purpose of the school and the character of its work were set forth by the legislature as follows (section 1106, Revised Code of 1905):

SECTION 1106. *Course of instruction.*—The object of such college shall be to afford practical instruction in agriculture and the natural sciences connected therewith, and in the sciences which bear directly upon all industrial arts and pursuits. The course of instruction shall embrace the English language and literature, military tactics, civil engineering, agricultural chemistry, animal and vegetable anatomy and physiology, the veterinary art, entomology, geology, and such other natural sciences as may be prescribed, political, rural, and household economy, horticulture, moral philosophy, history, bookkeeping, and especially the application of science and the mechanic arts to practical agriculture. A full course of study in the institution shall embrace not less than four years, and the college year shall consist of not less than nine calendar months, which may be divided into terms by the board of trustees as in its judgment will best secure the objects for which the college was founded.

The Morrill Land-Grant Act of July 2, 1862, under the provisions of which the North Dakota College of Agriculture was established, thus defines the character and scope of instruction intended:

The leading object shall be, without excluding other scientific and classical studies, and including military tactics, to teach such branches of learning as are related to agriculture and the mechanic arts, in such manner as the legislatures of the States may respectively prescribe, in order to promote the liberal and practical education of the industrial classes in the several pursuits and professions in life.

By the Session Laws of 1890, chapter 160, section 3, the management of the agricultural college was vested in a board of seven trustees, appointed by the governor for terms of two and four years,

40

all subsequent appointments to be for four years. The powers and duties of the board are outlined in section 6 of the same chapter. This method of control continued in force until the creation of the present State board of regents, in July, 1915.

The following sections of chapter 160 of the special laws of 1890 are of special interest in this study:

SECTION 11. *Duties of president.*—The president shall be the chief executive officer of the college, and it shall be his duty to see that all rules and regulations are executed, and the subordinate officers and employees not members of the faculty shall be under his direction and supervision.

SEC. 12. *Faculty to make annual report to board.*—The faculty shall make an annual report to the board of trustees on or before the first Monday of November of each year, showing the condition of the school, experiment station and farm, and the results of farm experiments, and containing such recommendations as the welfare of the institution demands.

EXPERIMENT STATION.

The establishment of the agricultural experiment station provided for in section 16, chapter 160, Session Laws of 1890, is reaffirmed in the Revised Code of 1905 and in the Compiled Laws of 1913, as follows:

SEC. 1619. *Experiment station.*—The agricultural experiment station heretofore established in connection with the agricultural college is continued, and the same shall be under fhe direction of the board of trustees of such college for the purpose of conducting experiments in agriculture according to the provisions of section 1 of the act of Congress approved March 2, 1887, entitled "An act to establish agricultural experiment stations in connection with the colleges established in the several States under the provisions of an act approved July 2, 1862, and of the acts supplementary thereto."

FEDERAL ENDOWMENT AND SUPPORT.

At the time North Dakota was admitted to the Union, November 2, 1889, 90,000 acres of land were set aside through the provisions of the Morrill Act of 1862, for the benefit of the agricultural college, and, by the enabling act, an additional 40,000 were for the same purpose provided, making a total of 130,000 acres.

By a wise provision of the enabling act, none of this land can be disposed of for less than $10 an acre. Up to this time (1915) the average sale price has been about $13. At this rate this land will afford the agricultural college an endowment considerably in excess of $2,000,000.

In 1890, Senator Justin S. Morrill secured an additional appropriation for the strengthening of the land-grant colleges. Beginning that year, $15,000 was granted to each State and Territory for the maintenance of its agricultural and mechanical college, and that sum was increased $1,000 each year until a maximum of $25,000 annually was reached. This maximum was reached in 1900.

The second Morrill Act, of 1890, providing for the further endowment of agricultural colleges, secures for the college of each State an annual income "to be applied only to instruction in agriculture, the mechanic arts, the English language, and the various branches of mathematical, physical, natural, and economic science, with special reference to their applications in the industries of life and to the facilities for such instruction."

The Nelson amendment of 1907, for the further endowment of agricultural colleges, provides "that said colleges may use a portion of this money for providing courses for the special preparation of instructors for teaching the elements of agriculture and the mechanic arts."

Under the Nelson amendment of 1907, which went into effect with the fiscal year ending June 30, 1908, the Federal appropriation of $25,000 for the agricultural college was increased by the sum of $5,000 annually until the total income arising from the Morrill-Nelson fund amounted to $50,000 annually.

The act of 1888 authorizes the President to detail an officer of the Army or Navy to act as professor of military tactics, and the Secretary of War to issue out of ordnance and ordnance stores belonging to the Government such equipment as may appear to be required for the military instruction of the students of the college.

The Hatch Act of 1887, establishing agricultural experiment stations in connection with agricultural colleges, provides:

SEC. 1. That in order to aid in acquiring and diffusing among the people of the United States useful and practical information on subjects connected with agriculture, and to promote scientific investigation and experiment respecting the principles and applications of agricultural science, there shall be established under direction of the college or colleges or agricultural department of colleges * * * a department to be known and designated as an "agricultural experiment station."

SEC. 2. That it shall be the object and duty of said experiment stations to conduct original researches or verify experiments on the physiology of plants and animals; the diseases to which they are severally subject, with the remedies of the same; the chemical composition of useful plants at their different stages of growth; the comparative advantages of rotative cropping as pursued under the varying series of crops; the capacity of new plants or trees for acclimation; the analysis of soils and water; the chemical composition of manures, natural or artificial, with experiments designed to test the comparative effects on crops of different kinds; the adaptation and value of grasses and forage plants; the composition and digestibility of the different kinds of food for domestic animals; the scientific and economic questions involved in the production of butter and cheese; and such other researches or experiments bearing directly on the agricultural industry of the United States as may in each case be deemed advisable, having due regard to the varying conditions and needs of the respective States or Territories.

The Adams Act of 1906, providing for the further endowment of agricultural experiment stations, stipulates that none of the annual appropriations from Congress for agricultural experiment stations "shall be applied, directly or indirectly, under any pretense whatever, to the purchase, erection, preservation, or repair of any building or buildings, or to the purchase or rental of land."

The total sum, $30,000, thus received from Congress for the North Dakota experiment station must be used for the development and diffusion in North Dakota of agricultural knowledge. Only 5 per cent of the total sum may be used for any other purpose.

The Smith-Lever Act of 1914 provides for extension work as follows:

That cooperative agricultural extension work shall consist of the giving of instruction and practical demonstrations in agriculture and home economics to persons not attending or resident in said colleges in the several communities, and imparting to such persons information on said subjects through field demonstrations, publications, and otherwise; and this work shall be carried on in such manner as may be mutually agreed upon by the Secretary of Agriculture and the State agricultural college or colleges receiving the benefits of this act.

The act further provides that no portion of the moneys received for extension work—

shall be applied, directly or indirectly, to the purchase, erection, preservation, or repair of any building or buildings, or the purchase or rental of land, or in college-course teaching, lectures in colleges, promoting agricultural trains, or any other purpose not specified in this act, and not more than five per centum of each annual appropriation shall be applied to the printing and distribution of publications.

The act making appropriations for the United States Department of Agriculture for the year ending June 30, 1915, provides for franking privilege in connection with the Smith-Lever Act.

TOTAL ANNUAL INCOME FROM NATIONAL GOVERNMENT.

In addition to the income from land grants, the North Dakota Agricultural College receives from the United States Government for the support of the agricultural college annually, $50,000; for the support of the experiment station, annually, $30,000; for extension work, Smith-Lever Act, for the year ending June 30, 1915, $10,000; total, $90,000.

The sum received from the Government for extension work will be increased from year to year until 1922, when $52,607 will be received, provided the proportion that the rural population of North Dakota bears to the total rural population of the United States remains as it is at present. In 1922, therefore, North Dakota will be receiving from the General Government for the support of the agricultural college in its several departments approximately $132,000 annually.

STATE SUPPORT.

The Legislative Assembly of North Dakota has appropriated funds for the establishment and maintenance of the agricultural college and experiment station from time to time as follows:

1891, $25,000 for the erection of an administration building.

1893, $55,000 for additional buildings and maintenance, which provided the Mechanics Art Building, the men's dormitory, now Francis Hall, the farm house, and a barn.

1895, $11,250 for miscellaneous expenses.

1897, $22,000 for buildings and maintenance; a wing to a proposed chemistry laboratory was constructed, which was later moved to another site, remodeled, and used as a music hall; $5,000 to cover a deficiency.

1899, $27,000 for maintenance, and for a small addition to the Mechanic Arts Building.

1901, $18,000 for maintenance.

Authority to issue bonds in the sum of $50,000, from the proceeds of which the south wing of Science Hall was built, also two barns to replace one that had burned the preceding winter; and a sewage system was installed.

Permanent income for maintenance was established by an act appropriating annually one-fifth of 1 mill tax upon the taxable property of the State.

1904, $15,000 to apply on installation of a new heating plant was authorized by the emergency board.

1905, $50,000 for the erection of a chemical laboratory. Gift of $18,400 from Andrew Carnegie for a library building.

1907, $108,000, of which $65,000 was used for the construction of an engineering building, $6,000 for a greenhouse, $10,000 for a seed barn and root cellar, $2,500 for an implement shed; the administration building was remodeled also, and the armory was remodeled and enlarged.

1909, $75,000 for the erection of a women's building, Ceres Hall; $30,000 for a veterinary science building; $12,000 for equipment, engineering laboratories; $10,000 for an electric-light plant; $3,000 for sidewalks.

1911, $65,000 for a chemical building, to replace the laboratory destroyed by fire in 1909; $40,000 for the completion of Ceres Hall; $15,000 for the purchase of additional land for the college farm.

In 1911 the legislative assembly established a permanent appropriation of $25,000 annually for the support of the agricultural college and experiment station. In 1915 there was apportioned to the college $61,800 out of the annual tax of $347,880 which was levied for the maintenance of the State educational institutions.

The income from the State for maintenance, for the year ended June 30, 1915, was $203,642.10; from "local receipts," $135,740.35; from the Federal Government, $90,000; total, $429,382.45.

Up to June 30, 1915, the total amount expended for buildings was $554,800; for equipment, $315,730. The institution has in campus and grounds 953.8 acres.

SUBSTATIONS, SPECIAL FUNDS, AND REGULATORY WORK.

In addition to the experiment station, the substations, and the enterprises usually committed to such institutions, the State of North

Dakota has created a number of special funds, investigations, and responsibilities, the administration of which is lodged with the agricultural college and experiment station at Fargo. These special funds, together with the provisions for the several substations, may be briefly summarized according to the provisions of the compiled laws of 1913, the date of the original enactment in each case being indicated in parentheses:

Section 1621 provides an annual appropriation of $5,000 for the maintenance of the subexperiment station at Edgeley, which is charged with the study of "agricultural, horticultural, and other problems peculiar to districts of the State where the soil and climatic conditions differ from those of that portion of the State known as the Red River Valley." (1903.)

Section 1622 provides an annual appropriation of $10,000, to be used for the further and better enforcement of the food laws, drug laws, formaldehyde and Paris green laws, the paint laws, and "such other food or drug laws as the said station may be charged with the enforcement of" by the legislature, and also for the dissemination of information through bulletins and reports. (1907.)

Section 1623 provides an annual appropriation of $12,000 for the purpose of continuing the 12 demonstration farms already established, for the establishment of not less than 6 nor more than 12 additional demonstration farms, for publishing the annual report of the demonstration farms and of the experiment stations and for printing additional bulletins, and "for complying with the provisions of the pure-paint law, Paris-green law, and formaldehyde law now on the statute books, and for making analysis of fertilizers and stock foods and for other experimental purposes."

.It is provided further that $2,000 of this amount shall be set aside for the sole purpose of installing and conducting demonstration farms near the village of McLeod "for making additional experiments with cereals, root crops, and tree culture, and for making experiments in the manufacture of denatured alcohol from by-products of the farm." (1909; supersedes an act passed in 1907.)

Section 1624 provides an annual appropriation of $12,000 "for the enforcement of the feeding stuffs, fertilizers, beverage and sanitary inspection laws, and such other enacted inspection laws as the food commissioner of this State may be authorized to enforce," and for the making of such investigations and the publishing of such bulletins and reports as are deemed necessary. Section 2920 provides that the "director of the North Dakota Government Agricultural Experiment Station, or his agent or deputy," is charged with the enforcement of the provisions of the laws referred to herein. (1907.)

Section 1625 provides that it shall be the duty of the experiment station at Fargo "to conduct experiments and determine the comparative milling values of the different grades and kinds of cereals and baking tests of the flours made therefrom," and to obtain, tabulate, and publish such other information with reference to cereals and their products as may be of value to the residents of the State. (1909.)

Sections 1626, 1626a, 1626b provide appropriations for the work specified in section 1625, as follows: Six thousand dollars for building and equipment (1907) ; $5,000 for additional equipment, purchasing and collecting samples of cereals, gathering information, and employing investigators (1909) ; $500 annually for maintenance of plant. (1907.)

Sections 1627 and 1628 provide an appropriation of $10,000 for establishing and conducting "an agricultural and grass experiment station," to be located at or near Dickinson, on condition that a suitable area of land not less than 160 acres be donated free of charge. The purpose of this station is to make experiments with native and other grasses and forage products as well as other agricultural products, "with a view of improving and enlarging the supply of forage of said district and extending and increasing the agricultural products thereof." One additional member of the board of trustees of the agricultural college and experiment station at Fargo is provided for, whose "authority on said board shall be limited to the considering of matters affecting the substation provided for in this article." (1905.)

Sections 1629 and 1630 provide for establishing and conducting "an irrigation and dry-farming experiment station," to be located at or near Williston, under conditions similar to those prescribed for the station at Dickinson, including the appointment of an additional member of the board of trustees of the agricultural college and experiment station at Fargo. (1907.)

Section 1631 provides for an initial appropriation of $4,000, and an annual appropriation of $3,000 thereafter, for establishing and maintaining the substation at Williston. (1907.)

Section 1632 provides an additional appropriation of $500 for each of the years 1909 to 1918, inclusive, "for the payment of the charges for water for irrigation, including construction, operation, and maintenance charges," for the substation at Williston. (1909.)

Sections 1633, 1634, and 1634a provide for an appropriation of $10,000 for the purpose of establishing and conducting "an agricultural and grass experiment station," to be located at or near Hannah or Langdon, under conditions similar to those prescribed for the substation at Dickinson, including the provision for an additional member of the board of trustees of the agricultural college at Fargo. (1907.)

Section 1635 provides that the subexperiment stations located at Dickinson, Williston, and Langdon, and such other agricultural subexperiment stations as may hereafter be established by law, shall be operated in connection with the North Dakota government experiment station at Fargo, and "under the exclusive management and control of the board of trustees of the agricultural college." (1909.)

Sections 1636 and 1637 outline the duties of the superintendents of the subexperiment stations, and provide for biennial reports by the superintendents "to the president of the agricultural college," which reports are to be kept separate and included by the board of trustees with its biennial report to the governor. (1907.)

Section 1638 provides an annual appropriation of $15,000, to be divided as follows: $5,000 annually for the support and maintenance of each of the three substations located at Dickinson, Williston, and Langdon. (1909.)

Sections 1639 and 1640 provide for the establishment of an agricultural experiment station at or near Harvey, "to make experiments with native and other grasses and forage products, as well as other agricultural products." (1909.)

Sections 1641 and 1642 provide for the establishment of "an agricultural, grass, and tree experiment station," to be located on the grounds of the State Reform School at Mandan, "provided, that all necessary labor in connection with said experiment station, except the services of an expert, shall be performed by the boys of the said reform school under the supervision of the officers of said school, and all surplus products of said experiment station shall apply on the maintenance of said reform school." (1909.)

Sections 1643 and 1644 provide an appropriation of $10,000 for establishing and conducting an agricultural experiment station at or near Hettinger, "to make experiments with native and other grasses and forage products, as well as other agricultural products," on conditions similar to those prescribed for the experiment station at Dickinson, except the provision for an additional member of the board of trustees of the agricultural college at Fargo. (1909.)

Sections 1657 and 1661 provide an annual appropriation of $3,000 for the establishment and maintenance of a "serum institute" at the agricultural college and experiment station, to be under the control and regulation of the board of trustees of the same. The professor of veterinary science is to be the director of the serum institute. (1909.)

Sections 1658 and 1659 outline the duties of the director of the serum institute: "To manufacture or cause to be manufactured vaccines, sera, and other agents for the prevention, eradication, cure, and control of tuberculosis, glanders, hog cholera, blackleg, and other infections or contagious diseases," and to distribute to residents of North Dakota, free of charge, the products referred to, under such conditions as may be prescribed by the live-stock sanitary board. (1909.)

Sections 1662, 1663, 1664, 1665 provide that the board of trustees of the North Dakota Agricultural College may cooperate with, and accept the cooperation of, the directors of the Federal surveys "in executing a topographic, economic, and agricultural survey and map of North Dakota," including also the collection of samples of all kinds of material and products of economic or scientific interest discovered during the survey, to be placed on exhibition in the museum of the agricultural college. (1901.)

Sections 1666, 1667, 1668 provide for publication of the maps and reports resulting from the survey, and for biennial reports to the governor on the progress of the work. (1901.)

Section 1670 provides for an annual appropriation of $1,000 for the work of the survey. (1901.)

Sections 1669, 1671, 1672 provide that the professor of geology of the North Dakota Agricultural College shall act as State director of this survey; that "this survey shall be known as the Agricultural College Survey of North Dakota," and that "this act is not to be construed as conflicting in any manner with or repealing the geological survey of North Dakota already established at the State university." (1901.)

COURSES OF INSTRUCTION.

The act establishing the agricultural college specified certain courses of instruction which should be offered, but when the college opened, in 1891, formal curricula were not immediately provided. The following subjects, which were later organized into courses of study, were taught: "Household economics, agriculture, chemistry, veterinary science, horticulture and forestry, botany, zoology, mechanics, mathematics, language, history, geography, geology, and military tactics." The first catalogue was issued for the year 1892–93.

The first real course of study formulated was known as the "general science course," and enabled students by election to specialize in chemistry or biology, as well as agriculture.

The list of courses of instruction announced for 1915–16 includes the following:

Division of Applied Agriculture.—Farm management, breeding, genetics, farm practices.

Division of Agronomy.—Farm crops, soil physics and management, soil fertility, crop production, methods of investigation.

Division of Animal Husbandry.—Judging live stock, breeds of live stock, feeds and feeding, animal nutrition, care and management, herd-book study.

Division of Dairy Husbandry.—Elements of dairying, buttermaking, ice cream, cheese making, dairy cattle and milk production, city market-milk supplies.

Division of Botany and Plant Pathology.—Seed analyses and seed testing, plant physiology and pathology, advanced botany and investigation, elementary pharmaceutical botany, botany (elements and structural).

Division of Zoology and Physiology.—Zoology foundations, embryology, animal histology, cytology, and microscopic anatomy, animal parasites, advanced vertebrate embryology, human physiology, advanced comparative physiology, economic zoology investigation.

Division of Bacteriology.—Bacteriology, pathogenic bacteriology, soil biology, dairy bacteriology, bacteriology of water and sewage, soil bacteriology.

Division of General and Historical Chemistry.—General chemistry, experimental chemistry, inorganic chemistry, qualitative chemistry.

Division of Agricultural Chemistry.—How crops grow, soils and feeding of plants, chemistry of soils, dairy chemistry.

Division of Quantitative, Organic, and Physical Chemistry.—Elementary quantitative chemistry, quantitative analysis, organic chemistry, organic preparations, physical chemistry.

Division of Food and Physiological Chemistry.—Veterinary chemistry, physiological chemistry, sanitary chemistry, chemistry of plant and animal life, toxicology and urinology, inorganic constituents, chemistry of food materials, food chemistry.

Division of Industrial Chemistry.—Industrial chemistry for engineers, inorganic industrial chemistry, organic industrial chemistry, technological analysis.

Division of Pharmacy.—Theory and practice of pharmacy, operative phar-
Division of Pharmacy.—Theory and practice of pharmacy, operative pharmacy and pharmaceutical preparations, pharmacopœial preparations, volumetric methods, alkaloidal analysis, pharmaceutical testing, prescription reading and writing and incompatibilities, prescription practice, drug assaying, United States Pharmacopœia and National Formulary, pharmaceutical research, veterinary pharmacy.

Division of Materia Medica and Therapeutics.—Materia medica, materia medica and therapeutics.

Division of Pharmacognosy and Pharmaceutical Problems.—Pharmacognosy (inorganic drugs), study of organic drugs, pharmaceutical and chemical problems, pharmaceutical Latin.

Department of Education.—History of education, psychology, childhood and adolescence, principles of teaching, agricultural and industrial education, education in the United States and educational administration, educational investigations, observation and practice, school law, the high school, education and society, rural education, current educational literature.

Division of Mechanical Engineering.—Wood shop, forge shop, machine shop, mechanical drawing, descriptive geometry, mechanical perspective, machine design, pattern shop, molding, internal-combustion engines and gas producers, manual training, testing laboratory, gas engineering, steam engineering, mechanism, mechanics of materials, analytical mechanics, materials of construction, heat engines, thermodynamics, electric machines, refrigeration and pneumatic machinery.

Division of Physics.—College physics, household physics.

Division of Civil Engineering.—Surveying, surveying for agricultural students, civil engineering drawing, land surveying, topographic surveying, railroad curves and earthwork, roads and pavements, railroad engineering, graphic statics, details, hydraulics, masonry construction, water-supply engineering, bridge stresses and details, bridge design, sewerage, engineering contracts and specifications, concrete and drainage for agricultural students, water purification, sewage disposal and sanitation, reinforced concrete design.

Division of Architecture and Architectural Engineering.—Elements, water color, free-hand drawing, architectural design, building construction and superintendence, clay modeling, history of architecture, plumbing, history of sculpture and painting, professional practice and inspection, railroad structures.

Free-hand Drawing and Industrial Art.—Elementary drawing, free-hand drawing, water color.

Department of English and Philosophy.—Exposition, argumentation, history of English literature, Milton, introduction to the drama, prose fiction, Wordsworth, Tennyson and Browning, essays, English scientific writers, advanced English composition, playwriting, logic, introduction to philosophic problems, ethics.

Department of Geology and Mineralogy.—Dynamic, physiographic, and structural geology, historical geology, economic and applied geology, practical field methods, formation of soils, glacial geology, descriptive mineralogy, determinative mineralogy and blowpipe analysis, metallurgy and assaying, meteorology, and climatology.

Department of History and Social Science.—Economic and social history of the United States, survey course in the history of agriculture and closely allied industries, agrarian history of the United States, history of Greek civilization and art, modern industrial history, American government and citizenship, sociology, political economy, rural sociology, current events, principles of cooperation, rural economics.

Department of Home Economics.—Food preparation, home architecture, foods and economic problems of food supply, economic uses of food, household management, therapeutic diet, dietetics, presentation of domestic science, theory and practice of teaching, social observances, household hygiene and sanitation, home nursing, institutional management, domestic art, drafting, undergarment making, dressmaking, millinery, textiles, presentation of domestic art, house decoration, domestic art design, art needlework.

Physical Training for Women.—Hygiene.

Department of Horticulture and Forestry.—Plant propagation, principles of plant culture, advanced general gardening, plant growth and improvement, landscape gardening, forestry, entomology, floriculture.

Department of Mathematics.—Descriptive astronomy, higher algebra, plane trigonometry, analytical geometry, differential calculus, integral calculus, biometry, slide rule, graphs, differential equations, mathematics of investment.

Department of Military Science and Tactics.—Target practice, military tactics.

Department of Modern Languages.—German: Grammar, reading and composition, modern prose, Schiller, comedies, Goethe, modern drama, Faust, Heine and the romantic school, modern fiction, lyric poems, scientific German, masterpieces in German literature, history of German literature. French: Grammar, reading and composition, modern prose, modern comedies, classic dramas, modern fiction, modern drama, lyric poems, journalistic French, history of French literature.

Department of Music.—Harmony, theory, musical history. Organizes cadet band, college orchestra, boys' glee club, girls' glee club, mixed chorus.

Department of Physical Training and Athletics.—Directs the athletic sports, and conducts classes in physical training.

Department of Public Discussion and Social Service.—Elementary public speaking, forensics, debate, ex tempore speech, community programs, dramatics; supervision of numerous literary contests.

Department of Veterinary Science.—Veterinary science, practical pathology and bacteriology, animal pathology, anatomy, hygiene, materia medica, pharmacy, physiology.

Agricultural and Manual Training High School.—Four-year high-school courses designated as follows: (1) Agriculture, (2) General science, (3) Mechanic arts, (4) Curriculum for rural teachers.

(1) Agriculture, (2) General science, (3) Mechanic arts, (4) Curriculum for rural teachers.

Industrial and Special Curricula.—The following special short courses are announced:

Names of courses.	Weeks in term.	From—	To—	Years required.
Farm husbandry	22	Oct. 11	Mar. 23	3
Homemakers'	22	...do....	...do....	3
Power machinery	22	...do....	...do....	3
Winter short courses	10	Jan. 2	Mar. 6	¹ 1
Pharmacy	36	Sept. 20	June 13	2
Draftsmen and builders	22	Oct. 11	Mar. 23	2

¹ Or more.

Department of College Extension.—Lists the following activities: Industrial contests, boys' and girls' institute, high-school lecture course, extension schools, public school cooperation, press service, assisting in organization of farmers' clubs or business associations, exhibits, package libraries.

SUMMARY OF CHRONOLOGICAL DEVELOPMENT.

The development of certain important features of the work of the agricultural college is set forth in the following summary:

1891. The North Dakota Agricultural College opened October 15, offering instruction in the following subjects: Household economics, agriculture, chemistry, veterinary science, horticulture and forestry, botany, zoology, mechanics, mathematics, language, history, geography, geology, military tactics.

1893. Four-year course in agriculture announced.

1896. Four-year course in mechanics announced. Prior to this date elective courses in wood shop and machine shop were offered as parts of a general course of study leading to the B. S. degree.

1897. Four-year course in mechanical engineering announced.

1898. Two-year course in steam engineering offered; separate organization of department of dairying.

1899. Department of history and social science organized, with one instructor in history and civics.

1902. Courses in pharmacy offered.

1908. Organized first two years of four-year course in veterinary medicine and surgery; department of education organized; course in civil engineering announced; two-year course in power machinery announced; agricultural students allowed to specialize in (1) agriculture, (2) agronomy, or (3) animal husbandry; department of public discussion and social service organized.

1909. Teachers' course added under course in agriculture.

1910. Course in chemical engineering announced.

1912. Short course in architecture announced; course in agricultural engineering announced.

1913. Two-year course for builders and contractors announced.

1914. Course in architectural engineering announced.

1915. Course in agricultural engineering transferred from department of agriculture to department of engineering and physics; two-year and four-year courses in pharmacy organized.

SUBSTATIONS, FARMS, ETC.

The long list of substations, experiment farms, surveys, and regulatory work provided by laws already cited make the field of operation of the agricultural college as wide as the State.

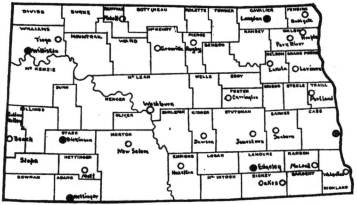

Fig. 9.—Demonstration work under the direction of the North Dakota Agricultural College.

○ Demonstration farms.
● Substation.
⊗ Experiment station.

In addition to the experiment station at Fargo, there are five substations—Williston, Dickinson, Hettinger, Langdon, and Edgeley—each having $5,000 a year for its support. There are also 22 demonstration farms, located at the following places: Bathgate, Beach, Carrington, Dawson, Granville, Hazleton, Hoople, Jamestown, Larimore, Lakota, McLeod, Mohall, Mott, New Salem, Oakes, Park River, Portland, Rugby, Sanborn, Tioga, Washburn, and Wahpeton. (See fig. 9.)

It is only a question of time when, under the provisions of the Smith-Lever bill, there will be an agricultural agent for each county in the State.

In the institutional farm at Fargo there are 953.8 acres, divided as follows:

	Acres.
Farming purposes	701. 0
Roads, fences, and right of way	40. 0
Campus	40. 2
Barns, yards, and farm buildings	50. 0
Experimental plats	97. 0
Garden and arboretum	25. 6
Total	953. 8

The 29 buildings at Fargo, including barns and sheds, have cost approximately $555,000; the value of equipment is estimated at $315,730; the annual income from all sources for the year ended June 30, 1915, was $429,382.45.[1]

The total income from producing lands to June 30, 1915, was $1,263,146.61.

ORGANIZATION.

It is explicitly provided in the laws establishing the North Dakota Agricultural College and Experiment Station, cited herein, that administrative authority for the entire institution is vested in the board of trustees, whose chief executive officer is the president of the college. During the early years of the institution, therefore, the president of the college was recognized as director of the experiment station also.

A department of college extension was organized by the faculty in 1910, which was formally recognized by vote of the board of trustees October 11, 1911. The legislative assembly of 1913 legalized the department of agricultural extension, and appropriated $20,000 for its maintenance for the following biennium. Although the governor vetoed the appropriation, the veto did not repeal the law establishing the department, and it was continued through the use of college funds for its maintenance.

The sections of the law relating to the faculty recognize the "institution" as embracing all college activities, including "the experiment station farm and results of farm experiments"; and all members of the station staff, as well as of the instructional force, are included in the term "faculty."

REORGANIZATION.

During the year 1911 the Better Farming Association was organized and financed by the lumber, elevator, railroad, and banking interests of Minnesota and North Dakota. The association was under

---

[1] For detailed statement of all these items, see Appendix V, Table 45, and IX, Tables 49–51.

the control of a board of directors, 21 in number, mostly North Dakota bankers.

On January 1, 1914, an arrangement was effected between the board of directors of the association and the board of trustees of the agricultural college by which the Better Farming Association was merged with the agricultural experiment station, and the secretary of the association became the director of the experiment station. The agreement between the two boards provided that the enterprises inaugurated by the Better Farming Association "shall be vigorously carried on in substantially the same manner and with no material curtailment" under the control of the director of the experiment station, "who shall be accountable only to the board of trustees of the North Dakota Agricultural College and Experiment Station, and such director shall also be in supreme charge of" the extension work and allied institutions started by the association.

It was further agreed that "the extension department of the institution shall be placed in the experiment station and that the director of the experiment station shall be made ex officio chief of said department or division," and that in administering the activities of the extension division the director shall be responsible only to the board of trustees of the college.

It appears, therefore, that there is now no official relationship between the college and the station, save that both are under the control of the same board. The organization provides for a president of the college and a director of the experiment station and extension division, coordinate in rank but with no mutual responsibilities. The existing arrangement is clearly not in accord with the meaning and evident intent of fundamental State law.[1]

The agricultural experiment station is the research department of the agricultural college, and the relation of the director of the experiment station to the president of the institution should be coordinate with that of the dean of agriculture.

There should be created the position of director of the extension division, coordinate with that of dean of agriculture, and that of director of experiment stations.[2] The extension work in North Dakota, as in other States, must grow in magnitude and importance.

[1] Since the date of the commission's investigation the plan of organization outlined above has been changed to comply with the law.

[2] The following extract from the Yearbook of the Department of Agriculture (1915) indicates that the authorities of agricultural colleges will find it necessary to coordinate the work of the experiment station and the extension organization :

"The institutions have created separate divisions or services and have brought under them all extension work in agriculture and home economics. Some of these divisions are not yet as clear-cut as they should be. In some cases laws or general administrative regulations adopted years ago have continued a confusing union of the extension organization with the experiment station. In 36 States a separate officer is in charge of the work, usually with the title of director ; in 9 this officer also is head of the experiment station or of the college of agriculture."

It will have a profound influence upon the experiment station itself, since the more the knowledge of scientific agriculture is extended among the farmers of the State, the more they will become interested in research problems.

According to the 1915 Report of the Secretary of Agriculture, 36 States have separate officers in charge of the extension work, usually with the title of director. In 9 States only is this officer also the head of the experiment station or of the college of agriculture.[1]

The extension work, therefore, is important enough and great enough to demand the entire time of an able scientist who is fitted by experience and training to bring to the farmers of the State the latest practical results of agricultural investigations, whether conducted in North Dakota or elsewhere. This officer should be in close touch with the director of the experiment station, the dean, and the president of the agricultural college, and also with the normal schools, the agricultural high schools, the granges, and other organizations of farmers, and all those engaged in agricultural pursuits.

The outline of organization of the work of the college, as given elsewhere, indicates a division of responsibility which the survey commission believes can not fail to prove a source of weakness. Power and efficiency would no doubt be promoted by closer organization and a larger grouping of these departments, divisions, schools, and courses under fewer responsible heads. The position of dean of biology, for instance, seems to be superfluous, inasmuch as the duties of this position fall more properly under the jurisdiction either of the dean of agriculture or the director of the experiment station.

TEACHING BY MEMBERS OF THE EXPERIMENT STATION STAFF.

The State suffers a great loss whenever a group of highly trained experts is assembled in connection with an experiment station if the duties of the members of the staff do not require or permit a reasonable amount of instruction of students. It is believed that a reasonable amount of teaching would not injure, but would improve, the scientific staff.

It is therefore recommended that, with a few exceptions for cause, at the discretion of the president, members of the staff of the experiment station be required to devote at least a certain designated minimum amount of time to the work of teaching and directing students. The amount for each investigator should be determined by the president of the institution, in consultation with the director in charge of research work.

This recommendation must not be understood to favor a plan whereby research work will be burdened with much teaching, to which research workers on an experiment station staff should prob-

---

[1] See footnote 1, p. 53.

ably devote not more than an hour or two daily. Sometimes, when important and engrossing work is under way, all teaching should be temporarily discontinued. The laboratories of the experiment station should be accessible to the teaching staff of the college.[1]

THE AGRICULTURAL AND MANUAL-TRAINING HIGH SCHOOL.

The agricultural and manual-training high school at the agricultural college was organized in 1909 to meet the legitimate demand which then existed for a preparatory school. But this was before the movement for the establishment and maintenance of high schools in city, town, and country was well under way. Because of the progress of this movement the demand for a preparatory school at the college is now less insistent than it was, and it should soon cease to exist. Indeed there is danger that the continuation of this school may retard, to some extent at least, the development of high schools throughout the State. Certainly it would do so if it drew.many of its students from the State at large. This, however, it does not do. Of the 138 students enrolled during the year 1914–15 in this preparatory school, 58, or 42 per cent of the whole, were from Cass County, and of the 94 enrolled in the first, second, and third years of this school 42, or nearly 45 per cent, were from this county. It is therefore evident that this preparatory school functions largely as a local high school in a county which is amply able to maintain high schools for all its boys and girls.

As a part of the work of this school, a course for rural teachers is offered. To this there is the same objection as to the low-grade courses for rural teachers at the normal schools. The agricultural college should, as elsewhere pointed out, prepare teachers of agriculture, home economics, and industrial subjects for the high schools and supervisors of these subjects for the elementary schools. But as the standard of requirements for teachers in the schools of the State is raised, there will be no demand for teachers of the low grade of preparation which this preparatory school now turns out.

The survey commission believes that this school should be discontinued as soon as the board of regents finds it practicable to do so.

---

[1] " According to the German idea, the university professor is both teacher and scientific investigator, and such emphasis is laid upon the latter function that one ought rather to say that in Germany the scientific investigators are also the instructors of the academic youth. * * * The important thing is not the student's preparation for a practical calling, but his introduction into scientific knowledge and research.—Paulsen's 'German Universities' (Thilly's translation).

" It is considered by all educational authorities that the investigator who is doing a limited amount of teaching does the best work for the advancement of science. Teaching makes it necessary for a man to go over his subject broadly, and the presence of young and earnest minds is always very stimulating to the investigator. The man who spends all his time in particular research too often loses his connection with everything else, with the result that he becomes buried in one subject. The greatest investigators have always been great teachers."—President CHARLES W. DABNEY.

The discontinuance should be gradual, as recommended in the summary of recommendations.

It is worthy of note that the agricultural college offers 27 courses in architecture and architectural engineering; that there were only 7 classes in these courses during the week of April 10, 1916, and that 4 of these classes had two attendants each and 3 had only one attendant each. It is not known how many of these were the same students enrolled in more than one class. Two of the classes were in freehand drawing, 2 in design, 1 in water color, 1 in the history of architecture, and 1 in the history of sculpture and painting. Evidently there is little demand for architecture and architectural engineering by the regular students of the college. It is doubtful if the demand is as yet sufficient to justify the expense, and it seems that the few students in these courses might better get the same instruction in the classes in these and similar subjects at the university, where the classes are larger than at the agricultural college, but still comparatively small.

SHORT COURSES.

The large attendance on the short courses at the agricultural college (in 1915–16, 195 for the four 22-weeks courses and 400 for the courses from 10 to 18 weeks in agriculture, engineering, and domestic science) shows a great demand for practical courses of such length and given at such times as make it possible for young men and women to attend without interfering to any large extent with their work on the farm. The experience of Minnesota and some other States shows the possibility, and the commission believes the advisability also, of organizing the 22-weeks courses into a school of agriculture, elementary mechanic arts, and household arts for those who do not expect to attend college or to become teachers. This school should, it is believed, offer courses of three years, and it is also believed it might be well worth while to try the experiment of repeating the winter courses with the necessary variations in a summer session. The shorter courses should be allowed to remain separate, as they are now. They should not, however, be taught as some of them now are in the regular classes of the college, of the agricultural and manual training high school, or of the longer 22-weeks courses. Those who come for these classes can be better served in classes planned for them alone, and the college can, it seems, well afford to provide such classes. If this separation of these classes from the regular departments of the college requires more instructors, then a larger draft might be made during these weeks on the time of experiment station men, and help might be had from extension workers and farm demonstration agents.

DISTRIBUTION OF ATTENDANCE.

That the agricultural college should extend its influence more largely into the western half of the State is shown clearly by the accompanying attendance map (fig. 10). No doubt in the case of both the college and the university the small attendance from this part of the State is due largely to the fact of its comparative newness and its lack of good high schools. The distance from the institutions also has its effect. Nevertheless, the fact remains that this part of the State both contributes its full share to the support of these institutions and is in no less need of its full share of their service than is the eastern half.

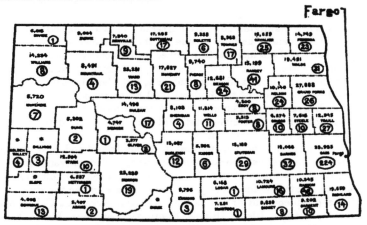

Fig. 10.—Distribution of resident students enrolled in the North Dakota Agricultural College at Fargo, exclusive of summer session, 1914–15. (See Table 31, p. 186.)

The figures above the county name in each case give the population in 1910. At that date the population of Golden Valley County (later subdivided into Golden Valley, Billings, and Slope Counties) was 10,186; and the population of Morton County (later subdivided into Morton and Sioux Counties) was 25,289.

The figures inclosed in the circle in each case indicate the number of students from the county who are enrolled at the agricultural college.

This institution drew 862 students from 49 of the 52 counties of North Dakota (of whom 25.9 per cent came from Cass County) and 174 from without the State; total, 1,036.

In 1910 the population of North Dakota was 577,056. Approximately 60 per cent of the population was found in the eastern half of the State (see note under fig. 8), and 40 per cent in the western half; whereas, of the North Dakota students in residence at the agricultural college, approximately 80 per cent came from the eastern half and only about 20 per cent from the western half.

Only 4 counties, outside of Cass County, sent more than 30 students each to the agricultural college; Minnesota sent 109; and Montana, South Dakota, and Wisconsin together sent 48.

Chapter V.

FUNCTION OF THE UNIVERSITY AND AGRICULTURAL COLLEGE.

HOW THE STATES HAVE ORGANIZED HIGHER EDUCATION.

The States have met in different ways the problem of maintaining higher education. Of the New England States, only Maine has established a State university. Vermont might be included, but Vermont divides its support for higher learning between a university and independent colleges.

New York maintains no State university in the usual sense of the word, but Cornell, having as one of its departments a college of agriculture and mechanic arts, receives for this college State support. Likewise, certain other New York colleges receive State appropriations for agriculture and other subjects, but Cornell receives all of New York's portion of the Federal land-grant funds.

The University of Pennsylvania is sometimes classed as a State institution, since it receives State aid for some of its departments, but it is not under State control.

In the foregoing States, and also in Rhode Island and New Jersey, there are no State-supported and State-controlled universities.

In the following 20 States the university and the agricultural college are located in the same place and both are under the direction of one president and of one board: Arizona, Arkansas, California, Florida, Georgia, Idaho, Illinois, Kentucky, Louisiana, Maine, Minnesota, Missouri, Nebraska, Nevada, Ohio, Tennessee, Vermont, West Virginia, Wisconsin, Wyoming.

In the following 19 States the agricultural college and the university are located in different places, have separate presidents, and usually separate boards of control: Alabama, Colorado, Indiana, Iowa, Kansas, Michigan, Mississippi, Montana, New Mexico, North Carolina, North Dakota, Oklahoma, Oregon, South Carolina, South Dakota, Texas, Utah, Virginia, Washington.

The following States have their institutions of higher education separated as follows: Missouri maintains, under one board, an agricultural college and university at Columbia, and at Rolla a school of mines which receives part of the Morrill fund; Michigan, Montana, New Mexico, Oklahoma, and Colorado have each three separate institutions, the university, the agricultural college, and the school of mines. Colorado and Montana maintain each four separate State institutions of higher learning, including a college of education. In some States, one or more normal schools, originally much below college rank, have been developed into colleges of education.

Illinois maintains a consolidated university at Urbana, and a medical school, a department of the university, in Chicago. The universities of several other States have medical or law schools at other places than that of the main seat of the university. Nebraska has an agricultural college and university in Lincoln, though they are not on the same campus, and a medical department in Omaha, all under the control of the same board. Similar conditions obtain in Minnesota, but all the university departments are in or near Minneapolis. Ohio has a university and agricultural college at Columbus, and universities at Oxford and Athens.

The foregoing statement indicates in a general way how the States have sought to meet the problem of the organization of higher education.

TWO FUNDAMENTAL CONCLUSIONS.

The development of higher education in so many Commonwealths which have sought each in its own way to solve its educational problems has furnished to students of education a fruitful field for study. From this study educational experts seem to have reached two fundamental conclusions touching higher education:

1. A State should, whenever possible and practicable, consolidate at one place in one university all higher education. This should not include normal schools whose purpose it is to prepare teachers for elementary schools.

2. When such consolidation is not practicable, as in States where two or more seats of higher learning have already been established, and developed at great expense, the work of these institutions should be so correlated as to promote cooperation and to prevent unnecessary and wasteful duplication of work.

The commission calls attention to a few of the reasons upon which these conclusions are based:

1. Higher education, especially graduate or research work, is expensive. To promote such work efficiently, costly laboratories are required and thoroughly trained experts who should command good salaries.

2. The number of students in these graduate courses is necessarily small and the duplication of work in them in two or more State-

supported schools would be wasteful, expensive, and unnecessary, and should not be permitted.

3. Professional schools, especially those of medicine, engineering, and agriculture, if high standards are set and maintained, are also very expensive. Even the largest and richest States would hesitate now to establish more than one such school of the highest grade, if the question were open for consideration.

Hence the commission is driven irresistibly to the conclusion that the maintenance in any State of two or more State-supported universities covering the same fields in graduate departments or of two or more professional schools of agriculture or engineering or medicine performing the same or similar service is expensive and unnecessary.

Hence it is that in States like California and Wisconsin, which have all higher education centered at one place in one university, the question of duplication is easy of solution. In States that maintain two or more seats of higher learning the question of duplication is difficult of solution and sometimes perplexing.

CONFLICT BETWEEN STATE UNIVERSITIES AND AGRICULTURAL COLLEGES.

In most States where the university is at one place and the agricultural college at another there is or has been more or less friction between the two institutions. This friction is intensified in States where two strong aggressive institutions have been developed, each striving to enlarge its field of operation. In some of these States the agricultural college has rapidly expanded into a technical university, while the university, striving to become a modern institution, to train men and women for practical pursuits and not alone for the older professions of law, medicine, and teaching, has also tended to become a technical university. Under such conditions conflict seems to be inevitable.

It is easy for the layman to see that the problem in these States is to eliminate, if possible, unnecessary duplication of work, with its accompanying inefficiency and waste of effort and money. Before this may be done a clear understanding of what duplication is and is not, when duplication is justifiable and when it is not justifiable, is essential to any satisfactory solution of the problem.

WHAT DUPLICATION IS NOT.

Because elementary and high schools are local, and because normal schools as recommended by the commission are mainly sectional or regional schools, the inclusion of the same subjects in a number of schools of the same kind is not duplication in the sense used in this report, but only repetition of facilities to meet the requirements of different communities or sections.

WHAT IS JUSTIFIABLE DUPLICATION?

During the first two years of college work there are certain funda- - mental branches that are common to several of the professional schools or colleges. The offering of these fundamental courses at more than one institution does not necessarily constitute unjustifiable or unduly expensive duplication. For example, such subjects as English, modern languages, mathematics, chemistry, physics, may usually be taught at two or more colleges at but little greater cost than at one, provided the equipment and teaching staff are utilized to anything like their capacity and class sections are not too small. It costs but very little more to offer five sections in mathematics at one institution, and five sections in the same course at another, than to offer ten sections at the same institution. The library and laboratory equipment for such students, in the introductory stages of these courses, is relatively inexpensive as compared with the equipment required for more advanced students, and especially for graduate students and professional students of medicine, law, and engineering. These considerations account for the recent pronounced tendency in the direction of the development of the junior college [1] in many States and municipalities.

UNJUSTIFIABLE DUPLICATION.

There is unjustifiable duplication of work when two or more institutions or departments are doing work which might be done, both more efficiently and more economically, and to the full extent required by the needs of the State, by one institution or department.

MAJOR AND SERVICE LINES OF WORK.

In dealing with the problem of duplication, the commission has been guided by what may be described as the principle of major and service lines of work.[2] In accordance with this principle each State institution should have assigned to it certain major fields which it should develop as fully as may be practicable. Literature, history, and philosophy at the university are such major lines; at the agricultural college, agriculture and home economics.

Service lines are such subordinate subjects as are essential to the proper cultivation of a major line. The amount required in these lines varies, but is generally not very full or comprehensive, being usually directed toward a special purpose. The modern languages are service lines at the agricultural college; home economics at the

---

[1] An institution doing two years' work beyond the high school, or freshman and sophomore years of the college.

[2] For a fuller discussion, see "State Higher Educational Institutions of Iowa," Bulletin, 1916, No. 19.

university. Institutions may well overlap as regards the relation of their service lines to one another and more particularly as regards the relation of their major to their service lines. English is a major line at the university, a service line at the agricultural college. There should be no material overlapping of major lines.

Certain subjects do not fall readily into line on such a principle of division. The detailed adjustments of these cases of overlapping, once the main principle has been accepted, seem capable of amicable settlement by means of a conference consisting of some convenient number of representatives of the faculties of the institutions affected (perhaps five from each), elected by the faculties and sitting with the State commissioner of education and a committee of members of the State board of regents. Such a conference might meet at stated periods, perhaps annually, to consider and adjust any difficulties that may arise from time to time. Meantime the principle of the major and the service lines will automatically settle the status of the larger number of subjects, and forthwith determine whether in a particular institution they shall be developed beyond their elementary stages.

If the principle of the establishment of major lines of work, forming the main structure in the curricula of the State institutions, be accepted, another principle will be at once clearly defined. All departments of an institution must be treated alike in the matter of thoroughly adequate provisions of men and apparatus with which to do the work required by the purposes of the college. All departments need not be treated alike, however, in facilities for expansion and outreach into graduate courses and research. A service department is a service department and not a major department, and it must so remain, if waste and unwarrantable duplication of effort and expenditure are to be avoided.[1]

THE PROBLEM IN NORTH DAKOTA.

In the light of the foregoing generally accepted conclusions and of the considerations set forth concerning major and service lines of work, the solution of the problem of duplication in North Dakota with its accompanying friction and waste of effort and money becomes, it is believed, easier of solution.

---

[1] Certain departments, like chemistry and botany, by their intimate and organic relation with the research work of the experimental stations, will need to develop specialised forms of work in the direction of major lines; for example, soil chemistry, organic chemistry, plant pathology, and dairy bacteriology. But in all such cases a clear differentiation of departmental functions should be enforced, for the State does not need two groups of research men and two research laboratories for plant pathology or dairy bacteriology. It is even conceivable that a strong man in one of the other State institutions might develop his talents along one of these lines to a point which would make it desirable to transfer him to the agricultural college staff instead of continuing his work on the old location.

MAIN PURPOSE OF THE UNIVERSITY AND THE COLLEGE.

GENERAL STATEMENT.

The main purpose of the university should be to give liberal training in literature, science, and the arts; to develop professional education in accordance with the needs of the State, and especially in the older professions of law, medicine, education, and engineering; to promote educational and scientific research; to conduct extension courses which do not duplicate the extension work of the agricultural college.

The main function of the agricultural college and experiment station should be to teach and to develop for the benefit of the people of the State the science of agriculture; to promote, as the needs of the State demand, agricultural, industrial, and technical education, as distinguished from the older professional education, for instance, of law and medicine; to conduct at the experiment station original investigations in agriculture and the allied arts and sciences; to carry to the people of the State through extension courses the results of research and experimental work beneficial to the farmers of the State.

DUPLICATION IN GRADUATE WORK.

It should not be difficult to determine the graduate work that should be undertaken at each of these institutions. The graduate department of the agricultural college, in so far as the college undertakes research, is the experiment station. All graduate work properly belonging to the Government experiment station in North Dakota should be conducted at Fargo or at the substations of the college. Should there be at the university professors interested in special problems connected with agriculture or allied subjects, they might be given an opportunity to conduct experiments at the laboratories of the experiment station, at the farms of the college, or at the substations. For the same reason, professors of the agricultural college who wish to undertake experiments that may be best conducted at the laboratories or stations of the university should be afforded opportunity to do so. In general, graduate work should be divided between the two institutions on the basis of major lines of work assigned to each, as recommended elsewhere. Graduate work at the university will naturally follow some of the lines of work pursued in the college of liberal arts and sciences. There is thus open to the university for research work vast fields that scarcely touch the domain of the agricultural college.

DUPLICATION IN THE COLLEGE OF LIBERAL ARTS.

In a number of agricultural colleges in other States courses in liberal arts and sciences leading to degrees are offered. Advanced courses in liberal arts and sciences, such courses as are given in the junior and senior years, and especially graduate courses, are necessarily expensive. Such courses should be offered only at the university. North Dakota should at this time maintain only one State college of liberal arts and sciences, and this should be at the university. Although it is declared in the charter establishing the agricultural college that the course of instruction shall embrace the English language and literature, moral philosophy, and history, and in the Morrill Act it is stated that the land-grant colleges are " to promote the liberal and practical education of the industrial classes in the several pursuits and professions in life," it clearly was not the intention either of Congress or of the Legislature of North Dakota to make training in the liberal arts and sciences the specific work of the agricultural college. While there is nothing in either Federal or State laws to prohibit its giving even extensive courses in liberal arts and science, it will promote efficiency and economy in both institutions if all advanced instruction in the liberal arts and the pure sciences is offered only at the university.

It will doubtless be practicable for the faculties of the two institutions so to coordinate their work that it may be possible for students who have taken such " liberal " courses as are offered at the agricultural college to enter the junior year of the college of arts and sciences at the university and to win in two years appropriate liberal arts degrees.

Here again cooperation is urged in the framing of courses and the exchange of students between the two higher institutions which by unity of effort may do the work undertaken in Minnesota, Illinois, and California by one consolidated university.

DUPLICATION IN THE INDUSTRIAL ARTS AND THE FINE ARTS.

In States where the agricultural college and the university are separated, the major work in the industrial arts would seem to belong to the agricultural college, the major work in the fine arts to the university. But in North Dakota conditions indicate a modification of such division.

In North Dakota are found extensive deposits of clays for brick, tile, and pottery; and the soil in the western part of the State is underlaid with lignite. The School of Mines and its stations, as authorized by law, are dealing with the problem of making use of these deposits. Its service to the State does not require that it should prepare engineers to deal with the problems of mining gold, silver, copper, iron, or other metals.

In consideration of these facts, the major work in industrial arts growing out of the manufacture of clay deposits and lignite belongs properly to the university; while the industrial arts related to agriculture, such for example as milling, canning vegetables, the manufacturing of cereals and starch, beet sugar, twine, paper, linen, dairying, and the preserving of dressed meats, may be taught best at the agricultural college.

In proportion as the manufacturing of clay products and lignite develop in the State, the college of education at the university will doubtless find it desirable, in cooperation with the School of Mines, to give instruction in industrial arts growing out of these industries; while the agricultural college will have a large field in training teachers of the industrial arts related to, or growing out of, agriculture.

In 1910 there were in North Dakota only 752 industrial establishments. These had a capital of $1,585,000. Only 4,148 persons were engaged in manufacturing. At that time only 960 persons were reported as engaged in mining. Consequently, it is not possible for the commission to predict what course of development manufacturing may take, or to what extent the State should make preparation for instruction in the industrial arts.

The university should in time develop a strong school of fine arts. American colleges and universities, interested in problems of pioneer life, have until now given comparatively little attention to the fine arts, but with the increase of wealth and the passing of pioneer conditions they will eventually turn their attention to these arts, which are no less essential to the largest and best interests of a democracy than are those things to which we have had to give first attention.

DUPLICATION IN MUSIC, HOME ECONOMICS, AND AGRICULTURE.

Both music and home economics should be taught in all State institutions of North Dakota. Home economics is a subject of universal interest to women, while music is, or should be, a subject of interest to all the people of the State; consequently some instruction in these subjects may well be offered at all the State institutions. The normal schools should continue to give in music, home economics, agriculture, and industrial arts, instruction suited to students preparing to be elementary teachers. Advanced or major courses, however, for experts in home economics, agriculture, and industrial arts related to, or growing out of, agriculture, should be given only at the agricultural college. The agricultural college should be thoroughly equipped both for the practical and scientific study of all these branches. It should be able, therefore, to train experts who should become teachers in high schools and normal schools, or engage in business related to its major lines of work.

Instruction in music, including special training in chorus, orchestra, and band, should be given both at the.university and at the agricultural college, but advanced and professional instruction in the higher forms of music should be given only at one place in the State, and that place should be the university.

DUPLICATION IN PHARMACY.

There is ground for the opinion that a school of pharmacy might best be developed in connection with the work of the medical college of the university. But inasmuch as it is necessary for the agricultural college to employ a number of expert pharmacists in connection with the food and drug inspection and other regulatory work of the State, the college is able to use these same experts without much additional expense as teachers in the school of pharmacy. Hence, the conclusion is reached that the school of pharmacy should remain at the agricultural college. Inasmuch, however, as it is necessary for physicians to have instruction in pharmacy, the medical school at the university will be forced to offer such instruction as may be necessary for prospective physicians.

DUPLICATION IN EXTENSION WORK.

The presidents of the State institutions, together with the State superintendent of public instruction and the director of the State library commission, should cooperate in formulating a plan for the efficient and economical organization of the extension work to be undertaken in the State. After due deliberation the committee thus constituted should submit to the State board of regents an outline for the accomplishment of the ends sought.

In general the extension work of the several institutions should be differentiated as follows: The university should limit its extension activities to those lines of popular interest that grow directly out of the university curriculum; the agricultural college should confine its activities to the great field of agriculture and rural life; the normal schools should confine their extension activities to work with teachers and should seek, through the more efficient organization of rural and elementary schools, to quicken popular interest in public education and social betterment; both the university and the agricultural college should foster the development of high schools and secondary education throughout the State; the schools at Wahpeton and Bottineau should limit their extension activities to the special fields suggested by their organization; the State library commission should follow the lines indicated in the chapter covering the work of the commission. .

It is to be noted that a very large part of extension work in North Dakota belongs properly to the agricultural college. All extension work coming under the provisions of the Smith-Lever Act of 1914 must be under the direction of the authorities of the agricultural college. North Dakota is at this time receiving from Congress $10,000 annually for extension work under the provisions of this act. In 1922, when the appropriation has reached its maximum, North Dakota will receive, upon the basis of her present rural population, $52,607. To receive this sum the State will have to provide its estimate, $42,607. Hence, North Dakota will have at that time $95,214, probably more, for extension work. This work at present includes (1) county agricultural agents, (2) boys' and girls' clubs, (3) movable schools, and (4) the supporting work of the college and department specialists. Since it has large funds for the purpose, the agricultural college will be expected to carry on this work.

The extension and correspondence work undertaken by the university should include, so far as may be practicable, all subjects not undertaken by the other institutions of the State. Lectures on general literature, on the liberal arts and sciences, on ethics and philosophy, history and government, on sanitation and hygiene, and providing public lyceum courses not closely related to the curricula of the agricultural college—this and much similar work may be carried on best by the university.

Correspondence and extension work are assuming large proportions in modern State universities and agricultural colleges. The aim of these schools seems to be, and rightly so, to extend their work to the utmost bounds of the State and to reach, directly or indirectly, all the people. Some States are spending large sums for extension and correspondence courses. The demand for such work in North Dakota will grow rapidly, if the State can afford to furnish the funds that are needed for its support.

DUPLICATION IN STATE SURVEYS.

The General Assembly has authorized a survey to be known as the Agricultural College Survey of North Dakota, and has also authorized the university to conduct a geological survey.

These two surveys would seem to cover in part the same work. There should at least be no conflict, and it is stated that there has been none. Cooperation on the part of the staffs of these surveys should be encouraged. There should be between the surveys, so far as may be practicable, an exchange of specimens collected for the use of museums at each institution, and there should be at least an annual conference of survey workers in order to secure cooperation and to prevent duplication of work and waste of effort.[1]

Both the university and the agricultural college are developing schools of engineering. The university has invested in buildings and equipment for engineering $129,313.95; the agricultural college, $135,200. Nothing either in State or Federal laws prevents either institution from establishing and developing such schools.

The enabling acts set aside 40,000 acres of land for the endowment of a school of mines which was located by the constitution at Grand Forks, the seat of the university. It would seem, therefore, mandatory that the State maintain a school of mines and engineering at the university.

On the other hand, North Dakota Agricultural College, like most of the separate land-grant colleges, has undertaken to maintain a department of "mechanic arts" and has interpreted "mechanic arts" to mean engineering of all kinds and all degrees of development.

Thus North Dakota has two colleges of engineering preparing to cover all subjects for which there is a demand, although there is no manifest need for more than one such school. Indeed, the question has been seriously raised whether North Dakota is at present justified in maintaining so expensive an institution as a college of engineering of first rank. The demand for professional engineers in a State so overwhelmingly agricultural is necessarily quite limited. At the same time, there is an impressive accumulation of facts pointing to the conclusion that there is need for the material extension of agricultural education in the State.

ENGINEERING AND AGRICULTURE.

There are educators of distinction who claim that, whenever professional engineering is strongly developed at the agricultural college, it invariably overshadows the agricultural work. The engineering

---

[1] "The geological survey (of the university) shall be carried on with a view to a complete account of the mineral kingdom, as represented in the State, including the number, order, dip, and magnitude of the several geological strata, their richness in ores, coals, clays, peats, salines and mineral waters, marls, cements, building stones, and other useful materials, the value of said substances for economical purposes, and their accessibility; also an accurate chemical analysis of the various rocks, soils, ores, clays, peats, marls, and other mineral substances of which a complete and exact record shall be made." Session Laws.

"It shall be the duty of the State director of this survey (the agricultural college) to collect, or cause to be collected, samples of all rocks, soils, coals, clays, minerals, fossils, plants, woods, skins and skeletons of native animals, and such other products of economic or scientific interest discovered during this survey, which, properly secured and labeled, shall be placed on exhibition in the museum of the North Dakota Agricultural College." Session Laws.

school, they claim, actually draws students from the agricultural courses. It is true that in many colleges of agriculture and mechanic arts there are far more students in engineering than in agriculture. If this is due to the fact that engineering is better supported than agriculture, the agricultural college would seem sometimes to suffer because of inadequate support when the two colleges are located on the same campus.

There is no reason, however, why an agricultural college should not be actually strengthened by reason of its location on the same campus with the engineering college. The real reason for the transfer of professional engineering unrelated to agriculture to the university is that the State can not afford to support, and does not need, two such schools of professional engineering.

AN AGRICULTURAL COLLEGE OF THE FIRST RANK AN IMPERATIVE NEED.

It will be apparent to thoughtful persons that if an agricultural college having only a limited amount of money devotes it all or the greater part to agriculture and allied arts and sciences, it may develop a stronger and a better school of agriculture than an institution similarly limited in funds which undertakes to maintain also professional schools not closely related to agriculture. For this reason Massachusetts has been able to maintain a good college of agriculture, because it devotes all available money to this one purpose. In Massachusetts the Morrill fund is divided between the agricultural college at Amherst and the Massachusetts Institute of Technology, at Boston, the former receiving two-thirds, the latter one-third, of the fund. But even if the college received all the Morrill fund it would seem better for the State to spend it all in developing a thoroughly efficient school of agriculture rather than two inefficient schools, one of agriculture and one of professional engineering which touches but slightly the problems of rural life.

Although, as elsewhere shown, the Agricultural College of North Dakota, including the experiment stations and regulatory work, already has a relatively large annual income—more than $400,000— this income is not yet large enough for the full support of such a college of agriculture as the State of North Dakota should have.

Since it is not possible, without a constitutional amendment, to center all engineering at either the college or the university, the commission is driven to the conclusion that the engineering work of the two institutions should be so divided as to prevent expensive and unnecessary duplication, the agricultural college to retain and to develop the courses related to agriculture and the industries growing out of agriculture, chemical engineering, and engineering courses designated industrial. (See recommendation 5, ch. 12.)

ENGINEERING AT THE COLLEGE.

The agricultural college should give such engineering as is related to agriculture—for example, surveying, road making, drainage, irrigation, water supply, drafting and designing to aid in the construction of rural buildings, such as farm houses and barns; engineering such as may be used in connection with the management of farm machinery, in the construction of agricultural manufactories, such as dairying, milling, canning, packing, refrigeration. In fact, the agricultural college, in proportion as its means permit and the needs of the State demand, should give instruction in all engineering that may help to lighten the burdens of the farm and the home or to aid in the development of industries connected with the farm and the manufacturing of the products of the farm.

ENGINEERING AT THE UNIVERSITY.

Both efficiency and economy demand that professional engineering such as is now generally given in the great engineering schools, demanding as. it does thorough training in the higher mathematics and physics and calling for expensive laboratories, and covering highly technical fields of work difficult to master without long and laborious application, should be centered at one place. These professional courses in mechanical, electrical, structural, and railroad engineering, which are very expensive, might be given at the University of North Dakota, but they should not be given at the agricultural college. All its available resources are needed to make it a great agricultural school. At any rate, North Dakota is not able to develop two such institutions. If the Massachusetts Institute of Technology and Harvard University found it worth while through cooperation to prevent waste and increase efficiency, what excuse can there be for the maintenance of two schools of professional engineering covering the same field, especially in a State having need for relatively few professionally trained engineers?

COOPERATION OF FACULTIES NEEDED.

It does not seem to be a difficult task to so divide the engineering work of these institutions as to prevent duplication in major and expensive lines. It is apart from the prime mission of the agricultural college to train men to build great office buildings for the city, to become marine or railroad engineers, electrical engineers (a profession split already into a score or more specialties), mining engineers—in short, to fit students for any of the highly specialized professions whose fields of operations are far removed from the needs of the farmers, from industries growing out of agriculture or the activities of the villages, towns, and small cities of North Dakota.

Nevertheless, the solution of the engineering problem in North Dakota is confronted by difficulties and calls for the cooperation of the faculties of the two schools. Civil engineering, highway engineering, some sanitary and municipal engineering, and chemical engineering fall naturally into the curricula of agricultural colleges. So closely is the work of the entomologists at the experiment station related to sanitation that the problem of eradicating "mountain fever" has been undertaken through the cooperative work of station entomologists and medical experts. One preparing to become a sanitary engineer might find it profitable to take courses in hygiene and sanitation at the medical college of the university, engineering courses both at the university and college, and courses in entomology and in veterinary science at the agricultural college. German students often spend a semester or more at two or three universities. Why should not North Dakota students find it advantageous in preparing for the professions to take some work both at the university and the college? Indeed, the State board of regents is especially authorized to provide for the exchange of students and instructors between the higher institutions of North Dakota.

Under the division proposed by the commission the college will still hold all the engineering courses related to agriculture and allied subjects. For these it needs not only the engineering buildings and equipment it now has, but in the near future it will need additional engineering equipment and buildings. It will continue to maintain courses in farm architecture, including the building of country homes, barns, cement construction, and possibly school houses; in power machinery, motor engines, dairy engineering, rural sanitation, and hydraulic engineering for farm purposes. These and other similar subjects have scarcely been touched by many of the agricultural colleges of the country.

The plan here outlined leaves undisturbed the following groups of subcollegiate students at the agricultural college: Drafting and building, 6; power machinery, 75; winter short course engineering, 204; engineering summer school students, 75; total 360. Courses of this type should not only be continued, but strengthened. With the approval of the board of regents advanced instruction in these branches might be continued through college courses and proper degrees granted upon their completion. At least one agricultural college is now granting a degree in agricultural engineering. Whether degrees should be given in what, for the lack of a better term, has been called "industrial" engineering, the board of regents and the faculty may be left to determine.

Under the plan here recommended only a very small number of students taking professional engineering courses such as are offered at the university would be affected—certainly not more than 22, and perhaps a much smaller number.

Indeed, it seems that the agricultural college should be happy to see such professional engineering courses as have little or no connection with agricultural development transferred to the university and the money thus saved devoted to more promising fields of endeavor. As agriculture grows more efficient it will grow more complex. The agricultural college will need large sums for extension work, for county agricultural agents, for cooperative work with consolidated rural schools, county high schools, and agricultural departments of normal schools.[1]

Without doubt it would be a waste of public money to maintain in North Dakota two colleges of professional engineering covering the same fields. Certainly many promising fields, as yet untouched, are open to the agricultural college. If it is urged that North Dakota needs two schools of professional engineering doing a similar service, more compelling reasons could be urged for the establishment of at least 10 colleges of agriculture. For every engineer needed in the State of North Dakota there is urgent need for at least 100 well-trained farmers. North Dakota, however, needs but one college of agriculture, but it can, and should be, made an institution of first rank.

AGRICULTURAL ENGINEERING.

The whole subject of agricultural engineering and rural arts is well covered by Prof. L. H. Bailey, formerly dean of the College of Agriculture of Cornell University in an article in the "Cyclopedia of American Agriculture."[2] The conclusions reached by Prof. Bailey are powerfully supported by facts presented in other parts of this report. These facts have been gathered by first-hand studies undertaken by the commission and may be understood by reference to maps and statistical tables. Again and again the commission is driven to the conclusion that the paramount problem of North Dakota is that of contributing to the health and happiness and prosperity, to the spiritual and intellectual life of the rural people.

---

[1] "There will be established," says Prof. Bailey, "out in the open country, plant doctors, plant breeders, soil experts, health experts, pruning and spraying experts, forest experts, farm-machinery experts, drainage and irrigation experts, recreation experts, market experts, and many others. There will be housekeeping experts or supervisors. There will be need for overseers of affiliated organizations and stock companies. These will all be needed for the purpose of giving special advice and direction. We shall be making new applications of rural law, of business methods for agricultural regions, new types of organization. The people will find that it will pay to support such professions or agents as these."

[2] See Appendix IV.

Chapter VI.

DEPARTMENTS OF EDUCATION AT THE UNIVERSITY AND THE AGRICULTURAL COLLEGE.

Elsewhere in this report it is urged that the normal schools of North Dakota shall limit their efforts to the preparation of teachers for the elementary schools of the State, that they shall gradually raise their standards to such degree as will enable them to give such preparation as should be required of teachers, both in urban and in rural elementary schools, that the normal schools now in existence should be given additional support, and that others shall be established to the end that a sufficient number of teachers may be prepared for all the elementary schools of the State. It is the task of the university and the agricultural college to give professional preparation for high-school teachers, teachers of special subjects, supervisors, superintendents and teachers in normal schools and colleges. Some of the graduates of these institutions and more who do a less amount of work than is required for graduation will, of course, become teachers in the elementary schools, but it should not be considered a part of the work of the college or university to prepare elementary teachers. The work of this kind now done at the university should be abandoned as soon as the normal schools are able to prepare all the teachers needed in the elementary schools of the State.

In addition to a knowledge of subjects taught, which should not be less than that represented by graduation from a standard college, teachers of youth in high schools should have a knowledge of economic, industrial, social, and civic life, an understanding of the relation of the subjects they teach to other subjects taught in the schools, and a breadth of culture which can be gained best at college or university. Principals and supervisors who must formulate, inspect, and direct the work of teachers under their charge, and superintendents who determine policies and administer the business affairs of city, county, and State school systems, need no less.

As elsewhere stated, the increase in the number of high schools in the State and the growing desire for better-trained superintendents and supervisors may be expected to make a steady demand for from

150 to 200 recruits from the university and college annually, at least until those entering this field of work remain in it much longer than they now do. At the University of North Dakota 208 students were enrolled in education during the year 1915–16; of these, 29 were in the senior class, 34 in the junior class, 72 in the sophomore class, 66 in the freshman class, and 7 were classed as specials. During the week of April 10–16, 65 of these attended a class in special methods in the elementary schools, and it may be supposed that most of these were preparing to become elementary teachers. At the agricultural college during the same week, 25 were in the senior class in education, 17 in one junior class, 16 in another, and 3 in a class the rank of which is not stated. Assuming that all the 29 seniors in education at the university and all the 25 at the agricultural college begin work as high-school teachers, superintendents, or supervisors in North Dakota at the beginning of the next school year, the total will be only 54, about 25 per cent of the number needed. Some will, of course, come from other States, but it is evident that the number of graduates in education from these two schools should be much larger than it now is, and that the school of education at the university and the department of education at the college should be largely increased. The interests not only of the high schools and the systems of elementary schools of the State, but the interests of the university, the college, and normal schools also depend upon it. The better and more numerous the high schools, the more. numerous and better prepared will be the students at the higher institutions.

Certainly the agricultural college might devote a larger amount of its funds to this purpose. The Nelson amendment to the Morrill Act, increasing by $25,000 the annual appropriation of the Federal Government to each of the land-grant colleges, provides that these colleges may use a part of this fund for the maintenance of courses for the preparation of teachers of agriculture and mechanic arts. The Commissioner of Education has interpreted this to include teachers of home economics, and has urged that a liberal portion of this fund be so used.

Both the school of education at the university and the department of education at the college should have for their use as laboratories schools of 12 grades, including both elementary and high schools. Such a school should be provided on the campus at each place, or arrangements should be made whereby the use of one or more schools can be had for this purpose in Grand Forks and in Fargo.

Chapter VII.

THE STATE NORMAL SCHOOLS.

THE SCHOOLS OF NORTH DAKOTA PREDOMINANTLY RURAL.

In 1910 nine-tenths of the children of school age in North Dakota lived in the open country or in villages and towns of less than 2,500 inhabitants, and were classed as rural in the United States census. Three-fourths of them lived outside of any incorporated place. The school problem of the State is therefore overwhelmingly a rural-school problem.

A very large majority of the men and women in the rural communities of the State are engaged directly in farming and in making country and village homes. Practically all the remainder of the rural population are directly interested in these occupations. The experiences of the children are almost all connected with the farm, and most of the children are looking forward to farming as their life work. For them it will be the means of making a living, of rendering service to State and society, and of self-expression. In so far, therefore, as education is vocational in North Dakota, it should, for a large majority of the children, prepare for farming, for home making in country, village, and small town, and for intelligent, joyous living under rural conditions. It would be easy to show that out of their rural life and occupations must come also a very large part of their cultural education, a very important element of which must consist in giving the power of understanding of and sympathy with the best in the life of the communities in which they live and of which they are a part.

In this implied plea for a larger amount of instruction in agriculture and home making for boys and girls in the rural schools of North Dakota it is not forgotten that those who live in the country and till the soil and make the country homes are also citizens and human beings, and that country children have the same right as have city children to such instruction and training as will prepare them for the duties and responsibilities of citizenship, develop most fully all their qualities of manhood and womanhood, and enable them to enjoy the finest and best in all the life of the world with which they may come in contact. Children in the country are not

75

to be trained into mere working cattle any more than children of
the city are to be made into mere productive machines, however intelligent, for the great industrial plants. It is remembered, however, that it is ever more and more important that the great mass
of country people should be intelligent about the life they live and
the work they do, and that all education to be most effective must
come out of and return into the life and work of those to be educated—" from life, through life, to life."

The schools for three-fourths of the children of North Dakota
must take hold of the life and work of the farm and the open
country. In them must be taught effectively what country people
living on and by their farms need to know. But schools are made
by their teachers, and teachers can not teach effectively that which
they themselves do not know. Therefore the schools in which
teachers are prepared must keep definitely in mind the work these
teachers are to do and use all possible means to prepare them for it.
In North Dakota they should prepare more than three-fourths of
their students who are prospective teachers to teach to country
children the things that as men and women living on North Dakota
farms and in North Dakota villages they will need to know, and also
teach them how to organize and manage country schools, not forgetting, of course, the needs of the smaller number who will teach in
the schools of towns and cities.

RURAL TEACHERS NEED NO LESS PREPARATION THAN CITY TEACHERS.

It is popularly supposed that teachers in one-room country schools
need less education and professional preparation than those who
teach in graded schools of the cities. A brief consideration of the
facts in the case will, however, show the fallacy of this supposition.
In the cities the schools are well organized, with expert superintendents, supervisors, and principals. Paid janitors and expert
health inspectors look after the heating, lighting, sanitation of
buildings, and the health of the children. Courses of study are carefully made out by subjects, grades, and years. Children are classified by principals, who also assist teachers in their more difficult
problems of discipline, as they and the special supervisors direct
and assist them in their classroom work. To the individual teacher
is assigned a group of children all of one grade, and she is given a
definitely prescribed kind and amount of work to do, or she may
be required to teach one or more closely allied subjects in two or
more grades. If she is weak in one subject or in any one phase of
school management, she can be given special help in it or be relieved
of it altogether. For the children and the older people of urban
communities there are many agencies of education other than the
schools, such as public libraries, museums, lecture courses. etc.

In the country it is far otherwise. The schools are not so well organized, and probably never can be. If the superintendents are expert, well educated, and highly trained, which is too often not the case, still they can visit any one school very seldom. In most counties there are few or no assistant superintendents or supervisors of special subjects. From the nature of the case, there can be no supervising principal in the one, two, or three teacher school. Frequently there is no trained janitor or expert health inspector. The teacher must be her own janitor, health inspector, truant officer, principal, supervisor, and to a large extent her own superintendent. She must organize and manage her own school, and teach unaided all the subjects to all the children in all the grades. If she fails in any particular, the failure can not be made good by anyone else. There are fewer educational agencies for children and older people in the country than in the city, and the function of the country school should, therefore, be much larger than that of the city school needs to be. The need for power of leadership in the country teacher is correspondingly greater than the need for such power in the city teacher.

NEED OF EQUAL PREPARATION FOR ALL SCHOOLS.

If there is need for well-educated, well-trained, and experienced teachers in the schools of one community there is equal need for such teachers in all communities. If the State taxes all the property and all the people of the State for the entire or partial support of all the schools of the State to the end that the State may have intelligent, virtuous, self-supporting citizens, then the State must require every community to put into its schools teachers who are prepared to do their work in such way that the money raised through the taxes of the people of the State may not be wasted and the State defrauded in the character of its citizenship.

If the people of all communities contribute to the support of the normal schools and other schools in which the teachers are prepared, then they have a right to demand that teachers be prepared in such way and in such numbers that there may be properly prepared teachers for the schools of each and every community and that no community may find it necessary to fill its schools with incompetent teachers at the risk of the loss of their money and the time and opportunity of their children. The State that assumes the responsibility of educating all its children at public expense must assume the accompanying responsibilities of determining standards of preparation for its teachers and of providing the means and opportunity of preparation for all the teachers needed in all its schools to the extent that they are not prepared elsewhere and by other means. Otherwise, the State is open to the charges of injustice and folly.

NUMBER OF TEACHERS.

In 1913 there were in North Dakota 171,872 children of legal school age. The rate of increase for the period of three years preceding 1913 was 11 per cent. At the same rate there should be approximately 190,700 children in 1916. In 1913 there were enrolled in the public schools of the State 142,434 children, and in approved private schools 2,611, a total of 145,045. Of these, 7,998 were in high-school grades. The total number of schools maintained in that year was 5,298, of which 464 were graded and 4,834 ungraded. Most of these ungraded schools were one-teacher schools. The total number of teachers employed was 7,911, of whom 7,396 were in elementary schools and 515 in high schools. The increase for the two preceding years was: Total, 342; elementary, 287; high schools, 55. At the same rate of increase there would be now (1916) a total of 8,253; elementary, 7,683; high schools, 570. Most of the high-school teachers are in cities and towns, since the development of the high schools in these began earlier and has gone forward much more rapidly than in the country, but a very large majority of the elementary teachers are in the rural schools and a still larger proportion of these are in ungraded one-teacher schools.

Since the rural schools have been distributed more or less evenly over the entire area of the State, and since the average enrollment in these schools is very small (only 16 to a teacher), future increase of rural population will not necessitate an equal increase in the number of rural elementary teachers. With proper care in guarding against an unnecessary increase in schoolhouses, and with due regard to the possibilities and advantages of consolidation, there will be need for very few more rural elementary teachers until after the rural population has become fully twice as large as it now is. But the movement for rural high schools has just begun, and the number of high-school teachers needed may be expected to increase more rapidly than the population. Indeed, it should and no doubt will come about within the next two decades, that there will be high schools within reach of all, and that a large majority of boys and girls of high-school age will attend them. There is now a definite movement in this direction in all parts of the United States, and nowhere stronger than in the West. For many years the increase in the number of elementary teachers in North Dakota has been far less in proportion than the increase in population, while the increase in the number of high-school teachers has been more than that of the population. For the five years 1911–1915, inclusive, the increase in the number of elementary teachers was a little less than 2 per cent, while the increase in number of high-school teachers was nearly 36 per cent. The increase in population from 1910 to 1915 is estimated at 23.6 per cent (United States census).

NUMBER OF NEW TEACHERS NEEDED ANNUALLY.

In response to a questionnaire sent to all elementary and high-school teachers in the State 4,981 replies were received and tabulated. Of those reporting 3,068 were rural teachers, 1,913 teachers in cities and towns. The average age of rural teachers reporting was 23 years, of teachers in cities and towns 28 years. The average time the rural teachers had been teaching was two years, city and town teachers 5.6 years. This indicates that approximately one-half of the rural teachers at the beginning of each school year are new and wholly inexperienced, while only about one-fifth of the teachers in urban communities are new. The summary of replies to the questionnaire reveals other facts of such general interest and such value to this discussion that it is inserted here. (Tables 15–17.)

TABLE 15.—*Birthplaces of teachers.*[1]

North Dakota	1, 635	Nebraska	57
Minnesota	1, 107	Other States	234
Iowa	412	Canada	87
Wisconsin	575	Norway	43
Indiana	221	Sweden	17
Illinois	154	Germany	20
South Dakota	169	Other countries	41
Michigan	90		
Ohio	78	Total reporting	4, 981
Kansas	41		

TABLE 16.—*Occupations of fathers of teachers.*[1]

Farmer	3, 078	Teacher	51
Merchant	306	Lawyer	40
Laborer	272	Physician	35
Contractor	177	Lumberman	34
Clergyman	118	Banker	32
Railroad man	118	Other occupations	535
Salesman	79		
Blacksmith	54	Total reporting	4, 981
Grain buyer	51		

[1] Based on replies from 4,981 teachers. See also Appendix X.

Table 17.—*Rural teachers and city teachers compared.*[1]

Teachers.	Rural teachers.	City teachers.
Number of teachers reporting	3,068	1,912
Average age reported	23	26
Average monthly salary in 1915–16	$56.39	$82.58
Number who were born in country	2,191	979
Number who were born in city	877	934
Amount of schooling:		
Graduated from eighth grade only	121	
Had 1 year of high school only	339	7
Had 2 years of high school	449	16
Had 3 years of high school	403	38
Had 4 years of high school	1,501	220
Normal school	241	1,070
College	14	560
Teachers' certificates:		
Second grade elementary	2,190	28
First grade elementary	621	248
Professional	257	1,540
Sex of teachers:		
Male	462	413
Female	2,606	1,500
Average number of years' experience in teaching	2	5.6
Average number of pupils enrolled	16	34

[1] Teachers employed in schools located in communities having a population of 2,500 or over are classified as "city teachers;" all others are classified as "rural teachers."

With teachers whose average age is 23, more than half being below this age, an average experience of less than 18 months of teaching, nearly half having had less than four years of high-school education, few having had any appreciable amount of professional training, and fewer still any definite preparation for the specific work which the country schools should do, the character and efficiency of the rural schools of the State must be far below the standards which all who are interested in the welfare of the State would like to see maintained; and little improvement may be expected until the conditions affecting teachers are much better than they are now. The points of attack for the improvement of the schools must be found in the raising of standards of requirements for the preparation of teachers and in providing the means for this better preparation.

No doubt most of the rural teachers quit teaching after one or two years of service because of their lack of preparation, their consequent lack of interest in their work, and their failure to attain sufficient success to create an interest in it. Many of them come from other States in which they have received whatever preparation for teaching they may have, but this type of teacher immigration will naturally grow less as the State grows older. Therefore, even with the longer terms of service which will come with the better preparation of teachers, the State must expect to have to furnish from its own schools approximately 1,000 elementary teachers and from 150 to 200 high-school teachers annually for many years to come. There will also be a demand for an increasing number of trained superintendents, principals, supervisors, and teachers of special subjects, such as drawing, music, agriculture, and domestic science.

REASONABLE STANDARDS OF PREPARATION.

As already pointed out, thè teachers in rural schools need no less ability, knowledge, and skill than teachers in city schools. For teachers in its elementary schools a rich and progressive State like North Dakota should demand as a minimum preparation graduation from a standard four-year high school and two full years of normal-school work, and it should encourage those preparing to teach in its elementary schools in the country to take still another year of normal-school preparation. It should require of teachers in its high schools graduation from its university or agricultural college, with a reasonable amount of pedagogical training. For superintendents and supervisors of special subjects should be chosen those who by their success as teachers have shown their fitness for such work, and who, after having gained experience as teachers, have fitted themselves by further study in university or college or by independent or prescribed study, as provided in the "Summary of recommendations and conclusions," for the work of administration and expert supervision. Of course full equivalents should be accepted in all cases. (See recommendation 27, ch. 12.)

The State should require of its rural teachers, both in elementary and high schools, such knowledge of rural life and rural industries as will enable them to inspire and direct the life of rural communities and to teach boys and girls the things they will need to know as men and women living and working in the country. It should also require of them the qualities of leadership necessary to enable them to assist in organizing, vitalizing, inspiring, and directing the life of rural communities. Policies of administration should be adopted looking toward longer terms of service and less moving of teachers from one school to another.

TABLE 18.—*Preparation of teachers in North Dakota.*

Amount of preparation.	Rural and city teachers.		Rural teachers.		City teachers.	
	Number.	Per cent.	Number.	Per cent.	Number.	Per cent.
College	574	11.5	14	0.4	560	29.2
Normal school	1,311	26.3	241	7.8	1,070	56.4
High school, 4 years	1,721	34.5	1,501	48.8	220	11.5
High school, 3 years	441	8.8	403	13.1	38	1.9
High school, 2 years	465	9.3	449	14.6	16	.8
High school, 1 year	346	6.9	339	11.0	7	.3
Eighth grade	121	2.4	121	3.9		
Total	4,981	100.0	3,068	100.0	1,913	100.0

The investigation referred to and other evidence at hand show that standards of preparation of teachers in North Dakota are at present far below those just set forth; see Table 18 and figure 11. Of the 3,068 rural teachers responding to the questionnaire, 121 have had only

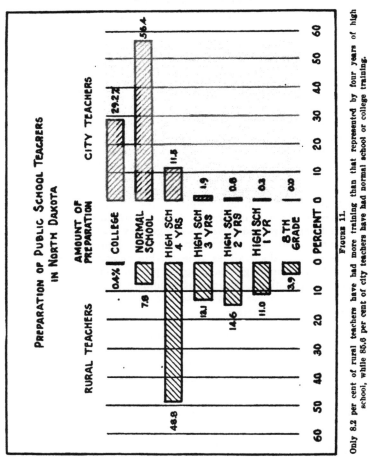

Figure 11.

Only 8.2 per cent of rural teachers have had more training than that represented by four years of high school, while 85.8 per cent of city teachers have had normal school or college training.

elementary school education and no professional training, except such as they may have gained by brief attendance on a summer school; 1,191 have had one, two, or three years of high-school education; 1,501 have had four years of high-school education; 241 have had some professional normal school training; 14 have spent some time in college. Fewer than one-twelfth (8.2 per cent) have had more training than that represented by four years in high school.

Those reported as having one, two, or three years in high school have had little or no professional training. Probably a good proportion of those who have had four years of high school have had some professional instruction in the last year of the high school, since many of them come from States in which "teacher training" is given in the last year of some of the high schools. It is quite certain that most of those reporting normal-school training have had only one year above the high school.

It is therefore safe to say that less than 5 per cent of teachers in the rural schools of the State have had such preparation as would be required by the standards assumed herein as being desirable and reasonable. Another indication of this is found in the fact that of the 3,068 rural teachers reporting, 2,190 held second-grade elementary certificates, 621 held first-grade certificates, and 257 held professional certificates. (See Table 19 and fig. 12.) The standard of requirements for the second-grade elementary certificate is indicated by the fact that it is given to those who, having graduated from the eighth grade of the public schools of North Dakota, take the $10\frac{1}{2}$ months' course in the normal schools of the State. Just what meaning is to be attached to graduation from the eighth grade of elementary schools taught by teachers most of whom have had only the preparation and experience indicated above must be quite indefinite.

That the low grade of preparation of the teachers is not due wholly or chiefly to laxness in examination, but to the want of a sufficient number of persons having the necessary preparation, is shown by the fact that at the four examinations for elementary certificates announced by the board of examiners in 1913, out of a total of 4,067 applicants, 460, or 11 per cent, received first-grade elementary certificates; 1,606, a little less than 40 per cent, received second-grade elementary certificates; and 2,001, or 51 per cent, failed in one or more subjects.

With teachers in city and town schools the case is much better. Of the total of 1,911 reporting, only 61 have had less than four years in high schools, 220 have had four years, 1,070 have had normal-school training, and 560 have had college training. Nearly seven-eighths (85.6 per cent) have had more preparation than that represented by four years in high school. (See Table 18 and fig. 11.) Only 23 hold second-grade elementary certificates, 248 hold first-grade elementary certificates, and 1,640 hold professional certificates. (See Table 19 and fig. 12.)

TABLE 19.--*Certificates held by North Dakota teachers.*

Grade of certificate.	Rural and city teachers.		Rural teachers.		City teachers.	
	Number.	Per cent.	Number.	Per cent.	Number.	Per cent.
Professional........................	1,897	38.1	257	8.3	1,640	85.8
First grade.........................	869	17.4	621	20.2	248	12.9
Second grade.......................	2,213	44.4	2,190	71.3	23	1.2
Total...........................	4,979	100.0	3,068	100.0	1,911	100.0

That the people of North Dakota believe in public education is shown by the magnitude of expenses for this purpose which they

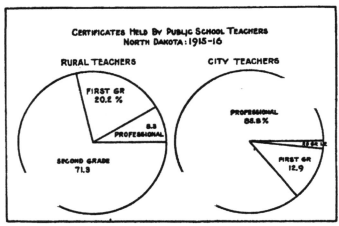

FIGURE 12.

Nearly three-fourths (71.3 per cent) of the rural teachers hold the lowest grade of certificate which will permit them to receive public money for teaching school, while nearly seven-eighths (85.8 per cent) of city teachers hold professional certificates.

have permitted in a State so new. Two years ago the total value of public-school property, as reported by the State superintendent of public instruction, was nearly ten and a half million dollars, equal to about 4 per cent of the assessable property of the State, and the total amount expended for the support of public schools was more than six millions, a larger amount per capita of adult male population than in any other State but one, and the State was ninth among the States in amount spent per capita of children of school age. Since the people willingly make these comparatively large expenditures for schools, it must be assumed that they desire the fullest possible returns for their money, and that they agree with Supt. Taylor's statement that the time has come when the people have a right to demand that those who offer themselves as public-school teachers shall be thoroughly qualified for their work. Certainly they should not employ those who are not qualified.

TEACHERS' CERTIFICATES IN NORTH DAKOTA.

The legal provisions governing the certification of teachers in the public schools of North Dakota, as set forth in the Compiled Laws of 1913, and amended by chapter 130 of the Laws of 1915, are as follows:

SEC. 1359. *Certificates.*—There shall be four regular grades of certificates issued by the board of examiners. * * *

(1) The second-grade elementary certificate.
(2) The first-grade elementary certificate.
(3) The second-grade professional certificate.
(4) The first-grade professional certificate.

SEC. 1360. *Second-grade elementary certificate.*—The second-grade elementary certificate shall be granted to those persons over 18 years of age who are found proficient in the following subjects: Reading, arithmetic, language and grammar, geography, United States history, physiology and hygiene (including physical culture), civil government, pedagogy, and any one of the following-named subjects: Music, drawing, agriculture, nature study, domestic science, manual training: *Provided*, That the board of examiners may, in their discretion, specify which of the above subjects may be required. The proficiency of the applicants in spelling and writing will be determined from the papers submitted by the applicants. The second-grade elementary certificate shall be valid for two years in any county in the State when recorded by the county superintendent of schools. It shall qualify the holder to teach in any grade in rural and graded schools up to and including the eighth grade, and may be renewable by the county superintendent of schools under rules prescribed by the board of examiners.

SEC. 1361. *First-grade elementary certificate.*—The first-grade elementary certificate shall be granted to those persons over 20 years of age who have had at least eight months' experience in teaching and who, in addition to those subjects required for a second-grade elementary certificate, are found proficient in elements of psychology and four of the following subjects of secondary grade: Elementary algebra, plane geometry, physics, physical geography, botany, the elements of agriculture, nature study, manual training, domestic science, and American literature. The first-grade elementary certificate shall be valid for three years in any county in the State when recorded by the county superintendent of schools. It shall qualify the holder to teach in any grade in any school in the State up to and including the eighth grade and in the ninth grade of schools doing not over one year of high-school work, and may be renewable by the county superintendent of schools under rules prescribed by the board of examiners.

SEC. 1362. *Second-grade professional certificate.*—The second-grade professional certificate shall be granted to those persons who are at least 20 years of age and who have had at least nine months' experience in teaching and have the qualifications necessary for a first-grade elementary certificate, and who in addition are found proficient in the following subjects of advanced grade: (1) Psychology; (2) the history of education; (3) the principles of education; (4) school administration; (5) methods in elementary subjects; (6) rhetoric and composition; (7) American or English literature; (8) Ancient, English, or American history; (9) some one natural science (which may include agriculture); (10) higher algebra, solid geometry, manual training, or domestic science. The second-grade professional certificate shall legally qualify the holder to teach in any of the common, graded, or high schools of the State, except in the high-school departments of schools doing four years of high-school work. It shall be valid for a period of five years and shall be renewable in the discretion of the board for a period of years or for life.

SEC. 1363. *First-grade professional certificate.*—The first-grade professional certificate shall be granted to those persons who have substantially the equivalent of a college education, and who have had at least 18 months' experience in teaching. They shall have all the qualifications necessary for a second-grade professional certificate and, in addition thereto, be found proficient in the following subjects: (1) Foreign language; (2) a natural science other than the one presented for the second-grade professional certificate; (3) ethics, logic, or sociology; (4) political science, economics, or domestic science; (5) any two subjects of college grade listed for the second-grade professional certificate and not previously offered by the applicant. The first-grade professional certificate shall qualify the holder to teach in all the common, graded, and high schools of the State, and shall be valid for five years or for life.

SEC. 1364. *Special certificates.*—The board may grant special certificates authorizing the holders to teach in any of the common, graded, or high schools, (1) drawing, (2) music, (3) kindergarten, or (4) primary subjects, to teachers holding at least a second-grade elementary certificate. Special certificates to teach (1) agriculture, (2) commercial subjects, (3) domestic science, or (4) manual and industrial training in the common, graded, or high schools of the State may be issued to applicants who possess qualifications equivalent to those required for a second-grade professional certificate. The applicant for a special certificate must satisfy the board by examination or otherwise of his proficiency in the subject which the holder is authorized to teach. Special certificates shall be valid for such a term of years as the board shall prescribe.

SEC. 1365. *Diplomas accredited.*—(1) The diplomas granted on the completion of the four-year curriculum of the teachers' college of the University of North Dakota shall be accredited as a first-grade professional certificate for two years, and after the holder has had nine months' successful experience in teaching, satisfactory evidence of which having been filed with the board, such diploma shall entitle the owner to a first-grade professional certificate for life.

(2) The diploma from the advanced or five-year curriculum of the State normal schools, or its equivalent, the two-year curriculum for high-school graduates, shall be accredited as a second-grade professional certificate for two years, and after the holder has had nine months' experience in teaching, satisfactory evidence of which having been filed with the board, such diploma shall entitle the holder to a second-grade professional certificate valid for life.

(3) The diploma from the four-year curriculum of the State normal schools or its equivalent, the one-year curriculum for high-school graduates, shall be accredited as a professional certificate of the second grade for two years, and after the holder has had nine months' successful experience in teaching, satisfactory evidence of which having been filed with the board, shall entitle the holder to a second-grade professional certificate, valid for five years, which certificate shall be renewable in the discretion of the board.

(4) The certificate of completion issued by the State normal schools to those who complete the 10½ months' curriculum of the State normal schools shall entitle the holder to a second-grade elementary certificate.

SEC. 1366. *Other diplomas accredited.*—Diplomas from institutions within or without the State shall be accredited, and professional certificates issued thereon upon the following basis: (a) The bachelor's diploma from a college of recognized standing shall be valid for a period of two years, after its presentation to the board, as a first-grade professional certificate: *Provided*, That the diploma implies at least two-year courses, or 16 semester hours, of professional preparation for teaching, or in lieu of such professional study that the holder of the diploma has had three years' successful experience in teaching or in administering schools after receiving such diploma; and after the holder has had nine months of successful experience in teaching, after the presentation of such diploma, satisfactory evidence of such experience having been filed with the board, he shall be entitled to a first-grade professional certificate which shall be valid for five years and which shall be renewed for life upon satisfactory evidence of successful experience of five years.

(b) The diploma or certificate from institutions whose curriculum is the equivalent of the four-year or the five-year curriculum of the State normal schools shall be valid for two years as a second-grade professional certificate: *Provided*, That the diploma or certificate implies at least two-year courses, or 16 semester hours, of professional preparation for teaching or, in lieu of such professional study, that the holder of the diploma has had three years of successful experience in teaching or in administering schools after receiving such diploma; and after the holder of such diploma has had nine months of successful experience in teaching after receiving such diploma, satisfactory evidence of such experience having been filed with the board, he shall be entitled to a second-grade professional certificate valid for five years or for life, respectively.

SEC. 1367. *Permits.*—A college graduate without experience or the required professional preparation may, for reasons satisfactory to the board, be granted a permit or probationary certificate, valid until such time, not to exceed six months, as shall be set by the board for his examination of the professional subjects, when, if successful, he may be granted a certificate, valid for a term of years or for life. Permits to teach till the next regular examination may be granted by the county superintendent of schools to any person applying at any time other than the regular examination who can show satisfactory reasons for not attending the previous examination and satisfactory evidence of qualification, subject to the rules and regulations of the board.

SEC. 1369. *High-school diplomas.*—Diplomas from North Dakota high schools doing four years' work, granted to graduates who have had psychology, school management, methods of instruction, and three senior review subjects, shall be accredited as second-grade elementary certificates; and if within two years from the date of the diploma the holder has had at least eight months' successful experience in teaching he shall be entitled to a first-grade elementary certificate.

SEC. 1372. *Qualifications of teachers.*—No certificate or permit to teach shall be issued to any person under 18 years of age, and no first-grade elementary certificate to any person who is under 20 years of age and who has not taught successfully eight months of school. First and second grade elementary certificates may be renewed without examination under such requirements as shall be imposed by the State board of examiners. The certificates issued by the State board of examiners shall be valid in any county in this State when recorded by the county superintendent of schools.

SEC. 1373. *Teacher must hold certificate to be recorded.*—No person shall be employed or permitted to teach in any of the public schools of the State, except those in cities organized for school purposes under special laws or organized as independent districts under the general school laws, who is not the holder of a lawful certificate of qualification or a permit to teach, and no teacher's certificate issued by the State board of examiners nor a teacher's diploma granted by any institution of learning in this State shall entitle a person to teach in such public school of any county unless such certificate or diploma shall have been recorded in the office of the county superintendent of the county in which the holder is engaged to teach, and it shall be the duty of the county superintendent to record such certificate or diploma.

DISSATISFACTION WITH PRESENT CONDITIONS.

That the people also believe that as a rule teachers in the rural schools are not qualified for the work they should do is indicated by replies received by the survey commission in response to questions sent to several hundreds of persons representing all classes and conditions of life in North Dakota. A majority of those who in these replies expressed opinions concerning rural schools and rural teachers thought that few competent teachers are to be found in the rural schools of North Dakota; that these teachers for the most part are not rural minded; that they have little knowledge of the needs of rural schools or ability to supply these needs; that they have little professional knowledge of teaching and frequently little ability in school organization and discipline; that as a rule they are incapable either of building up good country schools or of rendering much helpful service to country communities. Many of them also expressed the opinion that better schoolhouses should be provided; that homes should be built for the teachers; that efforts should be made to secure better attendance; and, finally, that the normal schools have failed to train adequately or in sufficient numbers teachers for rural schools.

ESTABLISHMENT OF NORMAL SCHOOLS.

North Dakota is one of the richest States in proportion to population in the Union, and may therefore be considered as able to provide fully for the support of such schools as may be necessary for the adequate preparation of all the teachers needed in its schools. That the people of the State understand the importance of this is shown by the fact that in the constitution adopted in 1889 they provided for three normal schools and an industrial school and school for manual training which has since become a normal school. They have recently amended the constitution to admit the establishment of a fifth normal school. Provision has also been made for the professional preparation of teachers in the State university and the State agricultural college. The three normal schools are located by the constitution at Valley City, in the county of Barnes; Mayville, in the county of Traill; and Minot, in the county of Ward. The industrial school and school for manual training, now the normal and industrial school, is at Ellendale, in the county of Dickey.

To the school at Valley City was apportioned 50,000 acres of public lands; to the school at Mayville, 30,000 acres; and to the school at Ellendale, 40,000 acres. The school at Minot has received no lands from State or Federal Government. For the further support of these schools the State granted a fairly liberal mill tax. In 1913 the millage for these schools was as follows: Valley City, fifteen hundredths of 1 mill; Mayville, twelve hundredths of 1 mill; Minot, thirteen and one-half hundredths of 1 mill; Ellendale, seven hundredths of 1 mill. By the session laws of 1915 a fixed amount of taxes levied upon all the property of the State was substituted for the millage tax for the support of State institutions. Of this fixed amount, the following sums were apportioned to the several normal schools: Valley City, $46,200; Mayville, $36,960; Minot, $41,580; Ellendale, $21,600. The total income of the schools for the year 1914–15, as shown in Table 36, page 143, was: Valley City, $120,192.96; Mayville, $61,779.86; Minot, $54,533.36; Ellendale, $48,197.20. For the average number and grade of students enrolled this is not an illiberal support, as compared with normal schools in other States. Table 20 shows that the values of buildings and equipment are about as large as the average for such schools throughout the country. But the schools must have more equipment and larger annual incomes before they can do fully and well the work which will be demanded of them when the standards of preparation for teachers recommended in this report have been adopted by the State.

TABLE 20.—*Per capita cost of maintenance of State normal schools in certain States, 1913–14.*

[Based on reported number of students enrolled, excluding duplications, and total income; Annual Report of Commissioner of Education, 1914, vol. 2, Ch. 6, pp. 364, 370.]

States.	Schools reporting.	Aggregate number of students.	Total income reported.		
			Amount.	Average per school.	Average per student.
Wisconsin	9	4,456	$1,465,962	$162,884	$329
California	8	3,985	1,056,244	132,030	265
South Dakota	4	1,239	279,976	69,994	225
Massachusetts	10	2,801	608,451	60,845	217
Illinois	6	7,840	1,186,840	197,806	151
Minnesota	5	4,166	559,878	111,975	134
Kansas	3	4,612	488,787	162,787	106
Missouri	6	6,461	599,105	98,184	86
Oklahoma	6	4,628	223,345	37,224	48
Total	57	40,188	6,428,588	112,782	159
North Dakota:					
In 1913–14 [1]	4	2,759	464,090	116,022	168
In 1914–15 [1]	4	2,725	284,703	71,175	104

[1] From reports to the survey commission.

Because of the fact that the school at Ellendale began its work as an industrial school and school for manual training, and has accumulated valuable equipment for work of this kind, and because of the peculiar needs of the people of the section which it serves directly, it should probably continue for the present to give instruction in these subjects in its regular and short courses for other than prospective teachers, but it should look to the discontinuance of work of this kind as the high schools of this section are more fully developed. It should, of course, cease at once to function as a local high school for the town of Ellendale. State funds appropriated for the support of schools for the use of the State as a whole should not be diverted to local use. This school, which has the necessary equipment for it, might, it is believed, well give a very few strong courses for teachers of industrial subjects, but it should not be permitted to let either of these phases of its work interfere with its regular work as a normal school for the preparation of teachers for the elementary schools of the State. To perform successfully this double or triple function this school will need a much larger income than it now has. It should immediately make some arrangement for practice teaching for its students. It might possibly arrange for the use of the elementary schools of the town of Ellendale for this purpose, as the school at Mayville has arranged for the use of the schools of that town.

Further discussion of this school is included in the following general discussion of normal schools.

COURSES OF STUDY.

The normal schools of North Dakota are authorized by law to offer the following courses:

1. A 10½-months course, known as the rural course, for graduates from the eighth grade of the public schools. Those who complete this course are entitled to a second-grade elementary certificate.

2. A four-year course for graduates from the eighth grade of the public schools.

3. A five-year course for graduates from the eighth grade of the public schools.

4. A one-year course for graduates from four-year high schools.

5. A two-year course, known as the advanced or standard course, for graduates from four-year high schools.

6. Several special two-year courses for graduates from four-year high schools. These special courses are intended for training teachers and supervisors for such special subjects as drawing, music, domestic

science, manual training, agriculture, and commercial courses. One school has given diplomas in 11 different special subjects.

Equivalents are accepted for admission in lieu of graduation from the eighth grade and from the four-year high schools.

In the beginning only courses 1, 2, and 4 were offered. Other courses were added later. Course 2 offers approximately three years of academic high-school work, supposed to be equivalent to four years of such work in the public high schools of the State and one year of professional work. Course 3 offers approximately four years of academic work, supposed to be equal to four years of high-school work and one year of advanced work and one year of professional work. Course 4 is made up principally of professional work. Course 5 is made up of approximately one year of academic work and one year of professional work. Courses 2 and 4 are supposed to have equal value and lead to graduation with a "first elementary" diploma which is accredited by the State as a professional certificate of the second grade, good for two years and renewable under certain conditions.[1] Courses 3 and 5 have equal value and lead to graduation with an "advanced" diploma, which is also accredited as a second-grade professional certificate, good for two years and renewable for life under certain conditions.[2] The two-year special courses offer one year of professional work and one year in the special subjects taken. Graduates from these courses receive a special diploma and seem to have the same privileges as to certification as do those who take the regular advanced course.

GRADE OF STUDENTS.

In the year 1915–16 more than 60 per cent of the students in the four schools were in classes of high-school grade. Less than 40 per cent, including those in the fourth year of the four-year course for eighth-grade graduates, were doing work in advance of the four-year high-school course. In two of the schools there were a few students below high-school grade. Apparently more than two-thirds of all students enter the normal schools with less than the preparation indicated by graduation from four-year high schools. These students average little more than 16 years of age. Graduates from accredited high schools and those entering with equivalent preparation average about 20 years. Nearly all graduates from the normal courses are students who have completed courses 2 and 4 and have received elementary diplomas.

Only at Valley City has there been any considerable number of graduates from courses 4, 5, and 6, and here the number of graduates from these courses has been only 14 per cent of the total from all

---

[1] See sec. 1365 (3), p. 86.   [2] See sec. 1365 (2), p. 86.

courses. Less than 10 per cent of the total number of graduates from all the schools have taken these courses. The president of the school at Mayville reports no advanced or special pupils and declares that it is useless to offer either of these courses or to make any attempt to give the training needed for rural school teachers as long as the certification laws of the State remain as they are. The president of the school at Minot reports only five or six in these courses.

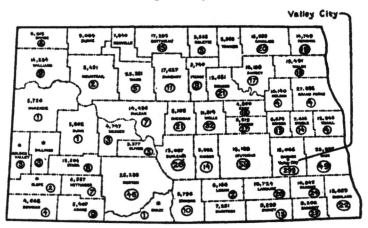

FIGURE 13.—Distribution of resident students enrolled in the State normal school at Valley City, including summer-school students, 1914–15. See Table 31, p. 136.

The figures above the county name in each case give the population in 1910. At that date the population of Golden Valley County (later subdivided into Golden Valley, Billings, and Slope Counties) was 10,186; and the population of Morton County (later subdivided into Morton and Sioux Counties) was 25,289.

The figures inclosed in the circle in each case indicate the number of students from the county who are enrolled at the State normal school at Valley City.

This institution drew 958 students from 48 of the 52 counties in North Dakota (of whom 31.2 per cent came from Barnes County) and 110 from without the State; total, 1,068.

Four counties, outside of Barnes County, sent more than 30 students each to Valley City; Minnesota sent 72.

It is evident that these normal schools are now practically only high schools with an additional year of study of elementary psychology, history of education, methods of teaching, etc., and some practice teaching under supervision. A study of attendance maps, figures 13–16, and Table 21, shows that they are very largely local high schools for the counties in which they are located and the adjacent counties. Indeed, the school at Ellendale has been providing two years of high-school work for the town at the expense of the State, thereby relieving the town of the expense of providing high-school facilities for its own children beyond the second year.

TABLE 21.—*Local attendance at normal schools.*

Normal schools.	Students from within the State.	Students from county in which school is located.	Percentage of local attendance.
Mayville	357	162	45.4
Valley City [1]	958	299	31.2
Ellendale	288	211	73.2
Minot	183	95	51.9
Total [2]	1,786	767	42.9

[1] Figures include students in summer session and institute.
[2] Figures include students in summer session and institute at Valley City, but not at the other schools.

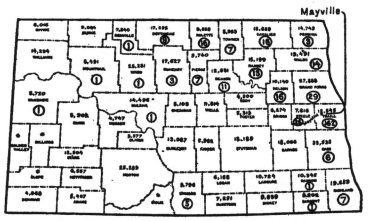

FIGURE 14.—Distribution of resident students enrolled in the State normal school at Mayville, exclusive of summer session, 1914–15. See Table 31, p. 136.

The figures above the county name in each case give the population in 1910.
The figures inclosed in the circle in each case indicate the number of students from the county who are enrolled at the State normal school at Mayville.
This institution drew 357 students from 24 of the 52 counties in North Dakota (of whom 45.8 per cent came from Traill County) and 28 from without the State; total, 385.
Only 9 counties, outside of Traill County, sent more than 7 students each to Mayville; Minnesota sent 14.

GRADUATES OF THE NORMAL SCHOOLS.

The total number of graduates of all kinds from all the schools up to the time of this survey is reported as 2,703, of whom approximately 1,575 are now teaching, and approximately 1,250 of these are teaching in North Dakota.[1] Thus after a quarter of a century from the

[1] These figures are based on the supposition that the percentage of graduates from the school at Mayville and the percentage of those graduates now teaching in North Dakota are approximately the same as for the other three schools.

opening of the first of these State normal schools, the number of
graduates of the grade indicated who are teaching in the schools of
the State is equal to about one-sixth of the total number of teachers
employed in the schools. As shown elsewhere in this report, practically all these graduates are teaching in city and town schools. The
number (366) graduated from the four schools in 1914–15 was
about one-eighth of the total number of new teachers employed in
the State the following year. It is about one-third. the number of
the elementary teachers that the State will probably have to supply
annually from its own schools when the more stable conditions are
realized, which will be brought about by the slackening in the tide

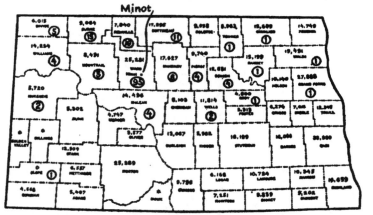

Figure 15.—Distribution of resident students enrolled in the State normal school at
Minot, exclusive of summer session, 1914–15. See Table 31, p. 136.

The figures above the county name in each case give the population in 1910.
The figures inclosed in the circle in each case indicate the number of students from
the county who are enrolled in the State normal school at Minot.
This institution drew 183 students from 20 of the 52 counties in North Dakota (of
whom 51.9 per cent came from Ward County) and 19 from without the State; total 202.
Only three counties, outside of Ward County, sent more than 10 students to Minot;
Minnesota sent 11.

of teacher immigration, which must surely come in a few years, and
the longer average term of service which will result from better
preparation of teachers.

Of course, these figures do not represent .all the service which the
normal schools have rendered and are now rendering to the schools
of the State. Every year many young men and women go out, not as
graduates, but from the lower classes of the normal schools to become teachers, especially in the rural schools. The general education of these is far below the standards which should be set for
teachers in the schools, and of professional training they have had

practically none. Also through their summer schools the normal schools give valuable help to many teachers already in service.

THE TASK OF THE NORMAL SCHOOLS.

This statement of facts is not made for the purpose of condemning the policy or the management of the normal schools in the past, and no adverse criticism of trustees or presidents is implied.[1] These schools have been serving pioneer communities in a new State under frontier conditions and have had to adapt themselves to the condi-

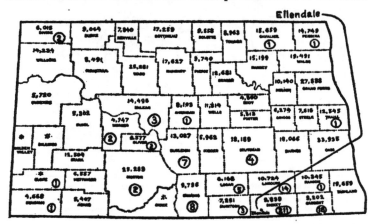

Figure 16.—Distribution of resident students enrolled in the State normal and industrial school at Ellendale, exclusive of summer session, 1914–15. See Table 31, p. 136.

The figures above the county name in each case give the population in 1910.

The figures inclosed in the circle in each case indicate the number of students from the county who are enrolled at the State normal and industrial school at Ellendale.

This institution drew 288 students from 20 of the 52 counties in North Dakota (of whom 73.2 per cent came from Dickey County) and 42 from without the State; total, 330.

Only 2 counties, outside of Dickey County, sent more than 8 students to Ellendale; South Dakota sent 23.

tions as they existed. Very naturally also they have followed the example of similar schools in other States. It would have been folly for them to attempt to impose standards of preparation for admission which the schools of the State could not meet or to attempt a type of work which the public sentiment of the State did not approve. The question is now, however, not of the past, but of the present and future.

---

[1] The commission wishes to express its appreciation of the spirit of service and devotion which it found to exist in all these schools, and of the high character of work they seem to be doing under present adverse conditions. The respects wherein they fail of rendering the service now needed by the State are due to the changing conditions and needs which must accompany the rapid transition through which the State is now passing.

As has already been pointed out, under the most favorable conditions which can reasonably be expected the State must train for its elementary schools 1,000 or more teachers every year. More than four-fifths of these will be needed in the rural schools. The normal schools are the proper agencies for training these teachers, and to this task they should devote themselves wholly and with all their energy and resources, resisting every temptation, however alluring,

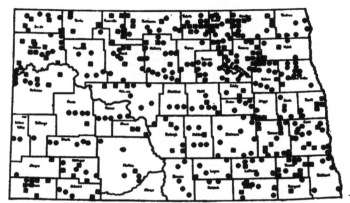

FIGURE 17.—Distribution of consolidated schools in North Dakota.

The number of consolidated schools grew from 114 in 1911 to 401 in 1916. The chief causes of growth, according to the State inspector of consolidated schools, were: (1) State aid; (2) educational campaign.

● Town (250).
■ Open country (151).
Total, 401.

to attempt any other task until this has been accomplished fully and well. Their courses of study should be adapted to this end, and all appropriations made to them should be made with the understanding that they may be used only for this purpose. Of course, some of the graduates may, by their native ability and through study at home and elsewhere, fit themselves for teachers of high-school grades connected with the elementary schools and even for work requiring still greater preparation, but this need not affect the work of the normal schools in any way. The consensus of the best opinion among school officers supports this view.[1]

---

[1] The survey commission submitted to the chief school officers of the several States of the Union this question: "What in your opinion should be the function of the normal school, the training of teachers for the elementary schools or the training of both elementary and high-school teachers?" A large majority of these chief school officers replied that in their opinion the normal schools should attempt to prepare teachers only for the elementary schools until that task has been accomplished, and that in agricultural States they should make it their chief concern to prepare teachers for the elementary rural schools. The report of the Survey of the Educational Institutions of the State of Washington (Educ. Bull. No. 26, 1916) points out that practically all the normal schools of the older States confine themselves to the task of preparing teachers for their elementary schools.

The standards of admission to the normal schools should be raised gradually, so that after the year 1923 graduation from a standard four-year high school or its equivalent shall be required for admission and two or more years of study shall be required for graduation, as set forth in the conclusions and recommendations included in this report. (See recommendation 22, ch. 12.)

The changing conditions of the State and the multiplication and standardization of high schools[1] now going on will soon make possible the higher standards of education without prejudice to any, and the sentiment of the State will beyond doubt approve the higher requirements for graduation and the changes in the laws for certification which, of course, should accompany pari passu the raising of the standards of the normal schools.

WILL RURAL SCHOOLS PAY?

It may be objected that the country schools will not pay sufficient salaries to entice and hold better-prepared teachers; but in answer it may be stated that the per capita wealth of the rural communities in North Dakota, as in many other Middle Western States, is larger than that of the urban communities, that living is cheaper in the country than in the city, that the purchasing power of salaries in the country is proportionately greater than that of salaries in the city, and that the State now pays its rural teachers much better than it pays its city teachers in proportion to their education, professional training, and experience, and it pays absolutely more per pupil taught.

In rural schools for teachers of an average age of 23 years, with one, two, three, or four years of high-school education, half as many having had only elementary school education as have had normal-school training, with an average of two years of experience and teaching an average of only 16 children, the average salary is $56.39 a month. In urban schools for teachers of an average age of 28 years, 85 per cent of whom have had normal school or college training, with an average of 5.6 years' experience and teaching an average of 34 children, the average salary is $82.58 a month.[2] The average per child for teachers' salaries in the rural schools is $3.40, in urban schools $2.43. As the population in the rural schools grows more

---

[1] In a letter of Sept. 24, 1916, to the survey commission, N. C. MacDonald, State inspector of consolidated, graded, and rural schools, states that in 1915–16 there were in the State 60 schools with a four-year high-school course, 90 with a three-year high-school course, 120 with a two-year high-school course, and 60 with a one-year high-school course, total 401, an increase of 252 per cent in five years. Of these, 250 were in towns, 151 in the open country. For distribution see map of consolidated schools in North Dakota, Fig. 17.

[2] See Table 17, p. 80.

dense, as school officers learn to consolidate their schools and build homes for teachers, and as teachers better prepared for the work of teaching in the country schools and for inspiring and directing country life can be had, the absolute difference in salaries may be expected to grow much less than it now is. It is not solely because of the larger salaries and the greater attractiveness of city life that teachers seek positions in city rather than country schools. In doing this they are influenced also by the better organization and the greater division of work which make the tasks of the teacher simpler and easier in the city than in the country. It is quite certain that if teachers had the kind and degree of preparation needed to assure success as teachers and leaders in country communities, many of the ablest of them would prefer to work in the country schools.

HOW CAN DEMANDS BE MET?

Assuming that these ideals are to be met, that the State is to have well-prepared teachers in all its schools, urban and rural, that rural teachers are to have preparation in harmony with the work they should do, and that the normal schools of the State are to furnish approximately 1,000 elementary teachers each year, what will be necessary to enable them to meet the demands?

BY RAISING STANDARDS.

By raising the standards for admission to graduation from an accredited four-year high school, or its equivalent, by eliminating their lower classes, and by concentrating their energies on two or three years of work of real normal school grade, the schools now in existence may be able to send out a larger number of graduates each year than they now do. Last year the total enrollment in these schools was 2,725. The enrollment for the three regular terms was: Fall, 1,113; winter, 1,354; spring, 1,154. The number present during the week of April 10–16, 1916, was 1,139—at Valley City, 539; at Mayville, 234; at Minot, 206; at Ellendale, 190—which is probably about the average weekly attendance for the year. Under the present plan of organization these students were spread over practically six years in some of the schools and seven years in others, counting the 10½ months rural course as different from the first year of the four-year and five-year courses. As a result, there was much duplication and much waste of time of teachers because of very small classes.

BY ELIMINATING SPECIAL COURSES.

The situation may be helped also by eliminating to a very large extent the special courses, in which few students are enrolled, and which add considerably to the number of very small classes. After all there is not much need of specialization in the preparation of teachers for elementary schools in a State so uniform in character as is North Dakota. The work of all elementary teachers is very much alike, except as it varies from city to country. It might easily be shown that much of the demand for specialization is based on false theory. Superintendents and supervisors should, as has already been pointed out, be chosen from those who have had experience as teachers and who have afterwards done advanced and special work in college or university or elsewhere. The few teachers of special subjects needed in the elementary schools might easily all be prepared in one normal school, or each school might add to its regular courses one such special subject. It would be much cheaper for all those wishing to specialize in any particular subject to go to the school in which that subject might be offered than to attempt to duplicate such courses.

That the demand for these courses is not great is shown by the fact that at Valley City, where they have been developed most fully, the number of students taking any one of them is very small.

TABLE 22.—*Graduates in special courses, Valley City, 1910–1915.*

Courses.	1910	1911	1912	1913	1914	1915	Total.
Music and art	4	4		5	4	4	21
Public school music	1	1			3	2	7
Public school art	1					1	2
Domestic science	1	7	11	10	32	17	78
Manual training	1	1	4	8	3	1	18
Physical education		1	1		1	1	4
Kindergarten			1	3	5	7	16
Agriculture					2		2
Commercial					1		1
Primary						3	3
Total	8	14	17	26	51	36	152
Elementary course	128	133	129	97	118	152	757
Standard two-year course	5	4	12	19	13	18	71
Total, all courses	141	151	158	142	182	206	980

Table 22 shows that in 10 special courses there have been only 152 graduates since these diplomas were first given in 1910. The number of graduates from the elementary course, and the "standard" two years' course (for high-school graduates) for the same years, 1910–1915, are given for comparison. From these figures it appears that the number of graduates of the nine special courses, 152, is only 15.5 per cent of the total number of graduates for the period in question, 980, and only 9.4 per cent of the total number of graduates of the institution from the beginning, 1,603. It will be noted that the number of graduates from the nine special courses for the six years is just equal to the number of graduates from the elementary course in 1915, namely, 152. The number of graduates for the "standard" two years' course, 71, is only 7.2 per cent of the total number of graduates for the six years, 980.

In Ellendale the numbers of graduates in the special courses from 1901 to 1915 have been as indicated in Table 23:

TABLE 23.—*Graduates, by courses and years, Ellendale.*

Courses.	Total.	1901	1902	1903	1904	1905	1906	1907	1908	1909	1910	1911	1912	1913	1914	1915
Mechanic arts	59	...	2	2	3	3	2	1	4	2	4	5	11	7	8	5
Home economics	63	3	3	...	2	4	2	...	4	3	5	3	11	9	8	6
Academic	100	...	7	3	8	6	5	1	8	6	12	12	8	4	7	13
Commercial	15				3	1	2		1				2	2	3	1
Fine arts	2			1			1									
Total	239	3	12	6	16	14	12	2	17	11	21	22	32	23	23	25
Normal course	106								5	5	11	13	15	10	20	27
Total, all courses [1]	345	3	12	6	16	14	12	2	22	16	32	35	47	33	43	52

[1] Counted more than once, 44

It is also worthy of note that a majority of those who have been prepared at Ellendale to teach manual training courses have gone to other States. Few have found positions in North Dakota schools. Possibly there should be a greater demand for manual training teachers in the schools of North Dakota, but it must not be forgotten that the first duty of the normal schools is to their own State. Of the total number of graduates of this school (88) who are now teaching, more than half (45) are teaching in other States than North Dakota.

Certain other subjects, as Latin and German and ancient history, taken by very few students might also be eliminated, unless the new conditions should produce a greater demand for them. The school at Mayville did drop Latin and German from its curriculum in 1913. It may be well for some normal school students in North Dakota to study these subjects while preparing to teach in the elementary schools, but it is far more important that all should have full opportunity for the best instruction in those subjects that have to do directly with their future work. The work done in these subjects is of high-school grade and may well be relegated to the high schools as they develop.

BY ELIMINATING SMALL CLASSES.

Reports of class attendance at Valley City for the week of April 10–16, 1916, Table 40, show a class in singing with only 4 students, a class in commercial law with 3 students, a class in mathematics with 1 student, one class in Latin with 3 students and another with 2, a class in German with 4 students, a class of 3 in manual-training methods, two classes of 3 each in mechanical drawing, a class of 1 in copper work, a class of 2 in physical education methods, a class of 4 in hygiene and sanitation (a subject which should be required of all who are preparing to teach). From Ellendale are reported three Latin classes, I, II, and III, of 1, 6, and 2 students, respectively, a class of 4 in "preparatory history." From Valley City 21 classes are reported as having 5 students or less, from Mayville one class, from Minot two, from Ellendale eight, though the average attendance in all classes of these schools was 18.8, 21.4, 24.4, and 12.7, respectively.

The 29 classes of 5 students or less at Valley City and Ellendale held during the week 124 meetings, with an aggregate attendance of 476 students, an average of only 3.8 students. In the higher classes of college, or in graduate work in university, conditions of this kind may not be objectionable, but certainly they should be avoided, if possible, in the normal schools of a State in which these schools are turning out less than one-eighth as many graduates each year as are needed to fill vacancies in the schools, and in which less than 10 per cent of the teachers in the rural schools have had more than a high-school education, and less than 8 per cent have had any professional normal-school training. The more important things should come first.

On the other hand, there are many classes in all these schools and especially in the schools at Valley City and Minot much larger than they should be. During the week referred to there were at Valley City 47 meetings of classes with from 40 to 49 students; at Minot, 25; at Mayville, 6; at Ellendale, 5. Of meetings of classes of 50 or more there were at Valley City 11; at Minot, 11; at Mayville, none; at Ellendale, none. The 94 class meetings of 40 or more students held at Valley City and Minot, during the week of April 10–16, had an aggregate attendance of 4,817, an average of 51.2, or 13.5 times as many as the average at meetings of classes of 5 or less at Valley City and Ellendale.

BY NARROWING VERTICAL AND HORIZONTAL SPREAD, ENLARGING SCHOOLS, AND INCREASING NUMBERS.

By narrowing both the vertical and the horizontal spread of their work, the four normal schools now in the State, which in April, 1916, had an attendance of 1,139, might well care for an average attendance of 1,600 students and graduate 650 annually from courses two and three years above the high school. For this they should have somewhat larger appropriations than they now have, but these the State can well afford. The normal school recommended to be established at Dickinson and a sixth school that should be established sooner or later somewhere in the western half of the State to help in meeting the needs of the people of that section, which is increasing rapidly in population, will, if established and maintained on a liberal scale, soon be able to turn out 300 graduates. The remaining teachers who will be needed according to estimates made herein may well come from the educational classes of the university and agricultural college and from the private colleges of the State.

No attempt should be made to increase the attendance at the normal schools much beyond the numbers they would have with the total attendance indicated above. There are fairly well-defined limits to the number of students which can be taught to advantage in a normal school under the conditions which obtain in North Dakota. To quote from the report of the survey of the educational institutions of the State of Washington made by the Bureau of Education:

There is a very definite limit to the number of students that can be taught to best advantage in the last year of the normal school. During his last year every student should teach under critical supervision at least an hour a day throughout the entire year, under conditions as nearly as possible like those which must be met in the schools of the State. As a rule, the opportunities for such practice teaching can not be multiplied indefinitely. For this and many other reasons the normal school should not be a large school. * * * In the normal schools of western European countries the attendance is limited.[1] When more teachers are needed the State establishes more schools, instead of increasing beyond desirable limits the attendance at the schools already in existence. In this country those States in which a similar policy is pursued appear to be more effectively served by their normal schools.

TABLE 24.—*Enrollment in non-State colleges—Students of collegiate rank.*

	Collegiate.	Graduate.	Professional.	Total.
1912.				
Fargo College	126	4		130
Jamestown College	71			71
Wesley College	31			31
1913.				
Fargo College	131			131
Jamestown College	40			40
Wesley College	12	3		15
1914.				
Fargo College	157			157
Jamestown College	44			44
Wesley College	37			37
1915.				
Fargo College				
Jamestown College	69			69
Wesley College	56			56

BY ADJUSTING WORK FOR RURAL TEACHERS.

Since four-fifths of the teachers prepared in normal schools should find their places in the rural schools, their courses of study should be made to conform to the needs of country teachers. This should not mean the elimination of many subjects now offered or a less

[1] The usual attendance is about 100.

THE STATE NORMAL SCHOOLS.

amount of them. It should mean, however, strengthening the courses in agriculture, horticulture, home making, and rural economics, strengthening the courses in physics, chemistry, and biology, and giving to them a more practical application to country life. It should mean such a treatment of all subjects and such a redirection of all work as to make students intelligent about rural life and occupations and to develop in them rural mindedness of the best type. It should also mean stronger courses in school organization and management, to give to students that power of independent action indispensable to success in rural-school work. Special effort should be made also to develop in students the power of community leadership which rural teachers should have.

Fortunately, these changes would better fit the schools also for the work of training teachers for the grades in the city schools. It is fundamental knowledge of this kind which they most need to start with. With it they may soon gain the necessary special knowledge of grade work, much of which may also be gained in the practice departments of the normal schools. It should also be remembered that much of the life of North Dakota cities and towns is rural and agricultural in its character and interests.

NEW SCHOOLS IN WESTERN PART OF STATE.

Need of more normal schools in the western part of the State is shown by the fact that although 40 per cent of the total population of the State in 1910 was in the half west of a line drawn between the counties of Rolette, Pierce, Wells, Kidder, Logan, and McIntosh on the east and Bottineau, McHenry, Sheridan, Burleigh, and Emmons on the west, and although the increase in population in this part of the State has been more rapid in the last five years than in the eastern half, and although, because of the distinctly rural character of this section, the number of teachers needed is larger in proportion to the population, still only 25 per cent of the students enrolled in the normal schools in 1915, including those in the summer session, were from this section of the State. From the 13 counties southwest of the Missouri River, with 11.4 per cent of the population in 1910, and a larger per cent in 1915, come only 7 per cent of the total number of normal-school students.

SHOULD NOT BECOME "COLLEGES."

When the normal schools have, as recommended, extended their courses to two and three years beyond high-school graduation they should not undertake to do any work of a higher grade than that required for their certificate or diploma. The argument frequently advanced that, the faculty already being engaged, a few students may be taken for advanced work with little or no additional cost is fallacious. Instructors should not attempt more work than they can do well. If they have time and energy not needed for the work they are already doing, this time and energy should be used in teaching more students rather than for a few students who might have better advantages elsewhere.

None of these schools should attempt to become a "teachers' college." There is no need for such an institution in North Dakota apart from the university and the agricultural college, and will probably not be for a half century yet, if ever. Neither should the normal schools attempt to become junior colleges, doing two years of academic work paralleling the academic work of the university or the agricultural college. Their legitimate work is the preparation of teachers for elementary schools, and they should hold to this, making their courses of study and adapting their methods of instruction to this end. If, after having taught a year or more, any of their graduates should wish to enter the university or the agricultural college of North Dakota, or similar institutions elsewhere, their earnestness, their greater maturity, and such studying as they may have done after leaving the normal school will quite certainly gain for them such advanced standing as they should have.

HELP FOR TEACHERS IN SERVICE.

When the recommendations looking to the establishment of higher and more definite standards of the academic and professional training of all public-school teachers in the State have been adopted the State must in justice to all those already in its service as teachers provide opportunity for them to meet the new requirements. This can be done by dividing the State into extension-service districts, one for each normal school, and requiring each normal school to organize for its district an extension service of such character as may be needed to enable teachers in service to meet the new demands and with special reference to the needs of the particular district. The extension service recently established by the State Teachers College of Iowa illustrates what is meant and might well be taken as a model.[1]

---

[1] The principal features of the Iowa system of normal-school extension, which is one of the best conceived and most successful, are as follows:

It is exclusively aimed to supplement the previous training of teachers. To this end, study centers are organized in as many localities as possible (94 out of 99 counties now have them). Meetings are held on Saturdays, usually at high-school buildings, and under the direction of the county superintendent of schools. About four hours in the morning and afternoon combined are devoted to the weekly sessions. Heads of departments at the State Teachers' College, and specially qualified local teachers, city superintendents, and other persons conduct instruction at these centers. The whole extension enterprise is under a director who is a member of the staff of the State Teachers' College. The subject matter studied comprises the usual subjects of the school curriculum.

For the next decade the summer schools for teachers held at the normal schools and elsewhere should maintain special classes for these teachers.

Graduation from a normal school or any other school, however good, is no guarantee that the graduate will finally succeed as a teacher. Therefore the practice of granting to graduates a life license to teach or a certificate which may be exchanged for a life license automatically after one or two years of service should be abandoned. Before being granted a life license to teach in the schools of the State, the graduate should prove both ability to teach and willingness and ability to carry forward cultural and professional studies without the constant oversight of teachers and other school helps.

ADVANCED WORK FOR GRADUATES.

Therefore, for all students who leave the normal schools with any kind of certificate or diploma which may be accepted as a license to teach in the schools of the State, the board of regents or the State board of education should, with the assistance of the presidents of the normal schools and the heads of the departments of education in the university and the agricultural college, prepare such courses of study, including both professional and cultural (scientific and literary) subjects, as may be completed within a period of three years by devoting to them not less than 10 hours per week for 10 months in each year. Examinations on portions of these courses should be held from time to time, and no person should be granted a permanent license to teach in the public schools of the State until after he has passed the final examination on all courses prescribed. The final examination should be passed not earlier than two nor later than five years after the time of leaving the normal school.

State, county, and city superintendents and supervisors should be required to give special attention to young teachers who are pursuing these prescribed courses of study and who have not yet been granted a permanent license to teach. Before granting a permanent license to any teacher there should also be required a specific statement from some qualified superintendent, supervisor, or inspector, that the teacher has taught satisfactorily not less than 16 months in the schools of the State, and this statement should be accompanied by a detailed record of work done, showing its excellence and its defects, in the last eight months.

A similar policy should, of course, apply to teachers entering the service from other States and from other schools than the State normal schools of this State. The first license granted to any such teacher should be a temporary license, and a permanent license should be granted in the same way as for the graduates of the State normal schools of this State. This policy should not prevent the adoption of any policy looking to the full accrediting of certificates or licenses issued in other States on the basis of requirements not below the standards of this State.

MINIMUM SALARIES.

To encourage young men and women of the best native ability to prepare themselves for and to enter and remain in the work of teaching in the schools of the State, the State should, when the standards of admission to and graduation from the normal schools have been adopted and when provisions have been made for continued study as recommended, fix by law minimum salaries for teachers holding normal school certificates and for teachers holding normal school diplomas, the difference between the minimum salaries of the two classes being such as may seem to be justified by their different degrees of preparation, and it should provide for a definite increase in minimum salaries of both classes of teachers when they have complied with the requirements for and have been granted permanent licenses. Such a law should be made to apply to teachers from other States and from other schools of this State, and should not be so construed as to discriminate on the one hand against teachers from the State normal schools or on the other hand to discourage good teachers from other States and schools from entering the service of this State.

PRACTICE SCHOOLS.

The practice school is the laboratory and training ground of the normal school, and it is most important that every normal school should have one or more such schools under its control. The practice school should be large enough to afford all students in the last year of their course in the normal school opportunity to teach at least an hour a day in classes of sufficient size to give experience in class management as well as in teaching subjects. This seems to be the case now with all the normal schools of North Dakota except the one at Ellendale, which as yet has no practice school. But the practice schools of all, except for a rural ungraded school used by the normal school at Mayville, are of the city-school type. Each of the normal schools should make some arrangement by which it may have the control of three or four or more rural schools for use as practice schools. If possible, some of these rural schools should be one-teacher schools, while others should be consolidated schools.

RURAL-SCHOOL COURSE.

In the raising of standards of admission to the normal schools the 10½ months' course now maintained for the training of teachers of rural schools, and to which students are admitted from the eighth grade of the public schools, will necessarily be abolished in the year 1918, as it should be. The State superintendent, the presidents and faculties of the normal schools, and educated men and women in the State agree in admitting that this course is unsatisfactory. Conditions in the State which called for its establishment have passed away. Its continuance under the title of " rural-school course " serves chiefly to keep alive the idea that teachers in rural schools need much less preparation than teachers in city schools.

TEACHERS IN NORMAL SCHOOLS.

Attention is called to the importance of scholarship and maturity of experience on the part of those who undertake the education and training of teachers. Not only do they need thorough scientific knowledge, but it is most important that they shall have such experience with elementary schools as will give them practical knowledge of their problems and their methods of work. The number of young and inexperienced instructors in normal schools should be reduced to the lowest possible minimum. Some of the schools of this State have, it appears to the commission, altogether too many instructors of this type. Of 100 instructors of all grades in the four normal schools, only 3 have the doctor's degree, only 17 have the master's degree, and 80 per cent have no degree showing evidence of work beyond that of the undergraduate in college or normal school.

In the practice of employing assistants at low salaries the several schools differ widely. The school at Mayville reports no assistant instructors. To obtain and retain the services of such instructors as the work of the normal school demands will require a higher scale of salaries than that which now obtains. There is at none of these schools a fixed schedule of salaries, but the average of salaries varies from $1,692.08 at Mayville, $1,383.13 at Minot, and $1,360 at Valley City, to $1,081.58 at Ellendale. Under present conditions in North Dakota it is believed that an average salary of $2,000 would not be unreasonable.

SHOULD EXCLUDE GENERAL STUDENTS.

The normal schools were established and are maintained " to prepare teachers in the science of education and the art of teaching for the public schools of the State." They should therefore exclude general students and refrain from establishing commercial courses and other courses not needed for their purpose.

TEACHER TRAINING IN HIGH SCHOOLS.

In some States, because of the failure of the normal schools to send teachers to the rural schools, the policy has been adopted of maintaining teacher-training classes in the high schools for the purpose of preparing teachers for the elementary schools, and North Dakota has adopted this policy to some extent. These classes serve a useful purpose temporarily, but they should be continued only until such time as the normal schools can prepare teachers in sufficient numbers for all schools. Reasons have already been given why rural teachers should have as extensive and thorough preparation as city teachers. Also there can be no justice in taxing all the people for the support of normal schools for the preparation of teachers for city schools only or chiefly, and then levying on country people another tax for the purpose of giving an inferior kind of preparation to the teachers of their schools.[1]

[1] Dr. Coffman dissents from some of the considerations implied in this paragraph.

Chapter VIII.

THE STATE SCHOOL OF FORESTRY AND THE STATE SCHOOL OF SCIENCE.

THE NEED FOR SPECIAL STATE SCHOOLS OF LESS THAN COLLEGE GRADE.

Rural high schools in North Dakota are of very recent development, and neither in these nor in the elementary schools are agriculture, farm mechanics, and subjects pertaining to rural home making taught except in a very meager way. For this reason there are now in the State, and must be for many years to come, many boys and girls and young men and young women who are to live in the country and engage in the pursuits of farming and home making who have had little or no opportunity for instruction in the principles and practices of these subjects, an understanding of which must be so vital to their success and happiness.

Even if good high schools could be established at once in all rural communities of the State, thousands of these persons are too old to be expected to attend the high schools and take the regular high-school courses for the sake of the little time which they might be permitted to devote to these practical subjects. Only the largest high schools could, as high schools are now organized, afford to offer opportunity for a sufficient amount of work in these subjects to take most of the time of any groups of students even for five or six months a year. Most of these persons, though of college age, are not prepared to enter college. Therefore opportunity for them to get any systematic and practical instruction in these subjects must come through schools organized for this particular purpose.

There is almost as much need for some special provision by which many young men and young women between the ages of 18 and 25, living in villages and small towns, may have an opportunity to attend for a few months in the year schools in which boys may be taught in a practical way carpentry, tinning, plumbing, and other forms of wood and metal work, steam fitting, the care and repair of gas engines, etc., and in which young women may be taught home making and the principles and practices of the occupations open for women in these communities.

These schools should admit boys and girls 16 years old and over who have completed elementary-school courses, and more mature young men and young women of even less school preparation. For the convenience of those boys and young men who must work on the farm during the spring and summer, the schools should offer short winter courses and courses of six months, as is now done in the agricultural schools of Minnesota and some other States and in the agricultural school of the North Dakota Agricultural College. For those girls and young women who can attend such a school more conveniently in the summer months, short courses and longer courses of four and a half or five months should be offered. The school should be opened for both sexes both winter and summer.

The survey commission believes the State School of Forestry, at Bottineau, and the State School of Science, at Wahpeton, should be reorganized on this basis and for these purposes. The school at Bottineau might well place most emphasis on agricultural subjects; the school at Wahpeton on mechanical and industrial subjects. Neither of these schools should undertake work of college grade in any of these subjects now nor until the State has become much more populous and the attendance at the State agricultural college has become much larger than it now is. When these conditions shall have come about, it may be found advisable for one or both of these schools and similar schools, which in the meantime may have been established in other parts of the State, to extend their courses so as to include one or two years of college work.

Although the practical subjects of farming and homemaking should take a much larger portion of the time and energies of students in these schools than in the regular high schools, their interest and work should not be limited entirely to these subjects. There should be systematic instruction in the elements of physics, chemistry, and biology as a basis for the more immediately practical work, and in literature, history, civics, and civil government for inspiration and direction in the duties of life and citizenship, but there should be no attempt at teaching foreign languages, ancient or modern. Many of the people of North Dakota who remember the so-called folk high schools and the agricultural schools of the Scandinavian countries from which they have come will understand at once the value of schools of this kind.

It is believed that schools organized on this basis and maintained liberally for these purposes would be largely attended, and that they would accomplish much good. In a State in which the great majority of farmers own and manage their own farms, as in North Dakota, and where there are few tenants and few large farms managed for absentee landlords, there is more need for schools of this kind than in States in which there are many tenants and many very large farms worked by hirelings directed by managers.

THE NORTH DAKOTA SCHOOL OF FORESTRY.

In the constitution of North Dakota (art. 6, sec. 216), adopted in 1889, provision is made as follows for the establishment of a school of forestry or some other institution somewhere in the group of counties constituting the north central part of the State:

> Fourth. The School of Forestry, or such other institution as the legislative assembly may determine, at such place in one of the counties of McHenry, Ward, Bottineau, or Rolette, as the electors of the said counties may determine by an election for that purpose to be held as provided by the legislative assembly.

The election was held on November 6, 1894, and resulted in the location of the School of Forestry at Bottineau, in the county of Bottineau. The school was opened January 7, 1907.

By an act approved March 19, 1907, the legislative assembly set forth the object of the school as follows: " To furnish the instruction and training contemplated in an agricultural high school, emphasizing those subjects that have a direct bearing on forestry and horticulture."

By an act approved March 11, 1913, the legislative assembly further provided that:

> The president of the School of Forestry shall have general supervision of the raising and distribution of seeds and forest-tree seedlings as hereinafter provided; shall promote practical forestry; compile and disseminate information relative thereto, and publish the results of such work by issuing and distributing bulletins, lecturing before farmers' institutes, associations, and other organizations interested in forestry, and in such other ways as will most practically reach the public. (S. L. 1913, art. 10, sec. 1679a.)

> There shall be established in connection with the State School of Forestry and under the direction of the State forester a forest-tree nursery for the propagation of seeds and forest-tree seedlings, which shall be best adapted to the climatic conditions of this State. For such purpose the board of trustees of the School of Forestry shall set apart a tract of not less than 10 acres of the lands belonging to such school. (Sec. 1679b.)

> Seeds and seedlings from such nursery shall be distributed to citizens and land owners of this State upon the payment of actual cost of transportation from the nursery to the place where the same are to be planted. As a condition precedent to such distribution, the citizen or land owner making application therefor must agree to plant the seeds and seedlings distributed under the direction of the State forester and in conformity with his instructions. (Sec. 1679c.)

> The State forester is required to furnish to each applicant for seeds or forest-tree seedlings, suitable directions for planting the same, and when requested so to do, shall furnish skilled assistants to supervise such work, and in the event that assistance is furnished the applicant therefor shall pay the expense thereof. (Sec. 1679d. Approved Mar. 11, 1913.)

In the Quarterly Bulletin of the school for May, 1915, it is stated that—

The aims of the school are twofold: (1) To provide practical and efficient instruction in forestry, horticulture, agriculture, nursery and greenhouse practice, manual training, household economics, and academic subjects; (2) as the North Dakota State Nursery to provide free of all expense, except that of transportation, forest trees, seeds, seedlings, and cuttings for planting within our State;

and it is further stated that—

In line with this work bulletins concerning windbreaks, shelter belts, the planting and caring for trees, etc., will be published as fast as possible.

NOT IN FACT A SCHOOL OF FORESTRY.

It seems that although established as a school of "forestry," the object of which should be "to furnish the instruction and training contemplated in an agricultural high school, emphasizing those subjects that have a direct bearing on forestry and horticulture," the school developed first as "a kind of business college," although it is located in a small town of only about 1,500 inhabitants, and although in the eight counties of Bottineau, Rolette, McHenry, Ward, Pierce, Renville, Benson, and Towner, which this school may be supposed to serve most directly, there is only one town, Minot, of more than 2,500 inhabitants, and only five (Minot included) of more than 1,000, the total population of the five towns in 1910 being less than 12,000. It is stated that when the people became dissatisfied with this type of development an attempt was made to develop in it general forestry, lumbering, and ranger courses, but there were few or no students for these courses. At one time, it is stated, the attendance dropped to less than a dozen students, though the total enrollment for that year is reported as more than 50. Recently the attendance has increased considerably. The total enrollment by years is as follows:

1906–7	82
1907–8	72
1908–9	74
1909–10	75
1910–11	64
1911–12	95
1912–13	52
1913–14	114
1914–15	187

These numbers include the totals for the fall, winter, spring, and summer terms and are much larger than the average attendance or the enrollment for any single term. During the week of April 10–16, 1916, the attendance was 105.

Beginning with 1910, the school has graduated 36 students, but 7 of the graduates received only the elementary certificate, and the majority of these 7 continued as students in the school. Of the remainder, 13 are reported as " advanced," 5 as " collegiate," 8 as " commercial," 3 as " domestic science." Of these graduates only 3 have become farmers, 7 are in business, 6 are teachers, 2 (married women) are home makers, 5 are in professions other than teaching, 12 (including those with elementary certificates) are students in this or other schools. Not one is reported as practicing forestry and only 1 is

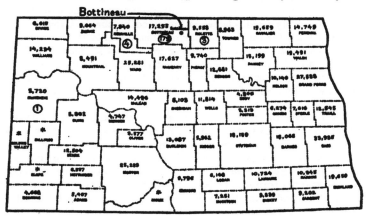

FIGURE 18.—Distribution of students enrolled in the State School of Forestry, 1914–15. See Table 31, p. 136.

The figures above the county name in each case give the population in 1910. At that date the population of Golden Valley County (later subdivided into Golden Valley, Billings, and Slope Counties) was 10,186; and the population of Morton County (later subdivided into Morton and Sioux Counties) was 25,289. The population of the State was 577,056.

The figures inclosed in the circle in each case indicate the number of students from the county who are enrolled at the School of Forestry.

This institution drew 187 students from 4 counties in North Dakota, and 8 students from without the State; of the entire number of sudents, 11 came from outside of Bottineau County.

reported as being a student at the North Dakota Agricultural College, although 3 are students at the University of North Dakota. Judged by the occupations of its graduates the school has functioned neither as a school of agriculture nor as a school of forestry. To a larger extent than any of the State schools under the immediate control of the board of regents the school at Bottineau is a local school. Of the 187 students enrolled from the State of North Dakota in 1914–15, 179 were from Bottineau County, 4 from Renville, 3 from Rolette, and 1 from McKenzie. Of those from Bottineau County a very large proportion were from the town of Bottineau.

The waste of time and energy of teachers because of the large number of very small classes reaches its maximum in this school. The average attendance of 132 class meetings held during the week of April 10–16, 1916, was only 6.1 students. Only 42—or 32 per cent— of the class meetings had an attendance of more than 5.[1] Only 22— or 16.6 per cent—had an attendance of 10 or more. At 85 class meetings of 18 classes having less than 5 students the total attendance was 237, an average of 2.8 students. There were 14 class meetings with only 1 student and 30 with only 2 students. The costliness of these excessively small classes is indicated by the fact that of each $100 expended for instruction during this week $59.10 was expended for the instruction of classes having less than 5 students and $83.30 for the instruction of classes having less than 10 students. (See Table 42 and fig. 23.) For students of the grade represented in this school so large a number of small classes must be considered as very wasteful.[2]

The reasons for the large number of very small classes in this school are: (1) The vertical spread from classes of elementary school grade through four years of high school and one or two of collegiate grade; and (2) the wide horizontal spread to include academic, agricultural, horticultural, forestry, commercial, domestic science, manual training, pedagogy, and music courses. Fortunately, many of the subjects offered, as Latin, German, advanced English, and courses in harmony, are not taken.

It should be noted that a majority of the students in elementary manual training classes are boys from the elementary grades of the public schools of Bottineau, who take one lesson a week, and more than half of the students taught by the teacher of household economics are in classes of fancy cooking and crocheting. Many of these are women in the town of Bottineau who take only a few lessons a year. These and similar facts account for the low average number of class meetings attended weekly by each student—only 7.7 during the week of April 10–16, as against averages of from 15.8 to 26.1 at other schools included in this survey.[3]

That there is no real demand for the commercial dpeartment in this school is indicated by the fact that, as President Smith says, the only distinctive things about the department, as it exists here, are stenography, typewriting, bookkeeping, and commercial law,

---

[1] See Table 39, p. 148.
[2] Of the 105 students present that week, 11 were above high-school grade, 70 in classes of high-school grade, 23 in classes below the high school, and 1 was classified as special.
[3] See Table 41, p. 151.

and that, in April, 3 classes in stenography had a total enrollment
of 8 students, 2 classes in typewriting a total of 12 students, and 1
class in bookkeeping 9 students.

During the year 1914–15 there were only 10 students in farm
forestry, including 4 in animal husbandry, and only 6 in pedagogy.
In April, 1916, there were only 2 students in advanced chemistry, 4
in college English, 1 in ancient history, etc. In no class above high
school grade were there more than 4 or 5 students. It would have
been much better for these students and much cheaper for the State
had those taking college subjects been taught in similar classes at
the university or at the agricultural college, and if those taking pedagogy had gone to one of the normal schools.

BUILDINGS AND GROUNDS.

The school of forestry has a main building valued at $55,000
and a greenhouse valued at $3,000. It has 35 acres of land used for
campus and nurseries, and a tract of 160 acres recently purchased
to be used for the development of nurseries. The equipment of the
school is valued at $7,756.90. The salary budget for the year 1915–16,
including the salaries of the president and the secretary, is $10,535.
The total income of the school for 1914–15 was:

Mill tax	$4, 283. 63
State warrants	6, 683. 76
Miscellaneous	1, 316. 12
Total	12, 288. 51

This is hardly enough for the support of a good agricultural
school of the kind recommended by the survey commission, but it
can be made to accomplish much more than it now does if only the
legitimate work of such a school is undertaken.

RECOMMENDATIONS.

A careful study of the history of this school makes it quite clear
that its difficulties have been due to the fact that there has been no
real demand here for most of the work which it has tried to do, and
to its attempt to cover too great a variety of subjects and to extend
its work over too many grades. Plainly the school will find itself
only when it abandons all other purposes and, fitting itself for it,
undertakes to do only the kind of work recommended in the first
part of this chapter, and in the "Summary of Conclusions and Recommendations.[1] Doing work of this kind, it should soon have
a reasonably large attendance from all the northern and central
counties of the State. The curriculum should not attempt to cover
more than three years and should be made as strong as possible

---

[1] See recommendations 32 and 33, ch. 12.

in practical agricultural subjects and in home economics. In this work it should have the constant advice and guidance of the agricultural college and the assistance of its extension workers and of farm demonstration and county agricultural agents of all kinds. Through the help of these it should enrich the work done within its walls and on its campus and farms by home projects carefully planned by the school and worked out by the students in their homes and on their home farms.

The survey commission agrees with Mr. Smith, the president of this school and the State forester, that the teaching of forestry and the management of nurseries should be transferred to the agricultural college, which .has the machinery and the organization whereby forestry work may be carried on successfully in the State. The college now has 5 substations and 22 model farms. The substation at Mandan is required by law to make experiments with trees, and other substations might well carry on similar experiments and conduct small nurseries. These nurseries should be located with reference to convenience of distribution. The fact that railroads from all parts of the State converge at Fargo makes this a convenient distributing center and would seem to make it advisable to establish large nurseries here. The college will in time have agricultural agents in all the counties of the State and will be sending out field workers in all forms of agriculture and home economics and also in other subjects. So important is the growing of trees to the State that the college might well consider the establishment of small nurseries, for local distribution, at other State institutions and at agricultural high schools. It is recommended that the nurseries already established at Bottineau be continued under the direction of the agricultural college.

It need hardly be said that the school of forestry which should be developed at the agricultural college for the service of the State of North Dakota should be quite different from schools of forestry in Montana, Washington, California, Oregon, New York, North Carolina, and other States having vast forests and timber industries. In these States the problems of forestry are largely of lumber engineering; but in North Dakota the problems are of tree planting, afforestation, providing windbreaks for homes and farms, conserving rainfall, and providing wood and timber for home and commercial use. In European countries this latter kind of forestry has received much attention and is in charge of highly trained experts. In New England the growing of timber for manufacturing purposes has begun to receive attention.[1]

The interest which the people of North Dakota are taking in this subject is attested by the fact that the legislative assembly has en-

---

[1] Dr. Liberty H. Bailey, of Cornell University, has emphasized the fact that timber growing is as much a proper agricultural interest as the growing of corn or potatoes.

acted a law providing a bounty, under certain conditions, for the planting and cultivation of trees.

THE NORTH DAKOTA STATE SCHOOL OF SCIENCE.

The constitution of North Dakota made it incumbent upon the legislative assembly of the State to provide for a scientific school or some other institution [1] at Wahpeton, in Richland County, and apportioned for the support of this school 40,000 acres of the congressional grant of public lands for institutions of higher learning in the State. The legislative act providing for this school was approved March 10, 1903, and the school was opened in September, 1904.

The first two years the school was held in rented buildings. In 1905 the trustees purchased for the use of the school the building and property of Red River Valley University. The present value of buildings is estimated at $113,020. The present value of equipment is estimated at $25,082.25.. The total income of the school for 1914–15 was:

Mill tax	$8, 552. 46
Interest and income	18, 335. 56
State appropriation	5, 000. 00
Fees	2, 392. 75
Total	84, 280. 77

The purpose of the school as defined by statute is—

to furnish such instruction in the pure and applied sciences, mathematics, languages, political sciences, and history as is usually given in schools of technology below the junior year, the chief object being the training of skilled workmen in the most practical phases of applied science.

The president of the school indicates the following as the classes of students the school desires to serve:

1. Students who are 16 years of age, who have no definite educational preparation, and yet feel the need of further vocational or industrial training.
2. Students who have finished the sixth grade or more in the rural schools and who, though bright but outclassed in age, desire to prepare for courses requiring eighth-grade preparation or for some vocational course.
3. Students who have graduated from the eighth grade and desire to take a vocational course immediately.
4. Students who have graduated from the eighth grade and desire vocational guidance and cultural courses.
5. Students who have graduated from high school and desire to learn a trade or vocation immediately.
6. Students who have graduated from high school and desire vocational training along with the higher cultural courses.
7. Students who have graduated from college and desire only the special technical training in a trade or vocational course.

---

[1] " Fifth. A scientific school, or such other educational or charitable institution as the legislative assembly may prescribe."

The president sums up the courses offered or that should be offered under the following heads:

	Courses.
Agriculture	3
Business and commerce	4
Home economics	3
Industrial arts	2
Industrial engineering	5
Special winter term	6
Teacher training	2
Trade	8
Vocational preparatory	4

The grade of students served by these courses extends from the seventh grade of the elementary schools through the second college year, a range of eight years.

Of 344 graduates to the end of the school year 1914–15, 219 have graduated in commercial subjects, 34 in domestic science, 48 in high-school academic courses, 22 in junior-college academic courses, and only 17 in all forms of engineering, as follows:

Steam engineering	6
Mechanical engineering	5
Electrical engineering	5
Chemical engineering	1

In electrical engineering there has been only one graduate in any one year. Of these 344 graduates, 137 were reported as engaged in business and 47 in farming. Only 12 are reported as engaged in any mechanical occupation involving applied science, as follows: Chemist, 1; mechanical engineers, 4; electrical workers, 7.

SMALL CLASSES.

As a result of the wide vertical and horizontal spread of the work in this school the faculty of 21, including president and secretary, were giving, in the spring of 1916, 92 different courses to 106 students. In 124 meetings of 27 classes having less than 5 students during the week of April 10–16, 1916, there was a total attendance of 362 students, an average of 2.9 students. Out of a total of 305 class meetings that week, 10 had 1 student, 53 had 2 students, 5 had 3 students, 36 had 4 students, and 25 had 5 students; 68.2 per cent of the class meetings were attended by less than 10 students. Among the small classes were 4 classes in German, with 8, 2, 2, and 4 students, respectively; a class in Latin, with 2 students; 3 classes in shorthand, with 4, 2, and 2 students, respectively; a class in dietetics, with 1 student; a class in textiles, with 1 student; a class in mechanism, with 2 students; and a class in education, with 8 students.

Of every $100 expended for instruction during that week, $34.10 was for classes of less than 5 students and $68.20 for classes of less than 10 students.

The attendance for 1914–15 was:

Fall term _____ 158
Winter term _____ 236
Spring term _____ 155
Summer term _____ 100

The average for the three regular terms was 180.' Of the 370 different students enrolled, 107 students entered with 15 or more units of preparation, 263 with less than 15 units. Of the 107 students entering with 15 or more units, only 78 were from North Dakota. If these had been cared for at the university and the agricultural college, they would have added very little to the burden of teaching in either institution.

SOURCE OF ATTENDANCE.

In any discussion of the place of the School of Science in the educational system of North Dakota and of the work it should undertake to do, it should be remembered that of the total attendance (in 1914–15) something more than 35 per cent were 'from other States than North Dakota, something more than 51 per cent from Richland County, and something less than 14 per cent from other North Dakota counties; that the school is located within easy reach by rail of the agricultural college, the university, and the normal schools at Mayville, Valley City, and Ellendale; and that, although this section of the State is a rich farming section, it is also the section having the largest per cent of urban population. (See Figure 19.)

RECOMMENDATIONS.

The survey commission believes that the school may find its greatest usefulness as a high-class industrial school, or school of mechanical trades, with such courses in agriculture as may seem advisable, but giving at present no work of college grade. It should give special attention to industrial subjects both for boys and girls, and it might be well to include also commercial subjects, such as bookkeeping and stenography, but it should avoid becoming a local elementary or high school. The commission recommends elsewhere that the State board of regents establish at Bottineau a six months' school especially adapted to needs of boys preparing to become farmers, and a four and one-half or five months' summer school especially suitable for girls wishing to study home economics and allied subjects, both the winter and summer schools, however, being open to both boys and girls. If the experiment at Bottineau proves

successful, a similar plan might also be tried at Wahpeton, which is
already fairly well equipped for the conduct of courses similar to
the courses below college grade offered at the agricultural college.

As already stated, with the increase in population and wealth of
the State and of attendance of students at the university and agricultural college, it may be well for the school at Wahpeton to become

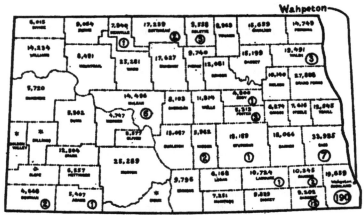

Figure 19.—Distribution of resident students enrolled in the North Dakota State School
of Science at Wahpeton, exclusive of summer session, 1914–15. See Table 31, p. 136.

The figures above the county name in each case give the population in 1910. At that
date the population of Golden Valley County (later subdivided into Golden Valley,
Billings, and Slope Counties) was 10,186; and the population of Morton County (later
subdivided into Morton and Sioux Counties) was 25,289.

The figures inclosed in the circle in each case indicate the number of students from
the county who are enrolled at the North Dakota State School of Science at Wahpeton.

This institution drew 238 students from 16 of the 52 counties in North Dakota (of
whom 79.8 per cent came from Richland County) and 132 from without the State;
total, 370.

Only 1 county, outside of Richland County, sent more than 7 students to Wahpeton;
Minnesota sent 105 and South Dakota sent 11.

a junior college of science and technology, but it does not appear to
the commission that there is at present any demand for a separate
school of science or of technology of junior college grade.

Chapter IX.

THE STATE LIBRARY COMMISSION.

Chapter 156, laws of 1909, assigns to the public library commission the following duties:

1. To administer the educational reference library.
2. To administer the traveling libraries.

It shall take over and add to the educational reference library and the system of traveling libraries, and shall continue the same, and, as its funds permit, shall increase the number and usefulness of the libraries. Any city, town, village, school district, or community within the State of North Dakota may borrow books under the rules and regulations of the State library commission. The commission shall catalogue and otherwise prepare said books for circulation and shall make rules and regulations according to which the business of the commission shall be done; and also such rules and regulations as shall insure the care, preservation, and safe return of all books loaned.

3. To establish and administer a legislative reference bureau.

The State library commission shall have the power and it shall be its duty to establish a legislative reference bureau for the information and assistance of the members of the legislative assembly in the work of legislation. The legislation of other States and information upon legal and economic questions shall be classified and catalogued in such a way as to render the same easy of access to members, thereby enabling them better to prepare for their work. It shall be the duty of the legislative librarian to assist in every way possible the members of the legislative assembly in obtaining information and in the preparation of bills.

4. To give advice in regard to the organization, maintenance, and administration of libraries.

The librarian or trustees of any free public library or the trustees of any village, town, or community entitled to borrow books from said traveling libraries may, without charge, ask and receive advice and instruction from said library commission upon any matter pertaining to the organization, maintenance, or administration of the libraries.

5. To aid in the formation of new libraries and the improvement of those already in existence.

And said commission shall, as far as possible, promote and assist by counsel and encouragement the formation of libraries where none exist, and the commission may also send its members to aid in organizing new libraries or improving those already established.

6. To collect statistics of the free public libraries of the State and to report its own activities.

The State library commission shall keep statistics of the free public libraries of North Dakota and a record of the work done and books loaned by said commission, and shall make a full report to each general session of the legislature of all expenditures by the commission, and of such statistics and records as shall show the work done by the commission and the use made of the traveling libraries and all other matters which they deem expedient for the information of the legislature.

These duties now devolve upon the board of regents, but they are discussed here as belonging to the library commission.

ORGANIZATION.

The commission has organized its work under the following divisions:

1. Educational reference department.
2. Traveling library system.
3. Legislative reference bureau.
4. Field work.

There are department heads for divisions 2 and 3. The secretary and director has immediate charge of divisions 1 and 4. The office of the commission is in the capitol at Bismarck. It appears that the secretary and director and the two heads of departments have the assistance of only one stenographer and one clerk, and that for lack of more assistance all the work of the commission is impeded. It also appears that the efficiency of the legislative reference bureau has been impaired because of lack of funds for printing bulletins on subjects of legislative interest to the people of the State and their representatives; that only slight additions have been made to the educational reference library and the traveling libraries within the last few years, and that the field work has been much less extensive and helpful than it might have been. Evidently there is need for considerable increase in the appropriations for all this library commission work if it is to accomplish for the State what was originally intended and meet fully the ever-larger demands of the rapidly increasing population and a constantly growing interest in all phases of the work.

The librarian of the legislative reference bureau reports that, in compliance with law, he has collected and compiled the laws of other States and information concerning questions of economic and legislative interest, has made files of bills introduced in the Legislative Assembly of North Dakota, and assisted legislators and legislative committees in drafting bills. The bureau now has a collection of 15.000 or more clippings arranged for the use of legislators. When the legislature is not in session, articles from the collections of this bureau are sent by the educational reference department to those who request them. The survey commission has made no detailed investigation of this bureau, and has no recommendations to make in regard to its work, except that the librarian should be given sufficient assistance to enable him to bring and keep up to date the work both of compiling and digesting laws and of cataloguing and indexing the collections, and that sufficient funds should be available to enable him to print necessary bulletins for the information of the people on questions of legislative interest.

The work of the educational reference division, formerly done by the department of public instruction, consists of correspondence with individuals, principally club women and teachers and pupils in the schools. It is especially helpful to rural homes and small communities without libraries. The reference library has something less than 4,000 volumes and about 15,000 mounted clippings from magazines and newspapers. It also uses the clippings of the legislative reference bureau when the legislature is not in session.

The traveling libraries, also especially helpful to rural communities, villages, and small towns, are of four kinds:

Community collections.
School collections.
Small school collections for grades below the sixth.
Farmers' libraries, consisting of technical books on agriculture.

Six sets of these last are reported. Of all these kinds of collections the traveling library system has between 300 and 400 sets. An inspection of the library map, page 126, shows that the traveling libraries reach all parts of the State, but, unfortunately, the number of these libraries is so small that only a very small per cent of the communities of the State can be served in any one year. Five or ten times as many could be used to great advantage.

The field work is supervision of all libraries in North Dakota and promotion of its library interests within and without the State. It includes fostering of library spirit, organization of new libraries, advice on technical and administrative problems, planning new buildings, selection of books and librarians, and instruction in library methods. There is a great need of field work among public libraries not able to employ trained librarians, in communities wishing to organize public libraries, and especially in school libraries. In an agricultural State destined to undergo the rural development fast coming to North Dakota, but still only sparsely settled, the furnishing of library facilities must long remain, in some communities, at least, with the school library, which also supplies community needs. Whether known as the school or township or county library, some agency must see that money is wisely spent in purchasing books, that the books when purchased are arranged and cared for so that their contents are easily available at the time needed, and that a uniform system is used, so that teachers and pupils from any school in the State will at once feel at home in any public library in the State. This work is a special province of the library commission.

The library in charge of the library commission not only ministers to the communities having no public libraries, but it supplements in an important way all the local public libraries of the State. With sufficient means to purchase some classes of books in sets of a half dozen or more, it might render great service in this last way.

INSTITUTION LIBRARIES.

It seems that the libraries of the university, the agricultural college, and the normal schools loan their books, to some extent, beyond their walls, as they should if they have the machinery for it. But the survey commission can see no danger of duplication or conflict of interests between these institutions and the library commission, so long as the libraries of the educational institutions resist all temptation to become circulating libraries, or to spend their incomes for books to be used only, or chiefly, for this purpose. In fact, the library commission might well arrange with these libraries to supplement the service of its educational reference library and refer to them requests for books not in this collection. These libraries, however, should avoid all effort to cover the general field of the library commission. They will need, no doubt, to use all their money and efforts in perfecting themselves for the immediate service of the institutions of which they are a part. Service beyond their walls should be only secondary, and to a large extent only supplementary, to the service of the library commission. In this secondary and supplementary service, each institutional library should have its own definite field.

The university library should be able to furnish to those who need them special and technical books upon subjects covered by the university curricula. The agricultural college should perform a similar service for students interested in special agricultural and other problems related to the work of that institution. The libraries of the normal schools should be rich in educational literature, dealing especially with the problems of elementary education, and these should be available both for teachers and for the people of the State interested in such problems.

The number of large libraries in North Dakota and the consequent demand for highly trained librarians are not now, nor will they be for some time, sufficiently large to justify extensive courses in library work at more than one institution, but there is need for instruction in the simplest and most elementary principles and practices of library work for those who have the care of the smaller libraries, and especially for teachers in the public schools who are responsible for the selection and care of books in the school libraries. Such instruction should be provided at the university and normal schools, and especially in the summer sessions of these schools. That there may be uniformity in this instruction, and therefore in library practice throughout the State, courses in library work should be planned by the secretary and director of the library commission, and the work inspected by her from time to time. She might also arrange for apprentice instruction at some of the larger libraries. The commission should have in its employ an organizer who should give most of her time to visiting schools and small libraries to give the prac-- tical help for which there are constant demands. When school boards understand more fully how important it is for teachers to have sufficient knowledge of the care and use of books to make the small school libraries most useful, and when they realize that money paid for books is practically thrown away unless the information contained in these books can be made available when needed, the demands for library instruction and for the help that such an organizer could give will be much greater than they are now.

LOCAL LIBRARIES.

The very liberal laws in North Dakota in regard to city, village, township, and school libraries show the intelligence of the people in regard to the value of books and of the habit of reading.

City councils and boards of villages and townships containing more than 400 inhabitants have the power to establish and maintain public libraries and reading rooms, and, when authorized by a vote of the people at a general election, may levy annually and cause to be collected taxes not exceeding 4 mills on the dollar for their support. In any city in which the sum of $400 or more has been donated for the benefit of a public library the council may appropriate to such library as much as $200 from the general fund without the authority of a vote. In like manner the board of trustees of a village or the board of supervisors of a township of not less than 400 inhabitants in each case may appropriate $100 from the general fund of the village or township for the use of a public library when the sum of $150 or more has been properly donated for the benefit of such library.

Section 1176 of the school laws requires the district school board to—

appropriate and expend each year not less than $10 nor more than $25 for each school of the district for the purpose of a school library, to be selected by the school board and the trustees from any list of books authorized by the superintendent of public instruction and forwarded by him to the county superintendent for that purpose * * * provided * * * that when a school board of a common school has purchased and has in their library 200 books as aforeprovided that the school board having such school under their supervision shall be obliged to expend not less than $5 annually until such library shall contain, in good condition, 300 volumes, after which said school board shall not be obliged to purchase so as to increase the number, but shall keep the books in good condition and replace annually as many books as may become lost or destroyed.

The large proportion of rural population in this State makes these laws in regard to village, township, and school libraries all the more desirable and beneficial, but the needs of the people for books and magazines can never be fully supplied by these small libraries, even when supplemented to the fullest possible extent by the traveling libraries of the library commission and by the circulation of books from the educational reference library. They are too small to supply more than the most elementary needs of the community. Though each of the 100 schools of a county might have its 300 volumes, making a total of 30,000 volumes in the school libraries of the county, and though these might be supplemented by a dozen or more small village and township libraries, still there would be available for the use of the people of any one community only a very

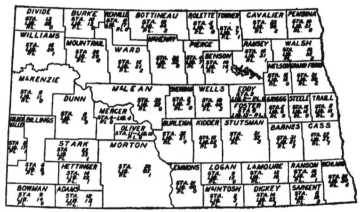

Fig. 20.—Distribution of traveling library stations (Sta.), traveling libraries (Lib.), and public libraries (P. L.) in North Dakota, by counties, 1914.

limited number and variety of books. To meet fully the needs of the people will require libraries larger than can be maintained by the small units of school district, village, and township. It will require the cooperation of county and State. In bringing about this the library commission should find its greatest opportunity for usefulness.

The fourth biennial report of the North Dakota State Library Commission (1912–1914) gives only 9 public libraries having 3,000 or more volumes on July 1, 1914, and only 28 having less than 3,000 volumes on the same date, a total of 37 public libraries of all sizes in the State. The 9 libraries having 3,000 or more volumes each had a total of less than 50,000 volumes and a total income of less than $30,000. The 9 towns which they serve had a population of less than

60,000 in 1910, probably less than 75,000 in 1914. The United States Bureau of education in 1916 reported 8 libraries in this State having more than 4,000 volumes each. These 8 reported a total of less than 50,000 volumes, a total income of less than $30,000, and less than $4,000 expended for books within the year. In 1916 there were only 4 libraries having as many as 5,000 volumes, and these served a total of not more than 50,000 of the 700,000 (estimated) people of the State. Less than 10 per cent of the people of the State have easy access to any adequate collection of books. (See Table 25 and fig. 20.)

TABLE 25.—*North Dakota public libraries, 1916.*

Location.	Name.	Librarian.	Number of volumes.	Accessions.	Income.	Book expenditures.
Devils Lake.....	Carnegie Library........	Dorothy Dodge........	4,253	392	$1,918	$228
Dickinson.......	Public Library..........	Helen F. Carleton.....	4,207	509	1,721	375
Fargo...........	....do.................	Winnie Bucklin.......	9,825	1,232	5,833	579
Grand Forks....	....do.................	Adah Durand.........	10,000	631	4,000	656
Jamestown......	....do.................	Alice M. Paddock.....	6,500	321	2,147	261
Minot...........	Free Public Library (1 station).	Margaret Greene......	6,000	870	4,500	785
Valley City.....	Carnegie Public Library.	Lillian E. Cook.......	4,652	617	2,666	696
Williston.......	James Memorial Library	Bessie R. Baldwin....	4,192	307	3,849	402
Total.....			49,629	4,879	26,634	3,982

[1]At Bowman, N. Dak., a new public library building was opened in January, 1916.

COUNTY LIBRARIES.

The taxable property of small towns, villages, townships, and rural school districts is not sufficient to enable them to support good public libraries alone. The public libraries owned and controlled by cities and towns seldom reach the people of these smaller communities. The only help for all is in the county library, supported by taxes levied on all the taxable property of the county, managed by a trained librarian, having branches in all the more important towns and villages of the county, and using the schools as distributing centers. Cooperation of smaller units through the larger units of which they are parts is as necessary for the best results in this as it is in all other matters of public welfare. That no county, however poor, may be without the means of supporting such a library, there should be State aid for public libraries just as there is for public schools. The people of no community should, through lack of means in that community, be deprived of free access to all the books of which they can make good use.

The survey commission recommends that the legislative assembly of the State be requested to make legal provision whereby counties may establish and maintain libraries to be administered and used as here suggested. It believes that this provision should contain some form of State aid for the support of these county libraries.

Under such provision the libraries already established in the larger
cities and towns of the State might be transformed immediately
into county libraries with larger support than the municipalities
alone are able to give them. This would not only extend the privileges of the libraries to all the people of the county, but would enhance
the value of them to the municipalities themselves. Libraries would
then no doubt be established in other counties, beginning with the
most populous and most wealthy and extending to the less populous
and less wealthy as rapidly as they could be induced to assume the
burden of their support. At present approximately one-third of the
counties of the State have a population of more than 15,000, and
more than one-half have a population of more than 10,000. It should
not be difficult for any of these counties to provide the funds for a
building, books, and their proper care and administration for a
library of 30,000 volumes. A library of this number of carefully
selected books would be amply sufficient for any county in the State,
and especially if many of the most popular books were owned in
sets of from three to six and if all the county libraries were supplemented by the educational reference library enlarged for this purpose.
For this supplementary work this reference library should have
many books on special subjects which might be called for sometimes,
but not frequently, in any county library, and which could be sent
to county libraries or to individual readers on request. Books of this
kind the educational reference library should have in sets of from
three to five. By this means the county libraries would be relieved
of the necessity of purchasing many costly books.

The county library should be located at the county seat, where the
roads converge—trolley lines sometimes, railroads frequently, country
roads always—and to which the people come to transact their legal
business and for other purposes. The libraries should be housed in
suitable buildings of a good and attractive style of architecture as
soon as means can be had for this, but the cost of buildings should not
be permitted to deter counties from establishing and maintaining
libraries, temporary quarters for which might usually be found in
the county courthouse or elsewhere at little expense. Books, and
proper care in their circulation, are more important than the buildings in which they are housed. In most counties, no doubt, money
could be had for buildings without the necessity of taxing the people
for them.

It is impossible to estimate the good that might come to the people
of North Dakota from such a system of libraries. It would increase
in large measure the value and effectiveness of the State's system of
public education. It would be especially helpful to those, the great
majority of the people of the State, who live in the open country
and in villages and small towns, and most helpful of all to those liv-

ing in remote, isolated farm homes. For many reasons these people have more time for reading than city people have. On Sundays, on rainy and snowy days when little or no work can be done outdoors, and on long winter evenings—very long in this northern latitude— much time for reading can be found by children and older people alike, and it comes in larger sections and with fewer interruptions than time for reading comes to those who live amid the distractions of city life. It is also true that country people will read, when they have opportunity, the best books with appreciation and profit. They read less for time-killing and mere entertainment and more for information and inspiration. Their close and familiar contact with nature and the simple fundamental things of life gives them more power of interpretation of the great literature of nature and life than city-bred people are likely to have. It should also be remembered that their opportunities for education in the schools and through lectures, plays, art galleries, museums, and other similar agencies being more limited than are those of the people of the cities, these country people have, therefore, the greater need of the services which only such a system of libraries as is here recommended can give.

The cost of upkeep of the libraries when once established will not be large. The total cost for all the counties would probably not exceed 6 or 7 per cent of the total annual expenditures for public schools.

46136°—Bull. 27—17——9

Chapter X.

STATISTICAL COMPARISONS.

A careful examination of the work of the several institutions, with the view to elimination of any unnecessary duplication of effort that might be found to exist, was emphasized in the outline of duties of the board of regents formulated by the legislature. To assist in an understanding of the problem, the tables in the following pages have been prepared. Since unnecessary duplication of work of college grade is presumably more expensive than is the case with courses of lower grade, and since normal schools and high schools are necessarily sectional or local schools of practically the same character and for the same purpose, respectively, special attention is given to a study of conditions in the university and the agricultural college.

EMPLOYEES AT UNIVERSITY AND AGRICULTURAL COLLEGE.

Table 26 presents a condensed summary of the employees for 1915–16 at the university and the agricultural college. With approximately the same number of resident students at each institution (see Table 28 for figures for 1914–15):

(1) The university makes use of an instructional staff nearly 60 per cent greater than that of the agricultural college (82 and 52, respectively). This difference may be explained partially by the fact that the university has a larger number of students in continuous residence than the agricultural college, approximately half of the resident student population at the latter institution being reported in special short-term classes.

(2) The number of employees classed as administrative and executive is more than twice as large at the agricultural college as at the university (13 and 6, respectively).

(3) The university employs twice as many engineers, janitors, and laborers as the agricultural college (22 and 11, respectively).

(4) Exclusive of those employed for the correspondence, extension, and research divisions, and for the summer session, the university staff is more than 50 per cent greater than that of the agricultural college (139 and 91, respectively).

A further analysis of the employees at the two institutions is given in Table 27. Attention is called particularly to the following points:

(1) With an enrollment of fewer than 100 students in engineering, the university maintains an instructional staff in this division of 17, including 2 deans.

(2) With a total instructional staff of 52, the agricultural college has only 5 assigned to agriculture, while 9 are assigned to engineering and 12 to general science. The number of instructors assigned to general science as compared with the number assigned to agriculture, which may properly be assumed to be the important department of the college, seems to the survey commission to be entirely out of due proportion.

TABLE 26.—*Employees at university and agricultural college, 1915-16.*

SUMMARY.

	University.	Agricultural college.
Instructional staff	82	52
Correspondence, extension, research	7	60
Administrative, executive	6	12
Clerks, librarians	15	18
Engineers, janitors, laborers	22	11
Commons employees	16	8
Total	148	162
Deduct those counted more than once	2	11
Net total	146	151
Summer session	22	11
Grand total	168	162

STUDENT ENROLLMENT AT UNIVERSITY AND AGRICULTURAL COLLEGE.

Table 28 presents a summary of the students enrolled for the year 1914-15 at the university and the agricultural college, classified according to departments. Attention is called to the following points:

(1) The numbers of students reported as entering with 15 high-school units of credit, line 2 of the table, is somewhat misleading, since a large number of those who entered the university with less than 15 credits were admitted with 14½ units, and none with less than 14 units, and at the agricultural college a considerable number of students were admitted to the special short courses without reference to scholastic attainments.

(2) Approximately one-half of the total enrollment at the university consists of regular-term students of college grade (675 out of 1,241), whereas the proportion of such students at the agricultural college is only a little more than one-fourth (319 out of 1,171).

(3) Two college departments at the university and seven at the agricultural college registered fewer than 10 students each.

TABLE 27.—*Employees at university and agricultural college, 1915–16.*

	University of North Dakota							North Dakota Agricultural College						
	Total	Deans	Professors	Associate professors	Assistant professors	Instructors	Assistants	Total	Deans	Professors	Associate professors	Assistant professors	Instructors	Assistants
I. Total, exclusive of names repeated	168							162						
II. Instructional staff (total, exclusive of summer session and names repeated)	82	7	21	5	15	23	11	52	4	20	2	12	12	2
(A) The colleges (total, exclusive of names repeated)	72	6	21	5	15	15	10	49	4	20	1	11	11	2
(1) Agriculture								5	1	3		1		
(2) Biology	3		1		1		1	5	1	1	1	1	1	
(3) Chemistry	5		1		1	2	1	5	1	3			1	
(4) Education	4	1	2		1			1		1				
(5) Engineering (total)	17	2	4		3	5	3	9	1	1		2	4	1
(a) Architecture								1					1	
(b) Chemical	2		1[1]		1[1]			1		1				
(c) Civil	1		1					1		1				
(d) Electrical	1													
(e) Mechanical	6	1	2[2]		1			2		2				
(f) Mining	7	1			1	2	3[3]							
(6) Home economics	3				1		2	5		1			3	1
(7) Law	6	1	2		1	2								
(8) Liberal arts, general science	34	1	12	4	7	5	5	12		6		4	2	
(9) Medicine	5	1	1	1	1	1								
(10) Military science								1		1				
(11) Pharmacy								2		1		1		
(12) Physical training								1		1				
(13) Veterinary medicine and surgery								3		1		2		
(B) High-school department	9					8	1	2		1		1		
(C) Not assigned to specific departments	1	1[*]						2						
III. Summer session	22							11						
IV. Correspondence division	1													
V. Extension division	1							21						
VI. Experiment station, research								39[7]						
VII. Administrative, executive	6[4]							13[6]						
VIII. Stenographers, clerks, librarians, etc.	15							18						
IX. Engineers, janitors, laborers (not including students)	22							11						
X. Common employees (not including students)	16							8						
XI. Counted more than once	2							11						

[1] Repeated in chemistry.
[2] Repeated in mining.
[3] One repeated in liberal arts.
[4] Two repeated in station and research.
[5] Repeated as assistant professor in liberal arts.
[6] One repeated as professor.
[7] Nine repeated elsewhere.
[8] Two repeated elsewhere.

TABLE 28.—*Summary of students at university and agricultural college, 1914–15.*

[According to figures verified by the registrars' offices.]

	University.	Agricultural college.
I. Grand total (excluding duplicates)	1,241	1,171
(1) Entered with 15 or more high school units	553	304
II. Graduate students	7	....
III. Students in the colleges (total)	675	319
(1) Agriculture	....	95
(2) Biology	....	1
(3) Chemistry	....	4
(4) Education	162	7
(5) Engineering (total)	83	36
(a) Architectural	....	7
(b) Architecture	....	5
(c) Chemical	....	2
(d) Civil	17	7
(e) Electrical	11	....
(f) Mechanical	6	15
(g) Mining	9	....
(h) Engineering, freshmen (unclassified)	40	....
(6) Home economics	....	74
(7) Law	92	....
(8) Liberal arts or general science	279	37
(9) Medicine	59	....
(10) Pharmacy	....	15
(11) Veterinary medicine and surgery	....	14
IV. Students in subcollegiate courses (total)	315	656
(1) Industrial and special (total)	....	242
(a) Drafting and building (22 weeks)	....	6
(b) Farm husbandry	....	118
(c) Power machinery	....	75
(d) Home making	....	26
(e) Pharmacy	....	17
(2) Winter short courses (total)	....	276
(a) Agriculture	....	50
(b) Engineering	....	204
(c) Domestic science	....	22
(3) High school	107	138
V. Students in summer session (total)	336	258
(1) Teachers summer school	....	36
(2) Engineering summer school	....	75
(3) Cass-Ransom Counties summer school	....	147
VI. Students in correspondence courses	116	....
VII. Names counted more than once	208	62

Table 29 presents an analysis of the student registration at the two institutions, exclusive of summer session, the percentage distribution being exhibited in figure 21. Approximately three-fourths of the regular year's work at the university is thus shown to be of college grade, compared with less than one-third at the agricultural college. Engineering constitutes less than 10 per cent of the total at the university and less than 4 per cent at the agricultural college. Work in agriculture of college grade involves only 10.1 per cent of the total registration at the agricultural college.

The analysis is carried still further in Table 30, in which only students of college grade, exclusive of summer session, are considered; see also figure 22. The department of liberal arts, with 41.3 per cent of the college students, is the core of the university, with the other departments in what seem to be reasonable proportions; while at the agricultural college, agriculture constitutes only about one-third (33.6 per cent) of the whole. Engineering occupies about the same relative space in the two institutions, 12.3 per cent and 12.7 per cent, respectively.

Instead of the department of agriculture dominating the situation at the agricultural college, as might naturally be expected, it is almost

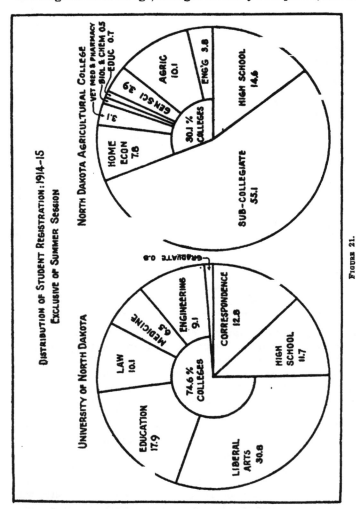

FIGURE 21.

Approximately three-fourths (74.6 per cent) of the students at the university are of college grade, as compared with less than one-third (30.1 per cent) at the agricultural college. Engineering constitutes less than 10 per cent of the work of the university and less than 4 per cent of that of the agricultural college.

equaled in importance by engineering, general science, education, and pharmacy, which, combined, register 33.3 per cent of the college students.

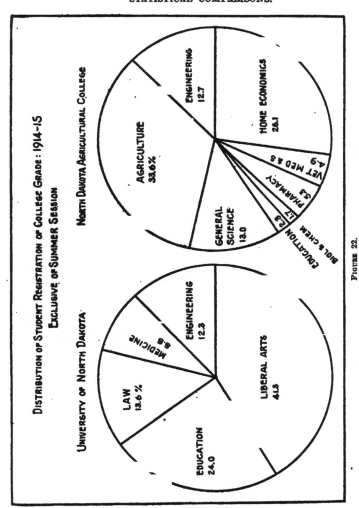

FIGURE 22.

A comparison of the student registrations of college grade only shows that 41.3 per cent of the university students are in liberal arts courses and only 33.6 per cent of the agricultural college are in agricultural courses. Engineering occupies about the same relative space in the two institutions, 12.3 per cent and 12.7 per cent, respectively.

TABLE 29.—*Distribution of student registration, 1914–15, exclusive of summer session.*

Departments.	University of North Dakota.		North Dakota Agricultural College.	
	Number.	Per cent.	Number.	Per cent.
Graduate	7	0.8		
Colleges	675	74.6	283	30.1
Subcollegiate			518	55.1
High school	107	11.7	138	14.6
Correspondence	116	12.8		
Total	905	100.0	939	100.0

TABLE 30.—*Distribution of student registration of college grade, 1914–15, exclusive of summer session.*

Departments.	University of North Dakota.		North Dakota Agricultural College.	
	Number.	Per cent.	Number.	Per cent.
Agriculture			95	33.6
Biology			1	.3
Chemistry			4	1.4
Engineering	83	12.3	36	12.7
Education	162	24.0	7	2.3
Home economics			74	26.1
Law	92	13.6		
Liberal arts, general science	279	41.3	37	13.0
Medicine	59	8.8		
Pharmacy			15	5.2
Veterinary medicine and surgery			14	4.9
Total	675	100.0	283	100.0

The geographical distribution of resident students enrolled in the eight institutions, exclusive of summer session, for the school year 1914–15 is shown in Table 31. The distribution by counties in North Dakota is exhibited also in figure 23.

TABLE 31.—*Distribution of resident students, exclusive of summer school (except at Valley City), eight institutions, 1914–15.*

Sources.	University.	Agricultural college.	Normal School, Valley City.	Normal School, Mayville.	Normal School, Minot.	Normal and Industrial School, Ellendale.	School of Science, Wahpeton.	School of Forestry, Bottineau.	Total, 8 institutions.
COUNTIES IN NORTH DAKOTA.									
Adams	1	2	9				1		13
Barnes	13	32	299						344
Benson	8	24	21	11	4				68
Billings	1	3	3						7
Bottineau	9	17	15	9	11		2	179	242
Bowman		13	4			1	2		20
Burke	5				15				20
Burleigh	5	12	26			7			50
Cass	16	234	49	6			7		302
Cavalier	15	25	20	16	1	1			78
Dickey	3	8	13			211			235
Divide	4	1	6		5	2			18
Dunn	2	2	1						5
Eddy	3	8	18		1		1		31
Emmons	2	3	10	5		8			28
Foster	8	8	27				3		46
Golden Valley	1	4	3						8
Grand Forks	194	26	4	29	1				254
Griggs	3	10	13						26
Hettinger		1	7						8
Kidder		6	14				2		22
Lamoure	9	16	26			14	1		66
Logan	1	1	2			5			9
McHenry	14	21	11	3	6				55
McIntosh		1				3			4
McKenzie	1	7	1	1	2			1	13
McLean		17	7	1	4	3	6		38
Mercer		1	3			2			6
Morton	8	19	46			2			75
Mountraill	1	4	2	1	5				13
Nelson	19	24	4	16					63
Oliver		3	5			2			10
Pembina	47	23	18	3		1			92
Pierce	1	8	3	7	4				23

TABLE 31.—*Distribution of resident students, exclusive of summer school (except at Valley City), eight institutions, 1914–15*—Continued.

Sources.	University.	Agricultural college.	Normal School, Valley City.	Normal School, Mayville.	Normal School, Minot.	Normal and Industrial School, Ellendale.	School of Science, Wahpeton.	School of Forestry, Bottineau.	Total, 8 institutions.
COUNTIES IN NORTH DAKOTA—continued.									
Ramsey	26	41	17	13	1			2		98
Ransom	9	48	24	1		1	2		85
Renville	5	9		1	19		1	4	39
Richland	10	14	22	7			190		243
Rolette	7	6	3	16			3	3	38
Sargent	2	10	29	1		18	13		73
Sheridan		4	21			1			26
Sioux			1						1
Slope			2		1	1			4
Stark	9	10	8						27
Steele	4	10	14	26					54
Stutsman	9	29	59			4	1		102
Towner	6	17		7	1				31
Traill	26	27	4	162		1			220
Walsh	38	31	18	14	1		3		105
Ward	19	13	5	1	95				133
Wells	3	11	32		2				48
Williams	16	8	9		4				37
OTHER STATES.									
Idaho	1								1
Illinois	4	3	1						8
Indiana	1	5	3	1	1				11
Iowa	1	5	5	2		1	1		15
Kansas	2				1		1		4
Kentucky		1	2	1					4
Maryland		1							1
Massachusetts	1		2			1			2
Michigan	1					1	4		7
Minnesota	67	109	72	14	11	8	105	1	387
Missouri	1	1			1				3
Montana	6	14	12	1	3	2	4		42
Nebraska			1					1	2
New Hampshire	1								1
New York	3		1						4
Oklahoma	1	1							2
Oregon	2								2
Pennsylvania	1								1
South Dakota	2	17	2	2		23	11		57
Texas							1		1
Washington	1	2				1			4
Wisconsin	4	12	7	4	2	4	1	1	35
OTHER COUNTRIES.									
Canada	2	1	2	1	1	1	1		9
England		1							1
Hawaii	1								1
Japan		1				1			3
Norway		1					2		3
Scotland	1								1
Sweden	1						1		2
SUMMARY.									
Counties of North Dakota	583	862	958	357	183	288	238	187	3,656
Other States	99	171	108	27	18	40	128	3	594
Other countries	5	3	2	1	1	2	4		18
Total outside of North Dakota	104	174	110	28	19	42	132	3	612
Grand total	687	1,036	1,068	385	202	330	370	190	4,268

TABLE 32.—*Number of graduates of the eight institutions.*

School years.	University.	Agricultural college.	Normal School, Valley City.	Normal School, Mayville.	Normal School, Minot.	Normal and Industrial School, Ellendale.	School of Science, Wahpeton.	School of Forestry, Bottineau.	Total, 8 institutions.
1900-1901	34	7	11	15	....	3	....	....	70
1901-2	28	4	18	22	....	12	....	....	84
1902-3	52	2	38	21	....	6	....	....	119
1903-4	62	7	23	26	....	16	....	....	144
1904-5	55	5	48	23	....	14	....	....	155
1905-6	62	8	69	54	....	12	....	....	205
1906-7	86	5	88	49	....	2	10	....	230
1907-8	93	12	109	51	....	22	19	....	306
1908-9	88	19	145	56	....	16	48	....	372
1909-10	99	10	133	40	....	33	44	5	362
1910-11	132	24	149	33	....	35	43	4	420
1911-12	83	23	160	62	....	47	50	6	431
1912-13	130	36	155	65	....	33	57	1	477
1913-14	120	37	185	75	16	43	34	11	521
1914-15	133	33	216	63	35	52	40	9	581
From date of opening to 1899-1900	140	15	46	71	....	....	....	....	278
1900-1901 to 1909-10, inclusive	659	79	692	367	....	135	121	5	2,053
1910-11 to 1914-15, inclusive	598	153	865	296	51	210	224	31	2,430
Total from date of opening to 1914-15, inclusive	1,397	247	1,603	736	51	345	345	36	4,760

Graduates.—The number of graduates annually since 1900-1901 is shown also (Table 32) so far as the figures are available.

There were 140 graduates from the university in the 16 years prior to 1900, 659 in the 10 years following, and 598 in the 5 years ending 1914-15; total, 1,397.

The agricultural college graduated 15 students during the first 10 years of its existence, 79 during the next 10 years, and 153 in the 5 years ending 1914-15; total, 247.

The Valley City Normal School graduated 46 students during its first 10 years, 692 during the next 10 years, and 865 during the 5 years ending 1914-15; total, 1,603.

The Mayville Normal School graduated 71 students during its first 10 years, 367 during the next 10 years, and 298 during the 5 years ending 1914-15; total, 736.

The Minot Normal School graduated 16 students the first year, and 35 the second; total, 51.

The number of graduates of the Ellendale school for the 10 years following 1900 is 135; for the 5 years ending 1914-15, 210; total, as reported, 345.

The total number of graduates from the School of Science at Wahpeton, as reported, is 345.

The School of Forestry at Bottineau has graduated 36 students in 6 years.

The total number of graduates of the 8 institutions, as reported, ranged from 70 in 1900-1901, and 420 in 1910-11, to 581 in 1914-15.

For the period preceding 1900, the graduates numbered 272; for the 10 years following, 2,058; for the 5 years ending 1914–15, 2,430; total, 4,760.

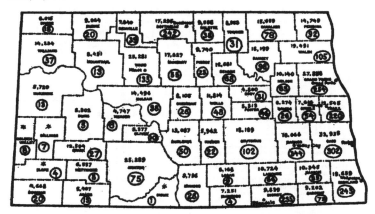

Fig. 23.—Distribution of resident students enrolled in 8 institutions in North Dakota, exclusive of summer session (except at Valley City, 1914–15). (See Table 31.)

The figures above the county name in each case give the population in 1910. At that date the population of Golden Valley County (later divided into Golden Valley, Billings, and Slope Counties) was 10,186; and the population of Morton County (later divided into Morton and Sioux Counties) was 25,289.

The figures inclosed in the circle in each case indicate the number of students from the county who are enrolled at the 8 institutions combined.

The 8 institutions drew 3,656 students from the 52 counties of North Dakota (of whom 53.9 per cent came from the 8 counties in which the institutions are located) and 612 from without the State; total, 4,268.

In 1910 the population of North Dakota was 577,056. Approximately 60 per cent (estimated 55 per cent in 1916) of the population were found in that portion of the State located east of the western boundary lines of the counties of Rolette, Pierce, Wells, Kidder, Logan, and McIntosh, which divide the State into two nearly equal parts, and 40 per cent were found in the portion west of this line; whereas, of the 3,656 North Dakota students in residence at the 8 institutions, approximately 76 per cent came from the territory east of the line indicated, and only about 24 per cent from west of this line.

A line drawn on the map from Grand Forks through Mayville, Valley City, and Ellendale to Wahpeton, together with the eastern boundary of the State, describes a territory which includes all of the educational institutions except those at Minot and Bottineau. The 10 counties included, with an aggregate of 7,506,560 acres, constitute 16.7 per cent of the area of the State, and with an aggregate population of 159,819 contain 27.7 per cent of the population of the State; on the other hand, these 10 counties furnish 1,876, or 51.3 per cent of all the students that North Dakota sends to the 8 institutions (3,656).

Outside of the 8 counties in which the institutions are located, only 18 counties are represented by more than 50 students per county at the 8 institutions combined.

Of the 52 counties, 22 have fewer than 30 students per county at the 8 institutions combined, and with an aggregate of 311 have fewer students in all of their own State institutions than the neighboring State of Minnesota, which is represented by 387 students in North Dakota.

Salaries.—The maximum salaries paid to members of the instructional staffs in the 8 institutions, exclusive of presidents, range from $1,500 at Bottineau to $3,700 at the agricultural college (Table 33).

The minimum salaries range from $100 at the university to $1,140 at Minot. The average salaries range from $991.66 at Bottineau to $1,870.54 at the agricultural college.

TABLE 33.—*Instructional staffs, eight institutions, 1914–15.*

	University.	Agricultural college.	Normal School, Valley City.	Normal School, Mayville.	Normal School, Minot.
1. Salaries of instructional staff, exclusive of president, 1914–15:					
a. Maximum salary paid	$3,200	$3,700	$2,500	$2,500	$2,000
b. Minimum salary paid	$100	$595	$585	$1,050	$1,140
c. Total amount paid for salaries	$126,437	$86,045	$64,920	$22,689.16	$20,757
d. Number of instructors reporting	70	47	48	14	15
e. Average salary	$1,806.24	$1,870.54	$1,360.00	$1,692.08	$1,383.13
2. Teaching activities of instructional staff, exclusive of president, 1914–15:					
a. Maximum number of class periods weekly	30	41	45	25	44
b. Minimum number of class periods weekly	3	5	16	5	10
c. Aggregate number of class periods weekly	1,269	1,092	1,279	245	424
d. Average number of class periods weekly	18.1	23.2	27.8	19.3	28.2
3. Education and professional preparation of members of instructional staff, exclusive of president, 1915–16:					
a. Number of instructors reporting	82	52	50	14	15
b. Number holding doctor's degree	23	7	2		1
c. Number holding master's degree	36	13	11	3	2
d. Number holding bachelor's degree	78	40	26	13	11
e. Number reporting college work, but without degree	3	6	6		2
f. Number of normal school graduates	16	7	31	5	9
g. Number reporting normal school work, but without graduating	4	5	6	7	2
h. Number reporting no education above high school		3			
4. Number of members of instructional staff, exclusive of president, who report giving public addresses, lectures, or recitals, Sept. 1, 1914, to Jan. 1, 1916	45	29	1	5	3
5. Aggregate number of addresses, lectures, and recitals reported	345	310	10	37	150

	Normal and Industrial School, Ellendale.	School of Science, Wahpeton.	School of Forestry, Bottineau.	Total, 8 institutions.
1. Salaries of instructional staff, exclusive of president, 1914–15:				
a. Maximum salary paid	$1,800	$1,800	$1,500	$3,700
b. Minimum salary paid	$300	$315	$675	$100
c. Total amount paid for salaries	$20,550	$22,500	$5,950	$370,848.16
d. Number of instructors reporting	19	19	6	238
e. Average salary	$1,061.58	$1,184.21	$991.66	$1,558.18
2. Teaching activities of instructional staff, exclusive of president, 1914–15:				
a. Maximum number of class periods weekly	45	40	45	45
b. Minimum number of class periods weekly	11	7	5	3
c. Aggregate number of class periods weekly	643	523	172	5,647
d. Average number of class periods weekly	33.8	27.5	28.6	23.7
3. Education and professional preparation of members of instructional staff, exclusive of president, 1915–16:				
a. Number of instructors reporting	21	19	7	260
b. Number holding doctor's degree				33
c. Number holding master's degree	1	4		70
d. Number holding bachelor's degree	13	9	4	194
e. Number reporting college work, but without degree	3	6	2	28
f. Number of normal school graduates	8	3		79
g. Number reporting normal school work, but without graduating	4	2	2	32
h. Number reporting no education above high school		2		6
4. Number of members of instructional staff, exclusive of president, who report giving public addresses, lectures, or recitals, Sept. 1, 1914, to Jan. 1, 1916	13	2	5	103
5. Aggregate number of addresses, lectures, and recitals reported	126	5	31	1,014

Teaching activities.—The maximum numbers of class periods taught weekly per instructor range from 25 at Mayville to 45 at Valley City, Ellendale, and Bottineau (Table 33). The minimum numbers of class periods range from 3 at the university to 16 at Valley City. The average numbers of class periods range from 18.1 at the university to 33.8 at Ellendale.

Professional preparation.—The standards of scholarship maintained in the 8 faculties are not high, so far as evidence is to be found in higher degrees held (Table 33). Of 260 instructors, only 33 hold the doctor's degree, 70 hold the master's degree, and 194 hold the bachelors degree. Only 53 of the 100 instructors in the four normal schools are normal-school graduates. Six instructors, in three institutions, report having had no schooling above high school.

Public addresses.—More than half of the instructors at the university and agricultural college report giving public addresses, lectures, and recitals; whereas, of the 100 instructors in the 4 normal schools, only 22 have been active recently in this kind of work (Table 33).

Student attendance.—The student attendance for the year 1914–15 is shown by terms (Table 34). Combining the first semester attendance at the university with the winter term attendance at the other seven institutions, including the winter short course students at the agricultural college, the maximum aggregate enrollment for any one period is 3,357.

TABLE 34.—*Student attendance, by terms, eight institutions, 1914–15.*

Terms.	University.	Agricultural college.	Normal School, Valley City.	Normal School, Mayville.	Normal School, Minot.	Normal and Industrial School, Ellendale.	School of Science, Wahpeton.	School of Forestry, Bottineau.	Total, 8 institutions
First semester	759								759
Second semester	708								708
Fall term		606	567	202	201	143	153	102	1,974
Winter term		607	624	224	201	305	226	125	2,322
Spring term		312	542	191	201	220	155	46	1,667
Summer term	336	111	423	190	330	212	100	5	1,707
Special or short terms		276							276

High-school credits.—Of the 2,768 students reported as entering the eight institutions in 1914–15, fewer than one-third, 881, presented 15 or more high-school credits; of these, 214 entered the university, 98 entered the agricultural college, and 449 entered the four normal schools (Table 35). Of the 1,887 students presenting less than 15 high-school credits, 30 entered the university, 252 entered the agricultural college, and 1,168 entered the four normal schools. The fact that the normal schools receive such large numbers of students of this class, of whom 339 average but 16 years of age and 162 average 16.3 years of age, suggests that these institutions are undertaking a difficult task in attempting to give professional training to young people of insufficient maturity and inadequate previous preparation.

TABLE 35.—*Numbers and average ages of students presenting specified number of high-school credits at entrance, eight institutions, 1914–15.*

	University.	Agricultural college.	Normal School, Valley City.	Normal School, Mayville.	Normal School, Minot.	Normal and Industrial School, Ellendale.	School of Science, Wahpeton.	School of Forestry, Bottineau.	Total, 8 institutions.
Number of students presenting 15 or more high-school credits at entrance..........	214	98	324	46	39	40	107	13	881
Average age of students entering with 15 or more high-school credits..years..	18.8	19.5	(1)	19.0	20.2	19.5	20.5	19.5	....
Number of students presenting less than 15 high-school credits at entrance..........	30	252	376	339	162	291	263	174	1,887
Average age of students entering with less than 15 high-school credits..years..	19.5	19.1	(1)	16.0	16.3	17.5	18.9	17.5	....

1 Not reported.

Permanent investment and maintenance costs.—The State of North Dakota has $2,150,730.02 invested in buildings and $749,076.31 invested in equipment in the eight institutions, averaging over $500 for each student enrolled during the school year 1914–15 (Table 36). The amounts invested in buildings at the university and agricultural college provide for other activities in addition to those directly involved in giving instruction to students, which necessarily bring up the average investment per student enrolled.

In the cases of the normal schools a relatively small enrollment at Mayville, and a new plant not yet utilized to capacity at Minot, explain in part the wide variation in investment in buildings per student enrolled. The amounts range from $217.44, at Valley City, to $708.56, at Minot. The amounts invested in equipment at the normal schools per student enrolled range from $9.98, at Mayville to $117.01, at Ellendale.

The amounts of total income of normal schools for 1914–15 per student enrolled range from $73.96, at Valley City, to $152.94, at Mayville.

TABLE 36.—*Investment in buildings and equipment and total income per student enrolled in 1914–15, eight institutions.*

	University.[1]	Agricultural College.[1]	Normal School, Valley City.	Normal School, Mayville.	Normal School, Minot.
Total investment to date in buildings.....	$508,597.05	$554,800.00	$353,350.00	$180,675.00	$255,712.00
Investment in buildings per student enrolled in 1914–15......................	409.82	473.78	217.44	447.21	708.56
Total investment to date in equipment, exclusive of grounds....................	272,069.54	315,730.00	59,504.67	4,032.95	27,337.00
Investment in equipment per student enrolled in 1914–15...................	219.23	269.62	36.61	9.98	75.56
Total income, school year 1914–15.........	400,743.55	439,382.45	120,192.96	61,779.86	54,533.36
Total income per student enrolled in 1914–15................................	322.91	366.59	73.96	152.94	145.42

	Normal and Industrial School, Ellendale.	School of Science, Wahpeton.	School of Forestry, Bottineau.	Total, 8 institutions.
Total investment to date in buildings...............	$126,575.97	$113,020.00	$58,000.00	$2,150,730.02
Investment in buildings per student enrolled in 1914–15	394.31	216.51	310.16	376.59
Total investment to date in equipment, exclusive of grounds...	37,563.00	25,082.25	7,756.90	749,076.31
Investment in equipment per student enrolled in 1914–15.....................................	117.01	48.05	41.48	131.16
Total income, school year 1914–15.....................	48,197.20	34,280.77	12,283.51	1,161,393.66
Total income per student enrolled in 1914–15........	150.14	65.67	65.69	203.36

[1] Includes experiment stations and other noninstructional activities, since it was impossible to distinguish clearly in the accounts as reported.

The School of Science and the School of Forestry have approximately the same amounts invested in equipment per student enrolled, $48.05 and $41.48, respectively, and the same total income per student, $65.67 and $65.69, respectively. The investment in buildings per student enrolled in 1914–15 was $216.51 at the School of Science and $310,16 at the School of Forestry.

DISTRIBUTION OF GRADUATES BY OCCUPATION.

The graduates of the six institutions reporting are summarized in Table 37 according to their present occupations. It is very unfortunate that records have not been kept to show the present occupations of the 1,397 graduates of the university and the 736 graduates of the normal school at Mayville. These two groups together constitute 45.1 per cent of the total number of graduates of the eight institutions, 4,729.

TABLE 37.—*Distribution of graduates by occupation.*[1]

Occupation groups.	Agricultural College, Fargo.	Normal School, Valley City.	Normal School, Minot.	Normal and Industrial School, Ellendale.	School of Science, Wahpeton.	School of Forestry, Bottineau.	Total, six institutions.
1. Agricultural pursuits	66			8	47	3	124
a. Farming	34			8	47	3	92
b. Investigation, extension, and station work	32						32
2. Professional pursuits	123	1,034	46	216	100	23	1,542
a. Teachers, school officers	79	964	41	126	50	6	1,266
b. Students	16	46	5	75	21	12	175
c. Engineering	18			6	11		35
d. Lawyers, political officers	1	11		5	9	2	28
e. Physicians, dentists, nurses	6	9		3	3	3	24
f. Other professional service	3	4		1	6		14
3. Commercial pursuits	31	58		31	137	7	264
a. In business	24	53		26	36	7	146
b. Banking	2	5		3	25		35
c. Stenographers, bookkeepers, clerks	5			2	76		83
4. Home makers, married (women)	20	381	3	79	53	2	538
5. Mechanics					3		3
6. Deceased	9			7			16
7. Occupation not reported		130	2	4	5		141
8. Total	249	1,603	51	345	345	35	2,628

[1] Records of the present occupations of 1,397 graduates of the university, and of the 736 graduates of the normal school at Mayville, are not available.

Of the 2,628 graduates of the six institutions for whom information is available, only 249 are contributed by the agricultural college; and of these only 66 are reported as engaged in agricultural pursuits. So far as its graduates are concerned, therefore, the agricultural college is not the factor in the vocational life of the people of the State that it should be. Three normal schools contribute 1,999 graduates, of whom 1,131 are teaching and 126 are students. More than one-tenth of all the graduates reported, 264, are engaged in commercial pursuits, and more than one-fifth, 538, are home makers.

The graduates of the university for the years 1888–89 to 1914–15, inclusive, classified by departments, are distributed as follows:

	Graduates.	Per cent.
Professional schools	985	70.5
Law	311	22.2
Engineering	107	7.6
Education	513	36.6
Medicine	14	1.0
School for nurses	3	.9
Graduate school	37	2.6
College of liberal arts	412	29.5
Grand total	1,397	100.0

The graduates of the agricultural college for the years 1894–95 to 1914–15, inclusive, classified by departments, are distributed as follows:

	Graduates.	Per cent.
Agriculture	75	30. 1
Engineering	38	15. 3
Science	75	30. 1
General science	61	24. 5
Chemistry	8	3. 2
Biology	3	1. 2
Pharmaceutical chemistry	3	1. 2
Home economics	57	22. 9
Education	4	1. 6
Total	249	100. 0

In figure 24 the percentage distribution of the graduates, by occupation, is compared with the census distribution of gainful occupations in North Dakota, 1910. The graduates of the six institutions are distributed as follows: Agricultural pursuits, 4.7 per cent; professional, 59.4 per cent; commercial, 10.1 per cent; mechanical, 0.1 per cent; home making, 20.7 per cent; all others, 4.9 per cent. According to the 1910 census the percentage distribution of persons engaged in gainful occupations in North Dakota was as follows: Agricultural pursuits (including " agriculture, forestry, and animal husbandry "), 60.2 per cent; professional (including " professional service " and " public service not elsewhere classified "), 5.2 per cent; commercial (including " trade " and " clerical service "), 10.1 per cent; mechanical (including " manufacturing and mechanical industries " and " extraction of minerals ") 10 per cent; home making, not enumerated; all others, 14.4 per cent.

The comparison emphasizes in a striking manner the fact that the State educational institutions in North Dakota are not adjusted to the vocational needs of the State, so far as the contributions made by the institutions are indicated in the occupations chosen by the graduates. Measured in these terms, North Dakota is spending approximately 60 per cent of her effort in State-supported educational institutions to prepare men and women for the *professions*, which represent only about 5 per cent of the vocational opportunities in the State, while devoting less than 5 per cent of her effort to preparation for *agricultural pursuits*, which represent 60 per cent of the occupations enumerated.

That this is a radical departure from the original policy which led to the founding of the institutions is apparent in the language used in the laws establishing them, and a study of the distribution of appropriations for the school year 1914–15 indicates that at the present time it is the evident intention of the State to give relatively less emphasis to preparation for the professions than actually is given. As shown in Table 38, 41 per cent of the cost of maintaining the eight institutions was definitely incurred for agricultural and industrial education. It is to be noted that in this table the Normal and Industrial School at Ellendale is included in the normal school

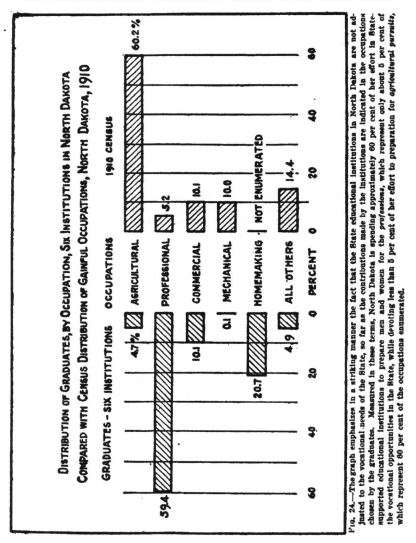

FIG. 24.—The graph emphasizes in a striking manner the fact that the State educational institutions in North Dakota are not adjusted to the vocational needs of the State, so far as the contributions made by the institutions are indicated in the occupations chosen by the graduates. Measured in these terms, North Dakota is spending approximately 60 per cent of her effort in State-supported educational institutions to prepare men and women for the *professions*, which represent only about 5 per cent of the vocational opportunities in the State, while devoting less than 5 per cent of her effort to preparation for *agricultural pursuits*, which represent 60 per cent of the occupations enumerated.

list, since the training of teachers appears to be its chief function at the present time, although it was originally established as an industrial school.

TABLE 38.—*Income of institutions for 1914–15.*

Institutions.	Amount.	Per cent.
University and normal schools:		
University	$400,743.55	
Valley City	120,192.96	
Mayville	61,779.86	
Minot	54,533.36	
Ellendale	48,197.20	
Total	685,446.66	59.0
Agricultural college and industrial schools:		
Agricultural college	429,382.45	
Wahpeton	34,280.77	
Bottineau	12,283.51	
Total	475,946.73	41.0
Grand total	1,161,393.66	100.0

It would be an error to conclude that the State institutions should prepare fewer persons for the professions. There is abundant evidence that the supply of trained teachers, especially, is entirely inadequate.

It would be an error also to assume that the facts presented are inconclusive with respect to the point here made, by reason of the omission of the records of 2,008 graduates of two institutions. If the present occupations of all the graduates of the university, including the graduates of the professional schools of law, medicine, engineering, and education, and of the graduates of the Mayville Normal School were known and added to the tabulation, it is reasonably certain that a far larger proportion of them would be classified under "professional pursuits" than under "agricultural pursuits." It can not be contended that in a distribution of the total number of graduates the "agricultural" group would probably constitute a materially greater percentage of the whole than is shown in figure 24, nor that the "professional" group would be much smaller proportionately than that indicated.

Further, it would be unfair to assume that the contribution made to agricultural education by the institutions in North Dakota is actually in proportion to the number of graduates who engage in agricultural pursuits, since many persons who are not graduates have received practical and helpful instruction in farming, and the agricultural interests of the State are benefited in many other ways than by the registration of students in agricultural courses.

After making due allowance for all of these considerations, however, the figures given emphasize the great need of agricultural education in North Dakota.

Some figures given in a recent study furnish additional evidence that the demand for higher education in North Dakota has not been fully met.[1] According to this study there were 213 young persons from North Dakota enrolled as students in 27 of the leading colleges and universities outside the State during the academic year 1914–15, as follows: University of California, 3; Cincinnati, 1; Columbia, 18; Cornell, 5; Harvard, 3; Illinois, 15; Iowa State, 4; Johns Hopkins, 4; Michigan, 8; Minnesota, 60; Missouri, 2; Northwestern, 38; Ohio State, 2; Stanford, 2; Syracuse, 2; Tulane, 4; Virginia, 1; Western Reserve, 1; Wisconsin, 25; Yale, 3; Dartmouth, 1; Massachusetts Institute of Technology, 3; Purdue, 3; Williams, 2; Smith, 1; Vassar, 1; Wellesley, 1; total, 213.

SIZE OF CLASSES AT EIGHT INSTITUTIONS.

At the request of the survey commission the president of each institution prepared a detailed report on the number of students in attendance during the week of April 10–16, 1916. A summary of these reports is presented in Table 39.

TABLE 39.—*Data on size of classes for the week of April 10–16, 1916.*

Number of students attending.	Meetings of classes.								
	Total.	University.	Agricultural college.	Valley City.	Mayville.	Minot.	Ellendale.	Wahpeton.	Bottineau.
1	143	47	55	11			6	10	14
2	195	60	35	13			4	53	30
3	116	37	33	24			4	5	13
4	208	47	50	27		5	22	36	21
5	139	34	29	18	5	5	11	25	12
6–9	553	162	93	89	11	20	79	79	20
10–14	537	122	68	101	44	36	93	66	7
15–19	414	86	41	138	56	29	47	12	5
20–29	588	148	35	203	89	28	61	19	5
30–39	187	50	10	39	38	44	1		5
40–49	94	9	2	47	6	25	5		
50 and over	39	14	3	11		11			
Total	3,213	816	454	721	249	203	333	305	132

During the week in question there were in the eight State institutions, 143 meetings of classes at which only 1 student was in attendance, 195 meetings at which 2 students were present, 116 meetings at which 3 students were present, and 208 meetings at which 4 students were present; a total of 662 meetings of classes in the 8 institutions having less than 5 students in attendance. These 662 meetings of classes constitute slightly more than one-fifth, 20.6 per cent, of the entire number meeting during the week, 3,213.

That is, assuming an average cost per meeting of class, 20.6 per cent of the cost of instruction for the week was incurred for the maintenance of classes having less than 5 students each. Or, to put

[1] J. C. Burg: The Geographical Distribution of the Student Body at a Number of Universities and Colleges; *School and Society*, Nov. 6, 1915, pp. 676–683.

it in another way, of every dollar expended for. instruction, 20.6 cents was expended for meetings of classes of 1 to 4 students each. ·

Considerable variation among the institutions in this respect is disclosed by the table, ranging from no meetings of less than 5 students at the State Normal School at Mayville, to more than one-half the entire number at the School of Forestry at Bottineau.

Combining the figures for meetings of classes of less than 10 students, an equally startling situation is disclosed. Of a total of 3,213 meetings of classes, 1,354 or 42.1 per cent, were attended by less than 10 students.

Table 40 presents a list of classes attended by not more than 5 students at any meeting of the class during the week in question.

TABLE 40.—*Meetings of classes attended by not more than five students during the week April 10–16, 1916.*

[This list does not include any class reporting an attendance of six or more students at any meeting of the class during the week.]

Subjects and catalogue numbers.	Number of sessions.	Number of students.	Subjects and catalogue numbers.	Number of sessions.	Number of students.
UNIVERSITY.			UNIVERSITY—continued.		
Biology 6	1	3	Sociology 4	2	4
Biology 24	1	1	Sociology 14	4	3
Botany 16	5	1	Education 110	1	4
Botany 8	4	4-5	Education 112	1	4
Botany 20	1	1	Education	2	2
Chemistry 18	2	2	Education 108	2	3
Do	3	2	Education 158	2	2
Graduate chemistry	4	1	Education 152	2	4
Chemistry 14	2	3	Principles of nursing	2	3-4
Glass working	1	1	Mechanical engineering 8 (4)	2	5
Economics 28	2	3	Mechanical engineering 10	5	1
Economics 54	2	1	Mechanical engineering X 34	1	5
Labor problems	2	5	Architectural drawing	2	2
History of socialism	4	1	Electrical engineering 2	4	2
Economic theory	1	1	Electrical engineering 14	3	1
Education specials	1	2	Electrical engineering thesis	1	3
Education 20	2	4	Mechanical engineering X 36 (2)	1	2
Do	2	3	Mechanical engineering X 36 (1)	1	4
English 20	1	3	Mechanical engineering 32	1	1
English 24	4	1-5	Mechanical engineering X 44	1	5
English 32	2	5	Mechanical engineering 6	2	1
English 6	2	4	Machine shop 8	2	1
English 10	2	3	Machine shop 6	2	2
English 30	2	2	Machine shop 5	2	4
Geology 10	2	4	Industrial engineering chemistry	2	4
Geology 8	3	2	Graduate chemistry	4	1
Geology 22	1	5	Ceramics	2	4
German 15	3	3	Mining engineering 2	3	4
Greek 2	4	5	Do	2	2
Greek 4	4	4-5	Metallurgy 2	4	2-5
Greek 10	2	4	Ore treatment	5	2-3
History 7	3	5	Experimental testing	6	2
History 18	2	3-4	Industrial engineering chemistry 10	4	4
Latin 2	4	4	Industrial engineering chemistry 12	4	2
Latin 6	3	3	Analytical work	6	2
Latin 8	1	4	Ceramics 6 (a)	2	3
Latin 10	4	4-5			
Manual training II	5	4	AGRICULTURAL COLLEGE.		
Manual training III	5	2			
Manual training advanced	3	2	Thesis class (agronomy)	2	2
Mathematics 8	2	1	Dairying 5	2	4
Physics 6	2	1	Dairying 6	2	4
Physics 12	4	1	Dairying 8	3	4
Physics 14	1	1			
Physics 16	3	3			
French 6	3	2			
Norse 160	1	1			
Swedish 11, 12	2	1			

TABLE 40.—*Meetings of classes attended, etc.*—Continued.

Subjects and catalogue numbers.	Number of sessions.	Number of students.	Subjects and catalogue numbers.	Number of sessions.	Number of students.
AGRICULTURAL COLLEGE—con.			STATE NORMAL SCHOOL, VALLEY CITY—continued.		
Animal husbandry 9	3	4-5	Mechanical drawing 1	5	3
Agronomy 8	2	3	Mechanical drawing 2	5	1
Agronomy 9	2	3	Copperwork	5	1
Agronomy 10	2	2-3	Shopwork	5	4
Thesis class (agronomy)	3	2	Physical education methods	3	3
Botany 3	2	3	Methods of coaching	3	3
Botany 18	2	2	Hygiene and sanitation	5	4
Botany 13	1	1	Apparatus work (gymnasium)	2	2
Botany 17 (1)	5	1	STATE NORMAL SCHOOL, MAYVILLE.		
Botany 17 (2)	3	1			
Bacteriology 13	3	4	General English literature	5	5
Bacteriology 9	3	4	STATE NORMAL SCHOOL, MINOT.		
Bacteriology 10	2	3			
Bacteriology 12	4	1	Household management	5	4
Bacteriology 11	4	5	School administration	5	5
Chemistry 13	3	3	STATE NORMAL AND INDUSTRIAL SCHOOL, ELLENDALE.		
Chemistry 8 (2)	3	4			
Chemistry 24	5	1	Civics	5	4
Pharmacy 12	4	3-4	Latin I	5	1
Education 14	1	3	Latin III	5	1-2
English 15	4	3-5	Qualitative chemistry	3	4-5
Philosophy 3	4	3-4	Trigonometry, surveying	5	4
English 21	4	4-5	Preparatory English	5	5
Special work (English)	3	2-3	Preparatory arithmetic	5	5
Mechanical engineering 38	4	2	Preparatory history	5	3-4
Civil engineering 4	4	1	STATE SCHOOL OF SCIENCE, WAHPETON.		
Civil engineering 4 (1)	4	1			
Civil engineering 17	4	1	College algebra	5	5
Civil engineering 19	4	1	Physics I	5	3-4
Civil engineering 8	5	3	Mechanism	5	2
Mechanical engineering 15	3	3	Botany	5	2
Mechanical engineering 29	2	3	German b	5	2
Mechanical engineering 23	2	4	German I	5	2
Mechanical engineering 28	2	3	German II	5	4
Mechanical engineering 3	2	1	Latin a	5	2
Mechanical engineering 39	5	1	Telephony	5	2-3
Mechanical engineering 9	2	5	Wireless telegraphy	5	2
Mechanical engineering 10	2	3-5	Machine shop	2	4
Mechanical engineering 7	5		Wood shop	2	4
Mechanical engineering 11	3	1	Dietetics	5	1
Mechanical engineering 14	1	1	Textiles	5	2
Architecture 19	2	1	Home nursing 2	5	4
Architecture 15	2	1	Food study	5	4
Architecture 16	2	1	Plain sewing 1	5	5
Architecture 6	2	2	Plain sewing 2	5	5
Architecture 13	2	2	Dressmaking	2	5
Architecture 18	5	1	Senior cooking	3	4
Architecture 9	2	2	Millinery	5	4
Domestic science 18	2	3	Shorthand 1	5	4
Mathematics 14	2	4	Shorthand 2	5	2
Mathematics 17	2	2	Shorthand 3	5	4
Mathematics 16	2	5	Typewriting 1	5	4
German 9	2	2-3	Typewriting 2	5	2
French 6	4	2-4	Typewriting 6	5	2
Public speaking 1	3	2	STATE SCHOOL OF FORESTRY, BOTTINEAU.		
Public speaking 6	2	4			
Public speaking 7	3	3	Sewing 1	5	3-4
Veterinary science 13	5	4-5	Cookery 1	5	4
Veterinary science 15	3	4	Shorthand I 1	5	2
Harmony	3	4	Shorthand II 1	5	5
Musical history	2	2	Typewriting II	5	5
Gymnasium 5	2	3	Mechanical drawing	5	5
Gymnasium 6	3	1	English I	5	1-2
STATE NORMAL SCHOOL, VALLEY CITY.			English II	5	1-2
			Advanced chemistry	5	2
Psychology 51a	5	5	College English	5	2-4
Singing method	3	4	Expression	5	2-3
Writing	3	5	United States history	4	2
Commercial law	2	3-4	Ancient history	4	1
Mathematics 21	4	1	Poultry	5	1
Latin 23	5	3	Elementary woodwork	2	4
Latin 33	5	2	Wireless telegraphy	5	3
German 33	5	4	Music	5	1-5
English expression	4	4-5	Physiology	4	3-4
Expression	2	1-2			
Stenography 23	5	4			
Typewriting and transcribing 2	5	5			
Manual training methods	5	3			

ATTENDANCE.

Table 41 presents a summary of the reports on students attendance for the week of April 10–16, 1916. The total number of students reported as being in attendance upon one or more classes during the week is 2,259. The sum of the numbers of students attending all classes for the week is 46,617, an average of 20.6 times present per student. Only two institutions fall below this average, the university and the School of Forestry. Concerning the university, it may be noted that an average of nearly 16 meetings of classes per student per week accords with the conditions prevailing in college and university work. The low average per student for the School of Forestry, 7.7 classes per week, has been explained elsewhere (see p. 114).

TABLE 41.—*Data on attendance for the week of Apr. 10–16, 1916.*

	Total.	University.[1]	Agricultural college.[2]	Valley City.[3]	Mayville.[3]	Minot.[3]	Ellendale.	Wahpeton.	Bottineau.
Number of students reported..................	2,259	706	203	539	204	206	190	106	105
Aggregate number times present..................	46,617	11,174	4,187	13,542	5,389	4,958	4,249	2,351	817
Average number times present per student......	20.6	15.8	20.6	25.1	26.1	24.0	22.3	22.1	7.7
Aggregate number meetings of classes............	3,213	816	454	721	249	203	333	305	132
Average student attendance per class............	14.5	13.7	9.2	18.8	21.4	24.4	12.7	7.7	6.1

[1] Exclusive of students in model high school.
[2] Exclusive of students in agricultural and manual training high school.
[3] Exclusive of children in training school.

By dividing the number representing the aggregate number of times present during the week by the number of meetings of classes, an average number of students in attendance per class is obtained, 14.5. Two institutions fall very much below this average, the School of Science and the School of Forestry. The figures in Table 41, taken in conjunction with those in Table 42, suggest the desirability of further investigation to determine the justification for the continuance of small classes.

The figures for two institutions, on the other hand, show averages considerably in excess of the general average, the Normal Schools at Mayville and Minot. One fact partially explaining the high average of the Normal School at Minot does not appear in the summary; namely, in a considerable proportion of cases (approximately 40 per cent of the entire number of classes) students of high-school grade are admitted to the same classes in which graduates of accredited high schools are receiving instruction. This practice serves to keep down the number of separate courses and classes, and is perhaps not objectionable in certain subjects. Careful inquiry should be made

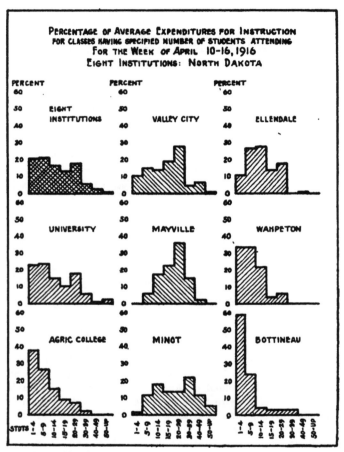

FIG. 25.—The wide range in the proportion of students taught in classes of one to four may be noted by comparing the height of the first left-hand rectangles in the distributions for Minot and Bottineau, respectively. Compare also the "20-29 students" rectangles at Mayville and Bottineau, respectively.

here to determine the point beyond which economy in this respect is detrimental to the interests of the real work of the normal school.

The facts set forth in Tables 39, 40, and 41 are reduced to a cost basis in Table 42, and presented in graphic form in figures 25 and 26.

TABLE 42.—*Relative cost of instruction for the week of Apr. 10–16, 1916.*

Number of students attending.	Of each dollar expended for instruction, the amount expended on classes having specified number of students.								
	Average.	University.	Agricultural college.	Valley City.	Mayville.	Minot.	Ellendale.	Wahpeton.	Bottineau.
1 to 4	$0.206	$0.234	$0.381	$0.104	....	$0.024	$0.108	$0.341	$0.501
5 to 9	.215	.240	.267	.148	$0.064	.123	.270	.341	.242
10 to 14	.167	.149	.149	.140	.176	.177	.279	.216	.053
15 to 19	.128	.105	.090	.191	.224	.142	.141	.039	.037
20 to 29	.183	.181	.077	.281	.361	.138	.183	.062	.037
30 to 39	.058	.061	.022	.054	.152	.216	.003	....	.037
40 to 49	.029	.011	.004	.065	.024	.123	.015	....	....
50 and over	.012	.017	.006	.015	....	.054	....	....	....

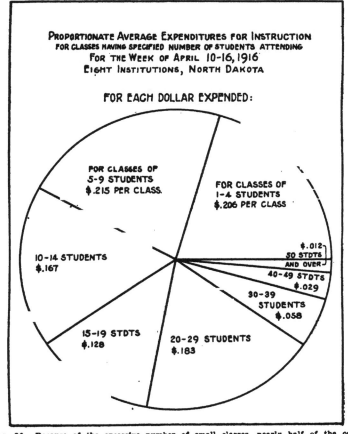

FIG. 26.—Because of the excessive number of small classes, nearly half of the cost of instruction is absorbed by classes having fewer than 10 students—$42.10 out of each $100.

Hasty conclusions should not be drawn from these figures (Table 42). The information available does not warrant arbitrary recommendations concerning the abolition of any or all of these small classes. The maintenance of a small class is a matter of internal administration, and frequently of expediency, and the decision should be reached only after careful examination of the facts in each case.

It seems evident, however, that there are in the eight institutions a number of courses the demand for which is not sufficient to justify their maintenance. The presidents of the institutions should be requested to scrutinize these lists with the greatest care for the purpose of eliminating all courses for which clear cases of necessity or expediency can not be made out.

If many courses essentially the same are given in two or more institutions with very small numbers taking them, it becomes desirable to consider carefully the relative need for such courses and the advisability of eliminating them from some of the institutions in the interest of economy to the end that the State may receive the largest possible service from its institutions. This is a matter for the cooperation of the board of regents and the administrative officers of the institutions concerned.

Chapter XI.

DUPLICATION OF COURSES AND CLASSES AT THE UNIVERSITY AND THE AGRICULTURAL COLLEGE.

In Table 43 is presented a list of the classes, arranged by departments, at the university and the agricultural college which held meetings during the week of April 10–16, 1916. At this time comparatively few irregular and short-course students were present at any of the institutions, but it is assumed that at all the institutions a very large majority of the students who attended through the year were present. The various courses are arranged in parallel columns to show to what extent there is duplication of work at the two institutions. Were all the courses outlined in the catalogues of the two institutions included, the table would be still more instructive; but so many of those offered had no students taking them that it is thought best to omit them from the table.[1] As noted elsewhere, the amount of objectionable duplication of work does not constitute a serious problem at the present time; it is not nearly so serious as that of the maintenance of a large number of very small classes. Some of these small classes, especially in the higher courses, are necessary and are not to be considered objectionable; but it is believed that, in the interest of efficiency, economy, and the best service of the State, this table should be studied very carefully both by the board of regents and by the executive officers and faculties of the institutions. The future of the two institutions must depend on a clear definition of their respective fields of effort, and a complete mutual understanding of their major aims and purposes.

If the recommendations made in this report for the avoidance of duplication at the university and the agricultural college had been made in April, 1916, only 11 classes and 30 students at the college would have been affected, counting the total number of attendants in all these classes and counting two or more times all such students as were enrolled in more than one of these classes.[2] Of these 30 students, 25 were in 7 junior classes and 5 in 4 senior classes. The commission is not sure that the courses designated as M. E. 15 and M. E. 29 might not be included under industrial engineering, as defined in this report. If they should be so included, then the total number of classes affected would have been only 9 and the total of class attendants only 24. No students of the university would have been affected.

---

[1] See Tables 55 and 56, Appendix XI.   [2] See Table 44.

TABLE 43.—*Meetings of classes held during the week*

University.				
Course number.	Subject.	Rank of instructor.	Meet-ings.	Students at-tending.
AGRICULTURE.				
ART AND DESIGN.				
Art and design... 2	Art and design	Instructor and assistant.	5	16,17,16,16,17
4	....do	Assistant	5	10,10,10,10,10
6	....do	Instructor	3	9,9,9
8	....do	...do	2	9,9
10	Art for teachers	...do	3	11,11,11
12	Applied art	...do	1	16
14	History of painting	...do	2	11,11
16	Appreciation of pictures	...do	1	12
BIOLOGY.				
Biology... 2	Evolution and heredity	Professor	2	16,16
6	Biological seminar	...do	1	3
22	Vertebrate comparative anatomy	...do	5	22,21,23,22,23
24	Research	...do	1	1
Botany... 8	Elementary plant physiology	Assistant professor	4	5,5,5,4
10	General botany	...do	4	6,6,7,7
16	Plant physiology	...do	5	1,1,1,1,1
20	Research	...do	1	1
CHEMISTRY.				
Chemistry... 2	General chemistry, lecture	Professor	3	54,111,53
2	General chemistry	Assistant professor	4	24,26,23,24
2 (1)	....do	Instructor	4	14,15,14,16
2 (2)	....do	...do	4	20,23,20,21
2 (3)	....do	...do	4	17,21,21,21
2	....do	...do	2	18,18
2 (e)	General chemistry, for engineering students.	Assistant professor	4	13,14,14,14
4 (1)	Quantitative analysis	...do	4	11,13,13,13
4 (2)	....do	...do	4	5,4,6,6
6	Chemistry of foods	Professor	2	21,21
6	....do	Instructor	3	21,12,8
8	Organic chemistry	...do	3	18,19,8
16	Individual research, recitation	Professor	1	6
16	Individual research, laboratory	...do	3	6,2,2
14	Photo-chemistry	Assistant professor	2	3,3
18	Recitation	Professor	2	2,2
18	....do	...do	3	2,2,2
	Chemistry seminar	...do	1	9
	Graduate course	...do	4	1,1,1,1
	Glass working	Instructor	1	1
	Industrial engineering chemistry for mining engineering students.	Professor	2	4,4

of April 10–16, 1916—University and agricultural work.

	Agricultural College.					
Course number.	Subject.	Rank of instructor.	Meetings.	Students attending.	Year of course.	

AGRICULTURE.

Course	Subject	Rank of instructor	Meetings	Students attending	Year of course
Horticulture. 2	Plant propagation............	Professor..........	4	26, 26, 26, 26....	Freshman.
6	Horticultural elective.........	....do........	3	5, 5, 5...........	
10	Forestry....................	....do........	2	7, 7.............	
Agronomy...1	Farm crops.................	....do........	2	18, 18...........	Do.
2	Crops laboratory............	....do........	1	18...............	Do.
	Thesis class...............	....do........	2	2, 2.............	Senior.
Dairy....... 5	Ice cream.................	....do........	2	4, 4.............	Junior.
6	Cheese making.............	....do........	2	4, 4.............	Do.
8	City market milk supplies....	....do........	3	4, 4, 4..........	Senior.
Anim. husb. 3	Breeds of live stock.........	....do........	5	27, 27, 26, 27, 27.	Freshman.
4	Judging live stock..........	....do........	2	24, 22..........	Do.
8	Care and management.......	....do........	3	9, 11, 11........	Junior.
9	Care and management, practice work.	....do........	3	6, 6, 6..........	Do.
9	.....do.....	....do........	3	5, 5, 4..........	Do.
10	Herd-book study...........	....do........	2	6, 6.............	Do.
Agronomy.. 7	Soil physics and management.	Assistant professor	3	18, 18, 19........	Soph.
8	Soil management laboratory...	....do........	2	3, 3.............	Do.
8	.....do.....	....do........	1	15..............	Do.
9	Soil fertility..............	....do........	2	3, 3.............	Junior.
10	Soil fertility laboratory......	....do........	2	2, 3.............	Do.
	Thesis class.............	....do........	3	2, 2, 2..........	Senior.

ARCHITECTURE.

Course	Subject	Rank of instructor	Meetings	Students attending	Year of course
Architecture. 6	Design....................	Instructor..........	2	2, 2.............	Soph.
9	Free-hand drawing.........	....do........	2	2, 2.............	Do.
15	.....do.....	....do........	2	1, 1.............	Junior.
16	Water color..............	....do........	2	1, 1.............	Do.
18	Design...................	....do........	5	1, 1, 1, 1, 1.....	Do.
13	History of architecture......	....do........	2	2, 2.............	Soph.
19	History of sculpture and painting.	....do........	2	2, 2.............	Junior.

BIOLOGY.

Course	Subject	Rank of instructor	Meetings	Students attending	Year of course
Botany..... 3	General introductory botany..	Associate professor	3	22, 22, 22.......	Freshman.
3	.....do.....	....do........	2	3, 3.............	Do.
13	Plant physiology and pathology.	....do........	1	1...............	Senior.
17	Advanced botany and investigation.	....do........	5	1, 1, 1, 1, 1.....	Do.
17	.....do.....	....do........	3	1, 1, 1..........	Do.
18	Elementary pharmaceutical botany.	....do........	3	7, 7, 7..........	Soph.
18	.....do.....	....do........	2	2, 2.............	Do.
20	Botany for home economics students.	....do........	4	14, 14, 15, 15....	Freshman.
Zoology..... 3	Zoological foundations........	Professor..........	3	6, 19, 19........	Do.
8	Animal parasites............	....do........	5	6, 6, 6, 6, 6.....	Soph.
12	Human physiology..........	....do........	3	16, 16, 16.......	Junior.

CHEMISTRY.

Course	Subject	Rank of instructor	Meetings	Students attending	Year of course
Chemistry. 3(2)	Inorganic chemistry...:.....	Professor..........	3	9, 9, 9..........	Freshman.
3 (2)	.....do.....	....do........	2	40, 40..........	Do.
4 (2)	Qualitative chemistry........	....do........	3	14, 14, 14.......	Do.
4 (2)	.....do.....	....do........	3	39, 39, 39.......	Do.
8 (2)	Elementary quantitative chemistry.	....do........	3	4, 4, 4..........	Soph.
9 (2)	Organic chemistry..........	....do........	3	17, 17, 17.......	Do.
10 (2)	Organic preparations........	....do........	2	15, 13..........	Do.
13	Elementary physical chemistry.	....do........	3	3, 3, 3..........	Junior.
21	Industrial chemistry for engineering students.	....do........	4	6, 6, 6, 6.......	Soph.
24	Organic industrial chemistry..	....do........	5	1, 1, 1, 1, 1.....	Senior.
33	Elementary physiological chemistry for home economics students.	....do........	3	39, 38, 38.......	Soph.
28	Inorganic constituents for home economics students.	....do........	3	20, 20, 20.......	Freshman.
7 (3)	General chemistry for students in veterinary science.	....do........	5	7, 8, 8, 8, 8.....	Do.
27	Toxicology and urinology.....	....do........	5	6, 7, 7, 7, 7.....	Senior.

TABLE 43.—*Meetings of classes held during the week of April*

		University.		
Course number.	Subject.	Rank of Instructor.	Meetings.	Students attending.
CHEMISTRY—Con.				
Chemistry........10	Industrial engineering chemistry..	Instructor........	4	4, 4, 4, 4........
12	.....do.....	...do......	4	2, 2, 2, 2........
EDUCATION.	Analytical work.................	...do........	6	2, 2, 2, 2, 2, 2........
	Theory and practice of teaching—			
Education.......102	English in high schools........	Instructor........	2	7, 7........
110	German.................	...do.....	1	4.
112	Latin.................	...do.....	1	4.
	History.................	...do.....	3	2, 2.
108	Mathematics..........	...do.....	2	3, 3.
156	Chemistry.....	Professor.....	1	9.
158	Stenography..........	Instructor.....	2	2, 2.
152	Manual training..........	...do.....	2	4, 4.
162	Music.........	Associate professor	2	5, 8.
2a	Philosophy of education..........	Professor..........	2	25, 25.
	Child study..........	...do.....	4	55, 52, 56, 53.
10	History of education..........	...do.....	4	8, 8, 8, 8.
16	Educational classics..........	...do.....	2	6, 5.
18	Secondary education..........	...do.....	2	16, 17.
	Special course..........	...do.....	1	2.
	History of education..........	Assistant professor	4	21, 20, 20, 21.
4	Special methods in the elementary school.	Professor.....	4	62, 65, 65, 65.
8	School supervision and administration.	...do.....	3	10, 10, 10.
20	School administration seminary...	...do.....	2	4, 4.
20	School in absentia..........	...do.....	2	3, 3.
ENGINEERING.				
CIVIL ENGINEERING.				
Surveying.........2	Elementary surveying..........	Professor..........	2	10, 10.
2	.....do..........	...do.....	2	9, 9.
4	Surveying..........	...do.....	3	10, 10, 10.
8	Topography..........	...do.....	2	6, 6.
8	.....do..........	...do.....	2	8, 8.
12	Mining surveying..........	...do.....	2	4, 4.
	Reinforced concrete..........	...do.....	4	7, 7, 7, 7.
	Structural design..........	...do.....	4	8, 8, 8, 8.
M. E. X..........44	Hydraulic laboratory..........	...do.....	1	5.
X..................44	.....do..........	Instructor........	1	5.
ELECTRICAL ENGINEERING.				
M. E. X..........42	Dynamo laboratory..........	Professor..........	1	6.
X..................42	.....do..........	Assistant professor	1	6.
E E.............2	Direct current machinery..........	...do.....	4	2, 2, 2, 2.
8	Electrical design..........	...do.....	4	6, 6, 6, 6.
10	Electrical engineering..........	...do.....	4	6, 6, 6, 6.
14	Electrical machinery..........	...do.....	3	1, 1, 1.
	Thesis in electrical engineering..........	...do.....	1	3.
ENGINEERING DRAWING.				
	Architectural drawing..........	Professor..........	2	2, 2.
M. E.............2	Mechanical drawing..........	Assistant professor	3	6, 6, 6.
2	.....do..........	...do.....	3	9, 9, 9.
4	Mechanical drawing, civil engineering students.	...do.....	2	8, 8.
4	Mechanical drawing, mechanical and electrical engineering students.	...do.....	2	11, 11.
M. E.............4	Machine design..........	Instructor........	2	12, 12.
6	.....do..........	...do.....	1	1.
6	.....do..........	...do.....	1	1.
10	.....do..........	Professor..........	5	1, 1, 1, 1, 1.
Min. E..........2	Mining engineering drawing........	Assistant professor	2	2, 3.

10–16, 1916—University and agricultural college—Continued.

	Agricultural College.				
Course number.	Subject.	Rank of Instructor.	Meetings.	Students attending.	Year of course.
EDUCATION.					
Education...4	Principles of teaching.........	Instructor.........	4	23, 24, 24, 25....	Senior.
5	Agricultural and industrial education.	.....do............	3	17, 17, 17.......	Junior.
9	School law...................	.....do............	2	16, 18...........	Do.
14	Current educational literature.	.....do............	1	3.............	
ENGINEERING.					
CIVIL ENGINEERING.					
C. E..... 1 (1)	Surveying for agricultural students.	Instructor.........	2	14, 14..........	Soph.
4	Roads and pavements..........	.....do............	4	1, 1, 1, 1........	Junior.
4 (1)	Roads...................	.....do............	2	1, 1............	Do.
15	Concrete and drainage for agricultural students.	.....do............	4	7, 7, 8, 8........	Senior.
17	Water purification, sewage disposal, sanitation.	.....do............	4	1, 1, 1, 1........	Do.
8	Hydraulics..................	Assistant professor.	5	4, 4, 4, 4, 4......	Junior.
19	Bridge design................	Professor.........	4	1, 1, 1, 1........	Senior.
ELECTRICAL ENGINEERING.					
ENGINEERING DRAWING.					
M. E.........7	Mechanical drawing..........	Instructor.........	5	3, 3, 3, 5, 5......	Freshman.
11	.....do..........	.....do............	3	1, 1, 1.........	Soph.
9	Descriptive geometry.........	.....do............	2	5, 5............	Freshman.
10	Mechanical perspective........	.....do............	2	5, 5............	Do.
38	Machine design..............	Professor.........	2	2, 2............	Senior.

TABLE 43.—*Meetings of classes held during the week of April*

University.

Course number.	Subject.	Rank of instructor.	Meetings.	Students attending.
MECHANICAL ENGINEERING.				
M. E........8 (2)	Thermodynamics.................	Professor........	4	6, 6, 6, 6...............
8 (4)	Power-plant problems............	...do............	2	5, 5...................
12	Design of pumping plants.........	...do............	4	6, 6, 6, 6...............
62	Mechanics of engineering.........	...do............	5	11, 11, 11, 11, 11......
X............36 (2)	Mechanical laboratory............	Instructor........	1	2......................
X............36 (1)	...do............	...do............	1	4......................
32	...do............	...do............	1	1......................
MINING ENGINEERING				
	Building materials................	Professor........	4	7, 7, 7, 7.............
	Ceramics........................	...do............	2	4, 4...................
Min. E...........2	Lecture.........................	Assistant professor	3	4, 4, 4................
Metall...........2	Metallurgy lecture................	...do............	2	7, 7...................
2	Metallurgy laboratory.............	...do............	4	2, 2, 5, 5.............
	Ore treatment, lecture............	...do............	1	3......................
	Ore treatment, laboratory and mill	...do............	4	3, 3, 2, 3.............
	Graduate course.................	Professor........	4	1, 1, 1, 1.............
SHOP PRACTICE.				
4	Pattern-making..................	Instructor........	2	9, 9..................
2A	Forge-shop......................	...do............	3	10, 10, 10............
2B	...do............	...do............	3	10, 10, 10............
5	Machine-shop...................	...do............	2	4, 4..................
6	...do............	...do............	2	2, 2..................
8	...do............	...do............	2	1, 1..................
HOME ECONOMICS.				
	Textiles and needlework..........	Assistant........	4	16, 16, 16, 16........
	...do............	...do............	4	18, 18, 18, 18........
	Food and cooking................	Instructor........	4	15, 16, 14, 16........
	...do............	...do............	4	10, 10, 10, 9.........
	Nutrition.......................	...do............	2	10, 10................
	Methods........................	...do............	1	20....................
	Nutrition.......................	Assistant........	1	10....................
LANGUAGE.				
English 2	Advanced rhetoric...............	Professor........	5	27, 24, 27, 27, 22.....
2	...do............	Associate professor	5	22, 22, 21, 22, 21.....
2	...do............	Assistant professor	5	29, 30, 28, 29, 29.....
2	...do............	...do............	5	35, 35, 35, 35, 35.....
2	...do............	Instructor........	5	46, 46, 43, 45, 44.....
2	...do............	...do............	5	16, 16, 16, 16, 16.....
2	...do............	Assistant........	5	26, 26, 26, 26, 26.....
2	...do............	...do............	4	22, 21, 21, 22........
4	Public address..................	Assistant professor	4	13, 13, 13, 13........
4a	Public speaking, for law students..	...do............	2	13, 13................
6	Journalism......................	...do............	2	4, 4..................
8	English composition, for engineering students.	Instructor........	4	14, 14, 14, 13........
10	The short story..................	...do............	2	3, 3..................
12		Professor........	3	6, 6, 6...............
14	Shakespeare....................	Associate professor	5	24, 24, 22, 24, 24.....
16	English poets of the nineteenth century.	Professor........	5	25, 25, 25, 25, 25.....
20	English seminar.................	...do............	1	3.....................
24	Modern drama..................	Associate professor	4	5, 5, 4, 1............
28	Interpretive reading.............	Assistant professor	2	22, 22................
30	The English novel...............	Instructor........	2	2, 2..................
32	Technic of the drama............	Associate professor	2	5, 5..................

*10–16, 1916—University and agricultural college—*Continued.

Agriculture College.					
Course number.	Subject.	Rank of instructor.	Meet-ings.	Students at-tending.	Year of course.
MECHANICAL ENGINEERING.					
M. E....... 15	Internal combustion engines...	Assistant professor	3	3, 3, 3..........	Junior.
39	Heat engines..............	...do...	5	1, 1, 1, 1, 1.....	Senior.
28	Mechanism...............	...do...	3	2, 2, 2..........	Soph.
29	Mechanics of materials.......	...do...	2	3, 3............	Junior.
23	Materials testing laboratory....	...do...	2	4, 4............	Do.
32	Materials of construction......	...do...	4	6, 6, 6, 6........	Do.
MINING ENGINEERING.					
SHOP PRACTICE.					
M. E........ 2	Forge shop...............	Instructor..........	3	6, 6, 6..........	Freshman.
3	Machine shop.............	Assistant professor	2	1, 1............	Soph.
14	Molding.................	Instructor..........	1	1..............	Do.
HOME ECONOMICS.					
Dom. Art... 3	Undergarment making........	Instructor..........	2	12, 10..........	Freshman.
4	Domestic art..............	...do...	2	12, 12..........	Soph.
8	Millinery................	...do...	2	12, 14..........	Junior.
10	Teaching domestic art........	...do...	2	8, 8............	Do.
11	Advanced dressmaking........	...do...	2	11, 11..........	Senior.
Dom. Sci.... 1	Food preparation...........	...do...	3	6, 6, 6..........	Soph.
8	Economic uses of food........	...do...	5	19, 19, 19, 19, 19.	Junior.
15	Teaching domestic science.....	...do...	2	13, 13..........	Do.
16	Theory and practice of teaching	...do...	2	6, 6............	Senior.
18	Social observances..........	...do...	2	3, 3............	Junior.
20	Home nursing.............	...do...	3	13, 14, 13.......	Senior.
21	Institutional management.....	...do...	2	24, 24..........	Do.
21	...do...	...do...	1	12..............	Do.
21	...do...	...do...	1	12..............	Do.
LANGUAGE.					
English..... 8	Argumentation............	Professor..........	4	11, 11, 11, 11....	Freshman.
9	History of English literature...	Assistant professor	4	11, 11, 10, 11....	Do.
15	Essays..................	Professor..........	4	4, 3, 5, 5........	
21	Playwriting..............	Assistant professor	4	4, 5, 5, 5........	
Pub. Spk... 1	Elementary public speaking....	Professor..........	5	12, 14, 12, 14, 12.	
1	...do...	...do...	3	2, 2, 2..........	
6	Community programs........	...do...	2	4, 4............	
7	Dramatics...............	...do...	3	3, 3, 3..........	
	Special work.............	Assistant professor	3	2, 2, 3..........	

TABLE 43.—*Meetings of classes held during the week of April*

	University.			
Course number.	Subject.	Rank of instructor.	Meetings.	Students attending.
LANGUAGE— Continued.				
German..........2	Beginning course in German......	Professor..........	4	24, 25, 23, 22.
3	....do....	Assistant professor	4	17, 18, 18, 18.
4	Reading, syntax, composition.....	Professor..........	4	26, 37, 35, 36.
4	....do....	Assistant professor	4	27, 29, 31, 31.
4b	Intermediate course...............	....do....	4	17, 17, 17, 17.
6	Advanced reading course...........	....do....	4	24, 24, 24, 24.
10	Scientific German.................	Professor..........	4	26, 23, 26, 25.
14	Goethe............................	....do....	3	7, 7, 7.
15	Lessing...........................	....do....	3	3, 3, 3.
Greek...........2	Introductory course.	Professor..........	4	5, 5, 5, 5.
4	Attic prose and epic poetry.......	....do....	4	5, 5, 4, 5.
8	Greek literature in English translation.	....do....	4	12, 12, 12, 10.
10	Greek archeology.................	....do....	2	4, 4.
11	Greek mythology..................	....do....	2	12, 13.
	Greek literature for teachers......	....do....	2	10, 10.
Latin...........2	Cicero............................	Assistant professor	4	4, 4, 4, 4.
4	Virgil's Aeneid...................	....do....	4	6, 6, 6, 6.
6	Horace: Odes.....................	....do....	3	3, 3, 3.
8	Latin prose composition...........	....do....	1	4.
10	Livy.............................	....do....	4	5, 5, 4, 5.
French..........2	Intermediate French..............	Professor..........	4	18, 17, 19, 19.
4	Modern French poetry and drama	....do....	4	14, 15, 15, 15.
6	Seventeenth century prose........	....do....	3	2, 2, 2.
10	Outlines French literature in English.	....do....	2	6, 6.
Spanish..........2	Intermediate Spanish.............	....do....	4	18, 18, 17, 18.
Norse...........2	Beginning Norse..................	....de....	4	22, 21, 22, 22.
4	Advanced Norse..................	....do....	4	14, 14, 14, 14.
8	Norse literature..................	....do....	4	5, 5, 6, 6.
16	Bjornson's dramas...............	....do....	2	3, 3.
160	Theory and practice of teaching the Scandinavian languages.	....do....	1	1.
Swedish........12	Beginning Swedish...............	....do....	2	1, 1.
LAW.				
	Code pleading....................	Professor..........	2	30, 29.
	Evidence.........................	....do....	4	29, 28, 28, 28.
	Practice court....................	....do....	3	19, 18, 18.
	Bailments and carriers...........	....do....	4	16, 16, 16, 16.
	Brief making.....................	....do....	1	21.
	Damages.........................	....do....	3	26, 25, 25.
	Contracts........................	....do....	3	29, 29, 28.
	Equity...........................	....do....	4	19, 20, 20, 20.
	Trusts...........................	....do....	2	18, 18.
	Real property....................	Instructor.........	3	32, 33, 33.
	Agency..........................	Assistant professor	3	33, 32, 32.
	Wills............................	....do....	2	17, 17.
	Torts............................	....do....	2	22, 22.
	Quasi-contracts..................	....do....	2	8, 8.
	Documents.......................	Instructor.........	1	16.
	Procedure........................	....do....	2	25, 25.
MANUAL TRAINING.				
II	Woodwork........................	Instructor.........	5	4, 4, 4, 4, 4.
III	....do....	....do....	5	2, 2, 2, 2, 2.
	Advanced woodwork..............	....do....	3	2, 2, 2.
V	Mechanical drawing..............	....do....	5	9, 8, 8, 8, 9.
MATHEMATICS.				
Math............2	Analytical geometry..............	Professor..........	4	11, 11, 11, 11.
2	....do....	....do....	4	8, 8, 8, 8.
2	....do....	....do....	5	15, 16, 16, 16, 16.
4	Calculus.........................	....do....	4	29, 29, 29, 29.
8	Theory of equations..............	....do....	2	1, 1.
18	Teachers' course.................	....do....	3	6, 6, 6.
	Solid geometry...................	....do....	1	10.

10–16, 1916—University and agricultural college—Continued.

		Agricultural College.				
Course number.	Subject.	Rank of instructor.	Meetings.	Students attending.	Year of course.	
LANGUAGE—Continued.						
German..... 6	German comedies..............	Professor...........	4	12,13,13,11....	Soph.	
9	Faust.................	....do.............	2	3,2.............	Junior.	
French...... 3	Reading and composition.....	Professor...........	4	7,7,5,5.......	Freshman.	
6	Classic French dramas........	....do.............	4	4,4,2,2.......	Soph.	
LAW.						
MANUAL TRAINING.	Manual training for teachers...	Instructor........	5	8,8,8,2,2......		
MATHEMATICS.						
Math........ 9	Higher algebra.................	Professor...........	4	6,7,6,5.......	Freshman.	
10	......do.....	Assistant professor	4	6,6,6,6.......	Do.	
11	Plane trigonometry	.....do.............	2	14,15.........	Do.	
14	Integral calculus	Professor...........	4	4,4,4,4.......	Soph.	
16	Slide rule....................	Assistant professor	2	5,5.............	Freshman.	
17	Graphs......................	......do............	2	2,2.............	Soph.	
19	Mathematics of investment.....	......do............	3	11,11,11.......	Freshman.	

TABLE 43.—*Meetings of classes held during the week of April*

	University.			
Course number.	Subject.	Rank of instructor.	Meetings.	Students attending.
MEDICINE.				
Anat............ 2	Neurology...............	Professor.........	6	11, 11, 11, 11, 11, 11..
4	Dissection.............	...do............	6	11, 11, 11, 11, 11, 11..
	Public hygiene and sanitation......	...do..........	2	9, 9............
Phys............. 2	Digestion...............	Associate professor	2	13, 13..........
2	Digestion, laboratory.............	...do..........	1	13.
2a	Bio-chemistry.............	...do..........	1	13..............
2a	Bio-chemistry, laboratory.........	...do..........	1	13.............
4	Nervous system............	...do..........	2	9, 9............
4	Nervous system, laboratory.........	...do..........	2	9, 9............
6	Pharmacology.............	...do..........	3	10, 10, 10......
6	Pharmacology, laboratory............	...do..........	2	10, 10..........
	Pathology.............	Assistant professor	5	9, 9, 9, 9, 9........
	Principles of nursing............	Instructor.........	3	7, 7, 7.........
	Principles of nursing, laboratory...	...do........	1	4..............
	....do...........	...do........	1	3..............
	General physiology............	...do........	4	19, 19, 20, 20......
MILITARY DRILL.				
MUSIC.				
Music............ 2	Harmony.............	Associate professor	2	6, 5............
6	History of music.............	...do..........	2	8, 6............
8	Vocal sight reading.............	...do..........	1	9.............
12	Choral singing, men.............	...do..........	2	28, 28..........
12	Choral singing, women.............	...do..........	2	33, 36..........
14	Orchestra.............	...do..........	1	12.............
16	Musical appreciation............	...do..........	1	6.............
18	Elements and principles............	...do..........	1	8.............
10	Band.............	Assistant.........	2	28, 28..........
PHILOSOPHY.				
Philos............ 2	Ethics.............	Professor.........	4	9, 9, 8, 8........
2	....do.............	Assistant professor	4	15, 15, 15, 15......
4	Abnormal psychology............	Professor.........	4	12, 11, 12, 12......
8	Introduction to philosophy........	...do........	3	6, 6, 5.........
	Educational psychology............	Assistant professor	4	7, 7, 7, 6..........
PHYSICAL TRAINING.				
Physical education 2	Physical education, for men........	Assistant professor	2	32, 32..........
2	....do.............	...do..........	2	42, 42..........
2	....do.............	...do..........	2	33, 33..........
4	....do.............	...do..........	2	23, 23..........
170	Teaching physical education.........	...do..........	1	3.............
	Track athletics.............	...do..........	6	25, 25, 25, 25, 25, 25.
	Base ball.............	Instructor.........	6	35, 35, 35, 35, 35, 35.
2	Physical education, for women.....	...do..........	2	26, 26..........
2	....do.............	...do..........	2	40, 40..........
2	....do.............	...do..........	2	30, 33..........
4	....do.............	...do..........	2	35, 34..........
4	....do.............	...do..........	2	24, 24..........
6	....do.............	...do..........	2	10, 10..........
10	Esthetic dancing, women............	...do..........	2	7, 9...........
12	Playgrounds, women.............	...do..........	2	6, 6...........
PHYSICS.				
Physics............1	General physics, lecture, experiments.	Associate professor	3	31, 31, 31.........
1	General physics, recitation.........	...do..........	2	17, 14..........
2	General physics, laboratory.......	Assistant professor	2	14, 14..........
2	....do.............	...do..........	2	17, 17..........
4	Engineering physics.............	Professor.........	4	25, 25, 25, 25.......
4	Engineering physics, laboratory..	Assistant professor	1	15..............

10–16, 1916—University and agricultural college—Continued.

Agricultural College.					
Course number.	Subject.	Rank of instructor.	Meet-ings.	Students at-tending.	Year of course.
PHARMACY, ETC.					
Pharm...... 4	Pharmacopœial preparations..	Assistant professor	4	11, 11, 11, 11....	Soph.
5	Operative pharmacy, etc......	.....do.............	2	10, 10............	Do.
9	Drug assaying..............	.....do.............	3	7, 7, 7............	Junior.
10	United States Pharmacopœia, etc.	.....do.............	5	6, 7, 7, 7, 7......	Do.
12	Veterinary pharmacy........	.....do.............	4	4, 3, 4, 4.........	Soph.
M. M........ 2	Materia medica and thera-peutics.	Professor............	4	6, 7, 7, 7.........	Do.
	Pharmaceutical Latin........	.....do.............	4	10, 10, 10, 9.....	Do.
	Pharmaceutical problems	.....do.............	3	10, 10, 10........	Do.
Bact 9	General bacteriological tech-nic.	Assistant professor	3	4, 4, 4............	Do.
13	General bacteriological tech-nic for home economic stu-dents.	.....do.............	3	4, 4, 4............	Do.
10	Pathogenic bacteriology......	.....do.............	2	3, 3..............	Senior.
11	Dairy bacteriology..........	.....do.............	4	5, 5, 5, 5.........	Do.
12	Bacteriological research......	.....do.............	4	1, 1, 1, 1.........	Do.
Vet. sci..... 3	Veterinary science..........	Professor............	5	7, 8, 8, 8, 8....	Soph.
10	Veterinary anatomy..........	Assistant professor	5	8, 8, 8, 8, 9......	Freshman.
13	Veterinary hygiene..........	.....do.............	5	5, 5, 5, 4, 5......	Soph
15	Materia medica............	.....do.............	5	4, 4, 4, 4, 4......	Do.
18	Physiology..............	.....do.............	5	8, 8, 8, 8, 9......	Freshman.
MILITARY DRILL.					
	Military drill.................	Professor............	3	51, 50, 52.......	
MUSIC.					
	Band....................	Director............	3	21, 20, 22.......	
	Harmony.................	.....do.............	3	4, 4, 4..........	
	Musical history...........	.....do.............	2	2, 2.............	
PHILOSOPHY.					
Philos....... 3	Ethics....................	Professor............	4	3, 4, 4, 4........	
PHYSICAL TRAINING.					
Gymnastics ..1	Gymnasium.................	Instructor...........	3	16, 15, 16.......	
2	.....do....	.....do.............	3	14, 14, 14.......	
3	.....do....	.....do.............	2	19, 18...........	
4	.....do....	.....do.............	2	14, 15...........	
5	.....do....	.....do.............	2	3, 3.............	
6	.....do....	.....do.............	3	1, 1, 1..........	
	Physical training.............	Director...........	5	25, 25, 25, 25, 25.	
PHYSICS.					
Physics......6	Magnetism and electricity.....	Professor............	2	18, 18...........	Soph.
6	Magnetism and electricity, laboratory.	.....do.............	2	12, 12...........	Do.
8	Household physics..............	.....do.	4	32, 32, 32, 32....	Do.

TABLE 43.—*Meetings of classes held during the week of April*

	University.			
Course number.	Subject.	Rank of instructor.	Meetings.	Students attending.
PHYSICS—Contd.				
Physics............4	Engineering physics, laboratory...	Assistant professor	2	11, 11.............
6	Variable currents.................	Professor............	2	2, 2.............
12	Graduate research................	....do.............	4	1, 1, 1, 1.........
14	Graduate colloquium.............	....do.............	1	1.................
POLITICAL AND SOCIAL SCIENCE.				
Economics........2	Banking....................	Professor............	4	26, 27, 26, 25......
28	Agricultural economics..............	....do.............	4	7, 7, 7, 6..........
28	Taxation................	....do.............	2	2, 3..........
Political science..32	American government.............	....do.............	2	18, 19...........
34	City government................	....do.............	2	7, 6...........
Economics.......54	Graduate course.............	....do.............	2	1, 1.............
NOT OTHERWISE CLASSIFIED.				
	Library science.................	Assistant professor	1	7.................
Geology...........1	General geology.............	Professor............	5	18, 26, 25, 25, 11...
4	Physiography...................	Associate professor	3	53, 53, 53.........
4	....do............	....do....	2	25, 29...........
8	Economic geology.............	Professor............	3	2, 2, 2...........
10	Petrology.............	....do.............	2	4, 4...........
14	Geographic influences..............	Associate professor	3	6, 6, 6...........
22	Geological seminar.............	....do.............	1	5.................
Ceramics..........4	Clay work laboratory, handicraft course.	Instructor.........	2	8, 8.............
6	Clay work laboratory.............	....do.............	1	3.............
6	....do.	....do.............	1	3.............
8	....do.	....do.............	1	10.............
8	....do.	....do.............	1	9.............
10	....do.	....do.............	1	8.............
12	....do.	....do.............	1	7.............

10-16. 1916—University and agricultural college—Continued.

Agricultural College.					
Course number.	Subject.	Rank of instructor.	Meetings.	Students attending.	Year of course.
PHYSICS—Con.					
POLITICAL AND SOCIAL SCIENCE.					
History.....12	History of Greek civilization and art.	Professor..........	4	13, 12, 13, 13....	
Social science 4	Sociology.....................	.....do.............	4	25, 29, 26, 28....	Freshman.
8	Current events...............	.....do........,..	1	4...............	
10	Rural economics...............	.....do.............	4	16, 15, 18, 15....	Junior.
NOT OTHERWISE CLASSIFIED.	Library methods..............	Assistant librarian.	1	6..............	

TABLE 44.—*Courses offered at the agricultural college in April, 1916, that would have been discontinued if the recommendation made in this report had been in effect.*

Junior year: Students involved.
Arch.	19. History of sculpture and painting	2
C. E.	8. Hydraulics	4
M. E.	15. Internal combustion engines	8
M. E.	29. Mechanics of materials	8
M. E.	23. Materials testing laboratory	4
M. E.	32. Materials of construction	6
German	9. Faust	8

                                            Total class attendance _____ 25
Senior year:
C. E.	17. Water purification, sewage disposals, and sanitation	1
C. E.	19. Bridge design	1
M. E.	38. Machine design	2
M. E.	39. Heat engines	1

                                            Total class attendance _____ 5

The number of students involved is negligible when compared with the saving in cost of instruction and the time, energy, and equipment now devoted to these small classes, which would be released for more economical and more efficient service in other directions. (See also, in this connection, Tables 55 and 56, Appendix XI.)

As bearing on statements elsewhere in this report in regard to the need and demand for courses in the various forms of engineering, the danger of excessive division of the subject, and of unnecessary costly duplication, the number and size of classes reported at the university and college should be given careful study. It should be noted that each institution reports six classes in engineering with only 1 student each, that all the classes at both institutions are small, and that in all forms of engineering at the agricultural college there are reported only 25 students in junior classes and 13 in senior classes, repeaters included. Of the 13 seniors, 8 were taking the course in "concrete and drainage for agricultural students."

In relation to the assumed principle that a subject for which there is not sufficient demand to justify its being included in the curriculum of more than one institution should be given at the institution which already and for other reasons offers the necessary courses in accompanying and supporting subjects, and further in relation to the commission's recommendation [1] as to the distribution of engineering between the two institutions, the courses and the size of classes in mathematics, physics, chemistry, and biology should be carefully studied.

---

[1] See recommendation 5, ch. 12.

The basis of the recommendation[2] of the commission that languages and literature be considered only as service courses at the agricultural college, and that degree courses in these subjects be offered only at the university, is found in the comparison of the courses taken and the size of courses at the two institutions. Apparently there were in April at the agricultural college only two students of these subjects in classes above the second year, the two German students taking the course in Faust in the junior year.

That the agricultural college is not yet performing its function as an agricultural college as fully as the agricultural college of such a State as North Dakota should is shown by the fact, revealed by this table, that in April, when at least a large majority of all the regular students of the college were present, the aggregate number of attendants at all of the 21 classes in agriculture which met during that week was only 211. Only 42 of these were in junior classes and only 4 were in senior classes. Since most of the students were counted two or more times each, the actual numbers of individuals involved are much smaller than the figures given. Plainly all these numbers should be very much larger, and the college should put forth every effort to bring more students into this department of its work. The number of graduates of the institution who are now engaged in agricultural pursuits also supports this contention.

---

[2] See recommendation 9, ch. 12.

Chapter XII.

SUMMARY OF RECOMMENDATIONS.

PRESUPPOSITIONS.

In making these recommendations it is assumed:

1. That all the institutions to which they refer belong alike to all the people of the State and constitute an integral part of the system of public education, and that no one of them is thought of as belonging to any particular class of people—as the poor or the rich, the people of the country or the people of the city, the farming or the industrial or the professional classes.

2. That each institution has its own particular function or group of functions to perform and finds its greatest usefulness in rendering to the people of the State its own peculiar service.

3. That all these forms of service are equally worthy and dignified if performed equally well.

4. That the officers of no one of these institutions desire to magnify for itself alone the institution for which they are responsible, but only to make it render most fully and most efficiently its particular service without encroaching upon the functions of any other institution.

5. That above all these institutions are the people of the State who have established them and who maintain them by their taxes, who are equally interested in them all, and who expect from all loyal service, each in its own field, and economical use of funds provided.

6. That the people of the State are both willing and able to provide all funds that may be needed by any institution for its legitimate work, but that they are neither willing nor able to provide funds for any one of the institutions to extend its work into fields covered by other institutions.

7. That the kind, degree, and quantity of higher education to be provided by a State at any time, particularly education of a vocational nature, should be shaped according to the character of the people, their social and political ideals, their occupations, and their vocational needs as determined by the natural resources of the State.

8. That in a State which has established more than one institution of higher learning the people and their responsible representatives

have the right and must face the obligation to apportion among these institutions the work of higher education in such way as will best serve all the interests of the State, and that it is their right and duty to change this apportionment whenever the public interest may demand such change, provided it may be done without violation of contract or of obligation to the Federal Government.

9. That the offering of the same subjects or the same or similar courses of study in the curricula of two or more institutions in the same State should be avoided as uneconomical and harmful duplication of effort: (a) When the total demand for such subjects or courses of study in the life of the State and the number of students applying therefor are not sufficient to justify the expense of giving instruction in them at more than one place; (b) when in the attempt to maintain such courses at any one of the institutions money, equipment, time, and energy are used that might be more profitably devoted to other purposes; (c) when the attempt to maintain such courses tends to confuse the purposes of the institution and to divert it from its more legitimate and immediate aims; and (d) when such division or duplication tends to detract from and weaken the courses in question as given at the institution in which they primarily and more legitimately belong.

10. That any subject which two or more institutions may desire to include in their curricula, but for which there is clearly not sufficient demand to justify its being offered by more than one institution, should be offered at that institution which already has in its curriculum as an essential part of its main purpose the necessary accompanying or supporting subjects, rather than at an institution in which such accompanying or supporting subjects would need to be provided for this particular purpose and without necessary relation to other subjects taught in that institution or to its main purposes; as, for examples, engineering courses dependent for their development on advanced courses in mathematics and physics, or other engineering courses dependent for their development on advanced courses in chemistry or biology.

11. That no institution established and maintained as a State institution should function chiefly as a local institution, appropriating State funds to purely local uses.

12. That the board of regents responsible for the general management of all the institutions included in this survey, while seeking to promote the harmonious cooperation of all as parts of one unified, flexible, adjustable, democratic system of education for the most efficient service of the State, desires also that the individuality, spirit, and best traditions of each institution shall be preserved.

RECOMMENDATIONS.

1. Education at the university and agricultural college. — The school of education at the university and the department of education at the agricultural college should be sufficiently enlarged to enable them to prepare high-school teachers, school superintendents, and supervisors for both elementary and high schools, and expert special teachers, in sufficient numbers to supply the demands of the schools of the State. Special teachers of agriculture, home economics, and industrial subjects should be prepared at the agricultural college. The university should prepare superintendents, high-school teachers, and supervisors in all subjects except agriculture, home economics, manual training, and other industrial subjects. The university should not undertake to prepare special teachers in home economics, but should give sufficient instruction in this subject and in methods of teaching it to enable young women to combine the teaching of this subject with other subjects in the high school. Neither the school of education at the university nor the department of education at the agricultural college should attempt to prepare teachers for the elementary schools.

2. The graduate schools. — Graduate work at the university and at the agricultural college should, for the present, continue to be limited to the requirements for the master's degree, and each institution should give graduate instruction only in those subjects which are considered major subjects at that institution. Graduate courses in education may be offered at each institution. The presidents of these institutions and the board of regents should work out plans for cooperation in graduate work where cooperation may be helpful. Duplication of graduate work would be unwarranted, costly, and wasteful.

3. Home economics. — Instruction in home economics should be given at both the university and the agricultural college. Except for the purpose of preparing teachers of home economics for high schools, as elsewhere indicated, there should be at the university only such courses in home economics as will fit young women for the duties of intelligent home making, or such as will function as service courses[1] for those taking the course for nurses and possibly some other subjects. The agricultural college should offer both major and normal courses in home economics.

4. Music. — Instruction in music and especially training in chorus, orchestra, and band, may be given at all the institutions, and instruction in singing should be given to all students at the normal schools

---

[1] " Service courses are such subordinate subjects as are essential to the proper cultivation of a major line." For a discussion of the principle of " major and service lines " of work, see p. 61.

to the extent needed for use in the elementary schools, but no attempt should be made to give advanced and professional instruction in music except at the university.

In all these schools there should be a strong cultural spirit, but only at the university should there be offered special or professional courses in the fine arts or degree courses in literature, languages, and pure science.

5. Engineering.—Mining engineering is placed at the university by the constitution of the State. Agricultural and what may be called industrial engineering, as defined in this section of these recommendations, should be given only at the agricultural college. Chemical engineering should also be given at the agricultural college when there is demand for its development in the State. Degree courses in other forms of engineering should be given only at the university. Except for mining engineering and agricultural and industrial engineering, the first two years of any engineering course may be given at either institution when authorized by the board of regents.

The courses in agricultural engineering and those which may be grouped under the term industrial engineering are recommended in order to meet the demands for practical engineering courses in connection with the industries growing out of or directly related to agriculture, and the large number of urban industries hitherto developed on an empirical basis, which are now undergoing a more scientific and technical development. To these latter courses the survey commission has for convenience given the designation industrial engineering, to distinguish them from the professional courses in mechanical, civil, and electrical engineering, which are already well organized in engineering schools. Such courses are given at the University of North Dakota and should not now, if ever, be duplicated at the agricultural college.

6. Reorganization of engineering at the university.—At the university all departments and courses of engineering, including mining, should be placed under the direction of one dean or other executive head.

7. Medical college.—Instruction in medicine at the university should continue to be given only in premedical courses and for the first two years' work of a medical college.

8. Instruction in agriculture.—Fully three-fourths of all the people of the State of North Dakota who are engaged in gainful pursuits are employed in agriculture or in occupations connected directly therewith. The agriculture of the State is carried on by farmers, a very large proportion of whom operate their own farms. These facts and others presented in this report indicate very clearly the importance of agriculture in the vocational education of the State and the need of instruction and training for large numbers of men

and women to the extent which will enable them to operate their
own farms intelligently and successfully, as well as the need of
highly technical training for a few. The agricultural college should
devote its energies and means to instruction in agriculture and the
immediately allied subjects in proportion to the needs herein
indicated.

9. Liberal arts and science at agricultural college.—Courses in
liberal arts and science at the agricultural college should be considered only as service courses,[1] and no degrees in the liberal arts
and sciences should be given here.

10. Architecture.—There does not seem to be at present sufficient
demand for architects and architectural engineers in the State of
North Dakota to justify the maintenance of a school or of extensive
courses in architecture or architectural engineering, either at the
university or at the agricultural college. Instruction in these subjects at the agricultural college should be only of an elementary
nature and should have special reference to farm buildings, ware-
houses, school buildings for rural and village communities, and other
similar buildings.

11. Pharmacy.—Instruction in pharmacy should be continued at
the agricultural college, and standards for admission to and graduation from this course should be raised as rapidly as possible to the
completion of a full high-school course of four years for admission
and a minimum of two years' instruction for graduation.

*12. Relation of president of agricultural college to experiment
station.*—The president of the agricultural college should have general control of the experiment station and of its branches and of the
extension department and be held responsible to the board of regents
for their management.

13. Teaching by members of research staff.—Investigators, men
and women engaged in research work, at the experiment station at
Fargo, should, except in case of those whose duties are such as to
make it inexpedient, be expected to teach some classes in the college;
and the experiment station and its farms and laboratories, as well
as the laboratories of the regulatory services, should be used under
necessary restrictions as teaching agencies for undergraduate college
students and as research agencies for graduate students.

14. Subexperiment stations and demonstration farms.—It is recommended that the board of regents cause a careful study to be made
of the operations of the subexperiment stations and demonstration
farms, with a view to determining whether or not much of the experimental work now under way might be carried on by farmers on
their own premises, without other expense to the State than that of
necessary supervision.

---

[1] See footnote on p. 172.

15. Commercial courses.—Commercial courses of higher or lower grade should be given in the university and the agricultural college; courses in farm accounting and rural economics should be given in the agricultural college, and probably also in the University. The normal schools should give courses in these subjects and in the simple forms of bookkeeping to the extent that they may be needed by teachers in the elementary schools; but the normal schools should not give commercial courses beyond the needs of these teachers.

16. Preparatory department at agricultural college.—The agricultural high school at the agricultural college should be discontinued as a preparatory school by dropping the lowest class each year beginning with 1917, so that after the beginning of the school year 1921 there will be no college preparatory classes at this institution.

17. School of agriculture, elementary mechanic arts, and home economics.—The 22-weeks courses at the agricultural college should be strengthened and organized into a school of agriculture, elementary mechanic arts, and home economics for young men and women who do not expect to attend college or to become teachers. This school should offer three-year courses, the sessions being held during the winter and lasting five and one-half or six months; and the desirability of repeating these courses with necessary variations in sessions of similar length in the summer months should be considered.

18. Special short courses.—The short winter courses in extension work for farmers and farmers' wives at the agricultural college are to be commended, but those attending these courses should not be taught in the regular classes of the college, of the agricultural high school, or of the 22-weeks courses as now conducted, or in the school of agriculture, elementary mechanic arts, and home economics, the formation of which is recommended elsewhere.

19. Extension courses.—Since Federal and State laws provide liberally for extension work in agriculture and home economics under the direction of the agricultural college, no other institution in the State should undertake extension work in these subjects. Any extension work done by instructors in agricultural schools in the State should be under the direction of the agricultural college. The normal schools should offer extension courses only for teachers, as explained elsewhere. Representatives of the university and of the agricultural college should confer with the board of regents for the purpose of determining the division of all other forms of extension work between the two institutions and of devising means for necessary cooperation. All extension work should be conducted with special reference to the instruction of the public in the subjects considered and not as a means of advertising the institutions.

20. Preparation of teachers for rural schools.—Since more than four-fifths of all the children of North Dakota live in the open country and in small villages, and only one-tenth live in places of 2,500 or more, all normal schools should, without neglecting the training of teachers for city schools, make it their chief purpose to prepare teachers for rural schools. Their courses of study and their practice and observation schools should be reorganized as may be necessary for this purpose. It should be recognized that teachers for the elementary rural schools need no less education, professional knowledge and skill, maturity and native ability than teachers of schools of the same grade in urban communities.

21. Preparation of teachers for elementary schools.—Until there is a sufficient number of well-prepared teachers for all the elementary schools of the State the normal schools should confine their activities to the preparation of teachers for these schools. In so far as possible they should exclude students who are not definitely preparing for teaching.

22. Standard of admission to normal school.—The standard of admission to the normal schools should be gradually raised to graduation from a standard high school of four years or its equivalent, or of six years when the high school is preceded by only six years of elementary schooling. It is recommended that this be done by requiring one year of high-school work for admission in 1918, two years in 1919, three years in 1921, and four years in 1923 and thereafter.

For the sake of teachers of low grade of preparation already engaged in the schools of the State, the summer sessions of the normal schools should continue to admit and form classes for teachers of all grades of preparation, but should not admit persons who have less preparation than is required at any given time for admission to regular classes in the school except those who have already been employed as teachers.

23. Minimum salaries for teachers.—When the normal schools have definitely established their standards at graduation from a high school of four years for admission, and at two years of work above the high school for the normal school certificate, and three years of work above the high school for the normal school diploma, as herein recommended, the State should fix by law minimum salaries for teachers holding normal school certificates and for teachers holding normal school diplomas; the difference between the minimum salaries of the two classes being such as may seem to be justified by the different degrees of preparation. It should also provide by law for a definite increase in the minimum salaries of both classes of teachers when they have complied with the requirements for, and have been granted, the permanent license.

The first license granted to a prospective teacher coming from without the State should be a temporary license, and the permanent license should be granted on the same terms as to those who have had corresponding training or experience in North Dakota.

24. Short course in normal schools.—The 10½-months course in the normal schools should be discontinued after the end of the summer term of 1917.

25. More normal schools needed.—A normal school should be established immediately at Dickinson or elsewhere in the southwestern quarter of the State, and steps should be taken for the establishment of another normal school somewhere in the western half of the State as soon as a constitutional amendment for that purpose can be obtained.

26. Requirements for teaching certificates to correspond with normal school standards.—Standards of requirements for certification to teach in the elementary schools of the State should be advanced to correspond with the standards set by the normal schools for the award of their certificates and diplomas.

27. Professional reading and study for teachers.—The State board of education, with the assistance of the presidents of the normal schools and the heads of departments of education at the university and the agricultural college, should prepare for all persons who leave the normal schools with any kind of certificate or diploma which may be accepted as a license to teach in the elementary schools of the State such courses of study, including both professional and cultural subjects, as can reasonably be completed within a period of three years by devoting to them not less than 10 hours per week for 10 months of each year. Examinations on given portions of these courses should be held from time to time, and no person should be granted a permanent license to teach in the public schools of the State until after having completed the courses prescribed, or their full equivalent, and after having passed satisfactorily final examinations on them.[1] The final examination should come not earlier than two nor later than five years after the time of leaving the normal school.

To any person of good moral character who holds a certificate or diploma of a normal school in this State, and who satisfactorily passes examinations in the courses of study outlined, and who.is certified by any qualified superintendent or supervisor as having taught satisfactorily not less than 16 months in the elementary schools of North Dakota, there should be issued a life license to teach in the elementary schools of the State.

---

[1] Nothing in this recommendation or in recommendation 23 should operate to prevent the State of North Dakota from accepting at their full value certificates issued in other States which maintain equally high standards.

28. Requirements for normal certificates and diplomas.—The standards of instruction required for certificates or diplomas from the normal schools should be raised as follows: In 1918 no certificate or diploma should be given for less than one year of work above the completion of a high-school course of four years; in 1920 no certificate or diploma should be given for less than two years of work above the completion of a high-school course of four years; in 1923 and thereafter the certificate of the normal school should be given for the completion of two full years of not less than 36 weeks each above the completion of a full high-school course of four years, and the diploma of the schools should be given for three full years of not less than 36 weeks above the completion of a high-school course of four years.

29. Graduates of university and agricultural college as teachers.— A policy similar to that recommended for the graduates of the normal schools, both in regard to advanced courses of study, examinations, and permanent licenses to teach in the schools of the State, or to hold positions as superintendents and supervisors, should apply to the graduates of the university and the agricultural college.

30. The normal and industrial school.—The normal and industrial school at Ellendale should prepare teachers for the elementary schools of the State on the same basis as other normal schools. In addition to its work as a normal school, it should, because of its equipment for instruction in industrial subjects, continue for the present to give instruction in these subjects, adapting this instruction to the special needs of the people of the south central counties which it serves.

31. The school of science.—For the present and until the State has become much more populous than it is now and the attendance in the lower classes of the university and the agricultural college much larger than at present, the school of science at Wahpeton should function only as a school of secondary grade in science, agriculture, mechanic arts, and household arts. It should give special attention to industrial subjects, both for boys and girls, and it might include commercial subjects, including bookkeeping, stenography, and similar subjects, but this and other State schools should avoid becoming local elementary or high schools. There can be no justification for local schools of this character maintained at the expense of the taxpayers of all the State. The board of regents should consider also the advisability of establishing here a school of the kind recommended for the agricultural college and at Bottineau.

32. The school of forestry.—The school of forestry at Bottineau does not now function as a school of forestry and has very few students other than local students of elementary and high-school grade or irregular students from the adult population of Bottineau. The constitution provides that the legislature may determine the kind of school to be maintained at Bottineau. The legislature has declared its function to be that of an agricultural high school, giving special attention to forestry and horticulture. The board of regents should consider the advisability of reorganizing this school, with one session of six months in winter and another of four and one-half or five months in summer, the work of both sessions to be made as practical as possible, offering opportunity for much outdoor farm work in the summer session. The courses of this school should be for three years, as recommended for the school of agriculture at the agricultural college.

33. Instruction in forestry.—The forestry and nursery work required of the school of foresty at Bottineau should be put under the direction of the agricultural college, and all instruction of college grade in forestry which may be thought needful for the State should be given at Fargo. It may be well to continue the nurseries at Bottineau, and to establish similar nurseries at other places in the State for convenience of distribution.

34. The library commission.—The library commission should be given the means of extending the kind of work it is now doing so as to serve a much larger number of people than it now serves, and it should begin a campaign for the establishment of a county library at the county seat of each county with branch libraries at smaller towns, and for the use of schools as distributing centers. Legislation should be requested providing for the establishment and maintenance of such county libraries.

35. Public school survey.—It is recommended that a careful and thorough survey be made of the elementary schools and high schools of the State for the purpose of determining details of necessary legislation for the improvement of these schools and also for the purpose of recommending changes in the courses of study, the local management, and internal organization of the schools, and of devising plans for the erection and equipment of school buildings and of meeting other ascertained needs of these schools. A conference of the State board of regents and the State board of education should be held to consider this matter.

36. Administration of State educational system.—It is believed that the entire system of education of the State of North Dakota might be unified and rendered more efficient if the board of regents were enlarged and given control of and responsibility for the management of all the public schools of the State. This board should elect a commissioner of education, and assistant commissioners for higher education, secondary education, elementary education, vocational education, library commission, and other assistants at fixed salaries and for specified terms of service, which should be comparatively long. It should be lawful for the board to elect commissioners and assistants either from the State of North Dakota or elsewhere, and these should be elected only for their fitness and definite preparation for the duties of their respective offices.

That portion of the constitution referring to the office of the State superintendent of public instruction should be so amended as to make possible the policy here recommended. It is believed also that there should be in each county a county board of education elected by the people or appointed in some way which will guarantee efficient service. This board should consist of five members; the term of office of each should be five years, and not more than two should be retired in any biennium. This board of education should have control of all the public schools of the county and should elect, subject to the approval of the State board of regents, and either from within or without the county, qualified superintendents, assistant superintendents, and supervisors.

37. Guide to the institutions.—The board of regents should have prepared for the use of prospective students in the State a pamphlet setting forth clearly and simply the purposes and aims of each of the several institutions, its courses of study, its requirements for admission and graduation, the cost of attendance, and other similar items, to the end that any prospective student may be able to determine as accurately as possible the special advantages to be had at each institution.

38. Building and campus plans.—That before other buildings are erected or additions made to the campus at any of the institutions now in existence, and before any buildings are erected at any institutions to be established in the future, the board of regents shall have made plans for campus and building development as has been done for the university, to the end that there may be a consistent and progressive policy of building for each of the institutions.

39. Vocational survey.—It is recommended that the board of regents, through its commissioner of education and with the cooperation of the university and the agricultural college, shall have made a careful and comprehensive survey of the industries and occupations of the people of the State, and a study in detail of the educational preparation needed for success in all the more important of them, and that the results of this survey be published for the guidance of young people in choosing their vocations and of the schools in making up their courses of study.

40. Institutional organization and administration.—The board of regents should cause to be made, through its commissioner of education or otherwise, a careful study of the organization and work of each of the institutions under its control, to ascertain—

(*a*) To what extent in any of them, if at all, an unnecessary division of subjects offered, and the offering of subjects for which there is little or no demand in the State, may result in a large number of small and costly classes which might be consolidated or eliminated without loss to the State, without injury to any large number of individuals, and with profit to the institution.

(*b*) Whether and to what extent, to the detriment of any institution, large numbers of students in the lower classes are taught by inexperienced teachers on low salaries, while the abler and more experienced teachers have only very few students in the higher classes.

(*c*) Whether or not too large a proportion of the faculties of some of the schools are made up of young and inexperienced teachers employed at low salaries. Such an investigation of some of the normal schools seems to the survey commission to be especially desirable.

(*d*) To what extent the efficiency of the work of teachers in the schools is lowered because of the large number of courses and of weekly class meetings for which they are responsible.

(*e*) Whether or not in some of these schools too large a proportion of the total expenditure is for administration and other non-instructional purposes.

(*f*) Whether or not it is desirable to establish a schedule of salaries in the normal schools and to increase to a considerable extent the average of salaries in these schools, to the end that they may more certainly be able to obtain and retain the services of teachers with the education, maturity, and experience necessary for those engaged in the task of instructing and training professional teachers for the elementary schools of the State.

It is believed that the executive officers and faculties of all these schools will welcome such a study and gladly assist in making it.

Several of these points are discussed more or less extensively in this report, but on none of them has the survey commission sufficient information to enable it to make formal and final recommendations.

APPENDIX.

I. THE MOST IMPORTANT PROVISIONS IN THE ACT CREATING THE STATE BOARD OF REGENTS, SESSION LAWS, 1915.

The State board of regents, consisting of five members appointed by the governor and confirmed by the senate, is created for the general control and administration of the following State educational institutions:

1. The State university and school of mines, at Grand Forks, with their substations.
2. The State agricultural college and experiment station, at Fargo, with their substations.
3. The school of science, at Wahpeton.
4. The State normal schools at Valley City, Mayville, and Minot.
5. The normal and industrial school, at Ellendale.
6. The school of forestry, at Bottineau.
7. The State library commission, at Bismarck.
8. And such other State educational institutions as may be hereafter established.

The State board of regents shall assume all the powers and perform all the duties now exercised or performed by the normal board of control and the several boards of trustees of the institutions included under this act.

The State board of regents first appointed shall, as soon as practicable after having organized, procure to be made by a competent expert, or experts, from without the State, an educational survey of all institutions under its control, for the purpose of ascertaining wherein the efficiency of the State educational institutions can be best served and economy in conducting the same be best practiced.

Upon the completion of such educational survey the State board of regents shall appoint from without the State a State commissioner of education, who shall perform such duties of examination, inspection, and visitation as the board may direct, and shall advise the board on all matters pertaining to the curricula, coordination, and correlating of work in the institutions under the control of such board, and he shall make a special study of the particular needs and requirements of each institution and shall report thereon to the board at such time as they shall direct.

The State board of regents shall coordinate and correlate the work in the different institutions so as to prevent wasteful duplication, and to develop cooperation among such institutions in the exchange of instructors and students, and shall fix a tuition to be paid in such institutions or any department thereof when not provided by law. It shall make recommendations in regard to needed legislation for the institutions under its control, prepare a budget setting forth the financial needs of all State educational institutions under its supervision and control for the period for which an appropriation is made.

182

In order to effect the greatest economy, efficiency, and facility in providing for the needs and work of the various institutions, the president of each institution shall submit to the State board of regents, at least once each year, a budget showing the needs and amounts recommended for the work of the various departments of the institutions, and for improvements, repairs, miscellaneous items of maintenance, and such other items as shall seem expedient.

There is hereby appropriated the sum of $18,000 annually, or as much thereof as may be necessary, to carry out the provisions of this act.

In conformity with the provisions of this bill, Hon. L. B. Hanna, governor of North Dakota, appointed the following persons members of the State board of regents:

> Ex-Gov. Frank White, Valley City.
> Dr. J. D. Taylor, Grand Forks.
> Mr. Emil Scow, Bowman.
> Mr. L. F. Crawford, Sentinel Butte.
> Mr. J. A. Power, Leonard.

After the presentation of draft of the report of the survey the board of regents appointed Dr. Edwin B. Craighead commissioner of education. Dr. Craighead took up the work of commissioner of education on August 1, 1916.

The State board of regents, the commissioner of education, and the secretary of the board of regents, Mr. Charles Brewer, have offices in the State capitol building, at Bismarck.

II. CONSTITUTIONAL PROVISIONS AND EDUCATIONAL LEGISLATION IN NORTH DAKOTA.

Below are given abstracts of the constitutional provisions relating to the State educational institutions:

ARTICLE VIII, SEC. 147. A high degree of intelligence, patriotism, integrity, and morality on the part of every voter in a government by the people being necessary in order to insure the continuance of that government and the prosperity and happiness of the people, the legislative assembly shall make provision for the establishment and maintenance of a system of public schools which shall be open to all children of the State of North Dakota and free from sectarian control. This legislative requirement shall be irrevocable without the consent of the United States and the people of North Dakota.

SEC. 149. In all schools instruction shall be given as far as practicable in those branches of knowledge that tend to impress upon the mind the vital importance of truthfulness, temperance, purity, public spirit, and respect for honest labor of every kind.

SEC. 150. A superintendent of schools for each county shall be elected every two years, whose qualifications, duties, powers, and compensation shall be fixed by law.

SEC. 151. The legislative assembly shall take such other steps as may be necessary to prevent illiteracy, secure a reasonable degree of uniformity in course of study, and to promote industrial, scientific, and agricultural improvements.

SEC. 152. All colleges, universities, and other educational institutions, for the support of which lands have been granted to this State, or which are supported by a public tax, shall remain under the absolute and exclusive control of the State. No money raised for the support of the public schools of the State shall be appropriated to or used for the support of any sectarian school * * *

ART. XVII, SEC. 209. The labor of children under 12 years of age shall be prohibited in mines, factories, and workshops in this State.

ART. XIX, SEC. 215. The following public institutions of the State are permanently located at the places hereinafter named, each to have the lands specifically granted to it by the United States, in the act of Congress, approved February 22, 1889, to be disposed of and used in such manner as the legislative assembly may prescribe, subject to the limitations provided in the article on school and public lands contained in this constitution: * * *

Second. The State university and the school of mines at the City of Grand Forks, in the County of Grand Forks.

Third. The agricultural college at the City of Fargo, in the County of Cass.

Fourth. A State normal school at the City of Valley City, in the County of Barnes; and the legislative assembly in apportioning the grant of 80,000 acres of land for normal schools made in the act of Congress referred to shall grant to the said normal school at Valley City as aforementioned 50,000 acres, and said lands are hereby appropriated to said institution for that purpose * * *

Seventh. A State normal school at the City of Mayville, in the County of Traill; and the legislative assembly in apportioning the grant of lands made by Congress in the act aforesaid for State normal schools shall assign 30,000 acres to the institution hereby located at Mayville, and said lands are hereby appropriated for said purpose. * * *

SEC. 216. The following-named public institutions are hereby permanently located as hereinafter provided, each to have so much of the remaining grant of 170,000 acres of land made by the United States for "other educational and charitable institutions" as is allotted by law, namely: * * *

Third. An industrial school and school for manual training, or such other educational or charitable institutions as the legislative assembly may provide, at the Town of Ellendale, in the County of Dickey, with a grant of 40,000 acres.

Fourth. A school of forestry, or such other institution as the legislative assembly may determine, at such place in one of the Counties of McHenry, Ward, Bottineau, or Rolette as the electors of the said counties may determine by an election for that purpose, to be held as provided by the legislative assembly.

Fifth. A scientific school, or such other educational or charitable institution as the legislative assembly may prescribe, at the City of Wahpeton, County of Richland, with a grant of 40,000 acres.

Sixth. A State normal school at the City of Minot, in the County of Ward: *Provided,* that no other institution of a character similar to any one of those located by this article shall be established or maintained without a revision of this constitution.

The Minot State Normal School was established, under constitutional amendment, approved March 10, 1913.

At the election in November, 1916, the people of North Dakota will vote upon a constitutional amendment, which has been passed by the legislature, locating a normal school at Dickinson.

SESSION LAWS OF 1915.

Section 1416. Maintenance of State educational institutions.—For the purpose of providing for the maintenance of the State university and school of mines at Grand Forks, the agricultural college at Fargo, the State normal school at Valley City, the State normal school at Mayville, the State normal school at Minot, the school for the deaf and dumb at Devil's Lake, the school of forestry at Bottineau, the North Dakota academy of science at Wahpeton, the normal and industrial school at Ellendale, as a part of the public school system of this State, there is hereby levied upon all the taxable property in the State, real and personal, an annual tax of $347,880.

This annual tax takes the place of the millage tax by which these institutions were formerly supported, and which was repealed by the act of 1915, of which this is a part. These schools and all other schools heretofore established, or that may be hereafter established, by law and maintained by public taxation constitute the system of "free public schools" of the State of North Dakota.

Section 1418. Taxes, how apportioned.—Such taxes levied shall be apportioned by the State treasurer to the several institutions herein mentioned as follows:

$102,720 to the State University and school of mines at Grand Forks;
$61,800 to the agricultural college at Fargo;
$41,580 to the State normal school at Minot;
$46,200 to the State normal school at Valley City;
$36,960 to the State normal school at Mayville;
$18,480 to the school for the deaf and dumb at Devil's Lake;
$6,180 to the school of forestry at Bottineau;
$21,600 to the normal and industrial school at Ellendale;
$12,360 to the school of science at Wahpeton:

Provided, That all moneys hereafter collected pursuant hereto shall be apportioned as herein provided.

III. DISTRIBUTION OF COURSES AMONG THE INSTITUTIONS.

On October 12, 1912, Dr. Kendric C. Babcock, specialist in higher education in the Bureau of Education, wrote to the temporary educational commission of North Dakota, created by act of the legislative assembly (Session Laws of 1911, Ch. IX), the following letter, which, before being sent, was submitted to the Commissioner of Education and received his approval. Except for the modification of Section C in so far as it applies to the preparation of superintendents and supervisors of elementary schools, indicated in the chapter on normal schools, page 96 of this report, the survey commission approves the spirit and purport of this letter and the apportionment of work which it would make among the several institutions:

[Letter of Dr. Babcock.]

This discussion of "a State system of education ideally outlined and operated" assumes (1) that such system should have the functions of its different parts so distributed as to insure unity, harmony, economy, and efficiency; (2) that its higher education has well-developed and coordinated elementary and secondary schools as a basis, with differentiation of secondary schools to meet the varying local needs for vocational instruction in agriculture, commerce, and industrial arts; (3) that the three groups of higher schools should admit only those students who have completed the course of one of the secondary schools. From present indications the vocational schools of elementary or secondary grade, even those of agriculture, will at an early day be distributed rather than centralized as a part of a single agricultural college.

A.

The function of the State university should be (1) to give standard liberalizing courses in arts and sciences, covering four years and leading to a bachelor's degree; (2) to give engineering and technological courses, including agriculture, unless the State has a separate agricultural college, covering four or five years and leading to a bachelor's degree in some applied science; in case of separation of the agricultural college and the university, possibly a civil-engineering course should be developed at the agricultural college; (3) to organize professional schools or some definite portion of a prescribed professional course, such professional work to have as its ultimate basis the first two years of the liberal arts or general science courses; (4) to develop a graduate school offering courses primarily for holders of bachelors degrees and leading to the degrees of master and doctor, where the requirements of the Commonwealth constitute a sufficient demand and the resources of the State will permit; (5) to develop a department of extramural relations for reaching with information and inspiration persons whose age and occupation preclude their taking work at the university. In such State universities there should be a department for secondary and higher schools in the State.

B.

The State agricultural college, when separate from a State university in which provision is made for standard engineering and technological instruction, should devote itself strictly and mainly to the development of courses in agriculture and such branches of engineering and mechanic arts as are allied to agriculture. The States are obliged, in accordance with the terms of the Federal grant of land and money, to maintain on an approximate parity instruction in agriculture and the mechanic arts, and it rests with the States to determine how the Federal funds shall be apportioned to accomplish this purpose. An ideally operated system involves the ultimate elimination from the agricultural college of work of a secondary grade and work purely vocational in its character. A second feature of the work of the agricultural college and the agricultural experiment station should be the development of summer and winter short courses, farmers' institutes, cooperative demonstration work, and general agricultural extension and propaganda.

The work of the agricultural college and the State university, in fundamental and general subjects, of the first year or the first two years should be so coordinated that students may at the end of either of these years change from one institution to the other, as their interest or inclination may dictate, and receive full credit for courses already taken, so far as these courses may be counted at all for a degree in the second institution. The duplication of courses of the first two years, which require merely teachers, classrooms, and modern equipment in laboratory and library—for example, in mathematics, English, general chemistry, biology, and economics—may go on indefinitely, provided, of course, that the faculty and plant necessary for the work in these fundamentals are fully employed. The wastefulness of duplication usually falls most heavily in the intermediate and advanced courses. Broadly speaking, 20 sections of freshman mathematics may be as economically administered in three places as in one.

C.

The State normal schools should be held to broad preparation of teachers and supervisors for the elementary schools. Such preparation should include some cultural and liberalizing elements, in addition to the grounding in the subject matter and methodology of elementary education. When the normal schools as a whole have thus provided the elementary schools of the cities, villages, and rural communities with well-trained teachers, supervisors, and superintendents, whose education and discipline represent substantially a high-school course plus two years of professional and general training, it will be time for them to request the privilege of further upward expansion and the power to grant standard degrees. It is an undeniable fact that in scarcely a single State are the normal schools at the present time supplying more than 40 per cent of the annual demand for new teachers in the public-school system.

D.

Provisions for trade, industrial, and commercial schools in a State essentially agricultural in its interests may safely be made in the differentiated secondary schools and in technological departments of the university and the agricultural college. The argument that a State should supply each of its citizens with any sort of an education that he may desire does not rest upon a logical basis, nor should it lead to the establishment of all sorts of specialized schools by each State. Cooperation between States and subsidies to promising students to seek their instruction in the best possible schools—for example, mining or textile engineering—may well be adopted as a policy rather than the establishment of various weak and spiritless schools. A student in North Dakota who desires advanced instruction in architecture, marine engineering, or industrial chemistry other than agricultural chemistry should expect to seek instruction outside the State. I see no sufficient justification for a "school of science" separate from the State university, agricultural college, and vocational schools in any State.

E.

The work in engineering should be done in connection with the university and agricultural college; generally speaking, it should be done at the university, with its highly equipped departments of pure science, since engineering professions show a marked tendency to emphasize severe training in the principles and fundamentals of engineering, which can best be taught in a university spirit and in a university atmosphere.

F.

In the original agriculture land-grant act of 1862 the terms "agriculture" and "the mechanic arts" are used coordinately. The Federal authorities are insistent that each State accepting the land grant, and later grants of money, must provide adequately for both forms of education. By common understanding the term mechanic arts has been interpreted to include all forms of engineering, though there is serious doubt in many quarters as to whether this was the original intent of the men who passed the act of 1862; in other words, the grade of instruction in agriculture and in mechanic arts should be the same; if one is of college grade, the other should be of college grade. While the vocational or industrial work both in agriculture and mechanic arts will continue to need attention from the agricultural colleges for some years to come, there is good reason to believe that this is a passing phase and that the localities will ultimately provide for the greater part of such instruction. The agricultural college must become a college in fact as well as in name, no matter how differentiated its function. It must not continue to undermine the work which the various communities and the State itself are doing to build up sound secondary education throughout the State.

G.

Neither efficiency nor economy dictates that the work of the normal schools should be extended under present conditions to include the preparation of teachers for secondary schools; on the other hand, the correlation between the normal schools and the State university and the agricultural college should be so worked out that students completing the normal school course and finding themselves eager for more thorough or specialized preparation could enter one of the other institutions with definite credits toward a degree.

By way of summary it should be said that it is high time, in the interests of efficiency and economy, that various States should think of their educational systems as a unity, subject to the sovereign wisdom of the State, and that the State itself should dictate a far-reaching policy of coordination and control.

K. C. Babcock,
Specialist in Higher Education.

October 12, 1912.

IV. AGRICULTURAL ENGINEERING AND RURAL ARTS.

By L. H. Bailey.

[See p. 72.]

Farm mechanics and machinery.—The use of machinery has now come to be a permanent part of the equipment for good agriculture, and the kinds of machines are legion. The principles that are involved in the construction of farm machinery, and the practice, can not be adequately discussed in most colleges of mechanic arts or engineering, for such colleges have another and special point of view.

Rural engineering.—Under this term are included such field engineering problems as have to do specially with agricultural enterprises, as surveying with reference to land measure, drainage, irrigation, road making, water supplies, and many of the lesser problems of bridge building, traction development, and other construction.

Nearly all the land of the open country is to be in farms (using the word farm to include organized and managed forests), and the complete utilization of this land will demand the expenditure of much engineering skill. The engineer will probably contribute as much as any other man to the making of the ideal country life. Professional engineering problems must be left to the technical engineering schools, but training must also be provided from the agricultural point of view and in connection with other agricultural studies. These agricultural engineering subjects are bound to multiply. Irrigation, for example, is not to be confined to arid regions; it must be added to humid regions, not only to overcome the effect of drought, but to cause the land to produce to its utmost. Irrigation for humid climates presents a special set of problems, for it must be intimately associated with drainage, and these problems are not yet well understood.

Rural art.—Almost from the first, agricultural colleges have included landscape gardening in their curricula. In fact, they are the only institutions that have taught it. The subject is considered to be their special province. To this day there is only one professional school in the United States covering this field, and that was recently organized at Harvard. At least 22 of the landgrant institutions are now giving instructions in these subjects.

As a country life and agricultural subject, landscape gardening (or landscape architecture) has to do primarily with the making of the farm property (both the home and the farm) attractive and artistic. In a larger way, it has to do with the preserving and improving of natural scenery, with village improvement, and with the general elevation of taste. The artistic handling of ordinary farm properties must be left largely to the agricultural schools and colleges, because it can not pay sufficient fees to warrant a professional man to undertake it; moreover, the desire for such handling must be aroused and fostered by educating the man who lives on the land. The entire farm area of a college or university should be laid out with reference to good taste, making it practically a rural park without in any way interfering with its agricultural utilization; in fact, such layout should increase its agricultural utility.

Rural architecture.—Rural architecture is for the most part hopelessly inefficient and therefore hopelessly inartistic. Real farm architecture will not be handled by professional architects because there are no fees in it; and, as in the case of rural art in general, the public sense must be quickened. Moreover, the problems in farm architecture are essentially agricultural problems. This is particularly true of barns and stables. Practically all farm buildings must be rebuilt on fundamentally new lines, if farming is to be an efficient business. In the past, barns and stables have been built merely to protect produce and animals, rather than to accomplish certain definite progressive ends. The modern ideas of sanitation, whereby dust is to be eliminated, are revolutionizing stable construction, to say nothing of means to securing cleanliness in other ways, of ventilation, of sunlight, water supplies, and other necessities.

Technology and other manufacture.—Several great departments or other kinds of work will develop in this field. Dairy manufacture has already reached a very high degree of development in several agricultural colleges, and is completely established in the public confidence, although it was a doubtful innovation only a few years ago. This intelligent dairy manufacture has had an immeasurable effect on dairy production and products. Therefore it is not too much to expect that comparable results will follow in other lines of agricultural manufacture, particularly in the making of commercial products and the utilization of waste in the great fruit industries. The technology of canning, evaporating, and preserving of fruit is much in need in the colleges. These institutions must also undertake the whole subject of the curing of meats and the manufacture of animal products. These subjects naturally lead to consideration of storage, refrigeration and the mechanics of transportation.

Domestic and personal questions.—The home as well as the land must be reached. The home questions are of two categories: The internal, comprising housekeeping and householding subjects; the external, in which the home is considered as part of the community in its relation to school, church, organizations, and various social questions. The farm home should be the ideal place in which to train boys and girls. It should be comfortable, attractive, and sanitary. Human food should receive scientific attention. Woman's work should be alleviated and elevated. The work needs reorganization. Mechanical appliances must be brought to its aid. The miscellaneous activities that center about the home have been assembled into courses of study. These courses have received various collective names, none of which is good, because the subjects are miscellaneous and not capable of being welded. Of these names, " home economics " seems now to be the oftenest preferred.

VI. THE UNIVERSITY OF NORTH DAKOTA—EDUCATIONAL SERVICE.

TABLE 46.

[Prepared by University of North Dakota.]

	Fiscal year.					
	1910–11	1911–12	1912–13	1913–14	1914–15	1915–16
Division of engineering:						
School of mines—						
Salaries, instruction	$4,000.00	$5,750.00	$5,950.00	$7,190.00	$7,910.00	$7,960.00
Salaries, clerical	183.71	612.38	293.79	862.47	540.00	540.00
Materials and supplies	738.65	576.72	616.41	1,449.75	1,817.92	1,555.00
Freight and express	97.60	47.29	90.81	201.07	251.56	....
Assistance by students in analysis and testing	465.79	168.73	148.47	472.10	243.80	470.00
Repairs	....	....	22.87	71.79	20.66	....
Museum	....	....	196.35	256.37	....	....
Salaries of dean and assistants	400.00	400.00	851.05	1,023.50	1,294.85	1,250.00
Total school of mines	5,885.75	7,556.12	8,170.75	11,534.05	12,078.79	11,775.00
Course in civil engineering—						
Salaries, instruction	....	....	....	....	2,500.00	2,500.00
Materials and supplies	....	....	....	....	46.80	125.00
Total course in civil engineering	....	....	....	....	2,546.80	2,625.00
College of mechanical and electrical engineering—						
Salaries, instruction	9,439.00	10,100.00	10,150.00	9,466.00	9,450.00	10,800.00
Salaries, office and clerical	424.18	30.75	12.50	3.56	....	....
Materials and supplies	1,717.51	616.93	539.72	752.94	769.09	750.00
Repairs	31.31	34.70	162.42	10.10	78.16	200.00
Freight and express	72.25	23.27	22.99	73.07	12.96	....
Salaries of dean and assistants	400.00	400.00	400.00	100.00	400.00	400.00
Total college of mechanical and electrical engineering	12,084.25	11,205.65	11,287.63	10,338.67	10,730.21	12,150.00
College of liberal arts:						
Graduate department	1,230.00	1,655.00	1,793.50	1,520.00	1,600.00	1,350.00
Art and design	....	....	....	....	1,708.53	2,200.00
Biology	5,257.67	5,187.36	6,050.37	6,487.03	4,150.62	4,240.00
Chemistry	4,460.19	4,644.94	5,242.11	7,369.29	8,344.62	8,300.00
Economics and political science	3,768.75	4,075.00	4,306.37	3,956.35	3,680.00	3,960.00
English	7,300.00	6,227.50	7,370.00	7,900.00	8,112.00	8,325.00
Geology	4,235.47	4,586.16	4,650.31	4,762.93	4,720.93	4,750.00
German	....	3,100.00	3,400.00	3,400.00	3,700.00	3,975.00
German and Scandinavian	4,100.00	....	....	....	....	....
Greek	2,368.15	2,424.84	2,500.00	2,500.00	2,500.00	2,525.00
History	3,965.61	4,027.26	3,216.55	3,761.94	3,655.50	3,710.00
Home economics	....	....	....	....	1,992.18	2,250.00
Latin	4,704.50	2,200.00	2,525.00	2,400.00	2,400.00	2,420.00
Mathematics and applied mathematics	3,997.16	4,068.29	4,050.78	4,137.29	1,700.00	1,850.00
Music	1,716.36	2,236.83	2,179.76	2,306.01	2,419.61	2,550.00
Physical training	8,966.26	4,404.66	4,299.55	5,465.78	4,792.80	5,375.00
Physics	5,604.49	5,697.36	6,274.16	6,582.65	6,453.51	7,110.00
Romance languages	2,100.00	2,200.00	2,300.00	2,022.23	2,166.88	2,375.00
Scandinavian	....	2,500.00	2,500.00	2,500.00	2,500.00	2,500.00
Sociology	2,435.06	2,590.87	3,351.13	3,630.54	3,882.39	3,980.00
Convocation lectures	320.59	492.20	401.47	348.09	141.25	400.00
Meteorology	174.06	....	....	....	....	....
Museum	....	1,330.12	306.34	....	....	....
Salaries of dean and assistants	400.00	200.00	400.00	350.00	200.00	200.00
Total college of liberal arts	62,107.56	63,848.39	67,117.40	71,402.02	70,815.82	74,345.00
Law school:						
Salaries, instruction	8,350.00	8,367.50	9,575.00	10,250.00	10,091.25	10,170.00
Salaries, office and clerical	1,166.28	1,168.96	473.13	491.90	761.60	835.00
Materials and supplies	222.49	228.84	309.21	273.79	589.60	750.00
Repairs	25.84	....	25.68	77.99	40.28	....
Rent of quarters	1,440.00	1,440.00	1,440.00	1,740.00	1,755.00	2,100.00
Books	418.29	870.82	900.17	2,348.25	1,662.26	500.00
Freight and express	2.58	....	3.26	9.64	3.66	....

TABLE 46—Continued.

	Fiscal year.					
	1910–11	1911–12	1912–13	1913–14	1914–15	1915–16
Law school—Continued.						
Traveling expenses...............		$73.82				
Salaries of dean and assistants....	$400.00	....	$960.00	$990.00	$300.00	$400.00
Total law school..........	12,025.48	12,149.96	13,716.45	16,181.57	15,208.65	14,755.00
School of education.	6,073.06	6,239.49	8,135.29	12,643.96		
Education and philosophy.......					8,677.12	8,630.00
Professional courses—						
Manual training.........					450.00	450.00
Commercial branches......					600.00	600.00
German.............					600.00	400.00
English.............						850.00
History.............						200.00
Mathematics.........						300.00
Total.................	6,073.06	6,239.49	8,135.29	12,643.96	10,327.12	11,930.00
Model high school—						
Salaries, instruction.......	11,842.00	13,427.50	13,003.41	11,768.30	10,182.50	9,020.00
Materials and supplies......	391.33	430.98	609.61	451.37	311.28	365.00
Repairs..................	4.80			18.00	4.07	
Freight and express........	19.56	7.40	20.18	21.34	12.07	
Salaries of dean and assistants...........:	400.00	400.00	400.00	500.00	500.00	400.00
Total school of education....	18,730.75	20,509.37	22,168.49	25,402.97	21,338.04	21,715.00
School of medicine:						
Salaries, instruction............	2,850.00	4,500.00	4,800.00	4,587.00	4,300.00	4,500.00
Salaries, clerical, etc..........	14.65	31.25	13.39	37.50	135.00	175.00
Materials and supplies..........	798.05	721.65	732.49	562.98	700.95	810.06
Repairs...................	110.88	55.42	16.19	5.99	37.84	
Freight and express...........	30.61		94.57	55.39	34.85	
Bacteriology and pathology.....	607.57	789.53	1,148.36	934.90	1,764.32	1,925.00
Nurses' course............	800.00	1,146.25	1,072.88	1,054.43	1,109.78	1,100.00
Infirmary and nursery..........	61.94	77.67				
Salaries of dean and assistants....	400.00			200.00	300.00	500.00
Total school of medicine....	5,673.70	7,321.77	7,877.88	7,438.17	7,032.74	8,810.00
Summer session (college section):						
Salaries.................	1,597.58	1,605.00	1,959.00	2,292.50	2,243.33	2,265.00
Materials and supplies..........	38.20	92.93	61.28	51.37	72.91	25.00
Printing..................			98.40	135.08	98.60	125.00
Total summer session.....	1,635.78	1,697.93	2,118.68	2,478.95	2,414.84	2,415.00
Extension division:						
Salaries direction, instruction, and lectures..............		1,399.92	2,182.50	3,700.44	4,395.59	3,300.00
Salaries, clerical...........	158.25	688.40	300.00	408.87	284.25	600.00
Materials and supplies.........	117.15	326.58		161.24	107.60	150.00
Repairs...................	26.05					
Traveling expenses of faculty lecturers and staff..............	856.24	1,667.48	2,420.87	1,885.33	669.04	1,350.00
Freight and express..........	22.69			34.74	50.30	
Printing and postage..........	193.20	539.59	545.42	385.87	830.69	750.00
Stationery and office supplies.....		232.62	129.61	167.24		
High-school contests...........			42.00		208.28	150.00
Refunds...................				49.82	18.00	
Total extension division....	1,373.58	4,854.59	5,620.40	6,793.55	6,563.74	6,300.00
Library:						
Salary, librarian..............	1,250.00	1,108.27	1,500.00	1,600.00	1,650.00	1,700.00
Salaries, clerical.............	2,238.98	2,555.07	2,776.44	3,158.10	3,385.98	3,210.00
Supplies..................	600.29	224.22	372.07	497.34	672.98	840.00
Freight and express...........	172.93	182.59	204.67	96.18	85.34	100.00
Books and periodicals..........	3,124.63	3,387.11	3,996.73	3,556.60	2,095.17	2,700.00
Total library............	7,386.83	7,457.26	8,849.91	8,908.22	7,889.47	8,550.00
Total educational service...	126,903.70	136,597.04	146,927.59	160,478.18	156,613.10	163,440.00

VII. UNIVERSITY PLANT.

TABLE 47.

Buildings.	Date built.	Cost.	Equipment.	Use.
Merrifield Hall...................	1883	$71,597.05	$9,575.00	Administration and recitations.
Davis Hall......................	1887	40,000.00	5,540.43	Women's dormitory.
Macnie Hall....................	1893	16,000.00	1,986.87	Do.
Budge Hall.....................	1899	27,000.00	1,905.50	Men's dormitory.
Science Hall....................	1901	47,000.00	30,099.15	Geology, biology, medicine, health, etc.
Mechanical engineering building.	1902	25,000.00	34,092.50	College of mechanical and electrical engineering.
President's residence...........	1902	25,000.00	898.25	
Library (gift of Andrew Carnegie).	1907	30,000.00	{[1] 57,168.50 [2] 7,232.66	
Gymnasium.....................	1907	28,000.00	1,201.00	Physical education.
Mining engineering building.....	1909–10	32,500.00	35,885.45	
Woodworth Hall................	1909–10	68,000.00	14,923.13	School of education; physical education for women; music.
School of law (rented quarters in city).			{[1] 27,375.50 [2] 1,531.37	
University Commons Building...	1910–1912	70,000.00	7,425.23	Dining hall.
Power plant....................	1909	8,500.00	15,644.90	
Plant house....................	1912–13	6,500.00		Green house.
Biological station building (Devils Lake).	1910	5,000.00	2,291.10	Biological research.
Mining station buildings (at Hebron).[3]		6,050.00	13,900.00	
Barn and carriage shed.........		1,900.00	} 2,703.20	
Carpenter shop, ice house, etc....		550.00		
Public health laboratory (branches at Bismarck and Minot).			689.80	
Total.......................		508,597.05	272,009.54	

[1] Library.   [2] Furniture.
[3] Office and laboratory, briqueting building; power and gas house, coal sheds, etc.

Campus, 80 acres (40 acres adjoining), with improvements worth $62,408.80.

SUMMARY.

College of liberal arts_____	$37,252.18
School of education and model high school_____	10,949.89
School of law_____	28,906.87
School of mines_____	22,005.00
School of medicine_____	4,394.03
College of mechanical and electrical engineering_____	34,092.50
Course in civil engineering_____	1,836.00

Total colleges _____		$139,436.42
Library_____	64,401.16	
Administrative offices_____	5,780.10	
Dormitories, president's residence, and commons_____	16,754.55	
Substations_____	18,258.60	
Museum _____	7,024.00	
Barn, power plant, mechanician, and weather bureau_____	20,414.71	134,608.42

SUMMARY OF LANDS, BUILDINGS, AND EQUIPMENT.

Estimated value of campus, 80 acres, and 40 acres adjoining_____	$50,000.00	
Campus improvements_____	62,408.80	
Buildings, book value_____	508,597.05	
Furniture, apparatus, and equipment_____	187,725.54	
Libraries (books)_____	84,344.00	
Land endowment:		
Funds invested _____	$1,163,019.78	
36,511.15 acres of unsold lands, estimated at $15 per acre _____	547,667.25	1,710,687.03
Total_____		2,603,762.42

46136°—Bull. 27—17——13

VIII. ITEMIZED STATEMENT OF INCOME OF THE UNIVERSITY, 1915-16.

TABLE 48.

INCOME—EDUCATIONAL.

Student fees	$22, 150. 00	
Mill tax, uncollected	4, 000. 00	
Mill tax, fixed sum	102, 720. 00	
Maintenance appropriation	25, 500. 00	
Reimbursement appropriation	36, 000. 00	
Appropriations for library, grounds, repairs, and summer session	7. 750. 00	
Interest and income	60, 000. 00	
Extension division:		
Appropriation	2, 500. 00	
Correspondence students	650. 00	
Lectures	1, 250. 00	
Lyceum fees, net	1, 250. 00	
Office of high-school examiner	900. 00	
Interest on bank balances	240. 00	
Miscellaneous receipts that reduce operating costs	5, 850. 00	
		$270, 760. 00

INCOME—NONEDUCATIONAL.

Appropriations for audit of accounts	2, 500. 00	
Insurance premiums and interest	13, 459. 95	
Commons equipment	4, 000. 00	
Medical-school equipment	1, 250. 00	
Re-wiring buildings	7, 500. 00	
		28, 709. 95
Stations:		
Mining substation	11, 000. 00	
Biological station	3, 678. 00	
Public-health laboratory	12, 340. 00	
Geological survey	616. 00	
		27, 634. 00
Dormitory rents	8, 925. 00	
University commons	54, 850. 00	
State oil inspection	3, 000. 00	
Athletic association (fees)	2, 800. 00	
County summer school	1, 925. 00	
Miscellaneous trust funds	2, 139. 60	
		78, 639. 60
		400, 743. 55

IX. BUILDINGS, EQUIPMENT, AND INCOME OF NORTH DAKOTA AGRICULTURAL COLLEGE.

TABLE 49.—*Buildings.*

Buildings.	Date of erection.	Construction.	Cost or estimate.	Uses.
Administration......	[1]1891	Brick.........	$34,000.00	Offices and classrooms, country theater.
Chemical.............	1910	Brick and concrete, fireproof.	110,000.00	Department chemistry and pharmacy, pure food laboratories.
Engineering.........	1907	Brick.........	59,000.00	Department engineering.
Mechanical Arts......	1893	.....do......	28,000.00	Shops.
Science Hall.........	1901	.....do......	20,000.00	Department biology and pure seed laboratory.
Francis Hall.........	1893	.....do......	20,000.00	Department agriculture and horticulture.
Veterinary...........	1909	.....do......	28,000.00	Department veterinary and State serum institute.
Dairy................	1913	Brick and concrete fireproof.	27,000.00	Department dairying and laboratories.
Music Hall...........	1897	Brick.........	3,700.00	Department music.
Ceres Hall...........	1909	.....do......	110,000.00	Department home economics and girls' dormitory.
Armory..............	[1]1897	Frame........	10,500.00	Department military drill and convocation hall.
Library..............	1905	Brick.........	22,000.00	Department library.
Experimental mill...	1907	Frame........	4,400.00	Experimental work in grains and flours.
Seed house..........	1907	Brick.........	9,500.00	Storage of grains and seed laboratory.
Greenhouse..........	[2]1907	Brick walls....	6,000.00	Greenhouse, garden and plants laboratory.
Farmhouse...........	1893	Frame........	4,000.00	Residence farm superintendent and farm laborers.
Horse barn..........	1901	.....do......	10,200.00	Horses.
Cow barn............	1901	.....do......	8,800.00	Cattle.
Sheep barn..........	1899	.....do......	3,000.00	Sheep.
Swine barn..........	1899	.....do......	1,500.00	Swine.
Dairy barn..........	1913	Concrete, frame roof.	110,500.00	Dairy cattle.
Milk house..........	1915	Concrete.....	1,500.00	For care of milk.
Poultry house No. 1..	1896	Frame........	1,800.00	Poultry.
Poultry house No. 2..	1895	.....do......	280.00	Do.
Machine shed No. 1..	1907	.....do......	2,200.00	Storage machinery.
Machine shed No. 2..	1900	.....do......	1,000.00	Do.
Garden house.......	1896	.....do......	220.00	Storage of garden tools.
Serum buildings (5)..	1909-15	.....do......	1,200.00	Manufacture of serum, and serum hog sheds.
Heating plant.......	[3]1905	Brick.........	10,500.00	Central heating plant for all buildings.
Total.............			554,800.00	

[1] Remodeled 1907.   [2] Addition 1913.   [3] Remodeled.

TABLE 50.—*Approximate value of equipment by departments.*

Department.	Equipment.	Department.	Equipment.
Agriculture...............	$74,360.00	Modern languages..............	$150.00
Engineering..............	45,000.00	Military......................	125.00
Biology..................	40,630.00	High school...................	110.00
Chemistry...............	33,700.00	Athletics.....................	530.00
Veterinary..............	26,240.00	President.....................	720.00
Home economics.........	7,000.00	Registrar.....................	1,170.00
Music...................	2,850.00	Secretary.....................	1,525.00
Public discussion........	2,500.00	Janitor.......................	1,960.00
Horticulture............	1,275.00	Director......................	2,700.00
Mathematics............	265.00	Power house..................	35,380.00
Education...............	250.00	Library.......................	37,990.00
English.................	150.00		
History.................	150.00	Total......................	315,730.00

Table 51.—*Statement of income, July 1, 1914, to June 30, 1915, inclusive.*

Name of fund.	Total.	United States.	State.	Local receipts.
United States Government	$50,000.00	$50,000.00		
Interest and income	59,830.81		$59,830.81	
Mill tax	42,811.29		42,811.29	
Building	5,501.74			$5,501.74
Miscellaneous and farm	19,942.73			19,942.73
Ceres Hall	¹18,326.47			18,326.47
Hatch	15,000.00	15,000.00		
Adams	15,000.00	15,000.00		
Smith Lever (United States)	10,000.00	10,000.00		
Extension	10,352.70		10,000.00	352.70
Maintenance	33,162.50		25,000.00	8,162.50
Smith Lever (State), available July 1, 1915				
Pure food	10,000.00		10,000.00	
Beverage	12,000.00		12,000.00	
Demonstration farms	12,295.13		12,000.00	295.13
Serum Institute	8,139.94		3,000.00	5,139.94
Pure seed	2,500.00		2,500.00	
Geological survey	1,000.00		1,000.00	
Mill maintenance	1,730.56		500.00	1,230.56
Development and research	15,148.37			15,148.37
Miscellaneous	38,449.99			38,449.99
Local income	16,096.90			16,096.90
Edgeley substation	5,694.53		5,000.00	694.53
Dickinson substation	5,727.96		5,000.00	727.96
Williston substation	8,508.35		5,000.00	3,508.35
Langdon substation	5,978.30		5,000.00	978.30
Hettinger substation	6,184.18		5,000.00	1,184.18
Total	429,382.45	90,000.00	203,642.10	135,740.35

¹ The income from Ceres Hall, $18,326.47, is not net and should be deducted from "Total," leaving $411,055.98.

X. PUBLIC SCHOOL TEACHERS IN NORTH DAKOTA.

Table 52.—*Number of teachers of specified ages of total of 4,981 teachers replying to questionnaire.*

	Less than 18	18	19	20	21	22	23	24	25	26
Ungraded schools	1	61	301	460	413	393	279	249	127	133
Graded elementary schools		3	18	53	98	114	123	149	94	101
High schools				1	10	10	28	42	31	42
Superintendents, principals, and supervisors			1	3	9	22	33	42	31	39
Total	1	64	320	517	530	539	463	482	283	315

	27	28	29	30	31	32	33	34	35	36
Ungraded schools	108	68	53	60	39	31	20	27	19	10
Graded elementary schools	78	60	43	59	31	25	20	11	17	12
High schools	20	23	16	12	6	11	8	1	6	3
Superintendents, principals, and supervisors	29	26	26	34	21	22	25	16	19	14
Total	235	177	138	165	97	89	73	55	61	39

	37	38	39	40	41	42	43	44	45	46
Ungraded schools	10	13	8	7	13	10	7	7	5	9
Graded elementary schools	8	7	9	13	4	5	4	3	1	6
High schools		2	1	1		2			3	
Superintendents, principals, and supervisors	10	10	5	13	5	5	3	8	1	4
Total	28	32	23	34	22	22	14	18	10	19

TABLE 52.—*Number of teachers of specified ages of total of 4,981 teachers replying to questionnaire*—Continued.

	47	48	49	50	51	52	53	54	55	56
Ungraded schools	7	5	7	2	3	6	2	2	1	2
Graded elementary schools	1	1	1	3	2	2	2	1	1	......
High schools	1	3	......	......	......	......	1	......	......	......
Superintendents, principals, and supervisors	2	7	5	4	1	2	4	2	2	1
Total	11	16	13	9	6	10	9	5	4	3

	57	58	59	60	61	62	63	64	65	66
Ungraded schools	1	......	......	2	1	2	1	3	......	......
Graded elementary schools	......	1	......	1	1	......	......	......	......	1
Superintendents, principals, and supervisors	1	......	......	......	......	......	......	......	......	1
Total	2	1	......	3	2	2	1	3	......	2

	67	68	70	81	Not reporting.	Totals.
Ungraded schools	1	1	......	......	4	2,994
Graded elementary schools	1	......	......	......	4	1,192
High schools	......	......	......	......	1	285
Superintendents, principals, and supervisors	......	1	......	......	1	510
Total	2	2	......	......	10	4,981

TABLE 53.—*Number of teachers who have taught specified number of years of total of 4,981 teachers replying to questionnaire.*

	Less than 1 year.	1	2	3	4	5	6	7	8
Ungraded schools	943	483	445	328	231	132	98	60	54
Graded elementary schools	140	112	161	149	121	100	98	50	60
High schools	42	47	42	36	27	24	25	8	7
Superintendents, supervisors, and principals	31	37	54	57	40	40	41	26	23
Total	1,156	679	702	570	419	296	262	144	144

	9	10	11	12	13	14	15	16	17
Ungraded schools	38	39	17	21	16	10	13	6	2
Graded elementary schools	48	28	27	18	16	8	10	5	8
High schools	5	5	5	3	2	1	1	1	2
Superintendents, supervisors, and principals	21	24	11	15	7	10	8	5	12
Total	112	96	60	57	41	29	31	17	24

	18	19	20	21	22	23	24	25	26
Ungraded schools	13	5	9	2	5	1	4	8	2
Graded elementary schools	4	6	5	3	5	1	3	......	1
High schools	......	1	......	......	......	......	......	......	......
Superintendents, supervisors, and principals	4	4	4	4	4	7	4	3	3
Total	21	16	18	9	14	9	11	11	6

TABLE 53.—*Number of teachers who have taught specified number of years of total of 4,981 teachers replying to questionnaire*—Continued.

	27	28	29	30	31	32	33	34	35
Ungraded schools	2	......	1	......	......	......	1	......	1
Graded elementary schools	1	......	1	......	......	1	......	1	......
High schools	......	......	1	......	......	......	......	......	......
Superintendents, supervisors, and principals	1	......	1	2	3	1	......	1	......
Total	4	......	4	2	3	2	1	2	1

	36	37	45	47	50	No report.	Totals.
Ungraded schools	......	3	......	1	1	......	2,994
Graded elementary schools	1	......	......	......	......	......	1,192
High schools	......	......	......	......	......	......	285
Superintendents, supervisors, and principals	......	1	1	......	......	......	510
Total	1	4	1	1	1	......	4,981

TABLE 54.—*Number of teachers who were appointed to their present positions within specified dates, of total of 4,981 teachers replying to questionnaire.*

	Since Jan. 1, 1916.	July 1 to Dec. 31, 1915.	Jan. 1 to June 30, 1915.	July 1 to Dec. 31, 1914.	Jan. 1 to June 30, 1914.	July 1 to Dec. 31, 1913.	Jan. 1 to June 30, 1913.
Ungraded schools	95	2,218	185	155	23	66	13
Graded elementary schools	12	364	289	169	89	66	49
High schools	1	92	63	51	21	15	8
Superintendents, supervisors, and principals	3	133	112	76	44	27	20
Total	111	2,807	649	451	177	174	81

	July 1 to Dec. 31, 1912.	Jan. 1 to June 30, 1912.	July 1 to Dec. 31, 1911.	Jan. 1 to June 30, 1911.	July 1 to Dec. 31, 1910.	Jan. 1 to June 30, 1910.	Jan. 1 to Dec. 31, 1909.
Ungraded schools	31	5	12	......	5	......	4
Graded elementary schools	27	5	10	7	15	3	15
High schools	6	3	4	1	4	1	2
Superintendents, supervisors, and principals	24	4	15	8	7	......	6
Total	88	17	41	16	31	4	27

	Jan. 1 to Dec. 31, 1908.	Jan. 1 to Dec. 31, 1907.	Jan. 1 to Dec. 31, 1906.	Jan. 1 to Dec. 31, 1905.	Jan. 1 to Dec. 31, 1904.	Jan. 1 to Dec. 31, 1903.	Jan. 1 to Dec. 31, 1902.
Ungraded schools	3	3	......	1	1	......	1
Graded elementary schools	5	1	4	3	1	1	1
High schools	2	......	......	......	......	......	......
Superintendents, supervisors, and principals	3	4	2	4	1	1	......
Total	13	8	6	8	3	2	3

TABLE 54.—*Number of teachers who were appointed to their present positions within specified dates, of 4,981 teachers replying to questionnaire*—Con.

	Jan. 1 to Dec. 31, 1901.	Jan. 1 to Dec. 31, 1900.	Jan. 1 to Dec. 31, 1899.	Jan. 1 to Dec. 31, 1898.	Jan. 1 to Dec. 31, 1897.	Jan. 1 to Dec. 31, 1896.	Not reported.	Totals.
Ungraded schools		1					172	2,994
Graded elementary schools				1		2	62	1,192
High schools							11	285
Superintendents, supervisors, and principals			1				5	510
Total		1	1	1		2	250	4,981

XI. COURSES FOR WHICH THERE IS LITTLE DEMAND.

TABLE 55.—*List of courses announced in the catalogue for the second semester, 1915–16, in which no classes were reported for the week of April 10–16, 1916: University of North Dakota.*

Figures following titles of courses indicate number of credit hours.

Since many courses are listed in the university catalogue according to a system of prerequisites rather than by years of the curriculum, it is impracticable to arrange the courses in the following list by years.

Astronomy 2_____Practical astronomy, 2.
Bacteriology 2_____General bacteriology, 4.
Biology 4_____Nature study, 2.
Botany 12_____Special morphology of bryophytes and pteridophytes, 4.
    14_____Special morphology of gymnosperms and angiosperms, 4.
    18_____Microscopical study of water and sewage, 3.
Ceramics 2_____Clay-working laboratory, 4.
Chemistry 12_____Water analysis, 1.
Commercial 2_____Bookkeeping, 4.
    4_____Shorthand and typewriting, 4.
    6_____Advanced bookkeeping and accounting, 4.
    8_____Stenography, 3.
    10_____Commercial law, 4.
Economics 8_____Tariff history of the United States, 4.
    10_____History of economic thought, 1.
    56_____Practical legislation and statutory construction, 2.
Education 6 A_____Sociology applied to education, 2.
    24_____Current educational literature, 2.
    104_____Theory and practice of teaching history, 2.
    106_____do., science, 2.
    154_____do., home economics, 1.
    156_____do., chemistry, 1.
    164_____do., art, 1.
    166_____do., physics, 2.
    168_____do., botany, 1.
Art and design 12 G_____History of Greek art, 2.
Geology 6_____Mineralogy, 4.
    12_____Applied geology, 2.
    16_____Historical geology, 2.
    18_____Geological research (hours to be arranged).
    20_____Climatology (2 or), 4.

German 12................German literature, land, and people, 3.
       16................Hauptmann and the modern German writers, 3.
       18................Hebbel, 2.
       20................Middle high German (can be arranged).
       22................Old high German (can be arranged).
Greek 6................Plato and dramatic poetry, 4.
History 6................Constitutional and political history of the United States, 3.
        12................Contemporary history, 3.
Latin 12................Roman comedy, 3.
       14................Roman life in the first century, 3.
Mathematics 6................Projective geometry, 3.
            14................Method of least squares, 2.
Philosophy 6................Experimental psychology, 3.
           10................History of modern philosophy, 3.
           12................Psychotherapy, 3.
Physics 8................Variable and alternating current measurements, 2.
        10................Mathematical physics, 2.
        20................Radio communication (hours to be arranged).
        22................Physical optics, 4.
French 12................Sixteenth century French, 2.
Spanish 4................Classic Spanish authors of the seventeenth century, 4.
Italian 2................Italian language and literature, 2.
Norse 6................History of Scandinavia, 2.
      10................Old Norse, 2.
Mining Engineering 4........Coal mining and handling, 4.
Surveying 10................Railway engineering, 2.
Mechanical Engineering X 34..Mechanical laboratory, 4.
Bridge Design 2.............Roof and bridge trusses, 2.
Sanitary Engineering 2......Elements of sanitary engineering, 2.
Mechanical Engineering X 38..Mechanical laboratory, 4.
                          84..Heating and ventilating, 2.
                          86..Railroad equipment, 2.
                          88..Waterworks plants, 2.
                          90..Mechanical engineering, 4.
                         100..Mechanical engineering thesis, 2 to 8.
Electrical Engineering 12....Electrical mining machinery, 2.
Municipal Engineering 2.....Municipal engineering, 2.
Water Supplies 2............Water supplies, 2.

If all the courses in the foregoing list were offered, there would be required 177 hours additional of instructors' time. At an average of 18.1 hours per week for each instructor (see Table 33, line 2d), more than nine additional instructors would be required.

TABLE 56.—*List of courses announced in the catalogue for the spring term, 1915–16, in which no classes were reported for the week of April 10–16, 1916: North Dakota Agricultural College.*

Figures following titles of courses indicate number of credit hours.

SENIOR YEAR.

Agronomy 11_____Crop production, 3.
     12_____Crop-production laboratory, 2.
Animal Husbandry 13_____Animal husbandry seminar, 1.
     15_____Animal husbandry elective, 2.
Dairy Husbandry 9_____Dairy seminar, 1.
Bacteriology 7_____Soil bacteriology, 4.
     8_____Sanitary bacteriology—water and sewage, 4.
Chemistry 18_____Chemistry of soils, 3.
     20_____Dairy chemistry, 3 or 5.
     35_____Physical chemistry laboratory, 3.
     31_____Technological analysis (hours to be arranged).
Pharmacy 11_____Pharmaceutical research, 2.
Mechanical Engineering 6___Machine-shop practice, 3.
     37___Electric machines, 4.
     38___Machine design, 5.
     40___Refrigeration and pneumatic machinery, 5.
Civil Engineering 13_____Sewerage, 3.
Architecture 23_____Architectural design, 10.
     26_____Architectural design, 4.
Geology 6_____Special senior geology, 4.
Domestic Science 20_____Home nursing, 3.

JUNIOR YEAR.

Zoology 11_____Advanced vertebrate embryology, 4.
     14_____Economic zoology investigation, 4.
Chemistry 19_____Chemistry laboratory investigation, 5.
     14_____Elementary physical chemistry laboratory, 4.
Pharmacy 7_____Pharmaceutical testing, 2.
Pharmacognosy 2_____Study of organic drugs, 4.
Drawing 2 (3)_____Freehand drawing, 1.
Geology 5_____Practical field methods in geology, 4.
Mineralogy 3_____Metallurgy and assaying, 5.
Domestic Art 5_____Dressmaking, 2.
German 9 (1)_____Advanced prose composition, 2.
     12_____Lyric poems, 2.
     15_____History of German literature, 2.
French 9_____Lyric poems, 2.
     12_____Advanced prose composition, 2.
Veterinary Science 4_____Veterinary science for agricultural students, 4.

SOPHOMORE YEAR.

Botany 9_____Seed analyses and seed testing, 4.
Zoology 7_____Animal histology and microscopic anatomy, 4.
Civil Engineering 3_____Land surveying, topographic surveying, railroad
     curves, and earth work, 3.

Architecture 7_____Water color, 1.
Drawing 3_____Freehand drawing—water color, 1.
English 12__ _____Prose fiction, 4.
Geology 1_____Dynamic, physiographic, and structural geology, 4.
      1 (1)_____do., advanced, 5.
      3_____Economic and applied geology, 5.
Veterinary Science 7_____Animal pathology (hours to be arranged).
      16_____Veterinary pharmacy, 4.

FRESHMAN YEAR.

Architecture 1_____Architectural elements, 5.
      2_____Water color, 1.
      3_____Freehand drawing, 1.
Drawing 3_____Elementary drawing, 2.
      2 (1)_____Freehand drawing, 1.
German 3_____Reading and composition, 4.

YEAR NOT SPECIFIED.

Mineralogy 4_____Meteorology and climatology, 4.
Horticulture 5_____Plant growth and improvement, 4.
Mathematics 5_____Descriptive astronomy (hours to be arranged).
Public Speaking 4_____Public speaking—debate, 3.

If all the courses in the foregoing list were offered, there would be required 180 hours additional of instructors' time. At an average of 23.2 hours per week for each instructor (see Table 33, line 2d), more than seven additional instructors would be required.

INDEX.

O

DEPARTMENT OF THE INTERIOR
BUREAU OF EDUCATION

BULLETIN, 1916, No. 28

THE SOCIAL STUDIES IN SECONDARY EDUCATION

A SIX-YEAR PROGRAM ADAPTED BOTH TO THE 6-3-3 AND THE 8-4 PLANS OF ORGANIZATION

REPORT OF THE COMMITTEE ON SOCIAL STUDIES OF THE
COMMISSION ON THE REORGANIZATION OF SECONDARY
EDUCATION OF THE NATIONAL EDUCATION ASSOCIATION

COMPILED BY

ARTHUR WILLIAM DUNN

Secretary of the Committee

WASHINGTON
GOVERNMENT PRINTING OFFICE
1916

ADDITIONAL COPIES
OF THIS PUBLICATION MAY BE PROCURED FROM
THE SUPERINTENDENT OF DOCUMENTS
GOVERNMENT PRINTING OFFICE
WASHINGTON, D. C.
AT
10 CENTS PER COPY

CONTENTS.

PREFACE.

The committee issues this report with the conviction that the secondary school teachers of social studies have a remarkable opportunity to improve the citizenship of the land. This conviction is based upon the fact that the million and a third secondary school pupils constitute probably the largest and most impressionable group in the country that can be directed to a serious and systematic effort, through both study and practice, to acquire the social spirit. If the two and a half million pupils of the seventh and eighth grades are included in the secondary group, according to the six-and-six plan, this opportunity will be very greatly increased.

The committee interprets this opportunity as a responsibility which can be realized only by the development in the pupil of a constructive attitude in the consideration of all social conditions. In facing the increasing complexity of society, it is most important that the youth of the land be steadied by an unwavering faith in humanity and by an appreciation of the institutions which have contributed to the advancement of civilization.

The following report is the result of three years of continuous inquiry by the committee whose membership is given on page 6. This committee as a whole has met at various times in each of these years for sessions of one or two days each, subcommittees have met on other occasions, and individual members designated by the committee have given prolonged service and made specific contributions to the general result. It has corresponded widely in search of suggestions and criticisms, and has conferred with many persons not members of the committee in various parts of the country. It has met in conference with representatives of the American Historical Association and the American Political Science Association. In short, the committee has sought for every available source of suggestion, criticism, and contribution of material that would aid it in formulating and explaining its conclusions.

In 1914 a preliminary report was prepared by the chairman of the committee and printed by the Bureau of Education in Bulletin, 1914, No. 41, together with other preliminary reports of the Commission on the Reorganization of Secondary Education. The report as presented herewith was compiled by Arthur William Dunn, who for the

5

past year has been the secretary of the committee. Mr. Dunn's pioneer service and long experience in civic education enabled him to make a very valuable contribution to the deliberations of the committee. His connection with the United States Bureau of Education as Special Agent in Civic Education has also given the committee unusual opportunity to keep in touch with the experience and thought of the entire country. The committee owes much to the cordial cooperation of the Bureau both in the preparation and in the publication of the report.

In 1915 the United States Bureau of Education published a bulletin on "The Teaching of Community Civics" (Bulletin, 1915, No. 23). This bulletin was prepared by J. Lynn Barnard, F. W. Carrier, Arthur W. Dunn, and Clarence D. Kingsley, who were constituted a special committee of the Committee on Social Studies for the purpose. This bulletin, which is referred to in the body of the present report, should be considered, therefore, as an integral part of the Report of the Committee on Social Studies.

The committee is fully conscious that available data derived from actual experience are not adequate for final judgments. It has endeavored at all points to avoid any suggestion of finality. It believes, however, that its report is more than a mere expression of personal opinion, in that the principles that it endeavors to formulate and illustrate are derived from an apparently clear and definite trend in actual practice.

A summary of this report has been approved by the Reviewing Committee of the Commission on the Reorganization of Secondary Education. This approval does not commit every member of the Reviewing Committee individually to every statement and every implied educational doctrine. It does, however, mean essential agreement as a committee with the general recommendations. On the basis of this summary, the Reviewing Committee has authorized the publication of the report by the Bureau of Education as one of the reports of the commission.

THOMAS JESSE JONES,
Chairman Committee on Social Studies.
CLARENCE D. KINGSLEY,
Chairman Reviewing Committee.

THE COMMITTEE ON SOCIAL STUDIES.

Thomas Jesse Jones, *chairman*, United States Bureau of Education, Washington, D. C.

Arthur William Dunn, *secretary*, United States Bureau of Education, Washington, D. C.

W. A. Aery, Hampton Institute, Hampton, Va.

J. Lynn Barnard, School of Pedagogy, Philadelphia, Pa.

George G. Bechtel, Principal, Northwestern High School, Detroit, Mich.

F. L. Boyden, Principal, High School, Deerfield, Mass.

E. C. Branson, University of North Carolina, Chapel Hill, N. C.

Henry R. Burch, West Philadelphia High School, Philadelphia, Pa.

F. W. Carrier, Somerville High School, Somerville, Mass.

Jessie C. Evans, William Penn High School for Girls, Philadelphia, Pa.

Frank P. Goodwin, Woodward High School, Cincinnati, Ohio.

W. J. Hamilton, Superintendent of Schools, Two Rivers, Wis.

Blanche C. Hazard, Cornell University, Ithaca, N. Y.

S. B. Howe, High School, Newark, N. J.

Clarence D. Kingsley, State High School Inspector, Boston, Mass.

J. Herbert Low, Manual Training High School, Brooklyn, N. Y.

William H. Mace, Syracuse University, Syracuse, N. Y.

William T. Morrey, Bushwick High School, Brooklyn, N. Y.

John Pettibone, High School, New Milford, Conn.

James Harvey Robinson, Columbia University, New York City.

William A. Wheatley, Superintendent of Schools, Middletown, Conn.

THE REVIEWING COMMITTEE.

(The Reviewing Committee consists of 26 members, of whom 16 are chairmen of committees and 10 are members at large.)

Chairman of the Commission and of the Reviewing Committee:

Clarence D. Kingsley, State High School Inspector, Boston, Mass.

Members at large:

Hon. P. P. Claxton, United States Commissioner of Education, Washington, D. C.

Thomas H. Briggs, Associate Professor of Education, Teachers College, Columbia University. New York City.

Alexander Inglis, Assistant Professor of Education, in charge of Secondary Education, Harvard University, Cambridge, Mass.

Henry Neumann, Ethical Culture School, New York City.

William Orr, Senior Educational Secretary, International Y. M. C. A. Committee, 104 East Twenty-eighth Street, New York City.

William B. Owen, Principal, Chicago Normal College, Chicago, Ill.

Edward O. Sisson, Commissioner of Education, Boise, Idaho.

Joseph S. Stewart, Professor of Secondary Education, University of Georgia, Athens, Ga.

Milo H. Stuart, Principal Technical High School, Indianapolis, Ind.

H. L. Terry, State High School Inspector, Madison, Wis.

Chairmen of committees:

Administration of High Schools—Charles Hughes Johnston, Professor of Secondary Education, University of Illinois, Urbana, Ill.

Agriculture—A. V. Storm, Professor of Agricultural Education, University of Minnesota, St. Paul, Minn.

Ancient Languages—Walter Eugene Foster, Stuyvesant High School, New York City.

Art Education—Henry Turner Bailey, Newton, Mass.

Articulation of High School and College—Clarence D. Kingsley, State High School Inspector, Boston, Mass.

Business Education—Cheesman A. Herrick, President Girard College, Philadelphia, Pa.

Chairmen of committees—Continued.

> English—James Fleming Hosic, Chicago Normal College, Chicago, Ill.
> (Address for 1916–17, 404 West One hundred and fifteenth Street, New
> York City.)
>
> Household Arts—Amy Louise Daniels, University of Wisconsin, Madison,
> Wis.
>
> Manual Arts—Wilson H. Henderson, Extension Division, University of
> Wisconsin, Milwaukee, Wis.
>
> Mathematics—William Heard Kilpatrick, Associate Professor of Educa-
> tion, Teachers College, Columbia University, New York City.
>
> Modern Languages—Edward Manley, Englewood High School, Chicago, Ill.
>
> Music—Will Earhart, Director of Music, Pittsburgh, Pa.
>
> Physical Education—James H. McCurdy, Director of Normal Courses of
> Physical Education, International Y. M. C. A. College, Springfield, Mass.
>
> Sciences—Otis W. Caldwell, School of Education, University of Chicago,
> Chicago, Ill.
>
> Social Studies—Thomas Jesse Jones, United States Bureau of Education,
> Washington, D. C.
>
> Vocational Guidance—Frank M. Leavitt, Professor of Industrial Education,
> University of Chicago, Chicago, Ill.

THE SOCIAL STUDIES IN SECONDARY EDUCATION.

PART I.—INTRODUCTION.

1. *Definition of the social studies.*—The social studies are understood to be those whose subject matter relates directly to the organization and development of human society, and to man as a member of social groups.

2. *Aims of the social studies.*—The social studies differ from other studies by reason of their social content rather than in social aim; for the keynote of modern education is "social efficiency," and instruction in all subjects should contribute to this end. Yet, from the nature of their content, the social studies afford peculiar opportunities for the training of the individual as a member of society. Whatever their value from the point of view of personal culture, unless they contribute directly to the cultivation of social efficiency on the part of the pupil they fail in their most important function. They should accomplish this end through the development of an appreciation of the nature and laws of social life, a sense of the responsibility of the individual as a member of social groups, and the intelligence and the will to participate effectively in the promotion of the social well-being.

More specifically, the social studies of the American high school should have for their conscious and constant purpose the cultivation of good citizenship. We may identify the "good citizen" of a neighborhood with the "thoroughly efficient member" of that neighborhood; but he will be characterized, among other things, by a loyalty and a sense of obligation to his city, State, and Nation as political units. Again, "society" may be interpreted to include the human race. Humanity is bigger than any of its divisions. The social studies should cultivate a sense of membership in the "world community," with all the sympathies and sense of justice that this involves as among the different divisions of human society. The first step, however, toward a true "neighborliness" among nations must be a realization of national ideals, national efficiency, national loyalty, national self-respect, just as real neighborliness among different family groups depends upon the solidarity, the self-respect, and the loyalty to be found within each of the component families.

High national ideals and an intelligent and genuine loyalty to them should thus be a specific aim of the social studies in American high schools.

8. *The point of view of the committee.*—(1) The committee adheres to the view that it was appointed, not to "obtain justice" for a group of social studies as against other groups, or for one social study as against others, but to consider wherein such studies might be made to contribute most effectively to the purposes of secondary education. It believes that the social studies require "socialization" quite as much as other studies, and that this is of greater moment than the number of social studies offered or the number of hours assigned to each.

The subject of civics may be taken to illustrate this point. Its avowed purpose is to train for citizenship. The various attempts to secure a more perfect fulfillment of this purpose by increasing the quantity offered, by making the subject required instead of elective, by transferring it from last year to first year of the high school or vice versa, by introducing it in the elementary course of study, by shifting the emphasis from the National Government to municipal government—such attempts have been more or less mechanical and superficial. Unless the subject matter and the methods of instruction are adapted to the pupil's immediate needs of social growth, such attempts avail little. What is true of civics is also true of the other social studies, such as history and economics.

(2) The committee has refrained from offering detailed outlines of courses, on the ground that they tend to fix instruction in stereotyped forms inconsistent with a real socializing purpose. The selection of topics and the organization of subject matter should be determined in each case by immediate needs. The attempt has been, therefore, to establish certain principles, to illustrate these as far as possible by examples from actual practice, and to stimulate initiative on the part of teachers and school administrators in testing proposed methods or in judicious experiments of their own.

No sensible teacher of history asks how many facts he is to teach. No two teachers—if good ones—would teach the same number of facts or just the same facts to the same pupils or class, and much less to different classes. No sensible teacher asks what kind of facts he shall teach, expecting to receive in answer a tabulation of his material. He knows that general rules accompanied by suitable illustrations are the only useful answer to these questions. (Elementary course of study in geography, history, and civics, Indianapolis.)

(3) One principle the committee has endeavored to keep before it consistently throughout this report because of its fundamental character. It is contained in the following quotation from Prof. Dewey:

We are continually uneasy about the things we adults know, and are afraid the child will never learn them unless they are drilled into him by instruction before he has any intellectual use for them. If we could really believe that attending to the needs of present growth would keep the child and teacher alike busy, and would also provide the best possible guarantee of the learning needed in the future, transformation of educational ideals might soon be accomplished, and other desirable changes would largely take care of themselves.

The high-school course has heretofore been determined too largely by supposed future needs and too little by present needs and past experience. The important fact is not that the pupil is getting ready to live, but that he is living, and in immediate need of such mental and social nourishment and training as will enable him to adjust himself to his present social environment and conditions. By the very processes of present growth he will make the best possible provision for the future. This does not mean that educational processes should have no reference to the future. It does not mean, to use a concrete illustration, that a boy should be taught nothing about voting until he is 21 and about to cast his first ballot. It means merely that such instruction should be given at the psychological and social moment when the boy's interests are such as to make the instruction function effectively in his processes of growth. A distinction should be made between the "needs of present growth" and immediate, objective utility. As a boy's mental and social horizon broadens with the processes of education, he will become inquisitive about facts and relations perhaps long before he has direct use for them in the affairs of life. The best question that can be asked in class is the question that the pupil himself asks because he wants to know, and not the question the teacher asks because he thinks the pupil some time in the future ought to know.

(4) For effective social training in the high school more consideration must be given to its organic continuity with the work of the elementary school in the same field. Opinion differs as to the grades when the social studies as such should be introduced, especially in the case of civics. This question is beyond the scope of this committee's consideration, except in its relation to the seventh and eighth years. These years are now in some places included with the ninth year in the junior high school, and must, therefore, be considered in any plan for the reorganization of secondary education. But even where the junior high-school plan is not adopted, the foundations of secondary education must be laid in the years preceding the present high school.

4. *General outline of social studies for secondary schools.*—Assuming that provision has been made for the social aspect of education

in Grades I–VI of the elementary school, the following general plan of social studies is proposed for the years VII–XII:

Junior cycle (years VII–IX):
  Geography.
  European history.
  American history.
  Civics.
Senior cycle (years X–XII):
  European history.
  American history.
  Problems of democracy—social, economic, and political.

5. *The "cycle" plan of organization—two three-year cycles preceded by an earlier six-year cycle.*—From the foregoing general outline it will be seen that the course of social studies proposed for the years VII–IX constitutes a cycle to be followed by a similar cycle in the years X–XII, and presumably preceded by another similar cycle in the six elementary grades. This grouping coincides roughly with the physiological periods of adolescence, but is based chiefly upon the practical consideration that large numbers of children complete their schooling with the sixth grade and another large contingent with the eighth and ninth grades. The course recommended in this report aims to provide a comprehensive, and in a sense complete, course of social study for each period. Those pupils who continue through the third period cover the same cycle provided for in the first and second periods, but with broader horizon, new relations, and more intensive study.

The Philadelphia course of study now in preparation and soon to be published, and the Indianapolis course of study described in Bulletin, 1915, No. 17, United States Bureau of Education, illustrate with variations the cycle organization of the six elementary grades. Within this period the pupils get at least some picture of the development of civilization as typified in the customs, historic personages and dramatic events of ancient and modern nations. They also acquire the simpler elements of American history from the period of exploration to the present time. This historical study is made in close relation with geographical study. Civic and social relations, beginning with the simple relations of home life in the first grade and gradually including the elemental relations of the larger community life, form a continuous phase of the work. In the sixth year of the Philadelphia course emphasis is placed upon economic or vocational relations, largely through a concrete study of occupations. In the Indianapolis course a similar though perhaps less intensive study of occupations is made, chiefly in connection with geography (general and local) and with especial emphasis in the fourth, fifth, and sixth years; while in the sixth year a somewhat systematic though elementary study is made of the more important "elements of community welfare."

With such a course of study, the pupil who leaves school after completing the sixth grade will have acquired some experience with practically the whole range of social studies—history (both ancient and modern, European and American); government in its relations to community welfare; economics in its simpler occupational relations, and also on the side of saving, thrift, conservation; and even sociology in very elementary and concrete terms. Elementary as the course is, and inadequate as it may be from the point of view of the pupil's future social efficiency, it is doubtless all that he can well assimilate at his stage of mental and social growth.

It will now require only a glance at the outline of courses suggested for the years VII–IX and X–XII on pages 12, 15, and 35 of this report to make apparent without further discussion the completeness with which the cycle organization is provided for.

6. *Differentiation of courses.*—The course of study outlined is flexible and permits of differentiation to any extent necessary to meet the needs of characteristic groups of pupils. It is an open question how far such differentiation is desirable, especially in the years VII–IX. It is a fallacy, for example, to imagine that the children of native-born Americans need civic education any less than the children of immigrants; or that the pupils of a school in a purely residential suburb require instruction in industrial history or vocational civics any less than the pupils of a school in an industrial district. But the scope and emphasis of such courses may well vary in the different cases. It is conceivable that in a class of immigrant children more emphasis might be given to American history and less to European history than in a class of native children. In both European and American history the selection of topics for emphasis should, within certain limits at least, be made to meet industrial or other specific needs. As suggested on pages 29–32, community civics needs special adaptation to rural conditions and requirements.

The committee can not emphasize too strongly its belief in the desirability of such careful adjustment of courses to local and current circumstances. It is believed that the flexibility of the course of social studies offered and the principles suggested for the organization of subject matter (see especially under the section on History, pp. 35–37), lend themselves readily to such adjustment.

7. *Adaptation to the 8–4 and 6–3–3 plans of organization.*—The validity of the committee's recommendations and suggestions is not dependent upon the adoption of the junior and senior high-school organization. There is only one point at which the adoption or nonadoption of this organization would seem to make any difference

in the completeness with which the course of social studies herein
proposed for the years VII–IX could be carried out. If it is true
that under the 8–4 organization more pupils are likely to leave
school at the end of the eighth year than would be the case under the
6–3–3 organization, it would mean simply that a larger percentage
of pupils would fail to complete the cycle of social studies provided
for the years VII–IX.

The committee believes, however, that the very nature of its proposed course in civics in the ninth year will tend to keep in school,
even under the 8–4 organization, many of those to whom the traditional history courses usually given in the ninth year would offer no
inducement to remain. However, it is partly to meet the needs of
those who, under either organization, leave school at the end of the
eighth year that the committee urgently recommends the inclusion
of an elementary course in community civics in that year. This
course, if planned with that end in view, will consummate a complete, though necessarily abbreviated, cycle in the years VII–VIII.
Let it be repeated, however, that one of the chief purposes of both
eighth and ninth year civics should be to provide the pupil with a
motive for the continuation of his education.

PART II.—SOCIAL STUDIES FOR THE SEVENTH, EIGHTH, AND NINTH YEARS.

(A) ADMINISTRATIVE FEATURES.

Geography, history, and civics are the social studies that find a proper place in the seventh, eighth, and ninth years. The geography should be closely correlated with the history and civics, and should be thoroughly socialized. The history should include European as well as American history. The civics should be of the "community civics" type (see pp. 22–32, following). In addition, it is desirable to emphasize the social aspects of other studies, such as hygiene or other science, and even arithmetic. (For a description of "community arithmetic" see "Civic Education in Elementary Schools as Illustrated in Indianapolis," Bulletin, 1915, No. 17, United States Bureau of Education, pp. 23–26.)

1. *Alternative programs for years VII–IX.*—Opinion and practice vary as to the organization of the social studies in these three years. It is the belief of the committee that the organization should be adapted to local circumstances, and that no one plan should be recommended as best for every case. The following alternative plans are suggested; it is not intended, however, to preclude the possibility of other adjustments that local conditions may require.

Seventh year:

    (1) Geography—½ year. ⎫ These two courses may be taught in se-
        European history—½ year. ⎭ quence, or parallel through the year.
        Civics—taught as a phase of the above and of other subjects, or segregated in one or two periods a week, or both.

Or, (2) European history—1 year.
        Geography—taught incidentally to, and as a factor in, the history.
        Civics—taught as a phase of the above and of other subjects, or segregated in one or two periods a week, or both.

Eighth year:

    American history—½ year. ⎫ These two courses may be taught in sequence,
    Civics—½ year. ⎭ or parallel through the year.
    Geography—taught incidentally to, and as a factor in, the above subjects.

Ninth year:

    (1) Civics: Continuing the civics of the preceding year, but with more emphasis upon State, national, and world aspects (see pp. 25, 26)—½ year.
        Civics: Economic and vocational aspects (see pp. 26–29)—½ year.
        History: Much use made of history in relation to the topics of the above courses.

Or, (2) Civics—economic and vocational. ⎫ 1 year, in sequence or parallel.
        Economic history. ⎭

15

2. *Organization of social studies in the seventh and eighth years.*—
The alternative programs given above suggest three methods of organizing the social studies in the seventh and eighth years.

(*a*) By the first method, the three social studies run parallel to each
other, with more or less direct dependence upon each other, and with
a good deal of one subject taught as an aspect of the other two. This
method is exemplified in the Indianapolis schools, according to their
course of study in geography, history, and civics published in 1914,
and explained in Bulletin, 1915, No. 17, United States Bureau of
Education. In the seventh year geography occupies three periods a
week throughout the year, alternating with European history on the
other two days. Civics is taught only as a phase of the geography,
history, and other subjects, with more or less attention to it in the
opening exercises. In the eighth year United States history occupies
three periods a week, alternating with civics on the other two days.
Geography is taught in this year only as a factor in the other two
subjects. It should be said in passing that while civics does not
appear as a distinct subject in the Indianapolis schools until the
eighth year, it is systematically taught as an aspect of other subjects
throughout the elementary grades beginning with the first.

The aim in the Indianapolis elementary schools seems to be to make of education, not a process of instruction in a variety of subjects, but a process of living,
of growth, during which the various relations of life are unfolded—civic, geographical, historical, ethical, vocational, etc. In the first grade, for example,
the pupil does not even study "English" or "language"; he merely does
things, and talks about things, and hears and tells stories about things, the
teacher alone being conscious that she is giving the child his first organized
lessons in civic life, as well as in the use of the English language. (Civic
Education in Elementary Schools as Illustrated in Indianapolis, Bulletin, 1915,
No. 17, United States Bureau of Education, p. 9.)

Even in the eighth year, where civics appears as a separate "subject," alternating throughout the year with American history, the
coordination is so close (in the hands of a skillful teacher) that
the pupils are hardly conscious that they are studying two "subjects." They are rather studying certain phenomena of life in two
aspects—historical and civic.

It is this aim that gives to the Indianapolis plan its chief distinction. It is perhaps an ideal aim. Its accomplishment, however,
requires skillful teaching. It is only fair to say that even in
Indianapolis there are principals and teachers who prefer the plan
which existed in that city prior to the adoption of the present plan
a year or two ago, and who, indeed, still follow it. This plan is
next described.

(*b*) By this second plan the social studies are taken up in
sequence. Civics occupies the entire attention (so far as the social
studies are concerned) five days in the week, in the last half of

the eighth year. It is preceded by the courses in history, and these in turn by geography. Of course geography also appears as an element in the history work, European and American. More or less civics instruction may be given prior to the last half of the eighth grade as a phase of history, geography, and other subjects.

The chief advantage claimed for this plan is the concentration and continuity of interest and attention. It is perhaps particularly important that attention be concentrated upon civics at the time just before the pupils enter high school or leave school altogether. This last argument may doubtless lose some of its force under the Junior High School plan of organization, if it be assumed that the latter would keep pupils in school at least a year longer and would provide further civic training in that year. At all events, of the two plans described, the second is perhaps more likely to be effective in the hands of the great majority of teachers, and especially of those who are inexperienced.

(c) A third general plan of organization, which admits of variations, is characterized by the introduction of civics as a distinct subject in the lower grades for one or more periods a week, and its continuation in increasing amount until the climax is reached in the seventh and eighth years. A plan of this kind is now being developed in Philadelphia. The advantages claimed for it are the cumulative effect of continuous civics instruction through the pupil's early years, and the definiteness secured by fixing attention upon the subject as such, even if for only one or two periods a week, instead of depending upon the interest and skill of the teacher to develop the subject incidentally to the teaching of other subjects.

Objections that have been raised to this plan are (1) the multiplication of " subjects " in the elementary curriculum; (2) the difficulty of maintaining interest and securing effective results from subjects taught one or two periods a week; (3) the belief that the very fact of designating a few periods a week for the study of " civics " would tend to the neglect of the civic aspects of instruction in other subjects. Data are not available to prove the validity of these objections.

3. *Time allotment for civics in years VII–IX.*—An objection has been raised to the amount of civics recommended for the years VII–IX on the ground that it is out of proportion to the time available for the social studies. This objection appears to be due in part to a misconception of the meaning of the term, and of the scope of the work intended to be included under it. The term " community civics " has arisen (it was not invented by this committee) to distinguish the new type of civics from the traditional " civil government," to which the name civics was also applied. Unfortunately,

the term has been interpreted by many as applying to a purely local study. From what is said on pages 23 and 25, it should be clear that the committee is not recommending a course, even in the eighth year, that is restricted to a study of "the pupil's own town"; and much less that it is recommending two consecutive years of such study. The proposed ninth year course (see pp. 25–29) is "civics" in that it is a specific course of training for citizenship; it is "community civics" solely in the sense of maintaining the point of view, the spirit, the general method, though not the same content in detail, which characterize the earlier course to which the name has been applied.

Although the committee recommends a course in civics in both eighth and ninth years, it does not necessarily follow that there must be or should be two full years of the subject. The committee has only suggested a half-year course in the eighth year (a daily period for one-half year, or two or three periods a week for the entire year). And while it has suggested a course for the ninth year that, in the committee's opinion, might well occupy the entire year under certain circumstances, this course is capable of adjustment to half-year requirements when conditions make it desirable. (See p. 15.)

(B) GEOGRAPHY AND HISTORY IN SEVENTH AND EIGHTH YEARS.

There are here given, with some comment, extracts from the course of study in geography and history in the sixth, seventh, and eighth grades of the Indianapolis schools, as published in 1914. These illustrate, as well as anything available to the committee, the socialization of geography and the coordination between geography, history, and civics. It has seemed well to include the sixth year in order to show the continuity of method from the elementary to the secondary period and because of its relation to the cycle organization.

Sixth-grade geography.—The geography of this year includes a study of Africa and South America in the first half and of the United States in the second half.

By the time children reach the sixth grade they are sufficiently mature to approach the study of a continent or country with some problem in-mind. Facts are needed in the solution of this problem; they should not, however, be given as isolated scraps of knowledge, but should be made to contribute to the working out of the problem.

The most vital problems, however, grow out of current events that stimulate questions in the minds of the children. Therefore problems may change from year to year.

The following may be taken as typical of the problems studied in this year:

1. Considering the proximity of Africa to Europe, why have there been so few settlements and explorations until recently?

2. Egypt was once the leading power of the world, to-day a country of little influence and under the domination of England. Why?

3. No part of the world is attracting more attention than South America. What are the reasons?

4. Brazil, a country nearly as large as the United States and known to European countries for over 400 years, has a population only one-fourth as large as that of the United States and is just beginning to take a prominent part in international affairs. Reasons?

5. What are the factors which have been largely influential in developing the United States into a great industrial nation?

To illustrate the method by which such problems are developed, the following suggestive outline for the fourth problem enumerated above is given:

I. Why was the development of Brazil so retarded?
   A. Character and policy of early settlers.
      1. Portuguese influence.
      2. Policy toward Indians.
      3. Introduction of slaves and consequent predominance of negro labor.
   B. Location and climate retarded development.
      1. Largely in Southern Hemisphere.
      2. Chiefly in Torrid Zone.
   C. Topography retarded development.
      1. Forests.
      2. Mountains parallel to southeastern coast.
      3. Great plateau beyond wall of woods and rock.
      4. Coastal plain very narrow.
   D. Drainage helped to retard development.
II. What factors are contributing to its great growth to-day?
   A. Its location.
      1. In South America.
         a. All but two countries of South America border on Brazil.
         b. Great extent of coast line.
      2. Nearer to Europe and North America than the other two progressive countries of South America.
   B. Topography and climate.
      1. Modification of climate by mountains and table-lands.
      2. Mountains accessible to short railroads connecting inland towns with coast.
      3. Southern part temperate and healthful.
   C. Character of later settlers.
      1. Over 200,000 Germans in Rio do Sul.
      2. Even greater number of Italians; work on and own coffee plantations.
      3. Portuguese, Spaniards, Syrians, etc.
   D. Great natural wealth.
      1. Forest resources.
      2. Mines.
      3. Agricultural resources.
      4. Grazing lands.

II.' What factors are contributing to its great growth to-day—Continued.
   E. Increased transportation facilities.
      1. Development of navigation on the Amazon.
      2. Navigation of Paraguay River.
      8. Few railroads, but increasing in number.
      4. Steamship lines to Europe and North America. Principal
        harbors and exports.

Sixth-grade history.—The prominence of the historical factor in the geography of this year will be suggested by the typical outline given above. In addition to this " incidental " historical study, the period of discovery and colonization is studied in story form parallel with the geography of the first half year, and that from the Revolution on in the second half year parallel with the geography of the United States. The stories of Livingstone, Cecil Rhodes, Stanley, and Kitchener are taken up along with the geography of Africa. A very elementary textbook in history is used for the first time in this grade.

It should be remarked that this sixth-year history work is the culmination of the elementary six-year cycle, which began with a study of the meaning of national holidays and of Hiawatha's childhood in the first two grades, was continued in the third and fourth grades with pioneer stories and biography from American history, and in the fifth grade with the elements of European and oriental history, based on " Ten Boys." In the fifth grade, also, the modern awakening of Japan is studied, with the story of " Perry and Japan " as a basis.

Seventh-grade geography.—The geography of the first half of the seventh grade is a study of " Some prominent nations of the world," including, for example, Holland, France, Italy, Austria, Hungary, Switzerland, China, Japan, Argentina, Brazil. In the second half of the year, " The world in general," " The conditions of commerce," and " Four great nations of the world—British Empire, German Empire, Russian Empire, the United States "—are the subjects of study. A general geography and a commercial geography are used as texts to supply the material for study. The method of study is the same as in the sixth year. Some typical problems are:

In spite of its size, Holland is one of the great mercantile nations of the world. Show why the Dutch were compelled to seek their fortunes in trade and why they were so successful.

The Argentine Republic has a better opportunity for future development than any other country of South America. Why?

The study of " The world in general " is organized around such topics as—

The sea, the great commercial highway.
Causes that give rise to commerce.
Natural conditions that affect commerce.
Human control of commerce.
Means of transportation.

The study of the British Empire is organized around the following main topics:

Size and population.
Wide distribution of territory.
Principal parts of the Empire.
, How the parts are helpful to one another.
Means of knitting the parts together.
Relation of the Empire to the rest of the world, especially to the United States.

Among the central topics for the study of the United States are:

What has caused it to become almost self-sustaining?
What has caused it to become one of the great commercial powers of the world?
Its present commercial status.
Conservation the great problem of the future if the present position at home and abroad is to be maintained.

Seventh-grade history.—Again the strong historical element in the geography of this year is to be noted. History, however, is also given a separate place throughout the year. In the history study geography becomes an essential factor.

Owing to the use of different texts, no attempt is made to outline the work in history of the 7B grade in detail. The point of view used in teaching this work should, however, be the same throughout.

In his "Moral principles in education" Dewey says: "History is vital or dead to the child according as it is, or is not, presented from the sociological standpoint. When treated simply as a record of what has passed and gone, it must be mechanical, because the past, as past, is remote. Simply as the past there is no motive for attending to it. The ethical value of history teaching will be measured by the extent to which past events are made the means of understanding the present." No history, therefore, should be treated as though it had meaning or value in itself, but should constantly be made to show its relation or contribution to the present. . . .

In the work of this grade make the children feel that the history of our country is a part of the history of the world and that it had its beginnings many centuries before its discovery. . . .

Accordingly, the elements of European history, which are studied throughout this grade, are organized under the general title, "European beginnings in American history," and are treated as such.

Eighth-grade history.—Geography has no place in this grade as a separate subject, though it is always an important factor in the study of history. The history of this year is American history, taken up systematically in connection with a text. A somewhat full suggestive outline is given in the course of study, but need not be repeated here. The spirit controlling the history instruction in this grade is the same as that which controls in the preceding grade.

The characteristic feature of this year is the introduction of "community civics" as a separate subject throughout the year, and its close coordination with the history. This means primarily that the history of the Nation is treated as the story of the growth of a national "community," involving all the "elements of welfare" with which the pupils are made familiar in their civics work, the same development of means of cooperation, especially through government, and so on. More particularly, it means that special aspects of civic life and organization are emphasized in connection with those periods of American history in which they are most significant. The pupils find, for example, that the motives that led to exploration and colonization (whether on the Atlantic coast or in the far West) were the same as those which have led to the development of their own local community and State, and that the process of development is the same in the one case as in the other. Advantage is taken of the period of development of transportation and communication to emphasize the importance of these factors from the point of view of the study of the same topics in civics.

Before leaving the subject of geography and history in the seventh and eighth years, attention should be called to the emphasis that is given in the Indianapolis course of study to economic facts and relations, not only in the subjects of geography and history, but also in civics. This has an important relation to the development of the same field of social study in the later cycle of the years X–XII (see pp. 36, 52).

(C) CIVICS FOR YEARS VII–IX.

1. *Special report on community civics.*—A special committee of the Committee on Social Studies has prepared a detailed report on the aims, methods, and content of community civics adapted particularly to the eighth and ninth grades.[1] This special report has been approved by the Committee on Social Studies, adopted as a part of its present general report, and issued as a manual on " The Teaching of Community Civics " in Bulletin, 1915, No. 23, United States Bureau of Education. Its availability in that bulletin makes unnecessary, in the present report, a detailed description of the course and its methods. Some of the essential features, however, are here summarized.

(a) *Significance of the term " community."*—Community civics lays emphasis upon the local community because (1) it is the community with which every citizen, especially the child, comes into most intimate relations, and which is always in the foreground of experience; (2) it is easier for the child, as for any citizen, to

---

[1] This committee consisted of J. Lynn Barnard, School of Pedagogy, Philadelphia; F. W. Carrier, Somerville (Mass.) High School; Arthur W. Dunn, specialist in civic education, United States Bureau of Education; and Clarence D. Kingsley, high-school inspector, Massachusetts Board of Education.

realize his membership in the local community, to feel a sense of personal responsibility for it, and to enter into actual cooperation with it, than is the case with the national community.

But our Nation and our State are communities, as well as our city or village, and a child is a citizen of the larger as of the smaller community. The significance of the term "community civics" does not lie in its geographical implications, but in its implication of community relations, of a community of interests. . . . It is a question of point of view, and community civics applies this point of view to the study of the national community as well as to the study of the local community.

(b) *Aims of community civics.*—The aim of community civics is to help the child to know his community—not merely a lot of facts about it, but the meaning of his community life, what it does for him, and how it does it, what the community has a right to expect from him, and how he may fulfill his obligation, meanwhile cultivating in him the essential qualities and habits of good citizenship.

More specifically this aim is analyzed as follows:

To accomplish its part in training for citizenship, community civics should aim primarily to lead the pupil (1) to see the importance and significance of the elements of community welfare in their relations to himself and to the communities of which he is a member; (2) to know the social agencies, governmental and voluntary, that exist to secure these elements of community welfare; (3) to recognize his civic obligations, present and future, and to respond to them by appropriate action.

A unique feature of the method of community civics described in this report lies in the fact that there is the closest relation between these three essential aims and the three steps by means of which each of the main topics is to be taught (see p. 24).

(c) *Content of community civics.*—A characteristic feature of community civics is that it focusses attention upon the "elements of community welfare" rather than upon the machinery of government. The latter is discussed only in the light of a prior study of the "elements of welfare," and in relation to them. The "elements of welfare" afford the organizing principle for this new type of civics.

It is suggested that the following elements of welfare be studied as topics: (1) Health; (2) Protection of life and property; (3) Recreation; (4) Education; (5) Civic beauty; (6) Wealth; (7) Communication; (8) Transportation; (9) Migration; (10) Charities; (11) Correction.

In addition, the course may well include the following topics dealing with the mechanism of community agencies: (12) How governmental agencies are conducted; (13) How governmental agencies are financed; (14) How voluntary agencies are conducted and financed.

(d) Methods of community civics.—I. Social facts upon which the method should be based:

(1) The pupil is a young citizen with real present interests at stake. . . . It is the first task of the teacher, therefore, not to create an interest for future use, but to demonstrate existing interests and present citizenship.

(2) The pupil as a young citizen is a real factor in community affairs. . . . Therefore it is a task of the teacher to cultivate in the pupil a sense of his responsibility, present as well as future.

(3) If a citizen has an interest in civic matters and a sense of his personal responsibility, he will want to act. Therefore the teacher must help the pupil to express his conviction in word and deed. He must be given an opportunity . . . to live his civics, both in the school and in the community outside.

(4) Right action depends not only upon information, interest, and will, but also upon good judgment. Hence the young citizen must be trained to weigh facts and to judge relative values, both in regard to what constitute the essential elements in a situation and in regard to the best means of meeting it.

(5) Every citizen possesses a large amount of unorganized information regarding community affairs. . . . It is, therefore, important to teach the pupils how to test and organize their knowledge.

(6) People are . . . most ready to act upon those convictions that they have helped to form by their own mental processes and that are based upon their own experience and observation. Hence the teacher should . . . lead the class: (1) To contribute facts from their own experience; (2) To contribute other facts gathered by themselves; (3) To use their own reasoning powers in forming conclusions; and (4) To submit these conclusions to criticism.

(7) The class has the essential characteristics of a community. Therefore the method by which the class exercises are conducted is of the utmost importance in the cultivation of civic qualities and habits. . . .

II. Three steps in teaching an element of welfare:

(1) *Approach to the topic.*—In beginning the study of an element of welfare the teacher should lead the pupils to realize its importance to themselves, to their neighborhood, and to the community, and to see the dependence of the individual upon social agencies. Much depends upon the method of approach. The planning of an approach appropriate to a given topic and applicable to a given class calls for ingenuity and resourcefulness. In this bulletin approaches to various topics are suggested by way of illustration, but the teacher should try to find another approach whenever he thinks the one suggested is not the best one for the class.

(2) *Investigation of agencies.*—The knowledge of the class should now be extended by a concrete and more or less detailed investigation of agencies such as those suggested in the bulletin. These investigations should consist largely of first-hand observation and study of local conditions. The agencies suggested under each topic are so many that no attempt should be made to have the class as a whole study them all intensively. Such an attempt would result in superficiality, kill interest, and defeat the purpose of the course. . . .

(3) *Recognition of responsibility.*—A lesson in community civics is not complete unless it leaves with the pupil a sense of his personal responsibility and results in right action. To attain these ends is perhaps the most difficult and delicate task of the teacher. It is discussed here as the third step in teaching an element of welfare; in practice, however, it is a process coincident with the first two steps and resulting from them. If the work suggested in the foregoing paragraphs on "Approach" and "Investigation of agencies" has been

well done, the pupil's sense of responsibility, his desire to act, and his knowledge of how to act will thereby have been developed. Indeed, the extent to which they have been developed is in a measure a test of the effectiveness of the approach and the study of agencies.

2. *Ninth-year civics.*—When provision is made for community civics in the eighth year the way is prepared for work in the ninth year that would not otherwise be possible. The work of the ninth year should build upon, or grow out of, the eighth-year course; but it should have a broader horizon, develop new points of view and new relations, and emphasize aspects of social and civic life that were only lightly touched upon or wholly omitted in the earlier course. Incidentally, also, this ninth-year course should lay substantial foundations for the social studies of succeeding years.

(*a*) *Amplification of national concepts.*—The reaction against the exclusive and formal study of national government and the increasing attention given to the study of local community relations have resulted in a noticeable tendency to minimize the study of civics in a national sense. It would be inexpressibly unfortunate if the study of local community life and local civic relations should supplant a study of national community life and national civic relations. The two aspects of civic life should clearly supplement each other. While we are impressing the pupil with the importance of his local civic relations and utilizing them as a means of cultivating fundamental civic concepts and habits, we should not allow this to divert attention from the increasingly intimate relations between local and national interests, and the increasing importance of a recognition by the individual of his responsibility for the national welfare.

It is extremely difficult for the average citizen in a democracy to think in terms of national interest, especially when there is any apparent conflict between it and the local or group interest. An illustration of this is seen in the local influence brought to bear upon the members of the National Congress which often prevent them from voting on public questions in the interest of the Nation as a whole when it seems to be antagonistic to the interests of the local districts. Questions of health, of education, of industry can no longer be considered in their local bearings alone, but must be dealt with in the light of national policy and to the end of national efficiency. As our population grows, means of communication perfected and the interests of the individual more closely interwoven with the interests of others, the opportunities for friction and conflict increase. So much the greater is the necessity for training the pupil to recognize the common general interest in the midst of conflicting group interests and for cultivating the will to subordinate the latter to the former.

On the other hand, there is another tendency which, though good in itself, sometimes has a tendency to undermine our sense of the importance of national solidarity. This is the conception of "internationalism," of "humanity as greater than its divisions," of a "world community." This conception indeed needs cultivation, as suggested in the following section; but it is necessary to keep our minds upon the elemental fact that before there can be effective "internationalism" there must be efficient and self-respecting nationalism; that the first step toward the realization of a "world community" must be the cultivation of sound ideals, and of efficiency in attaining these ideals, on the part of the several nations which must constitute the "world community."

The word "patriotism" has been much abused; but it is a good word. Instead of avoiding it because of its abuse, and instead of consciously or unconsciously giving young citizens the impression that the thing for which the word stands has somehow lost its significance, every effort should be made to imbue it with real meaning and to make it a potent influence in the development of a sound national life. The committee submits that this should be a definite aim of secondary education, and that one of the means of attaining it is by applying to the study of our national interests, activities, and organization the point of view, the spirit, and the methods of community civics. This may be done in some measure in the eighth year and earlier, but it may be accomplished more fully and more effectively in the ninth year, and later, on the basis of the earlier work.

(b) *Amplification of world interests.*—As individuals within a community, or local communities within a State, or the States constituting the Nation, are dependent upon one another and are bound together into the larger community life by their common interests and cooperative action, so it can easily be shown that nations are becoming more and more closely dependent upon each other. Common world interests need emphasis, world sympathies need cultivation. Pupils will be quite prepared for instruction to this end on the basis of the principles developed in community civics. Such study should be concrete and based upon current events and problems. It offers a socially important line of development, and every available opportunity to this end should be seized upon. (See also under "History," pp. 39, 40.)

(c) *Civic relations of vocational life.*—Still another opportunity presented in the ninth year is for the stressing of the civic relations of vocational life. There is evidence that, as a rule, ninth-year pupils have begun to think more or less earnestly about what they are "going to do," even though they may not have made any connection in their minds between their future vocations and the particular studies they are taking. Much of the mortality that occurs during the eighth and ninth years is due to the failure of pupils and parents to see the economic value of the high-school course. An opportunity exists to make high-school education seem "worth while" by taking the budding vocational or economic interest as one point of departure.

It is one of the essential qualities of the good citizen to be self-supporting, and through the activities necessary to his self-support to contribute efficiently to the world's progress. Not only is it important that this fact be emphasized in the civic education of the youth, but it is also appropriate that he be given as much enlightenment as possible to assist him in choosing his vocation wisely from the standpoint of social efficiency as well as from that of personal success.

The question of vocational guidance is very much in the foreground at present. While there is general agreement that the young need "guidance" for the vocational aspect of life, as for its other aspects, there is wide divergence of opinion as to the nature of this guidance and the means by which it may best be given. The committee on social studies believes that education as a whole should take account of vocational needs and should contribute to the preparation of the youth for an intelligent choice of vocation and for efficiency in it. As for the ninth-year study now under consideration, the committee is here interested in its vocational guidance aspect only as an incident to the broader social and civic training of the youth. If it can be made to contribute anything to his guidance toward a wise choice of vocation and intelligent preparation for it, it is that much gain.

The chief purpose of the phase of the ninth-year work now being emphasized should be the development of an appreciation of the social significance of all work; of the social value and interdependence of all occupations; of the social responsibility of the worker, not only for the character of his work but for the use of its fruits; of the opportunities and necessity for good citizenship in vocational life; of the duty of the community to the worker; of the necessity for social control, governmental and otherwise, of the economic activities of the community; and of the part that government actually plays in regulating the economic life of the community and of the individual. In other words, the work here proposed is an application of community civics to a phase of individual and community life that is now coming into the foreground of the pupil's interest. It has for its background the earlier work, and differs from it primarily in the larger emphasis given to the economic interest and its resulting activities. The other aspects of community life dealt with in the earlier course should receive renewed attention—the family, the protection of life, health, and property, education, recreation, etc.; but even they may be approached from the point of view of their relations to the activities and arrangements involved in "getting a living."

The term "vocational civics" has been suggested for this phase of the ninth-year work. The term is hardly adequate, however, since it is as important at this time to give instruction regarding the civic responsibility connected with the use of wealth as it is regarding responsibility in its production.

Community civics deals with real situations and relations in the pupil's own life. This vocational or economic phase of the subject should be no exception. It may well be approached through an examination of occupations or industries in which the pupils have some direct interest—those for which the several members of the class have a predilection, those in which their parents are engaged, or those of most importance in the immediate community.

Nowhere has a course in vocational civics been found that seems fully to satisfy the requirements postulated. Some steps have been taken in this direction, however, and, as an illustration of what has actually been done, reference may be made to the work of Supt. William A. Wheatley, of the Middletown (Conn.) public schools.

"*Vocational enlightenment*" *at Middletown, Conn.*—In the Middletown High School a half-year course has been introduced in the first year under the title of "A Survey of Vocations," or "Vocational Enlightenment." It consists of three parts:

1. Consideration of the importance of vocational information from the viewpoint of the individual and society, the characteristics of a good vocation, and how to study vocations.

2. Detailed treatment of 80 or 90 professions, trades, and occupations, grouped under agriculture, commerce, railroading, civil service, manufacturing, machine trades, engineering, building trades, learned professions, miscellaneous and new openings.

8. Practical discussion of choosing a life work, preparation for that work, securing a position, and efficient service and its reward.

In studying each of the vocations selected, we touch upon its healthfulness, remuneration, value to society, and social standing, as well as upon the natural qualifications, general education, and special preparation necessary for success. We investigate at first hand as many as possible of the vocations found in our city and vicinity. Each pupil is encouraged to bring from home first-hand and, as far as practicable, "inside" facts concerning his father's occupation. Local professional men, engineers, business men, manufacturers, mechanics, and agriculturists are invited to present informally and quite personally the salient features of their various vocations.

In the class exercise on the mechanical engineer such topics as these are discussed:

Which of the three engineers so far studied renders society the greatest service? Which is most necessary to your own community? Which one's work seems most attractive? What natural qualifications, general education, and special training are necessary? What subjects should constitute a high-school course preparatory to this profession? What subjects do the best technical schools demand for entrance? What advantages and disadvantages are there in preparing for this profession in a cooperative school and shop course? What kind of work during the summer would serve best to determine aptitude for it? Difference between expert machinist and mechanical engineer? What is a contracting engineer? etc.

Supt. Wheatley says of this course that—

Besides being intrinsically interesting to the pupils, it gives them greater respect for all kinds of honorable work, helps them to choose more wisely their life work, convinces them of the absolute necessity for a thorough preparation before entering any vocation, and holds to the end of the high-school course many who would otherwise drop out early in the race.

The committee would encourage experiment along this line. It would, however, repeat its suggestion that in the further development of such course particular attention be given to its broader social and civic implications; that instruction in vocations from the point of view of individual success be made not the end but a means to a more fundamental social education. The approach should be through a consideration of the services rendered by any particular vocation rather than from the point of view of remuneration. It is a principle no less important that the vocation, if it plays its true part in the life of the individual, is the chief means for the development of personality; consequently the pupil should be taught to seek a vocation that will call forth his best efforts. There should be something of the personal challenge in " vocational enlightenment."

3. *Adaptation of community civics to rural conditions.*—Community civics has been developed principally to meet urban needs. There is need for an adaptation of the subject to rural conditions. The community relations of the rural youth are different from those of the city youth. In a sense they are simpler. They also seem more vague. Their very simplicity apparently adds to the difficulty of developing a systematic course in community civics. Furthermore, the teachers in rural schools are often less experienced and less readily recognize the opportunities and materials for civic training.

Prof. J. F. Smith, of the Berea College (Ky.) Normal School has successfully developed a course in community civics to meet local rural conditions. One of his lesson plans on roads is given in Bulletin, 1915, No. 23, United States Bureau of Education, page 39, and is here reproduced because of its suggestiveness.

In this study numerous photographs were used, walks were taken over good and bad roads, and the pupils and teachers actually did a piece of road work.

Study and report on condition of roads in the community. Draw a map of the community, indicating roads. Which are dirt roads, rocky roads, other kinds? Which are well graded, well crowned? Note side ditches; are they adequate? Note culverts and bridges. Estimate miles of road in the community, public and private.

Study road-making material in the community. Note places where limestone is found; sandstone, slate, gravel. Are these materials accessible?

Find out cost of hauling in the community. Consult wagoners and learn charges per 100 pounds for freight and farm produce. Can farmers afford to market produce at present cost of cartage? Find out how much freight is hauled into the community annually and compute amount paid for this. How long will wagon and set of harness last on the roads? How long on good roads? Difference in cost for 10 years. How much could people who buy supplies afford to spend on road upkeep each year in order to cut down freight rates?

Compare cost of hauling here with cost in European countries where the best roads exist. What overtax do the people have to pay? Note that this overtax is in the form of higher prices for household necessities and in smaller profits for farm produce.

Road building: Determine kind of road; the location; grades; how grades affect the haul; the drainage level and steep roads, side ditches, culverts, subdrainage, crown; actual construction, tools, funds, means employed.

Road maintenance: Kind of material to use; regular attention necessary; the tools.

What good roads mean to a community; the economic problem. How they enhance the value of land. Means of communication. Better social life.

The history of the development of roads, canals, and railways in your State and in the Nation, in its relation to the growth of community spirit and cooperation, will be fruitful. What effect did the steam railway have upon the development of canals? Why? Show how the Panama Canal tends to unite our Nation more firmly. Study the problems of rapid transportation in cities and their relation to various phases of city life. Also the effects of the parcel post and of electric interurban lines on the welfare of farmers and city dwellers. Make a comprehensive study of the work of the Federal Government in promoting and safeguarding transportation. The ship-purchase bill and the Government ownership of railways and of street railway lines afford material for discussion and debate.

It is probable that the rural citizen comes into direct contact with State and National Governments with greater relative frequency than does the urban citizen, whose life is largely regulated by the municipality. Under the topic, "Protection of property," for example, the following discussion was introduced in rural classes in Delaware:

The United States Department of Agriculture, in a recent report, estimates that $795,100,000 worth of damage was done by insects to the crops of this country in a single year. What insects, birds, and animals are destructive of property in your community? What plant and animal diseases are prevalent in your locality or State? Investigate the work of your State agricultural college to prevent loss from these causes. (Get reports and other publications directly from the college. Ask the children whether their fathers receive publications.) Is there any department of your State government or any State officer whose work contributes to the protection of property against such enemies? Investigate and report on the work of the Federal Department of Agriculture for the protection of property against destruction by the causes named. Why should the Federal Government interest itself in this matter in your community? (Reports on this subject may be obtained directly from the department. These reports may also be in your local library.) Protection of birds; value to the farmer of insect-eating birds.

Under "Fire protection" the following topics were developed in the same classes:

Show how the farmer is largely dependent upon his own efforts and the friendly cooperation of neighbors. Contrast with the elaborate arrangement in cities. Why the difference? Point out the extreme importance of fire prevention in rural communities. Value of the telephone as a means of fire protection. If you live in a village or a small town, describe the arrangements for fire protection; method of alarm; water supply; bucket brigades; volunteer companies; etc. Compare with the conditions of the farm and of large cities. Have the children find out whether their fathers' property is insured. In what companies? Where are the main offices of these companies? (Probably in distant cities or · States.) Discuss the methods of insurance, to show the wide-spread cooperation through the payment of premiums. Is there a grange in your community? Does it provide a means of insurance? If so, describe it.

Under loss from storm, flood, frost, etc.:

Is it possible to get insurance against loss from such causes? Do any of your parents have insurance of this kind? What relation do the weather reports issued by the National Government have to the protection of property? Does your father receive weather reports by mail? If not, where may you find these reports? Investigate and report on the work of the Weather Bureau. (Information may be obtained directly from the Weather Bureau, Department of Agriculture, Washington.)

Urban conditions should not be entirely neglected even in rural schools, because rural life and urban life are closely dependent upon each other. The material selected for study, however, should be related to the child's experience as far as possible. For example, in rural schools in the neighborhood of Wilmington, Del., the following statement from the report of the Wilmington Board of Health was made a basis for discussion:

During the year 1914 there were 142 cases of typhoid fever, with 122 deaths. Our report for this year shows an increase of 76 cases over the previous year. This increase was due to the prevalence of typhoid in New Castle County, and we feel that Wilmington was particularly fortunate in not having an epidemic, as practically all milk and vegetable products supplied to Wilmington come from this agricultural district.

Again, from the report of the Wilmington City Board of Health was taken the classification of municipal waste into garbage, ashes, rubbish, and trade waste, with the requirement that these be kept separate:

Compare these provisions for the city of Wilmington with the needs and conditions of a small community like your own. Refer to what is said about other cities and compare with conditions and arrangements in your own town. How is the garbage from your home disposed of? Is it done by public provision or left to the individual householder? Whether it is done publicly or privately, note the necessity for cooperation on the part of the people. Is the garbage removed in a way to protect health and to avoid annoyance to your own families and neighbors? Is it important that garbage and other kinds of waste be kept separate in a small community? Are there laws or ordinances in your town to regulate the matter of garbage? What means can you think of to improve your own home methods of caring for garbage?

4. *Relation of civics to history.*—The coordination of geography, history, and civics instruction in the years VII–IX and earlier has been referred to in preceding pages (pp. 18–22). The application to instruction in history of the principles which have already vitalized instruction in civics is discussed in detail in later pages (pp. 38, 39). The principles there discussed, the committee believes, are equally pertinent to history instruction in both junior and senior cycles. The purpose of the present section is to emphasize the peculiar value of the civics proposed for the junior cycle from the standpoint of historical study.

History as it is usually taught in the first year of the high school is no better adapted to the educational requirements of that age than the old-time civil government. The committee further maintains that, even from the standpoint of the subsequent high-school courses in history, the latter should be preceded by a course in civics of the type described above. Children live in the present and not in the past. The past becomes educational to them only as it is related to the present. Hero stories and pioneer stories from history are of use in the early grades because children react naturally to them. Individuals are interested in the history of government, of education, of commerce, of industry, or of democracy, in proportion as they have a present interest in these things. Community civics endeavors to establish a consciousness of present community relations before discussing the more remote development of these relations.

On the other hand, the history of a thing may add to its present interest. Railroads assume a new significance when compared with the means of transportation in colonial times, or with the road system of the Roman Empire. Community civics affords opportunity for the actual use of much historical matter, for the development of the "historical sense," and for the creation of a desire to know more history. The best time to introduce history in the education of the child is when it is of immediate use. The traditional history course has given to the child a mass of facts, chronologically arranged, because, in the judgment of the adult, these facts may sometime be useful, or for the purposes of that vague thing, "general culture." Community civics affords opportunity to use history to illuminate topics of immediate interest.

Local history finds its best opportunity in connection with community civics. There is hardly a topic in community civics that may not be made clearer by looking back to the simpler stages of its development. For developing an appreciation of what history means and for giving historical perspective to the present, local history is as useful as any other history. The most effective courses in community civics make large use of local history. In 1910 the work of keeping Philadelphia clean was—

largely in the hands of a bureau of surveys, which has constructed over 1,200 miles of sewers at a cost of nearly $35,000,000, and of a bureau of highways and street cleaning, which, in 1909, employed a contractor to clean the streets of the city and to remove all ashes for $1,199,000; and to remove all garbage for $488,968.

Nothing could make so clear the statement that this complex and costly machinery of government is merely a means of citizen cooperation as the incident given in the autobiography of Benjamin Franklin, early citizen of Philadelphia:

One day I found a poor industrious man, who was willing to undertake keeping the pavement clean, by sweeping it twice a week, carrying off the dirt from before all the neighbors' doors, for the sum of sixpence per month, to be paid by each house. I then wrote and printed a paper setting forth the advantages to the neighborhood that might be obtained by this small expense; . . . I sent one of these papers to each house, and in a day or two went around to see who would subscribe an agreement to pay these sixpences; it was unanimously signed, and for a time well executed. This raised a general desire to have all the streets paved, and made the people more willing to submit to a tax for that purpose.

General history also finds its use. The topics set forth below are given as a mere suggestion.

Under the topic Health:

Conceptions of disease as found among uncivilized peoples, the ancients, and in mediæval times.

Alchemy and the development of a knowledge of medicine.

Development of sanitation; sanitary conditions in mediæval cities.

Greek ideal of physical development; gymnasiums and other means of perfecting the body.

Important discoveries: Circulation of the blood, surgery and anæsthetics, bacteria and germs, disinfectants.

Under the topic Education:

Of what the education of the youth consisted among savage, barbarous, and ancient peoples.

Among such peoples were all the youth educated or only certain classes?

Show how, among the savage Australians, the barbarous American Indians, the ancient Spartans, education was adapted to existing needs of life.

What kinds of schools existed among such peoples, and who were the teachers?

The part taken by the church in education in the Middle Ages.

Founding of the great universities in Europe and America.

Growth of public education in Europe and the United States.

How the decay of the apprentice system has led to a need for industrial education in the public schools.

Under the topic Recreation:

Primitive customs; dancing and music.
Public games in Greece and Rome.
Drama and the theater among the ancients.
Means of amusement in the Middle Ages.
Bards and troubadours.
Attitude of the Puritans toward recreation.
Comparison of forms of recreation in different countries.
Description and purposes of pageants.

Under the topics Transportation and Trade:

Early methods of trading and transportation; barter, market places, caravans, sailing vessel, etc.
The period of exploration and discovery.
Early trade routes and road building.
Periods of canal and railroad building.
Application of steam to land and water travel.
Discoveries and inventions relating to transportation and communication.

Under the topic Charities:

Provision made for widows, orphans, and the poor among the ancient Jews and Mohammedans.
Bread lines in Rome and their effects.
Treatment of beggars and diseased paupers in Eastern countries and in mediæval Europe and England.
Attitude of the church toward the poor.
Description of poorhouses by Dickens.
Condition of poorhouses in America 50 years ago.

5. *Summary.*—Community civics is a course of training in citizenship, organized with reference to the pupil's immediate needs, rich in its historical, sociological, economic, and political relations, and affording a logical and pedagogically sound avenue of approach to the later social studies.

PART III.—SOCIAL STUDIES FOR YEARS X–XII.

(A) GENERAL ADMINISTRATIVE FEATURES.

1. *General outline.*—The committee recommends as appropriate to the last three years of the secondary school the following courses:

I. *European history to approximately the end of the seventeenth century*—1 year. This would include ancient and oriental civilization, English history to the end of the period mentioned, and the period of American exploration.

II. *European history (including English history) since approximately the end of the seventeenth century*—1 (or ½) year.

III. *American history since the seventeenth century*—1 (or ½) year.

IV. *Problems of American democracy*—1 (or ½) year.

These courses clearly repeat the cycle of social study provided for in years VII–IX (see page 15). The principal of organization, suggested in the pages following for all of these courses makes them extremely flexible and easily adaptable to the special needs of different groups of pupils, or of different high-school curriculums (commercial, scientific, technical, agricultural, etc.).

2. *Time allotment and minimum essentials.*—The course of social studies here outlined would constitute, if all were taken, from 2½ to 4 units, dependent upon whether one or one-half year is allotted to each of the last three courses. The committee believes that there should be a social study in each year of the pupil's course. It is, however, conscious of the difficulty presented by the present requirements of the high-school program. The question then arises as to what would constitute a minimum course of social study under these existing conditions. To this question the committee would reply:

(*a*) The minimum essentials of the years X–XII should be determined by the needs of the particular pupil or group of pupils in question.

(*b*) Other things being equal, it would seem desirable for the pupil, whose time in the last three years is limited, to take those social studies which would most directly aid him to understand the relations of his own social life. If, for example, he had but one year out of the three for social study, and there were no special reason for deciding otherwise, it is probable that he might better take a half year of American history and a half year of European history (courses II and III); or, a half year of American history and a half year of the twelfth-year study of social problems (courses III and IV). The choice among these might be influenced by the trend taken by his social study in the ninth year (see the alternative possibilities of the ninth-year work, page 15).

(c) If the principles advocated in the following pages of this report for the organization of instruction in the social studies be adhered to, the apparent incompleteness of the cycle of social study, due to the impracticability of taking all the courses offered, will be in some degree obviated. Briefly stated, this means that any course of history instruction should be so organized that the pupil will inevitably acquire some familiarity with the economic, social, and civic factors in community life, just as in the study of civics or of social problems he should inevitably learn much history by using it. (See pages 32–34.)

(B) HISTORY.

I. GENERAL STATEMENT OF PRINCIPLES OF ORGANIZATION.

1. *Reasons for the proposed organization of history courses.*—The committee recommends the organization of the history course in two or three units as indicated in the general outline on page 35 in view of the following considerations:

(1) In small high schools more than two units of history are impracticable; and in large high schools, where more could be offered, few pupils would (or do) take more than two units, and these often unrelated.

(2) The long historical period included in course I offers a wide range of materials from which to select, and makes possible the development of topics continuously and unhampered by chronological and geographical limitations.

(3) The assignment of an equal amount of time (or twice the time if a year is given to each of courses II and III) to the period since the seventeenth century as to the period prior to that time, expresses the committee's conviction that recent history is richer in suitable materials for secondary education than the more remote periods, and is worthy of more intensive study.

(4) The history of any two years that a pupil may elect under this plan will be related; that of courses II and III is contemporaneous and presents many points of contact, and that of either course II or III is continuous with that of course I.

(5) Under the present four-unit plan a premium is placed upon ancient and American history, all that goes between being left largely to chance. Under the plan proposed by the committee a much larger proportion of the pupils will secure the benefits of a study of the essentials of European history.

(6) It is important to remember that the cycle of history provided for in the years X–XII will have been once traversed, on narrower lines, in the years VII–IX (see p. 12). Consequently, the pupil who for any reason can not complete the cycle in the years X–XII will not be wholly deficient in the knowledge of any of its parts.

(7) Although many teachers are at present inadequately prepared to follow the method of instruction advocated by the committee, which requires the selection of materials on the basis of the pupils' own immediate interests and of current problems (see below), the compression of a longer historical period into a briefer course will bring pressure to bear to induce a more careful selection of facts and events for emphasis.

2. *Organization of subject matter within history courses.*—Within each course the committee recommends—

(1) The adoption to the fullest extent possible of a "topical" method, or a "problem" method, as opposed to a method based on chronological sequence alone.

(2) The selection of topics or problems for study with reference to (a) the pupil's own immediate interest; (b) general social significance.

Concrete suggestion as to what the committee means by these criteria is given in the following pages, especially in the three type lessons on pages 44–47.

The organization of history instruction on this basis unquestionably requires greater skill on the part of the teacher than the traditional method, less dependence upon a single textbook of the types now existent, and larger use of many books, or of encyclopedic books, for reference purposes. If the selection of materials is to be determined by immediate interests and current problems, it is manifestly impossible to furnish in advance a detailed and complete outline of topics for universal and invariable use. To attempt to do so would be contrary to the very spirit of the method. Whether Miss Harris, for example, should dwell at length upon the War of 1812 and the subjects of the rights of neutrals (see p. 44), could not be determined for her in advance by a committee, nor even by an international lawyer to whom the question might seem of profound importance. The matter was determined for her by the exigencies of the hour and the interests of her pupils. So, also, was the method by which she approached and unfolded the subject.

On the other hand, there are certain topics that approach universality and invariability in their application. It is hardly conceivable, for example, that Miss Dilks could have omitted a study of "Athens—the City Beautiful" (see p. 45). The love for the beautiful is universal. In varied forms it is common to the pupils in the

class, and to all communities, nations, peoples, and times. Athens
represents a climax in the development of esthetics. But the feature
that especially characterizes Miss Dilks's lesson is the method by
which she brought "Athens—the City Beautiful" into the range of
the pupils' own interest and experience and made it a direct means
for the further cultivation of a fundamental interest in their lives.

In this there is suggested a possible organizing principle for history that is at once scientific and especially effective in teaching
pupils who have had a course in community civics of the type described earlier in this report. This organizing principle is found in
the "elements of welfare" or "fundamental interests," which afford
an effective basis for the organization of the latter subject. It is
a subjective rather than an objective basis. In the case just cited
the pupils themselves have a more or less developed esthetic interest,
which expresses itself in various elemental ways and reacts to conditions in the immediate community. This interest is common to all
mankind and finds expression in a great variety of ways. It expressed itself in a remarkable manner among the Greeks, who developed certain standards of beauty that have profoundly influenced
the world since their time.

Already the principle of organization here suggested is being
adopted more or less completely in the treatment of one great phase
of history—that which relates to the "economic interest" and is
expressed in economic or industrial history. Not all industrial history has been written on this basis of organization. Reference is
made to the type of industrial history to which Prof. Robinson evidently refers in the statement quoted on page 50 of this report and
which is clearly illustrated in the lesson described by Miss Hazard
(p. 47). The same principle is applied in the course suggested by
Dr. Leavitt and Miss Brown in their chapter on history in "Prevocational Education in the Public Schools."[1]

But boys and girls, even in vocational and prevocational classes,
have fundamental interests other than the economic. They are the
interests or "elements of welfare" that serve as the organizing
principle of community civics—physical, economic, intellectual, esthetic, religious, and social. Their relative prominence varies among
nations as among individuals, partly because of temperament and
partly because of physical and social influences; but the story of the
life of any nation is the story of effort to provide for them. The
life history of a nation, as of any community, consists of two great
lines of endeavor which are, of course, closely interrelated: (1) The
endeavor to establish permanent and definite relations with the land,
which involves the geographical factor, and (2) the endeavor to

---

[1] Leavitt and Brown, Prevocational Education in the Public Schools, chap. viii. Houghton Mifflin Co.

establish effective means of cooperation to provide for the " elements of welfare," which involves the evolution of a form of government. The committee merely raises the question as a basis for discussion and experiment whether the principle of organization here suggested may not do as much to vitalize instruction in history as it has already done to vitalize instruction in government under the name of community civics.

3. *Important aims in teaching history.*—(1) A primary aim of instruction in American history should be to develop a vivid conception of American nationality, a strong and intelligent patriotism, and a keen sense of the responsibility of every citizen for national efficiency. It is only on the basis of national solidarity, national efficiency (economic, social, political), and national patriotism that this or any nation can expect to perform its proper function in the family of nations (see pp. 25, 26).

(2) One of the conscious purposes of instruction in the history of nations other than our own should be the cultivation of a sympathetic understanding of such nations and their peoples, of an intelligent appreciation of their contributions to civilization, and of a just attitude toward them. So important has this seemed that a proposal has recently been made that one year of the history course be supplanted by a course to be known as "A Study of Nations." [1]

In suggesting such a study, Clarence D. Kingsley says:

The danger to be avoided above all others is the tendency to claim that one nation has a sweeping superiority over others. The claim of such superiority, as among individuals, is a sure cause of irreconcilable hatred. The cure for this narrow and partisan attitude is to be found in the broad conception that humanity is greater than any one nation. The idea should be developed that every nation has, or may have, something of worth to contribute to other nations, and to humanity as a whole. This conception when thoroughly inculcated would lead to a national respect for other nations, and to the belief that the continued existence and development of all nations are essential to the development of civilization. We can not expect that a principle so fundamental and comprehensive can be inculcated in the abstract; but through a specific study of many nations, the achievements and possibilities of each of which have been studied in the concrete, this idea may become established.

This conception of the supplementary value of the dissimilarities of the different nations and peoples, together with the ideal of human brotherhood, which is generally thought of in terms of essential similarity, should do much to establish genuine internationalism, free from sentiment, founded on fact, and actually operative in the affairs of nations.

This "Study of nations," as Mr. Kingsley sees it, instead of focusing attention upon the past, would start frankly with the present of typical modern nations—European, South American, oriental—and would use history in explanation of these nations and of clearly

[1] Kingsley, Clarence D., The Study of Nations: Its Possibilities as a Social Study in High Schools. School and Society, Vol. III, pp. 37–41, Jan. 8, 1916.

defined problems of supreme social importance at the present time.
Not only would the use of history organized in this way, according to
Mr. Kingsley, "tend to reduce friction in international relations, as
such friction often results from popular clamor, born of a lack of.
understanding of foreign nations," but "it would help to a truer
understanding and appreciation of the foreigners who come to our
shores," and "it would lead us to be more helpful in our relations
with backward peoples, because it would help us to value them on
the basis of their latent possibilities, rather than on the basis of
their present small achievements."

(3) In connection with the several history courses, and especially
in connection with courses II and III, due attention should be given
to Latin America and the Orient, especially Japan and China, and
to great international problems of social, economic, and political
importance to America and the world at large.

II. DETAILED DISCUSSION OF PRINCIPLES UNDERLYING HISTORY INSTRUCTION.

1. *The position of history in the curriculum.*—History, which has
long occupied the center of the stage among the social studies of the
high school, is facing competition not only from other branches of
study, such as science, but also from other social studies. The customary four units, which have been largely fixed in character by the
traditions of the historian and the requirements of the college, are
more or less discredited as ill adapted to the requirements of secondary education.

In a recent address Miss Jessie C. Evans, of the William Penn
High School for Girls, Philadelphia, said:

There is a growing danger that the traditional history course will only be
permitted to the college-preparatory student. I visited, the other day, one
of the largest high schools in the country and found that the majority of the
students took no history at all. The new definitions of culture and the new
demands for efficiency are causing very severe tests to be applied to any subject that would hold its own in our schools.

This statement suggests certain questions:

2. *To what extent and in what ways are college requirements
and life requirements mutually exclusive?*—In this connection the
words of Prof. Dewey quoted on page 11 are repeated with an
interpolation:

If we could really believe that attending to the needs of present growth
would keep the child and teacher alike busy and would also provide the best
possible guarantee of the learning needed in the future [in college or else-
where], transformation of educational ideals might soon be accomplished, and
other desirable changes would largely take care of themselves.

The problem of articulation between elementary and secondary schools, on the one hand, and between secondary schools and colleges, on the other, would take care of itself if elementary school, secondary school, and college would each give proper attention to the needs of present growth.

3. *To what extent does an increase in the amount of history offered insure more universal or better social education?*—The historical training acquired by the pupils is not proportional to the number of courses offered. Whether pupils elect history or not depends, first, upon whether they want it; and, second, upon the demands of other subjects upon their time. Those who are concerned for the prestige of history in the school program will find that their gains by adding courses are largely " on paper." In small high schools more than two or three units of history are impracticable; and in large schools few pupils take more than two units of the subject, these frequently disconnected; the majority take only what is required. Two or three units of history are ample in these years, provided they are adapted to the needs of the pupil and have been preceded by the cycle which this report recommends for the years VII–IX (see p. 12).

4. *What " tests " must the history course meet if it is "to hold its own in our schools "?*—It is true that " the new definitions of culture and the new demands for efficiency are causing very severe tests to be applied " to all subjects, and the traditional type of history is in danger because it fails to meet the tests.

The ideal history for each of us would be those facts of past human experience to which we should have recourse oftenest in our endeavors to understand ourselves and our fellows. No one account would meet the needs of all, but all would agree that much of what now passes for the elements of history meets the needs of none. No one questions the inalienable right of the *historian* to interest himself in any phase of the past that he chooses. It is only to be wished that a greater number of historians had greater skill in hitting upon those phases of the past which serve *us* best in understanding the most vital problems of the present.—(Prof. James Harvey Robinson, in The New History.)

The italics in this quotation are our own. It is the chief business of the maker of the course of study, the textbook writer, and the teacher to do what the historian has failed to do, viz, to " hit upon those phases of the past which serve us " (the high-school pupil) " best in understanding the most vital problems of the present." Further, " the most vital problems of the present " for the high-school pupil are the problems which he himself is facing now or which are of direct value to him in his present processes of growth.

Prof. Mace has made the following statement:

To connect events and conditions with life as the pupil knows it will make history more or less of a practical subject. The pupil will see where his knowledge turns up in the affairs of everyday life. He will really discover how present-day institutions came to be what they are. Whenever or wherever he strikes a point in history, in Egypt, Greece, Rome, England, or even America, the point must be connected with modern life. Otherwise it may have only a curious or perhaps an academic interest for him, or it may have no interest whatever.

This connection may be worked out in several ways. The Egyptians had certain ideas about immortality, and therefore certain customs of burial. The Greeks probably took these up and modified them. The Romans changed them still further, especially after the coming of Christ. The Roman Catholic Church made still greater changes. The Reformation introduced new conceptions of the soul after death, and to-day the great variety of ideas on the subject show the tremendous differentiations that have come since the days of old Egypt. Likewise, it shows how tenacious the idea has been—its continuity. How much interest is aroused if the student is put to working out this problem of the life development of an idea! What sort of history is this? It is neither ancient, medieval, or modern, but all these in one. It is the new kind of general history—the kind that socializes the student. It makes him feel that history has some meaning when he sees ancient ideas functioning in the present.

Not every idea in history lends itself to such treatment. Many facts have not preserved their continuity in as perfect a way, but seem to have lost it before modern life is reached. But there is another relation—that of similarity. The reforms of Solon in Greece and of the Gracchi in Rome, the causes of Wat Tyler's rebellion, the measures of Lloyd George in England to-day, and the social-justice idea of the Progressive platform in the Presidential campaign of 1912 bear striking resemblance to each other. While they can not be connected by progressive evolution, they are richly suggestive in the lessons they teach.

Again, many events whose continuity we may not be able to trace have valuable lessons growing out of their dissimilarity. By making note of their contrasts we may see their bearing on modern life. The terrible Thirty Years' War, the Puritan Revolution, the Revolution of 1688, the American Revolution, and finally the French Revolution, present such striking contrasts as to give the student some notion of what might have been avoided for the betterment of the people. This means that when one of these upheavals is studied the rest should be made to yield their particular points of contrast, to the end that the student may see the lessons they present.

Another contribution to the discussion is the following, by Prof. Robinson. A portion of this is italicized for future reference.

One of our chief troubles in teaching history comes from the old idea that history is a record of past events; whereas our real purpose nowadays is to present past conditions, explain them so far as we can, and compare them with our own. . . .

While events can be dealt with chronologically, conditions have to be presented topically if they are to become clear. For example, we can select the salient events of the Crusades, and tell them in the form of a story; but the medieval church, castle, monastery, and farm have to be described in typical forms, as they lasted several centuries. The older textbooks told the events more or less dryly, gave the succession of kings, and the battles and treaties of their respective reigns. It was not deemed necessary to describe conditions and institutions with any care, and such terms as pope, king, bishop, church, baron, alchemy, astrology, witchcraft, were used as if every boy or girl of 14 knew exactly what they were.

A still unsolved problem is to determine what conditions and institutions shall be given the preference, considering the capacity of the student on the one hand and the limitations of time on the other. The committee should not undertake to pronounce on this matter, but should urge that teachers and text-book writers should be constantly asking themselves whether what they are teaching seems to them worth while. . . .

All instruction is, so to speak, the function of three variables—the pupils, the teacher, and the textbook. Every teacher is aware that pupils differ a good deal according to their environment, and, as we develop industrial and other forms of special education, it will be necessary to select our material to meet the special needs of the pupils. As for the teacher, no satisfactory results will be obtained until he learns to outrun the textbook and becomes really familiar, through judicious reading or university instruction, with the institutions which he proposes to deal with. Teachers should learn to deal with their subject topically, and should not be contented with reading historical manuals, which are usually poor places to go for information in regard to conditions and institutions. They should turn to the articles in the Encyclopedia Britannica and other similar works and to special treatments.

5. *Two questions at issue.*—There is general agreement that history, to be of value in the education of the boy or girl, must "function in the present." Disagreement arises over two questions: (1) What is meant by "functioning in the present"? (2) How shall the material of history be organized to this end?

(1) *What is meant by functioning in the present?*—There are two interpretations of this phrase: (a) The sociological interpretation, according to which it is enough if history be made to explain present conditions and institutions; (b) the pedagogical interpretation, according to which history, to be of value educationally, must be related to the present interests of the pupil. Many present-day problems are as far removed from the interests and experience of youth as if they belonged to the most remote historical epoch. It is not that a past event has its results, or its counterpart, or its analogy, or its contrast, in the present that gives it its chief educational value, but that it "meets the needs of present growth" in the pupil. We have learned to use hero stories and pioneer stories from any epoch of history in certain elementary grades because there is something in children that makes them want such stories as food for growth.

Recent periods are doubtless richer in materials of present application than the more remote periods. But children have very little chronological perspective. As one star seems as far away as another, although millions of miles may intervene between them, so American colonization may seem as remote to the child as the period of Athenian supremacy. The relative educational value of the wars of 1775, 1812, and 1861 does not depend upon their remoteness or proximity. It does not necessarily follow from the fact that trusts are a live, present issue, and negro slavery came to an end 50 years ago, that the slavery agitation preceding the Civil War is of less educational value than the agitation regarding the control of trusts at the present time.

Do not these considerations suggest a basis for a partial answer at least to Prof. Robinson's "still unsolved problem," stated above (p. 43), viz, "to determine what conditions and institutions shall be given the preference," and to his question, "What is worth while?" The principle may be stated thus: *The selection of a topic in history and the amount of attention given to it should depend, not merely upon its relative proximity in time, nor yet upon its relative present importance from the adult or from a sociological point of view, but also and chiefly upon the degree to which such topic can be related to the present life interests of the pupil, or can be used by him in his present processes of growth.*

The committee does not imagine, however, that by stating this principle it has solved the problem of the organization of the history course. It has only recognized a new and most important factor in the problem. By so doing, it has even made the problem more difficult, for there are now raised the new questions, What history does meet the needs of the child's growth? and, How may a given topic be related to the child's interest? Acceptance of the principle throws the problem largely back upon the teacher, for the questions just stated are questions that she must answer for her particular group of pupils, and can not be disposed of once for all by a jury of historians or sociologists. The problem is only in part one of selection of topics; it is also one of method of approach. A topic that may be infused with vitality by a proper approach through the interests of the children may become perfectly barren of results through lack of such approach. (See discussion of the question of "Approach" in relation to the teaching of civics on p. 24 of this report).

Illustrations of the principle.—The following type lessons illustrate, more or less perfectly, the application of this principle. The first is given by Miss Hannah M. Harris, of the State Normal School at Hyannis, Mass., and illustrates both the selection of topic and the method of approach with reference to the pupils' immediate interest.

Ordinarily we have regarded the War of 1812 as not closely related to those interests (of the children) nor essential to the development of the central theme of the term, "The building of the Nation"; hence we have passed over the subject rather lightly, and have saved time for the more intensive study of the Revolution and the making of the Constitution, topics which are necessary to the central theme, and which can be made real to the children by means of their activities in a school club. This club makes and amends its own constitution, earns money, votes its expenditures; in short, manages its own affairs on democratic principles, and so brings home to its members the meaning of certain political terms and situations involved in these topics, such as taxation without representation, majority rule, compromises, etc.

In 1915, however, the subject of the War of 1812 appeared to us in a different light. The children were reading headlines in the newspapers in which the word "neutrality" had a conspicuous place. They heard the word repeated at home and on every street corner, and were beginning to use it themselves, though with but vague notions of its meaning. Consequently the preceding topic in the history course was less fully treated than in ordinary years, and time was appropriated for a study of the War of 1812.

The study was approached in the following way: What is meant by the expression "a neutral nation," "belligerent nation"? What nations are now belligerent? Which ones neutral? What are some of the ways in which the citizens of a neutral nation come into contact with the citizens or with the government of a belligerent nation? (Some of the answers: "Buy things of them"; "sell them goods"; "have our goods carried in their ships"; "travel in their countries.") So long as any nation remains neutral, what rights have its citizens in these matters and others? (So far answers all came from previous knowledge, casually acquired information.) Now, with some suggestions from the children and explanations from the teacher, the following outline was put upon the blackboard:

The main rights of neutrality:

1. To live peaceably at home; i. e., not to be forced to take sides in the war or to have life or property endangered by it.

2. To trade with any nation. Exceptions: Entrance to blockaded ports; dealing in contraband goods.

3. To travel peaceably on the high seas or anywhere permitted by existing treaties. Exceptions: Places in which belligerents are actually engaged in warfare.

The questioning was then resumed: Do neutral nations desire to keep up friendly relations with belligerents? What mistake on the part of a neutral nation may interfere with these friendly relations? (Showing more favor to one belligerent than to another.) Why does President Wilson ask us to be neutral (impartial, calm) in our talk and actions toward citizens of belligerent nations? What act on the part of a belligerent nation may interrupt these friendly relations? (The violation of any one of the rights of neutrality.)

The members of the class were referred to the textbook to find out how the United States tried in 1812 to maintain its neutrality and how it failed. The account in the textbook was found all too brief to satisfy the pupils' inquiries, and the study of the war was neither dry nor out of touch with reality.

Miss Clara G. Dilks, of Philadelphia, furnishes the following plan for a series of lessons on "Athens—the City Beautiful." Whatever we may eliminate from Greek history, it should not be Greek art, which has so profoundly influenced the world. But it is not merely that the influence of Greek art survives in modern architecture that gives this phase of Greek history its value; it is the additional fact that the æsthetic interest of children is strong and needs cultivation. We may assume that the following lessons had for a point of departure live interest on the part of the pupils in the beauty of their surroundings, perhaps specifically in a proposed city-planning movement or the erection of a new public building or, on the other hand, in the prevalence in the community of unsightly architecture.

Object of lesson:
1. To visualize Athens.
2. To stimulate the pupils to observe their own surroundings in comparison.
3. To give knowledge of the possibility of combining beauty and utility in building.

Method of assignment:
1. Give an outline that will fit the books available and the time of the pupils:
    (a) Topography of the Acropolis. Caution: Avoid affording pupils opportunity of making a mere catalogue of names. Let them imagine themselves visitors to the city.
    (b) Chief orders of Greek architecture.
    (c) Chief buildings—plan, material, decorations.
2. Assign problems, such as—
    (a) Examination of a principal street in the pupils' own community for—
        (1) Kind of buildings.
        (2) Uniformity in architectural scheme.
        (3) Attempts to combine beauty with utility.
    (b) Study of municipal buildings for—
        (1) Grouping or isolation.
        (2) Location with reference to business and residence sections.

Plan for teaching:
1. Question class as to characteristics of the Greeks that would influence their art. Compare characteristics of Americans and Greeks and draw conclusions.
2. Discuss orders of Greek architecture, compare them, and cite famous examples. Make use of pictures.
3. Application of orders to buildings.
4. Study of buildings. Use pictures.
    Note relative locations.
    Adaptation of form of buildings to geographical features.
    Decoration.
    Deduction as to whether architecture corresponds with the characteristics of the Greeks as noted.
5. Have pupils discover qualities in Greek architecture adaptable to all ages and countries.
6. Experience meeting regarding results of investigations by pupils in their own community and conclusions as to—
    (a) Presence of Greek influence.
    (b) Evidence of definite policy for beautifying pupils' own city. Compare with other American cities and European cities.
7. Conclusion of lesson:
    Is it possible to adapt the idealistic Greek art to a modern commercial city? Consider modern bridges, street lamps, public buildings.
    What is the best means of attaining this end?
        Development of general knowledge of good models and an artistic sense.
        Use of trained " city planners," art juries, etc.

Miss Blanche E. Hazard, of the department of home economics in the New York State Agricultural College, describes some work done by her when in the High School of Practical Arts, Boston. Her pupils were girls chiefly representing the "working classes." Neither they nor their parents looked with much favor upon an education that was not intensely "practical" from their point of view. Ancient and mediæval history made little appeal to them until—

The study of the mediæval craft guilds and of the development of crafts and commerce was taken up in connection with a close-at-hand examination of the present industries or occupations of their parents or other members of their families. Each father initiated his own daughter into the special mysteries of his craft: if a hod carrier, he sometimes had her await his freedom on Sunday, and then took her over the building where he was at work. The history of the craft, its problems, advantages and disadvantages, technique and conditions, in early times and in the nineteenth and twentieth centuries, were studied.

Not only did the girls take the keenest interest in this work, but their fathers also became so interested to know that Greeks and Romans, Germans in the thirteenth century, and Englishmen for the past ten centuries had been tailors, shoemakers, masons, or greengrocers, and to learn of their wares, tools, and methods, that there was a happy interchange of facts of past and present between father and daughter.

Six weeks were allowed for the work in this special industry and an oral report was made to the class. In some years, from 200 girls there would come reports on 75 different industries and occupations. Meanwhile instruction was given regarding general typical industries, such as weaving, printing, lumbering, etc.

The students became keen observers and asked foremen and guides intelligent questions. They came to have decided ideas as to monotonous work and dangerous occupations. They had in hand the history of the industries before and after the introduction of machinery; with and without the protection of legislation. From the mediæval craft guild to the present trade union faith and tenets, became an interesting mental road of travel for them, and linked the far-off history work in their vocational school with their fathers' daily life and interests. .

These three-type lessons illustrate the application to particular cases of the principle that history to function properly in the present must meet the needs of present growth in the pupils.

(2) *How shall the course in history be organised for the purposes of secondary education?*

Each new writer of a textbook is guided, consciously or unconsciously, in his choice of topics by earlier manuals which have established what teachers and the public at large are wont to expect under the caption "history."

Until recently the main thread selected was political. Almost everything was classified under kings' reigns, and the policy of their government, and the wars in which they became involved were the favorite subjects of discussion. . . . Political history is the easiest kind of history to write; it lends itself to accurate chronological arrangement just because it deals mainly with events rather than with conditions. (Prof. Robinson, in The New History, chapter on "History for the Common Man," p. 136.)

The substitution of a sociological point of view for that of the mere annalist has led to the introduction of new threads of human progress and the subordination of wars and political policies. It has also led to a partial, but only partial, breaking down of the purely chronological basis of organization. But no substitute for the chronological organization of history has been found that adequately meets the conditions and needs of secondary education.

It is not meant to suggest that chronology can be disregarded. The gradual and orderly evolution, step by step, of institutions and conditions is of the very essence of history. It would be impossible, were it thought desirable, to eliminate this element from historical study. But the principle of organization is antiquated which results in what some one has called the "what-came-next" plan of treatment, a mere succession of events; in the building of United States history on the framework of "administrations," and of English or Roman history on that of "reigns"; and in the organization of the entire history course in such a way that the pupil studies "ancient" history this year, "medieval" history next year, and "modern" history the year following—provided, indeed, that he happens to begin his history this year and continue it consecutively next year and the year following, which is by no means invariably true.

If, now, we accept the "pedagogical" interpretation of the principle that history must function in the present, namely, that history to be of educational value must relate to the present interests of the pupil, or meet the needs of present growth, in addition to explaining present-day conditions and institutions according to the sociological interpretation, what effect may this have upon the organization of the history course?

A statement by Miss Hannah M. Harris, of the State Normal School, at Hyannis, Mass., bears directly upon this question:

The moment we cut loose from the old method of trying to teach all the historical facts which may happen to be found between the covers of the textbook, the question of how to organize the material of history becomes an urgent one. The student of sociology desires to organize the subject matter primarily to exhibit some important phase or phases of the social evolution of the race or nation or of some smaller group. The student of children and their needs desires to start with their present interests and to select from the story of the past only such fragments as bear so close a relation to these interests that they are capable of being in some real sense understood by the children, and of proving incentives to further profitable interests and activities on their part. This second plan, if logically carried out, would leave the entire record of the past open as a field for selection at any stage of the child's education, and would thus impose upon the teacher a task immensely difficult if not impossible.

These two plans have a common purpose to make the study of history yield the help it should give in the social education of children and young people. Is it not possible to combine successfully certain features of both proposals?

Can we not heed the suggestions of modern pedagogy by starting with those contemporaneous matters in which the children have already some interest, and from this study of present-day community affairs be led naturally back into the past to find related material which is significant to the children because of this relationship, and valuable to them because it serves to make clearer or more interesting the present situation?

At the same time, can we not limit the field of history from which selection of material is to be made for any one year of school work to some one historical epoch, permitting the teacher free choice within these limits, the choice to be guided both by the present interests of the children and by the general rule that any historical facts considered must have some bearing upon the main lines of growth which are characteristic of the period being studied?

Plan of the University of Missouri elementary school.—One of the most radical experiments in the reorganization of history instruction to "meet the needs of present growth" is that of Prof. J. L. Meriam in the university elementary school of the University of Missouri. So far this experiment has been limited to the elementary school, but Dr. Meriam considers it a sufficient success to warrant its adaptation to the secondary school. He believes that "the present four units of history" in the secondary school are "quite out of date."

To quote from Dr. Meriam:

The university elementary school gives no instruction in history as such, although a great deal of historical material is very carefully studied. This policy is in accord with our policy in other subjects. We teach no arithmetic as such, but we do a great deal of arithmetical calculation in connection with special topics. We teach no geography as such, but we become acquainted with a great deal of geographical material in our study of various industrial and social activities. We teach no language as such, but language is in constant use in our efforts to express to the best of our ability the ideas we have in various other subjects.

History as usually taught is looked upon as a method of approach to the study of present-day problems. It is also used as a means of interpreting present-day problems. Thus history is usually studied before present-day problems. Further, history is usually studied by showing events in their chronological order. In the university elementary school no such purpose is present.

For us historical material is studied merely to satisfy interests and to further interests in present-day problems. Such study also provides at times inspiration and suggestion for the further study of problems that are of immediate interest. Such historical material frequently excites interest in reading and thus incidentally furnishes the pupil with certain information that may be of value later. This, however, must be looked upon as a mere by-product.

Thus, with us the study of historical material follows, rather than precedes, the study of similar events in the present, and there is no occasion for taking up these events in chronological order. The immature pupil is not yet prepared to understand and appreciate development of institutions merely because he has not yet had sufficient experience with details. He is, however, interested in isolated events, here and there, especially those which are similar in character to events taking place in the present time that are of interest to him. Thus we need no textbook as a guide, but we use many textbooks as mere reference books. Thus we have no course in history to follow and no given amount of historical study to complete. Within the elementary school field the pupil is not ready to summarize and organize this historical study.

One special illustration may be sufficient. In our sixth grade the subject of transportation is considered in so far as it is a present-day problem. Some eight weeks are spent on such topics as railways, steamship lines, public highways and animal power, use of electricity in travel, the automobile, the aeroplane. In the seventh or eighth grade the same topic is considered, but in certain historical aspects. For example, the growth of railways in the United States and elsewhere. Here would be considered change in the extent of mileage, change in location of roads as affected by needs in various parts of the country, change in the character of engines and cars as influenced by inventions, improvement made in roads, bridges, railway stations, and the like.

Such study calls for: (1) much reading; (2) geographical study concerning the trunk lines and lines of travel; (3) arithmetical calculations, especially in the change of mileage and the cost of construction of roads and trains; (4) some very elementary physics in the study of the steam engine, air brakes, and the like; (5) drawing as a means of illustration; (6) composition, spelling, and writing as a means of expression; (7) "history for the common boy and girl." (See Robinson's "The New History," chapter on "History for the Common Man.")

"History for the common man."—The chapter in Prof. Robinson's book to which Dr. Meriam alludes in the last clause constituted an address before a meeting of school superintendents at which the subject of discussion was industrial education. Prof. Robinson introduced his address as follows:

Should the student of the past be asked what he regarded as the most original and far-reaching discovery of modern times he might reply with some assurance that it is our growing realization of the fundamental importance and absorbing interest of common men and common things. Our democracy, with all its hopes and aspirations, is based on an appreciation of common men; our science, with all its achievements and prospects, is based on the appreciation of common things. . . . We have come together with a view of adjusting our education to this great discovery.

It is our present business to see what can be done for that very large class of boys and girls who must take up the burden of life prematurely and who must look forward to earning their livelihood by the work of their hands. But education has not been wont, until recently, to reckon seriously with the common man, who must do common things. It has presupposed leisure and freedom from the pressing cares of life. . . .

It is high time that we set to work boldly and without any timid reservation to bring our education into the closest possible relation with the actual life and future duties of the great majority of those who fill our public schools. . . .

History is what we know of the past. We may question it as we question our memory of our own personal acts and experiences. But those things that we recall in our own past vary continually with our moods and preoccupations. We adjust our recollection to our needs and aspirations, and ask from it light on the particular problems that face us. History, too, is not fixed and immutable, but ever changing. Each age has a perfect right to select from the annals of mankind those facts that seem to have a particular bearing on the matters it has at heart. . . .

So, in considering the place to be assigned to history in industrial education, I have no intention . . . of advocating what has hitherto commonly passed for an outline of history. On the contrary, I suggest that we take up the whole problem afresh, freed for the moment from our impressions of "history," vulgarly so called.

What Prof. Robinson suggests is that, given a group of boys and girls whose economic and social position is preordained to the ranks of the great majority of men and women " who do common things," the history instruction should be organized, not on the traditional basis of chronology and politics, but on that of their own immediate interests.

This is what Miss Hazard did in the case cited above (see p. 47). This is also what Dr. Meriam is doing—only he goes further. He maintains that, whether or not we know in advance that the pupils are to be "common men and women," they are at least "common boys and girls" with interests in the present. He would therefore organize all history instruction on the basis of these interests, selecting from any part of the past those facts that "meet the needs of present growth"; and he would utilize these facts at the time when the pupil has need for them in connection with any subject under discussion or any activity in progress.

Practical difficulties of radical reorganization.—It may be plausibly objected that, while such radical reorganization as that suggested by Dr. Meriam may succeed in a special experimental school under the direction of a Dr. Meriam and a well-trained, sympathetic staff, it could not succeed at present under the conditions of the ordinary school. Miss Harris refers to the difficulty (see p. 48, above) and proposes to meet it by a compromise between the "chronological" and "pedagogical" methods, restricting the field from which the teacher shall draw her materials in any given year to a particular historical epoch.

The limitation of the ground to be covered makes it practicable for the average grammar-school teacher, who, of course, is not a specialist in history, to become very familiar with the possibilities of the history of the period in question, as a mine of valuable material. And it is only this familiarity on the teacher's part that will make this sort of teaching a success.

The difficulty to which Miss Harris here refers—unpreparedness in history on the part of the teacher—is perhaps not so much of a factor in the secondary school, especially in cities, as in the elementary school. Unpreparedness of the high-school teacher is likely to be of another kind, namely, unpreparedness in the art of teaching. The college-trained high-school teacher may be a specialist in his subject, but have no training whatever as a teacher.

This unpreparedness of teachers, the lack of suitable textbooks, natural conservatism, and the opposition of those whose chief apparent interest is to maintain the supremacy of a "subject," or who see in the traditional methods of history instruction a means of "culture" that the schools can not dispense with, cause school authorities and teachers to hesitate "to work boldly and without timid reservation," or to "take up the whole matter afresh, freed . . . from the impression of 'history' . . . so called," and to seek rather to modify the existing course of study, incorporating in it as much as possible of the new ideas in the hope that as they prove their worth they will gain favor and open the way for further improvement. The committee has taken account of this fact in arriving at its conclusions, and has made its recommendations (pp. 35–39) in the hope that they will stimulate initiative and experiment rather than discourage effort at immediate improvement.

(C) PROBLEMS OF AMERICAN DEMOCRACY—ECONOMIC, SOCIAL, POLITICAL.

It is generally agreed that there should be a culminating course of social study in the last year of the high school, with the purpose of giving a more definite, comprehensive, and deeper knowledge of some of the vital problems of social life, and thus of securing a more intelligent and active citizenship. Like preceding courses, it should provide for the pupils' "needs of present growth," and should be founded upon what has preceded in the pupils' education, especially through the subjects of civics and history.

1. *Conflicting claims for the twelfth year.*—One fact stands out clearly in the present status of the twelfth-year problem, namely, the variety of opinion as to the nature of the work that should be offered in this year. Not to mention the claims of history, the principal claimants for position are political science (government, "advanced civics"), economics, and sociology in some more or less practical form.

A profitable course could be given in any one of these fields, provided only it be adapted to secondary-school purposes. Three alternatives seem to present themselves:

1. To agree upon some one of the three fields.

2. To suggest a type course in each of the three fields, leaving the choice optional with the local school.

3. To recommend a new course involving the principles and materials of all three fields, but adapted directly to the immediate needs of secondary education.

The traditional courses in civil government are almost as inadequate for the last as for the first year of the high school. Efforts to improve them have usually consisted of only slight modifications of the traditional course or of an attempted simplification of political science. The results have not met the needs of high-school pupils nor satisfied the demands of economists and sociologists.

A justifiable opinion prevails that the principles of economics are of such fundamental importance that they should find a more definite place in high-school instruction than is customary. Courses in economics are accordingly appearing in high-school curriculums with increasing frequency. To a somewhat less degree, and with even less unanimity as to nature of content, the claims of sociology are being pressed. A practical difficulty is presented by the resulting complexity of the course of study. The advocates of none of the social sciences are willing to yield wholly to the others, nor is it justifiable from the standpoint of the pupil's social education to limit his instruction to one field of social science to the exclusion of others. The most serious difficulty, however, is that none of the social sciences, as developed and organized by the specialists, is adapted to the requirements of secondary education, and all attempts to adapt them to such requirements have been obstructed by tradition, as in the case of history.

Is it not time, in this field as in history, " to take up the whole problem afresh, freed . . . from the impressions of " the traditional social sciences?

2. *Relation to preceding courses.*—The suggestion that follows with reference to the last-year course of social study must be consid-ered in the light of the recommendations for the preceding years. The courses in community civics and in history, if developed along the lines suggested in this report, are rich in their economic, sociological, and political connotations. Even if no provision be made in the last year for the further development of the special social sciences, the committee believes that its recommendations for the preceding years still provide as never before for the education of the pupil regarding the economic and social relations of his life.

3. *Concrete problems in varied aspects.*—The only feasible way the committee can see by which to satisfy in reasonable measure the demands of the several social sciences, while maintaining due regard for the requirements of secondary education, is to organize instruction, not on the basis of the formal social sciences, but on the basis of concrete problems of vital importance to society and of immediate interest to the pupil.

In other words, the suggestion is not to discard one social science in favor of another, nor attempt to crowd the several social sciences into this year in abridged forms; but to study actual problems, or issues, or conditions, as they occur in life, and in their several aspects, political, economic, and sociological. These problems or issues will naturally vary from year to year, and from class to class, but they should be selected on the ground (1) of their immediate interest to the class and (2) of their vital importance to society. The principle suggested here is the same as that applied to the organization of civics and history.

4. *Illustrations.*—In actual life, whether as high-school pupils or as adults, we face problems or conditions and not sciences. We use sciences, however, to interpret our problems and conditions. Furthermore, every problem or condition has many sides and may involve the use of various sciences. To illustrate the point we may take the cost of living, which is a vital problem from the standpoint of the individual and of society, and may readily have been forced upon the interest of the pupil through changes in mode of life, curtailment of allowance, sacrifice of customary pleasures, change in plans for education, etc. This problem involves, on the economic side, such fundamental matters as values, prices, wages, etc.; on the sociological side, such matters as standards of living, birth rate, etc.; on the political side, such matters as tariff legislation, control of trusts and the like, and the appropriate machinery of legislation, law enforcement, and judicial procedure.

The problem of immigration might impose itself upon attention for any one of a number of reasons. It will have been touched upon in an elementary way in community civics, and doubtless will have come up in a variety of ways in connection with history; but it may now be considered more comprehensively, more intensively, and more exhaustively. One of the chief aims should now be to organize knowledge with reference to the economic, sociological, and political principles involved.

Economic relations of immigration:

Labor supply and other industrial problems (on the side of "production").
Standards of living, not only of the immigrants, but also of native Americans as affected by immigration (on the side of "consumption").
Relation to the problem of land tenure in the United States.

Sociological relations of immigration:

Movements and distribution of population; congestion in cities; etc.
Assimilation of immigrant population; admixture of races.
Vital statistics, health problems, etc.
Educational and religious problems involved.
Social contributions of immigrants; art, science, ethics.

Political and governmental relations of immigration:

Political ideals of immigrants; comparison of their inherited political conceptions with those of the country of their adoption.
Naturalization; its methods, abuses, etc.
The courts in the light of the processes of naturalization.
Administration of immigration laws.
Defects and inconsistencies in the methods of our Government as shown in legislation regarding immigrants and in the administration of the laws.
Problems of municipal government arising from or complicated by immigration.

A study or series of studies of the type here suggested, developing from concrete issues, would afford opportunity to go as far as occa-

sion demands and time allows into the fundamental economic and
political questions of the time. In the field of political science, for
example, problems can readily be formulated on the basis of particular cases involving a study of legislative methods of Congress
and of State legislatures; the powers and limitations of Federal
and State executives; judicial machinery and procedure; lack of
uniformity in State legislation and its results; weakness of county
government; comparison of administration of cities in Europe, South
America, and the United States, etc.

There has not yet been the same insistent demand for sociology as
a science in the high school that there has been for economics and
the science of government. But there are many questions and principles of a more or less purely sociological character that are just as
important for the consideration of a high-school boy or girl as many
others of a more or less purely economic or political character. A
course of the kind suggested by the committee should doubtless
afford opportunity for some consideration of such vital social institutions as the family and the church. These institutions will, it is
hoped, have been studied in some of their aspects and relations in
connection with history courses and in community civics, but they
may now be considered from different angles, the point of departure
being some particular problem in the foreground of current attention,
such as, for example, the strength and weakness of the church as a
socializing factor in rural life, etc.

Again, there are certain facts relating to the "social mind" for
which the high-school boy and girl are quite ready, provided the
study has a sufficiently concrete foundation and a sufficiently direct
application. Any daily paper, indeed the life of any large school,
will afford numerous incidents upon which to base a serious consideration, for example, of the impulsive action of "crowds" in
contrast with the deliberative action of individuals and of the consequences of such action in social conduct. The power and effects of
tradition are another phenomenon of social psychology fully as
worthy of study in the high-school as many of the other social facts
and laws that seem indispensable; it is not necessary to go farther
than the curriculum which the pupil is following and the methods
by which he is instructed to find a starting point for a discussion of
this question and abundant material for its exemplification.

These two particular illustrations of expressions of the "social
mind" are taken from a description of the social studies in the curriculum of Hampton Institute.[1] It may be said in passing that this
committee has found no better illustration of the organization of
economic and sociological knowledge on a problem basis, and of the

---

[1] Jones, Thomas Jesse. "Social Studies in the Hampton Curriculum." Hampton Institute Press, 1908.

selection of problems for study with direct reference to the pupils'
immediate interests and needs than that offered in the work of this
institution.

5. *Summary of reasons for the proposed course.*—In making its
suggestion for this study of concrete problems of democracy in the
last year of the high school the committee has been particularly influenced by the following considerations:

(1) It is impracticable to include in the high-school program a
comprehensive course in each of the social sciences. And yet it is
unjust to the pupil that his knowledge of social facts and laws should
be limited to the field of any one of them, however important that
one may be.

(2) The purposes of secondary education and not the intrinsic
value of any particular body of knowledge should be the determining
consideration. From the standpoint of the purposes of secondary
education, it is far less important that the adolescent youth should
acquire a comprehensive knowledge of any or all of the social
sciences than it is that he should be given experience and practice in
the observation of social phenomena as he encounters them; that he
should be brought to understand that every social problem is many-
sided and complex; and that he should acquire the habit of forming
social judgments only on the basis of dispassionate consideration of
all the facts available. This, the committee believes, can best be
accomplished by dealing with actual situations as they occur and by
drafting into service the materials of all the social sciences as occasion demands for a thorough understanding of the situations in
question.

(3) The principles upon which such a course is based are the same
as those which have been successfully applied in community civics
and, to some extent in isolated cases, to the teaching of economics,
sociology, and even history.

6. *Experiment urged.*—The committee believes, however, that it
should at this time go no further than to define principles, with
such meager illustration as it has available, and to urge experiment.
It would especially urge that the methods and results of experiment,
either along the lines suggested in this report or in other directions,
be recorded by those who make them and reported for the benefit of
all who are interested.

PART IV.—STANDARDS—PREPARATION OF TEACHERS—AVAILABILITY OF MATERIAL.

I. STANDARDS BY WHICH TO TEST METHODS.

While the following statement [1] was made originally with specific reference to the teaching of civics, the committee sees in it a general application to all of the social studies.

While we are discussing ways and means of making the teaching of civics more effective, is it timely to consider by what standards we are to judge what is effective and what is not? If I examine your proposed course in civics, on what grounds shall I say that it is good or bad? If I visit your class and pronounce your teaching excellent or poor, by what standards do I estimate the value of your work? Why should you accept my judgment?. . . . Can standards be formulated so that we may have a common basis for comparison, and . . . so that any teacher may put her work to the test from day to day, or from week to week, and see, not whether it conforms to the opinions of some one, but whether it measures up to clearly recognized criteria?

There are those who say that we can not measure the results of teaching with a yardstick or a bushel measure. Neither can we so measure electricity or light. Nor, for that matter, do we measure potatoes with a yardstick nor cloth by the bushel. The standard must be appropriate to the commodity or force.

Those who say that the results of civics teaching can not be seen or measured until later years fall into one of the errors that have hindered the progress of civic education. This is the error of assuming that the child will be a citizen only at some future time; of forgetting that he is a citizen now, with real civic relations and interests. Civic education is a process of cultivating existing tendencies, traits, and interests. The gardener who cultivates a plant will, it is true, not know until the fullness of time how much fruit it will bear. Then he may measure his results by the bushel. But as he cultivates the plant day by day he appraises its growth by standards clearly recognized by all gardeners, and he varies his treatment according to the signs.

Civic education is . . . a cultivation of civic qualities which have already " sprouted ", and which will continue to grow under the eyes of the teacher. . . . The first step is to define the civic qualities whose resultant we recognize as good citizenship, and whose cultivation should be the aim of civics teaching. . . .

First in importance is interest in one's civic relations. . . . Bad citizenship is more often due to lack of interest than to lack of knowledge. . . . It follows that it should be an important part of civic education to cultivate an abiding civic interest. . . . The only way to do this is to *demonstrate* that these relations *are* of vital moment to the individual. The present interest of the child must be kept in mind, and not his probable or possible interest of 10 years hence. . . .

---

[1] Extract from an address by Arthur William Dunn on " Standards by which to Test the Value of Civics Instruction."

1. *Civics teaching is good in proportion as it makes its appeal definitely and constantly to the pupil's own present interest as a citizen.*

Interest is closely allied to motive. But real or apparent interest may lead to the setting up of wrong motives. . . . Good citizenship can only grow out of right motives. It follows that it should be a part of civic education to cultivate right motives. Pupils should be led both to *want to know* about their civic relations and to *want to do* something as good citizens.

2. *Civics teaching is good in proportion as it provides the pupil with adequate motives for studying civics and for seeking opportunity to participate in the civic life of the community of which he is a member.*

Community of interests implies community of effort. . . . The proper conception of government is that of a means of cooperation for the common wellbeing. No man can . . . be effective in civic life unless his "teamwork" is good. The possession of a spirit and habit of *cooperation* is an essential qualification for good citizenship. . . .

3. *Civics teaching is good in proportion as it stimulates cooperation among the pupils, and on the part of the pupils with others, for the common interest of the community (school, home, neighborhood, city, State, or Nation).*

Given an interest in civic affairs, a right motive, and a willingness to work with others, a man's citizenship will not count for a great deal unless he is able to sift out the essentials from the nonessentials of a situation and to decide wisely as to the best method of dealing with it; and unless he has power to initiate action. . . . Civic education ought to include the cultivation of civic judgment and civic initiative. . . .

4. *Civics teaching is good in proportion as it cultivates the judgment with reference to a civic situation and the methods of dealing with it; and in proportion as it cultivates initiative in the face of such situation.*

The only test that we have been in the habit of applying to our civics teaching is the informational test. We have contented ourselves with asking, How much do the children know? A certain fund of information is essential to good citizenship. But mere knowledge . . . will not make a good citizen. Ignorance of government is more often a result than a cause of civic inefficiency. . . . The problem which confronts the teacher and the maker of the course of study is, How much and what kind of information should be acquired by the pupil? This question can not be answered by an enumeration of topics of universal application. But, in general,

5. *Civics teaching is good in proportion as its subject matter is selected and organized on the basis of the pupil's past experience, immediate interests, and the needs of his present growth.*

It is not pretended that the standards here suggested are the only ones . . . to be adopted; it is hoped that better ones may be evolved. . . . It is not to be supposed that every half-hour class exercise will measure up to all of them. . . . What is suggested is that these or other standards be kept in view by every teacher as guides that will determine, with something like precision, the direction that he shall take.

II. THE PREPARATION OF THE TEACHER.

Probably the greatest obstacle to the vitalization of the social studies is the lack of preparation on the part of teachers. It is in part a lack of training in the facts and laws of social life as formulated in history and other social sciences. This is particularly true in the elementary schools and in rural schools. But there is an equally serious deficiency in the art of teaching these facts and laws, and this is as prevalent in large high schools and in colleges as in elementary schools, if not more so.

1. *In the high schools.*—One of the necessary steps for the adequate preparation of teachers of the social studies is the development of effective high-school courses of social study, which it is the purpose of this report to stimulate. Even for those teachers who have had higher education, the foundation should have been laid in the high school.

2. *In teacher-training schools.*—In the second place, more attention should be given in teacher-training schools of all kinds to the social studies and the methods of teaching them. Whatever is done in these schools in the fields of the social sciences as such, it is recommended that courses be given on the general lines recommended in this report for high schools, at least until the high schools shall have made adequate provision for them. In teacher-training schools, however, special attention should be given to methods by which instruction in the social studies may be made to meet the " needs of present growth" in pupils of elementary and high school age.

3. *In colleges and universities.*—Many high-school teachers come directly from the college or university with excellent equipment, so far as subject matter is concerned, but with no training whatever in methods of teaching. It is therefore recommended that colleges and universities that supply high schools with teachers provide courses in methods of teaching, in the sense indicated above in connection with teacher-training schools.

4. *In service.*—It will not do, however, to wait until teachers are trained especially for this work before making a beginning in the reorganization of secondary instruction in the social studies. The training schools for teachers are inclined not to introduce new courses until there is an evident demand for them. This is hardly as it should be, for these professional schools should be the leaders in experiment and in the discovery of more effective methods. A few such schools have recently introduced courses in method of teaching history, civics, and other social studies, in which such principles as those suggested in this report are being discussed and tested. But not much can be expected in this direction until the demand has been created by the public schools themselves.

Moreover, it is wholly practicable to train teachers for this work while they are in service. This has been demonstrated at least in the field of community civics. Teachers who have had no previous training for teaching that subject and to whom its spirit and methods were wholly new, have within a year of actual work become both skillful and enthusiastic in the work.

The committee urges that more attention be given to instruction in the social studies, from the point of view suggested in this report, in teachers' institutes and summer schools.

Finally, it is unquestionably true that the most effective teaching of the social studies can be secured where there is a supervisor or director trained in this particular field. It should be the duty of such director, in the first place, to study the particular problems that the several teachers in his charge have to encounter; to give personal assistance to them individually and to hold frequent conferences with them for the discussion of general and special features of their work. In addition to this, one of the most important services to be performed by such director is to act as a mediator between the teachers and the realities of the community life about which they are instructing the children. He may establish through a single channel relations with public and private agencies and gather much material for the general use of all teachers, instead of leaving it for them severally to establish their own relations and to gather their own material. Of course, each teacher will necessarily and advantageously do much of this work for herself, but where it is a question of establishing working relations with a public official or the busy office of a corporation the element of economy of time for the latter as well as for the teacher must be considered. In the few cases where such directors have been provided the development of community civics has progressed much more rapidly and effectively than could be expected otherwise.

III. AVAILABILITY OF TEXT MATERIALS.

The question will inevitably be raised, Where are the textbooks organized according to the principles and with the content proposed in this report? And unless such textbooks are forthcoming, how can inexperienced teachers, or teachers trained according to traditional methods, be expected to adopt the new methods with any chance of success?

Unquestionably there are very few textbooks prepared on the lines suggested in this report or that will be of any very direct help to the teacher in working out a course on these lines. Unquestionably, also, the lack of suitable texts is second only to the lack of preparation on the part of the teacher as an obstacle to the rapid reorganization of the subject matter and methods of instruction in history and the social sciences. The lack of teachers trained in the new methods and from the new viewpoint is more serious than the lack of suitable texts, because a skillful teacher can do much to vitalize instruction in spite of a poor text, while an unskillful teacher, even with an ideal text, may fail utterly to catch the spirit and the viewpoint, without which no teaching can be really successful.

The committee is making its report under no delusion that its recommendations in their entirety can be promptly adopted in all schools with the opening of the next school year. It is fully conscious of the difficulties presented by tradition, in the viewpoint and training of teachers and administrators and in the organization of textbooks and other aids. But neither the lack of trained teachers nor the paucity of suitable texts should deter from setting " to work boldly and without any timid reservations to bring our education into the closest possible relation with the actual life and future duties of the great majority of those who fill our public schools."

The teaching of community civics has progressed far beyond the experimental stage. A few textbooks are in the field that more or less closely represent the spirit, the viewpoint, and the method of social study as conceived by the committee and that are in successful use in many places. Other literature is also rapidly appearing that will do much to familiarize teachers with the methods of the subject, and that should make it comparatively easy to introduce this subject, at least, very generally.

The committee suggests, therefore, that a beginning be made toward reorganizing the social studies by introducing and developing community civics, to which there are no insuperable obstacles. Not only will this give to the pupil a point of view that will in itself tend to vitalize later social studies, but it will go far toward suggesting to teachers also a viewpoint and methods that may gradually influence the teaching of other subjects.

As for history and the other social studies, there will probably be no lack of textbooks when once our ideas are clarified as to the direction in which we want to go. Publishers are very much alive to the situation and eager to supply books to meet a real demand. Teachers and authors are experimenting, and here and there methods are being developed that give promise of better things to come. Already some texts in history and economics have appeared that show the influence of the new point of view and that have in a measure broken with tradition. Such books will multiply and improve as time goes on. Nothing will do more to hasten the production of books to meet the new needs than a prompt and accurate reporting by teachers and supervisors of new methods tried, and especially of the success or failure of such methods. One channel through which to report such matters is to be found in the educational journals. The United States Bureau of Education will also gladly receive and disseminate information relating to the subject.

It is the belief of the committee, based on the present trend of development as the committee sees it, that in the fields of history and other social sciences instruction in both elementary and secondary schools is going to be organized more and more definitely around the immediate interests and needs of the pupils. It must therefore vary, within limits, from term to term, from class to class, and even from pupil to pupil. The future textbook will accordingly be less and less a compendium of information and more and more a manual of method and illustrative material for the teacher and a guide to observation and study for the pupil. The particular information that a pupil or teacher needs at a given time for the satisfaction of a particular interest or for the illumination of a particular problem must be sought in many books or in books of encyclopedic scope.

There are two tendencies in connection with the use of textbooks, especially in the teaching of community civics, in regard to which the committee feels the need of a word of caution. The first is a tendency to dispense with a textbook altogether. This is doubtless due in part to dissatisfaction with available books. It is due also, however, to a growing appreciation of the fact that community civics, to be effective, must be a study of real community life and not merely of the pages of a text. In so far as the abandonment of textbooks is due to the latter influence, it is a sign of a wholesome development. But there is danger of going too far in this direction. Not only theoretical psychology, but also actual experiment seems to prove that a textbook is a positive aid to study and to teaching, provided, of course, that it is of the right kind and is rightly used. There may be exceptionally equipped and talented teachers who can do better without a textbook than they would do if they followed explicitly any existing text. Even such teachers will be more successful if their pupils have in their hands a well-planned text; and the great majority of teachers are not prepared to organize courses of their own. The teacher who is not able to use a fairly good text and to adapt it to the needs of his pupils to their great advantage can hardly be expected to be capable of devising a course independently of a text that would in any sense compensate for the loss of the recognized value of the best texts available.

The second tendency referred to is that toward dependence upon texts descriptive of the local communities in which they are used and prepared locally. This also has its favorable aspect. It indicates a recognition of the value of local life and conditions in the pupil's education. But it has its serious dangers. In the first place, it sometimes indicates a confusion between "community civics" as described in this report and purely local civics. As already pointed out in this report (p. 25), it will be a misfortune if the civic study of the pupil does not comprehend the larger life of the Nation along with that of the local communities which compose the Nation. But more serious than this is the fact that the great majority of such local "texts" are as devoid of the real spirit of community civics as the old-time "manuals" on the Constitution. Some of them merely substitute a description of the mechanism of the local government for the discarded description of the mechanism of the National Government. Others add to this description of govern-. mental machinery a catalogue of industries and public institutions, with more or less valuable statistical information. Still others are little more than a glorification of "our town" based too often on a false conception of "local patriotism." The fact must be recognized that comparatively few persons are competent to prepare a really good textbook even though it deal with purely local matters.

This is not to be taken, however, as a denial of the value of local materials compiled in available form. There is the utmost need for such materials, and in many places they are being collected and published to the great benefit of pupils and of the community at large. They constitute invaluable sources of information and are useful supplements to a good text. No better service can be performed for the schools by public libraries, chambers of commerce, women's clubs, and other civic agencies than to compile and publish in really available form local information of this kind. But it is rare indeed that such publications constitute suitable textbooks, or adequate substitutes for them.

O

DEPARTMENT OF THE INTERIOR
BUREAU OF EDUCATION

BULLETIN, 1916, No. 29

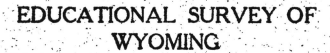

EDUCATIONAL SURVEY OF WYOMING

BY

A. C. MONAHAN
SPECIALIST IN RURAL SCHOOL ADMINISTRATION

AND

KATHERINE M. COOK
ASSISTANT IN RURAL EDUCATION, BUREAU OF EDUCATION

WASHINGTON
GOVERNMENT PRINTING OFFICE
1917

A WYOMING PUBLIC HIGH SCHOOL.

DEPARTMENT OF THE INTERIOR
BUREAU OF EDUCATION

BULLETIN, 1916, No. 29

EDUCATIONAL SURVEY OF WYOMING

BY

A. C. MONAHAN

SPECIALIST IN RURAL SCHOOL ADMINISTRATION

AND

KATHERINE M. COOK

ASSISTANT IN RURAL EDUCATION, BUREAU OF EDUCATION

WASHINGTON
GOVERNMENT PRINTING OFFICE
1917

ADDITIONAL COPIES

OF THIS PUBLICATION MAY BE PROCURED FROM
THE SUPERINTENDENT OF DOCUMENTS
GOVERNMENT PRINTING OFFICE
WASHINGTON, D. C.

AT

15 CENTS PER COPY

CONTENTS.

3

LETTER OF TRANSMITTAL.

DEPARTMENT OF THE INTERIOR,
BUREAU OF EDUCATION,
Washington, August 28, 1916.

SIR: At the request of the code committee appointed by the governor of the State of Wyoming in compliance with an act of the legislature of that State creating the committee for the purpose of studying the school system of the State and recommending new legislation, I detailed A. C. Monahan, specialist in agricultural education and rural school administration, and Katherine M. Cook, assistant in rural education in this bureau, to make a careful study of the laws of the State pertaining to education, the administration of the State school system and certain phases of the work of the schools, and to make such recommendations for the improvement of the schools through legislation and otherwise as the facts revealed by this study might seem to justify. This they have done, and the report submitted to the code committee has been approved by me. For the use of the people of the State of Wyoming and for the use of students of education throughout the country I recommend that this report, a copy of which I am transmitting herewith, be published as a bulletin of the Bureau of Education.

Respectfully submitted.

P. P. CLAXTON,
Commissioner.

The SECRETARY OF THE INTERIOR.

LETTER TO THE COMMISSIONER.

DEPARTMENT OF THE INTERIOR,
BUREAU OF EDUCATION,
Washington, May 26, 1916.

SIR: There are submitted herewith the results of a survey and study of the public-school system of Wyoming, with recommendations concerning the legislation needed for its improvement. This work was undertaken at your orders as a result of a request for assistance from the State of Wyoming. The thirteenth general assembly of the State, meeting in 1915, acting on the suggestion of prominent educators of the State under the leadership of the State superintendent of public instruction, enacted a law which provided for the formation of a school code committee to make a thorough investigation into the needs of the public schools of Wyoming and the laws under which they are organized and operated; to make a comparative study of such other public schools as may be advisable; and to report to the fourteenth Legislature of the State of Wyoming recommending a revised code of school laws.

In compliance with this act, the governor of the State appointed the following men and women to constitute the Wyoming school code committee: Miss Edith K. O. Clark, State superintendent of public instruction, Cheyenne, chairman; Miss Jennie McGuffey, county superintendent of schools, Park County, Cody; Mr. John T. Hawkes, principal of the Sheridan High School, Sheridan; Dean J. O. Creager, of the College of Education, State University, Laramie; and Mr. J. J. Underwood, ranchman, Underwood. The undersigned were designated as representatives from the Bureau of Education to assist in an investigation and to make a report with recommendations for transmittal to the committee. The first meeting of the school code committee was called at Laramie in July of 1915; all members but one were present. A representative of the Bureau of Education attended this meeting. After careful discussion of various plans and procedure, a general survey of educational conditions in the State was decided upon and tentative plans were laid for collecting material for such a survey.

Method and scope of the survey.—The school code committee held a second conference in Cheyenne early in November of the same year. All members and both representatives of the bureau were present.

Plans for the conduct of a careful survey of education in the State were presented and approved, as follows:

(a) A thorough investigation of grounds, buildings, water supply, etc., conducted through personal investigation and collection of information through questionnaires;

(b) A careful inquiry into the education and professional qualifications, living conditions, and salaries of teachers, conducted in the same manner;

(c) An intensive study of instruction offered in three counties selected as typical of general conditions made by personal investigation by members of the committee and representatives of the bureau;

(d) An investigation into qualifications and work of the county superintendents;

(e) A study of financial support, State, county, and local;

(f) General information concerning high-school and city-school systems.

The point of view which the investigators kept constantly in mind in these inquiries was that of general measurement of the system as a State system in terms of service to the State. In addition to the questionnaires, letters were sent through the county superintendents to several hundred prominent people in the State, setting forth the general purpose of the survey and asking for cooperation and suggestions.

In April, 1916, another meeting of the committee was held in Cheyenne. Reports showed that the plans formulated at preceding meetings were being successfully carried out. The general plans pursued had been discussed at the meeting of the State Teachers' Association at Thermopolis and progress was being made along all lines previously agreed upon. It was decided to ask that the governor appoint an auxiliary committee of 15 prominent citizens to act in conjunction with the school code committee; and that a general education conference be held in July at the University of Wyoming, to be called and presided over by the governor of the State, the purpose of which should be to discuss the recommendations submitted by the committee, to disseminate information concerning them, and to arouse public interest in better school conditions for Wyoming.

The survey from the beginning has had in view the single purpose of the educational welfare of the children of the State. There has been a spirit of cooperation, disinterested labor, and personal sacrifice on the part of members of the committee and others who have given of their time and service. Assisting in the survey, in addition to the members of the committee, were Miss Henrietta Kolshorn, Laramie; Supt. Ira Fee, of Cheyenne; Dr. J. E. Butterworth, of the University of Wyoming; and Supt. Joseph Burch, of Kemmerer. In addition, many county and city superintendents, teachers, and school officers responded to requests for information, and assisted in other ways; Dr. Harrison C. Dale, of the university, wrote the historical statement utilized in this report.

The material collected by the committee and other workers was turned over to the Bureau of Education. The accompanying report is made on the basis of these, of supplementary studies on Wyoming and education in Wyoming from all available sources, and on personal observations of instruction, supervision, and general educational conditions.

Respectfully submitted.

KATHERINE M. COOK,
Assistant in Rural Education.
A. C. MONAHAN,
Specialist in Rural School Administration.

The COMMISSIONER OF EDUCATION.

AN EDUCATIONAL SURVEY OF WYOMING.

I. A SKETCH OF THE HISTORY OF EDUCATION IN WYOMING.

The educational history of Wyoming dates from the creation of the Territory, July 25, 1868. When the first census was taken, in 1860, there were three groups of permanent settlements, two of some 100 or 150 each near Fort Bridger and Fort Laramie, and a few isolated ranches along the valley of the North Platte in what are now Platte and Goshen Counties. The total population of the Territory in 1860, including the wandering prospectors and trappers who occasionally pushed into the northern and western portions, numbered probably not more than 400. Within the next decade, however, because of the penetration of this region by the Union Pacific Railroad, the population increased rapidly.

The following table shows the population of Wyoming at various dates:

1860	[2] 400
1870	9,118
1875	[2] 14,951
1880	20,789
1885	[2] 31,391
1890	60,705
1900	92,531
1905	101,816
1910	[3] 145,965
1915	[3] 141,705

Provision for the regulation and maintenance of education was made in the first session of the Territorial assembly and approved December 10, 1869. According to provisions of the act the Territorial auditor was ex officio superintendent of public instruction, and his stipend for this service was $500. His duties as defined by the statutes were almost identically those of the present superintendent as outlined in the statutes now in force except that the apportionment was made on aggregate attendance instead of on the census basis.

---

[1] Digest from an article written by Harrison C. Dale, of the faculty of the State University.
[2] Estimated.
[3] The 1910 figures are from the Federal census, while the 1915 figures are from the State census, which was taken by the county assessors. It is estimated that the 1915 figures are incomplete by about 9,000.

A further act of the assembly created the office of county superintendent of schools, though no direct provision was made for the manner of election. The county tax for the maintenance of schools was fixed at not more than 2 mills on the dollar, and the county superintendents were required to report annually to the State superintendent. Should they fail to do so, they were to forfeit the sum of $100. It does not appear that this provision was ever enforced or even noticed, for year after year the State superintendent of public instruction in his annual report bemoaned the laxity of the county superintendents. The blame, no doubt, rested quite as much on the district clerks as upon the county superintendents, for the former were by law required to furnish annually a report of the affairs in their respective districts containing practically the same information which district clerks are now required to include in their reports to the county superintendent. Failure to make this report was punishable by a fine of $25. There is no record, however, that such a penalty was ever imposed.

A result of this carelessness is the absence of anything like adequate school statistics for many sections of the State. This accounts for many of the omissions and inadequacies of this history.

The board of district directors was empowered to determine the site of schoolhouses, the expenditures for the erection or rent of the same, and the curriculum to be followed in the lower schools. In the matter of secondary and high school education the determination of the last-mentioned feature was left to the county superintendent, acting in conjunction with the district board.

Provision was also made that, when there were 15 or more colored children within a specified district, the board might, with the approval of the county superintendent, provide a separate school. Apparently, however, no such segregated schools have ever been established, Negroes being admitted to the schools with whites.

The district treasurer was to keep two distinct funds, one called the "teachers' fund," comprising all moneys for school purposes, save only local taxes collected in the district, which comprised the "schoolhouse" fund.

The education act of 1869 remained in force two years, when a few minor changes were made. The State auditor was relieved of his ex officio duties as State superintendent of public instruction; the office was abolished for the time, the county superintendents reporting annually to the governor.

In the legislative session of 1873 the whole matter of education was reviewed and altered. The acts are of singular importance, being the true foundation of subsequent legislation and of the system now in force. The act of 1869 was in most respects repealed and provisions relative to the duties of the various school officers replaced by more explicit regulations.   The State librarian (an office created two years previously) was made ex officio State superintendent of public instruction.

The first report on public instruction was made in 1871 by Dr. J. H. Hayford, of Laramie, the Territorial auditor for the preceding biennium.   Dr. Hayford reported good schools in Albany and Laramie Counties, fair schools in Uinta and Carbon Counties, but in Sweetwater County neither superintendent nor schools.   The report embodied two summaries for Carbon and Uinta Counties, prepared by the respective county superintendents, Messrs. R. W. Baxter and R. H. Carter.   There were only five counties at that time.

Statistics of schools in Carbon and Uinta Counties in 1870.

Counties.	School-houses.	Teachers.		Pupils.
		Male.	Female.	
Carbon	1	2	1	74
Uinta	1	2	2	115

At this date (1870) Wyoming had only 9,118 inhabitants—8,726 whites, 183 colored, 66 Indians (outside the reservations), and 143 Chinese.   According to the report of the United States Commissioner of Education for 1873, the population was scattered along the Union Pacific Railroad for over 500 miles, with a school wherever enough children were congregated.   The provision for support was liberal; it came entirely from taxation, the school lands not yet having come into market.   The five counties had county superintendents.   Laramie city and Cheyenne had graded schools of three departments each, to which high schools were later to be added.   Schools in other districts, though small, were efficiently managed.

Beginning with the year 1883, statistical information becomes available.   The following figures are taken from the manuscript reports of the superintendents of public instruction preserved in the State archives at Cheyenne:

TABLE 1.—*Data on Wyoming schools.*

	1883	1885	1889
Number of schoolhouses	39	77	138
Number of schools taught	83	132	230
Number of pupils:			
Total	3,352	4,405	7,052
Male	1,675	2,252	3,492
Female	1,677	2,153	3,560
Number of teachers:			
Total	89	148	259
Male	19	32	58
Female	70	116	201
Cost per pupil per month	$2.87	[1] $4.14	$2.78

[1] For explanation of these cost figures see History of Education in Wyoming, by Dale, published by State department of education.

The character of the school buildings in this period may be gathered from the following list, incomplete and compiled from a variety of sources: Log building with a dirt room; upper room of a railroad section house; rented building; spare room of a ranch; vacant office of a mining company; blacksmith's shop; basement of the town hall; sheep wagon.

On July 10, 1890, Wyoming was admitted to the Union. The constitution and the first session of the State legislature virtually accepted the system of education in vogue during Territorial days. From this point the modern history of education in Wyoming may be said to date.

The following table shows the growth of schoolhouse construction, number of teachers, and number of pupils since 1875, by five-year periods:

TABLE 2.—*Schoolhouses and teachers in Wyoming.*

Year.	School-houses.	Number of teachers.			Pupils.
		Male.	Female.	Total.	
1875		7	16	23	1,222
1880		31	39	70	2,097
1885	77	40	150	190	4,988
1890	196	58	201	259	7,875
1895	305	112	362	474	11,253
1900	372	89	481	570	14,512
1905	503	107	690	797	18,823
1910	640	141	968	1,109	24,477
1915	952	223	1,411	1,634	30,816

Although the legislature in 1873 and in 1888 made efforts to establish uniform textbook adoptions, such regulations were not successfully carried out. The provision for free textbooks was adopted in 1901, and physiology and hygiene, with special reference to the use of alcohol and narcotics, were made compulsory subjects in 1885. In 1910 the study of humane treatment of animals was added and boards were required to purchase Coutant's *History of Wyoming* and Carroll's *The Sabbath as an American War Day.*

Certification.—In the education act of 1873 the county superintendent of schools was authorized—

to examine persons, and if in his opinion such persons were qualified to teach in public schools, to give a certificate, authorizing him or her to teach a public school in his county for one year. Whenever practicable, the examination of teachers shall be competitive, and the certificate shall be graded according to the qualifications of the applicant.

A law of 1876 empowered the Territorial superintendent of public instruction to grant honorary certificates of qualification to teachers of proper learning and ability and to regulate the grade of county certificates. These "honorary certificates" were granted primarily on the basis of continuous years of service. Forty were given between

1883 and 1887. At the same time the county superintendents were empowered to grant certificates for two-year periods. During the next 10 years little change was made in the matter of certification. In 1897–98 the State superintendent of public instruction recommended that graduates of the university, especially those having taken normal training, receive certificates without further examination. This change was made soon after.

State board of examiners.—In 1899 the State board of examiners was created. Their duty was to prepare uniform examination questions and to serve as a court of appeal from the decisions of the county superintendents. During the first year, under the presidency of Prof. C. B. Ridgaway, of the university, 16 sets of questions were prepared for the use of the county superintendents. The board also examined 33 applicants for certificates, recommended 16, and declined to recommend 17. Many of the applicants who were not favorably recommended were unable to comply with the requirement of ability to teach all of the subjects usually taught in high schools of the State. Under this system many third-grade certificates (valid for one year), and a fair number of second-grade certificates (valid for three years), were issued. Practically no first-grade certificates were issued.

In 1899 provision was made for issuing three grades of certificates and a professional or State certificate, the latter to be granted by the board of examiners. Examinations for the other three grades of certificates were still conducted by the county superintendents in subjects prescribed by law.

In 1907 the board was empowered to examine all candidates for certificates in the State. Examinations were conducted at stated intervals and the recipients of certificates were allowed to teach in any county of the State. In 1909 the subjects for examination in the three classes were more specifically fixed by law.

Teachers' institutes.—The education act of 1873 required the Territorial superintendent of public instruction to conduct annually a teachers' institute lasting not less than 4 nor more than 10 days. Its chief function was the selection of textbooks. In 1883 an appropriation of $1,500 was made to pay the traveling expenses of teachers attending institutes. Four years later the attendance of teachers was required by law; they were, however, to receive compensation for transportation. Provision was further made for the payment by the counties of expenses incidental to the holding of institutes, including the compensation of lecturers. The legislature of 1913 authorized the holding of joint institutes by two or more counties. The outcome of this was the act of 1915 providing for State institutes. These were to be maintained in part by nominal fees required of all teachers in the State. The State superintendent's biennial report for 1907–8 noted the tendency to make the county institutes a mere series of lectures. This has since been generally overcome by close attention at all meetings to the specific needs and problems of the teachers and the schools.

High schools.—The laws of the Territorial assembly provided for high schools, buildings, courses of study, etc., all to be determined by the county superintendent and board of directors. An enactment of the State legislature in 1905 provided for the creation of special high-school districts and the location of union district high-schools at specified places. In 1915 the people were empowered to lay a tax not exceeding 2 mills on the dollar for the payment of teachers' salaries and contingent expenses in such high schools and a total tax not exceeding 10 mills on the dollar in case of the construction of a building, provided such high schools maintained a four-year course qualifying for admission to the university.

The first high school established was at Cheyenne in 1875. This was followed by one at Buffalo, 1881; Newcastle, 1889; Rawlins, soon after; Lander, 1890; and Sheridan in 1893.

Kindergartens.—Kindergarten instruction began in private schools. In 1886 Mrs. F. D. M. Bratten established the Magic City Kindergarten in Cheyenne, charging a tuition fee of $4 a month. At the end of the first year she had 10 pupils. Subsequently other private kindergartens were opened in a number of communities in the State. In 1895, however, the legislature empowered the trustees of all school districts to establish free kindergartens for children between the ages of 4 and 6. Such schools were to be maintained out of the special school fund, and only graduates of approved kindergarten training schools were to be employed as teachers. In 1903 the State department reported 182 children attending kindergartens.

Private education.—In the beginning private schools exceeded in importance public schools. The census of 1870, for example, enumerated 4 public schools with 4 teachers (2 men and 2 women), while it listed 5 day and boarding schools with 11 teachers (5 men and 6 women). The public schools were attended by 175 pupils; the private schools by 130. The former had an income of $2,876, derived from taxation and public funds, while the latter had an income of $5,500, derived from tuition fees and other sources. The greater amount of income in addition to the relatively large number of teachers and small number of pupils probably indicates a higher quality of educational service on the part of the private schools.

With improvement in the standard of public education, the private schools became for a period less significant. One of the few to survive for a time was the Wyoming Institute, a Baptist school at Laramie, of which Rev. D. J. Pierce, A. M., was the first and only principal. It closed in 1873.

THE WYOMING INDUSTRIAL INSTITUTE, WORLAND, WYO. MAIN BUILDING AND POWER HOUSE.

BUREAU OF EDUCATION.

The teacher's saddle horse is on the right.

Pupils of school district No. 2.

Ranchester School, Sheridan County.

School No. 2, District 4, Albany County.

WYOMING RURAL SCHOOLS.

The educational traditions of Laramie, however, were maintained by St. Mary's School, a Roman Catholic institution, organized as far back as 1870, but not apparently making much headway till after a decade. By the year 1881 it had 4 teachers (women) and 73 pupils. In 1885 it was moved to Cheyenne. In 1890 there were 8 teachers and 60 pupils; in 1910, 13 teachers and 170 pupils; in 1915–16, 14 teachers and 210 pupils.

Another private institution was the Wyoming Collegiate Institute, at Big Horn, a Congregational school started in 1894–95 with 2 men and 1 woman teacher and an enrollment of 34 boys and 22 girls. The previous year, however, 1893, Sheridan Public High School had been started. The Wyoming Collegiate Institute declined and was soon closed.

In 1905 the Cheyenne Business College in Cheyenne was opened and, in the same year, Big Horn College, in Basin. The latter enterprise was financed by a number of prominent citizens of Big Horn. Its scope included commerce, music, and academic subjects.

In 1909 Jireh College was founded at Jireh, Niobrara County, under the auspices of the Christian Church. This institution offers courses in secondary subjects and some instruction of college grade.

The following table shows the enrollment in the private schools of the State since 1903:

Year.	Pupils.
1903	260
1905	259
1910	350
1914	262

The university.—Since 1878 the governor and commissioner of education had expressed the belief that the Territory needed a university and a normal school. On the 6th of September of 1887 a Territorial university was opened, and four years later provision was made for adequate normal instruction. In 1892 the university undertook to grant the degree of B. D. (Bachelor of Didactics) on completion of the normal course of two years beyond the grammar grades and the degree of L. I. (Licentiate of Instruction) on the completion of an additional year of graduate work. Prof. Henry Merz was the first principal of the normal school.

The university proper opened with a faculty of seven, including the president, ex-Gov. Hoyt. The first department organized was the college of liberal arts, the acknowledged nucleus of all university departments. A preparatory department was immediately added and preparations were made for all the schools essential to a State university. The two departments immediately organized thereafter were a school of mines and a school of agriculture, although the catalogue of 1890–91 announced also a department of law and a school of commerce. The college of agriculture was reorganized in 1891 and the division of mining the next year.

When Wyoming was admitted to the Union the constitutional convention made provision for the university. The first State legislature, which convened in Cheyenne, November 12, 1890, also passed an act to establish the Wyoming agricultural college, its location to be fixed by vote of the people, and created and named a board of five trustees to control this institution. At the same time, however, the legislature authorized the University of Wyoming at Laramie to accept the Federal appropriations for the support of agricultural colleges until such time as the agricultural college of Wyoming should be located and established. Thus an agricultural college was created at Laramie. In 1892 the question of the location of the agricultural college of Wyoming was submitted to the people, and by a plurality vote Lander was selected. No legislative enactment in conformity with this vote ensued, however, and accordingly the agricultural college remained at Laramie. In 1905 the legislature definitely fixed it at that place, repealing the act of 1891 and ignoring the popular vote of 1892. Thereupon the trustees of the "Agricultural College of Wyoming" brought suit against the treasurer of the State of Wyoming to prevent the execution of this act. The case was ultimately appealed to the Federal Supreme Court, which decided, May 13, 1907, that the popular vote of 1892 was purely advisory and that the agricultural college should remain at Laramie in conformity with the legislative act of 1905.

In 1891 the Wyoming Agricultural Experiment Station was established at Laramie and substations were located at Lander, Saratoga, Sheridan, Sundance, and Wheatland. The substations were abolished in 1897, in accordance with a ruling of the Federal Department of Agriculture.

The catalogue of 1891–92 announced provision for university extension whereby the whole State might share in the benefits of the institution, instead of those only who were so fortunate as to attend it in residence. Steps in this direction had already been taken by President Hoyt. Local extension "centers" were organized at Cheyenne with 65 members and at Laramie with 45 members and the Wyoming University extension association was formed. The following year another "center" was added at Rock Springs, with 14 members. The same year, also, a beginning of instruction by correspondence was made.

By 1893–94 the matter of preparation for the university was being more adequately handled by local high schools and a list of such accredited schools was compiled whose graduates might enter the university without further examination. The list, at this date, comprised Cheyenne, Evanston, Lander, Laramie, Rawlins, Rock Springs, and Sheridan.

In 1896–97 the college of agriculture was reorganized with a one-year course, a two-year course, and a four-year course. The last led to a degree and was supplemented by a graduate department in agriculture.

The following table shows the enrollment in all the departments of the university by five-year periods from 1890 to 1916:

Year.	Enrollment.
1890	82
1895	110
1900	187
1905	221
1910	315
1916	[1] 573

Finance.—The act of March, 1886, creating the university provided for its maintenance by a tax of one-fourth of 1 mill on all taxable property in the Territory. The first State legislature in 1891 undertook to offset the support granted by the agricultural college of the university under the land grant act of 1862, the Morrill Act and Hatch Act—whose terms were now complied with—by reducing the State appropriations from one-fourth to one-eighth of a mill. This remained the source of State support until 1905, when the rate was raised by the legislature to three-eighths of a mill and by the legislature of 1909 to one-half of a mill (but limited to $33,000 annually). In 1911 the amount was limited to $85,000. The legislature of 1913 fixed the tax at three-eighths of a mill, but without limitation. In 1915 an additional permanent building tax of one-eighth of a mill was voted. In addition to the income from Federal acts already noted, the agricultural college of the university and the agricultural experiment station have received appropriations from the Adams Act of 1906, the Nelson Act of 1907, and the Smith-Lever Act of 1915. By an act of the Wyoming Legislature in 1915, the university is to receive one-fourth of the income of 200,000 acres of Federal land granted to the State for "charitable, educational, penal, and reformatory institutions."

Buildings.—The first building erected was the liberal arts building, costing over $85,000, for which site and campus were in part donated by the city of Laramie and in part purchased from the Union Pacific Railroad. Since then the mechanical engineering building, Hall of Science, gymnasium and armory, heating plant, Woman's Hall, normal school building, and buildings for the agricultural college and experiment station have been erected at a total cost of $222,000. The grounds have been added to also by purchase and donation from

---

[1] Includes enrollment in all departments, including the summer school. See p. 25.

the Union Pacific Railroad and by the addition of the old penitentiary plant.

Miscellaneous.—Soon after the organization of the Territory some attempt was made to provide vocational education for the Indians. In 1870 the Protestant Episcopal Church maintained among the Shoshones an Indian school with 10 pupils. A few years later the school dwindled to 6 and in the year 1874 was abandoned. In 1878 a day

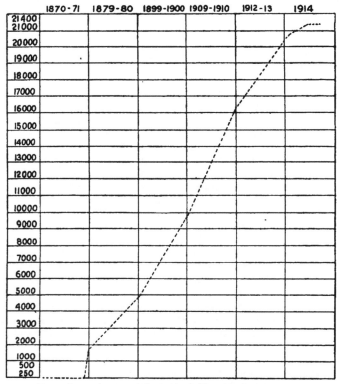

Fig. 1.—Increase in average daily attendance, Wyoming schools, 1870–1914.

school was established. More recently the task of educating the Indians has been undertaken seriously both by the churches and by the Federal Government.

The Territorial assembly in 1886 appropriated $8,000 to defray the expense of establishing a school for the blind and deaf for two years, not to be opened until there were 12 applicants for admission. The commission created under the act purchased a block of land and a building in Cheyenne for this purpose, but the school has never been opened.

An act of the legislature in 1907 created the Wyoming Home of the Feeble-Minded · and Epileptic, subsequently called the Wyoming School for Defectives, at Lander. The attendance in June, 1912, was 3, but by the end· of the year it had increased to 22. On January 1, 1916, there were 36 males and 22 females at the institution. The Wyoming Industrial Institute was established at Worland in 1913 and opened in 1915.

One of the purposes of the Wyoming University Extension Association, established 1891, was the organization of a State teachers' association. A step in this direction was taken by the publication for a time of the *Wyoming School Journal*, edited by Prof. Henry Merz, of the university. Meetings of the State teachers' association were held in Laramie, 1891; Cheyenne, 1892; Rawlins, 1893; Rock Springs, 1894; Evanston, 1895; and Laramie, 1897. The association, however, was already moribund and within five years succumbed. The State superintendent of public instruction in 1902 reported Wyoming as the only State without a teachers' association. Two years later (1904) a new State teachers' association was organized at a meeting of State educators in Casper. The association was formed in September, and in December appeared the first numbers of the new *Wyoming School Journal*, which is a monthly publication. The State teachers' association has met annually since its reorganization in 1904.

THE PRESENT SYSTEM.

The present school system of the State of Wyoming may be outlined briefly as follows:

There is a State department of education composed of a State superintendent of public instruction elected every four years by popular vote, assisted by a deputy State superintendent, and an office force of three clerks appointed by the State superintendent. The State superintendent is ex officio a member of the board of trustees of the State university, of the State board of charities and reforms, and of the State land board. From one-third to one-half the time of the State superintendent, deputy, and office force is required to perform the duties of these boards. There is no State board of education.

State superintendent.—The powers and duties conferred by law upon the State superintendent are as follows: He shall collect and file all papers, reports, and public documents transmitted to him by the school officers in the several counties each year, and keep a record of all matters pertaining to the business of his office. Upon these

matters he shall report biennially to the governor.   He shall apportion
State school funds to the counties in the manner prescribed by law,
prepare the State course of study, appoint the State board of examiners, and issue certificates on their recommendation, file and publish
price lists of textbooks of publishers complying with the requirements
of the law which make them eligible to do business in the State, and
make such other rules and regulations as may be necessary to carry
the law into effect according to its spirit and intent. ·In addition, he
shall have "general supervision of all the district schools of the State
and see that the school system is put into uniform operation as early
as practicable."   No means of putting this system into operation is
provided, and the law is therefore a dead letter.   No State superintendent has ever made any serious attempt to assume actual supervision of the school system.   The powers and duties are general and
indefinite and give the State superintendent little authority in the
educational development of the State.   The present superintendent
has been very active during her term of office in getting in touch with
the schools in all parts of the State through personal visits and various
forms of communication.

County superintendent.—Supervision of all schools, except those in
cities employing special superintendents, is in the hands of the county
superintendents, who are elected for two-year terms by popular vote.
In order to be eligible for election, candidates must have first-class
teachers' certificates.   These are issued to persons who pass examinations in elementary school subjects and the following: Elementary
algebra, English and American literature, elementary psychology,
physical geography, and two other subjects selected from a list of
those ordinarily taught in high-school courses.   One year of teaching
experience is required.   Salaries of superintendents in the State range
from $500 to $900 per year; the average is $710. Of the 21 superin-
tendents, 18 are women. The powers and duties of the county
superintendents as conferred upon them by law are not such as to
make them important factors in the schools. The county superintendent is required to collect school statistics and report to the State
superintendent; to distribute reports and circulars from the State
department; to apportion the county funds to the various school
districts as prescribed by law; to serve with the county civil commissioners as a district boundary board to fix or change boundaries,
consolidate or divide districts, and form new districts; to hold teachers'
institutes of from four to eight days in length each year; to visit each
school once a year; and to have general supervision over the schools
of the county.   The latter provision in practice means very little.
In addition, the superintendent is legally empowered to recommend
for dismissal all teachers who are incompetent.   Boards are not

required to comply with the recommendation, and the power is rarely used.

The district.—The State is divided into 365 school districts, containing 1,150 schools, taught by 1,533 teachers. Seven of these districts are city districts having a population of 2,500 or over, employing superintendents who devote their whole time to supervision. Many of the rural districts are large and employ a number of teachers; one district in Laramie County, for example, contains 27 schools, all of which are one-teacher rural schools. Each district is under the administration of a local board of three persons elected for three years, the term of one of whom expires each year. In districts of 1,000 population or over the board may be.increased to six. The directors have practically unlimited power to maintain the kind of schools they wish in their district with but little interference from higher authority. They are legally required to employ teachers certified by the State superintendent, to follow the course of study, and to maintain a minimum term of 120 days. No special provision is made to enforce these laws, however, and in many instances they are not complied with. There are no county boards of education.

Attendance in school is compulsory for all children between the ages of 7 and 14 during the entire time the school is in session. Districts with 2,500 population may appoint special truant officers; in other districts the county sheriff, deputies, and constables are assigned the duty of enforcing the compulsory attendance law. They may investigate cases of absence from school on their own knowledge or on the complaint of any resident or teacher in the county. The term varies in length throughout the State from 40 days to 220 days, the average being 163 days.

Support.—Schools are supported by funds from three sources—the State, the county, and the district. The State fund for 1915 amounted to approximately $334,110; the county funds to approximately $438,509; and the district funds to approximately $547,606. The annual State school fund is composed of the income from the sale and rent of State school lands and interest on State permanent school funds. By constitutional provision this fund is distributed to the counties in the State on the basis of the total number of children from 6 to 21 years old. The fund is reapportioned in the counties by the county superintendents to the various districts on the same basis. The State fund is increasing rapidly, and in 1915 amounted to $8.39 per capita of school population 6 to 21 years.

The county fund is composed of a $2 poll tax imposed on all persons 21 to 50 years of age, fines and forfeitures, and a tax on all taxable property in the county levied annually by the county commissioners "in an amount sufficient to raise $300 for each teacher, but not to exceed 3 mills." The county tax, with the exception of the poll tax, is distributed to the districts on the basis of the number of teachers employed; the polls are returned to the districts in which raised.

Local funds are levied only on vote of the taxpayers of the school districts, the maximum levy being 8½ mills. Some districts raise no local funds, maintaining such schools as are possible entirely from the money received from the State and county. The local tax when voted by taxpayers is collected by the county treasurer and paid over to the treasurer of the local district. Each board may audit its treasurer's account, or a district may vote an audit. There is no other way to secure an audit. Bonds for building purposes may be issued upon a majority vote of the taxpayers of the district, but the amount must not exceed 2 per cent of the valuation of the taxable property of the district.

Certification.—Certificates are issued by the State superintendent upon the recommendation of the State board of examiners. This board is composed of three persons engaged in school work in the State, appointed by the State superintendent. They formulate questions, examine and correct papers, and pass on credentials of such applicants as are legally entitled to certificates because of graduation from preparatory institutions of specified standing. The examinations are held in the different counties and are under the supervision of the county superintendents. Temporary certificates may be issued by the State superintendent, but are legally valid only until the first regular examination held after they are issued. In practice, many teachers are employed who hold only temporary certificates. Salaries of teachers vary throughout the State from $42 to $145 per month; the average is $82 for men, $58 for women.

High schools.—High schools may be established in any district in the State or in special "high-school districts," composed of "any number of present organized and constituted districts." Such high schools are administered by special boards of trustees, each composed of six persons elected by the voters of the high-school district. They are supported by local taxes on all taxable property in the high-school district, the amount of which taxation is determined by the board of trustees. A limit of 2 mills for teachers' salaries and contingent expenses is fixed by law. High schools receive a per capita apportionment from the State funds and $300 per teacher from the county funds. There are 26 schools in the State of secondary grade, giving four-year courses, and 22 giving from one to three year courses.

Higher education.—The State university is located at Laramie, Albany County, and includes among its departments the liberal arts college, the State college of agriculture, the college of engineering, the college of education, and the State normal school. The summary of registration for the year 1915–16, as reported in the university catalogue issued April, 1916, is given below:

STUDENTS IN RESIDENCE.

In graduate standing	14
Seniors	23
Juniors	40
Sophomores	58
Freshmen	77
Special	58
	270
University high school	43
Music (not taking other subjects)	25
Short course	11
Summer school of 1915	270
	349
	619
Less names counted more than once	46
	573

EXTENSION.

Correspondence study department	155
Extension center students (Cheyenne):	
English (Shakespeare)	10
Pedagogical principles	13
Mechanical drawing	20
Shop arithmetic	24
	67
Less names counted more than once	3
Total	46

Teacher training.—The State maintains but one institution for the professional training of teachers—the normal school and college of education of the State university. In practice this is an integral part of the university. The normal school pupils take all work except professional courses with the freshman and sophomore students of other departments of the university. Fifty students residing within the State were registered in the department of education in June, 1916. They were from the following counties: Albany County, 22; Big Horn, 4; Laramie, 4; Converse, 3; Crook, 3; Lincoln, 3; Niobrara, 2; Platte, 2; Sheridan 2; Weston, Sweetwater, Park, Hot Springs, and Fremont, each 1; total 50. There were 7 students from other States. These 57 are included in the enrollment of 270 given above.

TABLE 3.—*Data relative to Wyoming public schools, 1914–15.*

Counties.	Area (square miles).	Total population 6 to 21.	Districts.	School buildings.	Teachers employed.	Children enrolled.	Total expenditure.	Cost per pupil per month.
Albany............	4,436	2,049	25	65	133	1,452	$86,152	$8.02
Big Horn..........	3,185	2,401	32	45	74	1,819	66,495	5.67
Campbell.........	4,774	576	6	24	38	436	21,481	4.12
Carbon...........	8,016	2,093	35	47	80	1,641	71,457	6.52
Converse.........	4,176	945	16	27	44	663	29,915	6.61
Crook............	2,871	1,778	18	86	116	1,366	45,959	7.64
Fremont..........	12,198	1,839	39	52	87	1,501	60,238	5.92
Goshen...........	2,225	1,336	4	46	84	1,008	37,938	4.92
Hot Springs.......	2,018	675	14	14	35	569	23,371	6.52
Johnson..........	4,158	1,011	13	32	44	692	33,894	6.85
Laramie..........	2,704	4,147	10	118	174	3,005	156,025	9.49
Lincoln..........	8,974	4,321	24	63	129	3,431	122,502	5.59
Natrona..........	5,356	1,197	16	18	54	1,178	92,712	9.43
Niobrara.........	2,612	1,045	11	43	48	733	31,317	4.46
Park.............	5,248	1,477	23	33	57	1,247	52,245	12.37
Platte...........	2,117	1,581	8	63	112	1,462	88,224	14.48
Sheridan.........	2,522	4,101	36	67	119	3,035	138,090	5.76
Sweetwater.......	10,522	2,867	18	24	66	2,359	74,101	6.46
Uinta............	2,074	1,866	5	28	59	1,683	87,694	6.91
Washakie.........	2,265	523	8	19	26	463	16,705	9.00
Weston...........	3,054	1,328	4	38	54	1,098	44,262	13.00
Total..........	[1] 97,914	39,156	365	952	1,633	30,816	1,382,777	7.90

[1] Includes Yellowstone Park, 3,054 square miles.

II. EDUCATION IN THE STATE.

Education in the State will be treated as a matter affecting the State as a whole. It is not the function of the legislature to consider the efficiency of individual schools, but to provide machinery which will make it possible that such educational advantages as the State desires to furnish to its children shall be available to every boy and girl in the State. Clearly some communities will always be more law-abiding and more progressive than others, depending on individual ideals and community initiative. But clearly also the State must furnish legal machinery such that every community will have the possibility of being as orderly and law-abiding as the most progressive. It must also assume certain responsibilities that tend toward forcing the most unprogressive to reach definite minimum standards for law and order set up by the State government as necessary for the preservation of life and property. The State has a similar responsibility in providing for the education of its children. It should provide a minimum standard for all counties and should then initiate such steps as are necessary to enforce this provision. It should also encourage progress and stimulate such local effort as the intelligence and progressive spirit of different communities warrant.

The constitution of Wyoming asserts that the "legislature shall provide for a complete and uniform system of public education, and shall make such provision by taxation or otherwise as to create and maintain a thorough and efficient system of public schools adequate to the proper instruction of all the youth of the State." That this may be complied with, the State must from time to time revise and adjust existing provisions according to changing conditions and growing needs. Such an adjustment necessitates a careful study of the educational situation in order that the provisions made may be exactly suited to educational needs. The study of the status of education in the State which follows is made in compliance with an act of the legislature previously explained, and represents, therefore, an effort on the part of the State of its own school system to make the kind of study indicated. The inquiry as made is not a criticism; it is merely a study of the system of education in the State as a whole. Its purpose is to set forth facts as they are, in order that such recommendations as are made may be based on actual needs and conditions and not on opinion or theory.

The efficiency of a school system may be judged by the results it achieves and by the way in which certain well-defined and established principles or standards in administration and management are adhered to. There must be included in any inquiry concerning it the various factors which make up the complete whole and which influence directly or indirectly the results obtained. These factors will be treated under the following heads: Buildings and equipment, enrollment and attendance, teaching corps, instruction, supervision, revenue and support.

School records and reports.—The statistics used in this report to the school code committee have been obtained through questionnaires sent to the various school officers, through personal visits and interviews, and from the reports of the State superintendents, county superintendents, county treasurers, the State examiner, the United States census, and annual reports of the Commissioner of Education.

Practically all data necessary for a careful investigation into school attendance should be contained in the records of the State and county education departments and should be available always. Other information of any nature concerning schools should be procurable from school officers on the request of the State department or other legally constituted authority, such for example as the Wyoming school code committee. While the investigators felt justified in expecting to obtain all necessary information in the manner thus described, unfortunately it has been impossible to do so. Of the 1,600 teachers to whom questionnaires were sent for information relative to their education, training, and experience, about two-thirds replied. Replies were received from 59 per cent of the 1,000 questionnaires sent out regarding buildings, while only 20 per cent of the school directors replied to the questionnaire concerning school expenditures. Of 21 county superintendents, 16 replied to one questionnaire sent out by the Bureau of Education for the school code committee. To another questionnaire sent to county superintendents directly from the State department in November only one reply was received up to April 1, when all data were expected in the Bureau of Education. In this latter case, as in the case of replies from school directors, the data obtained must be omitted, since the replies were too few to be representative. One county superintendent in the State failed to return to the State department any of the information requested regarding buildings and teaching qualifications. This county has, therefore, of necessity been omitted from the tables concerning these particular items.

This indicates a serious condition. The State superintendent should have authority to demand necessary reports on school conditions and power to withhold State funds if they are not received. Otherwise it follows that only the best qualified school officers will

reply, since they are most apt to be prompted by courtesy to
Reports most needed, namely, those from officers least qualified,
from districts in which the school situation is particularly bad, will
usually be missing, and conditions most needing investigation thereby
escape it. The first requisite in an organized system, either State or
county, is the authority to demand all necessary information concerning schools. Refusal on the part of any school officer to comply
with such legal demand should be followed by forfeiture of an adequate
bond or of the position held by the officer refusing.

BUILDINGS AND EQUIPMENT.

The problem of economic, convenient, and sanitary housing of
schools in Wyoming is unique and difficult. The population is
sparse and scattered, and schools must be relatively numerous, far
apart, and small in membership in many cases for some years to come.
In addition, the school population is shifting. Complaints in regard
to bad housing, inconvenient location, and lack of necessary equipment have been received in large numbers by the school code committee. From these and from the investigation it seems apparent
that the important matters of location, buildings, and equipment—
closely related to the physical, moral, and esthetic welfare of school
children—have hardly received the serious consideration which their
importance justifies.

All children should have an opportunity for an education at public
expense in schoolhouses reasonably accessible to their homes and in
buildings which insure at least convenience, comfort, and healthful
conditions. One need not travel far in Wyoming to find schoolhouses of the best and of the worst possible types. The greatest need
seems to be that the State or county should adopt some settled and
economical policy of schoolhouse construction which will provide
measures of general improvement for present conditions and certain
minimum standards for the future.

Distribution.—Schoolhouses should be so located that at least an ele-.
mentary school may be within walking or riding distance (probably
not to exceed 6 miles) of every child of school age. County superintendents and others report that there are now many children living
so far from any schoolhouse that they are deprived of opportunity
for education. Letters in the hands of the school code committee
show that in some cases children as old as 14 years have attended
school a few months only. One report cites the case of a schoolhouse which is located on one side of the river (where the majority
of the voters reside), while practically all the children of school age
in the district live on the other side. When it is necessary to cross
the river by bridge, many children must walk from 3 to 6 miles to
reach the schoolhouse. On the other hand, city superintendents

complain that many unnecessary country schools are maintained on account of the present system of distributing county money in proportion to the number of teachers and that some families are supplied with what practically amounts to a private governess and maid at public expense. Plainly, some of the schools now existing should be abandoned and others established where there are none.

Sanitary requirements.—It is evident that a satisfactory system of schools will provide comfortable and sanitary housing and such equipment as good work necessitates. Appropriateness to the purpose for which intended, convenience, and beauty are other important considerations. The schoolhouse and grounds should represent all that the intelligence, good taste, and financial ability of the community warrant. Recent investigations of the health of rural children and the comparisons made of health conditions in rural and city districts have aroused throughout the country a new interest in rural school buildings and equipment and their relation to the health of children. Results show that country children are not as healthy and have more physical defects than children of the cities, even including the children of the slums. The accompanying graph indicates a few of the conditions revealed by these investigations:

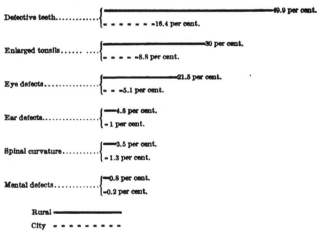

Defective teeth	49.9 per cent.
	16.4 per cent.
Enlarged tonsils	30 per cent.
	8.8 per cent.
Eye defects	21.5 per cent.
	5.1 per cent.
Ear defects	4.8 per cent.
	1 per cent.
Spinal curvature	3.5 per cent.
	1.3 per cent.
Mental defects	0.8 per cent.
	0.2 per cent.

Rural ————
City - - - - - - - -

According to a pamphlet recently distributed by the Bureau of Education:

Healthful and attractive rural schools are absolutely essential to the physical, mental, social, economic, and moral well-being of the nation as a whole. Country school children should have as sanitary and attractive schools and as intelligent and effective health care as school children in the cities.

This pamphlet proposes the following minimum health requirements for rural schools:

The *one-teacher* country school should contain in addition to the classroom:

(a) A small entrance hall, not less than 6 by 8 feet.

(b) A small retiring room, not less than 8 by 10 feet, to be used as an emergency room in case of illness or accident, for a teacher's conference room, for school library, and for health inspection, a feature now being added to the work of the rural school.

(c) A small room, not less than 8 by 10 feet, for a workshop, for instruction in cooking, and for the preparation of refreshments when the school is used, as it should be, for social purposes.

Classroom should not be less than 30 feet long, 20 feet wide, and 12 feet high. This will provide space enough for a maximum of 30 pupils.

VENTILATION AND HEATING.

The schoolroom should always receive fresh air coming directly from out of doors in one of the following arrangements:

(a) Through wide open windows in mild weather.

(b) Through window board ventilators under all other conditions, except when, with furnace or jacketed stove, special and adequate inlets and exits for air are provided.

Heating.—Unless furnace or some other basement system of heating is installed, at least a properly *jacketed stove* is required. (No unjacketed stove should be tolerated in any school.)

The jacketed stove should have a direct fresh-air inlet about 12 inches square, opening through the wall of the schoolhouse into the jacket against the middle or hottest part of the stove.

The exit for foul air should be through an opening at least 16 inches square on the wall near the floor on the same side of the room as the stove is located.

A fireplace with flue adjoining the stove chimney makes a good exit for bad air.[1]

Temperature.—Every school should have a thermometer, and the temperature in cold weather should be kept between 66° and 68° F.

LIGHTING.

The schoolroom should receive an abundance of light, sufficient for darkest days, with all parts of the room adequately illuminated.

The area of glass in windows should be from one-fifth to one-fourth of the floor area.

The best arrangement, according to present ideas, is to have the light come only from the left side of the pupils and from the long wall of the classroom. Windows may be allowed on rear as well as on the left side, but the sills of windows in the rear of the room should be not less than 7 feet above the floor. High windows not less than 7 feet from the floor may be permitted on the right side if thoroughly shaded as an aid to cross ventilation, but not for lighting.

There should be no trees or shrubbery near the schoolhouse which will interfere with the lighting and natural ventilation of the classroom.

The school building should so face that the schoolroom will receive the direct sunlight at some time during the day. The main windows of the schoolroom should not face either directly north or south. East or west facing is desirable.

Shades should be provided at tops and bottoms of windows with translucent shades at top, so that light may be properly controlled on bright days.

---

[1] The following arrangement for ventilating flue is required in one Western State: A circular sheet steel smoke flue, passing up in center of ventilating shaft (foul air exit) 20 inches square in the clear.

Schoolroom colors.—The best colors for the schoolroom in relation to lighting are:
Ceiling.—White or light cream.
Walls.—Light gray or light green.
Blackboards.—Black, but not glossy.

CLEANLINESS.

The schoolhouse and surroundings should be kept as clean as a good housekeeper keeps her home.

(a) No dry sweeping or dry dusting should be allowed.

(b) Floors and furniture should be cleaned with damp sweepers and oily cloths.

(c) Scrubbing, sunning, and airing are better than any form of fumigation.

DRINKING WATER.

Drinking water should be available for every pupil at any time of day which does not interfere with the school program.

Every rural school should have a sanitary drinking fountain located just inside or outside the schoolhouse entrance.

Drinking water should come from a safe source. Its purity should be certified by an examination by the State board of health or by some other equally reliable authority.

A common drinking cup is always dangerous and should never be tolerated.

Individual drinking cups are theoretically and in some conditions all right, but practical experience has proved that in schools individual cups, to be used more than once, are unsatisfactory and unhygienic. Therefore, they are not to be advocated nor approved for any school.

Sufficient pressure for running water for drinking fountain or other uses in the rural school may always be provided from any source without excessive expense by a storage tank or by pressure tank with force pump.

WATER FOR WASHING.

Children in all schools should have facilities for washing hands available at least:

(a) Always after the use of the toilet.

(b) Always before eating.

(c) Frequently after playing outdoors, writing on blackboard, or doing other forms of handwork connected with the school.

Individual clean towels should always be used.

Paper towels are the cheapest and most practicable.

The common towel is as dangerous to health as the common drinking cup.

FURNITURE.

School seats and desks should be hygienic in type and adjusted at least twice a year to the size and needs of growing children. Seats and desks should be individual, separate, adjustable, clean.

Books and other materials of instruction should not only be sanitary, but attractive enough to stimulate a wholesome response from the pupils.

TOILETS AND PRIVIES.

Toilets and privies should be sanitary in location, construction, and in maintenance.

(a) If water carriage system for sewage is available, separate toilets for boys and girls should be located in the schoolhouse, with separate entrances on different sides or corners of the school building.

BUREAU OF EDUCATION.

District No. 3, Washakie County, 40 miles from the railroad.

Buffalo Basin School, Crook County

Powell consolidated school, Park County.

Bennett Creek School, District No. 8.

A GROUP OF WYOMING SCHOOL BUILDINGS.

DISTRICT NO. 5, HOT SPRINGS COUNTY.

EMERSON SCHOOL, DISTRICT NO. 17, FREMONT COUNTY.

(b) If there is no water carriage system, separate privies should be located at least 50 feet in the different directions from the schoolhouse, with the entrances well screened.

(c) The privy should be rainproof, well ventilated, and one of the following types:

1. Dry-earth closet.
2. Septic-tank container.
3. With a water-tight vault or box.

All containers of excreta should be water-tight, thoroughly screened against insects, and easily cleaned at frequent intervals.

No cesspool should be used unless it is water-tight and easily emptied and cleaned.

All excreta should be either burned, buried, treated by subsoil drainage, reduced by septic-tank treatment, or properly distributed on tilled land as fertilizer.

All schoolhouses and privies.should be thoroughly and effectively screened against flies and mosquitoes.

.Schoolhouses and outhouses should be absolutely free from all defacing and obscene marks.

Buildings should be kept in good repair and with whole windows.

The tables which follow this section give a general idea of how Wyoming lives up to these minimum requirements in rural communities. The statistics include all school buildings, rural and urban, and therefore show a higher average than if rural schools alone were included. Table 4, which gives detailed data by counties, shows that many buildings are in bad condition inside and out. The exact percentage of districts having such buildings varies from 8 per cent of those reporting in one county to 66 per cent in another. A few excerpts from reports received by the code committee will show that these defects are often very serious ones:

1. Outside finish, mud; inside finish, mud; ventilation, door only.
2. Papered with newspapers; floors, poor.
3. Floor, rough; no paint, not ceiled overhead:
4. Inside finish, poor; large cracks in floor; plaster off the ceiling.
5. Cracked walls, uneven floor, ill-fitting windows.
6. Stove smokes, ventilated by cracks and broken window glass.
7. Building 25 years old, log, in wretched repair, stucco falling out, an abandoned cabin.
8. Cracks in walls, stuffed with rags.
9. Poor outside and inside; finished in rough logs and ventilated by cracks; no shades no ventilation, no outbuildings.
10. Schoolhouse in pasture, no fence, stock use house as windbreak.

Heating and lighting.—Over 73 per cent of the schools reporting are heated by ordinary stoves, about 10 per cent with jacketed stoves, and the others by furnace or steam. Steam-heated buildings and those provided with ventilating systems are confined to towns and cities. Windows are the only means of ventilating in 78 per cent of all the school buildings. At least three counties report all of their schools ventilated by windows only. This means that foul air is breathed by the children the greater part of the day, unless the teacher is trained in schoolroom ventilation and is unusually careful. Jacketed stoves with ventilating attachments in country schools mean reasonable comfort for the children, while rooms heated by unjacketed stoves are almost sure to be uncomfortably warm for those near the stove, and cold for those in the remote corners of the room. In the counties reporting, the number of buildings heated with jacketed stoves varies from 0 to 15 per cent of the total. Relatively few of the rural schools in the State are properly lighted. The country schoolhouses are usually of the box-car variety with windows on both sides or on three sides. Insufficient or cross lighting is reported in 61 per cent of the schools of the State.

Equipment.—The reports received indicate that the majority of rural schools in the State have little equipment. Every school should not only be supplied with cloakrooms, workrooms, adjustable desks, and the like, but with a liberal number of books for reference and supplementary reading, globes, maps, dictionaries, etc. These need not be expensive, but they should be carefully selected by those familiar with school work. Money should not be spent on useless material. One county reports only 10 per cent of schools supplied with books other than the basic texts, and 40 per cent of the schools in the State as a whole report similarly.

Sites and grounds.—The question of convenience of access is so important in deciding the location of schoolhouses that appropriateness in other respects must sometimes be lost sight of. The schoolhouse should be located in as healthful a place as exists in the community. The yard should always be well drained. In a few instances school grounds are reported as constantly flooded with waste water from irrigation. Very few reports indicate that any consideration whatever was given to drainage and soil in the selection of the school site. The reports show that very little attention is given to beautifying the school grounds in the rural districts and that there are practically no yards suitable or equipped for play except in cities and consolidated schools. The feeling is all too common in rural communities that country children have little need of play—that their out-of-door life and the healthful conditions which usually prevail in the country compensate for the lack of recreation. This is, of course, a mistaken view. Playground room and simple equipment are not luxuries, but necessities.

Water supply.—The water supply is a serious problem from the point of view of health and cleanliness. The table appended shows four counties in which none of the schools reporting have water on the school grounds; relatively few of the schools in the State (23 per cent) have water on the school grounds. In many cases the reports show that the teacher or children carry water for drinking long distances, often in open pails left uncovered throughout the day. Drinking water for children is so intimately related to their health that it deserves special attention. Lack of water, polluted water supply, insanitary arrangements for keeping water and for drinking it are fruitful sources of disease. There should be sanitary fountains on the school grounds where possible; but individual drinking cups, if kept clean and free from dust and germs, or paper cups— which are not costly—are also sanitary and satisfactory if the water is kept in covered jars. Some counties report no sanitary fountains or individual drinking cups in use. In the State as a whole about 9 per cent of the schools use sanitary fountains and 41 per cent individual drinking cups. Apparently little care is taken to see that the cups are kept clean and the water is rarely kept in covered receptacles. Not only should drinking water be available at all times, but water for washing and individual towels should also be furnished, and water for keeping the schoolhouse scrubbed and cleaned in order that it may be as sanitary and as wholesome as the best home in the community. Children should be taught hygiene and sanitation through example as well as precept. The difficulty of a satisfactory solution of this problem is fully realized. Wells can not always be provided on the school grounds, nor water piped there. Some arrangement for carrying it in large quantities and for properly storing it will be necessary in many cases. The important thing is that the matter of water supply be considered in the selection of a school site, and that some sanitary and adequate provision be made in the future before schoolhouses are definitely located. A competent administrative authority should have power to inspect and condemn sites and grounds as well as buildings when insanitary conditions prevail which can not be remedied.

Outbuildings.—The necessity of such supervisory control is still more apparent from an examination of reports concerning toilets. Some districts provide no toilets at all; in others one toilet is used by boys and girls and teacher. In many cases where two are supplied, they are, according to one local investigator, "dens of filth and neglect; they are not scrubbed, and pits are not cleaned or disinfected. Often the pits are full to overflowing, and often there are no doors." Over 50 per cent of the total number reporting from the State were reported as poor or in need of repairs; 4 per cent of the schools reported definitely that they had no outbuildings; and 28 per cent have but one. It need scarcely be added that such a condition needs immediate attention and is ample evidence of the need of an inspecting and supervisory control of buildings and grounds.

To summarize: It is very important that means be provided to insure adequate and sanitary buildings located on accessible and healthful sites where pure water can be had. Buildings, grounds, and outbuildings should be inspected and supervised by competent authorities and existing conditions remedied without unnecessary delay.

Report of school building survey.

	Number.	Per cent.
Total number of school buildings in State.	952	100
Total number of building reports received.	557	59
Number of school buildings built after 1900 and reported new.	383	*69
Number built before 1900 and reported old.	80	14
Number not reporting on this item.	94	17
Material in buildings:		
Brick or stone.	63	11
Log or sod.	141	25
Frame.	331	59
Number not reporting on this item.	22	4
Inside finish of buildings:		
Good.	316	55
Poor.	171	31
Number not reporting on this item.	70	13
Outside finish of buildings:		
Good.	314	56
Poor.	146	26
Number not reporting on this item.	97	17
Lighting:		
Side or rear lighting (good).	143	26
Insufficient or cross lighting (unsatisfactory).	342	61
Number not reporting on this item.	72	12
Heating:		
Steam or furnace.	44	8
Unjacketed stove.	406	73
Jacketed stove.	59	11
Both a jacketed and an unjacketed stove.	25	4
Number not reporting on this item.	23	4
Ventilation:		
Windows only means supplied.	438	79
Special provision.	79	14
Number not reporting on this item.	40	7
Kind of desks:		
Single.	365	66
Double.	109	20
Double and single reported.	58	10
No desks furnished.	7	1
Number not reporting on this item.	18	3
Adjustable.	223	40
Stationary.	257	46
Number not reporting on this item.	77	14
Buildings equipped with:		
Charts.	302	54
None.	255	46
Dictionaries.	369	66
None.	188	34
Supplementary books.	232	42
None.	325	58
Shades.	199	38
None.	358	64
Pictures.	214	38
None.	343	62
Sanitary fountains.	50	9
Individual cups.	226	41
No provision.	28	5
Number not reporting on this item.	253	45
Buildings employing janitor:		
Janitor employed.	89	16
Teacher acts as janitor.	438	79
Number not reporting on this item.	30	5
Buildings reporting:		
Assembly rooms.	16	
Gymnasiums.	11	
Work rooms.	39	
Rest or cloak rooms.	125	
Fence:		
Yards with fence.	183	33
No fence.	364	65
Irrigation:		
Irrigated.	54	10
Dry or not reporting on this item.	503	90
Trees:		
Trees.	71	13
No trees.	480	87

*In this and the following items, percentages are based on the number reporting, which is 59 per cent of the whole.

Report of school building survey—Continued

	Number.	Per cent.
Playground equipment:		
Number having equipment........................	54	10
Number not reporting any equipment...........................	503	90
Toilets:		
One only.................................	167	28
Two..................................	330	58
None..................................	23	4
Number not reporting on this item...........................	37	7
Condition of toilets:		
Good..................................	225	40
Poor or in need of repairs........................	302	54
Number not reporting on this item........................	30	5
Free from obscene markings........................	367	....
Connected with sewers............................	10	....
Water source:		
Well..................................	100	18
Water piped.............................	36	6
Carried from home, springs, or river by pupils....................	201	36
Number not reporting on this item....................	220	39

Outbuilding report from one county.

Schools reported	51	Condition of repair:		Free from markings.........	32
One outhouse only...........	14	Good....................	17	Not free from markings.... .	4
Two.........................	20	Poor....................	16	No report................. ..	15
None.......................	4	Not given...............	18		
No report received...........	13				

TABLE 4.—*Schoolhouses, grounds, and equipment*

[The numbers in all figure columns except the first, "Number reporting," indicate per cents.]

County	Number reporting.	Buildings relatively new.	Buildings of brick or stone.	Buildings of log or sod.	Buildings of wood.	Inside poor.	Outside poor.	Good, side or rear.	Poor, crosslighting.	Steam.	Stove, jacketed.	Stove, not jacketed.	Ventilation, no means provided.	Desks, double, old.	Charts furnished.	Dictionary.	Books supplied.	Walls decorated.	Shades.	Pictures.	Janitor furnished.	Assembly room.	Gymnasium.	Workroom.	Cloakroom.	Sanitary fountain.	Individual cups.	Fenced.	Trees.	Play equipment.	One only.	None.	Condition good.	Water on grounds.
Albany [1]	35	80	23	25	43	8	8	26	76	6	12	83	80	70	60	85	64	8	33	24	21	3	3	8	36	6	40	14	17	17	26	0	40	37
Big Horn	12	100	0	25	66	16	16	16	84	0	17	83	100	84	66	58	16	0	50	17	0	0	0	0	8	8	42	33	8	17	25	0	67	25
Campbell	23	66	33	33	33	66	66	61	43	0	46	50	87	33	50	70	76	0	66	17	4	0	0	0	51	30	66	33	13	8	23	8	43	30
Carbon	37	40	30	16	34	18	18	14	49	4	18	73	90	33	55	90	16	0	43	41	4	3	0	16	21	0	43	24	8	4	24	8	21	17
Converse	60	50	0	13	77	20	20	14	86	4	8	80	77	60	51	55	25	0	21	51	8	0	0	2	0	0	30	33	8	4	33	15	30	17
Crook	57	66	7	80	93	20	20	25	95	12	13	76	66	33	15	40	28	0	66	24	8	0	0	0	20	0	56	15	8	5	36	10	40	33
Fremont	30	100	0	33	66	20	64	5	95	9	20	100	100	48	10	53	33	7	33	71	20	0	0	0	28	0	36	67	0	0	26	10	100	80
Goshen	9	40	0	28	60	8	16	10	72	0	0	86	66	12	0	30	0	0	26	41	3	0	0	12	38	12	36	53	0	0	13	0	30	0
Johnson	11	40	0	7	93	16	16	26	75	0	8	91	83	26	67	83	33	0	26	27	37	0	0	0	18	3	18	67	9	8	45	15	30	18
Laramie	16	60	18	18	63	60	50	5	80	0	6	85	81	14	43	25	25	0	26	25	12	0	0	18	19	0	12	25	0	0	43	12	38	23
Lincoln	17	88	0	40	42	14	28	10	75	0	11	84	68	20	38	47	58	0	43	17	16	2	0	0	14	9	35	23	0	12	33	13	38	0
Natrona	25	88	18	20	70	58	58	20	70	0	11	84	84	12	80	66	21	50	16	66	12	0	0	12	32	11	29	24	28	26	33	4	17	24
Niobrara	11	80	0	33	68	33	26	26	80	8	18	76	68	8	26	66	80	8	32	33	9	0	0	19	40	7	27	15	18	7	55	4	21	0
Park	90	66	0	20	80	88	88	33	56	8	10	78	88	11	66	86	66	5	26	48	12	0	0	0	52	17	73	52	0	20	53	0	17	28
Platte	66	66	0	40	88	20	20	26	90	4	11	87	72	66	66	66	35	0	43	22	9	4	4	0	40	7	17	20	28	16	33	4	51	30
Sheridan	23	55	11	18	55	26	18	26	78	0	11	85	62	18	58	84	70	11	18	33	15	0	0	0	40	7	73	47	15	13	53	9	31	10
Sweetwater	33	65	11	4	85	55	16	25	75	4	10	86	68	12	76	88	50	0	43	44	27	3	3	3	40	7	28	25	7	0	25	0	21	7
Uinta	28	85	9	4	85	55	16	26	86	7	10	85	62	18	55	84	76	18	16	27	21	0	4	3	40	7	38	47	7	13	9	28	26	13
Weston	26	50	0	4	76	50	50	38	61	17	8	85	81	12	25	50	24	15	50	27	19	4	4	4	13	4	44	37	20	8	27	19	28	43

[1] No replies.

ENROLLMENT AND ATTENDANCE.

The data on enrollment and attendance herein submitted are gathered principally from reports of the county superintendents to the State superintendent. Unfortunately these reports are very incomplete, and do not contain many of the most important items concerning attendance. To illustrate: Nearly 85 per cent of the schools of Wyoming are one-teacher schools. In some cases many of them are included in one district; one district in Laramie County has 27. The county superintendents' reports give only averages by districts. Averages do not show the actual conditions, for in single districts there are schools in session a short term only, with teachers paid low salaries and the attendance very small, while there are others exactly opposite in each of these particulars. The average shows conditions somewhere between the two, or something which does not exist at all. A feature of the superintendent's report should be the presentation of such discrepancies. Data were not obtainable in the time at our disposal to show with any accuracy how many small, short-term schools having poorly paid teachers there are in the State, or in how many schools the percentage of attendance is very low.

Reliable data relative to the percentage of enrollment could not be obtained in spite of the importance of such information. An efficient school system enrolls all children of actual school age (approximately 6 to 18[1] years of age, if high schools are maintained), and holds them in school until they have finished both elementary and high schools. However effective may be the instruction furnished, unless the children are enrolled and attend school regularly the result is unsatisfactory. The "census" as given in the county superintendents' reports is the number of all children 6 to 21 years of age. No figures are available to show the number of children of actual school age, generally 6 to 18[1] years. Percentage of enrollment should be computed on the basis of the number of actual school age and the actual enrollment. The figures given for actual enrollment in the county superintendents' reports are evidently not reliable. This is due to the lack of system in keeping records on the part of the school district trustees, from whom the county superintendents collect the data. According to the county superintendents' reports for the year 1915, 78 per cent of the census children (6 to 21 years) were enrolled in school. This means an enrollment equal to the total number of children of actual school age (6 to 18[1] years), which is, of course, not probable. The United States Census of 1910 reported 35,776 children from 6 to 21 years of age in Wyoming, with 64 per cent enrolled in school. This is probably more nearly correct. The estimate made by the bureau is given in the appendix.

---

[1]Inclusive.

Other important data not available in State, county, or district records (except in a few districts) are these: Percentage of enrollment in average daily attendance; number of eighth-grade graduates; census of children of high-school age and percentage of these children enrolled in high school; census of children of high-school age in districts where high schools are not available; number of children of elementary school age not attending full term taught in the district as specified by the compulsory attendance law; and age-grade data. All of these items should be available for each school and for each district, and averages by counties should be made only when needed for special purposes. The last item—age-grade data—doubtless needs a little explanation. Experience proves that over-age shortens school life. Especially is this true when children are two years or more over-age; children three years over-age rarely attend school beyond the sixth grade. Information concerning age grade of children enrolled in school is, therefore, valuable in checking up the efficiency of the school system. As soon as a more centralized county system is organized and a reasonable degree of uniformity of grading is assured, the forms filed in the office of the county superintendent should contain information concerning the number of children in every grade, with their ages, lists of promotions by grades, and information as detailed as possible concerning children who leave school at the close of the compulsory school period.

The following table shows the census, the total enrollment, the high-school enrollment, and the number between 7 and 14 [1] years of age not enrolled in any school:

TABLE 5.—*Census and enrollment, 1914–15.*

Counties.	Census (6–21).	Enroll-ment.	Per capita cost per month (average).[2]	Attending high school.	Number between 7 and 14 years of age not attending school.
Albany	2,049	1,452	$8.02	180	122
Big Horn	2,401	1,819	5.67	146	60
Campbell	576	436	4.12	28	9
Carbon	2,093	1,641	6.52	148	11
Converse	945	663	6.61	89	4
Crook	1,778	1,358	7.64	51	58
Fremont	1,839	1,501	5.92	161	119
Goshen	1,336	984	4.92	52	50
Hot Springs	675	569	6.52	45	17
Johnson	1,011	692	6.85	76	17
Laramie	4,147	3,005	9.49	366	65
Lincoln	4,321	3,431	5.59	294	93
Natrona	1,197	1,176	9.43	131	23
Niobrara	1,045	733	4.46	45	51
Park	1,477	1,247	12.37	157	41
Platte	1,581	1,462	14.48	133	7
Sheridan	4,101	3,035	5.76	343	5
Sweetwater	2,867	2,343	6.46	260	10
Uinta	1,866	1,683	6.91	89	29
Washakie	523	436	9.00	47	13
Weston	1,328	1,098	13.00	72	5
Total					809

[1] Inclusive.   [2] Based on enrollment.

These figures are taken from the county superintendents' reports and show that 809 children between 7 and 14 years of age are not enrolled in any school. This is probably a low estimate, since, as explained above, the United States census report for 1910 shows a much larger number than the State superintendent's report, and the present meth:d of estimating information for school purposes leaves room for errors and omissions. In Albany County 10 per cent of the census children between the ages of 7 and 14 years are not enrolled in school. This may be due to laxity on the part of the attendance officer, or it may be due to the fact that some children live so far from school that they are unable to attend.

Though there are no available data to show what percentage of actual school population is enrolled in school and how regularly those enrolled attend school, it is, however, possible to obtain from the county superintendents' reports the average number of days attended by each pupil enrolled and the maximum and minimum terms by districts. In a few rural districts schools are maintained but two months, in others three, four, or five months, and a six months' term seems to be relatively prevalent. Practically all cities and towns maintain schools nine and one-half months. Nine months (180 school days) should be the minimum term in any district. The variation indicates that gross injustice is suffered by some children, since they have a possibility of only a few months of school per year. It also shows the inequality of opportunity offered under the existing system of school management.

A similar irregularity and consequent injustice is shown in the average number of days attended. Even in a county in which the minimum length of term is six months, or 120 days, the average number of days actually attended by each child enrolled is but 89. Schools in this county are evidently not holding pupils in school during the full term, even when the term is a short one, and, consequently, it is evident that the attendance law is not being enforced. The school term should be increased throughout the State to 180 days, and schools should be so respected in the various communities and should so appeal to the interests of the children that all those enrolled would attend regularly, except when kept away because of illness or other unavoidable reasons.

Regularity of attendance influences the cost of schooling. Data available do not show the cost per pupil on attendance basis, which really represents the actual cost. The per capita cost on enrollment basis, which now varies according to the table from a minimum of $4.12 per month in Campbell County to a maximum of $14.50 in Platte County, is much lower than if computed on an attendance basis. If attendance were better for each district, the actual cost per district would be no greater than now, the per capita cost smaller, and the educational results far more satisfactory.

Summary.—The reports of all school officers to the county superintendents and State superintendent should be revised to include important items of information now omitted. A follow-up system should be in force, so that these reports may be filed with the proper authorities at specified times. The present laxity in the enforcement of the compulsory-attendance law should be remedied and better attendance encouraged by State and county.[1]

Secondary schools.—The percentage of pupils enrolled (based on total census children of high-school age), the average daily attendance, the number of teachers, the branches taught, and other important data regarding high schools could not be obtained. Except for the item of total enrollment, no available reports give separate data for high schools either in regard to census and attendance or number and qualifications of teachers. Although two different attempts were made by the State superintendent to obtain information from 47 reported high schools (State superintendent's annual report) in the State, only 17 replied—a number not large enough to be representative of the State as a whole. From information obtainable from the State department, State university, and the United States Bureau of Education, there are 26 high schools giving a four-year course and 21 others giving some high-school work from one to three years.

The enrollment in all but a few of these is very small and the number of teachers small. In some cases four-year high schools are conducted by one teacher. In a few cases rural teachers are attempting to teach some high-school work in connection with their regular elementary classes. Taking time for this is unjust to the elementary pupils and the work is probably of little value to those taking secondary subjects.

If it were possible to ascertain the number of children of high-school age not enrolled in any high school, indications are that it would be very large. The city of Cheyenne, with a total enrollment of 1,909 (county superintendent's report, 1915), enrolls 288 pupils in the high school. This is 15 per cent of the total district enrollment. The State at large, with a total enrollment of 30,816, enrolls 2,912 in high schools, only 9 per cent of the total enrollment. This estimate includes the cities of Cheyenne, Sheridan, Laramie, and others, where high-school enrollment is relatively large. The indications are, therefore, that a very small percentage, probably not more than 5 or 6 per cent of the total enrollment in rural communities, is in high schools. Estimating from figures in the report of the Commissioner of Education for 1911, there were in Wyoming,

---

[1] For detailed suggestions, see p. 91.

in 1910, 10,951 pupils of high-school age (14–18 [1]). The increase in total school census for 1915 over 1910 is about 9 per cent. Using this as a basis of estimate, there were in Wyoming the present year 11,937 children of high-school age; 2,912 of these are enrolled in high schools, leaving a remainder of 8,925 children of high-school age not enrolled in high schools. While this, of course, is only an estimate, it is approximately correct.

So far as can be ascertained, vocational subjects in the Wyoming high schools receive little attention. Here and there attention is given to fitting boys and girls for a place in industrial life and an effort made to give some kind of vocational guidance, but no systematic State-wide effort is being made either to encourage a greater number of high schools or to assist in bringing those which now exist nearer to the industrial interests of the people. More high schools are needed, and they should be located in such a way as to serve the largest possible number of children. The courses of study need revision, particularly with respect to vocational training. High schools should file separate reports with the State and county superintendents. The State department of education should be equipped to have general supervision over the high schools and to give them advice and assistance.

TEACHING CORPS.

The most important consideration in the efficiency of any school is the teacher. If she is well qualified for her work, trained, experienced, and capable, many handicaps can be overcome. This is especially true in the rural schools. As the teacher, so is the school. Few, if any, interfere with her sway. She makes the course of study, outlines the program, selects the books, often without restraint or advice, and is the organizer and general administrative officer of the classroom. These responsibilities demand ability of a high order and such academic and professional training as give preparation proportional to the importance of the work pursued. It occasionally happens that teachers are "born;" that is, one of unusual native ability becomes a successful teacher through experience rather than through special preparation. Probably, however, the percentage of born teachers is as small as the percentage of born doctors, lawyers, or ministers. There is now general agreement among educators and laymen that the best assurance of good teaching consists in adequate preparation on the part of the teacher.

The training of the teacher is usually thought of as made up of two elements—general or academic education and special or professional training. In addition, a study of the qualifications of the

---

[1] Inclusive.

teaching force should consider such professional activities, graduate study, summer-school attendance, educational reading, etc., as show a progressive attitude and a professional spirit. Experience is another important factor. In order that the teaching body may be a homogeneous group with certain standard qualifications, most States have some system of certification by which the teachers are classified according to educational qualifications, generally measured by (1) examination or (2) evidence of graduation from schools of specified class and standard. The teaching force of Wyoming has therefore been considered (1) as to certification, (2) as to general education, (3) as to professional training and experience, and (4) as to professional spirit as evidenced in the manner above suggested.

Certification.—The State of Wyoming recognizes eight different kinds of teaching certificates, obtainable either on examination or on satisfactory evidence of graduation from approved schools. Legally the holders of higher-grade certificates have no advantage in appointment or salary over holders of lower-grade certificates. Briefly, the qualifications represented by both forms are as follows:

TABLE 6.—*Requirements for teaching certificates*

Class of certificates.	Requirements by examination.	Requirements by credentials.
(1) Third-grade certificate (valid one year, not renewable).	The common branches, including no high-school subjects, but including agriculture, Wyoming and United States civics, and obtaining an average of 70 per cent; no subject lower than 50.	Graduation from a four-year high school.
(2) Second-grade certificate (valid two years; renewable for two years by reading-circle work).	Rhetoric and composition, and the theory and practice of teaching, in addition to examinations required for third-class certificates.	Graduation from a four-year high school, with 18 weeks' additional work at a standard normal school.
(3) First-grade certificate (valid four years, renewable for four years by reading-circle work).	Algebra, English, and American literature, elementary psychology, physical geography, and two additional high-school subjects, in addition to examinations required for second-class certificate.	Graduation from a four-year high school and an additional full year at a standard normal school.
(4) Professional second-class (valid for life).	School management, pedagogy, methods, and history of education, the subjects required for a first-class certificate, and two additional high-school subjects.	Graduation from a regular two-year normal school, with one year's experience in teaching.
(5) Professional first-class (valid for life).	Issued to holders of professional second-class certificates on passing additional examinations in advanced psychology and school supervision, after three years' successful teaching experience.	Graduation from the college of liberal arts of the State university or institution of the same standing, provided one-fifth of the course pursued was in education, and two years' successful experience in teaching.
(6) Diploma certificate.....	Issued to graduates of the State normal school or the State university and held while gaining experience required for the above professional certificates.	
(7) Special certificates......	Issued to primary, kindergarten, and special technical teachers upon credentials or examinations.	
(8) Temporary certificates..	Issued to persons engaged to teach, but hold no certificate in force, but who have at some time held a teaching certificate. Requests must be indorsed by county superintendents and show "good and sufficient reasons." They are good legally only until next regular examination.	

It is evident that the two requirements for the same certificate, one by examination and one by presentation of satisfactory evidence of graduation from specified schools, are not equivalent. For instance, the lowest certificate (the third-grade certificate) requires graduation from a four-year high school, if obtained by credentials, but it may be obtained on examination by a person with no high-school education. The first-grade certificate requires graduation from a one-year standard normal school on credentials, but it may be obtained on examination by high-school graduates who have studied outside of school certain professional works on education. In fact, a study of the education of the individual teachers now holding first-grade certificates shows many with no education beyond high school, and a large number with even less general education.

As stated in a previous section, all kinds of certificates are issued by the State superintendent of public instruction on the recommendation of the State board of examiners, which consists of three members appointed by the State superintendent of public instruction from among high-school principals, city and county superintendents of the State, and the faculty of the State university. This sort of board was undoubtedly satisfactory when the number of teachers in the State was much fewer than at present. Now, however, that the work is more arduous, it is difficult to find education officers who can give enough time to the work to assure promptness in correcting examinations, passing upon credentials of education, and issuing certificates. Many complaints have been received because teachers are required to wait a seemingly unreasonable time for their certificates. Greater satisfaction would undoubtedly result if the board were abolished and a division of certification, with a permanent chief, created in the State department of education.

The following table shows the kind of certificates held by all teachers in the State at the end of the school year 1914–15, as taken from the records of the county superintendents, and those held by 1,077 teachers at work in the fall of 1915 as reported to the State department on the special inquiry for information for this report. It is interesting to note that while there were 10 per cent of the teachers without regular certificates in October of the year 1915, there were only 2 per cent the preceding spring. It indicates that a large number of teachers holding no certificates are employed each fall in the expectation that there will be no difficulty in securing certificates later.

Certificates of teachers in 1914–15.

Kinds of certificates.	Spring of 1915.	Fall of 1915.
	Per cent.	Per cent.
First professional certificates	6.4	7.4
Second professional certificates	16.8	20.2
First-grade certificates	16.5	13.4
Second-grade certificates	44.6	32.5
Third-grade certificates	10.4	11.2
Diploma certificates	2.5	1.7
Special certificates	.0	3.7
Temporary certificates	2.3	3.0
Those not reporting any grade of certificate	.0	6.9

The figures for the fall of 1915 show that more than half of the teachers of the State reporting hold either second or third grade certificates or none at all and 10 per cent hold temporary certificates or none. The first-grade certificate, held by 13 per cent of the teachers, is not a high grade of certificate, especially when obtained by examination. None of these three grades of certificate when obtained on examination necessarily represents any professional training worth while. Nearly 60 per cent of the total number of certificates issued during 18 months preceding June, 1916, were issued on examination. Data showing the exact number of each grade issued in this way are not available. However, of the 40 per cent issued on credentials, a large number were given on high-school diplomas and represent no professional training. Only 29 per cent of the total number of teachers now in the State (diploma and first and second professional certificates) hold certificates representing worthy attempts toward preparing for their chosen profession, and this 29 per cent in reality should be reduced by the consideration that a large portion of them were obtained by examination.

It is obvious that the professional status is low. It can be raised by legislation requiring of all teachers after a certain date, say 1922, a definite amount of professional training as a prerequisite for any type of certificate. This plan is being adopted in other States, and seems to be necessary, if trained teachers are to be secured.

Another point relating to certificates is noteworthy in these figures. Three per cent of the total number of teachers included in this report (1,077) hold temporary certificates, and 7 per cent held, at the time the questionnaires were sent out in October, none at all. Taking this as a basis of computation, it would appear that about 50 teachers in the State hold temporary certificates and more than 100 none at all. That is, approximately 150 teachers (or 10 per cent of the total) were teaching in the month of October holding no legal papers authorizing them to draw their salaries. The blame for this condition must be distributed among three classes of people, namely, the teachers themselves, those who employ them, and the State board of examiners. To remedy this, it should be illegal, as it is now in many States, for any teacher or any employing board or officer to enter into a teaching contract until the teacher holds a certificate.

A very interesting fact uncovered by this investigation is the surprising variation among counties as to the grades of certificates held by teachers. The county reporting the highest percentage of life certificates is Natrona, the percentage being 41.8. The one showing the lowest percentage (Campbell) reports no teachers holding life certificates. Thus we have a variation in the number of life certificates ranging from 0 in one county to 41.8 per cent in another. Likewise the variation in third-grade certificates (the lowest class of certificate) runs from 0 in Washakie to 25 per cent in Campbell. Similarly the average number of years of professional training varies from two-tenths of a year in Campbell to 1.9 years in Hot Springs County. No teachers holding degrees are reported in Big Horn, Crook, Niobrara, and Hot Springs, while Laramie County, containing the city of Cheyenne, excels on this point.

Variation in grades of certificates among counties.

	Per cent.
Largest percentage of life certificates, Natrona County	41.8
Smallest percentage of life certificates, Campbell County	0.0
Largest percentage of third-grade certificates, Campbell County	25.0
Smallest percentage of third-grade certificates, Washakie County	0.0

What is the cause of this rather striking variation? Professional schools for teachers as at present conducted do not prepare for rural-school work; hence trained teachers gravitate to the city. But the matter must also be traced largely to those who select teachers. In the four or five largest towns or cities in Wyoming the power to select teachers is usually given to the city superintendent. In small towns and rural schools the boards still perform this function. The table shows, for example, that the county in which Casper is situated, and in which there are few small town and rural schools, has a high percentage of life certificates. Sheridan County (containing the city of Sheridan) reports 110 teachers, 42 of whom hold life certificates and only 10 of whom hold third-grade certificates. Laramie County (containing Cheyenne) shows 46 life certificates out of a total of 123 certificates and only 7 third-grade certificates. The conclusion is inevitable that wherever the power of selecting teachers is left to the proper supervisory officer, instead of to school boards, much better teachers will be found. This is but natural. In many States county boards of education and county superintendents must approve all teachers appointed before the district receives any portion of the county funds.

General education.—Ability to teach can be judged better from the applicant's education and training than from the grade of certificate held. Too many elements of chance enter into the examination method of judging qualifications, and too much encouragement is given by such a system for cramming subject matter at the expense of time which could be spent better in preparation for work in the schoolroom.

An attempt was made to obtain information giving the exact education, both general and professional, of every teacher in the State; however, only 66 per cent replied, and in many cases the returns on normal and college training were so indefinite that it is impossible to say whether the work reported was done in standard normal school or college courses or in preparatory department courses. The following table gives the number of the 1,077 reporting who had elementary education only, partial secondary education, and complete secondary education. Many of those with complete secondary school work went to normal school or college; 495 reported that they had attended such institutions, more than the number reporting attendance at high schools; many of these did not report whether or not they had any secondary school work. In such cases their so-called college work was in fact secondary work. Many normal schools in the United States and many institutions known as colleges require little or no high-school work for entrance.

General education, elementary and secondary.

	Number.	Per cent.
Total number of teachers in State	1,633	....
Total number of teachers reporting	1,077	....
Teachers having elementary education only	70	6.5
Having some secondary, averaging in amount 2.2 years	273	25.3
Having some secondary, amount not reported	297	27.6
Full 4-year secondary (including those who have additional college training)	437	40.6
Total	1,077	100.0

Professional training and experience.—Fifty-four per cent of the total number of teachers report no professional training of any kind. This shows a lower percentage of professionally trained teachers than exists in many other States. Those reporting professional training did not in all cases designate the amount. They reported, however, attendance in courses which included professional education in normal schools and colleges as given below. It must be clearly understood that the institutions attended were not institutions necessarily requiring any high-school education for entrance; they include all kinds, from those that require none to those that require the full four-year high-school course.

Professional training.

Training.	Number.	Per cent.
One year (normal or college)	153	14
Two years	162	15
Three years	58	5
Four years or more	122	11
Reporting none or not reporting	582	54
Total	1,077	99

From these figures it is a fair inference that at least half of the teachers of the State have not completed a high-school course, and many have gone into teaching directly from the eighth grade. If reports had been obtained from all teachers, the percentage with less

"LONE STAR SCHOOL," DISTRICT NO. 1, SHERIDAN COUNTY.

DIFFICULTY GRAMMAR SCHOOL, DISTRICT NO. 32.

GRAMMAR SCHOOL, BASIN, WYO.

HIGH SCHOOL, GUERNSEY, WYO.

than a full high-school education and the percentage with elementary education only would probably be greater. Experience in collecting information from teachers in other States, particularly that relating to their education and training, shows that a larger percentage of those with poor training fail to reply than of those with good training.

A remedy for this condition in the general education of teachers is to make a four-year high-school course a prerequisite for examination for all grades of certificate and for entrance to all teacher-training courses. While this arrangement might seem to be inexpedient, because of the difficulty of obtaining teachers with higher standards than those at present employed, other States which have by legislation established such a standard as described above find that the supply rises to the demand in a few years.

While experience does not compensate for lack of professional training, it is evident that, other things being equal, a teacher without experience is not so well qualified as a teacher who has had successful experience. If the experience is obtained in a well-organized city system under expert supervision, it is of greater value than if obtained in rural districts without this advantage. However, experience without supervision is a factor in the efficiency of the teacher. The complete data on experience compiled from the replies to the questionnaires are somewhat unreliable, a few teachers having misinterpreted the question. According to it, of the 1,077 teachers, nearly 200 were teaching their first year. The remainder report experience varying from 1 year to 40 years, the average of those so reporting being 5 years. When extremes are so great, it is obvious that an average means little. Statistics are given concerning the teachers in one county which are far more accurate and are probably typical of conditions in the majority of counties in the State. This table shows that more than half the teachers have had no previous experience and that only a very small percentage, about 9, have had three years' experience or more. Three years may well be considered as the smallest possible amount of time necessary before one may be classed as following teaching as a serious life business.

Experience of the teachers of one county in Wyoming.

Experience.	Number.	Per cent.
Number of teachers in Laramie County	123	
Number teaching first year	67	54.4
Number teaching second year	27	21.9
Number teaching third year	20	16.3
Number teaching fourth year	3	2.4
Number teaching fifth year	2	1.6
Number teaching sixth year	1	.9
Number teaching seventh year	2	1.6
Number teaching more than seven years	1	.9

Progressiveness and professional spirit.—The table at the close of
this section shows data concerning summer school and correspondence courses and professional reading. Such items measure somewhat the teachers' ability to progress and to retain a professional
attitude toward her work. The majority of the teachers in Wyoming
do not attend summer schools; only 6 per cent of those replying
report attendance at one or more. The actual total number is
undoubtedly somewhat greater. About 6 per cent of the total
number reporting had taken some correspondence work; 16 per
cent had read no professional books, 35 per cent had read three such
books, and 32 per cent had read fewer than three books; only 8.6
per cent of the teachers report that they read professional magazines. It can not be concluded that this lack of professional spirit
is confined to immature and untrained teachers. Teachers who
hold normal-school diplomas often look upon them with a satisfied
sense of finality—in fact, the problem of training teachers is probably
matched by the equally great one of keeping them in training.
Perhaps the only remedy for this is professional supervision. This
is treated in a later chapter. In addition, renewal of certificates
should probably depend on evidence of professional progress, as shown
by the completion of reading-circle work, success grades given by the
supervising officer, or by some similar requirement.

The following table is a summary of the data relative to the 1,077
teachers reporting on the various items discussed in the preceding
pages:

TABLE 7.—Data concerning Wyoming teachers.

County	Number teachers in county, 1914-16.	Number teachers reporting.	Average age of those reporting age.	Number married.	Single or widows.	City grades per teacher	Rural grades per teacher	Number teaching in 1-teacher buildings.	First professional.	Second professional.	First class.	Second class.	Third class.	Diploma.	Special.	Temporary.	Elementary school only.	Some secondary, but less than 4 years.	Some secondary, but amount not reported.	Four years, secondary.	Number of teachers with degrees from college or normal schools.	Attendance in college or normal schools 1 to 4 years.	Number having attended summer schools.	Correspondence courses.	No book.	1 or 2 books.	3 books.	3 or more books.	Number reading professional magazines.	Teaching first year.	Teaching second year.	Teaching third year.	Teaching 4 years or more.
1 Albany	133		26	16		2	5	11	2	4	8			1	4	9	13	20		29		4		27		14	42	8	46	19	9	9	25
2 Big Horn	74	63	28	16	47	2	5	11	2	12	14	7	12	1	2	7	2	18	5	5	3	28	10	2		13	15	5	1	11	10	9	4
3 Campbell	38	51	25	8	41	1	7	20	5	5	1	16	3	3		7	1	17	7	20	3	45		2	13	6	5	5	1	11	10	8	37
4 Carbon	80	66	25	2	58	2	5	18	2	3	21	10	6	8	1	14	2	31	11	20	6	11		2	7	6	4	4	6	6	7	4	11
5 Converse	44	28	28	3	20	3	7	33	8	3	11	30	4		1	3	3	15	3	36	8	31	10	2	2	18	24	19	1	6	6	4	6
6 Crook	116	89	26	20	69	2	6	22	4	4	9	24	6		2	5	10	10	7	28	6	18	2	2	2	35	15	7		12	10	10	6
7 Fremont	89	54	25	15	39	1	6	18	4	2	9	9	7		2	6	1	9	0	28	6	12		2		36	9	4		10	5	6	25
8 Goshen	84	51	26	6	30	2	5	20	1	7	3	13	6		7	3	9	13	1	13	3	12	1	1	1	26	9	8	2	5	8	4	22
9 Hot Springs	35	31	25	4	27	1	5	17	8	3	10	13	2		3	2	2	13	9	13		12	4		2	12	5	4		5	11	4	15
10 Johnson	144	123	28	18	27	1	4	21	8	38	9	41	4	1		10	9	29	44	41	16	74	5	3	9	36	42	5	8	13	18	11	81
11 Laramie	174	102	28	9	53	2	5	18	3	20	10	16	2		2	8	2	14	24	22	4	35	8	1	3	13	13	6	2	13	14	13	28
12 Lincoln	129	62	28	8	104	1	5	17	4	12	8	18	4		7	3	1	26	24	26	5	33	8	1		22	12	9		13	8	2	27
13 Natrona	54	49	27	6	53	2	6	25	3	35	4	9	2	1	1	9	2	17	17	12	4	57	8		2	12	12	2		22	8	2	28
14 Niobrara	48	10	26	4	40	1	5	20	8	20	7	4	1	3	2	7	2	8	29	33	5	20	4		3	11	13	8	2	10	6	2	28
15 Park	157	104	27	11	93	2	6	18	4	17	10	18	1	1	10	2	6	14	17	26	8	62	8	1	21	32	36	6	1	23	17	17	84
16 Platte	112	110	25	11	104	1	6	17	3	12	8	14	5		1	10	1	31	20	26	6	25	3	1	3	12	8	8		22	16	6	28
17 Sheridan	119	51	27	7	60	2	6	15	7	35	10	18	2	2	2	4	1	18	15	28	7	25	4		2	16	14	8	1	12	9	5	29
18 Sweetwater	66	57	25	6	50	1	5	16	3	6	8	14	2		10	2	1	12	5	16	6	17	3		2	13	8	3		9	5	6	14
19 Uinta	59	67	25	6	48	1	6	18	3	6	10	18	1		1	3	2	16	9	9	7	22	3		3	16	14	7		11	9	5	29
20 Washakie	26	24	24	4	20	1	4	15	2	2	10	7			2	7	2	6	16	10	4	25	4		12	12	9	3	1	10	3	1	14
21 Weston	64	38	27	7	31	2	5	18	3	7	7	11	7		1	3	2	10	16	10	4	13	3	1	9	15	14	5	1	7	5	5	21
Total	1,633	1,077	66.0	164	913			541	80	217	144	350	120	18	40	105	70	273	297	437	87	495	67	64	170	337	278	170	93	198	156	139	544
Per cent		66.0		15.2	84.8			50.2	7.4	20.1	13.4	32.5	11.2	1.7	3.7	9.9	6.5	25.3	27.6	40.6	8.0	45.0	6.2	6.1	16.6	31.7	25.7	16.1	8.6	18.4	14.5	12.8	

Provision for teacher training.—At present the university is the only institution in the State preparing teachers for service in the public schools. The total enrollment in the normal-school department and college of education of the University of Wyoming for 1916 was 57. In 1914 there were 16 graduates from these two departments, 11 prepared especially for elementary and 5 for high-school work; in 1915 there were 15 graduates, 9 prepared for elementary and 6 for high-school work; in 1916 there were 23 graduates, 17 with preparation for elementary schools and 6 for high schools. Other graduates of the university are prepared to teach. The following is quoted from President Duniway:

Under our system graduates of the college of liberal arts who have taken requisite courses in professional education are equally entitled with the graduates of the college of education to teach in Wyoming schools. As a matter of fact, in 1916, six of the graduates of the college of liberal arts have been teachers or have prepared to be teachers. Furthermore, under our system the six graduates of the department of home economics have all been trained specifically to be teachers of home economics in high schools. * * * If we go beyond the matter of graduation, a great deal more in the way of teacher-training work is done by the University of Wyoming through its college of education. A considerable number of teachers take a course of one year and therefore do not graduate. A very much larger number come to summer schools or take correspondence study courses in professional subjects.

It is evident that the State is preparing a very small number of teachers for a Commonwealth with over 1,600 teachers in service. Unfortunately, data received from the teachers is too indefinite to make possible an accurate statement of the exact number of new teachers necessary each year to recruit the ranks of the teaching staff. The approximate number may be estimated, however, from experience in other States. An analysis of practically complete reports from the State of North Dakota shows that the average length of service of rural teachers in that State is two years; of those in cities and towns, five and one-half years. An estimate may be made also from the experience data of one county in Wyoming given on page 49 and from the results of the study of instruction in three counties given elsewhere in this report. From the first of these it appears that 54 per cent of the teachers in the county studied are inexperienced, and from the latter that 70 per cent of the teachers are employed for the first time in their respective districts. It is probable that, estimating very conservatively, one-fourth of the 1,600 teachers change each year. The State therefore undoubtedly requires not less than 400 new teachers each year. From the studies made it appears that not more than half of this number can be expected to come from other States. This leaves on the State of Wyoming the burden of preparing at least 200 teachers each year. At present it prepares from 15 to 20 per cent of that number.

As pointed out elsewhere in this report, untrained teachers are rarely able to conduct an efficient school. It may be reasonably expected that so long as such teachers are employed the money spent on schools is in a large measure wasted. The State must devise some means of offering professional training within reach of young people who desire to become teachers in order that the supply of adequately trained persons will at least approach the number demanded by annual changes in the force. It may be possible that the university, which is at present the teacher-training institution for the State, can make such adjustments as will enable it to meet this difficulty. But the committee, remembering the urgency of this need, and keeping in mind that it is the paramount duty of the State to remedy present conditions, must recommend a solution either through the university itself or by establishing additional normal schools to be conveniently located in different parts of the State under the management and direction of the State board of education.

INSTRUCTION.

It is recognized in the compilation of this report that no phase of school efficiency is more difficult to evaluate fairly, and that none is more difficult to express in terms which have real significance to the general observer, than the quality of the instruction. To visit every teacher in the State would be as easily possible as to judge fairly the work by such visit. It is possible, however, to make a reasonably careful study of relatively small territories more or less typical of general conditions in the State; and it is fair to assume that what is true in these sections will be a fair criterion by which to measure conditions throughout the State where in general the governing factors are similar. It is also possible to lay down certain necessary principles of instruction and certain defects in teaching which are so obvious and whose recognition is so widespread that, unless the former are adhered to and the latter avoided, only inefficiency can result. A large number of teachers in three widely separated counties were carefully observed by members of the committee and a representative of the bureau after certain well-defined principles of judgment had been agreed upon. Only the more obvious and generally accepted of these principles will be discussed.

Personality.—It is generally conceded among educators and laymen that a teacher, in order to be successful, should have certain personal qualities which help her to be an inspiration to the pupils and an example worthy of emulation, at least in so far as academic matters, such as the correct use of English, and general matters, such as good health, neatness of person, and similar factors, are concerned; similarly, that she should be an active and sympathetic member of the community in which she teaches, and should possess some qualities of leadership, at least sufficient to arouse interest in the school and make it something vital and positive to the community. This attitude may be shown in different ways—in the organization of boys' and girls' clubs, literary societies, and playground activities. The rural-school teacher ought to be far more a leader in the community than is here suggested, but at least this minimum may reasonably be required. It represents only the essentials, if the teacher is to have the respect and influence necessary to make her school worth while. It may be said of the teachers visited that they were in almost all cases young men or women physically fitted for their work, careful about personal neatness, habits, and manners, and conscientious in their desire to give good service. Unfortunately, when judged in regard to community service, such favorable conditions are not apparent. In not more than 10 per cent of the cases investigated was there any marked indication of leadership. Generally the attitude of the teacher is negative or at least passive. He or she considers that the four walls of the schoolroom should bound the legitimate activities of the teacher and the school. The school is an isolated institution, rather than a vital part of the community's life. The teacher comes into the community for a year, is a passive observer only, then moves on to another field, with no apparent desire to enter into the life of the people or to exert any influence more lasting than is left by the routine work of the schoolroom.

It must not be supposed that this unfortunate condition is always the fault of the teacher. There are factors governing the matter which only strong personalities can overcome. These lie dormant in the system itself and must be eliminated before the resulting conditions can be improved. Those relating to administration will be discussed later; it is sufficient to say here that living conditions and the existing method of selecting teachers are very potent factors. Of the teachers now under discussion, 70 per cent are teaching their first year in the district—an indication of a condition of constant change which makes real community interest and understanding quite out of the question. Nearly half (47 per cent) come from outside the State of Wyoming, and only a relatively few (less than 30 per cent) live in or near the district in which they teach.

Living conditions in the particular sections under consideration are better than in many of the more isolated and poorer districts in counties other than those visited. Yet 25 per cent have either no rooms of their own or no suitable place where they can retire, in comfort and quiet away from the family, for such study and preparation for school work as even well-trained modern teachers find necessary. Such conditions, for which the teachers are not immediately responsible, are not conducive to efficiency. No one does good work until living conditions are such as make for contentment, comfort, and happiness in one's work.

Again, the teacher can not create the community life, nor is it possible for her to play her own part in activities when the community itself is indifferent. There is practically no evidence of organized interest in the rural schools in the counties studied. While there are a few organizations, such as farmers' unions, the grange, women's clubs, and parent-teacher organizations, none of them are reported as cooperating helpfully for school improvement in the schools visited. In many places in the State they do cooperate, according to the statement of the State superintendent. In the particular communities under consideration such gatherings as are held in the schoolhouse—socials, dances, church, and Sunday school—are entirely isolated from school interests. This use of the schoolhouse is good, but it does not go far enough; it does not make the school the community center. In communities in which the people are indifferent the school directors are not as actively interested in school progress as they might be; they are indifferent to the general appearance and cleanliness of the house and grounds, and are parsimonious in supplying equipment. The majority of directors of the schools have children of their own in the school. Their immediate welfare, therefore, is concerned, yet two-thirds of them are reported as indifferent by the teachers. Their attitude is due not only to indifference, but to absorption in other interests and to a lack of knowledge as to what constitutes a good school. These conditions all have direct bearing on the attitude of the teachers and pupils, the discipline of the school, and the place of the school in the opinions and interests of parents and children. So long as these conditions are unchanged, the teachers, even if well qualified and experienced, will be handicapped in conducting efficient schools.

The teacher's ability to instruct.—Ability to instruct is governed by two main factors—(1) the material offered, or content of instruction, and (2) the manner or method in which it is presented. Practically all of the teachers visited nominally use the State course of study, but in reality they follow quite literally the arrangement of topics set forth in the particular text in use rather than the course of study. Since there is very little uniformity of books, there is also little uniformity in the work or in the grading. This is inevitable in a system in which each school is under the administration of a separate board of trustees. Each individual district is an entity in itself; the only connecting link is the county superintendent, and, as pointed out elsewhere, this official has under the present system practically no authority.

Legally the textbooks are selected by the board of trustees; in practice the teacher usually makes the selection. Some districts change books as often as they change teachers, generally annually: while in others, where the directors are either less accommodating or less generous or, as sometimes happens, have distinct opinions of their own, the books are rarely changed at all. Of course some county superintendents prevail upon school directors to select books in such a way that there is some uniformity in the county, and in like manner guide the teachers to follow an outlined course, but this is by no means universal. A study of the content of courses of study for the State, therefore, would mean practically a study for each particular district.

Since the schools visited were limited in number, only a few general conclusions will be drawn regarding the content of instruction. Modern practice in education assumes, since education is primarily for the purpose of preparing for definite life needs, that the subject matter of the curriculum should be closely related to the vocational life of the community and should be taught in terms that the children understand. For example, in rural communities arithmetic should not be presented through problems in shipbuilding or lumbering or manufacturing so much as through practical problems in farming, such as measuring the amount of hay in a stack, or computing the percentage of butter fat found in milk tested with the Babcock tester. Moreover, topics in the various subjects which have no relation to actual needs as represented by community interests—such, for example, as bank discount, cube and square root, in a farming community—are now omitted from the curriculum. These examples from arithmetic will serve to indicate what the material taught in this and other subjects should be. The survey committee finds little evidence of any effort to relate the subject matter of the course of study and textbooks to the life of the children. In geography, for example, the children were studying industries in the United States with little idea of what are the leading industries in the State of Wyoming. They were studying other States in the Union, but were unable to say whether these States are north, east, west, or south of the State in which they live. The arithmetic lessons observed were taken directly from the book, and the principles studied were not even illustrated in terms of familiar things. The history and geography consisted almost entirely of memorizing facts exactly as given in the book and then reproducing these in recitation. In this respect Wyoming country schools differ little from unsupervised schools in other States. Not all teaching was of this kind. One lesson in grammar will serve as an illustration, the exception. In this class the children were not learning rules or definitions from any book; they were simply learning to speak and write correctly short sentences and paragraphs concerning things with which they were familiar. The cow one milked and cared for, the pet lamb another was raising on a bottle, are examples. Such work, however, was rare. At least 90 per cent of the teaching observed showed a blind following of the textbook.

There was similar lack of adaptation on the basis of different tastes, changing interests, and varied abilities of children. In reading, for example, successive lessons in the textbook were followed. One lesson as numbered in the book seemed to be the standard day's work. In some cases the children observed read fluently and understandingly and could very well have read another selection, or, better, could have found more material on the same subject from other books; yet when the lesson was completed, the children, without being directed to do so, went back to the beginning of the lesson and reread it. Evidently this had become the fixed plan and needed no explanation. In other cases the children read poorly and apparently with very little understanding of the content of the material read, yet the reading went on as before, each pupil taking his turn, being corrected in pronunciation now and then, but with no apparent effort made to enlist the interest or to consider the abilities of the children in any case. Similar work was found in spelling. The words in the book were followed whether they were such as the children used in their ordinary writing vocabularies or not. If the lesson in the book consisted of 10 words, 10 words were given out regardless of the difficulty of the words or of the ability of the children to learn more or less than a lesson of that particular length.

Methods.—Some idea of the teaching method will be gained from the foregoing. Indeed, content and method are so closely related that in any discussion they will of necessity overlap. Here again, only a few of the most obvious principles will be discussed. It is a well-accepted idea in education that the schools should develop power, initiative, judgment, ability to select the important and omit the trivial, should impart economical methods of study, ability to read understandingly and rapidly, and similar qualities which need not be enumerated here. These do not include mere memorizing of facts as set down in the textbook without regard to their use and as if all facts were of equal importance; though this was the kind of lesson heard almost invariably. If any effort is made in the schools visited to develop the abilities mentioned above, it was not apparent during the visits made, at least not in any but exceptional cases. Although there was every evidence that the children were unable to select important facts from the book and organize details in reference to these, not a single lesson was heard in which such organization was taught or suggested. Practically every class showed lack of ability to study intelligently; yet no study lessons were seen or reported. Questions were formulated directly from the book and were answered

either by yes or no or by a quotation from the text. Usually the
questions were asked in the order in which they appeared in the book,
and it was practically always necessary for the teacher to keep the
book open constantly. It is uncertain whether this was in order not
to omit anything in its exact book sequence or because the teacher
was so unfamiliar with the text as to need the book for her own reference. Assignments were usually given as so many pages, occasionally so many topics, in the same order as given in the book, and
showed neither thought nor preparation on the part of the teacher.

The teachers observed showed very little appreciation of the fact
that the aim or purpose of a lesson should govern the way in which
it is taught. Literature was oftener word pronunciation than a lesson for appreciation or joy in the reading. History was drill in facts
or an exercise in memory more often than a study of life and institutions. In short, the recitations in general were merely question
and answer methods of finding how familiar the children had become
with the particular pages assigned in the textbook.

It should be added that here again, in method as in content, there
are exceptions. Many teachers in Wyoming are doing excellent
work. For example, one school visited presented an attractive appearance, of which any community might be proud. The teacher
was teaching her third successive year in the district, was well trained,
and had had successful experience elsewhere previous to her engage-
ment in that district. The school was equipped with simple apparatus for manual training and cooking, placed inconspicuously in the
rear of the room. There was every indication that the methods and
discipline and influence of this teacher were without exception good.
Only a few miles from this school is located one of the poorest of
those visited in the county. Here was found an untrained, inexperienced, indifferent teacher; the house and grounds were dirty and in
bad condition. There were no signs of orderliness or efficiency.

The difference between these two schools located so close together
merely illustrates the fact that each individual district in Wyoming
is a law unto itself, free to have as poor schools as the community
will endure. There is no system of equality either of opportunity
for the children or of expense in conducting the school for the patron.
Doubtless the children in the latter district were much the same in
all substantial ways as those of the former. Both will help to make
up the citizenship of the county and the State.

Summary.—The constitution of the State of Wyoming guarantees
an adequate education to *all*, not *some* of its children; yet glaring
inequalities exist. Here and there may be found children attending
good schools and enjoying the comfort, convenience, and benefit of
modern equipment and competent teachers; but while these advan-

tages are available to a small percentage of the children, a great many (probably 70 per cent is a conservative estimate if the groups visited are any criterion) have none or only a few of these advantages, and such as they have are available not regularly, but only accidentally, during a year or two of their school lives.

These conditions can be remedied only by a systematic reform in several different directions.

(1) A better method of selecting teachers should be practiced, in order that educational qualifications and professional training may be given more consideration, and tenure during good service assured. It has been pointed out that lack of training on the part of teachers is obvious in the majority of the rural schools. Unless teachers have a general education at least four years in advance of the grades they are to teach, they can scarcely be expected to have broad enough foundation for satisfactory school instruction. Unless they are trained for the profession of teaching in the fundamental aims of education and how they are accomplished, as well as in the understanding of the physical and mental nature and interests of children, they are unable either to instruct pupils or to organize and discipline a school. In order to supply better trained teachers, the State must furnish better facilities than at present exist for training teachers, especially for work in ungraded schools. There are few cities in the State, and the rural teachers outnumber those of the cities greatly; consequently special training for rural work is the important need under existing conditions.

(2) The problem of supervision will be discussed later and need only be referred to here as a necessary factor in good instruction. One feels in visiting them that the teachers now in service would do far better work if they were directed by trained, experienced supervisors.

(3) Centralization of administrative authority is necessary. At present the selection of books, the outlining of the course of study, and the administration of other strictly educational matters are in the hands of laymen instead of experienced educators. The units of administration are too small and too widely scattered to make for system, uniformity, or efficiency. There should be a more detailed and better adapted course of study, and teachers should be taught the best methods of using it through preliminary training and through associations for training in service. More uniformity should be secured in the school books used, either through county or State adoption of textbooks.

(4) Better living conditions should be provided for teachers. Either teachers' cottages should be erected on the school grounds or living rooms should be provided as additions to schoolhouses,

unless satisfactory boarding places can be found in the homes of the people.

SUPERVISION.

It is not within the province or scope of this report to discuss the necessity of adequate supervision in school systems. It is sufficient to say that modern school practice assumes it to be a necessity, that practically all of the towns in the United States of 2,500 or over in population have provided for it, and that many of the progressive States in the Union have made or are making provision to extend such facilities to rural communities. Wyoming is especially in need of adequate supervision for its country schools, because there are so many inexperienced and untrained teachers employed, because teachers and schools are isolated by great distances, and because the teaching corps is largely recruited from outside the State. Such teachers need in a special manner professional advice and instruction to help them to organize and conduct schools successfully and to make such adaptations of school subjects to community needs as modern ideas of education demand. This direction only experienced supervisors — well-trained and mature persons familiar with the State—can give.

Such supervision as Wyoming rural schools have is now given by the county superintendents. The efficiency of county supervision is conditioned by many factors, a few of which will be discussed here. It is evident that the superintendent must be a mature and experienced person, trained for the particular field of supervision, if he is to be able to give expert advice to the teachers under his jurisdiction. It follows, then, that the manner of selecting the superintendents, the salaries offered, and tenure, should be such as to attract the most capable men and women to enter and remain in this field. These factors will be considered first.

Selection.—The county superintendents of Wyoming are elected by popular vote at the regular general election. The laws covering election, salary, powers, and duties of county superintendents were made many years ago. Not only conditions, but educational ideals and practice, have changed materially, and however well these laws may have answered at that time the purposes for which they were made, their adequacy is entirely outgrown at the present time. Education has now become an established profession; the county superintendent must be an educator, not a politician, and must be selected because of professional fitness. So long as he is elected at a general political election every two years, depending for success upon his ability to get votes instead of on his ability to supervise schools, the position will not appeal to many competent persons trained in the educational field.

Salary.—Another equally unfortunate factor—the salary—increases the difficulty of obtaining and retaining efficient superintendents. The constitution limits the salary of the county superintendent to $1,000 a year, and by legislative enactment which fixes the salaries all counties pay less even than this. Of the 21 superintendents in the State, seven receive $900, seven $750, and seven $500, the average salary for the State being $717 per year. Many teachers of the State receive more, and the anomalous situation of a subordinate receiving a higher salary than his supervising officer is not uncommon in Wyoming. The average salary of city superintendents in the six largest cities of Wyoming is $2,340.

Tenure.—The inadequate salary and the method of selection would alone be sufficient obstacles to securing competent superintendents, but the tenure is equally unsatisfactory. Good work is not always rewarded at popular elections. Two years is too short a time in which to carry out educational reforms, especially when the superintendent's function is advisory only, and these reforms must come about through his ability to persuade a large number of directors, three for each district, to adopt them. Even the misfortune of accepting persons not specially trained in supervision would be overcome in some degree if the incumbents of the county superintendencies remained long enough, so that experience in the position would compensate in some measure for lack of training. In actual practice, however, this does not happen. Of the superintendents replying to questionnaires sent out by the Bureau of Education, exactly one-half are serving their first term. A study of the records seems to show that the time of service is shorter in recent years than in the earlier period of Statehood.

TABLE 8.—*Length of service, in years, of county superintendents in Wyoming since January, 1891,[1] including term of present incumbents, ending Jan. 1, 1917.*

Counties.	Number years organized.	Number of different superintendents.[2]	Average tenure, in years.	Counties.	Number years organized.	Number of different superintendents.[2]	Average tenure, in years.
Albany	26	6	4.3	Lincoln	4	1	4.0
Big Horn	20	5	4.0	Natrona	26	10	2.6
Campbell	4	2	2.0	Niobrara	4	1	4.0
Carbon	26	5	5.1	Park	8	2	4.0
Converse	26	7	3.7	Platte	4	1	4.0
Crook	26	11	2.4	Sheridan	26	8	3.2
Fremont	26	7	3.7	Sweetwater	26	9	2.9
Goshen	4	1	4.0	Uinta	26	8	3.2
Hot Springs	4	1	4.0	Washakie	4	1	4.0
Johnson	26	9	2.9	Weston	26	7	3.7
Laramie	26	4	6.5				

[1] Wyoming became a State in July, 1890. The first county superintendents elected since that time took office January, 1891.
[2] These numbers are approximately correct. No records could be obtained for one 2-year period, and the names of one or two superintendents are not included in the report of the State department in several instances.

Training.—With all these adverse conditions, it would be strange, indeed, if Wyoming were able to secure for its county superintendencies many men and women professionally prepared for their work. The necessity for careful training and special preparation for supervisors and teachers both is now fully established in progressive communities. Teaching is a profession as well defined in its function as that of the law, medicine, or engineering, and one should as readily, and could as safely, trust an untrained person with the care of his ill child as with that child's training and education. Wherever adequate expert supervision is provided for rural districts, as in Ohio and in New England, in the small cities of the United States, and in the cities of the State of Wyoming itself, not less than eight years of secondary and higher education is considered necessary preparation for this work. Wyoming has not yet reached the place where training of this kind can be demanded or expected of rural supervisors. An earnest attempt was made to secure information from the 21 county superintendents now in office relative to their general education, professional education, and experience. The information was given by 16 of the superintendents. From the other 5 no answers were received, although three separate requests were sent, two from the Bureau of Education and one from the State superintendent's office. If experience in collecting similar data elsewhere is of any value the five not reporting are below the standards of the others in training and education.

The 16 report on general education as follows:

Elementary school only.. 3
Some high school, but less than four years. 3
High school, but no further.. 1
High school and less than one year of college................................... 6
High school and two years of college 2
High school and four years of college... 1

Only a higher salary, assured tenure, a method of selection which will give consideration to educational qualifications rather than political ones, can be expected to improve this condition.

No consideration of the office of county superintendent is complete which does not recognize the difficulties of the work itself under existing conditions, regardless of the qualifications, salary, tenure, etc., of the persons selected. The size of the territory to cover, the number of buildings and teachers to visit, in conjunction with the traveling allowance and assistance available, are important factors in efficiency. Where there is a large percentage of inexperienced or untrained teachers, or where special difficulties are being met or experiments carried on, the superintendent must make frequent visits. If distances are great, as in Wyoming, assistants are necessary. The counties in Wyoming vary in area from 2,000 to 12,000 square miles. The average size is 4,500 square miles. The number of teachers to be supervised varies from 26 to 130, averaging 55; and the number of buildings to be visited varies from 14 to 115, averaging 45. On an average the county superintendents in Wyoming pay one visit to each teacher a year, and the average time spent in each schoolroom each year is one and one-half hours. It would seem to be a physical impossibility for one superintendent to cover a territory af 12,000 square miles, visit 73 teachers in 50 different buildings, even if there were no further handicaps. Add to this the fact that the mileage allowance in the county referred to is small, entirely inadequate, indeed, to cover necessary expenses of travel, that no supervisory assistants are furnished, and the difficulty is practically insurmountable. Very few superintendents have an adequate mileage allowance. The system itself, which permits a board [1] not primarily interested in schools, the very nature of whose duties makes economy the desideratum, to fix the travel allowance, is sufficient evidence that a change is imperative. The county superintendent is the only person who can judge when and how often the schools should be visited. There is no possibility of visiting them too often under present conditions.

Some idea of the relative attractiveness as to salaries, number of assistants, tenure, etc., of the city and county superintendencies in Wyoming, as well as the probable efficiency of the teaching force supervised (and therefore the necessity of close supervision), as judged from educational qualifications in city and county, may be had from the following comparison. The statistics given represent the average in five of the seven cities in Wyoming which have a population greater than 2,500 in column marked "City" and the average for 16 counties in the State in the column marked "County." These include all the superintendents who reported.

TABLE 9.—*Comparison of statistics concerning county and city superintendents in Wyoming.*

	City.	County.
Average time in present position..........................years..	6	2
Average number of assistant superintendents or supervisory assistants..............	4	0
Average number of teachers per supervisor.................................	23	55
Average number of visits to each teacher by supervising officers (per year).........	50	1
Average salary of superintendent...	$2,340	$743
TEACHERS.		
Minimum professional training required....................................years..	2	0
Teachers engaged having professional training.........................per cent..	92	[2] 40
Teachers having full 4 years of higher education..............................do....	60	[2].5

[1] Allowance for traveling expenses is made by the county commissioners.
[2] Estimated from tabulations made from reports of 1,000 teachers.

Summary.—It is evident that insufficient salary, uncertain tenure, the manner of selection, and size of the territory conspire to render real supervision a practical impossibility.

The county superintendent in an occasional friendly visit to the school can encourage and help the teacher and the pupils. He can inspect the building and grounds and often interview the directors and persuade them to do many things for the good of the school that would otherwise be neglected. There is no disposition to underestimate the benefit of such work, but it can not be classed as professional supervision. There is little reason to doubt the spirit, devotion, and conscientiousness which characterize the present body of county superintendents, but they are too much handicapped to do effective work.

Table 10 shows the maximum, minimum, and average salaries paid county superintendents in six Western States. These will offer a basis of comparison for salaries paid similar officers in Wyoming.

Table 11 is inserted to show what is possible in rural supervision when conditions as to selection, tenure, salary, etc., are such as to attract professionally trained supervisors. The counties are the first 16 counties in order on the tabulation sheets in the office of the Bureau of Education, and were compiled from reports sent in from the county superintendents.

In Maine the territory is small, enabling supervisors to visit frequently. In Ohio the assistant supervisors are numerous enough to insure adequate supervision, though the table does not show this in the number of visits made, because the system was just being inaugurated (under provision of a new law) when the reports were sent in.

TABLE 10.—*Salaries of county superintendents in 7 Western States reporting to Bureau of Education.*

States.	Maximum.	Minimum.	Average.
California	$4,000	$700	$2,300
Washington	2,100	700	1,280
Colorado	2,800	100	1,200
Utah	3,400	1,500	2,300
Nevada	2,000	2,000	2,000
Idaho	2,000	1,100	1,320
Nebraska	2,200	700	1,400
Montana	1,500	900	1,430
Oregon	1,800	1,200	1,500
Wyoming	900	500	717

DISTRICT SCHOOL, WARREN, MONT.

TABLE 11.—*Sixteen rural superintendents of Ohio, Maine, and Wyoming.*

[Includes all reporting from Wyoming and the first 16 in bureau lists from the other States.]

		Education and training.				School buildings.	One-teacher building.	Teachers.	Area.	Assistants.	
	Salary.	High school[1]	Normal.	College.	Degree.					Supervisory.	Clerical.
Ohio (County superintendents.)	2,300	X	....	X	A. B.	98	71	164	500	4	1
	3,000	X	....	X	A. B., A. M.	141	110	242	640	9	
	2,000	X	X	....	A. B.	109	98	155	400	6	
	2,000	X		X	B. S.	138	120	196	....	4	
	1,500	X		X	B. S., M. S.	130	170	188	625	6	
	2,000	X		X	A. B., A. M.	84	63	150	400	4	
	2,500	X		5(S)		130	120	617	325	10	
	1,200	X		X	A. B.	90	75	240	1,200	1	
	1,900	X		X	Ph. B., Ph. M.	103	52	173	401	6	
	2,000	X		X	Ph. B.	....	92	140	350	3	
	2,340	X		X	A. B.	55	38	130	420	3	
	2,000	X		X	A. B., A. M.	136	129	175	430	5	
	2,300	X		X	A. B.	125	110	190	424	8	
	2,100	X		X	A. B., A. M.	102	90	154	432	2	
	2,500	X		X	A. M.	116	96	282	414	11	
	2,500	X		X	A. B., A. M.	126	107	177	400	6	
Maine (Union district superintendents.)	1,550	X	2	X	A. B.	20	11	56	72		
	1,550	X		X	A. B.	23	11	45	100		
	1,575	X		X	A. B.	18	11	33	....		
	1,800	X	2			36	31	57	108		
	1,200	X		X	A. B.	18	12	25	108	2	
	1,500	X	1½			19	9	45	40		
	300	X				9	5	15	60		
	1,200	X			A. M.	22	21	25	108		
	1,750	X	5	X	A. B.	14	9	31	45		
	300	X		8	A. B., M. D.	19	18	21	100		
	1,300	X		X	A. B.	25	19	29	....		
	1,200	X	2	1	B. Pd.	10	7	29	70		
	1,225	X	X			46	41	59	216		
	1,400	X		X	Ph. B.	27	7	34	70		
	1,510	X	2 S	X	A. B.	20	7	32	60		
	2,300	X		X	A. B.	18	15	46	80		
Wyoming (County superintendents.)	750	X				29	15	61	2,000		
	600	X		2	2 S	19	17	26	2,300		4 1
	900		2½		3 C	61	36	120	12,000		
	750	X	X	½		40	25	78	2,880		
	750	X		X	A. B.	36	31	54	4,040		
	750					50	45	73	20,000		
	600	1				25	23	40	3,125		
	600		X	1	1	130	126	140	2,800		
	600	2		2 S		41	38	54	2,500		
	900	X		2 S		45	33	71	9,000		
	600					46	38	87	2,100		
	600	X		2		27	26	45	6,000		
	900					100	80	160	4,200		4 1
	900	3	2	2		19	17	52	5,200		
	600	X				19	16	37	1,800		
	750	X				38	35	57	4,900		4 1

[1] Cross indicates full 4 years; figures, number of years if more or less than 4.
[2] S means attended summer school.
[3] C, correspondence work.
[4] Part time.

III. REVENUE FOR THE SUPPORT OF SCHOOLS.[1]

Wyoming is a State of scattered population and of rich and undeveloped resources. In the last decade vast mineral and oil deposits have been opened up. Irrigation and reclamation projects involving a large amount of capital have been initiated, railroads and auto roads projected, and a new era of development has begun. This has been accompanied by a corresponding increase in population. The United States Census reports of 1910 show a population of 145,965, an increase of 57.7 per cent over 1900, while the total increase for the United States was 21 per cent. Wyoming is, therefore, growing in population nearly three times as rapidly as the country as a whole.

The rural population of the State is correspondingly prosperous and growing and constitutes 65.7 per cent of the total population. The value of farm property increased during the 10-year period 1900 to 1910 approximately 148 per cent; 92 per cent of the total number of farms in the State are operated by owners, and 80 per cent of these owned farms are free from mortgage; 57 per cent of the total number of farms in the State are irrigated.

The percentage of increase in irrigation works, in the output of mines and wells, in manufacturing and industries, corresponds to the increase in farm values. Wyoming has no State debt, is prosperous and growing, and can provide liberally for the education of its children. It should take such anticipatory measures as will insure adequate facilities for the future, as well as for the immediate present.

The State has a higher property valuation per school child than any State of the North Atlantic, South Atlantic, or South Central groups; higher than four States in the Western group and higher than any in the North Central group except Nebraska, North Dakota, and Iowa. There are 269 adults in Wyoming to bear the expense of educating each group of 100 children between the ages of 5 and 18 years, a larger number than in any other State in the Union except California. Of adult men 21 years and over Wyoming has 179 for every 100 children between 5 and 18 years—more than any State in the Union except Nevada. A comparison of Wyoming with the States bordering it in these three particulars follows:

[1] Figures in this section were taken from the reports of the State superintendent of public instruction, the State auditor, special reports to the bureau made by county superintendents, and by a few district boards. The figures on Lincoln County were prepared by Supt. Burch, of Kemmerer, as were also some of those on other counties, the information resulting from a questionnaire sent by Mr. Burch for the committee to all county superintendents.

Value of property for each school child:[1]

Idaho	$5,900
Utah	6,300
South Dakota	7,500
Wyoming	**10,200**
Nebraska	10,700
Colorado	11,100
Montana	12,300

Number of adults for each 100 children 5 to 18 years of age:

Utah	160
South Dakota	175
Nebraska	182
Idaho	190
Colorado	231
Montana	261
Wyoming	**269**

Number of men 21 or over for each 100 children 5 to 18 years of age:

Utah	85
Nebraska	95
South Dakota	96
Idaho	113
Colorado	125
Montana	165
Wyoming	**179**

A growing and progressive, and therefore a rapidly changing State must look forward if it would be ready to provide for emergencies as they arise. Such anticipatory provision is especially necessary in considering financial support for public schools. In no particular is a rapid increase in population more noticeable or more difficult to provide for than in proper and adequate education. Wyoming has had this situation to meet, as may be seen from diagrams 1, 2, and 3, which indicate graphically the increase in attendance, the per capita expenditure, and the total expenditure. That the situation has not always been met satisfactorily has already been indicated in the section devoted to instruction and supervision. As was pointed out in that section, this is partly due to lack of adequate financial support, as well as to other causes mentioned.

Wyoming must provide, for the present at least, for conditions brought about by scattered population and highly differentiated local valuations. Rich coal region districts, containing valuable improvements, machinery, railroad terminals, etc., constitute a school unit immediately adjoining large tracts of unproductive land whose value

---

[1] This means that an average school district of 40 children in Idaho, for example, would have behind it property valued at $236,000, and 76 adult men and women, 45 of whom would be men 21 years of age and over. In Wyoming the average school of this size would have behind it property valued at $408,000, and 108 adults, 76 of whom would be men 21 years of age and over.

and corresponding assessable possibilities are negligible. It is evident that if local taxation alone is to be depended upon for school support there can be no equality of burdens for the tax payer except at the expense of school facilities. But education is a State function, as necessary to the preservation of the State's integrity and progress as are the capitol building and the legislature itself. The State must therefore devise means to equalize educational opportunity and expense within its borders. The legislature has made attempts to do this, notably in passing a law providing that districts receive $300 from the county for every teacher employed, regardless of the size of the district. Other steps in the same direction are necessary, however.

Sources of revenue.—The schools of Wyoming derive their support from three sources, the State school fund, the county general tax, and the special local levy. In addition there are rentals from forest reserves, the penal fund, and revenue from poll taxes. In this report these will not be considered separately, however, but as part of the special and county fund, nor will the expense of collecting and the loss from failure to collect the tax be considered.

Revenue from the State.—The permanent State school fund from the sale of school lands, escheats, forfeitures, grants, gifts, etc., amounts to $1,015,364.84. Approximately two-thirds of this is invested in school funds drawing 5 or 6 per cent interest, and about one-third is deposited in banks drawing 3 per cent interest. There are approximately 3,450,000 acres of land for the support of the elementary and secondary schools of the State. Approximately three-fourths of the yearly income from the State comes from the rentals of these lands. The total income for the year ended March, 1916, from the above-named sources (interest on permanent funds and rentals) was $332,132, or $8.39 per school child, there being 39,584 between 6 and 21 years of age in the State in 1915. Under Federal regulations 25 per cent of the money derived from leasing the forest reserve lands and the sale of timber thereon must be turned over to the State for the benefit of the schools and public roads of the county or counties in which the reserve is situated. The commissioners of the respective counties decide how much of this fund shall be used for each of the two purposes, 5 per cent being the minimum amount which can be used for either.

Revenue from the county.—The county commissioners of each county are required by law to levy a general county school tax sufficient to raise $300 for each teacher employed in the county, provided that for each teacher for which credit is claimed there is an average attendance of 6 in "grade schools"[1] and 10 in high schools, and pro-

---

[1] Interpreted by the Supreme Court not to refer to ungraded one-teacher country schools.

vided also that there is a minimum term of six months. It is the duty of the commissioners to levy a poll tax of $2 for each person between the ages of 21 and 50, to be used for school purposes only and for the exclusive use of the school fund in the district in which the same is located. All fines and penalties under the general laws of the State go into the public school fund of the respective districts.

Revenue from the district.—The property owners in a school district may, at the annual district meeting, vote a special tax of 3½ mills for school purposes. An additional amount not exceeding 5 mills on all the taxable property of the district may be voted at any regular or special meeting, provided 30 days' notice has been given.

Bonds.—The board of school trustees may submit to the property owners of the school district the question of authorizing the board to issue coupon bonds, not to exceed 2 per cent of the taxable property in the district, at a rate of interest not higher than 6 per cent, for a period not longer than 25 years, for the purpose of building schoolhouses and providing the necessary furniture or for refunding outstanding indebtedness.

INEQUALITY OF THE PRESENT SYSTEM OF TAXATION.

State support.—From the standpoint of a State the question of financing schools centers about these considerations: (1) Is the revenue provided sufficient to insure at least reasonable minimum school facilities? (2) Are the provisions for raising and distributing it equitable? (3) Are the several units from which funds come, State, county, and school district, all bearing their proper share of the burden?

That the first consideration is not satisfactorily met is apparent from the preceding chapters on instruction, supervision, and teaching corps. In addition it may be of interest to compare Wyoming with other Western States as to per capita expenditure and expenditure per $100 of assessed valuation. The following statement shows that in 1912-13 Wyoming spent less per capita of school population than eight other Western States. In 1913-14 an encouraging improvement was made, but the State is still near the bottom of the list. Later figures are not available.

TABLE 12.—*Per capita expenditures for schools.*

States.	In 1912-13.	In 1913-14.	States.	In 1912-13.	In 1913-14.
Wyoming	$31.37	$33.13	Nevada	$40.24	$40.72
Colorado	31.58	31.02	Washington	42.76	40.57
Utah	34.26	34.66	Montana	48.99	41.48
Idaho	36.11	33.71	California	49.28	49.58
Oregon	36.39	34.63			

The following table shows how much several Western States spent on education per $100 of assessed valuation. The figures are for 1912, the latest available. A comparison on *true* valuation is given elsewhere in this report. (See p. 94.)

TABLE 13.—*Wealth and school expenditure in 1902 and 1912.*

States.	Assessed valuation of all property subject to ad valorem taxation, 1912.	Expenditure for public schools, excluding debt paid, 1912.	Expended for public schools on each $100 of assessed valuation of all property.	
			1902	1912
			Cents.	Cents.
United States................................	$69,452,936,104	$482,886,793	66.6	69.5
Western Division:				
Montana..............................	346,550,585	3,354,934	47.4	96.8
Wyoming..............................	180,750,690	997,022	58.5	55.2
Colorado..............................	422,330,199	6,527,569	87.6	154.6
New Mexico...........................	72,457,454	1,112,840	62.4	153.6
Arizona...............................	140,338,191	1,321,631	96.4	94.2
Utah..................................	200,299,207	3,626,686	118.6	181.1
Nevada...............................	101,087,082	625,562	71.4	61.9
Idaho.................................	167,512,157	2,959,194	112.4	176.7
Washington............................	1,005,086,251	10,526,981	107.5	104.7
Oregon................................	905,011,679	6,095,111	121.7	67.3
California.............................	2,921,277,451	23,978,621	59.0	82.1

The inefficiency of administration and the inequitable distribution of funds are responsible for much waste, and these administrative agencies are so closely connected with the financial agencies that it is difficult to differentiate clearly and show just how much is due to lack of economical administration and how much to insufficient funds. But the poor buildings and equipment, low salaries, etc., described in preceding chapters, indicate that, for the immediate present at least, more money will be needed to provide adequate educational facilities and that the State itself will need to aid more substantially than it has in the past. This may be justified on the basis of fairness as well as necessity, because of scattered population and because so much of the wealth of the State (coal and oil, for example) really contribute to State as well as to local prosperity. The exact methods of accomplishing this will be discussed later in the report.

The second and third considerations regarding the raising and distributing of the revenue will be more fully described under county and special taxation and will be referred to only briefly here. In a State in which the district system prevails, as in Wyoming, a just distribution of school expense is best attained when the State pays approximately one-third, the county one-third, the local district one-third. Many districts in the State have a low property valuation and a large school population, and even with a high special levy are unable to provide good schools. Other districts have a large valuation, few school children, and little or no special levy. The State, while assuming its share of educational burdens, must see to it that the local district also does its share, and likewise the county assumes a fair share of the burden. Table 14 shows the percentage of total income received from each of the three different sources in all of the counties of the State. The State fund is now distributed on a per capita basis, and, as would be expected under such a system, some counties are receiving from the State a far higher percentage of their total school expenditure than others. Three counties receive one-third or over, two receive but one-sixth, and the others receive amounts varying between these extremes. Later in this report [1] it will be shown that the unfairness of distribution is even more marked when considered from a district standpoint than when considered from a county standpoint.

TABLE 14.—*Sources of school funds in Wyoming.*

Counties.	Amount received from—			Per cent received from—		
	State.	County.	Local.	State.	County.	Local.
Albany	$17,191	$31,863	$36,133	20.18	37.40	42.42
Big Horn	20,144	21,630	26,646	29.44	31.62	38.94
Carbon	17,560	23,462	26,567	25.98	34.71	39.31
Campbell	4,833	11,906	12,828	16.35	40,26	43.39
Converse	7,929	12,641	20,064	19.51	31.11	49.38
Crook	18,506	18,418	17,553	33.97	33.81	32.22
Fremont	15,429	24,977	23,494	24.15	39.06	36.77
Goshen	11,209	13,709	13,308	29.32	35.86	34.82
Hot Springs	5,663	4,080	17,437	20.84	15.01	64.15
Johnson	8,482	12,072	11,283	26.64	37.92	35.44
Laramie	34,793	55,079	65,973	22.33	35.34	42.33
Lincoln	36,253	36,695	27,453	36.11	36.55	27.34
Natrona	10,043	16,471	35,671	16.15	26.49	57.36
Park	8,768	14,022	17,096	21.96	35.16	42.86
Platte	12,392	16,660	25,902	22.55	30.32	47.13
Sheridan	13,265	26,695	33,149	18.14	36.52	45.34
Sweetwater	34,407	35,275	62,711	25.99	26.64	47.37
Uinta	26,054	19,574	20,423	39.45	29.63	30.92
Washakie	15,655	18,150	28,746	25.03	29.02	45.95
Weston	4,388	8,700	8,868	19.98	39.63	40.39
	11,142	16,432	16,303	25.39	37.45	37.16
State	....	....	....	25.31	33.22	41.47

It is obvious that when population is scattered, as in Wyoming, and ranches are isolated, there will be certain communities in which schools will have a very small enrollment. However, the expense of maintaining a school, including the salary of the teacher, is practically the same whether 5 or 25 children are enrolled, yet the one receives from the State approximately one-fifth as much as the other. Again, the State apportionment is made on a basis of district census, which includes all children in the district from 6 to 21 years of age. The expense of maintaining school is concerned only with those children between 6 and 14 [2] where elementary schools only are supported and those between 6 and 18 [2] years of age where there are high schools. There is no apparent reason for giving school money to young men and women who have finished school, some of whom are now married and have children of their own. Further-

---

[1] See tables concerning Lincoln county.   [2] Inclusive.

more, distribution on a per capita basis has no educational significance, because it places no premium on local effort unless it stimulates each community to get names on the census list. The tendency is to cause districts to rely entirely on State and county funds, and to reduce salaries and term of school so that the total expenditure is within the amount so received.

An apportionment based one-half on number of teachers and one-half on the aggregate daily attendance would be a far more equitable one in Wyoming and would give individual communities an incentive to work for better school attendance and longer terms. Aggregate attendance is the average daily attendance multiplied by the number of days in the annual school session. There is the possible objection that such a distribution, if large enough to pay the entire salary of the teacher, may encourage districts to engage more teachers than are needed. This possibility would be avoided if funds were distributed to approved schools only, as suggested in another portion of this report.[1]

Not only is it good policy on the part of a State to encourage local initiative, but statistics given show that in Wyoming it seems absolutely essential to force certain backward communities to assume a just share of educational expenditure. Seventy per cent of the counties in the State contain some districts which make no local tax levy; on the other hand many communities with low taxable valuation and a large number of children enrolled in school are paying a very high levy and still are unable to provide satisfactory school facilities. The State could profitably increase its school fund by a special State tax. Part of this should be added to the income of the permanent fund as already constituted and part should form a reserve fund under the jurisdiction of the State board of education. This reserve fund should be apportioned to deserving districts for certain needs which can not be met locally when the maximum special levy has been made. A considerable amount of this reserve fund should also be available for assisting schools which make special effort in any direction recommended by the State board—such as the establishment of secondary schools or the introduction of special subjects like agriculture, cooking, and sewing.

The advantages of State over county taxation are the same as those of the county over the district. By a partial pooling of effort, longer terms and better teachers can be secured throughout the State than if each district were left entirely to itself.

Perhaps all children can not have absolutely equal advantages, but it is the duty of the State to secure a certain agreed-upon *minimum*, and to encourage communities to extend their educational energies as far as possible to new and desirable undertakings. Such advan-

---

[1] See recommendations relative to county board of education.

tages as the State deems absolutely necessary it must require and
must help the communities to finance.

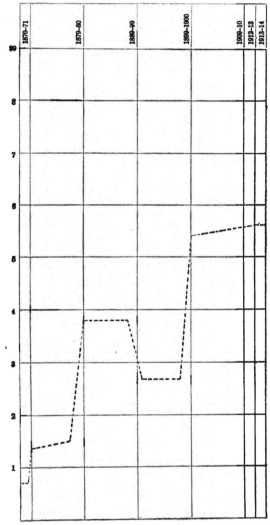

Fig. 2.—Increase in per capita expenditure of total population for schools
in Wyoming, 1870-1914.

Other things being equal, in an equitably adjusted system (always
omitting buildings and permanent improvements) the tax levy for

school maintenance should be approximately the same in all districts, and the income per school unit (that is, one teacher and the group of children under her charge) should approximate uniformity. In any classification made as to administration and taxation, these considerations, together with the fact that it is the paramount duty of the State to provide adequate education for all its children, should be carefully observed. It is important to see how nearly Wyoming approaches such a standard.

County and district support.—Table 15 shows the assessed valuation, county, general, and special local tax levies, census valuation per school child, and approximate State apportionment. It will be seen from this table that the different counties bear very unequal shares of total school expenditure through county general taxation and, consequently, must either have poor schools or force too high local levies on the individual districts. Presumably the county levies should be the same or about the same, assuming that valuations are equalized; yet as the table shows, they vary from 0.97 of a mill in Sweetwater County to the maximum of 3 mills in Big Horn, Crook, Goshen, Niobrara, Platte, and Weston Counties. The valuation of taxable property per school child varies from $2,783 in Crook County to $11,466 in Natrona County. This means that every school child in Crook County can draw on a valuation of $2,783 for the expense of its education, while every child in Natrona has a like income drawing possibility of $11,466. Since the State gives the same amount per capita in both cases, it is evident that either the education of the children in Crook County suffers materially, or the special tax rate must be approximately four times as great if the same educational advantages are offered.

TABLE 15.—*Income and tax rates, by counties.*

Counties.	Assessed valuation.[1]	School census.	Valuation per census child.	State apportionment.	General county school tax.[1]		Special school tax.[1]	
					Mills levy.	Amount of tax.	Average mills levy.[2]	Amount of tax.
Albany	$14,683,263	2,049	$7,117	$17,191	2.17	$31,862.68	2.743	$36,132.92
Big Horn	7,209,937	2,401	3,003	20,144	3.00	21,629.81	3.525	26,646.17
Carbon	16,068,704	2,093	7,678	17,560	1.46	23,461.77	2.530	26,567.23
Campbell	4,762,344	576	8,268	4,833	2.50	11,905.86	2.666	12,826.12
Converse	8,155,482	945	8,630	7,029	1.55	12,641.00	2.010	20,063.62
Crook	6,139,427	2,206	2,783	18,508	3.00	18,418.28	3.500	17,552.65
Fremont	10,407,092	1,839	5,659	15,429	2.40	24,977.02	2.744	23,494.39
Goshen	4,569,712	1,336	3,420	11,209	3.00	13,709.14	2.750	13,307.88
Hot Springs	4,080,902	675	6,046	5,663	1.00	4,080.90	4.340	17,437.11
Johnson	5,748,608	1,011	5,687	8,482	2.10	12,072.08	1.605	11,282.74
Laramie	23,437,704	4,147	5,652	34,793	2.35	55,078.61	3.013	65,972.61
Lincoln	14,334,018	4,321	3,317	36,253	2.56	36,695.09	3.644	27,452.56
Natrona	13,725,804	1,197	11,467	10,043	1.20	16,470.97	1.415	35,670.66
Niobrara	4,673,897	1,045	4,473	8,768	3.00	14,021.69	3.500	17,096.30
Park	6,664,058	1,477	4,512	12,392	2.50	16,660.15	3.654	25,901.91
Platte	8,898,194	1,581	5,628	13,265	3.00	26,694.57	3.290	33,148.56
Sheridan	19,170,942	4,101	4,675	34,407	1.84	35,274.53	2.723	62,710.55
Sweetwater	20,179,091	2,867	7,038	26,054	.97	19,573.72	1.856	20,422.62
Uinta	8,642,738	1,866	4,632	15,656	2.10	18,149.75	3.100	28,746.18
Washakie	3,480,125	523	6,654	4,388	2.50	8,700.31	2.760	8,868.23
Weston	5,477,168	1,328	4,124	11,142	3.00	16,431.50	2.000	16,302.89

[1] Reported to the State examiner for the year 1915.   [2] Many districts have no special tax.

TABLE 16.—*Taxation statistics, Lincoln County, Wyo.; also, for comparative purposes, statistics regarding pupil and teachers.*

School district No.—	Valuation	Special levy, in mills	Received from special levy and polls	Received from county	Received from State	Bond indebtedness	Teachers actually employed	Special levy necessary to raise $200 per teacher employed	Census, 6-21	Enrollment	Average daily attendance	Valuation per school child	Amt. spent per school child	Number of eighth-grade graduates (1915)	Number of teachers	Amount spent per teacher	Qualifications and certificates of teachers	Salary, per month	School months
1	$3,267,482	3.50	$13,809	$8,961	$8,533	$36,000	30	1.8	1,017	934	644	$3,225	$30.77	24	30	$1,043.12	Professional training required; first-grade certificate at least.	1 $75-$100 2 $65-90	9 10
2	1,994,981	1.51	4,484	3,516	3,815	0	11	1.1	419	413	283	4,761	27.48	14	11	1,046.90	All first grade except superintendent, first professional.	2 70- 80	9
3	574,500	.00	679	1,918	3,037	0	6	2.0	362	250	197	1,567	15.56	13	6	989.07	1 certificate; 2 professional; second grade; 1 primary.	70- 75	9
5	2,804,855	.00	760	2,328	2,299	4,000	7	.5	274	(*)	(*)	10,236	19.66	2	7	769.51	3 first grade; 4 second grade.	65- 80	9
6	1,241,520	.00	370	2,557	730	0	8	1.2	87	(*)	(*)	15,419	42.08	5	8	457.18	Second grade.	50 50	7-8 8
7	180,674	.00	53	320	176	0	1	1.1	21	(*)	(*)	6,691	26.15	2	1	549.22	Third grade.	50	8
8	900,678	3.00	2,940	1,598	915	10,000	5	1.9	109	(*)	(*)	8,263	50.02	1	5	1,090.61	3 second grade; 1 third grade; first professional.	50 *95	6
9	520,162	.00	189	1,288	529	0	4	1.5	63	(*)	(*)	8,256	31.88	0	4	501.36	Second grade.	55 60	6 6-9
10	220,205	.00	114	959	293	0	3	2.7	35	(*)	(*)	6,291	39.08	1	3	341.57			
19	1,546,995	3.50	6,114	11,828	12,384	29,010	42	5.4	1,476	(*)	(*)	1,007	20.54	74	42	819.61	Nearly all second grade; high school at least first grade.	3 60- 65 4 90-100	6-8
20	480,194	7.00	3,390	1,598	1,696	5,800	5	2.0	182	136	95	2,632	36.18	8	5	1,317.00	1 second grade; 1 first grade.	2 70- 80	6-9
21	356,890	3.50	1,563	969	998	0	5	2.5	119	(*)	(*)	2,974	29.83	4	3	1,183.50	2 second grade; 1 first grade.	60- 70	6
22	165,590	.00	185	639	628	0	2	3.6	75	(*)	(*)	2,207	19.38	0	2	726.27	Second grade.	55- 65	9
23	79,124	3.50	470	639	688	0	2	7.5	82	63	37	964	21.92	0	2	886.86	....do.....	50- 75	6

1 High school.   2 Grade.   3 Principal.   4 Grade.

* No information in the office of the county superintendent.

NOTE.—The amount received from the special levy makes up 24.8 per cent of whole amount. The amount received from the State makes up 32.8 per cent of whole amount. The amount received from the county and poll makes up 42.4 per cent of whole amount. In order to raise $200 per teacher, levy would vary from 0.5 mill in district 5 to 7.5 mills in district 23, because of unequal distribution of property valuation among districts.

Four-year high school, 5 or more teachers, Kemmerer, district 1.
Four-year high school, 5 or more teachers, Afton, district 19.
Four-year high school, 1 teacher, Big Piney, district 8.
Two-year high school, 1 teacher, Cokeville, district 5.
One-year high school, 1 teacher, Jackson, district 20.
One-year high school, 1 teacher, Diamondville, district 2.

However, special-tax burdens are much further from being equitable. The table shows also that the average special district tax varies from 1.4 mills in Natrona (a county with a high per capita valuation as noticed above) to 4.3 mills in Hot Springs County. The facts are that some districts which have large valuation need a very small levy for reasonably good schools, and other districts with small valuations must levy a high rate in order to provide even meagerly for the children. The small levy or the lack of any levy at all may also be due to the fact that the community is too indifferent to the necessity of education to care properly for the expense of good school facilities. The following shows the percentage of districts which make no special levy for each of 18 counties of the State from which data were obtained

	Per cent.		Per cent.		Per cent.
Albany	60	Weston	25	Laramie	0
Lincoln	50	Sheridan	25	Fremont	0
Washakie	37½	Park	20	Campbell	0
Crook	36	Carbon	14¾	Unita	0
Converse	33⅓	Big Horn	12½	Hot Springs	0
Johnson	31	Niobrara	9¹⁄₁₁	Natrona	0

Table 16 is a detailed study of one county showing special district levies, the amount received from special levy and polls, the amount from county general tax, and the amount from the State. Fifty per cent of the districts in this county levy no special tax, but depend upon the State and county for the entire support of their schools (excepting the small amount from polls). Reference to Table 16 will verify in part the statement of one investigator that these schools usually have poorly qualified teachers, with low salaries, short terms, poor buildings and equipment. So indifferent are some of these districts that data on enrollment and attendance are not available in the office of the county superintendent. In contrast to these, district No. 20 levies a tax of 7 mills, employs five teachers, enrolls 75 per cent of its census children, pays $70 to $80 to its teachers, and has a six or nine months' term. This district pays 52 per cent of its total school expenditure by local tax and receives approximately 24 per cent from the county and the same from the State.

The following shows the percentages of total expenditure for schools coming from local, county, and State sources in Lincoln County:

TABLE 17.—*Per cent of taxes from various sources in Lincoln County.*

Districts.	Local.	County.	State.
No. 1..	44	29	27
2..	39	31	31
3..	12	34	54
5..	14	43	43
6..	10	70	20
7..	10	58	32
8..	54	29	17
9..	9	64	26
10..	8	70	21
19..	20	39	41
20..	51	24	24
21..	45	27	28
22..	13	44	43
23..	26	35	38

District 1, with a special levy of 3½ mills, pays 44 per cent of the total expenditure through special levy and receives approximately 28 per cent each from the county and State. Districts Nos. 19, 21, and 23, with the same special levy of 3½ mills, pay from local sources, respectively, 20 per cent, 45 per cent, and 26 per cent of the total expenditure. The county and the State each contribute approximately one-half of the remaining 80 per cent, 65 per cent, and 74 per cent, respectively. These districts, though paying the same tax levy, raise thereby very different amounts (see Table 16), spend different amounts of money per teacher, and have different tax-levying wealth per child. For example, district 21 has more than twice the wealth per child that district 23 has. The wealth per teacher employed varies as greatly in these districts as shown in Table 18.

TABLE 18.—*Valuation per teacher and child in Lincoln County.*

Districts.	Valuation per teacher.	Valuation per school child.	Amount received from State divided by the number of teachers employed.
No. 1....	$108,916	$3,225	$284
2....	181,693	4,761	319
3....	95,759	1,587	506
5....	400,693	10,236	328
6....	155,188	15,419	91
7....	180,674	6,691	176
8....	180,135	8,263	182
9....	150,040	8,256	132
10....	73,401	6,291	98
19....	36,833	1,007	296
20....	96,039	2,632	319
21....	118,966	2,974	333
22....	83,794	2,207	314
23....	39,562	964	344

The difference in valuation per school child for the different districts in the county is shown also in the table referred to. This in itself is not always a fair method of judging the ability of a district to maintain necessary schools. As previously stated, one teacher

is needed for a school of 5 as well as for one of 25 children, and he
should be as well qualified and therefore receive as much salary.
The wealth per teacher is a fairer basis of judgment than the wealth
per child. The table shows that the two valuations do not always
correspond. In the county studied the wealth per teacher varies
from $36,833 in No. 19 to $400,693 in No. 5. This difference in
valuation indicates how much more in proportion to wealth some
communities must pay for education than others. The table shows
also the amount received from the State divided by number of
teachers employed. The county fund is now distributed on this
basis.

It is fair also to consider what the different districts in the county
contribute to the county funds and the relation of this contribution
to the amount they receive in return from the county. Table 19
makes such a comparison.

TABLE 19.—*Amounts received from and paid to the county general fund by districts in one county.*[1]

Districts.	Received from county.	Paid to county.	Paid more or less than received.
No. 1...	$3,951.04	$3,364.75	$586.29 less.
2...	3,516.48	5,107.15	1,590.67 more.
3...	1,918.08	1,470.87	447.21 less.
5...	2,327.76	7,180.43	4,852.67 more.
6...	2,557.44	3,178.19	620.75 more.
7...	319.68	462.53	142.85 more.
8...	1,598.40	1,305.94	292.46 less.
9...	1,287.72	1,331.61	43.89 more.
10...	959.04	563.72	396.32 less.
19...	11,828.16	3,960.31	7,967.85 less.
20...	1,598.40	1,229.30	369.10 less.
21...	959.04	913.66	45.38 less.
22...	639.36	424.91	214.45 less.
23...	639.36	202.56	436.80 less.

[1] No allowance made for loss from uncollected taxes or for cost of collection.

It is not advocated that these should be equal, as the purpose of
county aid is not to equalize total amounts, but to equalize tax
burdens and educational opportunities. In a general way the county
tax in this county is fairly distributed; that is, those districts which
received from the county more than they paid are usually the districts with the heaviest burdens and high levies, while those contributing more than they received have small local levies or relatively
small local expenditures. More specifically stated, of districts Nos.
2, 5, 6, 7, and 9, which pay more than they receive, No. 2 has a special
levy of only 1½ mills and the others none. Of those which receive
more than they pay, Nos. 1, 8, 19, 20, 21, and 23 have a special levy
of 3 mills or more. If State aid and local tax were equalized as well
as county tax, in this county at least, school taxation would be
reasonably fair to all districts. That the State fund does not tend
to equalize the expense of teaching is shown in Table 17. As will

be seen from that table, the amount per teacher varies in this county from $91¼ in district 6 to $506 in district 3; that is, the State helps one district to the extent of contributing $91 a year to the salary of each teacher employed, and helps the other district to the extent of contributing $506 each year for each teacher employed.

In addition to the discrepancy already mentioned, the amount spent in the education of each child varies from $15 in district 3 to $50 in district 8 (see Table 16). Unless the money is very well managed in one case and very badly managed in another, the children in district 8 will receive three times as much in educational value as those in district 3. The amount spent per teacher (see Table 16) varies from $341.50 in district 10 to $1,317 in district 20. Is the teaching in district 20 worth four times as much as that in district 10? What of the children in the 50 per cent of the districts from which enrollment and attendance statistics were not obtainable from the county superintendent, and the investigator says "probably not from the districts themselves"? Of the total school expenditure of the county studied, 24.8 per cent comes from special district tax, 42.4 from the county, and 32.8 from the State.

The figures given show that the district unit for taxation and administration tends to make very unequal burdens of taxation and very unequal educational opportunities for children. This is not true in Wyoming alone; it has been found almost universally true in States organized on this basis. Not only is this not an equitable basis among rural districts themselves, but it usually causes a wide discrepancy in the kind and amount of education furnished to rural and city children. An investigation recently made of school taxation in Colorado shows that rural districts pay about half as much in local taxation as city districts. For every dollar of special taxes spent on a child in the city 54 cents is spent on a child in the country—this in spite of the fact that the wealth per capita is greater in rural districts throughout the State than in city districts. Indications from data obtainable are that Wyoming conditions are similar.

Table 20 shows special levy, school census, and other data for 16 districts in the State which maintain high schools. The special tax rate in these districts varies from 2.7 to 10.5 mills, averaging about 5 mills. This should be contrasted with the levies in the county studied (Table 16), in which the highest rate is 7 mills and in which 50 per cent of the districts have no special levy whatever. Generally speaking, cities pay higher school tax, better salaries, have better buildings and equipment, and spend more per child on education than rural districts. Rural districts in the State are not doing their share in levying special taxes. The 16 districts referred to above enroll 32 per cent of all the children in school in the State, and they raise 41 per cent of all money raised in the State by special tax levies.

This is not because country districts are less able to afford taxation than city districts. Although detailed data for the whole State are not available, Table 21 shows valuation, school census, and per capita wealth for the three largest cities in the State and corresponding figures for the other districts in the counties in which they are located, after deducting census and valuation of cities from the county totals. Not only is the wealth per school child greater in each case in the county than in the city, but the combined valuation is such that rural districts could afford to provide not only elementary education, but high-school education as well, without increasing the tax rate above the average city rate (this estimate is made on a basis of a 5-mill levy, and presupposes some assistance from the State and county on the per capita teacher basis). While the conditions shown in this table may not hold in exactly the same way throughout the State, it illustrates the fact that a change in present methods of taxation is necessary if an equitable adjustment is to be accomplished and adequate educational facilities, including high schools, are to be furnished to children in the rural districts.

TABLE 20.—*School census, valuation, and special taxes in school districts in which cities with high schools are located.*[1]

Cities.	Counties.	School census.	Tax property valuation.	Amount raised by special tax, per child.	Special district tax, in mills.
Cheyenne	Laramie	2,718	$10,260,138	$10.31	2.73
Sheridan	Sheridan	2,272	7,732,150	17.01	5.00
Laramie	Albany	1,371	5,477,339	21.79	5.45
Kemmerer	Lincoln	1,013	3,267,481	11.28	3.50
Newcastle	Weston	1,013	4,313,674	14.90	3.50
Evanston	Uinta	800	3,505,217	13.78	3.50
Rawlins	Carbon	532	3,924,991	25.08	3.49
Powell	Park	498	871,638	19.64	10.50
Lander	Fremont	453	1,526,436	13.60	4.19
Lovell	Big Horn	444	479,896	9.19	8.59
Cody	Park	345	1,482,527	25.79	6.00
Lusk	Niobrara	318	1,201,804	15.09	4.00
Cowley	Big Horn	316	401,687	7.63	6.00
Basin	do	273	1,305,581	14.85	3.19
Gillette	Campbell	252	1,319,957	34.08	6.50
Thermopolis	Hot Springs	241	1,147,095	24.29	5.19

[1] Incomplete information prevented the giving of all. The average amount raised by special tax in the cities of the State is $17.35 per child. The average special tax rate is 4.95 mills.

TABLE 21.—*Valuation and census for the given cities.*

	Valuation.	School census.	Per capita wealth.[1]
Laramie County (Cheyenne city excluded)	$13,177,566	1,429	$9,221
Cheyenne (city of)	10,260,138	2,718	3,513
Albany County (Laramie city excluded)	9,205,924	678	13,578
Laramie (city of)	5,477,339	1,371	3,994
Sheridan County (Sheridan city excluded)	11,438,702	1,829	6,254
Sheridan (city of)	7,732,150	2,272	3,403
State as a whole (16 cities excluded)	163,292,519	26,635	6,137
Sixteen cities maintaining high schools	48,217,691	12,949	3,723

[1] On the basis of school population.

It is true that while an apportionment on per capita basis works a hardship on the rural districts, apportionment on a per teacher basis is a hardship on the cities. It is for this reason that a consideration of number of teachers, plus aggregate daily attendance, is usually fairer to all concerned. However, the country usually contributes to the taxable wealth of cities in such a way that the cities can afford to make some recompense. For example, most of the cities in Wyoming would not be favored with railroad terminals and shops, sugar-beet factories, and other taxable corporation property were it not for the industry of the people in the surrounding rural districts. Therefore, the country districts may justly partake of some of the benefits coming from a tax on these corporation properties. Moreover, under the existing system, the injustice done cities through the county method of distribution is largely compensated by the State method of distribution. Let us take, for example, the actual situation in the three largest cities of the State, Cheyenne, Sheridan, and Laramie. According to the report of the board of trustees of the city of Cheyenne, the city received from the county general tax $18,000 and paid into the county fund $31,000, an excess of about $13,000 in favor of the rural districts. Cheyenne received from the State $22,800, the remainder of the county $12,000, an excess over the rural districts of about $10,800 in favor of the city. While these funds do not exactly balance in amount, it should be remembered that the city of Cheyenne, employing 40 teachers for its elementary schools, receives from the State an amount equal to approximately $570 [1] for each elementary teacher employed, in addition to $300 from the county fund, while the rural schools in Laramie County, employing 104 teachers in elementary schools, receive only $115 from the State for each teacher, in addition to $300 from the county. Since the true expense of maintaining schools is based on the number of teachers necessary rather than on the number of children attending, the cities really receive from the State and county combined more aid in proportion to their needs than rural districts.[1]

The city of Laramie receives from the State $11,500, an amount equal to approximately $575 for each of 20 teachers employed in the elementary schools and the junior high school, in addition to $300 per teacher from the county fund. The rural schools receive from the State only $5,695 for 52 teachers in elementary schools, or about $109 per teacher, in addition to $300 from the county. The city of Laramie pays into the county fund about $11,000 and receives therefrom about $9,000. Here again this excess of $2,000

---

[1] If high-school teachers, special supervisors, and the city superintendent are included, the amount received would be $428 for each. High schools are omitted in the calculation because the country districts have no high schools.

paid to the county is more than balanced by the excess received
from the State ($5,808).

The city of Sheridan receives from the county fund $13,500 and
pays into the same fund $6,495. The country districts therefore,
through county tax as well as the State through apportionment,
are helping the district of Sheridan to maintain its schools. (These
figures are only approximately correct, because actual statistics
were not available. Those given are obtained by multiplying valuation by tax levy in mills in the one case and multiplying census by
$8.39—the State per capita apportionment—in the other. They
do not allow for uncollected taxes and the expense of collection.
They are, however, nearly correct, the proportions are right, and
the conclusions are practically true.)

One important consideration in the whole question of the support of education is the method of bookkeeping in the various school
units. Each board at present elects one of its members treasurer.
He keeps the board's accounts in his own way, although a special
clerk's and treasurer's record book is recommended by the State superintendent. Each board may audit its treasurer's accounts if it sees
fit to do so, or the district may vote an audit. No other agency has
power, however, to examine the records of the treasurer. As a matter of fact, very few accounts are ever audited and information concerning them is difficult to obtain. It was obtained for this report
in relatively few cases. Instances similar to the following are reported as common by the county superintendents. One district in reporting to the county superintendent shows a balance on hand at the
beginning of the fiscal year, May 1, 1915, of more than $500 less than
the balance on hand at the close of the preceding year as given in
the preceding annual report. On one report from a large district
the balance on hand at the close of the year was approximately
$5,000 less than the difference between the expenditures and the
receipts for the year including balance brought over from preceding
year.

An inquiry was sent to the clerks of 359 boards asking for definite
information of their accounting systems and of the general conduct
of the business side of their work. The answers received were in
nearly all cases vague, indicating very clearly the decided need of
more businesslike methods of handling school funds and accurate
methods of bookkeeping. It is recommended in another section that
all school funds be left in the county treasury, credited to the various
districts, and paid out by the treasurer on warrants signed by two
members of any board. The county treasurer thus acts as a banker
for the funds, and his accounts with the individual districts necessarily
show the expenditures of the districts and the purposes for which
made.

IV. MOVEMENTS IN OTHER STATES AS OUTLINED IN RECOMMENDATIONS FOR WYOMING.[1]

State administration.—In Wyoming, as in older States, there is a growing feeling that the State must assume more and better supervision over the public schools, so that the State school funds shall be expended in the best possible way. This does not mean that the State should attempt to administer the entire school system in all of its details from a central office. There is always a tendency toward a mechanical system in school affairs when a central office has a large amount of detail administrative work to handle. County management and a certain amount of local district management are desirable for this and other reasons of even more importance. However, there should be enough control from the State to assure that each local unit provides satisfactory education for its children and expends the State funds wisely.

As the population of a State increases, with the resulting growth in the school system, and as the work of education becomes more and more complex, the need of well-organized State leadership becomes greater. A State should establish a general educational policy and provide means for carrying it out consistently. To do this the leadership must be continuous. Older States than Wyoming have provided continuous leadership by creating a nonpolitical, continuing State board of education and a State department of education under the immediate management of a professionally qualified State superintendent of education selected by the board. In 37 of the 48 States of the Union there are such boards with functions relative to the public schools. In 15 of the States the State superintendents of public instruction are appointed officers, not affiliated with politics nor with political parties.

The composition of the State boards of education varies greatly in different States. In eight States the boards are made up ex officio of State officers, usually including the governor, the superintendent of public instruction, and one or more other State officers. Such boards have shown themselves to be of relatively little value. In 10 other States the boards are composed of ex officio members and members appointed at discretion by the governor. In several States the boards are made up ex officio of persons engaged in education. Neither plan gives a wholly satisfactory board. The drift is toward

---

[1] This section was prepared and included at the request of members of the State School Code Committee.—A. C. M.

the board appointed by the governor and composed of broad-minded men and women of affairs who may or may not be engaged in educational work, but who are particularly adapted to the position in personality and experience. The recent change to State boards of this type in Vermont and California is an indication of the trend.

Appointment of the board by the governor has a twofold merit:

(1) It recognizes the executive head of the State as responsible to the people for the efficiency of every department of public service; it tends to make the board responsible to the public.

(2) It centers responsibility where it can be definitely located, as can not be done where the board is elected by the legislature or by the people.

The size of the board, the term of office, and mode of retiring are all important factors. The board should be large enough so that a death or resignation occurring at the time of the expiration of the term of any of its members would not change the majority of the board; and the term of office should be long enough, with not over one-fifth expiring any year, so that the board may be continuous. A board of seven or eight members, holding office from six to nine years, with one term expiring each year or two terms each biennium, fulfills these conditions. Such a board would guarantee that degree of continuity in service without which no business can be successfully administered, and it could not be changed to satisfy the caprice of any individual or to meet the political needs of any State administration. A larger board means additional expense to the State, additional difficulty in determining policies, and difficulty in securing a quorum to do ordinary routine business. The best boards are those whose members serve without pay except for necessary expenses incurred in conducting the business of the board.

The preference in the various States seems to be for a State board with duties and powers which make it responsible for the efficiency of the whole State elementary and secondary systems. The duties and powers actually given vary all the way from almost no control to almost complete control of the public schools. The consensus of opinion in the United States seems to be that the board should have definite functions concerning the regular public schools of elementary and secondary grade, advisory control of all special schools of elementary or secondary grade, such as schools for the education of delinquents or of the blind and deaf, and of special State vocational schools; also control of the preparation and certification of teachers for the public schools. Otherwise its policies in regard to school management can be carried out only with difficulty.

Between the State board of education and the State superintendent there need be no clash. The functions of the board, apart from appointing the superintendent, and therefore approving or disapproving his acts, should be largely legislative and advisory. When it has determined upon a general policy or a particular action to be put into immediate operation, the execution should be left to the superintendent as executive officer. Such assistants as may be necessary to enable the superintendent to carry out his work should be selected by him, final appointment resting in the board. The board in reality passes upon his use of the selective power to obtain the right kind of persons rather than upon the persons themselves. This power of the board prevents a new superintendent from appointing a new set of assistants if those already employed are doing satisfactory work.

The State department of education, to be effective, must command the respect of local school officers and teachers and it must have legal authority to require that legislation relative to education be observed. To secure these conditions there must be a chief State school officer of high standing in educational work retained in office as long as satisfactory services are rendered; an officer who, with his assistants, by visiting all parts of the State and coming into contact with school authorities and schools, will know at first-hand the use made of State funds and the kind of educational opportunities offered.

The size of the State departments in the various States measured in terms of the number of employees varies from 2 in Delaware—a commissioner of education and a stenographer—to nearly 400 in New York—a commissioner, 3 assistant commissioners, 20 chiefs of division, 17 field inspectors, and over 300 clerks, all housed in a special State education building.

Wyoming stands next to Delaware in the size of its department, with a State superintendent, one deputy, and three clerks, at least one-half of the time of the office force being required for the work of the State board of charities and reforms and the land board. The size of the departments in a few other States with systems not highly centralized is given below:

Alabama employs a superintendent, a deputy superintendent, a chief examiner for certification of teachers, four field agents, and seven clerks.

California employs a superintendent, a deputy, a statistician, a commissioner of secondary schools, a commissioner of elementary schools, a commissioner of industrial schools, and eight clerks.

Indiana employs a superintendent, an assistant superintendent, a deputy superintendent, four field agents, head of a manuscript department, and five clerks.

Massachusetts employs a commissioner of education, 2 deputy commissioners, 8 field agents, and 12 clerks.

Minnesota employs a superintendent, two assistant superintendents, a director of the teachers' employment bureau, six field agents, and several office clerks. The six field agents are an inspector of high schools, an inspector of graded schools, a supervisor of teacher-training schools, a commissioner of rural schools, a commissioner of school buildings, and a commissioner of school libraries.

The cost of maintaining the Wyoming State department is also less than any other except Delaware. The State superintendent is paid $3,000 a year, which is the same salary as paid to 16 other State superintendents. In 23 States larger salaries are paid, 2 paying $10,000 a year. The salaries in 8 are less than those in Wyoming. None, however, pays its deputy superintendent so little.

Nonpolitical officers.—To give the office the standing that it should have, so that it may be regarded as the leading authority on school affairs in the State, it must be made nonpolitical, with its head no longer identified with party politics. So long as the people look upon it as a political office, they will not turn to it for advice in educational matters. In 15 States the chief school officer is now appointed; undoubtedly in many others a change would have been made before this time if a constitutional amendment were not required to make the change. In the States where the State superintendents are appointed, they may be selected from the country at large, in most instances paid whatever salary is necessary to get the best person obtainable, and retained in service as long as the work is effective. Of the 23 States paying greater salaries than Wyoming, the State superintendents are appointed in 12.

In several of the States with appointive State superintendents the selection and appointment is made by the governor. There are several objections to this method, and two States—Tennessee and Maryland—have since 1914 abandoned it and vested the appointment in the State board. If the State board is to be made responsible for the State's educational business, it would seem that it ought to have the selection of its own executive officer, particularly as when the appointment is by the governor there is a tendency to make the office a political one and to subject it to the fluctuations of party and factional politics.

The length of service of the State superintendent in Wyoming and in a few States where appointive officers are found is given below. Wyoming has not, of course, had as many changes as many other States where the State superintendent is elected for a two-year term instead of a four-year term. Since 1890, when Wyoming became a State, there have been nine superintendents, including the present officer, who began service in 1915. Six of these served one term of four years each, one served two terms or eight years, two served two years each. Of the following six States in which the State superintendents are appointed, terms have been as follows:

Pennsylvania has had one superintendent continuously since 1893.

Vermont had three superintendents from 1892 to July 1, 1916; the third served 16 years.

Maryland has had its present superintendent since 1900.

Massachusetts had four superintendents or commissioners between 1890 and 1916, the first serving 4 years, the second 10, the third 5, and the fourth 7 years.

New Jersey has had three since 1892; the first served 4 years, the second 15 years, the third since his appointment in 1911.

What has been said in regard to making the office of the State superintendent appointive applies equally as well to the office of county superintendent. This is quite generally appreciated, and considerable activity is evident in all parts of the United States to bring this condition about. In 23 States the rural superintendents are now appointed, in the other 25 they are still elected.

The rural superintendents of New England are township or union district officers and are appointed, except in Vermont, by the "town school committees" for whom they work. In Vermont they are selected and appointed by the State board of education. In New York the rural superintendents are appointed by a board composed of two persons elected from each township in the supervisory district; in Virginia, by the State board of education. Rural supervision in Nevada is under five deputy State superintendents appointed by the State board of education. The county superintendents of Delaware are appointed by the governor; those of New Jersey by the State commissioner of education; those of Alabama, Indiana, Louisiana, North Carolina, Ohio, Utah, and part of those in Georgia by the county boards of education; those of Tennessee by the county court; and those of Pennsylvania, Iowa, and Indiana by a county meeting of school officers representing the townships in the county. The consensus of opinion seems to be very strongly in favor of the appointment by a county board of education representing the people of the county. The superintendent should be selected from within or without the county for special fitness and retained as long as the services rendered are satisfactory. A study of the rural superintendents and the length of the terms of service and their education, training, and experience, recently made in the Bureau of Education, shows that the term of service in the States in which they are appointed is much longer than in the States in which they are elected, and that men and women with more general education and teaching experience are selected than when the superintendents are elected by popular vote. For instance, among the appointed county superintendents, 36 per cent are serving their first term, 29 per cent their second term, and 35 per cent their third or more than the third term. Among the elected superintendents 52 per cent are serving their first term, 28 per cent their second term, and 19 per cent their third term. This

omits the rural superintendents of New England, many of whom
have served many years, the district superintendents of New York,
and also the county superintendents of Ohio, who on account of the
change in the State school code are all serving their first term. As
to education, approximately 83 per cent of the superintendents in
New England have had four years of college education, requiring
four years of high school for entrance, and an additional 12 per cent
have had at least two years of college work. All have had at least a
complete high-school course, only 3 per cent having no college work.
In New York State 32 per cent have had complete college education
and an additional 50 per cent have had from one to three years of
college. Among the county superintendents appointed in various
ways 1.7 per cent have had elementary education only, while among
those elected by the people for four-year terms 9.1 per cent have had
elementary education only, and those elected for two-year terms 6.6
per cent. Among the appointed superintendents 44 per cent have
had full standard college education and 32 per cent from one to three
years of college work; among those elected for four years 12 per cent
are college graduates and 38 per cent have had from one to three
years; among those elected for two-year terms 17 per cent are college graduates and 33 per cent have had from one to three years of
college work.

Supervision.—Throughout the United States there is a growing
feeling that the county superintendent of schools should be a man
or woman of training and experience and should be assisted by a
competent corps of supervisors. Many States are now making provision for these supervisors.

In the New England States the supervisory district is always
small, being composed of from one to five townships, employing as a
rule 40 to 50 teachers. In New York the average supervisory district is one-fourth of the county, or approximately 200 square miles
of territory. In several States, such as Pennsylvania, Wisconsin,
and others, counties with more than a fixed number of teachers are
required to employ assistant superintendents. In Ohio, West Virginia, and Oregon counties are divided into supervisory districts, and
special supervisors as assistants to the county superintendents are
employed in each district. This is a mandatory law in Ohio, the 88
county superintendents being assisted by approximately 500 district
superintendents. In West Virginia it is a permissive law, but has
proved so successful that practically one-half of the teachers in the
State are teaching in districts supervised by district superintendents
under the general oversight of the county superintendent. The
supervisory system of Oregon is, all things being considered, probably
better suited for Wyoming than the others mentioned.

Oregon in 1911 passed an act providing for compulsory supervision. It required the county superintendent in every county with 60 or more school districts to appoint a county board of education, to be composed of four persons and the county superintendent. The majority of rural districts in Oregon contain but one school. This board was required to divide the county into supervisory districts, each to contain from 20 to 50 school districts (practically 20 to 50 teachers), and to appoint a district supervisor for each district so created. The district supervisors are required to devote their entire time to supervision for at least 10 months in each year. They are county officers, responsible to the counties through the county superintendents, and are paid by the county. The county superintendent of schools may be supervisor of one of these districts. If a similar plan be adopted in Wyoming, there seems to be no reason why the county superintendent could not receive special pay for his services as supervisor of one of the supervisory districts until such time as a constitutional amendment can be adopted making possible more adequate salaries than are now fixed by the constitution. Wyoming would require approximately 40 supervisors; the minimum salary should be $1,000, half of which should be paid by the State. The State would then be in a position to see that proper persons are appointed and to control their work sufficiently to assure satisfactory service. The district superintendents of Maine, Massachusetts, Vermont, Connecticut, and New York receive part or all of their salaries from the State; the county superintendents of New Jersey are paid by the State; those of Tennessee and Ohio receive part of their salary from the State; the assistant superintendents of Pennsylvania are paid from State funds. This indicates the trend.

In West Virginia many of the district superintendents who happen to be qualified for the work have been made organizers of boys' and girls' agricultural and canning clubs, devoting part of their time to the work, particularly during the summer months, and are paid for this by the State agricultural college. The result has been very satisfactory, in that it has made the club work a definite part of the regular school work, so that full advantage may be taken of it in the work of the school.

Organization for local administration.—Three distinct rural school units of organization are found in the United States—the district, the township, and the county. In addition, there are several instances of mixed systems, in which the responsibility for management is divided between the district and the township, the district and the county, or the township and the county. There is also some variety in the details of the township systems and much variety in those of the county systems.

The district system was adopted in practically all States in the early days of settlement and was probably the only system possible when the population was grouped in a comparatively few settlements scattered over a large section of country. With the increase of population it is passing away, being replaced by the township or the county system. Indiana, in 1852, was probably the first State to give it up.

Long before the abolishing of the district system in States which have adopted the township or county system, and in States which still have the district system, its weaknesses became apparent to those seeing the product of the system from the standpoint of the State, and State laws have been passed taking away from the local districts many of the powers and privileges formerly left with them. The requirement that none but State certified teachers be employed, that approved textbooks be purchased, that a State course of study be used, that certain sanitary measures be taken, are a few instances of this.

The township system prevails in New England and in New Jersey, Pennsylvania, Indiana, and parts of Michigan, North Dakota, and Iowa. It is particularly satisfactory in the States where the township is the principal unit for civil government, and not so satisfactory in others. For Wyoming and practically all of the West it would not be satisfactory for school administration.

Either the county or semicounty system, where the responsibility for the management is divided between the county or township and district, is found in 18 States. Maryland adopted the county system in 1865, the other States since that time. In the straight county system, such as Utah, Tennessee, etc., the schools of the county, except those in independent cities, are under the management of a single board and are supported by State and county funds expended by the board for schools in different parts of the county according to their needs. In other words, the schools of the county are handled by a single board in exactly the same way as are the schools of any large city system. The superintendent is appointed by the board and is its executive officer. As a rule, local trustees are appointed by the board or elected by the patrons of each school to act as custodians of the building and to represent the people before the county board. Under the system, the location of the schools is determined by the county board; usually, however, the territory in the county is divided by the board into school districts as a matter of convenience, so that children may know which school to attend, and in some cases the local districts are allowed to levy and collect a local tax to be used in supplementing the county funds in maintaining a better school than would be possible otherwise.

Wyoming, however, is probably not yet ready to adopt a county system, on account of the size of the present counties and the sparse population. A semicounty system would probably be more effective. It would seem advisable to provide in each county by election a con - tinuing county board of education and give to this board the management of those functions of education which can be best managed by the larger unit, leaving to the local communities all other functions. In this, Wyoming would be following the example of other States, not only those definitely known as county-unit States, but many others, for there are county educational boards of various kinds in 30 States. These include boards for supervisory purposes, for the examination of teachers, for the selection of textbooks, for the control of special schools, high schools, etc.

Support of schools.—The best way to raise and distribute funds for the support of public education is by no means definitely decided, and space can not be taken here for an extended discussion of the subject. In no two States is there uniformity. All States contribute some State funds to public elementary and secondary education, the amount varying from less than 1 per cent of the total cost of the schools in Massachusetts to 55 per cent of the total expenditure for all school purposes in Alabama. The Massachusetts State funds are used only for special purposes, such as the payment of the salaries of rural superintendents, the support of vocational schools, and for assistance to the poorer towns, which have less than a fixed valuation and are raising by local tax a specified amount. In Alabama all but a small amount of the State funds are distributed to the counties in proportion to the school population and are expended in the counties by the county boards in such a way as to assure as nearly as possible equal educational opportunities in all parts of the county. One-third of the counties depend entirely for the support of the schools on the money received from the State, the other third raise money by county taxation to supplement the State fund. Between these two extremes are all sorts of variations.

For the local support various States rely upon the county, township, or district as the unit of taxation—in many cases on two distinct units. In 24 States the local tax is from the county and local district; in 10 States from the township; in the others from the district only. The amount being raised on the county basis is constantly increasing; for instance, the New Mexico Legislature in 1915 placed practically the entire burden of support on the county rather than the local district.

The present practice in the distribution of the principal part of the State funds to the counties or townships or local communities is as follows:

32 on the basis of school population.
1 on the basis of valuation of taxable property.
5 on the basis of attendance of pupils.
3 on the basis of number of teachers.
2 on the basis of attendance and number of teachers.
1 on the basis of inverse ratio of property valuation.
2 on the basis of number of teachers and school population.
1 on the basis of number of schools and school population.
1 on the basis of attendance and property valuation.

County funds are distributed to local districts in many different ways similar to those stated above. In the States with the straight county system the county funds are expended by the county boards of education according to the needs of the individual schools, so that there will be furnished as nearly as possible equal educational opportunities in all parts of the county. Township funds are in practically all cases expended in the same way.

Special purposes for which State aid is given, either in specified amounts for the fulfillment of definite requirements set by legislation or in varying amounts for special needs at the discretion of the State board of education, are of considerable number, among them being the following:

(1) Maintenance of school to increase the length of term or the teacher's salary.
(2) Teachers' salaries when qualified teachers are employed.
(3) Minimum salary in poor district.
(4) School libraries.
(5) Erecting schoolhouses.
(6) Free textbooks.
(7) Salaries of county and other rural superintendents.
(8) Vocational education.
(9) Aiding schools for deaf, blind, and crippled children.
(10) Evening schools.
(11) Medical inspection.
(12) General improvement of rural schools.
(13) Consolidated rural schools.
(14) Transportation of children.
(15) Teachers' institutes.

Several plans of distributing State funds will illustrate the problem. The State school fund of Tennessee is 33⅓ per cent of the gross receipts of the State for all purposes. This education fund is divided as follows:

Sixty-one per cent is apportioned to the counties on the basis of school population 6 to 21 years of age.

Ten per cent is set aside, apportioned by the State board to counties which levy for public school purposes a tax of not less than 40 cents on each $100 of taxable property and a poll tax of $2 per poll to pay half the salary of the county superintendents up to a certain minimum,[1] one-half the salary of supervisors employed as assistants to county superintendents, and to assist the establishment of consolidated schools and transportation of pupils. Any surplus is distributed in the discretion of the State board among the counties according to their educational needs.

Six per cent constitutes a high-school fund distributed to the public county high schools in proportion to the amount of money received by each from local sources.

One per cent is used to encourage the maintenance of libraries in public schools under general rules and regulations of the State board.

Thirteen per cent is used for the support of the four State normal schools.

Seven per cent for the support of the State university.

Two per cent for the support of the Tennessee Polytechnic Institute.

California pays from the State funds to each county and city $250 for each teacher on the basis of 1 teacher to every 35 children in average daily attendance. The remainder of the fund is distributed according to the average daily attendance. This money and the county funds are then distributed to each district in an amount equal to $550 for each teacher employed.

Missouri apportions $50 of the State fund to the districts for each teacher employed, the rest on the basis of the actual number of days' attendance of all pupils, that is, the aggregate attendance.

These illustrations are sufficient to show how State funds are distributed in other States to help equalize the burden of education. If the Wyoming State funds were distributed on the basis suggested in the recommendations (see p. 101), each district would receive $100 for each teacher employed and $166,066 would be distributed in proportion to the aggregate daily attendance.

Resources and school support in the various States.

States.	Total value of taxable property, in millions of dollars (1912).	Value of property for each child 5–18 years old (1913).	Number of adults for each 100 children 5–18 years old (1910).	Number of men 21 years and over for each 100 children 5–18 years old (1910).
United States	175,425	$7,337		107
North Atlantic Division:				
Maine	1,030	5,900	241	120
New Hampshire	613	6,300	262	122
Vermont	797	9,500	237	119
Massachusetts	5,753	7,300	246	116
Rhode Island	823	6,600	231	111
Connecticut	2,154	7,900	231	115
New York	21,913	9,900	239	117
New Jersey	5,362	8,100	222	110
Pennsylvania	14,137	6,900	208	105

[1] All counties may participate in this one item.

Resources and school support in the various States—Continued.

States.	Total value of taxable property, in millions of dollars (1912).	Value of property for each child 5-18 years old (1913).	Number of adults for each 100 children 5-18 years old (1910).	Number of men 21 years and over for each 100 children 5-18 years old (1910).
North Central Division:				
Ohio	8,552	$7,300	227	113
Indiana	4,951	7,300	211	108
Illinois	14,596	10,000	213	108
Michigan	5,100	7,100	214	108
Wisconsin	4,282	6,400	183	98
Minnesota	5,267	8,900	185	98
Iowa	7,437	12,700	195	98
Missouri	5,546	6,300	195	98
North Dakota	2,038	10,900	166	98
South Dakota	1,331	7,500	175	96
Nebraska	3,605	10,700	182	95
Kansas	4,394	9,400	190	98
South Atlantic Division:				
Delaware	294	5,700	215	107
Maryland	2,002	5,700	196	94
Virginia	2,175	3,400	153	74
West Virginia	2,180	5,800	161	84
North Carolina	1,745	2,200	123	63
South Carolina	1,301	2,500	124	58
Georgia	2,299	2,600	137	66
Florida	1,015	4,300	165	87
District of Columbia	767	16,369	....	144
South Central Division:				
Kentucky	2,152	3,100	160	79
Tennessee	1,834	2,700	152	74
Alabama	2,050	2,900	138	67
Mississippi	1,306	2,100	160	65
Louisiana	2,057	3,800	144	70
Texas	6,552	5,000	142	72
Arkansas	1,758	3,400	139	70
Oklahoma	4,321	7,300	145	78
Western Division:				
Montana	1,113	12,300	261	165
Wyoming	345	10,200	260	179
Colorado	2,286	11,100	231	125
New Mexico	502	4,700	162	88
Arizona	487	8,600	213	129
Utah	735	6,300	160	85
Nevada	441	28,400	269	180
Idaho	591	5,900	190	113
Washington	3,055	10,400	255	151
Oregon	1,843	11,100	253	148
California	8,023	15,500	301	169

Teaching corps.—The amount of general education and professional training required for teaching is being raised rapidly throughout the country as more and more trained persons become available. Very few cities in the United States employ teachers who have not had the equivalent of a standard high-school course and two years of normal-school work. Those with less training have found employment in country schools. In order to force the employment of better qualified teachers in rural districts, State laws have been passed in several States prohibiting the employment of persons with less than a specified amount of general and professional education after certain dates. Ohio, for instance, in 1913, enacted the following law:

Unless said applicant is a graduate of a college or university of approved educational standing, shall possess an amount of professional training consisting of classroom instruction in a recognized institution for the training of teachers, not less than the following: After January 1, 1916, such applicant shall possess not less than 6 weeks of such instruction; after January 1, 1917, not less than 12 weeks of such instruction; after January 1, 1918, not less than 18 weeks of such instruction; after January 1, 1919, not less than 24 weeks of such instruction; after January 1, 1920, not less than 30 weeks of such instruction; after January 1, 1921, not less than one year of such class-room instruction in a recognized school for the training of teachers.

The result was an exceedingly large attendance in the six-week summer schools in the summer of 1913 and succeeding summers. It may be noted that the law is such that teachers already in service may meet the requirements by attending summer schools annually if at the time of the enactment of the law they possessed less than the required amount of professional training. Several other States have passed similar laws with practically the same result. Wyoming should pass such a law; it would make it necessary to establish several summer schools in various parts of·the State. These schools should be under the management of the State board of education, and for their support money now used for county institutes might be used, attendance at summer school being substituted for the institutes.

States having continuing boards of education with permanent administrative officers find that certification is far more satisfactory when controlled by the board than when subject to the changes and revisions which legislative control makes necessary. These States award certificates on a basis of education and professional training more often than on success in examination. In connection with the certification departments, employment bureaus are maintained at relatively slight expense. A State employment bureau is a saving to teachers, who now pay a percentage of their annual salary to a private bureau, and it enables school authorities to get impartial accounts of a teacher's efficiency. This plan is in successful operation in several States, notably Massachusetts and Minnesota.

V. RECOMMENDATIONS.[1]

As a result of the study of the school system of Wyoming the following recommendations are offered:

I. Provision for a State Board of Education as the responsible head of the educational system, the executive officer of the board to be the State superintendent of public instruction.

The board should be composed of men and women of affairs, scholarship, business ability, and broadmindedness, but not necessarily engaged in education; they should be appointed from various parts of the State by the governor with the approval of the senate, or elected by the people at large. A satisfactory number of members is seven, the term of office eight years, not more than two terms expiring each biennium. In this way a continuity of service and freedom from political interference may be secured. The members should serve without pay (or receive a small per diem), but should be paid their actual traveling and other expenses in attending board meetings. Four fixed meetings should be held each year and provision made for special meetings on the call of the governor, the State superintendent, or a majority of the members.

The powers and duties of the State board of education should be clearly defined by law and should include the following:

1. To advise the State superintendent of public instruction in the duties conferred upon him by constitution or law.

2. To have general charge of the educational interests of the State,[2] determining educational policies, particularly in organization and administration and concerning the general scope of the public-school system.

3. To appoint a State superintendent of public instruction (as soon as a constitutional amendment permitting can be obtained), and upon the recommendation of the State superintendent to appoint all assistants and employees of the State department of education; to fix the salaries and terms of office of the State superintendent and all assistants; to approve the appointment of all district supervisors in the counties as recommended below, who may be paid in whole or in part from State funds.

---

[1] The Wyoming school code committee met in Cheyenne on July 8, 9, and 10, 1916, and adopted the report of the bureau as its report and the recommendations of the bureau as its recommendations, with certain exceptions, all of which are noted above and in the following pages as footnotes.—A. C. M.

[2] Without reference to the State University, which is not included in this survey.

4. To advise the regents of the university relative to the content and administration of the course of study in the State normal school at the State university, and to have complete administrative control of all other State teacher-training schools that may be established by the State.

5. To have general oversight of vocational or other special schools or departments of schools receiving State aid or Federal or other financial aid given through the State, whether established by the State or established by local authorities and under immediate local control.

6. To control and manage State institutions for the care and education of orphans, the deaf or blind, feeble-minded, or other special classes that may be established, and to exercise general oversight of any similar institutions established by local communities and under immediate local control if they receive State aid.

7. To apportion the State school funds to the counties and to enforce State laws and regulations by withholding from any county the pro rata share of any school district maintaining a school violating such regulations.

8. To approve the charters of all higher education institutions that may be established in the State and to determine standards on which degrees may be conferred, always under the provision of statute law.

9. To exercise the functions, powers, and duties now conferred upon the State board of examiners; transferring the work to the State department of education and providing assistants, upon the recommendation of the State superintendent, to correct and grade examination papers and to recommend certification.

10. To maintain a State teachers' employment bureau in connection with the certification division of the State department of education to assist local authorities in securing teachers.

11. To approve the courses of study prepared for the schools of the State by the State superintendent, and the lists of textbooks that may be used as basic texts in public schools.

II. Reorganization of the State Department of Public Instruction.

The department should be strengthened (1) by having the functions, powers, and duties of the State superintendent of public instruction clearly defined by legislative enactment; (2) by relieving the State superintendent from service as secretary of the State board of charities and reforms so that practically his entire time may be given to the school system; (3) by making the position appointive instead of elective (see p. 83); (4) by adding to the department at least two efficient field agents to act as inspectors of secondary schools, vocational schools, and special schools receiving State aid, and as advisers and assistants to the State superintendent in the performance of his duties; (5) by providing an annual State appropriation to be expended by the State board of education on the recommendations of the State superintendent for assisting in paying the salaries of district supervisors employed in the counties, and for assisting industrial and vocational education, and for similar purposes that may be authorized by law.

The powers and duties conferred by law upon the State superintendent of public instruction should include the following:

1. To supervise all educational work supported in whole or in part by the State (the State university excepted) and report thereon to the board and to the United States Commissioner of Education.

2. To visit different parts of the State to assist educational work and collect and diffuse information in school affairs.

3. To prepare, publish, and distribute matter for the promotion of public-school work.

4. To collect reports from county and city superintendents and from private institutions, and to prepare and publish a complete report biennially on the status of education in the State and an annual statistical report.

5. To prepare blank forms for use by county superintendents in collecting data from districts, forms for the use of county treasurers and district treasurers in keeping account of the school receipts and expenditures, registration blanks and card records for use in all schools in the State, forms to be used in calling school meetings; and all other forms necessary for the use of school officials.

6. To compile and publish the school laws of the State.

7. To prepare courses of study for the public schools and to approve courses of study in all special schools receiving State aid.

8. To examine and approve textbooks and to publish lists of books which may be used in the State as basic texts such lists having first been approved by the State board of education.

9. To enforce State laws and regulations by withholding from any county the pro rata share of any school district maintaining a school violating such regulations until the State board of education takes action.

10. To hold an annual State teachers' institute and an annual convention of county and of city superintendents, and to approve the program of all regular county institutes.

11. To prepare or have prepared examination questions for teachers' certificates; to issue all teachers' certificates.

12. To prepare and publish plans and specifications for school buildings.

13. To interpret school laws and to advise school officers and teachers on all matters relative to the conduct of the schools.

14. To perform such duties as may be prescribed by law and, as executive officer of the State board, to perform such duties as the board may direct.

III. Nonpolitical School Officers.

The State superintendent of public instruction and his assistants should be selected and appointed by the State board of education, and the county superintendents by county boards of education in a manner similar to the method of selection and appointment of city superintendents by city boards of education and of college presidents by college boards of trustees.

These State and county education officers should be selected for their particular fitness for the positions to be filled, regardless of whether or not they are residents of the State, or of the county which they serve. Appointment should be for specified terms sufficiently long to insure the most effective service, the boards having power to remove from office for inefficiency or malfeasance. State and county officers so appointed would become the actual heads of the State and county systems, first in responsibility and opportunity, and able to count on long and definite terms of office by rendering good service.

IV. Provision for Expert Supervision of Rural Schools.

Each county with more than 40 teachers, not including those in supervised city systems, should be divided into supervisory districts containing approximately 30 teachers each,[1] and a supervisor for each district appointed, whose entire time should be devoted to the supervision of the schools in his district.[2] The salary for the supervisory work should be paid by the State and by the county in equal amounts. Minimum general education, professional education, and successful teaching experience should be required. The supervisors should be directly responsible to the county superintendent for their work, should be appointed on the recommendation of the county superintendent, and hold office while giving satisfactory service. The supervisory districts should be created and the supervisors appointed by a county board of education, and should remain in office until resigning or until removed by the board for cause. Each county superintendent, when eligible as far as general education, professional education, and successful teaching experience is concerned, should serve as supervisor of one district in his county and should

---

[1] The State school code committee recommend that the first sentence to this point should read: "Provision for expert supervision of rural schools by dividing each county, exclusive of supervised city systems, into supervisory districts containing approximately 20 teachers each." It also recommends that provision should be made so that two counties may maintain a joint supervisory district.

[2] It would be advisable to have these supervisors, when qualified for the work, serve also as boys' and girls' agricultural and canning club agents for the extension department of the State agricultural college. The summer months would be free to devote to the club work supervising the home projects. Whenever such arrangement is made, an equitable part of the total salary should be paid by the extension department.

receive the extra pay for this work.[1]   This would increase the income
of county superintendents, so that the position would be more
desirable than at present.

V. A County Board of Education.

To divide the county into supervisory districts and appoint supervisors as recommended above, provision should be made in each
county for a county board of education. The board should appoint
the county superintendent also. (See p. 88.) The board should
consist of five persons, not more than two of whom should be
residents of incorporated cities with independent systems employing
school superintendents. The members should be elected by popular
vote for six-year terms, two of which would expire each biennium.
Members should serve without pay, but should receive necessary
expenses.

The county board should have also the following additional functions, powers, and duties:

1. To advise the county superintendent in the duties conferred
upon him by constitution or law.

2. To exercise the functions, powers, and duties now conferred
upon "the district boundary board," viz, full authority to determine
the number and the boundaries of local districts into which the
county is divided.

3. To exercise the functions, powers, and duties now conferred
upon the board of directors of the county library, so that the schools
may be branch libraries, and the benefits of the libraries may be
available both for the children and the adults living outside of the
county seat.[2]

4. To fix the county school levy within statutory limits and
apportion the county school funds in whatever way may be provided by law. A recommendation concerning the manner of apportionment is given below.

5. To approve the location and plans of all schools that receive
any portion of the county funds for any purposes.

6. To purchase or direct the purchase of all textbooks and instructional supplies, such as maps and charts, upon the recommendation
of the county superintendent and the district supervisors and in
accordance with the regulations of the State board of education.

7. To assume full control and management of all high schools in the
county except those in independent incorporated city systems
employing superintendents. The high schools under the control of
the county board should be supported entirely from county funds
(plus the State apportionment). They should be free to residents of

---

[1] This is suggested as a temporary arrangement, to be in effect only until the constitutional limit to
county superintendents' salaries is removed.

[2] The School Code Committee do not adopt this recommendation.

the county, and children attending who live more than 5 miles from any high school should receive from the county school funds an amount sufficient to pay in part for transportation for days actually attended or for board and lodging near the school, in the discretion of the board. High schools in incorporated districts employing superintendents should receive from county funds a per capita amount based on the aggregate daily attendance not greater than the per capita cost of maintenance on the same basis of the high schools of the county under the county board.[1]

8. To approve the appointment and salaries of teachers employed in the county (except those in independent incorporated city districts under superintendents) who receive their salary in whole or in part from county funds, with full power to dismiss teachers for cause.

9. To provide adequate clerical assistants to county superintendents.

VI. Independent Supervision of City Districts.

It should be provided that incorporated city districts employing superintendents devoting half or more than half of their time to supervision may, on the approval of the State board of education, be independent of the authority of the county board and of the county superintendent in so far as the administration of the schools is concerned. They should be required to make to the county superintendent such reports as may be required by the county board and the State department of education; also before receiving any portion of the State or county funds to submit to the county board satisfactory evidence that schools have been maintained the minimum required term and taught by teachers holding certificates issued by the State department, and that all other regulations of the State have been complied with.

VII. A More Equitable Distribution of the Burden of the Support of Education.

Provision should be made for a constitutional amendment so that the State school funds may be distributed to the counties, one-half in proportion to the number of teachers employed and one-half on the aggregate daily attendance,[2] and reapportioned in the county as the legislature may determine from time to time as conditions change. Apportionment of the State funds by the counties to the districts

---

[1] The school code committee recommend this paragraph to read as follows: "7. To assume full control and management of all high schools in the county except those in independent incorporated city systems employing superintendents. The high schools under the control of the county board should be supported by a county high-school tax assessed on all taxable property in the county except that included in independent incorporated city districts supporting high schools. The county high-school tax may be used in the discretion of the board for paying tuition of pupils attending high schools in independent districts or in adjacent counties. The county high schools should be free of tuition to residents of the county."

[2] The State school code committee insert here the words "double amount being given for high-school teachers and attendance."

on the same basis suggested would be advisable until conditions change materially.

A continuing State fund should be provided by appropriation or by millage tax which, together with the income from the permanent school funds and school lands, would constitute an annual school fund equal in amount to approximately one-third of the total cost of maintenance of schools, and distributed as above. Before distribution a portion should be reserved for the employment of assistants in the State department of education, the partial payment of the salaries of supervisors employed in the counties, and for special aid to assist in the support of vocational agricultural schools and courses, domestic science schools and courses, trade schools, and other institutions.

A larger part of the support of schools should come from State and county and a smaller part from local districts. This may be accomplished by increasing the county school tax to an amount equal to $500[1] multiplied by the number of teachers. This should be apportioned by the county board to the various districts in proportion to the number of approved teachers employed. In determining the number of teachers to be used as a basis of distribution, only those should be counted whose appointment and salary have been approved by the county board and who are teaching in schools which the board has specifically authorized to be held and which have maintained the prescribed minimum term, with such minimum attendance as the board may prescribe; further, no district should receive from county funds (State apportionment not included) a sum more than twice as great as the amount raised by local district tax, unless the local tax is the maximum allowed by law. Before distribution the amount required for high-school purposes and a portion sufficient to pay the expenses of the county board of education and the salary and traveling expenses of the district supervisors should be set aside.

Local districts should continue to tax themselves as at present, the amount to be collected by the county treasurer and held in the county treasury to the credit of the district.

The county treasurer should be custodian of all school funds, whether county or local, holding such funds to the credit of the individual districts and paying warrants drawn upon them only when signed by two members of the local board. His accounts of receipts and disbursements of all school funds should be audited by the county board or its agent.

---

[1] The State school code committee recommend an amount equal to $400 multiplied by the number of elementary teachers; also that the words "the amount required for high-school purposes and" be omitted. Both of these changes result from the changed suggestion in regard to the support of high schools. (See p. 101.)

VIII. Requirements for a Higher Standard of General and Professional Education for Teachers.

The legislature should fix an early date after which no teacher should be engaged who has not an education equivalent to graduation from a four-year high school and a minimum of professional work in some approved school. The requirement for the professional preparation should be increased, so that on and after the 1st of September, 1922, it will include graduation from a two-year course in a standard normal school whose entrance requirements presuppose four years of standard high-school work or its equivalent.

The county institute should be replaced by a two-day teachers' conference with the county superintendent and supervisors, the money now appropriated for institutes being used for the support of summer schools with sessions four to six weeks in length and under the control of, and at such places as may be determined by, the State board of education.[1]

IX. Provision for Professional Training for Teachers.

Provision should be made for securing a larger proportion of professionally trained persons to teach in the public schools. At present the State university is the only institution in the State which gives such professional training. It may be possible that the university can make such adjustments as will enable it fully to meet the demands. The need must be met either through the university itself or by establishing additional normal schools to be conveniently located in different parts of the State and under the management and direction of the State board of education.

X. Reorganization of the Plan of Certification of Teachers.

Provision should be made for transferring to the State board of education the administration of the certification of teachers. A division of the department of education should be created as a Teachers' Employment and Certification Bureau. The division should be under the immediate charge of a chief appointed by the State board on the recommendation of the State superintendent. It should have on file a register of available teachers with qualifications, etc., and be ready to recommend teachers for vacancies upon request. It should hold teachers' examinations for certificates or examine credentials relative to their education, training, and experience, and recommend candidates to the State superintendent for certification.

The rules and regulations relative to certification requirements, the kinds of certificates to be issued, and the requirements for each cer-

---

1 The State school code committee recommend this paragraph to read as follows: "The county institutes should be replaced by a two-day rural teachers' conference with the county superintendent and supervisors. Provision should also be made for summer schools under the control of and at such places as may be determined by the State board of education."

tificate should be left entirely to the State board of education, acting upon recommendation of the State superintendent.

XI. Provision for Vocational Education.

Vocational courses in agriculture, household science, and the more usual trades for both boys and girls should be established in special departments in selected high schools in the State. This work should be under the direct supervision of the State department of education and should receive annually from the State department special State financial aid, as experience in other States has shown that satisfactory vocational work will not be established otherwise, and to be satisfactory must be properly supervised.

XII. Control of Special State Institutions by the State Board.

The State School for the Blind and Deaf, at Cheyenne; the Wyoming School for Defectives, at Lander; and the Wyoming Industrial Institute, at Worland, should be under the complete administrative control and management of the State board of education.

APPENDIX.—STATISTICAL COMPARISON.

Per cent of school population (5 to 18 years of age) enrolled, 1913–14.

United States—74 per cent.

North Atlantic Division:
Rhode Island—63 per cent.
New Hampshire—65 per cent.
New York—68 per cent.
Pennsylvania—68 per cent.
Massachusetts—72 per cent.
New Jersey—74 per cent.
Connecticut—77 per cent.
Vermont—77 per cent.
Maine—88 per cent.

North Central Division:
Wisconsin—66 per cent.
Illinois—71 per cent.
South Dakota—71 per cent.
Ohio—75 per cent.
Minnesota—76 per cent.
North Dakota—77 per cent.
Michigan—78 per cent.
Indiana—79 per cent.
Missouri—80 per cent.
Kansas—83 per cent.
Nebraska—85 per cent.
Iowa—87 per cent.

South Atlantic Division:
Virginia—66 per cent.
Delaware—69 per cent.
Georgia—69 per cent.
Maryland—70 per cent.
South Carolina—73 per cent.
Florida—76 per cent.
West Virginia—78 per cent.
North Carolina—79 per cent.
District of Columbia—80 per cent.

South Central Division:
Louisiana—51 per cent,
Texas—62 per cent.
Alabama—66 per cent.
Kentucky—77 per cent.
Mississippi—80 per cent.
Oklahoma—80 per cent.
Arkansas—84 per cent.
Tennessee—88 per cent.

Western Division:
New Mexico—60 per cent.
Nevada—72 per cent.
Arizona—77 per cent.
Washington—77 per cent.
Oregon—78 per cent.
Utah—80 per cent.
Idaho—82 per cent.
Colorado—84 per cent.
WYOMING—84 per cent.
Montana—87 per cent.
California—90 per cent.

Number attending daily for each 100 pupils enrolled, 1913–14.

United States—74.

North Atlantic Division:

New Jersey—77.

Maine—78.

Vermont—79.

Rhode Island—79.

Connecticut—79.

New Hampshire—79.

Pennsylvania—80.

New York—81.

Massachusetts—85.

North Central Division:

North Dakota—69.

Missouri—73.

Wisconsin—74.

Iowa—74.

Nebraska—75.

South Dakota—76.

Michigan—77.

Minnesota—78.

Kansas—79.

Indiana—80.

Ohio—81.

Illinois—87.

South Atlantic Division:

Delaware—63.

Georgia—65.

Maryland—65.

Virginia—66.

South Carolina—66.

North Carolina—68.

West Virginia—70.

Florida—71.

District of Columbia—82.

South Central Division:

Kentucky—55.

Mississippi—61.

Alabama—62.

Oklahoma—65.

Texas—67.

Arkansas—68.

Louisiana—69.

Tennessee—73.

Western Division:

Colorado—67.

Arizona—68.

Nevada—73.

New Mexico—74.

Montana—74.

Idaho—75.

Washington—76.

California—78.

WYOMING—82.

Utah—82.

Oregon—92.

Average number of days attended by every child 5 to 18 years of age, 1913–14.

United States—87.

North Atlantic Division:
New Hampshire—88.
Pennsylvania—94.
Rhode Island—96.
New Jersey—104.
New York—104.
Vermont—106.
Massachusetts—111.
Connecticut—113.
Maine—116.

North Central Division:
Wisconsin—81.
North Dakota—86.
South Dakota—88.
Minnesota—95.
Missouri—95.
Indiana—99.
Illinois—99.
Ohio—103.
Michigan—104.
Nebraska—106.
Kansas—113.
Iowa—115.

South Atlantic Division:
South Carolina—50.
Virginia—59.
Georgia—63.
North Carolina—65.
Florida—66.
Delaware—74.
West Virginia—74.
Maryland—81.
District of Columbia—115.

South Central Division:
Louisiana—46.
Alabama—51.
Texas—55.
Kentucky—60.
Mississippi—60.
Oklahoma—70.
Arkansas—73.
Tennessee—77.

Western Division:
New Mexico—61.
Arizona—81.
Nevada—85.
Idaho—93.
Colorado—96.
WYOMING—96.
Washington—103.
Montana—105.
Utah—107.
Oregon—111.
California—122.

Number of pupils in high schools per 1,000 in elementary schools, 1913–14.

United States—76.

North Atlantic Division:
Pennsylvania—71.
New Jersey—80.
Connecticut—94.
Rhode Island—95.
New York—98.
Maine—112.
Vermont—113.
Massachusetts—131.
New Hampshire—132.

North Central Division:
North Dakota—63.
Missouri—66.
South Dakota—74.
Illinois—77.
Michigan—93.
Wisconsin—93.
Minnesota—94.
Ohio—94.
Indiana—101.
Iowa—102.
Nebraska—103.
Kansas—117.

South Atlantic Division:
South Carolina—29.
Florida—33.
West Virginia—35.
North Carolina—35.
Georgia—36.
Maryland—57.
Virginia—58.
Delaware—66.
District of Columbia—152.

South Central Division:
Mississippi—25.
Arkansas—26.
Kentucky—32.
Alabama—36.
Louisiana—36.
Tennessee—41.
Oklahoma—41.
Texas—54.

Western Division:
New Mexico—37.
Arizona—60.
WYOMING—67.
Montana—78.
Idaho—82.
Nevada—91.
Colorado—100.
Utah—118.
Washington—125.
Oregon—125.
California—134.

Number of pupils in colleges per 1,000 in elementary schools, 1913–14.

United States—19.

North Atlantic Division:

New Jersey—10.

Rhode Island—18.

Vermont—20.

Pennsylvania—20.

Connecticut—21.

Maine—22.

New Hampshire—24.

New York—25.

Massachusetts—35.

North Central Division:

North Dakota—14.

Missouri—20.

Ohio—21.

Minnesota—21.

Iowa—21.

South Dakota—22.

Michigan—25.

Kansas—27.

Indiana—28.

Nebraska—29.

Illinois—30.

Wisconsin—30.

South Atlantic Division:

Delaware—4.

Florida—7.

West Virginia—9.

North Carolina—10.

Georgia—10.

South Carolina—11.

Virginia—15.

Maryland—22.

District of Columbia—103.

South Central Division:

Arkansas—4.

Mississippi—7.

Alabama—9.

Oklahoma—9.

Kentucky—11.

Tennessee—11.

Louisiana—12.

Texas—13.

Western Division:

New Mexico—5.

WYOMING—6.

Montana—9.

Idaho—11.

Arizona—14.

Utah—20.

Colorado—24.

Washington—25.

Nevada—27.

Oregon—28.

California—35.

NOTE.—It should be remembered in the interpretation of this data that such States as New York, Massachusetts, and California have many nonresident students enrolled in colleges within their borders.

Number of men 21 years and over for each 100 children 5 to 18 years old (1910).

United States—107.
   North Atlantic Division:
Pennsylvania—105.
New Jersey—110.
Rhode Island—111.
Connecticut—115.
Massachusetts—116.
New York—117.
Vermont—119.
Maine—120.
New Hampshire—123.
   North Central Division:
North Dakota—93.
Wisconsin—93.
Nebraska—95.
South Dakota—96.
Kansas—98.
Iowa—98.
Missouri—98.
Minnesota—99.
Indiana—106.
Illinois—108.
Michigan—109.
Ohio—113.
   South Atlantic Division:
South Carolina—55.
North Carolina—63.
Georgia—66.
Virginia—74.
West Virginia—84.
Florida—87.
Maryland—94.
Delaware—107.
District of Columbia—144.
   South Central Division:
Mississippi—65.
Alabama—67.
Louisiana—70.
Arkansas—70.
Texas—72.
Tennessee—74.
Oklahoma—78.
Kentucky—79.
   Western Division:
Utah—85.
New Mexico—88.
Idaho—113.
Colorado—125.
Arizona—129.
Oregon—148.
Washington—151.
Montana—165.
California—169.
WYOMING—179.
Nevada—180.

Value of property for each child 5–18 years old (1913).

United States—$7,337.

North Atlantic Division:
Maine—$5,900.

New Hampshire—$5,300.

Rhode Island—$6,600.

Pennsylvania—$6,900.

Massachusetts—$7,300.

Connecticut—$7,900.

New Jersey—$8,100.

Vermont—$9,500.

New York—$9,900.

North Central Division:
Missouri—$6,300. ,

Wisconsin—$6,400.

Michigan—$7,100. ,

Indiana—$7,200. ,

Ohio—$7,300.

South Dakota—7,500.

Minnesota—$8,900.

Kansas—$9,400.

Illinois—$10,000.

Missouri—$10,700.

North Dakota—$10,900.

Iowa—$12,700.

South Atlantic Division:
District of Columbia—$16,369.

North Carolina—$2,200.

South Carolina—$2,500.

Georgia—$2,600.

Virginia—$3,400.

Florida—$4,300.

Delaware—$5,700.

Maryland—$5,700.

West Virginia—$5,800.

South Central Division:
Mississippi—$2,100.

Tennessee—$2,700.

Alabama—$2,900.

Kentucky—$3,100.

Arkansas—$3,400.

Louisiana—$3,800.

Texas—$5,000.

Oklahoma—$7,300.

Western Division:
New Mexico—$4,700.

Idaho—$5,900.

Utah—$6,300.

Arizona—$8,600.

WYOMING—$10,200.

Washington—$10,400.

Oregon—$11,100.

Colorado—$11,100.

Montana—$12,300.

California—$15,500.

Nevada—$28,400.

Expenditure for school purposes per $10,000 of estimated wealth, 1911–12.

United States—$25.7.

North Atlantic Division:
New York—$23.2.

Rhode Island—$24.8.

Connecticut—$27.2.

Pennsylvania—$27.5.

New Hampshire—$28.1.

Maine—$29.5.

Vermont—$34.4.

New Jersey—$35.5.

Massachusetts—$35.7.

North Central Division:
Iowa—$18.6.

Illinois—$22.1.

Nebraska—$23.1.

Kansas—$24.2.

Missouri—$25.2.

North Dakota—$25.5.

Wisconsin—$26.2.

Minnesota—$27.4.

South Dakota—$29.4.

Michigan—30.8.

Indiana—$31.7.

Ohio—$32.4.

South Atlantic Division:
South Carolina—$17.6.

Maryland—$19.

Delaware—$19.6.

North Carolina—$20.9.

Georgia—$21.4.

West Virginia—$21.8.

Florida—$22.2.

Virginia—$23.

District of Columbia—$25.5

South Central Division:
Oklahoma—$16.6.

Alabama—$17.4.

Mississippi—$20.9.

Arkansas—$21.

Texas—$21.1.

Louisiana—$21.3.

Tennessee—$28.8.

Kentucky—$29.5.

Western Division:
Nevada—$18.7.

New Mexico—$21.7.

Arizona—$26.3.

Colorado—$27.3.

WYOMING—$28.2.

California—$28.3.

Montana—$29.2.

Oregon—$31.3.

Washington—$32.7.

Utah—$46.4.

Idaho—$48.6.

Average value of school property per child of school age, 1913–14.

United States—$55.

North Atlantic Division:

Vermont—$55.

Maine—$57.

New Hampshire—$62.

Pennsylvania—$62.

Rhode Island—$66.

Connecticut—$82.

New Jersey—$85.

New York—$100.

Massachusetts—$109.

North Central Division:

Wisconsin—$36.

South Dakota—$52.

Missouri—$55.

Kansas—$57.

North Dakota—$60.

Michigan—$61.

Iowa—$62.

Nebraska—$66.

Indiana—$71.

Minnesota—$75.

Ohio—$78.

Illinois—$81.

South Atlantic Division:

North Carolina—$12.

South Carolina—$12.

Georgia—$15.

Virginia—$19.

Florida—$21.

Maryland—$31.

West Virginia—$33.

Delaware—$62.

District of Columbia—$151.

South Central Division:

Mississippi—$5.

Alabama—$13.

Kentucky—$19.

Louisiana—$19.

Tennessee—$21.

Arkansas—$21.

Texas—$23.

Oklahoma—$34.

Western Division:

New Mexico—$22.

Arizona—$35.

WYOMING—$68.

Utah—$75.

Idaho—$76.

Colorado—$79.

Montana—$86.

Oregon—$91.

Nevada—$97.

Washington—$101.

California—$128.

Total expenditure per capita based on average daily attendance, 1913–14.

United States—$39.04.

North Atlantic Division:
Maine—$34.27.
New Hampshire—$37.08.
Vermont—$38.28.
Rhode Island—$42.08.
Pennsylvania—$45.71.
Connecticut—$48.24.
Massachusetts—$52.36.
New York—$53.47.
New Jersey—$60.92.

North Central Division:
Missouri—$33.37.
Kansas—$39.29.
Michigan—$42.63.
Wisconsin—$42.75.
Iowa—$42.82.
Illinois—$42.92.
Indiana—$45.21.
South Dakota—$45.80.
Nebraska—$47.14.
Ohio—$48.82.
Minnesota—$52.08.
North Dakota—$64.45.

South Atlantic Division:
South Carolina—$11.65.
North Carolina—$12.39.
Georgia—$13.70.
Virginia—$19.78.
Florida—$21.88.
West Virginia—$25.96.
Delaware—$37.04.
Maryland—$34.46.
District of Columbia—$57.84.

South Central Division:
Mississippi—$9.30.
Tennessee—$13.61.
Arkansas—$14.60.
Alabama—$15.39.
Kentucky—$23.90.
Oklahoma—$24.46.
Louisiana—$24.68.
Texas—$25.88.

Western Division:
New Mexico—$26.88.
WYOMING—$48.88.
Oregon—$48.46.
Utah—$52.73.
Idaho—$55.05.
Colorado—$55.49.
Montana—$64.54.
Washington—$69.44.
California—$70.96.
Arizona—$71.39.
Nevada—$77.14.

Expenditure per capita based on average daily attendance; salaries only.

United States—$22.76.

North Atlantic Division:
Maine—$19.63.

Pennsylvania—$21.19.

Vermont—$21.22.

New Hampshire—$21.42.

Connecticut—$24.87.

Rhode Island—$25.37.

Massachusetts—$29.58.

New Jersey—$29.91.

New York—$35.97.

North Central Division:
Missouri—$21.84.

Illinois—$23.63.

Michigan—$23.92.

Ohio—$24.75.

Indiana—$25.26.

Kansas—$25.53.

Wisconsin—$26.33.

Iowa—$27.37.

Nebraska—$27.63.

Minnesota—$27.64.

South Dakota—$28.23.

North Dakota—$33.50.

South Atlantic Division:
North Carolina—$7.51.

South Carolina—$8.38.

Georgia—$10.36.

Virginia—$12.32.

Florida—$12.99.

West Virginia—$16.50.

Delaware—$18.40.

Maryland—$20.41.

District of Columbia—$40.

South Central Division:
Mississippi—$7.20.

Tennessee—$9.36.

Arkansas—$11.01.

Alabama—$11.71.

Kentucky—$13.56.

Louisiana—$16.13.

Oklahoma—$16.32.

Texas—$17.52.

Western Division:
New Mexico—$16.57.

Utah—$23.31.

Arizona—$25.60.

Montana—$25.87.

Oregon—$29.55.

Idaho—$29.80.

WYOMING—$31.28.

Colorado—$34.51.

Washington—$39.27.

California—$43.57.

Nevada—$48.79.

Average annual salary of all teachers, 1913-14.

United States—$525.

  North Atlantic Division:

Maine—$399.

Vermont—$405.

New Hampshire—$413.

Pennsylvania—$459.

Connecticut—$599.

Rhode Island—$702.

Massachusetts—$729.

New Jersey—$851.

New York—$941.

  North Central Division:

North Dakota—$416.

Ohio—$454.

South Dakota—$456.

Minnesota—$469.

Missouri—$500.

Iowa—$508.

Wisconsin—$517.

Michigan—$519.

Nebraska—$525.

Indiana—$594.

Kansas—$622.

Illinois—$690.

  South Atlantic Division:

North Carolina—$243.

South Carolina—$273.

Georgia—$306.

Virginia—$307.

Florida—$327.

West Virginia—$350.

Delaware—$381.

Maryland—$545.

District of Columbia—$1,005.

  South Central Division:

Mississippi—$234.

Arkansas—$317.

Tennessee—$321.

Alabama—$343.

Kentucky—$359.

Louisiana—$413.

Texas—$422.

Oklahoma—$422.

  Western Division:

WYOMING—$435.

New Mexico—$437.

Oregon—$523.

Idaho—$586.

Colorado—$593.

Montana—$636.

Utah—$656.

Arizona—$699.

Nevada—$738.

Washington—$800.

California—$871.

Length of term in days, 1913–14.

United States—159.

North Atlantic Division:
Maine—168.

New Hampshire—172

Pennsylvania—172.

Vermont—173.

New Jersey—183.

Massachusetts—184.

Connecticut—185.

New York—190.

Rhode Island—194.

North Central Division:
Indiana—156.

North Dakota—159.

Minnesota—160.

Illinois—161.

South Dakota—163.

Missouri—163.

Wisconsin—168.

Ohio—169.

Nebraska—170.

Kansas—172.

South Atlantic Division:
South Carolina—104.

North Carolina—122.

Florida—123.

Virginia—136.

West Virginia—137.

Georgia—140.

Delaware—170.

District of Columbia—174.

Maryland—178.

South Central Division:
Tennessee—122.

Mississippi—123.

Alabama—125.

Arkansas—130.

Louisiana—130.

Texas—132.

Oklahoma—136.

Kentucky—140.

Western Division:
New Mexico—135.

WYOMING—139.

Idaho—152.

Oregon—155.

Arizona—156.

Nevada—160.

Utah—163.

Montana—168.

Colorado—171.

California—174.

Washington—177.

INDEX.

O

DEPARTMENT OF THE INTERIOR
BUREAU OF EDUCATION

BULLETIN, 1916, No. 30

UNIVERSITY TRAINING FOR PUBLIC SERVICE

A REPORT OF THE MEETING OF THE ASSOCIATION OF URBAN UNIVERSITIES, NOVEMBER 15-17, 1915

WASHINGTON
GOVERNMENT PRINTING OFFICE
1916

DEPARTMENT OF THE INTERIOR
BUREAU OF EDUCATION

BULLETIN, 1916, No. 30

UNIVERSITY TRAINING FOR PUBLIC SERVICE

A REPORT OF THE MEETING OF THE ASSOCIATION OF URBAN UNIVER- SITIES, NOVEMBER 15–17, 1915

WASHINGTON
GOVERNMENT PRINTING OFFICE
1916

ADDITIONAL COPIES
OF THIS PUBLICATION MAY BE PROCURED FROM
THE SUPERINTENDENT OF DOCUMENTS
GOVERNMENT PRINTING OFFICE
WASHINGTON, D. C.
AT
15 CENTS PER COPY

CONTENTS.

Average annual salary of all teachers, 1913–14.

United States—$525.

North Atlantic Division:

Maine—$399.
Vermont—$405.
New Hampshire—$418.
Pennsylvania—$459.
Connecticut—$599.
Rhode Island—$702.
Massachusetts—$729.
New Jersey—$851.
New York—$941.

North Central Division:

North Dakota—$416.
Ohio—$454.
South Dakota—$456.
Minnesota—$469.
Missouri—$500.
Iowa—$508.
Wisconsin—$517.
Michigan—$519.
Nebraska—$526.
Indiana—$594.
Kansas—$622.
Illinois—$690.

South Atlantic Division:

North Carolina—$243.
South Carolina—$273.
Georgia—$306.
Virginia—$307.
Florida—$327.
West Virginia—$350.
Delaware—$381.
Maryland—$545.
District of Columbia—$1,005.

South Central Division:

Mississippi—$234.
Arkansas—$317.
Tennessee—$321.
Alabama—$343.
Kentucky—$359.
Louisiana—$418.
Texas—$422.
Oklahoma—$422.

Western Division:

WYOMING—$435.
New Mexico—$437.
Oregon—$523.
Idaho—$586.
Colorado—$593.
Montana—$636.
Utah—$656.
Arizona—$699.
Nevada—$738.
Washington—$900.
California—$871.

Length of term in days, 1913–14.

United States—159.

  North Atlantic Division:
Maine—168.

New Hampshire—172

Pennsylvania—172.

Vermont—173.

New Jersey—183.

Massachusetts—184.

Connecticut—185.

New York—190.

Rhode Island—194.

  North Central Division:
Indiana—156.

North Dakota—159.

Minnesota—160.

Illinois—161.

South Dakota—163.

Missouri—163.

Wisconsin—168.

Ohio—169.

Nebraska—170.

Kansas—172.

  South Atlantic Division:
South Carolina—104.

North Carolina—122.

Florida—123.

Virginia—126.

West Virginia—137.

Georgia—140.

Delaware—170.

District of Columbia—174.

Maryland—178.

  South Central Division:
Tennessee—122.

Mississippi—123.

Alabama—125.

Arkansas—130.

Louisiana—130.

Texas—132.

Oklahoma—136.

Kentucky—140.

  Western Division:
New Mexico—135.

WYOMING—139.

Idaho—152.

Oregon—155.

Arizona—156.

Nevada—160.

Utah—163.

Montana—163.

Colorado—171.

California—174.

Washington—177.

ing officers now leaves much to be desired, conditions are improving; and, furthermore, the training has educational value, if it does not lead immediately to an official position.

IV. The training should be concrete and replete with field work in bureaus and departments of the city. Methods similar to those used in cooperative engineering, pedagogical, medical, and other professional courses should be employed.

V. Various ways of organizing, conducting, and crediting this field work have been devised and are now in operation, but the whole technique is in need of standardization.

VI. It was resolved that the work of the year for the association would be to make a thorough study of field work. A committee was appointed to do this, and its report will be the basis of much of the discussion at the next meeting. Committee: Chairman, President Parke R. Kolbe, of the Municipal University of Akron; President William T. Foster, of Reed College; Prof. Augustus R. Hatton, of Western Reserve University; President Charles William Dabney, of the University of Cincinnati; President Godfrey, of Drexel Institute; Dean Otis W. Caldwell, of the University of Chicago; Dean Everett W. Lord, of Boston University; Prof. James Q. Dealey, of Brown University; Prof. Philip A. Parsons, of Syracuse University.

Officers were elected as follows:

President.—Sidney Edward Mezes, LL. D., president of the College of the City of New York, for a term of one year.

Vice president.—Augustus R. Hatton, Ph. D., professor of political science, Western Reserve University, for a term of two years.

Secretary-treasurer.—Frederick B. Robinson, Ph. D., director of the evening session and municipal courses, College of the City of New York, for a term of three years.

The growing interest in the work of the Association of Urban Universities is indicated by the increase in membership and by the notable gathering of educators at the conference. Membership is by institution. The first 16 following are charter members, and the rest joined at the second conference: Boston University; The College of the City of New York; Hunter College of the City of New York: Johns Hopkins University, Baltimore, Md.; Municipal University of Akron, Akron, Ohio; New York University; Northwestern University, Evanston, Ill.; Reed College, Portland, Oreg.; Temple University, Philadelphia, Pa.; Toledo University; University of Buffalo; University of Cincinnati; University of Louisville; University of Pennsylvania, Philadelphia, Pa.; University of Pittsburgh; Washington University, St. Louis, Mo.; Brown University, Providence, R. I.; Case School of Applied Sciences, Cleveland, Ohio; Clark University, Worcester, Mass.; Drexel Institute, Philadelphia, Pa.; University of Tennessee, Knoxville, Tenn.; University of Toronto, Canada; University of Vermont, Burlington, Vt.; University of Washington, Seattle, Wash.; University College of the University of Chicago; University of Denver; University of Rochester; Syracuse University; Vanderbilt University, Nashville, Tenn.; Western Reserve University, Cleveland, Ohio; Ohio State University, Columbus, Ohio; Harvard University, Cambridge, Mass.; University of Minnesota, Minneapolis, Minn.

The following educators were present at the conference:

Morton A. Aldrich, dean of the College of Commerce, Tulane University; representing also the New Orleans Association of Commerce, New Orleans, La.

William H. Allen, Plandome, New York.

W. M. Anderson, professor of physics, University of Louisville, Louisville, Ky.

Charles A. Andrews, Manufacturers' Equipment Co., Waban, Mass.

S. W. Atkin, National Cash Register Co., Dayton, Ohio.

Frederick E. Ayer, dean of the College of Engineering, Municipal University of Akron, Akron, Ohio.

Brown Ayres, president of the University of Tennessee, Knoxville, Tenn.

Will P. Blair, secretary of National Paving Brick Manufacturers' Association, Cleveland, Ohio.

Leonard Blakey, Carnegie Institute of Technology, Pittsburgh, Pa.

Edgar E. Brandon, dean of the College of Liberal Arts, Miami University, Oxford, Ohio.

E. S. Brandt, promotion secretary, Northwestern University, Evanston, Ill.

E. J. Brown, superintendent of Dayton public schools, Dayton, Ohio.

Edward L. Burchard, secretary of the Civic Extension Commission, Chicago, Ill.

Allen T. Burns, director of the Cleveland Foundation, Cleveland, Ohio.

Otis W. Caldwell, dean of University College, University of Chicago, Chicago, Ill.

C. E. Chadsey, superintendent of public schools, Detroit, Mich.

A. E. Claggett, principal of Parker High School, Dayton, Ohio.

Walter E. Clark, professor of political science, the College of the City of New York.

Robert T. Crane, professor of political science, University of Michigan, Ann Arbor, Mich.

Allan R. Cullimore, dean of the College of Industrial Science, Toledo University; also representing Society for the Promotion of Engineering Education, Toledo, Ohio.

Charles William Dabney, president of the University of Cincinnati.

Dwight T. Davis, City Plan Commission, St. Louis, Mo.

J. Q. Dealey, professor of social and political science, Brown University, Providence, R. I.

W. E. Dorland, Chamber of Commerce of the United States of America, New York City.

Rev. Arthur Dumper, Dayton, Ohio.

G. W. Dyer, professor of economics, Vanderbilt University, Nashville, Tenn.

John W. Fahey, president of Chamber of Commerce of the United States of America, Boston, Mass.

Robert A. Falconer, president of the University of Toronto, Canada.

A. N. Farmer, National Cash Register Co., Dayton, Ohio.

Charles E. Ferris, dean of the College of Engineering, University of Tennessee, Knoxville, Tenn.

Edward A. Fitzpatrick, Society for the Promotion of Training for Public Service, Madison, Wis.

John S. Fletcher, associate professor of political science, University of Chattanooga, Chattanooga, Tenn.

George W. Forbes, professor of philosophy, University of Rochester, N. Y.

A. Y. Ford, president of the board of trustees, University of Louisville, Louisville, Ky.

William T. Foster, president of Reed College, Portland, Oreg.

Hollis Godfrey, president of Drexel Institute; also representing the city of Philadelphia, Philadelphia, Pa.

F. H. Hankins, department of economics and sociology, Clark University; also representing Clark College, Worcester, Mass.

J. M. Hanson, Charity Organization Society, Youngstown, Ohio.

Mrs. L. G. Hartman, registrar of the University of Cincinnati; representing also the National Association of Registrars.

Augustus R. Hatton, professor of political science, Western Reserve University, Cleveland, Ohio.

C. R. Hebble, National Society for the Promotion of Industrial Education, Cincinnati, Ohio.

C. N. Hitchcock, Akron Bureau of Municipal Research, Akron, Ohio.

George W. Hoke, professor of geography, Miami University, Oxford, Ohio.

Charles S. Howe, president of the Case School of Applied Science, Cleveland, Ohio.

Sydney D. M. Hudson, New York School of Philanthropy, New York City.

Lauder W. Jones, professor of chemistry, University of Cincinnati; representing also Williams College; Cincinnati, Ohio.

Clyde L. King, assistant professor of political science, University of Pennsylvania; also representing city of Philadelphia, Pa.

Thomas J. Knight, Louisville People's Forum and Louisville Commercial Club, Louisville, Ky.

Parke R. Kolbe, president of the Municipal University of Akron, Ohio.

Daniel Laurence, secretary of the University of Cincinnati; representing also the Association of Business Officers of Universities.

John H. Leets, dean of the School of Applied Science, Carnegie Institute of Technology, Pittsburgh, Pa.

S. B. Linhart, secretary of the University of Pittsburgh, Pittsburgh, Pa.

Milton E. Loomis, registrar of New York University, New York City.

Everett W. Lord, dean of the College of Business Administration, Boston University, Boston, Mass.

S. Gale Lowrie, professor of political science, University of Cincinnati.

Arch N. Mandel, Dayton Bureau of Municipal Research, Dayton, Ohio.

Leon C. Marshall, dean of the College of Commerce, University of Chicago, Chicago, Ill.

Walter Matscheck, Wisconsin Efficiency Bureau, Madison, Wis.

Sidney E. Mezes, president of the College of the City of New York.

W. E. Morrow, Louisville Board of Trade, Louisville, Ky.

Henry Moskowitz, president of the New York Civil Service Commission, New York.

Edwin L. Miller, Detroit, Mich.

L. H. Murlin, president of Boston University, Boston, Mass.

Charles P. Norton, chancellor of the University of Buffalo, Buffalo, N. Y.

O. E. Olin, professor of economics, Municipal University of Akron, Ohio.

Frances Parrott, Dayton, Ohio.

John L. Patterson, dean of the College of Liberal Arts, University of Louisville; also representing the Association of Colleges and Secondary Schools of the Southern States; Louisville, Ky.

J. J. Pettijohn, director of extension division, Indiana University, Bloomington, Ind.

L. C. M. Reed, Chamber of Commerce of the United States of America, Washington, D. C.

C. E. Rightor, director of the Dayton Bureau of Municipal Research, Dayton, Ohio.

Frederick B. Robinson, director of the evening session, College of the City of New York, New York City.

Frederick W. Roman, professor of economics, University of Syracuse; also representing the city of Syracuse, N. Y.

James Hardy Ropes, Hollis professor of divinity, Dexter lecturer on Biblical literature, and dean in charge of university extension, Harvard University, Cambridge, Mass.

Herman Schneider, dean of the College of Engineering, University of Cincinnati, Cincinnati, Ohio.

J. A. Shawan, superintendent of the Columbus public schools; representing also the National Council of Education; Columbus, Ohio.

A. I. Spanton, professor of English, Municipal University of Akron, Ohio.

Henry Russell Spencer, professor of political science, Ohio State University, Columbus, Ohio.

Arthur E. Swanson, assistant professor of economics and business organization, and director of evening classes, Northwestern Univerity, Evanston, Ill.

L. D. Upson, executive secretary, National Cash Register Co., Dayton, Ohio.

George R. Wallace, Pittsburgh, Pa.

G. A. Warfield, dean of the School of Commerce, University of Denver, Denver, Colo.

George F. Willett, Norwood Civic Association, Norwood, Mass.

C. H. Winder, superintendent of the city schools, Chattanooga, Tenn.

John W. Withers, principal Harris Teachers' College; also representing the St. Louis public schools, St. Louis, Mo.

Howard Woodhead, department of sociology, University of Pittsburgh; also representing the American Sociological Society, Pittsburgh, Pa.

S. M. Woodward, professor of mechanics and hydraulics, College of Applied Science, State University of Iowa, Iowa City, Iowa.

Victor S. Yarros, Chicago School of Civics and Philanthropy, Chicago, Ill.

L. S. Young, associate professor of political science, University of Minnesota, Minneapolis, Minn.

Besides these educators a large representation from the instructional staff of the University of Cincinnati attended the conference. The Cincinnati Chamber of Commerce and business organizations of the city sent delegates and did much to help in making various arrangements for meetings and entertainment.

The first president of the association, Dr. Charles William Dabney, president of the University of Cincinnati, welcomed the conference to Cincinnati and to the university and presided at most of the meetings. He and Prof. S. Gale Lowrie, as secretary of the committee of arrangements, had organized a most interesting program of visitation which demonstrated the remarkable work of the University of Cincinnati in cooperation with the educational, business, and governmental agencies of the city. Probably more than in any other single place, the ideals for which the Association of Urban Universities stands are being realized in Cincinnati.

FREDERICK B. ROBINSON,
Secretary, The College of the City of New York.

1. THE GENERAL RELATION OF THE UNIVERSITY TO THE CITY.

WELCOME.

By Hon. FREDERICK S. SPIEGEL,
Mayor of Cincinnati.

Training for public service, long established in Germany, has been considered only for a few decades within the boundaries of the United States. Heretofore, in America, faith has been not so much in training for public service as in the old German proverb, "To him to whom the dear Lord gives an office he will also give the necessary sense to conduct it properly."

It is good to know that we have indeed come to a realization of the necessity of training properly for public service. This necessity is emphasized in our own case by the fact that our city, to which I take more than ordinary pleasure in welcoming you, is expending almost eight million dollars a year for the welfare of its citizens. Since this amount must be raised by taxation, its expenditure in various departments should be conducted wisely and judiciously. Under our plan of government the mayor is responsible for every act of his subordinates. When once you realize the amount of work that he is expected to do, you will understand what the duties of a mayor presiding over a corporation of this kind are; and you will also agree that two years is not enough time to train him to discharge properly the duties of his office. Thus, you will see how absolutely appropriate it is that in your discussions here in one of the metropolises of the State of Ohio you should give serious consideration to this matter of training for public service. In your endeavor to solve this question satisfactorily, I wish you all success in the world.

What I particularly desire is this, that you will impress upon the people the need of giving greater liberty to the cities of the different States, in order that they may become at least what they are in Europe, each a free state within a state; in order that the city may be able to conduct not merely its educational, but all of its enterprises without being circumscribed by laws, and by being compelled to go to the State legislature, as undoubtedly you have had

11

to do in New York, Pennsylvania, Ohio, or in any other State of the Union. As the creature of the State, each city must ask permission to tax itself and to spend its own money in furtherance of the higher ideals of this century.

Furthermore, the time has passed for us to discuss simply the Constitution; the time has come in this great day of progress when we should consider the details of administration, realizing that the proper functioning of these details is more necessary to our welfare than an academic discussion of the Constitution.

RESPONSE.

By CHARLES P. NORTON,
Chancellor of the University of Buffalo, Buffalo, N. Y.

We have come with peculiar eagerness to Cincinnati because here in Cincinnati is an organization at work demonstrating that one of the great problems of the day, the training of Americans for public service, is being solved, and solved well. I come from the city of Buffalo. Buffalo is like so many cities of the United States which have sprung into being as the creation and result of the joining of the great railroads and the industries, and the imperious demand of them both for labor. To Buffalo, as to Cincinnati, there have come the children of the nations of the earth who have heard in their distant lands the mighty call of the voice of a new era whose name is Freedom. They have come with freedom as a new concept to them, confusing it, too often, with wealth and easy living, bringing the inheritance that their forefathers passed on to them, with the notions of government prevalent in their own countries. And among this huge host there were but few, very few, trained to regard the real basic principles of democracy as living forces for the guidance of communities.

On the other hand, they have come to America, bringing to it a wealth of excellent traits. Thousands of Germans have come, bringing the idealism of their race; thousands of Irish, bringing their ready wit and humor and loyalty. The French have brought their charming manners, their grace, their æstheticism; the Jew and the nations of the East their spiritual perception which men of other races have wondered at, but to which they have never attained. On the basic characteristic of the first English settlers, the civic structure is founded in the English sense of fairness and of love of order and of law and of liberty. Italians are here, with their love of grace, art, and music. Yes, each nation has come to my city, has come to every city in this country, bringing to it its best for the making of the character of a new type of man. It is for us educators to develop their traits and add to these qualities, thus making the new man one who is generous, patient, humble minded, strong, brave, wise, and merciful. And then, when we have trained this composite type of man, we shall christen him with a new and glorious name in history as the citizen who is the evolution of the ages; and the name we shall give him will be "American." This new man looks upon a new world, with new work laid ready to his hand.

In the latter part of the eighteenth century an epoch was entered marked by many distinctions, but most strikingly by what may be called the transformation of the world. The generations before that time, whether ancient or modern, had found the world in which they lived much the same, so far as concerns the common conditions of life; but for us of the present age it has been utterly transformed. Its distances mean nothing that they formerly did; its terrifying pestilences have been half subdued, by discovery of the germs from which they spring; its very storms, by being sentineled, have lost half their power to surprise us in our travels or our work. Netting the earth with steam and electric railways, seaming it with canals, wire-stringing it with telegraphic and telephonic lines; ferrying its oceans with swift, steam-driven ships; ploughing, planting, harvesting, spinning, weaving, knitting, sewing, writing, printing, doing everything, with cunning machines and with tireless forces borrowed from coal mines and from waterfalls, men are making a new world for themselves out of that in which they lived at the dawn of the era of mechanism and steam.

These, however, are but outward features of the change that is being wrought in the world. Socially, politically, morally, it has been undergoing, in this epoch, a deeper change. The growth of fellow-feeling that began in the last century has been an increasing growth. It has not ended war, nor the passions that cause war, but it is rousing an opposition which gathers strength every year, and it is forcing nations to settle their disputes by arbitration, more and more. It has made democratic institutions of government so common that the few arbitrary governments now remaining in civilized countries seem disgraceful to the people who endure them so long. It has broken many of the old yokes of conquest, and revived the independence of many long-subjugated States. It has swept away unnatural boundary lines which separated peoples of kindred language and race. It is pressing long-neglected questions of right and justice on the attention of all classes of men everywhere, and requiring that answers shall be found.

Even these are but minor effects of the prodigious change that the nineteenth century has brought into the experience of mankind.

Far beyond them all in importance are the new conceptions of the universe, the new suggestions and inspirations to all human thought that science has been giving in these later years. If we live in a world that is different from that which our ancestors knew, it is still more the fact that we think of a different universe, and feel differently in our relations to it.

We are the vedettes of a host which shall come to its work of serving and developing the mighty forces that the age in which we live has called into being. And one of the chiefest of them is this governmental experiment, the municipality which we are now considering. The population of the United States at the time of the formation of the Constitution was rural. It is now urban. At the time of the formation of the Constitution the little town meeting was the fundamental idea upon which the Constitution rested, and it was administered by men trained in the English common law and the English constitution, of which it was in fact the outgrowth. To-day the intellectual forces that create the American Constitution no longer are the inheritance of the majority of American citizens. Especially is this the case in the city, and in the cities one of the works of most importance is to either teach the citizens of cities the principles of democracy embodied in the American Constitution, or else to teach them principles evolved out of the great principles of human brotherhood which shall be better than the principles which the founders of the Constitution taught.

We are coming to try and find ways and means to develop the cosmopolitan man, the American, and to make him worthy of the new day that in our own time has dawned so splendidly upon humanity. And the true ultimate of this democracy, if we can develop this cosmopolitan man to grow up to it and adapt him to this new world, is that brotherhood of man which Christ founded so many years ago.

Cincinnati has been for generations an intellectual center, and, if you will allow me to be hackneyed, a veritable Athens of the West. It is fitting that this city should initiate and put into practical shape these principles of cooperation which are to work here. It is fitting that she should initiate and seek out a practical method to apply the higher education and developed knowledge to training her citizens for the service of democracy. In giving to the sons and daughters of men of small incomes the opportunity of strengthening themselves in their various livelihoods; in causing the cooperation between your university and their professions or business or conduct of life, Cincinnati is giving that equality of opportunity which shall cherish the new birth of freedom. In training educated and patriotic citizens for public service she is lessening the chances of defeat in this trial of the theory of the government of the people, by the people, for the people. . .

RESPONSE.

By ROBERT A. FALCONER,

President of the University of Toronto.

We have all heard for long of certain of the German urban universities which have had close connection with their cities; and some of us know very well the great provincial universities of England, such as Leeds, Manchester, Liverpool, Birmingham, and others in which similar results have been wrought out with great success; but I think that it is to the honor of the University of Cincinnati to have performed a unique function on this continent in being probably the most representative of these urban universities and an exemplar in more or less close similitude of the universities of the older countries.

How full of romance is the history of universities, and how splendidly the institution has adapted itself to the needs of the age. The university has been for the most part creative, rather than imitative. It has been the home of the pioneer thinker and the far-sighted investigator, from whom the generous youth has caught a new vision that caused alarm in the breast of the comfortable conservative, but which became the dogma of a succeeding age. The university has done much to give birth to the spirit of each new era. It has, indeed, served at times to enslave a people to false current conceptions, but most frequently it has stimulated them to noble patriotism and has been the home of quickening ideals which were cherished by its educated youth before their contemporaries were prepared to understand them and adopt them as the ruling conception of the Nation.

We must, therefore, expect that the university of the last quarter of the nineteenth and the first part of the twentieth century will have been modified very greatly from any earlier type. This period has been the age of science, of industrialism, and of cities. Ideas, methods, and discoveries, many of them by no means new or recent, suddenly burst into flower and fruit under the ripening atmosphere of the age. Physical science grew apace. Applications of scientific results to industry created new industries or revolutionized old ones. Inventions and discoveries flowered thick and fast. The means of communication also have been transformed, and new parts of the world have been explored. So ramified the land has been with railways, so furrowed the ocean with steamships, that the conception of distance has been modified and the mystery of the world has in part vanished.

Another result of these improved means of communication and of the industrial changes that have come is the shifting of population. Villages have become towns; towns have become cities; cities have begun to rank by the half million inhabitants' standard. The urban population in most civilized countries has increased so rapidly that in some countries one-half in others three-fourths, are now to be found in cities and towns.

The town as we know it in America differs from the old town in Europe. It differs in affairs municipal, in affairs industrial, and in affairs educational. Social change has demanded modifications in all directions. Old methods and systems have disappeared, and new ones have taken their place.

In municipal affairs the change is obvious. What was once performed or neglected by guilds is now done by the city itself under its own officials, who do work for the city as a whole and not for any one class. The expert engineer is one of the officials of greatest influence in the counsels of the city.

In affairs industrial the change is marked by the disappearance of tradesmen, craftsmen, and guilds, who had their privileges, who trained for the trade, and who transmitted their privileges to others, and who thus kept alive powerful associations of producers. Not only has the accumulation of men in cities produced new industries, but it has led to social changes, through the necessity of caring for the comfort and health of peoples who have thus been gathered together. A sense of community life has been diffused through the State, the city being regarded as an organism, and part of the higher organism of the State. Everywhere there is an increasing demand for standards, which have to be observed; standards in education, standards in sanitary conditions, and standards in the means of livelihood. Minima are required: The minimum wage, the minimum in education, and the minimum as regards housing. This development in the character of the town has had its effect also on the industrial development.

As you think of the manufactures of the country, two classes stand out before your mind. There is the directing mind, and the executing arm; the engineer who plans, the artisan who works as he is told. There is the engineer who has planned the bridge, built the railway, excavated the foundations; the architect who has designed the building with its thousands of rooms; the chemist who has discovered the new methods and valuable by-products; the miner who lays out the mine. All these are the mind, the controlling thought of our industrial life. Through them and on their advice the energy and will of the capitalist set into motion the machinery of our modern world.

And how complex is the modern world! What skilled directors it demands! It is true that the men who constructed the pyramids, erected the aqueducts, chiseled the marble of the Parthenon and placed it in position combined science and art and engineering skill in a fashion that challenges our admiration. It is true that those who designed and built the Gothic and Norman cathedrals were master workmen who need not fear the judgment of any age; but in variety of activity, in ingenuity, in the range of application of scientific principles to industry, the modern world stands by itself. This variety, this multiplicity, demands as never before a multitude of skilled directors of industry. Wealth would be idle without them, an inert mass, blind, and groping darkly.

Now, during the past generation our universities have served the life of the Nation well in supplying the country with these skilled leaders of industry. Every large university has its faculty of applied science, and in most this is the faculty that is growing fastest. Yet, we do not hear that of the graduates who are sent forth every spring, like a fleet from our harbor into the ocean of life, there are many derelicts. They get employment soon; with their good theory and their scientific training they pick up through practical experience the principles of their industry or trade, and soon step into positions of command.

Every year we have requests from some source for expansions or for new departments. We endeavor to supply the greatest needs of the country, but it is hard to keep up with the industrial demands of a growing nation.

But what about the noncommissioned officers and men of this industrial army? What of the foreman and the average artisan? Less has been done as yet for them than for their leaders. Let me not, however, allow you to fall into the error of thinking that by curtailing the education of the leaders you will further that of the men. Too much has not been done for the former. More must be done for the latter. Doubtless, the cry has often been heard in this city, as in others, urging that elementary education should be furthered and that too much is being spent on higher education. But the two must go together. A highly educated, well-trained leadership is bound to provide for a well-trained workman. Good engineers require good foremen and good artisans. So in this indirect way the university contributes through its standards in applied science to the creation of an industrial education for the workman.

The skilled engineer, the responsible head of an industrial concern, is well aware that his results can only be attained by means of skilled foremen and intelligent workmen. The higher the attainment and the more outreaching and ambitious the proposals of the directing head, the more earnest will he be to secure the best possible men to cooperate with him in carrying out his plans. The necessary complement to a well-equipped school of practical science or faculty of applied science in which the leaders of our industries are trained is a system of secondary industrial education for the training of

45424°—16——2

those who are to carry into execution their instructions or designs. Thus, the university indirectly contributes to the whole industrial life of the Nation by creating a need for industrial schools through its demand for efficiency in the workman to carry out the work assigned him by the engineer. In those States and Provinces where professional education is highest will good secondary education be called for soonest.

There is another important aspect of the work of the university in the city life. Thus far we have considered the function of the university in the actual preparation of the engineer by instruction in scientific principles, and indirectly and even directly in doing something for those in the employ of the engineer, the great multitude of workmen. But we must not overlook the character of a university. In a modern State or city its service is not to be confined to any one class; it is for the people, not for any one section of the people. It is not for the city man alone, but also for him who comes from the village or countryside. In politics city may be ranged against country, farmer against manufacturer; in a university never. We must endeavor to look at life steadily and, if possible, look at it whole.

A university stands for the advancement of science, knowledge, the humanities, those principles that are concerned with the constitution of man as a physical being in a physical environment, as a being with a mind, a memory, an imagination, and hope, as a member of a society in which alone he attains to what on this earth we call life. By the books a man reads, by the friendly chats with his neighbors, by his thought on the problems of the State, above all by his kindly deeds in his own home or circle, and his aspirations Godward, he finds life filled with a reasonable and satisfactory content. The function of a university can be fulfilled only in a social atmosphere in which the worth of a human life stands forth clear and luminous. There are hours of work and hours of freedom from labor; the day or most of it may be spent in what is often drudgery in order to get our living, or it may be absorbed in the interest of our work. But too much work stales the mind; the body needs rest or change of occupation; man should call into exercise other powers than those of intellect or affection. Man will forever go forth to his work and to his labor until the evening; but it concerns us in the university to ask in what spirit he fares forth to his work, to what home he returns, and with what measure of intelligence he occupies his evening hours. It is by this extra accomplishment that man refreshes his spirit and with the returning day returns renewed to the round of his toil. Nor is the fullness of life for the rich alone and for the highly trained professional man. It is the right and privilege of all. Our social advancement will be measured by the extent of opportunity for this self-development and its range among the classes of the people. Social advancement will manifest itself in industrial efficiency. From intelligent people will come a grade of industry immeasurably beyond the work of the dull driven slave.

So the university, open to all and to every class of the community, aiming only at the pursuit of truth in as wide a field as possible, must by its liberal studies and its broadly human view endeavor to set clearly before the people the varied phases of life in its truest aspects—man's history, his endeavors to understand himself, the laws of his mind, his principles of conduct, his social efforts, his scientific interpretation of the universe, and his marvelous control of nature through the accurate intuition of its character and his own powers. Whatever dignifies and ennobles man is a theme for our consideration. Therewith labor, one of man's worthiest expressions, in any and every form, will be invested with a new dignity, and the contempt under which it suffered through the dark centuries, yea, millenia, when manual toil fell to the lot of the underworld of slaves, will be replaced by the self-respect of the intelligent workman who will find his pride in sharing with his sympathetic director the credit of bringing to pass those results which with comprehension he sees shaping under his hand.

II. NEEDS FOR COOPERATION.

CAN BUSINESS METHODS BE APPLIED TO THE CONDUCT OF MUNICIPAL AFFAIRS?

By George F. Willett,

Of Willett, Sears & Co., Boston.

The achievement of a democracy like ours can be no higher than the standard of its citizenship as expressed not only in the conduct of its business affairs but also in the government of the city, the State, and the Nation. Indeed, the conduct of our Government itself should be on such a plane that it would serve as the best example and the highest source of inspiration to our business and commercial interests rather than merit their disdain. We have the power within us, because knowledge is power, but as we look about us we have good reason to pause and wonder whether we can so apply it that we may attain the necessary standard.

It is acknowledged the world over that our most successful American industrial concerns are attaining the very best business methods. We may well learn to apply them also to the conduct of the affairs of the Government.

There is no business in the world that is more efficiently managed—taking its size into consideration—than the United States Steel Corporation, the largest of our industrial groups. The ownership of this company lies within a large group of stockholders. They choose by ballot a board of directors, who, in turn, choose an executive committee for the closer counsel and guidance of their chairman, Judge Gary, who stands at the head of this general executive department which determines the plans and policies of the business. These plans and policies are carried out by the administrative department, which consists of as many operating units—with an expert in that particular line at the head of each—as are required to give every part of the business competent leadership and oversight; all brought together as a disciplined, homogeneous group under one administrative or operating head, President Farrell. He, with the.heads of the accounting and financial divisions, makes contact with the executive head, Judge Gary, at a single centralized point.

The difference between these two men is typical of the personnel of the distinct branches which they represent. Judge Gary, trained as a lawyer, holds his place at the head of the organization because his unusual executive qualities fit him to represent ably the interests of the directors and the stockholders; President Farrell is a business expert strong in practical knowledge of the operating end of the steel business, in which he has grown up. Those who best know the methods of this organization believe that they are so sound and effective that, if the company were to become twice as large, it would be just as effectively administered as it is to-day. Its ownership is steadily going into the hands of its employees and into the hands of the general citizenship of the country at large; but, despite this ever-widening ownership, the business itself is wisely and successfully carried on.

It is a simple application of this functional idea of organization that we have followed in Norwood, Mass. Ten years ago the situation in Norwood was inexcusably bad. We had the highest tax rate in the State of Massachusetts, $25.60 per thousand. With the exception of a memorial library, given by a private citizen, we had no public buildings except our schoolhouses, which were wooden and of indifferent style and construction. Although abounding in splendid natural advantages, Norwood had no parks or playgrounds, no hospitals or similar institutions. The railroad station was a disgrace, although within a few miles of the station are located some of the largest industries of their particular kind in the world.

By a more rigid enforcement of the antiquated Massachusetts tax laws, it became imperative for certain people in Norwood to move away. It was apparent that those who remained would have a still heavier burden of taxation to bear, and the prospects of the town became critical. Under these circumstances the responsibility of the citizens asserted itself. There came the realization among all classes that the town is a unit and that this idea should control the conduct of its common interests, political and otherwise.

When we began to study our situation from this new point of view and sought to improve it, it became apparent to us that: First, the form of town government that the old New England methods prescribed by law for all Massachusetts towns did not secure unified, efficient, economical administration of public affairs; second, there did not exist any single organization capable of looking out for the nonpolitical and yet common interests of the citizens in matters civic, charitable, and educational in the broadest sense, in such a way as to avoid duplication and waste and to secure efficient and unified handling of them; third, in order to make the town planning effective—to establish parks, boulevards, playgrounds, and improve the style and method of building construction and housing conditions—it was wise and necessary to control the ownership of certain real estate situated at strategic points.

As a first result of this awakened interest, subcommittees were formed, reassessments of property were made, economies in appropriation were introduced, and the matter of devising a business management was taken vigorously in hand. We soon found that in assessing our taxes we were merely distributing the burden of the support of government. The vital matter was to determine how to get the most for the money that was spent.

As a result of several years of study and hard work, a new charter was adopted which went into effect about a year ago. The principal feature of this new charter is the separation of the government into the executive and administrative divisions to which reference has already been made. The executive or official division is composed of the elected officials of the town. Various unwieldy boards and commissions, such as are usually found in municipal governments, have been consolidated into one board of five members (called the selectmen), the chairman of which is the head of the government. This board performs its duties in the same way as a board of directors and devotes itself to seeing that the policies of the town as expressed by the citizens in town meeting are properly carried out. As a part of their duties they appoint the board of assessors and the board of relief (one of the latter board may be a woman), each consisting of three members. In making these appointments the idea is carried out that such boards should be comprised only of those especially fitted for the duties involved and that on this account the members can be better selected by a small deliberative commission than by general vote of the citizens.

Besides the board of five selectmen, the citizens elect a finance commission of three members which makes a general audit of all expenditures and prepares the town budget, and a school commission, which, as formerly, handles school affairs through a paid superintendent.

The members of the boards of the official division receive no salary. Under the new method a comparatively small amount of time—and that mainly in the evening—is required of them, because the actual performance of the work is delegated to the administrative division.

At the head of this division is a general manager. He is chosen by the selectmen on the basis of merit and fitness alone, and he is obliged to choose his subordinates on the same basis. He is in charge of all public work and of the police and fire departments, and it is his duty to organize and direct this work along standardized business lines. He is retained in office only so long as he performs his work efficiently and well. He is assisted by an expert accountant who fills the office of town clerk and whose duty it is to keep a complete record of all transactions and their costs of operation. Every dollar spent must be accounted for as in any well-conducted business, so that every citizen may know what is being done and what it costs.

The second task before the citizens in the regeneration of the town was to create a central community and civic organization; in fact, it was very nearly necessary to create a civic sense. A start was made by inviting to a conference representatives from the various social and civic bodies of the town—the board of trade, woman's club, fraternal organizations, and the like. This finally resulted in the organization of the Norwood Civic Association. Such property as the civic association acquires is to be held for all time by nine trustees for the benefit of the community as a whole. Its management is in the hands of a board of 27 governors, who are chosen by an election committee consisting of the trustees, selectmen, and school committee; so that its control rests with the elected representatives of the people. There is also a woman's standing committee of 21 members, which deals with those matters which are of particular interest to the women of the community and the home. Its purpose, as set forth in its articles of organization, is to promote—

the welfare of the town of Norwood, Mass., and to improve the morality, industry, thrift, health, cleanliness, education, and good citizenship of its inhabitants.

There was some hesitancy over the word "civic," but when it was found that its inherent meaning is "belonging to the people," it was accepted as the best possible name.

The clubhouse has a floor space of some thirty thousand square feet. It contains an auditorium, gymnasium, swimming pool, bowling alleys, a billiard room, game rooms for the children, a social hall, and various rooms used for the meetings of outside organizations. The town meetings are held at the clubhouse, and its auditorium is in frequent use for concerts, lectures, and other public assemblies.

Gymnasium classes for young and old of both sexes are conducted under the supervision of trained leaders for physical development and recreation, and every opportunity is taken to stimulate high standards of character. Exhibitions and contests are held at intervals. In the summer the athletic field and tennis courts are in constant use. One of the most important features of this physical work is in connection with a fully equipped corrective room in which cases of malformation, including spinal and foot troubles, are treated by the physical directors, under the supervision of physicians. By arrangement with the school department the physical training of school children is carried on at the clubhouse and the physical directors coach the school athletic teams. There is now under way a plan for a closer union of the schools with the work of the civic association, so that the school work, conducted along the lines of work at Gary, Ind., may help the children best to meet their opportunities in life.

In addition to its work at the clubhouse, the civic association is doing extension work in outlying parts of the town; social centers are being developed as places of instruction and inspiration for its neighborhood. Within a few months the civic association has acquired ownership of an unused hall in one of the outlying parts of the town, and in still another section the town itself is turning over to the association an old school building.

In one corner of the grounds is the Corner House, so called because of its location. This is the health center. Here is a small hospital with a fully equipped operating room, and it is also the headquarters of the district and school nurses. A new and larger hospital is now being built. There are conducted regularly in the present hospital a dental clinic and an eye clinic, each in the care of a competent specialist. The entire work is under the general care of the women's standing committee, with the practical operation under a trained supervisor.

The supervisor is a graduate nurse and a student in social service, and she has under her a corps of trained assistants—both graduate nurses for service with physicians and attendant nurses for general nursing and home-keeping work. They all live together at the Corner House. They come in daily contact with the everyday life of numberless homes, and their influence is gradually manifesting itself. Norwood has to-day the lowest death rate in Massachusetts. The supervisor of the Corner House is the agent of the board of relief and helps to look after the dispensation of its funds; she serves to help the unemployed. There is also a fund at the Corner House to assist young men and women to obtain higher educational advantages than are offered in the town itself.

Then, there is the Model House. This is a small dwelling beside the Corner House. It is modestly furnished as an example and illustration of an attractive home within the possibilities of all who are capable of appreciating it.

It should be noted that the civic association is an organization for the purpose of centralizing in some one place the various community activities, rather than a social organization for the purpose of bringing all of the townspeople together on a common social basis. That would be clearly impossible. Each social group is bound to have its own activities, and the natural social life of the churches, lodges, and other organizations is not rivaled in the slightest degree. We must learn to get effective cooperation of our existing social groups. In our community center we are striving to create and arouse this cooperative spirit.

We have a town-planning committee which is following the best practice in town planning, along familiar lines. The Norwood Housing Association has been formed for the purpose of holding various parcels of property—both unimproved land in the outlying districts and improved properties in the residential and business sections of the town. Something like this is quite essential to make effective the best development of the community. Land is held for factory sites, so that the industrial development may be furthered; and, as the demand arises, it is planned to build houses in such number and under such modern standardized methods as to secure the best results at the minimum cost.

The Norwood Housing Association also has in mind the need of centers of recreation and is providing them. It has control of the entire shores of a lake nearly 2 miles long and half a mile wide, which lies on the outskirts of the town. Here it is proposed to build bathhouses, boathouses, and such additional buildings as will contribute to the pleasure of the greatest number of people. One portion of the shore is being set aside for bungalows, so that those who are able to do so may have comfortable homes there during the summer.

All of this brings in revenue; in fact, it is expected that from the development of this property the housing committee will secure very handsome returns and a large increase on its investment. This increased investment becomes an endowment fund for the civic association. It has been carefully worked out in this way: For the land deeded to it, the housing association issues its securities to the full extent of its cost or assessed value; mortgage bonds paying 5 per cent are issued for 60 per cent; preferred stock paying 6 per cent is issued for the next 20 per cent, and the common stock holds the remaining 20 per cent, which carries the entire equity of both the property and its earnings. Arrangements have been made by which the whole of this common stock may become the property of the civic association. As the town grows and its real estate develops, the civic association will thus find itself the beneficiary in a financial way of the development which it has helped make possible. Within a few years it should have sufficient income from this source alone to meet its entire running expenses. It is expected that this endowment fund, started with this common stock of the housing association, will be increased from time to time by legacies from public-spirited men and women in the community who have come to recognize the value of the work of the civic association and who will welcome the opportunity to aid in its continuance. The bonds and preferred stock of the housing association offer a safe and attractive investment for the townspeople, and at the same time serve to stimulate their interest in the whole undertaking.

As you well know, this idea of the housing association is not a new one. There are over 100 cities in Germany which have no municipal taxes, because all the money for public expenditures which would otherwise have to be met by taxes comes from the leased property which the cities have held for years.

Norwood appears to have made a real beginning. By assigning the duties of the town government to these two classes of men— one, honorable officials serving without salary, meeting at convenient intervals and giving to the town the same sort of attention that they would give to a private enterprise of which they were trustees or directors, and the other, business experts, chosen by careful methods of selection—we have established a well-ordered, economically conducted government. We have secured greater democracy, because we have broadened the field of citizenship from which these officials may be chosen; and we have gained greater efficiency, inasmuch as it is now possible to introduce the best possible methods.

The same principle of committee representation, working through paid experts, is giving us and our general community work the same splendid results. For a given amount of money we are, in my opinion, accomplishing very much more than formerly. It is astounding to consider what savings and gains could be effected by a similar centralization under expert management in a place the size of Boston, which now has scores and hundreds of charitable and civic organizations. It is true that many of these organizations perform efficient service, but the duplication and confusion occasioned by their great number mean undue expense and only partial handling of the whole task.

There is scarcely a limit to the things which can be done by a community which will find ways of uniting its powers and developing methods for expressing in action and deeds its ideals. Insurance against sickness and the loss of employment will go far toward removing a great fear from many households. We expect that we can work out in terms of the community some such form of insurance; and other problems are, we believe, capable of solution when once the community shall have appreciated its needs and its power to achieve.

In all these matters we are simply making effective in an old-fashioned New England community the same principles that have made German municipal management the most efficient in the world, and we are doing it by the cooperative effort of its citizens under the guidance of leaders of their own choice and kind. If we in Norwood, with no university to lead us, have made some progress in the direc-. tion of efficient democracy, how great are the possibilities of the cities of this country in which are established great universities, dedicated as they are to sound scholarship and lofty ideals of citizenship.

THE DEMAND FOR TRAINING FOR PUBLIC SERVICE.

By GEORGE R. WALLACE,
Pittsburgh Chamber of Commerce.

The time has not yet come for the urban universities to conduct an aggressive and insistent campaign to secure the employment of trained men in the public service. Something, of course, can be done; more in some cities than in others; but we have not yet reached the time for reaping the harvest of expert and efficient public service. We are rather still in the process of breaking the ground and sowing the seed. Expert public service will come only when there is a demand for it—not a theoretical demand that we ought to have expert service, but an economic demand, an actual desire on the part of city administrations to secure trained and efficient workers and to establish a permanent administrative organization on this basis.

City government is the product of the social and economic forces working in a community. In order to understand why a people which has developed great efficiency in its private affairs has failed to do so in its city administration, it is necessary to make some analysis of these forces.

Our city populations may be roughly divided for our purposes into three groups. There is, first, the general group of the average, nonpolitical citizen—the man who is earning from $700 or $800 a year to $5,000 or $10,000 a year. This group will constitute about half of our city population. It is composed of men who are essentially private men. They are absorbed in their private business and family affairs. Many of them, if not natives of other places, were born in what was practically an overgrown country town, for a generation ago most of our large cities were little more than that. These men have no inherited loyalty to their city. Very few of them feel that the city government is of any vital importance to them. Perhaps a majority of them regard politics as something more or less alien to their real interests. They distinguish between business and politics, and many of them pride themselves on knowing nothing about the affairs of their city government and of taking no interest in them. Although there is a constantly growing sentiment among these people for better conditions in city service, they are unorganized, without power of effective action, without leadership, without the means of securing the very considerable funds which are necessary for successful civic campaigns. They are the easy victims of trumped-up issues, popular slogans, and appeals to party loyalty.

It is true that from time to time they grumble about high taxes, bad streets, poor fire and police protection, and occasionally, under the impulse of some dramatic happening, they unite and sweep their representatives into power. The result is almost always disappointing. The men elected, with the best of intentions, are utterly unskilled in city administration, lacking technical knowledge, uninformed as to the real purposes of city government, and are subject to pressures which greatly embarrass and hinder their successes, while the mass of the population, after such an election, relapses into indifference. Most men of this class come to regard present civic conditions as natural and inevitable, for they have no knowledge of city government in other countries and no point of view for comparison.

Above this group is a small group of men representing large economic units, who are intensely interested in city government, but in a private and personal way. The public utilities of most of our cities are owned and operated not by the city but by corporations. Those who are responsible to the stockholders of these corporations are primarily interested in the success and earning power of the corporation. This success and earning power is very greatly affected by the city government. These corporations must have franchises, as required, on satisfactory terms, privileges of opening streets, placing wires and conduits, regulations of surface openings, of questions affecting the cleaning and maintenance of streets, etc. A hostile city government can do them vast injury. By the very pressure of economic necessity they have been driven into city politics.

There are other groups in the city which necessarily, as a matter of business, are vitally interested in the city government. The liquor dealers, for instance, can have their profits greatly affected by the attitude of the police department. There are city contractors, and there are the men on the shady side of the law, whose very existence depends upon a friendly administration.

In the American political system city government is inextricably enmeshed with the State and National Governments, and larger groups interested in State and National legislation and administration feel themselves compelled to protect their interests by taking a strong hand in the affairs of the city administration.

Below the great middle class lies the submerged class, the unskilled workmen, the thousands of foreigners, men without friends. without resources, without any economic strength, and therefore without any political strength. Perhaps 25 per cent or more of the actual voters in our large cities may be included in this class of helpless voters. The law gives them a ballot, but their economic position deprives them of it. They are at the mercy of the police and the police magistrates. They buy peace in the easiest way—by taking orders. There are precincts in many of our large cities where the mass of the voters are so helpless that they can not even protect their registration or secure the counting of their ballots. Then there is the large and increasing public pay roll. In many cities nearly 10 per cent of the actual voters are on some governmental pay roll. Economic necessity controls most of these votes, and the votes of men in their families.

There are also in our cities many men of narrow circumstances to whom politics afford an excitement, a recreation. It is to them the greatest national sport, after baseball. They love the fight. They are open to appeals of factional loyalty. Many of them aspire to city employment as a signal honor to be achieved. They are a great force in the recurring contests for the control of the city, and as a rule have no conception of what these contests are really about.

Now, out of these conditions there grows the actual thing which we call American city government. The powerful economic groups, vitally interested from a personal and business point of view in the conduct of city government, by a more or less conscious organization, and by the expenditure of large sums of money, when necessary, are back of most successful tickets in city elections. Their funds and their economic power are used to direct the vote of the helpless group. The great middle class, more or less indifferent and uninformed, confused by long ballots and the multiplicity of campaign cries, are generally divided and ineffective.

It is not the purpose of this paper to pillory the controlling group here described. Many of them are men of high character and real patriotism, but they are absorbed in business, they have never studied the problems of government, they have grown up under the system, they know no other way, and very often they are largely themselves ignorant of what they are really doing.

Suppose they have secured, for instance, as mayor a business man of high standing and character, who really desires to install business methods in the city administration. Almost inevitably he finds himself unable to do it to any extent. In the first place, he is himself without any technical knowledge or any clear views of what the city government is for. The conception of community activity for community ends is vague and faint in his mind. He is subjected to great pressure; his army of supporters is demanding recognition and employment. He is told that he must preserve the political organization which put him in. He is bombarded every day, and often from high and influential sources, to give certain persons employment; while the great mass of voters lies silent, dormant, inarticulate, there is pressure from the other side. Almost inevitably he yields, perhaps to his own discontent and disgust.

Furthermore, the maintenance of the controlling political organization is expensive. The natural impulse of those who support it financially is to pay as little of that expense as possible themselves, and to distribute as much as possible among the general body of the taxpayers. It is, from their point of view, profitable to have an inefficient and overloaded pay roll, because in this way the tax of supporting the organization is not all paid by themselves, but is partly paid by the taxpayers generally, and the advantages which they reap in their own private business more than compensate for the increased taxation which they have to pay.

We have, therefore, an actual government in cities which is of necessity inimical to a permanent, efficient, expert body of public servants. If a university in a city so governed, with whatever diplomacy and tact, offers itself for the training of public servants, and endeavors to insist upon their employment, it will meet three difficulties.

In the first place, if it becomes too insistent, it will be looked upon as meddling with affairs which do not concern it, and the plausible greetings with which its first efforts may be met will soon change into opposition more or less expressed.

In the second place, it will be very difficult to get intelligent young men to enter the city's services under these conditions, because it does not offer them a career. The exigencies of politics may throw them out at any time. They can not count upon rising step by step through a lifetime, as a reward of merit.

In the third place, most universities are in constant need of funds. These funds can be secured only from men of large means, and a university which presses this matter to a point where it becomes troublesome will be very apt to receive intimations that it is going outside of its proper sphere of influence, should stay out of politics, and confine itself to education.

There is another barrier in the way. The organization of cities under the charters in force in most of them makes expert public service difficult, if not impossible. We have been cursed in this country by the adoption of the political theories of the eighteenth century French philosophers. We owe a great debt to Montesquieu, Rousseau, and others for preaching the gospel of freedom, but their views of governmental organization have proven to be hopelessly wrong, and yet they are the basis underlying most city charters. We elect all manner of men for short terms, and in particular we elect the chief administrator, the mayor. Almost inevitably he is either a politician, bred in the old school, or a business man, unskilled in city government. In the former, he has no sympathy with efficiency. If the latter, he finds himself thrown into an occupation which is strange and new to him. He is necessarily cautious, timid, and uncertain. He is surrounded by great pressures. If he has the right stuff in him, after struggling for several years he does acquire some degree of knowledge and skill, and then his term has expired and the charter generally provides that he can not be a candidate for reelection. With an inefficient, confused, and constantly changing head, no administrative organization can rise very high. We must learn a lesson from the splendid city governments of Germany and other European countries. We must elect a council which shall serve as a board of directors, and let that council select the mayor or the bürgermeister on a basis of expert knowledge and ability, maintaining him in power so long as he renders good service. With a permanent and efficient head, there is a possibility of obtaining efficiency throughout the organization.

I do not paint this picture for the purpose of encouraging pessimism or discouraging the urban universities from attempting a great service to their cities. Conditions are rapidly improving, have improved enormously during the last 20 years. In many cities a foothold has been obtained for expert service. Some very gratifying results have been obtained in Pittsburgh, but after all, they are more or less sporadic and exigent. At present, the main fight should be waged in another place, where the universities can perform a great public service, greatly advance the day of real efficiency, and eventually put themselves in the place where they will be called upon by the cities to train men for city service.

Every year thousands of our most promising young men go through our urban universities. They go from them into the thick of city life. The work must begin with them. They must be given such instruction that they will be centers for the development of that intelligent public sentiment which is a necessary precursor of the thing we desire. Let no university undertake to serve its community unless it has that infinite patience which is willing to dig to the bottom of things and build slowly and solidly upon the rock foundation.

Now, what are these boys to be taught? The merely altruistic and emotional appeal is not enough. Our people mean well enough. What they need to learn is the tremendous, vital stake which they have as individuals and as communities in the conduct of their city government. The controlling facts must first be thoroughly learned by the universities themselves, and then taught to their students.

Why is it that we are so far behind European cities in this respect? Primarily because we have only recently become a city-dwelling people. We know little about cities. They are largely foreign to our processes of thought. At the time of the Revolutionary War there were only 12 or 15 chartered cities in the United States. The largest of them, Philadelphia, was not as big as many city wards to-day. In fact, the great growth of our cities has come since the close of the Civil War. Into them have been poured men from all sections of the country who have come into them indifferent and unconcerned, having no knowledge or conception of large community life, and the vast distinction between the country dweller and the city dweller.

It is a fact that in the small community the local government is not of much importance. The farmer or the villager does everything for himself. If he wants water, he digs a well or a cistern, and he has his water. The city dweller can not do this. The city provides him with water; and this is so whether the city owns the waterworks or makes a contract with some private organization for that purpose. The city likewise provides light and transportation. The man in the small community has little need of police protection, but lawless men accumulate and operate in the cities, and protection must be furnished by the city itself.

The rural man can protect his own health. The city man can not. The infected water, the poisonous sweatshop, the filthy slum may strike down his nearest and dearest, and he is helpless unless the city itself protects him. The city dweller has no protection for his children against moral infection. The plague spots will exist and contaminate unless the city government stamps them out. The business development of the city dweller is largely dependent upon the city government. The merchants may compete with each other for all the business there is in the community, but they can not enlarge the city. The city with high taxes, bad housing conditions, poor water, poor schools, poor traction service, poor opportunities for recreation is undesirable to live in, undesirable to establish plants in, while the city in the reverse condition is constantly drawing new populations, new consumers, and new capital, and so enlarging the opportunity of every dweller in the city for either employment or business. In every respect the city, and the larger the city the more true this is, is the factor most largely controlling the social and economic environment of the citizen.

Let the universities give sound, fundamental instruction to the constant stream of young men passing through them, so that they shall come out with some conception of what community activity is, of how important it is, with a breadth of view and a grasp of the larger relations of things, and a situation will soon be produced which will enable the universities to render a service greatly needed and increasingly desired in the training of men to the honorable career of efficient and expert service to the city.

A SEARCH FOR THE MAXIMUM CAPACITY FOR SERVICE.

By Dr. Hollis Godfrey,
President of Drexel Institute, Philadelphia, Pa.

THREE PRIMARY PURPOSES OF A TEACHING INSTITUTION.

The cooperation of any college with its community provides a problem with most complex factors and with an amazing number of variants. Because of that very complexity, effective cooperation demands the determination of a clear-cut general policy which can be clearly expressed to the community. Such a policy can only be effective when based on decisions which result from carefully made studies. Such studies can be accepted as guides only when they are made with a full understanding of the purposes of a teaching institution.

The primary purpose of a teaching institution to-day, as in the days of Plato's academy, is to transfer a vital thought from the mind of the teacher to the mind of the scholar. Any study has lost the essential touchstone of inherent truth which does not bear in mind continually as a fundamental concept the thought that any change made as a result of study which retards or blocks the transference of the vital thought is a loss, while every change so made which aids in that transference is a gain. No one can recognize more clearly than the trained and experienced engineer that efficiency is but one factor in economy, and that any economy which does not include spiritual and human factors is not true economy.

The administrators of any educational trust have, however, second and third purposes to carry out which are as basic as the first. Like any other trustees, they are given certain funds to administer. It must be their ideal to see that no dollar of the funds is wasted. Every student who comes to the institution gives to the keeping of the trustees many hours of his life. Consequently the third ideal of the trustees must be to see that no hour of the student's time is wasted through their fault. The term "trustees" in this connection includes not only those technically so named, but also every member of the teaching and administrative staff.

THE METHOD OF ATTACK UPON THE PROBLEM.

Three fundamental purposes of college investigations having been defined; the method of attack comes next. Fortunately, we have for this certain clear lines of procedure, based on analogies from the industrial world. If a thoroughly modern bank desires to have a complete report on a given business project, it requests reports not only from men trained in the special trade, craft, or art which it is proposed to establish, but it also seeks the advice of consulting engineers and lawyers. Only after the reports of all three groups are in can a complete picture, sufficient to warrant the investment of funds, be secured.

When that is true where funds and their investment are alone to be considered, how much more is it true where the investment includes the precious hours of thousands of men and women.

THE DREXEL INSTITUTE'S SPECIFIC PROBLEM.

With the three primary purposes and the known method of attack on industrial problems as starting points, we have been endeavoring to answer this question: How could the Drexel Institute, a small college type of technical school, giving day and evening instruction in three schools—engineering, domestic science, and arts and secretarial—give by means of its courses the best cooperation with the community factors of Philadelphia and at the same time carry out certain expressed desires of its founders?

In the attempt to answer this question, up to the present time 39 specific researches have been begun and continued for at least one year. Some 16 others have been begun during the last year and are now in various stages of development. Of this group there have been selected for the purposes of this paper brief statements of certain factors concerned in the studies made of the following subjects: Admission requirements; the institute catalogue; the distribution of scholarship funds; curricula; graduate work of the staff; teaching services of undergraduates; the employment of graduates and undergraduates.

ADMISSION REQUIREMENTS.

That upon the rock of entrance requirements the good ship "Cooperation" may be in dire peril of shipwreck goes without saying. We considered this question of what should be done about entrance requirements, therefore, with the utmost care, and finally answered it by means of the following methods and in the following ways:

First, the admission requirements of every institution of collegiate grade in and around Philadelphia, were obtained and analyzed.

Second, the entrance requirements of 230 colleges in the United States were analyzed.

Third, there are 119 four-year high and preparatory schools from whose districts students may take trolley or train to Philadelphia daily. Sixty of these were visited personally, and in each the principal of the school was asked to give us his or her best thought on the relation of admission requirements to the problem of cooperation between the high schools of greater Philadelphia and the Drexel Institute.

Fourth, a group of the men who have had the most experience with admission requirements were chosen and brought to the institute to aid us with their advice. We also took the data obtained to other experts who could not come to the institute.

Fifth, the results of all these studies were briefed and charted and submitted to the admission committee and then to the major faculty of the institute, who passed upon them.

The result of the studies outlined above showed, first, that the tendency of all the colleges in our field to require specific subjects for admission generally forced the student to decide the course he was to take at least by the end of the first year in the high school, or else to take more than the usual four years.

Second, that a considerable number of colleges of the first rank in the United States were giving admission on the basis of high-school graduation requiring work of high quality, but not specifying any given subjects.

Third, that the principals of the high schools in greater Philadelphia felt almost unanimously that there was great need for some collegiate institution to grant admission to high-school graduates of high quality who had not planned to go to college until the second or third year of their course and who would be debarred from entrance at the end of the four-year course because of that delay in decision.

Fourth, that every man consulted who had had to do with entrance requirements believed our wisest course would be to insist on quality, rather than on specific subjects, provided high-school graduation was secured and provided the proper safeguards be put around the admission of the entering student.

The result of this policy, so far as the quality and preparation of the students entering the institute is concerned, has been admirable. Of the freshman class last year, 95 per cent were high-school graduates. This year 94 per cent were high-school graduates, and no conditional student is admitted unless we can see a specific reason in his or her case for such admission.

So far as our relations with other institutions are concerned, the result has been most satisfactory.

THE COLLEGE CATALOGUE.

No single factor more advances cooperative action between the college and the community than clear expression of the opportunities that the college offers. Every college should place before its community those instructional opportunities which a part of the community desires or should desire. From the educational standpoint, however, it seems eminently wise to throw the emphasis on the fact that the college offers an apportunity to the student, rather than that the student grants an opportunity to the college when he enters it. For that reason the Drexel Institute limits its public statements to its own publications. Its belief that simple, honest statements of the work done, coupled with the best possible printing, were the most effective publicity program that could be secured, provided the basis for the next research mentioned here. This research was undertaken to determine the best expression of the facts about the institute. One part of it took this form: What is the most effective form for the college catalogue? To determine the answer to this question, the following methods were employed:

First, 420 college catalogues were examined and their main points noted and analyzed.

Second, the best catalogue work of certain industrial lines, such as the automobile line, which have come to recognize the value of good printing, were examined and analyzed.

Third, a group of experts in the printing art, including some of the best-known printers in America, were asked to the institute to go through it and to assist in writing specifications for the make-up of a catalogue which should properly express the institute to the community.

Fourth, as a result of the suggestion of those experts, 18 type pages were set up, one after another, and submitted to the printing experts, to oculists, and to illuminating engineers. The eighteenth page set was the one finally accepted. The catalogue as last issued is the result of this research.

The writing of the catalogue has been quite as carefully considered as its format. Each year it has been written by one man, but this man's work has been criticized by three trained writers and editorially amended and checked. The catalogue is now in its third form.

Style, however, is less important than directness and simple honesty. In order to obtain these things, all the essential facts in the

catalogue are placed for inspection in the hands, first, of the major
faculty; second, of the minor faculty; third, of the upper classes of
the institute. All of these groups meet in conference to go over the
facts in the catalogue, with the request that they criticize freely any
word or phrase which is in any way untrue or in any way misrepre-
sents the facts about the institute.

We can scarcely emphasize too strongly the value of this research
as shown in the educational results to students and faculty and as
regards the cooperative results with the community. There is no
single factor which has caused more vagueness in the efforts for
cooperation than ineffective and confused expression of educational
aims and opportunities.

THE DISTRIBUTION OF SCHOLARSHIP FUNDS.

In the two preceding researches the work was accomplished by the
cooperation of outside expert assistants and inside experienced effort.
In the next research, to determine the best use of scholarship funds,
the third of the three factors mentioned earlier, the legal factor,
appears. This research passed through the following stages:

First, examination and classification of all applications for financial help from students received during a given period of time.

Second, personal interviews with older students and their parents
to find where, if anywhere, financial pressure was most evident.

Third, the designing of a policy as regards scholarship funds
which should be equitable to all and do the greatest good to the
greatest number.

Fourth, consultation with the corporation counsel to obtain an
opinion as to whether or not the policy proposed carried out our legal
and moral obligations.

As a result of investigations one and two, it was found, first, that
a large percentage of the students who had held scholarships preferred to give work in exchange for financial aid, provided this were
possible, and second, that one of the most serious handicaps to the
planning of individual student finances was the uncertainty of the
one who paid the bills concerning the cost of books and supplies.

The plan finally proposed solved these difficulties. Exact studies
showed that by using the existing scholarship funds to purchase the
more expensive technical works required, it would be possible to
guarantee every entering regular student that his or her maximum
cost of books and supplies not representing permanent investment
would not exceed $25. An amount of work commanding a wage
equal to the scholarship funds then granted was at the same time
opened to student assistance.

The plan outlined was submitted to the corporation counsel, who
decided that it legally and morally carried out the purposes for

which the funds were given. This has meant a marked step forward in the clarification of our relations with the community.

CURRICULA.

Our use of the usual principles of the perpetual audit and of the perpetual inventory, with daily reports of the financial and educational state of the institute, has had the unusual effect of initiating studies which have resulted in three of the most fundamentally cooperative polices we have undertaken.

The first of these policies is the complete differentiation of our curricula from the curricula of any other institution in our territory.

Second, the development of the group of the night school, in which 1,500 men and women are now entered for continuous balanced courses of from two to seven years.

Third, the development of our plan of offering to any 16 persons any course given in the institute at any time when a teacher is unoccupied and a classroom or a laboratory is vacant.

As a result of these policies, we are rapidly reaching a point where some classes are working in the institute every hour of the day from 9 in the morning to 9.30 at night.

OTHER STUDIES.

In order to encourage graduate work, the institute pays the first fee of any member of its staff who desires to take courses at the University of Pennsylvania or Columbia. Last year 23 availed themselves of this opportunity, and 29 are doing graduate work this year.

As a result of an extensive study, we determined upon the policy of using the teaching powers of the upper classes for community service. The school of domestic science and arts furnishes teachers, free of charge, from among the ranks of the older students to charitable institutions in Philadelphia. The control of this outside work is vested in three members of the instructional staff, who are given specific hours to care for the effectiveness of the service.

The study concerning the employment of graduates and undergraduates has found effective form through the activities of the bureau of recommendations. Up to the present time these studies have been concerned chiefly with work open to graduates, vacation work open to undergraduates, and employment for undergraduates which can be carried on together with their academic work.

We have postponed, up to the present time, two vital studies which are now beginning: That of bettering the employment of the older graduates, and that of the employment of students in the night course.

Studies were made of the specific employment needs of the members of the national engineering societies in Philadelphia, certain branches of the iron and steel industry, the public service corporation, and the engineering branches of the city. On the women's side studies were made of the employment needs of hospitals, institutions, and schools, and especially of the executive who employs the women graduates of our secretarial school.

Our efforts have been very successful. Of 154 graduates of last year, all but one who desired positions are well placed. Over 30 per cent more good positions were available than we had graduates to place. Between 80 per cent and 90 per cent of our upper classmen worked last summer at employments closely related to their professional training. Their average for the summer was approximately $145.

In concluding this brief report of some phases of the continuous and arduous work of two years, certain facts should be noted. First, we are fully convinced that any problem will yield to this treatment, given the right conditions. Second, we have to-day more research work and we see our problem as a whole and the relation of each part to the whole more clearly than at any previous period. Third, we are more open-minded than ever before and more anxious for every possible type of assistance which may aid us in the definition and solution of our problems. Fourth, we really believe we can see marked gains in our cultivation of that rare flower—common sense.

But, beside all this, our statement would be incomplete did it not bear witness to the spiritual values which have come from the combined effort of a devoted group, each member eager to bear his or her full part in our research to determine the maximum capacity for service of the institute. Nothing is clearer to those of us who have taken part in this work than that it has affected us all in such a way as to give us greater pride in our great art of teaching, greater pride in our institution, greater pride in the community of which we are a part.

———

COOPERATION WITH BUSINESS ORGANIZATIONS.

By Mr. JOHN W. FAHEY,
President of the National Chamber of Commerce.

Organizations of business men have been undergoing a rather thorough reform. The old-time commercial organizations, chambers of commerce, boards of trade, and commercial clubs we have had with us from the first days of the Republic; but until recent years these organizations lacked the breadth of view which should characterize the work of modern business men—men realizing that there are problems of great importance affecting business and the common prosperity which have to do with the welfare of the city and its social progress and which do not come directly across the desk of the business man in his daily work.

But now, in nearly every one of these organizations, greater emphasis has been laid upon civic activity than ever before. In one city after another the business men have finally overcome the old-time suspicion of the professor as a theorist. And on the other side colleges and universities have come to see that the business man was not quite so intensely practical and ultraselfish as he was assumed to be, but that he had something of idealism and even altruism about him; that he was anxious to be of real service, realizing that the broad path to public confidence for the business man lies through service, and through service alone.

In training for public service an important point is that while we train young men as efficient public servants, as experts in municipal affairs, we must understand that they are going to have difficulty in holding their places and going on in their useful careers, unless they have the backing of intelligent citizenship—a citizenship that is based on leadership. So far as this leadership is concerned, there is a large amount of useful material among business men as a group.

Another part of the problem will depend for solution upon the upbuilding of schools of commerce. To support municipal efficiency, the business organization of a city must itself be efficient and prosperous. We need better training for business, better commercial training. We may say that there is nothing like practical experience in making the best type of business man, but business men are beginning to understand to-day that they can not have too much training in intelligence that can be utilized and adapted in daily practice.

_____

THE NEED FOR FURTHER INVESTIGATION OF THE PROBLEMS OF TRAINING FOR PUBLIC SERVICE.

By LEON C. MARSHALL,

Dean of the College of Commerce and Administration, University of Chicago.

We are in a very puzzled and mixed frame of mind concerning the whole question of public service and the training for public service. Good intentions we have by the wagonload; ideals we have in even greater abundance; but clean-cut policies, cool decision, these we sadly lack at the present stage of our undertaking.

A few months ago the former president of De Pauw University illustrated what different people do at times of mental indecision. He told of a group who were making their way through an uncharted wilderness. Just when they were in what seemed to them the hardest part of their journey, all at once a fog settled down and blotted out all of the landmarks with which they had become familiar. Thereupon one collection of that group of travelers said: "The only thing that we can do now is to retrace our steps and get back to high ground from which we can take another look and see if we can. discover the old landmarks back there, set our stakes, and make this journey over again, and perhaps the next time we can go on a little farther." Whereupon they retraced their steps. Another group felt not at all that way. They said: "There is no use going back over the territory that we have covered. This fog will soon lift; it will be dispelled by the sun, and we will be able to go on. Let us sit down and patiently wait, and meanwhile we will regain some of our strength; and when the fog lifts we will have recovered from our fatigue due to the journey that we have already made, and then we can go on with confidence." The third group would have none of that. They said: "No; let us plunge ahead. We will not know where we are going—that is true—but we will be on the way." So this third group plunged ahead through the fog; they tore their clothes on the briars and brambles, bumped themselves against logs and stumps that lay in their way, encountered various difficulties, and very likely some of them did push through; but the group became separated, and few, if any, of them ever reached their journey's end. But there was a fourth group that said: "It is no use for us to go back over the ground we have already traversed; we could not find the landmarks there if we did go back. Let us calmly consider and take stock of the situation as it is. We will reflect from what direction we were coming when we were stopped by this fog; where the sun was the last time we saw it; what the general lay of the land is, to the best of our knowledge; and on the basis of all the investigating and thinking over the matter that we can do we will proceed cautiously, moving slowly ahead all the time, meanwhile keeping close connection with each other, and see if we can not arrive at the promised land in that way."

This seems to depict fairly accurately the situation with reference to the training for public service. We must proceed slowly anyway, and we shall certainly be more comfortable if we are a little patient in the situation in which we find ourselves. The development of institutions should be lessons for us.

Take, for example, the modern college of commerce. The college of commerce originated in this country in the eighties. One educator generations ago outlined a program of training for commercial purposes, but there were no colleges of commerce established as the result of his outline. The time was not yet ripe. Many things had to occur before the time was ripe. The same thing was true of institutes of technology. They had to be preceded by a period of preparation which was upon the whole quiet preparation. The same thing was certainly true of the "industrial revolution" as a whole. We say it occurred after 1750; but if there is any one thing that is certain in human history, it is that the "industrial revolution" began before the year 1300 and was in process of preparation for five hundred years before a few inventors struck the match to the powder and gave us the explosion that has been called the "industrial revolution."

No human institution is perfect. If Frederick W. Taylor could, as he did when he was alive, step into the best shops in the United States—not the poorest shops, but the best shops—and with the same equipment increase their output anywhere from 100 to 1,100 per cent; if the steam engine to-day makes available but a small percentage of the energy that is in coal; if it is true that even according to present knowledge the human race is sometimes like one-quarter of 1 per cent efficient; if there is even a modicum of truth in these general propositions, we may well judge this movement of training for public service not by some absolute standards but by what may reasonably be expected of human beings in matters of this sort. We shall need to keep a calm and sane perspective and accumulate our powder until later or somebody shall be able to set the match to it. It may be that we shall not have to wait long. But only when we have arrived at the full consciousness of our needs in this country may we expect rapid progress to occur in training for public service; consequently patience seems to be one of the virtues that we may well cultivate for the next few years.

Another thing it seems to me would be highly important, namely, that we do not overlook the necessity of laying a good, firm foundation. The public servant is like a physician—indeed, he is a physician to society. In sending out these physicians to society we must recognize that the social organism is quite as complex as the human organism. Would it not be well, therefore, for us to make certain that our physicians go forth knowing first the physiology of the social organism; knowing, second, the pathology of the social organism, and possessing, finally, all the administrative qualities and all of the technique that we can crowd in behind? It is through technique, as has been very properly said, that much of the physiology can be taught, but let us make certain that we are giving these people a knowledge of the physiology of American society.

We have gone so far in our development of specialized studies since the great Civil War in this country that we have never had time to take stock of our situation. A man who is willing to take stock may by radicals be called "academic." That name does not frighten me, because that sort of work must be performed if we are to have well-rounded preparation. Our undergraduates do not need more courses in money, more courses in banking, more courses in trusts, more courses in railroading, more courses in municipal government; what they need is correlation. If we provide this correlation and then turn out students who have an appreciation of the structure and function of organized society, we shall be prepared to train a technical body of public servants properly.

III. METHODS OF TRAINING FOR PUBLIC SERVICE.

METHODS OF TRAINING FOR PUBLIC SERVICE.

By CHARLES A. BEARD,
Director of the New York Training School for Public Service.

An industrial democracy can not long endure without a sound and efficient public service. In older and simpler days when this was a nation of farmers, and the functions of government were largely limited to national defense, the repression of crime, and the collection of taxes, it mattered little if waste and folly and jobbery accompanied every public enterprise. The great economic processes of the Nation, even if somewhat hampered by the muddling methods of the State, could go on in the general tenor of their way in spite of the spoils system, rotation in office, and ignorance in public service. The slogan that "any man can fill any office that he can get, whether trained for it or not," although foolish enough in those days, was at least not criminal.

Signs are not wanting, however, that our generation is becoming keenly alive to the problems of public service presented by the new order. It is no mere coincidence that it was largely due to the inspiration of the great organizing genius of his time, Mr. E. H. Harriman, that the training school for public service, initiated by Mrs. Harriman in 1911, owes its origin.

From that hour the idea has taken firmer and firmer root in the American public mind. In 1912, the American Political Science Association appointed a committee to study the relation of the universities to public service, and its reports resulted in the stimulation of widespread interest inside and outside of academic circles. In 1914 the association's committee, on the invitation of Mayor Mitchel, held an important conference in New York, which was attended by representatives of the leading colleges and universities in the country. Since that time, Michigan, Texas, Indiana, Harvard, and Minnesota Universities, and the College of the City of New York have taken steps toward the assumption of strict responsibility in the matter of training for public service.

We may rest secure in the faith that our colleges and universities will respond to every real call for help—so secure in fact that we may now turn from the work of exhortation to that of adjusting our actual program of instruction to such opportunities as the public service at present offers. This adjustment involves two things: First, a regrouping of courses and the addition of new courses which will afford the requisite general foundation and the proper special discipline; and, secondly, the granting of academic credit for field or observation work in government and administration.

The granting of academic credit is undoubtedly a serious matter and must be closely controlled, but it is fundamental to any real advance in training for public service. That it can be done without impairment of academic standards seems certain. We shall have no difficulty in securing academic recognition for field work if we can show that the control over it is such as to guarantee its solid character.

While gaining at the hands of institutions of learning a proper grouping of courses of instruction and due credit for laboratory or field work, we must also devote ourselves assiduously to another more formidable task—that of educating the American public to appreciate trained service, to demand more of it, and to insist upon an adjustment of our civil-service organization and methods to our magnificent educational system. Every year thousands of young men and women are coming out of our schools filled with enthusiasm and high hopes. Plenty of them are ready to serve the state with the loyalty and zeal of the soldier if the state will open the door to them and make the way clear, even though narrow and rough.

The essential part of the program of those who are seeking to improve the public service by securing trained servants is as follows:

1. It is the function of politics to determine what should be done; it is the function of the trained expert to carry out the public will with all the instruments and methods which modern science, natural and social, can command.

2. A larger number of the exempt positions in civil service must be put upon a merit basis. In other words, in every division of government there should be permanent under secretaries whose experience and training will secure continuity in the particular field. Under such a system, the young man or woman entering public service could thus look forward to securing, by the display of genuine talents, positions of dignity, power, and responsibility.

3. There must be created some system of junior offices in the several great branches of administration, which offices will be open to properly qualified young men and women, and which will give them further practical training and open a gateway through promotion for loyal and efficient labor to the higher posts. At the present

time practically nothing has been done to link up the public service directly with our splendid system of education.

4. The residence qualification as a requirement for admission to public service must be abolished or seriously modified, thus widening the opportunities for careers in the public service by making it possible for able and devoted civil servants to move from city to city, or even State to State.

5. The term "examination" must be extended to include more laboratory or field experience, in addition to academic training, thus facilitating promotion and transfers in the public service, and recognizing practical work, such as is given in the training school for public service, and may be provided in connection with most colleges and universities. It is gratifying to note that our most enlightened civil-service commissioners are giving an increasing weight to experience.

Here we might inquire whether schools undertaking this training can hope to place their graduates in positions to which their abilities and labors may entitle them. They probably can. On surveying the public service to-day, we find it falls into what may be called two broad divisions: 1. Official public service. 2. Unofficial public service.

The first of these divisions—the official public service—may be subdivided according to method of appointment into exempt and classified positions. With reference to the exempt group, there is an inveterate suspicion that trained men and women can not look forward to permanent careers in that branch of the public service. To a considerable extent the suspicion is justified.

That branch of the civil service which is open through competitive examination is not only more extensive, but includes most of the positions for which technical training is actually required. The existence of a large number of "cramming" schools for Federal, State, and municipal service is an indication that some kind of special preparation is a gateway to that service. Since this is so, it is evident that high schools, colleges, and universities might, if they would put their minds to the problem, develop courses of instruction which would better equip their students for specified lines of the classified positions, thus encouraging them to enter the service of the State and cooperate in raising the standards of that service.

From the point of view of the nature of the positions, the official public service may be divided into two divisions—technical and professional, and nontechnical.

The first division includes those positions for which technical or professional training is required—engineers, physicians, chemists, foresters, accountants, geologists. For these positions the schools are giving reasonably satisfactory technical and professional instruction, but it would be an immense gain to the public service if they would add to their curricula courses in public administration involving the several specialties, taxation and finance, government and economics, institutional management, and other subjects calculated to broaden the horizon of the technical or professional student; and make it easier for him to fit into the complex scheme of public administration.

The nontechnical branch of the public service, whether exempt or under the merit system, includes a number of positions which are attractive to those who have had advanced university work in economics and political science, and particularly to those who supplement technical or professional education by such training. Among the positions of this type may be included the following: City managers and administrative officers; civil service examiners; directors of social centers; investigators for special staff bureaus, such as the Federal Trade Commission at Washington, or the Bureau of Standards in New York City; investigators for commissions, such as tax, public utility, insurance, industrial, and other commissions; reference librarians, municipal and State; secretaries and research agents for legislative committees or members; deputies and secretaries to executive officers.

The unofficial public service to which I referred above offers at the present time more available and attractive positions to trained men and women than the official service. One of the striking features of modern democracy is the constant cooperation of the citizens with the Government through civic organization. As the functions of government increase, the matters of these associations will increase and the work of those already in existence will extend. Indeed, our civic organizations are becoming, in fact, gateways to official public service in its higher ranges.

There is one branch of service which is so often treated apart from Government that it is frequently overlooked, namely, education. In the field of education there is a call for trained men and women capable of handling large administrative problems, as well as those of pedagogy. Our normal schools and teachers' colleges are, of course, giving a great deal of attention to this matter, and the time has now come to increase materially the amount of field work and observation. This is done in Massachusetts, where practical administration is counted toward the degree in education.

There is also a problem of educational policy which is vitally connected with the subject of the hour—that is, the training of teachers of government, civic and administrative. The neglect of these subjects, particularly in the high schools, is nothing short of a disgrace to the Republic.

There is another query, namely, is it possible to train men and women for the public service by what may be termed the laboratory method, which adds practical experience to book learning? This question will be answered by reference to the program and methods of instruction of the training school for public service.

The school insists that its students must have a broad foundation in general government, municipal science, administration, economics, and finance. The school does not at present offer formalized instruction in these subjects, and if an applicant has not already had these fundamental subjects in some college or university, he is required to secure this discipline before he is regarded as prepared for public service.

The school confines its attention largely to training the students in investigation of concrete civic problems, with New York City as the laboratory. The whole field is divided into several divisions, such as : Public finance and accounting; public works; public safety—police and fire administration; social service—the administration of health functions, charities, and correction, etc.; civil service and standardization of salaries and grades; central management and control, including executive, board, and staff organization and procedure.

In the course of his two years' residence the regular student passes through several, if not all, of these divisions. All contact with public officers and all reports of conferences with them are made under the direction of officers or staff members of the bureau of municipal research, who are responsible for statements of fact and conclusion reached. No member of the school is permitted to deal independently with public officers or to render independent reports. We control and check the students' work in many ways, in order to be able to form an accurate judgment as to quantity and quality.

Since the foundation of the school we have sent into the official and unofficial service more than 75 students—lawyers, doctors, accountants, engineers, teachers, and experts in public administration. While we have not escaped all the frailties of the flesh, we believe that the institution has justified the faith of the founders and has found a permanent place among the new professional schools of America. Having no cause to serve except that of wise and efficient administration, charging no tuition fees, seeking no private profit whatsoever, and asking no favors except a just recognition of the merits of its graduates, the training school hopes to command by good works the confidence and esteem of civic organization and authorities of State and to build the new profession of public service on a lasting foundation.

SOME PHASES OF FIELD WORK.

By PARKE R. KOLBE,

President of Municipal University of Akron, Ohio.

By field work is meant the activities of students sent out by a university department to get experience in the actual *doing* of some piece of extramural work. Visits of inspection or observation are not included under this term; they bear much the same relation to real field work as does the reading of a textbook to laboratory practice.

The traditions of education recognize three main factors in the formal training of the student—the recitation, the lecture, and the laboratory. The quiz, the conference, the demonstration, the examination, are only variants or tests of these three basic methods. The science of teaching has reduced them to an exact status. We may refer at any time to a multitude of books on pedagogy which will inform us as to the value or worthlessness of the many theories which have grown up about them. But neither books, professors nor schools have yet recognized the value of the newest factor in education, namely, field work. Few measures have been taken to insure its standardization in method or its efficiency in execution.

Certain standards of comparison may be laid down as basic and applicable to all forms of field work. Such are methods of supervision, means for testing results, and plan of accrediting. Other important factors are the assignment of work, coordination of theory and practice, remuneration for field workers, and practical usefulness of the work.

[Here President Kolbe enumerated forms of field work in various colleges. Then he proceeded to give typical plans of organization, as follows:]

One of the most broadly developed plans of sociological field work is found at Harvard under the department of social ethics. The following is quoted from a recent letter from Prof. James Ford:

Field work in this course has been undertaken in various forms. For example, in my class of last year six members made a thorough housing survey of several blocks in the city of Boston. Each man visited all the apartments within the blocks in his assigned section and filled out cards for each house and apartment. The investigations were made in the company of the regular municipal sanitary inspector of the district. Each student in the course of the term was assigned to several districts and thus to several inspectors. The students were made to summarize the findings of their investigations in different quarters of the city, together with comparative statistical tables and maps of their district. The findings were placed at the disposal of the municipal health department and were also put into the hands of the municipal city-planning commission to accompany a scheme privately projected for replanning of one of the areas inspected.

Two other students studied tenement-house fires, making their inspections in company with municipal and metropolitan fire inspectors.

Other students made maps showing the distribution of new buildings in the city of Cambridge, or distribution of three-deckers and the like, which have subsequently been utilized by the Cambridge city-planning commission.

The amount of supervision required necessarily depends upon the subject at which the student works. I permit no housing surveys to be made except where there is a reasonable assurance that the findings of the investigation will be utilized for the advantage of the municipality. Often there is some private body interested in the investigation made which provides a certain amount of supervision. Municipal supervision is, of course, provided. In addition, I require students to report to me at frequent intervals.

The grade is given for this work precisely as for other thesis work within the department. The student, in filling out housing investigation cards, is acquiring material which must be summarized and submitted in the form of a thesis which is graded in the usual manner. Some allowance is made in grading the cards for neatness and for accuracy of the results obtained. The latter is checked up by reinvestigation of selected portions of the districts examined by students. But the grade of the student for his research is determined primarily by the report submitted. In addition, of course, there are tests upon prescribed reading and lectures of the course which are large factors in determining the grade of the course.

Several interesting points occur in this account. Supervision of field work is here exercised entirely by the city authorities through municipal sanitary or fire inspectors. The findings of the students are primarily for practical usefulness, and serve as information for various city departments and commissions. Frequent reports to the professor in charge are required. Actual credit is given for the work done, the grade being based on the character of the report submitted. The accuracy of results is checked by reinvestigation. In addition lectures are held and reading is required, upon which tests are given. The system thus outlined may well serve as a model, since it meets all the requirements of strict supervision, careful coordination, and useful cooperation with civic interests.

A somewhat different kind of field work is illustrated by the activities of students in the settlement house maintained by the department of sociology of Syracuse University. The second annual report of this organization brings out the following facts:

The university settlement is located in the center of the fifteenth ward of Syracuse, in the heart of the most densely populated section of the city. This neighborhood presents, on a modified scale, practically all of the elements of the slums of a greater city. The social work is under the direction and management of the department of sociology of Syracuse University. The greater part of the work is being done by students who are doing major work in sociology at the university. Under the supervision of these a large number of other students assist with the work.

In connection with this settlement, a training class for social workers is carried on at the university in which students receive two hours per week credit for the year, four hours' actual work per week in addition to readings being required. No remuneration is given student workers.

In the Syracuse plan as above outlined the university not only has full supervision of student workers, but even controls the facilities under which the work is done, thus differing materially from the Harvard system. In both, however, the students are rewarded by college credit.

Different again is the plan of field work carried out by students of the Cleveland school of education under the direction of Dr. Jean Dawson in the antifly campaign waged in that city last summer. These girls were selected by Dr. Dawson for their peculiar fitness for the work, after preparation in courses specifically designed for this purpose. While not legally appointed sanitary inspectors, they were granted a definite badge by the city department of public welfare and were backed in every way by the various departments of the city. Their work was to make a thorough investigation of the city, and so far as possible to eliminate all places where flies could breed, reporting to the proper authorities those persons who failed to comply with their directions. For this work each girl received a remuneration of $7 per week, but no credit was given in the normal school nor was any effort apparently made to coordinate this field work with any concurrent course of study. This plan furnishes a still further variant from those in use at Harvard and Syracuse.

The brief survey just given shows a variety of methods now in actual use in the conduct of field work in colleges and universities in one department only—that of sociology. While fairly representative of methods in general, those just detailed are capable of considerable variation to meet the demands of subject and surrounding conditions. Without going into a broader field, it is interesting to summarize the variations on the basis of the standards of comparison as already indicated:

1. Method of supervision:
    a. By outside agencies (Pittsburgh, Harvard).
    b. By the college department (Pennsylvania, Syracuse).
2. Means of testing results:
    a. By personal conference (Pennsylvania).
    b. By direct personal supervision (Syracuse, Cleveland).
    c. By reinvestigation (Harvard).
    d. By reports, tests, classwork (Harvard, Pittsburgh).
3. Plan of accrediting:
    a. By giving college credit for field work alone (Pennsylvania).
    b. By giving college credit for field work with classwork (Harvard).
    c. By money remuneration with no college credit (Cleveland).

This all goes to show the utter lack of standardization in the realm of field work. It is quite possible that such standardization will never come; that it is not even desirable that it do come. Yet a conference of those under whose supervision such work is carried on would serve to eliminate much of the wide divergency in practice and to secure the universal adoption of certain desirable elements and the elimination of undesirable ones. I should not, however, like to leave you to-day with the inference that all those attending such a meeting would be professors of sociology. The scope of field work, while not universal, is much broader than the limits of any one department. The following enumeration, which is far from complete, is at least typical of the various kinds of efforts now made:

Practice teaching in city high schools.

Work of cooperative engineering students in industries and city departments.

Church work and preaching (Brown University).

In New York business firms (New York University).

Municipal sanitary inspection (College of the City of New York and School for Public Health Officers conducted by Harvard and Massachusetts Institute of Technology).

School nursing in New York public schools and settlements (Teachers College of Columbia University).

Home economics in New York public-school lunchrooms (Teachers College).

Cooperative law courses with practical law-office work (Georgetown University).

Assistants to city chemist (Akron).

In city offices under bureau of municipal research (Akron).

In addition also a large number of miscellaneous investigative efforts in the departments of political science, economics, and sociology.

It would be unjust to leave this subject without a brief mention of appreciation of the constructive suggestions in regard to supervision of field work by the American Political Science Association as outlined in the preliminary report of its committee on practical training for public service, pages 339–352. Equally enlightening are the remarks of Prof. Jenks, of New York University, before the First National Conference on Universities and Public Service, as reported in the proceedings of that meeting. The following statements quoted from this speech seem to define the essential points of cooperative field work:

It is probable that there has been too great readiness heretofore for teachers in all universities to emphasize the plan of inspection too much and actual work too little. Moreover, this looking things over does not give real training to students. Also, care must be taken to get always a scientific background for all the practical work done. Especially is this true if we are giving training to our graduate students with the idea that they are to occupy later high places in the city administration. There is much danger of the helter-skelter practice and not enough thorough training and supervision.

The keynote of the paragraph just quoted is a warning against lower standards in field work than in laboratory, lecture, or recitation. The problem of increasing the efficiency of field work is one of the most vital questions with which this movement will have to deal.[1]

---

[1] At the business meeting the association framed a resolution to appoint a committee to make a full report on field work. President Kolbe is chairman of that committee. President Kolbe took occasion to convert a misstatement which he had made concerning Hunter College, of the City of New York, and which appeared in the bulletin reporting the proceedings of the first meeting. He had referred to this institution as "Normal College," and as a normal school. He acknowledged his mistake and characterized the institution as a college.

IV. RESULTS OF COOPERATIVE TRAINING FOR PUBLIC SERVICE.

RESULTS OF COOPERATION BY THE MUNICIPALITY AND THE UNIVERSITY IN TRAINING FOR PUBLIC SERVICE.

By Lemuel Herbert Murlin,

President of Boston University.

Hitherto the consciousness of obligation to public service in education has been confined wholly to the State institutions, but even here it has been neither well-defined nor compelling. The normal school has, in a measure, felt its obligations to public service in training efficient teachers and competent administrators of public-school education. The agricultural colleges, also, diligently applied themselves to all aspects of rural welfare. The State university, at first content to be much like most other educational institutions, its only difference being that it drew its support from the State treasury, now enters into every activity of the life of the State.

Only within very recent years have institutions in or near cities begun to sense the fact that they owe a particular duty to serve the city in all its various forms of life, and that, at the same time, the city provides a unique opportunity for educational equipment, method, training, and service.

Hitherto our American colleges and universities have been located for the most part in the country, meeting the conditions of a social age whose population was largely rural. The rapid growth of cities has changed economic conditions so completely and rapidly that adjustments have not been able to keep pace. Democracy is now put to its supreme tests. We are far from demonstrating that a people can be free, intelligent, social, disinterested, and patriotic enough to govern themselves; and the stressing problem of a democratic civilization is the city. If the university of the twentieth century is to have that place of leadership in our age held by our institutions of learning in the eighteenth and nineteenth centuries, it must, as did these, be located among the people, seeking to clear their vision, to gird them for new tasks, and to enrich and nourish their lives. The municipal university is, therefore, natural and inevitable; its rise marks an era in the development of American education second only to the founding of the public school in the eighteenth century and opening of the State university in the nineteenth century.

Reference has already been made to the great equipment which a city offers a university located within or near its borders. Indeed, the city in itself is a library and a laboratory of manifold learning, literature, arts, and sciences; its libraries, factories, shops, offices, its vast commercial enterprises; its religious, moral, educational, social, philanthropic, and charitable undertakings; these the student may study at first hand in the very process of their making and onward movement; and he may have, in some small but important measure, a share in their actual development and conduct, thus uniting his thinking and doing, his learning and living, so important in efficient education.

It is rather early to enumerate results of such cooperation, much more so to evaluate. Many universities have been rendering a vast amount of public service without distinctly recognizing it as such. A few months ago the mayor of a certain city called together the heads of the various educational institutions in and about the city; he had just made the discovery that " The Municipality and the University," constituted a rather startling, interesting, and suggestive phrase which might have in it, if not political value,·at least good publicity value. There was a cordial response to his invitation; he read an interesting essay which made good material for the newspapers, and they published it in full. The responses of the presidents indicated that almost all, and in some aspects even more than the mayor had pointed out as possible, was being done; and every educator present was alive to the possibilities suggested, and ready to cooperate to any practicable degree desired by the city. Nor is this an exceptional case. In all communities institutions have quietly gone on, doing their work, responding to special calls for expert advice and service, giving them freely and gladly, as a natural expression of their ordinary activity, without taking any special accounting and without giving such service any name.

But far more important than the immediately and obviously practical service of the urban university to the problems of the daily ongoing life of the city has been the general service which the university has rendered in the kind of men and women it has given to the community. It should be distinctly understood that though we give to the city efficient practical workers and efficient practical service, nevertheless our largest opportunity still is, and ever will be, that we give to the city a sturdy, strong, conscientious manhood and womanhood. We must ever keep before us the vision of an ideal manhood and womanhood as our most worthy and most distinct contribution to the welfare of the city and Nation.

Granting all this, even holding it as a fundamental principle, at the same time we can not fail to see that for a large number of students the city and its institutions afford the need and the material and the opportunity for special aims and methods in education. It is, then, the duty of the urban university to undertake a distinct type of educational service, with new kinds of equipment, new methods of instruction, and new forms of administration.

It is, however, altogether too soon to enumerate the results of direct cooperation between the university and the city. We have as yet but the faintest gleams of the possibilities opening before us here; moreover, what cooperation we now have is so recent that we can not measure results. We must wait at least a generation before we begin to tabulate and evaluate the significance of what we are only beginning to see, and of what we have only very slightly begun to use. But we may reasonably suggest a few probable results.

First of all, there is the influence which such cooperation will have upon the colleges and universities. Their instruction will be vivified by immediate pragmatic tests. The reality thus given to the work of the classroom or seminar will arouse professor and student to best endeavor. They understand they are not merely pretending; they are in the midst of the veritable storm and stress of life itself. Now, it is thinking through the problem and doing the definite thing, tested out, tried, and found to be true, that is necessary to make the truly educated man; and a pragmatic test, applied to the student by the foreman in the shop, by the consumer of his product, by the editor of the magazine, or by anyone dealing directly with the ongoing of the practical affairs of life, lends reality, definiteness, vividness, accuracy, and richness to the work done in the university. "My business organization is as much an educational institution as your university," said a successful manager of several large corporations to a college president. There is so much of truth in his statement that educators can no longer overlook the value that will come to both the college and the business organization by hearty cooperation between them in the educational program.

Cooperation in education by the university and the municipality should mean, in the second place, that we shall have scholastic results superior to those which we now have. It is notorious that, save for a very few, there is little of the scholastic habit among college students. The president of a college in good standing, writing the other day, gave two lines to matters scholastic, while all the rest of the full-paged letter was devoted to an account of athletic achievements and outlook, closing with the assurance that the prospects of his institution were very bright! Better, if we must choose, is that statement of a western State university president who, in responding to a questionnaire on athletics, said:

I fear I can not give you any helpful information from our institution; college athletics we do have, but not in the sense that your questionnaire implies; our boys are too busy solving the problems of the desert to have any time for the prevalent type of college athletics.

"Solving the problems of the desert!" Their institution was located in the heart of that region which once appeared on the maps of American school geographies as "The Great American Desert." Ah! how numerous are the problems of civilization in the city, in the village, in the country, in the Nation! Look at our economic, social, educational, religious situation. It is a desert, challenging the best of heart and intellect for the solution of its problems.

We must be on guard, however, against the serious danger of the present tendency in education to meet the demand for so-called practical efficiency. Too often it means only industrial, material, mechanical efficiency. The following note of warning from the St. Louis Post-Dispatch finds much in our present tendency in education to justify itealf:

" Efficiency is 90 per cent " says a solemn bore who presides over a boiler factory full of men. Inside a boiler factory; yes, efficiency ought to be 90 per cent, and if possible 100 per cent of a man. But the inside factory point of view is prevailing too popularly outside. Wouldn't this be a dreary world if men were 100 per cent efficient and mere substitutes for machinery? Shall we have donkey engines conversing in the parlor and steam cranes in the pulpit? The whole human works would consist of interchangeable parts; we should have a standard type of man, and life would be literally a grind, The galley slave chained to the oar was a fair sample of 100 per cent efficiency. The man in the treadmill was likewise going some from the efficiency standpoint.

The ancient Greeks had standards of personal excellence and social worth which deserve meditation when our modern poise is threatened. The composite of these standards has rarely been attained, but he is a beautiful model. Olios represented wealth with grace, opulence, elegance, generosity, philanthropy, altruism—thus wealth the antithesis of plutocratic. Arete stood for what these times worship as efficiency; that is, capability, capacity, executive. Aldos was becoming ideal, a quality the precise opposite of " cheek." Sophrosyne elevated confidence and self-control. Kalokagathie fused into a single concept many notions of economic, esthetic, and moral good; and Eleutheros was the gentleman endowed with all admirable qualities—the noble rara avis whom our single aim of efficiency would slay and forget.

True the Greeks, as a historian has remarked, proved that people could sink very low while talking very high. But there is scarcely enough tall talk in our times to indicate our bare possession of ideals—the talk is mostly low-pitched, lumps men as a commercial asset, and lacks in sheer humanity as it does in grace and rhetoric. The world needs another education in the " humanities" such as it received in the Renaissance.

The question of its ideal man-as-he-should-be is the most vital, most fundamental, which concerns any organized society. It is for us of this day to consider: To what doom points a spirit of brutal crassness to which the nobler feelings and refinements are foreign? Shall we humans develop through survivals of the most efficient to become just units in a boiler factory world?

Happily, however, we do not have to descend to this crass standard of efficiency. We do not have to choose as between cultural education and vocational education. We may have both! It is a question of viewpoint and method during the educational process. A man's business in life ought to be a never-ending educational process in highest values; and he should be so educated as to see himself and his life work as a part of an ever-developing civilization whose chief concern, whose very life, depends upon the training and the use of the finer qualities of manhood and womanhood.

In the third place, cooperation between the university and the city in educational endeavor ought to result in a better citizenship. It will be a more intelligent citizenship, for the student's interest and initiative have been aroused to a purpose for nothing less than definiteness and accuracy in achievement. This practical experience in doing and learning in the city university and in the city's business, its industries and common welfare, will awaken in the student a sense of pride in the city that gave him his opportunity for gaining knowledge, and for the training and preparation which has fitted him for his life work. The experience will also awaken in him a sense of his obligation "to make good" in life by the service which he gives back to the city.

Then will we have citizens with a strong community consciousness; the very air they have breathed throughout their lives from primary school to university graduation has been that of men who see themselves as individuals and as integral parts of the whole community. No one of them can run his private business, not even his own home, as if he were the only one who is concerned; he sees at once that his own highest welfare is bound up in the welfare of his neighbors, and of all others whose industrial lives, as his, go to make the city.

In the best-governed city in the world there are 6,000 private citizens serving in unsalaried positions on committees or commissions, giving four to ten hours per week to the service of their city. They are lawyers, doctors, merchants, manufacturers, ministers, teachers, tradesmen, laboring men, each and all freely contributing their share to the common welfare. In such service they find their highest and best selves; they give to the city those fine qualities of personal character which unselfish service always develops in individuals. The city, after all, in its spirit and ideals, is but the average of the spirit and ideals of its individuals.

Let us hope that, along with engineers, doctors, ministers, educators, financiers, business administrators, and all other expert service required in our modern life, one of the first results—as it is the one most needed—of cooperation between the university and the city will be a still larger number of that type of good citizens who stand up and say "I am a citizen of no mean city," and by the quality and character of their own lives and the efficiency and sincerity of their voluntary service to the city have made it great and strong and beautiful in all the things that make for human betterment.

COOPERATION BETWEEN THE BUSINESS MEN OF NEW ORLEANS AND THE COLLEGE OF COMMERCE AND BUSINESS ADMINISTRATION OF THE TULANE UNIVERSITY OF LOUISIANA.

By MORTON A. ALDRICH,

Dean of the College of Commerce and Business Administration, Tulane University of Louisiana.

The business men of New Orleans realize the responsibility of their position at the gateway. Quietly and efficiently they are preparing to serve the growing commerce of the Mississippi Valley, and one of the responsibilities which they feel is that of providing adequate training for the young men who are preparing for a business career.

When a few representative New Orleans business men made up their minds that their city should have a college of commerce they found three groups of people to which they could turn for help. First, there was the city's organization of business men, the Association of Commerce; secondly, there was Tulane University; and, thirdly, there were those individual business men who were especially interested in the establishment of mature business education. Their problem was to mobilize and combine these forces. There was nothing unusual or peculiar to New Orleans, you see, either in the problem or the situation.

From the outset it was clearly understood that the college of commerce and business administration is one of the professional schools of Tulane University, and that the university has complete and undivided control of its appointments, of its policy and standards, and of its educational bill of fare.

But it was the ideal of those who took the lead in this movement that a truly substantial and adequate foundation for a college of commerce must include the active interest and support, not only of the university, but of every one of these three groups, and, moreover, that this support should be so organized that in each case the interest would be permanent.

Especially was it desirable that the individual business men who contributed money to the college should be organized in some way so that they would not feel that their responsibility ceased with the signing of a check. In all this cooperation it was not merely money that we were seeking, but solid, active, day-by-day interest, and helpful suggestions and support.

The business men of Germany have come to think of their colleges of commerce as an essential part of their commercial development. And in an American city a college of commerce can accomplish only a very little of what it might otherwise do to help unless the business men come to think of it, as they think of their exchanges and their railroads and their banks, as a natural and essential part of the city's business equipment and business life. We set out, therefore, to hook up with the college the interest of the business community. The result is that our college of commerce is to-day in the happy situation of having three parents solicitous for its welfare instead of one.

How is this cooperation between the business men and the college of commerce worked? What does the Association of Commerce do? On the material side, it provides ample quarters in its own building for the night courses which the college offers for business men and women (in addition to its four-year day course in the college buildings) and for the public informal Friday night talks. Furthermore, it advertises the college of commerce much as it advertises any other department of its work.

Another valuable result of the close connection between the college and the Association of Commerce is that more of the older members of the association and more of the members of its vigorous young men's department enroll in the business men's night courses of the college. There is no doubt that young business men are more likely to attend the courses of a college of commerce which is associated in their minds with the commercial organization of the older business men and has, therefore, an atmosphere of the right sort.

The public weekly informal Friday night talks of the college of commerce are plain business talks by business men on business subjects. They are short; they are informal; they are always followed by questioning and discussion; and they are largely attended by business men. One welcome result of these informal Friday night talks is that they bring the college to the attention of a large number of business men whom it would be difficult to reach in any other way. These talks are held under the joint auspices of the college and the Association of Commerce, with the result that we are developing in New Orleans, instead of occasional business talks at irregular intervals and at unexpected places, one strong business forum, to the success of which the Association of Commerce and its young men's branch, the college of commerce, and the business community generally unitedly contribute.

So much as to the cooperation of the Association of Commerce; let us turn to the cooperation of the individual citizens and business men. At the outset 104 of them combined to guarantee the expenses of the college. But the college needed from these business men their personal service as well as their money, and the danger was, as I have said, that they would feel that their responsibility, the need of their understanding of the work, and their possibilities of helpfulness to the college all ended with their signing of the guaranty.

One of the wisest and most far-reaching steps in the permanent coordination of all the groups interested in providing training preparing for a business career was the action of the board of administrators of Tulane University in requesting the members of this board of guarantors to elect officers and an executive committee and form a permanent organization, in order to make it possible to confer with them in regard to matters affecting the success of the college.

Not only do the officers and executive committee meet monthly to hear detailed reports of the work of the college and to lay plans for its future growth, but individually they and the other members of this board of guarantors stand ready to contribute their thought and time unselfishly, in all sorts of ways, to extend the usefulness of the college.

The professors of the college of commerce are in close association with the members of this board of guarantors and turn to them constantly for the results of their practical experience and for assistance and advice, and it is a great advantage to the teacher (and to his students) to be able to consult freely with business men who already are interested in helping the college and understand its work.

To cite one other evidence of their spirit, these business men guarantors soon realized that a main reason why more young men already in business were not attending our night classes was because their employers, in many cases, did not show them that they recognized the value of the work. The guarantors understood that if this business training is valuable for the students whom we had, it is equally valuable for ten times as many more. Consequently, they have set to work to talk with these employers, with the result that more and more the heads of our business houses and banks are advising their employees to attend the night classes, and frequently are offering to pay part or all of their tuition fees.

REED COLLEGE AND ITS COMMUNITY.

By WILLIAM T. FOSTER, LL. D.,

President of Reed College, Portland, Oreg.

Reed College is a small college, only four years old. It has started out in new fields. Its work is, therefore, largely tentative; the most it has to present is a suggestion here and there, and large hopes for the future.

For the instruction of college students who are later to take their places as citizens, indifferent or energetic, our methods should be those which, at the same time, will educate the adult population with respect to civic duties. A few such methods have been tried at Reed College.

We take our students in economics, government, education, psychology, and sociology out into the city, after their introductory courses in these fields, to find out what is actually going on in the laboratories of the city, in the health department, in the purchasing agent's office, in the police, fire, and finance departments, in the city employment agency, the tax bureau, the schools, and so on. The students have individual problems of investigation to carry on under the guidance of members of the faculty and at times with the faculty.

Much of the information thus assembled concerning the form and operation of the government of the city of Portland we arranged in a series of lectures, and the class in statistics, as laboratory work, endeavored to find means of graphically presenting the facts so as to make their meaning unmistakable and of interest to large numbers of citizens.

We thus got together about five hundred illustrations for a series of six lectures on "The Voter and His City." We then proceeded to try them on the voters. At the conclusion of each lecture we conducted discussions, partly to find out whether the lecture was understood, what pertinent questions remained unanswered, and how the practical value of the course might be increased. Our endeavor was, you see, to get before as many voters as possible nonpartisan, accurate, up-to-date, interesting, and immediately usable information about every aspect of the city government. Thus, for example, we explained how the new preferential voting system works, to what extent the city purchasing department saves money, the need of a campaign against the smoke nuisance, some of the mysteries of budget making, some of the wastes of the city administration, housing conditions, defects of the housing code, and the need of playground supervision. We treated 40 other topics without gloves, our sole purpose being to get information before the people.

When anybody objected to any statement, we asked, "Is it true?" If he could show that it was not true, we changed it; but, as a rule, the objection was merely that to make known these facts caused trouble. We replied that it is the business of a college to cause this kind of trouble.

It is gratifying to us that some unpleasant things which were true when we started that series of lectures are not true to-day. We had to change the lectures from time to time.

We have given the series in 15 different places, with a total attendance thus far of 3,740. Not only did our undergraduates prepare material for the lectures, but two students presented the course to all the classes in civil government in all the public schools in the city.

One of our faculty helped to organize and presided at the first meeting of a nonpartisan committee of 100 citizens, which recommended to the voters the men who were elected commissioners under the new city charter. That was the beginning of our cooperation with city officers. Our students and our faculty have been prominent in the movement for woman suffrage and for the extension of popular government; and a large number of our students, at least half of them, I think, and at least half of our faculty, were prominent in the campaign for the prohibition of the liquor traffic. Regardless of the merits of the question, this is indicative of what an institution can do if it is free from entangling alliances, independent of votes of city or State officers, and unhampered by traditional ideas of what a college should not do.

The mayor called upon the college to take charge of an investigation of public amusements in Portland. The students and faculty, with the aid of 40 other men and women, investigated the motion-picture and vaudeville houses of the city and published the results. Their recommendations were used in making new laws on the subject in various cities.

The college aided in the organization of the Oregon Civic League. One of our faculty was its first president. The college also works with the new Chamber of Commerce, an organization of 3,500 men. One of the faculty is in charge of the committee on city planning and the committee on city schools. Another professor is aiding .the chamber in an industrial survey of Oregon. The college and the chamber of commerce work together with mutual advantage. The same is true of all the libraries. Every one of them is as valuable a part of the Reed College equipment as if it were on our own campus.

In four years the number of individual attendants at extension-course lectures has increased from 3,000 to 15,000.

Our campus itself and our gymnasium and athletic field are put under the direction of the city department of parks and play-grounds as a free municipal playground all summer.

Another illustration of field work for the welfare of citizens and for the training of students who may at some time hold public office is in the field of social hygiene. In cooperation with a large number of citizens, students and faculty members conduct lectures and conferences and carry on a State-wide campaign. One of our faculty is president of the organization in charge of the work; one of our students is the executive secretary. We conducted an extension course for the preparation of workers in this field which was attended by 120 men and women. We published 705,000 circulars on 20 subjects. Besides giving lectures in 70 towns and cities, we prepared an exhibit which we have sent about the States and have shown to 113,000 people. We have maintained an advisory department, with a physician in charge. He has corresponded with 1,400 people in special need, and at his office 3,600 have called for help. We have obtained the cooperation of 57 business houses in the city. which have been sufficiently impressed with the value of this service to give their employees company time in order that they might profit by our instruction.

Another branch of · this work was the campaign against fake doctors and medical concerns, whose sole object is to get money from people whether they are diseased or not. Our first object was to cut off their means of circulating false information. This we did through the elimination of all such advertisements from the State of Oregon. It meant a great loss of revenue to the newspapers, yet they gave us their unqualified support.

Field work is necessary for students themselves; it gives them vital contact with the community; it is not purely academic. Second, it is necessary for the faculty, in order that they will not become "typical college professors." The traditional professor is said to be academic, impractical, uninteresting, completely lost when thrown into close contact with human beings outside the classroom or laboratory. He needs to know more of the world in order that his instruction may become vitalized.

Finally, such field work is necessary for the curriculum. There is something flabby, indeed almost immoral, about the teaching of ethics and sociology and government which issues into no grappling with immediate needs. Both teachers and students should appreciate actual conditions and should have immediate opportunity to act in response to emotions which they experience as a result of investigation or instruction.

It is partly because students have not had this vital training in college days that so many of them appear after graduation indifferent to the duties of a citizen. Often you can get better support for a program of municipal betterment from people who have not had a university education. That is a serious fact. The gentleman from Pittsburgh has rightly said that we must begin from the bottom with a new sort of education. We must offer new opportunities and create a new sense of civic responsibility in our schools and colleges if we are to create an effective demand for trained, devoted, and honest public servants in every branch of municipal affairs. Meantime, we must continue to strive for vital and continuous cooperation between the university and the municipality.

RESULTS OF COOPERATIVE TRAINING FOR PUBLIC SERVICE AT THE COLLEGE OF THE CITY OF NEW YORK.

By SIDNEY EDWARD MEZES,
President of the College of the City of New York.

We give cooperative instruction not only in order to train men to enter the service of the city, but also to improve the efficiency of those already in the service; we attempt to carry out investigations of a scientific character which will give dependable results, upon which city officials, and, incidentally, business men, may rely in conducting the enterprises in their charge; and our more experienced men are available as members of boards, commissions, and committees which are deliberating concerning the best method of conducting large undertakings.

Our college of arts and sciences is conducted both by day and by night. The standards of admission and graduation for day session and evening session are the same. We also have teachers' extension courses to give professional and cultural work to those in the city school system. Then there is a division of vocational subjects and civic administration, offering courses primarily for city employees in the college buildings and in the Municipal Building during afternoon and evening hours.

In the regular college course the cooperative work that comes first to mind is that connected with the chemistry department. The central testing laboratory of the city sends officially tested samples of materials which are to be purchased by the city to our instructor in municipal chemistry. He has his class perform the tests and checks their results by the official report. Students in this course are taken on inspection and observation trips to the city's laboratory, and they receive lectures from time to time from the directors of the laboratory and other municipal experts. There is a similar cooperative arrangement for courses in food inspection and analysis and municipal sanitation. Students preparing to enter the city education system as teachers in the grammar or high schools do practice teaching or pupil-teaching service in the system. These examples will show the general way in which undergraduates of the college are benefited by cooperation with city departments.

Now we turn to instruction of those already in the service. The largest single group of city employees improved by the college are the teachers, and in connection with courses provided for them it has been found necessary, in view of the large size and the generous spread of the City of New York, to have instruction not merely at the seat of the institution, but also at other centers in Manhattan and the other four boroughs of the city.

There are in attendance upon these particular courses which train or improve the training of the teachers in the public schools of the city at present over 5,000 teachers, and we think that is a service well worth rendering. The personnel of this student body changes from year to year, and it is safe to say that at a given time we have enough teachers in the service who have received our instruction to have contact, indirectly, with over 1,000,000 children, and we are to that extent helping those 1,000,000 children.

City employees in all of the other departments and those in the service of the State and Nation have the resources of the college placed at their disposal in a rather novel way. By virtue of their positions they are admitted to any course offered in the college which they are qualified to pursue. The general entrance requirements are waived. While such students are not candidates for degrees, they nevertheless receive much help from the courses. The effect of admitting these mature students with very definite and practical reasons for taking up studies has been most beneficial. In some cases the rather formal academic methods were modified and fresh ability and a new point of view were brought to the courses.

Special extra-curricula courses to meet the vocational needs of men in certain city departments were also established. There is the course in technical electricity, of especial interest to men in the department of water supply, gas, and electricity, and water-supply engineering for those in the same department or the board of water supply. Some of such special courses, as well as sections from the regular courses of study, were established in the Municipal Building, the governmental center of the City of New York. In giving these courses New York University cooperates with us. They are designed to meet the needs of three classes of employees.

First, there are those who are interested or occupied in engineering enterprises. New York City, like every large city, has a great deal of engineering work to do, and courses such as water-supply engineering, construction inspection, reinforced concrete construction, electrical engineering, draftsmanship of all kinds, engineering design, theory of stresses, and any matters of that general kind enable employees in engineering departments of the city government to become more efficient in doing their work and in serving the city. Then there is a large clerical business force engaged in the city, and members of it who wish appropriate instruction may take up English, accounting, economics, government, and allied studies. Those who are engaged in the great social services have courses in philanthropy, sociology, and various aspects of social work. Of course a great many of them have come into the service with a technical and legal rather than a broad social understanding and training for the work which they are to do. The courses tend to broaden them and render them more liberal and sympathetic in their dealings with the people.

There is also a certain number of elementary courses in the languages—Italian, for instance, and Spanish, and German, and Yiddish. The reason for giving these language courses to city employees is that many are inspectors employed to deal with the large foreign population of New York City. These courses make possible a means of communication between recent immigrants and the inspectors. We now instruct 270 city employees in the Municipal Building and over 300 in the main college buildings. This group of 600, together with the 5,000 teachers, makes a very respectable body of municipal students. And the body will grow.

We turn to an activity in another direction—namely, cooperation with business men. The evening session, as would be expected, is largely attended by business men, and these comprise engineers, lawyers, doctors, as well as men working in banks, in business establishments in stores—all sorts and conditions of men who are actually engaged or employed during the daytime. But the course which has just been instituted and which is intended for them specifically, and which is being carried on in the customs house with the cooperation of business men, is one on foreign markets. In a large exporting center like New York, obviously this is a very important thing. Certain business associations are cooperating with that course. They have joined together and have formed an advisory committee to aid the instructor in charge of the course. The course has to deal very practically with the subject of foreign markets.

The college also benefits persons employed by the city in laboratories. A few of them are given instruction so as to improve their technique in the matter of testing the city's supplies. They are as yet but a handful, but the course is prophetic, because it indicates that later on other men who may be engaged in this work for the city will not be asked to come out to the institution itself, but will have competent teachers come to them in their offices and workshops to give them the instruction necessary to increase their value to the city.

Another form of scientific cooperation is found in the psychological laboratory, or educational clinic. There are in all school systems children who do not get on. They are backward, or deficient, or unruly, and it is necessary that they be submitted to a very careful test to determine what is the matter with them. Of these children quite a number have to be dealt with by the courts of the city under certain circumstances, and the first thing to determine is whether they are responsible or irresponsible. For this purpose they are sent to our educational clinic to be examined mentally. If they are irresponsible they are sent to certain custodial institutions. If they are still irresponsible they are sent to truant schools. Obviously the number of examinations is great. For two or three days in the week there is a steady stream of children going through the clinic and being carefuly tested, and the cases are handled by experts who determine how best each child shall be treated. Incidentally much scientific information is gathered which is helpful to the schools of the city in dealing with their scholars.

There is also a survey which has been undertaken with a view of studying and deciding what kinds of further training are needed by the different groups of city employees. The city departments are cooperating most helpfully with the authorities of the college, and a small sum to finance this investigation has been appropriated. The departments of the city have been visited, with the cooperation of the heads of these departments, in order to find out just how the various employees of the city can be aided to become more efficient and give more to the city in return for the money that the city pays them. It is partly as a result of this that some of the courses I have mentioned have been already decided upon. We have, furthermore, a continuing investigation by men who are employed to keep these courses in touch with the needs as they ascertain these needs progressively of the various groups of city employees, so that courses and types of-training will never be much out of touch with real, existing needs.

Finally, our men have served on such commissions, for instance, as that on occupational disease. The board of health is constantly in cooperation with and is receiving advice from our men in chemistry, from our men in biology, and from our men in hygiene.

There was an investigation of mental deficiency and as to the best method of caring for the 1,750 defectives on Randalls Island, whose care has not been carried on, as was generally thought, quite as well as it might have been. One of the professors of the City College was on that commission. As a result of its recommendations some $600,000 was appropriated by the State to insure better attention to these unfortunates and to improve their surroundings.

Another board on which the college is represented is that which has charge of the factory inspection undertaken by the City of New York. All the factories were inspected to discover conditions existing in them, the nature of employment, and various problems of that kind. A report was published, which has been very helpful to us, and which will doubtless be helpful in other places.

Now, this very brief and very dry account will possibly give some notion of the types of cooperation under way. Only a beginning has been made. We do not go, for instance, as far as your local university goes in a number of directions. We do not go as far as we should in the training of many different groups of city employees. The city employee in New York has to come in contact with

45424°—16——5

very aggravated social conditions, and to try to better the environment of people who live in congested districts, in the way of housing facilities, sanitation, living facilities, food, and various other details of environment, all these men must be trained; they need the social spirit, a larger altruism, and a keener appreciation of neighborliness, and of civic obligation.

Moreover, a city government is only as good as public opinion will allow it to be. If the general mass or run of the citizens are not men with considerable information, with a large public spirit, with a vision of the future, with some notion of the significance of the latter-day municipal spirit, the government of the city can not be expected to rise very high above those people whom it governs.

So there is a large responsibility on the part of urban universities for disseminating information, for giving inspiration, for broadening the views, and lengthening the vision of the whole population, all of which can be done, and will be done more and more, as time goes on, by municipal institutions.

COOPERATIVE TRAINING FOR PUBLIC SERVICE IN NEW YORK CITY.

By HENRY MOSKOWITZ,

President of the Civil Service Commission, New York City.

The Municipal Civil Service Commission is deeply interested in recruiting trained public servants for the government of the city. It makes a considerable difference in the type of candidate if he has been trained in a cram school or in an institution with high educational ideals. When one considers such a service as the city of New York, with its 55,570 classified employees under the jurisdiction of the commission, with 21,631 applicants for positions in the competitive service in the past nine months, small wonder that a large number of schools have grown up under private auspices which prepare these candidates and which do a flourishing business. Some of these schools have high standards, but many are animated purely by business considerations and can be characterized as cram-factories. That many thrive is an indictment against our public educational system. If public schools and particularly high schools and colleges were alive to their responsibility they would, without sacrificing their educational ideals, equip public servants by supplying them with the necessary training for positions. These private schools meet a need which the public institutions have until very recently neglected.

But the civil-service problem is not restricted to examination of candidates before they enter the service. A vast and neglected field of civil-service administration relates to the galvanizing of the service after an employee has entered it. The civil-service law of the State of New York, which provides for promotion examinations wherever practicable, is typical of nearly every civil-service law in the country. This provision is necessary to insure that dignified and honorable career in the public service of which President Eliot has spoken. It is necessary to offer to those in the service a goal for their ambitions, a step-by-step advancement which means not only increased salaries but increased responsibilities, after an employee has demonstrated both by his record and by his examination that he has qualified for them. It is therefore proper that training for the public service. should meet not only the needs of the city for original entrance but for promotion as well.

New York City, recognizing this need, has cooperated with New York University and the College of the City of New York in a scheme of offering courses to city employees at a very nominal fee, which aim to equip them for the higher positions. They consist not only of general theoretical training, but of practical work based upon the duties of the various positions. Many of them are given in the Municipal Building. The government of the city has set apart certain rooms in the building for lecture purposes. Fifty-one such courses have been offered. They cover a very large field, from engineering English to philanthropy, the higher mathematics, such as algebra, plane geometry, solid geometry, trigonometry for engineering, engineering drawing, elementary surveying, advanced surveying, mechanics, nomographic charting, elementary structural detailing, elementary steel design, advanced structural design, masonry design and construction, reinforced concrete design and construction, materials of construction and construction inspection, production and use of engineering materials, water-supply engineering, sewerage and sewage disposal, highway engineering, engineering estimates and costs, engineering features of municipal contracts, technical electricity in laboratory Saturday afternoons, and advanced electricity. These courses are obviously designed to train employees in the engineering service. Some of the courses for those engaged in secretarial duties are as follows: English composition, advanced English composition, secretarial duties, advanced stenography, and stenotype. The accounting service is a very important one in our complex municipal government. Therefore, courses are offered in statistics, bookkeeping practice, principles of accounting, accounting practice, fund accounting, expenditure and revenue accounting, and cost accounting. There is also a course in the government of the city of New York and in the municipal functions of the city. There are courses in public speaking, Italian, French, German, Yiddish, German reports, economics, municipal sociology and philanthropy.

The fees are nominal. The lowest is $5 and the highest is $20.
Where the greatest sum is asked, not less than 60 hours and up to
150 are given. The courses were carefully thought out. In the
language of the mayor, " The courses were carefully considered not
only by the committee in charge but by the advisory committees,
consisting of those technically qualified to suggest desirable lines of
instruction in engineering and clerical subjects." The mayor requested his department heads to call the attention of employees to
these courses and to seek their cooperation. Last year a few courses
were given and have proved successful, and this year the elaborate
plan outlined by a committee of commissioners and educational
experts will be carried out if a sufficient number of employees are
interested.

This is a significant scheme for public training. It is significant
from the educational point of view because it is a practical application of the pregnant truth that education is a preparation for life.
While the foundations for education are laid in the elementary school
and the educators may differ as to vocational training even in the
high schools, no progressive educators to-day reject the conception
that the colleges and the universities must train for a life career.
The life-career motive in education is beginning to receive the
adequate consideration it deserves. The vocational motive in education has sometimes been interpreted in terms of manual training or
of trade education, but if it is expressed in terms of a life work
then the vocational conception of education assumes a richer meaning.
The life-career motive gives to education a definiteness of end which
very materially affects the methods of education.

But there is an added reason for a life-career motive in education
to-day, because industrialism, and its child, the modern industrial
city, exacts specialization. So great is the need of specialization
to-day that many of the vocations have become highly specialized.
Specialization makes for efficiency and for that perfection of service
in the narrow field which is deemed essential. We need trained
specialists in the public service and, assuming a broad educational
foundation, these specialists should be trained early enough to
prevent waste of energy and to take cognizance of the economic
needs of the students. This consideration is especially important
for urban universities. A university or a college which is supported
by the city attracts students from the middle classes, many of whom
come from the homes of artisans and workpeople. The student
body of the College of the City of New York, for example, does
not consist of scions of the rich, but of young men who are sent
there by their parents at great sacrifice. These young men can not
afford to indulge in a purely liberal education too long. They must

see some vocational goal in view. The College of the City of New York has trained many teachers who are now serving in the public schools of the city. If the college did not provide this life-career motive for a great many of the students, some of the very best graduates would not have been able to enjoy the privileges of the college. The practical courses which the college is giving will enable more students to prepare themselves for other careers than teachers. The city will be able to recruit many of these highly intelligent and serious-minded students who will be able to start a life career by earning enough as a result of their college education. They can not afford to indulge themselves in the luxury of a social college career; they are compelled to be earnest by their economic necessities. Therefore, it is peculiarly fitting that the urban universities and colleges supported by the people should offer the students an opportunity for sound theoretical and practical training. The urban universities, therefore, have an opportunity for training leaders in democracy; they can attract the serious bodies of students who can not afford to pay even the small tuition of an average private institution. They live near their schools and are thus relieved of the added expense of board and lodging. Many of the more gifted young men from the poor classes are thus enabled to take advantage of a college education.

The urban universities become in the truest sense of that term training colleges for leaders in a democracy, for they offer equal opportunities to the gifted sons of the people to equip themselves for such leadership. There is a growing need for trained public servants in the Government, for the modern industrial city has created a condition of interdependence which makes the individual dependent upon the action of the State for many of the most essential conditions of living. The industrial city is an organic fact which has led to an organic conception of life. Imagine the helplessness of a tenement dweller if a city government did not have a division of food inspection to inspect the milk which he buys, or a tenement department to inspect the sanitary conditions of the houses he must live in. These essential conditions of life can only be socially controlled; therefore, government has become more and more socialized, as a result of which the city government and city departments have expanded their functions and have become a positive instrument for social welfare. The city now provides for many of the social conditions of life which were heretofore the concern of private individuals or private groups. The city, therefore, needs trained social servants.

A progressive government like the city of New York requires social investigators in the charity departments, playground attendants in the park department, probation officers in the courts, attendance officers in the schools, tenements inspectors in the tenement house department, etc. Therefore, with the growing socializing of government new opportunities are offered for trained public servants and the urban universities are equipped both in plant, in their teaching staff, and in the education ideals which animate them to provide such trained public servants. They are the natural cooperators with city departments for apprenticeship during their educational training. The city university becomes the symbol of our modern civilization.

V. SUPPLEMENTARY REPORTS OF TYPICAL URBAN UNIVERSITIES.

Some of the charter members filed reports of their cooperative work last year and these reports were printed in Bulletin, 1915, No. 38. New members and those who were not represented the last time were invited to send accounts of their work for this publication. Opportunity was also given for a modification of the first descriptions, to bring them up to date. The following are the responses received.

MUNICIPAL UNIVERSITY OF AKRON.

By PARKE R. KOLBE, President.

The report of last year may be supplemented with the statement that we are further developing various forms of cooperation with the city departments.

The city's testing work is carried on entirely in the laboratories of the university, under the direction of a department called the bureau of city tests. Here is done the chemical testing of supplies purchased by various departments, bacteriological testing for the board of health and local physicians, and physical testing of paving brick, cement, etc.

The department of political science and sociology is cooperating with the board of health and the charity organization society in using students as workers and investigators in the city; also with the bureau of municipal research in the study of city departments. One of the fields now in prospect is that of training for public service. It is hoped eventually to establish a cooperative course for this purpose in connection with the department of political science, the engineering college, and the bureau of municipal research.

A step in advance has been taken by the establishment of a combination course in cooperation with the board of education, between the university and the city normal school for the training of teachers. Graduates of this course will receive preference in appointment to positions in the city school system.

Akron, being the center of the rubber industry, offers opportunity for specialization in the chemistry of rubber at the municipal university, which possesses the only fully equipped college laboratory for this purpose in the country.

The college of engineering is cooperating with nearly a dozen factories of the city where its students work in alternating two-week periods, also with various contracting firms and railroads. The college has also been active in the investigation of paving conditions in the city and has published a detailed report on the subject at the request of the city council.

Extension work is being carried on by means of a course of lectures offered by the university faculty to a number of clubs and organizations in the city. Late afternoon and evening classes have recently been organized and offer the opportunity for college work to teachers, employed persons, and citizens in general.

BROWN UNIVERSITY, PROVIDENCE, R. I.

By JAMES Q. DEALEY,

Professor of Social and Political Science.

Brown University is a private institution and derives no part of its income from municipal or State appropriations. Aside from the Rhode Island State College, at Kingston, there is no other institution of higher training in Rhode Island. The university, having a history of 150 years, has profoundly affected the State through its many alumni prominent in economic and civic life and through the natural influence exerted during these years by the members of its faculty on the community.

Within the past 25 years the university has to some extent laid stress on the policy of direct community service, and has slowly built up a series of connections between the institution and the city and State. At first this activity took the form of extension lectures given anywhere within the State; at present these are offered at special times on the campus, primarily to teachers, but in fact to all who care to register.

For 20 years a close connection has existed between the education department of the university and the public-school system. Students trained in educational courses are welcomed as visitors to classes

in the public schools, and selected persons are chosen to serve as
"pupil teachers" on half-time service with pay while completing
courses for the master's degree. A limited number of recommended
students who are preparing to become teachers may, by special arrangement, receive at State expense tuition scholarships while they
are candidates for advanced degrees. In addition may be mentioned
an annual meeting on the campus of a teachers' association made up
chiefly of those in the State or vicinity who are interested in the
problems arising from the relations of the university to secondary
education.

Through the department of social science, students are brought in
contact with the various philanthropic agencies of Providence and
assist in their work or in making special surveys of social conditions.
These surveys regularly have in mind some concrete practical problem, and have been helpful in formulating plans for social betterment. In political science, students have acquired practical knowledge in two ways: (1) Classes have been organized into conventions
for the purpose of preparing a city charter or a State constitution,
and (2) picked students have cooperated with the State legislative
reference bureau in the study of current legislation or with city
departments in respect to municipal questions. The economic department in a similar way uses its students in the investigation of
local and State civic economic studies. The department of biblical
literature cooperates with religious agencies for the better training
of Sunday-school teachers, in maintaining lecture courses on biblical
topics, and by offering courses aiming to prepare for churches social
workers and educational directors.

A great field of cooperation exists between the city and State and
the several departments of science. The department of biology
studies the conditions of the State shellfish industries and fisheries,
so as to conserve and build up these important sources of food supply.
Its study in respect to the rearing of young lobsters, for example,
has built up the Nation's supply of this important source of food.
Through its bacteriological experts, also, it is in close touch with
the health and milk departments in the State. The botanical department is in close touch with the botanical work of the public schools.
The National Government has a forestry laboratory on the campus,
so that an interest is developed in civic demands for information
regarding shade trees, tree surgery, and reforestation, and departmental studies of the diseases of trees are done under the direction
of the division of forest pathology of the United States Department
of Agriculture. The geological department assists in studies of soil
and geologic surveys, and its head is chairman of a State commission
on the conservation of natural resources. The astronomic department furnishes official time to the entire city and at frequent stated

intervals entertains at the observatory classes from the public schools. The engineering departments, electric, mechanical, and civil, maintain intimate relations of cooperation with kindred activities in city and State, and frequent conferences are held on the campus and addresses given to students in these branches by practical engineers. There are many other forms of cooperation that might be emphasized, such as the cooperation of the art department with the Rhode Island School of Design; the department of chemistry with the State college and with the textile industries of the State, or the many ways in which organizations of students cooperate with similar organizations in the city or State.

As already indicated, most of this activity has developed within the last 25 years. The amount of it is steadily increasing, as mutual needs arise and a cooperative interest develops. This growth in the cooperative spirit has come about almost unconsciously under the spirit of the times, and illustrates the inevitability of mutual relationships between a university with a civic spirit and a growing community in need of expert information and suggestion. Last spring this relationship was recognized by the appointment by the faculty, at the suggestion of President Faunce, of a committee on the relations of Brown University to the community. It is expected that this committee will systematize, unify, and enlarge the extramural work of the university so as to make it more effective.

UNIVERSITY OF DENVER, DENVER, COLO.

By GEORGE A. WARFIELD,

Dean of the School of Commerce.

Because of unusually close relations with the intellectual, social, and business life of the city the University of Denver is referred to as Denver's Municipal University.

The extension college serves especially the teachers of the public schools. Dr. Daniel E. Phillips taught the first class 18 years ago. The next year he had a faculty of three. Now a corps of a dozen or more teachers hold classes on Saturdays and on such afternoons and evenings as suit the largest number of students. This work is not confined to teachers, but business men and women, pastors, and serious-minded people of all occupations, attend in large numbers. More than 1,000 different teachers have attended these classes; 150 are now enrolled. Every school in the city has been strengthened and enriched.

All the professional colleges are closely allied with the professional men of the city. The Colorado College of Dental Surgery is one of the strongest institutions of its kind in the West. Its dental infirmary is completely equipped and always open for the use of the public. More than 12,000 patients are treated each year.

The school of commerce, accounts, and finance gives college instruction in commercial and financial subjects. Evening classes meet from 5.40 to 7.40, in the heart of the city. There is scarcely a large business office in Denver that is not represented by students. No department of the institution has a more direct influence upon the industrial and business life of Denver. The accountancy dispensary, established in 1914, has done much practical work free of charge for charitable, philanthropic, and religious societies of the city. Members of the faculty of the school of commerce do much extension work for business men and women. Courses are given in English, economics, money and banking, financial history of the United States, and business problems. One class of 200 pupils in the local factory of the Ford Motor Co. is studying the psychology of business under the instruction of a member of the faculty. For several years the classes conducted by the American Institute of Banking have been under the instruction of members of the school of commerce faculty. These courses have included business law, economics, finance, American financial history, foreign and domestic exchange, and the operation of the Federal Reserve Act.

The department of sociology has close relationship with the social and charitable agencies of Denver. Students are encouraged to work in settlements, make surveys and investigations, conduct classes and clubs. A special school for the Americanization of adult foreigners is being conducted under the supervision of the department. In cooperation with other social workers of Colorado, a summer school of civics and philanthropy was organized for the special benefit of charity workers and city employees. At the request of the city federation of charity this work is to be continued during the next school year.

The department of physical education has had notable success in cooperation with the city playground association. The university furnished an unusually choice corps of young men and women, well trained and competent, to supervise the parks and playgrounds of Denver.

THE UNIVERSITY OF MINNESOTA.

By JEREMIAH S. YOUNG,

Professor of Political Science.

The University of Minnesota is supported and controlled by the State. Most of the colleges are located in Minneapolis, but the college of agriculture is located in a suburb of St. Paul. The two plants are 3 miles apart, with an intercampus trolley connection. There is a population of more than half a million people within 20 miles of the university.   This fact emphasizes the urban location of the institution.

In the college of science, literature, and the arts, the department of sociology has courses of lectures this year by three representatives of charities and social-settlement organizations.   The department also sends a number of students for field work in connection with the University Hospital service.   Messrs. Crosgrave and James, under the direction of Prof. John H. Gray, head of the department of economics, are conducting surveys in connection with the civic and commerce association along the lines of unemployment.

The school of chemistry reports work in illuminating gas and water analysis.   Indeed, the gas department of Minneapolis was organized very largely by men in the school of chemistry.   A considerable amount of work along the line of testing paving material is being done.   The dean of the school entertains the hope that the chemistry laboratory will be a place where all technical control work can be done and where all disputes along industrial chemical lines between the city and the contractor may be settled.

The activities of the graduate school are numerous.   In 1913, when Prof. W. A. Schaper, of the department of political science, was a member of the commission to prepare a draft of a charter for Minneapolis, he made a direct study on the ground of some important experiments in commission form of government, his expenses being paid from the research funds.   This enabled him to put at the disposal of the city charter commission the results of his investigation.   The past year this same fund has been used to the extent of about $800 to aid in a vocational survey of the city of Minneapolis.   This survey was undertaken primarily by Prof. Prosser, head of the Dunwoody Institute.   This was a genuine piece of cooperative work, the university representative investigating commercial education in Minneapolis.   Mr. Gesell's monograph on Minnesota public utility rates was published from the research funds.   Certain studies are of municipal interest, such as Mr. Lampson's "The Spread of Tuberculosis in Families," William Anderson's "The Work of Public Service Commissions," and Prof. Weld's "Studies in Marketing and Farm Products."   This last study deals with such subjects as city markets, live-stock markets of South St. Paul, milk distribution in Minneapolis and St. Paul, and food-supply prices in the iron-range cities.   In this connection should be mentioned the publications of Messrs. McMillan and Shoop on "Concrete as a Structural Material."

The college of education carries on extension and correspondence courses, and enjoys the privilege of practice work in the city schools, together with cooperative research with the city teachers.   In this connection it should be noted that something like 115 courses of special interest to city teachers are offered at convenient hours, afternoons and Saturdays, with the local teachers especially in mind.

Many of the professors in the college of engineering render service for the city. Dean Shenehon is a member of the civic and commerce association committee on river development. Mr. Edward P. Burch is chairman of the committee on the high dam. Prof. Bass has been on the committee of public health. Prof. Cutler has been a member of the committee on abatement of railway noises, while many members of the faculty serve the city in technical civil-service examinations for city appointments. The college of engineering is raising the standard of the subordinates in many offices of architects, of workers in numerous industrial establishments, and in the offices of many practicing engineers.

The law school is engaged in a most interesting example of cooperation between the university law faculty and the associated charities of Minneapolis. This cooperation is concerned with the legal-aid bureau. The work is directed by a committee consisting of the president of the associated charities, the city attorney, and the dean of the university law school. This committee appoints a graduate of the law school at a stated annual salary. He acts as the attorney for the bureau and is also an instructor in practice in the law school. Two members of the senior class of the law school are assigned each week the duty of being present in the office of the legal-aid bureau from 1 to 6 p. m. each day. The students thus assigned are required to talk with clients as they come into the office and endeavor to determine in such conference the facts and the rights of the case and then report in writing to the attorney of the bureau, giving him the advice they think necessary in the circumstances. The attorney confirms or modifies the proposed advice. It usually happens that it is possible to settle these cases outside of court, but if no satisfactory settlement can be made, the student reporting the case will prepare, under the guidance of the bureau attorney, to institute such proceedings as may be necessary to secure the rights denied his client. At least once during each week one or more of the members of the law faculty visit the office of the legal-aid bureau and supervise the work. At the end of each week the attorney of the bureau makes a report of the two students to the law faculty. From April 15 to December 31, 1913, this bureau handled 1,039 cases and made collection of petty claims amounting to $4,184.95. From April to November, 1915, 2,554 cases were handled and $5,255.60 collected. This is a distinct piece of cooperation between the university and the city.

The university maintains two extension departments, one at the agricultural college, whose activities are confined to the rural parts of the State, and the other, the general extension division on the main campus, the bulk of whose work is done in Minneapolis and St. Paul through the evening extension classes. The·work of the general extension division falls under three main heads: College courses, business courses, and engineering courses. The registration in 1914–15 was as follows:

Registration in the general extension division, 1914–15.

Courses.	Minneapolis.	St. Paul.
Collegiate courses	861	218
Business courses	1,031	426
Engineering courses	311	16

These classes are conducted not only on the university campus, but also in the City Hall, the Public Library, and some of the schoolhouses. In St. Paul the work is done in cooperation with the St. Paul Institute. In addition to the classes conducted in the Twin Cities, the general extension division conducts classes in Duluth, St. Cloud, Winona, Albert Lea, Austin, and Northfield. The total registration of the towns above mentioned for the year was 3,850, or 2,508 different individuals. So far as possible, the general extension division has avoided duplicating the night-class work of the public schools, the Y. M. C. A., the Dunwoody Institute, and the St. Paul Institute. These institutions give elementary work for the most part, while the extension division gives the more advanced work, the effort being made to confine it to work of college grade. In addition to the class work, the division has been sponsor for courses of lectures in the Twin Cities. One notable series was that dealing with the European war and was given in the Central High School. Other lectures have been furnished for clubs, societies, and even for ward organizations. Another form of activity is through the league of Minnesota municipalities and the municipal reference bureau. During the year ending August 1, 1915, 80 villages and cities sent specific inquiries to the general extension division. In addition to this, there were over 200 letters of inquiry received from outside the State. The municipal reference bureau compiles statistics, makes researches, and furnishes information of all kinds to city officials. Moreover, it draws up model ordinances and makes itself useful in every way possible to officers of these municipalities.

The medical college renders a distinct public service through the hospital and dispensary. It is hoped to develop a closer working relation with the city hospitals.

The college of agriculture carries on many activities that, intended primarily for the rural population, still have a fairly direct bearing upon urban life. The university aids the civil-service commission of Minneapolis in many ways, not only in planning examinations and improving the methods of rating papers, but in gratuitously placing at the disposal of the commission the use of the gymnasium for examinations for firemen, the blacksmith shop at the university farm for the examinations for blacksmiths, the dairy laboratory for the examination of milk inspectors, and the use of the university equipment for examinations for various architectural and drafting positions.

This brief survey shows that the university conducts many differentiated lines of activity because of its urban location.

SYRACUSE UNIVERSITY, SYRACUSE, N. Y.

By Ross Jewell, Registrar.

In recognition of contributions toward campus improvement amounting to $20,000, the privileges of the 100-acre campus, with its notable rose garden, has been extended to the people of Syracuse. The music department gives free monthly recitals, the painting department two free exhibitions annually, and the medical college has a course in public health. The hospital has 150 beds, and a free dispensary has just been built. The professors of the several colleges speak before many city audiences, and expert services are frequently rendered gratis. The Young Women's Christian Association does city extension work, and 25 of the students have Sunday-school classes in one of the orphan homes. The university settlement is doing good work. We plan to open a night school next September.

WESTERN RESERVE UNIVERSITY.

In his last report to the trustees President Thwing enumerated the following direct services which his institution renders to the community:

In the first place, members of the faculty act as experts for public enterprises. The head of the department of biology identifies mineral and fossil specimens for those who make application, and also reports upon such matters as the rock structures underlying those portions of the city which now yield natural gas. He also assists the State biologist in investigating the Cleveland gas fields, thus saving the Government thousands of dollars which might otherwise be spent in unnecessary drilling. The head of the political science department served the city and State in like ways.

He was largely responsible for the framing and passage of the home-rule amendment of the Ohio constitution. He assisted materially in framing and getting passed a model municipal charter law in this State. Also, he advised several cities in the framing of their charter under the home-rule amendment. He was a member of the charter commission of Cleveland. He is president of the council of sociology and a member of the board of directors of the city club.

Other members of the department of political science are giving similar expert advice to various leagues and legislative bodies. The head of the department of sociology serves as vice chairman of the housing committee of the chamber of commerce. He and other members of his department act on numerous committees which are rendering effective help along sociological and philanthropic lines. The head of the department of chemistry of the college of women is serving on the filtration committee, and the head of the history department of the same college is on the executive committee of the civic league and Goodrich Social Settlement.

The department of romance languages is lending its efforts to cooperate with the Alliance Francaise in the extension of a knowledge of French outside the student body. Members of the various departments in the school of medicine are actively associated with the recent movement in the community for the study of eugenics. They also give expert advice to the authorities of the city in charge of the zoological collection concerning the care of animals. A member of the department of hygiene is city bacteriologist and also a member of the filtration commission.

The following communication, addressed to the trustees and quoted in the president's report, may be prophetic of some future development in direct service of a cooperative character:

Representing the will and wishes of 18 philanthropic organizations of Cleveland, we respectfully present the following for your consideration:

For at least 10 years there has been a growing conviction among the various public-welfare workers that there is in Cleveland a need and an opportunity for a school to teach sociological sciences. From time to time, as your president can relate to you, this need has been discussed by those interested in all kinds of welfare work, and plans for such a school have been considered. The recent increased demand for public and social service workers and the scarcity of tutored or practically trained candidates for these positions have compelled philanthropic organizations to give temporary courses of instruction that their workers might be at least partially trained; however, such courses have uniformly proven entirely inadequate, and no other result was ever expected. This condition and the constant stream of applications from high-grade, educated, and suitable, but entirely untrained persons for positions to do any and all kinds of social work have made these pleas for such a school more numerous and more emphatic.

Cleveland, with its great and varied business activities, its cosmopolitan population, and its rapid growth, is a fitting place to teach the sociologic sciences and to train in social work. No informed Clevelander will admit that any city has on the whole more advanced, varied, or active philanthropic institutions, municipal or private, or a more efficient fabric of social organizations working for the common welfare; and it is justly so. Therefore, no city offers greater opportunity for desirable practical experience, for popular extension courses, for properly supervised survey or original research work; no city has better material to study or from which to teach. Reserve has the necessary standing and prestige to attract properly prepared students to sociologic courses carrying university credits and leading to degrees. Reserve also has the confidence and the friendship of every social institution of Cleveland; so that practical extension courses could be given in co-operation with each and all of such institutions, and opportunity given to prepare for any special field of work. Such a combination of courses, academic, practical, liberal, we believe, would constitute a school in harmony with, but in advance of, the recent trend of sociologic teaching, and one more popular because more practical and of more value to promote public welfare, than the older established conventional schools of philanthropy.

We do, therefore, respectfully and earnestly ask that you give serious consideration to the needs of and the opportunities for such a school in Cleveland, and to the organization of this school as a part of Western Reserve University.

As a result of deliberations concerning this communication, the school of applied social sciences was organized; work will begin September, 1916.

UNIVERSITIES AND PUBLIC SERVICE: A BIBLIOGRAPHY, WITH SPECIAL REFERENCE TO THE PROBLEMS, FIELD WORK, AND COMMUNITY DUTIES OF URBAN UNIVERSITIES.

By Harry A. Rider,

Library of Research in Government Western Reserve University.

Akron, Ohio. Municipal university. Annual catalogue, 1st, 1914.
>Foundation, p. 15–16; aim, p. 16; social science courses of study in cooperation with the city, p. 84–85; College of Engineering, p. 110–111; Department of Civic Cooperation, p. 138–140.

——— Annual catalogue, 2d, 1915.
>Foundation, p. 15–16; aim, p. 16; Department of Civic Cooperation, p. 141–143.

——— Ordinance accepting the offer of the trustees of Buchtel to transfer and convey the entire property, assets, and endowments of said college to the city of. Akron for a municipal university. Ordinance No. 4050, approved August 25, 1913.

——— Ten reasons for the establishment of a municipal university in Akron.

Aley, R. J. Function of the university. *In* National Conference on Universities and Public Service. Proceedings, 1st, 1914. p. 27–30.
>The need of the university to enlarge its vision and its course of study.

American Political Science Association. Committee on practical training for public service. Preliminary report. *Also in* American Political Science Review (supplement), 8 : 301–356, February 1914.
>Investigation into the present efforts of cooperation between university and municipality in training public servants looking toward future advancement.

——— Proposed plan for training schools for public service. 1914.

Association of Urban Universities. *See* National Association of Municipal Universities.

Atkinson, F. M. Civic university constitution and its reform. English Review, 15 : 294–305, September 1913.
>Commentary on the government of civic universities in England.

Ayer, F. E. Akron pavements, a report of an investigation made by the municipal university of Akron, 1914.
>An example of university service to a municipality.

Baskerville, C. College of the City of New York. *In* National Association of Municipal Universities. Proceedings, 1st, 1914. p. 64–66.
>Cooperative work; municipal students; investigations; training for municipal service.

Beard, C. A. Methods of training for public service. School and Society, 2 : 904–911, December 25, 1915.

——— New York City as a political science laboratory. *In* National Conference on Universities and Public Service. Proceedings, 1st, 1914. p. 126–132.
>The opportunities in New York for the study of municipal government.

45424°—16——6

Beard, C. A. Problem of training for the public service. New York. Bureau of Municipal Research, 1915. p. 5–14. (Municipal Research, No. 68, December, 1915.)
    Outline of difficulties in organisation of training for public service with conclusions as to changes necessary.

——— Shadow and the substance. Public Servant, February 1916, p. 1.
    States necessity of academic credit as basis for real advance in training for public service.

——— Training for efficient public service. American Academy of Political and Social Science. Annals, 64: 215–226, March, 1916.

Benner, R. C., ed. Papers on the effect of smoke on building materials. Pittsburgh, 1913. (University of Pittsburgh. Mellon Institute of Industrial Research and School of Specific Industries. Smoke investigation bulletin, No. 6.)
    Investigation as to the waste caused by smoke in Pittsburgh.

Binkerd, R. S. New educational development. In National Conference on Universities and Public Service. Proceedings, 1st, 1914. p. 161–162.
    The interrelation of theory and practice.

Blackman, F. W. City manager a new career in public service. In National Conference on Universities and Public Service. Proceedings, 1st, 1914. p. 274–279.
    University training for city managers; establishment of permanent public service under this plant.

Breithut, F. E. Report of the committee of the College of the City of New York on municipal service survey. New York. Bureau of Municipal Research, p. 17–51. (Municipal Research, No. 68.)

Buchner, E. F. Johns Hopkins University, Baltimore, Md. In National Association of Municipal Universities. Proceedings, 1st, 1914. p. 50–52.
    Efforts of Johns Hopkins University at cooperation in the study of community problems.

Burris, W. P. Opportunity of a municipal university in relation to the city schools. School and Society, 1: 295–300, February 27, 1915.
    Interdependence of school system and university in Cincinnati.

——— Responsibility of a municipal university in relation to the city schools. In National Association of Municipal Universities. Proceedings, 1st, 1914. p. 27–33.
    The service of the municipal university in training teachers.

Burritt, B. B. Occupation of college graduates. In National Conference on Universities and Public Service. Proceedings, 1st, 1914. p. 85–88.
    The changing professions of college-trained men.

Butler, N. M. Suggestions and recommendations of the special committee on training for public service. Public Servant, March 1916. p. 27–30.

Carpenter, W. H. Privately endowed universities. In National Conference on Universities and Public Service. Proceedings, 1st, 1914. p. 169–175.
    The opportunities in community service by every American university.

——— Public service of Columbia university officers. Columbia University Quarterly, 16: 169–182, March 1914.
    Report on public service of the faculty of Columbia University.

Chamberlain, J. P. Training for public service. Survey, 33: 201–202, November 21, 1914.
    A letter regarding training for public service as outlined by E. A. Fitzpatrick (q. v.), taking issue with details as to method but agreeing on the main issue.

Cincinnati. Municipal reference bureau, University of Cincinnati. What it is, what it does, how it works. [1915.]

Cincinnati, University of. Announcement of the cooperative courses. College of Engineering, 1912–1913.

—— Annual catalogue, 1913–1914. University of Cincinnati Record, January 1914.
Foundation, p. 37–41. Municipal reference bureau, p. 44. College for teachers, p. 144. Cooperative system, p. 165–167. Hygiene, p. 243–244.

—— Annual catalogue, 1914–1915. University of Cincinnati Record, January 1915.
Foundation, p. 37–41. Municipal reference bureau, p. 44–45. College for teachers, p. 152. Cooperative system, p. 175–178. Hygiene, p. 253.

—— Annual report of the president, 1907.
Municipal university, p. 5–6.
College of engineering—cooperative courses, p. 12–16.

—— Condition and history of the university in 1912, including a sociological study of the student body. University of Cincinnati Record, August 1913.
Cooperation in the city departments, p. 13. Municipal exhibit, p. 13. Study of the student body, p. 18–31.

—— Cooperation in education at the University of Cincinnati. 1908.
From the annual reports of 1908; describes the cooperative work in the college for teachers and the college of engineering for the city.
Especially: City universities, p. 11–14; cooperative engineering course, p. 43–50; cooperation with the public schools, p. 58–62.

—— Educational system. [1915.]
Chart showing departments of Cincinnati educational system from public kindergartens to graduate school, including bureaus of municipal reference, vocational service, psychological research, and affiliated organizations like the City Club.

—— Education and cooperation in Cincinnati.
Descriptive pamphlet concerning the school system of Cincinnati from the grades to the university, and of other educational institutions of the city.

—— Exhibit of the University of Cincinnati. 1912.
Pamphlets of charts shown at the Budget Exhibit, illustrating cooperative work of the university.

—— How the university serves the city. [1911.]
Three charts, with explanations.

—— How the university serves the city. 1913.
Some facts from the exhibit of the University of Cincinnati at the municipal university.

—— Municipality owns university of nation-wide prominence.
Reprint of newspaper article. Describes the municipal university of Cincinnati.

—— Municipal university. 1911.
Income of the city, p. 8–10. College and the city, p. 12–18.

—— Municipal university devoted to the advancement of liberal and technical learning and to the service of the people of Cincinnati. July 1912.
Bulletin of information.

—— Organization and stations of cooperative work. [1914.]
Map showing 95 stations.

—— Our municipal courses. City College Quarterly, March 1916.

—— Progress of the university. 1909.
Needs of the university, p. 17–24.

—— Progress of the university and its needs.
Progress of the university, p. 14–18.

—— Service of the university to the city and its institutions. 1913.
Service of some of the departments, p. 9–11. Extramural work, p. 11–15. Municipal reference bureau, p. 15–16.

Cincinnati, University of. Service of the university to the city and the annual reports of the officers for 1913. University of Cincinnati Record, July 1914.
Passim, especially: Service of some of the departments, p. 12–14. Extramural work of the university, p. 14–16. Municipal reference bureau, p. 18, 59–60.

—— Service of the university to the city and the annual reports of the officers, 1914. University of Cincinnati Record, October 1915.
Passim, especially: Municipal reference bureau, p. 15–16, 76–77; bureau of city tests, p. 17, 80–82; evolution of cooperative system, college of engineering, p. 54–56.

—— Sociological study of the student body.
Brief statement of the investigation of the student body. See fuller accounts elsewhere in this list.

—— Study of the student body.
A full account of courses to train those in the employ of the City of New York. By Frederick B. Robinson, director of the division of vocational subjects and civic administration.

Claxton, P. P. Cooperative methods in education. In National Association of Municipal Universities. Proceedings, 1st, 1914. p. 18–25.
The municipal university and its problems.

—— Public service as a career. In National Conference on Public Service. Proceedings, 1st, 1914. p. 63–65.
Compares modern needs with old traditions.

—— Sound educational principle. In National Conference on Public Service. Proceedings, 1st, 1914. p. 22–23.
Lays down the fundamental principle that practical experience added to theory leads to a sounder educational policy.

Clevenger, J. F. Effect of the soot in smoke on vegetation. Pittsburgh, Pa. Mellon Institute of Industrial Research and School of Specific Industries, 1913. (Smoke investigation bulletin, No. 7.)
Illustrated. Investigation as to the injury to trees caused by the smoke nuisance in Pittsburgh.

Cockayne, C. Civic universities in Great Britain. In National Association of Municipal Universities. Proceedings, 1st. p. 33–37.
Brief historical account of the seven British municipal universities: Birmingham, Leeds, Liverpool, Sheffield, Bristol, National University of Ireland, and Belfast.

Colby, E. Call to battle. In National Conference on Universities and Public Service. Proceedings, 1st, 1914. p. 24–26.
Describes the change in university education.

College of the City of New York. Annual catalogue. Statement concerning municipal students and the evening session.

—— Department of chemistry. September 1912.
Introductory statement, p. 5–6.

—— Facts for students seeking a collegiate education. 1912.
History, p. 59–64.

—— Report of the committee on municipal service survey. December 31, 1915.
Report of ways in which the college might be of service to the New York city government, (1) in preparing future employees; (2) in improving efficiency of present employees.

Columbia University. Committee on training for public service. Report, March 27, 1915.
Arrangement of courses for training for public service.

Cooke, M. L. Cooperation of the University of Pennsylvania and the Philadelphia department of public works. In National Conference on Universities and Public Service. Proceedings, 1st, 1914. p. 191–197.
The work of the University of Pennsylvania in Philadelphia.

Coulter, J. M. University and research. University of Chicago Magazine. 8: 93–95, January 1916.

Crecraft, E. A. Municipal reference library. National Municipal Review, 2: 644–652, October 1913.
Includes municipal reference libraries of universities: Wisconsin, Kansas, Illinois, Cincinnati.

Curtis, M. M. Does Cleveland need a university? 1915. [Typewritten.]

Cutting, R. F. Democracy and a trained public service. In National Conference on Universities and Public Service. 1st, 1914. p. 117–119.
Training as an additional qualification for efficient public service.

Dabney, C. W. Movement for the modern city university in Germany. In National Association of Municipal Universities. Proceedings, 1st, 1914. p. 37–42.
Brief historical account of the development of German municipal universities: Frankfort-am-Main, Dresden, Cologne, Düsseldorf, Hamburg, and municipal training schools in Cologne, Berlin, and Düsseldorf.

—— Movement for the modern city university in Germany. School and Society, 1: 150–154, January 30, 1915.
Description of German city universities, with emphasis on the municipal universities.

—— Municipal university. Journal of Education. 81: 368–369, April 8, 1915.

—— Municipal university. In National Association of Municipal Universities. Proceedings, 1st, 1914. p. 7–15.
The need for the municipal university and its relation to other city departments and institutions.

—— Municipal university. Reprinted from the National Association of State Universities, 1914, v. 12.
Explains the service of the municipal university to the municipality.

—— Municipal university. School and society, 1: 73–80, January 16, 1915.
Compares the advantages of the municipal over the city university and its cooperative facilities with the city government.

—— Municipal university and its work. In National Education Association, 1912. p. 773–780.
Describes the University of Cincinnati and its cooperation with the city.

—— Study of the student body of the University of Cincinnati, a municipal institution. National Municipal Review, 3: 68–77, January 1914.
A sociological study of the student body.

—— University of Cincinnati. In National Association of Municipal Universities. Proceedings, 1st, 1914. p. 56–58.
Public service of the University of Cincinnati: Department of social science, Municipal reference bureau, City testing bureau, Industrial survey.

Daly, J. University of Cleveland. Cleveland Plain Dealer, February 22, 1914.

Dewey, J. Educational principles involved. In National Conference on Universities and Public Service. Proceedings, 1st, 1914. p. 249–254.
Discusses need for training for public service, with methods of coordinating theory and practice.

Düsseldorf's municipal college. National Municipal Review, 1: 306–307, April 1912.
Describes new school for training municipal officials. See also same magazine for April 1914 and July 1913.

Duggan, S. P. College of the City of New York and community service. In National Conference on Universities and Public Service. Proceedings, 1st, 1914. p. 156–160.
The opportunities for community service in New York.

Duncan, R. K. Industrial fellowship of the Mellon Institute. Science, n. s.
    39 : 672–678, May 8, 1914.

Feiker, F. M. Herman Schneider. System, 23 : 48–49, January 1913.
    Biographical sketch of the dean of the engineering department of the University
    of Cincinnati, who proposed the half-time plan of work and schooling.

Fellows, G. E. Millikin University, Decatur, Ill. In National Association
    of Municipal Universities. Proceedings, 1st, 1914. p. 54–55.
    Proposed cooperation between university and a small city.

Finley, J. H. Man and the job. 1910. Reprinted from City College Quarterly.
    Training for the city's young men is the function of the city college.

———— Spoken word. 1910. Reprinted from the City College Quarterly.
    New York City College—democracy's school.

———— Thirtieth man. 1911. Reprinted from the City College Quarterly,
    October 1911.
    One of every 30 men is a public servant. Education of young men of the city
    should include training for service to the community.

Fitzpatrick, E. A. Institute of political and administrative research. School
    and Society, 3 : 449–452, March 25, 1916.

———— Introduction. In National Conference on Universities and Public
    Service. Proceedings, 1st, 1914. p. 9–10.
    Explains purpose in the organization of this new association.

———— National program for training for public service. Public Servant, Feb-
    ruary 1916. p. 3–9.

———— Plan for a university extension department. Madison, Wis., Society
    for the Promotion of Training for Public Service, August 1915.

———— Progress of the movement for training for public service. Public
    Servant, March 1916. p. 19–26.
    Describes recent phases of the movement in the University of Illinois, University
    of Minnesota, Columbia University, University of Pennsylvania, University of Wis-
    consin, University of Missouri, University of Vermont, New York University, Uni-
    versity of Texas.

———— Universities and training for public service. Survey, 32 : 614–615, Sep-
    tember 19, 1914.
    The secretary of the committee on practical training of the American Political
    Science Association discusses the problem of training for public service by the
    universities.

———— University training for public service. American Political Science
    Review, 8 : 674–679, November 1914.
    Argues that practical training for public service should be conducted as a part
    of university work.

Foltz, E. B. K. Federal civil service as a career. New York, Putnam's Sons,
    1909.
    College graduate in public life, p. 307–319.

Foster, W. T. Reed College, Portland, Oreg. In National Association of
    Municipal Universities. Proceedings, 1st, 1914. p. 58–61.
    Cooperative studies : Motion picture shows, Unemployed, Faculty membership in
    vice commissions, Health bureaus, Social hygiene society, Establishment of clearing
    house for social, moral, economic, and political progress.

Gephart, W. F. Washington University, St. Louis, Mo. In National Associa-
    tion of Municipal Universities. Proceedings, 1st, 1914. p. 55–56.
    Cooperation between university and city, especially in school for social workers,
    special investigations, etc.

Gilbertson, H. S. City managership—a new career in public service. In
    National Conference on Universities and Public Service. Proceedings, 1st,
    1914. p. 89–112.
    University training of city managers, p. 89–94. Discussion, p. 95–112.

Gilman, D. C. Launching of a university and other papers; a sheaf of remembrances. New York, Dodd, Mead & Co., 1906.
> Chapter 14, Research, p. 235–251; chapter 15, Dawn of a university in the Western Reserve, p. 253–277, especially p. 267.

Gray, J. H. Public administration and practical training for public service. *In* National Conference on Universities and Public Service. Proceedings, 1st, 1914. p. 46–56.
> Reciprocal benefits of training for public service to city and university.

Greenough, M. B. Automobile as a factor in highway construction and maintenance. [Ohio] Motorist, December 1914. p. 5–11.
> Describes traffic census taken by students in civil engineering in Case School of Applied Sciences, Cleveland.

Gruener, H. Progress of water filtration, with special reference to Cleveland. Western Reserve University Bulletin, 16:159–171, November 1913.
> Investigation as to methods for securing a pure water supply for the city of Cleveland.

Haldane, R. B. Civic university. Hibbert Journal, 11:233–254, January 1913. Also reprinted, May 1913.
> An address to the citizens of Bristol, with mention of German and British municipal universities. Describes the functions of a modern city university: "Universities [are] becoming increasingly prominent in all municipal functions of a public character."

—— Civic university. Nature, 90:225–226, October 24, 1912.
> Extracts from Viscount Haldane's address.

Hamilton, F. W. How can class gifts to universities be made to emphasize the social function of the university and to stimulate training for public service? School and Society, 3:445–449, March 25, 1916.

Harper, W. R. Trend in higher education. Chicago, University of Chicago Press, 1905.
> Chapter 9, Urban university, p. 156–160.

Hasse, A. R. Schools giving instruction in municipal administration in Germany. National Municipal Review, 3:402–403, April 1914.
> A list of German schools for training city officials.

Heaton, J. P. School for mayors. Survey. 27:1340–1341, December 9, 1911.
> Discusses work of the Bureau of Municipal Research, New York, N. Y.

Hicks, F. C. Ideal municipal university. *In* National Conference on Universities and Public Service. Proceedings, 1st, 1914. p. 120–125.
> The ideals of the University of Cincinnati.

Holcombe, A. N. Harvard point of view. *In* National Conference on Universities and Public Service. Proceedings, 1st, 1914. p. 255–266.
> Practical training for public service, with discussion as to University credit, p. 255–259.
> Discussion, p. 260–266.

Horne, C. F. Sons of the city. Outlook, 104:706–712, July 26, 1913.
> Describes College of the City of New York—"New York City's most important manufactory . . . [whose product is] citizens."

Hotchkiss, W. E. Northwestern University, Evanston, Ill. *In* National Association of Municipal Universities. Proceedings, 1st, 1914. p. 62–64.
> Participation of this university in affairs of the community.

How the universities are helping. American City, 9:401–402, November, 1913.
> Describes three examples of increasing interest of American universities in cooperative community work. Cornell: Course in citizenship. Harvard: Sanitary commission of Cambridge. University of California: Bureau of municipal reference.

James, E. J. Professional training for important positions in the public service. *In* National Conference on Universities and Public Service. Proceedings, 1st, 1914. p. 269–273.
> Brief historical account; the German solution and the situation in the United States.

James, H. G. Announcement of courses in municipal administration at the University of Texas. Austin, University of Texas, 1914. (Municipal research series, No. 3, September 5, 1914.)
> University and the city, p. 5–8.

—— City's need, the university's opportunity. American City, 10: 247–249. March 1914.
> Adapting university to community needs.

—— Training for public service at the University of Texas. *In* National Conference on Universities and Public Service. Proceedings, 1st, 1914. p. 198–220.
> Describes the work of the University of Texas, in training men for the public service, with accounts of the Texas Bureau of Municipal Research and the proposed school of municipal administration, p. 198–205.
> Discussion, p. 206–220.

—— University training for municipal administration. Austin, University of Texas, 1915. (Municipal research series, No. 11, August 20, 1915.)
> The university as a training school for public service.

Jenks, J. W. Cooperation between city governments and universities. National Municipal Review, 3: 764–766, October 1914.
> Suggestions as to cooperative methods.

—— New York University, New York, N. Y. *In* National Association of Municipal Universities. Proceedings, 1st, 1914. p. 44–46.
> Brief description of cooperation between city and university.

—— University professors helping government—a brighter side. *In* National Conference on Universities and Public Service. Proceedings, 1st, 1914. p. 57–59.
> The influence of the college professor in actual governmental affairs.

—— What a college of administration might do for New York. *In* National Conference on Universities and Public Service. Proceedings, 1st, 1914. p. 146–155.
> Describes the need of a college of municipal administration in New York City for practical training of the city officials.

Kaiser, J. B. Law, legislative, and municipal reference libraries. Boston, Boston Book Co., 1914.
> Legislative reference in universities, p. 76–77, 232.
> List of municipal reference libraries, including university bureaus, p. 251–261.
> Municipal reference in universities, p. 243–245, 243n–245n.

—— Municipal reference libraries. Nation, 94: 109, February 1, 1912.
> A letter regarding the establishment of municipal reference libraries in cities and universities, to aid in the solution of municipal administrative problems.

Kimball, H. H. Meteorological aspect of the smoke problem. Pittsburgh, Pa., Mellon Institute of Industrial Research and School of Specific Industries, 1913. (Smoke investigation bulletin, No. 5.)
> Research work as to the effect of smoke on the climate and sunshine of Pittsburgh.

King, C. L. Cooperation between universities and cities. National Municipal Review, 5: 122–123, January 1916.
> Comment on second annual conference of the Association of Urban Universities.

—— Local residence requirement for public office. Public Servant, February 1916, p. 10–15.
> Shows the advantages of employing expert and efficient men without regard to residence.

King, C. L. Training for municipal service. Scientific American (supplement), 79 : 118–119, February 20, 1915.
  How public business is conducted efficiently and without waste in German cities.

——— Training for the municipal service in Germany. Reprint from the Journal of the American Society of Mechanical Engineers. 1914.
  Discusses the German State universities, urban universities, and municipal universities, and their work in relation to municipal service.

Klotz, O., *and* W. C. White, *eds.* Papers on the influence of smoke on health. Pittsburgh, Pa., Mellon Institute of Industrial Research and School of Specific Industries, 1914. (Smoke investigation bulletin, No. 9.)
  Investigation as to the effect of the smoke nuisance on the health of the city of Pittsburgh.

Kolbe, P. R. Civic investment. Popular Science Monthly, 87 : 250–253, September 1915.
  Gives two reasons for the foundation of the municipal university of Akron ·
  (1) Training of students. (2) Cooperation with city departments and activities.

——— Demonstration of university and governmental cooperation· and the next step. *In* National Conference on Universities and Public Service. Proceedings, 1st, 1914. p. 163–166.
  A brief word as to the prospects for the municipal and urban colleges in the United States.

——— History of the establishment of the municipal university of Akron. Akron, Ohio, Municipal university, 1914.
  Brief historical account, p. 3–20. Newspaper comment, p. 20–26.

——— Municipal university of Akron. *In* National Association of Municipal Universities. Proceedings, 1st, 1914. p. 42–44.
  Brief historical account of establishment and description of organisation.

———Municipal university of Akron; a history of its establishment. 1912.

——— Present status of the American municipal university. *In* National Association of Municipal Universities. Proceedings, 1st, 1914. p. 15–18.
  Gives an historical account of American municipal universities and their legal status.

——— Present status of the American municipal university. School and Society, 1 : 484–486, April 3, 1915.
  Discussion of city universities in United States. Two classes: (1) Municipal universities supported by cities. (2) Urban universities supported by private agencies.

——— Relation of the municipal university to the educational system. School and Society, 2 : 186–191, August 7, 1915.

Lavine, Morris. University and the police. Illustrated World, 24 : 816–821, February 1916.
  Describes courses in psychology given to the city police of Berkeley by the University of California.

Leathes, S. Universities and the public service. Nineteenth Century, 72 : 1260–1267, December 1912.
  Discusses the kind of education needed to train public men and public servants.

Levermore, C. H. Complete municipal university. North American, 196 : 705–713, November 1912.
  Describes a model university in a city and its work for the citizens.

Lindsay, S. M. New York as a sociological laboratory. *In* National Conference on Universities and Public Service. Proceedings, 1st, 1914. p. 133–138.
  The opportunities in New York for the study of social problems and their legislative aspects.

Linhart, S. B. University of Pittsburgh, Pittsburgh, Pa. *In* National Association of Municipal Universities. Proceedings, 1st, 1914. p. 46–48.
     Brief description of cooperative methods of this university, which though not a municipal university receives appropriations from the city.

Lord, E. W. Boston University, Boston, Mass. *In* National Association of Municipal Universities. Proceedings, 1st, 1914. p. 48–52.
     Brief account of university extension work and other methods of cooperation with city and State.

Louisville, University of. Catalogues, 1912–13, 1913–14, 1914–15.
     History, p. 7–9 ; 6–9 ; 7–10.

——— To supply Louisville's great need.
     Statement issued to acquaint the people with the history of the institution.

Mabie, H. W. University and research work. *In* his American ideals. p. 245–266.
     Discusses movement toward research in governmental fields which is gathering momentum in the United States.

Macadam, E. Universities and the training of the social worker. Hibbert Journal, 12 : 283–294, January 1914.

McCarthy, C. Plan of the committee on practical training for public service. *In* National Conference on Universities and Public Service. Proceedings, 1st, 1914. p. 243–248.
     Training for public service ; outline of a proposed plan.

——— Upbuilding of administration ; the greatest need of American democracy. *In* National Conference on Universities and Public Service. Proceedings, 1st, 1914. p. 33–45.
     Gives the reasons for practical training for public service from the administrative viewpoint.

McClelland, E. H. Bibliography of smoke and smoke prevention. Pittsburgh, Pa., Mellon Institute of Industrial Research and School of Specific Industries, 1913. (Smoke investigation bulletin, No. 2.)

McClure, S. S. Public service as a career. *In* National Conference on Universities and Public Service. Proceedings, 1st, 1914. p. 66–67.
     Efficient city government and a trained public service.

McCormick, S. B. Should universities organize institutes of political research on the plan of the Mellon Institute of Industrial Research? School and Society, 3 : 433–436, March 25, 1916.

McDougal, R. University research. School and Society, 1 : 793–800, June 5, 1915.
     Progress of university research in the United States, touching on the governmental field.

McVey, F. L. Relation of the universities to public service. School and Society, 3 : 411–416, March 18, 1916.

Manchester, University of. Municipal School of Technology. Prospectus of part-time courses in municipal and sanitary engineering, architecture, and building trades, 1913–14.

——— Prospectus of university courses, 1913–14, 1915–16.
     Municipal and sanitary engineering, p. 55–56. Syllabuses, p. 189–145 ; 136–142.

Mellon Institute of Industrial Research and School of Specific Industries, University of Pittsburgh, Pittsburgh, Pa. Industrial fellowships. 1914.
     "The Mellon institute . . . represents an alliance between industry and learning "—this is its purpose.

——— Some engineering phases of Pittsburgh's smoke problem. Smoke investigation bulletin, No. 8, 1914.
     Survey of field work done by the institute among the manufacturing plants of Pittsburgh.

Mitchel, J. P. Universities and the public service. *In* National Conference on Universities and Public Service. Proceedings, 1st, 1914. p. 19–21.

The mayor of New York City arrives at the conclusion that a closer cooperation between universities and city government is needed for three purposes: (1) To give university students practical knowledge of government; (2) to secure a trained public service; (8) to solve governmental problems.

Municipal university. Reprint.

Describes University of Cincinnati, with some mention of the other municipal universities in the United States and abroad.

Municipal university as a civic investment. Current Opinion, 59: 341, November 1915.

Describes the aims of Ohio's three municipal universities: Cincinnati, Toledo, Akron.

Munro, W. B. Bibliography of municipal government in the United States. Cambridge, Mass., Harvard University Press, 1915.

Agencies of instruction in municipal government, p. 387–390.

—— Instruction in municipal government in the universities and colleges of the United States. National Municipal Review, 2: 427–428, July 1913.

Résumé of college instruction in municipal government supplementary to report by author in 1908. (*See* National Municipal League. Proceedings, 1908. p. 848–866.)

—— Present status of instruction in municipal government in the universities and colleges of the United States. *In* National Municipal League. Proceedings, 1908. p. 848–866. Also reprinted.

Report of the committee on the coordination of instruction in municipal government.

Murlin, L. H. Results of cooperation by the municipality and the university in education. School and Society, 2: 911–917, December 25, 1915.

—— University and the city. *In* Inauguration of Lemuel Herbert Murlin as president of Boston University, October 20, 1911.

President Murlin's inaugural address; describes the problems of the city university and the need of practical cooperation with its influence on educational curricula.

National Conference on Universities and Public Service. College and the city. [Reprint of a part of the proceedings, 1st, 1914.] 1914.

—— Universities and public service. Proceedings, 1st, 1914.

Institutions represented, p. 13–15. Opening addresses, p. 16–30. Upbuilding of governmental administration, p. 31–60. Public service as a career, p. 61–112. Municipal universities, p. 113–166. Public service activities of universities, p. 167–220.

Should universities give credit for work done in governmental bureaus and other agencies, p. 241–226. Appendix, p. 267–280. Newspaper comment, p. 281–289. Articles indexed under names of authors.

National Education Association. Cincinnati. 1915.

An account of the school system of Cincinnati and the methods of cooperation between the university and the other educational forces of the city.

Public school system as a whole, p. 7–86. University of Cincinnati, p. 37–46.

New York City. Bureau of Municipal Research. Training for municipal service. Municipal research, No. 68, December 1915.

—— —— Training school for public service. Annual report, 1913. Efficient citizenship, No. 670, March 18, 1914.

Describes the field work of the school for which credit is given by Columbia University, New York University, and the University of Pennsylvania.

—— —— Training school for public service. Annual report, 1915. Municipal Research, Extra No. 1, August 1915.

Relations with universities, p. 24–25.

New York University. Health officers correspondence course in hygiene and sanitation. Calendar, September 11, 1915, p. 1-8.
Announcement of course in public health problems for health officers actually in service.

Norton, A. O. Readings in the history of education; Medieval universities. Cambridge, Mass., Harvard University Press, 1909.
Privileges granted by a municipality. p. 98-100.
Influence of medieval privileges on modern universities, p. 101-102.

Norton, C. P. University of Buffalo, Buffalo, N. Y. In National Association of Municipal Universities. Proceedings, 1st, 1914. p. 50.
Brief mention of an attempt to found a municipal college.

O'Connor, J. J. Economic cost of the smoke nuisance to Pittsburgh. Pittsburgh, Pa., Mellon Institute of Industrial Research and School of Specific Industries, 1913. (Smoke investigation bulletin No. 4.)
Investigation of the smoke nuisance in Pittsburgh, with statistics as to the financial loss to the city.

Ohio. Municipal universities in Ohio statutes. [Typewritten.]
A copy of the sections of the General Code relative to the powers of cities to establish and maintain municipal universities: Sections 4001-4003, 7902-7920.

Ohle, E. L. Smoke abatement—a report on recent investigations made at Washington University [St. Louis, Mo.]. Journal of the Association of Engineering Societies, 55:139-148, November, 1915.
Investigation as to methods for checking the smoke nuisance in St. Louis.

Patterson, J. L. University of Louisville and the municipal university. 1912.
Editorials from the Courier-Journal reprinted.

—— University of Louisville, Louisville, Ky. In National Association of Municipal Universities. Proceedings, 1st, 1914. p. 61-62.
Brief historical account of the municipal university and its cooperation with the city.

Paulsen, F. German universities; their character and historical development. New York, Macmillan, 1895.
Relations to the community, p. 105-125.
Social equality of educated men and nobility as a basis of public office holding.

Paxton, E. T. Street paving in Texas. Austin, University of Texas, 1915. (Municipal research bulletin, No. 9, May 5, 1915.)
Exposition of importance of street paving as a municipal problem, with information as to pavements in Texas cities and suggestions for the care and treatment of streets.

Pittsburgh, University of. Department of Industrial Research. Outline of the smoke investigation. Bulletin, No. 1, August 1912.
Announcement and outline of the smoke investigation undertaken by the University of Pittsburgh.

Reber, L. E. University extension—its scope and administration. School and Society, 2:145-152, July 31, 1915.

Reed, T. H. Government for the people. New York, B. W. Huebsch, 1915.
Place of experts in State and local administration, p. 194-214.

Relation of the university to the community. Education, 32:314-316, January 1912.
Summary of discussion at the educational conference held at New York University, November 10, 1911, on the problem of how the urban university can best study and meet the needs of its community.

Salt, E. M. Research and reference bureaus. National Municipal Review, 2:48-56, January 1913.
Gives a list of university bureaus, describing their functions.

Schneider, H. **Municipal universities.** *In* National Conference on Universities and Public Service. Proceedings, 1st, 1914. p. 184–188.
The coordination of theory and practice based on the University of Cincinnati system.

—— Philosophy of the cooperative method. *In* National Association of Municipal Universities. Proceedings, 1st, 1914. p. 25–26.
Reasons for extension of university's functions.

—— Field work. Announcement of the committee on field work for the Association of Urban Universities, by Frederick B. Robinson, secretary. 3 : 69, April 22.

Shaw, A. Knowledge in the guidance of committees. University of Cincinnati Record, July 1913.
Part played by university in affairs of the city in which it is located.

Shiels, A. Opportunity of the College of the City of New York. *In* National Conference on Universities and Public Service. Proceedings, 1st, 1914. p. 139–145.
Describes the opportunities of the college in New York City.

Sidlo. T. L. Teaching practical politics. Western Reserve University Bulletin, 13 : 105–116, November 1910.
Reciprocal valuable effect on colleges and politicians to be obtained by "calling in the men that play the game" to the classroom to expose their experiences.

Simon, A. City mind and the municipal university. June 18, 1913.

Smith, Z. D. Field work. *In* National Conference of Charities and Corrections, 1915. Reprint No. 49.
Necessity of combination of field work and class work in training for social work.

Society for the Promotion of Training for Public Service. Aims and purposes of the society. 1915.
Outlines the work of the society.

—— Constitution. [1915.]

Stevers, M. D. Let the expert do it! Illustrated World, 24 : 590–593, January 1916.

Stowe, A. M. Efficient womanhood; an open letter to the women of Toledo. [1914.]
A printed letter to the women of Toledo to attend the municipal university, with a list of courses.

—— Liberal education for workers? an open letter to Toledo workers.

—— Toledo University. *In* National Association of Municipal Universities. Proceedings, 1st, 1914. p. 52.
Plans for cooperation through a public service bureau.

—— Work of a municipal college of arts and sciences. School and Society, 2 : 786–788, November 27, 1915.

Toledo. City financial problems. [1914]
Campaign booklet advocating the Toledo University tax levy.

—— Futility of the attempt to establish a municipal university under the shadow of a great State university. [1914.]
Campaign booklet against the Toledo University tax levy.

—— Ordinance to provide for the establishment of the Toledo University. March 18, 1884.

Toledo University. Announcements; the college of arts and sciences and the college of industrial science. Bulletin, September 1912.
History, p. 5–8.

Toledo University. Announcements; the college of arts and sciences and college of industrial science. Bulletin, March 1913, p. 8–11.

> General statement, p. 5–7. Historical sketch, p. 8–11. Ordinance establishing university, p. 9–10.

The university and the municipality. Summary of proceedings of the first session of the National Association of Municipal Universities. Washington, Government Printing Office, 1915. (U. S. Bureau of Education. Bulletin, 1915, No. 38.)

University course in the valuation of public utilities. February 1914. p. 193.

> Announces course in University of Pittsburgh.

University training for public service. American Political Science Review, 8 : 674–679, November 1914.

Wallas, G. University and the nation in America and England. Contemporary Review. 105 : 783–790, June 1914.

> College men in public life in the United States and in England contrasted. "American distrust of the ' college-bred man ' is dying out."

Wallin, J. E. W. Psychological aspects of the problem of atmospheric smoke pollution. Pittsburgh, Pa., Mellon Institute of Industrial Research and School of Specific Industries, 1913. (Smoke investigation bulletin, No. 3.)

> Pt. 1, Pathology of smoke, p. 5–32. Pt. 2, Aesthetic aspects of smoke pollution, p. 33–43.

Washburn, W. S. College man in the public service. Bibliography. Science, 34 : 589–593, November 3, 1911.

> The increase of college men in the federal civil service leads to efficient and economical administration.

Wells, E. H. University of Cleveland. Cleveland Plain Dealer, February 6, 7, 9, 10, 1914.

> A series of four articles: (1) Some American examples of successful municipal universities. (2) Work and influence of a municipal university. (3) Loose ends in Cleveland educational system. (4) How Cleveland might get a university.

—— University of the City of Cleveland; report to Mayor Newton D. Baker. [Typewritten.] 1914.

> Brief digests of history of American municipal universities with recommendations showing advantages of establishing a municipal university in Cleveland and of cooperation between city and university.

Wisconsin Free Library Commission. Instruction in library administration and public service. 1913.

> Announcement of courses in the library school for public service training in municipal reference and public commission work.

Woodbridge, F. J. E. University and the public. Educational Review, 49 : 109–125, February 1915.

> The change in the viewpoints of the university and the public in respect to each other and the increased scope of university activity in recent years.

○

DEPARTMENT OF THE INTERIOR
BUREAU OF EDUCATION

BULLETIN, 1916, No. 31

MONTHLY RECORD
OF CURRENT EDUCATIONAL
PUBLICATIONS

NOVEMBER, 1916

WASHINGTON
GOVERNMENT PRINTING OFFICE
1916

ADDITIONAL COPIES
OF THIS PUBLICATION MAY BE PROCURED FROM
THE SUPERINTENDENT OF DOCUMENTS'
GOVERNMENT PRINTING OFFICE
WASHINGTON, D. C.
AT
5 CENTS PER COPY

MONTHLY RECORD OF CURRENT EDUCATIONAL PUBLICATIONS.

*Compiled by the Library Division, Bureau of Education.

CONTENTS.—Publications of associations—Educational history and biography—Current educational conditions—Educational theory and practice—Educational psychology: Child study—Special methods of instruction—Special subjects of curriculum—Kindergarten and primary school—Rural education—Secondary education— Teachers: Training and professional status—Higher education—School administration—School management—School hygiene and sanitation—Physical training—Play and playgrounds—Social aspects of education—Child welfare—Moral education—Religious education—Manual and vocational training—Vocational guidance—Home economics—Commercial education—Civic education—Military training—Education of woman—Negro education—Education of immigrants—Education of deaf—Exceptional children—Education extension—Libraries and reading—Bureau of Education: Recent publications—Bulletin of the Bureau of Education.

NOTE.

This office can not supply the publications listed in this bulletin, other than those expressly designated as publications of the Bureau of Education. Books, pamphlets, and periodicals here mentioned may ordinarily be obtained from their respective publishers, either directly or through a dealer, or, in the case of an association publication, from the secretary of the issuing organization. Many of them are available for consultation in various public and institutional libraries.

Publications intended for inclusion in this record should be sent to the library of the Bureau of Education, Washington, D. C.

PUBLICATIONS OF ASSOCIATIONS.

1256. **Associated academic principals and Council of elementary school principals and teachers.** Proceedings of the thirty-first annual meeting . . . Syracuse, 1915. 144 p. 8°. (Edward P. Smith, secretary, North Tonawanda, N. Y.)

Contains: 1. H. D. DeGroat: The weak teacher and the principal's responsibility, p. 2-7. 2. P. W. L. Cox: The relations of our present type of school organization to the socialization of education, p. 7-20. 3. H. H. Horner: The correlation of examinations and inspections, p. 21-35. 4. C. S. Wilson: Agriculture in our schools, p. 35-40. 5. Julia E. Crane: Music in the high school, p. 40-50. 6. George Works: Vocational work in the rural and village high school, p. 50-55. 7. William Wiener: Supervised study a social need of the high schools, p. 55-64. 8. F. W. Roman: A re-statement of the relation of vocational education to democracy, p. 64-69. 9. David Snedden: New problems in secondary education, p. 69-80. 10. H. N. MacCracken: Does the high school menace the college? p. 80-89. 11. Report of committee on visual instruction, p. 89-92. 12. R. B. Kelley: Elementary science in the grades, p. 113-21. 13. N. G. West: Some practical suggestions on the teaching of patriotism, p. 121-31. 14. P. M. Paine: The book, the teacher, and librarian, p. 131-42.

1277. **Gerson, Armand J.**   Appreciation; an educational aim.   Current education, 20 : 220–23, September 1916.

> The author says that "it is for our public schools to plant in the hearts of the new generation an appreciative attitude toward nature and art so that things of beauty may indeed be joys forever."

1278. **Greene, William Chase.**   Culture.   North American review, 204 : 610–15, October 1916.

> Writer says that our national culture should be the expression of a mature and well-balanced interest in humanity.

1279. **Hall, John William** *and* **Hall, Alice Cynthia King.**   The question as a factor in teaching.   Boston, New York [etc.] Houghton Mifflin company [1916] viii, 189 p.   12°.

> Contains such questions as the authors believe should be put in the teaching of certain well-known topics in various studies.   Furnishes a concrete basis for studying the general rank of the question in instruction, its peculiar purposes and possibilities, and its desirable characteristics.

1280. **Hewins, Nellie P.**   The doctrine of formal discipline in the light of experimental investigation.   Baltimore, Warwick & York, inc., 1916.   120 p.   illus.   12°.   (Educational psychology monographs, no. 16)

> Bibliography : p. 115–18.

1281. **Hosic, James Fleming.**   Waste in education.   School and society, 4 : 509–12, September 30, 1916.

> Given before the Department of classroom teachers of the National education association, July 6, 1916.

1282. **Temple, W.**   The objects and methods of education.   School and society, 4 : 471–85, October 14, 1916.

> Address of the president of the educational science section of the British association for the advancement of science, Newcastle-on-Tyne, 1916.

EDUCATIONAL PSYCHOLOGY: CHILD STUDY.

1283. **Anderson, Homer Willard.**   Measuring primary reading in the Dubuque schools.   The Harris-Anderson tests.   [Dubuque, Ia., 1916]   23 p.   12°.

1284. ———.   A study of handwriting in the public schools of Dubuque, Iowa.   1916.   James H. Harris, superintendent of schools; H. W. Anderson, director of school measurements.   [Dubuque, Ia., 1916]   [11] p.   tables, diagrs.   8°.

> The samples were gathered under the direction of Superintendent Harris and Mr. Anderson, and judged for quality on the Ayres scale by Mr. Anderson.   *cf.* p. [2]

1285. ——— *and* **Hilliard, George H.**   The standardization of certain mental tests for ten-year-old children.   Journal of educational psychology, 7 : 400–13, September 1916.

> A study from the Educational psychology seminar, 1914–1915, University of Iowa.
> "The tests employed were cancellation of A's, immediate memory for a group of pictures, opposites, association of numbers with geometrical forms, linguistic invention, Binet's rectangle test, selective judgment, and problem questions.   The subjects were one hundred and fifteen unselected public school children."

1286. **Bell, J. Carleton.**   Mental tests and college freshmen.   Journal of educational psychology, 7 : 381–99, September 1916.

> Bibliography: p. 399.
> "Nine mental tests were modified for use as mass tests and given to seven hundred freshmen at the University of Texas.   The article describes the modification of the tests, indicates the methods of scoring, gives percentile curves of the results, and presents the correlations of the tests with each other and with the marks obtained in class work."

1287. **Grove, C. C.** Mathematics and psychology. Mathematics teacher, 9 : 3–10, September 1916.

> Continued from page 182, vol. 8, and to be continued in the next issue.
> The mathematics of psychologists and the validity of their uses of its forms and processes.

1288. **Haberman, J. Victor.** The intelligence examination and evaluation; a study of the child's mind. Psychological review, 23 : 352–79, September 1916.

> To be continued.
> Second report, following "The intelligence examination and evaluation and a new intelligence examination sheet," in Journal of the American medical association, 65 : 399–404, July 31, 1915.

1289. **Haggerty, M. E.** Scales for reading vocabulary of primary children. Elementary school journal, 17 : 106–15, October 1916.

> Results of a test, used under the writer's direction, in a number of primary grades (I to III) of the Minneapolis schools and in the training school of one of the Wisconsin State normal schools. The test was proposed by Supt. R. G. Jones (14th yearbook of the National society for the study of education) for a standard minimum vocabulary for primary reading.

1290. **Johnston, Joseph Henry.** A brief tabular history of the movement toward standardization by means of scales and tests of educational achievement in the elementary school subjects. Educational administration and supervision, 2 : 483–92, October 1916.

1291. **Martin, A. Leila.** A contribution to the standardization of the De Sanctis tests. Training school bulletin, 13 : 93–110, June 1916.

1292. **Starch, Daniel.** Educational measurements. New York, The Macmillan company, 1916. 202 p. 8°.

1293. **Stewart, S. F.** A study of physical growth and school standing of boys. Journal of educational psychology, 7 : 414–26, September 1916.

> This study was made in connection with a course in experimental education under Dr. Frank N. Freeman of the University of Chicago. To him the writer is under obligations for suggestions and criticisms.
> "The study deals with two hundred and seven boys of the elementary and the high schools of the University of Chicago, whose records extend over a period of from four to seven years. The article gives charts of height and weight by ages and grades, and the rank correlations between these figures and school standing."

1294. **Whitney, F. L.** Measuring tidal memory content. Elementary school journal, 17 : 116–22, October 1916.

> Presents tables and charts representing an attempt (1) "to state in objective terms the fact that children invariably 'know something' of every unit of knowledge before they come into contact with it in formal school work. and (2) to measure roughly the permanent deposit and the fluctuating material in memory content "

1295. **Young, Herman H.** The Witmer formboard. Philadelphia, Pa., 1916. 93–111 p. 8°.

> Reprinted from the Psychological clinic, vol. 10, no 4, June 15, 1916.
> An abstract of a thesis presented to the faculty of the graduate school of the University of Pennsylvania in partial fulfilment of the requirements for the degree of Doctor of philosophy. Bibliography: p. 110–11.

SPECIAL METHODS OF INSTRUCTION.

1296. **Howard, Claud.** The use of pictures in teaching literature. English journal, 5 : 539–43, October 1916.

1297. **Stoner, Winifred Sackville.** Manual of natural education. Indianapolis, The Bobbs-Merrill company [1916] 216 p. illus. 12°.

SPECIAL SUBJECTS OF CURRICULUM.

1298. **Bagley, William Chandler** and **Rugg, Harold Ordway.** The content of American history as taught in the seventh and eighth grades; an analysis of typical school textbooks. [Urbana, The University of Illinois, 1916] 59 p. 8°. (University of Illinois bulletin. vol. XIII, August 21, 1916, no. 51)

"The textbooks represented in the study": p. 9-11.

1299. **Bartholomew, Wallace E.** Fundamental aims in the teaching of book-keeping. [New York] 1916. 4 p. 4°.

This paper was given as an address before the Business department of the National education association, July 4, 1916; it is a reprint from the Business journal.

1300. **Beaux, Cecilia.** What should the college A. B. course offer to the future artist? American magazine of art, 7 : 479–84, October 1916.

A paper presented at the annual meeting of the College art association of America, held in Philadelphia, April 20-22, 1916.

1301. **Bonham, Milledge L.** Recent history: to what extent to the exclusion of other history. [Baton Rouge, La., 1916] p. [307]-318. 8°. (University bulletin, Louisiana state university. vol. VII, n. s., no. 8, August 1916)

1302. **Bradbury, Robert H.** The future of chemistry in the high school. Journal of the Franklin institute, 182 : 229–47, August 1916.

1303. **Budington, Robert A.** Some consequences of biological study. School and society, 4 : 495–503, September 30, 1916.

An address given under the auspices of the department of biology, at Goucher college, November 5, 1915.

In conclusion the author says that "one of the semi-inevitable consequences of a study of biology is a more easy, a more natural, a more dispassionate, and a more sane estimate of all life, in all its various degrees of organization, in all its history, and in all its accomplishments, than can otherwise be attained."

1304. Bulletin of the University of Texas, 1916, no. 15. English bulletin. vol. 1, no. 2, March 1916. 49 p. 8°.

Contains: 1. T. E. Ferguson: Oral composition in school and college, p. 5-28. 2. Mary E. Johnson: English in the grades, p. 29-35. 3. A. C. Judson: On the teaching of college English, p. 36-43. 4. E. L. Bradsher: Notes on new textbooks, p. 44-49.

1305. **Chestnut, James Le C.** History from the viewpoint of the grammar-grade teacher. Education, 37 : 103–11, October 1916.

Gives an outline of the subject. Describes the teacher's preparation, the point of classroom attack, etc.

1306. **Collins, Joseph V.** Metric reform in the United States. Educational review, 52 : 265–71, October 1916.

Says that by comparison of American with foreign programs of studies, it is easy "to show that American children need about 7/4 as much time to learn their arithmetic as German and French children need." Advocates metric system.

1307. **Dynes, Sarah A.** Socializing the child; a guide to the teaching of history in the primary grades. Boston, New York [etc.] Silver, Burdett, and company [1916] 302 p. 12°.

"List of all references mentioned in the text": p. 282-94.

1308. **English, Harry.** College preparation: what is its effect on what you teach and how you teach it? Mathematics teacher, 9 : 21-32, September 1916.

Deals with high-school mathematics.

1309. **Goodell, Thomas D.** Greek in the new university. Yale review, 6 : 150–66, October 1916.

> Makes this forecast: "Greek will be learned by few, as it has always been. But they will learn it better, and with less of painful waste, than we and our predecessors, they will be more deeply influenced . . . they will be among the leading minds, the minds that will guide the generation next beyond."

1310. **Hunt, Everett Lee.** General specialists. Quarterly journal of public speaking, 2 : 253–63, July 1916.

> Discusses the question of specialists in the department of public speaking. The writer thinks that narrow specialization will not produce the best results.

1311. **Jessup, Walter A.** *and* **Coffman, Lotus D.** The supervision of arithmetic. New York, The Macmillan company, 1916. 225 p. 12°.

> Gives the supervisor certain criteria for judging his course of study in arithmetic, also certain tests for measuring the attainments of his pupils.

1312. **Keller, A. G.** The case of Latin. Yale review, 6 : 135–49, October 1916.

> Writer concludes that both Latin and mathematics, in particular Latin, "should be sustained pending the rise of a substitute of equal or superior disciplinary value along similar lines. In this rôle of a disciplinary study Latin shows itself worth the cost."

1313. **Llewelyn, E. J.** Reading in the Mt. Vernon (Indiana) city schools. Elementary school journal, 17 : 123–27, October 1916.

> Attempts to supply motivation for study and for interpretation of the printed page by means of questions and suggestions given by the teacher either orally or written upon the blackboard.

1314. **McLaughlin, Andrew C.** Teaching war and peace in American history. History teacher's magazine, 7 : 259–64, October 1916.

> Reprinted by permission from "The Journal of the New York state teachers' association," vol. 2, p. 290. An address to the history section of the New York state teachers' association, November 1915.

1315. **Munro, William B.** Instruction in municipal government in the universities and colleges of the United States. National municipal review, 5 : 565–73, October 1916.

> Results of questionnaire sent by the education committee of the National municipal league to American colleges and universities. Says that the teaching of municipal government is more effective than ever before. Gives table of statistics.

1316. The place of mathematics in the "secondary schools of tomorrow." School science and mathematics, 16 : 608–16, October 1916.

> This tentative report of a committee of mathematics teachers in Chicago is published as a basis for further investigation and deliberation.

1317. **Porterfield, Allen Wilson.** The study of German in the future. School and society, 4 : 473–80, September 23, 1916.

> Shows why a knowledge of German has been a valuable asset to the American student of the past and then speaks of the future of the study of German in this country.

1318. **Price, Andrew.** Teaching thrift as a branch of public instruction. Education, 37 : 116–21, October 1916.

> Advocates school savings banks as a most valuable aid in education. Gives statistics of savings in foreign countries.

1319. **Rabourn, Sara B. F.** "Boost mathematics." School science and mathematics, 16 : 595–602, October 1916.

> The first part of the article aims to inspire confidence in high-school teachers of mathematics for their subject, and to give them courage to "boost" the wonderful superiority of the mathematical province; the second part gives devices for stimulating the interest of pupils.

1320. **Smith, Irving W.** The future of Latin and Greek. Education, 37 : 95–102, October 1916.

> Writer declares that a well-rounded education should contain both "the humanities and the utilities, the word of God and bread." A compromise should then be made between the extreme classicists and the ultra vocationalists.

1321. **Spilman, Louise.** Composition in the first and second years of high school. English journal, 5 : 556–68, October 1916.

> Gives typical compositions by pupils. Takes issue with Dr. Judd's criticisms on teaching of English.

KINDERGARTEN AND PRIMARY SCHOOL.

1322. **Barbour, Marion B.** The influences of modern education upon handwork for young children. Kindergarten-primary magazine, 29 : 48–51, October 1916.

> Gives "a few of the possibilities of handwork with young children, meeting the requirements of child psychology and hygiene, and demanding of the child his interest, effort, and reflective thought."

1323. **Hill, Mary D.** The educational values which the child carries over from the kindergarten into the primary grades. Kindergarten-primary magazine, 29 : 53–56, October 1916.

> Paper before the joint meeting of the elementary and kindergarten departments of the National education association.

RURAL EDUCATION.

1324. **Ayer, Fred Carlton** *and* **Morse, Hermann N.** A rural survey of Lane County, Oregon. [Eugene, Oreg.] Extension division, University of Oregon [1916] 109 p. illus., maps, diagrs. 8°. (The University of Oregon bulletin. n. s., vol. XIII, no. 14, August 15, 1916)

> The survey of Lane County, Oregon, is the third survey made by the Presbyterian country church work on the Pacific coast. It was made in cooperation with the University of Oregon and under the local auspices of the committee representing the Interdenominational conference.

1325. **Bricker, Garland A.** The function of the rural teacher. Progressive teacher, 22 : 31–32, October 1916.

> The first of a series of articles on rural education for teachers.

1326. **Grote, Caroline.** The Illinois rural school survey. Illinois teacher, 5 : 27–33, October 1916.

> To be continued.
> In the rural school survey of Illinois the writer was assigned the rural schools of the Military Tract, a territory comprising 18 counties, wholly or partly, and more than 3,000 schools. The conditions brought to light by the survey are given in this article.

1327. **Harrington, J. B.** Hot lunches for rural schools. Forecast, 12 : 263–67, October 1916.

1328. **Mayne, D. D.** Farm boy cavaliers. School education, 36 : 3–4, October 1916.

> The Farm boy cavaliers is an organization that plans to do for the boy on the farm what the Boy scouts are doing for the boy in the city.

1329. **O'Shea, M. V.** The morals of the country school. Wisconsin journal of education, 48 : 213–15, October 1916.

> The evil influences of the rural school and what can be done to counteract them.

SECONDARY EDUCATION.

1330. **Abelson, Joseph.** A bibliography of the junior high school. Education, 37 : 122–29, October 1916.

1331. **Asplund, Rupert F.** The high school and after. New Mexico journal of education, 13 : 9–12, October 1916.

> Discusses the purposes and possible results of our high school and its place in modern education.

1332. **Baker, Thomas Stockham.** The place and mission of the private school. Educational foundations, 28 : 23–30, September 1916.

> The writer believes that there will be a decrease in the number of private day schools but an increase in the number of private boarding schools. The reasons that the private schools are likely to increase in importance in this country are, first, the growing utilitarian character of the public schools, and, second, the growing complexity of social conditions.

1333. **Cox, Philip W. L.** The Solvay junior high school. American education, 20 : 80–86, October 1916.

> Discusses the content of the curriculum, the readjustment grade, helping the pupils to help themselves, etc.

1334. **Cubberley, Ellwood P.** Some recent developments in secondary education in California. Education, 37 : 77–85, October 1916.

> Describes the growth of the California secondary schools; "their noteworthy means of support, the system employed for the certification of teachers," etc. Makes a plea for the junior college.

1335. **Griffin, Orwin Bradford.** The high-school principal. American school board journal, 53 : 17–18, 73–74, October 1916.

> The man, his duties and opportunities within the school and outside of it.

1336. **Luis-André, Eloy.** La educación de la adolescencia; estudio crítico del estado de la segunda enseñanza y de sus reformas más urgentes. Madrid, Imp. de "Alrededor del mundo," 1916. 256 p. 8°.

1337. **Martin, A. S.** A high-school day of six hours and directed study. American school board journal, 53 : 23, 71–72, October 1916.

> Gives the reasons for a longer school day in the high schools and tells of the experiment in Norristown, Pa., of the long school day and directed study.

1338. **Sanberg, G. H.** The high-school student's point of view. American schoolmaster, 9 : 315–21, September 1916.

> Gives data on the home life of high-school pupils and their attitude toward the school obtained from replies to a questionnaire given to the high-school pupils of Crookston, Minn.

1339. **Sisson, Edward O.** Some characteristics of the high-school movement in three far northwestern states. Inter-mountain educator, 12 : 11–17, September 1916.

> Tells of the high-school movement in Washington, Oregon, and Idaho. "A plain tale of the western high school, its natural history, its environment, its aims and spirit."

TEACHERS: TRAINING AND PROFESSIONAL STATUS.

1340. **Baker, George M.** Evidences of teaching ability. Kentucky high school quarterly, 2 : 16–26, October 1916.

> Takes up nine tangible evidences of teaching ability: scholarship, ability to properly take and make effective use of constructive criticism, tendency to keep growing mentally, objective rather than subjective attitude of mind, ability to harmonize, physical strength, resourcefulness, disposition, and good common sense.

1341. **Brown, George A.** The responsibility of school boards for the transient teacher. School and home education, 36 : 36–37, October 1916.

The writer says that teachers remain in school work an average of more than five years. In this time they teach in three or four different schools. He thinks the school board is responsible for this state of affairs.

1342. **Dewey, John.** Professional organization of teachers. American teacher, 5 : 99–101, September 1916.

From an address delivered at a mass meeting called by the American federation of teachers during the National education association convention, New York, July 6, 1916.

1343. **Hall-Quest, Alfred L.** The teacher's personality and efficiency. The importance of personality. Virginia journal of education, 10 : 26–29, September 1916.

1344. **Hart, Joseph K.** Can a college department of education become scientific? Scientific monthly, 3 : 377–84, October 1916.

Thinks that the great field of research in educational theory may yet come to be found in the social sources of educational experience. Presents a program.

1345. **Keating, J. F.** Tenure of teachers. Better schools, 2 : 172–75, September 1916.

Advocates permanency of tenure throughout the school system.

1346. **Stanley, Edward M.** Freedom in our schools. Industrial economist, 2 : 5–8, August 1916.

Advance pages.
In conclusion the writer says: "The activities of union leaders have been very great, but the schools should be free from their work, and the people should see to it that the classroom is kept free from the presence of the agitator, either in person or through his agent, the teacher, who is a member of a labor union."

HIGHER EDUCATION.

1347. The Christian college. New York, Cincinnati, The Methodist book concern [1916] 78 p. 12°.

CONTENTS.—1. The ideals and aims of the Christian college, by Herbert Welch. 2. The importance of the Christian college as a factor in the making of America, by Henry Churchill King. 3. The product of the Christian college in men and movements, by Thomas Nicholson.

1348. **Dexter, Franklin Bowditch,** ed. Documentary history of Yale university, under the original charter of the Collegiate school of Connecticut, 1701–1745. New Haven, Yale university press, 1916. 382 p. 4°.

1349. Educational biases. Unpopular review, 6 : 132–44, July–September 1916.

Writer condemns an anti-patriotic bias in favor of foreign educational systems. It is well if some of the excellences of a foreign system can be adapted to the local stock, but the one to do the adjusting must know that stock.

1350. **Fernald, Merritt Caldwell.** History of the Maine state college and the University of Maine. Orono, Me., University of Maine, 1916. 450 p. incl. front., plates, ports. 8°.

1351. **Hadley, Arthur T.** President Hadley's matriculation sermon, delivered in Woolsey Hall, Yale university, Sunday, October 1, 1916. Yale alumni weekly, 26 : 62–63, October 6, 1916.

President Hadley says self-control, intelligence, courtesy, devotion are the qualities which are to be learned at Yale if the course of study is to prepare for the larger duties of citizenship as well as the narrower ones of our several callings and professions.

1352. **Jastrow, Joseph.** Ten years of the Carnegie foundation. School and society, 4 : 533–51, October 7, 1916.

Considers the scope of the Foundation, its contribution to educational progress, and the management of the retiring allowances.

"While the reviewer aims to present opinion as objectively as the outlook which he commands makes possible, the individual angle as well as the personal organ of vision determines the perspective."

1353. **Patterson, John L.** Municipal universities in the United States. National municipal review, 5 : 553–64, October 1916.

Reviews the work of the municipal universities in this country, and commends the modern movement in the United States and abroad to develop such schools for the higher education of all classes of citizens.

1354. **Schumacher, Matthew.** What next? Catholic educational review, 12: 204–10, October 1916.

An address at the opening meeting of the college department of the Catholic educational association on the standardization of Catholic colleges.

1355. **Shields, Thomas Edward.** Standardization of Catholic colleges. Catholic educational review, 12 : 193–203, October 1916.

1356. **Sprague, Homer B.** President Sprague's administration of the University of North Dakota. Quarterly journal of the University of North Dakota, 7 : 3–28, October 1916.

The University of North Dakota from 1887–1891.

SCHOOL ADMINISTRATION.

1357. **Anderson, D. A.** The efficiency expert in education. Educational administration and supervision, 2 : 477–82, October 1916.

The duties and responsibilities of the efficiency expert in our school systems.

1358. **Case, Hiram C.** The uniform system for recording disbursements for school purposes as prescribed for New York state. American school board journal, 53 : 24–26, 68, October 1916.

1359. **Johnson, Harriet M.** The visiting teacher in New York city; a statement of the function and an analysis of the work of the visiting teacher staff of the Public education association from 1912 to 1915 inclusive. [New York] Public education association of the city of New York, 1916. 84 p. 8°.

1360. **Miller, William T.** A survey from within. American school board journal, 53 : 16, 73, October 1916.

Suggestions for a school survey by persons actually engaged in administering or teaching in the system they are examining.

1361. **Probst, Ella M.** The contributions of scientific studies to the value of supervision. School education, 36 : 7–9, October 1916.

The advantages of co-operative research and what experimental investigation has contributed to the field of supervision.

1362. **Savedge, L. N.** How should superintendents measure the work of teachers. Virginia journal of education, 10 : 9–13, September 1916.

Address delivered before Richmond conference of division superintendents, July 5, 1916.

1363. **Strayer, George Drayton.** Some problems in city school administration. Yonkers-on-Hudson, N. Y., World book company, 1916. 234 p. illus. 8°. (School efficiency series, ed. by P. H. Hanus)

Report of the Butte school survey.

1364. **Voorhees, Harvey Cortlandt.** The law of the public school system of the United States. Boston, Little, Brown, and company, 1916. lvii, 429 p. 8°.

1365. **Wirt, William Albert.** The official Wirt reports to the Board of education of New York city; comprising the official reports upon Public school 89, Brooklyn, and public schools 28, 2, 42, 6, 50, 44, 5, 53, 40, 32, 4 and 45, the Bronx, and an appendix showing the more extensive reorganization proposed. With an introduction by Howard W. Nudd. [New York] Public education association of the city of New York, 1916. 56 p. tables. 8°.

SCHOOL MANAGEMENT.

1366. **Du Shane, Donald.** The intermediate grades and departmentalization. Elementary school journal, 17 : 89–105, October 1916.

Suggests reforms. The writer expresses the hope that the time is near when "the tragedy of a school mortality of 50 per cent below the eighth grade will be deeply enough felt to secure a more purposeful school training of this important group of future American citizens." To be continued. •

1367. **Mackie, Ransom A.** Educators on election in education. Northwest journal of education, 28 : 80–85, October 1916.

Advocates the elective system and gives some of its advantages.

SCHOOL HYGIENE AND SANITATION.

1368. **Baker, S. Josephine.** The control of communicable diseases in schools. American journal of public health, 6 : 1078–82, October 1916.

Read before a general session of the American public health association, Rochester, N. Y., September 10, 1915.

Gives the wor ing program which has been followed by the Bureau of child hygiene of New York city for the past six years. Emphasizes the necessity of eeping children in school rather than closing schools in the presence of communicable diseases in a community.

1369. **Faulkner, James P.** Teaching health in the public schools. Forward, 1 : 29–36, July 1916.

Gives an outline of health instruction as developed during several years of experience in public health wor. in Kentuc .y.

1370. **Irwin, R. B.** Classes for the conservation of vision. Ohio teacher, 37 : 52–54, September 1916.

Describes the class opened in Cleveland three years ago for children having serious defects o vision.

1371. **Kingsley, Sherman C.** Open-air schools and open-window rooms—how to build and equip them. Journal of the outdoor life, 13 : 310–20, October 1916.

Concluded from September number. Gives plans of schools in various cities. Illustrated.

1372. **Redway, Jacques W.** The air of school buildings. Medical times, 44 : 309–10, October 1916.

Among other things the writer says that the humidifying of the air of school rooms is one of the most important problems in the sanitary regulation of school buildings.

1373. **Swinnerton, George G.** Medical supervision of country children. School education, 36 : 3–5, September 1916.

Wor. of the school physician in Koochiching county, Minnesota.

1374. **Tigert, John J.** The relation of defective vision to retardation. Kentucky high school quarterly, 2 : 3–12, October 1916.

Bibliography: p. 12.

1375. **Tomkins, Ernest.** What will the school board do with stammering? American school board journal, 53 : 30, 62–63, October 1916.

Spea s of the infectiousness of stammering and says that the school board should simply prohibit stammering on school property and require the stammering child to wait and calm himself, so that he can spea fluently, or to write or ma e signs or remain silent.

PHYSICAL TRAINING.

1376. Ehler, George W. Developing physical and moral vitality. A rational scheme. Playground, 10 : 232–44, October 1916.

Outlines a plan for an average elementary school with one or more rooms in each grammar grade with one hundred or more boys and as many girls in the four grades.
This is the third in a series of three articles dealing with the need for an adequate and rational system of physical education.

1377. McCord, Clinton P. State-wide physical training. American education, 20 : 76–79, October 1916.

The new physical training law of New York state, its general purpose and its main features.

1378. Warden, Randall D. Physical training. Mind and body, 23 : 246–49, October 1916.

Why it should be recognized as a necessary subject in a child's training for life, and why it should receive time and attention equal to that given to any of the other curricula subjects.
Read at the meeting of the American physical education association, Cincinnati, April 19–22, 1916.

1379. Ziegler, Carl. The preparation of the director of physical education. Mind and body, 23 : 210–17, September 1916.

Read at the convention of the American physical education association, Cincinnati, April 1916.

PLAY AND PLAYGROUNDS.

1380. Curtis, Henry S. Play and education. Teaching, 2 : 6–17, September 15, 1916.

Discusses the subject under the following headings: The message of the play movement to the teacher, Significance of the play movement, Play and recreation in the open country, The school as a social center.

SOCIAL ASPECTS OF EDUCATION.

1381. Arrick, Clifford. Recreational and educational activities of the Chicago telephone company employees. Social service review, 4 : 13–15, September 1916.

1382. Corson, O. T. The public school not a substitute for the home. Ohio educational monthly, 65 : 497–99, September 1916.

Says that the school should not be expected to introduce card games, pool tables, and dancing in order to counteract the evil influences outside the school, resulting from the indifference of parents. The school should always cooperate with the home, but it was never intended as a substitute for the home.

1383. Wisconsin. Department of education. Suggestive studies of school conditions; an outlined study in school problems for women's clubs, parent-teacher associations and community organizations. Madison, Wis., 1916. 101 p. illus. 8°.

Prepared by Janet R. Rankin, school service secretary, State department of education.

CHILD WELFARE.

1384. Gibson, H. W. Boyology; or, Boy analysis. New York [etc.] Association press, 1916. 294 p. front. 16°. (*On cover:* Boy life series)
Bibliography: p. 269–80.

1385. Koch, Felix J. Having the school children help in child welfare. Child-welfare magazine, 11 : 42–45, October 1916.

Unique toy-repair shops and toy factories, run by the boys and girls, in Cincinnati, for poor children.

MORAL EDUCATION.

1386. **Davis, Jesse B.** Moral training and instruction in high schools. *Religious education,* 11 : 394–402, October 1916.

A survey of progress since 1911 in the high schools.

1387. **Fisher,** *Mrs.* **Dorothea Frances (Canfield).** Self-reliance; a practical and informal discussion of methods of teaching self-reliance, initiative and responsibility to modern children. Indianapolis, The Bobbs-Merrill company [1916] 243 p. 12°. (Childhood and youth series)

Contains bibliographies.

RELIGIOUS EDUCATION.

1388. **Brown, Arlo Ayres.** Primer of teacher training. New York, Cincinnati, The Methodist book concern [1916] 168 p. 16°.

1389. **Brown, Frank L.** The Sunday school situation in China, Korea, and Japan. International review of missions (Edinburgh) 5 : 614–27, October 1916.

1390. **Hartshorne, Hugh.** Worship in connection with week-day religious instruction. Religious education, 11 : 419–34, October 1916.

1391. **Molloy, M. A.** The Winona plan for parochial schools. America, 15 : 625–26, October 7, 1916.

The Winona plan for parochial schools plans to take the rulings of the Minnesota State department of education with reference to the standardization of schools and adapt them as far as advisable to the parochial schools of the diocese.

MANUAL AND VOCATIONAL TRAINING.

1392. **Eastern arts association.** Proceedings seventh annual meeting, Springfield, Mass., April 20–22, 1916. 219 p. 8°. (Fred P. Reagle, secretary, Montclair, N. J.)

Contains: 1. David Snedden: Problems of art education, p. 7–23. 2. A new development in art training. An account of the Art high school department of the Ethical culture school, p. 24–33. 3. A. E. Dodd: What national aid to vocational education means to teachers of the arts, p. 36–42. 4. F. G. Bonser: Industrial education in present school problems, p. 43–51. 5. Sallie B. Tannahill: Art in lettering—selection of material and application to school problems, p. 52–62. 6. Helen R. Norton: What co-operation of the art school with the department store means to the public, p. 72–77. 7. F. E. Mathewson: The point of view. Some pertinent questions concerning industrial courses in high schools, p. 78–84. 8. K. V. Carman: Industrial work as a basis for other school subjects, p. 85–94. 9. W. R. Ward: The time factor in manual training in the elementary school, p. 95–99. 10. E. B. Kent: Some successful experiments in manual training, p. 100–108. 11. O. D. Evans: Compulsory continuation schools, p. 109–29. 12. R. O. Small: Abstract on present phases of vocational education in Massachusetts, p. 130–33. 13. W. E. Grady: The Ettinger plan of prevocational training, p. 134–40. 14. F. H. Perkins: Possibilities in industrial training for mentally deficient girls, p. 141–44. 15. Marie Sayles: Rural problem of household arts education, p. 145–49. 16. Lucia W. Dement: Illustration for elementary children, p. 158–62. 17. Final report of the committee on time allowance for the manual arts, p. 176–79.

1393. **Crouch, Calvin Henry.** Vocational training. Quarterly journal of the University of North Dakota, 7 : 29–39, October 1916.

Describes briefly the Boys trades school of Milwaukee, Wis., and tells how it is turning out skilled laborers rather than unskilled laborers.

1394. **Dodd, Alvin E.** Vocational training in the Army. School and society, 4 : 585–88, October 14, 1916.

Discusses the Army bill passed by Congress containing provision for the training of soldiers while in service so that when they return to civil life they will be prepared for more effective work in the industries. Formulates a plan for carrying out the provisions of the bill.

1395. **Farnum, Royal B.** Differentiation in art training to suit individual pupils' needs. Industrial-arts magazine, 5 : 432–37, October 1916.

    A paper read before the Department of vocational education and practical arts, National education association, New York city, July 7, 1916.

1396. **Harlan, Charles L.** Content of courses of study in handicrafts for elementary school pupils. School education, 36 : 6–8, September 1916.

    , A study of over two hundred elementary school courses.

1397. **Jensen, George Henry.** Commercial standards for woodwork in the schools. Industrial-arts magazine, 5 : 449–53, October 1916.

    Tells of the Department of industrial arts in the Stockton (Cal.) schools, and how building equipment and general repair work about the school buildings has taken the place of the traditional form of manual training.

1398. [The Opportunity school of Denver] Child welfare bulletin (Peoria) 4 : 183–85, September 1916.

    A free school for supplying special wants of boys and girls, men and women, who are working but who are held on low rungs of the ladder of success by lack of training and education.

1399. **Smith, Harry Bradley.** Establishing industrial schools. Boston, Houghton Mifflin company [1916] 167 p. 12°. (Riverside educational monographs, ed. by H. Suzzallo)

1400. A supervisor's quest for the real thing. By a supervisor of art instruction. School-arts magazine, 16 : 47–54, October 1916.

    The story of a supervisor who resigned her position, secured employment as a regular teacher in an ungraded school in the country, and proceeded to put her theories to the test.

1401. **White, Sophie D.** Experiments in industrial education in New York city. *In* National society for the promotion of industrial education. Newsletter no. 9, October 1916. p. 13–31.

    Reprinted from the Child labor bulletin for August 1916.
    Discusses the Schneider, Ettinger, Gary plans, etc.

1402. **Winslow, Leon Loyal.** Education through industrial arts. Ohio educational monthly, 65 : 511–16, October 1916.

    Read before the Northwestern Ohio teachers' association, Toledo, November 1915.

VOCATIONAL GUIDANCE.

1403. **Conley, C. C.** Vocational guidance. Associate teacher, 18 : 9–10, October 1916.

    A brief sketch of the vocational guidance movement.

1404. **Pressey, Park.** A vocational reader. Chicago, New York, Rand McNally & company [1916] 244 p. illus. 12°.

HOME ECONOMICS.

1405. **Hamilton, A. E.** Babies in the curriculum. Journal of heredity, 7 : 387–94, September 1916.

    Tells of a baby adopted by a girls' camp, who taught the girls more about mothercraft in a few weeks than they would have learned in as many years of the ordinary domestic science curriculum.

1406. **Read, Mary L.** The mothercraft manual. Boston, Little, Brown, and company, 1916. 440 p. illus. 12°.

COMMERCIAL EDUCATION.

1407. **Herrick, Cheesman A.** Commercial education in American secondary schools. Educational review, 52 : 247–64, October 1916.

Writer says that in dealing with the content of the high school commercial course "the aims should be social both in subjects selected and in the study of these. Studies that have to do with the science of society, such as economics and civics, should have a prominent place in the secondary commercial school."

CIVIC EDUCATION.

1408. **Dunn, Arthur W.** On civic education. Western journal of education, 22 : 9, September 1916.

Address before the San Francisco Congress of mothers, September 1, 1916.

1409. **Leonard, Russell B.** Civics as taught in the New Bedford industrial school. Education, 37 : 87–94, October 1916.

Says that the work in the New Bedford school is handled with the idea of no compulsory home work; but if a boy desires to do outside study or reading he is encouraged to do so. The method used is class discussion.

MILITARY TRAINING.

1410. **Ransom, William Lynn,** *ed.* Military training, compulsory or volunteer; a series of addresses and papers presented at the semiannual meeting of the Academy of political science in the city of New York, May 18, 1916. New York, The Academy of political science, Columbia university, 1916. 262 p. 8°. (Proceedings . . . vol. vi, no. 4)

Contains: The schoolmaster and military training, by A. Meiklejohn, p. 171–78.

1411. **Schaeffer, Nathan C.** Education and preparedness for war. Arizona teacher, 6 : 17–22, 24, September 1916.

Superintendent Schaeffer is not in favor of military drill in the public schools.

1412. **U. S. General staff. War college division.** Military training in public schools. Outline of a plan for military training in the public schools of the United States, being one of a series of supplements to "A statement of a proper military policy for the United States," together with a letter of the Department of public instruction of Wyoming, submitting certain data explaining the organization and control of the Cheyenne high school cadet corps. Washington, Government printing office, 1916. 8 p. 8°. (64th Cong., 1st sess. Senate. Doc. 452)

EDUCATION OF WOMEN.

1413. **Chapin, F. Stuart.** The budgets of Smith college girls. Quarterly publications of the American statistical association, 15 : 149–56, n. s. no. 114, June 1916.

1414. **Ellis, Havelock.** The mind of woman. Atlantic monthly, 118 : 366–74, September 1916.

1415. **Kelly, Jennie E.** Standards in dress for high school girls. Educator-journal, 17 : 68–73, October 1916.

1416. **Patterson, Herbert P.** The logical problem of coeducation. Education, 37 : 112-15, October 1916.

Writer after treating the psychological and physiological differences of the sexes comes to the conclusion that "complete separation in school is quite as illogical as complete coeducation, and the pendulum must never rest at either extreme position."

NEGRO EDUCATION.

1417. **Richardson, Clement.** Examining the near illiterate. Southern workman, 45 : 546–50, October 1916.

Negro education in the South.

1418. **Sutton, W. S.** The contributions of Booker T. Washington to the education of the negro. School and society, 4 : 457–63, September 23, 1916.

An address delivered April 19, 1916, in New Orleans before the Southern conference for education and industry.

EDUCATION OF IMMIGRANTS.

1419. The literacy test for immigrants; a debate. The constructive and rebuttal speeches of the representatives of the University of Chicago . . . in the eighteenth annual contests of the Central debating league, against Michigan and Northwestern, January 21, 1916. [Chicago] The Delta sigma rho, 1916. 62 p. front. (ports.) 8°.

Bibliography: p. 57–62.

1420. **Mason, Gregory.** "Americans first"; how the people of Detroit are making Americans of the foreigners in their city. Outlook, 114 : 193–201, September 27, 1916. illus.

EDUCATION OF DEAF.

1421. **Hansen, Anders.** The education of the deaf in the Scandinavian countries in 1916. Volta review, 18 : 407–13, October 1916.

Gives tables of statistics for Denmark, Norway, and Sweden, with other material, descriptive and historical.

1422. **Love, James K.** The aural school-clinique. Volta review, 18 : 413–16, October 1916.

Conditions in Glasgow, Scotland. Taken from the Glasgow medical journal, February 1916.

EXCEPTIONAL CHILDREN.

1423. **Browne, Blanche Van Leuven.** The cripple not an invalid. Van Leuven Browne national magazine, 5 : 7–8, October 1916.

1424. **Elliott, Charles M.** Administration of the special class. American school-master, 9 : 289–303, September 1916.

Outlines the necessary steps in the administration of special classes: the selection of children, the tests to be given, the grouping of atypical children, the program, the teacher and her training, supervision of special classes, the nurse and the field worker.

1425. **Henke, Francesca A.** The retarded pupil. Primary education, 24 : 484–85, 529, October 1916.

How to handle retarded pupils, methods of discipline, method of teaching reading, etc.

1426. **Meytrott, *Mrs.* Cornelia B.** What shall be done for the deficient child? Training school bulletin, 13 : 115–19, September 1916.

A Monmouth county experiment in coordination.
Read before the 1916 New Jersey state conference of charities and correction.

EDUCATION EXTENSION.

1427. **Perry, Clarence Arthur.** The quicksands of wider use. Playground, 10 : 200–208, September 1916.

Considers the defects in some of the schemes of plans for the administration of community centers.

1428. **Salser, Carl W.** Extension work in normal schools. Educational rev iew 52 : 272–83, October 1916.

    Writer says that by its attitude toward extension work a normal school determines largely whether "it is merely traditional in its policies or whether it is broad-gauged and aggressive." Shows what has been done by the Kansas State normal school.

LIBRARIES AND READING.

1429. **Dana, J. C.** *and* **Gardner, Blanche.** Aids in high school teaching; pictures and objects. Woodstock, Vt., The Elm tree press, 1916. 68 p. 8°. (Modern American library economy as illustrated by the Newark, N. J., Free public library, by John Cotton Dana. vol. 2, pt. XIX)

1430. **Legler, Henry E.** Library work with children: a synoptical criticism. Public libraries, 21 : 345–48, October 1916.

1431. **Schofield, F. A.** Outside reading in the Eugene (Oregon) high school. English journal, 5 : 544–48, October 1916.

    Shows results of credits given for outside reading. Lists 19 of the most popular books read, etc.

1432. **Wiswell, Leon Orlando.** How to use reference books. New York, Cincinnati [etc.] American book company [1916] 162 p. incl. front., diagr. 12°.

BUREAU OF EDUCATION: RECENT PUBLICATIONS.

1433. Accredited secondary schools in the United States; by Samuel P. Capen. Washington, 1916. 120 p. (Bulletin, 1916, no. 20)

1434. Answers to objections to the kindergarten. Prepared in the Kindergarten division, Bureau of education, in cooperation with the International kindergarten union. Washington, 1916. 4 p.

1435. Applied knowledge as a problem in negro education; by Hugh M. Browne. Washington, 1916. 6 p. (Miscellaneous publication, September 1916)

1436. Commercial education. A report on the commercial education subsection of the second Pan American scientific congress, December 1915–January 1916; by Glen Levin Swiggett. Washington, 1916. 96 p. (Bulletin, 1916, no. 25)

1437. Public facilities for educating the alien; prepared in the Division of immigrant education by F. E. Farrington. Washington, 1916. 51 p. (Bulletin, 1916, no. 18)

1438. Vocational secondary education. Prepared by the committee on vocational education of the National education association. Washington, 1916. 163 p. (Bulletin, 1916, no. 21)

BULLETIN OF THE UNITED STATES BUREAU OF EDUCATION.[1]

[NOTE.—Documents marked with an asterisk (*) may be obtained only from the Superintendent of Documents, Government Printing Office, Washington, D. C., at the price indicated. Remittances should be made direct to the Superintendent of Documents in coin, currency, or money order. Stamps are not accepted. Other publications will be sent free of charge upon application to the Commissioner of Education, as long as the limited supply lasts.]

1913.

*No. 1. Monthly record of current educational publications, January, 1913. 5 cts.
*No. 2. Training courses for rural teachers. A. C. Monahan and R. H. Wright. 5 cts.
*No. 3. The teaching of modern languages in the United States. Charles H. Handschin. 15 cts.
*No. 4. Present standards of higher education in the United States. George E. MacLean. 20 cts.
*No. 5. Monthly record of current educational publications. February, 1913. 5 cts.
*No. 6. Agricultural instruction in high schools. C. H. Robison and F. B. Jenks. 10 cts.
*No. 7. College entrance requirements. Clarence D. Kingsley. 15 cts.
*No. 8. The status of rural education in the United States. A. C. Monahan. 15 cts.
*No. 9. Consular reports on continuation schools in Prussia. 5 cts.
*No. 11. Monthly record of current educational publications, April, 1913. 5 cts.
*No. 12. The promotion of peace. Fannie Fern Andrews. 10 cts.
*No. 13. Standards and tests for measuring the efficiency of schools or systems of schools. 5 cts.
*No. 14. Agricultural instruction in secondary schools. 10 cts.
*No. 15. Monthly record of current educational publications, May, 1913. 5 cts.
*No. 16. Bibliography of medical inspection and health supervision. 15 cts.
*No. 17. A trade school for girls. 10 cts.
*No. 18. The fifteenth international congress on hygiene and demography. Fletcher B. Dresslar. 10 cts.
*No. 19. German industrial education and its lessons for the United States. Holmes Beckwith. 15 cts.
*No. 20. Illiteracy in the United States. 10 cts.
*No. 21. Monthly record of current educational publications, June, 1913. 5 cts.
*No. 22. Bibliography of industrial, vocational, and trade education. 10 cts.
*No. 23. The Georgia club at the State Normal School, Athens, Ga., for the study of rural sociology. E. C. Branson. 10 cts.
*No. 24. A comparison of public education in Germany and in the United States. Georg Kerschensteiner. 5 cts.
*No. 25. Industrial education in Columbus, Ga. Roland B. Daniel. 5 cts.
No. 26. Good roads arbor day. Susan B. Sipe.
*No. 28. Expressions on education by American statesmen and publicists. 5 cts.
*No. 29. Accredited secondary schools in the United States. Kendric C. Babcock. 10 cts.
*No. 30. Education in the South. W. Carson Ryan, jr. 10 cts.
*No. 31. Special features in city school systems. 10 cts.
*No. 34. Pension systems in Great Britain. Raymond W. Sies. 10 cts.
*No. 35. A list of books suited to a high-school library. 15 cts.
*No. 36. Report on the work of the Bureau of Education for the natives of Alaska, 1911-12. 10 cts.
*No. 37. Monthly record of current educational publications, October, 1913. 5 cts.
*No. 38. Economy of time in education. 10 cts.
*No. 40. The reorganized school playground. Henry S. Curtis. 10 cts.
*No. 41. The reorganization of secondary education. 10 cts.
*No. 42. An experimental rural school at Winthrop College. H. S. Browne. 10 cts.
*No. 43. Agriculture and rural-life day; material for its observance. Eugene C. Brooks. 10 cts.
*No. 44. Organized health work in schools. E. B. Hoag. 10 cts.
*No. 45. Monthly record of current educational publications, November, 1913. 5 cts.
*No. 46. Educational directory, 1913. 15 cts.
*No. 47. Teaching material in Government publications. F. K. Noyes. 10 cts.
*No. 48. School hygiene. W. Carson Ryan, jr. 15 cts.
*No. 49. The Farragut School, a Tennessee country-life high school. A. C. Monahan and Adams Phillips. 10 cts.

---

[1] For issues prior to 1913, see list "Available Publications of the United States Bureau of Education, October, 1916," which may be had on application. Numbers omitted are out of print.

* See note at top of p. 1.

* See note at top of p. I.

* See note at top of p. i.

O

SOME FACTS CONCERNING MANUAL ARTS AND HOME-MAKING SUBJECTS IN 156 CITIES.

The confused and chaotic condition which characterizes vocational and industrial education at the present time is evidence of the fact that certain far-reaching and fundamental adjustments are going on in the educational world. These adjustments involve, on the one hand, the school in all of its aspects and at all of its stages, and, on the other hand, the various industries and occupations with all of their social and economic implications. No one seems to know with any degree of certainty what solution the problem demands; nor is anyone able to predict with precision and accuracy what the outcome of the movement may be. Many interesting experiments have been and are now being carried on for the purpose of meeting present needs and satisfying various demands, but the problem in the large seems little nearer a satisfactory solution than when the experimentation began.

Educational, vocational, industrial, and social surveys are becoming common. These set forth the facts and make clear the existing conditions in each of these fields of activity. If carefully and scientifically conducted, the findings of survey commissions are valuable in determining needs and policies. It is on the basis of present practices and existing conditions that the needs and policies of the future must be determined.

It was the purpose of this investigation to determine the existing conditions and practices in the manual arts and homemaking subjects with reference to—

1. Nature and character of the work in the different grades and in the high school.

2. The number of minutes per week and the relative amount of time devoted to these subjects.

3. Methods used and their adaptation to age and grade of pupils.

4. Nature and amount of correlation with other subjects.

5. Methods of disposing of finished products of shops and kitchens.

6. The dominant aims in the teaching of these subjects and the prevalence of each.

7. Enrollment in vocational courses in elementary and in high schools.

8. Cost per pupil in different schools and cities.

9. Percentage of pupils entering work for which manual arts and homemaking courses prepared them.

10. Norms and standards of practice in all the above.

The method used in collecting the data was that of the questionnaire. A copy of the form used is here reproduced.

QUESTIONNAIRE ON THE TEACHING OF THE MANUAL ARTS, HOMEMAKING, AND VOCATIONAL SUBJECTS.

Name.................... *City*.................... *State*....................

1. Underline the courses offered in your schools and state the number of weeks in each course grade by grade.

GRADES.

	1	2	3	4	5	6	7	8	I	II	III	IV
Paper folding, cutting, etc.												
Cardboard construction.												
Raffia and basketry.												
Weaving and textiles.												
Knife work, coping saw, etc.												
Clay work, plasticine, etc.												
Leather work, etc.												
Art metal work.												
Jewelry.												
Printing and bookbinding.												
Joinery, cabinetmaking, carpentry.												
Wood turning, pattern making.												
Foundry.												
Machine shop.												
Forge shop.												
Concrete construction.												
Cooking.												
Sewing.												
Millinery.												

2. State the number of periods per week and total number of minutes per week given to manual arts and homemaking in the grades.

GRADES.

	1	2	3	4	5	6	7	8	I	II	III	IV
Periods per week.												
Total minutes per week to manual arts and homemaking.												
Total minutes per week to all subjects.												

3. Does the work consist of—

[a] Systematic graded exercises?.......................... In what grades?................
[b] Individual projects selected by pupils?................ In what grades?................
[c] Cooperative projects selected by class?................ In what grades?................
[d] Projects expressive of work in history, reading, language, or other subjects?..............
In what grades?......................

[Reverse of Questionnaire.]

4. Is the work in manual arts and homemaking correlated with the work in the subjects named below? State grade and subjects in form below.

GRADES.

	1	2	3	4	5	6	7	8	I	II	III	IV
Drawing												
Language												
History												
Reading												
Arithmetic												
Other subjects												

5. What disposal is made of the finished product?

[a] Kept by pupils?...In what grades?................
[b] Becomes property of the school?...........................In what grade?................
[c] Sold by school or pupils? ....In what grades?..........
[d] Other methods...

6. Underline *twice* the aim which dominates your teaching of the manual arts and home-making subjects, *once* the one which you consider of least importance.

[a] Cultural aim. [General: nonvocational, disciplinary, etc.]
[b] Vocational aim. [To give knowledge and skill of direct value upon immediate entrance into the trades or vocations.]
[c] Prevocational aim. [Giving knowledge and experiences of various occupations, materials, tools, etc.]
[d] Other aims...

7. What percentage of pupils, after leaving school, enter directly into the vocations for which the manual arts and home-making subjects prepared them?

8. Please state as accurately as possible:

[a] The value of the equipment of the shops and laboratories used for manual arts and home-making..
[b] The annual cost [last year] of supplying the manual arts and home-making courses [this includes teachers' salaries, materials, etc., but not new equipment]....................
In the elementary schools?......................
In the high schools?......................
[c] The total annual enrollment in manual arts and home-making courses·
In the elementary school...................
In the high school....................

Give below any additional information which you may consider important. ....

Responses were received from 156 superintendents, supervisors, and teachers in 39 States, furnishing usable returns from 156 city school systems. Of these cities, 13 offered no work in the manual arts and home-making subjects, leaving 143 cities reporting in full or in part on the conditions considered in the questionnaire.

The data on topics 4, 7, and 8 were so incomplete and unreliable that they are eliminated from this report.[1]

---

[1] The sources of error in the data are not numerous or serious, and great care has been taken in classifying and treating the returns, so that the results may be regarded as fairly reliable. It must be remembered, in interpreting the data, that the returns are for school systems and not for schools or pupils.

AIMS.

In the preparation of manual arts or home-making courses, and in the teaching of these subjects, some aim or purpose in the mind of the superintendent or supervisor dominates the selection of materials and the choice of methods to be used. It is quite possible that the aims or purposes may be complex and not clearly differentiated, and that no one aim predominates. It is more likely, however, that there is some one aim which outweighs all others, but which does not necessarily exclude all others. The nature of the work, its distribution throughout the grades, and the methods of presenting it are very largely determined by the purposes to be accomplished. A classification of aims, then, may help to discover the trend of vocational education in so far as it concerns manual arts and home-making subjects.

In the questionnaire the aims were arbitrarily classified as cultural, vocational, and prevocational, and an explanation was attached to each of these terms. The superintendents and supervisors making reply were asked to underline once the dominant aim, and twice the one of least importance. A summary of the results is given in Table 1.

TABLE 1.—*Aims as arranged by 112 superintendents, supervisors, and teachers (44 cities not reporting).*

	Dominant.		Secondary importance.		Least importance.	
	Number.	Per cent.	Number.	Per cent.	Number.	Per cent.
Cultural	44	39	25	22	43	38
Vocational	12	11	45	40	55	49
Prevocational	56	50	42	38	14	13
	112	100	112	100	112	100

The significant fact to be gained from Table 1 is that there is no general agreement as to the aim in presenting these subjects. The prevocational aim predominates in one-half of the schools, while the vocational aim ranks first in importance in only 11 per cent of the cities studied. There is some evidence, though not conclusive, that the present elementary and secondary schools are only incidentally vocational schools. The cultural aim ranks second as a dominant aim in a sufficient number of cities to indicate that the manual arts and homemaking subjects are still regarded largely as cultural and disciplinary subjects. Figure 1 represents graphically the reports of the 112 cities.

NATURE OF THE WORK.

The kind and variety of the work offered afford a partial indication of the extent to which the aims are being attained. If the culture aim dominates, one would expect to find wide variation in the work and the courses of long duration with more or less study and recitation accompanying the shop and laboratory work. If, on the other hand, the strictly vocational aim dominates, it would be

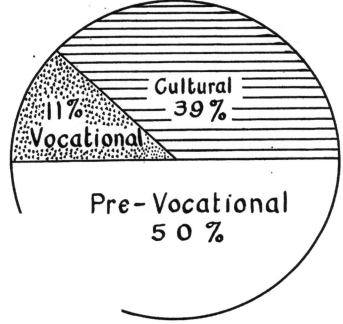

FIG. 1.—Distribution of cities as to dominant aim in manual arts and homemaking subjects, 112 cities (44 cities not reporting).

natural to find greater specialization and the greater portion of the work done in the shops and kitchens, all of it capable of application, more or less directly, in the trades and occupations. Work of a prevocational nature would possess in less degree some of the characteristics of both the cultural and vocational, but would be general in character and extensive in its scope. Some light is thrown on the nature of the work in terms of present practice by Tables 2 and 3.

Table 2.—*Nature of work and where offered, 142 cities (14 cities not reporting).*

Kind of work.	Grades.												Total.
	1	2	3	4	5	6	7	8	I	II	III	IV	
Paper folding, etc.	111	102	61	38	16	10	8	8					354
Cardboard construction	33	47	62	50	39	18	13	15	2	2	1	1	292
Raffia, basketry	23	27	38	51	44	31	12	12	4	1	2	3	248
Weaving, textiles	32	38	40	25	13	7	4	5	3	4	4	4	179
Knife, coping saw	2	2	4	8	30	28	14	12	1				101
Clay, plasticine	38	32	19	12	7	8	4	6	4	3	3	2	138
Leather, stamp, etc.			1		1	1	4	8	18	15	13	9	70
Art metal work				2	3	1		6	12	9	13	11	57
Jewelry								1	8	5	6	9	29
Printing, bookbinding			2	3	6	9	13	14	11	10	9	7	84
Joinery, cabinetmaking						12	53	93	98	91	56	33	32	468
Wood turning, pattern making						2	7	18	38	67	32	36	190
Foundry							1	1	2	4	10	11	7	36
Machine shop								2	4	7	22	24	59
Forge shop								1	7	13	16	6	43
Concrete construction							6	4	4	1	2	6	23
Cooking						6	24	62	91	86	68	43	39	422
Sewing	1	1	4	18	56	84	94	78	82	71	44	36	569
Millinery					1	1	1	3	16	14	27	19	82

The figures in Table 2 represent cities offering the stated kinds of work in each of the grades and in the high school. The totals represent the sum of all the courses offered in any kind of work in all grades and in all cities.

In order to make the figures for each grade comparable with those of other grades, there must be a common base. The total number of cities reporting (142) was used as the base for computing the percentages given in Table 3. Each per cent was computed to the nearest whole number.

Table 3.—*Figures of Table 2 reduced to percentages, based on 142 cities.*

Kinds of work.	Grades.											
	1	2	3	4	5	6	7	8	I	II	III	IV
Paper folding, etc.	78	72	43	27	11	7	6	6				
Cardboard construction	23	33	44	42	27	13	9	11	1	1	1	1
Raffia, basketry	16	19	27	36	31	22	8	8	3	1	1	2
Weaving, textiles	23	27	28	18	9	5	3	4	2	3	3	3
Knife, coping saw	1	1	3	6	21	20	10	8	1			
Clay, plasticine	27	23	13	8	5	6	3	4	3	2	2	1
Leather, stamp, etc.				1	1	1	4	6	13	11	9	6
Art metal work				1	2	1	4	8	6	9	8
Jewelry								1	6	4	4	6
Printing, bookbinding			1	2	4	6	9	10	8	7	6	5
Joinery, cabinetmaking					8	37	65	69	64	40	23	23
Wood turning, pattern making					1	5	13	27	47	23	18
Foundry						1	1	1	3	7	8	5
Machine shop							1	3	5	15	16
Forge shop							1	5	9	11	4
Concrete construction						4	3	3	1	1	4
Cooking					4	16	44	64	62	48	30	27
Sewing	1	1	3	13	40	59	66	55	58	50	31	25
Millinery					1	1	1	2	11	10	19	13

The variety in the kinds of work offered is an important fact to be gained from the tables. The fact that there are five kinds of work found in every grade and in the high school should also be noted.

Table 3 shows how the emphasis varies from grade to grade for the various lines of work. These facts are represented more clearly in figure 2.

From Tables 2 and 3 and from figure 2 the following general facts may be gained:

1. Many different kinds of work are given in the different grades, but those receiving the most attention are sewing, joinery and cabinetmaking, cooking, paper folding, cutting, etc., cardboard construction, and raffia and basketry.

2. The following kinds of work are offered in every grade and throughout the high school: Cardboard construction, raffia and basketry, weaving and textiles, clay, plasticine, etc., and sewing. These subjects are not given equal emphasis in each of the grades, however.

3. Paper folding, cutting, etc., joinery and cabinetmaking, cooking and sewing are the only kinds of work given in over 50 per cent of the cities reporting.

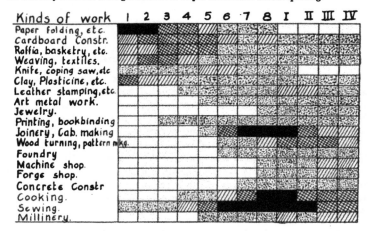

Fig. 2.—Percentage of cities offering work in different grades, 142 cities.

4. Grade eight is not only the grade in which the greatest emphasis is placed on manual arts and homemaking subjects, but it is the only grade in which every kind of work in these subjects is offered. The first high-school year ranks second in amount of emphasis and in variety of work.

5. The kinds of work receiving the least amount of attention are: Art metal, jewelry, printing and bookbinding, foundry, and concrete construction.

6. If the sanction of present practice be accepted, the following kinds of work are approved in—

Grades 1 to 5.—Paper, cardboard, raffia and reed, weaving textiles, clay and plasticine, and sewing.

Grades 6 to 8.—Knife and coping saw, joinery and cabinetmaking, cooking and sewing.

Grades I and II.—Leather stamping, etc., joinery and cabinetmaking, wood turning and pattern making, cooking and sewing.

Grades III and IV.—Machine shop, forge shop, cooking, sewing, and millinery.

In a general way these deductions should be of value to superintendents and supervisors who contemplate introducing the manual arts and homemaking subjects into their courses of study. To such persons the figures of Table 3 may serve as standards for the selection of material for courses of study and for the proper distribution of that material throughout the grades and the high school.

No attempt has been made to analyze the kinds of work reported. The details vary greatly in different localities. Even though designated by the same name in all the grades, there may be great variation in kind and amount of work done in the same subject in the different grades. Certainly the work with clay in the first grade differs much in character from work with the same material in the last year of the high school. A similar adaptation to the age and needs of pupils may be found in the other subjects. These details of variation can not be shown except in the general way indicated in the tables and figures.

TIME GIVEN TO THESE SUBJECTS.

It is generally conceded that when the work in the manual arts and homemaking courses is not correlated with other subjects it is better to have longer periods, even though fewer in number, than to have several short periods per week. The number of periods per week varies in different cities, and according to grades. In several cities the time is not distributed by periods in grades below the fifth. The work in manual arts and homemaking courses in these cities is taught incidentally and correlated with other subjects. The distribution of cities on the basis of the number of periods per week given to manual arts and homemaking subjects is shown in Table 4 for 56 cities.

TABLE 4.—*Number of periods per week, 56 cities (100 cities not reporting).*

Periods per week.	Grades.												
	1	2	3	4	5	6	7	8	I	II	III	IV	Total.
Undistributed	6	6	5	4	1	1	...	...	...	...	...	...	23
1	7	8	11	12	19	27	28	26	5	3	1	1	148
2	3	3	4	7	8	11	13	14	9	7	5	5	89
3	4	3	3	.4	2	...	1	4	3	2	...	...	26
4	1	1	...	1	2	3	3	3	2	3	4	4	27
5	7	7	5	1	2	1	1	1	14	12	12	12	75
6 or over				1	1	1	1	2	3	9	8	9	8	42
Total	28	28	28	30	35	44	48	51	42	35	31	39	430
Median	2	2	1	1	1	1	1	1	5	5	5	5	2

The median number of periods per week indicates the tendency to have fewer periods in the grades and a larger number in the high school.

Before the number of periods per week can have much significance, it is necessary to know something of the length of the periods. Table 5 represents the distribution of cities according to the total number of minutes per week given to the manual arts and homemaking subjects in 125 cities.

TABLE 5.—*Distribution of cities with reference to number of minutes per week given to manual arts and home-making subjects, 125 cities (31 cities not reporting).*

Minutes per week.	Grades.												
	1	2	3	4	5	6	7	8	I	II	III	IV	Total.
Less than 45	12	10	11	8	5	3	...	...	...	...	...	...	49
46 to 60	9	10	8	10	14	6	3	...	2	2	2	1	67
61 to 75	20	19	24	25	31	35	18	12	1	1	1	1	188
76 to 100	10	10	10	13	24	41	57	58	19	14	11	11	278
101 to 125	7	9	9	10	9	11	17	17	4	6	2	2	103
126 to 150	1	...	1	...	1	...	2	4	1	1	1	1	13
151 to 180	3	3	1	1	1	2	5	6	2	1	3	3	31
181 to 200	...	...	...	...	1	4	10	11	2	2	1	1	32
201 to 300	1	1	1	...	...	...	1	2	14	13	12	10	55
301 to 400	...	...	...	...	...	...	2	2	9	9	8	7	37
401 to 450	...	...	...	1	1	...	...	...	11	10	8	9	40
451 to 500	...	...	...	...	1	...	1	2	23	22	19	19	88
501 to 600	...	...	...	...	...	...	...	...	4	3	2	2	11
Over 600	...	...	...	...	...	...	...	...	3	3	3	2	11
Total	63	62	65	68	88	103	116	114	95	87	73	69	1,008
Lower quartile	53	54	57	60	69	69	79	83	114	122	161	161	72
Median	69	70	70	71	74	81	93	95	334	345	350	386	94
Upper quartile	91	96	91	94	93	97	116	124	464	468	469	468	190

This table should be read: Of the cities giving less than 45 minutes per week to the manual arts and home-making subjects, there are 12 in the first grade, 10 in the second grade, etc. In the first grade the middle 50 per cent of the cities give from 53 to 91 minutes per week to these subjects, the median being 69 minutes; in grade 2, from 54 to 96 minutes, with the median at 70, etc.

Figure 3 shows graphically the median amount of time given to the manual arts and home-making subjects, as well as the limits between which the middle 50 per cent of the cities fall. The extremes above and below the middle 50 per cent are not shown in this figure, but may be found by referring to Table 5.

The heavy vertical lines represent the time given in the middle 50 per cent of the cities reporting. The short horizontal lines represent the median number of minutes in these cities. The gradual rise in the median line after the fourth grade and the very abrupt rise after the eighth grade are significant. It must not be forgotten that in 25 per cent of the cities the time is greater than that represented by the black lines, and in 25 per cent of the cities it is less than here represented.

It is evident from Table 5 and figure 3 that there is great diversity in the amount of time given to these subjects. The number of minutes per week ranges from less than 45 to over 600. The limits of the middle 50 per cent, however, probably include those cities in which the number of minutes per week represents standard practice.

Given the number of periods per week and the total number of weekly minutes devoted to the manual arts and home-making subjects, it is still necessary to know what relation this time bears to the total school time. This can only be known by comparing the time given to these subjects with that given to all the school subjects.

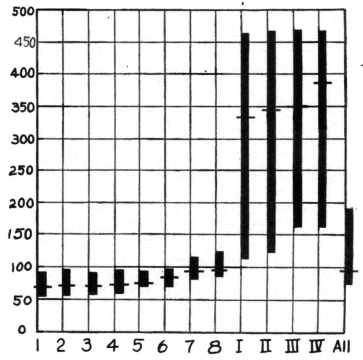

Fig. 3.—Median and middle 50 per cent of cities with reference to number of minutes per week given to manual arts and home-making subjects, 125 cities. Short horizontal bars represent medians; heavy vertical bars represent middle 50 per cent of cities.

The distribution of the 66 cities reporting with reference to the total school time is given in Table 6. The term "total school time" is here used to indicate the number of minutes per week that school is actually in session and does not include the time given to recesses and the noon intermission. It represents the number of minutes per week of actual schooling that a child may get provided he is in attendance at school for the entire week.

TABLE 6.—*Distribution of cities with reference to the total number of minutes per week given to all school subjects, exclusive of recesses and noon intermissions, 66 cities (90 cities not reporting).*

Minutes per week.	Grades.												
	1	2	3	4	5	6	7	8	I	II	III	IV	Total.
Less than 1,000.....	8	2	1	1	1	1	2	2	1	1	1	1	22
1,001 to 1,100........	1	.....	.....	.....	.....	1	1	1	1	1	.....	.....	6
1,101 to 1,200........	.....	.....	1	.....	1	1	1	1	2	2	.....	.....	10
1,201 to 1,250........	6	2	1	.....	.....	.....	.....	.....	2	2	2	2	17
1,251 to 1,350........	7	8	3	2	3	3	3	3	1	.....	.....	.....	34
1,351 to 1,400........	10	10	6	3	2	2	3	3	3	3	2	2	49
1,401 to 1,450........	2	3	2	4	6	6	6	5	1	1	1	.....	37
1,451 to 1,500........	.....	2	4	3	1	1	1	1	3	2	2	2	22
1,501 to 1,600........	12	15	21	22	23	26	23	28	19	18	15	15	236
1,601 to 1,800........	.....	.....	5	10	12	13	14	11	8	8	8	8	97
Over 1,800........	.....	.....	.....	1	1	3	3	4	8	8	9	9	46
Total........	46	42	44	47	50	57	56	59	49	47	40	39	567
Lower quartile.....	1,217	1,325	1,392	1,458	1,450	1,500	1,442	1,475	1,458	1,472	1,513	1,520	1,410
Median.............	1,355	1,395	1,520	1,548	1,550	1,554	1,550	1,550	1,558	1,556	1,580	1,547	1,539
Upper quartile.....	1,508	1,528	1,575	1,592	1,600	1,631	1,630	1,609	1,675	1,725	1,775	1,775	1,597

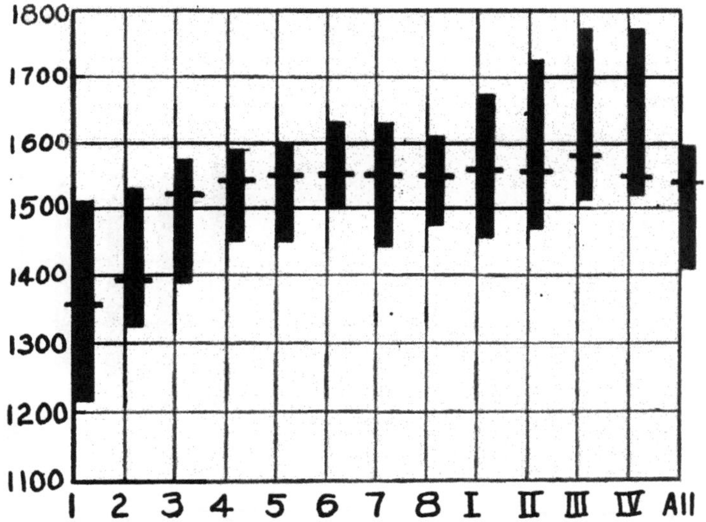

FIG. 4.—Median and middle 50 per cent of cities with reference to total number of minutes per week given to all subjects, 66 cities. Short horizontal bars represent medians; heavy vertical bars represent middle 50 per cent of cities.

The total school time varies greatly, the range being from less than 1,000 minutes per week to over 1,800 minutes per week. The limits for the middle 50 per cent of cities and the medians can best be represented graphically. Figure 4 shows these facts.

It will be noted from Table 6 and figure 4 that the total school time increases rapidly up to the third grade and that thereafter the increase is very slight.   The greatest amount of time is given to the subjects in the third year of the high school.

The figures of Table 6 were used as the base in computing the percentages given in Table 7, which shows the relation the manual arts and homemaking time bears to the total school time.   This table does not show the total distribution, but only the median percentages with the upper and lower limits of the middle 50 per cent of the cities reporting.

TABLE 7.—*Percentage that the time given to manual arts and homemaking subjects is of the total school time.*[1]

	Grades.												
	1	2	3	4	5	6	7	8	I	II	III	IV	Total.
Lower quartile............	4.4	4.1	4.1	4.1	4.7	4.6	5.5	5.6	7.8	8.0	10.6	10.6	5.1
Median...................	5.1	5.0	4.7	4.6	4.8	5.2	6.0	6.1	21.4	22.2	23.1	24.9	6.1
Upper quartile............	6.0	6.3	5.8	5.9	5.8	6.0	7.1	7.7	27.7	27.0	27.0	26.3	12.1

[1] In terms of medians and quartiles.

The figures of the above table are represented graphically in figure 5.

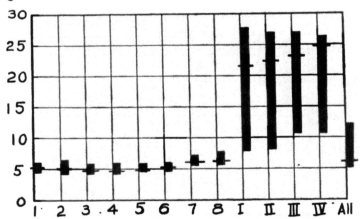

FIG. 5.—Median and middle 50 per cent of percentages of total school time given to manual arts, etc. Short horizontal bars represent medians, heavy vertical bars represent middle 50 per cent of cities.

Short horizontal bars represent medians, heavy vertical bars represent middle 50 per cent of cities.

From Table 7 and figure 5 it is evident that there is wide variation in the proportionate amount of time given to these subjects, especially in the high school.   Only about 5 per cent of the total school time is thus used in the first six grades.   This increases to 6 per cent in the seventh and eighth grades and to nearly one-fourth of all school time by the time the senior year of high school is reached.

The relative amount of time given to a subject is one indication of the educational value that is attributed to that subject. It will be seen that the proportion of time is about 1 to 20 in the grades and 1 to 4 in the high school. Is the work in the high school five times as valuable as that in the grades? In terms of present practice, as measured by the amount of time given to it, it is.

Relative to the time given to manual arts and homemaking subjects the data here presented justify the following conclusions:

1. The number of periods per week devoted to these subjects is one in the grades and five in the high school.

2. The time given to work of this kind amounts to about one and one-quarter hours per week in grades 1 to 5; one and one-half hours in grades 6 to 8; and nearly six hours per week in the high school.

3. The total school time varies greatly, but the median total time is 1,350 minutes in grade 1, 1,400 in grade 2, and about 1,550 minutes per week in all the other grades.

4. The time given to the manual arts and homemaking subjects is about 5 per cent of the total school time in the first six grades; about 6 per cent in the seventh and eighth grades, and nearly 25 per cent in the high school.

METHODS EMPLOYED.

The methods of presenting the work in manual arts and homemaking subjects and the nature of the work presented may be classified in general into four more or less distinct classes or groups—systematic, graded exercises; individual projects selected by the pupils; cooperative projects selected by the class; and projects expressive of the regular work in history, arithmetic, reading, and other subjects. It will be seen that several of these may be employed in one school in different grades; hence in actual practice there is a certain amount of overlapping of these methods. There is also a tendency to make use of the method adapted to the needs of children at various stages in their development, so that some of these methods are emphasized in a few grades and found scarcely at all in others.

Since the methods were classified in this way in the questionnaire, a brief explanation of each method is here given:

The *systematic graded exercise* plan is based largely on the Swedish sloyd, or some other system, in which the work is given with special reference to the sequence of the projects, tools, technical processes, construction, and finish. The chief aims are to develop skill and to make useful projects. Little attention is given to the interests of the pupils in those exercises. Exercise 6, or its equivalent, must be completed before exercise 7 is begun. Under this plan interest is maintained by the development of skill, by general interest in the use of tools and shaping materials, and by the desire to reach exercise 12, which may be the particular objective point in the course at that time.

Individual projects selected by the pupils have the advantage of making a direct appeal to the immediate interests of the pupils. Pupils, however, are apt to select projects that are beyond their capabilities, and because of this fact they may be disappointed in the finished project. This method presents many difficulties to the instructor, because in a class of 20 pupils there may be as many as 20 different projects under construction at one time. This plan seems to work successfully with mature pupils in the upper grades. When used alone, this plan sacrifices skill and well-finished products in order to secure temporary interest in a given project.

Cooperative projects selected by the pupils are designed to make an appeal to the group or cooperative instincts of the pupils. Frequently such projects are institutional projects, and if they are large jobs, interest is usually good. Boys will build boats, buildings, concrete walks, but interest lags when they are required to frame pictures, repair furniture, or construct some article of school equipment.

The making of projects expressive of some phase of subject matter in history, arithmetic, geography, or other subjects involves rather close correlation of manual arts and homemaking subjects with the regular school work in other subjects. This method makes the handwork incidental to the bookwork, and is merely a means of concrete expression of some of the ideas gained in the study of other phases of subject matter. When proper correlation exists the handwork may be made a strong incentive for better work in the other subjects.

Table 8 shows the prevalence of each method when used alone, also when used in combination with some other method.

TABLE 8.—*Methods used in presenting manual arts and homemaking subjects, 131 cities*
(25 cities not reporting).

	Cities.
A. Systematic graded exercises, and individual projects only	30
B. Systematic exercises, individual projects, and cooperative projects only	29
C. All four methods	28
D. Systematic graded exercises only	22
E. Systematic exercises, individual projects, and correlated projects	10
F. Systematic exercises and projects expressive of other work only	6
G. Individual projects, cooperative projects, and correlated projects	3
H. Individual projects only	2
I. Systematic exercises, cooperative projects, and correlated projects	1
Cities reporting	131

The single method in greatest favor among the cities reporting is that of the systematic graded exercises. This method combined with that of individual projects find greatest favor of all. These two methods combined with the cooperative project plan ranks second in importance, while a combination of all four methods ranks third. The figures of Table 8 above, when reduced to percentages, are represented graphically in figure 6.

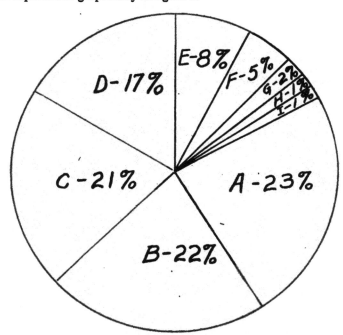

FIG. 6.—Methods used in presenting manual arts and homemaking subjects.

A. Systematic graded exercises, and individual projects only.
B. Systematic exercises, individual projects, and cooperative projects.
C. All four methods.
D. Systematic graded exercises only.
E. Systematic exercises, individual projects, and correlated projects.
F. Systematic exercises and projects expressive of other work only.
G. Individual projects, cooperative projects, and correlated projects.
H. Individual projects only.
I. Systematic exercises, cooperative projects, and correlated projects.

TABLE 9.—*Methods used in 131 cities, showing grades in which each is emphasized.*

	Grade.											
	1	2	3	4	5	6	7	8	I	II	III	IV
Systematic, graded exercises....................	72	70	70	76	87	99	105	104	80	71	64	63
Individual projects.............................	25	26	28	29	39	48	64	77	69	66	60	53
Cooperative projects...........................	22	21	22	22	25	26	35	38	39	39	40	39
Correlated projects.............................	37	37	37	38	27	27	26	26	15	17	16	16

The figures in Table 9 represent the number of cities using the method specified in each of the grades. The data of this table reduced to percentages are represented graphically in figure 7.

Regarding the methods of presenting the manual arts and homemaking subjects, the following general facts may be stated:

1. When any method is used alone, that of systematic, graded exercises leads all the rest, but combinations of two or more methods are more frequent than any one method used alone.

2. While each method is in use to some extent in every grade, that of systematic, graded exercises is most frequent in grades 6, 7, and 8; that of individual projects in grades 8, I, and II; that of cooperative projects in grades 7, 8, and through the high school; and that of projects expressive of work in history, geography, arithmetic, etc., in grades 1 to 4.

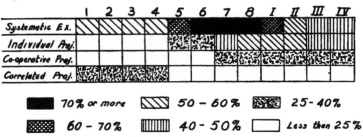

Fig. 7.—Methods used in different grades.

DISPOSAL OF PRODUCTS.

The method of disposing of the finished products of the manual arts and homemaking work depends somewhat upon the nature of the products. Obviously some of the products of the shop and kitchen have little or no market value, hence disposal by sale is not possible. Sometimes the materials are furnished by the school and used only as a means of training the pupils in the handling of tools and implements; in this case the products are retained by the school. In most cases, however, the pupils keep the products of their labor. Cooperative projects are likely to be of such a nature that the finished products are kept by the school. There are also combinations of the above methods and adaptations of each to the grade in which the work is done, to the nature of the product, and to the local demands for the output of the shops and kitchens. The methods of disposing of the products in the various cities are classified in Table 12.

TABLE 12.—*Methods of disposing of products, 130 cities (26 cities not reporting).*

	Cities.
Kept by pupils	52
Part kept by pupils, part by school	46
Part kept by pupils, part by school, part sold	19
Part kept by pupils, part sold	11
Given for charity, and exchanged with other schools	2
Total	130

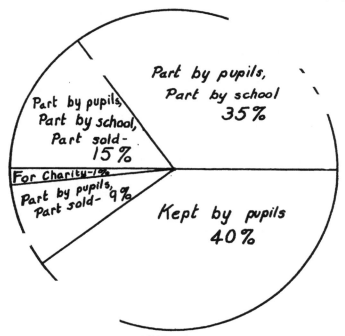

FIG. 8.—Methods of disposal of finished products.

The methods of disposal used in the different cities, grade by grade, are shown in Table 13.

TABLE 13.—*Number of cities using each method, grade by grade.*

Methods of disposal.	Grades.											
	1	2	3	4	5	6	7	8	I	II	III	IV
Kept by pupils	99	99	99	102	107	113	122	125	103	100	94	93
Kept by school	29	29	29	30	31	38	44	46	54	53	47	46
Sold by school or pupils	10	10	10	10	11	13	17	19	14	13	11	10

It will be noted that the method most commonly used is that of permitting the pupil to retain his project when completed. The combination nearly as popular is that of allowing part of the product to be kept by the pupil and the remainder by the school. Retention

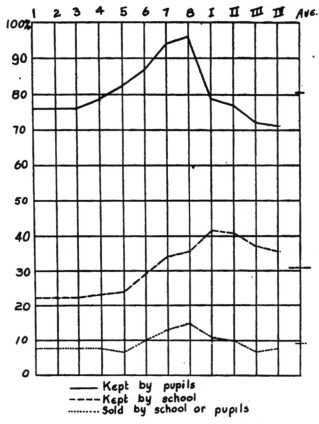

FIG. 9.—Methods of disposal of finished products by grades.

of products by pupils is found in the largest number of cities in the seventh and eighth grades. Retention by the school is most frequent in the first and second years of the high school, while disposal by sale is most frequent in grades seven and eight. Figure 9 shows in percentages the frequency of the use of each of these methods.

GENERAL SUMMARY.

In terms of the central tendencies represented by the data presented in the foregoing sections it is possible to state certain standards of practice in the teaching of manual arts and home-making subjects.

The dominant aim is prevocational in character. This means that the courses given are intended to give knowledge of and a low degree of facility in the use of tools, materials, and processes, some attention being given those phases of the work which have probability of usefulness in the arts and trades. It also implies that the work will be varied, covering as wide a range of tools, materials, and processes as possible in the time available.

There is great variety in the kinds of work offered, but the general tendency seems to lie in the direction of the following—work in paper in the primary grades, joinery and cabinet making for boys in the grammar grades, and sewing and cooking for girls in the grammar grades. These are also the lines of work receiving the greatest emphasis.

The time given to these subjects amounts to about 75 minutes per week in the lower grades, 90 minutes per week in the seventh and eighth grades, and over 300 minutes per week in the high school. This time is undistributed in the primary grades, is given in a single weekly period in the grammar grades, and in five weekly periods in the high school. The time given to these subjects is over 5 per cent of the total school time in the elementary school and over 25 per cent of the total time in the high school.

Although various methods of presenting the work are in use, that of systematic graded exercises is the one most frequently used. The type of method used varies somewhat with the grade in which the work is given, as well as with the aim dominating the teaching of these subjects.

The methods of disposing of the finished products are varied according to the nature of the product and according to the grade in which produced, but the one in most frequent use is that of permitting the pupil to keep the product of his handiwork.

The central tendencies obtained from a treatment of the data in this bulletin may be accepted as representative of the present status of the manual arts and home-making subjects in so far as they apply to the phases of the subjects studied and to the extent of the 156 cities reporting. The variations from these central tendencies, however, may be quite as important as the central tendencies themselves in determining future policies and reorganizations.

Cities and States represented in this study.

Alabama:
  Selma.
California:
  Alameda.
  Bakersfield.
  Berkeley.
  Los Angeles.
  Pasadena.
  San Jose.
Connecticut:
  Ansonia.
  Danbury.
  Meriden.
  Waterbury.
Colorado:
  Grand Junction.
  Greeley.
  Trinidad.
Georgia:
  Athens.
Idaho:
  Idaho Falls.
Illinois:
  Beardstown.
  Chicago Heights.
  Elgin.
  Freeport.
  Hinckley.
  Hoopestown.
  Joliet.
  Metroplis.
  Ottawa.
  Peoria.
  Quincy.
  East St. Louis.
Indiana:
  Crawfordsville.
  Indianapolis.
  Marion.
  Michigan City.
  Muncie.
  Oakland City.
  Peru.
  South Bend.
  Vincennes.
Iowa:
  Burlington.
  Clinton.
  Council Bluffs.
  Davenport.
  Keokuk.
  Ottumwa.

Iowa—Continued.
  Sioux City.
  Waterloo.
Kansas:
  Emporia.
  Kansas City.
  Leavenworth.
  Newton.
  Parsons.
  Topeka.
Kentucky:
  Bowling Green.
  Frankfort.
  Lexington.
  Winchester.
Louisiana:
  Baton Rouge.
  New Orleans.
Maine:
  Sanford.
Massachusetts.:
  Chelsea.
  Everett.
  Milford.
  Springfield.
  Waltham.
Michigan:
  Adrian.
  Benton Harbor.
  Calumet.
  Detroit.
  Muskegon.
Minnesota:
  Minneapolis.
Mississippi:
  Vicksburg.
Missouri:
  Hannibal.
  St. Louis.
  Webb City.
Montana:
  Great Falls.
  Missoula.
Nebraska:
  Beatrice.
  Lincoln.
  Omaha.
New Hampshire:
  Dover.
  Keene.
  Manchester.

New Jersey:
  Bayonne.
  East Orange.
  Elizabeth.
  Jersey City.
  Kearney..
  North Bergen.
  Rahway.
  Rutherford.
  Trenton.
  Plainfield.
New Mexico:
  Albuquerque.
New York:
  Cohoes.
  Dunkirk.
  Fulton.
  Gloversville.
  Harwell.
  Hudson Falls.
  Ithaca.
  Jamestown.
  Kingston.
  Newburgh.
  Oswego.
  Plattsburg.
  Rome.
  Syracuse.
  Utica.
  Yonkers.
North Carolina:
  Charlotte.
North Dakota: ·
  Bismarck.
  Fargo.
Ohio:
  Akron.
  Canton.
  Cincinnati.·
  Elyria.
  Hamilton.
  Lancaster.
  Norwood.
  Youngstown.
Oklahoma:
  Bartlesville.
  Chickasha.
Pennsylvania:
  Harrisburg.
  Indiana.
  Monessen.

Pennsylvania—Contd.
  Mount Carmel.
  Nanticoke.
  Phoenixville.
  Reading.
  Scranton.
  Sharon.
  Shenandoah.
  Tamaqua.
  West Chester..
Rhode Island:
  Central Falls.
  Providence.
South Carolina:
  Columbia.

South Dakota.
  Sioux Falls.
  Watertown.
Texas:
  Beaumont.
  Brownsville.
  El Paso.
  Galveston.
  Houston.
  Marshall.
  Sherman.
Utah:
  Ogden.
Vermont:
  Burlington.

Virginia:
  Richmond.
West Virginia:
  Huntington.
Wisconsin:
  Appleton.
  Racine.
  Superior.
  Wausaw.
  Sheboygan.
Wyoming:
  Cheyenne.
  Sheridan.

O

Lightning Source UK Ltd.
Milton Keynes UK
UKHW012133180219
337529UK00012B/1381/P